Commentary
on the
OLD TESTAMENT

Commentary on the

OLD TESTAMENT

IN TEN VOLUMES

by

C. F. KEIL and F. DELITZSCH

VOLUME X

Minor Prophets

by C. F. KEIL

Two Volumes in One

WILLIAM B. EERDMANS PUBLISHING COMPANY
Grand Rapids, Michigan

COMMENTARY ON THE OLD TESTAMENT
by C. F. Keil and F. Delitzsch
Translated from the German

Volumes translated by James Martin
THE PENTATEUCH
JOSHUA, JUDGES, RUTH
THE BOOKS OF SAMUEL
THE BOOKS OF THE KINGS
THE PROPHECIES OF ISAIAH
THE PROPHECIES OF EZEKIEL
THE TWELVE MINOR PROPHETS

Volumes translated by Andrew Harper
THE BOOKS OF THE CHRONICLES

Volumes translated by Sophia Taylor
THE BOOKS OF EZRA, NEHEMIAH, ESTHER

Volumes translated by Francis Bolton
THE BOOK OF JOB
THE PSALMS

Volumes translated by M. G. Easton
PROVERBS OF SOLOMON
THE SONG OF SONG AND ECCLESIASTES
THE BOOK OF DANIEL

Volumes translated by David Patrick
THE PROPHECIES OF JEREMIAH, VOL. I

Volumes translated by James Kennedy
THE PROPHECIES OF JEREMIAH, VOL. II

ISBN 0-8028-8044-4

Reprinted, February 1980

CONTENTS

———

JOEL.

AMOS.

OBADIAH.

JONAH.

MICAH

INTRODUCTION

TWELVE MINOR PROPHETS

———◆———

IN our editions of the Hebrew Bible, the book of Ezekiel is followed by the book of the Twelve Prophets (τῶν δώδεκα προφητῶν, Sir. xlix. 10; called שְׁנֵים עָשָׂר by the Rabbins; Chaldee, e.g. in the Masora, תְּרֵיסַר = תְּרֵי עָשָׂר), who have been called from time immemorial the smaller prophets (qᵉtannīm, minores) on account of the smaller bulk of such of their prophecies as have come down to us in a written form, when contrasted with the writings of Isaiah, Jeremiah, and Ezekiel.[1] On the completion of the canon these twelve writings were put together, so as to form *one* prophetic book. This was done " lest one or other of them should be lost on account of its size, if they were all kept separate," as Kimchi observes in his *Præf. Comm. in Ps.,* according to a rabbinical tradition. They were also reckoned as one book, μονόβιβλος, τὸ δωδεκαπρόφητον (see my *Lehrbuch der Einleitung in d. A. T.* § 156 and 216, Anm. 10 sqq.). Their authors lived and laboured as prophets at different periods, ranging from the ninth century B.C. to the fifth; so that in these prophetic books we have not only the earliest and

---

[1] Augustine (*De civit. Dei,* xviii. 29) observes: " *Qui propterea dicuntur minores, quia sermones eorum sunt breves in eorum comparatione, qui majores ideo vocantur, quia prolixa volumina condiderunt.*" Compare with this the notice from *b. Bathra* 14*b,* in Delitzsch on Isaiah, vol. i. p. 25, translation.

latest of the prophetic testimonies concerning the future history of Israel and of the kingdom of God, but the progressive
development of this testimony. When taken, therefore, in
connection with the writings of the greater prophets, they
comprehend all the essentials of that prophetic word, through
which the Lord equipped His people for the coming times of
conflict with the nations of the world, endowing them thus
with the light and power of His Spirit, and causing His servants to foretell, as a warning to the ungodly, the destruction of
the two sinful kingdoms, and the dispersion of the rebellious
people among the heathen, and, as a consolation to believers,
the deliverance and preservation of a holy seed, and the eventual
triumph of His kingdom over every hostile power.

In the arrangement of the twelve, the chronological principle has so far determined the order in which they occur, that
the prophets of the pre-Assyrian and Assyrian times (Hosea
to Nahum) are placed first, as being the earliest; then follow
those of the Chaldean period (Habakkuk and Zephaniah); and
lastly, the series is closed by the three prophets after the captivity (Haggai, Zechariah, and Malachi), arranged in the order
in which they appeared.[1] Within the first of these three
groups, however, the chronological order is not strictly preserved, but is outweighed by the nature of the contents. The
statement made by Jerome concerning the arrangement of the
twelve prophets—namely, that "the prophets, in whose books
the time is not indicated in the title, prophesied under the same
kings as the prophets, whose books precede theirs with the date
of composition inserted" (*Præf. in* 12 *Proph.*)—does not rest
"upon a good traditional basis," but is a mere conjecture, and
is proved to be erroneous by the fact that Malachi did not prophesy in the time of Darius Hystaspes, as his two predecessors
are said to have done. And there are others also, of whom it
can be shown, that the position they occupy is not chronologically correct. Joel and Obadiah did not first begin to prophesy
under Uzziah of Judah and Jeroboam II. of Israel, but commenced their labours before that time; and Obadiah prophesied before Joel, as is obvious from the fact that Joel (in
ch. ii. 32) introduces into his announcement of salvation the
words used by Obadiah in ver. 17, "and in Mount Zion shall

[1] Compare Delitzsch on Isaiah, vol. i. p. 25.

be deliverance," and does so with what is equivalent to a direct citation, viz. the expression " as the Lord hath said." Hosea, again, would stand after Amos, and not before him, if a strictly chronological order were observed; for although, according to the headings to their books, they both prophesied under Uzziah and Jeroboam II., Hosea continued prophesying down to the times of Hezekiah, so that in any case he prophesied for a long time after Amos, who commenced his work earlier than he. The plan adopted in arranging the earliest of the minor prophets seems rather to have been the following: Hosea was placed at the head of the collection, as being the most comprehensive, just as, in the collection of Pauline epistles, that to the Romans is put first on account of its wider scope. Then followed the prophecies which had no date given in the heading; and these were so arranged, that a prophet of the kingdom of Israel was always paired with one of the kingdom of Judah, viz. Joel with Hosea, Obadiah with Amos, Jonah with Micah, and Nahum the Galilean with Habakkuk the Levite. Other considerations also operated in individual cases. Thus Joel was paired with Hosea, on account of its greater scope; Obadiah with Amos, as being the smaller, or rather smallest book; and Joel was placed before Amos, because the latter commences his book with a quotation from Joel iii. 16, "Jehovah will roar out of Zion," etc. Another circumstance may also have led to the pairing of Obadiah with Amos, viz. that Obadiah's prophecy might be regarded as an expansion of Amos ix. 12, "that they may possess the remnant of Edom." Obadiah was followed by Jonah before Micah, not only because Jonah had lived in the reign of Jeroboam II., the contemporary of Amaziah and Uzziah, whereas Micah did not appear till the reign of Jotham, but possibly also because Obadiah begins with the words, "We have heard tidings from Judah, and a messenger is sent among the nations;" and Jonah was such a messenger (Delitzsch). In the case of the prophets of the second and third periods, the chronological order was well known to the collectors, and consequently this alone determined the arrangement. It is true that, in the headings to Nahum and Habakkuk, the date of composition is not mentioned; but it was evident from the nature of their prophecies, that Nahum, who predicted the destruction of Nineveh, the capital of the

Assyrian empire, must have lived, or at any rate have laboured, before Habakkuk, who prophesied concerning the Chaldean invasion. And lastly, when we come to the prophets after the captivity, in the case of Haggai and Zechariah, the date of their appearance is indicated not only by the year, but by the month as well; and with regard to Malachi, the collectors knew well that he was the latest of all the prophets, from the fact that the collection was completed, if not in his lifetime and with his co-operation, at all events very shortly after his death.

The following is the correct chronological order, so far as it can be gathered with tolerable certainty from the contents of the different writings, and the relation in which they stand to one another, even in the case of those prophets the headings to whose books do not indicate the date of composition :

1. Obadiah : in the reign of Joram king of Judah, between   .   .   .   889 and 884 B.C.
2. Joel : in the reign of Joash king of Judah, between   .   .   .   875 and 848 B.C.
3. Jonah : in the reign of Jeroboam II. of Israel, between   .   .   .   824 and 783 B.C.
4. Amos : in the reign of Jeroboam II. of Israel and Uzziah of Judah, between   .   810 and 783 B.C.
5. Hosea : in the reign of Jeroboam II. of Israel, and from Uzziah to Hezekiah of Judah, between   790 and 725 B.C.
6. Micah : in the reign of Jotham, Ahaz, and Hezekiah of Judah, between   .   . 758 and 710 B.C.
7. Nahum : in the second half of the reign of Hezekiah, between   .   .   . 710 and 699 B.C.
8. Habakkuk : in the reign of Manasseh or Josiah, between   .   .   .   650 and 628 B.C.
9. Zephaniah : in the reign of Josiah, between   628 and 623 B.C.
10. Haggai : in the second year of Darius Hystaspes, viz.   .   .   .   . 519 B.C.
11. Zechariah : in the reign of Darius Hystaspes, from   .   .   .   . 519 B.C.
12. Malachi : in the reign of Artaxerxes Longimanus, between   .   .   .   433 and 424 B.C.

Consequently the literature of the prophetic writings does not date, first of all, from the time when Assyria rose into an imperial power, and assumed a threatening aspect towards Israel, i.e. under Jeroboam the son of Joash king of Israel, and Uzziah king of Judah, or about 800 B.C., as is commonly supposed, but about ninety years earlier, under the two Jorams of Judah and Israel, while Elisha was still living in the kingdom of the ten tribes. But even in that case the growth of the prophetic literature is intimately connected with the development of the theocracy. The reign of Joram the son of Jehoshaphat was one of eventful importance to the kingdom of Judah, which formed the stem and kernel of the Old Testament kingdom of God from the time that the ten tribes fell away from the house of David, and possessed in the temple of Jerusalem, which the Lord Himself had sanctified as the dwelling-place of His name, and also in the royal house of David, to which He had promised an everlasting existence, positive pledges not only of its own preservation, but also of the fulfilment of the divine promises which had been made to Israel. Joram had taken as his wife Athaliah, a daughter of Ahab and of Jezebel the fanatical worshipper of Baal; and through this marriage he transplanted into Judah the godlessness and profligacy of the dynasty of Ahab. He walked in the way of the kings of Israel, and did what was evil in the sight of the Lord, as the house of Ahab did. He slew his brethren with the sword, and drew away Jerusalem and Judah to idolatry (2 Kings viii. 18, 19; 2 Chron. xxi. 4–7, 11). After his death, and that of his son Ahaziah, his wife Athaliah seized upon the government, and destroyed all the royal seed, with the exception of Joash, a child of one year old, who was concealed in the bed-chambers by the sister of Ahaziah, who was married to Jehoiada the high priest, and so escaped. Thus the divinely chosen royal house was in great danger of being exterminated, had not the Lord preserved to it an offshoot, for the sake of the promise given to His servant David (2 Kings xi. 1–3; 2 Chron. xxii. 10–12). Their sins were followed by immediate punishment. In the reign of Joram, not only did Edom revolt from Judah, and that with such success, that it could never be brought into subjection again, but Jehovah also stirred up the spirit of the Philistines and Petræan Arabians, so that they forced their way into Jerusalem, and carried off the treasures of the palace, as well as the wives and sons of the king, with the exception of Ahaziah, the youngest son (2 Kings viii. 20–22; 2 Chron. xxi. 8–10, 16, 17). Joram himself was very soon afflicted with a painful and revolting disease (2 Chron. xxi.

18, 19) ; his son Ahaziah was slain by Jehu, after a reign of rather less than a year, together with his brethren (relations) and some of the rulers of Judah ; and his wife Athaliah was dethroned and slain after a reign of six years (2 Kings ix. 27–29, xi. 13 sqq. ; 2 Chron. xxii. 8, 9, xxiii. 12 sqq.). With the extermination of the house of Ahab in Israel, and its off-shoots in Judah, the open worship of Baal was suppressed in both kingdoms ; and thus the onward course of the increasing religious and moral corruption was arrested. But the evil was not radically cured. Even Jehoiada, who had been rescued by the high priest and set upon the throne, yielded to the entreaties of the rulers in Judah, after the death of his de-liverer, tutor, and mentor, and not only restored idolatry in Jerusalem, but allowed them to stone to death the prophet Zechariah, the son of Jehoiada, who condemned this apostasy from the Lord (2 Chron. xxiv. 17–22). Amaziah, his son and successor, having defeated the Edomites in the Salt valley, brought the gods of that nation to Jerusalem, and set them up to be worshipped (2 Chron. xxv. 14). Conspiracies were organized against both these kings, so that they both fell by the hands of assassins (2 Kings xii. 21, xiv. 19 ; 2 Chron. xxiv. 25, 26, xxv. 27). The next two kings of Judah, viz. Uzziah and Jotham, did indeed abstain from such gross idolatry and sus-tain the temple worship of Jehovah at Jerusalem ; and they also succeeded in raising the kingdom to a position of great earthly power, through the organization of a powerful army, and the erection of fortifications in Jerusalem and Judah. But the internal apostasy of the people from the Lord and His law increased even in their reigns, so that under Ahaz the torrent of corruption broke through every dam ; idolatry prevailed throughout the entire kingdom, even making its way into the courts of the temple ; and wickedness reached a height un-known before (2 Kings xvi. ; 2 Chron. xxviii.). Whilst, there-fore, on the one hand, the godless reign of Joram laid the foundation for the internal decay of the kingdom of Judah, and his own sins and those of his wife Athaliah were omens of the religious and moral dissolution of the nation, which was arrested for a time, however, by the grace and faithfulness of the covenant God, but which burst forth in the time of Ahaz with terrible force, bringing the kingdom even then to the verge of destruction, and eventually reached the fullest height under Manasseh, so that the Lord could no longer refrain from pronouncing upon the people of His possession the judgment of rejection (2 Kings xxi. 10–16); on the other hand, the punishment inflicted upon Judah for Joram's sins, in the revolt of the Edomites, and the plundering of Jerusalem by Philistines and Arabians, were preludes of the rising up of the world of nations above and against the kingdom of God, in order, if possible, to destroy it. We may see clearly of what eventful importance the revolt of Edom was to the kingdom of Judah, from the remark made by the sacred historian, that Edom revolted from under the hand of Judah " unto this day " (2 Kings viii. 22 ; 2 Chron. xxi. 10), *i.e.* until the dissolution of the kingdom of Judah, for the victories of Amaziah and Uzziah over the Edomites did not lead to their subjugation ; and still more clearly from the description contained in Obad. 10–14, of the hostile acts of the Edomites towards Judah on the occasion of the taking of Jerusalem by the Philistines and Arabians ; from which it is evident, that they were not satisfied with having thrown off the hateful yoke of Judah, but proceeded, in their malignant pride, to attempt the destruction of the people of God.

In the kingdom of the ten tribes also, Jehu had rooted out the worship of Baal, but had not departed from the sins of Jeroboam the son of Nebat. Therefore even in his reign the Lord " began to cut off from Israel " and Hazael the Syrian smote it in all its coasts. At the prayer of Jehoahaz, his son and successor, God had compassion once more upon the tribes of this kingdom, and sent them deliverers in the two kings Joash and Jeroboam II., so that they escaped from the hands of the Syrians, and Jeroboam was able to restore the ancient boundaries of the kingdom (2 Kings x. 28–33, xiii. 3–5, 23–25, xiv. 25). Nevertheless, as this fresh display of grace did not bear the fruits of repentance and return to the Lord, the judgments of God burst upon the sinful kingdom after the death of Jeroboam, and hurried it on to destruction.

In this eventful significance of the reign of Joram king of Judah, who was related to the house of Ahab and walked in his ways, with reference to the Israelitish kingdom of God, we may doubtless discover the foundation for the change which occurred from that time forward in the development of prophecy:—namely, that the Lord now began to raise up prophets in the midst of His people, who discerned in the present the germs of the future, and by setting forth in this light the events of their own time, impressed them upon the hearts of their countrymen both in writing and by word of mouth. The difference between the *prophetæ priores*, whose sayings and doings are recorded in the historical books, and the *prophetæ posteriores*, who composed prophetic writings of their own, consisted, therefore, not so much in the fact that the former were prophets of " irresistible actions," and the latter prophets of " convincing words" (Delitzsch), as in the fact that the earlier prophets maintained the right of the Lord before the people and their civil rulers both by word and deed, and thereby exerted an immediate influence upon the development of the kingdom of God in their own time ; whereas the later prophets seized upon the circumstances and relations of their own times in the light of the divine plan of salvation as a whole, and whilst proclaiming both the judgments of God, whether nearer or more remote, and the future salvation, predicted the onward progress of the kingdom of God in conflict with the powers of the world, and through these predictions prepared the way for the revelation of the glory of the Lord in His kingdom, or the coming of the Saviour to establish a kingdom of righteousness and peace. This distinction has also been recognised by G. F. Oehler, who discovers the reason for the composition of separate prophetical books in the fact, that " prophecy now acquired an importance which extended far beyond the times then present ; inasmuch as the consciousness was awakened in the prophets' minds with regard to both kingdoms, that the divine counsels of salvation could not come to fulfilment in the existing generation, but that the present form of the theocracy must be broken to pieces, in order that, after a thorough judicial sifting, there might arise out of the rescued and purified remnant the future church of salvation ;" and who gives this explanation of the reason for committing the words of the prophets to writing, that " it was in order that, when fulfilled, they might prove to future generations the righteousness and faithfulness of the covenant God, and that they might serve until then as a lamp to the righteous, enabling them, even in the midst of the darkness of the coming times of judgment, to understand the ways of God in His kingdom." All the prophetical books subserve this purpose, however great may be the diversity in the prophetical word which they contain,—a diversity occasioned by the individuality of the authors and the special circumstances among which they lived and laboured.

For the exegetical writings on the Minor Prophets, see my *Lehrbuch der Einleitung*, p. 273 sqq.

HOSEA

INTRODUCTION.

1. THE PERSON OF THE PROPHET.—*Hosea*, הוֹשֵׁעַ, *i.e.*
help, deliverance, or regarding it as *abstractum pro
concreto*, helper, *salvator*, Ὡσηέ (LXX.) or Ὡσηέ
(Rom. ix. 20), *Osee* (Vulg.), the son of a certain
Beëri, prophesied, according to the heading to his book (ch. i. 1),
in the reigns of the kings Uzziah, Jotham, Ahaz, and Hezekiah
of Judah, and in that of king Jeroboam, son of Joash, of Israel;
and, as the nature of his prophecies clearly proves, he prophesied
not only concerning, but in, the kingdom of the ten tribes, so
that we must regard him as a subject of that kingdom. This
is favoured not only by the fact that his prophetic addresses
are occupied throughout with the kingdom of the ten tribes,
but also by the peculiar style and language of his prophecies,
which have here and there an Aramæan colouring (for example,
such forms as אֲמָאסָאֵך, ch. iv. 6 ; חַבֵּי (inf.), ch. vi. 9 ; קִימוֹשׁ for
קִמּוֹשׁ, ch. ix. 6 ; קָאם for קָם, ch. x. 14 ; תִּרְגַּלְתִּי, ch. xi. 3 ; אוֹכִיל
for אַאֲכִיל, ch. xi. 4 ; תְּלוֹא, in ch. xi. 7 ; יַפְרִיא for יַפְרֶה, ch.
xiii. 15; and such words as רְתֵת, ch. xiii. 1 ; אֱהִי for אַיֵּה, ch.
xiii. 10, 14), and still more by the intimate acquaintance with
the circumstances and localities of the northern kingdom apparent in such passages as ch. v. 1, vi. 8, 9, xii. 12, xiv. 6 sqq.,
which even goes so far that he calls the Israelitish kingdom
"the land" in ch. i. 2, and afterwards speaks of the king of
Israel as "our king" (ch. vii. 5). On the other hand, neither
the fact that he mentions the kings of Judah in the heading, to
indicate the period of his prophetic labours (ch. i. 1), nor the
repeated allusions to Judah in passing (ch. i. 7, ii. 2, iv. 15,
v. 5, 10, 12–14, vi. 4, 11, viii. 14, x. 11, xii 1, 3), furnish any
proof that he was a Judæan by birth, as Jahn and Maurer
suppose. The allusion to the kings of Judah (ch. i. 1), and

11

that before king Jeroboam of Israel, may be accounted for
not from any outward relation to the kingdom of Judah, but
from the inward attitude which Hosea assumed towards that
kingdom in common with all true prophets. As the separation
of the ten tribes from the house of David was in its deepest
ground apostasy from Jehovah (see the commentary on 1 Kings
xii.), the prophets only recognised the legitimate rulers of the
kingdom of Judah as true kings of the people of God, whose
throne had the promise of permanent endurance, even though
they continued to render civil obedience to the kings of the
kingdom of Israel, until God Himself once more broke up the
government, which he had given to the ten tribes in His anger
to chastise the seed of David which had fallen away from Him
(Hos. xiii. 11). It is from this point of view that Hosea, in
the heading to his book, fixes the date of his ministry according
to the reigns of the kings of Judah, of whom he gives a complete list, and whom he also places first; whereas he only
mentions the name of one king of Israel, viz. the king in whose
reign he commenced his prophetic course, and that not merely
for the purpose of indicating the commencement of his career
with greater precision, as Calvin and Hengstenberg suppose,
but still more because of the importance attaching to Jeroboam
II. in relation to the kingdom of the ten tribes.

Before we can arrive at a correct interpretation of the
prophecies of Hosea, it is necessary, as ch. i. and ii. clearly
show, that we should determine with precision the time when
he appeared, inasmuch as he not only predicted the overthrow
of the house of Jehu, but the destruction of the kingdom of
Israel as well. The reference to Uzziah is not sufficient for
this; for during the fifty-two years' reign of this king of Judah,
the state of things in the kingdom of the ten tribes was im-
mensely altered. When Uzziah ascended the throne, the Lord
had looked in mercy upon the misery of the ten tribes of Israel,
and had sent them such help through Jeroboam, that, after
gaining certain victories over the Syrians, he was able completely to break down their supremacy over Israel, and to restore
the ancient boundaries of the kingdom (2 Kings xiv. 25–27).
But this elevation of Israel to new power did not last long. In
the thirty-seventh year of Uzziah's reign, Zechariah, the son
and successor of Jeroboam, was murdered by Shallum after a

reign of only six months, and with him the house of Jehu was overthrown. From this time forward, yea, even from the death of Jeroboam in the twenty-seventh year of Uzziah's reign, the kingdom advanced with rapid strides towards utter ruin. Now, if Hosea had simply indicated the time of his own labours by the reigns of the kings of Judah, since his ministry lasted till the time of Hezekiah, we might easily be led to assign its commencement to the closing years of Uzziah's reign, in which the decline of the kingdom of Israel had already begun to show itself and its ruin could be foreseen to be the probable issue. If, therefore, it was to be made apparent that the Lord does reveal future events to His servants even "before they spring forth" (Isa. xlii. 9), this could only be done by indicating with great precision the time of Hosea's appearance as a prophet, *i.e.* by naming king Jeroboam. Jeroboam reigned contemporaneously with Uzziah for twenty-six years, and died in the twenty-seventh year of the reign of the latter, who outlived him about twenty-five years, and did not die till the second year of Pekah (see at 2 Kings xv. 1, 32). It is evident from this that Hosea commenced his prophetic labours within the twenty-six years of the contemporaneous reigns of Uzziah and Jeroboam, that is to say, before the twenty-seventh year of the former, and continued to labour till a very short time before the destruction of the kingdom of the ten tribes, since he prophesied till the time of Hezekiah, in the sixth year of whose reign Samaria was conquered by Shalmanezer, and the kingdom of Israel destroyed. The fact that of all the kings of Israel Jeroboam only is mentioned, may be explained from the fact that the house of Jehu, to which he belonged, had been called to the throne by the prophet Elisha at the command of God, for the purpose of rooting out the worship of Baal from Israel, in return for which Jehu received the promise that his sons should sit upon the throne to the fourth generation (2 Kings x. 30); and Jeroboam, the great-grandson of Jehu, was the last king through whom the Lord sent any help to the ten tribes (2 Kings xiv. 27). In his reign the kingdom of the ten tribes reached its greatest glory. After his death a long-continued anarchy prevailed, and his son Zechariah was only able to keep possession of the throne for half a year. The kings who followed fell, one after another, by conspiracies, so that the uninterrupted and regular succession to the throne ceased with the death of Jeroboam; and of the six rulers who came to the throne after his death, not one was called by God through the intervention of a prophet, and only two were able to keep possession of it for any length of time, viz. Menahem for ten years, and Pekah for twenty.

Again, the circumstance that Hosea refers repeatedly to Judah in his prophecies, by no means warrants the conclusion that he was a citizen of the kingdom of Judah. The opinion expressed by Maurer, that an Israelitish prophet would not have troubled himself about the Judæans, or would have condemned their sins less harshly, is founded upon the unscriptural assumption, that the prophets suffered themselves to be influenced in their prophecies by subjective sympathies and antipathies as mere *morum magistri*, whereas they simply proclaimed the truth as organs of the Spirit of God, without any regard to man at all. If Hosea had been sent out of Judah into the kingdom of Israel, like the prophet in 1 Kings xiii., or the prophet Amos, this would certainly have been mentioned, at all events in the heading, just as in the case of Amos the native land of the prophet is given. But cases of this kind formed very rare exceptions to the general rule, since the prophets in Israel were still more numerous than in the kingdom of Judah. In the reign of Jeroboam the prophet Jonah was living and labouring there (2 Kings xiv. 25); and the death of the prophet Elisha, who had trained a great company of young men for the service of the Lord in the schools of the prophets at Gilgal, Bethel, and Jericho, had only occurred a few years before. The fact that a prophet who was born in the kingdom of the ten tribes, and laboured there, alluded in his prophecies to the kingdom of Judah, may be accounted for very simply, from the importance which this kingdom possessed in relation to Israel as a whole, both on account of the promises it had received, and also in connection with its historical development. Whilst the promises in the possession of the Davidic government of the kingdom of Judah formed a firm ground of hope for godly men in all Israel, that the Lord could not utterly and for ever cast off His people; the announcement of the judgments, which would burst upon Judah also on account of its apostasy, was intended to warn the ungodly against false trust in the gracious promises of God, and to proclaim the severity and earnestness of the judgment of God. This also explains the fact that whilst, on the one hand, Hosea makes the salvation of the ten tribes dependent upon their return to Jehovah their God and David their king (ch. i. 7, ii. 2), and warns Judah against sinning with Israel (ch. iv. 15), on the other hand, he announces to Judah also that it is plunging headlong into the very same ruin as Israel, in consequence of its sins (ch. v. 5, 10 sqq., vi. 4, 11, etc.); whereas the conclusions drawn by Ewald from these passages—namely, that at first Hosea only looked at Judah from the distance, and that it was not till a later period that he became personally acquainted with it, and not till after he had laboured for a long time in the northern part of the kingdom that he came to Judah and composed his book—are not only at variance with the fact, that as early as ch. ii. 2 the prophet proclaims indirectly the expulsion of Judah from its own land into captivity, but are founded upon the false notion, that the prophets regarded their own subjective perceptions and individual judgments as inspirations from God.

According to the heading, Hosea held his prophetic office for about sixty or sixty-five years (viz. 27–30 years under Uzziah, 31 under Jotham and Ahaz, and 1–3 years under Hezekiah). This also agrees with the contents of his book. In ch. i. 4, the overthrow of the house of Jehu, which occurred about eleven or twelve years after the death of Jeroboam, in the thirty-ninth year of Uzziah (2 Kings xv. 10, 13), is foretold as being near at hand; and in ch. x. 14, according to the most probable explanation of this passage, the expedition of Shalmanezer into Galilee, which occurred, according to 2 Kings xvii. 3, at the commencement of the reign of Hoshea, the last of the Israelitish kings, is mentioned as having already taken place, whilst a fresh invasion of the Assyrians is threatened, which cannot be any other than the expedition of Shalmanezer against king Hoshea, who had revolted from him, which ended in the capture of Samaria after a three years' siege, and the destruction of the kingdom of the ten tribes in the sixth year of Hezekiah. The reproof in ch. vii. 11, "They call to Egypt, they go to Assyria," and that in ch. xii. 1, "They do make a covenant with the Assyrians, and oil is carried into Egypt," point to the same period; for they clearly refer to the time of Hoshea, who, notwithstanding the covenant that he had made with Asshur, *i.e.* notwithstanding the oath of fidelity rendered to Shalmanezer, purchased the assistance of the king of Egypt by means of presents, that he might be able to shake off the Assyrian yoke. The history knows nothing of any earlier alliances between Israel and Egypt; and the supposition that, in these reproaches, the prophet has in his mind simply two political parties, viz. an Assyrian and an Egyptian, is hardly reconcilable with the words themselves; nor can it be sustained by an appeal to Isa. vii. 17 sqq., or even to Zech. x. 9–11, at least so far as the times of Menahem are concerned. Nor is it any more possible to infer from ch. vi. 8 and xii. 11, that the active ministry of the prophet did not extend beyond the reign of Jotham, on the ground that, according to these passages, Gilead and Galilee, which were conquered and depopulated by Tiglath-pileser, whom Ahaz called to his help (2 Kings xv. 29), were still in the possession of Israel (Simson). For it is by no means certain that ch. xii. 11 presupposes the possession of Galilee, but the words contained in this verse might have been uttered even after the Assyrians had conquered the land to the east of the Jordan; and in that case, the book, which comprises the sum and substance of all that Hosea prophesied during a long period, must of necessity contain historical allusions to events that were already things of the past at the time when his book was prepared (Hengstenberg). On the other hand, the whole of the attitude assumed by Assyria towards Israel, according to ch. v. 13, x. 6, xi. 5, points beyond the times of Menahem and Jotham, even to the Assyrian oppression, which first began with Tiglath-pileser in the time of Ahaz. Consequently there is no ground whatever for shortening the period of our prophet's active labours. A prophetic career of sixty years is not without parallel. Even Elisha prophesied for at least fifty years (see at 2 Kings xiii. 20, 21). This simply proves, according to the apt remark of Calvin, "how great and indomitable were the fortitude and constancy with which he was endowed by the Holy Spirit." Nothing certain is known concerning the life of the prophet;[1] but his inner life lies before

---

[1] The traditional accounts are very meagre, and altogether unsupported. According to *Pseudepiphanius, De vitis prophet.* c. xi., *Pseudo-Doroth. De*

us in his writings, and from these we may clearly see that he had to sustain severe inward conflicts. For even if such passages as ch. iv. 4, 5, and ix. 7, 8, contain no certain indications of the fact, that he had to contend against the most violent hostilities as well as secret plots, as Ewald supposes, the sight of the sins and abominations of his countrymen, which he had to denounce and punish, and the outburst of the divine judgments upon the kingdom thus incessantly ripening for destruction, which he had to experience, could not fail to fill his soul, burning as it was for the deliverance of his people, with the deepest anguish, and to involve him in all kinds of conflicts.

2. Times of the Prophet.—When Hosea was called to be a prophet, the kingdom of the ten tribes of Israel had been elevated to a position of great earthly power by Jeroboam II. Even under Joash the Lord had had compassion upon the children of Israel, and had turned to them again for the sake of His covenant with Abraham, Isaac, and Jacob; so that Joash had been able to recover the cities, which Hazael of Syria had conquered in the reign of his father Jehoahaz, from Benhadad the son of Hazael, and to restore them to Israel (2 Kings xiii. 23-25). The Lord sent still further help through Jeroboam the son of Joash. Because He had not yet spoken to root out the name of Israel under heaven, He gave them victory in war, so that they were able to conquer Damascus and Hamath again, so far as they had belonged to Judah under David and Solomon, and to restore the ancient boundaries of Israel, from the province of Hamath to the Dead Sea, according to the word of Jehovah the God of Israel, which He had spoken through His servant the prophet Jonah (2 Kings xiv. 25-28). But this revival of the might and greatness of Israel was only the last display of divine grace, through which

prophetis, c. i., and in a Scholion before *Ephr. Syri Explan. in Hos.*, he sprang from *Belemoth*, or *Belemōn*, or *Beelmoth*, in the tribe of Issachar, and is said to have died and been buried there. On the other hand, according to a tradition current among the inhabitants of Thessalonica, found in שׁלשׁלת הקבלה, he died in Babylon. According to an Arabian legend, it was not far from Tripolis, viz. in the city of *Almenia;* whilst the Arabs also point out a grave, which is supposed to be his, in the land to the east of the Jordan, on the site of Ramoth Gilead; cf. Simson, *der Prophet Hosea*, p. 1 sqq.

the Lord sought to bring back His people from their evil ways, and lead them to repentance. For the roots of corruption, which the kingdom of Israel had within it from its very commencement, were not exterminated either by Joash or Jeroboam. These kings did not depart from the sins of Jeroboam the son of Nebat, who had caused Israel to sin, any more than their predecessors (2 Kings xiii. 11, xiv. 24). Jehu, the founder of this dynasty, had indeed rooted out Baal from Israel; but he had not departed from the golden calves at Bethel and Dan, through the setting up of which Jeroboam the son of Nebat had led Israel into sin (2 Kings x. 28, 29). Nor did his successors take any more care to walk in the law of Jehovah, the God of Israel, with all their heart. Neither the severe chastisements which the Lord inflicted upon the people and the kingdom, by delivering Israel up to the power of Hazael king of Syria and his son Benhadad, in the time of Jehu and Jehoahaz, causing it to be smitten in all its borders, and beginning to cut off Israel (2 Kings x. 32, 33, xiii. 3); nor the love and grace which He manifested towards them in the reigns of Joash and Jeroboam, by liberating them from the oppression of the Syrians, and restoring the former greatness of the kingdom,—were sufficient to induce the king or the people to relinquish the worship of the calves. This sin of Jeroboam, however, although it was Jehovah who was worshipped under the symbol of the calf, was a transgression of the fundamental law of the covenant, which the Lord had made with Israel, and therefore was a formal departure from Jehovah the true God. And Jeroboam the son of Nebat was not content with simply introducing images or symbols of Jehovah, but had even banished from his kingdom the Levites, who opposed this innovation, and had taken men out of the great body of the people, who were not sons of Levi, and made them priests, and had gone so far as to change the time of celebrating the feast of tabernacles from the seventh month to the eighth (1 Kings xii. 31, 32), merely for the purpose of making the religious gulf which separated the two kingdoms as wide as possible, and moulding the religious institutions of his kingdom entirely according to his own caprice. Thus the worship of the people became a political institution, in direct opposition to the idea of the kingdom of God; and the sanctuary of Jehovah was changed into a king's sanctuary (Amos vii. 13). But the consequences of this image-worship were even worse than these. Through the representation of the invisible and infinite God under a visible and earthly symbol, the glory of the one true God was brought down within the limits of the finite, and the God of Israel was placed on an equality with the gods of the heathen. This outward levelling was followed, with inevitable necessity, by an inward levelling also. The Jehovah worshipped under the symbol of an ox was no longer essentially different from the Baals of the heathen, by whom Israel was surrounded; but the difference was merely a formal one, consisting simply in a peculiar mode of worship, which had been prescribed in His revelation of Himself, but which could not lay the foundation of any permanently tenable party-wall. For, whilst the heathen were accustomed to extend to the national Deity of Israel the recognition which they accorded to the different Baals, as various modes of revelation of one and the same Deity; the Israelites, in their turn, were also accustomed to grant toleration to the Baals; and this speedily passed into formal worship. " Outwardly, the Jehovah-worship still continued to predominate; but inwardly, the worship of idols rose almost into exclusive supremacy. When once the boundary lines between the two religions were removed, it necessarily followed that that religion acquired the strongest spiritual force, which was most in accordance with the spirit of the nation. And from the very corruptions of human nature this was not the strict Jehovah religion, which being given by God did not bring down God to the low level of man, but sought to raise man up to its own lofty height, placing the holiness of God in the centre, and founding upon this the demand for holiness which it made upon its professors; but the voluptuous, sensual teaching of idolatry, pandering as it did to human corruption, just because it was from this it had originally sprung" (Hengstenberg's *Christology*). This seems to explain the fact, that whereas, according to the prophecies of Amos and Hosea, the worship of Baal still prevailed in Israel under the kings of the house of Jehu, according to the account given in the books of Kings Jehu had rooted out Baal along with the royal house of Ahab (2 Kings x. 28). Jehu had merely broken down the outward supremacy of the Baal-worship, and raised up the worship of

Jehovah once more, under the symbols of oxen or calves, into the state-religion. But this worship of Jehovah was itself a Baal-worship, since, although it was to Jehovah that the legal sacrifices were offered, and although His name was outwardly confessed, and His feasts were observed (Hos. ii. 13), yet in heart Jehovah Himself was made into a Baal, so that the people even called Him their Baal (Hos. ii. 16), and observed " the days of the Baals" (Hos. ii. 13).

This inward apostasy from the Lord, notwithstanding which the people still continued to worship Him outwardly and rely upon His covenant, had of necessity a very demoralizing influence upon the national life. With the breach of the fundamental law of the covenant, viz. of the prohibition against making any likeness of Jehovah, or worshipping images made by men, more especially in consequence of the manner in which this prohibition was bound up with the divine authority of the law, all reverence not only for the holiness of the law of God, but for the holy God Himself, was undermined. Unfaithfulness towards God and His word begot faithlessness towards men. With the neglect to love God with all the heart, love to brethren also disappeared. And spiritual adultery had carnal adultery as its inevitable consequence, and that all the more because voluptuousness formed a leading trait in the character of the idolatry of Hither Asia. Hence all the bonds of love, of chastity, and of order were loosened and broken, and Hosea uttered this complaint : " There is no truthfulness, and no love, and no knowledge of God in the land. Cursing, and murder, and stealing, and adultery ; they break out, and blood reaches to blood" (ch. iv. 1, 2). No king of Israel could put an effectual stop to this corruption. By abolishing the worship of the calves, he would have rendered the very existence of the kingdom doubtful. For if once the religious wall of division between the kingdom of Israel and the kingdom of Judah had been removed, the political distinction would have been in danger of following. And this was really what the founder of the kingdom of the ten tribes feared (1 Kings xii. 27), inasmuch as the royal family that occupied the throne had received no promise from God of permanent continuance. Founded as it was in rebellion against the royal house of David, which God Himself had chosen, it bore within itself from the very first the spirit of rebellion and revolution, and therefore the germs of internal self-destruction. Under these circumstances, even the long, and in outward respects very prosperous, reign of Jeroboam II. could not possibly heal the deep-seated evils, but only helped to increase the apostasy and immorality; since the people, whilst despising the riches of the goodness and mercy of God, looked upon their existing prosperity as simply a reward for their righteousness before God, and were therefore confirmed in their self-security and sins. And this was a delusion which false prophets loved to foster by predictions of continued prosperity (cf. ch. ix. 7). The consequence was, that when Jeroboam died, the judgments of God began to burst upon the incorrigible nation. There followed, first of all, an anarchy of eleven or twelve years; and it was not till after this that his son Zechariah succeeded in ascending the throne. But at the end of no more than six months he was murdered by Shallum, whilst he in his turn was put to death after a reign of one month by Menahem, who reigned ten years at Samaria (2 Kings xv. 14, 17). In his reign the Assyrian king Phul invaded the land, and was only induced to leave it by the payment of a heavy tribute (2 Kings xv. 19, 20). Menahem was followed by his son Pekachiah in the fiftieth year of Uzziah's reign; but after a reign of hardly two years he was murdered by his charioteer, Pekah the son of Remaliah, who held the throne for twenty years (2 Kings xv. 22–27), but who accelerated the ruin of his kingdom by forming an alliance with the king of Syria to attack the brother kingdom of Judah (Isa. vii.). For king Ahaz, when hard pressed by Pekah and the Syrians, called to his help the Assyrian king Tiglath-pileser, who not only conquered Damascus and destroyed the Syrian kingdom, but took a portion of the kingdom of Israel, viz. the whole of the land to the east of the Jordan, and carried away its inhabitants into exile (2 Kings xv. 29). Hoshea the son of Elah conspired against Pekah, and slew him in the fourth year of the reign of Ahaz; after which, an eight years' anarchy threw the kingdom into confusion, so that it was not till the twelfth year of Ahaz that Hoshea obtained possession of the throne. Very shortly afterwards, however, he came into subjection to the Assyrian king Shalmanezer, and paid him tribute. But after a time, in reliance upon the help of Egypt, he broke his oath of fealty to

the king of Assyria; whereupon Shalmanezer returned, conquered the entire land, including the capital, and led Israel
captive into Assyria (2 Kings xv. 30, xvii. 1–6).

3. THE BOOK OF HOSEA.—Called as he was at such a time
as this to proclaim to his people the word of the Lord, Hosea
necessarily occupied himself chiefly in bearing witness against
the apostasy and corruption of Israel, and in preaching the judgment of God.   The ungodliness and wickedness had become
so great, that the destruction of the kingdom was inevitable ;
and the degenerate nation was obliged to be given up into the
power of the Assyrians, the existing representatives of the
heathen power of the world.   But as God the Lord has no
pleasure in the death of the sinner, but that he should turn and
live, He would not exterminate the rebellious tribes of the
people of His possession from the earth, or put them away for
ever from His face, but would humble them deeply by severe
and long-continued chastisement, in order that He might bring
them to a consciousness of their great guilt and lead them to
repentance, so that He might at length have mercy upon them
once more, and save them from everlasting destruction.   Consequently, even in the book of Hosea, promises go side by side
with threatenings and announcements of punishment, and that
not merely as the general hope of better days, kept continually
before the corrected nation by the all-pitying love of Jehovah,
which forgives even faithlessness, and seeks out that which
has gone astray (Sims.), but in the form of a very distinct
announcement of the eventual restoration of the nation, when
corrected by punishment, and returning in sorrow and repentance to the Lord its God, and to David its king (ch. iii. 5),—
an announcement founded upon the inviolable character of the
divine covenant of grace, and rising up to the thought that the
Lord will also redeem from hell and save from death, yea, will
destroy both death and hell (ch. xiii. 14).   Because Jehovah
had married Israel in His covenant of grace, but Israel, like an
unfaithful wife, had broken the covenant with its God, and gone
a whoring after idols, God, by virtue of the holiness of His
love, must punish its unfaithfulness and apostasy.   His love,
however, would not destroy, but would save that which was
lost.   This love bursts out in the flame of holy wrath, which

burns in all the threatening and reproachful addresses of Hosea. In this wrath, however, it is not the consuming fire of an Elijah that burns so brightly; on the contrary, a gentle sound of divine grace and mercy is ever heard in the midst of the flame, so that the wrath but gives expression to the deepest anguish at the perversity of the nation, which will not suffer itself to be brought to a consciousness of the fact that its salvation rests with Jehovah its God, and with Him alone, either by the severity of the divine chastisements, or by the friendliness with which God has drawn Israel to Himself as with cords of love. This anguish of love at the faithlessness of Israel so completely fills the mind of the prophet, that his rich and lively imagination shines perpetually by means of changes of figure and fresh turns of thought, to open the eyes of the sinful nation to the abyss of destruction by which it is standing, in order if possible to rescue it from ruin. The deepest sympathy gives to his words a character of excitement, so that for the most part he merely hints at the thoughts in the briefest possible manner, instead of carefully elaborating them, passing with rapid changes from one figure and simile to another, and moving forward in short sentences and oracular utterances rather than in a calmly finished address, so that his addresses are frequently obscure, and hardly intelligible.[1]

His book does not contain a collection of separate addresses delivered to the people, but, as is generally admitted now, a general summary of the leading thoughts contained in his public addresses. The book is divisible into two parts, viz. ch. i.–iii. and iv.–xiv., which give the kernel of his prophetic labours, the one in a more condensed, and the other in a more elaborate form. In the *first* part, which contains the " beginning of the word of

---

[1] Jerome says of him, " *commaticus est et quasi per sententias loquens;* " and Ewald discovers in his style " a kernel-like fulness of language, and, notwithstanding many strong figures, which indicate not only poetical boldness and originality but also the tolerably upright thought of those times, a very great tenderness and warmth of language." His diction is distinguished by many peculiar words and forms, such as נַאֲפוּפִים (ch. ii. 4), אָהֲבוּ הֵבוּ (ch. iv. 18), נֵהָה (ch. v. 13), שַׁעֲרִירִיָה (ch. vi. 10), הַבְהָבִים (ch. viii. 13), תַּלְאוּבֹת (ch. xiii. 5) ; and by peculiar constructions, such as לֹא עָל (ch. vii. 16), אֶל-עָל (ch. xi. 7), מְרִיבֵי כֹהֵן (ch. iv. 4), and many others.

Jehovah by Hosea" (ch. i. 2), the prophet first of all describes, in the symbolical form of a marriage, contracted by the command of God with an adulterous woman, the spiritual adultery of the ten tribes of Israel, *i.e.* their falling away from Jehovah into idolatry, together with its consequences,—namely, the rejection of the rebellious tribes by the Lord, and their eventual return to God, and restoration to favour (ch. i. 2, ii. 3). He then announces, in simple prophetic words, not only the chastisements and punishments that will come from God, and bring the people to a knowledge of the ruinous consequences of their departure from God, but also the manifestations of mercy by which the Lord will secure the true conversion of those who are humbled by suffering, and their eventual blessedness through the conclusion of a covenant founded in righteousness and grace (ch. ii. 4–25); and this attitude on the part of God towards His people is then confirmed by a symbolical picture in ch. iii.

In the second part, these truths are expanded in a still more elaborate manner; but the condemnation of the idolatry and moral corruption of Israel, and the announcement of the destruction of the kingdom of the ten tribes, predominate,—the saving prediction of the eventual restoration and blessedness of those, who come to the consciousness of the depth of their own fall, being but briefly touched upon. This part, again, cannot be divided into separate addresses, as there is an entire absence of all reliable indices, just as in the last part of Isaiah (ch. xl.–lxvi.); but, like the latter, it falls into three large, unequal sections, in each of which the prophetic address advances from an accusation of the nation generally and in its several ranks, to a description of the coming punishment, and finishes up with the prospect of the ultimate rescue of the punished nation. At the same time, an evident progress is discernible in the three, not indeed of the kind supposed by Ewald, namely, that the address contained in ch. iv.–ix. 9 advances from the accusation itself to the contemplation of the punishment proved to be necessary, and then rises through further retrospective glances at the better days of old, at the destination of the church, and at the everlasting love, to brighter prospects and the firmest hopes; nor in that proposed by De Wette, viz. that the wrath becomes more and more threatening from ch. viii. onwards, and the destruction of Israel comes out more and more clearly before the reader's eye. The relation in which the three sections stand to one another is rather the following: In the first, ch. iv.–vi. 3, the religious and moral degradation of Israel is exhibited in all its magnitude, together with the judgment which follows upon the heels of this corruption; and at the close the conversion and salvation aimed at in this judgment are briefly indicated. In the second and much longer section, ch. vi. 4–xi. 11, the incorrigibility of the sinful nation, or the obstinate persistence of Israel in idolatry and unrighteousness, in spite of the warnings and chastisements of God, is first exposed and condemned (ch. vi. 4–vii. 16); then, secondly, the judgment to which they are liable is elaborately announced as both inevitable and terrible (ch. viii. 1–ix. 9); and thirdly, by pointing out the unfaithfulness which Israel has displayed towards its God from the very earliest times, the prophet shows that it has deserved nothing but destruction from off the face of the earth (ix. 10–xi. 8), and that it is only the mercy of God which will restrain the wrath, and render the restoration of Israel possible (ch. xi. 9–11). In the third section (ch. xii.–xiv.) the ripeness of Israel for judgment is confirmed by proofs drawn from its falling into Canaanitish ways, notwithstanding the long-suffering, love, and fidelity with which God has always shown Himself to be its helper and redeemer (ch. xii. xiii.). To this there is appended a solemn appeal to return to the Lord; and the whole concludes with a promise, that the faithful covenant God will display the fulness of His love again to those who return to Him with a sincere confession of their guilt, and will pour upon them the riches of His blessing (ch. xiv.).

This division of the book differs, indeed, from all the attempts that have previously been made; but it has the warrant of its correctness in the three times repeated promise (vi. 1–3, xi. 9–11, and xiv. 2–9), by which each of the supposed sections is rounded off. And within these sections we also meet with pauses, by which they are broken up into smaller groups, resembling strophes, although this further grouping of the prophet's words is not formed into uniform strophes.[1] For further remarks on this point, see the Exposition.

[1] All attempts that have been made to break up the book into different prophecies, belonging to different periods, are wrecked upon the contents

From what has been said, it clearly follows that Hosea himself wrote out the quintessence of his prophecies, as a witness of the Lord against the degenerate nation, at the close of his prophetic career, and in the book which bears his name. The preservation of this book, on the destruction of the kingdom of the ten tribes, may be explained very simply from the fact that, on account of the intercourse carried on between the prophets of the Lord in the two kingdoms, it found its way to Judah soon after the time of its composition, and was there spread abroad in the circle of the prophets, and so preserved. We find, for example, that Jeremiah has used it again and again in his prophecies (compare Aug. Kueper, *Jeremias librorum ss. interpres atque vindex.* Berol. 1837, p. 67 seq.). For the exegetical writings on Hosea, see my *Lehrbuch der Einleitung,* p. 275.

EXPOSITION.

I. ISRAEL'S ADULTERY.—CHAP. I.-III.

On the ground of the relation hinted at even in the Pentateuch (Ex. xxxiv. 15, 16; Lev. xvii. 7, xx. 5, 6; Num. xiv. 33; Deut. xxxii. 16–21), and still further developed in the Song of Solomon and Ps. xlv., where the gracious bond existing between the Lord and the nation of His choice is represented under the figure of a marriage, which Jehovah had contracted with Israel, the falling away of the ten tribes of Israel from Jehovah into idolatry is exhibited as whoredom and adultery, in the following manner. In the *first* section (i. 2–ii. 3), God commands the prophet to marry a wife of whoredoms with children of whoredoms, and gives names to the children born to the prophet by this wife, which indicate the fruits of idolatry,

of the book itself; single sections being obliged to be made into prophetic addresses, or declared to be such, and the period of their origin being merely determined by arbitrary conjectures and assumptions, or by fanciful interpretations, *e.g.* as that of the *chōdesh*, or new moon, in ch. v. 7, which is supposed to refer to the reign of Shallum, who only reigned one month.

viz. the rejection and putting away of Israel on the part of God (ch. i. 2–9), with the appended promise of the eventual restoration to favour of the nation thus put away (ch. ii. 1–3). In the *second* section (ch. ii. 4–25), the Lord announces that He will put an end to the whoredom, *i.e.* to the idolatry of Israel, and by means of judgments will awaken in it a longing to return to Him (vers. 4–15), that He will thereupon lead the people once more through the wilderness, and, by the renewal of His covenant mercies and blessings, will betroth Himself to it for ever in righteousness, mercy, and truth (vers. 16–25). In the *third* section (ch. iii.) the prophet is commanded to love once more a wife beloved of her husband, but one who had committed adultery; and after having secured her, to put her into such a position that it will be impossible for her to carry on her whoredom any longer. And the explanation given is, that the Israelites will sit for a long time without a king, without sacrifice, and without divine worship, but that they will afterwards return, will seek Jehovah their God, and David their king, and will rejoice in the goodness of the Lord at the end of the days. Consequently the falling away of the ten tribes from the Lord, their expulsion into exile, and the restoration of those who come to a knowledge of their sin—in other words, the guilt and punishment of Israel, and its restoration to favour—form the common theme of all three sections, and that in the following manner : In the first, the sin, the punishment, and the eventual restoration of Israel, are depicted symbolically in all their magnitude; in the second, the guilt and punishment, and also the restoration and renewal of the relation of grace, are still further explained in simple prophetic words; whilst in the third, this announcement is visibly set forth in a new symbolical act.

In both the first and third sections, the prophet's announcement is embodied in a symbolical act; and the question arises here, Whether the marriage of the prophet with an adulterous woman, which is twice commanded by God, is to be regarded as a marriage that was actually consummated, or merely as an internal occurrence, or as a parabolical representation.[1] The

[1] Compare on this point the fuller discussion of the question by John Marck, *Diatribe de muliere fornicationum*, Lugd. B. 1696, reprinted in his *Comment. in 12 proph. min.*, ed. Pfaff. 1734, p. 214 sqq. ; and Hengsten-

supporters of a marriage outwardly consummated lay the principal stress upon the simple words of the text. The words of ver. 2, "Go, take unto thee a wife of whoredoms," and of ver. 3, "So he went and took Gomer . . . which conceived," etc., are so definite and so free from ambiguity, that it is impossible, they think, to take them with a good conscience in any other sense than an outward and historical one. But since even Kurtz, who has thrown the argument into this form, feels obliged to admit, with reference to some of the symbolical actions of the prophets, *e.g.* Jer. xxv. 15 sqq. and Zech. xi., that they were not actually and outwardly performed, it is obvious that the mere words are not sufficient of themselves to decide the question *à priori*, whether such an action took place in the objective outer world, or only inwardly, in the spiritual intuition of the prophet himself.[1] The reference to Isa. vii. 3, and viii. 3, 4, as analogous cases, does apparently strengthen the conclusion that the occurrence was an outward one; but on closer exami-

---

berg's *Christology*, i. p. 177 sqq., translation, in which, after a historical survey of the different views that have been expressed, he defends the opinion that the occurrence was real, but not outward; whilst Kurtz (*Die Ehe des Propheten Hosea*, 1859) has entered the lists in defence of the assumption that it was a marriage actually and outwardly consummated.

[1] It is true that Kurtz endeavours to deprive this concession of all its force, by setting up the canon, that of all the symbolical actions of the prophets the following alone cannot be interpreted as implying either an outward performance or outward experience; viz. (1) those in which the narration itself expressly indicates a visionary basis or a parabolical fiction, and (2) those in which the thing described is physically impossible without the intervention of a miracle. But apart from the arbitrary nature of this second canon, which is apparent from the fact that the prophets both performed and experienced miracles, the symbolical actions recorded in Jer. xxv. and Zech. xi. do not fall under either the first or second of these canons. Such a journey as the one which Jeremiah is commanded to take (Jer. xxv.), viz. to the kings of Egypt, of the Philistines, the Phœnicians, the Arabians, the Edomites, the Ammonites, the Syrians, of Media, Elam, and Babylon, cannot be pronounced an absolute impossibility, however improbable it may be. Still less can the taking of two shepherds' staves, to which the prophet gives the symbolical names Beauty and Bands, or the slaying of three wicked shepherds in one month (Zech. xi.), be said to be physically impossible, notwithstanding the assertion of Kurtz, in which he twists the fact so clearly expressed in the biblical text, viz. that "a staff Beauty does not lie within the sphere of physically outward existence, any more than a staff Bands."

nation, the similarity between the two passages in Isaiah and the one under consideration is outweighed by the differences that exist between them. It is true that Isaiah gave his two sons names with symbolical meanings, and that in all probability by divine command; but nothing is said about his having married his wife by the command of God, nor is the birth of the first-named son ever mentioned at all. Consequently, all that can be inferred from Isaiah is, that the symbolical names of the children of the prophet Hosea furnish no evidence against the outward reality of the marriage in question. Again, the objection, that the command to marry a wife of whoredoms, if understood as referring to an outward act, would be opposed to the divine holiness, and the divine command, that priests should not marry a harlot, cannot be taken as decisive. For what applied to priests cannot be transferred without reserve to prophets; and the remark, which is quite correct in itself, that God as the Holy One could not command an immoral act, does not touch the case, but simply rests upon a misapprehension of the divine command, viz. upon the idea that God commanded the prophet to beget children with an immoral person without a lawful marriage, or that the " children of whoredom," whom Hosea was to take along with the " wife of whoredom," were the three children whom she bare to him (Hos. i. 3, 6, 8); in which case either the children begotten by the prophet are designated as " children of whoredom," or the wife continued her adulterous habits even after the prophet had married her, and bare to the prophet illegitimate children. But neither of these assumptions has any foundation in the text. The divine command, " Take thee a wife of whoredom, and children of whoredom," neither implies that the wife whom the prophet was to marry was living at that time in virgin chastity, and was called a wife of whoredom simply to indicate that, as the prophet's lawful wife, she would fall into adultery; nor even that the children of whoredom whom the prophet was to take along with the wife of whoredom are the three children whose birth is recorded in ch. i. 3, 6, 8. The meaning is rather that the prophet is to take, along with the wife, the children whom she already had, and whom she had born as a harlot before her marriage with the prophet. If, therefore, we assume that the prophet was commanded to take this woman and her children, for the purpose, as Jerome has explained it, of rescuing the woman from her sinful course, and bringing up her neglected children under paternal discipline and care; such a command as this would be by no means at variance with the holiness of God, but would rather correspond to the compassionate love of God, which accepts the lost sinner, and seeks to save him. And, as Kurtz has well shown, it cannot be objected to this, that by such a command and the prophet's obedience on his first entering upon his office, all the beneficial effects of that office would inevitably be frustrated. For if it were a well-known fact, that the woman whom the prophet married had hitherto been leading a profligate life, and if the prophet declared freely and openly that he had taken her as his wife for that very reason, and with this intention, according to the command of God; the marriage, the shame of which the prophet had taken upon himself in obedience to the command of God, and in self-denying love to his people, would be a practical and constant sermon to the nation, which might rather promote than hinder the carrying out of his official work. For he did with this woman what Jehovah was doing with Israel, to reveal to the nation its own sin in so impressive a manner, that it could not fail to recognise it in all its glaring and damnable character. But however satisfactorily the divine command could be vindicated on the supposition that this was its design, we cannot found any argument upon this in favour of the outward reality of the prophet's marriage, for the simple reason that the supposed object is neither expressed nor hinted at in the text. According to the distinct meaning of the words, the prophet was to take a "wife of whoredom," for the simple purpose of begetting children by her, whose significant names were to set before the people the disastrous fruits of their spiritual whoredom. The behaviour of the woman after the marriage is no more the point in question than the children of whoredom whom the prophet was to take along with the woman; whereas this is what we should necessarily expect, if the object of the marriage commanded had been the reformation of the woman herself and of her illegitimate children. The very fact that, according to the distinct meaning of the words, there was no other object for the marriage than to beget children, who should receive significant names, renders the assumption of a real marriage, *i.e.* of a marriage outwardly contracted and consummated, very improbable.

And this supposition becomes absolutely untenable in the case of ch. iii., where Jehovah says to the prophet (ver. 1), " Go again, love a woman beloved by the husband, and committing adultery ;" and the prophet, in order to fulfil the divine command, purchases the woman for a certain price (ver. 2). The indefinite expression *'isshâh*, a wife, instead of thy wife, or at any rate the wife, and still more the purchase of the woman, are quite sufficient of themselves to overthrow the opinion, that the prophet is here directed to seek out once more his former wife Gomer, who has been unfaithful, and has run away, and to be reconciled to her again. Ewald therefore observes, and Kurtz supports the assertion, that the pronoun in " I bought *her* to me," according to the simple meaning of the words, cannot refer to any adulteress you please who had left her husband, but must refer to one already known, and therefore points back to ch. i. But with such paralogisms as these we may insert all kinds of things in the text of Scripture. The suffix in וָאֶכְּרֶהָ, " I bought *her*" (ver. 2), simply refers to the " woman beloved of her friend" mentioned in ver. 1, and does not prove in the remotest degree, that the " woman beloved of her friend, yet an adulteress," is the same person as the Gomer mentioned in ch. i. The indefiniteness of *'isshâh* without the article, is neither removed by the fact that, in the further course of the narrative, this (indefinite) woman is referred to again, nor by the examples adduced by Kurtz, viz. יִקַּח־לֵב in ch. iv. 11, and הָלַךְ אַחֲרֵי־צָו in ch. v. 11, since any linguist knows that these are examples of a totally different kind. The perfectly indefinite אִשָּׁה receives, no doubt, a more precise definition from the predicates אֲהֻבַת רֵעַ וּמְנָאָפֶת, so that we cannot understand it as meaning any adulteress whatever ; but it receives no such definition as would refer back to ch. i. A woman beloved of her friend, *i.e.* of her husband, and committing adultery, is a woman who, although beloved by her husband, or notwithstanding the love shown to her by her husband, commits adultery. Through the participles אֲהֻבַת and מְנָאָפֶת, the love of the friend (or husband), and the adultery of the wife, are represented as contemporaneous, in precisely the same manner as in the explanatory clauses which follow : " as

Jehovah loveth the children of Israel, and they turn to other
gods!" If the *'isshâh* thus defined had been the *Gomer* mentioned in ch. i., the divine command would necessarily have
been thus expressed : either, " Go, and love again the wife
beloved by her husband, who has committed adultery ;" or,
" Love again thy wife, who is still loved by her husband,
although she has committed adultery." But it is quite as evident that this thought cannot be contained in the words of the
text, as that out of two co-ordinate participles it is impossible
that the one should have the force of the future or present, and
the other that of the pluperfect. Nevertheless, Kurtz has
undertaken to prove the possibility of the impossible. He
observes, first of all, that we are not justified, of course, in
giving to " love" the meaning " love again," as Hofmann does,
because the husband has never ceased to love his wife, in spite
of her adultery ; but for all that, the explanation, *restitue
amoris signa* (restore the pledges of affection), is the only
intelligible one ; since it cannot be the love itself, but only the
manifestation of love, that is here referred to. But the idea
of " again" cannot be smuggled into the text by any such
arbitrary distinction as this. There is nothing in the text to
the effect that the husband had not ceased to love his wife, in
spite of her adultery ; and this is simply an inference drawn
from ch. ii. 11, through the identification of the prophet with
Jehovah, and the tacit assumption that the prophet had withdrawn from Gomer the expressions of his love, of all which
there is not a single syllable in ch. i. This assumption, and
the inference drawn from it, would only be admissible, if the
identity of the woman, beloved by her husband and committing
adultery, with the prophet's wife Gomer, were an established
fact. But so long as this is not proved, the argument merely
moves in a circle, assuming the thing to be demonstrated as
already proved. But even granting that " love" were equivalent to " love again," or " manifest thy love again to a woman
beloved of her husband, and committing adultery," this could
not mean the same thing as " go to thy former wife, and prove
to her by word and deed the continuance of thy love," so long
as, according to the simplest rules of logic, " a wife" is not
equivalent to " thy wife." And according to sound logical
rules, the identity of the *'isshâh* in ch. iii. 1 and the *Gomer* of

ch. i. 3 cannot be inferred from the fact that the expression used in ch. iii. 1 is, " Go love a woman," and not " Go take a wife," or from the fact that in ch. i. 2 the woman is simply called a whore, not an adulteress, whereas in ch. iii. 1 she is described as an adulteress, not as a whore. The words " love a woman," as distinguished from " take a wife," may indeed be understood, apart from the connection with ver. 2, as implying that the conclusion of a marriage is alluded to ; but they can never denote " the restoration of a marriage bond that had existed before," as Kurtz supposes. And the distinction between ch. i. 2, where the woman is described as " a woman of whoredom," and ch. iii. 1, where she is called " an adulteress," points far more to a distinction between Gomer and the adulterous woman, than to their identity.

But ch. iii. 2, " I bought her to me for fifteen pieces of silver," etc., points even more than ch. iii. 1 to a difference between the women in ch. i. and ch. iii. The verb *kârâh*, to purchase or acquire by trading, presupposes that the woman had not yet been in the prophet's possession. The only way in which Kurtz is able to evade this conclusion, is by taking the fifteen pieces of silver mentioned in ver. 2, not as the price paid by the prophet to purchase the woman as his wife, but in total disregard of וָאֹמַר אֵלֶיהָ, in ch. iii. 3, as the cost of her maintenance, which the prophet gave to the woman for the period of her detention, during which she was to sit, and not go with any man. But the arbitrary nature of this explanation is apparent at once. According to the reading of the words, the prophet bought the woman to himself for fifteen pieces of silver and an ephah and a half of barley, *i.e.* bought her to be his wife, and then said to her, " Thou shalt sit for me many days ; thou shalt not play the harlot," etc. There is not only not a word in ch. iii. about his having assigned her the amount stated for her maintenance ; but it cannot be inferred from ch. ii. 9, 11, because there it is not the prophet's wife who is referred to, but Israel personified as a harlot and adulteress. And that what is there affirmed concerning Israel cannot be applied without reserve to explain the symbolical description in ch. iii., is evident from the simple fact, that the conduct of Jehovah towards Israel is very differently described in ch. ii., from the course which the prophet is said to have observed towards his wife in ch. iii. 3.

In ch. ii. 7, the adulterous woman (Israel) says, " I will go and return to my former husband, for then was it better with me than now ;" and Jehovah replies to this (ch. ii. 8, 9), "Because she has not discovered that I gave her corn and new wine, etc.; therefore will I return, and take away my corn from her in the season thereof, and my wine," etc. On the other hand, according to the view adopted by Kurtz, the prophet took his wife back again because she felt remorse, and assigned her the necessary maintenance for many days.

From all this it follows, that by the woman spoken of in ch. iii., we cannot understand the wife Gomer mentioned in ch. i. The " wife beloved of the companion (*i.e.* of her husband), and committing adultery," is a different person from the daughter of Diblathaim, by whom the prophet had three children (ch. i.). If, then, the prophet really contracted and consummated the marriage commanded by God, we must adopt the explanation already favoured by the earlier commentators, viz. that in the interval between ch. i. and ch. iii. Gomer had either died, or been put away by her husband because she would not repent. But we are only warranted in adopting such a solution as this, provided that the assumption of a marriage consummated outwardly either has been or can be conclusively established. And as this is not the case, we are not at liberty to supply things at which the text does not even remotely hint. If, then, in accordance with the text, we must understand the divine commands in ch. i. and iii. as relating to two successive marriages on the part of the prophet with unchaste women, every probability is swept away that the command of God and its execution by the prophet fall within the sphere of external reality. For even if, in case of need, the first command, as explained above, could be vindicated as worthy of God, the same vindication would not apply to the command to contract a second marriage of a similar kind. The very end which God is supposed to have had in view in the command to contract such a marriage as this, could only be attained by *one* marriage. But if Hosea had no sooner dissolved the first marriage, than he proceeded to conclude a second with a person in still worse odour, no one would ever have believed that he did this also in obedience to the command of God. And the divine command itself to contract this second marriage, if it was

intended to be actually consummated, would be quite irreconcilable with the holiness of God. For even if God could command a man to marry a harlot, for the purpose of rescuing her
from her life of sin and reforming her, it would certainly be
at variance with the divine holiness, to command the prophet
to marry a person who had either broken the marriage vow
already, or who would break it, notwithstanding her husband's
love; since God, as the Holy One, cannot possibly sanction
adultery.[1] Consequently no other course is left to us, than to
picture to ourselves Hosea's marriages as internal events, *i.e.*
as merely carried out in that inward and spiritual intuition in
which the word of God was addressed to him; and this removes
all the difficulties that beset the assumption of marriages contracted in outward reality. In occurrences which merely happened to a prophet in spiritual intercourse with God, not only
would all reflections as to their being worthy or not worthy of
God be absent, when the prophet related them to the people,
for the purpose of impressing their meaning upon their hearts,
inasmuch as it was simply their significance, which came into
consideration and was to be laid to heart; but this would also
be the case with the other difficulties to which the external view
is exposed—such, for example, as the questions, why the prophet
was to take not only a woman of whoredom, but children of
whoredom also, when they are never referred to again in the
course of the narrative; or what became of Gomer, whether
she was dead, or had been put away, when the prophet was
commanded the second time to love an adulterous woman—since
the sign falls back behind the thing signified.

But if, according to this, we must regard the marriages

---

[1] This objection to the outward consummation of the prophet's marriage
cannot be deprived of its force by the remark made by the older Rivetus,
to the effect that " things which are dishonourable in themselves, cannot
be honourable in vision, or when merely imaginary." For there is an
essential difference between a merely symbolical representation, and the
actual performance of anything. The instruction given to a prophet to
set forth a sin in a symbolical form, for the purpose of impressing upon
the hearts of the people its abominable character, and the punishment it
deserved, is not at variance with the holiness of God; whereas the command to commit a sin would be. God, as the Holy One, cannot abolish
the laws of morality, or command anything actually immoral, without
contradicting Himself, or denying His own nature.

enjoined upon the prophet as simply facts of inward experience, which took place in his own spiritual intuition, we must not set them down as nothing more than parables which he related to the people, or as poetical fictions, since such assumptions as these are at variance with the words themselves, and reduce the statement, " God said to Hosea," to an unmeaning rhetorical phrase. The inward experience has quite as much reality and truth as the outward; whereas a parable or a poetical fiction has simply a certain truth, so far as the subjective imagination is concerned, but no reality.

Ch. i. 1 contains the *heading* to the whole of the book of Hosea, the contents of which have already been discussed in the Introduction, and defended against the objections that have been raised, so that there is no tenable ground for refusing to admit its integrity and genuineness. The *t*e*chillath dibber-Y*e*hōvâh* with which ver. 2 introduces the prophecy, necessarily presupposes a heading announcing the period of the prophet's ministry; and the " twisted, un-Hebrew expression," which Hitzig properly finds to be so objectionable in the translation, " in the days of Jeroboam, etc., was the commencement of Jehovah's speaking," etc., does not prove that the heading is spurious, but simply that Hitzig's construction is false, *i.e.* that *t*e*chillath dibber-Y*e*hōvâh* is not in apposition to ver. 1, but the heading in ver. 1 contains an independent statement; whilst the notice as to time, with which ver. 2 opens, does not belong to the heading of the whole book, but simply to the prophecy which follows in ch. i.–iii.

ISRAEL THE ADULTERESS, AND HER CHILDREN.—CHAP. I.
2–II. 3.

For the purpose of depicting before the eyes of the sinful people the judgment to which Israel has exposed itself through its apostasy from the Lord, Hosea is to marry a prostitute, and beget children by her, whose names are so appointed by Jehovah as to point out the evil fruits of the departure from God. Ver. 2. " *At first, when Jehovah spake to Hosea, Jehovah said to him, Go, take thee a wife of whoredom, and children of whoredom; for whoring the land whoreth away from Jehovah.*" The marriage which the prophet is commanded to contract, is to

set forth the fact that the kingdom of Israel has fallen away
from the Lord its God, and is sunken in idolatry. Hosea is to
commence his prophetic labours by exhibiting this fact. תְּחִלַּת
דִּבֶּר יְיָ': literally, "at the commencement of 'Jehovah spake,'"
i.e. at the commencement of Jehovah's speaking (*dibber* is not
an infinitive, but a perfect, and *t^echillath* an accusative of time
(Ges. § 118, 2); and through the constructive the following
clause is subordinated to *t^echillath* as a substantive idea: see
Ges. § 123, 3, Anm. 1; Ewald, § 332, *c*.). דִּבֶּר with בְּ, not to
speak to a person, or through any one (בְּ is not = אֶל), but
to speak with (lit. in) a person, expressive of the inwardness
or urgency of the speaking (cf. Num. xii. 6, 8; Hab. ii. 1;
Zech. i. 9, etc.). "Take to thyself:" *i.e.* marry (a wife).
אֵשֶׁת זְנוּנִים is stronger than זוֹנָה. A woman of whoredom, is a
woman whose business or means of livelihood consists in prostitution. Along with the woman, Hosea is to take children of
prostitution as well. The meaning of this is, of course, not
that he is first of all to take the woman, and then beget children of prostitution by her, which would require that the two
objects should be connected with קַח *per zeugma*, in the sense of
"*accipe uxorem et suscipe ex ea liberos*" (Drus.), or "*sume tibi
uxorem forn. et fac tibi filios forn.*" (Vulg.). The children begotten by the prophet from a married harlot-wife, could not be
called *yaldē z^enūnīm*, since they were not illegitimate children,
but legitimate children of the prophet himself; nor is the
assumption, that the three children born by the woman, according to vers. 3, 6, 8, were born in adultery, and that the
prophet was not their father, in harmony with ver. 3, "he took
Gomer, and she conceived and bare him a son." Nor can this
mode of escaping from the difficulty, which is quite at variance
with the text, be vindicated by an appeal to the connection
between the figure and the fact. For though this connection
"necessarily requires that both the children and the mother
should stand in the same relation of estrangement from the
lawful husband and father," as Hengstenberg argues; it
neither requires that we should assume that the mother had
been a chaste virgin before her marriage to the prophet, nor
that the children whom she bare to her husband were begotten
in adultery, and merely palmed off upon the prophet as his
own. The marriage which the prophet was to contract, was

simply intended to symbolize the relation already existing between Jehovah and Israel, and not the way in which it had
come into existence.   The "wife of whoredoms" does not represent the nation of Israel in its virgin state at the conclusion
of the covenant at Sinai, but the nation of the ten tribes in its
relation to Jehovah at the time of the prophet himself, when
the nation, considered as a whole, had become a wife of whoredom, and in its several members resembled children of whoredom. The reference to the children of whoredom, along with
the wife of whoredom, indicates unquestionably *à priori*, that
the divine command did not contemplate an actual and outward marriage, but simply a symbolical representation of the
relation in which the idolatrous Israelites were then standing to
the Lord their God.   The explanatory clause, "for the land
whoreth," etc., clearly points to this. הָאָרֶץ, "the land," for the
population of the land (cf. ch. iv. 1). זָנֹה מֵאַחֲרֵי יי, to whore
from Jehovah, *i.e.* to fall away from Him (see at ch. iv. 12).

Ver. 3. *"And he went and took Gomer, the daughter of
Diblaim; and she conceived, and bare him a son."*   *Gomer* does
indeed occur in Gen. x. 2, 3, as the name of a people; but we
never meet with it as the name of either a man or a woman,
and judging from the analogy of the names of her children,
it is chosen with reference to the meaning of the word itself.
Gomer signifies perfection, completion in a passive sense, and
is not meant to indicate destruction or death (Chald. Marck),
but the fact that the woman was thoroughly perfected in her
whoredom, or that she had gone to the furthest length in prostitution.   *Diblaim,* also, does not occur again as a proper name,
except in the names of Moabitish places in Num. xxxiii. 46
('*Almon-diblathaim*) and Jer. xlviii. 22 (*Beth-diblathaim*); it is
formed from *dᵉbhēlâh,* like the form 'Ephraim, and in the sense
of *dᵉbhēlīm,* fig-cakes. "Daughter of fig-cakes," equivalent to
liking fig-cakes, in the same sense as "loving grape-cakes" in
ch. iii. 1, viz. *deliciis dedita.*[1]   The symbolical interpretation of
these names is not affected by the fact that they are not explained, like those of the children in vers. 4 sqq., since this

---

[1] This is essentially the interpretation given by Jerome : "Therefore is
a wife taken out of Israel by Hosea, as the type of the Lord and Saviour,
viz. one accomplished in fornication, and a perfect *daughter of pleasure*
(*filia voluptatis*), which seems so sweet and pleasant to those who enjoy it."

may be accounted for very simply from the circumstance, that the woman does not now receive the names for the first time, but that she had them at the time when the prophet married her.

Ver. 4. *"And Jehovah said to him, Call his name Jezreel; for yet a little, and I visit the blood of Jezreel upon the house of Jehu, and put an end to the kingdom of the house of Israel."* The prophet is directed by God as to the names to be given to his children, because the children, as the fruit of the marriage, as well as the marriage itself, are instructive signs for the idolatrous Israel of the ten tribes. The first son is named *Jezreel*, after the fruitful plain of Jezreel on the north side of the Kishon (see at Josh. xvii. 16); not, however, with any reference to the appellative meaning of the name, viz. " God sows," which is first of all alluded to in the announcement of salvation in ch. ii. 24, 25, but, as the explanation which follows clearly shows, on account of the historical importance which this plain possessed for Israel, and that not merely as the place where the last penal judgment of God was executed in the kingdom of Israel, as Hengstenberg supposes, but on account of the blood-guiltiness of Jezreel, *i.e.* because Israel had there contracted such blood-guiltiness as was now speedily to be avenged upon the house of Jehu. At the city of *Jezreel*, which stood in this plain, Ahab had previously filled up the measure of his sin by the ruthless murder of Naboth, and had thus brought upon himself that blood-guiltiness for which he had been threatened with the extermination of all his house (1 Kings xxi. 19 sqq.). Then, in order to avenge the blood of all His servants the prophets, which Ahab and Jezebel had shed, the Lord directed Elisha to anoint Jehu king, with a commission to destroy the whole of Ahab's house (2 Kings ix. 1 sqq.). Jehu obeyed this command. Not only did he slay the son of Ahab, viz. king Joram, and cause his body to be thrown upon the portion of land belonging to Naboth the Jezreelite, appealing at the same time to the word of the Lord (2 Kings ix. 21–26), but he also executed the divine judgment upon Jezebel, upon the seventy sons of Ahab, and upon all the rest of the house of Ahab (ch. ix. 30–x. 17), and received the following promise from Jehovah in consequence : "Because thou hast done well in executing that which is right in mine eyes, because thou hast done to the house of Ahab according to all that was in mine heart, sons of thine of the fourth generation shall sit upon the throne of Israel" (ch. x. 30). It is evident from this that the blood-guiltiness of Jezreel, which was to be avenged upon the house of Jehu, is not to be sought for in the fact that Jehu had there exterminated the house of Ahab; nor, as Hitzig supposes, in the fact that he had not contented himself with slaying Joram and Jezebel, but had also put Ahaziah of Judah and his brethren to death (2 Kings ix. 27, x. 14), and directed the massacre described in ch. x. 11. For an act which God praises, and for which He gives a promise to the performer, cannot be in itself an act of blood-guiltiness. And the slaughter of Ahaziah and his brethren by Jehu, though not expressly commanded, is not actually blamed in the historical account, because the royal family of Judah had been drawn into the ungodliness of the house of Ahab, through its connection by marriage with that dynasty; and Ahaziah and his brethren, as the sons of Athaliah, a daughter of Ahab, belonged both in descent and disposition to the house of Ahab (2 Kings viii. 18, 26, 27), so that, according to divine appointment, they were to perish with it. Many expositors, therefore, understand by "the blood of Jezreel," simply the many acts of unrighteousness and cruelty which the descendants of Jehu had committed in Jezreel, or "the grievous sins of all kinds committed in the palace, the city, and the nation generally, which were to be expiated by blood, and demanded as it were the punishment of bloodshed" (Marck). But we have no warrant for generalizing the idea of $d^e m\bar{e}$ in this way; more especially as the assumption upon which the explanation is founded, viz. that Jezreel was the royal residence of the kings of the house of Jehu, not only cannot be sustained, but is at variance with 2 Kings xv. 8, 13, where Samaria is unquestionably described as the royal residence in the times of Jeroboam II. and his son Zechariah. The blood-guiltinesses ($d^e m\bar{e}$) at Jezreel can only be those which Jehu contracted at Jezreel, viz. the deeds of blood recorded in 2 Kings ix. and x., by which Jehu opened the way for himself to the throne, since there are no others mentioned. The apparent discrepancy, however, that whereas the extermination of the royal family of Ahab by Jehu is commended by God in the second book of Kings, and Jehu is promised the possession of

the throne even to the fourth generation of his sons in
consequence, in the passage before us the very same act is
charged against him as an act of blood-guiltiness that has to
be punished, may be solved very simply by distinguishing
between the act in itself, and the motive by which Jehu was
instigated. In itself, *i.e.* regarded as the fulfilment of the
divine command, the extermination of the family of Ahab was
an act by which Jehu could not render himself criminal. But
even things desired or commanded by God may become crimes in
the case of the performer of them, when he is not simply carrying out the Lord's will as the servant of God, but suffers himself to be actuated by evil and selfish motives, that is to say,
when he abuses the divine command, and makes it the mere
cloak for the lusts of his own evil heart. That Jehu was
actuated by such motives as this, is evident enough from the
verdict of the historian in 2 Kings x. 29, 31, that Jehu did
indeed exterminate Baal out of Israel, but that he did not
depart from the sins of Jeroboam the son of Nebat, from
the golden calves at Bethel and Dan, to walk in the law of
Jehovah the God of Israel with all his heart. " The massacre,
therefore," as Calvin has very correctly affirmed, " was a crime
so far as Jehu was concerned, but with God it was righteous
vengeance." Even if Jehu did not make use of the divine
command as a mere pretext for carrying out the plans of
his own ambitious heart, the massacre itself became an act
of blood-guiltiness that called for vengeance, from the fact
that he did not take heed to walk in the law of God with all
his heart, but continued the worship of the calves, that fundamental sin of all the kings of the ten tribes. For this reason,
the possession of the throne was only promised to him with a
restriction to sons of the fourth generation. On the other
hand, it is no argument against this, that " the act referred to
cannot be regarded as the chief crime of Jehu and his house,"
or that " the bloody act, to which the house of Jehu owed its
elevation, never appears elsewhere as the cause of the catastrophe which befell this house; but in the case of all the
members of his family, the only sin to which prominence is
given in the books of Kings, is that they did not depart from
the sins of Jeroboam (2 Kings xiii. 2, 11, xiv. 24, xv. 9)."
(Hengstenberg). For even though this sin in connection with

religion may be the only one mentioned in the books of Kings, according to the plan of the author of those books, and though this may really have been the principal act of sin; it was through that sin that the bloody deeds of Jehu became such a crime as cried to heaven for vengeance, like the sin of Ahab, and such an one also as Hosea could describe as the blood-guiltiness of Jezreel, which the Lord would avenge upon the house of Jehu at Jezreel, since the object in this case was not to enumerate all the sins of Israel, and the fact that the apostasy of the ten tribes, which is condemned in the book of Kings as the sin of Jeroboam, is represented here under the image of whoredom, shows very clearly that the evil root alone is indicated, out of which all the sins sprang that rendered the kingdom ripe for destruction. Consequently, it is not merely the fall of the existing dynasty which is threatened here, but also the suppression of the kingdom of Israel. The "kingdom of the house of Israel" is obviously not the sovereignty of the house of Jehu in Israel, but the regal sovereignty in Israel. And to this the Lord will put an end מְעַט, *i.e.* in a short time. The extermination of the house of Jehu occurred not long after the death of Jeroboam, when his son was murdered in connection with Shallum's conspiracy (2 Kings xv. 8 sqq.). And the strength of the kingdom was also paralyzed when the house of Jehu fell, although fifty years elapsed before its complete destruction. For of the five kings who followed Zechariah, only one, viz. Menahem, died a natural death, and was succeeded by his son. The rest were all dethroned and murdered by conspirators, so that the overthrow of the house of Jehu may very well be called "the beginning of the end, the commencement of the process of decomposition" (Hengstenberg: compare the remarks on 2 Kings xv. 10 sqq.).

Ver. 5. "*And it cometh to pass in that day, that I break in pieces the bow of Israel in the valley of Jezreel.*" The indication of time, "in that day," refers not to the overthrow of the house of Jehu, but to the breaking up of the kingdom of Israel, by which it was followed. The bow of Israel, *i.e.* its might (for the bow, as the principal weapon employed in war, is a synecdochical epithet, used to denote the whole of the military force upon which the continued existence of the kingdom depended (Jer. xlix. 35), and is also a symbol of strength generally; *vid.*

Gen. xlix. 24, 1 Sam. ii. 4), is to be broken to pieces in the valley of Jezreel. The paronomasia between Israel and Jezreel is here unmistakeable. And here again Jezreel is not introduced with any allusion to its appellative signification, *i.e.* so that the mention of the name itself is intended to indicate the dispersion or breaking up of the nation, but simply with reference to its natural character, as the great plain in which, from time immemorial, even down to the most recent period, all the great battles have been fought for the possession of the land (cf. v. Raumer, *Pal.* pp. 40, 41). The nation which the Lord had appointed to be the instrument of His judgment is not mentioned here. But the fulfilment shows that the Assyrians are intended, although the brief historical account given in the books of Kings does not notice the place in which the Assyrians gained the decisive victory over Israel; and the statement made by Jerome, to the effect that it was in the valley of Jezreel, is probably simply an inference drawn from this passage.

With the name of the first child, *Jezreel*, the prophet had, as it were with a single stroke, set before the king and the kingdom generally the destruction that awaited them. In order, however, to give further keenness to this threat, and cut off every hope of deliverance, he now announces two other births. Ver. 6. "*And she conceived again, and bare a daughter. And He (Jehovah) said to him, Call her name Unfavoured; for I will no more favour the house of Israel, that I should forgive them.*" The second birth is a female one, not in order to symbolize a more degenerate race, or the greater need of help on the part of the nation, but to get a name answering to the idea, and to set forth, under the figure of sons and daughters, the totality of the nation, both men and women. *Lŏ' ruchâmâh,* lit. she is not favoured; for *ruchâmâh* is hardly a participle with the מ dropped, since לֹא is never found in close connection with the participle (Ewald, § 320, *c.*), but rather the third pers. perf. fem. in the pausal form. The child receives this name to indicate that the Lord will not continue (אוֹסִיף) to show compassion towards the rebellious nation, as He hitherto has done, even under Jeroboam II. (2 Kings xiii. 23.) For the purpose of strengthening לֹא אֲרַחֵם, the clause כִּי נָשֹׂא וגו' is added. This can hardly be understood in any other way than in the sense of נָשֹׂא עָוֹן לְ, viz. to take away sin or guilt, *i.e.* to forgive it (cf.

Gen. xviii. 24, 26, etc.). The explanation, " I will take away from them, *sc.* everything" (Hengstenberg), has no tenable support in ch. v. 14, because there the object to be supplied is contained in the context, and here this is not the case.

Ver. 7. " *And I will favour the house of Judah, and save them through Jehovah their God; and I will not save them through bow, and sword, and war, through horses and through horsemen.*" By a reference to the opposite lot awaiting Judah, all false trust in the mercy of God is taken away from the Israelites. From the fact that deliverance is promised to the kingdom of Judah through Jehovah its God, Israel is to learn that Jehovah is no longer its own God, but that He has dissolved His covenant with the idolatrous race. The expression, " through Jehovah their God," instead of the pronoun " through me" (as, for example, in Gen. xix. 24), is introduced with special emphasis, to show that Jehovah only extends His almighty help to those who acknowledge and worship Him as their God.[1] And what follows, viz. " I will not save them by bow," etc., also serves to sharpen the punishment with which the Israelites are threatened; for it not only implies that the Lord does not stand in need of weapons of war and military force, in order to help and save, but that these earthly resources, on which Israel relied (ch. x. 13), could afford no defence or deliverance from the enemies who would come upon it. *Milchâmâh,* " war," in connection with bow and sword, does not stand for weapons of war, but " embraces everything belonging to war—the skill of the commanders, the bravery of heroes, the strength of the army itself, and so forth" (Hengstenberg). Horses and horsemen are specially mentioned, because they constituted the main strength of an army at that time. Lastly, whilst the threat against Israel, and the promise made to Judah, refer primarily, as ch. ii. 1–3 clearly show, to the time immediately approaching, when the judgment was to burst upon the kingdom of the ten tribes, that is to say, to that attack upon Israel and Judah on

---

[1] " The antithesis is to be preserved here between false gods and Jehovah, who was the God of the house of Judah. For it is just as if the prophet had said : Ye do indeed put forward the name of God ; but ye worship the devil, and not God. For ye have no part in Jehovah, *i.e.* in that God who is the Creator of heaven and earth. For He dwells in His temple ; He has bound up His faith with David," etc.—CALVIN.

the part of the imperial power of Assyria, to which Israel succumbed, whilst Judah was miraculously delivered (2 Kings xix.; Isa. xxxvii.); it has also a meaning which applies to all times, namely, that whoever forsakes the living God, will fall into destruction, and cannot reckon upon the mercy of God in the time of need.

Vers. 8, 9. " *And she weaned Unfavoured, and conceived, and bare a son. And He said, Call his name Not-my-people; for ye are not my people, and I will not be yours.*" If weaning is mentioned not merely for the sake of varying the expression, but with a deliberate meaning, it certainly cannot indicate the continued patience of God with the rebellious nation, as Calvin supposes, but rather implies the uninterrupted succession of the calamities set forth by the names of the children. As soon as the Lord ceases to compassionate the rebellious tribes, the state of rejection ensues, so that they are no longer " my people," and Jehovah belongs to them no more. In the last clause, the words pass with emphasis into the second person, or direct address, " I will not be to you," *i.e.* will no more belong to you (cf. Ps. cxviii. 6; Ex. xix. 5; Ezek. xvi. 8). We need not supply *Elohim* here, and we may not weaken לֹא אֶהְיֶה לָכֶם into " no more help you, or come to your aid." For the fulfilment, see 2 Kings xvii. 18.

Vers. 10, 11 (Heb. Bib. ch. ii. 1–3). To the symbolical action, which depicts the judgment that falls blow after blow upon the ten tribes, issuing in the destruction of the kingdom, and the banishment of its inhabitants, there is now appended, quite abruptly, the saving announcement of the final restoration of those who turn to the Lord.[1]

Ver. 10 (Heb. Bib. ch. ii. 1). " *And the number of the sons*

[1] The division adopted in the Hebrew text, where these verses are separated from the preceding ones, and joined to the next verse, is opposed to the general arrangement of the prophetic proclamations, which always begin with reproving the sins, then describe the punishment or judgment, and close with the announcement of salvation. The division adopted by the LXX. and Vulg., and followed by Luther (and Eng. ver.: TR.), in which these two verses form part of the first chapter, and the new chapter is made to commence with ver. 3 (of the Hebrew), on account of its similarity to ver. 4, is still more unsuitable, since this severs the close connection between the subject-matter of ver. 2 and that of ver. 3 in the most unnatural way.

of Israel will be as the sand of the sea, which is not measured and not counted; and it will come to pass at the place where men say to them, Ye are not my people, it will be said to them, Sons of the living God." It might appear as though the promise made to the patriarchs, of the innumerable increase of Israel, were abolished by the rejection of the ten tribes of Israel predicted here. But this appearance, which might confirm the ungodly in their false security, is met by the proclamation of salvation, which we must connect by means of a " nevertheless" with the preceding announcement of punishment. The almost verbal agreement between this announcement of salvation and the patriarchal promises, more especially in Gen. xxii. 17 and xxxii. 13, does indeed naturally suggest the idea, that by the " sons of Israel," whose innumerable increase is here predicted, we are to understand all the descendants of Jacob or of Israel as a whole. But if we notice the second clause, according to which those who are called " not-my-people" will then be called " sons of the living God;" and still more, if we observe the distinction drawn between the sons of Israel and the sons of Judah in ver. 11, this idea is proved to be quite untenable, since the " sons of Israel" can only be the ten tribes. We must assume, therefore, that the prophet had in his mind only one portion of the entire nation, namely, the one with which alone he was here concerned, and that he proclaims that, even with regard to this, the promise in question will one day be fulfilled. In what way, is stated in the second clause. At the place where (בִּמְקוֹם אֲשֶׁר does not mean " instead of" or " in the place of," as the Latin *loco* does; cf. Lev. iv. 24, 33 ; Jer. xxii. 12 ; Ezek. xxi. 35 ; Neh. iv. 14) men called them *Lŏ'-'ammī*, they shall be called sons of the living God. This place must be either Palestine, where their rejection was declared by means of this name, or the land of exile, where this name became an actual truth. The correctness of the latter view, which is the one given in the Chaldee, is proved by ver. 11, where their coming up out of the land of exile is spoken of, from which it is evident that the change is to take place in exile. Jehovah is called *El chai*, the living God, in opposition to the idols which idolatrous Israel had made for itself; and " sons of the living God" expresses the thought, that Israel would come again into the right relation to the true God, and reach the goal of its divine calling. For the whole nation was called and elevated into the position of sons of Jehovah, through its reception into the covenant with the Lord (compare Deut. xiv. 1, xxxii. 19, with Ex. iv. 22).

The restoration of Israel will be followed by its return to the Lord. Ver. 11. *" And the sons of Judah and the sons of Israel gather together, and appoint themselves one head, and come up out of the land; for great is the day of Jezreel."* The gathering together, *i.e.* the union of Judah and Israel, presupposes that Judah will find itself in the same situation as Israel; that is to say, that it will also be rejected by the Lord. The object of the union is to appoint themselves *one* head, and go up out of the land. The words of the two clauses recal to mind the departure of the twelve tribes of Israel out of Egypt. The expression, to appoint themselves a head, which resembles Num. xiv. 4, where the rebellious congregation is about to appoint itself a head to return to Egypt, points back to Moses; and the phrase, " going up out of the land," is borrowed from Ex. i. 10, which also serves to explain הָאָרֶץ with the definite article. The correctness of this view is placed beyond all doubt by ch. ii. 14, 15, where the restoration of rejected Israel is compared to leading it through the desert to Canaan; and a parallel is drawn between it and the leading up out of Egypt in the olden time. It is true that the banishment of the sons of Israel out of Canaan is not predicted *disertis verbis* in what precedes; but it followed as clearly as possible from the banishment into the land of their enemies, with which even Moses had threatened the people in the case of continued apostasy (Lev. xxvi. and Deut. xxviii.). Moses had, in fact, already described the banishment of rebellious Israel among the heathen in so many words, as carrying them back into Egypt (Deut. xxviii. 68), and had thereby intimated that Egypt was the type of the heathen world, in the midst of which Israel was to be scattered abroad. On the basis of these threatenings of the law, Hosea also threatens ungodly Ephraim with a return to Egypt in ch. viii. 13 and ch. ix. 3. And just as in these passages Egypt is a type of the heathen lands, into which Israel is to be driven away on account of its apostasy from the Lord; so, in the passage before us, Canaan, to which Israel is to be led up out of Egypt, is a type of the land of the Lord, and the guidance of them to Canaan a figurative representation of the reunion of

Israel with its God, and of its reinstatement in the full enjoyment of the blessings of salvation, which are shadowed forth
in the fruits and productions of Canaan. (For further remarks,
see vers. 14, 15.) Another point to be noticed is the use of
the word 'echâd, one (single) head, i.e. one prince or king. The
division of the nation into two kingdoms is to cease; and the
house of Israel is to turn again to Jehovah, and to its king
David (ch. iii. 5). The reason assigned for this promise, in the
words " for great is (will be) the day of Jezreel," causes no
little difficulty; and this cannot be removed by giving a different meaning to the name Jezreel, on the ground of vers. 24,
25, from that which it has in ch. i. 4, 5. The day of Jezreel
can only be the day on which the might of Israel was broken
in the valley of Jezreel, and the kingdom of the house of Israel
was brought to an end (ch. i. 4). This day is called great, i.e.
important, glorious, because of its effects and consequences in
relation to Israel. The destruction of the might of the ten
tribes, the cessation of their kingdom, and their expulsion into
exile, form the turning-point, through which the conversion of
the rebellious to the Lord, and their reunion with Judah, are
rendered possible. The appellative meaning of יִזְרְעֶאל, to which
there was no allusion at all in ch. i. 4, 5, is still kept in the
background to a great extent even here, and only so far slightly
hinted at, that in the results which follow to the nation, from
the judgment poured out upon Israel in Jezreel, the valley of
Jezreel becomes a place in which God sows seed for the renovation of Israel.

To confirm the certainty of this most joyful turn of events,
the promise closes with the summons in ch. ii. 1: " *Say ye to
your brethren: My people; and to your sisters, Favoured.*" The
prophet " sees the favoured nation of the Lord (in spirit) before
him, and calls upon its members to accost one another joyfully
with the new name which had been given to them by God"
(Hengstenberg). The promise attaches itself in form to the
names of the children of the prophet. As their names of ill
omen proclaimed the judgment of rejection, so is the salvation
which awaits the nation in the future announced to it here by
a simple alteration of the names into their opposite through the
omission of the לֹא.

So far as the fulfilment of this prophecy is concerned, the

fact that the patriarchal promise of the innumerable multiplication of Israel is to be realized through the pardon and restoration of Israel, as the nation of the living God, shows clearly enough that we are not to look for this in the return of the ten tribes from captivity to Palestine, their native land. Even apart from the fact, that the historical books of the Bible (Ezra, Nehemiah, and Esther) simply mention the return of a portion of the tribes of Judah and Benjamin, along with the priests and Levites, under Zerubbabel and Ezra, and that the numbers of the ten tribes, who may have attached themselves to the Judæans on their return, or who returned to Galilee afterwards as years rolled by, formed but a very small fraction of the number that had been carried away (compare the remarks on 2 Kings xvii. 24) ; the attachment of these few to Judah could not properly be called a union of the sons of Israel and of the sons of Judah, and still less was it a fulfilment of the words, "They appoint themselves one head." As the union of Israel with Judah is to be effected through their gathering together under one head, under Jehovah their God and under David their king, this fulfilment falls within the Messianic times, and hitherto has only been realized in very small beginnings, which furnish a pledge of their complete fulfilment in the last times, when the hardening of Israel will cease, and all Israel be converted to Christ (Rom. xi. 25, 26). It is by no means difficult to bring the application, which is made of our prophecy in 1 Pet. ii. 10 and Rom. ix. 25, 26, into harmony with this. When Peter quotes the words of this prophecy in his first epistle, which nearly all modern commentators justly suppose to have been written to Gentile Christians, and when Paul quotes the very same words (ch. ii. 1, with ch. i. 10) as proofs of the calling of the Gentiles to be the children of God in Christ ; this is not merely an application to the Gentiles of what is affirmed of Israel, or simply the clothing of their thoughts in Old Testament words, as Huther and Wiesinger suppose, but an argument based upon the fundamental thought of this prophecy. Through its apostasy from God, Israel had become like the Gentiles, and had fallen from the covenant of grace with the Lord. Consequently, the re-adoption of the Israelites as children of God was a practical proof that God had also adopted the Gentile world as His children. "Because

God had promised to adopt the children of Israel again,
He must adopt the Gentiles also. Otherwise this resolution
would rest upon mere caprice, which cannot be thought of in
God" (Hengstenberg). Moreover, although membership in
the nation of the Old Testament covenant rested primarily
upon lineal descent, it was by no means exclusively confined
to this; but, from the very first, Gentiles also were received
into the citizenship of Israel and the congregation of Jehovah
through the rite of circumcision, and could even participate in
the covenant mercies, namely, in the passover as a covenant
meal (Ex. xii. 14). There was in this an indirect practical
prophecy of the eventual reception of the whole of the Gentile
world into the kingdom of God, when it should attain through
Christ to faith in the living God. Even through their adoption
into the congregation of Jehovah by means of circumcision,
believing Gentiles were exalted into children of Abraham, and
received a share in the promises made to the fathers. And
accordingly the innumerable multiplication of the children of
Israel, predicted in ver. 10, is not to be restricted to the actual
multiplication of the descendants of the Israelites now banished
into exile; but the fulfilment of the promise must also include
the incorporation of believing Gentiles into the congregation of
the Lord (Isa. xliv. 5). This incorporation commenced with
the preaching of the gospel among the Gentiles by the apostles;
it has continued through all the centuries in which the church
has been spreading in the world; and it will receive its final
accomplishment when the fulness of the Gentiles shall enter
into the kingdom of God. And as the number of the children
of Israel is thus continually increased, this multiplication will
be complete when the descendants of the children of Israel,
who are still hardened in their hearts, shall turn to Jesus Christ
as their Messiah and Redeemer (Rom. xi. 25, 26).

CHASTISEMENT OF IDOLATROUS ISRAEL, AND ITS CONVERSION
AND FINAL RESTORATION.—CHAP. II. 2–23 (HEB. BIB.
II. 4–25).

What the prophet announced in ch. i. 2–ii. 1, partly by a
symbolical act, and partly also in a direct address, is carried
out still further in the section before us. The close connection

between the contents of the two sections is formally indicated by the simple fact, that just as the first section closed with a summons to appropriate the predicted salvation, so the section before us commences with a call to conversion. As Rückert aptly says, " The significant pair give place to the thing signified; Israel itself appears as the adulterous woman." The Lord Himself will set bounds to her adulterous conduct, *i.e.* to the idolatry of the Israelites. By withdrawing the blessings which they have hitherto enjoyed, and which they fancy that they have received from their idols, He will lead the idolatrous nation to reflection and conversion, and pour the fulness of the blessings of His grace in the most copious measure upon those who have been humbled and improved by the punishment. The threatening and the announcement of punishment extend from ver. 2 to ver. 13; the proclamation of salvation commences with ver. 14, and reaches to the close of ver. 23. The threatening of punishment is divided into two strophes, viz. vers. 2–7 and vers. 8–13. In the first, the condemnation of their sinful conduct is the most prominent; in the second, the punishment is more fully developed.

Ver. 2. " *Reason with your mother, reason! for she is not my wife, and I am not her husband: that she put away her whoredom from her countenance, and her adultery from between her breasts.*" Jehovah is the speaker, and the command to get rid of the whoredom is addressed to the Israelites, who are represented as the children of the adulterous wife. The distinction between mother and children forms part of the figurative drapery of the thought; for, in fact, the mother had no existence apart from the children. The nation or kingdom, regarded as an ideal unity, is called the mother; whereas the several members of the nation are the children of this mother. The summons addressed to the children to contend or reason with this mother, that she may give up her adultery, presupposes that, although the nation regarded as a whole was sunken in idolatry, the individual members of it were not all equally slaves to it, so as to have lost their susceptibility for the divine warning, or the possibility of conversion. Not only had the Lord reserved to Himself seven thousand in Elijah's time who had not bowed their knees to Baal, but at all times there were many individuals in the midst of the corrupt mass,

who hearkened to the voice of the Lord and abhorred idolatry.
The children had reason to plead, because the mother was no
longer the wife of Jehovah, and Jehovah was no longer her
husband, *i.e.* because she had dissolved her marriage with the
Lord; and the inward, moral dissolution of the covenant of
grace would be inevitably followed by the outward, actual dissolution, viz. by the rejection of the nation. It was therefore
the duty of the better-minded of the nation to ward off the
coming destruction, and do all they could to bring the adulterous wife to desist from her sins. The object of the pleading
is introduced with וְתָסֵר. The idolatry is described as whoredom
and adultery. Whoredom becomes adultery when it is a wife
who commits whoredom. Israel had entered into the covenant
with Jehovah its God; and therefore its idolatry became a breach
of the fidelity which it owed to its God, an act of apostasy from
God, which was more culpable than the idolatry of the heathen.
The whoredom is attributed to the face, the adultery to the
breasts, because it is in these parts of the body that the want
of chastity on the part of a woman is openly manifested, and
in order to depict more plainly the boldness and shamelessness
with which Israel practised idolatry.

The summons to repent is enforced by a reference to the
punishment. Ver. 3. " *Lest I strip her naked, and put her
as in the day of her birth, and set her like the desert, and make
her like a barren land, and let her die with thirst.*" In the first
hemistich the threat of punishment corresponds to the figurative representation of the adulteress; in the second it proceeds
from the figure to the fact. In the marriage referred to, the
husband had redeemed the wife out of the deepest misery, to
unite himself with her. Compare Ezek. xvi. 4 sqq., where the
nation is represented as a naked child covered with filth, which
the Lord took to Himself, covering its nakedness with beautiful
clothes and costly ornaments, and entering into covenant with
it. These gifts, with which the Lord also presented and
adorned His wife during the marriage, He would now take
away from the apostate wife, and put her once more into a
state of nakedness. The day of the wife's birth is the time of
Israel's oppression and bondage in Egypt, when it was given
up in helplessness to its oppressors. The deliverance out of
this bondage was the time of the divine courtship; and the

conclusion of the covenant with the nation that had been brought out of Egypt, the time of the marriage. The words, "I set (make) her like the desert," are to be understood as referring not to the land of Israel, which was to be laid waste, but to the nation itself, which was to become like the desert, *i.e.* to be brought into a state in which it would be destitute of the food that is indispensable to the maintenance of life. The dry land is a land without water, in which men perish from thirst. There is hardly any need to say that these words do not refer to the sojourn of Israel in the Arabian desert; for there the Lord fed His people with manna from heaven, and gave them water to drink out of the rock.

Ver. 4. " *And I will not have compassion upon her children, for they are children of whoredom.*" This verse is also dependent, so far as the meaning is concerned, upon the *pen* (lest) in ver. 3; but in form it constitutes an independent sentence. *B^enē z^enūnīm* (sons of whoredoms) refers back to *yaldē z^enūnīm* in ch. i. 2. The children are the members of the nation, and are called " sons of whoredom," not merely on account of their origin as begotten in whoredom, but also because they inherit the nature and conduct of their mother. The fact that the children are specially mentioned after and along with the mother, when in reality mother and children are one, serves to give greater keenness to the threat, and guards against that carnal security, in which individuals imagine that, inasmuch as they are free from the sin and guilt of the nation as a whole, they will also be exempted from the threatened punishment.

Ver. 5. " *For their mother hath committed whoredom; she that bare them hath practised shame: for she said, I will go after my lovers, who give (me) my bread and my water, my wool and my flax, my oil and my drink.*" By *kī* (for) and the suffixes attached to *'immām* (*their* mother) and *hŏrāthām* (that bare them), the first clauses are indeed introduced as though simply explanatory and confirmatory of the last clause of ver. 4; but if we look at the train of thought generally, it is obvious that ver. 5 is not merely intended to explain the expression sons of whoredom, but to explain and vindicate the main thought, viz. that the children of whoredom, *i.e.* the idolatrous Israelites, will find no mercy. Now, as the mother and children are identical, if we trace back the figurative drapery to its actual basis, the punishment with which the children are threatened applies to the mother also; and the description of the mother's whoredom serves also to explain the reason for the punishment with which the mother is threatened in ver. 3. And this also accounts for the fact that, in the threat which follows in ver. 6, "I hedge up thy way," the mother herself is again directly addressed. The *hiphil hōbhīsh*, which is traceable to *yâbhēsh*, so far as the form is concerned, but derives its meaning from בּוֹשׁ, is not used here in its ordinary sense of being put to shame, but in the transitive sense of practising shame, analogous to the transitive meaning "to shame," which we find in 2 Sam. xix. 5. To explain this thought, the coquetting with idols is more minutely described in the second hemistich. The delusive idea expressed by the wife (אָמְרָה, in the *perfect*, indicates speaking or thinking which stretches from the past into the present), viz. that the idols give her food (bread and water), clothing (wool and flax), and the delicacies of life (oil and drink, *i.e.* wine and must and strong drink), that is to say, "everything that conduces to luxury and superfluity," which we also find expressed in Jer. xliv. 17, 18, arose from the sight of the heathen nations round about, who were rich and mighty, and attributed this to their gods. It is impossible, however, that such a thought can ever occur, except in cases where the heart is already estranged from the living God. For so long as a man continues in undisturbed vital fellowship with God, "he sees with the eye of faith the hand in the clouds, from which he receives all, by which he is guided, and on which everything, even that which has apparently the most independence and strength, entirely depends" (Hengstenberg).

Ver. 6. "*Therefore* (because the woman says this), *behold, thus will I hedge up thy way with thorns, and wall up a wall, and she shall not find her paths.*" The hedging up of the way, strengthened by the similar figure of the building of a wall to cut off the way, denotes her transportation into a situation in which she could no longer continue her adultery with the idols. The reference is to distress and tribulation (compare ch. v. 15 with Deut. iv. 30, Job iii. 23, xix. 8, Lam. iii. 7), especially the distress and anguish of exile, in which, although Israel was in the midst of idolatrous nations, and therefore had even more outward opportunity to practise idolatry, it learned the worthlessness of all trust in idols, and their utter inability to help, and was thus impelled to reflect and turn to the Lord, who smites and heals (ch. vi. 1).

This thought is carried out still further in ver. **7**: "*And she will pursue her lovers, and not overtake them; and seek them, and not find them: and will say, I will go and return to my first husband, for it was better with me then than now.*" Distress at first increases their zeal in idolatry, but it soon brings them to see that the idols afford no help. The failure to reach or find the lovers, who are sought with zeal (*riddēph, piel* in an intensive sense, to pursue eagerly), denotes the failure to secure what is sought from them, viz. the anticipated deliverance from the calamity, which the living God has sent as a punishment. This sad experience awakens the desire to return to the faithful covenant God, and the acknowledgment that prosperity and all good things are to be found in vital fellowship with Him.

The thought that God will fill the idolatrous nation with disgust at its coquetry with strange gods, by taking away all its possessions, and thus putting to shame its delusive fancy that the possessions which it enjoyed really came from the idols, is still further expanded in the second strophe, commencing with the eighth verse. Ver. 8. "*And she knows not that I have given her the corn, and the must, and the oil, and have multiplied silver to her, and gold, which they have used for Baal.*" Corn, must, and oil are specified with the definite article as being the fruits of the land, which Israel received from year to year. These possessions were the foundation of the nation's wealth, through which gold and silver were multiplied. Ignorance of the fact that Jehovah was the giver of these blessings, was a sin. That Jehovah had given the land to His people, was impressed upon the minds of the people for all time, together with the recollection of the mighty acts of the Lord, by the manner in which Israel had been put in possession of Canaan; and not only had Moses again and again reminded the Israelites most solemnly that it was He who gave rain to the land, and multiplied and blessed its fruitfulness and its fruits (compare, for example, Deut. vii. 13, xi. 14, 15), but this was also perpetually called to their remembrance by the law concerning the offering of the first-fruits at the feasts. The words '*āsū labbaʿal* are to be taken as a relative clause without 'asher, though not in the sense of "which they have made into Baal," i.e. out of which they have made Baal-images (Chald., Rabb., Hitzig, Ewald, and others); for even though עָשָׂה לְ occurs in this sense in Isa. xliv. 17, the article, which is wanting in Isaiah, and also in Gen. xii. 2 and Ex. xxxii. 10, precludes such an explanation here, apart from the fact that habba'al cannot stand by itself for a statue of Baal. Here עָשָׂה לְ has rather the general meaning "apply to anything," just as in 2 Chron. xxiv. 7, where it occurs in a perfectly similar train of thought. This use of the word may be obtained from the meaning "to prepare for anything," whereas the meaning "to offer," which Gesenius adopts ("which they have offered to Baal"), is untenable, since עָשָׂה simply denotes the preparation of the sacrifice for the altar, which is out of the question in the case of silver and gold. They had applied their gold and silver to Baal, however, not merely by using them for the preparation of idols, but by employing them in the maintenance and extension of the worship of Baal, or even by regarding them as gifts of Baal, and thus confirming themselves in the zealous worship of that god. By habba'al we are not simply to understand the Canaanitish or Phœnician Baal in the stricter sense of the word, whose worship Jehu had exterminated from Israel, though not entirely, as is evident from the allusion to an Asherah in Samaria in the reign of Jehoahaz (2 Kings xiii. 6); but Baal is a general expression for all idols, including the golden calves, which are called other gods in 1 Kings xiv. 9, and compared to actual idols.

Ver. 9. "Therefore will I take back my corn at its time, and my must at its season, and tear away my wool and my flax for the covering of her nakedness." Because Israel had not regarded the blessings it received as gifts of its God, and used them for His glory, the Lord would take them away from it. אָשׁוּב וְלָקַחְתִּי are to be connected, so that אָשׁוּב has the force of an adverb, not however in the sense of simple repetition, as it usually does, but with the idea of return, as in Jer. xii. 15, viz. to take again = to take back. "My corn," etc., is the corn, the must, which I have given. "At its time," i.e. at the time when men expect corn, new wine, etc., viz. at the time of harvest, when men feel quite sure of receiving or possessing it. If God suddenly takes away the gifts then, not only is the loss more painfully felt, but regarded as a punishment far more than when they have been prepared beforehand for a bad harvest by the failure of the crop. Through the manner in which God takes the fruits of the land away from the people, He designs to show them that He, and not Baal, is the giver and the taker also. The words "to cover her nakedness" are not dependent upon הִצַּלְתִּי, but belong to צַמְרִי וּפִשְׁתִּי, and are simply a more concise mode of saying, "Such serve, or are meant, to cover her nakedness." They serve to sharpen the threat, by intimating that if God withdraw His gifts, the nation will be left in utter penury and ignominious nakedness (*'erváh, pudendum*).

Ver. 10. "*And now will I uncover her shame before her lovers, and no one shall tear her out of my hand.*" The ἁπ. λεγ. נַבְלוּת, lit. a withered state, from נָבֵל, to be withered or faded, probably denotes, as Hengstenberg says, *corpus multa stupra passum*, and is rendered freely in the LXX. by ἀκαθαρσία. "Before the eyes of the lovers," *i.e.* not so that they shall be obliged to look at it, without being able to avoid it, but so that the woman shall become even to them an object of abhorrence, from which they will turn away (comp. Nahum iii. 5; Jer. xiii. 26). In this concrete form the general truth is expressed, that "whoever forsakes God for the world, will be put to shame by God before the world itself; and that all the more, the nearer it stood to Him before" (Hengstenberg). By the addition of the words "no one," etc., all hope is cut off that the threatened punishment can be averted (cf. ch. v. 14).

This punishment is more minutely defined in vers. 11–13, in which the figurative drapery is thrown into the background by the actual fact. Ver. 11. "*And I make all her joy keep holiday (i.e. cease), her feast, and her new moon, and her sabbath, and all her festive time.*" The feast days and festive times were days of joy, in which Israel was to rejoice before the Lord its God. To bring into prominence this character of the feasts, כָּל־מְשׂושָׂהּ, "all her joy," is placed first, and the different festivals are mentioned afterwards. *Chág* stands for the three principal festivals of the year, the Passover, Pentecost, and the feast of Tabernacles, which had the character of *chág, i.e.* of feasts of joy *par excellence*, as being days of commemoration of the great acts of mercy which the Lord performed on behalf of His people. Then came the day of the new moon every

month, and the Sabbath every week. Finally, these feasts are
all summed up in כָּל־מוֹעֲדָהּ; for מוֹעֵד, מוֹעֲדִים is the general expression for all festive seasons and festive days (Lev. xxiii. 2, 4).
As a parallel, so far as the facts are concerned, comp. Amos
viii. 10, Jer. vii. 34, and Lam. i. 4, v. 15.

The Lord will put an end to the festive rejoicing, by taking
away the fruits of the land, which rejoice man's heart. Ver.
12. "*And I lay waste her vine and her fig-tree, of which she
said, They are lovers' wages to me, which my lovers gave me; and
I make them a forest, and the beasts of the field devour them.*"
Vine and fig-tree, the choicest productions of the land of
Canaan, are mentioned as the representatives of the rich means
of sustenance with which the Lord had blessed His people (cf.
1 Kings v. 5; Joel ii. 22, etc.). The devastation of both of
these denotes the withdrawal of the possessions and enjoyments
of life (cf. Jer. v. 17; Joel i. 7, 12), because Israel regarded
them as a present from its idols. אֶתְנָה, softened down from אֶתְנַן
(ch. ix. 1), like שִׂרְיָה, in Job xli. 18, from שִׂרְיָן (1 Kings xxii.
34; cf. Ewald, § 163, *h*), signifies the wages of prostitution
(Deut. xxiii. 19). The derivation is disputed and uncertain,
since the verb תָּנָה cannot be shown to have been used either
in Hebrew or the other Semitic dialects in the sense of *dedit,
dona porrexit* (Ges.), and the word cannot be traced to תָּנַן, to
extend; whilst, on the other hand, the verb הִתְנָה, תָּנָה (ch. viii.
9, 10) is most probably a denominative of אֶתְנָה. Consequently,
Hengstenberg supposes it to be a bad word formed out of the
question put by the prostitute, מַה תִּתֶּן לִי, and the answer given
by the man, אָנֹכִי אֶתֵּן לָךְ (Gen. xxxviii. 16, 18), and used in the
language of the brothel in connection with an evil deed. The
vineyards and fig-orchards, so carefully hedged about and cultivated, are to be turned into a forest, *i.e.* to be deprived of their
hedges and cultivation, so that the wild beasts may be able to
devour them. The suffixes attached to שַׂמְתִּים and אֲכָלָתַם refer
to גֶּפֶן וּתְאֵנָה (the vine and fig-tree), and not merely to the fruit.
Comp. Isa. vii. 23 sqq. and Mic. iii. 12, where a similar figure
is used to denote the complete devastation of the land.

In this way will the Lord take away from the people their
festivals of joy. Ver. 13. "*And I visit upon her the days of
the Baals, to which she burned incense, and adorned herself with
her ring and her jewels, and went after her lovers; and she hath

forgotten me, is the word of Jehovah." The days of the Baals
are the sacred days and festive seasons mentioned in ver. 13,
which Israel ought to have sanctified and kept to the Lord its
God, but which it celebrated in honour of the Baals, through
its fall into idolatry. There is no ground for thinking of special
feast-days dedicated to Baal, in addition to the feasts of Jehovah
prescribed by the law. Just as Israel had changed Jehovah
into Baal, so had it also turned the feast-days of Jehovah into
festive days of the Baals, and on those days had burned incense,
i.e. offered sacrifice to the Baals (cf. ch. iv. 13 ; 2 Kings xvii.
11). In ver. 8 we find only הַבַּעַל mentioned, but here בְּעָלִים in
the plural, because Baal was worshipped under different modifi-
cations, from which *Beʿâlīm* came to be used in the general
sense of the various idols of the Canaanites (cf. Judg. ii. 11 ;
1 Kings xviii. 18, etc.). In the second hemistich this spiritual
coquetry with the idols is depicted under the figure of the outward coquetry of a woman, who resorts to all kinds of outward
ornaments in order to excite the admiration of her lovers (as in
Jer. iv. 30 and Ezek. xxiii. 40 sqq.). There is no ground for
thinking of the wearing of nose-rings and ornaments in honour
of the idols. The antithesis to this adorning of themselves is
" forgetting Jehovah," in which the sin is brought out in its
true shape. On נאם יהוה, see Delitzsch on Isa. i. 24.

In ver. 14 the promise is introduced quite as abruptly as in
ver. 1, that the Lord will lead back the rebellious nation step
by step to conversion and reunion with Himself, the righteous
God. In two strophes we have first the promise of their conversion (vers. 14–17), and secondly, the assurance of the renewal
of the covenant mercies (vers. 18-23). Vers. 14, 15. " *Therefore, behold, I allure her, and lead her into the desert, and speak
to her heart. And I give her her vineyards from thence, and the
valley of Achor (of tribulation) for the door of hope ; and she
answers thither, as in the days of her youth, and as in the day
when she came up out of the land of Egypt.*" לָכֵן, therefore (not
utique, profecto, but, nevertheless, which *lâkhēn* never means),
is co-ordinate with the *lâkhēn* in vers. 6 and 9, and is connected primarily with the last clause of ver. 13. "Because
the wife has forgotten God, He calls Himself to her remembrance again, first of all by punishment (vers. 6 and 9) ; then,
when this has answered its purpose, and after she has said, I

will go and return (ver. 7), by the manifestations of His love"
(Hengstenberg). That the first clause of ver. 14 does not refer
to the flight of the people out of Canaan into the desert, for
the purpose of escaping from their foes, as Hitzig supposes, is
sufficiently obvious to need no special proof. The alluring of
the nation into the desert to lead it thence to Canaan, presupposes that rejection from the inheritance given to it by
the Lord (viz. Canaan), which Israel had brought upon itself
through its apostasy. This rejection is represented as an expulsion from Canaan to Egypt, the land of bondage, out of
which Jehovah had redeemed it in the olden time. פָּתָה, in the
piel to persuade, to decoy by words ; here *sensu bono*, to allure
by friendly words. The desert into which the Lord will lead
His people cannot be any other than the desert of Arabia,
through which the road from Egypt to Canaan passes. Leading
into this desert is not a punishment, but a redemption out of
bondage. The people are not to remain in the desert, but to
be enticed and led through it to Canaan, the land of vineyards.
The description is typical throughout. What took place in the
olden time is to be repeated, in all that is essential, in the time
to come. Egypt, the Arabian desert, and Canaan are types.
Egypt is a type of the land of captivity, in which Israel had
been oppressed in its fathers by the heathen power of the world.
The Arabian desert, as the intervening stage between Egypt
and Canaan, is introduced here, in accordance with the importance which attached to the march of Israel through this desert
under the guidance of Moses, as a period or state of probation
and trial, as described in Deut. viii. 2–6, in which the Lord
humbled His people, training it on the one hand by want and
privation to the knowledge of its need of help, and on the other
hand by miraculous deliverance in the time of need (*e.g.* the
manna, the stream of water, and the preservation of their
clothing) to trust to His omnipotence, that He might awaken
within it a heartfelt love to the fulfilment of His commandments and a faithful attachment to Himself. Canaan, the
land promised to the fathers as an everlasting possession, with
its costly productions, is a type of the inheritance bestowed by
the Lord upon His church, and of blessedness in the enjoyment of the gifts of the Lord which refresh both body and
soul. דִּבֶּר עַל לֵב, to speak to the heart, as applied to loving,

comforting words (Gen. xxxiv. 3, l. 21, etc.), is not to be restricted to the comforting addresses of the prophets, but denotes a comforting by action, by manifestations of love, by which her grief is mitigated, and the broken heart is healed. The same love is shown in the renewed gifts of the possessions of which the unfaithful nation had been deprived. In this way we obtain a close link of connection for ver. 15. By נָתַתִּי . . . מִשָּׁם, " I give from thence," *i.e.* from the desert onwards, the thought is expressed, that on entering the promised land Israel would be put into immediate possession and enjoyment of its rich blessings. Manger has correctly explained מִשָּׁם as meaning " as soon as it shall have left this desert," or better still, " as soon as it shall have reached the border." " Its vineyards" are the vineyards which it formerly possessed, and which rightfully belonged to the faithful wife, though they had been withdrawn from the unfaithful (ver. 12). The valley of *Achor*, which was situated to the north of Gilgal and Jericho (see at Josh. vii. 26), is mentioned by the prophet, not because of its situation on the border of Palestine, nor on account of its fruitfulness, of which nothing is known, but with an evident allusion to the occurrence described in Josh. vii., from which it obtained its name of ʿ*Akhōr, Troubling.* This is obvious from the declaration that this valley shall become a door of hope. Through the sin of Achan, who took some of the spoil of Jericho which had been devoted by the ban to the Lord, Israel had fallen under the ban, so that the Lord withdrew His help, and the army that marched against Ai was defeated. But in answer to the prayer of Joshua and the elders, God showed to Joshua not only the cause of the calamity which had befallen the whole nation, but the means of escaping from the ban and recovering the lost favour of God. Through the name *Achor* this valley became a memorial, how the Lord restores His favour to the church after the expiation of the guilt by the punishment of the transgressor. And this divine mode of procedure will be repeated in all its essential characteristics. The Lord will make the valley of troubling a door of hope, *i.e.* He will so expiate the sins of His church, and cover them with His grace, that the covenant of fellowship with Him will no more be rent asunder by them; or He will so display His grace to the sinners, that compassion

will manifest itself even in wrath, and through judgment and
mercy the pardoned sinners will be more and more firmly
and inwardly united to Him. And the church will respond to
this movement on the part of the love of God, which reveals
itself in justice and mercy. It will answer to the place, whence
the Lord comes to meet it with the fulness of His saving
blessings. עָנָה does not mean "to sing," but "to answer;"
and שָׁמָּה, pointing back to מִשָּׁם, must not be regarded as equivalent to שָׁם. As the comforting address of the Lord is a
sermo realis, so the answer of the church is a practical response
of grateful acknowledgment and acceptance of the manifestations of divine love, just as was the case in the days of the
nation's youth, *i.e.* in the time when it was led up from Egypt
to Canaan. Israel then answered the Lord, after its redemption from Egypt, by the song of praise and thanksgiving at
the Red Sea (Ex. xv.), and by its willingness to conclude the
covenant with the Lord at Sinai, and to keep His commandments (Ex. xxiv.).

Ver. 16. "*And it comes to pass in that day, is the saying of
Jehovah, thou wilt call, My husband; and thou wilt no more call
to me, My Baal.*" The church will then enter once more into
the right relation to its God. This thought is expressed thus,
that the wife will no more call her husband Baal, but husband.
Ba'al is not to be taken as an appellative in the sense of master,
as distinguished from '*ish*, man, *i.e.* husband, for *ba'al* does not
mean master or lord, but owner, possessor; and whenever it is
applied to a husband in an appellative sense, it is used quite
promiscuously with '*ish* (*e.g.* 2 Sam. xi. 26, Gen. xx. 3). Moreover, the context in this instance, especially the *B^eâlim* in ver.
19, decidedly requires that *Ba'al* should be taken as a proper
name. Calling or naming is a designation of the nature or the
true relation of a person or thing. The church calls God her
husband, when she stands in the right relation to Him; when
she acknowledges, reveres, and loves Him, as He has revealed
Himself, *i.e.* as the only true God. On the other hand, she
calls Him Baal, when she places the true God on the level of
the Baals, either by worshipping other gods along with Jehovah,
or by obliterating the essential distinction between Jehovah and
the Baals, confounding together the worship of God and idolatrous worship, the Jehovah-religion and heathenism.

Ver. 17. "*And I put away the names of the Baals out of her mouth, and they are no more remembered by their name.*" As soon as the nation ceases to call Jehovah Baal, the custom of taking the names of the Baals into its mouth ceases of itself. And when this also is mentioned here as the work of God, the thought is thereby expressed, that the abolition of polytheism and mixed religion is a work of that divine grace which renews the heart, and fills with such abhorrence of the coarser or more refined forms of idolatry, that men no longer dare to take the names of the idols into their lips. This divine promise rests upon the command in Ex. xxiii. 13, "Ye shall make no mention of the names of other gods," and is repeated almost word for word in Zech. xiii. 2.

With the complete abolition of idolatry and false religion, the church of the Lord will attain to the enjoyment of undisturbed peace. Ver. 18. "*And I make a covenant for them in that day with the beasts of the field, and the fowls of heaven, and the moving creatures of the earth: and I break in pieces bow, and sword, and battle out of the land, and cause them to dwell securely.*" God makes a covenant with the beasts, when He imposes the obligation upon them to hurt men no more. "*For them:*" *lâhem* is a *dat. comm.*, for the good of the favoured ones. The three classes of beasts that are dangerous to men, are mentioned here, as in Gen. ix. 2. "Beasts of the field," as distinguished from the same domestic animals (*b^ehēmâh*), are beasts that live in freedom in the fields, either wild beasts, or game that devours or injures the fruits of the field. By the "fowls of heaven," we are to understand chiefly the birds of prey. *Remes* does not mean reptiles, but that which is active, the smaller animals of the land which move about with velocity. The breaking in pieces of the weapons of war and of battle out of the land, is a pregnant expression for the extinction not only of the instruments of war, but also of war itself, and their extermination from the land. *Milchâmâh*, war, is connected with *shâbhar per zeugma*. This promise rests upon Lev. xxvi. 3 sqq., and is still further expanded in Ezek. xxxiv. 25 sqq. (Compare the parallels in Isa. ii. 4, xi., xxxv. 9, and Zech. ix. 10.)

Ver. 19. "*And I betroth thee to myself for ever; and I betroth thee to myself in righteousness, and judgment, and in*

grace and pity. Ver. 20. *And I betroth thee to myself in faithfulness; and thou acknowledgest Jehovah."* אֵרֶשׂ לִי, to betroth
to one's self, to woo, is only applied to the wooing of a maiden,
not to the restoration of a wife who has been divorced, and is
generally distinguished from the taking of a wife (Deut. xx. 7).
אֵרַשְׂתִּיךְ therefore points, as Calvin observes, to an entirely new
marriage. "It was indeed great grace for the unfaithful wife
to be taken back again. She might in justice have been put
away for ever. The only valid ground for divorce was there,
since she had lived for years in adultery. But the grace of God
goes further still. The past is not only forgiven, but it is also
forgotten" (Hengstenberg). The Lord will now make a new
covenant of marriage with His church, such as is made with a
spotless virgin. This new and altogether unexpected grace He
now directly announces to her: "I betroth thee to myself;" and
repeats this promise three times in ever fresh terms, expressive of the indissoluble character of the new relation. This is
involved in לְעוֹלָם, "for ever," whereas the former covenant had
been broken and dissolved by the wife's own guilt. In the
clauses which follow, we have a description of the attributes
which God would thereby unfold in order to render the covenant indissoluble. These are, (1) righteousness and judgment;
(2) grace and compassion; (3) faithfulness. *Tsedeq = tsᵉdâqâh*
and *mishpât* are frequently connected. *Tsedeq,* "being right,"
denotes subjective righteousness as an attribute of God or
man; and *mishpât,* objective right, whether in its judicial execution as judgment, or in its existence in actual fact. God
betroths His church to Himself in righteousness and judgment,
not by doing her justice, and faithfully fulfilling the obligations
which He undertook at the conclusion of the covenant (Hengstenberg), but by purifying her, through the medium of just
judgment, from all the unholiness and ungodliness that adhere
to her still (Isa. i. 27), that He may wipe out everything that
can injure the covenant on the part of the church But with
the existing sinfulness of human nature, justice and judgment
will not suffice to secure the lasting continuance of the covenant; and therefore God also promises to show mercy and
compassion. But as even the love and compassion of God have
their limits, the Lord still further adds, "in faithfulness or constancy," and thereby gives the promise that He will no more

withdraw His mercy from her. בֶּאֱמוּנָה is also to be understood of the faithfulness of God, as in Ps. lxxxix. 25, not of that of man (Hengstenberg). This is required by the parallelism of the sentences. In the faithfulness of God the church has a certain pledge, that the covenant founded upon righteousness and judgment, mercy and compassion, will stand for ever. The consequence of this union is, that the church knows Jehovah. This knowledge is "real." "He who knows God in this way, cannot fail to love Him, and be faithful to Him" (Hengstenberg); for out of this covenant there flows unconquerable salvation.

Vers. 21, 22. "*And it comes to pass in that day, I will hear, is the word of Jehovah; I will hear heaven, and it hears the earth. And the earth will hear the corn, and the new wine, and the oil; and they will hear Jezreel (God sows)."* God will hear all the prayers that ascend to Him from His church (the first אֶעֱנֶה is to be taken absolutely; compare the parallel in Isa. lviii. 9), and cause all the blessings of heaven and earth to flow down to His favoured people. By a prosopopeia, the prophet represents the heaven as praying to God, to allow it to give to the earth that which is requisite to ensure its fertility; whereupon the heaven fulfils the desires of the earth, and the earth yields its produce to the nation.[1] In this way the thought is embodied, that all things in heaven and on earth depend on God; "so that without His bidding not a drop of rain falls from heaven, and the earth produces no germ, and consequently all nature would at length be barren, unless He gave it fertility by His blessing" (Calvin). The promise rests upon Deut. xxviii. 12, and forms the antithesis to the threat in Lev. xxvi. 19 and Deut. xxviii. 23, 24, that God will make the heavens as brass, and the earth as iron, to those who despise His name. In the last clause the prophecy returns to its starting-point with the words, "Hear Jezreel." The blessing which flows down from heaven to earth flows to *Jezreel*, the nation which "God sows." The name Jezreel, which symbolizes the judgment about to burst upon the kingdom of Israel, according to the historical signification

---

[1] As Umbreit observes, "It is as though we heard the exalted harmonies of the connected powers of creation, sending forth their notes as they are sustained and moved by the eternal key-note of the creative and moulding Spirit."

of the name in ch. i. 4, 11, is used here in the primary sense
of the word, to denote the nation as pardoned and reunited to
its God.

This is evident from the explanation given in ver. 23: "*And
I sow her for myself in the land, and favour Unfavoured, and say
to Not-my-people, Thou art my people; and it says to me, My
God.*" זָרַע does not mean " to strew," or scatter (not even in
Zech. x. 9; cf. Koehler on the passage), but simply " to sow."
The feminine suffix to זְרַעְתִּיהָ refers, *ad sensum*, to the wife
whom God has betrothed to Himself for ever, *i.e.* to the favoured
church of Israel, which is now to become a true *Jezreel*, as a
rich sowing on the part of God. With this turn in the guidance of Israel, the ominous names of the other children of the
prophet's marriage will also be changed into their opposite, to
show that mercy and the restoration of vital fellowship with the
Lord will now take the place of judgment, and of the rejection
of the idolatrous nation. With regard to the fulfilment of the
promise, the remarks made upon this point at ch. i. 11 and ii. 1
(pp. 49, 50), are applicable here, since this section is simply a
further expansion of the preceding one.

THE ADULTERESS AND HER FRESH MARRIAGE.—CHAP. III.

" The significant pair are introduced again, but with a fresh
application." In a second symbolical marriage, the prophet
sets forth the faithful, but for that very reason chastising and
reforming, love of the Lord to rebellious and adulterous Israel.
By the command of God he takes a wife, who lives in continued
adultery, notwithstanding his faithful love, and places her in a
position in which she is obliged to renounce her lovers, that he
may thus lead her to return. Vers. 1–3 contain the symbolical
action; vers. 4, 5 the explanation, with an announcement of
the reformation which this proceeding is intended to effect.

Ver. 1. "*And Jehovah said to me, Go again, and love a
woman beloved of her companion, and committing adultery, as
Jehovah loveth the children of Israel, and they turn to other gods,
and love raisin-cakes.*" The purely symbolical character of this
divine command is evident from the nature of the command
itself, but more especially from the peculiar epithet applied to
the wife. עוֹד is not to be connected with וַיֹּאמֶר, in opposition to

the accents, but belongs to לֹו, and is placed first for the sake of emphasis. Loving the woman, as the carrying out of the divine command in ver. 2 clearly shows, is in fact equivalent to taking a wife; and *'âhabh* is chosen instead of *lâqach*, simply for the purpose of indicating at the very outset the nature of the union enjoined upon the prophet. The woman is characterized as beloved of her companion (friend), and committing adultery. רֵעַ denotes a friend or companion, with whom one cherishes intercourse and fellowship, never a fellow-creature generally, but simply the fellow-creature with whom one lives in the closest intimacy (Ex. xx. 17, 18, xxii. 25, etc.). The רֵעַ (companion) of a woman, who loves her, can only be her husband or paramour. The word is undoubtedly used in Jer. iii. 1, 20, and Song of Sol. v. 16, with reference to a husband, but never of a fornicator or adulterous paramour. And the second epithet employed here, viz. " committing adultery," which forms an unmistakeable antithesis to אהבת רע, requires that it should be understood in this instance as signifying a husband; for a woman only becomes an adulteress when she is unfaithful to her loving husband, and goes with other men, but not when she gives up her beloved paramour to live with her husband only. If the epithets referred to the love shown by a paramour, by which the woman had annulled the marriage, this would necessarily have been expressed by the perfect or pluperfect. By the participles אֲהֻבַת and מְנָאֶפֶת, the love of the companion and the adultery of the wife are supposed to be continued and contemporaneous with the love which the prophet is to manifest towards the woman. This overthrows the assertion made by Kurtz, that we have before us a woman who was already married at the time when the prophet was commanded to love her, as at variance with the grammatical construction, and changing the participle into the pluperfect. For, during the time that the prophet loved the wife he had taken, the רֵעַ who displayed his love to her could only be her husband, *i.e.* the prophet himself, towards whom she stood in the closest intimacy, founded upon love, *i.e.* in the relation of marriage. The correctness of this view, that the רֵעַ is the prophet as husband, is put beyond all possibility of doubt by the explanation of the divine command which follows. As Jehovah loves the sons of Israel, although or whilst they turn to other gods, *i.e.* break

their marriage with Jehovah; so is the prophet to love the
woman who commits adultery, or will commit adultery, notwithstanding his love, since the adultery could only take place
when the prophet had shown to the woman the love commanded, *i.e.* had connected himself with her by marriage. The
peculiar epithet applied to the woman can only be explained
from the fact intended to be set forth by the symbolical act
itself, and, as we have already shown at p. 31, is irreconcilable with the assumption that the command of God refers to
a marriage to be really and outwardly consummated. The
words כְּאַהֲבַת יי recal Deut. vii. 8, and וְהֵם פָּנִים וגו' Deut. xxxi.
18. The last clause, "and loving grape-cakes," does not apply
to the idols, who would be thereby represented either as lovers
of grape-cakes, or as those to whom grape-cakes were offered
(Hitzig), but is a continuation of פָּנִים, indicating the reason
why Israel turned to other gods. Grape or raisin cakes (on
'ăshīshâh, see at 2 Sam. vi. 19) are delicacies, figuratively representing that idolatrous worship which appeals to the senses,
and gratifies the carnal impulses and desires. Compare Job
xx. 12, where sin is figuratively described as food which is
sweet as new honey in the mouth, but turns into the gall of
asps in the belly. Loving grape-cakes is equivalent to indulging in sensuality. Because Israel loves this, it turns to other
gods. "The solemn and strict religion of Jehovah is plain but
wholesome food; whereas idolatry is relaxing food, which is
only sought after by epicures and men of depraved tastes"
(Hengstenberg).

Ver. 2. "*And I acquired her for myself for fifteen pieces of
silver, and a homer of barley, and a lethech of barley.*" אֶכְּרֶהָ,
with *dagesh lene* or *dirimens* (Ewald, § 28, *b*), from *kârâh*, to
dig, to procure by digging, then generally to acquire (see at
Deut. ii. 6), or obtain by trading (Job vi. 27, xl. 30). Fifteen
keseph are fifteen shekels of silver; the word *shekel* being
frequently omitted in statements as to amount (compare Ges.
§ 120, 4, Anm. 2). According to Ezek. xlv. 11, the *homer*
contained ten baths or ephahs, and a *lethech* (ἡμίκορος, LXX.)
was a half homer. Consequently the prophet gave fifteen
shekels of silver and fifteen ephahs of barley; and it is a very
natural supposition, especially if we refer to 2 Kings vii. 1,
xvi. 18, that at that time an ephah of barley was worth

a shekel, in which case the whole price would just amount to the sum for which, according to Ex. xxi. 32, it was possible to purchase a slave, and was paid half in money and half in barley. The reason for the latter it is impossible to determine with certainty. The price generally, for which the prophet obtained the wife, was probably intended to indicate the servile condition out of which Jehovah purchased Israel to be His people; and the circumstance that the prophet gave no more for the wife than the amount at which a slave could be obtained, according to Ex. xxi. 32 and Zech. xi. 12, and that this amount was not even paid in money, but half of it in barley—a kind of food so generally despised throughout antiquity (*vile hordeum;* see at Num. v. 15)—was intended to depict still more strikingly the deeply depressed condition of the woman. The price paid, moreover, is not to be regarded as purchase money, for which the wife was obtained from her parents; for it cannot be shown that the custom of purchasing a bride from her parents had any existence among the Israelites (see my *Bibl. Archäologie,* ii. § 109, 1). It was rather the marriage present (*mōhar*), which a bridegroom gave, not to the parents, but to the bride herself, as soon as her consent had been obtained. If, therefore, the woman was satisfied with fifteen shekels and fifteen ephahs of barley, she must have been in a state of very deep distress.

Ver. 3. "*And I said to her, Many days wilt thou sit for me: and not act the harlot, and not belong to a man; and thus will I also towards thee.*" Instead of granting the full conjugal fellowship of a wife to the woman whom he had acquired for himself, the prophet puts her into a state of detention, in which she was debarred from intercourse with any man. Sitting is equivalent to remaining quiet, and ל indicates that this is for the husband's sake, and that he imposes it upon her out of affection to her, to reform her and train her up as a faithful wife. הָיָה לְאִישׁ, to be or become a man's, signifies conjugal or sexual connection with him. Commentators differ in opinion as to whether the prophet himself is included or not. In all probability he is not included, as his conduct towards the woman is simply indicated in the last clause. The distinction between זָנָה and הָיָה לְאִישׁ, is that the former signifies intercourse with different paramours, the latter conjugal intercourse; here adulterous intercourse with a single man. The last words, " and I also to thee" (towards thee), cannot have any other meaning, than that the prophet would act in the same way towards the wife as the wife towards every other man, *i.e.* would have no conjugal intercourse with her. The other explanations that have been given of these words, in which *v⁰gam* is rendered " and yet," or " and then," are arbitrary. The parallel is not drawn between the prophet and the wife, but between the prophet and the other man ; in other words, he does not promise that during the period of the wife's detention he will not conclude a marriage with any other woman, but declares that he will have no more conjugal intercourse with her than any other man. This thought is required by the explanation of the figure in ver. 4. For, according to the former interpretation, the idea expressed would be this, that the Lord waited with patience and long-suffering for the reformation of His former nation, and would not plunge it into despair by adopting another nation in its place. But there is no hint whatever at any such thought as this in vers. 4, 5 ; and all that is expressed is, that He will not only cut off all intercourse on the part of His people with idols, but will also suspend, for a very long time, His own relation to Israel.

Ver. 4. *" For the sons of Israel will sit for many days without a king, and without a prince, and without slain-offering, and without monument, and without ephod and teraphim."* The explanation of the figure is introduced with פִּי, because it contains the ground of the symbolical action. The objects, which are to be taken away from the Israelites, form three pairs, although only the last two are formally connected together by the omission of אֵין before תְּרָפִים, so as to form one pair, whilst the rest are simply arranged one after another by the repetition of אֵין before every one. As king and prince go together, so also do slain-offering and memorial. King and prince are the upholders of civil government ; whilst slain-offering and memorial represent the nation's worship and religion. מַצֵּבָה, monument, is connected with idolatrous worship. The " monuments" were consecrated to Baal (Ex. xxiii. 24), and the erection of them was for that reason prohibited even in the law (Lev. xxvi. 1 ; Deut. xvi. 22 : see at 1 Kings xiv. 23) ; but they were widely spread in the kingdom of Israel (2 Kings iii. 2, x.

26-28, xvii. 10), and they were also erected in Judah under idolatrous kings (1 Kings xiv. 23; 2 Kings xviii. 4, xxiii. 14; 2 Chron. xiv. 2, xxxi. 1). The *ephod* and *teraphim* did indeed form part of the apparatus of worship, but they are also specially mentioned as media employed in searching into the future. The *ephod*, the shoulder-dress of the high priest, to which the Urim and Thummim were attached, was the medium through which Jehovah communicated His revelations to the people, and was used for the purpose of asking the will of God (1 Sam. xxiii. 9, xxx. 7); and for the same purpose it was imitated in an idolatrous manner (Judg. xvii. 5, xviii. 5). The *teraphim* were Penates, which were worshipped as the givers of earthly prosperity, and also as oracular deities who revealed future events (see my *Bibl. Archäol.* § 90). The prophet mentions objects connected with both the worship of Jehovah and that of idols, because they were both mixed together in Israel, and for the purpose of showing to the people that the Lord would take away both the Jehovah-worship and also the worship of idols, along with the independent civil government. With the removal of the monarchy (see at ch. i. 4), or the dissolution of the kingdom, not only was the Jehovah-worship abolished, but an end was also put to the idolatry of the nation, since the people discovered the worthlessness of the idols from the fact that, when the judgment burst upon them, they could grant no deliverance; and notwithstanding the circumstance that, when carried into exile, they were transported into the midst of idolaters, the distress and misery into which they were then plunged filled them with abhorrence of idolatry (see at ch. ii. 7).

This threat was fulfilled in the history of the ten tribes, when they were carried away with the Assyrian captivity, in which they continue for the most part to the present day without a monarchy, without Jehovah-worship, and without a priesthood. For it is evident that by Israel the ten tribes are intended, not only from the close connection between this prophecy and ch. i., where Israel is expressly distinguished from Judah (ch. i. 7), but also from the prospect held out in ver. 5, that the sons of Israel will return to David their king, which clearly points to the falling away of the ten tribes from the house of David. At the same time, as the carrying away of

Judah also is presupposed in ch. i. 7, 11, and therefore what is
said of Israel is transferred *implicite* to Judah, we must not
restrict the threat contained in this verse to the Israel of the
ten tribes alone, but must also understand it as referring to the
Babylonian and Roman exile of the Jews, just as in the time of
king Asa (2 Chron. xv. 2–4). The prophet Azariah predicted
this to the kingdom of Judah in a manner which furnishes an
unmistakeable support to Hosea's prophecy.

Ver. 5. " *Afterward will the sons of Israel turn and seek
Jehovah their God, and David their king, and will go trembling
to Jehovah and to His goodness at the end of the days.*" This
section, like the previous one, closes with the announcement of
the eventual conversion of Israel, which was not indicated in
the symbolical action which precedes it, but is added to complete the interpretation of the symbol. Seeking Jehovah their
God is connected with seeking David their king. For just as
the falling away of the ten tribes from the royal house of David
was merely the sequel and effect of their inward apostasy from
Jehovah, and was openly declared in the setting up of the
golden calves; the true return to the Lord cannot take place
without a return to David their king, since God has promised
the kingdom to David and his seed for ever (2 Sam. vii. 13, 16),
and therefore David is the only true king of Israel (*their* king).
This King David, however, is no other than the Messiah. For
although David received the promise of the everlasting continuance of his government, not with reference to his own
person, but for his seed, *i.e.* his family; and on the ground of
this promise, the whole of the royal house of David is frequently embraced under the expression " King David," so that
we might imagine that David is introduced here, not as an
individual, but as signifying the Davidic family; yet we must
not understand it on this account as referring to such historical
representatives of the Davidic government as Zerubbabel, and
other earthly representatives of the house of David, since the
return of the Israelites to " their King David" was not to take
place till *'achărīth hayyâmīm* (the end of the days). For " the
end of the days" does not denote the future generally, but
always the closing future of the kingdom of God, commencing
with the coming of the Messiah (see at Gen. xlix. 1; Isa. ii. 2).
Pâchad 'el Yᵉhōváh, to shake or tremble *to* Jehovah, is a preg-

nant expression for " to turn to Jehovah with trembling;"
i.e. either trembling at the holiness of God, in the consciousness of their own sinfulness and unworthiness, or else with
anguish and distress, in the consciousness of their utter helplessness. It is used here in the latter sense, as the two parallels,
ch. v. 15, " in their affliction they will seek me," and ch. xi. 11,
" they shall tremble as a bird," etc., clearly show. This is also
required by the following expression, וְאֶל־טוּבוֹ, which is to be
understood, according to ch. ii. 7, as denoting the goodness of
God manifested in His gifts. Affliction will drive them to
seek the Lord, and His goodness which is inseparable from
Himself (Hengstenberg). Compare Jer. xxxi. 12, where " the
goodness of the Lord" is explained as corn, new wine, oil, lambs,
and oxen, these being the gifts that come from the goodness of
the Lord (Zech. ix. 17 ; Ps. xxvii. 13, xxxi. 20). He who has
the Lord for his God will want no good thing.

II. THE UNGODLINESS OF ISRAEL. ITS PUNISHMENT, AND FINAL DELIVERANCE.—Chap. iv.–xiv.

The spiritual adultery of Israel, with its consequences, which
the prophet has exposed in the first part, and chiefly in a symbolical mode, is more elaborately detailed here, not only with
regard to its true nature, viz. the religious apostasy and moral
depravity which prevailed throughout the ten tribes, but also in
its inevitable consequences, viz. the destruction of the kingdom
and rejection of the people ; and this is done with a repeated
side-glance at Judah. To this there is appended a solemn
appeal to return to the Lord, and a promise that the Lord will
have compassion upon the penitent, and renew His covenant of
grace with them.

I. THE DEPRAVITY OF ISRAEL, AND ITS EXPOSURE TO PUNISHMENT.—CHAP. IV.–VI. 3.

The first section, in which the prophet demonstrates the
necessity for judgment, by exposing the sins and follies of

Israel, is divided into two parts by the similar openings, " Hear
the word of the Lord" in ch. iv. 1, and " Hear ye this" in
ch. v. 1.   The distinction between the two halves is, that in
ch. iv. the reproof of their sins passes from Israel as a whole,
to the sins of the priests in particular ; whilst in ch. v. it
passes from the ruin of the priesthood to the depravity of the
whole nation, and announces the judgment of devastation upon
Ephraim, and then closes in ch. vi. 1–3 with a command to
return to the Lord.   The contents of the two chapters, however, are so arranged, that it is difficult to divide them into
strophes.

The Sins of Israel and the Visitation of God.—Chap. iv.

Vers. 1–5 form the first strophe, and contain, so to speak,
the theme and the sum and substance of the whole of the
following threatening of punishment and judgment.   Ver. 1.
" *Hear the word of Jehovah, ye sons of Israel! for Jehovah
has a controversy with the inhabitants of the land ; for there is
no truth, and no love, and no knowledge of God in the land.*"
Israel of the ten tribes is here addressed, as ver. 15 clearly
shows.   The Lord has a controversy with it, has to accuse and
judge it (cf. Mic. vi. 2), because truth, love, and the knowledge
of God have vanished from the land.   '*Emeth* and *chesed* are
frequently associated, not merely as divine attributes, but also
as human virtues.   They are used here in the latter sense, as
in Prov. iii. 3.   " There is no '*emeth, i.e.* no truthfulness, either
in speech or action, no one trusting another any more" (cf. Jer.
ix. 3, 4).   *Chesed* is not human love generally, but love to
inferiors, and to those who need help or compassionate love.
Truth and love are mutually conditions, the one of the other.
" Truth cannot be sustained without mercy ; and mercy without truth makes men negligent ; so that the one ought to be
mingled with the other" (Jerome).   They both have their roots
in the knowledge of God, of which they are the fruit (Jer. xxii.
16 ; Isa. xi. 9) ; for the knowledge of God is not merely " an
acquaintance with His nature and will" (Hitzig), but knowledge of the love, faithfulness, and compassion of God, resting
upon the experience of the heart.   Such knowledge not only
produces fear of God, but also love and truthfulness towards

brethren (cf. Eph. iv. 32, Col. iii. 12 sqq.). Where this is wanting, injustice gains the upper hand.

Ver. 2. " *Swearing, and lying, and murdering, and stealing, and committing adultery; they break in, and blood reaches to blood.*" The enumeration of the prevailing sins and crimes commences with *infin. absoll.*, to set forth the acts referred to as such with the greater emphasis. *'Aláh*, to swear, in combination with *kichēsh*, signifies false swearing (= אָלוֹת שָׁוְא in ch. x. 4; compare the similar passage in Jer. vii. 9); but we must not on that account take *kichēsh* as subordinate to *'aláh*, or connect them together, so as to form one idea. Swearing refers to the breach of the second commandment, stealing to that of the eighth; and the infinitives which follow enumerate the sins against the fifth, the seventh, and the sixth commandments. With *pârâtsū* the address passes into the finite tense (Luther follows the LXX. and Vulg., and connects it with what precedes; but this is a mistake). The perfects, *pârâtsū* and *nâgâ'ū*, are not preterites, but express a completed act, reaching from the past into the present. *Pârats* to tear, to break, signifies in this instance a violent breaking in upon others, for the purpose of robbery and murder, " *grassari* as פריצים, *i.e.* as murderers and robbers" (Hitzig), whereby one bloody deed immediately followed another (Ezek. xviii. 10). *Dâmīm*: blood shed with violence, a bloody deed, a capital crime.

These crimes bring the land to ruin. Ver. 3. " *Therefore the land mourns, and every dweller therein, of beasts of the field and birds of the heaven, wastes away; and even the fishes of the sea perish.*" These words affirm not only that the inanimate creation suffers in consequence of the sins and crimes of men, but that the moral depravity of men causes the physical destruction of all other creatures. As God has given to man the dominion over all beasts, and over all the earth, that he may use it for the glory of God; so does He punish the wickedness of men by pestilences, or by the devastation of the earth. The mourning of the earth and the wasting away of the animals are the natural result of the want of rain and the great drought that ensues, such as was the case in the time of Ahab throughout the kingdom of the ten tribes (1 Kings xvii. 18), and judging from Amos i. 2, viii. 8, may have occurred repeatedly with the continued idolatry of the people. The verbs are not

futures, in which case the punishment would be only threatened, but aorists, expressing what has already happened, and
will continue still.   כָּל־יוֹשֵׁב בָּהּ (every dweller therein) : these
are not the men, but the animals, as the further definition
בְּחַיַּת וגו' shows.   בְּ is used in the enumeration of the individuals,
as in Gen. vii. 21, ix. 10.   The fishes are mentioned last, and
introduced with the emphasizing וְגַם, to show that the drought
would prevail to such an extent, that even lakes and other waters
would be dried up.   הָאָסֵף, to be collected, to be taken away, to
disappear or perish, as in Isa. xvi. 10, lx. 20, Jer. xlviii. 33.

Notwithstanding the outburst of the divine judgments, the
people prove themselves to be incorrigible in their sins.   Ver. 4.
" *Only let no man reason, and let no man punish ; yet thy people
are like priest-strivers.*"   אַךְ is to be explained from the tacit
antithesis, that with such depravity there would be much to
punish ; but this would be useless.   The first clause contains a
desperatæ nequitiæ argumentum.   The notion that the second
'*ish* is to be taken as an object, is decidedly to be rejected, since
it cannot be defended either from the expression אִישׁ בְּאִישׁ in
Isa. iii. 5, or by referring to Amos ii. 15, and does not yield any
meaning at all in harmony with the second half of the verse.
For there is no need to prove that it does not mean, " Every
one who has a priest blames the priest instead of himself when
any misfortune happens to him," as Hitzig supposes, since עַם
signifies the nation, and not an individual.   וְעַמְּךָ is attached
adversatively, giving the reason for the previous thought in the
sense of " since thy people," or simply " thy people are surely
like those who dispute with the priest."   The unusual expression, priest-disputers, equivalent to quarrellers with the priest,
an analogous expression to boundary-movers in ch. v. 10, may
be explained, as Luther, and Grotius, and others suppose, from
the law laid down in Deut. xvii. 12, 13, according to which
every law-suit was to be ultimately decided by the priest and
judge as the supreme tribunal, and in which, whoever presumes
to resist the verdict of this tribunal, is threatened with the
punishment of death.   The meaning is, that the nation resembled those who are described in the law as rebels against
the priest (Hengstenberg, *Dissertations on Pentateuch*, vol. i.
p. 112, translation).   The suffix " thy nation" does not refer
to the prophet, but to the sons of Israel, the sum total of whom

constituted their nation, which is directly addressed in the following verse.

Ver. 5. "*And so wilt thou stumble by day, and the prophet with thee will also stumble by night, and I will destroy thy mother.*" *Kâshal* is not used here with reference to the sin, as Simson supposes, but for the punishment, and signifies to fall, in the sense of to perish, as in ch. xiv. 2, Isa. xxxi. 3, etc. הַיּוֹם is not to-day, or in the day when the punishment shall fall, but " by day," *interdiu*, on acccount of the antithesis לַיְלָה, as in Neh. iv. 16. נָבִיא, used without an article in the most indefinite generality, refers to false prophets—not of Baal, however, but of Jehovah as worshipped under the image of a calf—who practised prophesying as a trade, and judging from 1 Kings xxii. 6, were very numerous in the kingdom of Israel. The declaration that the people should fall by day and the prophets by night, does not warrant our interpreting the day and night allegorically, the former as the time when the way of right is visible, and the latter as the time when the way is hidden or obscured; but according to the parallelism of the clauses, it is to be understood as signifying that the people and the prophets would fall at all times, by night and by day. "There would be no time free from the slaughter, either of individuals in the nation at large, or of false prophets" (Rosenmüller). In the second half of the verse, the destruction of the whole nation and kingdom is announced ('*ēm* is the whole nation, as in ch. ii. 2, Heb. 4.).

This thought is carried out still further in the second strophe, vers. 6–10. Ver. 6. "*My nation is destroyed for lack of knowledge; for thou, the knowledge hast thou rejected, and so do I reject thee from being a priest to me. Thou didst forget the law of thy God; thy sons will I also forget.*" The speaker is Jehovah: *my* nation, that is to say, the nation of Jehovah. This nation perishes for lack of the knowledge of God and His salvation. *Hadda'ath* (*the* knowledge) with the definite article points back to *da'ath Elōhīm* (knowledge of God) in ver. 1. This knowledge Israel might have drawn from the law, in which God had revealed His counsel and will (Deut. xxx. 15), but it would not. It rejected the knowledge and forgot the law of its God, and would be rejected and forgotten by God in consequence. In '*attâh* (*thou*) it is not the priests who are addressed— the custodians of the law and promoters of divine knowledge

in the nation—but the whole nation of the ten tribes which adhered to the image-worship set up by Jeroboam, with its illegal
priesthood (1 Kings xii. 26–33), in spite of all the divine threats
and judgments, through which one dynasty after another was
destroyed, and would not desist from this sin of Jeroboam. The
Lord would therefore reject it from being priest, *i.e.* would
deprive it of the privilege of being a priestly nation (Ex. xix. 6),
would strip it of its priestly rank, and make it like the heathen.
According to Olshausen (*Heb. Gram.* p. 179), the anomalous
form אמאסאָך is only a copyist's error for אֶמְאָסְךָ; but Ewald
(§ 247, *e*) regards it as an Aramæan pausal form. "Thy sons,"
the children of the national community, regarded as a mother,
are the individual members of the nation.

Ver. 7. "*The more they increased, the more they sinned against
me; their glory will I change into shame.*" כְּרֻבָּם, "according
to their becoming great," does not refer to the increase of the
population only (ch. ix. 11), but also to its growing into a
powerful nation, to the increase of its wealth and prosperity,
in consequence of which the population multiplied. The progressive increase of the greatness of the nation was only
attended by increasing sin. As the nation attributed to its own
idols the blessings upon which its prosperity was founded, and
by which it was promoted (cf. ch. ii. 7), and looked upon them
as the fruit and reward of its worship, it was strengthened
in this delusion by increasing prosperity, and more and more
estranged from the living God. The Lord would therefore
turn the glory of Ephraim, *i.e.* its greatness or wealth, into
shame. כְּבוֹדָם is probably chosen on account of its assonance
with כְּרֻבָּם. For the fact itself, compare ch. ii. 3, 9–11.

Ver. 8. "*The sin of my people they eat, and after their transgression do they lift up their soul.*" The reproof advances from
the sin of the whole nation to the sin of the priesthood. For
it is evident that this is intended, not only from the contents of
the present verse, but still more from the commencement of
the next. *Chatta'th 'ammī* (the sin of my people) is the sin-
offering of the people, the flesh of which the priests were commanded to eat, to wipe away the sin of the people (see Lev. vi.
26, and the remarks upon this law at Lev. x. 17). The fulfilment of this command, however, became a sin on the part of
the priests, from the fact that they directed their soul, *i.e.* their

longing desire, to the transgression of the people; in other words, that they wished the sins of the people to be increased, in order that they might receive a good supply of sacrificial meat to eat. The prophet evidently uses the word *chattā'th*, which signifies both sin and sin-offering, in a double sense, and intends to designate the eating of the flesh of the sin-offering as eating or swallowing the sin of the people. נָשָׂא נֶפֶשׁ אֶל, to lift up or direct the soul after anything, *i.e.* to cherish a longing for it, as in Deut. xxiv. 15, etc. The singular suffix attached to *naphshō (his* soul) is to be taken distributively : "(they) every one his soul." [1]

Ver. 9. " *Therefore it will happen as to the people so to the priest; and I will visit his ways upon him, and I repay to him his doing.*" Since the priests had abused their office for the purpose of filling their own bellies, they would perish along with the nation. The suffixes in the last clauses refer to the priest, although the retribution threatened would fall upon the people also, since it would happen to the priest as to the people. This explains the fact that in ver. 10 the first clause still applies to the priest ; whereas in the second clause the prophecy once more embraces the entire nation.

Ver. 10. " *They will eat, and not be satisfied; they commit whoredom, and do not increase: for they have left off taking heed to Jehovah.*" The first clause, which still refers to the priests on account of the evident retrospect in וְאָכְלוּ to יֹאכֵלוּ in ver. 8, is taken from the threat in Lev. xxvi. 16. The following word *hiznū*, to practise whoredom (with the meaning of the *kal* intensified as in ver. 18, not to seduce to whoredom), refers to the whole nation, and is to be taken in its literal sense, as the antithesis לֹא יִפְרֹצוּ requires. *Pârats*, to spread out, to increase in number, as in Ex. i. 12 and Gen. xxviii. 14. In the last clause לִשְׁמֹר belongs to Jehovah : they have given up keeping Jehovah, *i.e.* giving heed to Him (cf. Zech. xi. 11). This applies to the priests as well as to the people. Therefore God withdraws His blessing from both, so that those who eat are not satisfied, and those who commit whoredom do not increase.

The allusion to whoredom leads to the description of the

---

[1] It is evident from this verse, that the sacrificial worship was maintained in the kingdom of Israel according to the ritual of the Mosaic law, and that the Israelitish priests were still in possession of the rights conferred by the Pentateuch upon Levitical priests.

idolatrous conduct of the people in the third strophe, vers.
11–14, which is introduced with a general sentence. Ver. 11.
" *Whoring and wine and new wine take away the heart (the understanding* ").   Z^enūth is licentiousness in the literal sense of the
word, which is always connected with debauchery. What is
true of this, namely, that it weakens the mental power, shows
itself in the folly of idolatry into which the nation has fallen.
Ver. 12. " *My nation asks its wood, and its stick prophesies to it:
for a spirit of whoredom has seduced, and they go away whoring
from under their God.*"   שָׁאַל בְּעֵצוֹ is formed after שָׁאַל בַּיהוָה, to
ask for a divine revelation of the idols made of wood (Jer. x. 3;
Hab. ii. 19), namely, the teraphim (cf. ch. iii. 4, and Ezek.
xxi. 26). This reproof is strengthened by the antithesis *my*
nation, *i.e.* the nation of Jehovah, the living God, and *its* wood,
the wood made into idols by the people.   The next clause,
" and its stick is showing it," *sc.* future events (*higgīd* as in Isa.
xli. 22, 23, etc.), is supposed by Cyril of Alexandria to refer to
the practice of rhabdomancy, which he calls an invention of the
Chaldæans, and describes as consisting in this, that two rods
were held upright, and then allowed to fall while forms of incan-
tation were being uttered; and the oracle was inferred from the
way in which they fell, whether forwards or backwards, to the
right or to the left.   The course pursued was probably similar
to that connected with the use of the wishing rods.[1]   The
people do this because a spirit of whoredom has besotted them.

By *rūăch z^enūnīm* the whoredom is represented as a demoniacal power, which has seized upon the nation. *Z^enūnīm*
probably includes both carnal and spiritual whoredom, since
idolatry, especially the Asherah-worship, was connected with
gross licentiousness.   The missing object to הִתְעָה may easily
be supplied from the context. זָנָה מִתַּחַת אֱל', which differs from
זָנָה מֵאַחֲרֵי (ch. i. 2), signifies " to whore away from under God,"
i.e. so as to withdraw from subjection to God.

This whoredom is still further explained in the next verse.
Ver. 13. " *They sacrifice upon the tops of the mountains, and
upon the hills they burn incense, under oak and poplar and*

----

[1] According to Herod. iv. 67, this kind of soothsaying was very common
among the Scythians (see at Ezek. xxi. 26). Another description of rhabdomancy is described by Abarbanel, according to Maimonides and Moses
Mikkotz: cf. Marck and Rosenmüller on this passage.

terebinth, for their shadow is good; therefore your daughters commit whoredom, and your daughters-in-law commit adultery." Mountain-tops and hills were favourite places for idolatrous worship; because men thought, that there they were nearer to heaven and to the deity (see at Deut. xii. 2). From a comparison of these and other passages, *e.g.* Jer. ii. 20 and iii. 6, it is evident that the following words, "under oak," etc., are not to be understood as signifying that trees standing by themselves upon mountains and hills were selected as places for idolatrous worship; but that, in addition to mountains and hills, green shady trees in the plains and valleys were also chosen for this purpose. By the enumeration of the oak, the poplar (*libhneh*, the white poplar according to the Sept. *in loc.* and the Vulg. at Gen. xxxvii. 30, or the storax-tree, as the LXX. render it at Gen. xxxvii. 30), and the terebinth, the frequent expression "under every green tree" (Deut. xii. 2, 1 Kings xiv. 23, Jer. ii. 20, iii. 6) is individualized. Such trees were selected because they gave a good shade, and in the burning lands of the East a shady place fills the mind with sacred awe. עַל־כֵּן, therefore, on that account, *i.e.* not because the shadow of the trees invites to it, but because the places for idolatrous worship erected on every hand presented an opportunity for it; therefore the daughters and daughters-in-law carried on prostitution there. The worship of the Canaanitish and Babylonian goddess of nature was associated with prostitution, and with the giving up of young girls and women (compare Movers, *Phönizier*, i. pp. 583, 595 sqq.).

Ver. 14. "*I will not visit it upon your daughters that they commit whoredom, nor upon your daughters-in-law that they commit adultery; for they themselves go aside with harlots, and with holy maidens do they sacrifice: and the nation that does not see is ruined.*" God would not punish the daughters and daughters-in-law for their whoredom, because the elder ones did still worse. "So great was the number of fornications, that all punishment ceased, in despair of any amendment" (Jerome). With כִּי הֵם God turns away from the reckless nation, as unworthy of being further addressed or exhorted, in righteous indignation at such presumptuous sinning, and proceeds to speak about it in the third person: for "*they* (the fathers and husbands, not 'the priests,' as Simson supposes,

since there is no allusion to them here) go," etc. פָּרַד, *piel* in
an intransitive sense, to separate one's self, to go aside for the
purpose of being alone with the harlots. Sacrificing with the
qᵉdēshōth, i.e. with prostitutes, or *Hetairai* (see at Gen. xxxviii.
14), may have taken its rise in the prevailing custom, viz. that
fathers of families came with their wives to offer yearly sacrifices, and the wives shared in the sacrificial meals (1 Sam. i.
3 sqq.). Coming to the altar with *Hetairai* instead of their
own wives, was the climax of shameless licentiousness. A
nation that had sunk so low and had lost all perception must

perish. לָבַט = لبط : to throw to the earth ; or in the *niphal*, to

cast headlong into destruction (Prov. x. 8, 10).

A different turn is now given to the prophecy, viz. that if
Israel would not desist from idolatry, Judah ought to beware
of participating in the guilt of Israel ; and with this the fourth
strophe (vers. 15–19) is introduced, containing the announcement of the inevitable destruction of the kingdom of the ten
tribes. Ver. 15. *" If thou commit whoredom, O Israel, let not
Judah offend ! Come ye not to Gilgal, go not up to Bethaven,
and swear ye not by the life of Jehovah."* אָשֵׁם, to render one's
self guilty by participating in the whoredom, *i.e.* the idolatry, of
Israel. This was done by making pilgrimages to the places of
idolatrous worship in that kingdom, viz. to *Gilgal, i.e.* not the
Gilgal in the valley of the Jordan, but the northern Gilgal
upon the mountains, which has been preserved in the village of
Jiljilia to the south-west of Silo (Seilun ; see at Deut. xi. 30
and Josh. viii. 35). In the time of Elijah and Elisha it was the
seat of a school of the prophets (2 Kings ii. 1, iv. 38) ; but it
was afterwards chosen as the seat of one form of idolatrous
worship, the origin and nature of which are unknown (compare
ch. ix. 15, xii. 12 ; Amos iv. 4, v. 5). *Bethaven* is not the place
of that name mentioned in Josh. vii. 2, which was situated to
the south-east of Bethel ; but, as Amos iv. 4 and v. 5 clearly
show, a name which Hosea adopted from Amos v. 5 for *Bethel*
(the present *Beitin*), to show that *Bethel,* the house of God, had
become Bethaven, a house of idols, through the setting up of the
golden calf there (1 Kings xii. 29). Swearing by the name of
Jehovah was commanded in the law (Deut. vi. 13, x. 20 ; compare Jer. iv. 2) ; but this oath was to have its roots in the fear

of Jehovah, to be simply an emanation of His worship. The worshippers of idols, therefore, were not to take it into their mouths. The command not to swear by the life of Jehovah is connected with the previous warnings. Going to Gilgal to worship idols, and swearing by Jehovah, cannot go together. The confession of Jehovah in the mouth of an idolater is hypocrisy, pretended piety, which is more dangerous than open ungodliness, because it lulls the conscience to sleep.

The reason for this warning is given in vers. 16 sqq., viz. the punishment which will fall upon Israel. Ver. 16. "*For Israel has become refractory like a refractory cow; now will Jehovah feed them like a lamb in a wide field.*" סוֹרֵר, unmanageable, refractory (Deut. xxi. 18, cf. Zech. vii. 11). As Israel would not submit to the yoke of the divine law, it should have what it desired. God would feed it like a lamb, which being in a wide field becomes the prey of wolves and wild beasts, *i.e.* He would give it up to the freedom of banishment and dispersion among the nations.

Ver. 17. "*Ephraim is joined to idols, let it alone.*" חֲבוּר עֲצַבִּים, bound up with idols, so that it cannot give them up. Ephraim, the most powerful of the ten tribes, is frequently used in the loftier style of the prophets for Israel of the ten tribes. הַנַּח־לוֹ, as in 2 Sam. xvi. 11, 2 Kings xxiii. 18, let him do as he likes, or remain as he is. Every attempt to bring the nation away from its idolatry is vain. The expression *hannach-lō* does not necessitate the assumption, however, that these words of Jehovah are addressed to the prophets. They are taken from the language of ordinary life, and simply mean: it may continue in its idolatry, the punishment will not long be delayed.

Ver. 18. "*Their drinking has degenerated; whoring they have committed whoredom; their shields have loved, loved shame.* Ver. 19. *The wind has wrapt it up in its wings, so that they are put to shame because of their sacrifices.*" סָר from סוּר, to fall off, degenerate, as in Jer. ii. 21. סֹבֵא is probably strong, intoxicating wine (cf. Isa. i. 22; Nah. i. 10); here it signifies the effect of this wine, viz. intoxication. Others take *sâr* in the usual sense of departing, after 1 Sam. i. 14, and understand the sentence conditionally: "when their intoxication is gone, they commit whoredom." But Hitzig has very properly objected to this, that it is intoxication which leads to licentiousness, and not temperance. Moreover, the strengthening of *hiznû* by the *infin. abs.* is not in harmony with this explanation. The *hiphil hiznâh* is used in an emphatic sense, as in ver. 10. The meaning of the last half of the verse is also a disputed point, more especially on account of the word הֵבוּ, which only occurs here, and which can only be the imperative of יָהַב (הֵבוּ for הֲבוּ), or a contraction of אָהֲבוּ. All other explanations are arbitrary. But we are precluded from taking the word as an imperative by קָלוֹן, which altogether confuses the sense, if we adopt the rendering " their shields love ' Give ye'—shame." We therefore prefer taking הֵבוּ as a contraction of אָהֲבוּ, and אָהֲבוּ הֵבוּ as a construction resembling the pealal form, in which the latter part of the fully formed verb is repeated, with the verbal person as an independent form (Ewald, § 120), viz. "their shields loved, loved shame," which yields a perfectly suitable thought. The princes are figuratively represented as *shields*, as in Ps. xlvii. 10, as the supporters and protectors of the state. They love shame, inasmuch as they love the sin which brings shame. This shame will inevitably burst upon the kingdom. The tempest has already seized upon the people, or wrapt them up with its wings (cf. Ps. xviii. 11, civ. 3), and will carry them away (Isa. lvii. 13). צָרַר, literally to bind together, hence to lay hold of, wrap up. *Rûăch*, the wind, or tempest, is a figurative term denoting destruction, like רוּחַ קָדִים in ch. xiii. 15 and Ezek. v. 3, 4. אוֹתָהּ refers to Ephraim represented as a woman, like the suffix attached to מַגִּנֶּיהָ in ver. 18. יֵבֹשׁוּ מִזִּבְחוֹתָם, to be put to shame on account of their sacrifices, *i.e.* to be deceived in their confidence in their idols (*bôsh* with *min* as in ch. x. 6, Jer. ii. 36, xii. 13, etc.), or to discover that the sacrifices which they offered to Jehovah, whilst their heart was attached to the idols, did not save from ruin. The plural formation זְבָחוֹת for זְבָחִים only occurs here, but it has many analogies in its favour, and does not warrant our altering the reading into מִזְבְּחֹתָם, after the Sept. ἐν τῶν θυσιαστηρίων, as Hitzig proposes; whilst the inadmissibility of this proposal is sufficiently demonstrated by the fact that there is nothing to justify the omission of the indispensable מִן, and the cases which Hitzig cites as instances in which *min* is omitted (viz. Zech. xiv. 10, Ps. lxviii. 14, and Deut. xxiii. 11) are based upon a false interpretation.

The Judgment.—Chap. v.-vi. 3.

With the words " Hear ye this," the reproof of the sins of Israel makes a new start, and is specially addressed to the priests and the king's house, *i.e.* the king and his court, to announce to the leaders of the nation the punishment that will follow their apostasy from God and their idolatry, by which they have plunged the people and kingdom headlong into destruction. Vers. 1–5 form the first strophe. Ver. 1. " *Hear ye this, ye priests; and give heed thereto, O house of Israel; and observe it, O house of the king! for the judgment applies to you; for ye have become a snare at Mizpah, and a net spread upon Tabor.*" By the word " *this*," which points back to ver. 4, the prophecy that follows is attached to the preceding one. Beside the priests and the king's house, *i.e.* the royal family, in which the counsellors and adjutants surrounding the king are probably included, the house of Israel, that is to say, the people of the ten tribes regarded as a family, is summoned to hear, because what was about to be announced applied to the people and kingdom as a whole. There is nothing to warrant our understanding by the " house of Israel," the heads of the nation or elders. *Lâkhem hammishpât* does not mean, It rests with you to know or to defend the right; nor, " Ye ought to hear the reproof," as Hitzig explains it, for *mishpât* in this connection signifies neither " the maintenance of justice " nor " a reproof," but the judgment about to be executed by God, τὸ κρίμα (LXX.). The thought is this, The judgment will fall upon you; and *lâkhem* refers chiefly to the priests and the king's house, as the explanatory clause which follows clearly shows. It is impossible to determine with certainty what king's house is intended. Probably that of Zechariah or Menahem; possibly both, since Hosea prophesied in both reigns, and merely gives the quintessence of his prophetical addresses in his book. Going to Asshur refers rather to Menahem than to Zechariah (comp. 2 Kings xv. 19, 20). In the figures employed, the bird-trap (*pach*) and the net spread for catching birds, it can only be the rulers of the nation who are represented as a trap and net, and the birds must denote the people generally who are enticed into the net of destruction and

caught (cf. ch. ix. 8).[1] *Mizpah*, as a parallel to Tabor, can only
be the lofty *Mizpah* of Gilead (Judg. x. 17, xi. 29) or Ramah-
Mizpah, which probably stood upon the site of the modern
es-Salt (see at Deut. iv. 43); so that, whilst Tabor represents
the land on this side of the Jordan, Mizpah, which resembled
it in situation, is chosen to represent the land to the east of the
river.[2] Both places were probably noted as peculiarly adapted
for bird-catching, since Tabor is still thickly wooded. The
supposition that they had been used as places of sacrifice in
connection with idolatrous worship, cannot be inferred from
the verse before us, nor is it rendered probable by other
passages.

This accusation is still further vindicated in vers. 2 sqq.,
by a fuller exposure of the moral corruption of the nation.
Ver. 2. "*And excesses they have spread out deeply; but I am
a chastisement to them all.*" The meaning of the first half
of the verse, which is very difficult, and has been very differently interpreted by both ancient and modern expositors,
has been brought out best by Delitzsch (Com. on Ps. ci. 3),
who renders it, "they understand from the very foundation
how to spread out transgressions." For the word שֵׂטִים the
meaning transgressions is well established by the use of סֵטִים in
Ps. ci. 3, where Hengstenberg, Hupfeld, and Delitzsch all
agree that this is the proper rendering (see Ewald's philological
defence of it at § 146, *e*). In the psalm referred to, however,
the expression עָשֹׂה סֵטִים also shows that *shachătâh* is the inf.
piel, and *sētīm* the accusative of the object. And it follows
from this that *shachătâh* neither means to slaughter or slaughter
sacrifices, nor can be used for שׁחתה in the sense of acting
injuriously, but that it is to be interpreted according to the
shâchūth in 1 Kings x. 16, 17, in the sense of stretching,
stretching out; so that there is no necessity to take שׁחט in the

---

[1] Jerome has given a very good explanation of the figure: "I have
appointed you as watchmen among the people, and set you in the highest
place of honour, that ye might govern the erring people; but ye have
become a trap, and are to be called sportsmen rather than watchmen."

[2] As Tabor, for instance, rises up as a solitary conical hill (see at Judg.
iv. 6), so *es-Salt* is built about the sides of a round steep hill, which rises
up in a narrow rocky valley, and upon the summit of which there stands
a strong fortification (see Seetzen in Burckhardt's *Reisen in Syrien*, p.
1061).

sense of שׁטח, as Delitzsch does, though the use of עָלְוָה for עֹלָה in ch. x. 9 may no doubt be adduced in its support. שֵׂטִים, from שָׂטָה (to turn aside, Num. v. 12, 19), are literally digressions or excesses, answering to the *hiznâh* in ver. 3, the leading sin of Israel. "They have deepened to stretch out excesses," *i.e.* they have gone to great lengths, or are deeply sunken in excesses,—a thought quite in harmony with the context, to which the threat is appended. "I (Jehovah) am a chastisement to them all, to the rulers as well as to the people;" *i.e.* I will punish them all (cf. ver. 12), because their idolatrous conduct is well known to me. The way is thus prepared for the two following verses.

Ver. 3. "*I know Ephraim, and Israel is not hid from me: for now, O Ephraim, thou hast committed whoredom; Israel has defiled itself.* Ver. 4. *Their works do not allow to return to their God, for the spirit of whoredom is in them, and they know not Jehovah.*" By עַתָּה, the whoredom of Ephraim is designated as in fact lying before them, and therefore undeniable; but not, as Hitzig supposes, an act which has taken place once for all, viz. the choice of a king, by which the severance of the kingdoms and the previous idolatry had been sanctioned afresh. נִטְמָא, defiled by whoredom, *i.e.* idolatry. Their works do not allow them to return to their God, because the works are merely an emanation of the character and state of the heart, and in their hearts the demon of whoredom has its seat (cf. ch. iv. 12), and the knowledge of the Lord is wanting; that is to say, the demoniacal power of idolatry has taken complete possession of the heart, and stifled the knowledge of the true God. The rendering, "they do not direct their actions to this," is incorrect, and cannot be sustained by an appeal to the use of נָתַן לֵב in Judg. xv. 1 and 1 Sam. xxiv. 8 sqq., or to Judg. iii. 28.

Ver. 5. "*And the pride of Ephraim will testify against its face, and Israel and Ephraim will stumble in their guilt; Judah has also stumbled with them.*" As the meaning "to answer," to bear witness against a person, is well established in the case of עָנָה בְ (cf. Num. xxxv. 30, Deut. xix. 18, and Isa. iii. 9), and עָנָה בְּפָנִים also occurs in Job xvi. 8 in this sense, we must retain the same meaning here, as Jerome and others have done. And there is the more reason for this, because the explanation based upon the LXX., καὶ ταπεινωθήσεται ἡ ὕβρις, "the haughtiness of Israel will be humbled," can hardly be reconciled with בְּפָנָיו. "The pride of Israel," moreover, is not the haughtiness of Israel, but that of which Israel is proud, or rather the glory of Israel. We might understand by this the flourishing condition of the kingdom, after Amos vi. 8; but it would be only by its decay that this would bear witness against the sin of Israel, so that "the glory of Israel" would stand for "the decay of that glory," which would be extremely improbable. We must therefore explain "the glory of Israel" here and in ch. vii. 10 in accordance with Amos viii. 7, *i.e.* we must understand it as referring to Jehovah, who is Israel's eminence and glory; in which case we obtain the following very appropriate thought: They know not Jehovah, they do not concern themselves about Him; therefore He Himself will bear witness by judgments, by the destruction of their false glory (cf. ch. ii. 10–14), against the face of Israel, *i.e.* bear witness to their face. This thought occurs without ambiguity in ch. vii. 10. Israel will stumble in its sin, *i.e.* will fall and perish (as in ch. iv. 5). Judah also falls with Israel, because it has participated in Israel's sin (ch. iv. 15).

Israel, moreover, will not be able to avert the threatening judgment by sacrifices. Jehovah will withdraw from the faithless generation, and visit it with His judgments. This is the train of thought in the next strophe (vers. 6–10). Ver. 6. *" They will go with their sheep and their oxen to seek Jehovah, and will not find Him: He has withdrawn Himself from them. Ver. 7. They acted treacherously against Jehovah, for they have born strange children: now will the new moon devour them with their fields."* The offering of sacrifices will be no help to them, because God has withdrawn Himself from them, and does not hear their prayers; for God has no pleasure in sacrifices which are offered in an impenitent state of mind (cf. ch. vi. 6; Isa. i. 11 sqq.; Jer. vii. 21 sqq.; Ps. xl. 7, l. 8 sqq.). The reason for this is given in ver. 7. *Bâgad,* to act faithlessly, which is frequently applied to the infidelity of a wife towards her husband (*e.g.* Jer. iii. 20; Mal. ii. 14; cf. Ex. xxi. 8), points to the conjugal relation in which Israel stood to Jehovah. Hence the figure which follows. "Strange children" are such as do not belong to the home (Deut. xxv. 5), *i.e.* such as have not sprung from the conjugal union. In actual fact, the expression is equivalent to בְּנֵי זְנוּנִים in ch. i. 2, ii. 4, though *zâr* does not expressly mean " adulterous." Israel ought to have begotten children of God in the maintenance of the covenant with the Lord; but in its apostasy from God it had begotten an adulterous generation, children whom the Lord could not acknowledge as His own. " The new moon will devour them," viz. those who act so faithlessly. The meaning is not, " they will be destroyed on the next new moon ;" but the new moon, as the festal season, on which sacrifices were offered (1 Sam. xx. 6, 29 ; Isa. i. 13, 14), stands here for the sacrifices themselves that were offered upon it. The meaning is this : your sacrificial feast, your hypocritical worship, so far from bringing you salvation, will rather prove your ruin. חֶלְקֵיהֶם are not sacrificial portions, but the hereditary portions of Israel, the portions of land that fell to the different families and households, and from the produce of which they offered sacrifices to the Lord.[1]

The prophet sees in spirit the judgment already falling upon the rebellious nation, and therefore adddresses the following appeal to the people. Ver. 8. *"Blow ye the horn at Gibeah, the trumpet at Ramah ! Raise the cry at Bethaven, Behind thee, Benjamin !"* The blowing of the *shōphâr*, a far-sounding horn, or of the trumpet[2] (*chătsōtsᵉrâh*), was a signal by which the invasion of foes (ch. viii. 1 ; Jer. iv. 5, vi. 1) and other calamities (Joel. ii. 1, cf. Amos iii. 6) were announced, to give the inhabitants warning of the danger that threatened them. The words therefore imply that foes had invaded the land. *Gibeah* (of Saul ; see at Josh. xviii. 28) and *Ramah* (of Samuel ; see at Josh. xviii. 25) were two elevated places on the northern boundary of the tribe of Benjamin, which were well adapted for signals, on account of their lofty situation. The introduction of these particular towns, which did not belong to the tribe of Israel, but to that of Judah, is intended to intimate that the enemy has already conquered the kingdom of the ten tribes,

---

[1] It is very evident from this verse, that the feasts and the worship prescribed in the Mosaic law were observed in the kingdom of the ten tribes, at the places of worship in Bethel and Dan.

[2] " The *sophar* was a shepherd's horn, and was made of a carved horn ; the *tuba* (*chătsōtsᵉrâh*) was made of brass or silver, and sounded either in the time of war or at festivals."—JEROME.

and has advanced to the border of that of Judah. הָרִיעַ, to make
a noise, is to be understood here as relating to the alarm given
by the war-signals already mentioned, as in Joel ii. 1, cf. Num.
x. 9. *Bethaven* is Bethel (Beitin), as in ch. iv. 15, the seat of
the idolatrous worship of the calves ; and בֵּית is to be taken in
the sense of בְּבֵית (according to Ges. § 118, 1). The difficult
words, " behind thee, Benjamin," cannot indicate the situation
or attitude of Benjamin, in relation to Bethel or the kingdom
of Israel, or show that " the invasion is to be expected to start
from Benjamin," as Simson supposes. For the latter is no
more appropriate in this train of thought than a merely geographical or historical notice. The words are taken from the
ancient war-song of Deborah (Judg. v. 14), but in a different
sense from that in which they are used there. There they
mean that Benjamin marched behind Ephraim, or joined it in
attacking the foe ; here, on the contrary, they mean that the
foe is coming behind Benjamin—that the judgment announced
has already broken out in the rear of Benjamin. There is no
necessity to supply " the enemy rises" behind thee, O Benjamin,
as Jerome proposes, or " the sword rages," as Hitzig suggests ;
but what comes behind Benjamin is implied in the words, " Blow
ye the horn," etc. What these signals announce is coming
after Benjamin ; there is no necessity, therefore, to supply anything more than " it is," or " it comes." The prophet, for
example, not only announces in ver. 8 that enemies will invade
Israel, but that the hosts by which God will punish His rebellious
people have already overflowed the kingdom of Israel, and are
now standing upon the border of Judah, to punish this kingdom
also for its sins. This is evident from vers. 9, 10, which contain the practical explanation of ver. 8.

Ver. 9. "*Ephraim will become a desert in the day of punishment: over the tribes of Israel have I proclaimed that which
lasts.* Ver. 10. *The princes of Judah have become like boundary-movers ; upon them I pour out my wrath like water.*" The
kingdom of Israel will entirely succumb to the punishment. It
will become a desert—will be laid waste not only for a time, but
permanently. The punishment with which it is threatened will
be נֶאֱמָנָה. This word is to be interpreted as in Deut. xxviii. 59,
where it is applied to lasting plagues, with which God will
chastise the obstinate apostasy of His people. By the perfect

הוֹדַעְתִּי, what is here proclaimed is represented as a completed event, which will not be altered. *B*e*shibhtē*, not in or among the tribes, but according to עָנָה בְ, in ver. 5, against or over the tribes (Hitzig). Judah also will not escape the punishment of its sins. The unusual expression *massīgē g*e*bhūl* is formed after, and to be explained from Deut. xix. 14, " Thou shalt not remove thy neighbour's landmark;" or xxvii. 17, " Cursed be he that removeth his neighbour's landmark." The princes of Judah have become boundary-removers, not by hostile invasions of the kingdom of Israel (Simson); for the boundary-line between Israel and Judah was not so appointed by God, that a violation of it on the part of the princes of Judah could be reckoned a grievous crime, but by removing the boundaries of right which had been determined by God, viz. according to ch. iv. 15, by participating in the guilt of Ephraim, *i.e.* by idolatry, and therefore by the fact that they had removed the boundary between Jehovah and Baal, that is to say, between the one true God and idols. " If he who removes his neighbour's boundary is cursed, how much more he who removes the border of his God!" (Hengstenberg.) Upon such men the wrath of God would fall in its fullest measure. כַּמַּיִם, like a stream of water, so plentifully. For the figure, compare Ps. lxix. 25, lxxix. 6, Jer. x. 25. Severe judgments are thus announced to Judah, viz. those of which the Assyrians under Tiglath-pileser and Sennacherib were the instruments; but no ruin or lasting devastation is predicted, as was the case with the kingdom of Israel, which was destroyed by the Assyrians.

From these judgments Israel and Judah will not be set free, until in their distress they seek their God. This thought is expanded in the next strophe (vers. 11–15). Ver. 11. *" Ephraim is oppressed, broken in pieces by the judgment; for it has wished, has gone according to statute."* By the participles *'āshūq* and *rātsūts*, the calamity is represented as a lasting condition, which the prophet saw in the spirit as having already begun. The two words are connected together even in Deut. xxviii. 33, to indicate the complete subjection of Israel to the power and oppression of its foes, as a punishment for falling away from the Lord. *R*e*tsūts mishpât* does not mean " of broken right," or " injured in its right" (Ewald and Hitzig), but " broken in pieces by the judgment" (of God), with a *geni-*

tivum efficientis, like *mukkēh Elōhīm* in Isa. liii. 4. For it liked to walk according to statute. For הָלַךְ אַחֲרֵי compare Jer. ii. 5 and 2 Kings xviii. 15. *Tsav* is a human statute; it stands both here and in Isa. xxviii. 10, 13, the only other passages in which it occurs, as an antithesis to the word or commandment of God. The statute intended is the one which the kingdom of Israel upheld from beginning to end, viz. the worship of the calves, that root of all the sins, which brought about the dissolution and ruin of the kingdom.

Ver. 12. "*And I am like the moth to Ephraim, and like the worm to the house of Judah.*" The moth and worm are figures employed to represent destructive powers; the moth destroying clothes (Isa. l. 9, li. 8; Ps. xxxix. 12), the worm injuring both wood and flesh. They are both connected again in Job xiii. 28, as things which destroy slowly but surely, to represent, as Calvin says, *lenta Dei judicia.* God becomes a destructive power to the sinner through the thorn of conscience, and the chastisements which are intended to effect his reformation, but which lead inevitably to his ruin when he hardens himself against them. The preaching of the law by the prophets sharpened the thorn in the conscience of Israel and Judah. The chastisement consisted in the infliction of the punishments threatened in the law, viz. in plagues and invasions of their foes.

The two kingdoms could not defend themselves against this chastisement by the help of any earthly power. Ver. 13. "*And Ephraim saw his sickness, and Judah his abscess; and Ephraim went to Asshur, and sent to king Jareb (striver): but he cannot cure you, nor drive the abscess away from you.*" By the imperfects, with *Vav rel.*, וַיַּרְא, וַיֵּלֶךְ, the attempts of Ephraim and Judah to save themselves from destruction are represented as the consequence of the coming of God to punish, referred to in ver. 12. Inasmuch as this is to be seen, so far as the historical fulfilment is concerned, not in the present, but in the past and future, the attempts to obtain a cure for the injuries also belong to the present (? past) and future. *Māzōr* does not mean a bandage or the cure of injuries (Ges., Dietr.), but is derived from זוּר, to squeeze out (see Del. on Isa. i. 6), and signifies literally that which is pressed out, *i.e.* a festering wound, an abscess. It has this meaning not only here, but also in Jer. xxx. 13, from which the meaning bandage has been derived. On the figure employed, viz. the disease of the body politic, see Delitzsch on Isa. i. 5, 6. That this disease is not to be sought for specially in anarchy and civil war (Hitzig), is evident from the simple fact, that Judah, which was saved from these evils, is described as being just as sick as Ephraim. The real disease of the two kingdoms was apostasy from the Lord, or idolatry with its train of moral corruption, injustice, crimes, and vices of every kind, which destroyed the vital energy and vital marrow of the two kingdoms, and generated civil war and anarchy in the kingdom of Israel. Ephraim sought for help from the Assyrians, viz. from king *Jareb,* but without obtaining it. The name *Jareb, i.e.* warrior, which occurs here and at ch. x. 6, is an epithet formed by the prophet himself, and applied to the king of Assyria, not of Egypt, as Theodoret supposes. The omission of the article from מֶלֶךְ may be explained from the fact that *Jârēbh* is, strictly speaking, an appellative, as in לְמוּאֵל מֶלֶךְ in Prov. xxxi. 1. We must not supply *Y*ᵉ*hūdáh* as the subject to *vayyishlach.* The omission of any reference to Judah in the second half of the verse, may be accounted for from the fact that the prophecy had primrily and principally to do with Ephraim, and that Judah was only cursorily mentioned. The ἀπ. λεγ. יִגְהֶה from גָּהָה, in Syriac to be shy, to flee, is used with *min* in the tropical sense of removing or driving away.

No help is to be expected from Assyria, because the Lord will punish His people. Ver. 14. *" For I am like a lion to Ephraim, and like the young lion to the house of Judah: I, I tear in pieces, and go; I carry away, and there is no deliverer.* Ver. 15. *I go, return to my place, till they repent and shall seek my face. In their affliction they will seek me early."* For the figure of the lion, which seizes it prey, and tears it in pieces without deliverance, see ch. xiii. 7 and Isa. v. 29. אֶשָּׂא denotes the carrying away of booty, as in 1 Sam. xvii. 34. For the fact itself, compare Deut. xxxii. 39. The first clause of ver. 15 is still to be interpreted from the figure of the lion. As the lion withdraws into its cave, so will the Lord withdraw into His own place, viz. heaven, and deprive the Israelites of His gracious, helpful presence, until they repent, *i.e.* not only feel themselves guilty, but feel the guilt by bearing the punishment.

Suffering punishment awakens the need of mercy, and impels them to seek the face of the Lord. The expression, " in the distress to them," recals בַּצַּר לְךָ in Deut. iv. 30. *Shichēr* is to be taken as a denom. of *shachar*, the morning dawn (ch. vi. 3), in the sense of early, *i.e.* zealously, urgently, as the play upon the word כְּשַׁחַר in ch. vi. 3 *unmistakeably* shows. For the fact itself, compare ch. ii. 9 and Deut. iv. 29, 30.

Chap. vi. 1–3. To this threat the prophet appends in the concluding strophe, both the command to return to the Lord, and the promise that the Lord will raise His smitten nation up again, and quicken them anew with His grace. The separation of these three verses from the preceding one, by the division of the chapters, is at variance with the close connection in the actual contents, which is so perfectly obvious in the allusion made in the words of ver. 1, " Come, and let us return," to those of ch. v. 15, " I will go, and return," and in טָרַף וְיִרְפָּאֵנוּ (ver. 1) to the similar words in ch. v. 13*b* and 14. Ver. 1. " *Come, and let us return to Jehovah: for He has torn in pieces, and will heal us ; He has smitten, and will bind us up.* Ver. 2. *He will quicken us after two days ; on the third He will raise us up, that we may live before Him."* The majority of commentators, following the example of the Chald. and Septuagint, in which לֵאמֹר, λέγοντες, is interpolated before לְכוּ, have taken the first three verses as an appeal to return to the Lord, addressed by the Israelites in exile to one another. But it would be more simple, and more in harmony with the general style of Hosea, which is characterized by rapid transitions, to take the words as a call addressed by the prophet in the name of the Lord to the people, whom the Lord had smitten or sent into exile. The promise in ver. 3 especially is far more suitable to a summons of this kind, than to an appeal addressed by the people to one another. As the endurance of punishment impels to seek the Lord (ch. v. 15), so the motive to return to the Lord is founded upon the knowledge of the fact that the Lord can, and will, heal the wounds which He inflicts. The preterite *târaph*, as compared with the future *'etrōph* in ch. v. 14, presupposes that the punishment has already begun. The following יַךְ is also a preterite with the *Vav consec.* omitted. The Assyrian cannot heal (ch. v. 13) ; but the Lord, who manifested Himself as Israel's physician in the time of Moses

(Ex. xv. 26), and promised His people healing in the future also (Deut. xxxii. 39), surely can. The allusion in the word יִרְפָּאֵנוּ to this passage of Deuteronomy, is placed beyond all doubt by ver. 2. The words, "He revives after two days," etc., are merely a special application of the general declaration, "I kill, and make alive" (Deut. xxxii. 39), to the particular case in hand. What the Lord there promises to all His people, He will also fulfil upon the ten tribes of Israel. By the definition "after two days," and "on the third day," the speedy and certain revival of Israel is set before them. Two and three days are very short periods of time; and the linking together of two numbers following one upon the other, expresses the certainty of what is to take place within this space of time, just as in the so-called numerical sayings in Amos i. 3, Job v. 19, Prov. vi. 16, xxx. 15, 18, in which the last and greater number expresses the highest or utmost that is generally met with. הֵקִים, to raise the dead (Job xiv. 12; Ps. lxxxviii. 11; Isa. xxvi. 14, 19). "That we may live before Him:" i.e. under His sheltering protection and grace (cf. Gen. xvii. 18). The earlier Jewish and Christian expositors have taken the numbers, "after two days, and on the third day," chronologically. The Rabbins consequently suppose the prophecy to refer either to the three captivities, the Egyptian, the Babylonian, and the Roman, which has not ended yet; or to the three periods of the temple of Solomon, of that of Zerubbabel, and of the one to be erected by the Messiah. Many of the fathers, on the other hand, and many of the early Lutheran commentators, have found in them a prediction of the death of Christ and His resurrection on the third day. Compare, for example, *Calovii Bibl. illustr. ad h. l.*, where this allusion is defended by a long series of undeniably weak arguments, and where a fierce attack is made, not only upon Calvin, who understood these words as "referring to the liberation of Israel from captivity, and the restoration of the church after two days, *i.e.* in a very short time;" but also upon Grotius, who found, in addition to the immediate historical allusion to the Israelites, whom God would soon liberate from their death-like misery after their conversion, a foretype, in consequence of a special divine indication, of the time "within which Christ would recover His life, and the church its hope." But any direct allusion in the hope here uttered to the death and resurrection of Christ, is proved to be untenable by the simple words and their context. The words primarily hold out nothing more than the quickening of Israel out of its death-like state of rejection from the face of God, and that in a very short period after its conversion to the Lord. This restoration to life cannot indeed be understood as referring to the return of the exiles to their earthly fatherland; or, at all events, it cannot be restricted to this. It does not occur till after the conversion of Israel to the Lord its God, on the ground of faith in the redemption effected through the atoning death of Christ, and His resurrection from the grave; so that the words of the prophet may be applied to this great fact in the history of salvation, but without its being either directly or indirectly predicted. Even the resurrection of the dead is not predicted, but simply the spiritual and moral restoration of Israel to life, which no doubt has for its necessary complement the reawakening of the physically dead. And, in this sense, our passage may be reckoned among the prophetic utterances which contain the germ of the hope of a life after death, as in Isa. xxvi. 19–21, and in the vision of Ezekiel in Ezek. xxxvii. 1–14.

That it did not refer to this in its primary sense, and so far as its historical fulfilment was concerned, is evident from the following verse. Ver. 3. "*Let us therefore know, hunt after the knowledge of Jehovah. His rising is fixed like the morning dawn, that He may come to us like the rain, and moisten the earth like the latter rain.*" וְנֵדְעָה נִר' corresponds to לְכוּ וְנָשׁוּבָה in ver. 1. The object to נדעה is also אֶת־יְהוָֹה, and נדעה is merely strengthened by the addition of נִרְדְּפָה לָדַעַת. The knowledge of Jehovah, which they would hunt after, *i.e.* strive zealously to obtain, is a practical knowledge, consisting in the fulfilment of the divine commandments, and in growth in the love of God with all the heart. This knowledge produces fruit. The Lord will rise upon Israel like the morning dawn, and come down upon it like fertilizing rain. מוֹצָאוֹ, His (*i.e.* Jehovah's) rising, is to be explained from the figure of the dawn (for יָצָא applied to the rising of the sun, see Gen. xix. 23 and Ps. xix. 7). The dawn is mentioned instead of the sun, as the herald of the dawning day of salvation (compare Isa. lviii. 8 and lx. 2). This salvation which dawns when the Lord appears, is represented in the last clause as a shower of rain that fertilizes the land. יוֹרֶה is hardly a *kal* participle, but rather the imperfect *hiphil* in the sense of sprinkling. In Deut. xi. 14 (cf. xxviii. 12 and Lev. xxvi. 4, 5), the rain, or the early and latter rain, is mentioned among the blessings which the Lord will bestow upon His people, when they serve Him with all the heart and soul. This promise the Lord will so fulfil in the case of His newly quickened nation, that He Himself will refresh it like a fertilizing rain. This will take place through the Messiah, as Ps. lxxii. 6 and 2 Sam. xxiii. 4 clearly show.

II. THE RIPENESS OF ISRAEL FOR THE JUDGMENT OF DESTRUCTION.—CHAP. VI. 4–XI. 11.

Just as, in the middle section of the first part of our book (ch. ii. 2–23), the symbolical announcements of judgment contained in ch. i. were more fully elaborated and explained; so again, in the second part, after the shorter description of the corruption and culpability of Israel contained in ch. iv. v., we find in the second or middle section, viz. ch. vi. 4–xi. 11, a longer account both of the religious apostasy and moral corruption which have become so injurious, and also of the judgment about to fall upon the sinful kingdom and people. In this, the condemnation of sin and threatening of punishment follow one another throughout; but in such a way that in this longer exposition the progressive development of these truths is clearly indicated in the fact, that in the first section (ch. vi. 4–vii. 16) the description of the religious and moral degradation of the nation and its princes prevails; in the second (ch. viii. 1–ix. 9) the threatening of judgment comes into the foreground; and in the third (ch. ix. 10–xi. 11) evidence is adduced, how, from time immemorial, Israel has resisted the gracious guidance of God, so that nothing but the compassion of God can preserve it from utter annihilation. Each of these divisions may be subdivided again into three strophes.

The Incurableness of the Corruption.—Chap. vi. 4–vii. 16.

The prophet's address commences afresh, as in ch. ii. 4, without any introduction, with the denunciation of the incurability of the Israelites. Vers. 4–11 form the first strophe.

Ver. 4. *" What shall I do to thee, Ephraim? what shall I do to thee, Judah? for your love is like the morning cloud, and like the dew which quickly passes away."* That this verse is not to be taken in connection with the preceding one, as it has been by Luther *("* how shall I do such good to thee?") and by many of the earlier expositors, is evident from the substance of the verse itself. For *'âsâh*, in the sense of doing good, is neither possible in itself, nor reconcilable with the explanatory clause which follows. The *chesed*, which is like the morning cloud, cannot be the grace of God; for a morning cloud that quickly vanishes away, is, according to ch. xiii. 3, a figurative representation of that which is evanescent and perishable. The verse does not contain an answer from Jehovah, *"* who neither receives nor repels the penitent, because though they love God it is only with fickleness," as Hitzig supposes; but rather the thought, that God has already tried all kinds of punishment to bring the people back to fidelity to Himself, but all in vain (cf. Isa. i. 5, 6), because the piety of Israel is as evanescent and transient as a morning cloud, which is dispersed by the rising sun. Judging from the *chesed* in ver. 6, *chasdᵉkhem* is to be understood as referring to good-will towards other men flowing out of love to God (see at ch. iv. 1).

Ver. 5. *" Therefore have I hewn by the prophets, slain them by the words of my mouth: and my judgment goeth forth as light."* *'Al-kēn*, therefore, because your love vanishes again and again, God must perpetually punish. חָצַב בְּ does not mean to strike in among the prophets (Hitzig, after the LXX., Syr., and others); but בְּ is instrumental, as in Isa. x. 15, and *châtsabh* signifies to hew, not merely to hew off, but to hew out or carve. The *nᵉbhî'îm* cannot be false prophets, on account of the parallel *"* by the words of my mouth," but must be the true prophets. Through them God had hewed or carved the nation, or, as Jerome and Luther render it, *dolavi*, *i.e.* worked it like a piece of hard wood, in other words, had tried to improve it, and shape it into a holy nation, answering to its true calling. *"* Slain by the words of my mouth," which the prophets had spoken; *i.e.* not merely caused death and destruction to be proclaimed to them, but suspended judgment and death over them—as, for example, by Elijah—since there dwells in the word of God the power to kill and to make alive (compare Isa. xi. 4, xlix. 2). The last clause, according to the Masoretic pointing and division of the words, does not yield any appropriate meaning. מִשְׁפָּטֶיךָ could only be the judgments inflicted upon the nation; but neither the singular suffix ךָ for כֶם (ver. 4), nor אוֹר יֵצֵא, with the singular verb under the כ *simil.* omitted before אוֹר, suits this explanation. For אוֹר יֵצֵא cannot mean "to go forth to the light;" nor can אוֹר stand for לָאוֹר. We must therefore regard the reading expressed by the ancient versions,[1] viz. מִשְׁפָּטִי כָאוֹר יֵצֵא, "my judgment goeth forth like light," as the original one. My penal judgment went forth like the light (the sun); *i.e.* the judgment inflicted upon the sinners was so obvious, so conspicuous (clear as the sun), that every one ought to have observed it and laid it to heart (cf. Zeph. iii. 5). The Masoretic division of the words probably arose simply from an unsuitable reminiscence of Ps. xxxvii. 6.

The reason why God was obliged to punish in this manner is given in the following verses. Ver. 6. "*For I take pleasure in love, and not in sacrifices; and in the knowledge of God more than in burnt-offerings.* Ver. 7. *But they have transgressed the covenant like Adam: there have they acted treacherously towards me.*" *Chesed* is love to one's neighbour, manifesting itself in righteousness, love which has its roots in the knowledge of God, and therefore is connected with "the knowledge of God" here as in ch. iv. 1. For the thought itself, compare the remarks on the similar declaration made by the prophet Samuel in 1 Sam. xv. 22; and for parallels as to the fact, see Isa. i. 11–17, Mic. vi. 8, Ps. xl. 7–9, and Ps. l. 8 sqq., in all which passages it is not sacrifices in themselves, but simply the heartless sacrifices with which the wicked fancied they could cover their sins, that are here rejected as displeasing to God, and as abominations in His eyes. This is apparent also from the antithesis in ver. 7, viz. the reproof of their transgression of the covenant. הֵמָּה (they) are Israel and Judah, not the priests, whose sins are first referred to in ver. 9. כְּאָדָם, not "after the manner of men," or "like ordinary men,"—for this explanation would only be admissible if הֵמָּה referred to the priests or prophets, or if a contrast were drawn between the rulers

[1] The Vulgate in some of the ancient MSS. has also *judicium meum*, instead of the *judicia tua* of the Sixtina. See Kennicott, *Diss. gener.* ed. Bruns. p. 55 sqq.

and others, as in Ps. lxxxii. 7,—but " like Adam," who transgressed the commandment of God, that he should not eat of
the tree of knowledge.   This command was actually a covenant,
which God made with him, since the object of it was the preservation of Adam in vital fellowship with the Lord, as was
the case with the covenant that God made with Israel (see Job
xxxi. 33, and Delitzsch's Commentary).   The local expression
" there," points to the place where the faithless apostasy had
occurred, as in Ps. xiv. 5.   This is not more precisely defined,
but refers no doubt to Bethel as the scene of the idolatrous
worship.   There is no foundation for the temporal rendering
" then."

The prophet cites a few examples in proof of this faithlessness in the two following verses.   Ver. 8. " *Gilead is a city of
evil-doers, trodden with blood.*   Ver. 9. *And like the lurking
of the men of the gangs is the covenant of the priests; along
the way they murder even to Sichem : yea, they have committed
infamy.*"   *Gilead* is not a city, for no such city is mentioned in
the Old Testament, and its existence cannot be proved from
Judg. xii. 7 and x. 17, any more than from Gen xxxi. 48, 49,[1]
but it is the name of a district, as it is everywhere else ; and
here in all probability it stands, as it very frequently does,
for the whole of the land of Israel to the east of the Jordan.
Hosea calls Gilead a city of evil-doers, as being a rendezvous
for wicked men, to express the thought that the whole land
was as full of evil-doers as a city is of men.   עֲקֻבָּה: a denom. of
עָקֵב, a footstep, signifying marked with traces, full of traces of

---

[1] The statement of the *Onomast.* (*s. v.* Γαλααδ), that there is also a
city called Galaad, situated in the mountain which Galaad the son of
Machir, the son of Manasseh, took from the Amorite, and that of Jerome,
"from which mountain the city built in it derived its name, viz. that which
was taken," etc., furnish no proof of the existence of a city called *Gilead*
in the time of the Israelites ; since Eusebius and Jerome have merely
inferred the existence of such a city from statements in the Old Testament, more especially from the passage quoted by them just before, viz.
Jer. xxii. 6, *Galaad tu mihi initium Libani,* taken in connection with Num.
xxxii. 39–42, as the words "which Gilead took" clearly prove.   And with
regard to the ruined cities *Jelaad* and *Jelaud,* which are situated, according
to Burckhardt (pp. 599, 600), upon the mountain called Jebel Jelaad or
Jelaud, it is not known that they date from antiquity at all.   Burckhardt
gives no description of them, and does not even appear to have visited
the ruins.

blood, which are certainly not to be understood as referring to idolatrous sacrifices, as Schmieder imagines, but which point to murder and bloodshed. It is quite as arbitrary, however, on the part of Hitzig to connect it with the murder of Zechariah, or a massacre associated with it, as it is on the part of Jerome and others to refer it to the deeds of blood by which Jehu secured the throne. The bloody deeds of Jehu took place in Jezreel and Samaria (2 Kings ix. x.), and it was only by a false interpretation of the epithet applied to Shallum, viz. *Ben-yâbhēsh*, as signifying citizens of Jabesh, that Hitzig was able to trace a connection between it and Gilead.—Ver. 9. In these crimes the priests take the lead. Like highway robbers, they form themselves into gangs for the purpose of robbing travellers and putting them to death. חַכֵּי, so written instead of חַכֵּה (Ewald, § 16, *b*), is an irregularly formed infinitive for חַכּוֹת (Ewald, § 238, *e*). *'Ish gᵉdūdīm*, a man of fighting-bands, *i.e.* in actual fact a highway robber, who lies in wait for travellers.[1] The company (*chebher*, gang) of the priests resembled such a man. They murder on the way (*derekh*, an adverbial accusative) to Sichem. *Sichem*, a place on Mount Ephraim, between Ebal and Gerizim, the present Nablus (see at Josh. xvii. 7), was set apart as a city of refuge and a Levitical city (Josh. xx. 7, xxi. 21); from which the more recent commentators have inferred that priests from Sichem, using the privileges of their city to cover crimes of their own, committed acts of murder, either upon fugitives who were hurrying thither, and whom they put to death at the command of the leading men who were ill-disposed towards them (Ewald), or upon other travellers, either from avarice or simple cruelty. But, apart from the fact that the Levitical cities are here confounded with the priests' cities (for Sichem was only a Levitical city, and not a priests' city at all), this conclusion is founded upon the

---

[1] The first hemistich has been entirely misunderstood by the LXX., who have confounded כְּחַכֵּי with כֹּחֲךָ, and rendered the clause καὶ ἡ ἰσχύς σου ἀνδρὸς πειρατοῦ· ἔκρυψαν (חבןֹ or חבאו instead of חבר) ἱερεῖς ὁδόν. Jerome has also rendered כחבי strangely, *et quasi fauces* (כְּחַכֵּי) *virorum latronum particeps sacerdotum.* Luther, on the other hand, has caught the sense quite correctly on the whole, and simply rendered it rather freely : " And the priests with their mobs are like footpads, who lie in wait for people."

erroneous assumption, that the priests who were taken by
Jeroboam from the people generally, had special places of
abode assigned them, such as the law had assigned for the
Levitical priests.   The way to Sichem is mentioned as a place
of murders and bloody deeds, because the road from Samaria
the capital, and in fact from the northern part of the kingdom
generally, to Bethel the principal place of worship belonging to
the kingdom of the.ten tribes, lay through this city.   Pilgrims
to the feasts for the most part took this road; and the priests,
who were taken from the dregs of the people, appear to have
lain in wait for them, either to rob, or, in case of resistance,
to murder.   The following פִּי carries it still higher, and adds
another crime to the murderous deeds.   *Zimmâh* most probably
refers to an unnatural crime, as in Lev. xviii. 17, xix. 29.

Thus does Israel heap up abomination upon abomination.
Ver. 10. " *In the house of Israel I saw a horrible thing: there
Ephraim practises whoredom: Israel has defiled itself.*"   The
house of Israel is the kingdom of the ten tribes.   שַׁעֲרוּרִיָה, a
horrible thing, signifies abominations and crimes of every kind.
In the second hemistich, *z^enûth, i.e.* spiritual and literal whoredom, is singled out as the principal sin.   *Ephraim* is not the
name of a tribe here, as Simson supposes, but is synonymous
with the parallel *Israel.*

In conclusion, Judah is mentioned again, that it may not
regard itself as better or less culpable.   Ver. 11. " *Also, O
Judah, a harvest is appointed for thee, when I turn the imprisonment of my people.*"   Judah stands at the head as an absolute
noun, and is then defined by the following לְךָ.   The subject to
shâth cannot be either Israel or Jehovah.   The first, which Hitzig
adopts, " Israel has prepared a harvest for thee," does not
supply a thought at all in harmony with the connection ; and
the second is precluded by the fact that Jehovah Himself is
the speaker.   *Shâth* is used here in a passive sense, as in Job
xxxviii. 11 (cf. Ges. § 137, 3*).   קָצִיר, harvest, is a figurative
term for the judgment, as in Joel iv. 13, Jer. li. 33.   As
Judah has sinned as well as Israel, it cannot escape the punishment (cf. ch. v. 5, 14).   שׁוּב שְׁבוּת never means to bring back
the captives; but in every passage in which it occurs it simply
means to turn the captivity, and that in the figurative sense of
restitutio in integrum (see at Deut. xxx. 3).   '*Ammî*, my people,

i.e. the people of Jehovah, is not Israel of the ten tribes, but the covenant nation as a whole. Consequently *sh^ebhūth 'ammī* is the misery into which Israel (of the twelve tribes) had been brought, through its falling away from God, not the Assyrian or Babylonian exile, but the misery brought about by the sins of the people. God could only avert this by means of judgments, through which the ungodly were destroyed and the penitent converted. Consequently the following is the thought which we obtain from the verse : " When God shall come to punish, that He may root out ungodliness, and bring back His people to their true destination, Judah will also be visited with the judgment." We must not only reject the explanation adopted by Rosenmüller, Maurer, and Umbreit, " when Israel shall have received its chastisement, and be once more received and restored by the gracious God, the richly merited punishment shall come upon Judah also," but that of Schmieder as well, who understands by the " harvest" a harvest of joy. They are both founded upon the false interpretation of *shūbh sh^ebhūth*, as signifying the bringing back of the captives ; and in the first there is the arbitrary limitation of *'ammī* to the ten tribes. Our verse says nothing as to the question when and how God will turn the captivity of the people and punish Judah ; this must be determined from other passages, which announce the driving into exile of both Israel and Judah, and the eventual restoration of those who are converted to the Lord their God. The complete turning of the captivity of the covenant nation will not take place till Israel as a nation shall be converted to Christ its Saviour.

Chap. vii. In the first strophe (vers. 1–7) the exposure of the moral depravity of Israel is continued. Ver. 1. " *When I heal Israel, the iniquity of Ephraim reveals itself, and the wickedness of Samaria : for they practise deceit ; and the thief cometh, the troop of robbers plundereth without.* Ver. 2. *And they say not in their heart, I should remember all their wickedness. Now their deeds have surrounded them, they have occurred before my face.* Ver. 3. *They delight the king with their wickedness, and princes with their lies.*" As the dangerous nature of a wound is often first brought out by the attempt to heal it, so was the corruption of Israel only brought truly to light by the effort to stem it. The first hemistich of ver. 1 is not to be referred to the future, nor is the healing to be understood as signifying punishment, as Hitzig supposes; but the allusion is to the attempts made by God to put a stop to the corruption, partly by the preaching of repentance and the reproofs of the prophets, and partly by chastisements designed to promote reformation. The words contain no threatening of punishment, but a picture of the moral corruption that had become incurable. Here again Ephraim is not the particular tribe, but is synonymous with Israel, the people or kingdom of the ten tribes; and Samaria is especially mentioned in connection with it, as the capital and principal seat of the corruption of morals, just as Judah and Jerusalem are frequently classed together by the prophets. The lamentation concerning the incurability of the kingdom is followed by an explanatory notice of the sins and crimes that are openly committed. *Sheqer*, lying, *i.e.* deception both in word and deed towards God and man, theft and highway robbery, and not fear of the vengeance of God. "*Accedit ad hæc facinora securitas eorum ineffabilis*" (Marck). They do not consider that God will remember their evil deeds, and punish them; they are surrounded by them on all sides, and perform them without shame or fear before the face of God Himself. These sins delight both king and prince. To such a depth have even the rulers of the nation, who ought to practise justice and righteousness, fallen, that they not only fail to punish the sins, but take pleasure in their being committed.

To this there is added the passion with which the people make themselves slaves to idolatry, and their rulers give them-selves up to debauchery (vers. 4–7). Ver. 4. "*They are all adulterers, like an oven heated by the baker, who leaves off stirring from the kneading of the dough until its leavening. Ver. 5. In the day of our king the princes are made sick with the heat of wine : he has stretched out his hand with the scorners. Ver. 6. For they have brought their heart into their ambush, as into the oven ; the whole night their baker sleeps ; in the morning it burns like flaming fire. Ver. 7. They are all red-hot like the oven, and con-sume their judges : all their kings have fallen ; none among them calls to me.*" "All" (*kullâm :* ver. 4) does not refer to the king and princes, but to the whole nation. נָאַף is spiritual adultery, apostasy from the Lord; and literal adultery is only so far to be thought of, that the worship of Baal promoted licentiousness.

In this passionate career the nation resembles a furnace which a baker heats in the evening, and leaves burning all night while the dough is leavening, and then causes to burn with a still brighter flame in the morning, when the dough is ready for baking. בֹּעֵרָה מֵאֹפֶה, burning from the baker, *i.e.* heated by the baker. בֹּעֵרָה is accentuated as *milel*, either because the Masoretes took offence at תַּנּוּר being construed as a feminine (Ges. *Lehrgeb.* p. 546; Ewald, *Gramm.* p. 449, note 1), or because *tiphchah* could not occupy any other place in the short space between *zakeph* and *athnach* (Hitzig). הֵעִיר, *excitare*, here in the sense of stirring. On the use of the participle in the place of the infinitive, with verbs of beginning and ending, see Ewald, § 298, *b.*

Both king and princes are addicted to debauchery (ver. 5). "The day of our king" is either the king's birthday, or the day when he ascended the throne, on either of which he probably gave a feast to his nobles. יוֹם is taken most simply as an adverbial *accus. loci.* On this particular day the princes drink to such an extent, that they become ill with the heat of the wine. הֶחֱלוּ, generally to make ill, here to make one's self ill. Hitzig follows the ancient versions, in deriving it from חלל, and taking it as equivalent to הֵחֵלּוּ, "they begin," which gives a very insipid meaning. The difficult expression מָשַׁךְ יָדוֹ אֶת־לֹ, "he draws his hand with the scoffers," can hardly be understood in any other way than that suggested by Gesenius (*Lex.*), "the king goes about with scoffers," *i.e.* makes himself familiar with them, so that we may compare שׁוּת יָדוֹ עִם (Ex. xxiii. 1). The scoffers are drunkards, just as in Prov. xx. 1 wine is directly called a scoffer. In vers. 6, 7, the thought of the fourth verse is carried out still further. כִּי introduces the explanation and ground of the simile of the furnace; for ver. 5 is subordinate to the main thought, and to be taken as a parenthetical remark. The words from כִּי קֵרְבוּ to בְּאָרְבָּם form one sentence. קֵרֵב is construed with בְּ *loci*, as in Judg. xix. 13, Ps. xci. 10: they have brought their heart near, brought them into their craftiness. "Like a furnace" (כְּתַנּוּר) contains an abridged simile. But it is not their *heart* itself which is here compared to a furnace (their heart = themselves), in the sense of "burning like a flaming furnace with base desires," as Gesenius supposes; for the idea of bringing a furnace into an 'ōrebh would be unsuitable and unintelligible. "The furnace is rather '*orbâm* (their ambush), that which they have in common, that which keeps them together; whilst the fuel is *libbâm*, their own disposition" (Hitzig). Their baker is the *machinator doli*, who kindles the fire in them, *i.e.* in actual fact, not some person or other who instigates a conspiracy, but the passion of idolatry. This sleeps through the night, *i.e.* it only rests till the opportunity and time have arrived for carrying out the evil thoughts of their heart, or until the evil thoughts of the heart have become ripe for execution. This time is described in harmony with the figure, as the morning, in which the furnace burns up into bright flames (הוא points to the more remote *tannûr* as the subject). In ver. 7 the figure is carried back to the literal fact. With the words, "they are all hot as a furnace," the expression in ver. 4, "adulterous like a furnace," is resumed; and now the fruit of this conduct is mentioned, viz. "they devour their judges, cast down their kings." By the judges we are not to understand the *sârîm* of ver. 5, who are mentioned along with the king as the supreme guardians of the law; but the kings themselves are intended, as the administrators of justice, as in ch. xiii. 10, where *shôph'tîm* is also used as synonymous with מֶלֶךְ, and embraces both king and princes. The clause, "all their kings are fallen," adds no new feature to what precedes, and does not affirm that kings have also fallen in addition to or along with the judges; but it sums up what has been stated already, for the purpose of linking on the remark, that no one calls to the Lord concerning the fall of the kings. The suffix בָּהֶם does not refer to the fallen kings, but to the nation in its entirety, *i.e.* to those who have devoured their judges. The thought is this: in the passion with which all are inflamed for idolatry, and with which the princes revel with the kings, they give no such heed to the inevitable consequences of their ungodly conduct, as that any one reflects upon the fall of the kings, or perceives that Israel has forsaken the way which leads to salvation, and is plunging headlong into the abyss of destruction, so as to return to the Lord, who alone can help and save. The prophet has here the times after Jeroboam II. in his mind, when Zechariah was overthrown by Shallum, Shallum by Menahem, and Menahem the son of Pekahiah by Pekah, and that in the most rapid succession (2 Kings. xv. 10, 14, 25), together with the eleven years' anarchy between Zechariah and Shallum (see at 2 Kings xv. 8–12). At the same time, the expression, " all their kings have fallen," shows clearly, not only that the words are not to be limited to these events, but embrace all the earlier revolutions, but also and still more clearly, that there is no foundation whatever for the widespread historical interpretation of these verses, as relating to a conspiracy against the then reigning king Zechariah, or Shallum, or Pekahiah, according to which the baker is either Menahem (Hitzig) or Pekah (Schmidt).

In the next strophe (vers. 8–16) the prophecy passes from the internal corruption of the kingdom of the ten tribes to its worthless foreign policy, and the injurious attitude which it had assumed towards the heathen nations, and unfolds the disastrous consequences of such connections. Ver. 8. *"Ephraim, it mixes itself among the nations ; Ephraim has become a cake not turned.* Ver. 9. *Strangers have devoured his strength, and he knoweth it not; grey hair is also sprinkled upon him, and he knoweth it not."* יִתְבּוֹלָל, from בָּלַל, to mix or commingle, is not a future in the sense of "it will be dispersed among the Gentiles;" for, according to the context, the reference is not to the punishment of the dispersion of Israel among the nations, but to the state in which Israel then was. The Lord had separated Israel from the nations, that it might be holy to Him (Lev. xx. 24, 26). As Balaam said of it, it was to be a people dwelling alone (Num. xxiii. 9). But in opposition to this object of its divine calling, the ten tribes had mingled with the nations, *i.e.* with the heathen, learned their works, and served their idols (cf. Ps. cvi. 35, 36). The mingling with the nations consisted in the adoption of heathen ways, not in the penetration of the heathen into Israelitish possessions (Hitzig), nor merely in the alliances which it formed with heathen nations. For these were simply the consequence of inward apostasy from its God, of that inward mixing with the nature of heathenism which had already taken place. Israel had thereby become a cake not turned. עֻגָּה, a cake baked upon hot ashes or red-hot stones, which, if it be not turned, is burned at the bottom, and not baked at all above. The meaning of this figure is explained by ver. 9. As the fire will burn an ash-cake when it is left unturned, so have foreigners consumed the strength of Israel, partly by devastating wars, and partly by the heathenish nature which has penetrated into Israel in their train. "Greyness is also sprinkled upon it;" *i.e.* the body politic, represented as one person, is already covered with traces of hoary old age, and is ripening for destruction. The object to לֹא יָדַע may easily be supplied from the previous clauses, namely, that strangers devour its strength, and it is growing old. The rendering *non sapit* is precluded by the emphatic וְהוּא, and he knoweth it not, *i.e.* does not perceive the decay of his strength.

Ver. 10. "*And the pride of Israel beareth witness to his face, and they are not converted to Jehovah their God, and for all this they seek Him not.*" The first clause is repeated from ch. v. 5. The testimony which the pride of Israel, *i.e.* Jehovah, bore to its face, consisted in the weakening and wasting away of the kingdom as described in ver. 9. But with all this, they do not turn to the Lord who could save them, but seek help from their natural foes.

Ver. 11. "*And Ephraim has become like a simple dove without understanding; they have called Egypt, they are gone to Asshur.* Ver. 12. *As they go, I spread my net over them; I bring them down like fowls of the heaven; I will chastise them, according to the tidings to their assembly.*" The perfects in ver. 11 describe the conduct of Israel as an accomplished fact, and this is represented by וַיְהִי as the necessary consequence of its obstinate impenitence. The point of comparison between Israel and the simple dove, is not that the dove misses its proper dwelling and resting-place, and therefore goes fluttering about (Ewald); nor that, in trying to escape from the hawk, it flies into the net of the bird-catcher (Hitzig); but that when flying about in search of food, it does not observe the net that is spread for it (Rosenmüller). אֵין לֵב is to be taken as a predicate to *Ephraim* in spite of the accents, and not to *yōnâh phōthâh* (a simple dove), since *phōthâh* does not require either strengthening or explaining. Thus does Ephraim seek help from Egypt and Assyria. These words do not refer to the fact that there were two parties in the nation—an Assyrian and an Egyptian. Nor do they mean that the whole nation applied at one time to Egypt to get rid of Asshur, and at another time to Asshur to escape from Egypt. "The situation is rather this: the people being sorely pressed by Asshur, at one time seek help from

Egypt against Asshur; whilst at another they try to secure the friendship of the latter" (Hengstenberg, *Christology*, i. p. 164 transl.). For what threatened Israel was the burden of the "king of princes" (ch. viii. 10), *i.e.* the king of Asshur. And this they tried to avert partly by their coquettish arts (ch. viii. 9), and partly by appealing to the help of Egypt; and while doing so, they did not observe that they had fallen into the net of destruction, viz. the power of Assyria. In this net will the Lord entangle them as a punishment. As they go thither, God will spread His net over them like a bird-catcher, and bring them down to the earth like flying birds, *i.e.* bring them down from the open air, that is to say, from freedom, into the net of captivity, or exile. אֲיִסִירֵם, a rare *hiphil* formation with *Yod mobile*, as in Prov. iv. 25 (see Ewald, § 131, *c*). "According to the tidings (announcement) to their assembly:" *i.e.* in accordance with the threatening already contained in the law (Lev. xxvi. 14 sqq.; Deut. xxviii. 15 sqq.), and repeatedly uttered to the congregation by the prophets, of the judgments that should fall upon the rebellious, which threatening would now be fulfilled upon Ephraim.

Ver. 13. "*Woe to them! for they have flown from me; devastation to them! for they have fallen away from me. I would redeem them, but they speak lies concerning me.* Ver. 14. *They did not cry to me in their heart, but howl upon their beds; they crowd together for corn and new wine, and depart against me.*" The Lord, thinking of the chastisement, exclaims, Woe to them, because they have fled from Him! *Nâdad*, which is applied to the flying of birds, points back to the figures employed in vers. 11, 12. *Shôd*, used as an exclamation, gives the literal explanation of *'ôi* (woe). The imperfect *'ephdēm* cannot be taken as referring to the redemption out of Egypt, because it does not stand for the preterite. It is rather voluntative or optative. "I would (should like to) redeem them (still); but they say I cannot and will not do it." These are the lies which they utter concerning Jehovah, partly with their mouths and partly by their actions, namely, in the fact that they do not seek help from Him, as is explained in ver. 14. They cry to the Lord; yet it does not come from the heart, but (פִּי after לֹא) they howl (יְיֵלִילוּ, cf. Ges. § 70, 2, note) upon their beds, in unbelieving despair at the distress that has come upon them.

What follows points to this. *Hithgōrēr*, to assemble, or crowd
together (Ps. lvi. 7, lix. 4; Isa. liv. 15); here to gather in
troops or crowd together for corn and new wine, because their
only desire is to fill their belly. Thus they depart from God.
The construction of סוּר with בְּ, instead of with מִן or מֵאַחֲרֵי, is
a pregnant one : to depart and turn against God.

Vers. 15, 16. Yet Jehovah has done still more for Israel.
Ver. 15. *" And I have instructed, have strengthened their arms,
and they think evil against me.* Ver. 16. *They turn, but not
upwards : they have become like a false bow. Their princes will
fall by the sword, for the defiance of their tongue : this is their
derision in the land of Egypt."* יִסַּר here is not to chastise, but
to instruct, so that זְרוֹעֹתָם (their arms) is to be taken as the
object to both verbs. Instructing the arms, according to the
analogy of Ps. xviii. 35, is equivalent to showing where and how
strength is to be acquired. And the Lord has not contented
Himself with merely instructing. He has also strengthened
their arms, and given them power to fight, and victory over
their foes (cf. 2 Kings xiv. 25, 26). And yet they think evil
of Him; not by speaking lies (ver. 13), but by falling away
from Him, by their idolatrous calf-worship, by which they rob
the Lord of the glory due to Him alone, practically denying
His true divinity. This attitude towards the Lord is summed
up in two allegorical sentences in ver. 16, and the ruin of their
princes is foretold. They turn, or turn round, but not upwards
(עַל, an adverb, or a substantive signifying height, as in ch. xi. 7,
2 Sam. xxiii. 1, not " the Most High," *i.e.* God, although turning upwards is actually turning to God). From the fact that
with all their turning about they do not turn upwards, they
have become like a treacherous bow, the string of which has lost
its elasticity, so that the arrows do not hit the mark (cf. Ps.
lxxviii. 57). And thus Israel also fails to reach its destination.
Therefore its princes shall fall. The *princes* are mentioned as
the originators of the enmity against God, and all the misery
into which they have plunged the people and kingdom. זַעַם,
fury, here defiance or rage. Defiance of tongue the princes
showed in the lies which they uttered concerning Jehovah
(ver. 13), and with which they blasphemed in a daring manner
the omnipotence and faithfulness of the Lord. זוּ stands,
according to a dialectical difference in the mode of pronuncia-

tion, for זֶה, not for זֹאת (Ewald, § 183, *a*). This, namely their
falling by the sword, will be for a derision to them in the land
of Egypt: not because they will fall in Egypt, or perish by the
sword of the Egyptians; but because they put their trust in
Egypt, the derision of Egypt will come upon them when they
are overthrown (cf. Isa. xxx. 3, 5).

The Judgment consequent upon Apostasy.—
Chap. viii.–ix. 9.

The coming judgment, viz. the destruction of the kingdom
of the ten tribes, is predicted in three strophes, containing a
fresh enumeration of the sins of Israel (ch. viii. 1–7), a reference to the fall of the kingdom, which is already about to
commence (vers. 8–14), and a warning against false security
(ch. ix. 1–9).

Ch. viii. 1–7. The prophecy rises with a vigorous swing, as
in ch. v. 8, to the prediction of judgment. Ver. 1. " *The
trumpet to thy mouth! Like an eagle upon the house of Jehovah!
Because they transgressed my covenant, and trespassed against
my law.* Ver. 2. *To me will they cry: My God, we know Thee,
we Israel!*" The first sentence of ver. 1 is an exclamation,
and therefore has no verb. The summons issues from Jehovah,
as the suffixes in the last sentences show, and is addressed to the
prophet, who is to blow the trumpet, as the herald of Jehovah,
and give the people tidings of the approaching judgment (see
at ch. v. 8). The second sentence gives the alarming message
to be delivered: like an eagle comes the foe, or the judgment upon the house of Jehovah. The simile of the eagle,
that shoots down upon its prey with the rapidity of lightning,
points back to the threat of Moses in Deut. xxviii. 49. The
" *house of Jehovah*" is neither the temple at Jerusalem (Jerome,
Theod., Cyr.), the introduction of which here would be at
variance with the context; nor the principal temple of Samaria,
with the fall of which the whole kingdom would be ruined
(Ewald, Sims.), since the temples erected for the calf-worship
at Dan and Bethel are called *Bēth bâmōth*, not *Bēth Yᵉhōvâh;*
nor even the land of Jehovah, either here or at ch. ix. 15
(Hitzig), for a land is not a house; but Israel was the house of
Jehovah, as being a portion of the congregation of the Lord.

as in ch. ix. 15, Num. xii. 7, Jer. xii. 7, Zech. ix. 8 ; cf. οἶκος Θεοῦ in Heb. iii. 6 and 1 Tim. iii. 15. The occasion of the judgment was the transgression of the covenant and law of the Lord, which is more particularly described in ver. 4. In this distress they will call for help to Jehovah : " My God (*i.e.* each individual will utter this cry), we know Thee !" *Israel* is in apposition to the subject implied in the verb. They know Jehovah, so far as He has revealed Himself to the whole nation of Israel ; and the name Israel is in itself a proof that they belong to the people of God.

But this knowledge of God, regarded simply as a historical acquaintance with Him, cannot possibly bring salvation. Ver. 3. " *Israel dislikes good ; let the enemy pursue it.*" This is the answer that God will give to those who cry to Him. טוֹב denotes neither " Jehovah as the highest good" (Jerome) or as " the good One" (Sims.), nor " the good law of God" (Schmieder), but the good or salvation which Jehovah has guaranteed to the nation through His covenant of grace, and which He bestowed upon those who kept His covenant. Because Israel has despised this good, let the enemy pursue it.

The proof of Israel's renunciation of its God is to be found in the facts mentioned in ver. 4. " *They have set up kings, but not from me, have set up princes, and I know it not : their silver and their gold they have made into idols, that it may be cut off.*" The setting up of kings and princes, not from Jehovah, and without His knowledge, *i.e.* without His having been asked, refers chiefly to the founding of the kingdom by Jeroboam I. It is not to be restricted to this, however, but includes at the same time the obstinate persistence of Israel in this ungodly attitude on all future occasions, when there was either a change or usurpation of the government. And the fact that not only did the prophet Ahijah foretel to Jeroboam I. that he would rule over the ten tribes (1 Kings xi. 30 sqq.), but Jehu was anointed king over Israel by Elisha's command (2 Kings ix.), and therefore both of them received the kingdom by the express will of Jehovah, is not at variance with this, so as to require the solution, that we have a different view here from that which prevails in the books of Kings,—namely, one which sprang out of the repeated changes of government and anarchies in this kingdom (Simson). For neither the divine promise of the throne, nor the anointing performed by the command of God, warranted their forcibly seizing upon the government,— a crime of which both Jeroboam and Jehu rendered themselves guilty. The way in which both of them paved the way to the throne was not in accordance with the will of God, but was most ungodly (see at 1 Kings xi. 40). Jeroboam was already planning a revolt against Solomon (1 Kings xi. 27), and led the gathering of the ten tribes when they fell away from the house of David (1 Kings xii. 2 sqq.). Of Jehu, again, it is expressly stated in 2 Kings ix. 14, that he conspired against Joram. And the other usurpers, just like the two already named, opened the way to the throne by means of conspiracies, whilst the people not only rebelled against the rightful heir to the throne at Solomon's death, from pure dislike to the royal house of David, which had been appointed by God, and made Jeroboam king, but expressed their approval of all subsequent conspiracies as soon as they had been successful. This did not come from Jehovah, but was a rebellion against Him—a transgression of His covenant. To this must be added. the further sin, viz. the setting up of the idolatrous calf-worship on the part of Jeroboam, to which all the kings of Israel adhered. It was in connection with this, that the application of the silver and gold to idols, by which Israel completely renounced the law of Jehovah, had taken place. It is true that silver was not used in the construction of the golden calves ; but it was employed in the maintenance of their worship. לְמַעַן יִכָּרֵת: that it (the gold and silver) may be destroyed, as more fully stated in ver. 6. לְמַעַן describes the consequence of this conduct, which, though not designed, was nevertheless inevitable, as if it had been distinctly intended.

Ver. 5. " *Thy calf disgusts, O Samaria; my wrath is kindled against them: how long are they incapable of purity ?* Ver. 6. *For this also is from Israel: a workman made it, and it is not God; but the calf of Samaria will become splinters.*" *Zânach* (disgusts) points back to ver. 3. As Israel felt disgust at what was good, so did Jehovah at the golden calf of Samaria. It is true that *zânach* is used here intransitively in the sense of smelling badly, or being loathsome ; but this does not alter the meaning, which is obvious enough from the context, namely, that it is Jehovah whom the calf disgusts. The calf of Samaria is not a golden calf set up in the city of Samaria; as there is no allusion in history to any such calf as this. Samaria is simply mentioned in the place of the kingdom, and the calf is the one that was set up at Bethel, the most celebrated place of worship in the kingdom, which is also the only one mentioned in ch. x. 5, 15. On account of this calf the wrath of Jehovah is kindled against the Israelites, who worship this calf, and cannot desist. This is the thought of the question expressing disgust at these abominations. How long are they incapable of נִקָּיֹן, *i.e.* purity of walk before the Lord, instead of the abominations of idolatry (cf. Jer. xix. 4); not "freedom from punishment," as Hitzig supposes. To לֹא יֻכְלוּ, "they are unable," we may easily supply "to bear," as in Isa. i. 14 and Ps. ci. 5. "For" (*kī*, ver. 6) follows as an explanation of the main clause in ver. 5, "Thy calf disgusts." The calf of Samaria is an abomination to the Lord, for it is also out of Israel (Israel's God out of Israel itself!); a workman made it,—what folly! וְהוּא is a predicate, brought out with greater emphasis by ו, *et quidem*, in the sense of *iste*. Therefore will it be destroyed like the golden calf at Sinai, which was burnt and ground to powder (Ex. xxxii. 20; Deut. ix. 21). The ἅπ. λεγ. שְׁבָבִים, from ‫سَبَّ‬ to cut, signifies ruins or splinters.

This will Israel reap from its ungodly conduct. Ver. 7. "*For they sow wind, and reap tempest: it has no stalks; shoot brings no fruit; and even if it brought it, foreigners would devour it.*" With this figure, which is so frequently and so variously used (cf. ch. x. 13, xii. 2; Job iv. 8; Prov. xxii. 8), the threat is accounted for by a general thought taken from life. The harvest answers to the sowing (cf. Gal. vi. 7, 8). Out of the wind comes tempest. *Wind* is a figurative representation of human exertions; the *tempest*, of destruction. Instead of *rūăch* we have אָוֶן, עָמָל, עוֹלָה (nothingness, weariness, wickedness) in ch. x. 13, Job iv. 8, and Prov. xxii. 8. In the second hemistich the figure is carried out still further. קָמָה, "seed standing upon the stalk," is not to *it* (viz. that which has been sowed). *Tsemach* brings no *qemach*,—a play upon the words, answering to our shoot and fruit. *Qemach*: generally meal, here probably the grain-bearing ear, from which the meal is obtained. But even if the shoot, when grown, should yield some meal, strangers, *i.e.* foreigners, would consume it. In these words not only are the people threatened with failure of the crop; but the failure and worthlessness of all that they do are here predicted. Not only the corn of Israel, but Israel itself, will be swallowed up.

With this thought the still further threatening of judgment in the next strophe is introduced. Ver. 8. "*Israel is swallowed up; now are they among the nations like a vessel, with which there is no satisfaction.*" The advance in the threat of punishment lies less in the extension of the thought, that not only the fruit of the field, but the whole nation, will be swallowed up by foes, than in the perfect נִבְלַע, which indicates that the time of the ripening of the evil seeds has already begun (Jerome, Simson). עַתָּה הָיוּ, now already have they become among the nations like a despised vessel, which men cast away as useless (cf. Jer. xxii. 28, xlviii. 38). This lot have they prepared for themselves.

Ver. 9. "*For they went up to Asshur; wild ass goes alone by itself; Ephraim sued for loves.* Ver. 10. *Yea, though they sue among the nations, now will I gather them, and they will begin to diminish on account of the burden of the king of the princes.*" Going to Assyria is defined still further in the third clause as suing for loves, *i.e.* for the favour and help of the Assyrians. The folly of this suing is shown in the clause, " wild ass goes by itself alone," the meaning and object of which have been quite mistaken by those who supply a כְּ *simil.* For neither by connecting it with the preceding words thus, " Israel went to Asshur, like a stubborn ass going by itself" (Ewald), nor by attaching it to those which follow, "like a wild ass going alone, Ephraim sued for loves," do we get any suitable point of comparison. The thought is rather this : whilst even a wild ass, that stupid animal, keeps by itself to maintain its independence, Ephraim tries to form unnatural alliances with the nations of the world, that is to say, alliances that are quite incompatible with its vocation. *Hithnâh,* from *tânâh,* probably a denom. of '*ethnâh* (see at ch. ii. 14), to give the reward of prostitution, here in the sense of bargaining for *amours,* or endeavouring to secure them by presents. The *kal yithnû* has the same meaning in ver. 10. The word אֲקַבְּצֵם, to which different renderings have been given, can only have a

threatening or punitive sense here; and the suffix cannot refer
to בַּגּוֹיִם, but only to the subject contained in *yithnu*, viz. the
Ephraimites. The Lord will bring them together, *sc.* among
the nations, *i.e.* bring them all thither. קִבֵּץ is used in a similar
sense in ch. ix. 6. The more precise definition is added in the
next clause, in the difficult expression וַיָּחֵלּוּ מְעָט, in which וַיָּחֵלּוּ
may be taken most safely in the sense of "beginning," as in
Judg. xx. 31, 2 Chron. xxix. 17, and Ezek. ix. 6, in all of which
this form occurs, and מְעָט as an *adject. verb.*, connected with
הֵחֵל like the adjective כֵּהוֹת in 1 Sam. iii. 2: "They begin to be,
or become, less (*i.e.* fewer), on account of the burden of the
king of princes," *i.e.* under the oppression which they will suffer
from the king of Assyria, not by war taxes or deportation, but
when carried away into exile. מֶלֶךְ מַלְכִים = מֶלֶךְ שָׂרִים is a term
applied to the great Assyrian king, who boasted, according to
Isa. x. 8, that his princes were all kings.

This threat is accounted for in vers. 11 sqq., by an allusion
to the sins of Israel. Ver. 11. "*For Ephraim has multiplied
altars for sinning, the altars have become to him for sinning.*
Ver. 12. *I wrote to him the fulnesses of my law; they were
counted as a strange thing.*" Israel was to have only one altar,
and that in the place where the Lord would reveal His name
(Deut. xii. 5 sqq.). But instead of that, Ephraim had built
a number of altars in different places, to multiply the sin of
idolatry, and thereby heap more and more guilt upon itself.
לַחֲטֹא is used, in the first clause, for the act of sin; and in the
second, for the consequences of that act. And this was not
done from ignorance of the divine will, but from neglect of the
divine commandments. אֶכְתּוֹב is a historical present, indicating
that what had occurred was continuing still. These words
refer unquestionably to the great number of the laws written in
the Mosaic *thorah.* רבו, according to the *chethib* רֻבּוֹ, with ת
dropped, equivalent to רְבָבָה, as in 1 Chron. xxix. 7, ten thousand, myriads. The Masoretes, who supposed the number to be
used in an arithmetical sense, altered it, as conjecturally unsuitable, into רֻבֵּי, multitudes, although רֹב does not occur anywhere
else in the plural. The expression "the myriads of my law" is
hyperbolical, to indicate the almost innumerable multitude of
the different commandments contained in the law. It was also
in a misapprehension of the nature of the hyperbole that the

supposition originated, that אֶכְתּוֹב was a hypothetical future (Jerome). כְּמוֹ זָר, like something foreign, which does not concern them at all.

Ver. 13. " *Slain-offerings for gifts they sacrifice; flesh, and eat: Jehovah has no pleasure in them: now will He remember their transgression, and visit their sins: they will return to Egypt.* Ver. 14. *And Israel forgot its Creator, and built palaces: and Judah multiplied fortified cities: and I shall send fire into its cities, and it will devour its castles.*" With the multiplication of the altars they increased the number of the sacrifices. הַבְהָבַי is a noun in the plural with the suffix, and is formed from יהב by reduplication. The slain-offerings of my sacrificial gifts, equivalent to the gifts of slain-offerings presented to me continually, they sacrifice as flesh, and eat it; that is to say, they are nothing more than flesh, which they slay and eat, and not sacrifices in which Jehovah takes delight, or which could expiate their sins. Therefore the Lord will punish their sins; they will return to Egypt, *i.e.* be driven away into the land of bondage, out of which God once redeemed His people. These words are simply a special application of the threat, held out by Moses in Deut. xxviii. 68, to the degenerate ten tribes. Egypt is merely a type of the land of bondage, as in ch. ix. 3, 6. In ver. 14 the sin of Israel is traced back to its root. This is forgetfulness of God, and deification of their own power, and manifests itself in the erection of הֵיכָלוֹת, palaces, not idolatrous temples. Judah also makes itself partaker of this sin, by multiplying the fortified cities, and placing its confidence in fortifications. These castles of false security the Lord will destroy. The '*armânōth* answer to the *hēkhâloth*. The suffixes attached to בְּעָרָיו and אַרְמְנֹתֶיהָ refer to both kingdoms: the masculine suffix to Israel and Judah, as a people; the feminine to the two as a land, as in Lam. ii. 5.

Ch. ix. 1–9. Warning against false security. The earthly prosperity of the people and kingdom was no security against destruction. Because Israel had fallen away from its God, it should not enjoy the blessing of its field-produce, but should be carried away to Assyria, where it would be unable to keep any joyful feasts at all. Ver. 1. " *Rejoice not, O Israel, to exult like the nations: for thou hast committed whoredom against thy God: hast loved the wages of whoredom upon all corn-floors.*

Ver. 2. *The threshing-floor and press will not feed them, and the new wine will deceive it."* The rejoicing to which Israel was not to give itself up was, according to ver. 2, rejoicing at a plentiful harvest. All nations rejoiced, and still rejoice, at this (cf. Isa. ix. 2), because they regard the blessing of harvest as a sign and pledge of the favour and grace of God, which summon them to gratitude towards the giver. Now, when the heathen nations ascribed their gifts to their gods, and in their way thanked them for them, they did this in the ignorance of their heart, without being specially guilty on that account, since they lived in the world without the light of divine revelation. But when Israel rejoiced in a heathenish way at the blessing of its harvest, and attributed this blessing to the Baals (see ch. ii. 7), the Lord could not leave this denial of His gracious benefits unpunished. אֶל־גִּיל belongs to תִּשְׂמַח, heightening the idea of joy, as in Job iii. 22. כִּי זָנִיתָ does not give the object of the joy ("that thou hast committed whoredom:" Ewald and others), but the reason why Israel was not to rejoice over its harvests, namely, because it had become unfaithful to its God, and had fallen into idolatry. זָנָה מֵעַל, to commit whoredom out beyond God (by going away from Him). The words, "thou lovest the wages of whoredom upon all corn-floors," are to be understood, according to ch. ii. 7, 14, as signifying that Israel would not regard the harvest-blessing upon its corn-floors as gifts of the goodness of its God, but as presents from the Baals, for which it had to serve them with still greater zeal. There is no ground for thinking of any peculiar form of idolatry connected with the corn-floors. Because of this the Lord would take away from them the produce of the floor and press, namely, according to ver. 3, by banishing the people out of the land. Floor and press will not feed them, *i.e.* will not nourish or satisfy them. The floor and press are mentioned in the place of their contents, or what they yield, viz. for corn and oil, as in 2 Kings vi. 27. By the press we must understand the oil-presses (cf. Joel ii. 24), because the new wine is afterwards specially mentioned, and corn, new wine, and oil are connected together in ch. ii. 10, 24. The suffix בָּהּ refers to the people regarded as a community.

Ver. 3. "*They will not remain in the land of Jehovah: Ephraim returns to Egypt, and they will eat unclean things in the land of Asshur.* Ver. 4. *They will not pour out wine to Jehovah, and their slain-offerings will not please Him: like bread of mourning are they to Him; all who eat it become unclean: for their bread is for themselves, it does not come into the house of Jehovah.*" Because they have fallen away from Jehovah, He will drive them out of His land. The driving away is described as a return to Egypt, as in ch. viii. 13; but Asshur is mentioned immediately afterwards as the actual land of banishment. That this threat is not to be understood as implying that they will be carried away to Egypt as well as to Assyria, but that Egypt is referred to here and in ver. 6, just as in ch. viii. 13, simply as a type of the land of captivity, so that Assyria is represented as a new Egypt, may be clearly seen from the words themselves, in which eating unclean bread in Assyria is mentioned as the direct consequence of their return to Egypt; whereas neither here nor in ver. 6 is their being carried away to Assyria mentioned at all; but, on the contrary, in ver. 6, *Egypt* only is introduced as the place where they are to find their grave. This is still more evident from the fact that Hosea throughout speaks of Asshur alone, as the rod of the wrath of God for His rebellious people. The king of Asshur is king *Jareb* (striver), to whom Ephraim goes for help, and by whom it will be put to shame (ch. v. 13, x. 6); and it is from the Assyrian king *Salman* that devastation and destruction proceed (ch. x. 14). And, lastly, it is expressly stated in ch. xi. 5, that Israel will not return to Egypt, but to Asshur, who will be its king. By the allusion to Egypt, therefore, the carrying away to Assyria is simply represented as a state of bondage and oppression, resembling the sojourn of Israel in Egypt in the olden time, or else the threat contained in Deut. xxviii. 68 is simply transferred to Ephraim. They will eat unclean things in Assyria, not only inasmuch as when, under the oppression of their heathen rulers, they will not be able to observe the laws of food laid down in the law, or will be obliged to eat unclean things from simple want and misery; but also inasmuch as all food, which was not sanctified to the Lord by the presentation of the first-fruits, was unclean food to Israel (Hengstenberg). In Assyria these offerings would cease with the whole of the sacrificial ritual; and the food which was clean in itself would thereby become unclean outside the land of Jehovah (cf. Ezek. iv. 13). This explanation of טָמֵא is required by ver. 4, in which a further reason is assigned for the threat. For what we have there is not a description of the present attitude of Israel towards Jehovah, but a picture of the miserable condition of the people in exile. The verbs are pure futures. In Assyria they will neither be able to offer wine to the Lord as a drink-offering, nor such slain-offerings as are well-pleasing to Him. For Israel could only offer sacrifices to its God at the place where He made known His name by revelation, and therefore not in exile, where He had withdrawn His gracious presence from it. The drink-offerings are mentioned, as *pars pro toto*, in the place of all the meat-offerings and drink-offerings, *i.e.* of the bloodless gifts, which were connected with the *z^ebhâchīm*, or burnt-offerings and thank-offerings (*sh^elâmīm*, Num. xv. 2–15, xxviii., xxix.), and could never be omitted when the first-fruits were offered (Lev. xxiii. 13, 18). "Their sacrifices:" *zibhchĕhem* belongs to יֶעֶרְבוּ־לֹו (shall be pleasing to Him), notwithstanding the previous *segholta*, because otherwise the subject to יערבו would be wanting, and there is evidently quite as little ground for supplying נִסְכֵּיהֶם from the preceding clause, as Hitzig proposes, as for assuming that עָרַב here means to mix. Again, we must not infer from the words, "their slain-offerings will not please Him," that the Israelites offered sacrifices when in exile. The meaning is simply that the sacrifices, which they might wish to offer to Jehovah there, would not be well-pleasing to Him. We must not repeat וּבחיהם as the subject to the next clause לָהֶם . . . בְּלֶחֶם, in the sense of "their sacrifices will be to them like mourners' bread," which would give no suitable meaning; for though the sacrifices are called bread of God, they are never called the bread of men. The subject may be supplied very readily from *k^elechem* (like bread) thus: their bread, or food, would be to them like mourners' bread; and the correctness of this is proved by the explanatory clause, "for their bread," etc. *Lechem 'ōnīm*, bread of affliction, *i.e.* of those who mourn for the dead (cf. Deut. xxvi. 14), in other words, the bread eaten at funeral meals. This was regarded as unclean, because the corpse defiled the house, and all who came in contact with it, for seven days (Num. xix. 14). Their bread would resemble bread of this kind, because it had not been sanctified by the offering of the first-fruits. " For their bread will not come into the house of Jehovah," viz. to be sanctified, " for their souls," *i.e.* to serve for the preservation of their life.

Their misery will be felt still more keenly on the feast-days. Ver. 5. " *What will ye do on the day of the festival, and on the day of the feast of Jehovah?* Ver. 6. *For behold they have gone away because of the desolation: Egypt will gather them together, Memphis bury them: their valuables in silver, thistles will receive them; thorns in their tents.*" As the temple and ritual will both be wanting in their exile, they will be unable to observe any of the feasts of the Lord. No such difference can be shown to exist between *yōm mōʻēd* and *yōm chag Yᵉhōvâh*, as would permit of our referring *mōʻēd* to feasts of a different kind from *chag*. In Lev. xxiii., all the feasts recurring at a fixed period, on which holy meetings were held, including the Sabbath, are called מוֹעֲדֵי יְהֹוָה; and even though the three feasts at which Israel was to appear before the Lord, viz. the passover, pentecost, and the feast of tabernacles, are described as *chaggīm* in Ex. xxxiv. 18 sqq., every other joyous festival is also called a *chag* (Ex. xxxii. 5; Judg. xxi. 19). It is therefore just as arbitrary on the part of Grotius and Rosenmüller to understand by *mōʻēd* the three yearly pilgrim-festivals, and by *chag Yᵉhōvâh* all the rest of the feasts, including the new moon, as it is on the part of Simson to restrict the last expression to the great harvest-feast, *i.e.* the feast of tabernacles (Lev. xxiii. 39, 41). The two words are synonymous, but they are so arranged that by *chag* the idea of joy is brought into greater prominence, and the feast-day is thereby designated as a day of holy joy before Jehovah; whereas *mōʻēd* simply expresses the idea of a feast established by the Lord, and sanctified to Him (see at Lev. xxiii. 2). By the addition of the *chag Yᵉhōvâh*, therefore, greater emphasis is given to the thought, viz. that along with the feasts themselves all festal joy will also vanish. The perfect הָלְכוּ (ver. 6) may be explained from the fact, that the prophet saw in spirit the people already banished from the land of the Lord. הָלַךְ, to go away out of the land. Egypt is mentioned as the place of banishment, in the same sense as in ver. 3. There will they all find their graves. קִבֵּץ in combination with קָבַר is the gathering together of the dead for a common burial, like אָסַף in Ezek. xxix. 5, Jer. viii. 2, xxv. 33. מֹף, or נֹף, as in

Isa. xix. 13, Jer. ii. 16, xliv. 1, Ezek. xxx. 13, 16, probably
contracted from מֹנִף, answers rather to the Coptic *Membe*,
Memphe, than to the old Egyptian *Men-nefr*, *i.e. mansio bona*,
the profane name of the city of *Memphis*, the ancient capital of
Lower Egypt, the ruins of which are to be seen on the western
bank of the Nile, to the south of Old Cairo. The sacred name
of this city was *Hă-ka-ptah*, *i.e.* house of the worship of Phtah
(see Brugsch, *Geogr. Inschriften*, i. pp. 234–5). In their own
land thorns and thistles would take the place of silver valuables.
The suffix attached to יִירָשֵׁם refers, *ad sensum*, to the collective
מַחְמַד לְכַסְפָּם, the valuables in silver. These are not " silver
idols," as Hitzig imagines, but houses ornamented and filled
with the precious metal, as בְּאָהֳלֵיהֶם in the parallel clause clearly
shows. The growth of thorns and thistles presupposes the utter
desolation of the abodes of men (Isa. xxxiv. 13).

Ver. 7. " *The days of visitation are come, the days of retribution are come; Israel will learn: a fool the prophet, a madman
the man of spirit, for the greatness of thy guilt, and the great
enmity.* Ver. 8. *A spy is Ephraim with my God: the prophet
a snare of the bird-catcher in all his ways, enmity in the house of
his God.* Ver. 9. *They have acted most corruptly, as in the days
of Gibeah: He remembers their iniquity, visits their sins.*" The
perfects in ver. 7 are prophetic. The time of visitation and
retribution is approaching. Then will Israel learn that its
prophets, who only predicted prosperity and good (Ezek. xiii.
10), were infatuated fools. אֱוִיל וגו׳ introduces, without *kī*, what
Israel will experience, as in ch. vii. 2, Amos v. 12. It does
not follow, from the use of the expression '*īsh rŭăch*, that the
reference is to true prophets. '*Ish rŭăch* (a man of spirit) is
synonymous with the '*īsh hōlēkh rŭăch* (a man walking in the
spirit) mentioned in Mic. ii. 11 as prophesying lies, and may
be explained from the fact, that even the false prophets stood
under the influence of a superior demoniacal power, and were
inspired by a *rŭăch sheqer* (" a lying spirit," 1 Kings xxii. 22).
The words which follow, viz. " a fool is the prophet," etc., which
cannot possibly mean, that men have treated, despised, and per-
secuted the prophets as fools and madmen, are a decisive proof
that the expression does not refer to true prophets. עַל רֹב עֲוֹנְךָ
is attached to the principal clauses, בָּאוּ . . . . הֻשְׁלַּם. The punishment and retribution occur because of the greatness of the guilt

of Israel. In וְרַבָּה the preposition עַל continues in force, but as a conjunction : " and because the enmity is great" (cf. Ewald, § 351, a). *Mastēmâh*, enmity, not merely against their fellow-men generally, but principally against God and His servants the true prophets. This is sustained by facts in ver. 8. The first clause, which is a difficult one and has been interpreted in very different ways, " spying is Ephraim עִם אֱלֹהָי " (with or by my God), cannot contain the thought that Ephraim, the tribe, is, according to its true vocation, a watchman for the rest of the people, whose duty it is to stand with the Lord upon the watch-tower and warn Israel when the Lord threatens punishment and judgment (Jerome, Schmidt); for the idea of a prophet standing with Jehovah upon a watch-tower is not only quite foreign to the Old Testament, but irreconcilable with the relation in which the prophets stood to Jehovah. The Lord did indeed appoint prophets as watchmen to His people (Ezek. iii. 17); but He does take His own stand upon the watch-tower with them. *Tsâphâh* in this connection, where prophets are spoken of both before and after, can only denote the eager watching on the part of the prophets for divine revelations, as in Hab. ii. 1, and not their looking out for help ; and עִם אֱלֹהָי cannot express their fellowship or agreement with God, if only on account of the suffix " *my* God," in which Hosea contrasts the true God as His own, with the God of the people. The thought indicated would require אֱלֹהָיו, a reading which is indeed met with in some codices, but is only a worthless conjecture. עִם denotes outward fellowship here : " with " = by the side of. Israel looks out for prophecies or divine revelations with the God of the prophet, *i.e.* at the side of Jehovah; in other words, it does not follow or trust its own prophets, who are not inspired by Jehovah. These are like snares of a bird-catcher in its road, *i.e.* they cast the people headlong into destruction. נָבִיא stands at the head, both collectively and absolutely. In all its ways there is the trap of the bird-catcher : *i.e.* all its projects and all that it does will only tend to ensnare the people. Hostility to Jehovah and His servants the true prophets, is in the house of the God of the Israelites, *i.e.* in the temple erected for the calf-worship; a fact of which Amos (vii. 10–17) furnishes a practical example. Israel has thereby fallen as deeply into abomination and sins as in the days of Gibeah, *i.e.* as at the time when the abominable conduct of the men of Gibeah in connection with the concubine of a Levite took place, as related in Judg. xix. sqq., in consequence of which the tribe of Benjamin was almost exterminated. The same depravity on the part of Israel will be equally punished by the Lord now (cf. ch. viii. 13).

The Degeneracy of Israel, and Ruin of its Kingdom.— Chap. ix. 10–xi. 11.

In this section the arrangement of the contents in strophes becomes very apparent. Three times (viz. ch. ix. 10, x. 1, and xi. 1) does the prophet revert to the early days of Israel, and show how Israel has been unfaithful to its divine calling, and from time immemorial has responded to all the manifestations of the love and grace of God by apostasy and idolatry, so that the Lord is obliged to punish the degenerate and obstinate nation with banishment into exile and the destruction of the kingdom. Nevertheless, as the Holy One, and for the sake of His own unchangeable covenant faithfulness, He will not utterly eradicate it.

Chap. ix. 10–17. Ver. 10. "*I found Israel like grapes in the desert, I saw your fathers like early fruit on the fig-tree in the first shooting; but they came to Baal-Peor, and consecrated themselves to shame, and became abominations like their lover.*" Grapes in the desert and early figs are pleasant choice fruits to whoever finds them. This figure therefore indicates the peculiar pleasure which Jehovah found in the people of Israel when He led them out of Egypt, or the great worth which they had in His eyes when He chose them for the people of His possession, and concluded a covenant with them at Sinai (Theod., Cyr.). *Bammidbâr* (in the desert) belongs, so far as its position is concerned, to *'ănâbhīm*: grapes in the dry, barren desert, where you do not expect to find such refreshing fruit; but, so far as the fact is concerned, it also refers to the place in which Israel was thus found by God, since you can only find fruit in the desert when you are there yourself. The words, moreover, evidently refer to Deut. xxxii. 10 ("I found him (Israel) in the wilderness," etc.), and point *implicite* to the helpless condition in which Israel was when God first adopted it. The suffix to *bᵉrēʾshīthāh* (at *her* beginning) refers to תְּאֵנָה, the first-fruit, which the fig-tree bears in its first time, at the first shooting. But Israel no longer answered to the good pleasure of God. They came to Baal-Peor. בַּעַל־פְּעוֹר without the preposition אֶל is not the idol of that name, but the place where it was worshipped, which was properly called *Beth-Peor* or *Peor* (see at Num. xxiii. 28 and xxv. 3). יִנָּזְרוּ is chosen instead of יִצָּמֶד (Num. xxiii. 3, 5), to show that Israel ought to have consecrated itself to Jehovah, to have been the *nazir* of Jehovah. *Bōsheth* (shame) is the name given to the idol of Baal-Peor (cf. Jer. iii. 24), the worship of which was a shame to Israel. *ʾOhabh*, the paramour, is also Baal-Peor. Of all the different rebellions on the part of Israel against Jehovah, the prophet singles out only the idolatry with Baal-Peor, because the principal sin of the ten tribes was Baal-worship in its coarser or more refined forms.

It is very evident that this is what he has in his mind, and that he regards the apostasy of the ten tribes as merely a continuation of that particular idolatry, from the punishment which is announced in vers. 11, 12, as about to fall upon Ephraim in consequence. Ver. 11. "*Ephraim, its glory will fly away like a bird; no birth, and no pregnancy, and no conception.* Ver. 12. *Yea, though they bring up their sons, I make them bereft, without a man; for woe to them when I depart from them!*" The glory which God gave to His people through great multiplication, shall vanish away. The licentious worship of luxury will be punished by the diminution of the numbers of the people, by childlessness, and the destruction of the youth that may have grown up. מִלֵּדָה, so that there shall be no bearing. בֶּטֶן, the womb, for pregnancy or the fruit of the womb. Even (*kī* emphatic) if the sons (the children) grow up, God will make them bereft, מֵאָדָם, so that there shall be no men there. The grown-up sons shall be swept away by death, by the sword (cf. Deut. xxxii. 25). The last clause gives the reason for the punishment threatened. גַּם adds force; it usually stands at the head of the sentence, and here belongs to לָהֶם: Yea, woe to them, if I depart from them, or withdraw my favour from them! שׂוּר stands for סוּר, according to the interchangeableness of שׂ and ס (Aquila and Vulg.). This view has more to support it than the supposition that שׂוּר is an error of the pen for שׁוּר (Ewald, Hitzig, etc.), since שׁוּר, to look, construed with מִן, in the sense of to look away from a person, is never met with, although the meaning is just the same.

The vanishing of the glory of Ephraim is carried out still further in what follows. Ver. 13. " *Ephraim as I selected it for a Tyre planted in the valley; so shall Ephraim lead out its sons to the murderer.* Ver. 14. *Give them, O Jehovah: what shalt Thou give him? Give them a childless womb and dry breasts.*" In ver. 13 *Ephraim* is the object to רָאִיתִי (I have seen), but on account of the emphasis it is placed first, as in ver. 11; and רָאָה with an accusative and לְ signifies to select anything for a purpose, as in Gen. xxii. 8. The Lord had selected Ephraim for Himself to be a Tyre planted in the meadow, *i.e.* in a soil adapted for growth and prosperity, had intended for it the bloom and glory of the rich and powerful Tyre; but now, for its apostasy, He would give it up to desolation, and dedicate its sons, *i.e.* its people, to death by the sword. The commentators, for the most part, like the LXX., have overlooked this meaning of ראה, and therefore have not only been unable to explain *l*ᵉ*tsōr* (for a Tyre), but have been driven either to resort to alterations of the text, like *l*ᵉ*tsūrâh,* " after the form" (Ewald), or to arbitrary assumptions, *e.g.* that *tsōr* signifies " palm" after the Arabic (Arnold, Hitzig), or that *l*ᵉ*tsōr* means " as far as Tyre" (לְ = עַד), in order to bring a more or less forced interpretation into the sentence. The *Vav* before '*Ephraim* introduces the apodosis to כַּאֲשֶׁר : " as I have selected Ephraim, so shall Ephraim lead out," etc. On the construction לְהוֹצִיא, see Ewald, § 237, *c*. In ver. 14 the threat rises into an appeal to God to execute the threatened punishment. The excited style of the language is indicated in the interpolated *mah-tittēn* (what wilt Thou give ?). The words do not contain an intercessory prayer on the part of the prophet, that God will not punish the people too severely but condemn them to barrenness rather than to the loss of the young men (Ewald), but are expressive of holy indignation at the deep corruption of the people.

The Lord thereupon replies in ver. 15 : " *All their wickedness is at Gilgal; for there I took them into hatred: for the evil of their doings will I drive them out of my house, and not love them any more; all their princes are rebellious.*" How far all the wickedness of Ephraim was concentrated at Gilgal it is impossible to determine more precisely, since we have no historical accounts of the idolatrous worship practised there (see at ch. iv. 15). That Gilgal was the scene of horrible human sacrifices, as Hitzig observes at ch. xii. 12, cannot be proved from ch. xiii. 2. שָׂנֵא is used here in an inchoative sense, viz. to conceive hatred. On account of their wickedness they should be expelled from the house, *i.e.* the congregation of Jehovah (see at ch. viii. 1). The expression "I will drive them out of my house" (*mibbēthī 'ăgârᵉshēm*) may be explained from Gen. xxi. 10, where Sarah requests Abraham to drive (*gârash*) Hagar her maid out of the house along with her son, that the son of the maid may not inherit with Isaac, and where God commands the patriarch to carry out Sarah's will. The expulsion of Israel from the house of the Lord is separation from the fellowship of the cove-nant nation and its blessings, and is really equivalent to loving it no longer. There is a play upon words in the last clause שָׂרֵיהֶם סוֹרְרִים.

Ver. 16. "*Ephraim is smitten: their root is dried up; they will bear no fruit: even if they beget, I slay the treasures of their womb.* Ver. 17. *My God rejects them: for they have not hearkened to Him, and they shall be fugitives among the nations.*" In ver. 16a Israel is compared to a plant, that is so injured by the heat of the sun (Ps. cxxi. 6, cii. 5), or by a worm (Jonah iv. 7), that it dries up and bears no more fruit. The perfects are a prophetic expression, indicating the certain execution of the threat. This is repeated in ver. 16b in figurative language; and the threatening in vers. 11, 12, is thereby strengthened. Lastly, in ver. 17 the words of threatening are rounded off by a statement of the reason for the rejection of Israel; and this rejection is described as banishment among the nations, accord-ing to Deut. xxviii. 65.

Ch. x. In a fresh turn the concluding thought of the last strophe (ch. ix. 10) is resumed, and the guilt and punishment of Israel still more fully described in two sections, vers. 1–8 and 9–15. Ver. 1. "*Israel is a running vine; it set fruit for itself: the more of its fruit, the more altars did it prepare; the better its land, the better pillars did they make.* Ver. 2. *Smooth was their heart, now will they atone. He will break in pieces their altars, desolate their pillars.* Ver. 3. *Yea, now will they say, No king to us! for we feared not Jehovah; and the king, what shall he do to us?"* Under the figure of a vine running luxuriantly, which did indeed set some good fruit, but bore no sound ripe grapes, the prophet describes Israel as a glorious plantation of God Himself, which did not answer the expectations of its Creator. The figure is simply sketched in a few bold lines. We have an explanatory parallel in Ps. lxxx. 9–12. The participle *bōqēq* does not mean " empty" or " emptying out" here; for this does not suit the next clause, according to which the fruit was set, but from the primary meaning of *bâqaq*, to pour out, pouring itself out, overflowing, *i.e.* running luxuriantly. It has the same meaning, therefore, as סֹרַחַת 'ג in Ezek. xvii. 6, that which extends its branches far and wide, that is to say, grows most vigorously. The next sentence, " it set fruit," still belongs to the figure; but in the third sentence the figure passes over into a literal prophecy. According to the abundance of its fruit, Israel made many altars; and in proportion to the goodness of its land, it made better מַצֵּבוֹת, Baal's pillars (see at 1 Kings xiv. 23); *i.e.* as Israel multiplied, and under the blessing of God attained to prosperity, wealth, and power in the good land (Ex. iii. 8), it forgot its God, and fell more and more into idolatry (cf. ch. ii. 10, viii. 4, 11). The reason of all this was, that their heart was smooth, *i.e.* dissimulating, not sincerely devoted to the Lord, inasmuch as, under the appearance of devotedness to God, they still clung to idols (for the fact, see 2 Kings xvii. 9). The word *châlâq*, to be smooth, was mostly applied by a Hebrew to the tongue, lip, mouth, throat, and speech (Ps. v. 10, xii. 3, lv. 22 ; Prov. v. 3), and not to the heart. But in Ezek. xii. 24 we read of *smooth*, *i.e.* deceitful prophesying; and there is all the more reason for retaining the meaning " smooth" here, that the rendering " their heart is divided," which is supported by the ancient versions, cannot be grammatically defended. For *châlâq* is not used in *kal* in an intransitive sense; and the active rendering, " He (*i.e.* God) has divided their heart" (Hitzig), gives an unscriptural thought. They will now atone for this, for God will destroy their altars and pillars. עָרַף, " to break the neck of the altars," is a bold expression, applied to the destruction of the altars by breaking off the horns (compare Amos iii. 14). Then will the people see and be compelled to confess that it has no longer a king, because it has not feared the Lord, since the king who has been set up in opposition to the will of the Lord (ch. viii. 4) cannot bring either help or deliverance (ch. xiii. 10). עָשָׂה, to do, *i.e.* to help or be of use to a person (cf. Eccles. ii. 2).

The thoughts of vers. 2, 3 are carried out still further in vers. 4–7. Ver. 4. " *They have spoken words, sworn falsely, made treaties: thus right springs up like darnel in the furrows of the field.* Ver. 5. *For the calves of Beth-Aven the inhabitants of Samaria were afraid: yea, its people mourn over it, and its sacred ministers will tremble at it, at its glory, because it has strayed from them.* Ver. 6. *Men will also carry it to Asshur, as a present for king Jareb: shame will seize upon Ephraim, and Israel will be put to shame for its counsel.*" The dissimulation of heart (ver. 3) manifested itself in their speaking words which were nothing but words, *i.e.* in vain talk (cf. Isa. lviii. 13), in false swearing, and in the making of treaties. אָלוֹת, by virtue of the parallelism, is an infin. abs. for אָלֹה, formed like כָּרֹת, analogous to שְׁתוֹת (Isa. xxii. 13 ; see Ewald, § 240, *b*). כָּרַת בְּרִית, in connection with false swearing, must signify the making of a covenant without any truthfulness in it, *i.e.* the conclusion of treaties with foreign nations—for example, with Assyria—which they were inclined to observe only so long as they could promise themselves advantages from them. In consequence of this, right has become like a bitter plant growing luxuriantly (רוֹשׁ = רֹאשׁ ; see at Deut. xxix. 17). *Mishpát* does not mean judgment here, or the punitive judgment of God (Chald. and many others), for this could hardly be compared with propriety to weeds running over everything, but *right* in its degeneracy into wrong, or right that men have turned into bitter fruit or poison (Amos vi. 12). This spreads about in the kingdom, as weeds spread luxuriantly in the furrows of the field (שָׂדַי a poetical form for שָׂדֶה, like Deut. xxxii. 13, Ps. viii. 8). Therefore the judgment cannot be delayed, and is already approaching in so threatening a manner, that the inhabitants of Samaria tremble for the golden calves. The plural '*eglóth* is used with indefinite generality, and gives no warrant, therefore, for the inference that there were several golden calves set up in Bethel. Moreover, this would be at variance with the fact, that in the sentences which follow we find " *the* (one) calf " spoken of. The feminine form '*eglóth*, which only occurs here, is also probably connected with the abstract use of the plural, inasmuch as the feminine is the proper form for abstracts. *Bēth-'âven* for *Bēth-'ēl*, as in ch. iv. 15. *Shâkhēn* is construed with the plural, as an adjective used in a collective sense. כִּי (ver. 5) is emphatic, and the suffixes attached to עַמּוֹ and כְּמָרָיו do not refer to Samaria, but to the idol, *i.e.* the calf, since the prophet distinctly calls Israel, which ought to have been the nation of Jehovah, the nation of its calf-idol, which mourned with its priests (*k*emârîm, the priests appointed in connection with the worship of the calves : see at 2 Kings xxiii. 5) for the carrying away of the calf to Assyria. גִּיל does not mean to exult or rejoice here, nor to tremble (applied to the leaping of the heart from fear, as it does from joy), but has the same meaning as חִיל in Ps. xcvi. 9. עָלָיו is still further defined by עַל־כְּבוֹדוֹ, " for its glory," *i.e.* not for the temple-treasure at Bethel (Hitzig), nor the one glorious image of the calf, as the symbol of the state-god (Ewald, Umbreit), but the calf, to which the people attributed the glory of the true God. The perfect, *gâlâh*, is used prophetically of that which was as good as complete and certain (for the *fut exact.*, cf. Ewald, § 343, *a*). The golden calf, the glory of the nation, will have to wander into exile. This cannot even save itself ; it will be taken to Assyria, to king *Jareb* (see at ch. v. 13), as *minchâh*, a present or tribute (see 2 Sam. viii. 2, 6; 1 Kings v. 1). For the construing of the passive with אֵת, see Ges. § 143, 1, *a*. Then will Ephraim (= Israel) be seized by reproach and shame. *Boshnâh*, a word only met with here ; it is formed from the masculine *bōshen*, which is not used at all (see Ewald, § 163, 164).

With the carrying away of the golden calf the kingdom of Samaria also perishes, and desert plants will grow upon the places of idols. Vers. 7, 8. " *Destroyed is Samaria; her king like a splinter on the surface of the water. And destroyed are the high places of Aven, the sin of Israel : thorn and thistle will rise up on their altars ; and they will speak to the mountains, Cover us ! and to the hills, Fall on us !*" שֹׁמְרוֹן מַלְכָּהּ is not an asyndeton, " Samaria and its king ;" but *Shōm*erōn is to be taken absolutely, " as for Samaria," although, as a matter of fact, not only Samaria, the capital of the kingdom, but the kingdom itself, was destroyed. For *malkâh* does not refer to any particular king, but is used in a general sense for " the king that

Samaria had," so that the destruction of the monarchy is here predicted (cf. ver. 15). The idea that the words refer to one particular king, is not only at variance with the context, which contains no allusion to any one historical occurrence, but does not suit the simile : like a splinter upon the surface of the water, which is carried away by the current, and vanishes without leaving a trace behind. *Qetseph* is not "foam" (Chald., Symm., Rabb.), but a broken branch, a fagot or a splinter, as *q*ᵉ*tsâphâh* in Joel i. 7 clearly shows. *Bâmōth 'âven* are the buildings connected with the image-worship at Bethel (*'âven = Bēth-'ēl*, ver. 5), the temple erected there (*bēth bâmōth*), together with the altar, possibly also including other illegal places of sacrifice there, which constituted the chief sin of the kingdom of Israel. These were to be so utterly destroyed, that thorns and thistles would grow upon the ruined altars (cf. Gen. iii. 18). " The sign of extreme solitude, that there are not even the walls left, or any traces of the buildings" (Jerome). When the kingdom shall be thus broken up, together with the monarchy and the sacred places, the inhabitants, in their hopeless despair, will long for swift death and destruction. Saying to the mountains, " Cover us," etc., implies much more than hiding themselves in the holes and clefts of the rocks (Isa. ii. 19, 21). It expresses the desire to be buried under the falling mountains and hills, that they may no longer have to bear the pains and terrors of the judgment. In this sense are the words transferred by Christ, in Luke xxiii. 30, to the calamities attending the destruction of Jerusalem, and in Rev. vi. 16 to the terrors of the last judgment.

Vers. 9–15. After the threatening of punishment has thus been extended in ver. 8, even to the utter ruin of the kingdom, the prophet returns in ver. 9 to the earlier times, for the purpose of exhibiting in a new form the deeply rooted sinfulness of the people, and then, under cover of an appeal to them to return to righteousness, depicting still further the time of visitation, and (in vers. 14, 15) predicting with still greater clearness the destruction of the kingdom and the overthrow of the monarchy. Ver. 9. " *Since the days of Gibeah hast thou sinned, O Israel : there have they remained : the war against the sons of wickedness did not overtake them at Gibeah.* Ver. 10. *According to my desire shall I chastise them; and nations will be*

*gathered together against them, to bind them to their two trans-
gressions.*" Just as in ch. ix. 9, the days of Gibeah, *i.e.* the
days when that ruthless crime was committed at Gibeah upon
the concubine of the Levite, are mentioned as a time of deep
corruption ; so are those days described in the present passage
as the commencement of Israel's sin. For it is as obvious that
מִימֵי is not to be understood in a comparative sense, as it is
that the days of Gibeah are not to be taken as referring to the
choice of Saul, who sprang from Gibeah, to be their king
(Chald.). The following words, שָׁם עָמְדוּ וגו׳, which are very
difficult, and have been variously explained, do not describe
the conduct of Israel in those days ; for, in the first place, the
statement that the war did not overtake them is by no means
in harmony with this, since the other tribes avenged that crime
so severely that the tribe of Benjamin was almost exterminated;
and secondly, the suffix attached to תַּשִּׂיגֵם evidently refers to
the same persons as that appended to אֶפְרַם in ver. 10, *i.e.* to
the Israelites of the ten tribes, to which Hosea foretels the
coming judgment. These are therefore the subject to עָמְדוּ,
and consequently עמד signifies to stand, to remain, to persevere
(cf. Isa. xlvii. 12, Jer. xxxii. 14). There, in Gibeah, did they
remain, that is to say, they persevered in the sin of Gibeah,
without the war at Gibeah against the sinners overtaking them
(the imperfect, in a subordinate clause, used to describe the
necessary consequence ; and עלוה transposed from עוֹלָה, like זַעֲוָה
in Deut. xxviii. 25 for זְוָעָה). The meaning is, that since the
days of Gibeah the Israelites persist in the same sin as the
Gibeahites ; but whereas those sinners were punished and
destroyed by the war, the ten tribes still live on in the
same sin without having been destroyed by any similar war.
Jehovah will now chastise them for it. בְּאַוָּתִי, in my desire,
equivalent to according to my wish, — an anthropomorphic
description of the severity of the chastisement. וָאֶסְּרֵם from
יָסַר (according to Ewald, § 139, *a*), with the *Vav* of the
apodosis. The chastisement will consist in the fact, that
nations will be gathered together against Israel בְּאָסְרָם, *lit.* at
their binding, *i.e.* when I shall bind them. The *chethib* עינתם
cannot well be the plural of עַיִן, because the plural עינות is not
used for the eyes ; and the rendering, " before their two eyes,"
in the sense of " without their being able to prevent it "

(Ewald), yields the unheard-of conception of binding a person before his own eyes; and, moreover, the use of שְׁתֵּי עֵינוֹת instead of the simple dual would still be left unexplained. We must therefore give the preference to the *keri* עוֹנֹת, and regard the *chethib* as another form, that may be accounted for from the transition of the verbs עי into עו, and עוֹנֹת as a contraction of עוֹנֹת, since עוֹנָה cannot be shown to have either the meaning of "furrow" (Chald., A. E.), or that of the severe labour of "tributary service." And, moreover, neither of these meanings would give us a suitable thought; whilst the very same objection may be brought against the supposition that the doubleness of the work refers to Ephraim and Judah, which has been brought against the rendering "to bind to his furrows," viz. that it would be *non solum ineptum, sed locutionis monstrum.* לִשְׁתֵּי עוֹנֹתָם, "to their two transgressions" to bind them: *i.e.* to place them in connection with the transgressions by the punishment, so that they will be obliged to drag them along like beasts of burden. By the two transgressions we are to understand neither the two golden calves at Bethel and Dan (Hitzig), nor unfaithfulness towards Jehovah and devotedness to idols, after Jer. ii. 13 (Cyr., Theod.); but their apostasy from Jehovah and the royal house of David, in accordance with ch. iii. 5, where it is distinctly stated that the ultimate conversion of the nation will consist in its seeking Jehovah and David their king.

In the next verse the punishment is still further defined, and also extended to Judah. Ver. 11. "*And Ephraim is an instructed cow, which loves to thresh; and I, I have come over the beauty of her neck: I yoke Ephraim; Judah will plough, Jacob harrow itself.*" *M⁰lummádáh*, instructed, trained to work, received its more precise definition from the words "loving to thresh" (*'óhabhtī*, a participle with the connecting *Yod* in the constructive: see Ewald, § 211, *b*), not as being easier work in comparison with the hard task of driving, ploughing, and harrowing, but because in threshing the ox was allowed to eat at pleasure (Deut. xxv. 4), from which Israel became fat and strong (Deut. xxxii. 15). Threshing, therefore, is a figurative representation not of the conquest of other nations (as in Mic. iv. 13, Isa. xli. 15), but of pleasant, productive, profitable labour. Israel had accustomed itself to this, from the fact that God had bestowed His blessing upon it (ch. xiii. 6). But it would be different now. עָבַרְתִּי עַל, a prophetic perfect: I come over the neck, used in a hostile sense, and answering to our "rushing in upon a person." The actual idea is that of putting a heavy yoke upon the neck. not of putting a rider upon it. אַרְכִּיב, not to mount or ride, but to drive, or use for drawing and driving, *i.e.* to harness, and that, as the following clauses show, to the plough and harrow, for the performance of hard field-labour, which figuratively represents subjugation and bondage. Judah is also mentioned here again, as in ch. viii. 14, vi. 11, etc. *Jacob,* in connection with Judah, is not a name for the whole nation (or the twelve tribes), but is synonymous with Ephraim, *i.e.* Israel of the ten tribes. This is required by the correspondence between the last two clauses, which are simply a further development of the expression ארכיב אפ׳, with an extension of the punishment threatened against Ephraim to Judah also.

The call to repentance and reformation of life is then appended in vers. 12, 13, clothed in similar figures. Ver. 12. "*Sow to yourselves for righteousness, reap according to love; plough for yourselves virgin soil: for it is time to seek Jehovah, till He come and rain righteousness upon you.* Ver. 13. *Ye have ploughed wickedness, ye have reaped crime: eaten the fruit of lying: because thou hast trusted in thy way, in the multitude of thy mighty men.*" Sowing and reaping are figures used to denote their spiritual and moral conduct. לִצְדָקָה, for righteousness, is parallel to לְפִי חֶסֶד; *i.e.* sow that righteousness may be able to spring up like seed, *i.e.* righteousness towards your fellow-men. The fruit of this will be *chesed,* condescending love towards the poor and wretched. *Nīr nīr,* both here and in Jer. iv. 3 to plough virgin soil, *i.e.* to make land not yet cultivated arable. We have an advance in this figure: they are to give up all their previous course of conduct, and create for themselves a new sphere for their activity, *i.e.* commence a new course of life. וְעֵת, and indeed it is time, equivalent to, for it is high time to give up your old sinful ways and seek the Lord, till (עַד) He come, *i.e.* till He turn His grace to you again, and cause it to rain upon you. *Tsedeq,* righteousness, not salvation, a meaning which the word never has, and least of all here, where *tsedeq* corresponds to the *tsᵉdáqáh* of the first clause. God causes righteousness to rain, inasmuch as He not only gives strength to secure it, like rain for the growth of the seed (cf. Isa. xliv. 3), but must also generate and create it in man by His Spirit (Ps. li. 12). The reason for this summons is given in ver. 13, in another allusion to the moral conduct of Israel until now. Hitherto they have ploughed as well as reaped unrighteousness and sin, and eaten lies as the fruit thereof,—lies, inasmuch as they did not promote the prosperity of the kingdom as they imagined, but only led to its decay and ruin. For they did not trust in Jehovah the Creator and rock of salvation, but in their way, *i.e.* their deeds and their might, in the strength of their army (Amos vi. 13), the worthlessness of which they will now discover.

Ver. 14. "*A tumult will arise against thy peoples, and all thy fortifications are laid waste, as Shalman laid Beth-Arbeel waste in the day of the war: mother and children are dashed to pieces.* Ver. 15. *Thus hath Bethel done to you because of the wickedness of your wickedness: in the morning dawn the king of Israel is cut off, cut off.*" קאם with א as *mater lect.* (Ewald, § 15, *e*), construed with ב: to rise up against a person, as in Ps. xxvii. 12, Job xvi. 8. שָׁאוֹן, war, tumult, as in Amos ii. 2. בְּעַמֶּיךָ: against thy people of war. The expression is chosen with a reference to *rōbh gibbōrīm* (the multitude of mighty men), in which Israel put its trust. The meaning, countrymen, or tribes, is restricted to the older language of the Pentateuch. The singular יוֹשֵׁר refers to כֹּל, as in Isa. lxiv. 10, contrary to the ordinary language (cf. Ewald, § 317, *c*). Nothing is known concerning the devastation of Beth-Arbeel by Shalman; and hence there has always been great uncertainty as to the meaning of the words. *Shalman* is no doubt a contracted form of *Shalmanezer*, the king of Assyria, who destroyed the kingdom of the ten tribes (2 Kings xvii. 6). *Bēth-'arbē'l* is hardly Arbela of Assyria, which became celebrated through the victory of Alexander (Strab. xvi. 1, 3), since the Israelites could scarcely have become so well acquainted with such a remote city, as that the prophet could hold up the desolation that befel it as an example to them, but in all probability the *Arbela* in *Galilœa Superior*, which is mentioned in 1 Macc. ix. 2, and very frequently in Josephus, a place in the tribe of Naphtali, between Sephoris and Tiberias (according to Robinson, *Pal.* iii. pp. 281-2, and *Bibl. Researches*, p. 343 : the modern *Irbid*). The objection offered by Hitzig,—viz. that *shōd* is a noun in ch. ix. 6, vii. 13, xii. 2, and that the infinitive construct, with ל prefixed, is written לִשְׁדֹּד in Jer. xlvii. 4 ; and lastly, that if *Shalman* were the subject, we should expect the preposition אֶת before בֵּית,—is not conclusive, and the attempt which he makes to explain *Salman-Beth-Arbel* from the Sanscrit is not worth mentioning. The clause " mother and children," etc., a proverbial expression denoting inhuman cruelty (see at Gen. xxxii. 12), does not merely refer to the conduct of Shalman in connection with Beth-Arbel, possibly in the campaign mentioned in 2 Kings xvii. 3, but is also intended to indicate the fate with which the whole of the kingdom of Israel was threatened. In ver. 16 this threat concludes with an announcement of the overthrow of the monarchy, accompanied by another allusion to the guilt of the people. The subject to בְּכָה עָשָׂה is *Beth-el* (Chald.), not Shalman or Jehovah. Bethel, the seat of the idolatry, prepares this lot for the people on account of its great wickedness. עָשָׂה is a *perf. proph.*; and רָעַת רָעַתְכֶם, wickedness in its second potency, extreme wickedness (cf. Ewald, § 313, c). *Basshachar*, in the morning-dawn, *i.e.* at the time when prosperity is once more apparently about to dawn, *tempore pacis alluscente* (Cocc., Hgst.). The gerund נִדְמֹה adds to the force ; and מֶלֶךְ יִשׂ' is not this or the other king, but as in ver. 7, the king generally, *i.e.* the monarchy of Israel.

Ch. xi. The prophet goes back a third time (cf. ch. x. 1, ix. 10) to the early times of Israel, and shows how the people had repaid the Lord, for all the proofs of His love, with nothing but ingratitude and unfaithfulness; so that it would have merited utter destruction from off the earth, if God should not restrain His wrath for the sake of His unchangeable faithfulness, in order that, after severely chastening, He might gather together once more those that were rescued from among the heathen. Ver. 1. " *When Israel was young, then I loved him, and I called my son out of Egypt. Ver. 2. Men called to them; so they went away from their countenance: they offer sacrifice to the Baals, and burn incense to the idols.*" Ver. 1 rests upon Ex. iv. 22, 23, where the Lord directs Moses to say to Pharaoh, " Israel is my first-born son ; let my son go, that he may serve me." Israel

was the son of Jehovah, by virtue of its election to be Jehovah's
peculiar people (see at Ex. iv. 22). In this election lay the
ground for the love which God showed to Israel, by bringing it
out of Egypt, to give it the land of Canaan, promised to the
fathers for its inheritance. The adoption of Israel as the son
of Jehovah, which began with its deliverance out of the bondage
of Egypt, and was completed in the conclusion of the covenant
at Sinai, forms the first stage in the carrying out of the divine
work of salvation, which was completed in the incarnation of
the Son of God for the redemption of mankind from death and
ruin. The development and guidance of Israel as the people
of God all pointed to Christ; not, however, in any such sense
as that the nation of Israel was to bring forth the Son of God
from within itself, but in this sense, that the relation which the
Lord of heaven and earth established and sustained with that
nation, was a preparation for the union of God with humanity,
and paved the way for the incarnation of His Son. by the fact
that Israel was trained to be a vessel of divine grace. All
essential factors in the history of Israel point to this as their
end, and thereby become types and material prophecies of the
life of Him in whom the reconciliation of man to God was to
be realized, and the union of God with the human race to be
developed into a personal unity. It is in this sense that the
second half of our verse is quoted in Matt. ii. 15 as a prophecy
of Christ, not because the words of the prophet refer directly
and immediately to Christ, but because the sojourn in Egypt,
and return out of that land, had the same significance in relation to the development of the life of Jesus Christ, as it had to
the nation of Israel. Just as Israel grew into a nation in Egypt,
where it was out of the reach of Canaanitish ways, so was the
child Jesus hidden in Egypt from the hostility of Herod. But
ver. 2 is attached thus as an antithesis: this love of its God
was repaid by Israel with base apostasy. קָרְאוּ, they, viz. the
prophets (cf. ver. 7; 2 Kings xvii. 13; Jer. vii. 25, xxv. 4;
Zech. i. 4), called to them, called the Israelites to the Lord and
to obedience to Him; but they (the Israelites) went away from
their countenance, would not hearken to the prophets, or come
to the Lord (Jer. ii. 31). The thought is strengthened by כֵּן,
with the כַּאֲשֶׁר of the protasis omitted (Ewald, § 360, a): as the
prophets called, so the Israelites drew back from them, and

served idols. בְּעָלִים as in ch. ii. 15, and פְּסִלִים as in 2 Kings xvii. 41 and Deut. vii. 5, 25 (see at Ex. xx. 4).

Nevertheless the Lord continued to show love to them. Vers. 3, 4, " *And I, I have taught Ephraim to walk : He took them in His arms, and they did not know that I healed them. I drew them with bands of a man, with cords of love, and became to them like a lifter up of the yoke upon their jaws, and gently towards him did I give* (him) *food.*" תִּרְגַּלְתִּי, a *hiphil*, formed after the Aramæan fashion (cf. Ges. § 55, 5), by hardening the ה into ת, and construed with לְ, as the *hiphil* frequently is (*e.g.* ch. x. 1 ; Amos viii. 9), a *denom.* of רֶגֶל, to teach to walk, to guide in leading-strings, like a child that is being trained to walk. It is a figurative representation of paternal care for a child's prosperity. קָחָם, *per aphæresin*, for לְקָחָם, like קַח for לְקַח in Ezek. xvii. 5. The sudden change from the first person to the third seems very strange to our ears ; but it is not uncommon in Hebrew, and is to be accounted for here from the fact, that the prophet could very easily pass from speaking in the name of God to speaking of God Himself. קָח cannot be either an infinitive or a participle, on account of the following word זְרוֹעֹתָיו, *his* arms. The two clauses refer chiefly to the care and help afforded by the Lord to His people in the Arabian desert ; and the prophet had Deut. i. 31 floating before his mind : " in the wilderness the Lord thy God bare thee, as a man doth bear his son." The last clause also refers to this, רְפָאתִים pointing back to Ex. xv. 26, where the Lord showed Himself as the physician of Israel, by making the bitter water at Marah drinkable, and at the same time as their helper out of every trouble. In ver. 4, again, there is a still further reference to the manifestation of the love of God to Israel on the journey through the wilderness. חַבְלֵי אָדָם, cords with which men are led, more especially children that are weak upon their feet, in contrast with ropes, with which men control wild, unmanageable beasts (Ps. xxxii. 9), are a figurative representation of the paternal, humane guidance of Israel, as explained in the next figure, " cords of love." This figure leads on to the kindred figure of the yoke laid upon beasts, to harness them for work. As merciful masters lift up the yoke upon the cheeks of their oxen, *i.e.* push it so far back that the animals can eat their food in comfort, so has the Lord made the yoke of the law, which

has been laid upon His people, both soft and light.　As הֵרִים עַל עַל
does not mean to take the yoke away from (מֵעַל) the cheeks, but
to lift it above the cheeks, *i.e.* to make it easier, by pushing it
back, we cannot refer the words to the liberation of Israel from
the bondage of Egypt, but can only think of what the Lord
did, to make it easy for the people to observe the commandments imposed upon them, when they were received into His
covenant (Ex. xxiv. 3, 7), including not only the many manifestations of mercy which might and ought to have allured them
to reciprocate His love, and yield a willing obedience to His
commandments, but also the means of grace provided in their
worship, partly in the institution of sacrifice, by which a way of
approach was opened to divine grace to obtain forgiveness of
sin, and partly in the institution of feasts, at which they could
rejoice in the gracious gifts of their God.　וְאַט is not the first
pers. imperf. *hiphil* of נטה ("I inclined myself to him;" Symm.,
Syr., and others), in which case we should expect וָאַט, but an
adverb, softly, comfortably; and אֵלָיו belongs to it, after the
analogy of 2 Sam. xviii. 5.　אוֹכִיל is an anomalous formation for
אַאֲכִיל, like אוֹבִיד for אַאֲבִיד in Jer. xlvi. 8 (cf. Ewald, § 192, *d*;
Ges. § 68, 2, Anm. 1).　Jerome has given the meaning quite
correctly: "and I gave them manna for food in the desert,
which they enjoyed."

By despising this love, Israel brings severe punishment upon
itself.　Ver. 5. "*It will not return into the land of Egypt; but
Asshur, he is its king, because they refused to return.*　Ver. 6.
*And the sword will sweep round in its cities, and destroy its
bolts, and devour, because of their counsels.*　Ver. 7. *My people is
bent upon apostasy from me: and if men call it upwards, it does
not raise itself at all.*"　The apparent contradiction between
the words, "It will not return into the land of Egypt," and the
threat contained in ch. viii. 13, ix. 3, that Israel should return
to Egypt, ought not to lead us to resort to alterations of the
text, or to take לֹא in the sense of לֹ, and connect it with the
previous verse, as is done by the LXX., Mang., and others, or
to make an arbitrary paraphrase of the words, either by taking
לֹא in the sense of הֲלֹא, and rendering it as a question, "Should it
not return?" equivalent to "it will certainly return" (Maurer,
Ewald, etc.); or by understanding the return to Egypt as
signifying the longing of the people for help from Egypt

(Rosenmüller). The emphatic הוּא of the second clause is at variance with all these explanations, since they not only fail to explain it, but it points unmistakeably to an antithesis: "Israel will not return to Egypt; but Asshur, it shall be its king," *i.e.* it shall come under the dominion of Assyria. The supposed contradiction is removed as soon as we observe that in ch. viii. 13, ix. 3, 6, Egypt is a type of the land of bondage; whereas here the typical interpretation is precluded partly by the contrast to Asshur, and still more by the correspondence in which the words stand to ver. 1*b*. Into the land from which Jehovah called His people, Israel shall not return, lest it should appear as though the object, for which it had been brought out of Egypt and conducted miraculously through the desert, had been frustrated by the impenitence of the people. But it is to be brought into another bondage. וְאַשּׁוּר is appended adversatively. Asshur shall rule over it as king, because they refuse to return, *sc.* to Jehovah. The Assyrians will wage war against the land, and conquer it. The sword (used as the principal weapon, to denote the destructive power of war) will circulate in the cities of Israel, make the round of the cities as it were, and destroy its bolts, *i.e.* the bolts of the gates of the fortifications of Ephraim. *Baddīm*, poles (Ex. xxv. 13 sqq.), cross-poles or cross-beams, with which the gates were fastened, hence bolts in the literal sense, as in Job xvii. 16, and not tropically for "princes" (Ges.), *electi* (Jer., Chald., etc.). "On account of their counsels:" this is more fully defined in ver. 7. וְעַמִּי, *and* my people (= *since* my people) are harnessed to apostasy from me (*meshūbhāthī*, with an objective suffix). תְּלוּאִים, lit. suspended on apostasy, *i.e.* not "swaying about in consequence of apostasy or in constant danger of falling away" (Chald., Syr., Hengst.), since this would express too little in the present context and would not suit the second half of the verse, but impaled or fastened upon apostasy as upon a stake, so that it cannot get loose. Hence the constructing of תָּלָה with לְ instead of עַל or בְּ (2 Sam. xviii. 10), may be accounted for from the use of the verb in a figurative sense. אֶל־עַל, *upwards* (עַל as in ch. vii. 16), do they (the prophets: see ver. 2) call them; but *it* does not rise, *sc.* to return to God, or seek help from on high. רוֹמֵם *pilel,* with the meaning of the *kal* intensified, to make a rising, *i.e.* to rise up. This explana-

tion appears simpler than supplying an object, say "the soul"
(Ps. xxv. 1), or "the eyes" (Ezek. xxxiii. 25).

They deserved to be utterly destroyed for this, and would
have been if the compassion of God had not prevented it.
With this turn a transition is made in ver. 8 from threatening
to promise. Ver. 8. *" How could I give thee up, O Ephraim!
surrender thee, O Israel! how could I give thee up like Admah,
make thee like Zeboim! My heart has changed within me, my
compassion is excited all at once.* Ver. 9. *I will not execute the
burning heat of my wrath, I will not destroy Ephraim again:
for I am God, and not man, the Holy One in the midst of thee:
and come not into burning wrath."* "How thoroughly could I
give thee up!" *sc.* if I were to punish thy rebellion as it
deserves. *Nâthan,* to surrender to the power of the enemy,
like *miggēn* in Gen. xiv. 20. And not that alone, but I could
utterly destroy thee, like Admah and Zeboim, the two cities of
the valley of Siddim, which were destroyed by fire from heaven
along with Sodom and Gomorrha. Compare Deut. xxix. 22,
where Admah and Zeboim are expressly mentioned along with
the cities of Sodom and Gomorrha, which stand alone in Gen.
xix. 24. With evident reference to this passage, in which
Moses threatens idolatrous Israel with the same punishment,
Hosea simply mentions the last two as quite sufficient for his
purpose, whereas Sodom and Gomorrha are generally mentioned in other passages (Jer. xlix. 18; cf. Matt. x. 15, Luke
x. 12). The promise that God will show compassion is
appended here, without any adversative particle. My heart
has turned, changed in me (עַל, lit. upon or with me, as in the
similar phrases in 1 Sam. xxv. 36, Jer. viii. 18). יַחַד נִכְמְרוּ, in
a body have my feelings of compassion gathered themselves
together, *i.e.* my whole compassion is excited. Compare Gen.
xliii. 30 and 1 Kings iii. 26, where, instead of the abstract
nichămīm, we find the more definite *rachămīm,* the bowels as
the seat of the emotions. עָשָׂה חֲרוֹן אַף, to carry out wrath, to
execute it as judgment (as in 1 Sam. xxviii. 18). In the expression לֹא אָשׁוּב לְשַׁחֵת, I will not return to destroy, שׁוּב may be
explained from the previous נֶהְפַּךְ לִבִּי. After the heart of God
has changed, it will not return to wrath, to destroy Ephraim;
for Jehovah is God, who does not alter His purposes like a man
(cf. 1 Sam. xv. 29, Num. xxiii. 19, Mal. iii. 6), and He shows

Himself in Israel as the Holy One, *i.e.* the absolutely pure and perfect one, in whom there is no alternation of light and darkness, and therefore no variableness in His decrees (see at Ex. xix. 6; Isa. vi. 3). The difficult expression בְּעִיר cannot mean "into a city," although it is so rendered by the ancient versions, the Rabbins, and many Christian expositors; for we cannot attach any meaning to the words "I do not come into a city" at all in harmony with the context. עִיר signifies here *æstus iræ*, the heat of wrath, from עוּר, *effervescere*, just as in Jer. xv. 8 it signifies the heat of alarm and anxiety, *æstus animi*.

Ver. 10. "*They will go after Jehovah; like a lion will He roar; for He will roar: and sons will tremble from the sea.* Ver. 11. *Tremble like birds out of Egypt, and like doves out of the land of Asshur: and I cause them to dwell in their houses, is the saying of Jehovah.*" When the Lord turns His pity towards the people once more, they will follow Him, and hasten, with trembling at His voice, from the lands of their banishment, and be reinstated by Him in their inheritance. The way for this promise was opened indeed by ver. 9, but here it is introduced quite abruptly, and without any logical particle of connection, like the same promise in ch. iii. 5. הָלַךְ אַחֲרֵי יי, to walk after the Lord, denotes not only "obedience to the gathering voice of the Lord, as manifested by their drawing near" (Simson), but that walking in true obedience to the Lord which follows from conversion (Deut. xiii. 5; 1 Kings xiv. 8), so that the Chaldee has very properly rendered it, "They will follow the worship of Jehovah." This faithfulness they will exhibit first of all in practical obedience to the call of the Lord. This call is described as the roaring of a lion, the point of comparison lying simply in the fact that a lion announces its coming by roaring, so that the roaring merely indicates a loud, far-reaching call, like the blowing of the trumpet in Isa. xxvii. 13. The reason for what is affirmed is then given: "for He (Jehovah) will really utter His call," in consequence of which the Israelites, as His children, will come trembling (*chârēd* synonymous with *pâchad*, ch. iii. 5). מִיָּם, from the sea, *i.e.* from the distant islands and lands of the west (Isa. xi. 11), as well as from Egypt and Assyria, the lands of the south and east. These three regions are simply a special form of the idea, "out of all quarters of the globe;" compare the more

complete enumeration of the several remote countries in Isa.
xi. 11. The comparison to birds and doves expresses the swiftness with which they draw near, as doves fly to their dovecots
(Isa. lx. 8). Then will the Lord cause them to dwell in their
houses, *i.e.* settle them once more in their inheritance, in His
own land (cf. Jer. xxxii. 37, where לָבֶטַח is added). On the
construing of הוֹשִׁיב with עַל, cf. 1 Kings xx. 43, and the German
auf der Stube sein. The expression נְאֻם יְיָ affixes the seal of
confirmation to this promise. The fulfilment takes place in the
last days, when Israel as a nation shall enter the kingdom of God.
Compare the remarks on this point at ch. ii. 1–3 (pp. 49, 50).

III. ISRAEL'S APOSTASY AND GOD'S FIDELITY.—
CHAP. XII.–XIV.

For the purpose of proving that the predicted destruction
of the kingdom is just and inevitable, the prophet now shows,
in this last division, first that Israel has not kept the ways of
its father Jacob, but has fallen into the ungodly practice of
Canaan (ch. xii.) ; and secondly, that in spite of all the manifestations of love, and all the chastisements received from its
God, it has continued its apostasy and idolatry, and therefore
perfectly deserves the threatened judgment. Nevertheless the
compassion of God will not permit it to be utterly destroyed,
but will redeem it even from death and hell (ch. xiii.–xiv. 1).
To this there is appended, lastly, in ch. xiv. 2–9, a call to conversion, and a promise from God of the forgiveness and abundant blessing of those who turn to the Lord. With this the
book closes (ch. xiv. 10). Thus we find again, that the contents
of this last division fall very evidently into three parts (ch. xii.
13, 14, and xiv. 2–10), each of which is still further divisible
into two strophes.

Israel's Degeneracy into Canaanitish Ways.—Chap. xii.
(Eng. Ver. xi. 12–xii.)

The faithlessness of Israel and Judah's resistance to God
bring righteous punishment upon the entire posterity of Jacob
(xi. 12–xii. 2); whereas the example of their forefather ought to
have led them to faithful attachment to their God (vers. 3–6).

But Israel has become Canaan, and seeks its advantage in deception and injustice, without hearkening to its God or to the voice of its prophets, and will be punished for its idolatry (vers. 7–11). Whereas Jacob was obliged to flee, and to serve for a wife in Aram, Jehovah led Israel out of Egypt, and guarded it by prophets. Nevertheless this nation has excited His wrath, and will have to bear its guilt (vers. 12–14). The two strophes of this chapter are xi. 12–xii. 6 and 7–14.

Ch. xi. 12 (Heb. Bib. xii. 1). "*Ephraim has surrounded me with lying, and the house of Israel with deceit: and Judah is moreover unbridled against God, and against the faithful Holy One.* Ch. xii. 1 (Heb. Bib. 2). *Ephraim grazeth wind, and hunteth after the east: all the day it multiplies lying and desolation, and they make a covenant with Asshur, and oil is carried to Egypt.* Ver. 2. *And Jehovah has a controversy with Judah, and to perform a visitation upon Jacob, according to his ways: according to his works will He repay him.*" In the name of Jehovah, the prophet raises a charge against Israel once more. Lying and deceit are the terms which he applies, not so much to the idolatry which they preferred to the worship of Jehovah (ψευδῆ καὶ δυσσεβῆ λατρείαν, Theod.), as to the hypocrisy with which Israel, in spite of its idolatry, claimed to be still the people of Jehovah, pretended to worship Jehovah under the image of a calf, and turned right into wrong.[1] *Bēth Yisrā'ēl* (the house of Israel) is the nation of the ten tribes, and is synonymous with Ephraim. The statement concerning Judah has been interpreted in different ways, because the meaning of רָד is open to dispute. Luther's rendering, " but Judah still holds fast to its God," is based upon the rabbinical interpretation of רוּד, in the sense of רָדָה, to rule, which is decidedly false. According to the Arabic راد, the meaning of *rūd* is to ramble about (used of cattle that have broken loose, or have not yet been fastened up,

---

[1] Calvin explains סְבָבֻנִי correctly thus: " that He (*i.e.* God) had experienced the manifold faithlessness of the Israelites in all kinds of ways." He interprets the whole sentence as follows: " The Israelites had acted unfaithfully towards God, and resorted to deceits, and that not in one way only, or of only one kind; but just as a man might surround his enemy with a great army, so had they gathered together innumerable frauds, with which they attacked God on every side."

as in Jer. ii. 31) ; *hiphil,* to cause to ramble about (Gen. xxvii. 40 ; Ps. lv. 3). Construed as it is here with עִם, it means to ramble about in relation to God, *i.e.* to be unbridled or unruly towards God. עִם, as in many other cases where reciprocal actions are referred to, standing towards or with a person : see Ewald, § 217, *h.* קְדוֹשִׁים נֶאֱמָן, the faithful, holy God. *Q⁰dōshīm* is used of God, as in Prov. ix. 10 (cf. Josh. xxiv. 19), as an intensive *pluralis majestatis,* construed with a singular adjective (cf. Isa. xix. 4 ; 2 Kings xix. 4). נֶאֱמָן, firm, faithful, trustworthy ; the opposite of *râd.* Judah is unbridled towards the powerful God (*'El*), towards the Holy One, who, as the Faithful One, also proves Himself to be holy in relation to His people, both by the sanctification of those who embrace His salvation, and also by the judgment and destruction of those who obstinately resist the leadings of His grace. In ver. 1 the lying and deceit of Israel are more fully described. רֹעֶה רוּחַ is not to entertain one's self on wind, *i.e.* to take delight in vain things ; but רָעָה means to eat or graze spiritually ; and *rūăch,* the wind, is equivalent to emptiness. The meaning therefore is, to strive eagerly after what is empty or vain ; synonymous with *râdaph,* to pursue. קָדִים, the east wind, in Palestine a fierce tempestuous wind, which comes with burning heat from the desert of Arabia, and is very destructive to seeds and plants (compare Job xxvii. 21, and Wetzstein's Appendix to Delitzsch's *Commentary on Job*). It is used, therefore, as a figurative representation, not of vain hopes and ideals, that cannot possibly be reached, but of that destruction which Israel is bringing upon itself. "All the day," *i.e.* continually, it multiplies lying and violence, through the sins enumerated in ch. iv. 2, by which the kingdom is being internally broken up. Added to this, there is the seeking for alliances with the powers of the world, viz. Assyria and Egypt, by which it hopes to secure their help (ch. v. 13), but only brings about its own destruction. Oil is taken to Egypt from the land abounding in olives (Deut. viii. 8 ; 1 Kings v. 25), not as tribute, but as a present, for the purpose of securing an ally in Egypt. This actually took place during the reign of Hoshea, who endeavoured to liberate himself from the oppression of Assyria by means of a treaty with Egypt (2 Kings xvii. 4).[1]

[1] Manger has given the meaning correctly thus : " He is looking back to the ambassadors sent by king Hoshea with splendid presents to the king

The Lord will repay both kingdoms for such conduct as this. But just as the attitude of Judah towards God is described more mildly than the guilt of Israel in ch. xi. 12, so the punishment of the two is differently described in ver. 2. Jehovah has a trial with Judah, *i.e.* He has to reprove and punish its sins and transgressions (ch. iv. 1). Upon Jacob, or Israel of the ten tribes (as in ch. x. 11), He has to perform a visitation, *i.e.* to punish it according to its ways and its deeds (cf. ch. iv. 9). לִפְקֹד, it is to be visited, *i.e.* He must visit.

Ver. 3. " *He held his brother's heel in the womb, and in his man's strength he fought with God.* Ver. 4. *He fought against the angel, and overcame ; wept, and prayed to Him : at Bethel he found Him, and there He talked with us.* Ver. 5. *And Jehovah, God of hosts, Jehovah is His remembrance.*" The name Jacob, which refers to the patriarch himself in ver. 3, forms the link between vers. 2 and 3. The Israelites, as descendants of Jacob, were to strive to imitate the example of their forefather. His striving hard for the birthright, and his wrestling with God, in which he conquered by prayer and supplication, are types and pledges of salvation to the tribes of Israel which bear his name.[1] עָקַב, a denom. from עָקֵב, "to hold the heel" = אָחַז בְּעֲקֵב in Gen. xxv. 26, which the prophet has in his mind, not "to overreach," as in Gen. xxvii. 36 and Jer. ix. 3. For the wrestling with God, mentioned in the second clause of the verse, proves most indisputably that Jacob's conduct is not held up before the people for a warning, as marked by cunning or deceit, as Umbreit and Hitzig suppose, but is set before them for their imitation, as an eager attempt to secure the birthright and the

---

of Egypt, to bring him over to his side, and induce him to send him assistance against the king of Assyria, although he had bound himself by a sacred treaty to submit to the sovereignty of the latter." Compare also Hengstenberg's *Christology*, vol. i. p. 164 transl., where he refutes the current opinion, that the words refer to two different parties in the nation, viz. an Assyrian and an Egyptian party, and correctly describes the circumstances thus : " The people being severely oppressed by Asshur, sometimes apply to Egypt for help against Asshur, and at other times endeavour to awaken friendly feelings in the latter."

[1] " He shows what good Jacob received, and the son is named in the father : he calls to remembrance the ancient history, that they may see both the mercy of God towards Jacob, and his resolute firmness towards the Lord."—JEROME.

blessing connected with it. This shows at the same time, that the holding of the heel in the mother's womb is not quoted as a proof of the divine election of grace, and, in fact, that there is no reference at all to the circumstance, that " even when Jacob was still in his mother's womb, he did this not by his own strength, but by the mercy of God, who knows and loves those whom He has predestinated" (Jerome). בְּאוֹנוֹ, in his manly strength (cf. Gen. xlix. 3) he wrestled with God (Gen. xxxii. 25–29). This conflict (for the significance of which in relation to Jacob's spiritual life, see the discussion at Gen. *l.c.*) is more fully described in ver. 4, for the Israelites to imitate. מַלְאָךְ is the angel of Jehovah, the revealer of the invisible God (see the *Commentary on the Pentateuch,* vol. i. p. 126 transl.). וַיָּכֹל is from Gen. xxxii. 29. The explanatory clause, " he wept, and made supplication to Him" (after Gen. xxxii. 27), gives the nature of the conflict. It was a contest with the weapons of prayer; and with these he conquered. These weapons are also at the command of the Israelites, if they will only use them. The fruit of the victory was, that he (Jacob) found Him (God) at Bethel. This does not refer to the appearance of God to Jacob on his flight to Mesopotamia (Gen. xxviii. 11), but to that recorded in Gen. xxxv. 9 sqq., when God confirmed his name of Israel, and renewed the promises of His blessing. And there, continues the prophet, He (God) spake with us; *i.e.* not there He speaks with us still, condemning by His prophets the idolatry at Bethel (Amos v. 4, 5), as Kimchi supposes; but, as the imperfect יְדַבֵּר corresponds to יִמְצָאֶנּוּ, " there did He speak to us through Jacob," *i.e.* what He there said to Jacob applies to us.[1] The explanation of this is given in ver. 5, where the name is recalled in which God revealed Himself to Moses, when He first called him (Ex. iii. 15), *i.e.* in which He made known to him His true nature. *Yᵉhōvâh zikhrō* is taken literally from זֶה זִכְרִי לְדֹר דֹּר; but there the name *Jehovah* is still further defined by " the God of Abraham, Isaac, and Jacob," here by

[1] " Let it be carefully observed, that God is said to have talked at Bethel not with Jacob only, but with all his posterity. That is to say, the things which are here said to have been done by Jacob, and to have happened to him, had not regard to himself only, but to all the race that sprang from him, and were signs of the good fortune which they either would, or certainly might enjoy" (Lackemacher in Rosenmüller's *Scholia*).

"the God of hosts." This difference needs consideration. The Israelites in the time of Moses could only put full confidence in the divine call of Moses to be their deliverer out of the bondage of Egypt, on the ground that He who called him was the God who had manifested Himself to the patriarchs as the God of salvation ; but for the Israelites of Hosea's time, the strength of their confidence in Jehovah arose from the fact that Jehovah was the God of hosts, *i.e.* the God who, because He commands the forces of heaven, both visible and invisible, rules with unrestricted omnipotence on earth as well as in heaven (see at 1 Sam. i. 3).

To this God Israel is now to return. Ver. 6. "*Ana thou, to thy God shalt thou turn : keep love and right, and hope continually in thy God.*" שׁוּב with בְּ is a pregnant expression, as in Isa. x. 22 : "so to turn as to enter into vital fellowship with God ;" *i.e.* to be truly converted. The next two clauses, as the omission of the copula before *chesed* and the change in the tense clearly show, are to be taken as explanatory of תָּשׁוּב. The conversion is to show itself in the perception of love and right towards their brethren, and in constant trust in God. But Israel is far removed from this now. This thought leads the way to the next strophe (vers. 8–15), which commences afresh with a disclosure of the apostasy of the people.

Ver. 7. "*Canaan, in his hand is the scale of cheating : he loves to oppress.* Ver. 8. *And Ephraim says, Yet I have become rich, have acquired property : all my exertions bring me no wrong, which would be sin.*" Israel is not a Jacob who wrestles with God ; but it has become Canaan, seeking its advantage in deceit and wrong. Israel is called *Canaan* here, not so much on account of its attachment to Canaanitish idolatry (cf. Ezek. xvi. 3), as according to the appellative meaning of the word *Kᵉnaʿan*, which is borrowed from the commercial habits of the Canaanites (Phœnicians), viz. merchant or trader (Isa. xxiii. 8 ; Job xl. 30), because, like a fraudulent merchant, it strove to become great by oppression and cheating ; not "because it acted towards God like a fraudulent merchant, offering Him false show for true reverence," as Schmieder supposes. For however thoroughly this may apply to the worship of the Israelites, it is not to this that the prophet refers, but to fraudulent weights, and the love of oppression or violence. And this points not to their attitude towards God, but to their conduct towards their fellow-men, which is the very opposite of what, according to the previous verse, the Lord requires (*chesed ûmishpât*), and the very thing which He has forbidden in the law, in Lev. xix. 36, Deut. xxv. 13–16, and also in the case of *'áshaq*, violence, in Lev. vi. 2–4, Deut. xxiv. 14. Ephraim prides itself upon this unrighteousness, in the idea that it has thereby acquired wealth and riches, and with the still greater self-deception, that with all its acquisition of property it has committed no wrong that was sin, *i.e.* that would be followed by punishment. אוֹן does not mean " might" here, but wealth, *opes*, although as a matter of fact, since Ephraim says this as a nation, the riches and power of the state are intended. כָּל־יְגִיעַי is not written at the head absolutely, in the sense of " so far as what I have acquired is concerned, men find no injustice in this ;" for if that were the case, בִּ would stand for לְ ; but it is really the subject, and יִמְצְאוּ is to be taken in the sense of acquiring = bringing in (cf. Lev. v. 7, xii. 8, etc.).

Ver. 9. " *Yet am I Jehovah thy God, from the land of Egypt hither: I will still cause thee to dwell in tents, as in the days of the feast.* Ver. 10. *I have spoken to the prophets ; and I, I have multiplied visions, and spoken similitudes through the prophets.* Ver. 11. *If Gilead* (is) *worthlessness, they have only come to nothing : in Gilgal they offered bullocks : even their altars are like stone-heaps in the furrows of the field.*" The Lord meets the delusion of the people, that they had become great and powerful through their own exertion, by reminding them that He (וְאָנֹכִי is adversative, yet I) has been Israel's God from Egypt hither, and that to Him they owe all prosperity and good in both past and present (cf. ch. xiii. 4). Because they do not recognise this, and because they put their trust in unrighteousness rather than in Him, He will now cause them to dwell in tents again, as in the days of the feast of Tabernacles, *i.e.* will repeat the leading through the wilderness. It is evident from the context that *mo'ēd* (the feast) is here the feast of Tabernacles. יְמֵי מוֹעֵד (the days of the feast) are the seven days of this festival, during which Israel was to dwell in booths, in remembrance of the fact that when God led them out of Egypt He had caused them to dwell in booths (tabernacles, Lev. xxiii. 42, 43). עֹד אוֹשִׁיבְךָ stands in antithesis to הוֹשַׁבְתִּי

in Lev. xxiii. 43. " The preterite is changed into a future
through the ingratitude of the nation" (Hengstenberg). The
simile, " as in the days of the feast," shows that the repetition
of the leading through the desert is not thought of here merely
as a time of punishment, such as the prolongation of the
sojourn of the Israelites in the wilderness for forty years really
was (Num. xiv. 33). For their dwelling in tents, or rather in
booths (*sukkōth*), on the feast of Tabernacles, was intended
not so much to remind the people of the privations of their
unsettled wandering life in the desert, as to call to their
remembrance the shielding and sheltering care and protection
of God in their wandering through the great and terrible
wilderness (see at Lev. xxiii. 42, 43). We must combine the
two allusions, therefore: so that whilst the people are threatened
indeed with being driven out of the good and glorious land,
with its large and beautiful cities and houses full of all that is
good (Deut. vi. 10 sqq.), into a dry and barren desert, they
have also set before them the repetition of the divine guidance
through the desert; so that they are not threatened with utter
rejection on the part of God, but only with temporary banishment into the desert. In vers. 10 and 11 the two thoughts of
ver. 9 are still further expanded. In ver. 10 they are reminded
how the Lord had proved Himself to be the God of Israel
from Egypt onwards, by sending prophets and multiplying
prophecy, to make known His will and gracious counsel to the
people, and to promote their salvation. דִּבֶּר with עַל, to speak
to, not because the word is something imposed *upon* a person,
but because the inspiration of God came down to the prophets
from above. אֲדַמֶּה, not " I destroy," for it is only the *kal* that
occurs in this sense, and not the *piel*, but " to compare," *i.e.*
speak in similes; as, for example, in ch. i. and iii., Isa. v. 1 sqq.,
Ezek. xvi. etc.: " I have left no means of admonishing them
untried" (Rosenmüller). Israel, however, has not allowed
itself to be admonished and warned, but has given itself up to
sin and idolatry, the punishment of which cannot be delayed.
Gilead and Gilgal represent the two halves of the kingdom of
the ten tribes; Gilead the land to the east of the Jordan,
and Gilgal the territory to the west. As Gilead is called
" a city (*i.e.* a rendezvous) of evil-doers " (פֹּעֲלֵי אָוֶן) in ch. vi. 8,
so is it here called distinctly אָוֶן, worthlessness, wickedness;

and therefore it is to be utterly brought to nought. אָוֶן and שָׁוְא are synonymous, denoting moral and physical nonentity (compare Job xv. 31). Here the two notions are so distributed, that the former denotes the moral decay, the latter the physical. Worthlessness brings nothingness after it as a punishment. אַךְ, only = nothing, but equivalent to utterly. The perfect הָיוּ is used for the certain future. Gilgal, which is mentioned in ch. iv. 15, ix. 15, as the seat of one form of idolatrous worship, is spoken of here as a place of sacrifice, to indicate with a play upon the name the turning of the altars into heaps of stones (*Gallim*). The desolation or destruction of the altars involves not only the cessation of the idolatrous worship, but the dissolution of the kingdom and the banishment of the people out of the land. שְׁוָרִים, which only occurs in the plural here, cannot of course be the dative (to sacrifice to oxen), but only the accusative. The sacrifice of oxen was reckoned as a sin on the part of the people, not on account of the animals offered, but on account of the unlawful place of sacrifice. The suffix to *mizb*ᵉ*chōthâm* (*their* sacrifices) refers to Israel, the subject implied in *zibbēchū*.

This punishment Israel well deserved. Ver. 12. "*And Jacob fled to the fields of Aram; and Israel served for a wife, and for a wife did he keep guard.* Ver. 13. *And through a prophet Jehovah brought Israel out of Egypt, and through a prophet was he guarded.* Ver. 14. *Ephraim has stirred up bitter wrath; and his Lord will leave his blood upon him, and turn back his shame upon him.*" In order to show the people still more impressively what great things the Lord had done for them, the prophet recals the flight of Jacob, the tribe-father, to Mesopotamia, and how he was obliged to serve many years there for a wife, and to guard cattle; whereas God had redeemed Israel out of the Egyptian bondage, and had faithfully guarded it through a prophet. The flight of Jacob to Aramæa, and his servitude there, are mentioned not " to give prominence to his zeal for the blessing of the birthright, and his obedience to the commandment of God and his parents" (Cyr., Theod., Th. v. Mops.); nor " to bring out the double servitude of Israel,—the first the one which the people had to endure in their forefather, the second the one which they had to endure themselves in Egypt" (Umbreit); nor " to lay stress

upon the manifestation of the divine care towards Jacob as
well as towards the people of Israel" (Ewald); for there is
nothing at all about this in ver. 12. The words point simply
to the distress and affliction which Jacob had to endure, according to Gen. xxix.–xxxi., as Calvin has correctly interpreted
them. "Their father Jacob," he says, "who was he? what
was his condition? . . . He was a fugitive from his country.
Even if he had always lived at home, his father was only a
stranger in the land. But he was compelled to flee into Syria.
And how splendidly did he live there? He was with his uncle,
no doubt, but he was treated quite as meanly as any common
slave: *he served for a wife.* And how did he serve? He was
the man who tended the cattle." *Shâmar*, the tending of
cattle, was one of the hardest and lowest descriptions of servitude (cf. Gen. xxx. 31, xxxi. 40; 1 Sam. xvii. 20). *S^edēh 'ărâm*
(the field of Aram) is no doubt simply the Hebrew rendering
of the Aramæan *Paddan-'ărâm* (Gen. xxviii. 2, xxxi. 18 : see at
Gen. xxv. 20). Jacob's flight to Aramæa, where he had to
serve, is contrasted in ver. 10 with the leading of Israel, the
people sprung from Jacob, out of Egypt by a prophet, *i.e.* by
Moses (cf. Deut. xviii. 18); and the guarding of cattle by
Jacob is placed in contrast with the guarding of Israel on the
part of God through the prophet Moses, when he led them
through the wilderness to Canaan. The object of this is to
call to the nation's remembrance that elevation from the lowest
condition, which they were to acknowledge with humility every
year, according to Deut. xxvi. 5 sqq., when the first-fruits were
presented before the Lord. For Ephraim had quite forgotten
this. Instead of thanking the Lord for it by love and faithful
devotedness to Him, it had provoked Him in the bitterest
manner by its sins (הִכְעִים, to excite wrath, to provoke to anger:
tamrūrīm, an adverbial accusative = bitterly). For this should
its blood-guiltiness remain upon it. According to Lev. xx. 9 sqq.,
dâmīm denotes grave crimes that are punishable by death.
Nâtash, to let a thing alone, as in Ex. xxiii. 11 ; or to leave
behind, as in 1 Sam. xvii. 20, xxii. 28. Leaving blood-guiltiness upon a person, is the opposite of taking away (נָשָׂא) or
forgiving the sin, and therefore inevitably brings the punishment after it. *Cherpâthō* (its reproach or dishonour) is the
dishonour which Ephraim had done to the Lord by sin and

idolatry (cf. Isa. lxv. 7). And this would be repaid to it by its Lord, *i.e.* by Jehovah.

Israel's deep Fall.—Chap. xiii.–xiv. 1.

Because Israel would not desist from its idolatry, and entirely forgot the goodness of its God, He would destroy its might and glory (vers. 1–8). Because it did not acknowledge the Lord as its help, its throne would be annihilated along with its capital; but this judgment would become to all that were penitent a regeneration to newness of life. Ver. 1. " *When Ephraim spake, there was terror; he exalted himself in Israel; then he offended through Baal, and died.* Ver. 2. *And now they continue to sin, and make themselves molten images out of their silver, idols according to their understanding: manufacture of artists is it all: they say of them, Sacrificers of men: let them kiss calves.*" In order to show how deeply Israel had fallen through its apostasy, the prophet points to the great distinction which the tribe of Ephraim formerly enjoyed among the tribes of Israel. The two clauses of ver. 1*a* cannot be so connected together as that נָשָׂא should be taken as the continuation of the infinitive דַּבֵּר. The emphatic הוּא is irreconcilable with this. We must rather take רְתֵת (*ἅπ. λεγ.*, in Aramæan = רְטַט, Jer. xlix. 24, terror, *tremor*) as the apodosis to *kᵉdabbēr 'Ephraim* (when Ephraim spake), like שְׂאֵת in Gen. iv. 7: " As Ephraim spake there was terror," *i.e.* men listened with fear and trembling (cf. Job xxix. 21). נָשָׂא is used intransitively, as in Nahum i. 5, Ps. lxxxix. 10. Ephraim, *i.e.* the tribe of Ephraim, " exalted itself in Israel,"—not " it was distinguished among its brethren" (Hitzig), but " it raised itself to the government." The prophet has in his mind the attempts made by Ephraim to get the rule among the tribes, which led eventually to the secession of the ten tribes from the royal family of David, and the establishment of the kingdom of Israel by the side of that of Judah. When Ephraim had secured this, the object of its earnest endeavours, it offended through Baal; *i.e.* not only through the introduction of the worship of Baal in the time of Ahab (1 Kings xvi. 31 sqq.), but even through the establishment of the worship of the calves under Jeroboam (1 Kings xii. 28), through which Jehovah was

turned into a Baal. וַיָּמָת, used of the state or kingdom, is equivalent to " was given up to destruction" (cf. Amos ii. 2). The
dying commenced with the introduction of the unlawful worship
(cf. 1 Kings xii. 30). From this sin Ephraim (the people of
the ten tribes) did not desist: they still continue to sin, and
make themselves molten images, etc., contrary to the express
prohibition in Lev. xix. 4 (cf. Ex. xx. 4). These words are not
merely to be understood as signifying, that they added other
idolatrous images in Gilgal and Beersheba to the golden calves
(Amos viii. 14); but they also involve their obstinate adherence
to the idolatrous worship introduced by Jeroboam (compare
2 Kings xvii. 16). כִּתְבוּנָם from תְּבוּנָה, with the feminine termination dropped on account of the suffix (according to Ewald,
§ 257, d; although in the note Ewald regards this formation
as questionable, and doubts the correctness of the reading):
" according to their understanding," i.e. their proficiency in art.
The meaning of the second hemistich, which is very difficult,
depends chiefly upon the view we take of זֹבְחֵי אָדָם, viz. whether
we render these words " they who sacrifice men," as the LXX.,
the fathers, and many of the rabbins and Christian expositors
have done; or " the sacrificers of (among) men," as Kimchi,
Bochart, Ewald, and others do, after the analogy of אֶבְיוֹנֵי אָדָם in
Isa. xxix. 19. Apart from this, however, zōbhᵉchē 'âdâm cannot
possibly be taken as an independent sentence, such as " they
sacrifice men," or " human sacrificers are they," unless with the
LXX. we change the participle זבחי arbitrarily into the perfect
זָבְחוּ. As the words read, they must be connected either with
what follows or with what precedes. But if we connect them
with what follows, we fail to obtain any suitable thought,
whether we render it " human sacrificers (those who sacrifice
men) kiss calves," or " the sacrificers among men kiss calves."
The former is open to the objection that human sacrifices were
not offered to the calves (i.e. to Jehovah, as worshipped under
the symbol of a calf), but only to Moloch, and that the worshippers of Moloch did not kiss calves. The latter, " men who
offer sacrifice kiss calves," might indeed be understood in this
sense, that the prophet intended thereby to denounce the great
folly, that men should worship animals; but this does not suit
the preceding words הֵם אֹמְרִים, and it is impossible to see in what
sense they could be employed. There is no other course left,

therefore, than to connect *zōbhᵉchē 'âdâm* with what precedes, though not in the way proposed by Ewald, viz. " even to these do sacrificers of men say." This rendering is open to the following objections : (1) that הֵם after לָהֶם would have to be taken as an emphatic repetition of the pronoun, and we cannot find any satisfactory ground for this ; and, (2) what is still more important, the fact that *'âmar* would be used absolutely, in the sense of " they speak in prayer," which, even apart from the "prayer," cannot be sustained by any other analogous example. These difficulties vanish if we take *zōbhᵉchē 'âdâm* as an explanatory apposition to *hēm :* " of them (the *'ătsabbīm*) they say, viz. the sacrificers from among men (*i.e.* men who sacrifice), Let them worship calves." By the apposition *zōbhᵉchē 'âdâm,* and the fact that the object *'ăgâlīm* is placed first, so that it stands in immediate contrast to *'âdâm,* the absurdity of men kissing calves, *i.e.* worshipping them with kisses (see at 1 Kings xix. 18), is painted as it were before the eye.

They prepare for themselves swift destruction in consequence. Ver. 3. " *Therefore will they be like the morning cloud, and like the dew that passes early away, as chaff blows away from the threshing-floor, and as smoke out of the window.*" *Lâkhēn,* therefore, viz. because they would not let their irrational idolatry go, they would quickly perish. On the figures of the morning cloud and dew, see at ch. vi. 4. The figure of the chaff occurs more frequently (*vid.* Isa. xvii. 13, xli. 15, 16 ; Ps. i. 4, xxxv. 5, etc.). יְסֹעֵר is used relatively : which is stormed away, *i.e.* blown away from the threshing-floor by a violent wind. The threshing-floors were situated upon eminences (compare my *Bibl. Archäol.* ii. p. 114). " Smoke out of the window," *i.e.* smoke from the fire under a saucepan in the room, which passed out of the window-lattice, as the houses were without chimneys (see Ps. lxviii. 3).

Ver. 4. " *And yet I am Jehovah thy God from the land of Egypt hither ; and thou knowest no God beside me, and there is no helper beside me.* Ver. 5. *I knew thee in the desert, in the land of burning heats.*" As in ch. xii. 10, a contrast is drawn here again between the idolatry of the people and the uninterrupted self-attestation of Jehovah to the faithless nation. From Egypt hither Israel has known no other God than Jehovah, *i.e.* has found no other God to be a helper and

Saviour. Even in the desert He knew Israel, *i.e.* adopted it in love. יָדַע, to know, when applied to God, is an attestation of His love and care (compare Amos iii. 2 ; Isa. lviii. 3, etc.). The ἀπ. λεγ. תַּלְאֻבֹת, from לאב, لب, *med. Vav*, to thirst, signifies burning heat, in which men famish with thirst (for the fact, compare Deut. viii. 15).

But prosperity made Israel proud, so that it forgot its God. Ver. 6. " *As they had their pasture, they became full ; they became full, and their heart was lifted up : therefore have they forgotten me.*" This reproof is taken almost word for word from Deut. viii. 11 sqq. (cf. ch. xxxi. 20, xxxii. 15 sqq.). כְּמַרְעִיתָם, answering to their pasture, *i.e.* because they had such good pasture in the land given them by the Lord. The very thing of which Moses warned the people in Deut. viii. 11 has come to pass. Therefore are the threats of the law against the rebellious fulfilled upon them.

Ver. 7. " *And I became like a lion to them ; as a leopard by the wayside do I lie in wait. Ver. 8. I fall upon them as a bear robbed of its young, and tear in pieces the enclosure of their heart, and eat them there like a lioness : the beast of the field will tear them in pieces.*" The figure of the pasture which made Israel full (ver. 6) is founded upon the comparison of Israel to a flock (cf. ch. iv. 16). The chastisement of the people is therefore represented as the tearing in pieces and devouring of the fattened flock by wild beasts. God appears as a lion, panther, etc., which fall upon them (cf. ch. v. 14). וָאֱהִי does not stand for the future, but is the preterite, giving the consequence of forgetting God. The punishment has already begun, and will still continue ; we have therefore from אָשׁוּר onwards imperfects or futures. אָשׁוּר, from שׁוּר, to look round, hence to lie in wait, as in Jer. v. 26. It is not to be changed into '*Asshur*, as it is by the LXX. and Vulgate. סְגוֹר לִבָּם, the enclosure of their heart, *i.e.* their breast. *Shâm* (there) points back to ʿ*al-derekh* (by the way).

Ver. 9 commences a new strophe, in which the prophet once more discloses to the people the reason for their corruption (vers. 9–13) ; and after pointing to the saving omnipotence of the Lord (ver. 14), holds up before them utter destruction as the just punishment for their guilt (ver. 15 and ch. xiv. 1).

Ver. 9. " *O Israel, it hurls thee into destruction, that thou (art)*
against me, thy help. Ver. 10. *Where is thy king? that he may*
help thee in all thy cities: and (where) thy judges? of whom
thou saidst, Give me king and princes! Ver. 11. *I give thee*
kings in my anger, and take them away in my wrath." שִׁחֶתְךָ
does not combine together the verbs in ver. 8, as Hitzig supposes; nor does ver. 9 give the reason for what precedes, but
shichethkhâ is explained by ver. 10, from which we may see that
a new train of thought commences with ver. 9. *Shichēth* does
not mean to act corruptly here, as in Deut. xxxii. 5, ix. 12, and
Ex. xxxii. 7, but to bring into corruption, to ruin, as in Gen.
vi. 17, ix. 15, Num. xxxii. 15, etc. The sentence כִּי בִי וגו׳
cannot be explained in any other way than by supplying the
pronoun אַתָּה, as a subject taken from the suffix to שִׁחֶתְךָ
(Marck, and nearly all the modern commentators). " This
throws thee into distress, that thou hast resisted me, who am
thy help." בְעֶזְרֶךָ: as in Deut. xxxiii. 26, except that ב is used
in the sense of against, as in Gen. xvi. 12, 2 Sam. xxiv. 17,
etc. This opposition did not take place, however, when all
Israel demanded a king of Samuel (1 Sam. viii. 5). For
although this desire is represented there (ver. 7) as the rejection of Jehovah, Hosea is speaking here simply of the Israel of
the ten tribes. The latter rebelled against Jehovah, when
they fell away from the house of David, and made Jeroboam
their king, and with contempt of Jehovah put their trust in
the might of their kings of their own choosing (1 Kings xii. 16
sqq.). But these kings could not afford them any true help.
The question, " Where " (*'ĕhī* only occurs here and twice in
ver. 14, for אִי or אַיֵּה, possibly simply from a dialectical variation
—*vid.* Ewald, § 104, *c*—and is strengthened by אֵפוֹא, as in Job
xvii. 15), " Where is thy king, that he may help thee?" does
not presuppose that Israel had no king at all at that time, and
that the kingdom was in a state of anarchy, but simply that it
had no king who could save it, when the foe, the Assyrian,
attacked it in all its cities. Before *shōphᵉteykhâ* (thy judges)
we must repeat *'ĕhī* (where). The *shōphᵉtīm*, as the use of the
word *sârīm* (princes) in its stead in the following clause clearly
shows, are not simple judges, but royal counsellors and ministers, who managed the affairs of the kingdom along with the
king, and superintended the administration of justice. The

saying, "Give me a king and princes," reminds us very forcibly of the demand of the people in the time of Samuel; but they really refer simply to the desire of the ten tribes for a king of their own, which manifested itself in their dissatisfaction with the rule of the house of David, and their consequent secession, and to their persistence in this secession amidst all the subsequent changes of the government. We cannot therefore take the imperfects אֶתֶּן and אֶקַּח in ver. 11 as pure preterites, *i.e.* we cannot understand them as referring simply to the choice of Jeroboam as king, and to his death. The imperfects denote an action that is repeated again and again, for which we should use the present, and refer to all the kings that the kingdom of the ten tribes had received and was receiving still, and to their removal. God in His wrath gives the sinful nation kings and takes them away, in order to punish the nation through its kings. This applies not merely to the kings who followed one another so rapidly through conspiracy and murder, although through these the kingdom was gradually broken up and its dissolution accelerated, but to the rulers of the ten tribes as a whole. God gave the tribes who were discontented with the theocratical government of David and Solomon a king of their own, that He might punish them for their resistance to His government, which came to light in the rebellion against Rehoboam. He suspended the division of the kingdom not only over Solomon, as a punishment for his idolatry, but also over the rebellious ten tribes, who, when they separated themselves from the royal house to which the promise had been given of everlasting duration, were also separated from the divinely appointed worship and altar, and given up into the power of their kings, who hurled one another from the throne; and God took away this government from them to chastise them for their sins, by giving them into the power of the heathen, and by driving them away from His face. It is to this last thought, that what follows is attached. The removal of the king in wrath would occur, because the sin of Ephraim was reserved for punishment.

Ver. 12. "*The guilt of Ephraim is bound together: his sin is preserved.* Ver. 13. *The pains of a travailing woman come upon him: he is an unwise son; that he does not place himself at the time in the breaking forth of children.*" Ver. 12 is a special application of Deut. xxxii. 34 to the ten tribes. *Tsârûr*, bound up in a bundle, like a thing which you wish to take great care of (compare Job xiv. 17; 1 Sam. xxv. 29). The same thing is applied in *tsâphûn*, hidden, carefully preserved, so as not to be lost (Job xxi. 19). "All their sins are preserved for punishment" (Chald.). Therefore will pains overtake Ephraim like a woman in labour. The pains of childbirth are not merely a figurative representation of violent agony, but of the sufferings and calamities connected with the refining judgments of God, by which new life was to be born, and a complete transformation of all things effected (cf. Mic. iv. 9, 10; Isa. xiii. 8, xxvi. 17; Matt. xxiv. 8). He cannot be spared these pains, for he is a foolish son (cf. Deut. xxxii. 6, 28 sqq.). But in what respect? This is explained in the words וגו עֵת כִּי, "for at the time," or as עֵת cannot stand for לְעֵת, more correctly "when it is time," he does not place himself in, *i.e.* does not enter, the opening of the womb. *Mishbar bânîm* is to be explained as in 2 Kings xix. 3 and Isa. xxxvii. 3; and *c*. ב עָמַד as in Ezek. xxii. 30. If the child does not come to the opening at the right time, the birth is retarded, and the life of both mother and child endangered. The mother and child are one person here. And this explains the transition from the pains of the mother to the behaviour of the child at the time of birth. Ephraim is an unwise son, inasmuch as even under the chastening judgment he still delays his conversion, and will not let himself be new-born, like a child, that at the time of the labour-pains will not enter the opening of the womb and so come to the birth.

But in order to preserve believers from despair, the Lord announces in ver. 14 that He will nevertheless redeem His people from the power of death. Ver. 14. "*Out of the hand of hell will I redeem them; from death will I set them free! Where are thy plagues, O death? where thy destruction, O hell! Repentance is hidden from mine eyes.*" The fact that this verse contains a promise, and not a threat, would hardly have been overlooked by so many commentators, if they had not been led, out of regard to vers. 13, 15, to put force upon the words, and either take the first clauses as interrogative, "Should I . . . redeem?" (Calvin and others), or as conditional, "I would redeem them," with "*si resipiscerent*" supplied·(Kimchi, Sal.

b. Mel. Ros., etc.). But apart from the fact that the words supplied are perfectly arbitrary, with nothing at all to indicate them, both of these explanation are precluded by the sentences which follow ; for the questions, " Where are thy plagues, O death ? " etc., are obviously meant to affirm the conquest or destruction of hell and death. And this argument retains its force even if we take אֱהִי as an optative from הָיָה, without regard to ver. 10, since the thought, " I should like to be thy plague, O death," presupposes that deliverance from the power of death is affirmed in what comes before. But, on account of the style of address, we cannot take אֱהִי even as an interrogative, in the sense of " Should I be," etc. And what would be the object of this gradation of thought, if the redemption from death were only hypothetical, or were represented as altogether questionable ? If we take the words as they stand, therefore, it is evident that they affirm something more than deliverance when life is in danger, or preservation from death. To redeem or ransom from the hand (or power) of hell, i.e. of the under world, the realm of death, is equivalent to depriving hell of its prey, not only by not suffering the living to die, but by bringing back to life those who have fallen victims to hell, i.e. to the region of the dead. The cessation or annihilation of death is expressed still more forcibly in the triumphant words : " Where are thy plagues (pestilences), O death ? where thy destruction, O hell ? " of which Theodoret has aptly observed, παιανίζειν κατὰ τοῦ θανάτου κελεύει. דְּבָרֶיךָ is an intensive plural of debher, plague, pestilence, and is to be explained in accordance with Ps. xci. 6, where we also find the synonym קֶטֶב in the form קֶטֶב, pestilence or destruction. The Apostle Paul has therefore very properly quoted these words in 1 Cor. xv. 55, in combination with the declaration in Isa. xxv. 8, " Death is swallowed up in victory," to confirm the truth, that at the resurrection of the last day, death will be annihilated, and that which is corruptible changed into immortality. We must not restrict the substance of this promise, however, to the ultimate issue of the redemption, in which it will receive its complete fulfilment. The suffixes attached to 'ephdēm and 'eg'âlēm point to Israel of the ten tribes, like the verbal suffixes in ver. 8. Consequently the promised redemption from death must stand in intimate connection with the threatened destruction of the

kingdom of Israel.   Moreover, the idea of the resurrection of
the dead was by no means so clearly comprehended in Israel at
that time, as that the prophet could point believers to it as a
ground of consolation when the kingdom was destroyed.   The
only meaning that the promise had for the Israelites of the
prophet's day, was that the Lord possessed the power even to
redeem from death, and raise Israel from destruction into newness of life ; just as Ezekiel (ch. xxxvii.) depicts the restoration
of Israel as the giving of life to the dry bones that lay scattered
about the field.   The full and deeper meaning of these words
was but gradually unfolded to believers under the Old Testament, and only attained complete and absolute certainty for
all believers through the actual resurrection of Christ.   But
in order to anticipate all doubt as to this exceedingly great promise, the Lord adds, " repentance is hidden from mine eyes,"
i.e. my purpose of salvation will be irrevocably accomplished.
The ἀπ. λεγ. *nōcham* does not mean " resentment" (Ewald),
but, as a derivative of *nicham*, simply consolation or repentance.
The former, which the Septuagint adopts, does not suit the
context, which the latter alone does.   The words are to be
interpreted in accordance with Ps. lxxxix. 36 and Ps. cx. 4,
where the oath of God is still further strengthened by the
words וְלֹא יִנָּחֵם, " and will not repent;" and לא ינחם corresponds to
אִם אֲכַזֵּב in Ps. lxxxix. 36 (Marck and Krabbe, *Quæstion. de Hos.
vatic. spec.* p. 47).   Compare 1 Sam. xv. 29 and Num. xxiii. 19.

Ver. 15. " *For he will bear fruit among brethren.   East
wind will come, a wind of Jehovah, rising up from the desert ;
and his fountain will dry up, and his spring become dried.   He
plunders the treasuries of all splendid vessels.*"   The connection
between the first clause and the previous verse has been correctly pointed out by Marck.   " Ver. 15," he says, " adduces
a reason to prove that the promised grace of redemption would
certainly stand firm."   כִּי cannot be either a particle of time or
of condition here (when, or if) ; for neither of them yields a
suitable thought, since Ephraim neither was at that time, nor
could become, fruit-bearing among brethren.   Ewald's hypothetical view, " Should Ephraim be a fruitful child," cannot be
grammatically sustained, since *kī* is only used in cases where a
circumstance is assumed to be real.   For one that is merely
supposed to be possible, אִם is required, as the interchange of

אִם and כִּי, in Num. v. 19, 20, for example, clearly shows. The meaning of יַפְרִיא is placed beyond all doubt by the evident play upon the name *Ephraim;* and this also explains the writing with א instead of ה, as well as the idea of the sentence itself: Ephraim will bear fruit among the brethren, *i.e.* the other tribes, as its name, double-fruitfulness, affirms (see at Gen. xli. 52). This thought, through which the redemption from death set before Israel is confirmed, is founded not only upon the assumption that the name must become a truth, but chiefly upon the blessing which the patriarch promised to the tribe of Ephraim on the ground of its name, both in Gen. xlviii. 4, 20, and Gen. xlix. 22 sqq. Because Ephraim possessed such a pledge of blessing in its very name, the Lord would not let it be overwhelmed for ever in the tempest that was bursting upon it. The same thing applies to the name Ephraim as to the name Israel, with which it is used as synonymous; and what is true of all the promises of God is true of this announcement also, viz. that they are only fulfilled in the case of those who adhere to the conditions under which they were given. Of Ephraim, those only will bear fruit which abides to everlasting life, who walk as true champions for God in the footsteps of faith and of their forefathers, wrestling for the blessing of the promises. On the other hand, upon the Ephraim that has turned into Canaan (ch. xii. 8) an east wind will come, a tempest bursting from the desert (see at ch. xii. 2), and that a stormy wind raised by Jehovah, which will dry up his spring, *i.e.* destroy not only the fruitful land with which God has blessed it (Deut. xxxiii. 13–16), but all the sources of its power and stability. Like the promise in ver. 14, the threatening of the judgment, to which the kingdom of Israel is to succumb, is introduced quite abruptly with the word יָבוֹא. The figurative style of address then passes in the last clause into a literal threat. הוּא, he, the hostile conqueror, sent as a tempestuous wind by the Lord, viz. the Assyrian, will plunder the treasure of all costly vessels, *i.e.* all the treasures and valuables of the kingdom. On *keli chemdâh* compare Nah. ii. 10 and 2 Chron. xxxii. 27. We understand by it chiefly the treasures of the capital, to which a serious catastrophe is more especially predicted in the next verse (ch. xiv. 1), which also belongs to this strophe, on account of its rebellion against God.

Ver. 16. (Heb. Bib. ch. xiv. 1). *" Samaria will atone, because it has rebelled against its God: they will fall by the sword; their children will be dashed to pieces, and its women with child ripped up."* אָשֵׁם, to atone, to bear the guilt, *i.e.* the punishment. It is not equivalent to *shâmēm* in Ezek. vi. 6, although, as a matter of fact, the expiation consisted in the conquest and devastation of Samaria by Shalmanezer. The subject to *yipp⁽ᵉ⁾lū* (will fall) is the inhabitants of Samaria. The suffix to הָרִיּוֹתָיו (*its* women, etc.) refers to the nation. The form הָרִיָּה is one derived from הָרָה, for הָרָה (Ewald, § 189, *c*). The construction with the masculine verb יְבֻקָּעוּ, in the place of the feminine, is an anomaly, which may be explained from the fact that feminine formations from the *plur. imperf.* are generally very rare (see Ewald, § 191, *b*). For the fact itself, compare ch. x. 14; 2 Kings viii. 12, xv. 16; Amos i. 13.

Israel's Conversion and Pardon.—Chap. xiv.

After the prophet has set before the sinful nation in various ways its own guilt, and the punishment that awaits it, viz. the destruction of the kingdom, he concludes his addresses with a call to thorough conversion to the Lord, and the promise that the Lord will bestow His grace once more upon those who turn to Him, and will bless them abundantly (vers. 1–8). Ver. 1. (Heb. Bib. ver. 2). *" Return, O Israel, to Jehovah thy God; for thou hast stumbled through thy guilt. Ver. 2. Take with you words, and turn to Jehovah; say ye to Him, Forgive all guilt, and accept what is good, that we may offer our lips as bullocks. Ver. 3. Asshur will not help us: we will not ride upon horses, nor say ' Our God' any more to the manufacture of our own hands; for with Thee the orphan findeth compassion."* There is no salvation for fallen man without return to God. It is therefore with a call to return to the Lord their God, that the prophet opens the announcement of the salvation with which the Lord will bless His people, whom He has brought to reflection by means of the judgment (cf. Deut. iv. 30, xxx. 1 sqq.). שׁוּב עַד יי, to return, to be converted to the Lord, denotes complete conversion; שׁוּב אֶל is, strictly speaking, simply to turn towards God, to direct heart and mind towards Him. By *kâshaltâ* sin is represented as a false step, which still leaves it possible to

return ; so that in a call to conversion it is very appropriately
chosen.   But if the conversion is to be of the right kind, it
must begin with a prayer for the forgiveness of sin, and attest
itself by the renunciation of earthly help and simple trust in the
mercy of God.   Israel is to draw near to God in this state of
mind.   " Take with you words," *i.e.* do not appear before the
Lord empty (Ex. xxiii. 15, xxxiv. 20) ; but for this ye do not
require outward sacrifices, but simply words, *sc.* those of confession of your guilt, as the Chaldee has correctly explained it.
The correctness of this explanation is evident from the confession of sin which follows, with which they are to come before
God.   In כָּל־תִּשָּׂא עָוֹן, the position of *col* at the head of the
sentence may be accounted for from the emphasis that rests
upon it, and the separation of *'āvōn*, from the fact that *col* was
beginning to acquire more of the force of an adjective, like our
all (thus 2 Sam. i. 9 ; Job xxvii. 3 : cf. Ewald, § 289, *a ;* Ges.
§ 114, 3, Anm. 1).   *Qach tōbh* means neither " accept goodness,"
i.e. let goodness be shown thee (Hitzig), nor " take it as good,"
sc. that we pray (Grotius, Ros.) ; but in the closest connection
with what proceeds : Accept the only good thing that we are able
to bring, viz. the sacrifices of our lips.   Jerome has given the
correct interpretation, viz. : " For unless Thou hadst borne away
our evil things, we could not possibly have the good thing which
we offer Thee ;" according to that which is written elsewhere
(Ps. xxxvii. 27), "Turn from evil, and do good."   וּנְשַׁלְּמָה... שְׂפָתֵינוּ,
literally, " we will repay (pay) as young oxen our lips," *i.e.*
present the prayers of our lips as thank-offerings.   The expression is to be explained from the fact that *shillēm*, to wipe
off what is owing, to pay, is a technical term, applied to the
sacrifice offered in fulfilment of a vow (Deut. xxiii. 22 ; Ps.
xxii. 26, l. 14, etc.), and that *pārīm*, young oxen, were the best
animals for thank-offerings (Ex. xxiv. 5).   As such thank-
offerings, *i.e.* in the place of the best animal sacrifices, they
would offer their lips, *i.e.* their prayers, to God (cf. Ps. li. 17-19,
lxix. 31, 32).   In the Sept. rendering, ἀποδώσομεν καρπὸν
χειλεων, to which there is an allusion in Heb. xiii. 15, פָּרִים has
been confounded with פְּרִי, as Jerome has already observed.   But
turning to God requires renunciation of the world, of its power,
and of all idolatry.   Rebellious Israel placed its reliance upon
Assyria and Egypt (ch. v. 13, vii. 11, viii. 9).   It will do this

no longer. The riding upon horses refers partly to the military force of Egypt (Isa. xxxi. 1), and partly to their own (ch. i. 7; Isa. ii. 7). For the expression, " neither will we say to the work of our hands," compare Isa. xlii. 17, xliv. 17. אֲשֶׁר בְּךָ, not " Thou with whom," but " for with Thee" ('ăsher as in Deut. iii. 24). The thought, " with Thee the orphan findeth compassion," as God promises in His word (Ex. xxii. 22; Deut. x. 18), serves not only as a reason for the resolution no longer to call the manufacture of their own hands God, but generally for the whole of the penitential prayer, which they are encouraged to offer by the compassionate nature of God. In response to such a penitential prayer, the Lord will heal all His people's wounds, and bestow upon them once more the fulness of the blessings of His grace. The prophet announces this in vers. 4–8 as the answer from the Lord.

Ver. 4. " *I will heal their apostasy, will love them freely: for my wrath has turned away from it.* Ver. 5. *I will be like dew for Israel: it shall blossom like the lily, and strike its roots like Lebanon.* Ver. 6. *Its shoots shall go forth, and its splendour shall become like the olive-tree, and its smell like Lebanon.* Ver. 7. *They that dwell in its shadow shall give life to corn again; and shall blossom like the vine: whose glory is like the wine of Lebanon.* Ver. 8. *Ephraim: What have I further with the idols? I hear, and look upon him: I, like a bursting cypress, in me is thy fruit found.*" The Lord promises first of all to heal their apostasy, *i.e.* all the injuries which have been inflicted by their apostasy from Him, and to love them with perfect spontaneity (*nᵉdâbhâh* an adverbial accusative, *promta animi voluntate*), since His anger, which was kindled on account of its idolatry, had now turned away from it (*mimmennū, i.e.* from Israel). The reading *mimmennī* (from me), which the Babylonian Codices have after the Masora, appears to have originated in a misunderstanding of Jer. ii. 35. This love of the Lord will manifest itself in abundant blessing. Jehovah will be to Israel a refreshing, enlivening dew (cf. Isa. xxvi. 19), through which it will blossom splendidly, strike deep roots, and spread its shoots far and wide. " Like the lily :" the fragrant white lily, which is very common in Palestine, and grows without cultivation, and " which is unsurpassed in its fecundity, often producing fifty bulbs from a single root" (Pliny *h. n.* xxi. 5).

" Strike roots like Lebanon," *i.e.* not merely the deeply rooted forest of Lebanon, but the mountain itself, as one of the "foundations of the earth" (Mic. vi. 2). The deeper the roots, the more the branches spread and cover themselves with splendid green foliage, like the evergreen and fruitful olive-tree (Jer. xi. 16; Ps. lii. 10). The smell is like Lebanon, which is rendered fragrant by its cedars and spices (Song of Sol. iv. 11). The meaning of the several features in the picture has been well explained by Rosenmüller thus: " The *rooting* indicates stability; the *spreading of the branches,* propagation and the multitude of inhabitants; the *splendour of the olive,* beauty and glory, and that constant and lasting; the *fragrance,* hilarity and loveliness." In ver. 7 a somewhat different turn is given to the figure. The comparison of the growth and flourishing of Israel to the lily and to a tree, that strikes deep roots and spreads its green branches far and wide, passes imperceptibly into the idea that Israel is itself the tree beneath whose shade the members of the nation flourish with freshness and vigour. יָשֻׁבוּ is to be connected adverbially with יְחַיּוּ. Those who sit beneath the shade of Israel, the tree that is bursting into leaf, will revive corn, *i.e.* cause it to return to life, or produce it for nourishment, satiety, and strengthening. Yea, they themselves will sprout like the vine, whose remembrance is, *i.e.* which has a renown, like the wine of Lebanon, which has been celebrated from time immemorial (cf. Plin. *h. n.* xiv. 7; Oedmann, *Verm. Sammlung aus der Naturkunde,* ii. p. 193; and Rosenmüller, *Bibl. Althk.* iv. 1, p. 217). The divine promise closes in ver. 9 with an appeal to Israel to renounce idols altogether, and hold fast by the Lord alone as the source of its life. *Ephraim* is a vocative, and is followed immediately by what the Lord has to say to Ephraim, so that we may supply *memento* in thought. מַה־לִּי עוֹד לָע׳, what have I yet to do with idols? (for this phrase, compare Jer. ii. 18); that is to say, not " I have now to contend with thee on account of the idols (Schmieder), nor "do not place them by my side any more" (Ros.); but, " I will have nothing more to do with idols," which also implies that Ephraim is to have nothing more to do with them. To this there is appended a notice of what God has done and will do for Israel, to which greater prominence is given by the emphatic אֲנִי: *I,* I hearken (*ánîthî* a prophetic perfect), and look upon him. שׁוּר, to look about for a person, to be anxious about him, or care for him, as in Job xxiv. 15. The suffix refers to Ephraim. In the last clause, God compares Himself to a cypress becoming green, not only to denote the shelter which He will afford to the people, but as the true tree of life, on which the nation finds its fruits—a fruit which nourishes and invigorates the spiritual life of the nation. The salvation which this promise sets before the people when they shall return to the Lord, is indeed depicted, according to the circumstances and peculiar views prevailing under the Old Testament, as earthly growth and prosperity; but its real nature is such, that it will receive a spiritual fulfilment in those Israelites alone who are brought to belief in Jesus Christ.

Ver. 9 (10) contains the epilogue to the whole book. *" Who is wise, that he may understand this? understanding, that he may discern it? For the ways of Jehovah are straight, and the righteous walk therein: but the rebellious stumble in them."* The pronoun אֵלֶּה and the suffix to יְדָעֵם refer to everything that the prophet has laid before the people in his book for warning, for reproof, for correction, for chastening in righteousness. He concludes by summing up the whole substance of his teaching in the one general sentence, which points back to Deut. xxxii. 4: The ways of the Lord are straight. " The ways of Jehovah " (*darkhē Yᵉhōvāh*) are the ways taken by God in the guidance and government of men ; not only the ways which He prescribes for them, but also His guidance of them. These ways lead some to life and others to death, according to the different attitudes which men assume towards God, as Moses announced to all the Israelites that they would (Deut. xxx. 19, 20), and as the Apostle Paul assured the church at Corinth that the gospel of Jesus also would (1 Cor. i. 18).

JOEL

INTRODUCTION.

1. **P**ERSON AND TIMES OF THE PROPHET JOEL.—
Joel (יוֹאֵל, *i.e.* whose God is Jehovah, Ἰωήλ) is
distinguished from other men of the same name,
which occurs very frequently (*e.g.* 1 Sam. viii. 2;
1 Chron. iv. 35, v. 4, viii. 12, vi. 21, vii. 3; 2 Chron. xxix. 12;
Neh. xi. 9), by the epithet "son of *Pethuel*" (פְּתוּאֵל, the open-
heartedness or sincerity of God). Nothing is known of the
circumstances connected with his life, since the traditional
legends as to his springing from *Bethom* (Βηθών, *al.* Θεβυράν in
Ps. Epiph.), or *Bethomeron* in the tribe of Reuben (*Ps. Doroth.*),
are quite unsupported. All that can be inferred with any
certainty from his writings is, that he lived in Judah, and in
all probability prophesied in Jerusalem. The date of his
ministry is also a disputed point; though so much is certain,
namely, that he did not live in the reign of Manasseh or
Josiah, or even later, as some suppose, but was one of the
earliest of the twelve minor prophets. For even Amos (i. 2)
commences his prophecy with a passage from Joel (iii. 16),
and closes it with the same promises, adopting in ch. ix. 13 the
beautiful imagery of Joel, of the mountains dripping with new
wine, and the hills overflowing (Joel iii. 18). And Isaiah,
again, in his description of the coming judgment in ch. xiii.,
had Joel in his mind; and in ver. 6 he actually borrows a
sentence from his prophecy (Joel i. 15), which is so peculiar
that the agreement cannot be an accidental one. Consequently, Joel prophesied before Amos, *i.e.* before the twenty-
seven years of the contemporaneous reigns of Uzziah and
Jeroboam II. How long before, can only be inferred with any
degree of probability from the historical circumstances to which

169

he refers in his prophecy. The only enemies that he mentions besides Egypt and Edom (ch. iii. 19), as those whom the Lord would punish for the hostility they had shown towards the people of God, are Tyre and Zidon, and the coasts of Philistia (ch. iii. 4); but not the Syrians, who planned an expedition against Jerusalem after the conquest of Gath, which cost Joash not only the treasures of the temple and palace, but his own life also (2 Kings xii. 18 sqq.; 2 Chron. xxiv. 23 sqq.), on account of which Amos predicted the destruction of the kingdom of Syria, and the transportation of the people to Assyria (Amos i. 3–5). But inasmuch as this expedition of the Syrians was not "directed against the Philistines, so that only a single detachment made a passing raid into Judah on their return," as Hengstenberg supposes, but was a direct attack upon the kingdom of Judah, to which the city of Gath, that Rehoboam had fortified, may still have belonged (see at 2 Kings xii. 18, 19), and inflicted a very severe defeat upon Judah, Joel would surely have mentioned the Syrians along with the other enemies of Judah, if he had prophesied after that event. And even if the absence of any reference to the hostility of the Syrians towards Judah is not strictly conclusive when taken by itself, it acquires great importance from the fact that the whole character of Joel's prophecy points to the times before Amos and Hosea. We neither meet with any allusion to the sins which Hosea and Amos condemn on the part of Judah, and which brought about the Assyrian judgment; nor is idolatry, as it prevailed under Joram, Ahaziah, and Athaliah, ever mentioned at all; but, on the contrary, the Jehovah-worship, which Jehoiada the high priest restored when Joash ascended the throne (2 Kings xi. 17 sqq.; 2 Chron. xxiii. 16 sqq.), is presupposed with all its well-regulated and priestly ceremonial. These circumstances speak very decidedly in favour of the conclusion that the first thirty years of the reign of Joash, during which the king had Jehoiada the high priest for his adviser, are to be regarded as the period of Joel's ministry. No well-founded objection can be brought against this on account of the position which his book occupies among the minor prophets, since there is no ground for the opinion that the writings of the twelve minor prophets are arranged with a strict regard to chronology.

2. THE BOOK OF JOEL.—The writings of Joel contain a connected prophetic proclamation, which is divided into two equal halves by ch. ii. 18 and 19a. In the first half the prophet depicts a terrible devastation of Judah by locusts and scorching heat; and describing this judgment as the harbinger, or rather as the dawn, of Jehovah's great day of judgment, summons the people of all ranks to a general day of penitence, fasting, and prayer, in the sanctuary upon Zion, that the Lord may have compassion upon His nation (ch. i. 2–ii. 17). In the second half there follows, as the divine answer to the call of the people to repentance, the promise that the Lord will destroy the army of locusts, and bestow a rich harvest blessing upon the land by sending early and latter rain (ch. ii. 19b–xxvii.), and then in the future pour out His Spirit upon all flesh (ch. ii. 28–32), and sit in judgment upon all nations, who have scattered His people and divided His land among them, and reward them according to their deeds; but that He will shelter His people from Zion, and glorify His land by rivers of abundant blessing (ch. iii.). These two halves are connected together by the statement that Jehovah manifests the jealousy of love for His land, and pity towards His people, and answers them (ch. ii. 18, 19a). So far the commentators are all agreed as to the contents of the book. But there are differences of opinion, more especially as to the true interpretation of the first half,—namely, whether the description of the terrible devastation by locusts is to be understood literally or allegorically.[1] The decision of this question depends upon the reply that is given to the prior question, whether ch. i. 2–

---

[1] The allegorical exposition is found even in the Chaldee, where the four names of the locusts are rendered literally in ch. i. 4, whereas in ch. ii. 25 we find hostile tribes and kingdoms instead; also in Ephraem Syrus, Cyril of Alex., Theodoret, and Jerome, although Theodoret regards the literal interpretation as also admissible, and in Abarb., Luther, and many other expositors. And lately it has been vigorously defended by Hengstenberg in his *Christology* (i. p. 302 translation), and by Hävernick (*Introduction*, ii. 2, p. 294 sqq.), who both of them agree with the fathers in regarding the four swarms of locusts as representing the imperial powers of Chaldea, Medo-Persia, Greece, and Rome. On the other hand, Rufinus, Jarchi, Ab. Ezra, Dav. Kimchi, support the literal view that Joel is describing a terrible devastation of the land by locusts; also Bochart, Pococke, J. H. Michaelis, and in the most recent times, Hofmann and Delitzsch.

ii. 17 contains a description of a present or a future judgment.
If we observe, first of all, that the statement in ch. ii. 18 and
19*a*, by which the promise is introduced, is expressed in four
successive imperfects with *Vav consec.* (the standing form for
historical narratives), there can be no doubt whatever that this
remark contains a historical announcement of what has taken
place on the part of the Lord in consequence of the penitential
cry of the people. And if this be established, it follows still
further that the first half of our book cannot contain the prediction of a strictly future judgment, but must describe a
calamity which has at any rate in part already begun. This
is confirmed by the fact that the prophet from the very outset (ch. i. 2–4) describes the devastation of the land by locusts
as a present calamity, on the ground of which he summons
the people to repentance. As Joel begins with an appeal
to the old men, to see whether such things have happened in
their own days, or the days of their fathers, and to relate
them to their children and children's children, and then
describes the thing itself with simple perfects, 'וגו יֶתֶר הַגָּזָם אָכַל, it
is perfectly obvious that he is not speaking of something that
is to take place in the future, but of a divine judgment that
has been inflicted already.[1] It is true that the prophets frequently employ preterites in their description of future events,
but there is no analogous example that can be found of such a
use of them as we find here in ch. i. 2–4; and the remark
made by Hengstenberg, to the effect that we find the preterites
employed in exactly the same manner in ch. iii., is simply incorrect. But if Joel had an existing calamity before his eye, and
depicts it in ch. i. 2 sqq., the question in dispute from time immemorial, whether the description is to be understood allegorically
or literally, is settled in favour of the literal view. "An allegory must contain some significant marks of its being so. Where
these are wanting, it is arbitrary to assume that it is an allegory
at all." And we have no such marks here, as we shall show in
our exposition in detail. "As it is a fact established by the

---

[1] "Some imagine," as Calvin well observes, "that a punishment is here
threatened, which is to fall at some future time; but the context shows
clearly enough that they are mistaken and mar the prophet's true meaning. He is rather reproving the hardness of the people, because they do
not feel their plagues."

unanimous testimony of the most credible witnesses, that wherever swarms of locusts descend, all the vegetation in the fields immediately vanishes, just as if a curtain had been rolled up; that they spare neither the juicy bark of woody plants, nor the roots below the ground; that their cloud-like swarms darken the air, and render the sun and even men at a little distance off invisible; that their innumerable and closely compact army advances in military array in a straight course, most obstinately maintained; that it cannot be turned back or dispersed, either by natural obstacles or human force; that on its approach a loud roaring noise is heard like the rushing of a torrent, a waterfall, or a strong wind; that they no sooner settle to eat, than you hear on all sides the grating sound of their mandibles, and, as Volney expresses it, might fancy that you heard the foraging of an invisible army;—if we compare these and other natural observations with the statements of Joel, we shall find everywhere the most faithful picture, and nowhere any hyperbole requiring for its justification and explanation that the army of locusts should be paraphrased into an army of men; more especially as the devastation of a country by an army of locusts is far more terrible than that of an ordinary army; and there is no allusion, either expressed or hinted at, to a massacre among the people. And if we consider, still further, that the migratory locusts (*Acridium migratorium*, in Oken, *Allg. Naturgesch.* v. 3, p. 1514 sqq.) find their grave sometimes in dry and barren steppes, and sometimes in lakes and seas, it is impossible to comprehend how the promise in ch. ii. 20—one part of the army now devastating Judah shall be hurled into the southern desert, the van into the Dead Sea, and the rear into the Mediterranean—can harmonize with the allegorical view" (Delitzsch).[1] The only thing that appears to favour the idea that the locusts are used figuratively to represent hostile armies, is the circumstance that Joel discerns in the devastation of the locusts as depicted by him, the drawing near or coming of the day of the Lord (ch. i. 15, ii. 1), connected with the fact that Isaiah speaks of the judgment upon Baal, which was accomplished by

---

[1] Proofs of this have been collected in great numbers by Sam. Bochart (*Hieroz.*), and both Oedmann (*Vermischte Sammlungen*, ii. 76 sqq. and vi. 74 sqq.) and Credner (appendix to his *Commentary on Joel*) have contributed abundant gleanings gathered from the reports of travellers.

a hostile army, in the words of Joel (ch. i. 15; see Isa. xiii. 6). But on closer examination, this appearance does not rise into reality. It is true that by the "day of Jehovah" we cannot understand a different judgment from the devastation of the locusts, since such a supposition would be irreconcilable with ch. ii. 1 sqq. But the expression, "for the day of Jehovah is at hand, and as a destruction from the Almighty does it come," shows that the prophet did not so completely identify the day of the Lord with the plague of locusts, as that it was exhausted by it, but that he merely saw in this the approach of the great day of judgment, *i.e.* merely one element of the judgment, which falls in the course of ages upon the ungodly, and will be completed in the last judgment. One factor in the universal judgment is the judgment pronounced upon Babylon, and carried out by the Medes; so that it by no means follows from the occurrence of the words of Joel in the prophecy of Isaiah, that the latter put an allegorical interpretation upon Joel's description of the devastation by the locusts.

But even if there are no conclusive indications or hints, that can be adduced in support of the allegorical interpretation, it cannot be denied, on the other hand, that the description, as a whole, contains something more than a poetical painting of one particular instance of the devastation of Judah by a more terrible swarm of locusts than had ever been known before; that is to say, that it bears an ideal character surpassing the reality,—a fact which is overlooked by such commentators as can find nothing more in the account than the description of a very remarkable plague. The introduction, "Hear this, ye old men; and give ear, all ye inhabitants of the land: hath this been in your days, or in the days of your fathers? Tell ye your children of it, and let your children tell their children, and their children the following generation" (ch. i. 2, 3); and the lamentation in ver. 9, that the meat-offering and drink-offering have been destroyed from the house of Jehovah; and still more, the picture of the day of the Lord as a day of darkness and of gloominess like the morning red spread over the mountains; a great people and a strong, such as has not been from all eternity, and after which there will be none like it for ever and ever (ch. ii. 2),— unquestionably show that Joel not only regarded the plague of locusts that came upon Judah in the light of divine revelation,

and as a sign, but described it as the breaking of the Lord's
great day of judgment, or that in the advance of the locusts
he saw the army of God, at whose head Jehovah marched as
captain, and caused His voice, the terrible voice of the Judge
of the universe, to be heard in the thunder (ch. ii. 11), and
that he predicted this coming of the Lord, before which the
earth trembles, the heavens shake, and sun, moon, and stars
lose their brightness (ch. ii. 10), as His coming to judge the
world. This proclamation, however, was no production of
mere poetical exaggeration, but had its source in the inspiration of the Spirit of God, which enlightened the prophet; so
that in the terrible devastation that had fallen upon Judah
he discerned one feature of the day of judgment of the Lord,
and on the ground of the judgment of God that had been thus
experienced, proclaimed that the coming of the Lord to judgment upon the whole world was near at hand. The medium
through which this was conveyed to his mind was meditation
upon the history of the olden time, more especially upon the
judgments through which Jehovah had effected the redemption
of His people out of Egypt, in connection with the punishment
with which Moses threatened the transgressors of the law
(Deut. xxviii. 38, 39, 42),—namely, that locusts should devour
their seed, their plants, their fields, and their fruits. Hengstenberg has correctly observed, that the words of Joel in ch.
ii. 10, "There have not been ever the like," are borrowed from
Ex. x. 14; but it is not in these words alone that the prophet
points to the Egyptian plague of locusts. In the very introduction to his prophecy (ch. i. 2, 3), viz. the question whether
such a thing has occurred, and the charge, Tell it to your children, etc., there is an unmistakeable allusion to Ex. x. 2, where
the Lord charges Moses to tell Pharaoh that He will do signs,
in order that Pharaoh may relate it to his son and his son's son,
and then announces the plague of locusts in these words: "that
thy fathers and thy fathers' fathers have not seen such things
since their existence upon the earth" (Ex. x. 6). As the basis
of this judgment of God which fell upon Egypt in the olden
time, and by virtue of a higher illumination, Joel discerned in
the similar judgment that had burst upon Judah in his own
time, a type of the coming of Jehovah's great day of judgment,
and made it the substratum of his prophecy of the judgment of

the wrath of the Lord which would come upon Judah, to terrify
the sinners out of their self-security, and impel them by earnest
repentance, fasting, and prayer, to implore the divine mercy for
deliverance from utter destruction. This description of the
coming day of Jehovah, *i.e.* of the judgment of the world, for
which the judgment inflicted upon Judah of the devastation by
locusts prepared the way, after the foretype of these occurrences
of both the olden and present time, is no allegory, however, in
which the heathen nations, by whom the judgments upon the
covenant nation that had gone further and further from its
God would be executed in the time to come, are represented
as swarms of locusts coming one after another and devastating the land of Judah; but it has just the same reality as the
plague of locusts through which God once sought to humble
the pride of the Egyptian Pharaoh. We are no more at liberty
to turn the locusts in the prophecy before us into hostile
armies, than to pronounce the locusts by which Egypt was
devastated, allegorical figures representing enemies or troops of
hostile cavalry. Such a metamorphosis as this is warranted
neither by the vision in Amos vii. 1–3, where Amos is said to
have seen the divine judgment under the figure of a swarm of
locusts; nor by that described in Rev. ix. 3 sqq., where locusts
which come out of the bottomless pit are commanded neither
to hurt the grass nor any green thing, nor any tree, but only
to torment men with their scorpion-stings: for even in these
visions the locusts are not figurative, representing hostile nations;
but on the basis of the Egyptian plague of locusts and of Joel's
prophecy, they stand in Amos as a figurative representation of
the devastation of the land, and in the Apocalypse as the symbol
of a supernatural plague inflicted upon the ungodly. Lastly,
another decisive objection to the allegorical interpretation is to
be found in the circumstance, that neither in the first nor in
the second half of his book does Joel predict the particular
judgments which God will inflict in the course of time, partly
upon His degenerate people, and partly upon the hostile powers
of the world, but that he simply announces the judgment of
God upon Judah and the nations of the world in its totality,
as the great and terrible day of the Lord, without unfolding
more minutely or even suggesting the particular facts in which
it will be historically realized. In this respect, the ideality of

his prophecy is maintained throughout; and the only speciality given to it is, that in the first half the judgment upon the covenant people is proclaimed, and in the second the judgment upon the heathen nations: the former as the groundwork of a call to repentance; the latter as the final separation between the church of the Lord and its opponents. And this separation between the covenant nation and the powers of the world is founded on fact. The judgment only falls upon the covenant nation when it is unfaithful to its divine calling, when it falls away from its God, and that not to destroy and annihilate it, but to lead it back by means of chastisement to the Lord its God. If it hearken to the voice of its God, who speaks to it in judgments, the Lord repents of the evil, and turns the calamity into salvation and blessing. It was Joel's mission to proclaim this truth in Judah, and turn the sinful nation to its God. To this end he proclaimed to the people, that the Lord was coming to judgment in the devastation that the locusts had spread over the land, and by depicting the great and terrible day of the Lord, called upon them to turn to their God with all their heart. This call to repentance was not without effect. The Lord was jealous for His land, and spared His people (ch. ii. 18), and sent His prophets to proclaim the removal of the judgment and the bestowal of a bountiful earthly and spiritual blessing: viz., for the time immediately ensuing the destruction of the army of locusts, the sending of the teacher for righteousness, and a plentiful fall of rain for the fruitful supply of the fruits of the ground (ch. ii. 19, 27); and in the more remote future, the pouring out of His Spirit upon the whole congregation, and on the day of the judgment upon all nations the deliverance and preservation of His faithful worshippers; and finally, after the judgment, the transformation and eternal glory of Zion (ch. ii. 28–iii. 21). Here, again, the ideality of the prophetic announcement is maintained throughout, although a distinction is made between the inferior blessing in the immediate future, and the higher benediction of the church of God at a more distant period. The outpouring of the Spirit of God upon all flesh is followed, without any intervening link, by the announcement of the coming of the terrible day of the Lord, as a day of judgment upon all nations, including those who have shown themselves hostile to Judah, either in Joel's own time or a little while before. The nations are gathered together in the valley of Jehoshaphat, and there judged by Jehovah through His mighty heroes ; but the sons of Israel are delivered and sheltered by their God. Here, again, all the separate judgments, which fall upon the nations of the world that are hostile to God, during the many centuries of the gradual development of the kingdom of God upon earth, are summed up in one grand judicial act on the day of Jehovah, through which the separation is completely effected between the church of the Lord and its foes, the ungodly power of the world annihilated, and the kingdom of God perfected; but without the slightest hint, that both the judgment upon the nations and the glorification of the kingdom of God will be fulfilled through a succession of separate judgments.

The book of Joel, therefore, contains two prophetic addresses, which are not only connected together as one work by the historical remark in ch. ii. 18, 19a, but which stand in the closest relation to each other, so far as their contents are concerned, though the one was not delivered to the people directly after the other, but the first during the devastation by the locusts, to lead the people to observe the judgment of God and to assemble together in the temple for a service of penitence and prayer ; and the second not till after the priests had appointed a day of fasting, penitence, and prayer, in the house of the Lord, in consequence of His solemn call to repentance, and in the name of the people had prayed to the Lord to pity and spare His inheritance. The committal of these addresses to writing did not take place, at any rate, till after the destruction of the army of the locusts, when the land began to recover from the devastation that it had suffered. But whether Joel committed these addresses to writing just as he delivered them to the congregation, and merely linked them together into one single work by introducing the historical remark that unites them, or whether he merely inserted in his written work the essential contents of several addresses delivered after this divine judgment, and worked them up into one connected prophecy, it is impossible to decide with certainty. But there is no doubt whatever as to the composition of the written work by the prophet himself.— For the different commentaries upon the book of Joel, see my *Introduction to the Old Testament*.

EXPOSITION.

I. THE JUDGMENT OF GOD, AND THE PROPHET'S CALL TO REPENTANCE.—CHAP. I. 2-II. 17.

An unparalleled devastation of the land of Judah by several successive swarms of locusts, which destroyed all the seedlings, all field and garden fruits, all plants and trees, and which was accompanied by scorching heat, induced the prophet to utter a loud lamentation at this unparalleled judgment of God, and an earnest call to all classes of the nation to offer prayer to the Lord in the temple, together with fasting, mourning, and weeping, that He might avert the judgment. In the first chapter, the lamentation has reference chiefly to the ruin of the land (ch. i. 2–20); in the second, the judgment is depicted as a foretype and harbinger of the approaching day of the Lord, which the congregation is to anticipate by a day of public fasting, repentance, and prayer (ch. ii. 1–17); so that ch. i. describes rather the magnitude of the judgment, and ch. ii. 1–17 its significance in relation to the covenant nation.

LAMENTATION OVER THE DEVASTATION OF JUDAH BY LOCUSTS AND DROUGHT.—CHAP. I.

After an appeal to lay to heart the devastation by swarms of locusts, which has fallen upon the land (vers. 2–4), the prophet summons the following to utter lamentation over this calamity : first the drunkards, who are to awake (vers. 5–7); then the congregation generally, which is to mourn with penitence (vers. 8–12); and then the priests, who are to appoint a service of repentance (vers. 13–18). For each of these appeals he gives, as a reason, a further description of the horrible calamity, corresponding to the particular appeal; and finally, he sums up his lamentation in a prayer for the deliverance of the land from destruction (vers. 19, 20).

Ver. 1 contains the heading to the book, and has already been noticed in the introduction. Ver. 2. " *Hear this, ye old men ; and attend, all ye inhabitants of the land ! Has such a thing*

indeed happened in your days, or in the days of your fathers?
Ver. 3. *Ye shall tell your sons of it, and your sons their sons,
and their sons the next generation.* Ver. 4. *The leavings of the
gnawer the multiplier ate, and the leavings of the multiplier the
licker ate, and the leavings of the licker the devourer ate.*" Not
only for the purpose of calling the attention of the hearers to
his address, but still more to set forth the event of which he is
about to speak as something unheard of—a thing that has never
happened before, and therefore is a judgment inflicted by God
—the prophet commences with the question addressed to the
old men, whose memory went the furthest back, and to all the
inhabitants of Judah, whether they had ever experienced anything of the kind, or heard of such a thing from their fathers;
and with the command to relate it to their children, and grandchildren, and great-grandchildren.[1] "The inhabitants of the
land" are the inhabitants of Judah, as it was only with this
kingdom that Joel was occupied (cf. ver. 14 and ch. ii. 1). זאת
is the occurrence related in ver. 4, which is represented by the
question " Has this been in your days?" as a fact just experienced.   *Yether haggâzâm,* the leavings of the gnawer, *i.e.*
whatever the gnawer leaves unconsumed of either vegetables or
plants. The four names given to the locusts, viz. *gâzâm, 'arbeh,
yeleq,* and *châsîl,* are not the names applied in natural history
to four distinct species, or four different generations of locusts;
nor does Joel describe the swarms of two successive years, so
that *"gâzâm* is the migratory locust, which visits Palestine chiefly
in the autumn, *'arbeh* the young brood, *yeleq* the young locust
in the last stage of its transformation, or before changing its
skin for the fourth time, and *châsîl* the perfect locust after this
last change, so that as the brood sprang from the *gâzâm, châsîl*
would be equivalent to *gâzâm*" (Credner). This explanation is

---

[1] " As he is inquiring concerning the past according to the command
of Moses in Deut. xxxii. 7, he asks the old men, who have been taught by
long experience, and are accustomed, whenever they see anything unusual,
to notice that this is not according to the ordinary course of nature, which
they have observed for so many years. And since this existing calamity,
caused by the insects named, has lasted longer and pressed more heavily
than usual, he admonishes them to carry their memory back to the former
days, and see whether anything of the kind ever happened naturally before;
and if no example can be found, the prophet's advice is, that they should
recognise this as the hand of God from heaven."—TARNOV.

not only at variance with ch. ii. 25, where *gâzâm* stands last, after *châsîl*, but is founded generally merely upon a false interpretation of Nah. iii. 15, 16 (see the passage) and Jer. li. 27, where the adjective *sâmâr* (*horridus*, horrible), appended to *yeleq*, from *sâmar*, to shudder, by no means refers to the rough, horny, wing-sheath of the young locusts, and cannot be sustained from the usage of the language. It is impossible to point out any difference in usage between *gâzâm* and *châsîl*, or between these two words and *'arbeh*. The word *gâzâm*, from *gâzam*, to cut off (in Arabic, Ethiopic, and the Rabb.), occurs only in this passage, in ch. ii. 25, and in Amos iv. 9, where it is applied to a swarm of flying locusts, which leave the vine, fig-tree, and olive, perfectly bare, as it is well known that all locusts do, when, as in Amos, the vegetables and field fruits have been already destroyed. *'Arbeh*, from *râbhâh*, to be many, is the common name of the locust, and indeed in all probability of the migratory locust, because this always appears in innumerable swarms. *Châsîl*, from *châsal*, to eat off, designates the locust (*hâ'arbeh*), according to Deut. xxviii. 38, by its habit of eating off the field crops and tree fruits, and is therefore used in 1 Kings viii. 37, 2 Chron. vi. 28, Ps. lxxviii. 46, as synonymous with *hâ'arbeh*, and in Isa. xxxiii. 4 in its stead. *Yeleq*, from *yâlaq = lâqaq*, to lick, to lick off, occurs in Ps. cv. 34 as equivalent to *'arbeh*, and in Nahum as synonymous with it; and indeed it there refers expressly to the Egyptian plague of locusts, so that young locusts without wings cannot possibly be thought of. *Haggâzâm* the gnawer, *hayyeleq* the licker, *hechâsîl* the devourer, are therefore simply poetical epithets applied to the *'arbeh*, which never occur in simple plain prose, but are confined to the loftier (rhetorical and poetical) style. Moreover, the assumption that Joel is speaking of swarms of locusts of two successive years, is neither required by ch. ii. 25 (see the comm. on this verse), nor reconcilable with the contents of the verse itself. If the *'arbeh* eats what the *gâzâm* has left, and the *yeleq* what is left by the *'arbeh*, we cannot possibly think of the field and garden fruits of two successive years, because the fruits of the second year are not the leavings of the previous year, but have grown afresh in the year itself.[1] The

---

[1] Bochart (*Hieroz.* iii. p. 290, ed. Ros.) has already expressed the same opinion. "If," he says, "the different species had been assigned to so

thought is rather this : one swarm of locusts after another has invaded the land, and completely devoured its fruit. The use of several different words, and the division of the locusts into four successive swarms, of which each devours what has been left by its precursor, belong to the rhetorical drapery and individualizing of the thought. The only thing that has any real significance is the number four, as the four kinds of punishment in Jer. xv. 3, and the four destructive judgments in Ezek. xiv. 21, clearly show. The number four, " the stamp of œcumenicity" (Kliefoth), indicates here the spread of the judgment over the whole of Judah in all directions.

Vers. 5–7. In order that Judah may discern in this unparalleled calamity a judgment of God, and the warning voice of God calling to repentance, the prophet first of all summons the wine-bibbers to sober themselves, and observe the visitation of God. Ver. 5. " *Awake, ye drunken ones, and weep! and howl, all ye drinkers of wine! at the new wine; for it is cut off from your mouth.* Ver. 6. *For a people has come up over my land, a strong one, and innumerable: its teeth are lion's teeth, and it has the bite of a lioness.* Ver. 7. *It has made my vine a wilderness, and my fig-tree into sticks. Peeling, it has peeled it off, and cast it away : its shoots have grown white.*" הָקִיץ, to awake out of the reeling of intoxication, as in Prov. xxiii. 35. They are to howl for the new wine, the fresh sweet juice of the grape, because with the destruction of the vines it is taken away and destroyed from their mouth. Vers. 6 and 7 announce through whom. In the expression *gōi 'âlâh* (a people has come up) the locusts are represented as a warlike people,

---

many different years, the *'arbeh* would not be said to have eaten the leavings of the *gâzâm*, or the *yeleq* the leavings of the *'arbeh*, or the *châsîl* the leavings of the *yeleq;* for the productions of this year are not the leavings of last, nor can what will spring up in future be looked upon as the leavings of this. Therefore, whether this plague of locusts was confined to one year, or was repeated for several years, which seems to be the true inference from Joel ii. 25, I do not think that the different species of locusts are to be assigned to different years respectively, but that they all entered Judæa in the same year; so that when one swarm departed from a field, another followed, to eat up the leavings of the previous swarm, if there were any; and that this was repeated as many times as was necessary to consume the whole, so that nothing at all should be left to feed either man or beast."

because they devastate the land like a hostile army. *Gŏi* furnishes no support to the allegorical view. In Prov. xxx. 25, 26, not only are the ants described as a people ('*ám*), but the locusts also; although it is said of them that they have no king. And '*ám* is synonymous with *gŏi*, which has indeed very frequently the idea of that which is hostile, and even here is used in this sense; though it by no means signifies a heathen nation, but occurs in Zeph. ii. 9 by the side of '*ám*, as an epithet applied to the people of Jehovah (*i.e.* Israel: see also Gen. xii. 2). The weapons of this army consist in its teeth, its "bite," which grinds in pieces as effectually as the teeth of the lion or the bite of the lioness (מְתַלְּעוֹת; see at Job xxix. 17). The suffix attached to אַרְצִי does not refer to Jehovah, but to the prophet, who speaks in the name of the people, so that it is the land of the people of God. And this also applies to the suffixes in גַּפְנִי and תְּאֵנָתִי in ver. 7. In the description of the devastation caused by the army of locusts, the vine and fig-tree are mentioned as the noblest productions of the land, which the Lord has given to His people for their inheritance (see at Hos. ii. 14). לִקְצָפָה, εἰς κλασμόν, literally, for crushing. The suffix in *chăsâphâh* refers, no doubt, simply to the vine as the principal object, the fig-tree being mentioned casually in connection with it. *Châsaph*, to strip, might be understood as referring simply to the leaves of the vine (cf. Ps. xxix. 9); but what follows shows that the gnawing or eating away of the bark is also included. *Hishlīkh*, to throw away not merely what is uneatable, "that which is not green and contains no sap" (Hitzig), but the vine itself, which the locusts have broken when eating off its leaves and bark. The branches of the vine have become white through the eating off of the bark (*sârīgīm*, Gen. xl. 10).[1]

Vers. 8–12. The whole nation is to mourn over this devastation. Ver. 8. "*Lament like a virgin girded with sackcloth for the husband of her youth.* Ver. 9. *The meat-offering and the drink-offering are destroyed from the house of Jehovah. The*

---

[1] H. Ludolf, in his *Histor. Æthiop.* i. c. 13, § 16, speaking of the locusts, says: "Neither herbs, nor shrubs, nor trees remain unhurt. Whatever is either grassy or covered with leaves, is injured, as if it had been burnt with fire. Even the bark of trees is nibbled with their teeth, so that the injury is not confined to one year alone."

priests, the servants of Jehovah mourn. Ver. 10. *The field is laid waste, the ground mourns: for the corn is laid waste: the new wine is spoiled, the oil decays.* Ver. 11. *Turn pale, ye husbandmen; howl, ye vinedressers, over wheat and barley: for the harvest of the field is perished.* Ver. 12. *The vine is spoiled, and the fig-tree faded; the pomegranate, also the palm and the apple tree: all the trees of the field are withered away; yea, joy has expired from the children of men."* In ver. 8 Judah is addressed as the congregation of Jehovah. אֱלִי is the imperative of the verb אָלָה, equivalent to the Syriac ܐܠܐ, to lament. The verb only occurs here. The lamentation of the virgin for the בַּעַל נְעוּרֶיהָ, *i.e.* the beloved of her youth, her bridegroom, whom she has lost by death (Isa. liv. 6), is the deepest and bitterest lamentation. With reference to חֲגֹרַת־שַׂק, see Delitzsch on Isa. iii. 24. The occasion of this deep lamentation, according to ver. 9, is the destruction of the meat-offering and drink-offering from the house of the Lord, over which the servants of Jehovah mourn. The meat and drink offerings must of necessity cease, because the corn, the new wine, and the oil are destroyed through the devastation of the field and soil. *Hokhrath minchah* does not affirm that the offering of the daily morning and evening sacrifice (Ex. xxix. 38–42)—for it is to this that מִנְחָה וָנֶסֶךְ chiefly, if not exclusively, refers—has already ceased; but simply that any further offering is rendered impossible by the failure of meal, wine, and oil. Now Israel could not suffer any greater calamity than the suspension of the daily sacrifice; for this was a practical suspension of the covenant relation—a sign that God had rejected His people. Therefore, even in the last siege of Jerusalem by the Romans, the sacrificial worship was not suspended till it had been brought to the last extremity; and even then it was for the want of sacrificers, and not of the material of sacrifice (Josephus, *de bell. Jud.* vi. 2, 1). The reason for this anxiety was the devastation of the field and land (ver. 10); and this is still further explained by a reference to the devastation and destruction of the fruits of the ground, viz. the corn, *i.e.* the corn growing in the field, so that the next harvest would be lost, and the new wine and oil, *i.e.* the vines and olive-trees, so that they could bear no grapes for new wine, and no olives for oil. The verbs in ver. 11a are not

perfects, but imperatives, as in the fifth verse. הֹבִישׁ has the
same meaning as *bōsh*, as in Jer. ii. 26, vi. 15, etc., to stand
ashamed, to turn pale with shame at the disappointment of
their hope, and is probably written defectively, without וֹ, to
distinguish it from הוֹבִישׁ, the *hiphil* of יָבֵשׁ, to be parched or
dried up (vers. 10 and 12). The hope of the husbandmen was
disappointed through the destruction of the wheat and barley,
the most important field crops. The vine-growers had to
mourn over the destruction of the vine and the choice fruit-
trees (ver. 12), such as the fig and pomegranate, and even the
date-palm (*gam-tâmár*), which has neither a fresh green rind
nor tender juicy leaves, and therefore is not easily injured by
the locusts so as to cause it to dry up; and *tappūăch*, the
apple-tree, and all the trees of the field, *i.e.* all the rest of the
trees, wither. "All trees, whether fruit-bearing or not, are consumed by the devastating locusts" (Jerome). In the concluding
clause of ver. 12, the last and principal ground assigned for
the lamentation is, that joy is taken away and withered from
the children of men (*hōbhīsh min*, *constr. prægn.*). כִּי introduces a reason here as elsewhere, though not for the clause
immediately preceding, but for the הֹבִישׁוּ and הֵילִילוּ in ver. 11,
the leading thought in both verses; and we may therefore
express it by an emphatic *yea*.

Vers. 13–20. The affliction is not removed by mourning
and lamentation, but only through repentance and supplication
to the Lord, who can turn away all evil. The prophet therefore proceeds to call upon the priests to offer to the Lord penitential supplication day and night in the temple, and to call the
elders and all the people to observe a day of fasting, penitence,
and prayer; and then offers supplication himself to the Lord
to have compassion upon them (ver. 19). From the motive
assigned for this appeal, we may also see that a terrible drought
had been associated with the devastation by the locusts, from
which both man and beast had endured the most bitter suffering, and that Joel regarded this terrible calamity as a sign of
the coming of the day of the Lord. Ver. 13. "*Gird yourselves,
and lament, ye priests; howl, ye servants of the altar; come, pass
the night in sackcloth, ye servants of my God: for the meat-offering and drink-offering are withdrawn from the house of your God.
Ver. 14. Sanctify a fast, call out an assembly, assemble the*

elders, all ye inhabitants of the land, at the house of Jehovah your God, and cry to Jehovah." From what follows we must supply *bassaqqīm* (with sackcloth) to *chigrū* (gird yourselves). Gird yourselves with mourning apparel, *i.e.* put it on (see ver. 8). In this they are to pass the night, to offer supplication day and night, or incessantly, standing between the altar and the porch (ch. ii. 17). "Servants of *my* God," *i.e.* of the God whose prophet I am, and from whom I can promise you a hearing. The reason assigned for this appeal is the same as for the lamentation in ver. 9. But it is not the priests only who are to pray incessantly to the Lord; the elders and all the people are to do the same. קַדְּשׁוּ צוֹם, to sanctify a fast, *i.e.* to appoint a holy fast, a divine service of prayer connected with fasting. To this end the priests are to call an *'ătsârâh, i.e.* a meeting of the congregation for religious worship. *'Atsârâh,* or *'ătsereth, πανήγυρις,* is synonymous with מִקְרָא קוֹדֶשׁ in Lev. xxiii. 36 (see the exposition of that passage). In what follows, כָּל־יֹשְׁבֵי ה' is attached *ἀσυνδέτως* to זְקֵנִים; and the latter is not a vocative, but an accusative of the object. On the other hand, בֵּית יְהוָֹה is an *accus. loci,* and dependent upon אִסְפוּ. זָעַק, to cry, used of loud and importunate prayer. It is only by this that destruction can still be averted.

Ver. 15. "*Alas for the day! for the day of Jehovah is near, and it comes like violence from the Almighty.*" This verse does not contain words which the priests are to speak, so that we should have to supply לֵאמֹר, like the Syriac and others, but words of the prophet himself, with which he justifies the appeal in vers. 13 and 14. לַיּוֹם is the time of the judgment, which has fallen upon the land and people through the devastation by the locusts. This "day" is the beginning of the approaching day of Jehovah, which will come like a devastation from the Almighty. *Yŏm Yᵉhŏvâh* is the great day of judgment upon all ungodly powers, when God, as the almighty ruler of the world, brings down and destroys everything that has exalted itself against Him; thus making the history of the world, through His rule over all creatures in heaven and earth, into a continuous judgment, which will conclude at the end of this course of the world with a great and universal act of judgment, through which everything that has been brought to eternity by the stream of time unjudged and unadjusted, will be judged and adjusted once for all, to bring to an end the whole development of the world in accordance with its divine appointment, and perfect the kingdom of God by the annihilation of all its foes. (Compare the magnificent description of this day of the Lord in Isa. ii. 12–21.) And accordingly this particular judgment—through which Jehovah on the one hand chastises His people for their sins, and on the other hand destroys the enemies of His kingdom—forms one element of the day of Jehovah; and each of these separate judgments is a coming of that day, and a sign of His drawing near. This day Joel saw in the judgment that came upon Judah in his time, *keshōd misshaddai*, lit. like a devastation from the Almighty,—a play upon the words (since *shōd* and *shaddai* both come from *shâdad*), which Rückert renders, though somewhat too freely, by *wie ein Graussen vom grossen Gott.* כ is the so-called כ *veritatis*, expressing a comparison between the individual and its genus or its idea. On the relation between this verse and Isa. xiii. 6, see the Introduction.

Ver. 16. *" Is not the food destroyed before our eyes, joy and exulting from the house of our God? Ver. 17. The grains have mouldered under their clods, the storehouses are desolate, the barns have fallen down; because the corn is destroyed. Ver. 18. How the cattle groan! the herds of oxen are bewildered, for no pasture was left for them; even the flocks of sheep suffer."* As a proof that the day of the Lord is coming like a devastation from the Almighty, the prophet points in ver. 16 to the fact that the food is taken away before their eyes, and therewith all joy and exulting from the house of God. "The food of the sinners perishes before their eyes, since the crops they looked for are snatched away from their hands, and the locust anticipates the reaper" (Jerome). אֹכֶל, food as the means of sustenance; according to ver. 10, corn, new wine, and oil. The joy is thereby taken from the house of Jehovah, inasmuch as, when the crops are destroyed, neither first-fruits nor thank-offerings can be brought to the sanctuary to be eaten there at joyful meals (Deut. xii. 6, 7, xvi. 10, 11). And the calamity became all the more lamentable, from the fact that, in consequence of a terrible drought, the seed perished in the earth, and consequently the prospect of a crop the following year entirely disappeared. The prophet refers to this in ver. 17, which has

been rendered in extremely different ways by the LXX.,
Chald., and Vulg., on account of the ἀπ. λεγ. עָבְשׁוּ, פְּרֻדוֹת, and
מֶגְרְפוֹת (compare Pococke, *ad h. l.*). עָבַשׁ signifies to moulder
away, or, as the injury was caused by dryness and heat, to dry
up; it is used here of grains of corn which lose their germinating power, from the Arabic عبس, to become dry or withered,
and the Chaldee עֲפַשׁ, to get mouldy. *P^erudōth*, in Syriac,
grains of corn sowed broadcast, probably from *pârad*, to scatter
about. *Megrâphōth*, according to Ab. Esr., clods of earth
(compare جَرَف, *gleba terræ*), from *gâraph*, to wash away
(Judg. v. 21) a detached piece of earth. If the seed-corn
loses its germinating power beneath the clod, no corn-harvest
can be looked for. The storehouses (*'ōtsârōth;* cf. 2 Chron.
xxxii. 27) moulder away, and the barns (*mamm^egūrâh* with
dag. dirim. = *m^egūrâh* in Hag. ii. 19) fall, tumble to pieces,
because being useless they are not kept in proper condition.
The drought also deprives the cattle of their pasture, so that
the herds of oxen and flocks of sheep groan and suffer with
the rest from the calamity. בּוּךְ, *niphal*, to be bewildered with
fear. *'Ashēm*, to expiate, to suffer the consequences of men's
sin.

The fact, that even irrational creatures suffer along with
men, impels the prophet to pray for help to the Lord, who
helps both man and beast (Ps. xxxvi. 7). Ver. 19. "*To Thee,
O Jehovah, do I cry : for fire has devoured the pastures of the
wilderness, and flame has consumed all the trees of the field.*
Ver. 20. *Even the beasts of the field cry unto Thee ; for the
water-brooks are dried up, and fire has devoured the pastures of
the wilderness.*" Fire and flame are the terms used by the
prophet to denote the burning heat of the drought, which consumes the meadows, and even scorches up the trees. This is
very obvious from the drying up of the water-brooks (in ver.
20). For ver. 20*a*, compare Jer. xiv. 5, 6. In ver. 20*b* the
address is rhetorically rounded off by the repetition of וְאֵשׁ
אָכְלָה וגו' from ver. 19.

SUMMONS TO PENITENTIAL PRAYER FOR THE REMOVAL OF
THE JUDGMENT.—CHAP. II. 1-17.

This section does not contain a fresh or second address of
the prophet, but simply forms the second part of his sermon of
repentance, in which he repeats with still greater emphasis the
command already hinted at in ch. i. 14, 15, that there should
be a meeting of the congregation for humiliation and prayer,
and assigns the reason in a comprehensive picture of the approach of Jehovah's great and terrible judgment-day (vers.
1-11), coupled with the cheering assurance that the Lord will
still take compassion upon His people, according to His great
grace, if they will return to Him with all their heart (vers.
12–14); and then closes with another summons to the whole
congregation to assemble for this purpose in the house of the
Lord, and with instructions how the priests are to pray to the
Lord (vers. 15-17).

Vers. 1-11. By blowing the far-sounding horn, the priests
are to make known to the people the coming of the judgment,
and to gather them together in the temple to pray. Ver. 1.
" *Blow ye the trumpet upon Zion, and cause it to sound upon my*
holy mountain ! All the inhabitants of the land shall tremble ;
for the day of Jehovah cometh, for it is near." That this summons is addressed to the priests, is evident from ver. 15, compared with ver. 14. On *tiq'û shôphâr* and *hârî'û*, see at Hos. v. 8.
" Upon Zion," *i.e.* from the top of the temple mountain. Zion
is called the holy mountain, as in Ps. ii. 6, because the Lord
was there enthroned in His sanctuary, on the summit of Moriah,
which He claimed as His own. *Râgaz*, to tremble, *i.e.* to start
up from their careless state (Hitzig). On the expression, " for
the day of Jehovah cometh," see ch. i. 15. By the position
of בוֹא at the head of the sentence, and that in the perfect בָּא
instead of the imperfect, as in ch. i. 15, the coming of the day
of Jehovah is represented as indisputably certain. The addition of *kî qârôbh* (for it is near) cannot be accounted for, however, from the fact that in the spiritual intuition of the prophet
this day had already come, whereas in reality it was only
drawing near (Hengstenberg) ; for such a separation as this
between one element of prophesying and another is incon-

ceivable. The explanation is simply, that the day of the Lord runs throughout the history of the kingdom of God, so that it occurs in each particular judgment ; not, however, as fully manifested, but simply as being near or approaching, so far as its complete fulfilment is concerned. Joel now proclaims the coming of that day in its full completion, on the basis of the judgment already experienced, as the approach of a terrible army of locusts that darkens the land, at the head of which Jehovah is riding in all the majesty of the Judge of the world. The description is divided into three strophes thus : he first of all depicts the sight of this army of God, as seen afar off, and its terrible appearance in general (vers. 2b and 3) ; then the appearance and advance of this mighty army (vers. 4–6) ; and lastly, its irresistible power (vers. 7–11) ; and closes the first strophe with a figurative description of the devastation caused by this terrible army, whilst in the second and third he gives prominence to the terror which they cause among all nations, and over all the earth.   Ver. 2. " *A day of darkness and obscurity, a day of clouds and cloudy night : like morning dawn spread over the mountains, a people great and strong : there has not been the like from all eternity, nor will there be after it even to the years of generation and generation.* Ver. 3. *Before it burneth fire, and behind it flameth flame : the land before it as the garden of Eden, and behind it like a desolate wilderness ; and even that which escaped did not remain to it.*" With four words, expressing the idea of darkness and obscurity, the day of Jehovah is described as a day of the manifestation of judgment. The words חֹשֶׁךְ עָנָן וַעֲרָפֶל are applied in Deut. iv. 11 to the cloudy darkness in which Mount Sinai was enveloped, when Jehovah came down upon it in the fire ; and in Ex. x. 22, the darkness which fell upon Egypt as the ninth plague is called אֲפֵלָה. כְּשַׁחַר וגו׳ does not belong to what precedes, nor does it mean blackness or twilight (as Ewald and some Rabbins suppose), but " the morning dawn." The subject to *pârus* (spread) is neither *yōm* (day), which precedes it, nor *'am* (people), which follows ; for neither of these yields a suitable thought at all. The subject is left indefinite : " like morning dawn is it spread over the mountains." The prophet's meaning is evident enough from what follows. He clearly refers to the bright glimmer or splendour which is seen in the sky as a swarm of locusts ap-

proaches, from the reflection of the sun's rays from their wings.[1]
With עַם רַב וְעָצוּם (a people great and strong) we must consider
the verb בָּא (cometh) in ver. 1 as still retaining its force. *Yōm*
(day) and *'âm* (people) have the same predicate, because the
army of locusts carries away the day, and makes it into a day
of cloudy darkness. The darkening of the earth is mentioned
in connection with the Egyptian plague of locusts in Ex. x. 15,
and is confirmed by many witnesses (see the comm. on Ex. *l.c.*).
The fire and the flame which go both before and behind the
great and strong people, viz. the locusts, cannot be understood
as referring to the brilliant light kindled as it were by the
morning dawn, which proceeds from the fiery armies of the
vengeance of God, *i.e.* the locusts (Umbreit), nor merely to
the burning heat of the drought by which everything is consumed (ch. i. 19) ; but this burning heat is heightened here
into devouring flames of fire, which accompany the appearing
of God as He comes to judgment at the head of His army, after
the analogy of the fiery phenomena connected with the previous
manifestations of God, both in Egypt, where a terrible hail fell
upon the land before the plague of locusts, accompanied by
thunder and balls of fire (Ex. ix. 23, 24), and also at Sinai,
upon which the Lord came down amidst thunder and lightning,
and spoke to the people out of the fire (Ex. xix. 16–18 ; Deut.
iv. 11, 12). The land, which had previously resembled the
garden of paradise (Gen. ii. 8), was changed in consequence
into a desolate wilderness. פְּלֵיטָה does not mean escape or
deliverance, either here or in Ob. 17, but simply that which has
run away or escaped. Here it signifies that part of the land
which has escaped the devastation ; for it is quite contrary to
the usage of the language to refer לֹו, as most commentators do,
to the swarm of locusts, from which there is no escape, no
deliverance (cf. 2 Sam. xv. 14, Judg. xxi. 17, Ezra ix. 13, in

---

[1] The following is the account given by the Portuguese monk Francis
Alvarez, in his *Journey through Abyssinia* (Oedmann, *Vermischte Sammlungen*, vi. p. 75) : " The day before the arrival of the locusts we could
infer that they were coming, from a yellow reflection in the sky, proceeding
from their yellow wings. As soon as this light appeared, no one had the
slightest doubt that an enormous swarm of locusts was approaching." He
also says, that during his stay in the town of Barua he himself saw this
phenomenon, and that so vividly, that even the earth had a yellow colour
from the reflection. The next day a swarm of locusts came.

all of which ‫ל‬ refers to the subject, to which the thing that escaped was assigned). Consequently ‫לו‬ can only refer to ‫הָאָרֶץ‬. The perfect ‫הָיְתָה‬ stands related to ‫אַחֲרָיו‬, according to which the swarm of locusts had already completed the devastation.

In vers. 4–6 we have a description of this mighty army of God, and of the alarm caused by its appearance among all nations. Ver. 4. "*Like the appearance of horses is its appearance; and like riding-horses, so do they run.* Ver. 5. *Like rumbling of chariots on the tops of the mountains do they leap, like the crackling of flame which devours stubble, like a strong people equipped for conflict.* Ver. 6. *Before it nations tremble; all faces withdraw their redness.*" The comparison drawn between the appearance of the locusts and that of horses refers chiefly to the head, which, when closely examined, bears a strong resemblance to the head of a horse, as Theodoret has already observed; a fact which gave rise to their being called *Heupferde* (hay-horses) in German. In ver. 4*b* the rapidity of their motion is compared to the running of riding-horses (*pârâshĭm*); and in ver. 5 the noise caused by their springing motion to the rattling of chariots, the small two-wheeled war-chariots of the ancients, when driven rapidly over the rough mountain roads. The noise caused by their devouring the plants and shrubs is also compared to the burning of a flame over a stubble-field that has been set on fire, and their approach to the advance of a war force equipped for conflict. (Compare the adoption and further expansion of these similes in Rev. ix. 7, 9.) At the sight of this terrible army of God the nations tremble, so that their faces grow pale. '*Ammĭm* means neither people (see at 1 Kings xxii. 28) nor the tribes of Israel, but nations generally. Joel is no doubt depicting something more here than the devastation caused by the locusts in his own day. There are differences of opinion as to the rendering of the second hemistich, which Nahum repeats in ch. ii. 11. The combination of ‫פָּארוּר‬ with ‫פָּרוּר‬, a pot (Chald., Syr., Jer., Luth., and others), is untenable, since ‫פָּרוּר‬ comes from ‫פָּרַר‬, to break in pieces, whereas ‫פָּארוּר‬ (= ‫פָּאֲרוּר‬) is from the root ‫פאר‬, *piel*, to adorn, beautify, or glorify; so that the rendering, "they gather redness," *i.e.* glow with fear, which has an actual but not a grammatical support in Isa. xiii. 8, is evidently worthless. We therefore understand ‫פָּארוּר‬, as Ab. Esr., Abul Wal., and others have done, in the sense of *elegantia, nitor, pulchritudo,* and as referring to the splendour or healthy ruddiness of the cheeks, and take קָבַץ as an intensive form of קָבַץ, in the sense of drawing into one's self, or withdrawing, inasmuch as fear and anguish cause the blood to fly from the face and extremities to the inward parts of the body. For the fact of the face turning pale with terror, see Jer. xxx. 6.

In vers. 7–10 the comparison of the army of locusts to a well-equipped army is carried out still further; and, in the first place, by a description of the irresistible force of its advance. Ver. 7. " *They run like heroes, like warriors they climb the wall; every one goes on its way, and they do not change their paths.* Ver. 8. *And they do not press one another, they go every one in his path; and they fall headlong through weapons, and do not cut themselves in pieces.* Ver. 9. *They run about in the city, they run upon the wall, they climb into the houses, they come through the windows like a thief.*" This description applies for the most part word for word to the advance of the locusts, as Jerome (*in loc.*) and Theodoret (on ver. 8*a*) attest from their own observation.[1] They run like heroes—namely, to the assault: רוּץ referring to an attack, as in Job xv. 26 and Ps. xviii. 30, " as their nimbleness has already been noticed in ver. 4 " (Hitzig). Their climbing the walls also points to an assault. Their irresistible march to the object of their attack is the next point described. No one comes in another's way; they do not twist

---

[1] Jerome says: " We saw (*al.* heard) this lately in the province (Palestine). For when the swarms of locusts come and fill the whole atmosphere between the earth and sky, they fly in such order, according to the appointment of the commanding God, that they preserve an exact shape, just like the squares drawn upon a tesselated pavement, not diverging on either side by, so to speak, so much as a finger's breadth. ' And,' as he (the prophet) interprets the metaphor, ' *through the windows they will fall, and not be destroyed.*' For there is no road impassable to locusts; they penetrate into fields, and crops, and trees, and cities, and houses, and even the recesses of the bed-chambers." And Theodoret observes on ver. 8*a*: " For you may see the grasshopper like a hostile army ascending the walls, and advancing along the roads, and not suffering any difficulty to disperse them, but steadily moving forward, as if according to some concerted plan." And again, on ver. 9: " And this we have frequently seen done, not merely by hostile armies, but also by locusts, which not only when flying, but by creeping along the walls, pass through the windows into the houses themselves."

(עבט) their path, *i.e.* do not diverge either to the right hand or to the left, so as to hinder one another. Even the force of arms cannot stop their advance. שֶׁלַח is not a missile, *telum, missile* (Ges. and others), but a weapon extended or held in front (Hitzig); and the word is not only applied to a sword (2 Chron. xxiii. 10 ; Neh. iv. 11), but to weapons of defence (2 Chron. xxxii. 5). בִּצֵּעַ, not " to wound themselves " (= פָּצַע), but " to cut in pieces," used here intransitively, to cut themselves in pieces. This does no doubt transcend the nature even of the locust; but it may be explained on the ground that they are represented as an invincible army of God.[1] On the other hand, the words of ver. 9 apply, so far as the first half is concerned, both to the locusts and to an army (cf. Isa. xxxiii. 4 ; Nah. ii. 5) ; whereas the second half applies only to the former, of which Theodoret relates in the passage quoted just now, that he has frequently seen this occur (compare also Ex. x. 6).

The whole universe trembles at this judgment of God. Ver. 10. " *Before it the earth quakes, the heavens tremble: sun and moon have turned black, and the stars have withdrawn their shining.* Ver. 11. *And Jehovah thunders before His army, for His camp is very great, for the executor of His word is strong ; for the day of Jehovah is great and very terrible, and who can endure it ?*" The remark of Jerome on ver. 10, viz. that " it is not that the strength of the locusts is so great that they can move the heavens and shake the earth, but that to those who suffer

---

[1] The notion that these words refer to attempts to drive away the locusts by force of arms, in support of which Hitzig appeals to *Liv. hist.* xlii. 10, *Plinii hist. n.* xi. 29, and Hasselquist, *Reise nach Pal.* p. 225, is altogether inappropriate. All that Livy does is to speak of *ingenti agmine hominum ad colligendas eas* (*locustas*) *coacto ;* and Pliny merely says, *Necare et in Syria militari imperio coguntur.* And although Hasselquist says, "Both in Asia and Europe they sometimes take the field against the locusts with all the equipments of war," this statement is decidedly false so far as Europe is concerned. In Bessarabia (according to the accounts of eye-witnesses) they are merely in the habit of scaring away the swarms of locusts that come in clouds, by making a great noise with drums, kettles, hay-forks, and other noisy instruments, for the purpose of preventing them from settling on the ground, and so driving them further. Hass's account of a pasha of Tripoli having sent 4000 soldiers against the insects only a few years ago, is far too indefinite to prove that they were driven away by the force of arms.

from such calamities, from the amount of their own terror, the
heavens appear to shake and the earth to reel," is correct enough
so far as the first part is concerned, but it by no means exhausts
the force of the words. For, as Hitzig properly observes, the
earth could only quake because of the locusts when they had
settled, and the heavens could only tremble and be darkened
when they were flying, so that the words would in any case be
very much exaggerated. But it by no means follows from this,
that לְפָנָיו is not to be taken as referring to the locusts, like מִפָּנָיו
in ver. 6, but to the coming of Jehovah in a storm, and that it
is to be understood in this sense: " the earth quakes, the air
roars at the voice of Jehovah, *i.e.* at the thunder, and storm-
clouds darken the day." For although *nâthan qōlō* (shall utter
His voice) in ver. 11 is to be understood as referring to the
thunder, Joel is not merely describing a storm, which came when
the trouble had reached its height and put an end to the plague
of locusts (Credner, Hitzig, and others). לְפָנָיו cannot be taken
in any other sense than that in which it occurs in ver. 3; that is
to say, it can only refer to " the great people and strong," viz.
the army of locusts, like מִפָּנָיו. Heaven and earth tremble at
the army of locusts, because Jehovah comes with them to judge
the world (cf. Isa. xiii. 13; Nahum i. 5, 6; Jer. x. 10). The
sun and moon become black, *i.e.* dark, and the stars withdraw
their brightness ('*âsaph*, withdraw, as in 1 Sam. xiv. 19), *i.e.*
they let their light shine no more. That these words affirm
something infinitely greater than the darkening of the lights of
heaven by storm-clouds, is evident partly from the predictions
of the judgment of the wrath of the Lord that is coming upon
the whole earth, and upon the imperial power (Isa. xiii. 10;
Ezek. xxxii. 7), at which the whole fabric of the universe
trembles and nature clothes itself in mourning, and partly
from the adoption of this particular feature by Christ in His
description of the last judgment (Matt. xxiv. 29; Mark xiii. 24,
25). Compare, on the other hand, the poetical description of a
storm in Ps. xviii. 8 sqq., where this feature is wanting. (For
further remarks, see at ch. iii. 4.) At the head of the army
which is to execute His will, the Lord causes His voice of thunder to sound (*nâthan qōl*, to thunder; cf. Ps. xviii. 14, etc.).
The reason for this is given in three sentences that are introduced by *kī*. Jehovah does this because His army is very great;

because this powerful army executes His word, *i.e.* His command; and because the day of judgment is so great and
terrible, that no one can endure it, *i.e.* no one can stand before
the fury of the wrath of the Judge (cf. Jer. x. 10; Mal. iii. 1).

Vers. 12–14. But there is still time to avert the completion
of the judgment by sincere repentance and mourning; for God
is merciful, and ready to forgive the penitent. Ver. 12. *" Yet
even now, is the saying of Jehovah, turn ye to me with all your
heart, and with fasting, and with weeping, and with mourning.*
Ver. 13. *And rend your heart and not your garments, and turn
back to Jehovah your God; for He is gracious and merciful, long-
suffering, and great in kindness, and suffers Himself to repent of
the evil.* Ver. 14. *Who knoweth He turns and repents, and leaves
behind Him blessing, meat-offering and drink-offering for Jehovah
your God?"* As the plague of locusts was intended to bring the
people to reflect upon their conduct towards the Lord, so was
the announcement of the great day of judgment and all its
terrors made with no other object than to produce repentance
and conversion, and thereby promote the good of the people of
God. Joel therefore appends to the threatening of judgment
a summons to sincere conversion to the Lord; and this he does
by first of all addressing the summons to the people as a saying
of Jehovah (ver. 12), and then explaining this word of God in
the most emphatic manner (vers. 13, 14). The Lord God
requires conversion to Himself with all the heart (cf. 1 Sam.
vii. 3, and Deut. vi. 5; and for שׁוּב עַד, Hos. xiv. 2), associated
with deep-rooted penitence on account of sin, which is to be
outwardly manifested in fasting and mourning. But lest the
people should content themselves with the outward signs of
mourning, he proceeds in ver. 13 with the warning admonition,
"Rend your heart, and not your garments." Rending the heart
signifies contrition of heart (cf. Ps. li. 19; Ezek. xxxvi. 26).
He then assigns the motive for this demand, by pointing to the
mercy and grace of God, in the words of Ex. xxxiv. 6, with
which the Lord made known to Moses His inmost nature,
except that in the place of וֶאֱמֶת, which we find in this passage,
he adds, on the ground of the facts recorded in Ezek. xxxii. 14
and 2 Sam. xxiv. 16, וְנִחָם עַל הָרָעָה. On the strength of these
facts he hopes, even in the present instance, for forgiveness on
the part of God, and the removal of the judgment. " Who

knoweth?" equivalent to "perhaps;" not because "too confident a hope would have had in it something offensive to Jehovah" (Hitzig), but "lest perchance they might either despair on account of the magnitude of their crimes, or the greatness of the divine clemency might make them careless" (Jerome).[1] יָשׁוּב, to turn, *sc.* from coming to judgment. נִחַם as in ver. 13. הִשְׁאִיר אַחֲרָיו, to leave behind Him, *sc.* when He returns to His throne in heaven (Hos. v. 15). *Beràkhâh*, a blessing, viz. harvest-produce for a meat-offering and drink-offering, which had been destroyed by the locusts (ch. i. 9, 13).

Vers. 15-17. To make this admonition still more emphatic, the prophet concludes by repeating the appeal for the appointment of a meeting in the temple for prayer, and even gives the litany in which the priests are to offer their supplication. Ver. 15. "*Blow ye the trumpet in Zion, sanctify a fast, proclaim a meeting.* Ver. 16. *Gather the people together, sanctify an assembly, bring together the old men, gather together the children and sucklings at the breasts. Let the bridegroom go out of his chamber, and the bride out of her room.* Ver. 17. *Between the porch and the altar are the priests, the servants of Jehovah, to weep and say, Spare, O Jehovah, Thy people, and give not up Thine inheritance to shame, so that the heathen scoff at them. Wherefore should men say among the nations, Where is their God?*" Ver. 15 is a literal repetition from ver. 1 and ch. i. 14a; ver. 16 a more detailed expansion of ch. i. 14b, in which, first of all, the people generally (עָם) are mentioned, and then the object of the summons explained in the words קַדְּשׁוּ קָהָל, "Call a holy meeting of the congregation." But in order that none may think themselves exempt, the people are more precisely defined as old men, children, and sucklings. Even the bride and bridegroom are to give up the delight of their hearts, and take part in the penitential and mournful worship. No age, no rank, is to stay away, because no one, not even the suckling, is free from sin ; but all, without exception, are exposed to the judgment. "A

[1] "He speaks after the manner of a terrified conscience, which is lifted up again with difficulty after a season of affliction, and begins to aspire after hope and the mercy of God. Moreover, the expression 'who knoweth' is a Hebrew phrase, which does not indicate doubt, but rather affirmation, coupled with desire, as if we were to say, 'And yet surely God will turn again.' "—LUTHER, *Enarrat. in Joelem, Opp.*, Jena 1703, p. iii.

stronger proof of the deep and universal guilt of the whole
nation could not be found, than that on the great day of penitence and prayer, even new-born infants were to be carried
in their arms" (Umbreit). The penitential supplication of the
whole nation is to be brought before the Lord by the priests as
the mediators of the nation. יִבְכּוּ in ver. 17 is jussive, like יֵצֵא
in ver. 16, though Hitzig disputes this, but on insufficient
grounds. The allusion to the priests in the former could only
be unsuitable, if they were merely commanded to go to the
temple like the rest of the people. But it is not to this that
ver. 17 refers, but to the performance of their official duty,
when the people had assembled for the penitential festival.
They were to stand between the porch of the temple and the
altar of burnt-offering, *i.e.* immediately in front of the door of
the holy place, and there with tears entreat the Lord, who was
enthroned in the sanctuary, not to give up the people of His
possession (*nachălâh* as in 1 Kings viii. 51; cf. Deut. iv. 20,
xxxii. 9) to the reproach of being scoffed at by the heathen.
לִמְשָׁל־בָּם גּוֹיִם is rendered by Luther and others, "that heathen
rule over them," after the ancient versions; and Ps. cvi. 41,
Deut. xv. 6, and Lam. v. 8, might be appealed to in support of
this rendering. But although grammatically allowable, it is not
required by the parallelism, as Hengstenberg maintains. For
even if the reproach of Israel could consist in the fact that they,
the inheritance of the Lord, were subjected to the government
of heathen, this thought is very remote from the idea of the
passage before us, where there is no reference at all in the
threatening of punishment to subjection to the heathen, but
simply to the devastation of the land. מָשַׁל with בְּ also signifies
to utter a proverb (= to scoff) at any one, for which Ezekiel
indeed makes use of מָשַׁל מָשָׁל (Ezek. xvii. 2, xviii. 2, and in xii.
23 and xviii. 3 construed with בְּ); but it is evident that *mâshal*
was sometimes used alone in this sense, from the occurrence of
mōshᵉlīm in Num. xxi. 27 as a term applied to the inventors of
proverbs, and also of *mᵉshōl* as a proverb or byword in Job xvii.
6, whether we take the word as an infinitive or a substantive.
This meaning, as Marck observes, is rendered probable both by
the connection with חֶרְפָּה, and also by the parallel clause which
follows, viz. "Wherefore should men among the heathen say,"
etc., more especially if we reflect that Joel had in his mind not

Deut. xv. 6, which has nothing in common with the passage before us except the verb *mâshal*, but rather Deut. xxviii. 37, where Moses not only threatens the people with transportation to another land for their apostasy from the Lord, and that they shall become "an astonishment, a proverb (*mâshâl*), and a byword" among all nations, but (vers. 38, 40–42) also threatens them with the devastation of their seed-crops, their vineyards, and their olive-grounds by locusts. Compare also 1 Kings ix. 7, 8, where not only the casting out of Israel among the heathen, but even the destruction of the temple, is mentioned as the object of ridicule on the part of the heathen; also the combination of לְחֶרְפָּה and לְמָשָׁל in Jer. xxiv. 9. But ver. 19 is decisive in favour of this view of לִמְשָׁל בָּם גּ. The Lord there promises that He will send His people corn, new wine, and oil, to their complete satisfaction, and no longer make them a reproach among the nations; so that, according to this, it was not subjugation or transportation by heathen foes that gave occasion to the scoffing of the nations at Israel, but the destruction of the harvest by the locusts. The saying among the nations, "Where is their God?" is unquestionably a sneer at the covenant relation of Jehovah to Israel; and to this Jehovah could offer no inducement, since the reproach would fall back upon Himself. Compare for the fact itself, Ex. xxxii. 12, Mic. vii. 10, and Ps. cxv. 2. Thus the prayer closes with the strongest reason why God should avert the judgment, and one that could not die away without effect.

II. THE PROMISE OF GOD TO AVERT THE JUDGMENT, AND BESTOW AN ABUNDANT BLESSING.—Chap. ii. 18–iii. 21.

The promise, which the Lord conveys to His people through the prophet in answer to the prayer of the priests, refers to the present and the future. In the first part, relating to the present and the times immediately following (ch. ii. 19–27), they are promised the destruction of the army of locusts, the gift of a teacher for righteousness, and the pouring out of a plentiful fall of rain for abundant harvests. To this there are appended, by means of the formula, "And it shall come to pass

afterward" (וְהָיָה אַחֲרֵי כֵן), in ch. ii. 28 (Heb. Bib. iii. 1), the
promise of a higher blessing through the outpouring of the Spirit
of God upon all flesh, the judgment upon the nations that are
hostile to Israel, and the eternal deliverance and benediction
of the church of God (ch. ii. 28–iii. 21). The blessing which
the Lord promises for the time just coming, and for the remote
future, is not a twofold one, so that the outpouring of the
fertilizing rain and the outpouring of the Spirit of God answer
to one another on the one hand, and the destruction of the
army of locusts and that of the army of men on the other, but
a threefold one, as v. Hofmann has shown, viz.: What the
raising up of the teacher for righteousness, the destruction of
the army of locusts, and the return of a fruitful season are to
the time present, that will the outpouring of the Spirit of God
upon all flesh, the judgment upon the army of the heathen
world, and the eternal salvation and glorification of the people
of God, be in the last times.

DESTRUCTION OF THE ARMY OF LOCUSTS, AND RENEWAL OF THE SPIRITUAL AND EARTHLY BLESSINGS.—CHAP. II. 18-27.

Vers. 18 and 19a contain the historical statement, that in
consequence of the penitential prayer of the priests, the Lord
displayed His mercy to His people, and gave them a promise,
the first part of which follows in vers. 19–27. Vers. 18, 19a.
" *Then Jehovah was jealous for His land, and had compassion
upon His people. And Jehovah answered, and said.*" The
grammar requires that we should take the imperfects with *Vav
consec.* in these clauses, as statements of what actually occurred.
The passages in which imperfects with *Vav cons.* are either
really or apparently used in a prophetic announcement of the
future, are of a different kind; *e.g.* in ver. 23, where we find
one in a subordinate clause preceded by perfects. As the verb
וַיַּעַן describes the promise which follows, as an *answer* given by
Jehovah to His people, we must assume that the priests had
really offered the penitential and supplicatory prayer to which
the prophet had summoned them in ver. 17. The circumstance
that this is not expressly mentioned, neither warrants us in
rendering the verbs in ver. 17 in the present, and taking them
as statements of what the priest really did (Hitzig), nor in

changing the historical tenses in vers. 18, 19 into futures. We
have rather simply to supply the execution of the prophet's command between vers. 17 and 18. קִנֵּא with לְ, to be jealous for a
person, *i.e.* to show the jealousy of love towards him, as in Ex.
xxxix. 25, Zech. i. 14 (see at Ex. xx. 5). חָמַל as in Ex. ii. 6,
1 Sam. xxiii. 21. In the answer from Jehovah which follows,
the three features in the promise are not given according to
their chronological order; but in order to add force to the
description, we have first of all, in ver. 19, a promise of the
relief of the distress at which both man and beast had sighed,
and then, in ver. 20, a promise of the destruction of the de-
vastator; and it is not till vers. 21–23*b* that the third feature
is mentioned in the further development of the promise, viz. the
teacher for righteousness. Then finally, in vers. 23*c*–27, the
fertilizing fall of rain, and the plentiful supply of the fruits of
the ground that had been destroyed by the locusts, are more
elaborately described, as the first blessing bestowed upon the
people.

The promise runs as follows. Ver. 19*b*. *" Behold, I send you*
the corn, and the new wine, and the oil, that ye may become satisfied
therewith; and will no more make you a reproach among the
nations. Ver. 20. *And I will remove the northern one far away*
from you, and drive him into the land of drought and desert;
its van into the front sea, and its rear into the hinder sea: and its
stink will ascend, and its corruption ascend, for it has done great
things." The Lord promises, first of all, a compensation for the
injury done by the devastation, and then the destruction of the
devastation itself, so that it may do no further damage. Ver. 19
stands related to ch. i. 11. *Shâlach*, to send: the corn is said
to be sent instead of given (Hos. ii. 10), because God sends the
rain which causes the corn to grow. Israel shall no longer be
a reproach among the nations, " as a poor people, whose God is
unable to assist it, or has evidently forsaken it" (Ros.). Marck
and Schmieder have already observed that this promise is related
to the prayer, that He would not give up His inheritance to the
reproach of the scoffings of the heathen (ver. 17: see the comm.
on this verse). הַצְּפוֹנִי, the northern one, as an epithet applied
to the swarm of locusts, furnishes no decisive argument in
favour of the allegorical interpretation of the plague of locusts.
For even if locusts generally come to Palestine from the south,

out of the Arabian desert, the remark made by Jerome, to the effect that " the swarms of locusts are *more* generally brought by the south wind than by the north," shows that the rule is not without its exceptions. " Locusts come and go with all winds" (Oedmann, ii. p. 97). In Arabia, Niebuhr (*Beschreib*. p. 169) saw swarms of locusts come from south, west, north, and east. Their home is not confined to the desert of Arabia, but they are found in all the sandy deserts, which form the southern boundaries of the lands that were, and to some extent still are, the seat of cultivation, viz. in the Sahara, the Libyan desert, Arabia, and Irak (Credner, p. 285); and Niebuhr (*l.c.*) saw a large tract of land, on the road from Mosul to Nisibis, completely covered with young locusts. They are also met with in the Syrian desert, from which swarms could easily be driven to Palestine by a north-east wind, without having to fly across the mountains of Lebanon. Such a swarm as this might be called the *ts^{e}phōnī*, *i.e.* the northern one, or northerner, even if the north was not its true home. For it cannot be philologically proved that *ts^{e}phōnī* can only denote one whose home is in the north. Such explanations as the Typhonian, the barbarian, and others, which we meet with in Hitzig, Ewald, and Meier, and which are obtained by alterations of the text or far-fetched etymologies, must be rejected as arbitrary. That which came from the north shall also be driven away by the north wind, viz. the great mass into the dry and desert land, *i.e.* the desert of Arabia, the van into the front (or eastern) sea, *i.e.* the Dead Sea (Ezek. xlvii. 18; Zech. xiv. 8), the rear into the hinder (or western) sea, *i.e.* the Mediterranean (cf. Deut. xi. 24). This is, of course, not to be understood as signifying that the dispersion was to take place in all these three directions at one and the same moment, in which case three different winds would blow at the same time; but it is a rhetorical picture of rapid and total destruction, which is founded upon the idea that the wind rises in the north-west, then turns to the north, and finally to the north-east, so that the van of the swarm is driven into the eastern sea, the great mass into the southern desert, and the rear into the western sea. The explanation given by Hitzig and others — namely, that *pānīm* signifies the eastern border, and *sōph* the western border of the swarm, which covered the entire breadth of the land, and was driven from north to south — cannot be sustained. Joel mentions both the van and the rear after the main body, simply because they both meet with the same fate, both falling into the sea and perishing there; whereupon the dead bodies are thrown up by the waves upon the shore, where their putrefaction fills the air with stench. The perishing of locusts in seas and lakes is attested by many authorities.[1] For עָלָה בָאְשׁוֹ, compare Isa. xxxiv. 3 and Amos iv. 10. צַחֲנָה is ἁπ. λεγ.; but the meaning corruption is sustained partly by the parallelism, and partly by the Syriac verb, which means to be dirty. The army of locusts had deserved this destruction, because it had done great things. הִגְדִּיל לַעֲשׂוֹת, to do great things, is affirmed of men or other creatures, with the subordinate idea of haughtiness; so that it not only means he has done a mighty thing, accomplished a mighty devastation, but is used in the same sense as the German *grossthun*, viz. to brag or be proud of one's strength. It does not follow from this, however, that the locusts are simply figurative, and represent hostile nations. For however true it may be that sin and punishment presuppose accountability (Hengst., Hävernick), the conclusion drawn from this—namely, that they cannot be imputed to irrational creatures—is incorrect. The very opposite is taught by the Mosaic law, according to which God will punish every act of violence done by beasts upon man (Gen. ix. 5), whilst the ox which killed a man was commanded to be stoned (Ex. xxi. 28-32).

This promise is carried out still further in what follows; and Joel summons the earth (ver. 21), the beasts of the field (ver. 22), and the sons of Zion (ver. 23) to joy and exultation at this mighty act of the Lord, by which they have been delivered from the threatening destruction. Ver. 21. *" Fear not, O earth! exult and rejoice : for Jehovah doeth great things!* Ver. 22. *Fear ye not, O beasts of the field! for the pastures of*

---

[1] Even Pliny says (*h. n.* xi. 29), *Gregatim sublato vento in maria aut stagna decidunt;* and Jerome has the following remarks on this verse: " Even in our own times we have seen the land of Judæa covered by swarms of locusts, which, as soon as the wind rose, were precipitated into the *first* and *latest* seas, *i.e.* the Dead Sea and the Mediterranean. And when the shores of both seas were filled with heaps of dead locusts, which the waters had thrown up, their corruption and stench became so noxious, that even the atmosphere was corrupted, and both man and beasts suffered from the consequent pestilence."

the desert become green, for the tree bears its fruit; fig-tree and vine yield their strength. Ver. 23. *And ye sons of Zion, exult and rejoice in the Lord your God; for He giveth you the teacher for righteousness, and causes to come down to you a rain-fall, early rain and latter rain, first of all."* The soil had suffered from the drought connected with the swarms of locusts (ch. i. 9); the beasts of the field had groaned on account of the destruction of all the plants and vegetation of every kind (ch. i. 18); the men had sighed over the unparalleled calamity that had befallen both land and people. The prophet here calls to all of them not to fear, but to exult and rejoice, and gives in every case an appropriate reason for the call. In that of the earth, he introduces the thought that Jehovah had done great things—had destroyed the foe that did great things; in that of the beasts, he points to the fresh verdure of the pastures, and the growth of the fruit upon the trees; in that of men, he lays stress upon a double fact, viz. the gift of a teacher for right-eousness, and the pouring out of a plentiful rain. In this description we have to notice the rhetorical individualizing, which forms its peculiar characteristic, and serves to explain not only the distinction between the earth, the beasts of the field, and the sons of Zion, but the distribution of the divine blessings among the different members of the creation that are mentioned here. For, so far as the fact itself is concerned, the threefold blessing from God benefits all three classes of the earthly creation: the rain does good not only to the sons of Zion, or to men, but also to animals and to the soil; and so again do the green of the pastures and the fruits of the trees; and lastly, even the הִגְדִּיל יי׳ לַעֲשׂוֹת not only blesses the earth, but also the beasts and men upon it. It is only through over-looking this rhetorico-poetical distribution, that any one could infer from ver. 22*b*, that because the fruits are mentioned here as the ordinary food of animals, in direct contrast to Gen. i. 28, 29, where the fruit of the trees is assigned to men for food, the beasts of the field signify the heathen. The perfects in the explanatory clauses of these three verses are all to be taken alike, and not to be rendered in the preterite in ver. 21, and in the present in vers. 22 and 23. The perfect is not only applied to actions, which the speaker looks upon from his own standpoint as actually completed, as having taken place, or as things belonging to the past, but to actions which the will or the lively fancy of the speaker regards as being as good as completed, in other words, assumes as altogether unconditional and certain, and to which in modern languages we should apply the present (Ewald, § 135, *a*, etc.).   The latter is the sense in which it is used here, since the prophet sets forth the divine promise as a fact, which is unquestionably certain and complete, even though its historical realization has only just begun, and extends into the nearer or more remote future. The divine act over which the prophet calls upon them to rejoice, is not to be restricted to the destruction of those swarms of locusts that had at that time invaded Judah, and the revivi-fication of dying nature, but is an act of God that is being constantly repeated whenever the same circumstances occur, or whose influence continues as long as this earth lasts ; since it is a tangible pledge, that to all eternity, as is stated in vers. 26, 27, the people of the Lord will not be put to shame.   The " sons of Zion" are not merely the inhabitants of Zion itself, but the dwellers in the capital are simply mentioned as the representa-tives of the kingdom of Judah.   As the plague of locusts fell not upon Jerusalem only, but upon the whole land, the call to rejoicing must refer to all the inhabitants of the land (ch. i. 2, 14).   They are to rejoice in Jehovah, who has proved Himself to be their God by the removal of the judgment and the bestowal of a fresh blessing.   This blessing is twofold in its nature.   He gives them אֶת־הַמּוֹרֶה לִצְדָקָה.   From time immemo-rial there has been a diversity of opinion as to the meaning of these words.   Most of the Rabbins and earlier commentators have followed the Chaldee and Vulgate, and taken *mōreh* in the sense of " teacher ;" but others, in no small number, have taken it in the sense of " early rain," *e.g.* Ab. Ezra, Kimchi, Tanch., Calvin, and most of the Calvinistic and modern com-mentators.   But although *mōreh* is unquestionably used in the last clause of this verse in the sense of early rain ; in every other instance this is called *yōreh* (Deut. xi. 14 ; Jer. v. 24) ; for Ps. lxxxiv. 7 cannot be brought into the account since the meaning is disputed.   Consequently the conjecture is a very natural one, that in the last clause of the verse Joel selected the form *mōreh*, instead of *yōreh*, to signify early rain, simply on account of the previous occurrence of *hammōreh* in the sense of " teacher," and for the sake of the unison. This rendering of *hammōreh* is not only favoured by the article placed before it, since neither *mōreh* = *yōreh* (early rain), nor the corresponding and tolerably frequent *malqōsh* (latter rain), ever has the article, and no reason can be discovered why *mōreh* should be defined by the article here if it signified early rain; but it is decisively confirmed by the following word לִצְדָקָה, which is quite inapplicable to early rain, since it cannot mean either " in just measure," or " at the proper time," or " in becoming manner," as *tsᵉdâqâh* is only used in the ethical sense of righteousness, and is never met with *sensu physico*, neither in 2 Sam. xix. 29, Neh. ii. 20, nor in Ps. xxiii. 3 and Lev. xix. 36, where moreover צֶדֶק occurs. For מַעְגְּלֵי צֶדֶק (in the Psalm) are not straight or right ways, but ways of righteousness (spiritual ways); and although אַבְנֵי צֶדֶק, מֹאזְנֵי צֶדֶק, are no doubt really correct scales and weight-stones, this is simply because they correspond to what is ethically right, so that we cannot deduce from this the idea of correct measure in the case of the rain. Ewald and Umbreit, who both of them recognise the impossibility of proving that *tsᵉdâqâh* is used in the physical sense of correctness or correct measure, have therefore adopted the rendering " rain for justification," or " for righteousness;" Ewald regarding the rain as a sign that they are adopted again into the righteousness of God, whilst Umbreit takes it as a manifestation of eternal righteousness in the flowing stream of fertilizing grace. But apart from the question, whether these thoughts are in accordance with the doctrine of Scripture, they are by no means applicable here, where the people have neither doubted the revelation of the righteousness of God, nor prayed to God for justification, but have rather appealed to the compassion and grace of God in the consciousness of their sin and guilt, and prayed to be spared and rescued from destruction (vers. 13, 17). By the " teacher for righteousness," we are to understand neither the prophet Joel only (v. Hofmann), nor the Messiah directly (Abarbanel), nor the ideal teacher or collective body of messengers from God (Hengstenberg), although there is some truth at the foundation of all these suppositions. The direct or exclusive reference to the Messiah is at variance with the context, since all the explanatory clauses in vers. 21–23 treat of blessings or gifts of

God, which were bestowed at any rate partially at that particular
time. Moreover, in ver. 23, the sending of the rain-fall is represented by וַיּוֹרֶד (imperf. *c. Vav cons.*), if not as the consequence
of the sending of the teacher for righteousness, at any rate
as a contemporaneous event. These circumstances apparently
favour the application of the expression to the prophet Joel.
Nevertheless, it is by no means probable that Joel describes
himself directly as the teacher for righteousness, or speaks of
his being sent to the people as the object of exultation. No
doubt he had induced the people to turn to the Lord, and to
offer penitential supplication for His mercy through his call to
repentance, and thereby effected the consequent return of rain
and fruitful seasons; but his address and summons would
not have had this result, if the people had not been already
instructed by Moses, by the priests, and by other prophets before
himself, concerning the ways of the Lord. All of these were
teachers for righteousness, and are included under *hammōreh*.
Still we must not stop at them. As the blessings of grace, at
the reception of which the people were to rejoice, did not
merely consist, as we have just observed, in the blessings which
came to it at that time, or in Joel's days, but also embraced
those which were continually bestowed upon it by the Lord;
we must not exclude the reference to the Messiah, to whom
Moses had already pointed as the prophet whom the Lord
would raise up unto them, and to whom they were to hearken
(Deut. xviii. 18, 19), but must rather regard the sending of
the Messiah as the final fulfilment of this promise. This view
answers to the context, if we simply notice that Joel mentions
here both the spiritual and material blessings which the Lord
is conveying to His people, and then in what follows expounds
the material blessings still further in vers. 23c–27, and the
spiritual blessings in vers. 28–32 and ch. iii. They are both of
them consequences of the gift of the teacher for righteousness.
Hence the expansion of the earthly saving gifts is attached by
וַיּוֹרֶד with *Vav cons.* Joel mentions first of all *geshem*, a rain-fall,
or plentiful rain for the fertilizing of the soil, and then defines
it more exactly as early rain, which fell in the autumn at the
sowing time and promoted the germination and growth of the
seed, and latter rain, which occurred in the spring shortly
before the time of harvest and brought the crops to maturity

(see at Lev. xxvi. 3). בְּרִאשׁוֹן, in the beginning, *i.e.* first (=רִאשֹׁנָה
in Gen. xxxiii. 2, just as כְּרִאשׁוֹן is used in Lev. ix. 15 for
בָּרִאשֹׁנָה in Num. x. 13), not in the first month (Chald., etc.),
or in the place of כְּבָרִאשֹׁנָה, as before (LXX., Vulg., and others).
For בְּרִאשׁוֹן corresponds to אַחֲרֵי־כֵן in ver. 28 (Heb. iii. 1), as
Ewald, Meier, and Hengstenberg admit. *First of all* the pouring out of a plentiful rain (an individualizing expression for all
kinds of earthly blessings, chosen here with reference to the
opposite of blessing occasioned by the drought) ; and *after that*,
the pouring out of the spiritual blessing (ch. ii. 28–iii. 21).

Vers. 24–27. Effects of the rain. Ver. 24. "*And the barns
become full of corn, and the vats flow over with new wine and oil.*
Ver. 25. *And I repay to you the years which the locust has eaten,
the licker, and the devourer, and the gnawer, my great army which
I sent among you.* Ver. 26. *And ye will eat, eat and be satisfied,
and praise the name of Jehovah your God, who hath done
wondrously with you ; and my people shall not be put to shame to
all eternity.* Ver. 27. *And ye will know that I am in the midst
of Israel, and I (am) Jehovah your God, and none else, and my
people shall not be put to shame to all eternity.*" Ver. 24 is
practically the same as ver. 19*a*, and the counterpart to ch. i.
10–12. הֵשִׁיק from שׁוּק, to run, *hiphil* only here and ch. iv. 13,
to run over, to overflow ; *pilel*, Ps. lxv. 10, *shōqēq*, to cause to
overflow. יְקָבִים, the vats of the wine-presses, into which the
wine flows when trodden out ; here it also applies to the vats
of the oil-presses, into which the oil ran as it was pressed out.
Through these bountiful harvests God would repay to the
people the years, *i.e.* the produce of the years, which the
locusts ate. The plural, *shânîm*, furnishes no certain proof
that Joel referred in ch. i. to swarms of locusts of several successive years ; but is used either with indefinite generality, as
in Gen. xxi. 7, or with a distinct significance, viz. as a poetical
expression denoting the greatness and violence of the devastation. On the different names of the locusts, see at ch. i. 4.
It is to be observed here that the copula stands before the last
two names, but not before *yeleq*, so that the last three names
belong to one another as co-ordinates (Hitzig), *i.e.* they are
merely different epithets used for '*arbeh*, the locusts.—Ver. 26.
On the reception of these benefits the people will praise the
Lord, who has shown it such wondrous grace, *lit.* has acted

towards it even to the doing of wonders.—Ver. 27. They will learn thereby that Jehovah is present among His people, and the only true God, who does not suffer His people to be put to shame. The repetition of וְלֹא יֵבֹשׁוּ וְגוֹ, by which the promised grace is guaranteed to the people for all ages, serves as a rhetorical rounding off of the section (see at ch. ii. 20).

OUTPOURING OF THE SPIRIT OF GOD UPON ALL FLESH; JUDG-
MENT UPON THE WORLD OF NATIONS, AND ETERNAL
DELIVERANCE AND GLORIFICATION OF THE PEOPLE OF
GOD.—CHAP. II. 28–III. 21 (HEB. BIB. CHAP. III. AND IV.).

These three distinct features in the higher blessing set before the congregation of the Lord are practically connected very closely together: inasmuch as, with the outpouring of the Spirit of God upon all flesh, the judgment breaks upon the ungodly world; and with the judgment not only does the rescue of the true worshippers of God ensue, but the sanctification and glorification of the kingdom of God begin. Consequently we do not find these three features kept rigidly separate in the prophetic announcement; but just as in ch. ii. 28–32 (ch. iii. according to the ordinary division of the chapters) the signs of the dawning of the judgment are appended to the outpouring of the Spirit of God, so in ch. iii. (Heb. etc. ch. iv.) the description of the judgment is framed as it were in the prediction of the restoration of Judah (ver. 1), and of the salvation and transfiguration of Zion (vers. 16, 17); and in vers. 18–21 the eternal glorification of the kingdom of God is interwoven, by way of contrast, into the lasting devastation of the power of the world.

Vers. 28–32 (Heb. ch. iii.). OUTPOURING OF THE SPIRIT OF GOD, AND ANNOUNCEMENT OF JUDGMENT.[1]—Ver. 28. *" And it will come to pass afterwards, I will pour out my Spirit upon all flesh; and your sons and your daughters will prophesy, your old men will dream dreams, and your young men see visions. Ver. 29. And also upon the men-servants and maid-servants I will put out my Spirit in those days."* As 'achărē-khēn points back to

---

[1] Among other special expositions of these verses, see Hengstenberg's *Christology*, vol. i. p. 326 sqq. translation.

bârî'shōn in ver. 23, the formula *v^ehâyâh achărē-khēn* describes
the outpouring of the Spirit as a second and later consequence
of the gift of the teacher for righteousness. שָׁפַךְ, to pour out,
signifies communication in rich abundance, like a rain-fall or
water-fall.   For the communication of the Spirit of God was not
entirely wanting to the covenant nation from the very first.   In
fact, the Spirit of God was the only inward bond between the
Lord and His people; but it was confined to the few whom God
endowed as prophets with the gift of His Spirit.   This limitation was to cease in the future.[1]   What Moses expressed as a
wish—namely, that the people were all prophets, and the Lord
would put His Spirit upon them (Num. xi. 29)—was to be fulfilled in the future.   *Rŭăch Y^ehōvâh* is not the first principle
of the physico-creaturely life (*i.e.* not equivalent to *rŭăch
Elōhīm* in Gen. i. 2), but that of the spiritual or ethical and
religious life of man, which filled the prophets under the Old
Testament as a spirit of prophecy; consequently Joel describes
its operations under this form.   "All flesh" signifies all men.
The idea that it embraces the irrational animals, even the
locusts (Credner), is rejected with perfect justice by Hitzig as
an inconceivable thought, and one unheard-of in the Bible;
but he is wrong in adding that the Old Testament does not
teach a communication of the Spirit of God to all men, but
limits it to the people of Israel.   A decided protest is entered
against this by Gen. vi. 3, where Jehovah threatens that He
will no longer let His Spirit rule *bâ'âdâm, i.e.* in the human
race, because it has become *bâsâr* (flesh).   *Bâsâr*, as contrasted
with *rŭăch Y^ehōvâh*, always denotes human nature regarded
as incapacitated for spiritual and divine life.   Even in this
verse we must not restrict the expression "all flesh" to the
members of the covenant nation, as most of the commentators
have done; for whatever truth there may be in the remark

---

[1] "There is no doubt that the prophet promises something greater here
than the fathers had experienced under the law.   We know that the grace
of the Holy Spirit flourished even among the ancient people; but the
prophet promises here not what the faithful had formerly experienced, but
something greater.   And this may be gathered from the verb 'to pour'
which he employs.   For שָׁפַךְ does not mean merely to give in drops, but
to pour out in great abundance.   But God did not pour out the Holy Spirit
so abundantly or copiously under the law, as He has since the manifestation of Christ."—CALVIN.

made by Calovius and others (compare Hengstenberg, *Christol.* i. p. 328 transl.), that the following clause, "your sons, your daughters, your old men, your young men, and men-servants and maid-servants," contains a specification of כָּל־בָּשָׂר, it by no means follows with certainty from this, that the word *all* does not do away with the limitation to one particular nation, but merely that in this one nation even the limits of sex, age, and rank are abolished; since it cannot be proved that the specification in vers. 2 and 3 is intended to exhaust the idea of "all flesh." Moreover, as the prophecy of Joel had respect primarily to Judah, Joel may primarily have brought into prominence, and specially singled out of the general idea of *kolbâsâr* in vers. 28 and 29, only those points that were of importance to his contemporaries, viz. that all the members of the covenant nation would participate in this outpouring of the Spirit, without regard to sex, age, or rank; and in so doing, he may have looked away from the idea of the entire human race, including all nations, which is involved in the expression "all flesh." We shall see from ver. 32 that this last thought was not a strange one to the prophet. In the specification of the communication of the Spirit, the different forms which it assumes are rhetorically distributed as follows: to the sons and daughters, prophesying is attributed; to the old, dreams; to the young, sights or visions. But it by no means follows from this, that each of these was peculiar to the age mentioned. For the assertion, that the Spirit of God only manifests itself in the weakened mind of the old man by dreams and visions of the night; that the vigorous and lively fancy of the youth or man has sights by day, or true visions; and lastly, that in the soul of the child the Spirit merely works as *furor sacer* (Tychs., Credner, Hitzig, and others), cannot be historically sustained. According to Num. xii. 6, visions and dreams re the two forms of the prophetic revelation of God; and נִבָּא is the most general manifestation of the prophetic gift, which must not be restricted to the ecstatic state associated with prophesying. The meaning of this rhetorical individualizing, is simply that their sons, daughters, old persons, and youths, would receive the Spirit of God with all its gifts. The outpouring of the Spirit upon slaves (men-servants and maidens) is connected by *v^egam*, as being something very extraordinary, and under existing circumstances not to be expected. Not a single case occurs in the whole of the Old Testament of a slave receiving the gift of prophecy. Amos, indeed, was a poor shepherd servant, but not an actual slave. And the communication of this gift to slaves was irreconcilable with the position of slaves under the Old Testament. Consequently even the Jewish expositors could not reconcile themselves to this announcement. The LXX., by rendering it ἐπὶ τοὺς δούλους μου καὶ ἐπὶ τὰς δούλας μου, have put servants of God in the place of the slaves of men; and the Pharisees refused to the ὄχλος even a knowledge of the law (John vii. 49). The gospel has therefore also broken the fetters of slavery.

Judgment upon all nations goes side by side with the outpouring of the Spirit of God. Ver. 30. "*And I give wonders in the heavens and on earth, blood, fire, and pillars of smoke.* Ver. 31. *The sun will turn into darkness, and the moon into blood, before the day of Jehovah, the great and terrible (day), comes.* Ver. 32. *And it comes to pass, every one who shall call upon the name of Jehovah will be saved; for on Mount Zion and in Jerusalem will be fugitives, as Jehovah hath said, and among those that are left will be those whom Jehovah calls.*" With the word וְנָתַתִּי, ver. 3 is attached to ver. 2 as a simple continuation (Hitzig). The wonders which God will give in the heavens and upon earth are the forerunners of judgment. *Mōphethīm* (see at Ex. iv. 21) are extraordinary and marvellous natural phenomena. The wonders on earth are mentioned first, in ver. 30*b*; then in ver. 31 those in the heavens. Blood and fire recal to mind the plagues which fell upon Egypt as signs of the judgment: the blood, the changing of the water of the Nile into blood (Ex. vii. 17); the fire, the balls of fire which fell to the earth along with the hail (Ex. ix. 24). Blood and fire point to bloodshed and war. *Timrōth ʿâshân* signifies cloud-pillars (here and in Song of Sol. iii. 6), whether we regard the form *timrōth* as original, and trace it to *timrâh* and the root *tâmar*, or prefer the reading תִּימְרוֹת, which we meet with in many codices and editions, and take the word as a derivative of *yâmar = mūr*, as Hengstenberg does (*Christol.* i. p. 334 transl.). This sign has its type in the descent of Jehovah upon Sinai, at which the whole mountain smoked, and its smoke ascended like the smoke of a smelting-furnace (Ex. xix. 18). We have not to think, therefore, of columns of cloud ascending from basons of fire, carried in front of caravans or armies on the march to show the way (see at Song of Sol. iii. 6), but of pillars of cloud, which roll up from burning towns in time of war (Isa. ix. 17). Ver. 31. In the heavens the sun is darkened, and the moon assumes a dull, blood-red appearance. These signs also have their type in the Egyptian plague of darkness (Ex. x. 21 sqq.). The darkening and extinction of the lights of heaven are frequently mentioned, either as harbingers of approaching judgment, or as signs of the breaking of the day of judgment (it was so in ch. ii. 2, 10, and is so again in ch. iii. 14 : see also Isa. xiii. 10, xxxiv. 4; Jer. iv. 23; Ezek. xxxii. 1–8; Amos viii. 9; Matt. xxiv. 29; Mark xiii. 24; Luke xxi. 25). What we have to think of here, is not so much periodically returning phenomena of nature, or eclipses of the sun and moon, as extraordinary (not ecliptic) obscurations of the sun and moon, such as frequently occur as accompaniments to great catastrophes in human history.[1] And these earthly and celestial phenomena are forerunners and signs of the approaching or bursting judgment; not only so far as subjective faith is concerned, from the impression which is made upon the human mind by rare and terrible phenomena of nature, exciting a feeling of anxious expectation as to the things that are about to happen,[2] but also in their real connection with the onward progress of humanity towards its divinely appointed goal, which may be explained from the calling of man to be the

[1] Compare O. Zoeckler, *Theologia Natural.* i. p. 420, where reference is made to Humboldt (*Kosmos*, iii. 413–17), who cites no fewer than seventeen extraordinary cases of obscuration of the sun from the historical tradition of past ages, which were occasioned, not by the moon, but by totally different circumstances, such as diminished intensity in the photosphere, unusually large spots in the sun, extraneous admixtures in our own atmosphere, such as trade-wind dust, inky rain, sand rain, etc.; and many of which took place in most eventful years, such as 45 B.C., A.D. 29 (the year of the Redeemer's death), 358, 360, etc.

[2] Calvin has taken too one-sided and subjective a view of the matter, when he gives the following explanation of ver. 31 : " What is said here of the sun and moon—namely, that the sun will be turned into darkness, and the moon into blood—is metaphorical, and signifies that the Lord will fill the whole universe with signs of His wrath, which will paralyze men with fear, as if all nature were changed into a thing of horror. For just as the sun and moon are witnesses of the paternal favour of God towards us, while they give light in their turns to the earth, so, on the

lord of the earth, though it has not yet received from science its due recognition and weight; in accordance with which connection, they show " that the eternal motion of the heavenly worlds is also appointed by the world-governing righteousness of God; so that the continued secret operation of this peculiar quality manifests itself through a strong cosmico-uranian symbolism, in facts of singular historical significance" (Zoeckler, *l. c.*).　For ver. 31*b*, see at ch. ii. 1, 11.　But it is only by the world and its children that the terrible day of the Lord is to be feared; to the children of God it brings redemption (Luke xxi. 28).　Whoever calls upon the name of Jehovah, *i.e.* the believing worshippers of the Lord, will be exempted from the judgment.　" Calling upon the name of Jehovah" signifies not only the public worship of God, but inward worship also, in which the confession of the mouth is also an expression of the heart. Upon Mount Zion will be *p^elētâh,* *i.e.* not deliverance, but that which has escaped, or, in a collective sense, those who have escaped the judgment, as the synonym *s^erīdīm,* which follows, clearly shows.　Mount Zion and Jerusalem are not mentioned here as the capital of the kingdom of Judah, but, according to their spiritual significance, as the place where the Lord was enthroned in the sanctuary in the midst of His people; that is to say, as the central spot of the kingdom of God.　Consequently it is not " to the whole nation of Judah as such that deliverance is promised, on the assumption that in those times of distress the population of the land would have streamed to

other hand, the prophet affirms that they will be the heralds of an angry and offended God. . . . By the darkness of the sun, the turning of the moon into blood, and the black vapour of smoke, the prophet meant to express the thought, that wherever men turned their eyes, everywhere, both above and below, many things would meet the eye that would fill them with terror. So that it is just as if he had said, that there had never been such a state of misery in the world, nor so many fierce signs of the wrath of God." For example, the assertion that they " are metaphorical expressions" cannot possibly be sustained, but is at variance with the scriptural view of the deep inward connection between heaven and earth, and more particularly with the scriptural teaching, that with the last judgment the present heavens and present earth will perish, and the creation of a new heaven and new earth will ensue. Moreover, the circumstance that a belief in the significance of these natural phenomena is met with in all nations, favours their real (not merely imaginary) connection with the destinies of humanity.

Jerusalem" (Hitzig), but only to those who call upon the name of the Lord, *i.e.* to the true worshippers of God, upon whom the Spirit of God is poured out. The words כַּאֲשֶׁר אָמַר יְיָ are not synonymous with נְאֻם יְיָ or כִּי דִּבֶּר יְיָ (ch. iv. 8; Isa. i. 20, xl. 5, etc.), but point to a prophetic word already known, viz. to Ob. 17, where the saying of the Lord, that in the midst of the judgment there would be rescued ones upon Mount Zion, occurs word for word. וּבַשְּׂרִידִים also depends upon תִּהְיֶה . . . כִּי: " and among those that remain will be those whom Jehovah calls." *Sârîd* is one who is left after a judgment or a battle; hence in Jer. xlii. 17 and Josh. viii. 22 it is connected with *pâlît* (one who has escaped from destruction), so that here *s͏ͤrîdîm* and *p͏ͤlētâh* are actually alike, the *s͏ͤrîdîm* being just the escaped ones upon Mount Zion. Through this clause there is appended to what precedes the fresh definition, that among the saved will be found those whom the Lord calls. These may either be the believing portion of Judah, or believers from among the heathen. If we adopted the first view, the sentence would simply contain a more precise definition of the thought, that none are saved but those who call upon the name of the Lord, and therefore would preclude the possibility of including all the inhabitants of Judah among those who call upon the Lord. If we took the second view, the sentence would add this new feature to the thought contained in the first hemistich, that not only citizens of Jerusalem and Judah would be saved in the time of judgment, but all who called upon the Lord out of every nation. The latter view deserves the preference, because the expression קרא בשם יְיָ did not need a more precise definition. The salvation of believers from the heathen world is implied in the first half of the verse, since it is simply connected with calling upon the name of the Lord. The Apostle Paul has quoted it in this sense in Rom. x. 13, as a proof of the participation of the heathen in the Messianic salvation.

If we proceed now to seek for the fulfilment of this prophecy, the Apostle Peter quoted the whole of these verses (28–32), with the exception of ver. 32*b*, after the outpouring of the Holy Spirit upon the disciples, on the first Whitsuntide feast of the apostolical church, as having been fulfilled by that Whitsuntide miracle (Acts ii. 17-21); and in his subsequent reference to this fulfilment in ch. ii. 39, "For the promise is unto you and to your children, and to all that are afar off, even as many as the Lord our God shall call," he even adds the closing words of Joel (ver. 32b).[1] Consequently the Christian church from time immemorial has recognised in the miracle of Pentecost the outpouring of the Spirit of God predicted in vers. 1, 2 :[2] so that the only point upon which there has been a division of opinion has been, whether the fulfilment is to be confined to the feast of Pentecost (as nearly all the fathers and earlier Lutheran commentators suppose) ; or is to be sought for in certain events of Joel's own time, as well as the first feast of Pentecost (Ephr. Syr., Grot., and others); or, lastly, whether the occurrence at the first feast of Pentecost is to be regarded as simply the beginning of the fulfilment which has continued throughout the whole of the Christian era (Calov., Hengstenberg, and many others). Even the Rabbins, with the exception of *R. Mose hakkohen* in *Aben Ezra,* who sees only a reference to some event in Joel's own time, expect the fulfilment to take place in the future on the advent of the Messiah (Yarchi, Kimchi, Abarb.). Of the three views expressed by Christian commentators, the third is the only one that answers to the nature of the prophecy as correctly interpreted. The outpouring of the Spirit of God, or the communication of it in all its fulness to the covenant nation, without any limitation whatever, is a standing mark with the prophets of the Messianic times (compare Isa. xxxii. 15 with xi. 9 and liv. 13) or new covenant (Jer. xxxi. 33, 34 ; Ezek. xxxvi. 26 sqq.; Zech. xii. 10). And even if the way was opened and prepared for this by the prophetic endowment of particular members of the old

---

[1] In quoting this passage Peter follows the LXX. on the whole, even in their deviations from the original text, viz. in ἀπὸ τοῦ πνεύματός μου instead of רוּחִי (vers. 28, 29), in the addition of μου to ἐπὶ τοὺς δούλους and δούλας (ver. 29b), in ἐπιφανῆ for נוֹרָא (ver. 4), because these differences were of no consequence, so far as his object was concerned. On the other hand, he has interpreted καὶ ἔσται μετὰ ταῦτα (וְהָיָה אַחֲרֵי כֵן) by καὶ ἔσται ἐν ταῖς ἐσχάταις ἡμέραις, and added for the same purpose, λέγει ὁ Θεός. He has also transposed the two clauses καὶ οἱ πρεσβύτεροι . . . and καὶ οἱ νεανίσκοι, probably simply for the purpose of letting the youths follow the sons and daughters, and placing the old men in the third row ; and lastly, he has added ἄνω to ἐν τῷ οὐρανῷ . . . , and κάτω to ἐπὶ τῆς γῆς, to give greater prominence to the antithesis.

[2] See Hengstenberg, *Christol.* i. pp. 345, 346, translation.

covenant, these sporadic communications of the Spirit of God
in the Old Testament times cannot be regarded as the first
steps in the fulfilment of our prophecy, since they were not
outpourings of the Spirit of God. This first took place when
Christ Jesus the Son of God had completed the work of redemption, *i.e.* on the first feast of Pentecost after the resurrection and ascension of Christ. Previous to this the words of
John vii. 39 applied: οὔπω ἦν πνεῦμα ἅγιον, ὅτι ὁ Ἰησοῦς
οὐδέπω ἐδοξάσθη. The reference in this prophecy to the
founding of the new covenant, or Christian church, is also
evident from the words, " And it shall come to pass afterwards,"
for which Peter substituted, " And it shall come to pass in the
last days," interpreting אחרי כן, the use of which was occasioned
by the retrospective reference to בְּרִאשׁוֹן in ch. ii. 23, with perfect
correctness so far as the fact was concerned, by the formula
answering to באחרית הימים, viz. ἐν ταῖς ἐσχάταις ἡμέραις, which
always denotes the Messianic future, or times of the completion
of the kingdom of God. And just as *achărē khēn* precludes
any reference to an event in Joel's own time, so does ἐν ταῖς
ἐσχάταις ἡμέραις preclude any fulfilment whatever in the times
before Christ. But however certain it may be that the fulfilment first took place at the first Christian feast of Pentecost,
we must not stop at this one pentecostal miracle. The address
of the Apostle Peter by no means requires this limitation, but
rather contains distinct indications that Peter himself saw
nothing more therein than the commencement of the fulfilment, " but a commencement, indeed, which embraced the
ultimate fulfilment, as the germ enfolds the tree." We see
this in ver. 38, where he exhorts his hearers to repent and be
baptized, and adds the promise, " and ye shall receive the gift
of the Holy Ghost ;" and again in ver. 39, where he observes,
" The promise belongs to you and to your children, and to all
that are afar off (τοῖς εἰς μακράν), as many as the Lord our
God will call." For if not only the children of the apostle's contemporaries, but also those that were afar off—*i.e.* not foreign
Jews, but the far-off heathen—were to participate in the gift
of the Holy Spirit, the outpouring of the Holy Spirit which
commenced at Pentecost must continue as long as the Lord
shall receive into His kingdom those who are still standing afar
off, *i.e.* until the fulness of the Gentiles shall have entered the

kingdom of God. See Hengstenberg, *Christology*, i. pp. 326 sqq. transl., where further reasons are adduced for taking this to be the allusion in the prophecy.

There is far greater diversity in the opinions entertained as to the fulfilment of vers. 30–32 : some thinking of the destruction of Jerusalem by the Chaldeans (Grotius, Turretius, and the Socinians) ; others of judgments upon the enemies of the covenant nation shortly after the return from the Babylonian exile (Ephr. Syr. and others) ; others, again, of the last judgment (Tertull., Theod., Crus.), or the destruction of Jerusalem and the last judgment (Chrys.). Of all these views, those which refer to events occurring before the Christian era are irreconcilable with the context, according to which the day of the Lord will come after the outpouring of the Spirit of God. Even the wonders connected with the death of Christ and the outpouring of the Holy Spirit upon the apostles, of which some have thought, cannot properly be taken into account, although the marvellous phenomena occurring at the death of Christ— the darkening of the sun, the shaking of the earth, and the rending of the rocks—were harbingers of the approaching judgment, and were recognised by the ὄχλοις as warnings to repent, and so escape from the judgment (Matt. xxvii. 45, 51 ; Luke xxiii. 44, 48). For the signs in heaven and earth that are mentioned in vers. 30 and 31 were to take place before the coming of the terrible day of the Lord, which would dawn after the outpouring of the Spirit of God upon all flesh, and which came, as history teaches, upon the Jewish nation that had rejected its Saviour on the destruction of Jerusalem by the Romans, and upon the Gentile world-power in the destruction of the Roman empire, and from that time forward breaks in constant succession upon one Gentile nation after another, until all the ungodly powers of this world shall be overthrown (cf. ch. iii. 2). On account of this internal connection between the day of Jehovah and the outpouring of the Spirit upon the church of the Lord, Peter also quoted vers. 30–32 of this prophecy, for the purpose of impressing upon the hearts of all the hearers of his address the admonition, " Save yourselves from this perverse generation" (Acts ii. 40), and also of pointing out the way of deliverance from the threatening judgment to all who were willing to be saved.

Chap. iii. (Heb. Bib. ch. iv.) JUDGMENT UPON THE WORLD OF NATIONS, AND GLORIFICATION OF ZION.—Vers. 1, 2. "*For, behold, in those days, and in that time, when I shall turn the captivity of Judah and Jerusalem, I will gather together all nations, and bring them down into the valley of Jehoshaphat, and will contend with them there concerning my people and my inheritance Israel, which they have scattered among the nations, and my land have they divided.* Ver. 3. *And for my people they cast the lot; and gave the boy for a harlot, and the maiden they have sold for wine, and drunk (it).*" The description of the judgment-day predicted in ch. ii. 31 commences with an explanatory כִּי. The train of thought is the following: When the day of the Lord comes, there will be deliverance upon Zion only for those who call upon the name of the Lord; for then will all the heathen nations that have displayed hostility to Jehovah's inheritance be judged in the valley of Jehoshaphat. By *hinnēh*, the fact to be announced is held up as something new and important. The notice as to the time points back to the "afterward" in ii. 28 : "in those days," viz. the days of the outpouring of the Spirit of God. This time is still further described by the apposition, "at that time, when I shall turn the captivity of Judah," as the time of the redemption of the people of God out of their prostrate condition, and out of every kind of distress. שׁוּב אֶת שְׁבוּת is not used here in the sense of "to bring back the prisoners," but, as in Hos. vi. 11, in the more comprehensive sense of *restitutio in integrum*, which does indeed include the gathering together of those who were dispersed, and the return of the captives, as one element, though it is not exhausted by this one element, but also embraces their elevation into a new and higher state of glory, transcending their earlier state of grace. In וְקִבַּצְתִּי the prediction of judgment is appended to the previous definition of the time in the form of an apodosis. The article in כָּל־הַגּוֹיִם (all *the* nations) does not refer to "all those nations which were spoken of in ch. i. and ii. under the figure of the locusts" (Hengstenberg), but is used because the prophet had in his mind all those nations upon which hostility towards Israel, the people of God, is charged immediately afterwards as a crime : so that the article is used in much the same manner as in Jer. xlix. 36, because the notion, though in itself an indefinite one, is more fully defined in what follows (cf. Ewald,

§ 277, *a*). The valley of *Y^ehŏshâphât, i.e.* Jehovah judges, is not the valley in which the judgment upon several heathen nations took place under Jehoshaphat (2 Chron. xx.), and which received the name of *Valley of blessing,* from the feast of thanksgiving which Jehoshaphat held there (2 Chron. xx. 22–26), as Ab. Ezra, Hofmann, Ewald, and others suppose; for the " Valley of blessing" was not " the valley of Kidron, which was selected for that festival in the road back from the desert of Tekoah to Jerusalem" (see Bertheau on 2 Chron. *l.c.*), and still less "the plain of Jezreel" (Kliefoth), but was situated in the neighbourhood of the ruins of *Bereikût,* which have been discovered by Wolcott (see Ritter, *Erdkunde,* xv. p. 635, and Van de Velde, *Mem.* p. 292). On the other hand, the valley of Jehoshaphat is unquestionably to be sought for, according to this chapter (as compared with Zech. xiv. 4), in or near Jerusalem; and the name, which does not occur anywhere else in either the Old or New Testament, excepting here and in ver. 12, is formed by Joel, like the name *'ēmeq hechârûts* in ver. 14, from the judgment which Jehovah would hold upon the nations there. The tradition of the church (see Euseb. and Jerome in the *Onom. s.v. κοιλάς, Cœlas,* and *Itiner. Anton.* p. 594; cf. Robinson, *Pal.* i. pp. 396, 397) has correctly assigned it to the valley of the Kidron, on the eastern side of Jerusalem, or rather to the northern part of that valley (2 Sam. xviii. 18), or valley of *Shaveh* (Gen. xiv. 17). There would the Lord contend with the nations, hold judgment upon them, because they had attacked His people (*nachălâthĭ,* the people of Jehovah, as in ch. ii. 17) and His kingdom (*'artsĭ*). The dispersion of Israel among the nations, and the division (חלק) of the Lord's land, cannot, of course, refer to the invasion of Judah by the Philistines and Arabians in the time of Joram (2 Chron. xxi. 16, 17). For although these foes did actually conquer Jerusalem and plunder it, and carried off, among other captives, even the sons of the king himself, this transportation of a number of prisoners cannot be called a dispersion of the people of Israel among the heathen; still less can the plundering of the land and capital be called a division of the land of Jehovah; to say nothing of the fact, that the reference here is to the judgment which would come upon all nations after the outpouring of the Spirit of God upon all flesh, and that it is not till vers. 4–8 that Joel proceeds to speak of the calamities which neighbouring nations had inflicted upon the kingdom of Judah. The words presuppose as facts that have already occurred, both the dispersion of the whole nation of Israel in exile among the heathen, and the conquest and capture of the whole land by heathen nations, and that in the extent to which they took place under the Chaldeans and Romans alone. In vers. 2 and 3 Joel is speaking not of events belonging to his own time, or to the most recent past, but of that dispersion of the whole of the ancient covenant nation among the heathen, which was only completely effected on the conquest of Palestine and destruction of Jerusalem by the Romans, and which continues to this day; though we cannot agree with Hengstenberg, that this furnishes an argument in favour of the allegorical interpretation of the army of locusts in ch. i. and ii. For since Moses had already foretold that Israel would one day be driven out among the heathen (Lev. xxvi. 33 sqq.; Deut. xxviii. 36 sqq.), Joel might assume that this judgment was a truth well known in Israel, even though he had not expressed it in his threatening of punishment in ch. i. and ii. Ver. 3 depicts the ignominious treatment of Israel in connection with this catastrophe. The prisoners of war are distributed by lot among the conquerors, and disposed of by them to slave-dealers at most ridiculous prices,—a boy for a harlot, a girl for a drink of wine. Even in Joel's time, many Israelites may no doubt have been scattered about in distant heathen lands (cf. ver. 5); but the heathen nations had not yet cast lots upon the nation as a whole, to dispose of the inhabitants as slaves, and divide the land among themselves. This was not done till the time of the Romans.[1] But, as many of the

[1] After the conquest and destruction of Jerusalem, Titus disposed of the prisoners, whose number reached 97,000 in the course of the war, in the following manner: Those under seventeen years of age were publicly sold; of the remainder, some were executed immediately, some sent away to work in the Egyptian mines, some kept for the public shows to fight with wild beasts in all the chief cities of Rome; and only the tallest and most handsome for the triumphal procession in Rome (compare Josephus, de bell. Jud. vi. 9, 2, 3). And the Jews who were taken prisoners in the Jewish war in the time of Hadrian, are said to have been sold in the slave-market at Hebron at so low a price, that four Jews were disposed of for a measure of barley. Even in the contests of the Ptolemæans and Seleucidæ for the possession of Palestine, thousands of Jews were sold as prisoners of

earlier commentators nave clearly seen, we must not stop even at this. The people and inheritance of Jehovah are not merely the Old Testament Israel as such, but the church of the Lord of both the old and new covenants, upon which the Spirit of God is poured out; and the judgment which Jehovah will hold upon the nations, on account of the injuries inflicted upon His people, is the last general judgment upon the nations, which will embrace not merely the heathen Romans and other heathen nations by whom the Jews have been oppressed, but all the enemies of the people of God, both within and without the earthly limits of the church of the Lord, including even carnally-minded Jews, Mohammedans, and nominal Christians, who are heathens in heart.[1]

Before depicting the final judgment upon the hostile nations of the world, Joel notices in vers. 4–8 the hostility which the nations round about Judah had manifested towards it in his own day, and foretels to these a righteous retribution for the crimes they had committed against the covenant nation. Ver. 4. *"And ye also, what would ye with me, O Tyre and Sidon, and all ye coasts of Philistia? will ye repay a doing to me, or do anything to me? Quickly, hastily will I turn back your doing upon your head.* Ver. 5. *That ye have taken my silver and my gold, and have brought my best jewels into your temples.* Ver. 6. *And the sons of Judah and the sons of Jerusalem ye have sold to the sons of Javan, to remove them far from their border.* Ver. 7. *Behold, I waken them from the place whither ye have sold them, and turn back your doing upon your head.*

war. Thus, for example, the Syrian commander Nicanor, in his expedition against the Jews in the Maccabæan war, sold by anticipation, in the commercial towns along the Mediterranean, such Jews as should be made prisoners, at the rate of ninety prisoners for one talent; whereupon 1000 slave-dealers accompanied the Syrian army, and carried fetters with them for the prisoners (1 Macc. iii. 41; 2 Macc. viii. 11, 25; Jos. *Ant.* xii. 7, 3).

[1] As J. Marck correctly observes, after mentioning the neighbouring nations that were hostile to Judah, and then the Syrians and Romans: "We might proceed in the same way to all the enemies of the Christian church, from its very cradle to the end of time, such as carnal Jews, Gentile Romans, cruel Mohammedans, impious Papists, and any others who either have borne or yet will bear the punishment of their iniquity, according to the rule and measure of the restitution of the church, down to those enemies who shall yet remain at the coming of Christ, and be overthrown at the complete and final redemption of His church."

Ver. 8. *And sell your sons and your daughters into the hand of Javan, and they sell them to the Sabæans, to a people far off; for Jehovah has spoken it."* By v⁵gam the Philistines and Phœnicians are added to the *gōyim* already mentioned, as being no less culpable than they; not, however, in the sense of, "and also if one would inquire more thoroughly into the fact" (Ewald), or, "and even so far as ye are concerned, who, in the place of the friendship and help which ye were bound to render as neighbours, have oppressed my people" (Rosenmüller), for such additions as these are foreign to the context; but rather in this sense, "and yea also . . . do not imagine that ye can do wrong with impunity, as though ye had a right so to do." מַה־אַתֶּם לִי does not mean, "What have I to do with you?" for this would be expressed differently (compare Josh. xxii. 24; Judg. xi. 12); but, "What would ye with me?" The question is unfinished, because of its emotional character, and is resumed and completed immediately afterwards in a disjunctive form (Hitzig). Tyre and Sidon, the two chief cities of the Phœnicians (see at Josh. xix. 29 and xi. 8), represent all the Phœnicians. כֹּל גְּלִילוֹת פְּל׳, "all the circles or districts of the Philistines," are the five small princedoms of Philistia (see at Josh. xiii. 2). גְּמוּל, the doing, or inflicting (*sc.* of evil), from *gâmal*, to accomplish, to do (see at Isa. iii. 9). The disjunctive question, "Will ye perhaps repay to me a deed, *i.e.* a wrong, that I have done to you, or of your own accord attempt anything against me?" has a negative meaning: "Ye have neither cause to avenge yourselves upon me, *i.e.* upon my people Israel, nor any occasion to do it harm. But if repayment is the thing in hand, I will, and that very speedily (*qal mᵉhērâh*, see Isa. v. 26), bring back your doing upon your own head" (cf. Ps. vii. 17). To explain what is here said, an account is given in vers. 5, 6 of what they have done to the Lord and His people, —namely, taken away their gold and silver, and brought their costly treasures into their palaces or temples. These words are not to be restricted to the plundering of the temple and its treasury, but embrace the plundering of palaces and of the houses of the rich, which always followed the conquest of towns (cf. 1 Kings xiv. 26; 2 Kings xiv. 14). הֵיכְלֵיכֶם also are not temples only, but palaces as well (cf. Isa. xiii. 22; Amos viii. 3; Prov. xxx. 28). Joel had no doubt the plundering of Judah and Jerusalem by the Philistines and Arabians in the time of Jehoram in his mind (see 2 Chron. xxi. 17). The share of the Phœnicians in this crime was confined to the fact, that they had purchased from the Philistines the Judæans who had been taken prisoners by them, and sold them again as slaves to the sons of Javan, *i.e.* to the Ionians or Greeks of Asia Minor.[1] The clause, " that ye might remove them far from their border," whence there would be no possibility of their returning to their native land, serves to bring out the magnitude of the crime. This would be repaid to them according to the true *lex talionis* (vers. 7, 8). The Lord would raise up the members of His own nation from the place to which they had been sold, *i.e.* would bring them back again into their own land, and deliver up the Philistines and Phœnicians into the power of the Judæans (*mâkhar b'yâd* as in Judg. ii. 14, iii. 8, etc.), who would then sell their prisoners as slaves to the remote people of the Sabæans, a celebrated trading people in Arabia Felix (see at 1 Kings x. 1). This threat would certainly be fulfilled, for Jehovah had spoken it (cf. Isa. i. 20). This occurred partly on the defeat of the Philistines by Uzziah (2 Chron. xxvi. 6, 7) and Hezekiah (2 Kings xviii. 8), where Philistian prisoners of war were certainly sold as slaves ; but principally after the captivity, when Alexander the Great and his successors set many of the Jewish prisoners of war in their lands at liberty (compare the promise of King Demetrius to Jonathan, "I will send away in freedom such of the Judæans as have been made prisoners, and reduced to slavery in our land," Josephus, *Ant.* xiii. 2, 3), and portions of the Philistian and Phœnician lands were for a time under Jewish sway ; when Jonathan besieged Ashkelon and Gaza (1 Macc. x. 86, xi. 60) ; when King Alexander (Balas) ceded Ekron and the district of Judah (1 Macc. x. 89); when the Jewish king Alexander Jannæus conquered Gaza, and destroyed it (Josephus, *Ant.* xiii. 13, 3 ; *bell. Jud.* i. 4, 2) ; and when, subsequent to the cession of Tyre, which had been conquered by Alexander the Great, to the Seleucidæ, Antiochus the younger appointed Simon commander-in-chief from the Ladder of Tyre to the border of Egypt (1 Macc. xi. 59).

[1] On the widespread slave-trade of the Phœnicians, see Movers, *Phönizier*, ii. 3, p. 70 sqq.

Vers. 9–17. Fulfilment of the judgment upon all the heathen predicted in ver. 2. Compare the similar prediction of judgment in Zech. xiv. 2 sqq. The call is addressed to all nations to equip themselves for battle, and march into the valley of Jehoshaphat to war against the people of God, but in reality to be judged by the Lord through His heavenly heroes, whom He sends down thither. Ver. 9. *"Proclaim ye this among the nations; sanctify a war, awaken the heroes, let all the men of war draw near and come up! Ver. 10. Forge your coulters into swords, and your vine-sickles into spears : let the weak one say, A hero am I. Ver. 11. Hasten and come, all ye nations round about, and assemble yourselves! Let thy heroes come down thither, O Jehovah! Ver. 12. The nations are to rise up, and come into the valley of Jehoshaphat; for there shall I sit to judge all the heathen round about."* The summons to prepare for war (ver. 9) is addressed, not to the worshippers of Jehovah or the Israelites scattered among the heathen (Cyr., Calv., Umbreit), but to the heathen nations, though not directly to the heroes and warriors among the heathen, but to heralds, who are to listen to the divine message, and convey it to the heathen nations. This change belongs to the poetical drapery of the thought, that at a sign from the Lord the heathen nations are to assemble together for war against Israel. קַדְּשׁ מִלְחָמָה does not mean "to declare war" (Hitzig), but to consecrate a war, *i.e.* to prepare for war by sacrifices and religious rites of consecration (cf. 1 Sam. vii. 8, 9; Jer. vi. 4). הָעִירוּ : waken up or arouse (not wake up) the heroes from their peaceful rest to battle. With יִגְּשׁוּ the address passes over from the second person to the third, which Hitzig accounts for on the ground that the words state what the heralds are to say to the nations or heroes; but the continuance of the imperative *kōttū* in ver. 10 does not suit this. This transition is a very frequent one (cf. Isa. xli. 1, xxxiv. 1), and may be very simply explained from the lively nature of the description. עָלָה is here applied to the advance of hostile armies against a land or city. The nations are to summon up all their resources and all their strength for this war, because it will be a decisive one. They are to forge the tools of peaceful agriculture into weapons of war (compare Isa. ii. 4 and Mic. iv. 3, where the Messianic times of peace are depicted as the turning of weapons of war into instruments of agriculture). Even the weak one is to rouse himself up to be a hero, " as is generally the case when a whole nation is seized with warlike enthusiasm" (Hitzig). This enthusiasm is expressed still further in the appeal in ver. 11 to assemble together as speedily as possible. The ἅπ. λεγ. עוּשׁ is related to חוּשׁ, to hasten; whereas no support can be found in the language to the meaning " assemble," adopted by the LXX., Targ., etc. The expression כָּל־הַגּוֹיִם by no means ne-cessitates our taking these words as a summons or challenge on the part of Joel to the heathen, as Hitzig does ; for this can be very well interpreted as a summons, with which the nations call one another to battle, as the following וְנִקְבָּצוּ requires ; and the assumption of Hitzig, Ewald, and others, that this form is the imperative for הִקָּבְצוּ, cannot be sustained from Isa. xliii. 9 and Jer. l. 5. It is not till ver. 11b that Joel steps in with a prayer addressed to the Lord, that He will send down His heavenly heroes to the place to which the heathen are flowing together. *Hanchath* an *imper. hiph.*, with *pathach* instead of *tzere*, on account of the guttural, from *náchath*, to come down. The heroes of Jehovah are heavenly hosts, or angels, who exe-cute His commands as *gibbōrē khŏăch* (Ps. ciii. 20, cf. lxxviii. 25). This prayer is answered thus by Jehovah in ver. 12 : " Let the nations rise up, and come into the valley of Jehosha-phat, for there will He hold judgment upon them." יֵעוֹרוּ cor-responds to הָעִירוּ in ver. 9; and at the close, " all the heathen round about" is deliberately repeated. Still there is no an-tithesis in this to " all nations " in ver. 2, as though here the judgment was simply to come upon the hostile nations in the neighbourhood of Judah, and not upon all the heathen univer-sally (Hitzig). For even in ver. 2 כל הגוים are simply all the heathen who have attacked the people of Jehovah—that is to say, all the nations round about Israel. Only these are not merely the neighbouring nations to Judah, but all heathen nations who have come into contact with the kingdom of God, *i.e.* all the nations of the earth without exception, inasmuch as before the last judgment the gospel of the kingdom is to be preached in all the world for a testimony to all nations (Matt. xxiv. 14; Mark xiii. 10).

It is to the last decisive judgment, in which all the single judgments find their end, that the command of Jehovah to

His strong heroes refers.   Ver. 13. *" Put ye in the sickle; for the harvest is ripe: come, tread, for the wine-press is full, the vats overflow: for their wickedness is great."*   The judgment is represented under the double figure of the reaping of the fields and the treading out of the grapes in the wine-press.   The angels are first of all summoned to reap the ripe corn (Isa. xvii. 5; Rev. xiv. 16), and then commanded to tread the wine-presses that are filled with grapes.   The opposite opinion expressed by Hitzig, viz. that the command to tread the wine-presses is preceded by the command to cut off the grapes, is supported partly by the erroneous assertion, that *bâshal* is not applied to the ripening of corn, and partly upon the arbitrary assumption that *qâtsîr*, a harvest, stands for *bâtsîr*, a vintage; and *maggâl*, a sickle (cf. Jer. l. 16), for *mazmērâh*, a vine-dresser's bill.   But *bâshal* does not mean " to boil," either primarily or literally, but to be done, or to be ripe, like the Greek πέσσω, πέπτω, to ripen, to make soft, to boil (see at Ex. xii. 9), and hence in the *piel* both to boil and roast, and in the *hiphil* to make ripe or ripen (Gen. xl. 10), applied both to grapes and corn.   It is impossible to infer from the fact that Isaiah (xvi. 9) uses the word *qâtsîr* for the vintage, on account of the alliteration with *qayits*, that this is also the meaning of the word in Joel.   But we have a decisive proof in the resumption of this passage in Rev. xiv. 15 and 18, where the two figures (of the corn-harvest and the gathering of the grapes) are kept quite distinct, and the clause כִּי בָשַׁל קָצִיר is paraphrased and explained thus: " The time is come for thee to reap, for the harvest of the earth is ripe."   The ripeness of the corn is a figurative representation of ripeness for judgment.   Just as in the harvest—namely, at the threshing and winnowing connected with the harvest—the grains of corn are separated from the husk, the wheat being gathered into the barns, the husk blown away by the wind, and the straw burned; so will the good be separated from the wicked by the judgment, the former being gathered into the kingdom of God for the enjoyment of eternal life,—the latter, on the other hand, being given up to eternal death.   The harvest field is the earth (ἡ γῆ, Rev. xiv. 16), *i.e.* the inhabitants of the earth, the human race.   The ripening began at the time of the appearance of Christ upon the earth (John iv. 35; Matt. ix. 38).   With the preaching of the gospel among all nations, the judgment of separation and decision (ἡ κρίσις, John iii. 18–21) commenced; with the spread of the kingdom of Christ in the earth it passes over all nations; and it will be completed in the last judgment, on the return of Christ in glory at the end of this world. Joel does not carry out the figure of the harvest any further, but simply presents the judgment under the similar figure of the treading of the grapes that have been gathered. רְדוּ, not from *yârad*, to descend, but from *râdâh*, to trample under foot, tread the press that is filled with grapes. הֵשִׁיקוּ הַיְקָבִים is used in ch. ii. 24 to denote the most abundant harvest; here it is figuratively employed to denote the great mass of men who are ripe for the judgment, as the explanatory clause, for "their wicked (deed) is much," or "their wickedness is great," which recals Gen. vi. 5, clearly shows. The treading of the wine-press does not express the idea of wading in blood, or the execution of a great massacre; but in Isa. lxiii. 3, as well as in Rev. xiv. 20, it is a figure denoting an annihilating judgment upon the enemies of God and of His kingdom. The wine-press is "the wine-press of the wrath of God," *i.e.* "what the wine-press is to ordinary grapes, the wrath of God is to the grapes referred to here" (Hengstenberg on Rev. xiv. 19).

The execution of this divine command is not expressly mentioned, but in ver. 14 sqq. the judgment is simply depicted thus: first of all we have a description of the streaming of the nations into the valley of judgment, and then of the appearance of Jehovah upon Zion in the terrible glory of the Judge of the world, and as the refuge of His people. Ver. 14. "*Tumult, tumult in the valley of decision: for the day of Jehovah is near in the valley of decision.*" *Hămōnīm* are noisy crowds, whom the prophet sees in the Spirit pouring into the valley of Jehoshaphat. The repetition of the word is expressive of the great multitude, as in 2 Kings iii. 16. עֵמֶק הֶחָרוּץ, not valley of threshing; for though *chârûts* is used in Isa. xxviii. 27 and xli. 15 for the threshing-sledge, it is not used for the threshing itself, but valley of the deciding judgment, from *chârats*, to decide, to determine irrevocably (Isa. x. 22; 1 Kings xx. 40), so that *chârûts* simply defines the name *Jehoshaphat* with greater precision. כִּי קָרוֹב וגו׳ (compare ch. i. 15, ii. 1) is used here to denote the immediate proximity of the judgment, which bursts at once, according to ver. 15.

Ver. 15. *" Sun and moon have become black, and the stars have withdrawn their shining.* Ver. 16. *And Jehovah roars out of Zion, and He thunders out of Jerusalem ; and heaven and earth quake : but Jehovah is a refuge to His people, and a stronghold to the sons of Israel.* Ver. 17. *And ye will perceive that I Jehovah am your God, dwelling upon Zion, my holy mountain : and Jerusalem will be a sanctuary, and strangers will not pass through it any more."* On the forebodings of the judgment in ver. 15, see at ch. ii. 10. Out of Zion, the place of His throne, will Jehovah cause His thunder-voice to sound, will roar like a lion which is rushing upon its prey (Hos. v. 14 ; Amos iii. 4), so that heaven and earth tremble in consequence. But it is only to His enemies that He is terrible ; to His people, the true Israel, He is a refuge and strong tower. From the fact that He only destroys His enemies, and protects His own people, the latter will learn that He is their God, and dwells upon Zion in His sanctuary, *i.e.* that He there completes His kingdom, that He purifies Jerusalem of all foes, all the ungodly through the medium of the judgment, and makes it a holy place which cannot be trodden any more by strangers, by Gentiles, or by the unclean of either Gentiles or Israelites (Isa. xxxv. 8), but will be inhabited only by the righteous (Isa. lx. 21; Zech. xiv. 21), who, as Rev. xxi. 27 affirms, are written in the Lamb's book of life. For Zion or Jerusalem is of course not the Jerusalem of the earthly Palestine, but the sanctified and glorified city of the living God, in which the Lord will be eternally united with His redeemed, sanctified, and glorified church. We are forbidden to think of the earthly Jerusalem or the earthly Mount Zion, not only by the circumstance that the gathering of all the heathen nations takes place in the valley of Jehoshaphat, *i.e.* in a portion of the valley of the Kidron, which is a pure impossibility, but also by the description which follows of the glorification of Judah.

Vers. 18–21. After the judgment upon all nations, the land of the Lord will overflow with streams of divine blessing ; but the seat of the world-power will become a barren waste. Ver. 18. *" And it comes to pass in that day, the mountains will trickle down with new wine, and the hills flow with milk, and all the*

*brooks of Judah flow with water; and a fountain will issue
from the house of Jehovah, and water the Acacia valley.* Ver. 19.
*Egypt will become a desolation, and Edom a barren waste, for
the sin upon the sons of Judah, that they have shed innocent
blood in their land.* Ver. 20. *But Judah, it will dwell for ever,
and Jerusalem from generation to generation.* Ver. 21. *And I
shall expiate their blood that I have not expiated: and Jehovah
dwelleth upon Zion.*" The end of the ways of the Lord is
eternal blessing for His people, whilst the enemies of His kingdom fall victims to the curse. This thought is expressed in
figures taken from the state of the covenant land of the Old
Testament, and those of the bordering kingdoms of Egypt and
Edom which were hostile to Israel. If we bear this in mind,
we shall not fall into Volck's error, of seeking in this description for a clear statement as to the transfiguration of the land
of Israel during the thousand years' reign, whilst the rest of the
earth is not yet glorified; for it is evident from ver. 18, as
compared with the parallel passages, viz. Zech. xiv. 6 sqq. and
Ezek. xlvii. 1–12, that this passage does not teach the earthly
glorification of Palestine, and desolation of Egypt and Idumæa,
but that Judah and Jerusalem are types of the kingdom of God,
whilst Egypt and Edom are types of the world-powers that are
at enmity against God; in other words, that this description is
not to be understood literally, but spiritually. " In that day,"
viz. the period following the final judgment upon the heathen,
the mountains and hills of Judah, *i.e.* the least fruitful portions
of the Old Testament kingdom of God in the time of the
prophet, will overflow with new wine and milk, and all the
brooks of water be filled, *i.e.* no more dry up in the hot season
of the year (ch. i. 20). Thus will the fruitfulness of Canaan,
the land of the Lord, flowing with milk and honey, come forth
in all its potency. Even the unfruitful acacia valley will be
watered by a spring issuing from the house of Jehovah, and
turned into a fruitful land. The valley of *Shittim* is the barren
valley of the Jordan, above the Dead Sea. The name *Shittim*,
acacia, is taken from the last encampment of the Israelites in
the steppes of Moab, before their entrance into Canaan (Num.
xxv. 1; Josh. iii. 1), and was chosen by the prophet to denote
a very dry valley, as the acacia grows in a dry soil (cf. Celsii,
Hierob. i. p. 500 sqq.). The spring which waters this valley,

and proceeds from the house of Jehovah, and the living water that flows from Jerusalem, according to Zech. xiv. 8, are of course not earthly streams that are constantly flowing, as distinguished from the streams caused by rain and snow, which very soon dry up again, but spiritual waters of life (John iv. 10, 14, vii. 38) ; and, in fact, as a comparison of Ezek. xlvii. 7–12 with Rev. xxii. 1, 2 clearly shows, the " river of the water of life, clear as a crystal," which in the New Jerusalem coming down from God upon the earth (Rev. xxi. 10) proceeds out of the throne of God and of the Lamb, and on both sides of which there grows the tree of life, that bears its fruit twelve times a-year, or every month, and the leaves of which are for the healing of the nations. The partially verbal agreement between the description of this river of water in Rev. xxii. 2, and that in Ezek. xlvii. 12, overthrows the millenarian view, that the glorification of Judah and Jerusalem, predicted by Joel, Zechariah, and Ezekiel, will be a partial glorification of the earth, viz. of the Holy Land, which takes place before the creation of the new heaven and the new earth.—Ver. 19. On the other hand, the curse of desolation will fall upon Egypt and Edom, on account of the sin which they have committed upon the sons of Judah. חֲמַס בְּנֵי, with the genitive of the object, as in Ob. 10, Hab. ii. 8, 17, etc. This sin is then more precisely defined, as consisting in the fact that they had shed innocent blood of the sons of Judah, *i.e.* of the people of God, in their land (*'artsâm*, the land of the Egyptians and Edomites, not of the Judæans) : that is to say, in the Egypt in the olden time, more especially by the command to slay all the Hebrew boys (Ex. i. 16), and in the Edom of more recent times, probably when throwing off the dominion of Judah (see at Amos i. 11 and Ob. 10). These nations and lands had both thereby become types of the power of the world in its hostility to God, in which capacity they are mentioned here, and Edom again in Isa. xxxiv. and lxiii.; cf. Jer. xlix. 7 sqq. and Ezek. xxxv.—Ver. 20. On the other hand, Judah and Jerusalem shall dwell for ever,—a poetical expression for " be inhabited," both land and city being personified, as in Isa. xiii. 20, etc. Thus will Jehovah, by means of the final judgment upon the heathen, wipe away the blood-guiltiness that they have contracted in their treatment of His people, and manifest Himself as King of Zion. With these thoughts the prophecy of Joel closes (ver. 21). The verb *niqqâh*, to cleanse, with *dâm*, to wipe away or expunge blood-guiltiness by punishment, is chosen with reference to דָּם נָקִיא in ver. 19 ; and לֹא נִקֵּיתִי, which follows, is to be taken in a relative sense : so that there is no need to alter וְנִקֵּיתִי into וְנִקַּמְתִּי (Ges.); and the latter has no critical support in the Septuagint rendering καὶ ἐκζητήσω, which merely reproduces the sense.—Ver. 21*a* does not contain the announcement of a still further punishment upon Egypt and Edom, but simply the thought with which the proclamation of the judgment closes,—namely, that the eternal desolation of the world-kingdoms mentioned here will wipe out all the wrong which they have done to the people of God, and which has hitherto remained unpunished. But Zion will rejoice in the eternal reign of its God. Jehovah dwells upon Zion, when He manifests Himself to all the world as the King of His people, on the one hand by the annihilation of His foes, and on the other hand by the perfecting of His kingdom in glory.

AMOS

INTRODUCTION.

1. **T**HE PROPHET.—*Amos* (עָמוֹס, *i.e.* Bearer or Burden), according to the heading to his book, was "among the shepherds (*nōqᵉdīm*) of Tekoah" when the Lord called him to be a prophet; that is to say, he was a native of Tekoah, a town situated on the borders of the desert of Judah, two hours to thé south of Bethlehem, the ruins of which have been preserved under the ancient name (see at Josh. xv. 59, LXX.), and lived with the shepherds who fed their sheep in the steppe to the east of Tekoah ; of course not as a rich owner of flocks, but simply as a shepherd. For even though *nōqēd* is applied to the Moabitish king in 2 Kings iii. 4 as a rich owner of a choice breed of sheep and goats, the word properly signifies only a rearer of sheep, *i.e.* not merely the owner, but the shepherd of choice sheep, as Bochart (*Hieroz.* i. p. 483, ed. Ros.) has proved from the Arabic. But Amos himself affirms, in ch. vii. 14, that he was a simple shepherd. He there replies to the priest at Bethel, who wanted to prevent him from prophesying in the kingdom of Israel : " I am not a prophet, nor yet a prophet's pupil, but a herdman (*bōqēd*) am I, and *bōlēs shiqmīm*, a gatherer of sycamores" (see at ch. vii. 14),—*i.e.* one who fed upon this fruit, which resembles figs, and is described by Pliny (*Hist. n.* 13, 14) as *prædulcis*, but which, according to Strabo, xvii. 823 (ἄτιμος κατὰ τὴν γεῦσιν), was very lightly esteemed as food, and also, according to Dioscor., was ἄτιμος καὶ κακοστόμαχος, and which is only used in Egypt as the food of the common people (Norden, *Reise*, p. 118). Consequently we have to regard Amos as a shepherd living in indigent circumstances, not as a prosperous man possessing both a flock of sheep and a sycamore plantation, which many commentators, following the Chaldee

and the Rabbins, have made him out to be.   Without having
dedicated himself to the calling of a prophet, and without even
being trained in the schools of the prophets, he was called by
the Lord away from the flock to be a prophet, to prophesy
concerning Israel (ch. vii. 14, 15), under the Judæan king
Uzziah and the Israelitish king Jeroboam II., *i.e.* within the
twenty-six years of the contemporaneous rule of these two
kings, or between 810 and 783 B.C.   Amos therefore commenced his prophetic labours about the same time as Hosea,
probably a few years earlier, and prophesied in Bethel, the
chief seat of the Israelitish image-worship (ch. vii. 10).   We
cannot fix with any greater exactness either the time of his
appearing or the duration of his ministry ; for the notice in ch.
i. 1, "two years before the earthquake," furnishes no chronological datum, because the time of the earthquake is unknown.
It is never mentioned in the historical books of the Old Testament, though it can hardly be any other than the terrible earthquake in the time of Uzziah, which the people had not forgotten
even after the captivity, inasmuch as Zechariah was able to
recal the flight that took place on that occasion (Zech. xiv. 5).
As Amos has not given the date of the earthquake, his evident
intention was not to fix the time when his ministry commenced,
or when his book was composed, but simply to point to the internal
connection between this event and his own prophetic mission.
According to the teaching of Scripture, the earth quakes when
the Lord comes to judgment upon the nations (see at ch. viii. 8).
The earthquake which shook Jerusalem two years after the
appearance of Amos as prophet, was a harbinger of the judgment threatened by Him against the two kingdoms of Israel
and the surrounding nations,—a practical declaration on the part
of God that He would verify the word of His servant ; and
the allusion to this divine sign on the part of the prophet was
an admonition to Israel to lay to heart the word of the Lord
which he had announced to them.   So far as the explanation
and importance of his prophecies were concerned, it was enough
to mention the kings of Judah and Israel in whose reigns he
prophesied.

Under these kings the two kingdoms stood at the summit
of their prosperity.   Uzziah had completely subdued the Edomites, had subjugated the Philistines, and had even made the

Ammonites tributary. He had also fortified Jerusalem strongly, and had raised a powerful army; so that his name reached as far as Egypt (2 Chron. xxvi.). And Jeroboam had completely overcome the Syrians, and restored the original borders of the kingdom from the country of Hamath to the Dead Sea (2 Kings xiv. 25–28). After the power of the Syrians had been broken, Israel had no longer any foe to fear, for Assyria had not yet arisen as a conquering power. The supposition that Calneh or Ctesiphon is represented in ch. vi. 2 as having already been taken (by the Assyrians), rests upon an incorrect interpretation, and is just as erroneous as the inference, also drawn from the same passage, that Hamath was conquered and Gath destroyed. Amos does not mention the Assyrians at all; although in ch. i. 5 he threatens the Syrians with transportation to Kir, and in ch. v. 27 predicts that the Israelites will be carried into captivity beyond Damascus. In the existing state of things, the idea of the approaching fall or destruction of the kingdom of Israel was, according to human judgment, a very improbable one indeed. The inhabitants of Samaria and Zion felt themselves perfectly secure in the consciousness of their might (ch. vi. 1). The rulers of the kingdom trusted in the strength of their military resources (ch. vi. 13), and were only concerned to increase their wealth by oppressing the poor, and to revel in earthly luxuries and pleasures (ch. ii. 6–8, v. 11, 12, vi. 4–6); so that the prophet denounces woes upon those who are in security upon Zion and without care upon the mountain of Samaria (ch. vi. 1), and utters the threat that the Lord will cause the sun to set at noon, and bring darkness over the land in broad daylight (ch. viii. 9).

It was at such a time as this that the plain shepherd of Tekoah was sent to Bethel, into the kingdom of the ten tribes, to announce to the careless sinners the approach of the divine judgment, and the destruction of the kingdom. And whilst it was in itself a strange event for a prophet to be sent out of Judah into the kingdom of the ten tribes,—so strange, in fact, that in all probability it had never occurred since the kingdom had been founded, or at any rate, that no second instance of the kind is recorded, from the time when the man of God was sent out of Judah to Bethel in the reign of Jeroboam I. (1 Kings xiii.), down to the time of Amos himself,—it must have attracted

universal attention, for a man to rise up who belonged to the
rank of a shepherd, who had had no training at all for a prophet's vocation, but who nevertheless proved, by the demonstration of the Spirit, that he was a prophet indeed, and who
foretold, in the strength of God, what destruction awaited the
covenant people, before there was the slightest human probability of any such catastrophe.

The prophet's style of composition does indeed betray the
former shepherd in the use of certain words, which evidently
belonged to the dialect of the common people,—*e.g.* מֵעִיק for מֵצִיק
(ch. ii. 13), בּוֹשֵׁם for בּוֹסֵם (ch. v. 11), מְתָאֵב for מְתַעֵב (ch. vi. 8),
מְסָרֵף for מִשְׂרֵף (ch. vi. 10), יְשָׂחֵק for יִצְחָק (ch. vii. 9, 16), נִשְׁקָה
for נִשְׁקְעָה (ch. viii. 8), and in many figures and similes drawn
from nature and rural life ; but for the rest, it indicates a close
acquaintance on the part of the prophet with the Mosaic law
and the history of his nation, and also considerable rhetorical
power, wealth and depth of thought, vivacity and vigour, more
especially in the use of bold antitheses, and a truly poetical
roll, which rises by no means unfrequently into actual rhythm ;
so that Lowth has already expressed the following opinion concerning him (*De poesi sacr.* ed. Mich. p. 433): "*Æquus judex,
de re non de homine quæsiturus, censebit, credo, pastorem nostrum
μηδὲν ὑστερηκέναι τῶν ὑπερλίαν προφητῶν, ut sensuum elatione
et magnificentia spiritus prope summis parem, ita etiam dictionis
splendore et compositionis elegantia vix quoquam inferiorem.*"
Beyond these facts, which we gather from the prophet's own
writings, nothing further is known of the circumstances connected with his life. After fulfilling his mission, he probably
returned to Judah, his native land, where his prophecies were
most likely first committed to writing. The apocryphal
accounts of his death, in Pseud.-Epiphanius, c. 12, and Pseudo-
Doroth. (see Carpzov, p. 319), have no historical value whatever.

2. The Book.—Although Amos was sent by the Lord to
Bethel, to prophesy to the people of Israel there, he does not
restrict himself in his prophecy to the kingdom of the ten tribes,
but, like his younger contemporary Hosea, notices the kingdom
of Judah as well, and even the surrounding nations, that were
hostile to the covenant nation. His book is not a mere col-

lection of the addresses delivered in Bethel, but a carefully planned, complete work, in which Amos, after the occurrence of the earthquake in the time of Uzziah, gathered together all the essential contents of the prophecies he had previously uttered at Bethel. It consists of a lengthy introduction (ch. i. ii.) and two parts, viz. simple prophetic addresses (ch. iv.–vi.), and visions with short explanations (ch. vii.–xix.). In the introduction the prophet proclaims, in the following manner, the judgment about to fall upon Damascus, Philistia, Tyre, Edom, Ammon, Moab, Judah, and Israel. The storm of the Lord, which bursts upon all these kingdoms, remains suspended over the kingdom of Israel, which is mentioned last. This is evident from the fact, that the sin of Israel is depicted more fully than that of the other nations; and the threatening of judgment is couched in such general terms, that it can only be regarded as a provisional announcement, or as the introduction to the body of the book by which it is followed. The *first* part contains an extended address, divided into three sections by the recurrence of שִׁמְעוּ (hear ye) in ch. iii. 1, iv. 1, and v. 1. The address consists of a " great warning to repent," in which the prophet holds up before the sinful Israelites, especially the rulers of the kingdom, the arts of injustice and wickedness that are current among them, and proclaims a judgment which embraces the destruction of the palaces and holy places, the overthrow of the kingdom, and the transportation of the people. In ch. iii. the sin and punishment are described in the most general form. In ch. iv. the prophet sweeps away from the self-secure sinners the false ground of confidence afforded by their own worship, recals to their mind the judgments with which God has already visited them, and summons them to stand before God as their judge. In ch. v. and vi., after a mournful elegy concerning the fall of the house of Israel (ch. v. 1–3), he points out to the penitent the way to life, coupled with the repeated summons to seek the Lord, and that which is good (ch. v. 4, 6, 14); and then, in the form of a woe, for which a double reason is assigned (ch. v. 18, vi. 1), he takes away all hope of deliverance from the impenitent and hardened. Throughout the whole of this address Amos prophesies chiefly to the ten tribes, whom he repeatedly addresses, predicting ruin and exile. At the same time, he not only addresses

his words in the introduction (ch. iii. 1, 2) to all Israel of the
twelve tribes, whom Jehovah brought out of Egypt, but he also
pronounces the last woe (ch. vi. 1) upon the secure ones on
Zion, and the careless ones on the mountain of Samaria; so
that his prophecy also applies to the kingdom of Judah, and
sets before it the same fate as that of the kingdom of the ten
tribes, if it should fall into the same sin. The *second* part
contains five visions, and at the close the proclamation of salvation. The first two visions (ch. vii. 1–3 and 4–6) threaten
judgments; the next two (ch. vii. 7–9, viii. 1–3) point out the
impossibility of averting the judgment, and the ripeness of the
people for it. Between these, viz. in ch. vii. 10–17, the conversation between the prophet and the chief priest at Bethel is
related. The substance of the fourth vision is carried out still
further, in a simple prophetic address (ch. viii. 4–14). Lastly,
the fifth vision (ch. ix. 1) shows the overthrow and ruin of the
whole of Israel, and is also still further expanded in a plain
address (ch. ix. 2–10). To this there is appended the promise
of the restoration of the fallen kingdom of God, of its extension
through the adoption of the Gentiles, and of its eternal glorification (ch. ix. 11–15). This conclusion corresponds to the
introduction (ch. i. and ii.). Like all the nations that rise up
in hostility to the kingdom of God, even Judah and Israel shall
fall victims to the judgment, on account of their unrighteousness and idolatry, in order that the kingdom of God may be
purified from its dross, be exalted to glory, and so be made
perfect. This is the fundamental thought of the writings of
Amos, who was called by the Lord to preach this truth to the
nation of Israel. And just as the close of his book points back
to the introduction (ch. i. and ii.), so also do the visions of the
second part correspond to the addresses of the first, embodying
the substance of the addresses in significant symbols. The
parallel between the fifth vision and the elegy struck up in ch.
v. 1 is very conspicuous; and it is also impossible to overlook
the material agreement between the first and second visions and
the enumeration in ch. iv. 6–11, of the divine visitations that
had already fallen upon Israel; whilst the third and fourth
visions set clearly before the eye the irrevocable character of
the judgments with which careless and wanton sinners are
threatened in ch. iii.–vi.

There is evidently no foundation for the assumption that the second part contains "the true kernel of his work," namely, "the addresses which Amos originally delivered at Bethel;" and that the first part, together with the introduction (ch. i.–vi.) and the Messianic conclusion (ch. ix. 11–15), is purely a written description, composed by Amos after his return from Bethel to Judah, to give a further expansion to his original utterances (Ewald, Baur). This by no means follows, either from the fact that the account of what the prophet experienced at Bethel is inserted in the series of visions, as it moves on step by step, and that the place in which it occurs (viz. ch. vii.) is evidently its original position, or from the circumstance that Amos commences his work with a saying of Joel (compare ch. i. 2 with Joel iv. 16), and evidently refers to Joel (iii. 18) even in the promise at the close (ch. ix. 13). For the position of this account in ch. vii. proves nothing further than that Amos related those visions in Bethel; and the allusion to Joel simply presupposes an acquaintance with the predictions of this prophet. If there were no previous addresses, the visions in ch. vii. and viii. would have nothing to explain their occurrence, and would also be lacking in the requisite clearness. Moreover, the work of Amos in Bethel cannot possibly be limited to ch. vii.–ix. And lastly, the addresses in ch. iv.–vi. are throughout so individual, so full of life, and so impressive, that they clearly reflect the original oral delivery, even though it may be nothing more than the essential substance of what was orally delivered, that has been given here. Only ch. i. and ii. appear to have been really conceived in the form of a written composition, and placed at the head of the book at the time when it was first compiled, although certain thoughts that had been orally expressed may lie at the foundation even there.

For the exegetical writings upon Amos, see my *Lehrbuch der Einleitung*, pp. 284–5.

EXPOSITION.

I. THE APPROACHING JUDGMENT.—CHAP. I. AND II.

Starting from the saying of Joel (iii. 16), "Jehovah will roar out of Zion, and utter His voice from Jerusalem," Amos announces the wrath of the Lord, which will discharge itself upon Damascus (i. 3–5), Philistia (i. 6–8), Tyre (i. 9, 10), Edom (i. 11, 12), Ammon (i. 13–15), Moab (ii. 1–3), Judah (ii. 4, 5), and Israel (ii. 6–16). The announcement of this judgment maintains a certain uniformity throughout; every one of these nations being threatened with the destruction of the kingdom, or with ruin and exile, "for three or four transgressions;" and the threat, as Rückert has well expressed it, "rolling like a storm, in strophe after strophe, over all the surrounding kingdoms," touching Judah as it passes along, and eventually resting over Israel. The six heathen nations mentioned, three of which are related to the covenant nation, represent all the Gentile nations, which rise up in hostility to the people or kingdom of God. For the sins on account of which they are to be punished, are not certain general breaches of morality, but crimes which they have committed against the people of God; and in the case of Judah, contempt of the commandments of the Lord, and idolatry. The whole section, not merely ch. i. 2–ii. 5, but also ch. ii. 6–16, has an introductory character. Whilst, on the one hand, the extension of the prediction of judgment to the Gentile nations indicates the necessity and universality of the judgment, which is sent to promote the interests of the kingdom of God, and preaches the truth that every one will be judged according to his attitude towards the living God; on the other hand, the place assigned to the Gentile nations, viz. before the covenant nation, not only sharpened the conscience, but taught this lesson, that if even the nations which had only sinned indirectly against the living God were visited with severe punishment, those to whom God had so gloriously revealed Himself (ch. ii. 9–11, iii. 1) would be punished still more surely for their apostasy (ch. iii. 2). It is with this design that Judah is also mentioned along with Israel, and in fact before it.

"The intention was to impress this truth most strongly upon the people of the ten tribes, that not even the possession of such glorious prerogatives as the temple and the throne of David could avert the merited punishment. If this be the energy of the justice of God, what have we to look for?" (Hengstenberg.)

Ch. i. Ver. 1 contains the heading, which has already been discussed in the Introduction; and אֲשֶׁר חָזָה ("which he saw") refers to דִּבְרֵי עָמוֹס (the words of Amos). Ver. 2 forms the Introduction, which is attached to the heading by וַיֹּאמַר, and announces a revelation of the wrath of God upon Israel, or a theocratic judgment. Ver. 2. "Jehovah roars out of Zion, and He utters His voice from Jerusalem; and the pastures of the shepherds mourn, and the head of Carmel withers." The voice of Jehovah is the thunder, the earthly substratum in which the Lord manifests His coming to judgment (see at Joel iii. 16). By the adoption of the first half of the verse word for word from Joel, Amos connects his prophecy with that of his predecessor, not so much with the intention of confirming the latter, as for the purpose of alarming the sinners who were at ease in their security, and overthrowing the delusive notion that the judgment of God would only fall upon the heathen world. This delusion he meets with the declaration, that at the threatening of the wrath of God the pastures of the shepherds, i.e. the pasture-ground of the land of Israel (cf. Joel i. 19), and the head of the forest-crowned Carmel, will fade and wither. Carmel is the oft-recurring promontory at the mouth of the Kishon on the Mediterranean (see the comm. on Josh. xix. 26 and 1 Kings xviii. 19), and not the place called Carmel on the mountains of Judah (Josh. xv. 55), to which the term ראֹשׁ (head) is inapplicable (vid. ch. ix. 3 and Mic. vii. 14). Shepherds' pastures and Carmel individualized the land of Israel in a manner that was very natural to Amos the shepherd. With this introduction, Amos announces the theme of his prophecies. And if, instead of proceeding at once to describe still further the judgment that threatens the kingdom of Israel, he first of all enumerates the surrounding nations, including Judah, as objects of the manifestation of the wrath of God, this enumeration cannot have any other object than the one described in our survey of the contents of the book. The enumeration opens with the kingdoms of Aram, Philistia.

and Tyre (Phœnicia), which were not related to Israel by any ties of kinship whatever.

Vers. 3–5. ARAM-DAMASCUS.—Ver. 3. "*Thus saith Jehovah, For three transgressions of Damascus, and for four, I shall not reverse it, because they have threshed Gilead with iron rollers, Ver. 4. I send fire into the house of Hazael, and it will eat the palaces of Ben-hadad, Ver. 5. And break in pieces the bolt of Damascus, and root out the inhabitant from the valley of Aven, and the sceptre-holder out of Beth-Eden: and the people of Aram will wander into captivity to Kir, saith Jehovah.*" In the formula, which is repeated in the case of every people, "for three transgressions, and for four," the numbers merely serve to denote the multiplicity of the sins, the exact number of which has no bearing upon the matter. "The number four is added to the number three, to characterize the latter as simply set down at pleasure; in other words, it is as much as to say that the number is not exactly three or four, but probably a still larger number" (Hitzig). The expression, therefore, denotes not a small but a large number of crimes, or "ungodliness in its worst form" (Luther; see at Hos. vi. 2[1]). That these numbers are to be understood in this way, and not to be taken in a literal sense, is unquestionably evident from the fact, that in the more precise account of the sins which follows, as a rule, only one especially grievous crime is mentioned by way of example. לֹא אֲשִׁיבֶנּוּ (I will not reverse it) is inserted before the more minute description of the crimes, to show that the threat is irrevocable. הֵשִׁיב signifies to turn, *i.e.* to make a thing go back, to withdraw it, as in Num. xxiii. 20, Isa. xliii. 13. The suffix attached to אֲשִׁיבֶנּוּ refers neither to *qōlō* (his voice), nor "to the idea of דָּבָר which is implied in כֹּה אָמַר (thus saith), or the substance of the threatening thunder-voice" (Baur); for *hēshībh dābhâr* signifies to give an answer, and never to make a word ineffectual. The reference is to the punishment threatened afterwards, where the masculine stands in the place of the neuter. Consequently the close of the verse contains the epexegesis of

---

[1] J. Marck has correctly explained it thus: "When this perfect number (*three*) is followed by *four*, by way of gradation, God not only declares that the measure of iniquity is full, but that it is filled to overflowing and beyond all measure."

the first clause, and vers. 4 and 5 follow with the explanation of
לא אשׁיבנו (I will not turn it). The threshing of the Gileadites
with iron threshing-machines is mentioned as the principal
transgression of the Syrian kingdom, which is here named after
the capital Damascus (see at 2 Sam. viii. 6). This took place
at the conquest of the Israelitish land to the east of the Jordan
by Hazael during the reign of Jehu (2 Kings x. 32, 33, cf.
ch. xiii. 7), when the conquerors acted so cruelly towards the
Gileadites, that they even crushed the prisoners to pieces with
iron threshing-machines, according to a barbarous war-custom
that is met with elsewhere (see at 2 Sam. xii. 31). *Chârûts*
(= *chârîts*, 2 Sam. xii. 31), lit. sharpened, is a poetical term
applied to the threshing-roller, or threshing-cart (*môrag chârûts*,
Isa. xli. 15). According to Jerome, it was "a kind of cart
with toothed iron wheels underneath, which was driven about
to crush the straw in the threshing-floors after the grain had
been beaten out." The threat is individualized historically
thus: in the case of the capital, the burning of the palaces is
predicted; and in that of two other places, the destruction of
the people and their rulers; so that both of them apply to
both, or rather to the whole kingdom. The palaces of Hazael
and Benhadad are to be sought for in Damascus, the capital
of the kingdom (Jer. xlix. 27). Hazael was the murderer of
Benhadad I., to whom the prophet Elisha foretold that he
would reign over Syria, and predicted the cruelties that he
would practise towards Israel (2 Kings viii. 7 sqq.). Benhadad
is generally regarded as his son; but the plural "palaces" leads
us rather to think of both the first and second Benhadad, and
this is favoured by the circumstance that it was only during
his father's reign that Benhadad II. oppressed Israel, whereas
after his death, and when he himself ascended the throne, the
conquered provinces were wrested from him by Joash king of
Israel (2 Kings xiii. 22-25). The breaking of the bar (the
bolt of the gate) denotes the conquest of the capital; and the
cutting off of the inhabitants of *Biq'ath-Aven* indicates the
slaughter connected with the capture of the towns, and not
their deportation; for *hikhrîth* means to exterminate, so that
gâlâh (captivity) in the last clause applies to the remainder of
the population that had not been slain in war. In the parallel
clause תוֹמֵךְ שֵׁבֶט, the sceptre-holder, *i.e.* the ruler (either the

king or his deputy), corresponds to *yōshēbh* (the inhabitant); and
the thought expressed is, that both prince and people, both high
and low, shall perish.   The two places, *Valley-Aven* and *Beth-
Eden*, cannot be discovered with any certainty; but at any rate
they were capitals, and possibly they may have been the seat of
royal palaces as well as Damascus, which was the first capital
of the kingdom.   בִּקְעַת אָוֶן, valley of nothingness, or of idols, is
supposed by Ewald and Hitzig to be a name given to Heliopolis or Baalbek, after the analogy of Beth-Aven = Bethel (see
at Hos. v. 8).   They base their opinion upon the Alex. rendering ἐκ πεδίου Ὤν, taken in connection with the Alex. interpretation of the Egyptian *On* (Gen. xli. 45) as Heliopolis.   But
as the LXX. have interpreted אָוֶן by Heliopolis in the book of
Genesis, whereas here they have merely reproduced the Hebrew
letters אָוֶן by Ὤν, as they have in other places as well (*e.g.* Hos.
iv. 15, v. 8, x. 5, 8), where Heliopolis cannot for a moment be
thought of, the πεδίον Ὤν of the LXX. furnishes no evidence
in favour of Heliopolis, still less does it warrant an alteration of
the Hebrew pointing (into אוֹן).   Even the Chaldee and Syriac
have taken בִּקְעַת אָוֶן as a proper name, and Ephraem Syrus
speaks of it as "a place in the neighbourhood of Damascus,
distinguished for idol-chapels."   The supposition that it is a
city is also favoured by the analogy of the other threatenings,
in which, for the most part, cities only are mentioned.   Others
understand by it the valley near Damascus, or the present
Bekaa between Lebanon and Antilibanus, in which Heliopolis
was always the most distinguished city, and Robinson has pronounced in favour of this (*Bibl. Res.* p. 677).   *Bēth-ʿEden, i.e.*
house of delight, is not to be sought for in the present village
of Eden, on the eastern slope of Lebanon, near to the cedar
forest of Bshirrai, as the Arabic name of this village اهدن has
nothing in common with the Hebrew עֶדֶן (see at 2 Kings xix.
12); but it is the Παράδεισος of the Greeks, which Ptolemy
(v. 15, 20) places ten degrees south and five degrees east of
Laodicea, and which Robinson imagines that he has found in
Old Jusieh, not far from Ribleh, a place belonging to the
times before the Saracens, with very extensive ruins (see *Bibl.
Researches*, pp. 542–6, and 556).   The rest of the population
of Aram would be carried away to *Kir, i.e.* to the country on

the banks of the river *Kur*, from which, according to ch. ix. 7, the Syrians originally emigrated. This prediction was fulfilled when the Assyrian king Tiglath-pileser conquered Damascus in the time of Ahaz, and broke up the kingdom of Syria (2 Kings xvi. 9). The closing words, *'âmar Y'hōvâh* (saith the Lord), serve to add strength to the threat, and therefore recur in vers. 8, 15, and ch. ii. 3.

Vers. 6–8. PHILISTIA.—Ver. 6. "*Thus saith Jehovah, For three transgressions of Gaza, and for four, I shall not reverse it, because they carried away captives in full number to deliver them up to Edom, Ver. 7. I send fire into the wall of Gaza, and it will eat their palaces; Ver. 8. And I exterminate the inhabitant from Ashdod, and the sceptre-holder from Askelon, and turn my hand against Ekron, and the remnant of the Philistines will perish, saith the Lord Jehovah.*" Instead of the Philistines generally, the prophet mentions *Gaza* in ver. 6. This is still a considerable town, bearing the old name *Guzzeh* (see the comm. on Josh. xiii. 3), and was the one of the five capitals of the Philistines which had taken the most active part as a great commercial town in handing over the Israelitish prisoners to the Edomites. For it is evident that Gaza is simply regarded as a representative of Philistia, from the fact that in the announcement of the punishment, the other capitals of Philistia are also mentioned. *Gâlûth sh'lēmâh* is correctly explained by Jerome thus: "a captivity so perfect and complete, that not a single captive remained who was not delivered to the Idumæans." The reference is to captive Israelites, who were carried off by the Philistines, and disposed of by them to the Edomites, the arch-enemies of Israel. Amos no doubt had in his mind the invasion of Judah by the Philistines and tribes of Arabia Petræa in the time of Joram, which is mentioned in 2 Chron. xxi. 16, and to which Joel had already alluded in Joel iv. 3 sqq., where the Phœnicians and Philistines are threatened with divine retribution for having plundered the land, and sold the captive Judæans to the Javanites (Ionians). But it by no means follows from this, that the "sons of Javan" mentioned in Joel iv. 6 are not Greeks, but the inhabitants of the Arabian *Javan* noticed in Ezek. xxvii. 19. The fact was simply this: the Philistines sold one portion of the many prisoners, taken at that time, to the Edomites, and the rest to the Phœnicians, who disposed of them again to the Greeks. Joel simply mentions the latter circumstance, because, in accordance with the object of his prophecy, his design was to show the wide dispersion of the Jews, and their future gathering out of all the lands of their banishment. Amos, on the other hand, simply condemns the delivering of the captives to Edom, the arch-foe of Israel, to indicate the greatness of the sin involved in this treatment of the covenant nation, or the hatred which the Philistines had displayed thereby. As a punishment for this, the cities of Philistia would be burned by their enemies, the inhabitants would be exterminated, and the remnant perish. Here again, as in vers. 4, 5, the threat is rhetorically individualized, so that in the case of one city the burning of the city itself is predicted, and in that of another the destruction of its inhabitants. (On Ashdod, Askelon, and Ekron, see the comm. on Josh. xiii. 3.) הֲשִׁיב יָד, to return the hand, *i.e.* to turn or stretch it out again (see comm. on 2 Sam. viii. 3). The use of this expression may be explained on the ground, that the destruction of the inhabitants of Ashdod and Askelon has already been thought of as a stretching out of the hand. The fifth of the Philistian capitals, Gath, is not mentioned, though not for the reason assigned by *Kimchi*, viz. that it belonged to the kings of Judah, or had been conquered by Uzziah, for Uzziah had not only conquered Gath and Jabneh, but had taken Ashdod as well, and thrown down the walls (2 Chron. xxvi. 6), and yet Amos mentions Ashdod; nor because Gath had been taken by the Syrians (2 Kings xii. 18), for this Syrian conquest was not a lasting one, and in the prophet's time (cf. ch. vi. 2), and even later (cf. Mic. i. 10), it still maintained its independence, and was a very distinguished city; but for the simple reason that the individualizing description given by the prophet did not require the complete enumeration of all the capitals, and the idea of Gath being excepted from the fate with which the other cities are threatened, is precluded by the comprehensive terms in which the threat is concluded. For whilst "the remnant of the Philistines" does indeed denote "not the remaining Philistines who had not yet been named, but all that was still in existence, and had escaped destruction" (ch. ix. 12 and Jer. vi. 9), it nevertheless includes not merely the four states just named, but every part of Philistia that had hitherto escaped destruction, so that Gath must be included.

Vers. 9, 10. Tyre or Phœnicia.—Ver. 9. "*Thus saith Jehovah : For three transgressions of Tyre, and for four, I shall not reverse it, because they have delivered up prisoners in full number to Edom, and have not remembered the brotherly covenant,* Ver. 10. *I send fire into the wall of Tyrus, and it will devour their palaces.*" In the case of Phœnicia, the capital only (Tzōr, *i.e.* Tyrus ; see at Josh. xix. 29) is mentioned. The crime with which it is charged is similar to the one for which the Philistines were blamed, with this exception, that instead of עַל־הַגְלוֹתָם לְהַסְגִּיר (ver. 6) we have simply עַל־הַסְגִּירָם. If, therefore, Tyre is only charged with delivering up the captives to Edom, and not with having carried them away, it must have bought the prisoners from an enemy of Israel, and then disposed of them to Edom. From what enemy they were purchased, it is impossible to determine with certainty. Probably from the Syrians, in the wars of Hazael and Benhadad with Israel ; for there is nothing at variance with this in the fact that, when they purchased Israelitish captives in the time of Joram, they sold them to Javan. For a commercial nation, carrying on so extensive a trade as the Phœnicians did, would have purchased prisoners in more than one war, and would also have disposed of them as slaves to more nations than one. Tyre had contracted all the more guilt through this trade in Israelitish slaves, from the fact that it had thereby been unmindful of the brotherly covenant, *i.e.* of the friendly relation existing between Israel and itself—for example, the friendly alliance into which David and Solomon had entered with the king of Tyre (2 Sam. v. 11 ; 1 Kings v. 15 sqq.)—and also from the fact that no king of Israel or Judah had ever made war upon Phœnicia.

Vers. 11, 12. Edom.—Ver. 11. "*Thus saith Jehovah: For three transgressions of Edom, and for four, I shall not reverse it, because it pursues its brother with the sword, and stifles its compassion, and its anger tears in pieces for ever, and it keeps its wrath for ever,* Ver. 12. *I send fire into Teman, and it will*

devour the palaces of Bozrah." Edom and the two following
nations were related to Israel by lineal descent. In the case of
Edom, Amos does not condemn any particular sins, but simply
its implacable, mortal hatred towards its brother nation Israel,
which broke out into acts of cruelty at every possible opportunity. וְשִׁחֵת רַחֲמָיו, he annihilates, *i.e.* suppresses, stifles his
sympathy or his compassionate love; this is still dependent
upon עַל רָדְפוֹ, the preposition עַל continuing in force as a conjunction before the infinitive (*i.e.* as equivalent to עַל אֲשֶׁר), and
the infinitive passing into the finite verb (cf. ch. ii. 4). In the
next clause אַפּוֹ is the subject: its wrath tears in pieces, *i.e.*
rages destructively (compare Job xvi. 9, where *târaph* is applied to the wrath of God). In the last clause, on the other
hand, Edom is again the subject; but it is now regarded as a
kingdom, and construed as a feminine, and consequently עֶבְרָתוֹ
is the object, and placed at the head as an absolute noun.
שְׁמָרָה, with the tone upon the *penult. (milel)* on account of *netsach*,
which follows with the tone upon the first syllable, stands for
שְׁמָרָהּ (it preserves it), the *mappik* being omitted in the toneless
syllable (compare Ewald, § 249, *b*). If עֶבְרָתוֹ were the subject,
the verb would have to be pointed שָׁמְרָה. Again, the rendering
proposed by Ewald, "his fury lies in wait for ever," is precluded by the fact that שָׁמַר, when applied to wrath in Jer.
iii. 5, signifies to keep, or preserve, and also by the fact that
lying in wait is generally inapplicable to an emotion. *Teman,*
according to Jerome (*ad h. l.*), is *Idumæorum regio quæ vergit
ad australem partem,* so that here, just as in ch. ii. 2 and 5,
the land is mentioned first, and then the capital.[1] *Bozrah,*
an important city, supposed to be the capital of Idumæa (see
comm. on Gen. xxxvi. 33). It was to the south of the
Dead Sea, and has been preserved in *el-Buseireh,* a village
with ruins in Jebâl (see Robinson, *Pal.* ii. p. 570), and must
not be confounded with *Bossra* in Hauran (Burckhardt, *Syr.*
p. 364).

[1] It is true that, according to Eusebius, Jerome does also mention in
the *Onom.* a *villa* (κώμη) named Teman, which was five Roman miles from
Petra, and in which there was a Roman garrison; and also that there is a
Teman in Eastern Hauran (see Wetzstein in Delitzsch's *Comm. on Job,*
i. 73); but in the Old Testament Teman is never to be understood as referring to a city.

Vers. 13–15. AMMON.—Ver. 13. *"Thus saith Jehovah:
For three transgressions of the sons of Ammon, and for four,
I shall not reverse it, because they have ripped up the pregnant
women of Gilead, to widen their border,* Ver. 14. *I kindle fire in
the wall of Rabbah, and it will devour its palaces, with the war-
cry on the day of slaughter, in the storm on the day of the tempest.*
Ver. 15. *And their king shall go into captivity, he and his princes
all at once, saith Jehovah."* The occasion on which the Ammonites were guilty of such cruelty towards the Israelites as
is here condemned, is not recorded in the historical books of
the Old Testament; possibly during the wars of Hazael with
Israel, when they availed themselves of the opportunity to
widen their territory by conquering back the land which had
been wrested from them by Sihon king of the Amorites, and
was then taken possession of by the Israelites, when he was
overcome by them,—a thing which they had attempted once
before in the time of Jephthah the judge (Judg. xi. 12 sqq.).
We may see from Jer. xlix. 1 sqq. that they had taken possession of the territory of the tribe of Gad, which lay nearest to
them, though probably not till after the carrying away of the
tribes beyond Jordan by the Assyrians (2 Kings xv. 29). The
ripping up of the women with child (see at 2 Kings viii. 12)
is singled out as the climax of the cruelties which the Ammonites inflicted upon the Israelites during the war. As a
punishment for this, their capital was to be burned, and the
king, with the princes, to wander into exile, and consequently
their kingdom was to be destroyed. *Rabbâh, i.e.* the great one,
is the abbreviated name of the capital; Rabbah of the children
of Ammon, which has been preserved in the ruins of *Aurân*
(see at Deut. iii. 11). The threat is sharpened by the clause
בִּתְרוּעָה וגו׳, at the war-cry on the field of battle, *i.e.* an actual
fact, when the enemy shall take the city by storm. בְּסַעַר וגו׳ is
a figurative expression applied to the storming of a city carried
by assault, like בְּסוּפָה in Num. xxi. 14. The reading מַלְכָּם,
" their (the Ammonites') king," is confirmed by the LXX. and
the Chaldee, and required by וְשָׂרָיו (cf. ch. ii. 3), whereas
Μαλχόμ, *Melchom,* which is found in Aq., Symm., Jerome, and
the Syriac, rests upon a false interpretation.

Chap ii. Vers. 1–3. MOAB.—Ver. 1. *"Thus saith Jehovah:*

*For three transgressions of Moab, and for four, I shall not reverse
it, because it has burned the bones of the king of Edom into lime,*
Ver. 2. *I send fire into Moab, and it will devour the palaces of
Kirioth, and Moab will perish in the tumult, in the war-cry, in
the trumpet-blast.* Ver. 3. *And I cut off the judge from the
midst thereof, and all its princes do I strangle with it, saith
Jehovah.*" The burning of the bones of the king of Edom is
not burning while he was still alive, but the burning of the
corpse into lime, *i.e.* so completely that the bones turned into
powder like lime (D. Kimchi), to cool his wrath still further
upon the dead man (cf. 2 Kings xxiii. 16). This is the only
thing blamed, not his having put him to death. No record has
been preserved of this event in the historical books of the Old
Testament; but it was no doubt connected with the war referred to in 2 Kings iii., which Joram of Israel and Jehoshaphat of Judah waged against the Moabites in company with
the king of Edom; so that the Jewish tradition found in
Jerome, viz. that after this war the Moabites dug up the bones
of the king of Edom from the grave, and heaped insults upon
them by burning them to ashes, is apparently not without foundation. As Amos in the case of all the other nations has mentioned only crimes that were committed against the covenant
nation, the one with which the Moabites are charged must have
been in some way associated with either Israel or Judah, that
is to say, it must have been committed upon a king of Edom,
who was a vassal of Judah, and therefore not very long after
this war, since the Edomites shook off their dependence upon
Judah in less than ten years from that time (2 Kings viii. 20).
As a punishment for this, Moab was to be laid waste by the
fire of war, and Keriyoth with its palaces to be burned down.
הַקְּרִיּוֹת is not an appellative noun (τῶν πόλεων αὐτῆς, LXX.),
but a proper name of one of the chief cities of Moab (cf. Jer.
xlviii. 24, 41), the ruins of which have been discovered by
Burckhardt (*Syr.* p. 630) and Seetzen (ii. p. 342, cf. iv. p.
384) in the decayed town of *Kereyat* or *Körriât.* The application of the term מֵת to Moab is to be explained on the supposition that the nation is personified. שָׁאוֹן signifies war
tumult, and בִּתְרוּעָה is explained as in ch. i. 14 by בְּקוֹל שׁוֹפָר,
blast of the trumpets, the signal for the assault or for the commencement of the battle. The judge with all the princes shall

be cut off *miqqirbâh*, *i.e.* out of the land of Moab. The feminine suffix refers to Moab as a land or kingdom, and not to Keriyoth. From the fact that the *shōphēt* is mentioned instead of the king, it has been concluded by some that Moab had no king at that time, but had only a *shōphēt* as its ruler ; and they have sought to account for this on the ground that Moab was at that time subject to the kingdom of the ten tribes (Hitzig and Ewald). But there is no notice in the history of anything of the kind, and it cannot possibly be inferred from the fact that Jeroboam restored the ancient boundaries of the kingdom as far as the Dead Sea (2 Kings xiv. 25). *Shōphēt* is analogous to *tōmēkh shēbhet* in ch. i. 5, and is probably nothing more than a rhetorical expression applied to the מֶלֶךְ, who is so called in the threat against Ammon, and simply used for the sake of variety. The threatening prophecies concerning all the nations and kingdoms mentioned from ch. i. 6 onwards were fulfilled by the Chaldeans, who conquered all these kingdoms, and carried the people themselves into captivity. For fuller remarks upon this point, see at Jer. xlvii. 49 and Ezek. xxv. 28.

Vers. 4, 5. JUDAH.—Ver. 4. " *Thus saith Jehovah : Fc three transgressions of Judah, and for four, I shall not reverse it, because they have despised the law of Jehovah, and have not kept His ordinances, and their lies led them astray, after which their fathers walked,* Ver. 5. *I send fire into Judah, and it will devour the palaces of Jerusalem.*" With the announcement that the storm of the wrath of God will also burst upon Judah, Amos prepares the way for passing on to Israel, the principal object of his prophecies. In the case of Judah, he condemns its contempt of the law of its God, and also its idolatry. *Tōrâh* is the sum and substance of all the instructions and all the commandments which Jehovah had given to His people as the rule of life. *Chuqqīm* are the separate precepts contained in the *thōrâh*, including not only the ceremonial commands, but the moral commandments also ; for the two clauses are not only parallel, but synonymous. כִּזְבֵיהֶם, their lies, are their idols, as we may see from the relative clause, since " walking after" (*hâlakh 'achărē*) is the standing expression for idolatry. Amos calls the idols *lies*, not only as *res quœ fallunt* (Ges.), but as fabrications and nonentities (*'ĕlīlīm* and *hăbhâlīm*);

having no reality in themselves, and therefore quite unable to perform what was expected of them. The "fathers" who walked after these lies were their forefathers generally, since the nation of Israel practised idolatry even in the desert (cf. ch. v. 26), and was more or less addicted to it ever afterwards, with the sole exception of the times of Joshua, Samuel, David, and part of the reign of Solomon, so that even the most godly kings of Judah were unable to eradicate the worship upon the high places. The punishment threatened in consequence, namely, that Jerusalem should be reduced to ashes, was carried out by Nebuchadnezzar.

Vers. 6–16. After this introduction, the prophet's address turns to Israel of the ten tribes, and in precisely the same form as in the case of the nations already mentioned, announces the judgment as irrevocable. At the same time, he gives a fuller description of the sins of Israel, condemning first of all the prevailing crimes of injustice and oppression, of shameless immorality and daring contempt of God (vers. 6–8); and secondly, its scornful contempt of the benefits conferred by the Lord (vers. 9–12), and threatening inevitable trouble in consequence (vers. 13–16). Ver. 6. *"Thus saith Jehovah: For three transgressions of Israel, and for four, I shall not reverse it, because they sell the righteous for money, and the poor for a pair of shoes. Ver. 7. They who pant after dust of the earth upon the head of the poor, and bend the way of the meek: and a man and his father go to the same girl, to desecrate my holy name. Ver. 8. And they stretch themselves upon pawned clothes by every altar, and they drink the wine of the punished in the house of their God."* The prophet condemns four kinds of crimes. The *first* is unjust treatment, or condemnation of the innocent in their administration of justice. Selling the righteous for silver, *i.e.* for money, refers to the judges, who were bribed to punish a man as guilty of the crime of which he was accused, when he was really *tsaddīq, i.e.* righteous in a judicial, not in a moral sense, or innocent of any punishable crime. *Bakkeseph*, for money, *i.e.* either to obtain money, or for the money which they had already received, viz. from the accuser, for condemning the innocent. בַּעֲבוּר, on account of, is not synonymous with בְּ *pretii*; for they did not sell the poor man merely to get a pair of sandals for him, as the worst

possible slave was certainly worth much more than this (cf.
Ex. xxi. 32); but the poor debtor who could not pay for a pair
of shoes, *i.e.* for the merest trifle, the judge would give up to
the creditor for a slave, on the strength of the law in Lev.
xxv. 39 (cf. 2 Kings iv. 1). As a *second* crime, Amos reproves
in ver. 7*a* their thirst for the oppression of the quiet in the
land. דַּלִּים, ταπεινοί, and עֲנָוִים, πραεῖς. The address is carried
on in participles, in the form of lively appeal, instead of quiet
description, as is frequently the case in Amos (cf. ch. v. 7, vi.
3 sqq., 13, viii. 14), and also in other books (cf. Isa. xl. 22, 26 ;
Ps. xix. 11). In the present instance, the article before the
participle points back to the suffix in מִכְרָם, and the finite verb
is not introduced till the second clause. שָׁאַף, to gasp, to pant,
to long eagerly for earth-dust upon the head of the poor, *i.e.* to
long to see the head of the poor covered with earth or dust, or
to bring them into such a state of misery, that they scatter
dust upon their head (cf. Job ii. 12 ; 2 Sam. i. 2). The explanation given by Hitzig is too far-fetched and unnatural,
viz. that they grudge the man in distress even the handful of
dust that he has strewn upon his head, and avariciously long
for it themselves. To bend the way of the meek, *i.e.* to bring
them into a trap, or cast them headlong into destruction by
impediments and stumblingblocks laid in their path. The way
is the way of life, their outward course. The idea that the
way refers to the judgment or legal process is too contracted.
The *third* crime is their profanation of the name of God by
shameless immorality (ver. 7*b*) ; and the *fourth*, desecration of
the sanctuary by drinking carousals (ver. 8). A man and his
father, *i.e.* both son and father, go to the girl, *i.e.* to the prostitute. The meaning is, to one and the same girl; but 'achath
is omitted, to preclude all possible misunderstanding, as though
going to different prostitutes was allowed. This sin was tantamount to incest, which, according to the law, was to be
punished with death (cf. Lev. xviii. 7, 15, and xx. 11). Temple
girls (*q°dēshōth*) are not to be thought of here. The profanation of the name of God by such conduct as this does not
indicate prostitution in the temple itself, such as was required
by the licentious worship of Baal and Asherah (Ewald, Maurer,
etc.), but consisted in a daring contempt of the commandments
of God, as the original passage (Lev. xxii. 32) from which

Amos took the words clearly shows (cf. Jer. xxxiv. 16). By *l^ema'an*, in order that (not "so that"), the profanation of the holy name of God is represented as intentional, to bring out the daring character of the sin, and to show that it did not arise from weakness or ignorance, but was practised with studious contempt of the holy God. *B^egâdîm chăbhulîm*, pawned clothes, *i.e.* upper garments, consisting of a large square piece of cloth, which was wrapt all around, and served the poor for a counterpane as well. If a poor man was obliged to pawn his upper garment, it was to be returned to him before night came on (Ex. xxii. 25), and a garment so pawned was not to be slept upon (Deut. xxiv. 12, 13). But godless usurers kept such pledges, and used them as cloths upon which they stretched their limbs at feasts (*yattû, hiphil*, to stretch out, *sc.* the body or its limbs); and this they did by every altar, at sacrificial meals, without standing in awe of God. It is very evident that Amos is speaking of sacrificial feasting, from the reference in the second clause of the verse to the drinking of wine in the house of God. עֲנוּשִׁים, punished in money, *i.e.* fined. Wine of the punished is wine purchased by the produce of the fines. Here again the emphasis rests upon the fact, that such drinking carousals were held in the house of God. *'Elôhêhem*, not their gods (idols), but their God; for Amos had in his mind the sacred places at Bethel and Dan, in which the Israelites worshipped Jehovah as their God under the symbol of an ox (calf). The expression *col-mizbêăch* (every altar) is not at variance with this; for even if *col* pointed to a plurality of altars, these altars were still *bāmōth*, dedicated to Jehovah. If the prophet had also meant to condemn actual idolatry, *i.e.* the worship of heathen deities, he would have expressed this more clearly; to say nothing of the fact, that in the time of Jeroboam II. there was no heathenish idolatry in the kingdom of the ten tribes, or, at any rate, it was not publicly maintained.

And if this daring contempt of the commandments of God was highly reprehensible even in itself, it became perfectly inexcusable if we bear in mind that Israel was indebted to the Lord its God for its elevation into an independent nation, and also for its sacred calling. For this reason, the prophet reminds the people of the manifestations of grace which it had received from its God (vers. 9–11). Ver. 9. "*And yet I destroyed the Amorite before them, whose height was like the height of the cedars, and who was strong as the oaks; and I destroyed his fruit from above, and his roots from beneath.* Ver. 10. *And yet I brought you up from the land of Egypt, and led you forty years in the desert, to take possession of the land of the Amorite.*" The repeated וְאָנֹכִי is used with peculiar emphasis, and serves to bring out the contrast between the conduct of the Israelites towards the Lord, and the fidelity of the Lord towards Israel. Of the two manifestations of divine grace to which Israel owed its existence as an independent nation, Amos mentions first of all the destruction of the former inhabitants of Canaan (Ex. xxiii. 27 sqq., xxxiv. 11); and secondly, what was earlier in point of time, namely, the deliverance out of Egypt and guidance through the Arabian desert; not because the former act of God was greater than the latter, but in order to place first what the Lord had done for the nation, and follow that up with what He had done to the nation, that he may be able to append to this what He still continues to do (ver. 11). The nations destroyed before Israel are called Amorites, from the most powerful of the Canaanitish tribes, as in Gen. xv. 16, Josh. xxiv. 15, etc. To show, however, that Israel was not able to destroy this people by its own strength, but that Jehovah the Almighty God alone could accomplish this, he proceeds to transfer to the whole nation what the Israelitish spies reported as to their size, more especially as to the size of particular giants (Num. xiii. 32, 33), and describes the Amorites as giants as lofty as trees and as strong as trees, and, continuing the same figure, depicts their utter destruction or extermination as the destruction of their fruit and of their roots. For this figure of speech, in which the posterity of a nation is regarded as its fruit, and the kernel of the nation out of which it springs as the root, see Ezek. xvii. 9, Hos. ix. 16, Job xviii. 16. These two manifestations of divine mercy Moses impressed more than once upon the hearts of the people in his last addresses, to urge them in consequence to hold fast to the divine commandments and to the love of God (cf. Deut. viii. 2 sqq., ix. 1–6, xxix. 1–8).

But Jehovah had not only put Israel into possession of Canaan; He had also continually manifested Himself to it as the founder and promoter of its spiritual prosperity. Ver. 11. *"And I raised up some of your sons as prophets, and some of your young men as dedicated ones (Nazirœans). Ah, is it not so, ye sons of Israel? is the saying of Jehovah.* Ver. 12. *But ye made the dedicated drink wine, and ye commanded the prophets, saying, Ye shall not prophesy."* The institution of prophecy and the law of the Nazarite were gifts of grace, in which Israel had an advantage over every other nation, and by which it was distinguished above the heathen as the nation of God and the medium of salvation. Amos simply reminds the people of these, and not of earthly blessings, which the heathen also enjoyed, since the former alone were real pledges of the covenant of grace made by Jehovah with Israel; and it was in the contempt and abuse of these gifts of grace that the ingratitude of the nation was displayed in the most glaring light. The Nazarites are placed by the side of the prophets, who proclaimed to the nation the counsel and will of the Lord, because, although as a rule the condition of a Nazarite was merely the consequence of his own free will and the fulfilment of a particular vow, it was nevertheless so far a gift of grace from the Lord, that the resolution to perform such a vow proceeded from the inward impulse of the Spirit of God, and the performance itself was rendered possible through the power of this Spirit alone. (For a general discussion of the law of the Nazarite, see the commentary on Num. vi. 2-12, and my *Biblical Antiquities,* § 67.) The raising up of Nazarites was not only intended to set before the eyes of the people the object of their divine calling, or their appointment to be a holy nation of God, but also to show them how the Lord bestowed the power to carry out this object. But instead of suffering themselves to be spurred on by these types to strive earnestly after sanctification of life, they tempted the Nazarites to break their vow by drinking wine, from which they were commanded to abstain, as being irreconcilable with the seriousness of their sanctification (see my *Bibl. Ant.* § 67); and the prophets they prohibited from prophesying, because the word of God was burdensome to them (cf. ch. vii. 10 sqq.; Mic. ii. 6).

This base contempt of their covenant mercies the Lord would visit with a severe punishment. Ver. 13. *" Behold, I will press you down, as the cart presses that is filled with sheaves.*

Ver. 14. *And the flight will be lost to the swift, and the strong one will not fortify his strength, and the hero will not deliver his soul.* Ver. 15. *And the carrier of the bow will not stand, and the swift-footed will not deliver, and the rider of the horse will not save his soul.* Ver. 16. *And the courageous one among the heroes will flee away naked in that day, is the saying of Jehovah."* The Lord threatens as a punishment a severe oppression, which no one will be able to escape. The allusion is to the force of war, under which even the bravest and most able heroes will succumb. הֵעִיק, from עוּק, Aramæan for צוּק, to press, construed with *tachath*, in the sense of κατά, downwards, to press down upon a person, *i.e.* to press him down (Winer, Ges., Ewald). This meaning is established by עָקָה in Ps. lv. 4, and by מוּעָקָה in Ps. lxvi. 11; so that there is no necessity to resort to the Arabic, as Hitzig does, or to alterations of the text, or to follow Baur, who gives the word the meaning, " to feel one's self pressed under another," for which there is no foundation in the language, and which does not even yield a suitable sense. The comparison instituted here to the pressure of a cart filled with sheaves, does not warrant the conclusion that Jehovah must answer to the cart; the simile is not to be carried out to this extent. The object to תָּעִיק is wanting, but may easily be supplied from the thought, namely, the ground over which the cart is driven. The לְ attached to הַמְלֵאָה belongs to the latitude allowed in ordinary speech, and gives to מָלֵאָה the reflective meaning, which is full in itself, has quite filled itself (cf. Ewald, § 315, *a*). In vers. 14-16 the effects of this pressure are individualized. No one will escape from it. אָבַד מָנוֹס, flight is lost to the swift, *i.e.* the swift will not find time enough to flee. The allusion to heroes and bearers of the bow shows that the pressure is caused by war. קַל בְּרַגְלָיו belong together: "He who is light in his feet." The swift-footed will no more save his life than the rider upon a horse. נַפְשׁוֹ in ver. 15 belongs to both clauses. אַמִּץ לִבּוֹ, the strong in his heart, *i.e.* the hearty, courageous. עָרוֹם, naked, *i.e.* so as to leave behind him his garment, by which the enemy seizes him, like the young man in Mark xiv. 52. This threat, which implies that the kingdom will be destroyed, is carried out still further in the prophet's following addresses.

II. PROPHECIES CONCERNING ISRAEL.—Chap. III.-VI.

Although the expression "Hear this word," which is repeated at the commencement of ch. iii. iv. and v., suggests the idea of three addresses, the contents of these chapters show that they do not contain three separate addresses delivered to the people by Amos at different times, but that they group together the leading thoughts of appeals delivered by word of mouth, so as to form one long admonition to repentance. Commencing with the proofs of his right to predict judgment to the nation on account of its sins (ch. iii. 1–8), the prophet exposes the wickedness of Israel in general (ch. iii. 9–iv. 3), and then shows the worthlessness of the nation's trust in idolatry (ch. iv. 4–13), and lastly announces the destruction of the kingdom as the inevitable consequence of the prevailing injustice and ungodliness (ch. v. and vi.).

ANNOUNCEMENT OF THE JUDGMENT.—CHAP. III.

Because the Lord has chosen Israel to be His people, He must visit all its sins (ver. 2), and has commissioned the prophet to announce this punishment (vers. 3–8). As Israel has heaped up oppression, violence, and wickedness, an enemy will come upon the land and plunder Samaria, and cause its inhabitants to perish, and demolish the altars of Bethel, and destroy the capital (vers. 9–15).

Vers. 1 and 2 contain the introduction and the leading thought of the whole of the prophetic proclamation. Ver. 1. *" Hear this word which Jehovah speaketh concerning you, O sons of Israel, concerning the whole family which I have brought up out of the land of Egypt, saying :* Ver. 2. *You only have I acknowledged of all the families of the earth ; therefore will I visit all your iniquities upon you."* The word of the Lord is addressed to all the family of Israel, which God had brought up out of Egypt, that is to say, to all the twelve tribes of the covenant nation, although in what follows it is the ten tribes of Israel alone who are primarily threatened with the destruction of the kingdom, to indicate at the very outset that Judah might anticipate a similar fate if it did not turn to its God with sincerity. The threat is introduced by the thought that its divine election would not secure the sinful nation against punishment, but that, on the contrary, the relation of grace into which the Lord had entered with Israel demanded the punishment of all evil deeds. This cuts off the root of all false confidence in divine election. "To whomsoever much is given, of him shall be much required. The greater the measure of grace, the greater also is the punishment if it is neglected or despised." This is the fundamental law of the kingdom of God. יָדַע does not mean to know, to become acquainted with, or to take knowledge of a person (Hitzig), but to acknowledge. Acknowledgment on the part of God is not merely taking notice, but is energetic, embracing man in his inmost being, embracing and penetrating with divine love; so that ידע not only includes the idea of love and care, as in Hos. xiii. 5, but expresses generally the gracious fellowship of the Lord with Israel, as in Gen. xviii. 19, and is practically equivalent to electing, including both the motive and the result of election. And because Jehovah had acknowledged, *i.e.* had singled out and chosen Israel as the nation best fitted to be the vehicle of His salvation, He must of necessity punish all its misdeeds, in order to purify it from the dross of sin, and make it a holy vessel of His saving grace.

Vers. 3–8. But this truth met with contradiction in the nation itself. The proud self-secure sinners would not hear such prophesying as this (compare ch. ii. 4, vii. 10 sqq.). Amos therefore endeavours, before making any further announcement of the judgment of God, to establish his right and duty to prophesy, by a chain-like series of similes drawn from life. Ver. 3. *"Do two walk together without having agreed?* Ver. 4. *Does the lion roar in the forest, and he has no prey? does the young lion utter his cry out of his den, without having taken anything? Ver. 5. Does the bird fall into the trap on the ground, when there is no snare for him? does the trap rise up from the earth without making a capture? Ver. 6. Or is the trumpet blown in the city, and the people are not alarmed? or does misfortune happen in the city, and Jehovah has not done it? Ver. 7. For the Lord Jehovah does nothing at all, without having revealed His secret to His servants the prophets. Ver. 8. The lion has roared; who does not fear? the Lord Jehovah hath spoken; who must not*

prophesy?" The contents of these verses are not to be reduced to the general thought, that a prophet could no more
speak without a divine impulse than any other effect could
take place without a cause. There was certainly no need for
a long series of examples, such as we have in vers. 3-6, to
substantiate or illustrate the thought, which a reflecting hearer
would hardly have disputed, that there was a connection between
cause and effect. The examples are evidently selected with the
view of showing that the utterances of the prophet originate
with God. This is obvious enough in vers. 7, 8. The first
clause, " Do two men walk together, without having agreed as
to their meeting?" (*nō'ad*, to betake one's self to a place, to
meet together at an appointed place or an appointed time ;
compare Job ii. 11, Josh. xi. 5, Neh. vi. 2 ; not merely to
agree together), contains something more than the trivial truth,
that two persons do not take a walk together without a previous
arrangement. The two who walk together are Jehovah and
the prophet (Cyril) ; not Jehovah and the nation, to which the
judgment is predicted (Cocceius, Marck, and others). Amos
went as prophet to Samaria or Bethel, because the Lord had
sent him thither to preach judgment to the sinful kingdom.
But God would not threaten judgment if He had not a nation
ripe for judgment before Him. The lion which roars when
it has the prey before it is Jehovah (cf. ch. i. 2 ; Hos. xi. 10,
etc.). טֶרֶף אֵין לוֹ is not to be interpreted according to the
second clause, as signifying "without having got possession of
its prey" (Hitzig), for the lion is accustomed to roar when it
has the prey before it and there is no possibility of its escape,
and before it actually seizes it (cf. Isa. v. 29).[1] On the contrary, the perfect *lākhad* in the second clause is to be interpreted
according to the first clause, not as relating to the roar of satisfaction with which the lion devours the prey in its den (Baur),
but as a perfect used to describe a thing which was as certain
as if it had already occurred. A lion has made a capture not

[1] The most terrible feature in the roaring of a lion is that with this
clarigatio, or, if you prefer it, with this *classicum*, it declares war. And
after the roar there immediately follows both slaughter and laceration.
For, as a rule, it only roars with that sharp roar when it has the prey in
sight, upon which it immediately springs (Bochart, *Hieroz.* ii. 25 seq., ed.
Ros.).

merely when it has actually seized the prey and torn it in pieces, but when the prey has approached so near that it cannot possibly escape. *K^ephīr* is the young lion which already goes in pursuit of prey, and is to be distinguished from the young of the lion, *gūr* (*catulus leonis*), which cannot yet go in search of prey (cf. Ezek. xix. 2, 3). The two similes have the same meaning. The second strengthens the first by the assertion that God not only has before Him the nation that is ripe for judgment, but that He has it in His power. The similes in ver. 5 do not affirm the same as those in ver. 4, but contain the new thought, that Israel has deserved the destruction which threatens it. *Pach*, a snare, and *mōqēsh*, a trap, are frequently used synonymously; but here they are distinguished, *pach* denoting a bird-net, and *mōqēsh* a springe, a snare which holds the bird fast. The earlier translators have taken *mōqēsh* in the sense of *yōqēsh*, and understand it as referring to the bird-catcher; and Baur proposes to alter the text accordingly. But there is no necessity for this; and it is evidently unsuitable, since it is not requisite for a bird-catcher to be at hand, in order that the bird should be taken in a snare. The suffix *lâh* refers to *tsippōr*, and the thought is this: in order to catch a bird in the net, a springe (gin) must be laid for it. So far as the fact itself is concerned, *mōqēsh* is "evidently that which is necessarily followed by falling into the net; in this instance it is sinfulness" (Hitzig); so that the meaning of the figure would be this: "Can destruction possibly overtake you, unless your sin draws you into it?" (cf. Jer. ii. 35.) In the second clause *pach* is the subject, and יַעֲלֶה is used for the ascent or springing up of the net. Hitzig has given the meaning of the words correctly: "As the net does not spring up without catching the bird, that has sent it up by flying upon it, can ye imagine that when the destruction passes by, ye will not be seized by it, but will escape without injury?" (cf. Isa. xxviii. 15.) Jehovah, however, causes the evil to be foretold. As the trumpet, when blown in the city, frightens the people out of their self-security, so will the voice of the prophet, who proclaims the coming evil, excite a salutary alarm in the nation (cf. Ezek. xxxiii. 1–5). For the calamity which is bursting upon the city comes from Jehovah, is sent by Him as a punishment. This thought is explained in vers. 7, 8, and with this explanation the whole series of

figurative sentences is made perfectly clear.   The approaching
evil, which comes from the Lord, is predicted by the prophet,
because Jehovah does not carry out His purpose without
having (כִּי אִם, for when, except when he has, as in Gen. xxxii.
27) first of all revealed it to the prophets, that they may warn
the people to repent and to reform.   *Sôd* receives a more precise
definition from the first clause of the verse, or a limitation to
the purposes which God is about to fulfil upon His people.
And since (this is the connection of ver. 8) the judgment with
which the Lord is drawing near fills every one with fear, and
Jehovah has spoken, *i.e.* has made known His counsel to the
prophets, they cannot but prophesy.

Amos has thus vindicated his own calling, and the right of
all the prophets, to announce to the people the judgments of
God; and now (vers. 9–15) he is able to proclaim without
reserve what the Lord has resolved to do upon sinful Israel.
Ver. 9. " *Make it heard over the palaces in Ashdod, and over
the palaces in the land of Egypt, and say, Assemble yourselves
upon the mountains of Samaria, and behold the great tumult in the
midst thereof, and the oppressed in the heart thereof.*   Ver. 10.
*And they know not to do the right, is the saying of Jehovah, who
heap up violence and devastation in their palaces.*"   The speaker
is Jehovah (ver. 10), and the prophets are addressed.   Jehovah
summons them to send out the cry over the palaces in Ashdod
and Egypt (עַל as in Hos. viii. 1), and to call the inhabitants of
these palaces to hear, (1) that they may see the acts of violence,
and the abominations in the palaces of Samaria; and (2) that
they may be able to bear witness against Israel (ver. 13).   This
turn in the prophecy brings out to view the overflowing excess
of the sins and abominations of Israel.   The call of the prophets,
however, is not to be uttered upon the palaces, so as to be heard
far and wide (Baur and others), but over the palaces, to cause
the inhabitants of them to draw near.   It is they alone, and
not the whole population of Ashdod and Egypt, who are to be
called nigh; because only the inhabitants of the palace could
pronounce a correct sentence as to the mode of life commonly
adopted in the palaces of Samaria.   Ashdod, one of the Philistian capitals, is mentioned by way of example, as a chief city of
the uncircumcised, who were regarded by Israel as godless
heathen; and Egypt is mentioned along with it, as the nation

whose unrighteousness and ungodliness had once been experienced by Israel to satiety. If therefore such heathen as these
are called to behold the unrighteous and dissolute conduct to
be seen in the palaces, it must have been great indeed. The
mountains of Samaria are not the mountains of the kingdom of
Samaria, or the mountains upon which the city of Samaria was
situated—for Samaria was not built upon a plurality of mountains, but upon one only (ch. iv. 1, vi. 1)—but the mountains
round about Samaria, from which you could look into the city,
built upon one isolated hill. The city, built upon the hill of
Semer, was situated in a mountain caldron or basin, about two
hours in diameter, which was surrounded on all sides by lofty
mountains (see at 1 Kings xvi. 24).[1] *Mᵉhûmâh*, noise, tumult,
denotes a state of confusion, in which everything is topsy-turvy,
and all justice and order are overthrown by open violence
(Maurer, Baur). *'Ashûqîm*, either the oppressed, or, taken as
an abstract, the oppression of the poor (cf. ch. ii. 6). In ver.
10 the description is continued in the finite verb : they do not
know how to do right; that is to say, injustice has become their
nature ; they who heap up sins and violence in their palaces
like treasures.

Thus do they bring about the ruin of the kingdom. Ver. 11.
" *Therefore thus saith the Lord Jehovah, An enemy, and that
round about the land; and he will hurl down thy glory from thee,
and thy palaces are plundered.* Ver. 12. *Thus saith Jehovah,
As the shepherd delivers out of the mouth of the lion two shin-
bones or an ear-lappet, so will the sons of Israel deliver themselves ; they who sit on the corner of the couch and on the damask
of the bed.*" The threat is introduced in the form of an aposiopesis. צָר, enemy, וּסְבִיב הָאָרֶץ, and indeed round about the land
(ו explic. as in ch. iv. 10, etc.; and סָבִיב in the construct state
construed as a preposition), *i.e.* will come, attack the land on
all sides, and take possession of it. Others regard צַר as an
abstract : oppression (from the Chaldee) ; but in this case we
should have to supply *Jehovah* as the subject to וְהוֹרִיד ; and
although this is probable, it is by no means natural, as Jehovah
is speaking. There is no foundation, on the other hand, for the

[1] " As the mountains round the hill of *Semer* are loftier than this hill
itself, the enemy might easily discover the internal state of besieged
Samaria."—V. DE VELDE, *R.* i. p. 282.

remark, that if *tsar* signified the enemy, we should either find the plural צָרִים, or הַצָּר with the article (Baumgarten). The very indefiniteness of *tsar* suits the sententious brevity of the clause. This enemy will hurl down the splendour of Samaria, "which ornaments the top of the mountain like a crown, Isa. xxviii. i. 3" (Hitzig : עֹז, might, with the subordinate idea of glory), and plunder the palaces in which violence, *i.e.* property unrighteously acquired, is heaped up (ver. 10). The words are addressed to the city of Samaria, to which the feminine suffixes refer. On the fall of Samaria, and the plundering thereof, the luxurious grandees, who rest upon costly pillows, will only be able to save their life to the very smallest extent, and that with great difficulty. In the simile used in ver. 12 there is a slight want of proportion in the two halves, the object of the deliverance being thrown into the background in the second clause by the passive construction, and only indicated in the verb, to deliver themselves, *i.e.* to save their life. "A pair of shin-bones and a piece (בְּדַל ἅπαξ λεγ.), *i.e.* a lappet, of the ear," are most insignificant remnants. The grandees of Samaria, of whom only a few were to escape with their life, are depicted by Amos as those who sit on costly divans, without the least anxiety. פְּאַת מִטָּה, the corner of the divan, the most convenient for repose. According to ch. vi. 4, these divans were ornamanted with ivory, and according to the verse before us, they were ornamented with costly stuffs. דְּמֶשֶׁק comes from דַּמֶּשֶׂק, Damascus, and signifies *damask*, an artistically woven material (see Ges. *Thes.* p. 346). This brings the visitation of God to an end. Even the altars and palaces are to be laid in ruins, and consequently Samaria will be destroyed.

This feature in the threat is brought out into peculiar prominence by a fresh introduction. Ver. 13. "*Hear ye, and testify it to the house of Jacob, is the utterance of the Lord, Jehovah, the God of hosts: Ver.* 14. *That in the day when I visit the transgressions of the house of Israel upon it, I shall visit it upon the altars of Bethel; and the horns of the altar will be cut off, and fall to the ground.* Ver. 15. *And I smite the winter-house over the summer-house, and the houses of ivory perish, and many houses vanish, is the saying of Jehovah.*" The words "Hear ye" cannot be addressed to the Israelites, for they could not bear witness against the house of Israel, but must either refer to the prophets, as in ver. 9*a* ("publish ye"), or to the heathen, in which case they correspond to "assemble yourselves and behold" in ver. 9*b*. The latter assumption is the only correct one, for the context does not assign a sufficient motive for an address to the prophets. On the other hand, as the heathen have been summoned to convince themselves by actual observation of the sins that prevail in Samaria, it is perfectly in keeping that they should now hear what is the punishment that God is about to inflict upon Israel in consequence, and that they should bear witness against Israel from what they have heard. הָעִיד בּ, to bear witness towards or against (not "in," as Baur supposes). The house of Jacob is the whole of Israel, of the *twelve* tribes, as in ver. 1; for Judah was also to learn a lesson from the destruction of Samaria. As the appeal to the heathen to bear witness against Israel indicates the greatness of the sins of the Israelites, so, on the other hand, does the accumulation of the names of God in ver. 13*b* serve to strengthen the declaration made by the Lord, who possesses as God of hosts the power to execute His threats. כִּי introduces the substance of what is to be heard. The punishment of the sins of Israel is to extend even to the altars of Bethel, the seat of the idolatrous image-worship, the hearth and home of the religious and moral corruption of the ten tribes. The smiting off of the horns of the altar is the destruction of the altars themselves, the significance of which culminated in the horns (see at Ex. xxvii. 2). The singular *hammizbēăch* (*the altar*) preceded by a plural is the singular of species (cf. Ges. § 108, 1), and does not refer to any particular one—say, for example, to the principal altar. The destruction of the palaces and houses (ver. 15) takes place in the capital. In the reference to the winter-house and summer-house, we have to think primarily of the royal palace (cf. Jer. xxxvi. 22); at the same time, wealthy noblemen may also have had them. עַל, lit. over, so that the ruins of one house fall upon the top of another; then "together with," as in Gen. xxxii. 12. בָּתֵּי שֵׁן, ivory houses, houses the rooms of which are decorated by inlaid ivory. Ahab had a palace of this kind (1 Kings xxii. 39, compare Ps. xlv. 9). בָּתִּים רַבִּים, not the large houses, but many houses; for the description is rounded off with these words. Along with the palaces, many houses will also fall to the ground. The ful-

filment took place when Samaria was taken by Shalmanezer
(2 Kings xvii. 5, 6).

THE IMPENITENCE OF ISRAEL.—CHAP. IV.

The voluptuous and wanton women of Samaria will be
overtaken by a shameful captivity (vers. 1–3). Let the Israelites only continue their idolatry with zeal (vers. 4, 5), the Lord
has already visited them with many punishments without their
having turned to Him (vers. 6–11); and therefore He must
inflict still further chastisements, to see whether they will not
at length learn to fear Him as their God (vers. 12, 13).

Ver. 1. "*Hear this word, ye cows of Bashan, that are upon
the mountain of Samaria, that oppress there the humble and
crush the poor, that say to their lords, Bring hither, that we may
drink.* Ver. 2. *The Lord Jehovah hath sworn by His holiness: behold, days come upon you, that they drag you away
with hooks, and your last one with fish-hooks.* Ver. 3. *And ye
will go out through breaches in the wall, every one before him,
and be cast away to Harmon, is the saying of Jehovah.*" The
commencement of this chapter is closely connected, so far as
the contents are concerned, with the chapter immediately preceding. The prophet having there predicted, that when the
kingdom was conquered by its enemies, the voluptuous grandees
would perish, with the exception of a very few who would hardly
succeed in saving their lives, turns now to the voluptuous
women of Samaria, to predict in their case a shameful transportation into exile. The introduction, "Hear this word," does
not point therefore to a new prophecy, but simply to a fresh
stage in the prophecy, so that we cannot even agree with Ewald
in taking vers. 1–3 as the conclusion of the previous prophecy
(ch. iii.). The cows of Bashan are well-fed, fat cows, βόες
εὔτροφοι, *vaccæ pingues* (Symm., Jer.), as Bashan had fat pastures, and for that reason the tribes that were richest in flocks
and herds had asked for it as their inheritance (Num. xxxii.).
The fuller definitions which follow show very clearly that by
the cows of Bashan, Amos meant the rich, voluptuous, and
violent inhabitants of Samaria. It is doubtful, however, whether
he meant the rich and wanton wives of the great, as most of
the modern commentators follow Theodor., Theodoret, and

others, in assuming; or "the rulers of Israel, and all the leading men of the ten tribes, who spent their time in pleasure and robbery" (Jerome); or "those rich, luxurious, and lascivious inhabitants of the palace of whom he had spoken in ch. iii. 9, 10" (Maurer), as the Chald., Luther, Calvin, and others suppose, and whom he calls cows, not oxen, to denote their effeminacy and their unbridled licentiousness. In support of the latter opinion we might adduce not only Hos. x. 11, where Ephraim is compared to a young heifer, but also the circumstance that from ver. 4 onwards the prophecy refers to the Israelites as a whole. But neither of these arguments proves very much. The simile in Hos. x. 11 applies to Ephraim as a kingdom or people, and the natural personification as a woman prepares the way for the comparison to an 'eglâh; whereas voluptuous and tyrannical grandees would be more likely to be compared to the bulls of Bashan (Ps. xxii. 13). And so, again, the transition in ver. 4 to the Israelites as a whole furnishes no help in determining more precisely who are addressed in vers. 1–3. By the cows of Bashan, therefore, we understand the voluptuous women of Samaria, after the analogy of Isa. iii. 16 sqq. and xxxii. 9–13, more especially because it is only by forcing the last clause of ver. 1 that it can be understood as referring to men. שִׁמְעוּ for שְׁמַעְנָה, because the verb stands first (compare Isa. xxxii. 11). The mountain of Samaria is mentioned in the place of the city built upon the mountain (see at ch. iii. 9). The sin of these women consisted in the tyrannical oppression of the poor, whilst they asked their lords, i.e. their husbands, to procure them the means of debauchery. For עָשַׁק and רָצַץ, compare Deut. xxviii. 33 and 1 Sam. xii. 3, 4, where the two words are already connected. הָבִיאָה stands in the singular, because every wife speaks in this way to her husband. The announcement of the punishment for such conduct is introduced with a solemn oath, to make an impression, if possible, upon the hardened hearts. Jehovah swears by His holiness, i.e. as the Holy One, who cannot tolerate unrighteousness. כִּי (for) before הִנֵּה introduces the oath. Hitzig takes וְנִשָּׂא as a niphal, as in the similar formula in 2 Kings xx. 17; but he takes it as a passive used impersonally with an accusative, after Gen. xxxv. 26 and other passages (though not Ex. xiii. 7). But as נָשָׂא unquestionably occurs as a piel in 1 Kings ix. 11, it is more natural to take

the same form as a *piel* in this instance also, and whilst interpreting it impersonally, to think of the enemy as understood.
Tsinnōth = *tsinnīm*, Prov. xxii. 5, Job v. 5, צִנָּה = צֵן, thorns,
hence hooks; so also *sīrōth* = *sīrīm*, thorns, Isa. xxxiv. 13,
Hos. ii. 8. *Dūgáh*, fishery; hence *sīrōth dūgáh*, fish-hooks.
'Achărīth does not mean posterity, or the young brood that has
grown up under the instruction and example of the parents
(Hitzig), but simply "the end," the opposite of *rē'shīth*, the
beginning. It is "end," however, in different senses. Here
it signifies the remnant (Chaldee), *i.e.* those who remain and
are not dragged away with *tsinnōth;* so that the thought expressed is "all, even to the very last" (compare Hengstenberg, *Christology,* i. p. 368). אַחֲרִיתְכֶן has a feminine suffix,
whereas masculine suffixes were used before (עֲלֵיכֶם, אֶתְכֶם); the
universal gender, out of which the feminine was first formed.
The figure is not taken from animals, into whose noses hooks
and rings are inserted to tame them, or from large fishes that
are let down into the water again by nose-hooks; for the
technical terms applied to these hooks are חָח, חוֹחַ, and חַכָּה
(cf. Ezek. xxix. 4; Job xl. 25, 26); but from the catching of
fishes, that are drawn out of the fish-pond with hooks. Thus
shall the voluptuous, wanton women be violently torn away or
carried off from the midst of the superfluity and debauchery
in which they lived as in their proper element. פְּרָצִים תֵּצֶאנָה, to
go out of rents in the wall, יָצָא being construed, as it frequently
is, with the accusative of the place; we should say, "through
rents in the wall," *i.e.* through breaches made in the wall at
the taking of the city, not out at the gates, because they had
been destroyed or choked up with rubbish at the storming of
the city. "Every one before her," *i.e.* without looking round
to the right or to the left (cf. Josh. vi. 5, 20). The words
וְהִשְׁלַכְתֶּנָה הַהַרְמוֹנָה are difficult, on account of the ἅπ. λεγ.
הַהַרְמוֹנָה, and have not yet been satisfactorily explained. The
form הִשְׁלַכְתֶּנָה for הִשְׁלַכְתֶּן is probably chosen simply for the
purpose of obtaining a resemblance in sound to תֵּצֶאנָה, and is
sustained by אַתֵּנָה for אַתֵּן in Gen. xxxi. 6 and Ezek. xiii. 11.
הִשְׁלִיךְ is applied to thrusting into exile, as in Deut. xxix. 27.
The ἅπ. λεγ. הַהַרְמוֹנָה with ה loc. appears to indicate the place
to which they were to be carried away or cast out. But the
hiphil הִשְׁלַכְתֶּנָה does not suit this, and consequently nearly all

the earlier translators have rendered it as a passive, ἀπορριφή-
σεσθε (LXX.), *projiciemini* (Jerome); so also the Syr. and
Chald. וְיִגְלוּ יַתְהֹן, "men will carry them away captive." One
Hebrew codex actually gives the *hophal*. And to this reading
we must adhere ; for the *hiphil* furnishes no sense at all, since
the intransitive or reflective meaning, to plunge, or cast one's
self, cannot be sustained, and is not supported at all by the
passages quoted by Hitzig, viz. 2 Kings x. 25 and Job xxvii.
22 ; and still less does *haharmōnâh* denote the object cast away
by the women when they go into captivity.[1] The literal meaning of *harmōnâh* or *harmōn* still remains uncertain. According
to the etymology of הרם, to be high, it apparently denotes a
high land : at the same time, it can neither be taken as an
appellative, as Hesselberg and Maurer suppose, "the high
land;" nor in the sense of *'armōn*, a citadel or palace, as
Kimchi and Gesenius maintain. The former interpretation is
open to the objection, that we cannot possibly imagine why
Amos should have formed a word of his own, and one which
never occurs again in the Hebrew language, to express the
simple idea of a mountain or high land ; and the second to
this objection, that "the citadel" would require something to
designate it as a citadel or fortress in the land of the enemy.

[1] The Masoretic pointing probably originated in the idea that *harmōnâh*, corresponding to the talmudic *harmânâ'*, signifies royal power or
dominion, and so Rashi interprets it : "ye will cast away the authority,
i.e. the almost regal authority, or that pride and arrogance with which
you bear yourselves to-day" (Ros.). This explanation would be admissible, if it were not that the use of a word which never occurs again in
the old Hebrew for a thing so frequently mentioned in the Old Testament,
rendered it very improbable. At any rate, it is more admissible than the
different conjectures of the most recent commentators. Thus Hitzig, for
example (*Comm.* ed. 3), would resolve *haharmōnâh* into *hâhâr* and *mōnâh*
= *me'ōnâh* (" and ye will plunge headlong to the mountain as a place of
refuge"). The objections to this are, (1) that *hishlikh* does not mean to
plunge headlong ; (2) the improbability of *me'ōnâh* being contracted into
mōnâh, when Amos has *me'ōnâh* in ch. iii. 4 ; and lastly, the fact that
me'ōnâh means simply a dwelling, not a place of refuge. Ewald would
read *hâhâr rimmōnâh* after the LXX., and renders it, "ye will cast Rimmonah to the mountain," understanding by Rimmonah a female deity of
the Syrians. But antiquity knows nothing of any such female deity ; and
from the reference to a deity called *Rimmon* in 2 Kings v. 18, you cannot
possibly infer the existence of a goddess *Rimmonah*. The explanation given
by Schlottmann (*Hiob*, p. 132) and Paul Bötticher (*Rudimenta mythologiæ*

The unusual word certainly points to the name of a land or district, though we have no means of determining it more precisely.[1]

Vers. 4, 5. After this threat directed against the voluptuous women of the capital, the prophecy turns again to all the people. In bitter irony, Amos tells them to go on with zeal in their idolatrous sacrifices, and to multiply their sin. But they will not keep back the divine judgment by so doing. Ver. 4. "*Go to Bethel, and sin; to Gilgal, multiply sinning; and offer your slain-offerings in the morning, your tithes every three days. Ver. 5. And kindle praise-offerings of that which is leavened, and cry out freewill-offerings, proclaim it; for so ye love it, O sons of Israel, is the saying of the Lord, of Jehovah.*" "Amos here describes how zealously the people of Israel went on pilgrimage to Bethel, and Gilgal, and Beersheba, those places of sacred associations; with what superabundant diligence they offered sacrifice and paid tithes; how they would rather do too much than too little, so that they even burnt upon the altar a portion of the leavened loaves of the praise-offering, which were only intended for the sacrificial meals, although none but unleavened bread was allowed to be offered; and lastly, how in their pure zeal for multiplying the works of piety, they so completely mistook

semit. 1848, p. 10)—namely, that *harmōnâh* is the Phœnician goddess *Chusarthis*, called by the Greeks Ἀρμονία—is still more untenable, since Ἀρμονία is no more derived from the talmudic *harmân* than this is from the Sanscrit *pramāna* (Bötticher, *l.c.* p. 40); on the contrary, *harmân* signifies loftiness, from the Semitic root הרם, to be high, and it cannot be shown that there was a goddess called *Harman* or *Harmonia* in the Phœnician worship. Lastly, the fanciful idea of Bötticher, that *harmōnâh* is contracted from *hâhar rimmōnâh*, and that the meaning is, "and then ye throw, *i.e.* remove, the mountain (your Samaria) to Rimmon, that ancient place of refuge for expelled tribes" (Judg. xx. 45 sqq.), needs no refutation.

[1] Even the early translators have simply rendered *haharmōnâh* according to the most uncertain conjectures. Thus LXX., εἰς τὸ ὄρος τὸ Ῥομμάν (*al.* Ῥεμμάν); Aq., *mons Armona*; Theod., *mons Mona*; the *Quinta*: *excelsus mons* (according to Jerome); and Theodoret attributes to Theodot. ὑψηλὸν ὄρος. The Chaldee paraphrases it thus: לְהַלְאָה מִן טוּרֵי הַרְמֵינִי, "far beyond the mountains of Armenia." Symmachus also had *Armenia*, according to the statement of Theodoret and Jerome. But this explanation is probably merely an inference drawn from 2 Kings xvii. 23, and cannot be justified, as Bochart supposes, on the ground that *mōnâh* or *mōn* is identical with *minni*.

their nature, as to summon by a public proclamation to the presentation of freewill-offerings, the very peculiarity of which consisted in the fact that they had no other prompting than the will of the offerer" (v. Hofmann, *Schriftbeweis*, ii. 2, p. 373). The irony of the summons to maintain their worship comes out very distinctly in the words וּפִשְׁעוּ, and sin, or fall away from God. הַגִּלְגָּל is not a nominative absolute, " as for Gilgal," but an accusative, and בֹּאוּ is to be repeated from the first clause. The absence of the copula before הַרְבּוּ does not compel us to reject the Masoretic accentuation, and connect הַגִּלְגָּל with פִּשְׁעוּ, as Hitzig does, so as to obtain the unnatural thought, " sin ye towards Gilgal." On Gilgal mentioned along with Bethel as a place of idolatrous worship (here and ch. v. 5, as in Hos. iv. 15, ix. 15, and xii. 12), see at Hos. iv. 15. Offer your slain-offerings *labbōqer*, for the morning, *i.e.* every morning, like *layyōm* in Jer. xxxvii. 21. This is required by the parallel *lishlōsheth yâmîm*, on the three of days, *i.e.* every three days. הָבִיאוּ . . . זְבָחִים does not refer to the morning sacrifice prescribed in the law (Num. xxviii. 3)—for that is always called *'ōlâh*, not *zebach*—but to slain sacrifices that were offered every morning, although the offering of *z^ebhâchîm* every morning presupposes the presentation of the daily morning burnt-offering. What is said concerning the tithe rests upon the Mosaic law of the second tithe, which was to be brought every three years (Deut. xiv. 28, xxvi. 12 ; compare my *Bibl. Archäol.* § 71, Anm. 7). The two clauses, however, are not to be understood as implying that the Israelites had offered slain sacrifices every morning, and tithe every three days. Amos is speaking hyperbolically, to depict the great zeal displayed in their worship ; and the thought is simply this : "If ye would offer slain sacrifices every morning, and tithe every three days, ye would only thereby increase your apostasy from the living God." The words, " kindle praise-offerings of that which is leavened," have been misinterpreted in various ways. קַטֵּר, an *inf. absol.* used instead of the *imperative* (see Ges. § 131, 4, *b*). According to Lev. vii. 12–14, the praise-offering (*tōdâh*) was to consist not only of unleavened cakes and pancakes with oil poured upon them, but also of cakes of leavened bread. The latter, however, were not to be placed upon the altar, but one of them was to be assigned to the priest who sprinkled the blood, and the rest to be eaten at the sacrificial meal. Amos now charges the people with having offered that which was leavened instead of unleavened cakes and pancakes, and with having burned it upon the altar, contrary to the express prohibition of the law in Lev. ii. 11. His words are not to be understood as signifying that, although outwardly the praise-offerings consisted of that which was unleavened, according to the command of the law, yet inwardly they were so base that they resembled unleavened cakes, inasmuch as whilst the material of the leaven was absent, the true nature of the leaven—namely, malice and wickedness—was there in all the greater quantity (Hengstenberg, *Dissertations*, vol. i. p. 143 translation). The meaning is rather this, that they were not content with burning upon the altar unleavened cakes made from the materials provided for the sacrifice, but that they burned some of the leavened loaves as well, in order to offer as much as possible to God. What follows answers to this: call out *nᵉdâbhōth*, *i.e.* call out that men are to present freewill-offerings. The emphasis is laid upon קְרָאוּ, which is therefore still further strengthened by הַשְׁמִיעוּ. Their calling out *nᵉdâbhōth*, *i.e.* their ordering freewill-offerings to be presented, was an exaggerated act of zeal, inasmuch as the sacrifices which ought to have been brought out of purely spontaneous impulse (cf. Lev. xxii. 18 sqq.; Deut. xii. 6), were turned into a matter of moral compulsion, or rather of legal command. The words, "for so ye love it," show how this zeal in the worship lay at the heart of the nation. It is also evident from the whole account, that the worship in the kingdom of the ten tribes was conducted generally according to the precepts of the Mosaic law.

Vers. 6–11. But as Israel would not desist from its idolatrous worship, Jehovah would also continue to visit the people with judgments, as He had already done, though without effecting any conversion to their God. This last thought is explained in vers. 6–11 in a series of instances, in which the expression וְלֹא שַׁבְתֶּם עָדַי (and ye have not returned to me), which is repeated five times, depicts in the most thorough manner the unwearied love of the Lord to His rebellious children.

Ver. 6. "*And I have also given you cleanness of teeth in all your towns, and want of bread in all your places: and ye have not returned to me, is the saying of Jehovah."* The strongly adversative וְגַם אֲנִי forms the antithesis to כֵּן אֲהַבְתֶּם : Ye love to persist in your idolatry, and yet I have tried all means of turning you to me. Cleanness of teeth is explained by the parallel "want of bread." The first chastisement, therefore, consisted in famine, with which God visited the nation, as He had threatened the transgressors that He would do in the law (Deut. xxviii. 48, 57). For שׁוּב עַד, compare Hos. xiv. 2.

Ver. 7. "*And I have also withholden the rain from you, in yet three months to the harvest; and have caused it to rain upon one city, and I do not cause it to rain upon another. One field is rained upon, and the field upon which it does not rain withers.* Ver. 8. *And two, three towns stagger to one town to drink water, and are not satisfied: and ye have not returned to me, is the saying of Jehovah."* The second punishment mentioned is the withholding of rain, or drought, which was followed by the failure of the harvest and the scarcity of water (cf. Lev. xxvi. 19, 20; Deut. xxviii. 23). The rain "in yet (*i.e.* at the time when there were yet) three months to the harvest" is the so-called latter rain, which falls in the latter half of February and the first half of March, and is of the greatest importance to the vigorous development of the ears of corn and also of the grains. In southern Palestine the harvest commences in the latter half of April (Nisan), and falls for the most part in May and June; but in the northern part of the land it is from two to four weeks later (see my *Archäologie,* i. pp. 33, 34, ii. pp. 113, 114), so that in round numbers we may reckon three months from the latter rain to the harvest. But in order to show the people more clearly that the sending and withholding of rain belonged to Him, God caused it to rain here and there, upon one town and one field, and not upon others (the imperfects from '*amtīr* onwards express the repetition of a thing, what generally happens, and *timmâtēr,* third pers. fem., is used impersonally). This occasioned such distress, that the inhabitants of the places in which it had not rained were obliged to go to a great distance for the necessary supply of water to drink, and yet could not get enough to satisfy them. נוּעַ, to stagger, to totter, expresses the insecure and trembling walk of a man almost fainting with thirst.

Ver. 9. "*I have smitten you with blight and yellowness; many of your gardens, and of your vineyards, and of your fig-trees, and of your olive-trees, the locust devoured; and ye have not returned to me, is the saying of Jehovah."* The third chastisement consisted in the perishing of the corn by blight, and by the ears turning yellow, and also in the destruction of the produce of the gardens and the fruits of the trees by locusts. The first is threatened in Deut. xxviii. 22, against despisers of the commandments of God; the second points to the threatenings in Deut. xxviii. 39, 40, 42. The *infin. constr. harbōth* is used as a substantive, and stands as a noun in the construct state before the following words; so that it is not to be taken adverbially in the sense of many times, or often, as though used instead of *harbēh* (cf. Ewald, § 280, *c*). On *gâzâm*, see at Joel i. 4. The juxtaposition of these two plagues is not to be understood as implying that they occurred simultaneously, or that the second was the consequence of the first; still less are the two to be placed in causal connection with the drought mentioned in vers. 7, 8. For although such combinations do take place in the course of nature, there is no allusion to this in the present instance, where Amos is simply enumerating a series of judgments, through which Jehovah had already endeavoured to bring the people to repentance, without any regard to the time when they occurred.

The same thing may be said of the fourth chastisement mentioned in ver. 10, " *I have sent pestilence among you in the manner of Egypt, have slain your young men with the sword, together with the booty of your horses, and caused the stench of your camps to ascend, and that into your nose; and ye have not returned to me, is the saying of Jehovah."* In the combination of pestilence and sword (war), the allusion to Lev. xxvi. 25 is unmistakeable (compare Deut. xxviii. 60, where the rebellious are threatened with all the diseases of Egypt). בְּדֶרֶךְ מִצְרַיִם, in the manner (not in the road) of Egypt (compare Isa. x. 24, 26; Ezek. xx. 30), because pestilence is epidemic in Egypt. The idea that there is any allusion to the pestilence with which God visited Egypt (Ex. ix. 3 sqq.), is overthrown by the circumstance that it is only a dreadful murrain that is mentioned there. The slaying of the youths or young men points to overthrow in war, which the Israelites endured most grievously in the wars with the Syrians (compare

2 Kings viii. 12, xiii. 3, 7). עִם שְׁבִי סוּסֵיכֶם does not mean together with, or by the side of, the carrying away of your horses, *i.e.* along with the fact that your horses were carried away; for שְׁבִי does not mean carrying away captive, but the captivity, or the whole body of captives. The words are still dependent upon הִרְגְתִּי, and affirm that even the horses that had been taken perished,—a fact which is also referred to in 2 Kings xiii. 7. From the slain men and animals forming the camp the stench ascended, and that into their noses, " as it were, as an '*azkârâh* of their sins" (Hitzig), but without their turning to their God.

Ver. 11. " *I have destroyed among you, like the destruction of God upon Sodom and Gomorrah, and ye were like a brand plucked out of the fire; and ye have not returned to me, is the saying of Jehovah.*" Proceeding from the smaller to the greater chastisements, Amos mentions last of all the destruction similar to that of Sodom and Gomorrah, *i.e.* the utter confusion of the state, by which Israel was brought to the verge of ruin, so that it had only been saved like a firebrand out of the fire. הָפַכְתִּי does not refer to an earthquake, which had laid waste cities and hamlets, or a part of the land, say that mentioned in ch. i. 1, as Kimchi and others suppose; but it denotes the desolation of the whole land in consequence of devastating wars, more especially the Syrian (2 Kings xiii. 4, 7), and other calamities, which had undermined the stability of the kingdom, as in Isa. i. 9. The words כְּמַהְפֵּכַת אֱלֹהִים וגו׳ are taken from Deut. xxix. 22, where the complete desolation of the land, after the driving away of the people into exile on account of their obstinate apostasy, is compared to the destruction of Sodom and Gomorrah. By thus playing upon this terrible threat uttered by Moses, the prophet seeks to show to the people what has already happened to them, and what still awaits them if they do not eventually turn to their God. They have again been rescued from the threatening destruction like a firebrand out of the fire (Zech. iii. 2) by the deliverer whom the Lord gave to them, so that they escaped from the power of the Syrians (2 Kings xiii. 5). But inasmuch as all these chastisements have produced no fruit of repentance, the Lord will now proceed to judgment with His people.

Ver. 12. " *Therefore thus will I do to thee, O Israel; because*

I will do this to thee, prepare to meet thy God, O Israel. Ver. 13.
*For, behold, He that formeth the mountains, and createth the wind,
and maketh known to man what is his thought; who maketh dawn,
darkness, and goeth over the high places of the earth, Jehovah
God of hosts is His name."* The punishment which God is now
about to inflict is introduced with *lâkhēn* (therefore). כֹּה אֶעֱשֶׂה
cannot point back to the punishment threatened in vers. 2, 3,
and still less to the chastisements mentioned in vers. 6–11; for
lâkhēn kōh is always used by Amos to introduce what is about to
ensue, and any retrospective allusion to vers. 6–11 is precluded
by the future אֶעֱשֶׂה. What Jehovah is now about to do is not
expressed here *more iratorum*, but may clearly be discerned from
what follows. "When He has said, '*This will I do to thee,*' He
is silent as to what He will do, in order that, whilst Israel is left
in uncertainty as to the particular kind of punishment (which
is all the more terrible because all kinds of things are imagined), it may repent of its sins, and so avert the things which
God threatens here" (Jerome). Instead of an announcement of
the punishment, there follows in the words, "Because I will
do this to thee (זֹאת pointing back to כֹּה), prepare to meet thy
God," a summons to hold themselves in readiness *liqra'th
'ĕlōhīm* (*in occursum Dei*), *i.e.* to stand before God thy judge.
The meaning of this summons has been correctly explained by
Calvin thus: "When thou seest that thou hast resorted in vain
to all kinds of subterfuges, since thou never wilt be able to
escape from the hand of thy judge; see now at length that
thou dost avert this last destruction which is hanging over
thee." But this can only be effected "by true renewal of
heart, in which men are dissatisfied with themselves, and submit with changed heart to God, and come as suppliants, praying
for forgiveness." For if we judge ourselves, we shall not be
judged by the Lord (1 Cor. xi. 31). This view is shown to be
the correct one, by the repeated admonitions to seek the Lord
and live (ch. v. 4, 6; cf. ver. 14). To give all the greater
emphasis to this command, Amos depicts God in ver. 13 as the
Almighty and Omniscient, who creates prosperity and adversity. The predicates applied to God are to be regarded as
explanations of אֵלֶיךָ, prepare to meet thy God; for it is He
who formeth mountains, etc., *i.e.* the Almighty, and also He
who maketh known to man מַה־שֵּׂחוֹ, what man thinketh, not

what God thinketh, since שֵׂחַ = שִׂיחַ is not applicable to God, and is only used ironically of Baal in 1 Kings xviii. 27. The thought is this: God is the searcher of the heart (Jer. xvii. 10; Ps. cxxxix. 2), and reveals to men by prophets the state of their heart, since He judges not only the outward actions, but the inmost emotions of the heart (cf. Heb. iv. 12). עֹשֶׂה שַׁחַר עֵיפָה might mean, He turns morning dawn into darkness, since עֹשֶׂה may be construed with the accusative of that into which any-thing is made (compare Ex. xxx. 25, and the similar thought in ch. v. 8, that God darkens the day into night). But both of these arguments simply prove the possibility of this explana-tion, not that it is either necessary or correct. As a rule, where עָשָׂה occurs, the thing into which anything is made is introduced with לְ (cf. Gen. xii. 2; Ex. xxxii. 10). Here, therefore, לְ may be omitted, simply to avoid ambiguity. For these reasons we agree with Calvin and others, who take the words as asyndeton. God makes morning-dawn and dark-ness, which is more suitable to a description of the creative omnipotence of God; and the omission of the *Vav* may be explained very simply from the oratorical character of the prophecy. To this there is appended the last statement: He passes along over the high places of the earth, *i.e.* He rules the earth with unlimited omnipotence (see at Deut. xxxii. 13), and manifests Himself thereby as the God of the universe, or God of hosts.

THE OVERTHROW OF THE KINGDOM OF THE TEN TRIBES.— CHAP. V. AND VI.

The elegy, which the prophet commences in ver. 2, upon the fall of the daughter of Israel, forms the theme of the admonitory addresses in these two chapters. These addresses, which are divided into four parts by the admonitions, " Seek Jehovah, and live," in vers. 4 and 6, " Seek good " in ver. 14, and the two woes (*hōi*) in ch. v. 18 and vi. 1, have no other purpose than this, to impress upon the people of God the im-possibility of averting the threatened destruction, and to take away from the self-secure sinners the false foundations of their trust, by setting the demands of God before them once more. In every one of these sections, therefore, the proclamation of

the judgment returns again, and that in a form of greater and
greater intensity, till it reaches to the banishment of the whole
nation, and the overthrow of Samaria and the kingdom (ch.
v. 27, vi. 8 sqq.).

Vers. 1–3. The Elegy.—Ver. 1. *" Hear ye this word, which
I raise over you ; a lamentation, O house of Israel.* Ver. 2. *The
virgin Israel is fallen ; she does not rise up again ; cast down
upon her soil ; no one sets her up.* Ver. 3. *For thus saith the
Lord Jehovah, The city that goes out by a thousand will retain a
hundred, and that which goes out by a hundred will retain ten, for
the house of Israel."* הַדָּבָר הַזֶּה is still further defined in the relative clause אֲשֶׁר וגו' as קִינָה, a mournful song, *lit.* a lamentation or
dirge for one who is dead (cf. 2 Sam. i. 17 ; 2 Chron. xxxv. 25).
אֲשֶׁר is a relative pronoun, not a conjunction (for) ; and *qīnáh*
is an explanatory apposition : which I raise or commence as
(or " namely ") a lamentation. " House of Israel " is synonymous with " house of Joseph " (ver. 6), hence Israel of the ten
tribes. The lamentation follows in ver. 2, showing itself to be
a song by the rhythm and by its poetical form. נָפַל, to fall,
denotes a violent death (2 Sam. i. 19, 25), and is here a figure
used to denote the overthrow or destruction of the kingdom.
The expression virgin Israel (an epexegetical genitive, not " of
Israel") rests upon a poetical personification of the population
of a city or of a kingdom, as a daughter, and wherever the
further idea of being unconquered is added, as a virgin (see at
Isa. xxiii. 12). Here, too, the term " virgin " is used to indicate the contrast between the overthrow predicted and the
original destination of Israel, as the people of God, to be unconquered by any heathen nation whatever. The second clause
of the verse strengthens the first. נָטַשׁ, to be stretched out or
cast down, describes the fall as a violent overthrow. The third
verse does not form part of the lamentation, but gives a brief,
cursory vindication of it by the announcement that Israel will
perish in war, even to a very small remnant. יָצָא refers to their
marching out to war, and מֵאָה, אֶלֶף is subordinated to it, as a
more precise definition of the manner in which they marched
out (cf. Ewald, § 279, *b*).

Vers. 4–12. The short, cursory explanation of the reason for
the lamentation opened here, is followed in vers. 4 sqq. by the
more elaborate proof, that Israel has deserved to be destroyed,

because it has done the very opposite of what God demands of His people. God requires that they should seek Him, and forsake idolatry, in order to live (vers. 4–6); but Israel, on the contrary, turns right into unrighteousness, without fearing the almighty God and His judgment (vers. 7–9). This unrighteousness God must punish (vers. 10–12). Ver. 4. "*For thus saith Jehovah to the house of Israel, Seek ye me, and live.* Ver. 5. *And seek not Bethel, and come not to Gilgal, and go not over to Beersheba: for Gilgal repays it with captivity, and Bethel comes to nought.* Ver. 6. *Seek Jehovah, and live; that He fall not upon the house of Joseph like fire, and it devour, and there be none to quench it for Bethel.*" The *kī* in ver. 4 is co-ordinate to that in ver. 3, "Seek me, and live," for "Seek me, so shall ye live." For this meaning of two imperatives, following directly the one upon the other, see Gesenius, § 130, 2, and Ewald, § 347, *b*. חָיָה, not merely to remain alive, not to perish, but to obtain possession of true life. God can only be sought, however, in His revelation, or in the manner in which He wishes to be sought and worshipped. This explains the antithesis, "Seek not Bethel," etc. In addition to Bethel and Gilgal (see at ch. iv. 4), Beersheba, which was in the southern part of Judah, is also mentioned here, being the place where Abraham had called upon the Lord (Gen. xxi. 33), and where the Lord had appeared to Isaac and Jacob (Gen. xxvi. 24 and xlvi. 1; see also at Gen. xxi. 31). These sacred reminiscences from the olden time had caused Beersheba to be made into a place of idolatrous worship, to which the Israelites went on pilgrimage beyond the border of their own kingdom (עָבַר). But visiting these idolatrous places of worship did no good, for the places themselves would be given up to destruction. Gilgal would wander into *captivity* (an expression used here on account of the similarity in the ring of גָּלָה and נָּלָה יִגְלֶה). Bethel would become '*âven*, that is to say, not "an idol" here, but "nothingness," though there is an allusion to the change of *Beth-el* (God's house) into *Beth-'âven* (an idol-house; see at Hos. iv. 15). The Judæan Beersheba is passed over in the threat, because the primary intention of Amos is simply to predict the destruction of the kingdom of the ten tribes. After this warning the prophet repeats the exhortation to seek Jehovah, and adds this threatening, "that Jehovah come not like fire upon the house of Joseph" (*tsâlach*, generally construed with *'al* or *'el*, cf. Judg. xiv. 19, xv. 14, 1 Sam. x. 6 ; here with an accusative, to fall upon a person), "and it (the fire) devour, without there being any to extinguish it for Bethel." Bethel, as the chief place of worship in Israel, is mentioned here for the kingdom itself, which is called the "house of Joseph," from Joseph the father of Ephraim, the most powerful tribe in that kingdom.

To add force to this warning, Amos (vers. 7–9) exhibits the moral corruption of the Israelites, in contrast with the omnipotence of Jehovah as it manifests itself in terrible judgments. Ver. 7. *" They that change right into wormwood, and bring righteousness down to the earth.* Ver. 8. *He that maketh the seven stars and Orion, and turneth the shadow of death into morning, and darkeneth day to night : that calleth to the waters of the sea, and poureth them over the surface of the earth ; Jehovah is His name.* Ver. 9. *Who causeth desolation to flash upon the strong, and desolation cometh upon the fortress."* The sentences in vers. 7 and 8 are written without any connecting link. The participle in ver. 7 cannot be taken as an address, for it is carried on in the third person (*hinnīchŭ*), not in the second. And *hahōphᵉkhīm* (who turn) cannot be in apposition to *Beth-el*, since the latter refers not to the inhabitants, but to the houses. As Amos is generally fond of a participial construction (cf. ch. ii. 7, iv. 13), so in a spirited address he likes to utter the thoughts one after another without any logical link of connection. As a matter of fact, *hahōphᵉkhīm* is connected with *bēth-yōsēph* (the house of Joseph), " Seek the Lord, ye of the house of Joseph, who turn right into wrong ;" but instead of this connection, he proceeds with a simple description, " They are turning," etc. *La'ănâh*, wormwood, a bitter plant, is a figurative term denoting bitter wrong (cf. ch. vi. 12), the actions of men being regarded, according to Deut. xxix. 17, as the fruits of their state of mind. Laying righteousness on the ground (*hinnĭăch* from *nŭăch*) answers to our "trampling under feet." Hitzig has correctly explained the train of thought in vers. 7 and 8 : "They do this, whereas Jehovah is the Almighty, and can bring destruction suddenly upon them." To show this antithesis, the article which takes the place of the relative is omitted from the participles *'ōsēh* and *hōphēkh*. The description of the divine omnipotence com-

mences with the creation of the brightly shining stars; then
follow manifestations of this omnipotence, which are repeated
in the government of the world. *Kîmâh,* lit. the crowd, is the
group of seven stars, the constellation of the Pleiades. *K^{e}sîl,*
the gate, according to the ancient versions the giant, is the constellation of Orion. The two are mentioned together in Job
ix. 9 and xxxviii. 31 (see Delitzsch on the latter). And He
also turns the darkest night into morning, and darkens the
day into night again. These words refer to the regular interchange of day and night; for *tsalmâveth,* the shadow of death,
i.e. thick darkness, never denotes the regularly recurring
gloominess of night, but the appalling gloom of night (Job
xxiv. 17), more especially of the night of death (Job iii. 5, x. 21,
22, xxxviii. 17; Ps. xliv. 20), the unlighted depth of the heart
of the earth (Job xxviii. 3), the darkness of the prison (Ps.
cvii. 10, 14), also of wickedness (Job xii. 22, xxxiv. 22), of sufferings (Job xvi. 16; Jer. xiii. 16; Ps. xxiii. 4), and of spiritual
misery (Isa. ix. 1). Consequently the words point to the
judicial rule of the Almighty in the world. As the Almighty
turns the darkness of death into light, and the deepest misery
into prosperity and health,[1] so He darkens the bright day of
prosperity into the dark night of adversity, and calls to the
waters of the sea to pour themselves over the earth like the
flood, and to destroy the ungodly. The idea that by the waters
of the sea, which pour themselves out at the call of God over
the surface of the earth, we are to understand the moisture
which rises from the sea and then falls upon the earth as rain, no
more answers to the words themselves, than the idea expressed
by Hitzig, that they refer to the water of the rivers and brooks,
which flow out of the sea as well as into it (Eccles. i. 7). The
words suggest the thought of terrible inundations of the earth
by the swelling of the sea, and the allusion to the judgment of
the flood can hardly be overlooked. This judicial act of the
Almighty, no strong man and no fortress can defy. With the
swiftness of lightning He causes desolation to smite the strong
man. *Bâlag,* lit. *micare,* used in the Arabic to denote the

---

[1] Theodoret has given a correct explanation, though he does not quite
exhaust the force of the words: "It is easy for Him to turn even the greatest
dangers into happiness; for by the shadow of death he means great dangers.
And it is also easy to bring calamity upon those who are in prosperity."

lighting up of the rays of the dawn, *hiphil* to cause to light up,
is applied here to motion with the swiftness of lightning; it is
also employed in a purely metaphorical sense for the lighting
up of the countenance (Ps. xxxix. 14; Job ix. 27, x. 20). In
ver. 9*b* the address is continued in a descriptive form; יָבוֹא has
not a causative meaning. The two clauses of this verse point to
the fate which awaits the Israelites who trust in their strength
and their fortifications (ch. vi. 13). And yet they persist in
unrighteousness.

Ver. 10. " *They hate the monitor in the gate, and abhor him
that speaketh uprightly.* Ver. 11. *Therefore, because ye tread
upon the poor, and take the distribution of corn from him, ye
have built houses of square stones, and will not dwell therein;
planted pleasant vineyards, and will not drink their wine.* Ver. 12.
*For I know how many are your transgressions, and how great
your sins; oppressing the righteous, taking atonement money; and
ye bow down the poor in the gate.*" However natural it may
seem to take מוֹכִיחַ and דֹּבֵר תָּמִים in ver. 10 as referring to prophets, who charge the ungodly with their acts of unrighteousness, as Jerome does, this explanation is precluded not only by
bassha'ar (in the gate), since the gate was not the meeting-place
of the people where the prophets were accustomed to stand, but
the place where courts of judgment were held, and all the public
affairs of the community discussed (see at Deut. xxi. 19); but
also by the first half of ver. 11, which presupposes judicial proceedings. *Mōkhūăch* is not merely the judge who puts down
unjust accusers, but any one who lifts up his voice in a court of
justice against acts of injustice (as in Isa. xxix. 21). דֹּבֵר תָּמִים,
he who says what is blameless, *i.e.* what is right and true: this
is to be taken generally, and not to be restricted to the accused
who seeks to defend his innocence. תִּעֵב is a stronger expression than שָׂנֵא. The punishment for this unjust oppression of
the poor will be the withdrawal of their possessions. The *ἀπ.
λεγ. bōshēs* is a dialectically different form for בּוֹסֵס, from בּוּס,
to trample down (Rashi, Kimchi), analogous to the interchange
of שִׁרְיוֹן and סִרְיוֹן, a coat of mail, although as a rule שׂ passes
into ס, and not ס into שׂ. For the derivation from בֹּשׁ, according to which בּוֹשֵׁס would stand for בּוֹשֵׁשׁ (Hitzig and Tuch on
Gen. p. 85), is opposed both to the construction with עַל, and
also to the circumstance that בּוֹשֵׁשׁ means to delay (Ex. xxxii. 1;

Judg. v. 28) ; and the derivation suggested by Hitzig from an Arabic verb, signifying to carry one's self haughtily towards others, is a mere loophole. Taking a gift of corn from the poor refers to unjust extortion on the part of the judge, who will only do justice to a poor man when he is paid for it. The main clause, which was introduced with *lākhēn*, is continued with בָּתֵּי גָזִית : "thus have ye built houses of square stones, and shall not dwell therein;" for "ye shall not dwell in the houses of square stones which ye have built." The threat is taken from Deut. xxviii. 30, 39, and sets before them the plundering of the land and the banishment of the people. Houses built of square stones are splendid buildings (see Isa. ix. 9). The reason for this threat is given in ver. 12, where reference is made to the multitude and magnitude of the sins, of which injustice in the administration of justice is again held up as the chief sin. The participles צֹרְרֵי and לֹקְחֵי are attached to the suffixes of פִּשְׁעֵיכֶם and חַטֹּאתֵיכֶם : *your* sins, who oppress the righteous, attack him, and take atonement money, contrary to the express command of the law in Num. xxxv. 31, to take no *kōpher* for the soul of a murderer. The judges allowed the rich murderer to purchase exemption from capital punishment by the payment of atonement money, whilst they bowed down the right of the poor. Observe the transition from the participle to the third person fem., by which the prophet turns away with disgust from these ungodly judges. Bowing down the poor is a concise expression for bowing down the right of the poor : compare ch. ii. 7 and the warnings against this sin (Ex. xxiii. 6 ; Deut. xvi. 19).

Vers. 13–17. With the new turn that all talking is useless, Amos repeats the admonition to seek good and hate evil, if they would live and obtain favour with God (vers. 13–15); and then appends the threat that deep mourning will arise on every hand, since God is drawing near to judgment. Ver. 13. "*Therefore, whoever has prudence at this time is silent, for it is an evil time.*" As *lākhēn* (therefore) always introduces the threatening of divine punishment after the exposure of the sins (cf. vers. 11, 16, ch. vi. 7, iv. 12, iii. 11), we might be disposed to connect ver. 13 with the preceding verse; but the contents of the verse require that it should be taken in connection with what follows, so that *lākhēn* simply denotes the close connection of the two turns of speech, *i.e.* indicates that the new command in vers. 14, 15 is a consequence of the previous warnings. *Hammaskîl*, the prudent man, he who acts wisely, is silent. בָּעֵת הַהִיא, at a time such as this is, because it is an evil time, not however "a dangerous time to speak, on account of the malignity of those in power," but a time of moral corruption, in which all speaking and warning are of no avail. It is opposed to the context to refer בעת ההיא to the future, *i.e.* to the time when God will come to punish, in which case the silence would be equivalent to not murmuring against God (Rashi and others). At the same time, love to his people, and zeal for their deliverance, impel the prophet to repeat his call to them to return.

Ver. 14. "*Seek good, and not evil, that ye may live; and so Jehovah the God of hosts may be with you, as ye say.* Ver. 15. *Hate evil, and love good, and set up justice in the gate; perhaps Jehovah the God of hosts will show favour to the remnant of Joseph.*" The command to seek and love good is practically the same as that to seek the Lord in vers. 4, 6; and therefore the promise is the same, "that ye may live." But it is only in fellowship with God that man has life. This truth the Israelites laid hold of in a perfectly outward sense, fancying that they stood in fellowship with God by virtue of their outward connection with the covenant nation as sons of Israel or Abraham (cf. John viii. 39), and that the threatened judgment could not reach them, but that God would deliver them in every time of oppression by the heathen (cf. Mic. iii. 11; Jer. vii. 10): Amos meets this delusion with the remark, "that Jehovah may be so with you as ye say." כֵּן neither means "in case ye do so" (Rashi, Baur), nor "in like manner as, *i.e.* if ye strive after good" (Hitzig). Neither of these meanings can be established, and here they are untenable, for the simple reason that כֵּן unmistakeably corresponds with the following כַּאֲשֶׁר. It means nothing more than "so as ye say." The thought is the following: "Seek good, and not evil: then will Jehovah the God of the heavenly hosts be with you as a helper in distress, so as ye say." This implied that in their present condition, so long as they sought good, they ought not to comfort themselves with the certainty of Jehovah's help. Seeking good is explained in ver. 15 as loving good, and this is still further defined as setting up justice in the gate, *i.e.* maintaining a righteous administration of justice at the place of judgment; and to this the hope, so humiliating to carnal security, is attached: perhaps God will then show favour to the remnant of the people. The emphasis in these words is laid as much upon *perhaps* as upon the remnant of Joseph. The expression "*perhaps* He will show favour" indicates that the measure of Israel's sins was full, and no deliverance could be hoped for if God were to proceed to act according to His righteousness. The "remnant of Joseph" does not refer to "the existing condition of the ten tribes" (Ros., Hitzig). For although Hazael and Benhadad had conquered the whole of the land of Gilead in the times of Jehu and Jehoahaz, and had annihilated the Israelitish army with the exception of a very small remnant (2 Kings x. 32, 33, xiii. 3, 7), Joash and Jeroboam II. had recovered from the Syrians all the conquered territory, and restored the kingdom to its original bounds (2 Kings xiii. 23 sqq., xiv. 26–28). Consequently Amos could not possibly describe the state of the kingdom of the ten tribes in the time of Jeroboam II. as "the remnant of Joseph." As the Syrians had not attempted any deportation, the nation of the ten tribes during the reign of Jeroboam was still, or was once more, all Israel. If, therefore, Amos merely holds out the possibility of the favouring of the remnant of Joseph, he thereby gives distinctly to understand, that in the approaching judgment Israel will perish with the exception of a remnant, which may possibly be preserved after the great chastisement (cf. ver. 3), just as Joel (iii. 5) and Isaiah (vi. 13, x. 21–23) promise only the salvation of a remnant to the kingdom of Judah.

This judgment is announced in vers. 16, 17. Ver. 16. "*Therefore thus saith Jehovah the God of hosts, the Lord: In all roads lamentation! and in all streets will men say, Alas! alas! and they call the husbandman to mourning, and lamentation to those skilled in lamenting. Ver. 17. And in all vineyards lamentation, because I go through the midst of thee, saith Jehovah.*" *Lâkhēn* (therefore) is not connected with the admonitions in vers. 14, 15, nor can it point back to the reproaches in vers. 7, 10–12, since they are too far off: it rather links on to the substance of ver. 13, which involves the thought that all admonition to return is fruitless, and the ungodly still persist in their unrighteousness,—a thought which also forms the background of vers. 14, 15. The meaning of vers. 16, 17 is, that mourning and lamentation for the dead will fill both city and land. On every hand will there be dead to weep for, because Jehovah will go judging through the land. The roads and streets are not merely those of the capital, although these are primarily to be thought of, but those of all the towns in the kingdom. *Mispēd* is the death-wail. This is evident from the parallel *'âmar hō hō*, saying, Alas, alas! *i.e.* striking up the death-wail (cf. Jer. xxii. 18). And this death-wail will not be heard in all the streets of the towns only, but the husbandman will also be called from the field to mourn, *i.e.* to weep for one who has died in his house. The verb קָרְאוּ, they call, belongs to מִסְפֵּד אֶל ', they call lamentation to those skilled in mourning: for they call out the word *mispēd* to the professional mourners; in other words, they send for them to strike up their wailing for the dead. יֹדְעֵי נֶהִי (those skilled in mourning) are the public wailing women, who were hired when a death occurred to sing mourning songs (compare Jer. ix. 16, Matt. ix. 23, and my *Bibl. Archäologie*, ii. p. 105). Even in all the vineyards, the places where rejoicing is generally looked for (ver. 11; Isa. xvi. 10), the death-wail will be heard. Ver. 17*b* mentions the event which occasions the lamentation everywhere. כִּי, for (not "if") I go through the midst of thee. These words are easily explained from Ex. xii. 12, from which Amos has taken them. Jehovah there says to Moses, "I pass through the land of Egypt, and smite all the first-born." And just as the Lord once passed through Egypt, so will He now pass judicially through Israel, and slay the ungodly. For Israel is no longer the nation of the covenant, which He passes over and spares (ch. vii. 8, viii. 2), but has become an Egypt, which He will pass through as a judge to punish it. This threat is carried out still further in the next two sections, commencing with *hōi*.

Vers. 18–27. The first turn.—Ver. 18. "*Woe to those who desire the day of Jehovah! What good is the day of Jehovah to you? It is darkness, and not light. Ver. 19. As if a man fleeth before the lion, and the bear meets him; and he comes into the house, and rests his hand upon the wall, and the snake bites him. Ver. 20. Alas! is not the day of Jehovah darkness, and not light; and gloom, and no brightness in it?*" As the Israelites rested their hope of deliverance from every kind of hostile oppression upon their outward connection with the covenant nation (ver. 14); many wished the day to come, on which Jehovah would judge all the heathen, and redeem Israel out of all distress, and exalt it to might and dominion above all nations, and bless it with honour and glory, applying the prophecy of Joel in ch. iii. without the least reserve to Israel as the nation of Jehovah, and without considering that, according to Joel ii. 32, those only would be saved on the day of Jehovah who called upon the name of the Lord, and were called by the Lord, *i.e.* were acknowledged by the Lord as His own. These infatuated hopes, which confirmed the nation in the security of its life of sin, are met by Amos with an exclamation of woe upon those who long for the day of Jehovah to come, and with the declaration explanatory of the woe, that that day is darkness and not light, and will bring them nothing but harm and destruction, and not prosperity and salvation. He explains this in ver. 19 by a figure taken from life. To those who wish the day of Jehovah to come, the same thing will happen as to a man who, when fleeing from a lion, meets a bear, etc. The meaning is perfectly clear: whoever would escape one danger, falls into a second; and whoever escapes this, falls into a third, and perishes therein. The serpent's bite in the hand is fatal. " In that day every place is full of danger and death; neither in-doors nor out-of-doors is any one safe: for out-of-doors lions and bears prowl about, and in-doors snakes lie hidden, even in the holes of the walls" (C. a. Lap.). After this figurative indication of the sufferings and calamities which the day of the Lord will bring, Amos once more repeats in ver. 20, in a still more emphatic manner (הלא, *nonne* = assuredly), that it will be no day of salvation, *sc.* to those who seek evil and not good, and trample justice and righteousness under foot (vers. 14, 15).

This threatening judgment will not be averted by the Israelites, even by their feasts and sacrifices (vers. 21, 22). The Lord has no pleasure in the feasts which they celebrate. Their outward, heartless worship, does not make them into the people of God, who can count upon His grace. Ver. 21. *" I hate, I despise your feasts, and do not like to smell your holy days. Ver. 22. For if ye offer me burnt-offerings, and your meat-offerings, I have no pleasure therein; and the thank-offering of your fatted calves I do not regard.* Ver. 23. *Put away from me the noise of thy songs; and I do not like to hear the playing of thy harps.* Ver. 24. *And let judgment roll like water, and righteousness like an inexhaustible stream.*" By the rejection of the *opus operatum* of the feasts and sacrifices, the roots are cut away from the false reliance of the Israelites upon their connection with the people of God. The combination of the words שָׂנֵאתִי מָאַסְתִּי expresses in the strongest terms the dislike of God to the feasts of those who were at enmity with Him. *Chaggīm* are the great annual feasts; *'ătsârōth,* the meetings for worship at those feasts, inasmuch as a holy meeting took place at the *'ătsereth* of the feast of Passover and feast of Tabernacles (see at Lev. xxiii. 36). *Rīăch,* to smell, is an expression of satisfaction, with an allusion to the רֵיחַ נִיחוֹחַ, which ascended to God from the burning sacrifice (see Lev. xxvi. 31). *Kī,* in ver. 22, is explanatory: " for," not " yea." The observance of the feast culminated in the sacrifices. God did not like the feasts, because He had no pleasure in the sacrifices. In ver. 23a the two kinds of sacrifice, *'ōlâh* and *minchâh,* are divided between the protasis and apodosis, which gives rise to a certain incongruity. The sentences, if written fully, would read thus: When ye offer me burnt-offerings and meat-offerings, I have no pleasure in your burnt-offerings and meat-offerings. To these two kinds the *shelem,* the health-offering or peace-offering, is added as a third class in ver. 22b. מְרִיאִים, fattened things, generally mentioned along with *bâqâr* as one particular species, for fattened calves (see Isa. i. 11). In הָסֵר (ver. 23) Israel is addressed as a whole. הֲמוֹן שִׁרֶיךָ, the noise of thy songs, answers to the strong expression הָסֵר. The singing of their psalms is nothing more to God than a wearisome noise, which is to be brought to an end. Singing and playing upon harps formed part of the temple worship (*vid.* 1 Chron. xvi. 40, xxiii. 5, and xxv.). Isaiah (Isa. i. 11 sqq.) also refuses the heartless sacrifice and worship of the people, who have fallen away from God in their hearts. It is very clear from the sentence which Amos pronounces here, that the worship at Bethel was an imitation of the temple service at Jerusalem. If, therefore, with ch. vi. 1 in view, where the careless upon Mount Zion and in Samaria are addressed, we are warranted in assuming that here also the prophet has the worship in Judah in his mind as well; the words apply primarily and chiefly to the worship of the kingdom of the ten tribes, and therefore even in that case they prove that, with regard to ritual, it was based upon the model of the temple service at Jerusalem. Because the Lord has no pleasure in this hypocritical worship, the judgment shall pour like a flood over the land. The meaning of ver. 24 is not, " Let justice and righteousness take the place of your sacrifices." *Mishpât* is not the justice to be practised by men; for " although Jehovah might promise that He would create righteousness in the nation, so that it would fill the land as it were like a flood (Isa. xi. 9), He only demands righteousness generally, and not actually in floods" (Hitzig). Still less can *mishpât ûtsᵉdâqâh* be understood as relating to the righteousness of the gospel which Christ has revealed. This thought is a very far-fetched one here, and is only founded upon the rendering given to יִגַּל, *et revelabitur* (Targ., Jerome, = יִגָּל), whereas יִגַּל comes from גָּלַל, to roll, to roll along. The verse is to be explained according to Isa. x. 22, and threatens the flooding of the land with judgment and the punitive righteousness of God (Theod. Mops., Theodoret, Cyr., Kimchi, and others).

Their heartless worship would not arrest the flood of divine judgments, since Israel had from time immemorial been addicted to idolatry. Ver. 25. " *Have ye offered me sacrifices and gifts in the desert forty years, O house of Israel?* Ver. 26. *But have ye borne the booth of your king and the pedestal of your images, the star of your gods, which ye made for yourselves?* Ver. 27. *Then I will carry you beyond Damascus, saith Jehovah; God of hosts is His name.*" The connection between these verses and what precedes is explained by Hengstenberg thus: " All this (the acts of worship enumerated in vers. 21–23) can no more be called a true worship, than the open idolatry in the wilderness. Therefore (ver. 17) as in that instance the outwardly idolatrous people did not tread the holy land, so now will the inwardly idolatrous people be driven out of the holy land" (*Dissertations on the Pentateuch*, vol. i. p. 157 transl.). But if this were the train of thought, the prophet would not have omitted all reference to the punishment of the idolatrous people in the wilderness. And as there is no such allusion here, it is more natural to take vers. 25 and 26, as Calvin does, and regard the reference to the idolatry of the people, which was practised even in the wilderness, as assigning a further reason for their exposure to punishment.[1] The question, "Have ye offered me sacrifices?" is equivalent to a denial, and the words apply to the nation as a whole, or the great mass of the people, individual exceptions being passed by. The *forty* years are used as a round number, to denote the time during which the people were sentenced to die in the wilderness after the rebellion at Kadesh, just as in Num. xiv. 33, 34, and Josh. v. 6, where this time, which actually amounted to only thirty-eight years, is given, as it is here, as forty years. And " the prophet could speak all the more naturally of forty years, since the germ of apostasy already existed in the great mass of the people, even when they still continued outwardly to maintain their fidelity to the God of Israel" (Hengstenberg). During that time even the circumcision of the children born in the thirty-eight years was suspended (see at Josh. v. 5–7), and the sacrificial worship prescribed by the law fell more and more into disuse, so that the generation that was sentenced to die out offered no more sacrifices. *Z*ᵉ*bhâchīm* (slain-offerings) and *min-châh* (meat-offerings), *i.e.* bleeding and bloodless sacrifices, are mentioned here as the two principal kinds, to denote sacrifices of all kinds. We cannot infer from this that the daily sacrificial worship was entirely suspended : in Num. xvii. 11, indeed, the altar-fire is actually mentioned, and the daily sacrifice assumed to be still in existence ; at the same time, the event there referred to belonged to the time immediately succeeding the passing of the sentence upon the people. Amos mentions the omission of the sacrifices, however, not as an evidence that the blessings which the Lord had conferred upon the people were not to be attributed to the sacrifices they had offered to Him,

---

[1] " In this place," says Calvin, " the prophet proves more clearly, that he is not merely reproving hypocrisy among the Israelites, or the fact that they only obtruded their external pomps upon the notice of God, without any true piety of heart, but he also condemns their departure from the precepts of the law. And he shows that this was not a new disease among the Israelitish people, since their fathers had mixed up such leaven as this with the worship of God from the very beginning, and had thereby corrupted that worship. He therefore shows that the Israelites had always been addicted to superstitions, and could not be kept in any way whatever to the true and innate worship of God."

as Ephraem Syrus supposes, nor to support the assertion that
God does not need or wish for their worship, for which Hitzig
appeals to Jer. vii. 22; but as a proof that from time immemorial Israel has acted faithlessly towards its God, in adducing
which he comprehends all the different generations of the
people in the unity of the house of Israel, because the existing
generation resembled the contemporaries of Moses in character
and conduct. Ver. 26 is attached in an adversative sense:
"To me (Jehovah) ye have offered no sacrifices, but ye have
borne," etc. The opposition between the Jehovah-worship
which they suspended, and the idol-worship which they carried
on, is so clearly expressed in the verbs הִגַּשְׁתֶּם and נְשָׂאתֶם, which
correspond to one another, that the idea is precluded at once as
altogether untenable, that "ver. 26 refers to either the present
or future in the form of an inference drawn from the preceding verse: therefore do ye (or shall ye) carry the hut of your
king," etc. Moreover, the idea of the idols being carried into
captivity, which would be the meaning of נָשָׂא in that case, is
utterly foreign to the prophetical range of thought. It is not
those who go into captivity who carry their gods away with
them; but the gods of a vanquished nation are carried away
by the conquerors (Isa. xlvi. 1). To give a correct interpretation to this difficult verse, which has been explained in various
ways from the very earliest times, it is necessary, above all
things, to bear in mind the parallelism of the clauses. Whereas
in the first half of the verse the two objects are connected
together by the copula ו (וְאֵת), the omission of both אֵת and the
copula ו before כּוֹכַב indicates most obviously that כּוֹכַב אֱלֹהֵיכֶם
does not introduce a third object in addition to the two preceding ones, but rather that the intention is to define those
objects more precisely; from which it follows still further, that
סִכּוּת מַלְכְּכֶם and כִּיּוּן צַלְמֵיכֶם do not denote two different kinds
of idolatry, but simply two different forms of the very same
idolatry. The two ἅπ. λεγ. sikkûth and kiyyûn are undoubtedly
appellatives, notwithstanding the fact that the ancient versions
have taken kiyyûn as the proper name of a deity. This is
required by the parallelism of the members; for צלמיכם stands
in the same relation to כיון as מלככם to סבות. The plural צלמיכם,
however, cannot be in apposition to the singular כיון (kiyyûn,
your images), but must be a genitive governed by it: "the

kiyyūn of your images." And in the same way מלככם is the
genitive after סכות : " the *sikkūth* of your king." *Sikkūth* has
been taken in an appellative sense by all the ancient translators.
The LXX. and Symm. render it τὴν σκηνήν ; the Peshito,
Jerome, and the Ar. *tentorium*. The Chaldee has retained
sikkūth. The rendering adopted by Aquila, συσκιασμός, is
etymologically the more exact; for *sikkūth*, from סָכַךְ, to shade,
signifies a shade or shelter, hence a covering, a booth, and
is not to be explained either from *sâkhath*, to be silent, from
which Hitzig deduces the meaning " block," or from the Syriac
and Chaldee word סכתא, a nail or stake, as Rosenmüller and
Ewald suppose. בִּין, from כּוּן, is related to כֵּן, *basis* (Ex. xxx.
18), and מְכוֹנָה, and signifies a pedestal or framework. The
correctness of the Masoretic pointing of the word is attested
by the *kiyyūn* of the Chaldee, and also by צַלְמֵיכֶם, inasmuch
as the reading בֵּין, which is given in the LXX. and Syr.,
requires the singular צַלְמְכֶם, which is also given in the Syriac.
צְלָמִים are images of gods, as in Num. xxxiii. 52, 2 Kings xi. 18.
The words כּוֹכַב אֱל׳ which follow are indeed also governed by
נְשָׂאתֶם ; but, as the omission of וְאֵת clearly shows, the connection is only a loose one, so that it is rather to be regarded as
in apposition to the preceding objects in the sense of " namely,
the star of your god;" and there is no necessity to alter the
pointing, as Hitzig proposes, and read כּוֹכָב, " a star was your
god," although this rendering expresses the sense quite correctly. כּוֹכַב אֱלֹהֵיכֶם is equivalent to the star, which is your god,
which ye worship as your god (for this use of the construct
state, see Ges. § 116, 5). By the star we have to picture to
ourselves not a star formed by human hand as a representation
of the god, nor an image of a god with the figure of a star upon
its head, like those found upon the Ninevite sculptures (see
Layard). For if this had been what Amos meant, he would
have repeated the particle וְאֵת before כּוֹכַב. The thought is
therefore the following : the king whose booth, and the images
whose stand they carried, were a star which they had made
their god, *i.e.* a star-deity (אֲשֶׁר refers to אֱלֹהֵיכֶם, not to כּוֹכָב).
This star-god, which they worshipped as their king, they had
embodied in *tsᵉlâmīm*. The booth and the stand were the
things used for protecting and carrying the images of the star-
god. *Sikkūth* was no doubt a portable shrine, in which the

image of the deity was kept. Such shrines (ναοί, ναΐσκοι) were used by the Egyptians, according to Herodotus (ii. 63) and Diodorus Sic. (i. 97): they were "small chapels, generally gilded and ornamented with flowers and in other ways, intended to hold a small idol when processions were made, and to be carried or driven about with it" (Drumann, *On the Rosetta Inscription*, p. 211). The stand on which the chapel was placed during these processions was called παστοφόριον (Drumann, p. 212); the bearers were called ἱεραφόροι or παστοφόροι (D. p. 226). This Egyptian custom explains the prophet's words: "the hut of your king, and the stand of your images," as Hengstenberg has shown in his *Dissertations on the Pentateuch*, vol. i. p. 161), and points to Egypt as the source of the idolatry condemned by Amos. This is also favoured by the fact, that the golden calf which the Israelites worshipped at Sinai was an imitation of the idolatry of Egypt; also by the testimony of the prophet Ezekiel (ch. xx. 7 sqq.), to the effect that the Israelites did not desist even in the wilderness from the abominations of their eyes, namely the idols of Egypt; and lastly, by the circumstance that the idea of there being any allusion in the words to the worship of Moloch or Saturn is altogether irreconcilable with the Hebrew text, and cannot be historically sustained,[1] whereas star-worship, or at any rate the

---

[1] This explanation of the words is simply founded upon the rendering of the LXX.: καὶ ἀνελάβετε τὴν σκηνὴν τοῦ Μολόχ καὶ τὸ ἄστρον τοῦ Θεοῦ ὑμῶν Ῥαιφάν, τοὺς τύπους οὓς ἐποιήσατε ἑαυτοῖς. These translators, therefore, have not only rendered מלככם erroneously as Μολόχ, but have arbitrarily twisted the other words of the Hebrew text. For the Hebrew reading מלככם is proved to be the original one, not only by the τοῦ βασιλέως ὑμῶν of Symm. and Theod., but also by the Μαλχόμ of Aquila and the ܡܠܟܟܘܢ of the Peshito; and all the other ancient translators enter a protest against the displacing of the other words. The name Ῥαιφάν (Ῥηφάν), or Ῥεμφάν (Acts vii. 43), however, owes its origin simply to the false reading of the unpointed כין as ריפן, inasmuch as in the old Hebrew writing not only is ב similar to ר, but ו is also similar to פ; and in 2 Sam. xxii. 12, where חשרת־מים is rendered σκοτός (i.e. חשכת) ὑδάτων, we have an example of the interchange of ב and ר. There was no god *Rephan* or *Rempha*; for the name never occurs apart from the LXX. The statement made in the Arabico-Coptic list of planets, edited by Ath. Kircher, that *Suhhel* (the Arabic name of Saturn) is the same as Ῥηφάν, and the remark found in a Coptic MS. on the Acts of the Apostles, "*Rephan*

worship of the sun, was widely spread in Egypt from the very earliest times. According to the more recent investigations into the mythology of the ancient Egyptians which have been made by Lepsius (*Transactions of the Academy of Science at Berlin*, 1851, p. 157 sqq.), "the worship of the sun was the oldest kernel and most general principle of the religious belief of Egypt;" and this "was regarded even down to the very latest times as the outward culminating point of the whole system of

deus temporis," prove nothing more than that Coptic Christians supposed the *Rephan* or *Remphan*, whose name occurred in their version of the Bible which was founded upon the LXX., to be the star Saturn as the god of time; but they by no means prove that the ancient Egyptians called Saturn *Rephan*, or were acquainted with any deity of that name, since the occurrence of the Greek names Ὑλια and Σελινη for sun and moon are a sufficient proof of the very recent origin of the list referred to. It is true that the Peshito has also rendered כִּיּוּן by כֵּ֫אוָן (כִּיּוּן), by which the Syrians understood Saturn, as we may see from a passage of Ephraem Syrus, quoted by Gesenius in his *Comm. on Isaiah* (ii. p. 344), where this father, in his *Sermones adv. hær.* s. 8, when ridiculing the star-worshippers, refers to the *Kevan*, who devoured his own children. But no further evidence can be adduced in support of the correctness of this explanation of כִּיּוּן. The corresponding use of the Arabic *Kaivân* for Saturn, to which appeal has also been made, does not occur in any of the earlier Arabic writings, but has simply passed into the Arabic from the Persian; so that the name and its interpretation originated with the Syrian church, passing thence to the Persians, and eventually reaching the Arabs through them. Consequently the interpretation of *Kevan* by Saturn has no higher worth than that of an exegetical conjecture, which is not elevated into a truth by the fact that בִּין is mentioned in the *Cod. Nazar.* i. p. 54, ed. Norb., in connection with Nebo, Bel, and Nerig (= Nergal). With the exception of these passages, and the gloss of a recent Arabian grammarian cited by Bochart, viz. "Keivan signifies Suhhel," not a single historical trace can be found of *Kevan* having been an ancient oriental name of Saturn; so that the latest supporter of this hypothesis, namely Movers (*Phönizier*, i. p. 290), has endeavoured to prop up the arguments already mentioned in his own peculiar and uncritical manner, by recalling the Phœnician and Babylonian names, *San-Choniâth*, *Kyn-el-Adan*, and others. Not even the Græco-Syrian fathers make any reference to this interpretation. Theodoret cannot say anything more about Μολόχ καὶ Ῥεφάν, than that they were εἰδώλων ὀνόματα; and Theod. Mops. has this observation on Ῥεμφάν: φασὶ δὲ τὸν ἑωσφόρον οὕτω κατὰ τὴν Ἑβραίων γλῶτταν. It is still very doubtful, therefore, whether the Alexandrian and Syrian translators of Amos really supposed Ῥαιφάν and כִּין to signify Saturn; and this interpretation, whether it originated with the translators named, or was first started by religion" (Lepsius, p. 193). The first group of deities of Upper and Lower Egypt consists of none but sun-gods (p. 188).[1] *Ra, i.e.* Helios, is the prototype of the kings, the highest potency and prototype of nearly all the gods, the king of the gods, and he is identified with Osiris (p. 194). But from the time of Menes, Osiris has been worshipped in This and Abydos; whilst in Memphis the bull Apis was regarded as the living copy of Osiris (p. 191). According to Herodotus (ii. 42), Osiris and Isis were the only gods worshipped by the ancient Egyptians; and, according to Diodorus Sic. (i. 11), the Egyptians were said to have had originally only two gods, Helios and Selene, and to have worshipped the former in Osiris, the latter in Isis. The *Pan* of *Mendes* appears to have also been a peculiar form of Osiris (cf. Diod. Sic. i. 25, and Leps. p. 175). Herodotus (ii. 145) speaks of this as of primeval antiquity, and reckons it

later commentators upon these versions, arose in all probability simply from a combination of the Greek legend concerning Saturn, who swallowed his own children, and the Moloch who was worshipped with the sacrifice of children, and therefore might also be said to devour children; that is to say, it was merely an inference drawn from the rendering of מלכבם as Μολόχ. But we are precluded from thinking of Moloch-worship, or regarding מלכבם, "your king," as referring to Moloch, by the simple circumstance that כּוֹכַב אֱלֹהֵיכֶם unquestionably points to the Sabæan (sidereal) character of the worship condemned by Amos, whereas nothing is known of the sidereal nature of Moloch; and even if the sun is to be regarded as the physical basis of this deity, as Münter, Creuzer, and others conjecture, it is impossible to discover the slightest trace in the Old Testament of any such basis as this.

The Alexandrian translation of this passage, which we have thus shown to rest upon a misinterpretation of the Hebrew text, has acquired a greater importance than it would otherwise possess, from the fact that the proto-martyr Stephen, in his address (Acts vii. 42, 43), has quoted the words of the prophet according to that version, simply because the departure of the Greek translation from the original text was of no consequence, so far as his object was concerned, viz. to prove to the Jews that they had always resisted the Holy Ghost, inasmuch as the Alex. rendering also contains the thought, that their fathers worshipped the στρατιᾷ τοῦ οὐρανοῦ.

[1] It is true, that in the first divine sphere *Ra* occupies the second place according to the Memphitic doctrine, namely, after *Phtha* (*Hephæstos*), and according to the Theban doctrine, *Amen* ("Αμων). Mentu and Atmu stand at the head (Leps. p. 186); but the two deities, *Mentu, i.e.* the rising sun, and *Atmu, i.e.* the setting sun, are simply a splitting up of *Ra;* and both *Hephæstos* and *Amon* (*Amon-Ra*) were placed at the head of the gods at a later period (Leps. pp. 187, 189).

among the eight so-called first gods; and Diodorus Sic. (i. 18)
describes it as διαφερόντως ὑπὸ τῶν Αἰγυπτίων τιμώμενον. It
was no doubt to these Egyptian sun-gods that the star-god
which the Israelites carried about with them in the wilderness
belonged. This is all that can at present be determined concerning it. There is not sufficient evidence to support Hengstenberg's opinion, that the Egyptian Pan as the sun-god was
the king worshipped by them. It is also impossible to establish
the identity of the king mentioned by Amos with the שְׂעִירִים in
Lev. xvii. 7, since these שְׂעִירִים, even if they are connected with
the goat-worship of Mendes, are not exhausted by this goat-
deity.

The prophet therefore affirms that, during the forty years'
journey through the wilderness, Israel did not offer sacrifices
to its true King Jehovah, but carried about with it a star made
into a god as the king of heaven. If, then, as has already been
observed, we understand this assertion as referring to the great
mass of the people, like the similar passage in Isa. xliii. 23, it
agrees with the intimations in the Pentateuch as to the attitude
of Israel. For, beside the several grosser outbreaks of rebellion against the Lord, which are the only ones recorded at all
circumstantially there, and which show clearly enough that it
was not devoted to its God with all its heart, we also find traces
of open idolatry. Among these are the command in Lev. xvii.,
that every one who slaughtered a sacrificial animal was to
bring it to the tabernacle, when taken in connection with the
reason assigned, namely, that they were not to offer their
sacrifices any more to the *Seʿīrīm*, after which they went a
whoring (ver. 7), and the warning in Deut. iv. 19, against
worshipping the sun, moon, and stars, even all the host of
heaven, from which we may infer that Moses had a reason for
this, founded upon existing circumstances. After this further
proof of the apostasy of Israel from its God, the judgment
already indicated in ver. 24 is still further defined in ver. 27
as the banishment of the people far beyond the borders of the
land given to it by the Lord, where *higlâh* evidently points
back to *yiggal* in ver. 24. מֵהָלְאָה לְ, lit. "from afar with regard
to," *i.e.* so that when looked at from Damascus, the place
showed itself afar off, *i.e.* according to one mode of viewing it,
"far beyond Damascus."

Ch. vi. The prophet utters the second woe over the careless heads of the nation, who were content with the existing state of things, who believed in no divine judgment, and who revelled in their riches (vers. 1-6). To these he announces destruction and the general overthrow of the kingdom (vers. 7-11), because they act perversely, and trust in their own power (vers. 12-14). Ver. 1. " *Woe to the secure upon Zion, and to the careless upon the mountain of Samaria, to the chief men of the first of the nations, to whom the house of Israel comes!* Ver. 2. *Go over to Calneh, and see; and proceed thence to Hamath, the great one: and go down to Gath of the Philistines: are they indeed better than these kingdoms? or is their territory greater than your territory?* Ver. 3. *Ye who keep the day of calamity far off, and bring the seat of violence near.*" This woe applies to the great men in Zion and Samaria, that is to say, to the chiefs of the whole of the covenant nation, because they were all sunk in the same godless security; though special allusion is made to the corrupt leaders of the kingdom of the ten tribes, whose debauchery is still further depicted in what follows. These great men are designated in the words נְקֻבֵי רֵאשִׁית הַגּוֹיִם, as the heads of the chosen people, who are known by name. As רֵאשִׁית הג׳ is taken from Num. xxiv. 20, so נקבי is taken from Num. i. 17, where the heads of the tribes who were chosen as princes of the congregation to preside over the numbering of the people are described as men אֲשֶׁר נִקְּבוּ בְּשֵׁמוֹת, who were defined with names, *i.e.* distinguished by names, that is to say, well-known men; and it is used here in the same sense. Observe, however, with reference to רֵאשִׁית הַגּוֹיִם, that in Num. xxiv. 20 we have not הַגּוֹיִם, but simply רֵאשִׁית גּוֹיִם. Amalek is so called there, as being the first heathen nation which rose up in hostility to Israel. On the other hand, ר׳ הגוים is the firstling of the nations, *i.e.* the first or most exalted of all nations. Israel is so called, because Jehovah had chosen it out of all the nations of the earth to be the people of His possession (Ex. xix. 5; cf. 2 Sam. vii. 23). In order to define with still greater precision the position of these princes in the congregation, Amos adds, "to whom the house of Israel cometh," namely, to have its affairs regulated by them as its rulers. These epithets were intended to remind the princes of the people of both kingdoms, " that they were the descendants of those tribe-

princes who had once been honoured to conduct the affairs of
the chosen family, along with Moses and Aaron, and whose
light shone forth from that better age as brilliant examples of
what a truly theocratical character was" (Hengstenberg, *Dissertations*, i. p. 148). To give still greater prominence to the
exalted calling of these princes, Amos shows in ver. 2 that
Israel can justly be called the firstling of the nations, since it
is not inferior either in prosperity or greatness to any of the
powerful and prosperous heathen states. Amos names three
great and flourishing capitals, because he is speaking to the
great men of the capitals of the two kingdoms of Israel, and
the condition of the whole kingdom is reflected in the circumstances of the capital. *Calneh* (= *Calno*, Isa. x. 9) is the later
Ctesiphon in the land of Shinar, or Babylonia, situated upon
the Tigris opposite to Seleucia (see at Gen. x. 10) ; hence the
expression עִבְרוּ, because men were obliged to cross over the
river (Euphrates) in order to get there. *Hamath* : the capital
of the Syrian kingdom of that name, situated upon the Orontes
(see at Gen. x. 18 and Num. xxxiv. 8.) There was not another
Hamath, as Hitzig supposes. The circumstance that Amos
mentions Calneh first, whereas it was much farther to the east,
so that Hamath was nearer to Palestine than Calneh was, may
be explained very simply, from the fact that the enumeration
commences with the most distant place and passes from the
north-east to the south-west, which was in the immediate
neighbourhood of Israel. *Gath* : one of the five capitals of
Philistia, and in David's time the capital of all Philistia (see at
Josh. xiii. 3, 2 Sam. viii. 1). The view still defended by Baur—
namely, that Amos mentions here three cities that had either lost
their former grandeur, or had fallen altogether, for the purpose
of showing the self-secure princes of Israel that the same fate
awaited Zion and Samaria—is groundless and erroneous ; for
although *Calneh* is spoken of in Isa. x. 9 as a city that had
been conquered by the Assyrians, it cannot be proved that this
was the case as early as the time of Amos, but is a simple inference drawn from a false interpretation of the verse before
us. Nor did Jeroboam II. conquer the city of Hamath on the
Orontes, and incorporate its territory with his own kingdom
(see at 2 Kings xiv. 25). And although the Philistian city
Gath was conquered by Uzziah (2 Chron. xxvi. 6), we cannot

infer from 2 Chron. xxvi. 6, or from the fact of Gath not being
mentioned in Amos i. 6–8, that this occurred before the time
of Amos (see at ch. i. 8).   On the other hand, the fact that it
is placed by the side of Hamath in the passage before us, is
rather a proof that the conquest did not take place till afterwards.   Ver. 2b states what the princes of Israel are to see in
the cities mentioned,—namely, that they are not better off (טוֹבִים
denoting outward success or earthly prosperity) than these two
kingdoms, *i.e.* the kingdoms of Judah and Israel, and that their
territories are not larger than theirs.   It is very evident that
this does not apply to cities that have been destroyed.   The
double question הַ . . . אִם requires a negative answer.   Ver. 3
assigns the reason for the woe pronounced upon the sinful
security of the princes of Israel, by depicting the godless conduct of these princes; and this is appended in the manner
peculiar to Amos, viz. in participles.   These princes fancy that
the evil day, *i.e.* the day of misfortune or of judgment and
punishment, is far away (מְנַדִּים, *piel* of נָדָה = נָדַד, to be far off,
signifies in this instance not to put far away, but to regard
as far off); and they go so far as to prepare a seat or throne
close by for wickedness and violence, which must be followed
by judgment.   הַגִּישׁ שֶׁבֶת, to move the sitting (*shebheth* from
yâshabh) of violence near, or better still, taking *shebheth* in
the sense of enthroning, as Ewald does, to move the throne of
violence nearer, *i.e.* to cause violence to erect its throne nearer
and nearer among them.

This forgetfulness of God shows itself more especially in
the reckless licentiousness and debauchery of these men.   Ver.
4. " *They who lie upon beds of ivory, and stretch themselves
upon their couches, and eat lambs from the flock, and calves
out of the fattening stall.   Ver. 5. Who prattle to the tune of the
harp ; like David, they invent string instruments.   Ver. 6. Who
drink wine out of sacrificial bowls, and anoint themselves with
the best oils, and do not afflict themselves for the hurt of Joseph.* "
They lie stretched, as it were poured out (סְרֻחִים), upon beds
inlaid with ivory, to feast and fill their belly with the flesh of
the best lambs and fattened calves, to the playing of harps and
singing, in which they take such pleasure, that they invent new
kinds of playing and singing.   The ἁπ. λεγ. *pârat*, to strew
around (cf. *peret* in Lev. xix. 10), in Arabic to throw many

useless words about, to gossip, describes the singing at the
banquets as frivolous nonsense. כְּלֵי שִׁיר, articles or instruments
of singing, are not musical instruments generally, but, as we
may see from 2 Chron. xxxiv. 12, compared with 2 Chron.
xxix. 26, 27, and 1 Chron. xxiii. 5, the stringed instruments that
were either invented by David (*e.g.* the *nebel*), or arranged by
him for the sacred song of the temple, together with the peculiar mode of playing them; in other words, "the playing upon
stringed instruments introduced by David." Consequently the
meaning of ver. 5 is the following: As David invented stringed
instruments in honour of his God in heaven, so do these princes
invent playing and singing for their god, the belly. The
meaning to invent or devise, which Baur will not allow to חָשַׁב,
is established beyond all doubt by Ex. xxxi. 4. They drink
thereby out of sacrificial bowls of wine, *i.e.* drink wine out of
sacrificial bowls. שָׁתָה with בְּ, as in Gen. xliv. 5. *Mizráq*, in
the plural *mizráqīm* and *mizráqōth*, from *záraq*, to sprinkle,
was the name given both to the vessels used for the sprinkling
of the blood, and also to the bowls made use of for pouring
the libation of wine upon the table of shew-bread (2 Chron.
iv. 8). This word is applied by Amos to the bowls out of
which the gluttons drank their wine; with special reference to
the offering of silver sacrificial bowls made by the tribe-princes
at the consecration of the altar (Num. vii.), to show that
whereas the tribe-princes of Israel in the time of Moses manifested their zeal for the service of Jehovah by presenting sacrificial bowls of silver, the princes of his own time showed just
as much zeal in their care for their god, the belly. *Mizráqīm*
does not mean "rummers, or pitchers used for mixing wine."
Lastly, Amos refers to their anointing themselves with the
firstling of the oils, *i.e.* the best oils, as a sign of unbridled
rejoicing, inasmuch as the custom of anointing was suspended
in time of mourning (2 Sam. xiv. 2), for the purpose of append-
ing the antithesis וְלֹא נֶחְלוּ, they do not afflict or grieve themselves for the ruin of Israel. *Shëbher*, breach, injury, destruction.
Joseph signifies the people and kingdom of the ten tribes.

Vers. 7-11. Announcement of Punishment. — Ver. 7.
"*Therefore will they now go into captivity at the head of the
captives, and the shouting of the revellers will depart.*" Because
these revellers do not trouble themselves about the ruin of

Israel, they will now be obliged to wander into captivity at the head of the people (cf. 1 Kings xxi. 9), when the approaching *shebher* occurs. גֹּלִים בְּרֹאשׁ is chosen with direct reference to רֵאשִׁית שְׁמָנִים, as Jerome has observed: "Ye who are *first* in riches will be the *first* to bear the yoke of captivity." *S²rūchīm* also points back to ver. 4, "those who are stretched upon their couches"—that is, the revellers; and it forms a play upon words with *mirzach*. מַרְזֵחַ signifies a loud cry, here a joyous cry, in Jer. xvi. 5 a cry of lamentation.

This threat is carried out still further in vers. 8–11. Ver. 8. "*The Lord Jehovah hath sworn by Himself, is the saying of Jehovah, the God of hosts: I abhor the pride of Jacob, and his palaces I hate; and give up the city, and the fulness thereof.* Ver. 9. *And it will come to pass, if ten men are left in a house, they shall die.* Ver. 10. *And when his cousin lifts him up, and he that burieth him, to carry out the bones out of the house, and saith to the one in the hindermost corner of the house, Is there still any one with thee? and he says, Not one; then will he say, Hush; for the name of Jehovah is not to be invoked.* Ver. 11. *For, behold, Jehovah commandeth, and men smite the great house to ruins, and the small house into shivers.*" In order to show the secure debauchees the terrible severity of the judgments of God, the Lord announces to His people with a solemn oath the rejection of the nation which is so confident in its own power (cf. ver. 13). The oath runs here as in ch. iv. 2, with this exception, that instead of בְּקָדְשׁוֹ we have בְּנַפְשׁוֹ in the same sense; for the *nephesh* of Jehovah, His inmost being or self, is His holiness. מְתָאֵב, with the guttural softened, for מְתָעֵב. The participle describes the abhorrence as a continued lasting feeling, and not a merely passing emotion. גְּאוֹן יַעֲקֹב, the loftiness or pride of Jacob, *i.e.* everything of which Jacob is proud, the true and imaginary greatness and pride of Israel, which included the palaces of the voluptuous great men, for which reason they are placed in parallelism with 'ע יי' נאון. This glory of Israel Jehovah abhors, and He will destroy it by giving up the city (Samaria), and all that fills it (houses and men), to the enemies to be destroyed. הִסְגִּיר, to give up to the enemy, as in Deut. xxxii. 30 and Ob. 14; not to surround, to which וּמִלְאָהּ is unsuitable. The words not only threaten surrounding, or siege, but also conquest, and (ver. 11) the destruction of the city. And then, even if there are ten in one house, they will all perish. אֲנָשִׁים : people, men. Ten in one house is a large number, which the prophet assumes as the number, to give the stronger emphasis to the thought that not one will escape from death. This thought is still further explained in ver. 10. A relative comes into the house to bury his deceased blood-relation. The suffix to נְשָׂאוֹ refers to the idea involved in מֵתוּ, a dead man. *Dōd,* literally the father's brother, here any near relation whose duty it was to see to the burial of the dead. מְסָרֵף for מְשָׂרֵף, the burner, *i.e.* the burier of the dead. The Israelites were indeed accustomed to *bury* their dead, and not to *burn* the corpses. The description of the burier as *m°sâreph* (a burner) therefore supposes the occurrence of such a multitude of deaths that it is impossible to bury the dead, whose corpses are obliged to be burned, for the purpose of preventing the air from being polluted by the decomposition of the corpses. Of course the burning did not take place at the house, as Hitzig erroneously infers from לְהוֹצִיא עֲצָמִים; for עֲצָמִים denotes the corpse here, as in Ex. xiii. 19, Josh. xxiv. 32, and 2 Kings xiii. 21, and not the different bones of the dead which remained without decomposition or burning. The burier now asks the last living person in the house, who has gone to the very back of the house in order to save his life, whether there is any one still with him, any one still living in the house beside himself, and receives the answer, אֶפֶס (adv.), "Nothing more;" whereupon he says to him, *has,* "Be still," answering to our Hush! because he is afraid that, if he goes on speaking, he may invoke the name of God, or pray for the mercy of God; and he explains his words by adding, "The name of Jehovah must not be mentioned." It is not Amos who adds this explanation, but the relation. Nor does it contain "the words of one who despairs of any better future, and whose mind is oppressed by the weight of the existing evils, as if he said, Prayers would be of no use, for we too must die" (Livel., Ros.). לֹא לְהַזְכִּיר, "it is not to (may not) be mentioned," would be unsuitable as an utterance of despair. It rather indicates the fear lest, by the invocation of the name of God, the eye of God should be drawn towards this last remaining one, and he also should fall a victim to the judgment of death. This judgment the Lord accomplishes not merely by a pestilence which breaks out during the siege, and rages all around (there is no ground for any such limitation of the words), but also by sword and plague during the siege and conquest of the town. For the reason assigned for the threat in ver. 11 points to the latter. כִּי links the words to the main thought in ver. 11, or even ver. 10*b* : " When the Lord delivers up the city and all that fills it, they will all perish ; for, behold, He commands, orders the enemy (the nation in ver. 14), and it will smite in pieces the houses, great and small." The singular הַבַּיִת is used with indefinite generality : every house, great and small (cf. ch. iii. 15).

Vers. 12–14. This judgment also, they, with their perversion of all right, will be unable to avert by their foolish trust in their own power. Ver. 12. *" Do horses indeed run upon the rock, or do men plough (there) with oxen, that ye turn justice into poison, and the fruit of righteousness into wormwood?* Ver. 13. *They who rejoice over what is worthless, who say : with our strength we make ourselves horns !* Ver. 14. *For, behold, I raise over you, O house of Israel, is the saying of Jehovah, the God of hosts, a nation ; and they will oppress you from the territory of Hamath to the brook of the desert."* To explain the threat in ver. 11, Amos now calls attention in ver. 12, under two different similes, to the perversity with which the haughty magnates of Israel, who turn right into bitter wrong, imagine that they can offer a successful resistance, or bid defiance with their own strength to the enemy, whom the Lord will raise up as the executor of His judgment. The perversion of right into its opposite can no more bring salvation than horses can run upon rocks, or any one plough upon such a soil with oxen. In the second question בַּסֶּלַע (on the rock) is to be repeated from the first, as the majority of commentators suppose. But the two questions are not to be taken in connection with the previous verse in the sense of " Ye will no more be able to avert this destruction than horses can run upon rocks," etc. (Chr. B. Mich.) They belong to what follows, and are meant to expose the moral perversity of the unrighteous conduct of the wicked. For הַפַכְתֶּם וגו', see ch. v. 7; and for רֹאשׁ, Hos. x. 4. The impartial administration of justice is called the " fruit of righteousness," on account of the figurative use of the terms darnel and wormwood. These great men, however, rejoice thereby in לֹא דָבָר, " a nothing," or a thing which has no existence. What the prophet refers to may be seen from the parallel clause, viz. their imaginary strength (*chōzeq*). They rested this hope upon the might with which Jeroboam had smitten the Syrians, and restored the ancient boundaries of the kingdom. From this might they would take to themselves (*lâqach*, to take, not now for the first time to create, or ask of God) the horns, to thrust down all their foes. *Horns* are signs and symbols of power (cf. Deut. xxxiii. 17; 1 Kings xxii. 11); here they stand for the military resources, with which they fancied that they could conquer every foe. These delusions of God-forgetting pride the prophet casts down, by saying that Jehovah the God of hosts will raise up a nation against them, which will crush them down in the whole length and breadth of the kingdom. This nation was Assyria. *Kī hinnēh* (for behold) is repeated from ver. 11; and the threat in ver. 14 is thereby described as the resumption and confirmation of the threat expressed in ver. 11, although the *kī* is connected with the perversity condemned in vers. 12, 13, of trusting in their own power. *Lâchats*, to oppress, to crush down. On the expression לְבוֹא חֲמָת, as a standing epithet for the northern boundary of the kingdom of Israel, see Num. xxxiv. 8. As the southern boundary we have נַחַל הָעֲרָבָה instead of יָם הָעֲרָבָה (2 Kings xiv. 25). This is not the willow-brook mentioned in Isa. xv. 7, the present Wady *Sufsaf,* or northern arm of the Wady *el-Kerek* (see Delitzsch on Isaiah, *l.c.*), nor the *Rhinokorura,* the present *el-Arish,* which formed the southern boundary of Canaan, because this is constantly called "the brook of Egypt" (see at Num. xxxiv. 5, Josh. xv. 4), but the present *el-Ahsy* (*Ahsa*), the southern border river which separated Moab from Edom (see at 2 Kings xiv. 25).

III. SIGHTS OR VISIONS.

The last part of the writings of Amos contains five visions, which confirm the contents of the prophetic addresses in the preceding part. The first four visions, however (ch. vii. and viii.), are distinguished from the fifth and last (ch. ix.) by the fact, that whereas the former all commence with the same formula, " Thus hath the Lord showed me," the latter commences with the words, " I saw the Lord," etc. They also differ in their contents, inasmuch as the former symbolize the judgments which have already fallen in part upon Israel, and in part have still to fall; whilst the latter, on the contrary, proclaims the overthrow of the old theocracy, and after this the restoration of the fallen kingdom of God, and its ultimate glory. And again, of these four, the first and second (ch. vii. 1–6) are distinguished from the third and fourth (ch. vii. 7–9, and viii. 1–3) by the fact, that whereas the former contain a promise in reply to the prophet's intercession, that Jacob shall be spared, in the latter any further sparing is expressly refused; so that they are thus formed into two pairs, which differ from one another both in their contents and purpose. This difference is of importance, in relation both to the meaning and also to the historical bearing of the visions. It points to the conclusion, that the first two visions indicate universal judgments, whilst the third and fourth simply threaten the overthrow of the kingdom of Israel in the immediate future, the commencement of which is represented in the fifth and last vision, and which is then still further depicted in its results in connection with the realization of the divine plan of salvation.

VISIONS OF THE LOCUSTS, THE FIRE, AND THE PLUMB-LINE. THE PROPHET'S EXPERIENCE AT BETHEL.—CHAP. VII.

Vers. 1–6. The first two visions.—Vers. 1–3. THE LO-CUSTS.—Ver. 1. " *Thus the Lord Jehovah showed me; and, behold, He formed locusts in the beginning of the springing up of the second crop; and, behold, it was a second crop after the king's mowing.* Ver. 2. *And it came to pass, when they had finished eating the vegetable of the land, I said, Lord Jehovah, forgive, I pray: how can Jacob stand? for he is small.* Ver. 3. *Jehovah repented of this: It shall not take place, saith Jehovah.*" The formula, " Thus the Lord Jehovah showed me," is common to this and the three following visions (vers. 4, 7, and ch. viii. 1), with this trifling difference, that in the third (ver. 7) the subject (the Lord Jehovah) is omitted, and '*Adōnāi* (the Lord) is inserted instead, after *v*ᵉ*hinnēh* (and behold). הִרְאַנִי denotes seeing with the eyes of the mind—a visionary seeing.

These visions are not merely pictures of a judgment which was ever threatening, and drawing nearer and nearer (Baur); still less are they merely poetical fictions, or forms of drapery selected arbitrarily, for the purpose of clothing the prophet's thoughts; but they are inward intuitions, produced by the Spirit of God, which set forth the punitive judgments of God. *Kōh* (*ita*, thus) points to what follows, and *v^ehinnēh* (and behold) introduces the thing seen. Amos sees the Lord form locusts. Baur proposes to alter יוֹצֵר (forming) into יֵצֶר (forms), but without any reason, and without observing that in all three visions of this chapter *hinnēh* is followed by a participle (קֹרֵא in ver. 4, and נִצָּב in ver. 7), and that the *'Adōnâi* which stands before נִצָּב in ver. 7 shows very clearly that this noun is simply omitted in ver. 1, because *'Adōnâi Y^ehōvâh* has immediately preceded it. גֹּבַי (a poetical form for גֹּבֶה, analogous to שָׂדַי for שָׂדֶה, and contracted into גּוֹב in Nah. iii. 17) signifies locusts, the only question being, whether this meaning is derived from

נּוּב = جاب, to cut, or from גֹּבֶה = جبا, to creep forth (out of the earth). The fixing of the time has an important bearing upon the meaning of the vision: viz. " at the beginning of the springing up of the second crop (of grass);" especially when taken in connection with the explanation, " after the mowings of the king." These definitions cannot be merely intended as outward chronological data. For, in the first place, nothing is known of the existence of any right or prerogative on the part of the kings of Israel, to have the early crop in the meadow land throughout the country mown for the support of their horses and mules (1 Kings xviii. 5), so that their subjects could only get the second crop for their own cattle. Moreover, if the second crop, " after the king's mowings," were to be interpreted literally in this manner, it would decidedly weaken the significance of the vision. For if the locusts did not appear till after the king had got in the hay for the supply of his own mews, and so only devoured the second crop of grass as it grew, this plague would fall upon the people alone, and not at all upon the king. But such an exemption of the king from the judgment is evidently at variance with the meaning of this and the following visions. Consequently the definition of the time must be interpreted spiritually, in accordance with the idea of the vision. The king, who has had the early grass mown, is Jehovah; and the mowing of the grass denotes the judgments which Jehovah has already executed upon Israel. The growing of the second crop is a figurative representation of the prosperity which flourished again after those judgments; in actual fact, therefore, it denotes the time when the dawn had risen again for Israel (ch. iv. 13). Then the locusts came and devoured all the vegetables of the earth. עֵשֶׂב הָאָרֶץ is not the second crop; for עֵשֶׂב does not mean grass, but vegetables, the plants of the field (see at Gen. i. 11). Vers. 2 and 3 require that this meaning should be retained. When the locusts had already eaten the vegetables of the earth, the prophet interceded, and the Lord interposed with deliverance. This intercession would have been too late after the consumption of the second crop. On the other hand, when the vegetables had been consumed, there was still reason to fear that the consumption of the second crop of grass would follow; and this is averted at the prophet's intercession. וְהָיָה for וַיְהִי, as in 1 Sam. xvii. 48, Jer. xxxvii. 11, etc. סְלַח־נָא, pray forgive, sc. the guilt of the people (cf. Num. xiv. 19). מִי יָקוּם, how (מִי qualis) can Jacob (the nation of Israel) stand (not arise), since it is small? קָטֹן, small, i.e. so poor in sources and means of help, that it cannot endure this stroke; not " so crushed already, that a very light calamity would destroy it" (Rosenmüller). For נִחַם עַל, see Ex. xxxii. 14. זֹאת (this) refers to the destruction of the people indicated in מִי יָקוּם; and זֹאת is also to be supplied as the subject to לֹא תִהְיֶה.

Vers. 4–6. THE DEVOURING FIRE.—Ver. 4. " *Thus the Lord Jehovah showed me: and, behold, the Lord Jehovah called to punish with fire; and it devoured the great flood, and devoured the portion.* Ver. 5. *And I said, Lord Jehovah, leave off, I pray: how can Jacob stand? for it is small.* Ver. 6. *Jehovah repented of this; this also shall not take place, said the Lord Jehovah.*" That the all-devouring fire represents a much severer judgment than that depicted under the figure of the locusts, is generally acknowledged, and needs no proof. But the more precise meaning of this judgment is open to dispute, and depends upon the explanation of the fourth verse. The object to קֹרֵא is לָרִיב בָּאֵשׁ, and רִיב is to be taken as an infinitive, as in Isa. iii. 13 : He called to strive (*i.e.* to judge or punish) with fire. There is no necessity to supply *ministros suos* here. The expression is a concise one, for " He called to the fire to punish with fire" (for the expression and the fact, compare Isa. lxvi. 16). This fire devoured the great flood. *T^ehōm rabbâh* is used in Gen. vii. 11 and Isa. li. 10, etc., to denote the un-fathomable ocean ; and in Gen. i. 2 *t^ehōm* is the term applied to the immense flood which surrounded and covered the globe at the beginning of the creation. וַאֹכְלָה, as distinguished from וַתֹּאכַל, signifies an action in progress, or still incomplete (Hitzig). The meaning therefore is, " it also devoured (began to devour) *'eth-hachēleq ;"* *i.e.* not the field, for a field does not form at all a fitting antithesis to the ocean ; and still less " the land," for *chēleq* never bears this meaning; but the inheritance or portion, namely, that of Jehovah (Deut. xxxii. 9), *i.e.* Israel. Conse-quently *t^ehōm rabbâh* cannot, of course, signify the ocean as such. For the idea of the fire falling upon the ocean, and consuming it, and then beginning to consume the land of Israel, by which the ocean was bounded (Hitzig), would be too mon-strous ; nor is it justified by the simple remark, that " it was as if the last great conflagration (2 Pet. iii. 10) had begun" (Schmieder). As the fire is not earthly fire, but the fire of the wrath of God, and therefore a figurative representation of the judgment of destruction ; and as *hachēleq* (the portion) is not the land of Israel, but according to Deuteronomy (*l.c.*) Israel, or the people of Jehovah ; so *t^ehōm rabbâh* is not the ocean, but the heathen world, the great sea of nations, in their rebellion against the kingdom of God. The world of nature in a state of agitation is a frequent symbol in the Scriptures for the agitated heathen world (*e.g.* Ps. xlvi. 3, xciii. 3, 4). On the latter passage, Delitzsch has the following apt remark : " The stormy sea is a figurative representation of the whole heathen world, in its estrangement from God, and enmity against Him, or the human race outside the true church of God ; and the rivers are figurative representations of the kingdoms of the world, *e.g.* the Nile of the Egyptian (Jer. xlvi. 7, 8), the Euphrates of the Assyrian (Isa. viii. 7, 8), or more precisely still, the arrow-swift Tigris of the Assyrian, and the winding Euphrates of the Babylonian (Isa. xxvii. 1)." This symbolism lies at the foundation of the vision seen by the prophet. The world of nations, in its rebellion against Jehovah, the Lord and King of the world, appears as a great flood, like the chaos at the beginning of the creation, or the flood which poured out its waves upon the globe in the time of Noah. Upon this flood of nations does fire from the Lord fall down and consume them; and after consuming them, it begins to devour the inheritance of Jehovah, the nation of Israel also. The prophet then prays to the Lord to spare it, because Jacob would inevitably perish in this conflagration; and the Lord gives the promise that "this shall not take place," so that Israel is plucked like a firebrand out of the fire (ch. iv. 11).

If we inquire now into the historical bearing of these two visions, so much is à priori clear,—namely, that both of them not only indicate judgments already past, but also refer to the future, since no fire had hitherto burned upon the surface of the globe, which had consumed the world of nations and threatened to annihilate Israel. If therefore there is an element of truth in the explanation given by Grotius to the first vision, "After the fields had been shorn by Benhadad (2 Kings xiii. 3), and after the damage which was then sustained, the condition of Israel began to flourish once more during the reign of Jeroboam the son of Joash, as we see from 2 Kings xiv. 15," according to which the locusts would refer to the invasion on the part of the Assyrians in the time of Pul; this application is much too limited, neither exhausting the contents of the first vision, nor suiting in the smallest degree the figure of the fire. The "mowing of the king" (ver. 1) denotes rather all the judgments which the Lord had hitherto poured out upon Israel, embracing everything that the prophet mentions in ch. iv. 6–10. The locusts are a figurative representation of the judgments that still await the covenant nation, and will destroy it even to a small remnant, which will be saved through the prayers of the righteous. The vision of the fire has a similar scope, embracing all the past and all the future; but this also indicates the judgments that fall upon the heathen world, and will only receive its ultimate fulfilment in the destruction of everything that is ungodly upon the face of the earth, when the Lord comes in fire to strive with all flesh (Isa. lxvi. 15, 16), and to burn up the earth and all that is therein, on the day of judgment and perdition of ungodly men (2 Pet. iii. 7, 10–13).

The removal of the two judgments, however, by Jehovah in consequence of the intercession of the prophet, shows that these judgments are not intended to effect the utter annihilation of the nation of God, but simply its refinement and the rooting out of the sinners from the midst of it, and that, in consequence of the sparing mercy of God, a holy remnant of the nation of God will be left. The next two visions refer simply to the judgment which awaits the kingdom of the ten tribes in the immediate future.

Vers. 7–9. The Third Vision.—Ver. 7. " *Thus he showed me : and, behold, the Lord stood upon a wall made with a plumb-line, and a plumb-line in His hand.* Ver. 8. *And Jehovah said to me, What seest thou, Amos? And I said, A plumb-line. And the Lord said, Behold, I put a plumb-line in the midst of my people Israel : I shall pass by it no more.* Ver. 9. *And the sacrificial heights of Isaac are laid waste, and the holy things of Israel destroyed; and I rise up against the house of Jeroboam with the sword.*" The word אֲנָךְ, which only occurs here, denotes, according to the dialects and the Rabbins, tin or lead, here a plumb-line. *Chōmath 'ănákh* is a wall built with a plumb-line, *i.e.* a perpendicular wall, a wall built with mechanical correctness and solidity. Upon this wall Amos sees, the Lord standing. The wall built with a plumb-line is a figurative representation of the kingdom of God in Israel, as a firm and well-constructed building. He holds in His hand a plumb-line. The question addressed to the prophet, " What does he see ? " is asked for the simple purpose of following up his answer with an explanation of the symbol, as in Jer. i. 11, 13, since the plumb-line was used for different purposes,—namely, not only for building, but partly also for pulling buildings down (compare 2 Kings xxi. 13; Isa. xxxiv. 11). Jehovah will lay it *bᵉqerebh 'ammī,* to the midst of His people, and not merely to an outward portion of it, in order to destroy this building. He will no longer spare as He has done hitherto. עָבַר לְ, to pass by any one without taking any notice of him, without looking upon his guilt or punishing him; hence, to spare,—the opposite of עָבַר בְּקֶרֶב in ch. v. 17. The destruction will fall upon the idolatrous sanctuaries of the land, the *bâmōth* (see at 1 Kings iii. 2), *i.e.* the altars of the high places, and the temples at

Bethel, at Dan (see at 1 Kings xii. 29), and at Gilgal (see ch.
iv. 4). Isaac (יִשְׂחָק, a softened form for יִצְחָק, used here and at
ver. 16, as in Jer. xxxiii. 26) is mentioned here instead of *Jacob*,
and the name is used as a synonym for *Israel* of the ten tribes.
Even the house of Jeroboam, the reigning royal family, is to
perish with the sword (קָם עַל as in Isa. xxxi. 2). Jeroboam
is mentioned as the existing representative of the monarchy,
and the words are not to be restricted to the overthrow of
his dynasty, but announce the destruction of the Israelitish
monarchy, which actually was annihilated when this dynasty
was overthrown (see p. 41). The destruction of the sacred
places and the overthrow of the monarchy involve the dissolution of the kingdom. Thus does Amos himself interpret
his own words in vers. 11 and 17.

Vers. 10–17. Opposition to the Prophet at Bethel.
—The daring announcement of the overthrow of the royal
family excites the wrath of the high priest at Bethel, so that
he relates the affair to the king, to induce him to proceed
against the troublesome prophet (vers. 10 and 11), and then
calls upon Amos himself to leave Bethel (vers. 12 and 13).
That this attempt to drive Amos out of Bethel was occasioned
by his prophecy in vers. 7–10, is evident from what Amaziah
says to the king concerning the words of Amos. " *The priest
of Bethel*" (*Kōhēn Bēth-ēl*) is the high priest at the sanctuary
of the golden calf at Bethel. He accused the prophet to the
king of having made a conspiracy (*qâshar ;* cf. 1 Kings xv. 27,
etc.) against the king, and that " in the midst of the house of
Israel," *i.e.* in the centre of the kingdom of Israel—namely
at Bethel, the religious centre of the kingdom—through all
his sayings, which the land could not bear. To establish this
charge, he states (in ver. 11) that Amos has foretold the death
of Jeroboam by the sword, and the carrying away of the
people out of the land. Amos had really said this. The fact
that in ver. 9 Jeroboam is named, and not the house of
Jeroboam, makes no difference ; for the head of the house is
naturally included in the house itself. And the carrying away
of the people out of the land was not only implied in the
announcement of the devastation of the sanctuaries of the
kingdom (ver. 9), which presupposes the conquest of the land

by foes; but Amos had actually predicted it in so many words
(ch. v. 27). And Amaziah naturally gave the substance of
all the prophet's addresses, instead of simply confining himself
to the last. There is no reason, therefore, to think of intentional slander.

Vers. 12, 13. The king appears to have commenced no
proceedings against the prophet in consequence of this denunciation, probably because he did not regard the affair as
one of so much danger. Amaziah therefore endeavours to
persuade the prophet to leave the country. "*Seer, go, and flee
into the land of Judah.*" בְּרַח־לְךָ, *i.e.* withdraw thyself by flight
from the punishment which threatens thee. "*There eat thy
bread, and there mayst thou prophesy:*" *i.e.* in Judah thou
mayst earn thy bread by prophesying without any interruption.
It is evident from the answer given by Amos in ver. 14, that
this is the meaning of the words: "*But in Bethel thou shalt no
longer prophesy, for it is a king's sanctuary* (*i.e.* a sanctuary
founded by the king; 1 Kings xii. 28), *and bēth mamlâkhâh,*"
house of the kingdom, *i.e.* a royal capital (cf. 1 Sam. xxvii. 5),
—namely, as being the principal seat of the worship which the
king has established for his kingdom. There no one could be
allowed to prophesy against the king.

Vers. 14, 15. Amos first of all repudiates the insinuation
that he practises prophesying as a calling or profession, by
which he gets his living. "*I am no prophet,*" *sc.* by profession, "*and no prophet's son,*" *i.e.* not a pupil or member of the
prophets' schools, one who has been trained to prophesy (on
these schools, see the comm. on 1 Sam. xix. 24); *but* (according
to my proper calling) a *bōqēr, lit.* a herdsman of oxen (from
bâqâr); then in a broader sense, a herdsman who tends the
sheep (צֹאן), a shepherd; and a *bōlēs shiqmīm, i.e.* one who
plucks sycamores or mulberry-figs, and lives upon them. The
ἀπ. λεγ. *bōlēs* is a denom. from the Arabic name for the mul-
berry-fig, and signifies to gather mulberry-figs and live upon
them; like συκάζειν and ἀποσυκάζειν, *i.e.* according to Hesych.
τὰ σῦκα τρώγειν, to eat figs. The rendering of the LXX.
κνίζων, Vulg. *vellicans*, points to the fact that it was a common
custom to nip or scratch the mulberry-figs, in order to make
them ripen (see Theophr. *Hist. plant.* iv. 2; Plin. *Hist. nat.*
13, 14; and Bochart, *Hieroz.* i. 384, or p. 406 ed. Ros.); but

this cannot be shown to be the true meaning of *bōlēs*. And even if the idea of nipping were implied in the word *bōlēs*, it would by no means follow that the possession of a mulberry plantation was what was intended, as many commentators have inferred ; for " the words contain an allusion to the ' eating of bread' referred to in ver. 12, and the fruit is mentioned here as the ordinary food of the shepherds, who lived at the pasture grounds, and to whom bread may have been a rarity" (Hitzig). From this calling, which afforded him a livelihood, the Lord had called him away to prophesy to His people Israel ; so that whoever forbade him to do so, set himself in opposition to the Lord God.

Vers. 16, 17. In return for this rebellion against Jehovah, Amos foretels to the priest the punishment which will fall upon him when the judgment shall come upon Israel, meeting his words, " *Thou sayst, Thou shalt not prophesy*," with the keen retort, " *Thus saith Jehovah.*" הִטִּיף, to drip, applied to prophesying here and at Mic. ii. 6, 11, and Ezek. xxi. 2, 7, is taken from Deut. xxxii. 2, " My teaching shall drip as the rain," etc. *Isaac* (*yischâq*) for Israel, as in ver. 9. The punishment is thus described in ver. 17 : " Thy wife will be a harlot in the city," *i.e.* at the taking of the city she will become a harlot through violation. His children would also be slain by the foe, and his landed possession assigned to others, namely, to the fresh settlers in the land. He himself, viz. the priest, would die in an unclean land, that is to say, in the land of the Gentiles,—in other words, would be carried away captive, and that with the whole nation, the carrying away of which is repeated by Amos in the words which the priest had reported to the king (ver. 11), as a sign that what he has prophesied will assuredly stand.

THE RIPENESS OF ISRAEL FOR JUDGMENT.—CHAP. VIII.

Under the symbol of a basket filled with ripe fruit, the Lord shows the prophet that Israel is ripe for judgment (vers. 1-3); whereupon Amos, explaining the meaning of this vision, announces to the unrighteous magnates of the nation the changing of their joyful feasts into days of mourning, as the punishment from God for their unrighteousness (vers. 4-10), and sets before them a time when those who now

despise the word of God will sigh in vain in their extremity
for a word of the Lord (vers. 11–14).

Vers. 1–3. Vision of a BASKET OF RIPE FRUIT.—Ver. 1.
" *Thus did the Lord Jehovah show me: and behold a basket with
ripe fruit.* Ver. 2. *And He said, What seest thou, Amos? And
I said, A basket of ripe fruit. Then Jehovah said to me, The
end is come to my people Israel; I will not pass by them any
more.* Ver. 3. *And the songs of the palace will yell in that day,
is the saying of the Lord Jehovah: corpses in multitude; in every
place hath He cast them forth; Hush!* " כְּלוּב from כָּלָה, to lay
hold of, to grasp, lit. a receiver, here a basket (of basket-work),
in Jer. v. 27 a bird-cage. קַיִץ: summer-fruit (see at 2 Sam.
xvi. 1); in Isa. xvi. 9, xxviii. 4, the gathering of fruit, hence
ripe fruit. The basket of ripe fruit (*qayits*) is thus explained
by the Lord: the end (*qēts*) is come to my people (cf. Ezek
vii. 6). Consequently the basket of ripe fruit is a figurative
representation of the nation that is now ripe for judgment,
although *qēts*, the end, does not denote its ripeness for judgment, but its destruction, and the word *qēts* is simply chosen
to form a paronomasia with *qayits*. לֹא אוֹסִיף וגו׳ as in ch. vii. 8.
All the joy shall be turned into mourning. The thought is
not that the temple-singing to the praise of God (ch. v. 23)
would be turned into yelling, but that the songs of joy (ch. vi. 5;
2 Sam. xix. 36) would be turned into yells, *i.e.* into sounds of
lamentation (cf. ver. 10 and 1 Macc. ix. 41), namely, because
of the multitude of the dead which lay upon the ground on
every side. הִשְׁלִיךְ is not impersonal, in the sense of " which
men are no longer able to bury on account of their great number, and therefore cast away in quiet places on every side;"
but Jehovah is to be regarded as the subject, viz. which God
has laid prostrate, or cast to the ground on every side. For
the adverbial use of הַס cannot be established. The word is an
interjection here, as in ch. vi. 10; and the exclamation, Hush!
is not a sign of gloomy despair, but an admonition to bow
beneath the overwhelming severity of the judgment of God, as
in Zeph. i. 7 (cf. Hab. ii. 20 and Zech. ii. 17).

Vers. 4–10. To this vision the prophet attaches the last
admonition to the rich and powerful men of the nation, to
observe the threatening of the Lord before it is too late, im-

pressing upon them the terrible severity of the judgment.
Ver. 4. " *Hear this, ye that gape for the poor, and to destroy
the meek of the earth,* Ver. 5. *Saying, When is the new moon
over, that we may sell corn? and the sabbath, that we may
open wheat, to make the ephah small, and the shekel great, and
to falsify the scale of deceit?* Ver. 6. *To buy the poor for silver,
and the needy for a pair of shoes, and the refuse of the corn will
we sell.*" The persons addressed are the הַשֹּׁאֲפִים אֶבְיוֹן, *i.e.* not
those who snort at the poor man, to frighten him away from
any further pursuit of his rights (Baur), but, according to ch.
ii. 6, 7, those who greedily pant for the poor man, who try to
swallow him (Hitzig). This is affirmed in the second clause of
the verse, in which שֹׁאֲפִים is to be repeated in thought before
לְהַשְׁבִּית: they gape to destroy the quiet in the land (עַנְוֵי־אֶרֶץ =
עֲנָוִים in ch. ii. 7), " namely by grasping all property for themselves, Job xxii. 8, Isa. v. 8 " (Hitzig). Vers. 5 and 6 show
how they expect to accomplish their purpose. Like covetous
usurers, they cannot even wait for the end of the feast-days to
pursue their trade still further. *Chōdesh,* the new moon, was a
holiday on which all trade was suspended, just as it was on the
Sabbath (see at Num. xxviii. 11 and 2 Kings iv. 23). הַשְׁבִּיר שֶׁבֶר,
to sell corn, as in Gen. xli. 57. פָּתַח בָּר, to open up corn, *i.e.* to
open the granaries (cf. Gen. xli. 56). In doing so, they wanted
to cheat the poor by small measure (ephah), and by making
the shekel great, *i.e.* by increasing the price, which was to be
weighed out to them; also by false scales (*'ivvēth,* to pervert,
or falsify the scale of deceit, *i.e.* the scale used for cheating),
and by bad corn (*mappal,* waste or refuse); that in this way
they might make the poor man so poor, that he would either be
obliged to sell himself to them from want and distress (Lev.
xxv. 39), or be handed over to the creditor by the court of
justice, because he was no longer able to pay for a pair of
shoes, *i.e.* the very smallest debt (cf. ch. ii. 6).

Such wickedness as this would be severely punished by the
Lord. Ver. 7. " *Jehovah hath sworn by the pride of Jacob,
Verily I will not forget all their deeds for ever.* Ver. 8. *Shall
the earth not tremble for this, and every inhabitant upon it mourn?
and all of it rises like the Nile, and heaves and sinks like the
Nile of Egypt.*" The pride of Jacob is Jehovah, as in Hos.
v. 5 and vii. 10. Jehovah swears by the pride of Jacob, as He

does by His holiness in ch. iv. 2, or by His soul in ch. vi. 8, *i.e.* as He who is the pride and glory of Israel: *i.e.* as truly as He is so, will He and must He punish such acts as these. By overlooking such sins, or leaving them unpunished, He would deny His glory in Israel. שָׁכַח, to forget a sin, *i.e.* to leave it unpunished. In ver. 8 the negative question is an expression denoting strong assurance. "For this" is generally supposed to refer to the sins; but this is a mistake, as the previous verse alludes not to the sins themselves, but to the punishment of them; and the solemn oath of Jehovah does not contain so subordinate and casual a thought, that we can pass over ver. 7, and take עַל זֹאת as referring back to vers. 4–6. It rather refers to the substance of the oath, *i.e.* to the punishment of the sins which the Lord announces with a solemn oath. This will be so terrible that the earth will quake, and be resolved, as it were, into its primeval condition of chaos. *Râgaz*, to tremble, or, when applied to the earth, to quake, does not mean to shudder, or to be shocked, as Rosenmüller explains it after Jer. ii. 12. Still less can the idea of the earth rearing and rising up in a stormy manner to cast them off, which Hitzig supports, be proved to be a biblical idea from Isa. xxiv. 20. The thought is rather that, under the weight of the judgment, the earth will quake, and all its inhabitants will be thrown into mourning, as we may clearly see from the parallel passage in ch. ix. 5. In ver. 8*b* this figure is carried out still further, and the whole earth is represented as being turned into a sea, heaving and falling in a tempestuous manner, just as in the case of the flood. כֻּלָּהּ, the totality of the earth, the entire globe, will rise, and swell and fall like waters lashed into a storm. This rising and falling of the earth is compared to the rising and sinking of the Nile. According to the parallel passage in ch. ix. 5, כְּאֹר is a defective form for כִּיאֹר, just as בֻּל is for יְבוּל in Job xl. 20, and it is still further defined by the expression כִּיאוֹר מִצְרַיִם, which follows. All the ancient versions have taken it as יְאוֹר, and many of the Hebrew codd. (in Kennicott and De Rossi) have this reading. *Nigrash*, to be excited, a term applied to the stormy sea (Isa. lvii. 20). נִשְׁקָה is a softened form for נִשְׁקְעָה, as is shown by שָׁקְעָה in ch. ix. 5.

Ver. 9. "*And it will come to pass on that day, is the saying of the Lord Jehovah, I cause the sun to set at noon, and make it dark to the earth in clear day.* Ver. 10. *And turn your feasts into mourning, and all your songs into lamentation: and bring mourning clothes upon all loins, and baldness upon every head; and make it like mourning for an only one, and the end thereof like a bitter day."* The effect of the divine judgment upon the Israelites is depicted here. Just as the wicked overturn the moral order of the universe, so will the Lord, with His judgment, break through the order of nature, cause the sun to go down at noon, and envelope the earth in darkness in clear day. The words of the ninth verse are not founded upon the idea of an eclipse of the sun, though Michaelis and Hitzig not only assume that they are, but actually attempt to determine the time of its occurrence. An eclipse of the sun is not the setting of the sun (בּוֹא). But to any man the sun sets at noon, when he is suddenly snatched away by death, in the very midst of his life. And this also applies to a nation when it is suddenly destroyed in the midst of its earthly prosperity. But it has a still wider application. When the Lord shall come to judgment, at a time when the world, in its self-security, looketh not for Him (cf. Matt. xxiv. 37 sqq.), this earth's sun will set at noon, and the earth be covered with darkness in bright daylight. And every judgment that falls upon an ungodly people or kingdom, as the ages roll away, is a harbinger of the approach of the final judgment. Ver. 10. When the judgment shall burst upon Israel, then will all the joyous feasts give way to mourning and lamentation (compare ver. 3 and ch. v. 16; Hos. ii. 13). On the shaving of a bald place as a sign of mourning, see Isa. iii. 24. This mourning will be very deep, like the mourning for the death of an only son (cf. Jer. vi. 26 and Zech. xii. 10). The suffix in שַׂמְתִּיהָ (I make *it*) does not refer to אֵבֶל (mourning), but to all that has been previously mentioned as done upon that day, to their weeping and lamenting (Hitzig). אַחֲרִיתָהּ, the end thereof, namely, of this mourning and lamentation, will be a bitter day (כְּ is *caph verit.*; see at Joel i. 15). This implies that the judgment will not be a passing one, but will continue.

Vers. 11–14. And at that time the light and comfort of the word of God will also fail them. Ver. 11. *"Behold, days come, is the saying of the Lord Jehovah, that I send a hungering into the land, not a hungering for bread nor a thirst for water, but to*

hear the words of Jehovah. Ver. 12. *And they will reel from,
sea to sea; and from the north, and even to the east, they sweep
round to seek the word of Jehovah, and will not find it.*" The
bitterness of the time of punishment is increased by the fact
that the Lord will then withdraw His word from them, *i.e.* the
light of His revelation. They who will not now hear His word,
as proclaimed by the prophets, will then cherish the greatest
longing for it. Such hunger and thirst will be awakened by
the distress and affliction that will come upon them. The
intensity of this desire is depicted in ver. 12. They reel (נוּעַ
as in ch. iv. 8) from the sea to the sea; that is to say, not "from
the Dead Sea in the east to the Mediterranean in the west," for
Joel ii. 20 and Zech. xiv. 8 are not cases in point, as the two
seas are defined there by distinct epithets; but as in Ps. lxxii. 8
and Zech. ix. 10, according to which the meaning is, from the
sea to where the sea occurs again, at the other end of the world,
"the sea being taken as the boundary of the earth" (Hupfeld).
The other clause, " from the north even to the east," contains
an abridged expression for " from north to south and from west
to east," *i.e.* to every quarter of the globe.

Ver. 13. " *In that day will the fair virgins and the young
men faint for thirst.* Ver. 14. *They who swear by the guilt of
Samaria, and say, By the life of thy God, O Dan! and by the
life of the way to Beersheba; and will fall, and not rise again.*"
Those who now stand in all the fullest and freshest vigour of
life, will succumb to this hunger and thirst. The virgins and
young men are individualized, as comprising that portion of
the nation which possessed the vigorous fulness of youth.   עָלַף,
to be enveloped in night, to sink into a swoon, *hithp.* to hide
one's self, to faint away.   הַנִּשְׁבָּעִים refers to the young men and
virgins; and inasmuch as they represent the most vigorous
portion of the nation, to the nation as a whole. If the strongest
succumb to the thirst, how much more the weak! *'Ashmath
Shōm^erōn*, the guilt of Samaria, is the golden calf at Bethel,
the principal idol of the kingdom of Israel, which is named
after the capital Samaria (compare Deut. ix. 21, " the sin of
Israel"), not the Asherah which was still standing in Samaria
in the reign of Jehoahaz (2 Kings xiii. 6); for apart from the
question whether it was there in the time of Jeroboam, this is
at variance with the second clause, in which the manner of

their swearing is given,—namely, by the life of the god at Dan, that is to say, the golden calf that was there; so that the guilt of Samaria can only have been the golden calf at Bethel, the national sanctuary of the ten tribes (cf. ch. iv. 4, v. 5). The way to Beersheba is mentioned, instead of the worship, for the sake of which the pilgrimage to Beersheba was made. This worship, again, was not a purely heathen worship, but an idolatrous worship of Jehovah (see ch. v. 5). The fulfilment of these threats commenced with the destruction of the kingdom of Israel, and the carrying away of the ten tribes into exile in Assyria, and continues to this day in the case of that portion of the Israelitish nation which is still looking for the Messiah, the prophet promised by Moses, and looking in vain, because they will not hearken to the preaching of the gospel concerning the Messiah, who appeared as Jesus.

DESTRUCTION OF THE SINFUL KINGDOM, AND ESTABLISHMENT OF THE NEW KINGDOM OF GOD.—CHAP. IX.

The prophet sees the Lord standing by the altar, and giving command to overthrow the temple, that the whole nation may be buried beneath the ruins (ver. 1). Should any one escape, the Lord will pursue him everywhere, and overtake and destroy him (vers. 2-4); for He is the Almighty God, and the Judge of the world (vers. 5 and 6); and Israel has become like the heathen, so that it deserves no sparing. Nevertheless it shall not be utterly destroyed, but simply sifted, and the sinful mass be slain (vers. 7-10). Then will the fallen tabernacle of David be raised up again, and the kingdom of God be glorified by the reception of all nations (ver. 12), and richly blessed with the fulness of the gifts of divine grace (vers. 13, 14), and never destroyed again (ver. 15). As the chapter gives the final development of the judgment threatened in the preceding one, so is it also closely attached in form to ch. vii. and viii., commencing with a vision just as they do. But whilst the preceding visions simply indicate the judgment which is to fall upon the sinful nation, and are introduced with the words, "The Lord showed me" (ch. vii. 1, 4, 7, viii. 1), this closing vision shows the Lord engaged in the execution of the judgment, and commences accordingly with the words, "I saw the Lord standing," etc.

Ver. 1. " *I saw the Lord standing by the altar; and He said, Smite the top, that the thresholds may tremble, and smash them upon the head of all of them; and I will slay their remnant with the sword: a fugitive of them shall not flee; and an escaped one of them shall not escape.*" The correct and full interpretation not only of this verse, but of the whole chapter, depends upon the answer to be given to the question, what altar we are to understand by *hammizbēăch*. Ewald, Hitzig, Hofmann, and Baur follow Cyril in thinking of the temple at Bethel, because, as Hitzig says, this vision attaches itself in an explanatory manner to the close of ch. viii. 14, and because, according to Hofmann, " if the word of the prophet in general was directed against the kingdom, the royal house and the sanctuary of the ten tribes, the article before *hammizbēăch* points to the altar of the sanctuary in the kingdom of Israel, to the altar at Bethel, against which he has already prophesied in a perfectly similar manner in ch. iii. 14." But there is no ground whatever for the assertion that our vision contains simply an explanation of ch. viii. 14. The connection with ch. viii. is altogether not so close, that the object of the prophecy in the one chapter must of necessity cover that of the other. And it is quite incorrect to say that the word of the prophet throughout is directed simply against the kingdom of the ten tribes, or that, although Amos does indeed reprove the sins of Judah as well as those of Israel, he proclaims destruction to the kingdom of Jeroboam alone. As early as ch. ii. 5 he announces desolation to Judah by fire, and the burning of the palaces of Jerusalem; and in ch. vi. 1, again, he gives utterance to a woe upon the self-secure in Zion, as well as upon the careless ones in Samaria. And lastly, it is evident from vers. 8–10 of the present chapter, that the sinful kingdom which is to be destroyed from the face of the earth is not merely the kingdom of the ten tribes, but the kingdoms of Judah and Israel, which are embraced in one. For although it is stated immediately afterwards that the Lord will not utterly destroy the house of Jacob, but will shake the house of Israel among all nations, the house of Jacob cannot mean the kingdom of Judah, and the house of Israel the kingdom of the ten tribes, because such a contrast between Judah and Israel makes the thought too lame, and the antithesis between the destruction of the sinful kingdom and the utter destruction of the nation is quite obliterated. Amos does not generally draw such a distinction between the house of Jacob and the house of Israel, as that the first represents Judah, and the second the ten tribes; but he uses the two epithets as synonymous, as we may see from a comparison of ch. vi. 8 with ch. vi. 14, where the rejection of the pride of Israel and the hating of its palaces (ver. 8) are practically interpreted by the raising up of a nation which oppresses the house of Israel in all its borders (ver. 14). And so also in the chapter before us, the "house of Israel" (ver. 9) is identical with "Israel" and the "children of Israel" (7), whom God brought up out of Egypt. But God brought up out of Egypt not the ten tribes, but the twelve. And consequently it is decidedly incorrect to restrict the contents of vers. 1–10 to the kingdom of the ten tribes. And if this be the case, we cannot possibly understand by *hammizbēăch* in ver. 1 the altar of Bethel, especially seeing that not only does Amos foretel the visitation or destruction of the *altars* of Bethel in ch. iii. 14, and therefore recognises not one altar only in Bethel, but a plurality of altars, but that he also speaks in ch. vii. 9 of the desolation of the high places and sanctuaries of Israel, and in ch. viii. 14 places the sanctuary at Dan on a par with that at Bethel; so that there was not any *one* altar in the kingdom of the ten tribes, which could be called *hammizbēăch*, the altar *par excellence*, inasmuch as it possessed from the very beginning two sanctuaries of equal dignity (viz. at Bethel and Dan). *Hammizbēăch*, therefore, both here and at Ezek. ix. 2, is the altar of burnt-offering in the temple at Jerusalem, the sanctuary of the whole of the covenant nation, to which even the ten tribes still belonged, in spite of their having fallen away from the house of David. So long as the Lord still continued to send prophets to the ten tribes, so long did they pass as still forming part of the people of God, and so long also was the temple at Jerusalem the divinely appointed sanctuary and the throne of Jehovah, from which both blessings and punishment issued for them. The Lord roars from Zion, and from Zion He utters His voice (ch. i. 2), not only upon the nations who have shown hostility to Judah or Israel, but also upon Judah and Israel, on account of their departure from His law (ch. ii. 4 and 6 sqq.).

The vision in this verse is founded upon the idea that the

whole nation is assembled before the Lord at the threshold of
the temple, so that it is buried under the ruins of the falling
building, in consequence of the blow upon the top, which
shatters the temple to its very foundations. The Lord appears
at the altar, because here at the sacrificial place of the nation
the sins of Israel are heaped up, that He may execute judgment upon the nation there. נִצָּב עַל, standing at (not upon)
the altar, as in 1 Kings xiii. 1. He gives commandment to
smite the top. The person who is to do this is not mentioned;
but it was no doubt an angel, probably the הַמַּלְאָךְ הַמַּשְׁחִית, who
brought the pestilence as a punishment at the numbering of the
people in the time of David (2 Sam. xxiv. 15, 16), who smote
the army of the Assyrian king Sennacherib before Jerusalem
(2 Kings xix. 35), and who also slew the first-born of Egypt
(Ex. xii. 13, 23) ; whereas in Ezek. ix. 2, 7, He is represented
as accomplishing the judgment of destruction by means of six
angels. *Hakkaphtōr*, the knob or top ; in Ex. xxv. 31, 33 sqq.,
an ornament upon the shaft and branches of the golden candlestick. Here it is an ornament at the top of the columns, and
not " the lintel of the door," or " the pinnacle of the temple with
its ornaments." For the latter explanation of *kaphtōr*, which
cannot be philologically sustained, by no means follows from
the fact that the antithesis to the *kaphtōr* is formed by the
sippīm, or thresholds of the door. The knob and threshold
simply express the contrast between the loftiest summit and
the lowest base, without at all warranting the conclusion that
saph denotes the base of the pillar which culminated in a knob,
or *kaphtōr*, the top of the door which rested upon a threshold.
The description is not architectural, but rhetorical, the separate
portions of the whole being individualized, for the purpose of
expressing the thought that the building was to be shattered to
pieces *in summo usque ad imum, a capite ad calcem*. Would
we bring out more clearly the idea which lies at the foundation
of the rhetorical mode of expression, we have only to think of
the capital of the pillars Jachin and Boaz, and that with
special reference to their significance, as symbolizing the stability of the temple. The smiting of these pillars, so that they
fall to the ground, individualizes the destruction of the temple,
without there being any necessity in consequence to think of
these pillars as supporting the roof of the temple hall. The

rhetorical character of the expression comes out clearly again in what follows, " and smash them to pieces, *i.e.* lay them in ruins upon the head of all,"[1] where the plural suffix attached to בִּצְעָם (with the toneless suffix for בְּצָעֵם ; see Ewald, § 253, *a*) cannot possibly be taken as referring to the singular *hakkaphtōr*, nor even to *hassippīm* alone, but must refer to the two nouns *hakkaphtōr* and *hassippīm*. The reference to *hassippīm* could no doubt be grammatically sustained; but so far as the sense is concerned, it is inadmissible, inasmuch as when a building falls to the ground in consequence of its having been laid in ruins by a blow from above, the thresholds of the entrance could not possibly fall upon the heads of the men who were standing in front of it. The command has throughout a symbolical meaning, and has no literal reference to the destruction of the temple. The temple symbolizes the kingdom of God, which the Lord had founded in Israel; and as being the centre of that kingdom, it stands here for the kingdom itself. In the temple, as the dwelling-place of the name of Jehovah, *i.e.* of the gracious presence of God, the idolatrous nation beheld an indestructible pledge of the lasting continuance of the kingdom. But this support to their false trust is taken away from it by the announcement that the Lord will lay the temple in ruins. The destruction of the temple represents the destruction of the kingdom of God embodied in the temple, with which indeed the earthly temple would of necessity fall to the ground. No one will escape this judgment. This is affirmed in the words which follow: And their last, their remnant (*'achărīth*, as in ch. iv. 2), I will slay with the sword; as to the meaning of which Cocceius has correctly observed, that the magnitude of the slaughter is increased *exclusione fugientium et eorum, qui videbantur effugisse.* The apparent discrepancy in the statement, that they will *all* be crushed to pieces by the ruins, and yet there will be fugitives and persons who have escaped, is removed at once if we bear in mind that the intention of the prophet is to cut off every loophole for carnal security, and that the meaning of the words is simply this : " And even if any should succeed in fleeing and

---

[1] Luther's rendering, " for their avarice shall come upon the head of all of them," in which he follows the Vulgate, arose from בְּצָעָם being confounded with בִּצְעָם.

escaping, God will pursue them with the sword, and slay them" (see Hengstenberg, *Christology*, on this passage).

The thought is still further expanded in vers. 2–6. Ver. 2. *"If they break through into hell, my hand will take them thence; and if they climb up to heaven, thence will I fetch them down.* Ver. 3. *And if they hide themselves upon the top of Carmel, I will trace them, and fetch them thence; and if they conceal themselves from before mine eyes in the bottom of the sea, thence do I command the serpent, and it biteth them.* Ver. 4. *And if they go into captivity before their enemies, I will command the sword thence, and it slayeth them; and I direct my eye upon them for evil, and not for good."* The imperfects, with אִם, are to be taken as futures. They do not assume what is impossible as merely hypothetical, in the sense of " if they should hide themselves;" but set forth what was no doubt in actual fact an impossible case, as though it were possible, in order to cut off every escape. For the cases mentioned in vers. 3*a* and 4*a* might really occur. Hiding upon Carmel and going into captivity belong to the sphere of possibility and of actual occurrence. In order to individualize the thought, that escape from the punishing arm of the Almighty is impossible, the prophet opposes the most extreme spaces of the world to one another, starting from heaven and hell, as the loftiest height and deepest depth of the universe, in doing which he has in all probability Ps. cxxxix. 7, 8 floating before his mind. He commences with the height, which a man cannot possibly climb, and the depth, to which he cannot descend, to show that escape is impossible. חָתַר, to break through, with בְּ, to make a hole into anything (Ezek. viii. 8, xii. 5, 7). According to the Hebrew view, Sheol was deep in the interior of the earth. The head of Carmel is mentioned (see at Josh. xix. 26). The reference is not to the many caves in this promontory, which afford shelter to fugitives; for they are not found upon the head of Carmel, but for the most part on the western side (see v. Raumer, *Pal.* p. 44). The emphasis lies rather upon the head, as a height overgrown with trees, which, even if not very high (about 1800 feet; see at 1 Kings xviii. 19), yet, in comparison with the sea over which it rises, might appear to be of a very considerable height; in addition to which, the situation of Carmel, on the extreme western border of the kingdom of Israel, might also be taken into consideration. "Whoever hides himself there, must assuredly know of no other place of security in the whole of the land besides. And if there is no longer any security there, there is nothing left but the sea." But even the deep sea-bottom will not shelter from the vengeance of God. God commands the serpent, or summons the serpent to bite him. *Nâchâsh*, here the water-serpent, called elsewhere *livyāthān* or *tannīn* (Isa. xxvii. 1), a sea-monster, which was popularly supposed to be extremely dangerous, but which cannot be more exactly defined. Even by going into captivity, they will not be protected from the sword. בַּשְּׁבִי, not into captivity, but *in statu captivitatis*: even if they should be among those who were wandering into captivity, where men are generally sure of their lives (see Lam. i. 5). For God has fixed His eye upon them, *i.e.* has taken them under His special superintendence (cf. Jer. xxxix. 12); not, however, to shelter, to protect, and to bless, but לְרָעָה, for evil, *i.e.* to punish them. "The people of the Lord remain, under all circumstances, the object of special attention. They are more richly blessed than the world, but they are also more severely punished" (Hengstenberg).

To strengthen this threat, Amos proceeds, in vers. 5, 6, to describe Jehovah as the Lord of heaven and earth, who sends judgments upon the earth with omnipotent power. Ver. 5. *" And the Lord Jehovah of hosts, who toucheth the earth, and it melteth, and all the inhabitants thereupon mourn; and the whole of it riseth like the Nile, and sinketh like the Nile of Egypt. Ver. 6. Who buildeth His stories in heaven, and His vault, over the earth hath He founded it; who calleth to the waters of the sea, and poureth them out over the earth: Jehovah is His name."* This description of God, who rules with omnipotence, is appended, as in ch. iv. 13 and v. 8, without any link of connection whatever. We must not render it, "The Lord Jehovah of hosts is He who toucheth the earth;" but we must supply the connecting thought, "And He who thus directeth His eye upon you is the Lord Jehovah of hosts, who toucheth the earth, and it melteth." The melting or dissolving of the earth is, according to Ps. xlvi. 7, an effect produced by the Lord, who makes His voice heard in judgments, or "the destructive effect of the judgments of God, whose instruments the conquerors are" (Hengstenberg), when nations reel and kingdoms totter. The

Lord therefore touches the earth, so that it melts, when He
dissolves the stability of the earth by great judgments (cf. Ps.
lxxv. 4). "Israel could not fail to test the truth of these words
by painful experience, when the wild hordes of Assyria poured
themselves over the western parts of Asia" (Hengstenberg).
The following words, depicting the dissolution of the earth, are
repeated, with very inconsiderable alterations, from ch. viii. 8 :
we have merely the omission of וְנִגְרְשָׁה, and the *kal* שָׁקְעָה substituted for the *niphal* נִשְׁקָה. In ver. 6 there is evidently an
allusion to the flood. God, who is enthroned in heaven, in the
cloud-towers built above the circle of the earth, possesses the
power to pour the waves of the sea over the earth by His
simple word. *Ma'ălōth* is synonymous with עֲלִיּוֹת in Ps. civ. 3 :
upper rooms, *lit.* places to which one has to ascend. *'Aguddâh*,
an arch or vault : that which is called *râqīă'*, the firmament, in
other places. The heaven, in which God builds His stories, is
the heaven of clouds; and the vault, according to Gen. i. 7,
is the firmament of heaven, which divided the water above the
firmament from the water beneath it. Consequently the upper
rooms of God are the waters above the firmament, in or out of
which God builds His stories (Ps. civ. 3), *i.e.* the cloud-tower
above the horizon of the earth, which is raised above it like a
vault. Out of this cloud-castle the rain pours down (Ps. civ.
13) ; and out of its open windows the waters of the flood
poured down, and overflowed the earth (Gen. vii: 11). When
God calls to the waters of the sea, they pour themselves over
the surface of the earth. The waves of the sea are a figurative
representation of the agitated multitude of nations, or of the
powers of the world, which pour their waves over the kingdom
of God (see at ch. vii. 4).

The Lord will pour out these floods upon sinful Israel,
because it stands nearer to Him than the heathen do. Ver. 7.
"*Are ye not like the sons of the Cushites to me, ye sons of Israel?
is the saying of Jehovah. Have I not brought Israel up out of
the land of Egypt, and the Philistines out of Caphtor, and Aram
out of Kir ?*" With these words the prophet tears away from
the sinful nation the last support of its carnal security, namely,
reliance upon its election as the nation of God, which the Lord
has practically confirmed by leading Israel up out of Egypt.
Their election as the people of Jehovah was unquestionably a

pledge that the Lord would not cast off His people, or suffer them to be destroyed by the heathen. But what the apostle says of circumcision in Rom. ii. 25 applied to this election also, namely, that it was of benefit to none but those who kept the law. It afforded a certainty of divine protection simply to those who proved themselves to be the children of Israel by their walk and conduct, and who faithfully adhered to the Lord. To the rebellious it was of no avail. Idolaters had become like the heathen. The Cushites are mentioned, not so much as being descendants of the accursed Ham, as on account of the blackness of their skin, which was regarded as a symbol of spiritual blackness (cf. Jer. xiii. 23). The expression " *sons* (children) of the Cushites" is used with reference to the title " sons (children) of Israel," the honourable name of the covenant nation. For degenerate Israel, the leading up out of Egypt had no higher signification than the leading up of the Philistines and Syrians out of their former dwelling-places into the lands which they at present inhabited. These two peoples are mentioned by way of example : the Philistines, because they were despised by the Israelites, as being uncircumcised; the Syrians, with an allusion to the threat in ch. i. 5, that they should wander into exile to Kir. On the fact that the Philistines sprang from Caphtor, see the comm. on Gen. x. 14.

Election, therefore, will not save sinful Israel from destruction. After Amos has thus cut off all hope of deliverance from the ungodly, he repeats, in his own words in vers. 8 sqq., the threat already exhibited symbolically in ver. 1. Ver. 8. " *Behold, the eyes of the Lord Jehovah are against the sinful kingdom, and I destroy it from off the face of the earth; except that I shall not utterly destroy the house of Jacob : is the saying of Jehovah.* Ver. 9. *For, behold, I command, and shake the house of Israel among all nations, as (corn) is shaken in a sieve, and not even a little grain falls to the ground.* Ver. 10. *All the sinners of my people will die by the sword, who say, The evil will not overtake or come to us.*" The sinful kingdom is Israel; not merely the kingdom of the ten tribes however, but all Israel, the kingdom of the ten tribes along with Judah, the house of Jacob or Israel, which is identical with the sons of Israel, who had become like the Cushites, although Amos had chiefly the people and kingdom of the ten tribes in his mind. *Bammamlâkhâh*, not upon the kingdom, but against the kingdom. The directing of the eye upon an object is expressed by עַל (ver. 4) or אֶל (cf. Ps. xxxiv. 16); whereas בּ is used in relation to the object upon which anger rests (Ps. xxxiv. 17). Because the Lord had turned His eye towards the sinful kingdom, He must exterminate it,—a fate with which Moses had already threatened the nation in Deut. vi. 15. Nevertheless (אֶפֶס כִּי, "only that," introducing the limitation, as in Num. xiii. 28, Deut. xv. 4) the house of Jacob, the covenant nation, shall not be utterly destroyed. The "house of Jacob" is opposed to the "sinful nation;" not, however, so that the antithesis simply lies in the kingdom and people (*regnum delebo, non populum*), or that the "house of Jacob" signifies the kingdom of Judah as distinguished from the kingdom of the ten tribes, for the "house of Jacob" is perfectly equivalent to the "house of Israel" (ver. 9). The house of Jacob is not to be utterly destroyed, but simply to be shaken, as it were, in a sieve. The antithesis lies in the predicate הַחַטָּאָה, the *sinful* kingdom. So far as Israel, as a kingdom and people, is sinful, it is to be destroyed from off the face of the earth. But there is always a divine kernel in the nation, by virtue of its divine election, a holy seed out of which the Lord will form a new and holy people and kingdom of God. Consequently the destruction will not be a total one, a הַשְׁמֵיד אַשְׁמִיד. The reason for this is introduced by *kî* (for) in ver. 9. The Lord will shake Israel among the nations, as corn is shaken in a sieve; so that the chaff flies away, and the dust and dirt fall to the ground, and only the good grains are left in the sieve. Such a sieve are the nations of the world, through which Israel is purified from its chaff, *i.e.* from its ungodly members. *Tsᵉrôr*, generally a bundle; here, according to its etymology, that which is compact or firm, *i.e.* solid grain as distinguished from loose chaff. In 2 Sam. xvii. 13 it is used in a similar sense to denote a hard piece of clay or a stone in a building. Not a single grain will fall to the ground, that is to say, not a good man will be lost (cf. 1 Sam. xxvi. 20). The self-secure sinners, however, who rely upon their outward connection with the nation of God (compare ver. 7 and ch. iii. 2), or upon their zeal in the outward forms of worship (ch. v. 21 sqq.), and fancy that the judgment cannot touch them (הַקְדִּים בְּעַד), to come to meet a person round about him, *i.e.* to come upon him from every side), will all perish by the sword. This threat is repeated at the close, without any formal link of connection with ver. 9, not only to prevent any abuse of the foregoing modification of the judgment, but also to remove this apparent discrepancy, that whereas in vers. 1–4 it is stated that not one will escape the judgment, according to ver. 8*b*, the nation of Israel is not to be utterly destroyed. In order to anticipate the frivolity of the ungodly, who always flatter them-selves with the hope of escaping when there is a threatening of any general calamity, the prophet first of all cuts off all possi-bilities whatever in vers. 1–4, without mentioning the excep-tions; and it is not till afterwards that the promise is introduced that the house of Israel shall not be utterly annihilated, whereby the general threat is limited to sinners, and the prospect of deliverance and preservation through the mercy of God is opened to the righteous. The historical realization or fulfil-ment of this threat took place, so far as Israel of the ten tribes was concerned, when their kingdom was destroyed by the Assyrians, and in the case of Judah, at the overthrow of the kingdom and temple by the Chaldeans; and the shaking of Israel in the sieve is still being fulfilled upon the Jews who are dispersed among all nations.

Vers. 11–15. THE KINGDOM OF GOD SET UP.—Since God, as the unchangeable One, cannot utterly destroy His chosen people, and abolish or reverse His purpose of salvation, after destroying the sinful kingdom, He will set up the new and genuine kingdom of God. Ver. 11. " *On that day will I set up the fallen hut of David, and wall up their rents; and what is destroyed thereof I will set up, and build it as in the days of eternity.* Ver. 12. *That they may take possession of the remnant of Edom, and all the nations upon which my name shall be called, is the saying of Jehovah, who doeth such things.*" "In that day," *i.e.* when the judgment has fallen upon the sinful kingdom, and all the sinners of the people of Jehovah are destroyed. *Sukkâh*, a hut, indicates, by way of contrast to *bayith*, the house or palace which David built for himself upon Zion (2 Sam. v. 11), a degenerate condition of the royal house of David. This is placed beyond all doubt by the predicate *nôpheleth*, fallen down. As the stately palace supplies a figurative representa-

tion of the greatness and might of the kingdom, so does the
fallen hut, which is full of rents and near to destruction, symbolize the utter ruin of the kingdom.   If the family of David
no longer dwells in a palace, but in a miserable fallen hut, its
regal sway must have come to an end.   The figure of the stem
of Jesse that is hewn down, in Isa. xi. 1, is related to this;
except that the former denotes the decline of the Davidic
dynasty, whereas the fallen hut represents the fall of the kingdom.   There is no need to prove, however, that this does not
apply to the decay of the Davidic house by the side of the
great power of Jeroboam (Hitzig, Hofmann), least of all under
Uzziah, in whose reign the kingdom of Judah reached the
summit of its earthly power and glory.   The kingdom of David
first became a hut when the kingdom of Judah was overcome
by the Chaldeans,—an event which is included in the prediction
contained in vers. 1 sqq., and hinted at even in ch. ii. 5.   But
this hut the Lord will raise up again from its fallen condition.
This raising up is still further defined in the three following
clauses : "I wall up their rents" (*pirtsēhen*).   The plural suffix
can only be explained from the fact that *sukkâh* actually refers
to the kingdom of God, which was divided into two kingdoms
("these kingdoms," ch. vi. 2), and that the house of Israel,
which was not to be utterly destroyed (ver. 8), consisted of the
remnant of the people of the two kingdoms, or the ἐκλογή of
the twelve tribes ; so that in the expression גָּדַרְתִּי פִרְצֵיהֶן there
is an allusion to the fact that the now divided nation would
one day be united again under the one king David, as Hosea
(ch. ii. 2, iii. 5) and Ezekiel (ch. xxxvii. 22) distinctly prophesy.
The correctness of this explanation of the plural suffix is confirmed by הֲרִסֹתָיו in the second clause, the suffix of which refers
to David, under whom the destroyed kingdom would rise into
new power.   And whilst these two clauses depict the restoration of the kingdom from its fallen condition, in the third
clause its further preservation is foretold.   בָּנָה does not mean
to "build" here, but to finish building, to carry on, enlarge,
and beautify the building.   The words כִּימֵי עוֹלָם (an abbreviated
comparison for "as it was in the days of the olden time") point
back to the promise in 2 Sam. vii. 11, 12, 16, that God would
build a house for David, would raise up his seed after him,
and firmly establish his throne for ever, that his house and his

kingdom should endure for ever before Him, upon which the whole of the promise before us is founded. The days of the rule of David and of his son Solomon are called " days of eternity," *i.e.* of the remotest past (compare Mic. vii. 14), to show that a long period would intervene between that time and the predicted restoration. The rule of David had already received a considerable blow through the falling away of the ten tribes. And it would fall still deeper in the future ; but, according to the promise in 2 Sam. vii., it would not utterly perish, but would be raised up again from its fallen condition. It is not expressly stated that this will take place through a shoot from its own stem ; but that is implied in the fact itself. The kingdom of David could only be raised up again through an offshoot from David's family. And that this can be no other than the Messiah, was unanimously acknowledged by the earlier Jews, who even formed a name for the Messiah out of this passage, viz. בר נפלים, *filius cadentium,* He who had sprung from a fallen hut (see the proofs in Hengstenberg's *Christology,* vol. i. p. 386 transl.). The kingdom of David is set up in order that they (the sons of Israel, who have been proved to be corn by the sifting, ver. 9) may take possession of the remnant of Edom and all the nations, etc. The Edomites had been brought into subjection by David, who had taken possession of their land. At a late period, when the hut of David was beginning to fall, they had recovered their freedom again. This does not suffice, however, to explain the allusion to Edom here ; for David had also brought the Philistines, the Moabites, the Ammonites, and the Aramæans into subjection to his sceptre,—all of them nations who had afterwards recovered their freedom, and to whom Amos foretels the coming judgment in ch. i. The reason why Edom alone is mentioned by name must be sought for, therefore, in the peculiar attitude which Edom assumed towards the people of God, namely, in the fact " that whilst they were related to the Judæans, they were of all nations the most hostile to them" (Rosenmüller). On this very ground Obadiah predicted that judgment would come upon the Edomites, and that the remnant of Esau would be captured by the house of Jacob. Amos speaks here of the " remnant of Edom," not because Amaziah recovered only a portion of Edom to the kingdom (2 Kings xiv. 7), as Hitzig

supposes, but with an allusion to the threat in ch. i. 12, that
Edom would be destroyed with the exception of a remnant.
The "remnant of Edom" consists of those who are saved in the
judgments that fall upon Edom.   This also applies to כָּל־הַגּוֹיִם.
Even of these nations, only those are taken by Israel, *i.e.* incorporated into the restored kingdom of David, the Messianic
kingdom, upon whom the name of Jehovah is called; that is
to say, not those who were first brought under the dominion of
the nation in the time of David (Hitzig, Baur, and Hofmann),
but those to whom He shall have revealed His divine nature,
and manifested Himself as a God and Saviour (compare Isa.
lxiii. 19, Jer. xiv. 9, and the remarks on Deut. xxviii. 10), so
that this expression is practically the same as אֲשֶׁר יְהֹוָה קֹרֵא
(whom Jehovah shall call) in Joel iii. 5.   The perfect נִקְרָא
acquires the sense of the *futurum exactum* from the leading
sentence, as in Deut. xxviii. 10 (see Ewald, § 346, *c*).   יִירְשׁוּ, to
take possession of, is chosen with reference to the prophecy of
Balaam (Num. xxiv. 18), that Edom should be the possession
of Israel (see the comm. on this passage).   Consequently the
taking possession referred to here will be of a very different
character from the subjugation of Edom and other nations to
David.   It will make the nations into citizens of the kingdom
of God, to whom the Lord manifests Himself as their God,
pouring upon them all the blessings of His covenant of grace
(see Isa. lvi. 6-8).   To strengthen this promise, נְאֻם יי וְגוֹ
(" saith Jehovah, that doeth this ") is appended.   He who says
this is the Lord, who will also accomplish it (see Jer. xxxiii. 2).

The explanation given above is also in harmony with the
use made by James of our prophecy in Acts xv. 16, 17, where
he derives from vers. 11 and 12 a prophetic testimony to the
fact that Gentiles who became believers were to be received
into the kingdom of God without circumcision.   It is true that
at first sight James appears to quote the words of the prophet
simply as a prophetic declaration in support of the fact related
by Peter, namely, that by giving His Holy Spirit to believers
from among the Gentiles as well as to believers from among
the Jews, without making any distinction between Jews and
Gentiles, God had taken out of the Gentiles a people ἐπὶ τῷ
ὀνόματι αὐτοῦ, " upon His name " (compare Acts xv. 14 with
Acts xv. 8, 9).   But as both James and Peter recognise in

this fact a practical declaration on the part of God that circumcision was not a necessary prerequisite to the reception of the Gentiles into the kingdom of Christ, while James follows up the allusion to this fact with the prophecy of Amos, introducing it with the words, " and to this agree the words of the prophets," there can be no doubt that James also quotes the words of the prophet with the intention of adducing evidence out of the Old Testament in support of the reception of the Gentiles into the kingdom of God without circumcision. But this proof is not furnished by the statement of the prophet, "through its silence as to the condition required by those who were pharisaically disposed" (Hengstenberg); and still less by the fact that it declares in the most striking way "what significance there was in the typical kingdom of David, as a prophecy of the relation in which the human race, outside the limits of Israel, would stand to the kingdom of Christ" (Hofmann, *Schriftbeweis*, ii. 2, pp. 84, 85). For the passage would contain nothing extraordinary concerning the typical significance possessed by the kingdom of David in relation to the kingdom of Christ, if, as Hofmann says (p. 84), the prophet, instead of enumerating all the nations which once belonged to the kingdom of David, simply mentions Edom by name, and describes all the others as the nations which have been subject like Edom to the name of Jehovah. The demonstrative force of the prophet's statement is to be found, no doubt, as Hofmann admits, in the words כָּל־הַגּוֹיִם אֲשֶׁר נִקְרָא שְׁמִי עֲלֵיהֶם. But if these words affirmed nothing more than what Hofmann finds in them—namely, that all the nations subdued by David were subjected to the name of Jehovah; or, as he says at p. 83, " made up, in connection with Israel, the kingdom of Jehovah and His anointed, without being circumcised, or being obliged to obey the law of Israel"—their demonstrative force would simply lie in what they do not affirm,—namely, in the fact that they say nothing whatever about circumcision being a condition of the reception of the Gentiles. The circumstance that the heathen nations which David brought into subjection to his kingdom were made tributary to himself and subject to the name of Jehovah, might indeed be typical of the fact that the kingdom of the second David would also spread over the Gentiles; but, according to this explanation, it would affirm nothing at all as to the internal relation of the Gentiles to Israel in the new kingdom of God. The Apostle James, however, quotes the words of Amos as decisive on the point in dispute, which the apostles were considering, because in the words, " all the nations upon whom my name is called," he finds a prediction of what Peter has just related,—namely, that the Lord has taken out of the heathen a people " upon His name," that is to say, because he understands by the calling of the name of the Lord upon the Gentiles the communication of the Holy Ghost to the Gentiles.[1]

To the setting up of the kingdom and its outward extension the prophet appends its inward glorification, foretelling the richest blessing of the land (ver. 13) and of the nation (ver. 14), and lastly, the eternal duration of the kingdom (ver. 15). Ver. 13. " *Behold, days come, is the saying of Jehovah, that the plough-man reaches to the reaper, and the treader of grapes to the sower of seed ; and the mountains drip new wine, and all the hills melt away.* Ver. 14. *And I reverse the captivity of my people Israel, and they build the waste cities, and dwell, and plant vineyards, and drink the wine thereof ; and make gardens, and eat the fruit thereof.* Ver. 15. *And I plant them in their land, and they shall no more be torn up out of their land which I have given them, saith Jehovah thy God.*" In the new kingdom of God the people of the Lord will enjoy the blessing, which Moses promised to Israel when faithful to the covenant. This blessing will be poured upon the land in which the kingdom is set up. Ver. 13a is formed after the promise in Lev. xxvi. 5, " Your thresh-ing shall reach unto the vintage, and the vintage shall reach unto the sowing-time ; " but Amos transfers the action to the

---

[1] Moreover, James (or Luke) quotes the words of Amos according to the LXX., even in their deviations from the Hebrew text, in the words ὅπως ἂν ἐκζητήσωσιν οἱ κατάλοιποι τῶν ἀνθρώπων με (for which Luke has τὸν κύριον, according to Cod. Al.), which rest upon an interchange of לְמַעַן יִרְשׁוּ אֶת־שְׁאֵרִית אֱדוֹם with לְמַעַן יִדְרְשׁוּ שְׁאֵרִית אָדָם ; because the thought upon which it turned was not thereby altered, inasmuch as the possession of the Gentiles, of which the prophet is speaking, is the spiritual sway of the people of the Lord, which can only extend over those who seek the Lord and His kingdom. The other deviations from the original text and from the LXX. (compare Acts xv. 16 with Amos ix. 11) may be ex-plained on the ground that the apostle is quoting from memory, and that he alters ἐν τῇ ἡμέρᾳ ἐκείνῃ ἀναστήσω into μετὰ ταῦτα ἀναστρέψω καὶ ἀνοικοδομήσω, to give greater clearness to the allusion contained in the pro-phecy to the Messianic times.

persons employed, and says, " The ploughman will reach to the reaper." Even while the one is engaged in ploughing the land for the sowing, the other will already be able to cut ripe corn; so quickly will the corn grow and ripen. And the treading of the grapes will last to the sowing-time, so abundant will the vintage be. The second half of the verse is taken from Joel iv. 18 ; and according to this passage, the melting of the hills is to be understood as dissolving into streams of milk, new wine, and honey, in which the prophet had the description of the promised land as a land flowing with milk and honey (Ex. iii. 8, etc.) floating before his mind. In the land so blessed will Israel enjoy unbroken peace, and delight itself in the fruits of its inheritance. On שׁוּב אֶת־שְׁבוּת, see the exposition of Hos. vi. 11. That this phrase is not used here to denote the return of the people from captivity, but the turning of misfortune and misery into prosperity and salvation, is evident from the context; for Israel cannot be brought back out of captivity *after* it has already taken possession of the Gentiles (ver. 12). The thought of ver. 14, as attached to ver. 13, is the following: As the land of Israel, *i.e.* the territory of the re-erected kingdom of David, will no more be smitten with the curse of drought and failing crops with which the rebellious are threatened, but will receive the blessing of the greatest fertility, so will the people, *i.e.* the citizens of this kingdom, be no more visited with calamity and judgment, but enjoy the rich beneficent fruits of their labour in blessed and unbroken peace. This thought is individualized with a retrospective glance at the punishment with which the sinners are threatened in ch. v. 11, —namely, as building waste cities, and dwelling therein, and as drinking the wine of the vineyards that have been planted; not building houses for others any more, as was threatened in ch. v. 11, after Deut. xxviii. 30, 39 ; and lastly, as laying out gardens, and eating the fruit thereof, without its being consumed by strangers (Deut. xxviii. 33). This blessing will endure for ever (ver. 15). Their being planted in their land denotes, not the settling of the people in their land once more, but their firm and lasting establishment and fortification therein. The Lord will make Israel, *i.e.* His rescued people, into a plantation that will never be torn up again, but strikes firm roots, sends forth blossom, and produces fruit. The words point back to 2 Sam. vii. 10, and declare that the firm planting of Israel which was begun by David will be completed with the raising up of the fallen hut of David, inasmuch as no further driving away of the nation into captivity will occur, but the people of the Lord will dwell for ever in the land which their God has given them. Compare Jer. xxiv. 6. This promise is sealed by אָמַר יי' אל'.

We have not to seek for the realization of this promise in the return of Israel from its captivity to Palestine under Zerubbabel and Ezra; for this was no planting of Israel to dwell for ever in the land, nor was it a setting up of the fallen hut of David. Nor have we to transfer the fulfilment to the future, and think of a time when the Jews, who have been converted to their God and Saviour Jesus Christ, will one day be led back to Palestine. For, as we have already observed at Joel iii. 18, Canaan and Israel are types of the kingdom of God and of the church of the Lord. The raising up of the fallen hut of David commenced with the coming of Christ and the founding of the Christian church by the apostles; and the possession of Edom and all the other nations upon whom the Lord reveals His name, took its rise in the reception of the Gentiles into the kingdom of heaven set up by Christ. The founding and building of this kingdom continue through all the ages of the Christian church, and will be completed when the fulness of the Gentiles shall one day enter into the kingdom of God, and the still unbelieving Israel shall have been converted to Christ. The land which will flow with streams of divine blessing is not Palestine, but the domain of the Christian church, or the earth, so far as it has received the blessings of Christianity. The people which cultivates this land is the Christian church, so far as it stands in living faith, and produces fruits of the Holy Ghost. The blessing foretold by the prophet is indeed visible at present in only a very small measure, because Christendom is not yet so pervaded by the Spirit of the Lord, as that it forms a holy people of God. In many respects it still resembles Israel, which the Lord will have to sift by means of judgments. This sifting will be first brought to an end through the judgment upon all nations, which will attend the second coming of Christ. Then will the earth become a Canaan, where the Lord will dwell in His glorified kingdom in the midst of His sanctified people.

OBADIAH

INTRODUCTION.

A S to the *person* and *circumstances* of Obadiah, nothing certain is known, since the heading to his prophecy simply contains the name עֹבַדְיָה, *i.e.* servant, worshipper of Jehovah ('Οβδιού *al.* 'Αβδιού, *sc.* ὅρασις, LXX.), and does not even mention his father's name. The name *Obadiah* frequently occurs in its earlier form 'Obadyâhû. This was the name of a pious governor of the palace under king Ahab (1 Kings xviii. 3 sqq.), of a prince of Judah under Jehoshaphat (2 Chron. xvii. 7), of a brave Gadite under David (1 Chron. xii. 9), of a Benjamite (1 Chron. viii. 38), of an Issacharite (1 Chron. vii. 3), of a Zebulunite (1 Chron. xxvii. 19), of several Levites (1 Chron. ix. 16, 44; 2 Chron. xxxiv. 12), and of different men after the captivity (1 Chron. iii. 21; Ezra viii. 9; Neh. x. 6). The traditional accounts of our prophet in the rabbins and fathers, some of whom identify him with Ahab's pious commander of the castle, others with the third captain sent by Ahaziah against Elisha (2 Kings i. 13), whilst others again make him an Edomitish proselyte (see Carpzov, *Introd.* p. 332 sqq., and Delitzsch, *de Habacuci vita atque ætate*, pp. 60, 61), are quite worthless, and evidently false, and have merely originated in the desire to know something more about him than the simple name (see C. P. Caspari, *Der Proph. Ob.* pp. 2, 3).

The *writing* of Obadiah contains but one single prophecy concerning the relation in which Edom stood to the people of God. It commences with the proclamation of the destruction with which the Lord has determined to visit the Edomites, who rely upon the impregnability of their rocky seat (vers. 1–9); and then depicts, as the cause of the divine judgment which

will thus suddenly burst upon the haughty people, the evil
which it did to Jacob, the covenant nation, when Judah and
Jerusalem had been taken by heathen nations, who not only
plundered them, but shamefully desecrated the mountain of
Zion (vers. 10-14). For this the Edomites and all nations
will receive retribution, even to their utter destruction in the
approaching day of the Lord (vers. 15, 16). But upon Mount
Zion there will be delivered ones, and the mountain will be
holy. The house of Jacob will take possession of the settlement of the Gentiles, and, in common with Israel, will destroy
the Edomites, and extend its territory on all sides (vers. 17–19).
That portion of the nation which has been scattered about in
heathen lands will return to their enlarged fatherland (ver. 20).
Upon Mount Zion will saviours arise to judge Edom, and the
kingdom will then be the Lord's (ver. 21). This brief statement of the contents is sufficient to show that Obadiah's prophecy does not consist of a mere word of threatening directed
against Edom, or treat of so special a theme as that his *châzōn*
could be compared to Ahijah's *nᵉbhū'âh*, and Yehdi's (Iddo's)
châzōth against Jeroboam I. (2 Chron. ix. 29); but that
Obadiah takes the general attitude of Edom towards the
people of Jehovah as the groundwork of his prophecy, regards
the judgment upon Edom as one feature in the universal
judgment upon all nations (cf. vers. 15, 16), proclaims in the
destruction of the power of Edom the overthrow of the power
of all nations hostile to God, and in the final elevation and re-
establishment of Israel in the holy land foretels the completion
of the sovereignty of Jehovah, *i.e.* of the kingdom of God, as
dominion over all nations; so that we may say with Hengstenberg, that " Obadiah makes the judgment upon the Gentiles
and the restoration of Israel the leading object of his prophetic
painting." Through this universal standpoint, from which
Edom is taken as a representative of the ungodly power of the
world, Obadiah rises far above the utterances of the earlier
prophets contained in the historical books of the Old Testament, and stands on a level with the prophets, who composed
prophetic writings of their own for posterity, as well as for their
own age; so that, notwithstanding the small space occupied by
his prophecy, it has very properly had a place assigned it in the
prophetic literature. At the same time, we cannot agree with

Hengstenberg, who gives the following interpretation to this view of the attitude of Edom towards the people of God, namely, that Obadiah simply adduces Edom as an example of what he has to say with regard to the heathen world, with its enmity against God, and as to the form which the relation between Israel and the heathen world would eventually assume, and therefore that his prophecy simply individualizes the thought of the universal dominion of the kingdom of God which would follow the deepest degradation of the people of God, the fullest and truest realization of which dominion is to be sought for in Christ, and that the germ of his prophecy is contained in Joel iii. 19, where Edom is introduced as an individualized example and type of the heathen world with its hostility to God, which is to be judged by the Lord after the judgment upon Judah. For, apart from the fact that Obadiah does not presuppose Joel, but *vice versa*, as we shall presently see, this mode of idealizing our prophecy cannot be reconciled with its concrete character and expression, or raised into a truth by any analogies in prophetic literature. All the prophecies are occasioned by distinct concrete relations and circumstances belonging to the age from which they spring. And even those which are occupied with the remote and remotest future, like Isa. xl.-lxvi. for example, form no real exception to this rule. Joel would not have mentioned Edom as the representation of the heathen world with its hostility to God (iii. 19), and Obadiah would not have predicted the destruction of Edom, if the Edomites had not displayed their implacable hatred to the people of God on one particular occasion in the most conspicuous manner. It is only in this way that we can understand the contents of the whole of Obadiah's prophecy, more especially the relation in which the third section (vers. 17-21) stands to the first two, and explain them without force.

The *time* of the prophet is so much a matter of dispute, that some regard him as the oldest of the twelve minor prophets, whilst others place him in the time of the captivity, and Hitzig even assigns him to the year 312 B.C., when prophecy had long been extinct. (For the different views, see my *Lehrbuch der Einleitung*, § 88.) That Obadiah does not belong to the prophets of the captivity, or to those after the captivity, but to the earlier prophets, may be generally inferred

from the position of his book in the collection of the twelve
minor prophets; for although the collection is not strictly
chronological, yet it is so arranged as a whole, that the writings
of the captivity and the times after the captivity occupy the
last places, whereas Obadiah stands among older prophets.
More precise information may be obtained from the contents
of his prophecy, more especially from the relation in which it
stands on the one hand to the prophecy of Jeremiah (xlix. 7–22)
concerning Edom, and on the other hand to the prophecy
of Joel. Obadiah so thoroughly coincides with these in a
number of characteristic thoughts and expressions, that the one
must have known the other. If we examine, first of all, the
relation which exists between Obadiah and Jeremiah (*l.c.*),
there can be no doubt, (and since the thorough investigations
of Caspari (p. 5 sqq.) it has been admitted by every one with
the exception of Hitzig,) that Obadiah did not use Jeremiah,
but that Jeremiah read and made use of Obadiah. This might
indeed be conjectured from the peculiar characteristic of Jeremiah, namely, that he leans throughout upon the utterances of
the earlier prophets, and reproduces their thoughts, figures, and
words (see A. Kueper, *Jeremias librorum ss. interpres atque
vindex*, 1837). Thus, for example, nearly all his prophecies
against foreign nations are founded upon utterances of the
earlier prophets: that against the Philistines (Jer. xlvii.) upon
Isaiah's prophecy against that people (Isa. xiv. 28–32); that
against the Moabites (Jer. xlviii.) upon that of Isaiah in ch.
xv. xvi.; that against the Ammonites (Jer. xlix. 1–6) upon
the prophecy of Amos against the same (Amos i. 13–15); that
against Damascus (Jer. xlix. 23–27) upon that of Amos against
this kingdom (Amos i. 3–5); and lastly, that against Babylon
(Jer. l. li.) upon the prophecy of Isaiah against Babylon in
Isa. xiii.–xiv. 23. To this we may add, (1) that the prophecy of Jeremiah against Edom contains a number of expressions peculiar to himself and characteristic of his style, not a
single one of which is to be found in Obadiah, whilst nothing
is met with elsewhere in Jeremiah of that which is common to
Obadiah and him (for the proofs of this, see Caspari, pp. 7, 8);
and (2) that what is common to the two prophets not only
forms an outwardly connected passage in Obadiah, whereas in
Jeremiah it occurs in several unconnected passages of his pro-

phecy (compare Obad. 1–8 with Jer. xlix. 7, 9, 10, 14–16), but, as the exposition will show, that in Obadiah it is more closely connected and apparently more original than in Jeremiah. But if it be a fact, as this unquestionably proves, that Obadiah's prophecy is more original, and therefore older, than that of Jeremiah, Obadiah cannot have prophesied after the destruction of Jerusalem by the Chaldeans, but must have prophesied before it, since Jeremiah's prophecy against Edom belongs to the fourth year of Jehoiakim (see Caspari, p. 14 sqq., and Graf's *Jeremias*, pp. 558–9, compared with p. 506).

The central section of Obadiah's prophecy (vers. 10–16) does not appear to harmonize with this result, inasmuch as the cause of the judgment with which the Edomites are threatened in vers. 1–9 is said to be their rejoicing over Judah and Jerusalem at the time of their calamity, when foreigners entered into his gates, and cast the lot upon Jerusalem ; and they are charged not only with looking upon the destruction of the brother nation with contemptuous pleasure, but with taking part themselves in the plundering of Judah, and murdering the fugitives, or giving them up to their enemies. These reproaches unquestionably presuppose a conquest of Jerusalem by foreign nations ; but whether it is the destruction of Jerusalem by the Chaldeans, is by no means so certain as many commentators imagine. It is true that Caspari observes (p. 18), that " every one who reads these verses would naturally suppose that they refer to that catastrophe, and to the hostilities shown by the Edomites to the Judæans on that occasion, to which those prophets who lived after the destruction of Jerusalem, viz. Jeremiah (Lam. iv. 21, 22), Ezekiel (ch. xxxv.), and the author of Ps. cxxxvii., refer to some extent in almost the same words in which Obadiah speaks of them." But of the passages cited, Lam. iv. 21, 22 cannot be taken into account at all, since it simply contains the thought that the cup (of affliction) will also reach to the daughter of Edom ; and that she will be intoxicated and stripped, and that Jehovah will punish her guilt. The other two are no doubt similar. The Psalmist in Ps. cxxxvii. utters this prayer in ver. 7 : " Remember, Jehovah, the children of Edom in the day of Jerusalem, who say, Strip, strip (*i.e.* demolish) even to the foundation thereof;" and Ezekiel threatens Edom with everlasting desolation, because

it has cherished everlasting enmity, and given up the sons of
Israel to the sword, בְּעֵת אֵידָם בְּעֵת עֲוֹן קֵץ (ver. 5), because it has
said, The two nations (Judah and Israel) shall be mine, we will
take possession of them (ver. 10); because it has cherished
hatred toward the sons of Israel, and spoken blasphemy against
the mountains of Israel, and said they are laid waste, they are
given to us for food (ver. 12); because it has taken pleasure in
the desolation of the inheritance of the house of Israel (ver. 15).
There is a most unambiguous allusion here to the desolating of
Judah and the destruction of Jerusalem, and to the hostilities
which the Edomites displayed when this calamity fell upon
Judah. On the other hand, Obadiah does not hint at the
destruction of Jerusalem in a single word. He neither speaks
of the *everlasting* enmity of Edom, nor of the fact that it wanted
to get possession of Judah and Israel for itself, but simply
of the hostile behaviour of the Edomites towards the brother
nation Judah, when enemies forced their way into Jerusalem
and plundered its treasures, and the sons of Judah perished.
Consequently Obadiah has before his eyes simply the conquest
and plundering of Jerusalem by foreign, *i.e.* heathen foes, but
not the destruction of Jerusalem by the Chaldeans. Even
Caspari is obliged to admit, that there is no necessity to understand most (or more correctly " any") of the separate expressions of Obadiah as referring to the destruction of Jerusalem
by the Chaldeans; but, in his opinion, this allusion is required
by " what is said in vers. 11–14 when taken all together,
inasmuch as the prophet there describes the day of Jerusalem
by the strongest possible names, following one upon another, as
the day of his people's rejection, the day of their distress (twice),
and the day of their calamity (three times)." But even this we
cannot regard as well established, since neither יוֹם נָכְרוֹ nor
יוֹם אֵידוֹ designates the calamitous day as a day of rejection; and
יוֹם אָבְדָם cannot possibly denote the utter destruction of all the
Judæans, but simply affirms that the sons of Judah perished
en masse. The other epithets, נֵכָר, אֵיד, צָרָה, do not enable us
to define more precisely the nature of the calamity which befel
Judah at that time; and the crowding together of these expressions simply shows that the calamity was a very great one,
and not that Jerusalem was destroyed and the kingdom of
Judah dissolved.

But before the destruction of Jerusalem by Nebuchadnezzar, it was several times taken and plundered by foes: viz. (1) by Shishak king of Egypt in the fifth year of Rehoboam (1 Kings xiv. 25, 26; 2 Chron. xii. 2 sqq.); (2) by the Philistines and Arabians in the time of Jehoram (2 Chron. xxi. 16, 17); (3) by the Israelitish king Joash in the reign of Amaziah (2 Kings xiv. 13, 14; 2 Chron. xxv. 23, 24); (4) by the Chaldeans in the time of Jehoiakim (2 Kings xxiv. 1 sqq.; 2 Chron. xxxvi. 6, 7); and (5) by the Chaldeans again in the reign of Jehoiachin (2 Kings xxiv. 10 sqq.; 2 Chron. xxxvi. 10). Of these different conquests, the first can have no bearing upon the question before us, inasmuch as in the time of Rehoboam the Edomites were subject to the kingdom of Judah, and therefore could not have attempted to do what Obadiah says they did; nor can the two Babylonian conquests under Jehoiakim and Jehoiachin, inasmuch as, according to the relation in which Obadiah stood to Jeremiah, as shown above, he must have prophesied before they occurred; nor can the conquest in the reign of Amaziah, because Obadiah describes the enemies as *zârîm* and *nokhrîm* (strangers and foreigners), which clearly points to Gentile nations (compare Joel iii. 17; Lam. v. 2; Deut. xvii. 15), and does not apply to the citizens of the kingdom of the ten tribes. Consequently there only remains the taking of Jerusalem by the Philistines and Arabians in the time of Jehoram; and the relation in which Obadiah stood to Joel clearly points to this.

There is so remarkable a coincidence between vers. 10–18 of Obadiah and ch. ii. 32 and ch. iii. of Joel, in a very large number of words, expressions, and thoughts, considering the smallness of the two passages, and especially of that of Obadiah, that the dependence of one upon the other must be universally acknowledged.[1] But this dependence is not to be sought for on the side of Obadiah, as Caspari and others suppose; for the fact that Joel bears the stamp of originality in a greater degree than any other prophet, and the circumstance

---

[1] Compare מֵחֲמַס אָחִיךָ יַעֲקֹב in Ob. 10 with מֵחֲמַס בְּנֵי יְהוּדָה in Joel iii. 19; וְעַל יְרוּשָׁלַ͏ִם יַדּוּ גוֹרָל in Ob. 11 with וְאֶל־עַמִּי יַדּוּ גוֹרָל in Joel iii. 3; כִּי־קָרוֹב יוֹם־יְהוָֹה עַל כָּל־הַגּוֹיִם in Ob. 15 and גְּמֻלְךָ יָשׁוּב בְּרֹאשֶׁךָ *ibid.* with כִּי קָרוֹב יוֹם יְהוָֹה בְּעֵמֶק הֶחָרוּץ (Joel iii. 14, compare i. 15, ii. 1, and iii. 12,

that we meet with references to him in not a few of the later prophets from Amos onwards, furnish no evidence that will bear a moment's test. " The originality of Joel," as Delitzsch observes, " is no disproof of his dependence; for, on the one hand, the reproduction of certain elements from Obadiah's prophecy does not in the least invalidate his originality, inasmuch as the reproduction is itself original; and, on the other hand, not one of the prophets with whom we are acquainted (not even Isaiah) is so original as that the prophecies of his predecessors are not echoed by him, just as Obadiah, even if he were original in relation to Joel, had the prophecies of Balaam as his original, and imitates them in several passages (compare Num. xxiv. 21, 18, 19 with Ob. 4, 18, 19)." But the fact that Joel rests upon Obadiah is proved in the most decisive manner by the expression in Joel ii. 32, " as the Lord hath said," where the foregoing thought, which is common both to Joel and Obadiah, viz. "in Mount Zion . . . shall be *pᵉlētâh*" (see Ob. 17), is described as a well-known word of·the Lord. Now Joel can only have taken this from Obadiah, for it occurs nowhere else; and the idea suggested by Ewald, that it is derived from an older oracle that has been lost, would only be feasible if the later date of Obadiah, or his dependence upon Joel, could be demonstrated by conclusive arguments, which is not the case.

A correct determination of the relation in which Obadiah stood to Joel, especially if we compare the prophecies of Amos, who also alludes to Joel (compare Joel iii. 16 with Amos i. 2, and Joel iii. 18 with Amos ix. 13), leads with the greatest probability to the conclusion that Obadiah reproaches the Edomites with the hostility which they displayed when Judah and Jerusalem were plundered by the Philistines and Arabians in the time of Jehoram. In the reign of Jehoram the Edomites threw off the Judæan supremacy (compare 2 Kings viii. 20–22, and 2 Chron. xxi. 8–10); and in connection with this rebellion, they appear to have planned a great massacre upon

---

בְּהַר צִיּוֹן (לִשְׁפֹּט אֶת־כָּל־הַגּוֹיִם) and אָשִׁיב גְּמֻלְכֶם בְּרֹאשְׁכֶם in Joel iii. 4, 7; כִּי בְּהַר־צִיּוֹן וּבִירוּשָׁלַםִ תִּהְיֶה פְלֵיטָה with Ob. 17 with וְהָיָה קֹדֶשׁ and תִּהְיֶה פְלֵיטָה in Joel ii. 32, and וְהָיְתָה יְרוּשָׁלַםִ קֹדֶשׁ in Joel iii. 17; and lastly, כִּי יְהֹוָה דִּבֵּר in Ob. 18 and Joel iii. 8.

the Judæans, who were in their land at the time (compare Joel iii. 19 with Amos i. 11). Libnah also fell away from Judah at the same time (2 Kings viii. 22; 2 Chron. xxi. 10), and Philistines and Arabians penetrated victoriously into Judah. This expedition of the Philistines and (Petræan) Arabians against Jerusalem was not merely "a passing raid on the part of certain of the neighbouring nations who had been made tributary by Jehoshaphat (2 Chron. xvii. 11), and had rebelled in the time of Jehoram," as Caspari says; but these hordes continued their ravages in the most cruel manner in Judah and Jerusalem. According to 2 Chron. xxi. 17, they burst into the land, forced their way into Jerusalem, plundered the royal palace, and carried away the children and wives of the king, so that only the youngest son, Jehoahaz or Ahaziah, was left behind. We also learn from Joel iii. 5 that they took away gold, silver, and jewels from the temple; and from Joel iii. 3, 6, that they carried on the vilest trade with the men and women of Judah, and sold the captives to the Greeks, and that, as we see from Amos i. 6, 9, through the medium of the Phœnicians and Edomites. This agrees perfectly with Ob. 10–14. For, according to this passage also, the Edomites themselves were not the enemies who conquered Jerusalem and plundered its treasures, but simply accomplices, who rejoiced in the doings of the enemy (vers. 11 sqq.), held carousals with them upon the holy mountain Zion (ver. 16), and sought, partly by rapine and partly by slaying or capturing the fugitive Judæans (ver. 14), to get as much gain as possible out of Judah's misfortune. We must therefore regard this event, as Hofmann and Delitzsch have done, as the occasion of Obadiah's prophecy, and that all the more, because the historical allusions which it contains can thereby be satisfactorily explained; whereas the other attempts at solving the difficulties, when we look at the thing more closely, prove to be either altogether untenable, or such as will not apply throughout.

Thus, for example, Ewald and Graf (on Jer. xlix. 7 sqq.) have endeavoured to reconcile the fact that Jeremiah had read the first part of Obadiah as early as the fourth year of Jehoiakim, and had made use of it in his prophecy, with the opinion that vers. 10–16 (Ob.) refer to the Chaldean conquest and destruction of Jerusalem, by the hypothesis that the first part of Obadiah, as we possess it, was founded upon an earlier prophecy, which was adopted by the later editor of our book, and incorporated in his writings, and which had also been made use of by Jeremiah. In support of this hypothesis, the circumstance has been adduced, that Jeremiah's references to Obadiah only extend to ver. 9, that the introductory words in Obadiah, "Thus saith the Lord Jehovah concerning Edom," do not stand in a close connection with what follows immediately after and thus appear to have been added at a later period, and that the rare word *tiphlatst^ekhâ* (Jer. xlix. 16), which is not met with anywhere else in Jeremiah, is wanting in Obadiah. But the first phenomenon may be explained very simply, from the fact that the remaining portion of Obadiah (vers. 10–21) furnished nothing which Jeremiah could make use of for his object, and that we have an analogy in the relation between Jer. xlviii. and Isaiah's prophecy concerning Moab (Isa. xv. xvi.), where in just the same manner certain portions, viz. Isa. xvi. 1–5, have not been made use of at all.   Again, the want of any closer logical connection between the introduction, "Thus hath the Lord said with regard to Edom," and what follows, "We have heard a rumour from Jehovah," arises from the circumstance that these introductory words do not apply exclusively to what follows immediately after, but belong to the whole of Obadiah's prophecy (see at ver. 1).   Moreover, these words could not have been wanting even in the supposed earlier or original prophecy, inasmuch as what follows would be unintelligible without them, since the name *Edom*, to which the suffixes and addresses in vers. 1c–5 apply, would be altogether wanting. And lastly, the word *tiphlatst^ekhâ*, which is otherwise strange to Jeremiah, proves nothing in favour of an earlier source, which both Obadiah and Jeremiah employed ; nor can we see any sufficient reason for its omission when the earlier oracle was adopted.   The other arguments adduced in support of this hypothesis are entirely without significance, if not absolutely erroneous.   The fact that from ver. 10 onwards, where Jeremiah ceases to make use of our prophecy, the connection between Obadiah and Joel commences, of which there is not the slightest trace in vers. 1–9, has its natural foundation in the contents of the two parts of Obadiah.   The announcement of the judgment upon the Edomites in Ob. 1–9 could not be made use of by Joel, because, with the exception of the casual allusion in ch. iii. 19, he does not treat of the judgment upon Edom at all. The contents of Ob. 1–9 also show the reason why no allusion whatever is made in these verses to Israel and Jerusalem. The judgment predicted here was not to be executed by either Israel or Judah, but by the nations. Graf's assertion, that ver. 7 contains an allusion to totally different circumstances from those referred to in vers. 10 sqq., as the verses mentioned relate to altogether disproportionate things, is decidedly incorrect. So also is Ewald's opinion, that half our present Obadiah, viz. vers. 1–10, and vers. 17a and 18, "clearly points to an earlier prophet in contents, language, and colour." Caspari has already replied to this as follows : " We confess, on the contrary, that we can discover no difference in colour and language between vers. 1–9 and 10–21. The latter has its ἅπαξ λεγόμενα and its rare words just like the former (compare חַגְוֵי סֶלַע ver. 3, נִבְעוּ ver. 6, מַצְפֻּנָיו ver. 6, מְזוֹר ver. 7, קְטֶל ver. 9, in the first paragraph; and נָכְרוֹ ver. 12, תִּשְׁלַחְנָה ver. 13, פֶּרֶק ver. 14, לָעוּ ver. 16, in the second) ; and precisely the same liveliness and boldness which distinguished the first part of the prophecy, prevail in the second also. Not a single later word, nor a single form of more recent date, is met with to indicate the later origin of the second part." Moreover, it is impossible to discover any well-established analogy in the prophetical writings of the Old Testament to support this hypothesis.

The attempt made by Caspari, Hengstenberg, and others, to reconcile the opinion, that Obadiah alludes in vers. 11 sqq. to the Chaldean destruction of Jerusalem, with the fact that Jeremiah has made use of our book of Obadiah in his prophecy against Edom, which was uttered in the reign of Jehoiakim, by the assumption that Obadiah is not describing something that has already happened, but giving a prophetic picture of the future, is wrecked on the wording of the verses in question. When Obadiah threatens Edom with shame and destruction on account of its wickedness towards its brother Jacob (ver. 10), and then describes this wickedness in preterites—" On the day of thy standing opposite when strangers had come into his gates and cast the lot upon Jerusalem " (ver. 11) ; and, " As ye have drunk upon my holy mountain, so will all the heathen drink," etc. (ver. 16)—no one would understand these preterites as used

prophetically, *i.e.* as referring to what was not to take place
till a far distant future, except on the most conclusive grounds.
Such grounds, however, some imagine that they can find in
vers. 12–14, where the prophet warns the Edomites not to
rejoice over their brother nation's day of calamity, or take
part in the destruction of Judah. Hengstenberg and Caspari
follow Theodoret, Michaelis, and others, in the opinion that
Obadiah is predicting the destruction of Jerusalem, and that
ver. 11 can only be interpreted prophetically, and cannot be
taken as referring to an ideal past. For, as Caspari adds
(p. 29), "I might very well be able to warn a person against an
act, even though he were just about to perform it, and I were
perfectly certain that he would perform it notwithstanding, and
my warning would be fruitless, and though I merely warned
him, that he might not perform it without warning; but to
warn a person against an act which he has already performed
would be a most marvellous thing, even though the warning
were only given in the spirit and with the deed standing out
as a present thing." No doubt it is perfectly true that "such
a warning after the deed was done would be quite out of place,"
if it had reference merely to one isolated act, a repetition of
which was not to be expected. But if the act already performed was but one single outbreak of a prevailing disposition,
and might be repeated on every fresh occasion, and possibly
had already shown itself more than once, a warning against
such an act could neither be regarded as out of place, nor as
particularly striking, even after the thing had been done. The
warnings in vers. 12–14, therefore, do not compel us to interpret
the preterites in vers. 11 and 16 prophetically, as relating to
some future deed. Moreover, "the repeated warnings against
so wicked a deed were simply the drapery in which the prophet
clothed the prediction of the certain coming of the day of
Jehovah, which would put an end to the manifestation of such
a disposition on the part of Edom" (Delitzsch). There is still
less ground for the further remark of Caspari, that the allusions
to Joel in Obadiah's description of the day of calamity (not
"of the destruction") of Jerusalem, unquestionably preclude
the supposition that he was an eye-witness of that event, and
require the hypothesis that he wrote either before or a long
time afterwards. For these allusions are not of such a nature

that Obadiah simply repeats and still further develops what Joel had already prophesied before him, but, on the contrary, of such a nature that Joel had Obadiah before his mind, and has expanded certain features of his prophecy still further in ch. iii. 3–6. The description of the hostilities of the Edomites towards Israel, Obadiah could not possibly take from either Joel, or Amos ix. 12, or the sayings of Balaam in Num. xxiv. 18, 19, as Caspari supposes; because neither of these prophets has depicted them any more fully, but can only have drawn it from his own experience, and from what he himself had seen, so that his prophecy is thereby proved to be the original, as compared with that of Joel and Amos.

All this leads to the conclusion, that we must regard Obadiah as older than Joel, and fix upon the reign of Joram as the date of his ministry, but without thereby giving him " an isolated position;" for, according to the most correct chronological arrangement of their respective dates, Joel prophesied at the most twenty years after him, and Hosea and Amos commenced their labours only about seventy-five years later. The calamitous event which burst upon Judah and Jerusalem, and gave occasion for Obadiah's prophecy, took place in the latter part of Joram's eight years' reign. Consequently Obadiah cannot have uttered his prophecy, and committed it to writing, very long before Jehoram's death. At the same time, it cannot have been at a later period; because, on the one hand, it produces the unquestionable impression, that the hostilities practised by the Edomites were still kept in the most lively remembrance; and on the other hand, it contains no hint of that idolatrous worship to which the ruthless Athaliah endeavoured to give the pre-eminence in Judah, after the one year's reign of Ahaziah, who succeeded Joram. For the commentaries on Obadiah, see my *Lehrbuch der Einleitung*, § 88.

EXPOSITION.

THE JUDGMENT UPON EDOM, AND THE ESTABLISHMENT OF THE KINGDOM OF GOD UPON ZION.

The prophecy of Obadiah, which is headed the *châzōn*, *visio* (see at Isa. i. 1), is divisible into three sections: vers. 1-9, 10-16, and 17-21. In the first section the prophet proclaims—

EDOM'S RUIN, setting forth, in the first place, the purpose of God to make Edom small through the medium of hostile nations, and to hurl it down from the impregnable heights of its rocky castles (vers. 1-4); and then depicting, in lively colours, how it will be plundered by enemies, forsaken and deceived by allies and friends, and perish in helplessness and impotence (vers. 5-9). Ver. 1 contains, in addition to the brief heading, the introduction to the prophecy, which gives in a brief form the substance of the first section : " *Thus hath the Lord Jehovah spoken of Edom, A report have we heard from Jehovah, and a messenger is sent among the nations : Up, and let us arise against it in battle.*" The first clause, כֹּה אָמַר ... לֶאֱדוֹם, does not harmonize with what follows, inasmuch as we should expect it to be followed with a declaration made by Jehovah Himself, instead of which there follow simply tidings heard from Jehovah. The difficulty cannot be removed by assuming that these introductory words are spurious, or were added by a later prophet (Eichhorn, Ewald, and others); for the interpolator could not fail to observe the incongruity of these words just as well as Obadiah. Moreover, לֶאֱדוֹם could not be omitted from the opening, because it is required not only by the suffix in עָלֶיהָ (against *her*), but also by the direct addresses in vers. 2 sqq. Nor is the assumption that the prophet suddenly altered the construction any more satisfactory, or that the declaration of Jehovah announced in כֹּה אָמַר וגו׳ (" thus saith the Lord") commences in ver. 2, and that the words from שְׁמוּעָה to the end of the verse form an explanatory parenthesis to כֹּה אָמַר וגו׳. For such an alteration of the construction at the very be-

ginning of the address is hardly conceivable; and the parenthetical explanation of the last three clauses of ver. 1 is at
variance with their contents, which do not form by any means
a subordinate thought, but rather the main thought of the
following address. No other course remains, therefore, than
to take these introductory words by themselves, as Michaelis,
Maurer, and Caspari have done, in which case כה אמר does not
announce the actual words of Jehovah in the stricter sense, but
is simply meant to affirm that the prophet uttered what follows
jussu Jehovæ, or *divinitus monitus*, so that כה אמר is really
equivalent to זֶה הַדָּבָר אֲשֶׁר דִּבֶּר in Isa. xvi. 13, as Theodoret has
explained it. לֶאֱדוֹם, not "to Edom," but with reference to, or
of, Edom. On the occurrence of *Yᵉhōvâh* after *'Adōnâi*, see
the comm. on Gen. ii. 4. What Obadiah saw as a word of the
Lord was the tidings heard from the Lord, and the divine
message sent to the nations to rise up for war against Edom.
The plural שָׁמַעְנוּ (*we* have heard) is communicative. The
prophet includes himself in the nation (Israel), which has heard
the tidings in him and through him. This implies that the
tidings were of the greatest interest to Israel, and would afford
it consolation. Jeremiah (xlix. 14) has removed the pregnant
character of the expression, by introducing the singular שָׁמַעְתִּי
(I have heard). The next clause, "and an ambassador," etc.,
might be taken, as it has been by Luther, as a statement of the
import of the news, namely, that a messenger had been sent;
inasmuch as in Hebrew a sentence is frequently co-ordinated
with the preceding one by *Vav cop.*, when it ought really to be
subordinated to it so far as the sense is concerned, from a simple
preference for the parallelism of the clauses. But the address
gains in force, if we take the clause as a co-ordinate one, just
as it reads, viz. as a declaration of the steps already taken by
the Lord for carrying out the resolution which had been heard
of by report. In this case the substance of the report is not
given till the last clause of the verse; the summons of the
ambassador sent among the nations, "to rise up for war against
Edom," indicating at the same time the substance of the report
which Israel has heard. The perfect *shullâch* with *qâmets* in the
pause, which is changed by Jeremiah into the less appropriate
passive participle *kal*, corresponds to שָׁמַעְנוּ, and expresses in
prophetic form the certainty of the accomplishment of the

purpose of God.   The sending of the messenger (*tsîr* as in Isa.
xviii. 2) among the nations (ב as in Judg. vi. 35) is an assurance that the nations will rise up at the instigation of Jehovah
to war against Edom (compare Isa. xiii. 17; Jer. li. 1, 11).
The plural *nâqûmâh* (let us rise up), in the words of the
messenger, may be explained on the simple ground that the
messenger speaks in the name of the sender.   The sender is
Jehovah, who will also rise up along with the nations for war
against Edom, placing Himself at their head as leader and
commander (compare Joel ii. 11; Isa. xiii. 4, 5).   עָלֶיהָ, against
Edom, construed as a land or kingdom, *gener. fœm.*   The fact
that it is the nations generally that are here summoned to make
war upon Edom, and not any one nation in particular, points
at once to the fact that Edom is regarded as a type of the
power of the world, and its hostility to God, the destruction of
which is here foretold.

Vers. 2–4.   The Lord threatens Edom with war, because
He has determined to reduce and humble the nation, which
now, with its proud confidence in its lofty rocky towers, regards
itself as invincible.   Ver. 2.   " *Behold, I have made thee small
among the nations; thou art greatly despised.   Ver. 3. The pride
of thy heart hath deceived thee; thou that dwellest in rocky castles,
upon its lofty seat; that saith in its heart, Who will cast me down
to the ground?   Ver. 4. If thou buildest high like the eagle, and
if thy nest were placed among stars, thence will I cast thee down,
is the saying of Jehovah.*"   Ver. 2 is correctly attached in Jeremiah (ver. 15) by כִּי, inasmuch as it contains the reason for
the attack upon Edom.   By *hinnēh* (behold), which points to
the fact itself, the humiliation of Edom is vividly presented to
the mind.   The perfect *nâthattî* " describes the resolution of
Jehovah as one whose fulfilment is as certain as if it had
already occurred" (Caspari).   What Jehovah says really takes
place.   קָטֹן refers to the number of the people.   The participle
בָּזוּי is perfectly appropriate, as expressing the ideal present,
i.e. the present which follows the קָטֹן נְתַתִּיךָ.   When the Lord
has made Edom small, it will be very much despised.   It is
only through an incorrect interpretation of the historical present
that Hitzig could possibly be led to regard the participle as
unsuitable, and to give the preference to Jeremiah's בָּזוּי בָּאָדָם.
Ver. 3 contains a consequence which follows from ver. 2.   Edom

will be unable to avert this fate: its lofty rocky castles will not
preserve it from the overthrow which has been decreed by the
Lord, and which He will carry out through the medium of the
nations. Edom has therefore been deceived by its proud reliance
upon these rocky towers. שֹׁכְנִי, with the connecting sound יִ
attached to the construct state (see at Gen. xxxi. 39), is a vocative. חַגְוֵי סֶלַע are rocky towers, though the primary meaning
of חגוי is open to dispute. The word is derived from the root
חָגָה, which is not used in Hebrew (like קְצָוֵי from קָצָה), and is
found not only here and in the parallel passage of Jeremiah,
but also in the Song of Sol. ii. 14, where it occurs in parallelism
with סֵתֶר, which points to the meaning *refugium, i.e.* asylum.
This meaning has also been confirmed by A. Schultens (*Anim-
adv. ad Jes.* xix. 17) and by Michaelis (*Thes. s.v. Jes.*), from

the Arabic حَجَا, *confugit,* and مَحْجَأ, *refugium.*[1] In the
expression מְרוֹם שִׁבְתּוֹ the ב is to be considered as still retaining its force from חגוי onwards (cf. Isa. xxviii. 7; Job xv. 3,
etc). The emphasis rests upon *high;* and hence the abstract
noun *mârōm,* height, instead of the adjective. The Edomites
inhabited the mountains of *Seir,* which have not yet been
carefully explored in detail. They are on the eastern side of
the Ghor (or Arabah), stretching from the deep rocky valley
of the Ahsy, which opens into the southern extremity of the
Dead Sea, and extending as far as *Æla* on the Red Sea, and
consist of mighty rocks of granite and porphyry, covered with
fresh vegetation, which terminate in the west, towards the
deeply intersected sand-sea of the Ghor and Arabah, in steep
and lofty walls of sandstone. The mountains are hardly accessible, therefore, on the western side; whereas on the east they

[1] The renderings adopted on the authority of the ancient versions, such
as clefts of the rock, *scissuræ,* jagged rocks, fissures (ὀπαί, LXX.), caves,
which are derived either from the supposed connection between חנה and

חקה, and the Arabic خَدَّ, *fidit, laceravit,* or from the Arabic وَجَخَ,
antrum (with the letters transposed), have far less to sustain them. For
the meanings assigned to these Arabic words are not the primary meanings,
but derivative ones. The former signifies literally *propulit,* the latter

confugit, iv. *effecit ut ad rem confugeret;* and مَوْجِخ means *refugium,*
asylum.

are gradually lost in the broad sandy desert of Arabia, without
any perceptible fall (see Burckhardt in v. Raumer's *Pal.* pp.
83–4, 86 ; and Robinson's *Palestine*, ii. p. 551 sqq.). They also
abound in clefts, with both natural and artificial caves ; and
hence its earliest inhabitants were Horites, *i.e.* dwellers in
caves ; and even the Edomites dwelt in caves, at least to some
extent.[1] The capital, *Sela* (*Petra*), in the Wady Musa, of
whose glory at one time there are proofs still to be found in
innumerable remains of tombs, temples, and other buildings,
was shut in both upon the east and west by rocky walls, which
present an endless variety of bright lively colours, from the
deepest crimson to the softest pale red, and sometimes passing
into orange and yellow ; whilst on the north and south it was
so encircled by hills and heights, that it could only be reached
by climbing through very difficult mountain passes and defiles
(see Burckhardt, *Syr.* p. 703 ; Robinson, *Pal.* ii. p. 573 ; and
Ritter, *Erdk.* xiv. p. 1103) ; and Pliny calls it *oppidum circum-
datum montibus inaccessis.* Compare Strabo, xvi. 779 ; and for
the different roads to Petra, Ritter, p. 997 sqq. Ver. 4 shows
the worthlessness of this reliance of the Edomites. The object
to תַּגְבִּיהַ, viz. קִנֶּךָ, does not follow till the second clause : If
thou makest thy nest high like the eagle, which builds its nest
upon the loftiest jagged rocks (Job xxxix. 27, 28). This
thought is hyperbolically intensified in the second clause : if
thy nest had been placed among stars. שִׂים is not an infinitive,
but a passive participle, as in the primary passage, Num. xxiv.
21, which Obadiah had before his mind, and in 1 Sam. ix. 24,
2 Sam. xiii. 32 ; but קִנֶּךָ is nevertheless to be taken as an accusative of the object, after the analogy of the construction of
passives *c. accus. obj.* (see Ges. § 143, *l, a.*)

Vers. 5–7. The prophet sees this overthrow of Edom from
its lofty height as something that has already happened, and
he now depicts the utter devastation of Edom through the
medium of the enemies whom Jehovah has summoned against
it. Ver. 5. "*If thieves had come to thee, if robbers by night,*

---

[1] Jerome observes on ver. 6 : " And indeed . . . throughout the whole
of the southern region of the Idumæans, from Eleutheropolis to Petra and
Hala (for this is a possession of Esau), there are small dwellings in caves ;
and on account of the great heat of the sun, since it is a southern province, subterranean huts are used."

*alas, how art thou destroyed! would they not steal their suffi-
ciency? If vine-dressers had come to thee, would they not leave
gleanings?* Ver. 6. *How have the things of Esau been explored,
his hidden treasures desired!* Ver. 7. *Even to the border have
all the men of thy covenant sent thee: the men of thy peace have
deceived thee, overpowered thee. They make thy bread a wound
under thee. There is no understanding in him.*" In order to
exhibit the more vividly the complete clearing out of Edom,
Obadiah supposes two cases of plundering in which there is
still something left (ver. 5), and then shows that the enemies
in Edom will act much worse than this. אִם with the perfect
supposes a case to have already occurred, when, although it
does not as yet exist in reality, it does so in imagination. גַּנָּבִים
are common thieves, and שֹׁדְדֵי לַיְלָה robbers by night, who carry
off another's property by force. With this second expression,
the verb בָּאוּ לְךָ must be repeated. " To thee," *i.e.* to do thee
harm ; it is actually equivalent to " upon thee." The following words אֵיךְ נִדְמֵיתָה cannot form the apodosis to the two previous clauses, because *nidmēthâh* is too strong a term for the
injury inflicted by thieves or robbers, but chiefly because the
following expression הֲלוֹא יִגְנְבוּ וגו' is irreconcilable with such an
explanation, the thought that thieves steal דַּיָּם being quite
opposed to *nidmâh*, or being destroyed. The clause "how art
thou destroyed" must rather be taken as pointing far beyond
the contents of vers. 5c and 6. It is more fully explained in
ver. 9, and is thereby proved to be a thought thrown in parenthetically, with which the prophet anticipates the principal fact
in his lively description, in the form of an exclamation of amazement. The apodosis to *'im gannábhīm* (if robbers, etc.) follows
in the words " do they not steal" (= they surely steal) *dayyám*,
i.e. their sufficiency (see Delitzsch on Isa. xl. 16); that is to
say, as much as they need, or can use, or find lying open before
them. The picture of the grape-gatherers says the same thing.
They also do not take away all, even to the very last, but leave
some gleanings behind, not only if they fear God, according to
Lev. xix. 10, Deut. xxiv. 21, as Hitzig supposes, but even if
they do not trouble themselves about God's commandments at
all, because many a bunch escapes their notice which is only
discovered on careful gleaning. Edom, on the contrary, is
completely cleared out. In ver. 6 the address to Edom passes

over into words concerning him. עֵשָׂו is construed as a collective with the plural. אֵיךְ is a question of amazement. *Châphas,* to search through, to explore (cf. Zeph. i. 12, 13). *Bâ'âh* (*nibh'û*), to beg, to ask; here in the *niphal* to be desired. *Matspōn, ἀπ. λεγ.* from *tsâphan,* does not mean a secret place, but a hidden thing or treasure (τὰ κεκρυμμένα αὐτοῦ, LXX.). Obadiah mentions the plundering first, because Petra, the capital of Edom, was a great emporium of the Syrio-Arabian trade, where many valuables were stored (*vid.* Diod. Sic. xix. 95), and because with the loss of these riches the prosperity and power of Edom were destroyed.[1]—Ver. 7. In the midst of this calamity Edom will be forsaken and betrayed by its allies, and will also be unable to procure any deliverance for itself by its own understanding. The allies send Edom even to the border. The meaning of this is not that they will not receive the Edomitish fugitives, but drive them back to the frontier, so that they fall into the hands of the enemy (Hitzig and others); for the suffix ךְ cannot refer to the small number of fugitives from Edom who have escaped the massacre, but applies to Edom as a nation. The latter seeks for help and support from their allies,—namely, through the medium of ambassadors whom it sends to them. But the ambassadors, and in their persons the Edomites themselves, are sent back to the frontier by all the allies, because they will not entangle themselves in the fate of Edom. Sending to the frontier, however, is not to be understood as signifying that the allies " send their troops with them as far as the frontier, and then order them to turn back," as Michaelis supposes; for " if the allies were unwilling to help, they would hardly call out the army to march as far as the frontier " (Hitzig). Nor is this implied either in שִׁלְּחוּךָ or הִשִּׁיאוּךָ; for *shilleâch* means to send away, to dismiss, and both here and in Gen. xii. 20 to send across the frontier. This was a deception of the expectation of the Edomites, although the words " have deceived thee" belong, strictly speaking, to what follows, and not to the conduct of the allies. אַנְשֵׁי שְׁלֹמֶךָ,

---

[1] Jeremiah (ch. xlix. 9) has greatly altered the words of Obadiah, dropping the comparison of the enemy to thieves and grape-gatherers, and representing the enemy as being themselves grape-gatherers who leave no gleaning, and thieves who waste till they have enough; and thereby considerably weakening the poetical picture.

an expression taken from Ps. xli. 10, both here and in Jer.
xxxviii. 22 (cf. xx. 10), the men or people with whom thou
didst live in peace, are probably neighbouring Arabian tribes,
who had made commercial treaties with the Edomites. They
deceived, or rather overpowered, Edom. יֻכְלוּ is the practical
explanation and more precise definition of הִשִּׁיאוּ. But the
answer to the question whether the overpowering was carried
out by cunning and deception (Jer. xx. 10, xxxviii. 22), or by
open violence (Gen. xxxii. 26; Ps. cxxix. 2), depends upon the
explanation given to the next sentence, about which there are
great diversities of opinion, partly on account of the different
explanations given of לַחְמְךָ, and partly on account of the
different renderings given to מָזוֹר. The latter occurs in Hos.
v. 13 and Jer. xxx. 13 in the sense of a festering wound or
abscess, and the rabbinical commentators and lexicographers
have retained this meaning in the passage before us. On the
other hand, the older translators have here ἔνεδρα (LXX.),

תַּקְלָא, offence, σκάνδαλον (Chald.), ܟܣܘ̈ܠܐ, insidiœ (Syr.), Aq.

and Symm. σύνδεσμος and ἐπίδεσις, Vulg. insidiœ; and hence
the modern rendering, they lay a snare, or place a trap under
thee. But this rendering cannot be vindicated etymologically,
since zūr (= zârar) does not mean to bind, but to press together
or squeeze out. Nor can the form mâzōr be taken as a contraction of mᵉzōrâh, as Hitzig supposes, since this is derived
from zârâh, to strew or scatter. And no weight is to be
attached to the opinion of Aquila with his literal translation,
for the simple reason that his rendering of Hos. v. 13 is
decidedly false. Ewald and Hitzig prefer the rendering
"net;" but this, again, cannot be sustained either from the
expression mᵉzōrâh hâresheth in Prov. i. 17 (Hitzig), or from
the Syriac mᵉzar, extendit (Ges. Addid. ad thes. p. 96). The
only meaning that can be sustained is abscess or wound. We
must therefore adhere to the rendering, "they make thy bread
a wound under thee." For the proposal to take lachmᵉkhâ (thy
bread) as a second genitive dependent upon 'anshē (the men),
is not only opposed to the accents and the parallelism of the
members, according to which 'anshē shᵉlōmekhâ (the men of thy
peace) must conclude the second clause, just as 'anshē bᵉrîthekhâ
(the men of thy covenant) closes the first; but it is altogether

unexampled, and the expression *'anshē lachmᵉkhâ* is itself unheard of. For this reason we must not even supply *'anshē* to *lach-mᵉkhâ* from the previous sentence, or make "the men of thy bread" the subject, notwithstanding the fact that the LXX., the Chald., the Syr., and Jerome have adopted this as the meaning. Still less can *lachmᵉkhâ* stand in the place of אֹכְלֵי לַחְמְךָ (they that eat thy bread), as some suppose. *Lachmᵉkhâ* can only be the first object to *yâsīmū*, and consequently the subject of the previous clause still continues in force : they who befriended thee make thy bread, *i.e.* the bread which they ate from thee or with thee, not "the bread which thou seekest from them" (Hitzig), into a wound under thee, *i.e.* an occasion for destroying thee. We have not to think of common meals of hospitality here, as Rashi, Rosenmüller, and others do; but the words are to be taken figuratively, after the analogy of Ps. xli. 10, which floated before the prophet's mind, " He that eateth bread with me hath lifted up the heel against me," as denoting conspiracies on the part of those who were allied to Edom, and drew their own sustenance from it, the rich trading nation, to destroy that very nation which was now oppressed by its foes. The only difficulty is in the word תַּחְתֶּיךָ, under thee, inasmuch as the meaning "without thy knowledge" (*clam te*), which Vatablus and Drusius adopt, cannot be sustained, and least of all from 2 Sam. iii. 12. We must connect תַּחְתֶּיךָ closely with מָזוֹר, in this sense, that the wound is inflicted upon the lower part of the body, to express its dangerous nature, inasmuch as wounds upon which one sits or lies are hard to heal. Consequently יָכְלוּ לָךְ (they prevail against thee) is to be understood as denoting conquest, not by an unexpected attack or open violence, but by cunning and deceit, or by secret treachery. The last clause, אֵין תְּבוּנָה וגו׳, does not give the reason why the thing described was to happen to the Edomites (Chald., Theod.); nor is it to be connected with *mâzōr* as a relative clause (Hitzig), or as explanatory of תַּחְתֶּיךָ, "to thee, without thy perceiving it, or before thou perceivest it" (Luther and L. de Dieu). The very change from the second person to the third (בּוֹ) is a proof that it introduces an independent statement,—namely, that in consequence of the calamity which thus bursts upon the Edomites, they lose their wonted discernment, and neither know what to do nor how to help themselves (Maurer and Caspari). This thought is expanded still further in vers. 8, 9.

Ver. 8. " *Does it not come to pass in that day, is the saying of Jehovah, that I destroy the wise men out of Edom, and discernment from the mountains of Esau?* Ver. 9. *And thy heroes despair, O Teman, that every one may be cut off by murder from the mountains of Esau.*" In order to give up the Edomites to destruction at that time, the Lord will take away discernment from their wise men, so that even they will not be able to help them. The destruction of the wise men is not to be understood as signifying that the wise men will all be slain, or slain before any others, but simply that they will be destroyed as wise men by the withdrawal or destruction of their wisdom. This meaning is sustained, not only by the fact that in the second clause *t^ebhūnáh* only is mentioned as that which is to be destroyed, but also by the parallel passages, Jer. xlix. 7, Isa. xix. 11, xxix. 14. Jeremiah mentions here the wisdom of the Temanites in particular. That they were celebrated for their wisdom, is evident not only from this passage, but also from the fact that Eliphaz, the chief opponent of Job in argument, was a Temanite (Job ii. 1, etc.). With this withdrawal of wisdom and discernment, even the brave warriors lose their courage. The heroes are dismayed (*chattū*), or fall into despair. *Tēmán*, which the Chaldee has rendered incorrectly as an appellative, viz. inhabitant of the south (*dârōmâ'*), is a proper name of the southern district of Idumæa (see at Amos i. 12), so called from Teman, a son of Eliphaz and grandson of Esau (Gen. xxxvi. 11, 15). *Gibbōrekhâ* (thy heroes), with the masculine suffix, the people inhabiting the district being addressed under the name of the district itself. God inflicts this upon Edom with the intention (*l^ema'an*, to this end) that all the Edomites should be cut off. *Miqqâtel*, from the murdering, by murder (compare Gen. ix. 11, where *min* occurs after *yikkârēth* in this sense); not "without conflict," as Ewald renders it, for *qetel* signifies slaying, and not conflict. The thought of connecting *miqqâtel* with what follows cannot for a moment be entertained (*vid.* LXX., Syr., Vulg.). It is opposed not only by the authority of the Masoretic punctuation, but still more decisively by the fact, that the stronger and more special word (*qetel*) cannot precede the weaker and more general one (*châmâs*), and that the murder of certain fugitives is placed first in the list of crimes committed by Edom upon the Israelites (vers. 10–14).

Vers. 10–16. The Cause of the Ruin of the Edomites is their wickedness towards the brother nation Jacob (vers. 10 and 11), which is still further exhibited in vers. 12–14 in the form of a warning, accompanied by an announcement of righteous retribution in the day of the Lord upon all nations (vers. 15, 16). Ver. 10. *"For the wickedness towards thy brother Jacob shame will cover thee, and thou wilt be cut off for ever. Ver. 11. In the day that thou stoodest opposite, in the day when enemies carried away his goods, and strangers came into his gates, and cast the lot upon Jerusalem, then even thou (wast) like one of them."* *Chămas 'âchĭkhâ*, wickedness, violent wrong towards (upon) thy brother (*genit. obj.* as in Joel iii. 19, Gen. xvi. 5, etc.). Drusius has already pointed out the peculiar emphasis on these words. Wrong, or violence, is all the more reprehensible, when it is committed against a brother. The fraternal relation in which Edom stood towards Judah is still more sharply defined by the name *Jacob*, since Esau and Jacob were twin brothers. The consciousness that the Israelites were their brethren, ought to have impelled the Edomites to render helpful support to the oppressed Judæans. Instead of this, they not only revelled with scornful and malignant pleasure in the misfortune of the brother nation, but endeavoured to increase it still further by rendering active support to the enemy. This hostile behaviour of Edom arose from envy at the election of Israel, like the hatred of Esau towards Jacob (Gen. xxvii. 41), which was transmitted to his descendants, and came out openly in the time of Moses, in the unbrotherly refusal to allow the Israelites to pass in a peaceable manner through their land (Num. xx.). On the other hand, the Israelites are always commanded in the law to preserve a friendly and brotherly attitude towards Edom (Deut. ii. 4, 5); and in Deut. xxiii. 7 it is enjoined upon them not to abhor the Edomite, because he is their brother. תְּכַסְּךָ בוּשָׁה (as in Mic. vii. 10), shame will cover thee, *i.e.* come upon thee in full measure,—namely, the shame of everlasting destruction, as the following explanatory clause clearly shows. וְנִכְרַתָּ with *Vav consec.*, but

with the tone upon the *penultima*, contrary to the rule (cf. Ges.
§ 49, 3; Ewald, § 234, *b* and *c*). In the more precise account
of Edom's sins given in ver. 11, the last clause does not answer
exactly to the first. After the words " in the day that thou
stoodest opposite," we should expect the apodosis " thou didst
this or that." But Obadiah is led away from the sentence
which he has already begun, by the enumeration of hostilities
displayed towards Judah by its enemies, so that he observes
with regard to Edom's behaviour : Then even thou wast as one
of them, that is to say, thou didst act just like the enemy.
עֲמָד מִגֶּנֶד, to stand opposite (compare Ps. xxxviii. 12), used here
to denote a hostile intention, as in 2 Sam. xviii. 13. They
showed this at first by looking on with pleasure at the misfor-
tunes of the Judæans (ver. 12), still more by stretching out
their hand after their possessions (ver. 13), but most of all by
taking part in the conflict with Judah (ver. 14). In the
clauses which follow, the day when Edom acted thus is described as a day on which Judah had fallen into the power of
hostile nations, who carried off its possessions, and disposed of
Jerusalem as their booty. *Zârîm* and *nokhrîm* are synonymous epithets applied to heathen foes. שָׁבָה generally denotes
the carrying away of captives ; but it is sometimes applied to
booty in cattle and goods, or treasures (1 Chron. v. 21; 2 Chron.
xiv. 14, xxi. 17). חַיִל is not used here either for the army, or
for the strength, *i.e.* the kernel of the nation, but, as חֵילוֹ in
ver. 13 clearly shows, for its possessions, as in Isa. viii. 4, x. 14,
Ezek. xxvi. 12, etc. שְׁעָרָו, his (Judah's) gates, used rhetorically for his cities. Lastly, Jerusalem is also mentioned as the
capital, upon which the enemies cast lots. The three clauses
form a climax : first, the carrying away of Judah's possessions,
that is to say, probably those of the open country ; then the
forcing of a way into the cities ; and lastly, arbitrary proceedings both in and with the capital. יַדּוּ גוֹרָל (*perf. kal* of
יָדָה=יָדד, not *piel* for יְַדּוּ, because the *Yod præf.* of the imperfect *piel* is never dropped in verbs פ'), to cast the lot upon
booty (things) and prisoners, to divide them among them (compare Joel iii. 3 and Nah. iii. 10). Caspari, Hitzig, and others
understand it here as in Joel iii. 3, as denoting the distribution
of the captive inhabitants of Jerusalem, and found upon this
one of their leading arguments, that the description given here

refers to the destruction of Jerusalem, which Obadiah either foresaw in the Spirit, or depicts as something already experienced. But this by no means follows from the fact that in Joel we have עַמִּי instead of יְרוּשָׁלֵם, since it is generally acknowledged that, when the prophets made use of their predecessors, they frequently modified their expressions, or gave them a different turn. But if we look at our passage simply as it stands, there is not the slightest indication that Jerusalem is mentioned in the place of the people. As שְׁבוֹת חֵילוֹ does not express the carrying away of the inhabitants, there is not a single syllable which refers to the carrying away captive of either the whole nation or the whole of the population of Jerusalem. On the contrary, in ver. 13 we read of the perishing of the children of Judah, and in ver. 14 of fugitives of Judah, and those that have escaped. From this it is very obvious that Obadiah had simply a conquest of Jerusalem in his eye, when part of the population was slain in battle and part taken captive, and the possessions of the city were plundered; so that the casting of the lot upon Jerusalem has reference not only to the prisoners, but also to the things taken as plunder in the city, which the conquerors divided among them. גַּם אַתָּה, even thou, the brother of Jacob, art like one of them, makest common cause with the enemy. The verb הָיִיתָ, thou wast, is omitted, to bring the event before the mind as something even then occurring. For this reason Obadiah also clothes the further description of the hostilities of the Edomites in the form of a warning against such conduct.

Ver. 12. "*And look not at the day of thy brother on the day of his misfortune; and rejoice not over the sons of Judah in the day of their perishing, and do not enlarge thy mouth in the day of the distress.* Ver. 13. *Come not into the gate of my people in the day of their calamity; thou also look not at his misfortune in the day of his calamity, and stretch not out thy hand to his possession in the day of his calamity:* Ver. 14. *Nor stand in the cross-road, to destroy his fugitives, nor deliver up his escaped ones in the day of distress.*" This warning cannot be satisfactorily explained either "on the assumption that the prophet is here foretelling the future destruction of Judah and Jerusalem" (Caspari), or "on the supposition that he is merely depicting an event that has already past" (Hitzig). If the taking and plundering of Jerusalem were an accomplished fact, whether in idea or in reality, as it is shown to be by the perfects בָּאוּ and יַדּוּ in ver. 11, Obadiah could not in that case warn the Edomites against rejoicing over it, or even taking part therein. Hence Drusius, Rosenmüller, and others, take the verbs in vers. 12–14 as futures of the past: "Thou shouldest not have seen, shouldest not have rejoiced," etc. But this is opposed to the grammar. אַל followed by the so-called *fut. apoc.* is jussive, and cannot stand for the *pluperf. conjunct.* And Maurer's suggestion is just as untenable, namely, that *yōm* in ver. 11 denotes the day of the capture of Jerusalem, and in vers. 12, 13 the period after this day; since the identity of יוֹם עֲמָדְךָ (the day of thy standing) in ver. 11 with יוֹם אָחִיךָ in ver. 12 strikes the eye at once. The warning in vers. 12–14 is only intelligible on the supposition, that Obadiah has not any particular conquest and plundering of Jerusalem in his mind, whether a future one or one that has already occurred, but regards this as an event that not only has already taken place, but will take place again: that is to say, on the assumption that he rises from the particular historical event to the idea which it embodied, and that, starting from this, he sees in the existing case all subsequent cases of a similar kind. From this ideal standpoint he could warn Edom of what it had already done, and designate the disastrous day which had come upon Judah and Jerusalem by different expressions as a day of the greatest calamity; for what Edom had done, and what had befallen Judah, were types of the future development of the fate of Judah and of the attitude of Edom towards it, which go on fulfilling themselves more and more until the day of the Lord upon all nations, upon the near approach of which Obadiah founds his warning in ver. 15. The warning proceeds in vers. 12–14 from the general to the particular, or from the lower to the higher. Obadiah warns the Edomites, as Hitzig says, "not to rejoice in Judah's troubles (ver. 12), nor to make common cause with the conquerors (ver. 13), nor to outdo and complete the work of the enemy (ver. 14)." By the cop. *Vav*, which stands at the head of all the three clauses in ver. 12, the warning addressed to the Edomites, against such conduct as this, is linked on to what they had already done. The three clauses of ver. 12 contain a warning in a graduated form against malicious pleasure. רְאֵה

with בְּ, to look at anything with pleasure, to take delight in it, affirms less than שָׂמַח בְּ, to rejoice, to proclaim one's joy without reserve. הִגְדִּיל פֶּה, to make the mouth large, is stronger still, like הִגְדִּיל בְּפֶה, to boast, to do great things with the mouth, equivalent to הִרְחִיב פֶּה עַל, to make the mouth broad, to stretch it open, over (against) a person (Ps. xxxv. 21 ; Isa. lvii. 4), a gesture indicating contempt and derision. The object of their malicious pleasure mentioned in the first clause is *yŏm 'ăchīkhâ*, the day of thy brother, *i.e.* the day upon which something strange happened to him, namely, what is mentioned in ver. 11. *Yŏm* does not of itself signify the disastrous day, or day of ruin, either here or anywhere else ; but it always receives the more precise definition from the context. If we were to adopt the rendering "disastrous day," it would give rise to a pure tautology when taken in connection with what follows. The expression *'ăchīkhâ* (*of thy brother*) justifies the warning. בְּיוֹם נָכְרוֹ is not in apposition to בְּיוֹם אָחִיךָ, but, according to the parallelism of the clauses, it is a statement of time. נֵכֶר, ἁπ. λεγ. = נֵכֶר (Job xxxi. 3), *fortuna aliena*, a strange, *i.e.* hostile fate, not "rejection" (Hitzig, Caspari, and others). The expression יוֹם אָבְדָם, the day of their (Judah's sons) perishing, is stronger still ; although the perishing (*'ăbhōd*) of the sons of Judah cannot denote the destruction of the whole nation, since the following word *tsârâh*, calamity, is much too weak to admit of this. Even the word אֵיד, which occurs three times in ver. 13, does not signify destruction, but (from the root אוּד, to fall heavily, to load) simply pressure, a burden, then weight of suffering, distress, misfortune (see Delitzsch on Job xviii. 12). In ver. 13 Obadiah warns against taking part in the plundering of Jerusalem. The gate of my people : for the city in which the people dwell, the capital (see Mic. i. 9). Look not thou also, a brother nation, upon his calamity, as enemies do, *i.e.* do not delight thyself thereat, nor snatch at his possessions. The form *tishlachnâh*, for which we should expect *tishlach*, is not yet satisfactorily explained (for the different attempts that have been made to explain it, see Caspari). The passages in which *nâh* is appended to the third pers. fem. sing., to distinguish it from the second person, do not help us to explain it. Ewald and Olshausen would therefore alter the text, and read תִּשְׁלַח יָד. But יָד is not absolutely necessary, since it is omitted in 2 Sam.

vi. 6, xxii. 17, or Ps. xviii. 17, where *shâlach* occurs in the sense
of stretching out the hand. חֵילוֹ, his possessions. On the fact
itself, compare Joel iv. 5. The prominence given to the day
of misfortune at the end of every sentence is very emphatic;
"inasmuch as the selection of the time of a brother's calamity,
as that in which to rage against him with such cunning and
malicious pleasure, was doubly culpable" (Ewald). In ver. 14
the warning proceeds to the worst crime of all, their seizing
upon the Judæan fugitives, for the purpose of murdering them
or delivering them up to the enemy. *Pereq* signifies here the
place where the roads break or divide, the cross-road. In Nah.
iii. 1, the only other place in which it occurs, it signifies tearing
in pieces, violence. *Hisgîr*, to deliver up (lit. *concludendum
tradidit*), is generally construed with אֶל (Deut. xxiii. 16) or
בְּיַד (Ps. xxxi. 9; 1 Sam. xxiii. 11). Here it is written absolutely with the same meaning: not "to apprehend, or so overpower that there is no escape left" (Hitzig). This would affirm
too little after the preceding הַכְרִית, and cannot be demonstrated
from Job xi. 10, where *hisgîr* means to keep in custody.

This warning is supported in ver. 15 by an announcement
of the day of the Lord, in which Edom and all the enemies of
Israel will receive just retribution for their sins against Israel.
Ver. 15. "*For the day of Jehovah is near upon all nations.
As thou hast done, it will be done to thee; what thou hast performed returns upon thy head.* Ver. 16. *For as ye have drunken
upon my holy mountain, all nations will drink continually, and
drink and swallow, and will be as those that were not.*" כִּי (for)
connects what follows with the warnings in vers. 12–14, but not
also, or exclusively, with vers. 10, 11, as Rosenmüller and others
suppose, for vers. 12–14 are not inserted parenthetically. "The
day of Jehovah" has been explained at Joel i. 15. The
expression was first formed by Obadiah, not by Joel; and Joel,
Isaiah, and the prophets that follow, adopted it from Obadiah.
The primary meaning is not the day of judgment, but the day
on which Jehovah reveals His majesty and omnipotence in a
glorious manner, to overthrow all ungodly powers, and to complete His kingdom. It was this which gave rise to the idea of
the day of judgment and retribution which predominates in the
prophetic announcements, but which simply forms one side of
the revelation of the glory of God, as our passage at once shows;

inasmuch as it describes Jehovah as not only judging all nations
and rewarding them according to their deeds (cf. vers. 15*b*, 16),
but as providing deliverance upon Zion (ver. 17), and setting
up His kingdom (ver. 21).   The retribution will correspond to
the actions of Edom and of the nations.   For וגו׳ גְּמֻלְךָ, compare
Joel iii. 4, 7, where (vers. 2–7) the evil deeds of the nations,
what they have done against the people of God, are described.
In ver. 16 Obadiah simply mentions as the greatest crime the
desecration of the holy mountain by drinking carousals, for
which all nations are to drink the intoxicating cup of the wrath
of God till they are utterly destroyed.   In *sh^ethīthem* (ye have
drunk) it is not the Judæans who are addressed, as many commentators, from Ab. Ezra to Ewald and Meier, suppose, but
the Edomites.   This is required not only by the parallelism of
כַּאֲשֶׁר שְׁתִיתֶם (as ye have drunk) and כַּאֲשֶׁר עָשִׂיתָ (as thou hast
done), but also by the actual wording and context.   כַּאֲשֶׁר שְׁתִיתֶם
עַל הַר cannot mean " as ye who are upon my holy mountain
have drunk ;" and in the announcement of the retribution
which all nations will receive for the evil they have done to
Judah, it is impossible that either the Judæans should be
addressed, or a parallel drawn between their conduct and that
of the nations.   Moreover, throughout the whole of the prophecy Edom only is addressed, and never Judah.   Mount Zion
is called " my holy mountain," because Jehovah was there
enthroned in His sanctuary.   The verb *shâthâh* is used in the
two clauses in different senses : viz. *sh^ethīthem*, of the drinking
carousals which the Edomites held upon Zion, like *yishtū* in
Joel iii. 3 ; and *shâthū*, in the apodosis, of the drinking of the
intoxicating goblet (cf. Isa. li. 17 ; Jer. xxv. 15, xlix. 12, etc.),
as the expression " they shall be as though they had not been"
clearly shows.   At the same time, we cannot infer from the
words " all nations will drink," that all nations would succeed
in taking Zion and abusing it, but that they would have to
taste all the bitterness of their crime ; for it is not stated that
they are to drink upon Mount Zion.   The fact that the anti-
thesis to שְׁתִיתֶם is not תִּשְׁתּוּ (" ye will drink") but יִשְׁתּוּ כָל־הַגּוֹיִם,
does not compel us to generalize *sh^ethīthem*, and regard all
nations as addressed *implicite* in the Edomites.   The difficulty
arising from this antithesis cannot be satisfactorily removed by
the remark of Caspari, that in consequence of the allusion to

the day of the Lord upon all nations in ver. 15, the judgment upon all nations and that upon the Edomites were thought of as inseparably connected, or that this induced Obadiah to place opposite to the sins of the Edomites, not their own punishment, but the punishment of all nations, more especially as, according to ver. 11, it must necessarily be assumed that the foreign nations participated in the sin of Edom. For this leaves the question unanswered, how Obadiah came to speak at all (ver. 15) of the day of the Lord upon all nations. The circumstance that, according to ver. 11, heathen nations had plundered Jerusalem, and committed crimes like those for which Edom is condemned in vers. 12–14, does not lead directly to the day of judgment upon *all* nations, but simply to a judgment upon Edom and the nations which had committed like sins. The difficulty is only removed by the assumption that Obadiah regarded Edom as a type of the nations that had risen up in hostility to the Lord and His people, and were judged by the Lord in consequence, so that what he says of Edom applies to all nations which assume the same or a similar attitude towards the people of God. From this point of view he could, without reserve, extend to all nations the retribution which would fall upon Edom for its sins. They should drink *tâmîd*, *i.e.* not at once, as Ewald has rendered it in opposition to the usage of the language, but "continually." This does not mean, however, that "there will be no time in which there will not be one of the nations drinking the intoxicating cup, and being destroyed by drinking thereof; or that the nations will come in turn, and therefore in a long immeasurable series, one after the other, to drink the cup of intoxication," as Caspari supposes, but "continually, so that the turn never passes from the heathen to Judah, Isa. li. 22, 23" (Hitzig). This drinking is more precisely defined as drinking and swallowing (לוע, in Syriac, to devour or swallow, hence לע, a throat, so called from the act of swallowing, Prov. xxiii. 2), *i.e.* drinking in full draughts; and the effect, "they will be like such as have not been, have never existed" (cf. Job x. 19), *i.e.* they will be utterly destroyed as nations.

Vers. 17–21. THE KINGDOM OF JEHOVAH ESTABLISHED UPON ZION.—The prophecy advances from the judgment upon all the heathen to the completion of the kingdom of God by the raising up of Israel to world-wide dominion. While the judgment is falling upon all the heathen nations, Mount Zion will be an asylum for those who are delivered. Judah and Israel will capture the possessions of the nations, destroy Edom, and extend its borders on every side (vers. 17–19). The Israelites scattered among the nations will return into their enlarged inheritances, and upon Zion will saviours arise, to judge Edom, and the kingdom will then be the Lord's (vers. 20, 21). This promise is appended as an antithesis to the proclamation of judgment in ver. 16. Ver. 17. *" But upon Mount Zion will be that which has been saved, and it will be a sanctuary, and the house of Jacob will take possession of their possessions."* Upon Mount Zion, which the Edomites have now desecrated by drinking carousals, there will then, when the nations are obliged to drink the cup of intoxication even to their utter destruction, be *peletáh*, that which has escaped, *i.e.* the multitude of those who have been rescued and preserved throughout the judgment. See the explanation of this at Joel ii. 32, where this thought is still further expounded. Mount Zion is the seat of the kingdom of Jehovah (cf. ver. 21). There the Lord is enthroned (Joel iii. 17), and His rescued people with Him. And it (Mount Zion) will be *qôdesh*, a sanctuary, *i.e.* inviolable; the heathen will no more dare to tread it and defile it (Joel iii. 17). It follows from this, that the rescued crowd upon it will also be a holy people ("a holy seed," Isa. vi. 13). This sanctified people of the Lord, the house of Jacob, will capture the possessions of their foes. The suffix attached to מוֹרָשֵׁיהֶם is supposed by many to refer to בֵּית יַעֲקֹב : those of the house of Jacob, *i.e.* the rescued Israelites, will take their former possessions once more. This view cannot be overthrown by the simple remark that *yârash* cannot mean to take possession again; for that meaning might be given to it by the context, as, for example, in Deut. xxx. 5. But it is a decisive objection to it, that neither in what precedes nor in what follows is there any reference to Israel as having been carried away. The penetration of foes into the gates of Jerusalem, the plundering of the city, and the casting of lots upon the booty and the prisoners (ver. 11), do not involve the carrying away of the whole nation into exile; and the *gâlûth* of the sons of Israel and Jerusalem in ver. 20 is clearly distinguished from the "house of Jacob" in ver. 18. And since we have first of all (vers. 18, 19) an announcement of the conquest of Edom by the house of Jacob, and the capture of the mountains of Esau, of Philistia, etc., by the inhabitants of the south-land, *i.e.* by Judæans; and then in ver. 20 the possession of the south-land is promised to the *gâluth* (captivity); this *gâluth* can only have been a small fragment of the nation, and therefore the carrying away can only have extended to a number of prisoners of war, whilst the kernel of the nation had remained in the land, *i.e.* in its own possessions. The objection offered to this, namely, that if we refer the suffix in *mōrâshēhem* (their possessions) to *kŏl-haggōyīm* (all nations), Judah would have to take possession of *all* nations, which is quite incredible and even at variance with vers. 19, 20, inasmuch as the only enemies' land mentioned there (ver. 19) is the territory of the Edomites and Philistines, whilst the other countries or portions of country mentioned there are not enemies' land at all. For there is no incredibility in the taking of the land of all nations by Judah, except on the assumption that Judah merely denotes the posterity or remnant of the citizens of the earthly kingdom of Judah. But this is not what Obadiah says. He does not mention Judah, but the house of Jacob, and means thereby not the natural Israel, but the people of God, who are eventually to obtain the dominion of the world. The discrepancy between ver. 17*b* and ver. 19 is not greater than that between שְׁתִיתֶם in ver. 16*a* and יִשְׁתּוּ כָל־הַגּוֹיִם in ver. 16*b*, and disappears if we only recognise the fact that Edom and the Philistines are simply mentioned in ver. 19 as types of the heathen world in its hostility to God. We therefore regard the application of the expression *mōrâ-shēhem* to the possessions of the heathen nations as the only correct one, and that all the more because the וְיָרְשׁוּ in ver. 19 is very clearly seen to be a more exact explanation of the וְיָרְשׁוּ in ver. 17*b*. In ver. 17 Obadiah gives, in a few brief words, the sum and substance of the salvation which awaits the people of the Lord in the future. This salvation is unfolded still further in what follows, and first of all in vers. 18, 19, by a fuller exposition of the thought expressed in ver. 17*b*.

Ver. 18. "*And the house of Jacob will be a fire, and the house of Joseph a flame, and the house of Esau for stubble. And they will burn among them, and consume them, and there will not be one left to the house of Esau, for Jehovah hath spoken.*" This verse not only resumes the discussion of the retribution, so that it corresponds to ver. 15, but it also affirms, as an appendix to ver. 17, that Edom is to be utterly destroyed. By the "house of Jacob" Judah is intended, as the co-ordination of the house of Joseph, *i.e.* of the ten tribes, clearly shows. The assumption that "house of Jacob" signifies all Israel, in connection with which that portion is also especially mentioned, which might be supposed to be excluded (Rosenmüller, Hengstenberg, and others), is at variance with such passages as Isa. xlvi. 3, "the house of Jacob, and all the remnant of the house of Israel," where the reason assigned for the co-ordination is not applicable. Obadiah uses the name Jacob for Judah, because ever since the division of the kingdoms Judah alone has represented the people of God, the ten tribes having fallen away from the kingdom of God for a time. In the future, however, Judah and Israel are to be united again (*vid.* Hos. ii. 2; Ezek. xxxvii. 16; Jer. xxxi. 18), and unitedly to attack and overcome their foes (Isa. xi. 13, 14). Obadiah distinctly mentions the house of Joseph, *i.e.* of the ten tribes, in this passage and in this alone, for the purpose of guarding against the idea that the ten tribes are to be shut out from the future salvation. For the figure of the flame of fire which consumes stubble, see Isa. v. 24 and x. 17. For the expression, "for Jehovah hath spoken," compare Joel iii. 8.

After the destruction of its foes the nation of God will take possession of their land, and extend its territory to every region under heaven. Ver. 19. "*And those towards the south will take possession of the mountains of Esau ; and those in the lowland, of the Philistines : and they will take possession of the fields of Ephraim, and the fields of Samaria ; and Benjamin (will take possession) of Gilead.* Ver. 20. *And the captives of this army of the sons of Israel (will take possession) of what Canaanites there are as far as Zarephath ; and the prisoners of Jerusalem that are in Sepharad will take possession of the cities of the south.*" In וְיָרְשׁוּ וגו' the expression וְיָרְשׁוּ בֵּית י' in ver. 17*b* is more precisely defined, and the house of Jacob, *i.e.* the kingdom of Judah, is divided into the Negeb, the Shephelah, and Benjamin, to each of which a special district is assigned,

of which it will take possession, the countries being mentioned
in the place of their inhabitants.   The *negebh,* or southern land
of Judah (see the comm. on Josh. xv. 21), *i.e.* the inhabitants
thereof, will take possession of the mountains of Esau, and
therefore extend their territory eastwards; whilst those of the
lowland (*sh°phēlâh;* see at Josh. xv. 33), on the Mediterranean,
will seize upon the Philistines, that is to say, upon their land,
and therefore spread out towards the west.   The subject to the
second וְיָרְשׁוּ is not mentioned, and must be determined from the
context : viz. the men of Judah, with the exception of the inhabitants of the *Negeb* and *Shephelah* already mentioned, that is
to say, strictly speaking, those of the mountains of Judah, the
original stock of the land of Judah (Josh. xv. 48–60).   Others
would leave *hannegebh* and *hassh°phēlâh* still in force as subjects;
so that the thought expressed would be this : The inhabitants of
the south land and of the lowland will also take possession in
addition to this of the fields of Ephraim and Samaria.   But not
only is the parallelism of the clauses, according to which one
particular portion of territory is assigned to each part, utterly destroyed, but according to this view the principal part of Judah is
entirely passed over without any perceptible reason.   *Sâdeh,* fields,
used rhetorically for land or territory.   Along with Ephraim
the land, Samaria the capital is especially mentioned, just as
we frequently find Jerusalem along with Judah.   In the last
clause יָרְשׁוּ (shall take possession of) is to be repeated after
Benjamin.   From the taking of the territories of the kingdom
of the ten tribes by Judah and Benjamin, we are not to infer
that the territory of the ten tribes was either compared to an
enemy's land, or thought of as depopulated; but the thought
is simply this: Judah and Benjamin, the two tribes, which
formed the kingdom of God in the time of Obadiah, will
extend their territory to all the four quarters of the globe, and
take possession of all Canaan beyond its former boundaries.
Hengstenberg has rightly shown that we have here simply an
individualizing description of the promise in Gen. xxviii. 14,
" thy seed will be as the dust of the ground; and thou breakest
out to the west and to the east, to the north and to the south,"
etc.; *i.e.* that on the ground of this promise Obadiah predicts
the future restoration of the kingdom of God, and its extension
beyond the borders of Canaan.   In this he looks away from

the ten tribes, because in his esteem the kingdom of Judah alone constituted the kingdom or people of God. But he has shown clearly enough in ver. 18 that he does not regard them as enemies of Judah, or as separated from the kingdom of God, but as being once more united to Judah as the people of God. And being thus incorporated again into the people of God, he thinks of them as dwelling with them upon the soil of Judah, so that they are included in the population of the four districts of this kingdom. For this reason, no other places of abode are assigned to the Ephraimites and Gileadites. The idea that they are to be transplanted altogether to heathen territory, rests upon a misapprehension of the true facts of the case, and has no support whatever in ver. 20. "The sons of Israel" in ver. 20 cannot be the ten tribes, as Hengstenberg supposes, because the other portion of the covenant nation mentioned along with them would in that case be described as Judah, not as Jerusalem. "The sons of Israel" answer to the "Jacob" in ver. 10, and the "house of Jacob" in ver. 17, in connection with which special prominence is given to Jerusalem in ver. 11, and to Mount Zion in ver. 17; so that it is the Judæans who are referred to,—not, however, as distinguished from the ten tribes, but as the people of God, with whom the house of Jacob is once more united. In connection with the *gâluth* (captivity) of the sons of Israel, the *gâluth* of Jerusalem is also mentioned, like the sons of Judah and the sons of Jerusalem in Joel iii. 6, of whom Joel affirms, with a glance at Obadiah, that the Phœnicians and Philistines have sold them to the sons of Javan. These citizens of Judah and Jerusalem, who have been taken prisoners in war, are called by Obadiah the *gâluth* of the sons of Israel and Jerusalem, the people of God being here designated by the name of their tribe-father Jacob or Israel. That we should understand by the "sons of Israel" Judah, as the tribe or kernel of the covenant nation, is required by the actual progress apparent in ver. 20 in relation to ver. 19. After Obadiah had foretold to the house of Jacob in vers. 17b–19 that it would take possession of the land of their enemies, and spread beyond the borders of Canaan, the question still remained to be answered, What would become of the prisoners, and those who had been carried away captive, according to vers. 11 and 14? This is explained in ver. 20. The

carrying away of the sons of Israel is restricted to a portion of
the nation by the words, "the captivity of *this* host" (*hachēl-
hazzeh*); no such carrying away of the nation as such had
taken place at that time as that which afterwards occurred at
the destruction of the kingdoms of Israel and Judah. The
enemies who had conquered Jerusalem had contented themselves with carrying away those who fell into their hands. The
expression *hachēl-hazzeh* points to this host which had been
carried away captive. חֵל, which the LXX. and some of the
Rabbins have taken as a verbal noun, ἡ ἀρχή, *initium*, is a
defective form of חַיִל, an army (2 Kings xviii. 7; Isa. xxxvi. 2),
like חֵק for חֵיק in Prov. v. 20, xvii. 23, xxi. 14, and is not to
be identified with חֵל, the trench of a fortification. The two
clauses in ver. 20 have only one verb, which renders the
meaning of אֲשֶׁר כ' . . . צָרְפַת ambiguous. The Chaldee (according to our editions, though not according to Kimchi's account)
and the Masoretes (by placing *athnach* under *sᵉphârâd*), also
Rashi and others, take אֲשֶׁר כְּנַעֲנִים as in apposition to the subject: those prisoners of the sons of Israel who are among the
Canaanites to Zarephath. And the parallelism to אֲשֶׁר בִּסְפָרַד
appears to favour this; but it is decidedly negatived by the
absence of ב before כנענים. אֲשֶׁר כ' can only mean, "who are
Canaanites." But this, when taken as in apposition to בְּנֵי יִשׂ',
gives no sustainable meaning. For the sons of Israel could
only be called Canaanites when they had adopted the nature of
Canaan. And any who had done this could look for no share
in the salvation of the Lord, and no return to the land of the
Lord. We must therefore take אשר כנענים as the object, and
supply the verb יִרְשׁוּ from the first clauses of the preceding verse.
Obadiah first of all expresses the verb twice, then omits it in
the next two clauses (ver. 19*d* and 20*a*), and inserts it again in
the last clause (ver. 20*b*). The meaning is, that the army of
these sons of Israel, who have been carried away captive, will
take possession of what Canaanites there are as far as *Zarephath*,
i.e. the Phœnician city of *Sarepta*, the present *Surafend*, between
Tyre and Sidon on the sea-coast (see comm. on 1 Kings xvii. 9).
The capture of the land of the enemy presupposes a return to
the fatherland. The exiles of Jerusalem shall take possession
of the south country, the inhabitants of which have pushed
forward into Edom. בִּסְפָרַד (in Sepharad) is difficult, and has

never yet been satisfactorily explained, as the word does not occur again. The rendering *Spain*, which we find in the Chaldee and Syriac, is probably only an inference drawn from Joel iii. 6 ; and the Jewish rendering *Bosphorus*, which is cited by Jerome, is simply founded upon the similarity in the name. The supposed connection between this name and the *ÇPaRaD*, or *Çparda*, mentioned in the great arrow-headed inscription of Nakshi Rustam in a list of names of tribes between *Katpadhuka* (Cappadocia) and *Yunâ* (Ionia), in which Sylv. de Sacy imagined that he had found our Sepharad, has apparently more to favour it, since the resemblance is very great. But if *Çparda* is the Persian form for *Sardis* (Σάρδις or Σάρδεις), which was written *Çvarda* in the native (Lydian) tongue, as Lassen maintains, *Sepharad* cannot be the same as *Çparda*, inasmuch as the Hebrews did not receive the name ספרד through the Persians ; and the native *Çvarda*, apart from the fact that it is merely postulated, would be written סורד in Hebrew. To this we may add, that the impossibility of proving that *Sardis* was ever used for Lydia, precludes our rendering *Çparda* by *Sardis*. It is much more natural to connect the name with Σπάρτη (*Sparta*) and Σπαρτιάται (1 Macc. xiv. 16, 20, 23, xii. 2, 5, 6), and assume that the Hebrews had heard the name from the Phœnicians in connection with Javan, as the name of a land in the far west.[1] The cities of the south country stand in antithesis to the Canaanites as far as Zarephath in the north ; and these two regions are mentioned synecdochically for all the countries round about Canaan, like " the breaking forth of Israel on the right hand and on the left, that its seed may inherit the Gentiles," which is promised in Isa. liv. 3. The description is rounded off by the closing reference to the south country, in which it returns to the point whence it started.

With the taking of the lands of the Gentiles, the full dis-

---

[1] The appellative rendering ἐν διασπορᾷ (Hendewerk and Maurer) is certainly to be rejected ; and Ewald's conjecture, סְפָרֵם, " a place three hours' journey from Acco," in support of which he refers to Niebuhr, *R.* iii. p. 269, is a very thoughtless one. For Niebuhr there mentions the village of *Serfati* as the abode of the prophet Elijah, and refers to Maundrell, who calls the village *Sarphan*, *Serephat*, and *Serepta*, in which every thoughtful reader must recognise the biblical Zarephath, and the present village of *Surafend*.

play of salvation begins in Zion. Ver. 21. " *And saviours go up on Mount Zion to judge the mountains of Esau; and the kingdom will be Jehovah's.*" עָלָה followed by בְ does not mean to go up to a place, but to climb to the top of (Deut. v. 5; Ps. xxiv. 3; Jer. iv. 29, v. 10), or into (Jer. ix. 20). Consequently there is no allusion in וְעָלוּ to the return from exile. Going up to the top of Mount Zion simply means, that at the time when Israel captures the possessions of the heathen, Mount Zion will receive and have saviours who will judge Edom. And as the mountains of Esau represent the heathen world, so Mount Zion, as the seat of the Old Testament kingdom of God, is the type of the kingdom of God in its fully developed form. מוֹשִׁעִים, which is written defectively מֹשִׁעִים in some of the ancient MSS., and has consequently been rendered incorrectly σεσωσμένοι and ἀνασωζόμενοι by the LXX., Aq., Theod., and the Syriac, signifies *salvatores*, deliverers, saviours. The expression is selected with an allusion to the olden time, in which Jehovah saved His people by judges out of the power of their enemies (Judg. ii. 16, iii. 9, 15, etc.). "The מוֹשִׁעִים are heroes, resembling the judges, who are to defend and deliver Mount Zion and its inhabitants, when they are threatened and oppressed by enemies" (Caspari). The object of their activity, however, is not Israel, but Edom, the representative of all the enemies of Israel. The mountains of Esau are mentioned instead of the people, partly on account of the antithesis to the mountain of Zion, and partly also to express the thought of supremacy not only over the people, but over the land of the heathen also. *Shâphat* is not to be restricted in this case to the judging or settling of disputes, but includes the conduct of the government, the exercise of dominion in its fullest extent, so that the " judging of the mountains of Esau" expresses the dominion of the people of God over the heathen world. Under the saviours, as Hengstenberg has correctly observed, the Saviour *par excellence* is concealed. This is not brought prominently out, nor is it even distinctly affirmed; but it is assumed as self-evident, from the history of the olden time, that the saviours are raised up by Jehovah for His people. The following and concluding thought, that the kingdom will be Jehovah's, *i.e.* that Jehovah will show Himself to the whole world as King of the world, and Ruler in His kingdom, and will be acknow-

ledged by the nations of the earth, either voluntarily or by
constraint, rests upon this assumption.   God was indeed King
already, not as the Almighty Ruler of the universe, for this is
not referred to here, but as King in Israel, over which His
kingdom did extend.   But this His royal sway was not acknowledged by the heathen world, and could not be, more especially
when He had to deliver Israel up to the power of its enemies,
on account of its sins.   This acknowledgment, however, He
would secure for Himself, by the destruction of the heathen
power in the overthrow of Edom, and by the exaltation of
His people to dominion over all nations.   Through this mighty
saving act He will establish His kingdom over the whole earth
(cf. Joel iii. 21 ; Mic. iv. 7 ; Isa. xxiv. 23).   " The coming of
this kingdom began with Christ, and looks for its complete
fulfilment in Him" (Hengstenberg).

If now, in conclusion, we cast another glance at the fulfilment of our whole prophecy; the fulfilment of that destruction
by the nations, with which the Edomites are threatened (vers.
1–9), commenced in the Chaldean period.   For although no
express historical evidence exists as to the subjugation of the
Edomites by Nebuchadnezzar, since Josephus (*Ant.* x. 9, 7)
says nothing about the Edomites, who dwelt between the
Moabites and Egypt, in the account which he gives of Nebuchadnezzar's expedition against Egypt, five years after the
destruction of Jerusalem, in which he subdued the Ammonites
and Moabites ; the devastation of Edom by the Chaldeans may
unquestionably be inferred from Jer. xlix. 7 sqq. and Ezek.
xxxv., when compared with Jer. xxv. 9, 21, and Mal. i. 3.   In
Jer. xxv. 21 the Edomites are mentioned among the nations
round about Judah, whom the Lord would deliver up into the
hand of His servant Nebuchadnezzar (Jer. xxv. 9), and to whom
Jeremiah was to present the cup of the wine of wrath from the
hand of Jehovah ; and they are placed between the Philistines
and the Moabites.   And according to Mal. i. 3, Jehovah made
the mountains of Esau into a wilderness ; and this can only
refer to the desolation of the land of Edom by the Chaldeans
(see at Mal. i. 3).   It is true, that at that time the Edomites
could still think of rebuilding their ruins ; but the threat of
Malachi, " If they build, I shall pull down, saith the Lord,"
was subsequently fulfilled, although no accounts have been

handed down as to the fate of Edom in the time of Alexander the Great and his successors. The destruction of the Edomites as a nation was commenced by the Maccabees. After Judas Maccabæus had defeated them several times (1 Macc. v. 3 and 65; Jos. *Ant.* xii. 18, 1), John Hyrcanus subdued them entirely about 129 B.C., and compelled them to submit to circumcision, and observe the Mosaic law (Jos. *Ant.* xiii. 9, 1), whilst Alexander Jannæus also subjugated the last of the Edomites (xiii. 15, 4). And the loss of their national independence, which they thereby sustained, was followed by utter destruction at the hands of the Romans. To punish them for the cruelties which they had practised in Jerusalem in connection with the Zelots, immediately before the siege of that city by the Romans (Josephus, *Wars of the Jews,* iv. 5, 1, 2), Simon the Gerasene devastated their land in a fearful manner (*Wars of the Jews,* iv. 9, 7); whilst the Idumæans in Jerusalem, who took the side of Simon (v. 6, 1), were slain by the Romans along with the Jews. The few Edomites who still remained were lost among the Arabs; so that the Edomitish people was " cut off for ever" (ver. 10) by the Romans, and its very name disappeared from the earth. Passing on to the rest of the prophecy, Edom filled up the measure of its sins against its brother nation Israel, against which Obadiah warns it in vers. 12–14, at the taking and destruction of Jerusalem by the Chaldeans (*vid.* Ezek. xxxv. 5, 10; Ps. cxxxvii. 7; Lam. iv. 22). The fulfilment of the threat in ver. 18 we cannot find, however, in the subjugation of the Edomites by the Maccabæans, and the devastating expedition of Simon the Gerasene, as Caspari and others do, although it is apparently favoured by the statement in Ezek. xxv. 14, that Jehovah would fulfil His vengeance upon Edom by the hand of His people Israel. For even if this prophecy of Ezekiel may have been fulfilled in the events just mentioned, we are precluded from understanding Ob. 18, and the parallel passages, Amos ix. 11, 12, and Num. xxiv. 18, as referring to the same events, by the fact that the destruction of Edom, and the capture of Seir by Israel, are to proceed, according to Num. xxiv. 18, from the Ruler to arise out of Jacob (the Messiah), and that they were to take place, according to Amos ix. 11, 12, in connection with the raising up of the fallen hut of David, and according to

Obadiah, in the day of Jehovah, along with and after the judgment upon all nations. Consequently the fulfilment of vers. 17–21 can only belong to the Messianic times, and that in such a way that it commenced with the founding of the kingdom of Christ on the earth, advances with its extension among all nations, and will terminate in a complete fulfilment at the second coming of our Lord.

JONAH

INTRODUCTION.

1. **T**HE PROPHET.—We know from 2 Kings xiv. 25 that *Jonah* the son of Amittai was born in Gath-Hepher, in the tribe of Zebulon, which was, according to Jewish tradition as given by Jerome, "*haud grandis viculus Geth*," to the north of Nazareth, on the road from Sephoris to Tiberias, on the site of the present village of Meshad (see at Josh. xix. 13); that he lived in the reign of Jeroboam II., and foretold to this king the success of his arms in his war with the Syrians, for the restoration of the ancient boundaries of the kingdom; and that this prophecy was fulfilled. From the book before us we learn that the same Jonah (for this is evident from the fact that the name of the father is also the same) received a command from the Lord to go to Nineveh, and announce the destruction of that city on account of its sins. This mission to Nineveh evidently falls later than the prophecy in favour of Jeroboam; but although it is quite possible that it is to be assigned to the time of Menahem, during the period of the first invasion of Israel by the Assyrians, this is by no means so probable as many have assumed. For, inasmuch as Menahem began to reign fifty-three years after the commencement of the reign of Jeroboam, and the war between Jeroboam and the Syrians took place not in the closing years, but in the very first years of his reign, since it was only the continuation and conclusion of the successful struggle which his father had already begun with these enemies of Israel; Jonah must have been a very old man when he was entrusted with his mission to Nineveh, if it did not take place till after the invasion of Israel by Pul. Nothing is known of the circumstances of Jonah's life apart from these biblical notices. The Jewish tradition mentioned by Jerome

in the *Prœm.* to Jonah, to the effect that Jonah was the son
of the widow at Zarephath, whom Elijah restored to life
(1 Kings xvii. 17–24), which has been still further expounded
by Ps. Epiph. and Ps. Doroth. (see Carpzov, *Introd.* ii. pp.
346–7), is proved to be nothing more than a Jewish Hagada,
founded upon the name "son of Amittai" (LXX. υἱοῦ ᾿Αμαθί),
and has just as much historical evidence to support it as the
tradition concerning the prophet's grave, which is pointed out
in Meshad of Galilee, and also in Nineveh in Assyria, for the
simple reason adduced by Jerome (*l.c.*) : *matre postea dicente
ad eum : nunc cognovi, quia vir Dei es tu, et verbum Dei in ore tuo
est veritas ; et ob hanc causam etiam ipsum puerum sic vocatum,
Amathi enim in nostra lingua veritatem sonat.*

2. The Book of Jonah resembles, in contents and form,
the narratives concerning the prophets in the historical books
of the Old Testament, *e.g.* the history of Elijah and Elisha
(1 Kings xvii.–xix.; 2 Kings ii. 4–6), rather than the writings
of the minor prophets. It contains no prophetic words concerning Nineveh, but relates in simple prose the sending of
Jonah to that city to foretel its destruction ; the behaviour of
the prophet on receiving this divine command ; his attempt to
escape from it by flight to Tarshish ; the way in which this
sin was expiated ; and lastly, when the command of God had
been obeyed, not only the successful result of his preaching of
repentance, but also his murmuring at the sparing of Nineveh
in consequence of the repentance of its inhabitants, and the
reproof administered by God to the murmuring prophet. If,
then, notwithstanding this, the compilers of the canon have
placed the book among the minor prophets, this can only have
been done because they were firmly convinced that the prophet
Jonah was the author. And, indeed, the objections offered to
the genuineness of the book, apart from doctrinal reasons for
disputing its historical truth and credibility, and the proofs
adduced of its having a much later origin, are extremely trivial,
and destitute of any conclusive force. It is said that, apart
from the miraculous portion, the narrative is wanting in clearness and perspicuity. "The author," says Hitzig, "leaps over
the long and wearisome journey to Nineveh, says nothing
about Jonah's subsequent fate, or about his previous abode, or

the spot where he was cast upon the land, or the name of the Assyrian king; in brief, he omits all the more minute details which are necessarily connected with a true history." But the assertion that completeness in all external circumstances, which would serve to gratify curiosity rather than to help to an understanding of the main facts of the case, is indispensable to the truth of any historical narrative, is one which might expose the whole of the historical writings of antiquity to criticism, but can never shake their truth. There is not a single one of the ancient historians in whose works such completeness as this can be found : and still less do the biblical historians aim at communicating such things as have no close connection with the main object of their narrative, or with the religious significance of the facts themselves. Proofs of the later origin of the book have also been sought for in the language employed, and in the circumstance that Jonah's prayer in ch. ii. 3–10 contains so many reminiscences from the Psalms, that Ph. D. Burk has called it *præstantissimum exemplum psalterii recte applicati.* But the so-called Aramaisms, such as הֵטִיל to throw (ch. i. 4, 5, 12, etc.), the interchange of סְפִינָה with אֳנִיָּה (ch. i. 5), מִנָּה to determine, to appoint (ch. ii. 1, iv. 6 sqq.), חָתַר in the supposed sense of rowing (ch. i. 13), הִתְעַשֵּׁת to remember (ch. i. 6), and the forms בְּשֶׁלְּמִי (ch. i. 7), בְּשֶׁלִּי (ch. i. 12), and שֶׁ for אֲשֶׁר (ch. iv. 10), belong either to the speech of Galilee or the language of ordinary intercourse, and are very far from being proofs of a later age, since it cannot be proved with certainty that any one of these words was unknown in the early Hebrew usage, and שֶׁ for אֲשֶׁר occurs as early as Judg. v. 7, vi. 17, and even שֶׁלִּי in Song of Sol. i. 6, viii. 12, whilst in the book before us it is only in the sayings of the persons acting (ch. i. 7, 12), or of God (ch. iv. 10), that it is used. The only non-Hebraic word, viz. טַעַם, which is used in the sense of command, and applied to the edict of the king of Assyria, was heard by Jonah in Nineveh, where it was used as a technical term, and was transferred by him. The reminiscences which occur in Jonah's prayer are all taken from the Psalms of David or his contemporaries, which were generally known in Israel long before the prophet's day.[1] Lastly, the statement in ch. iii. 3, that

---

[1] They are the following: ver. 3a is formed from Ps. xviii. 7 and cxx. 1; ver. 4b is taken literally from Ps. xlii. 8 ; ver. 5a from Ps. xxxi. 23, whilst

"Nineveh was an exceeding great city," neither proves that
Nineveh had already been destroyed at the time when this was
written, nor that the greatness of Nineveh was unknown to the
contemporaries of Jonah, though there would be nothing sur-
prising in the latter, as in all probability very few Israelites
had seen Nineveh at that time. הָיְתָה is the synchronistic imperfect, just as in Gen. i. 2. Nineveh was a great city of
three days' journey when Jonah reached it, *i.e.* he found it so,
as Staeudlin observes, and even De Wette admits.

The doctrinal objections to the miraculous contents of the
book appear to be much more weighty; since it is undeniable
that, if they were of the character represented by the opponents,
this would entirely preclude the possibility of its having been
composed by the prophet Jonah, and prove that it had originated in a mythical legend. "The whole narrative," says Hitzig
in his prolegomena to the book of Jonah, "is miraculous and
fabulous. But nothing is impossible with God. Hence Jonah
lives in the belly of the fish without being suffocated; hence
the *Qīqāyōn* springs up during the night to such a height that
it overshadows a man in a sitting posture. As Jehovah bends
everything in the world to His own purposes at pleasure, the
marvellous coincidences had nothing in them to astonish the
author. The lot falls upon the right man; the tempest rises
most opportunely, and is allayed at the proper time; and the
fish is ready at hand to swallow Jonah, and vomit him out again.
So, again, the tree is ready to sprout up, the worm to kill it,
and the burning wind to make its loss perceptible." But the
coarse view of God and of divine providence apparent in all this,
which borders very closely upon atheism, by no means proves
that the contents of the book are fabulous, but simply that the
history of Jonah cannot be vindicated, still less understood,
without the acknowledgment of a living God, and of His activity
in the sphere of natural and human life.[1] The book of Jonah

ver. 5*b* recals Ps. v. 8; ver. 6*a* is formed from Ps. lxix. 2 and xviii. 5;
ver. 8*a* from Ps. cxlii. 4 or cxliii. 4, whilst ver. 8*b* recals Ps. xviii. 7 and
lxxxviii. 3; ver. 9*a* is formed after Ps. xxxi. 7; and ver. 10 resembles Ps.
xlii. 5 and Ps. l. 14, 23.

[1] The offence taken at the miracles in the book originated with the
heathen. Even to Lucian they apparently presented an occasion for ridicule (see *Veræ histor.* lib. i. § 30 sq., ed. Bipont). With regard to the three

records miraculous occurrences; but even the two most striking miracles, the three days' imprisonment in the belly of the sea-fish, and the growth of a *Qīqāyōn* to a sufficient height to over-shadow a sitting man, have analogies in nature, which make the possibility of these miracles at least conceivable (see the comm. on ch. ii. 1 and iv. 6). The repentance of the Nine-vites in consequence of the prophet's preaching, although an unusual and extraordinary occurrence, was not a miracle in the strict sense of the word. At the same time, the possibility of this miracle by no means proves its reality or historical truth. This can only be correctly discerned and rightly estimated, from the important bearing of Jonah's mission to Nineveh and of his conduct in relation to this mission upon the position of Israel in the divine plan of salvation in relation to the Gentile world. *The mission of Jonah was a fact of symbolical and typical im-portance, which was intended not only to enlighten Israel as to the position of the Gentile world in relation to the kingdom of God, but also to typify the future adoption of such of the heathen, as should observe the word of God, into the fellowship of the salvation prepared in Israel for all nations.*

As the time drew nigh when Israel was to be given up into the power of the Gentiles, and trodden down by them, on account of its stiff-necked apostasy from the Lord its God, it was very natural for the self-righteous mind of Israel to regard the Gen-tiles as simply enemies of the people and kingdom of God, and not only to deny their capacity for salvation, but also to inter-pret the prophetic announcement of the judgment coming upon

---

days' imprisonment in the belly of the fish, and on the *Qīqāyōn*, Augustine in his Epist. 102 says, "I have heard this kind of inquiry ridiculed by pagans with great laughter;" and Theophylact also says, "Jonah is there-fore swallowed by a whale, and the prophet remains in it three days and the same number of nights; which appears to be beyond the power of the hearers to believe, chiefly of those who come to this history fresh from the schools of the Greeks and their wise teaching." This ridicule first found admission into the Christian church, when the rise of deism, naturalism, and rationalism caused a denial of the miracles and inspiration of the Scriptures to be exalted into an axiom of free inquiry. From this time forward a multitude of marvellous hypotheses and trivial ideas concerning the book of Jonah have been brought out, which P. Friedrichsen has collected and dis-cussed in a most unspiritual manner in his *Kritische Uebersicht der verschie-denen Ansichten von dem Buche Jona*.

the Gentiles as signifying that they were destined to utter
destruction. The object of Jonah's mission to Nineveh was to
combat in the most energetic manner, and practically to overthrow, a delusion which had a seeming support in the election
of Israel to be the vehicle of salvation, and which stimulated the
inclination to pharisaical reliance upon an outward connection
with the chosen nation and a lineal descent from Abraham.
Whereas other prophets proclaimed in words the position of
the Gentiles with regard to Israel in the nearer and more
remote future, and predicted not only the surrender of Israel to
the power of the Gentiles, but also the future conversion of the
heathen to the living God, and their reception into the kingdom
of God, the prophet Jonah was entrusted with the commission
to proclaim the position of Israel in relation to the Gentile
world in a symbolico-typical manner, and to exhibit both figuratively and typically not only the susceptibility of the heathen
for divine grace, but also the conduct of Israel with regard to
the design of God to show favour to the Gentiles, and the consequences of their conduct. The susceptibility of the Gentiles
for the salvation revealed in Israel is clearly and visibly depicted
in the behaviour of the Gentile sailors, viz. in the fact that
they fear the God of heaven and earth, call upon Him, present
sacrifice to Him, and make vows; and still more in the deep
impression produced by the preaching of Jonah in Nineveh,
and the fact that the whole population of the great city, with
the king at their head, repent in sackcloth and ashes. The
attitude of Israel towards the design of God to show mercy to
the Gentiles and grant them salvation, is depicted in the way
in which Jonah acts, when he receives the divine command,
and when he goes to carry it out. Jonah tries to escape from
the command to proclaim the word of God in Nineveh by flight
to Tarshish, because he is displeased with the display of divine
mercy to the great heathen world, and because, according to
ch. iv. 2, he is afraid lest the preaching of repentance should
avert from Nineveh the destruction with which it is threatened.
In this state of mind on the part of the prophet, there are reflected the feelings and the general state of mind of the Israelitish nation towards the Gentiles. According to his natural
man, Jonah shares in this, and is thereby fitted to be the representative of Israel in its pride at its own election. At the same

time, it is only in this state of mind that the old man, which rebels against the divine command, comes sharply out, whereas his better *I* hears the word of God, and is moved within; so that we cannot place him in the category of the false prophets, who prophesy from their own hearts. When the captain wakes him up in the storm upon the sea, and the lot shows that he is guilty, he confesses his fault, and directs the sailors to cast him into the sea, because it is on his account that the great storm has come upon them (ch. i. 10–12). The infliction of this punishment, which falls upon him on account of his obstinate resistance to the will of God, typifies that rejection and banishment from the face of God which Israel will assuredly bring upon itself by its obstinate resistance to the divine call. But Jonah, when cast into the sea, is swallowed up by a great fish; and when he prays to the Lord in the fish's belly, he is vomited upon the land unhurt. This miracle has also a symbolical meaning for Israel. It shows that if the carnal nation, with its ungodly mind, should turn to the Lord even in the last extremity, it will be raised up again by a divine miracle from destruction to newness of life. And lastly, the manner in which God reproves the prophet, when he is angry because Nineveh has been spared (ch. iv.), is intended to set forth as in a mirror before all Israel the greatness of the divine compassion, which embraces all mankind, in order that it may reflect upon it and lay it to heart.

But this by no means exhausts the deeper meaning of the history of Jonah. It extends still further, and culminates in the typical character of Jonah's three days' imprisonment in the belly of the fish, upon which Christ threw some light when He said, "As Jonah was three days and three nights in the whale's belly, so shall the Son of man be three days and three nights in the heart of the earth" (Matt. xii. 40). The clue to the meaning of this type, *i.e.* to the divinely-appointed connection between the typical occurrence and its antitype, is to be found in the answer which Jesus gave to Philip and Andrew when they told Him, a short time before His death, that there were certain Greeks among them that came up to worship at the feast who desired to see Jesus. This answer consists of two distinct statements, viz. (John xii. 23, 24): "The time is come that the Son of man should be glorified. Verily, verily,

I say unto you, Except the grain of wheat fall into the earth, and die, it abideth alone : but if it die, it bringeth forth much fruit;" and (ver. 32), "And I, if I be lifted up from the earth, will draw all men unto me." This answer of Jesus intimates that the time to admit the Gentiles has not yet come ; but the words, " the hour is come," etc., also contain the explanation, that " the Gentiles have only to wait patiently a little longer, since their union with Christ, with which the address concludes (ver. 32), is directly connected with the glorification of the Son of man" (Hengstenberg on John xii. 20). This assertion of the Lord, that His death and glorification are necessary in order that He may draw all men, even the heathen, to Himself, or that by His death He may abolish the wall of partition by which the Gentiles were shut out of the kingdom of God, at which He had already hinted in John x. 15, 16, teaches us that the history of Jonah is to be regarded as an important and significant link in the chain of development of the divine plan of salvation. When Assyria was assuming the form of a world-conquering power, and the giving up of Israel into the hands of the Gentiles was about to commence, Jehovah sent His prophet to Nineveh, to preach to this great capital of the imperial kingdom His omnipotence, righteousness, and grace. For although the giving up of Israel was inflicted upon it as a punishment for its idolatry, yet, according to the purpose of God, it was also intended to prepare the way for the spread of the kingdom of God over all nations. The Gentiles were to learn to fear the living God of heaven and earth, not only as a preparation for the deliverance of Israel out of their hands after it had been refined by the punishment, but also that they might themselves be convinced of the worthlessness of their idols, and learn to seek salvation from the God of Israel. But whilst this brings out distinctly to the light the deep inward connection between the mission of Jonah to Nineveh and the divine plan of salvation, the typical character of that connection is first made perfectly clear from what Jonah himself passed through. For whereas the punishment, which he brought upon himself through his resistance to the divine command, contained this lesson, that Israel in its natural nationality must perish in order that out of the old sinful nature there may arise a new people of God, which, being dead to the law, may serve the Lord in the willingness of the spirit, God also appointed the mortal anguish and the deliverance of Jonah as a type of the death and resurrection of Jesus Christ to be the Saviour of the whole world. As Jonah the servant of God is given up to death that he may successfully accomplish the work committed to him, namely, to proclaim to the Ninevites the judgment and mercy of the God of heaven and earth; so must the Son of God be buried in the earth like a grain of wheat, that He may bring forth fruit for the whole world. The resemblance between the two is apparent in this. But Jonah deserved the punishment of death; Christ, on the contrary, suffered as the innocent One for the sins of mankind, and went voluntarily to death as One who had life in Himself to accomplish His Father's will. In this difference the inequality appears; and in this the type falls back behind the antitype, and typifies the reality but imperfectly. But even in this difference we may perceive a certain resemblance between Jonah and Christ which must not be overlooked. Jonah died according to his natural man on account of the sin, which was common to himself and his nation; Christ died for the sin of His people, which He had taken upon Himself, to make expiation for it; but He also died as a member of the nation, from which He had sprung according to the flesh, when He was made under the law, that He might rise again as the Saviour of all nations.

This symbolical and typical significance of the mission of the prophet Jonah precludes the assumption that the account in his book is a myth or a parabolical fiction, or simply the description of a symbolical transaction which the prophet experienced in spirit only. And the contents of the book are at variance with all these assumptions, even with the last. When the prophets are commanded to carry out symbolical transactions, they do so without repugnance. But Jonah seeks to avoid executing the command of God by flight, and is punished in consequence. This is at variance with the character of a purely symbolical action, and proves that the book relates historical facts. It is true that the sending of Jonah to Nineveh had not its real purpose within itself; that is to say, that it was not intended to effect the conversion of the Ninevites to the living God, but simply to bring to light the truth that even the Gentiles were capable of receiving divine truth, and to exhibit the possibility of their eventual reception into the kingdom of God. But this truth could not have been brought to the consciousness of the Israelites in a more impressive manner than by Jonah's really travelling to Nineveh to proclaim the destruction of that city on account of its wickedness, and seeing the proclamation followed by the results recorded in our book. Still less could the importance of this truth, so far as Israel was concerned, be exhibited in a merely symbolical transaction. If the intended flight of the prophet to Tarshish and his misfortune upon the sea were not historical facts, they could only be mythical or parabolical fictions. But though myths may very well embody religious ideas, and parables set forth prophetical truths, they cannot be types of future facts in the history of salvation. If the three days' confinement of Jonah in the belly of the fish really had the typical significance which Christ attributes to it in Matt. xii. 39 sqq. and Luke xi. 29 sqq., it can neither be a myth or dream, nor a parable, nor merely a visionary occurrence experienced by the prophet; but must have had as much objective reality as the facts of the death, burial, and resurrection of Christ.[1]

But if it follows from what has been said, that our book contains facts of a symbolico-typical meaning from the life of the prophet Jonah, there is no tenable ground left for disputing the authorship of the prophet himself. At the same time, the fact that Jonah was the author is not in itself enough to explain the admission of the book among the writings of the minor prophets. This place the book received, not because it related historical events that had happened to the prophet Jonah, but because these events were practical prophecies. Marck saw this, and has the following apt remark upon this point: "The writing is to a great extent historical, but so that in the history itself there is hidden the mystery of a very great prophecy; and he proves himself to be a true

---

[1] Compare also the critical examination of the more recent views that have been published against the historical character of the book of Jonah, and the negative and positive vindication of the historical view, in Hävernick's *Handbuch der Einleitung in d. A. T.* ii. 2, p. 326 sqq.; and the discussions on the symbolical character of the book by Hengstenberg (*Christology*, vol. i. p. 404 sqq. translation), and K. H. Sack in his *Christliche Apologetik*, p. 343 sqq., ed. 2.

prophet quite as much by his own fate as he does by his prophecies."

For the exegetical literature on the book of Jonah, see my *Lehrbuch der Einleitung,* p. 291.

EXPOSITION.

MISSION OF JONAH TO NINEVEH—HIS FLIGHT AND PUNISHMENT.—Chap. i.

Jonah tries to avoid fulfilling the command of God, to preach repentance to the great city Nineveh, by a rapid flight to the sea, for the purpose of sailing to Tarshish (vers. 1–3); but a terrible storm, which threatens to destroy the ship, brings his sin to light (vers. 4–10); and when the lot singles him out as the culprit, he confesses that he is guilty; and in accordance with the sentence which he pronounces upon himself, is cast into the sea (vers. 11–16).

Vers. 1–3. The narrative commences with וַיְהִי, as Ruth (i. 1), 1 Samuel (i. 1), and others do. This was the standing formula with which historical events were linked on to one another, inasmuch as every occurrence follows another in chronological sequence; so that the *Vav* (and) simply attaches to a series of events, which are assumed as well known, and by no means warrants the assumption that the narrative which follows is merely a fragment of a larger work (see at Josh. i. 1). The word of the Lord which came to Jonah was this: "*Arise, go to Nineveh, the great city, and preach against it.*" עַל does not stand for אֶל (ch. iii. 2), but retains its proper meaning, *against,* indicating the threatening nature of the preaching, as the explanatory clause which follows clearly shows. The connection in ch. iii. 2 is a different one. *Nineveh,* the capital of the Assyrian kingdom, and the residence of the great kings of Assyria, which was built by Nimrod according to Gen. x. 11, and by Ninos, the mythical founder of the Assyrian empire, according to the Greek and Roman authors, is repeatedly called " the great city" in this book (ch. iii. 2, 3, iv. 11), and its size

is given as three days' journey (ch. iii. 3). This agrees with
the statements of classical writers, according to whom Νῖνος,
Ninus, as Greeks and Romans call it, was the largest city in
the world at that time.   According to Strabo (xvi. 1, 3), it was
much larger than Babylon, and was situated in a plain, Ἀτου-
ρίας, of Assyria, *i.e.* on the left bank of the Tigris. According
to Ctesias (in Diod. ii. 3), its circumference was as much as
480 stadia, *i.e.* twelve geographical miles; whereas, according
to Strabo, the circumference of the wall of Babylon was not
more than 365 stadia.   These statements have been confirmed
by modern excavations upon the spot. The conclusion to which
recent discoveries lead is, that the name Nineveh was used
in two senses: *first*, for one particular city; and *secondly*,
for a complex of four large primeval cities (including Nineveh
proper), the circumvallation of which is still traceable, and a
number of small dwelling-places, castles, etc., the mounds (Tell)
of which cover the land.   This Nineveh, in the broader sense,
is bounded on three sides by rivers—viz. on the north-west by
the Khosr, on the west by the Tigris, and on the south-west by
the Gazr Su and the Upper or Great Zab—and on the fourth
side by mountains, which ascend from the rocky plateau; and
it was fortified artificially all round on the river-sides with dams,
sluices for inundating the land, and canals, and on the land
side with ramparts and castles, as we may still see from the
heaps of ruins.   It formed a trapezium, the sharp angles of
which lay towards the north and south, the long sides being
formed by the Tigris and the mountains.   The average length
is about twenty-five English miles; the average breadth fifteen.
The four large cities were situated on the edge of the trapezium,
Nineveh proper (including the ruins of Kouyunjik, Nebbi
Yunas, and Ninua) being at the north-western corner, by the
Tigris; the city, which was evidently the later capital (Nimrud),
and which Rawlinson, Jones, and Oppert suppose to have been
Calah, at the south-western corner, between Tigris and Zab;
a third large city, which is now without a name, and has been
explored least of all, but within the circumference of which the
village of Selamiyeh now stands, on the Tigris itself, from three
to six English miles to the north of Nimrud; and lastly, the
citadel and temple-mass, which is now named Khorsabad, and
is said to be called Dur-Sargina in the inscriptions, from the

palace built there by Sargon, on the Khosr, pretty near to the north-eastern corner (compare M. v. Niebuhr, *Geschichte Assurs,* p. 274 sqq., with the ground-plan of the city of Nineveh, p. 284). But although we may see from this that Nineveh could very justly be called the great city, Jonah does not apply this epithet to it with the intention of pointing out to his countrymen its majestic size, but, as the expression *g^edôlâh lē'lōhīm* in ch. iii. 3 clearly shows, and as we may see still more clearly from ch. iv. 11, with reference to the importance which Nineveh had, both in the eye of God, and with regard to the divine commission which he had received, as the capital of the Gentile world, *quæ propter tot animarum multitudinem Deo curæ erat* (Michaelis). Jonah was to preach against this great Gentile city, because its wickedness had come before Jehovah, *i.e.* because the report or the tidings of its great corruption had penetrated to God in heaven (cf. Gen. xviii. 21; 1 Sam. v. 12).—Ver. 3. Jonah sets out upon his journey; not to Nineveh, however, but to flee to *Tarshish, i.e. Tartessus,* a Phœnician port in Spain (see at Gen. x. 4 and Isa. xxiii. 1), " *from the face of Jehovah,*" *i.e.* away from the presence of the Lord, out of the land of Israel, where Jehovah dwelt in the temple, and manifested His presence (cf. Gen. iv. 16); not to hide himself from the omnipresent God, but to withdraw from the service of Jehovah, the God-King of Israel.[1] The motive for this flight was not fear of the difficulty of carrying out the command of God, but, as Jonah himself says in ch. iv. 2, anxiety lest the compassion of God should spare the sinful city in the event of its repenting. He had no wish to co-operate in this; and that not merely because " he knew, by inspiration of the Holy Spirit, that the repentance of the Gentiles would be the ruin of the Jews, and, as a lover of his country, was actuated not so much by envy of the salvation of Nineveh, as by unwillingness that his own people should perish," as Jerome supposes, but also because he really grudged salvation

---

[1] Marck has already correctly observed, that " this must not be understood as flight from the being and knowledge of God, lest we should attribute to the great prophet gross ignorance of the omnipresence and omniscience of God; but as departure from the land of Canaan, the gracious seat of God, outside which he thought, that possibly, at any rate at that time, the gift and office of a prophet would not be conferred upon him."

to the Gentiles, and feared lest their conversion to the living
God should infringe upon the privileges of Israel above the
Gentile world, and put an end to its election as the nation of
God.[1] He therefore betook himself to *Yāphō*, *i.e.* Joppa, the
port on the Mediterranean Sea (*vid.* comm. on Josh. xix. 46),
and there found a ship which was going to Tarshish; and
having paid the *sᵉkhârâh*, the hire of the ship, *i.e.* the fare for
the passage, embarked " *to go with them* (*i.e.* the sailors) *to
Tarshish.*"

Vers. 4–10. Jonah's foolish hope of being able to escape
from the Lord was disappointed. "*Jehovah threw a great wind*
(*i.e.* a violent wind) *upon the sea.*" A mighty tempest (סַעַר,
rendered appropriately κλύδων by the LXX.) arose, so that
"*the ship thought to be dashed to pieces,*" *i.e.* to be wrecked
(חִשֵּׁב used of inanimate things, equivalent to "*was very nearly*"
wrecked). In this danger the seamen (*mallâch*, a denom. of
melach, the salt flood) cried for help, "*every one to his god.*"
They were heathen, and probably for the most part Phœnicians,
but from different places, and therefore worshippers of different
gods. But as the storm did not abate, they also resorted to

---

[1] Luther has already deduced this, the only true reason, from ch. iv., in
his *Commentary on the Prophet Jonah:* " Because Jonah was sorry that
God was so kind, he would rather not preach, yea, would rather die, than
that the grace of God, which was to be the peculiar privilege of the people
of Israel, should be communicated to the Gentiles also, who had neither
the word of God, nor the laws of Moses, nor the worship of God, nor
prophets, nor anything else, but rather strove against God, and His word,
and His people." But in order to guard against a false estimate of the
prophet, on account of these " carnal, Jewish thoughts of God," Luther
directs attention to the fact that " the apostles also held at first the carnal
opinion that the kingdom of Christ was to be an outward one; and even
afterwards, when they understood that it was to be a spiritual one, they
thought that it was to embrace only the Jews, and therefore ' preached
the gospel to the Jews only' (Acts viii.), until God enlightened them by a
vision from heaven to Peter (Acts x.), and by the public calling of Paul
and Barnabas (Acts xiii.), and by wonders and signs; and it was at last
resolved by a general council (Acts xv.), that God would also show mercy
to the Gentiles, and that He was the God of the Gentiles also. For it was
very hard for the Jews to believe that there were any other people outside
Israel who helped to form the people of God, because the sayings of the
Scripture stop there and speak of Israel and Abraham's seed; and the
word of God, the worship of God, the laws and the holy prophets, were with
them alone."

such means of safety as they had at command. They "*threw the wares in the ship into the sea, to procure relief to themselves*" (לְהָקֵל מֵעֲלֵיהֶם as in Ex. xviii. 22 and 1 Kings xii. 10). The suffix refers to the persons, not to the things. By throwing the goods overboard, they hoped to preserve the ship from sinking beneath the swelling waves, and thereby to *lighten, i.e.* diminish for themselves the danger of destruction which was so burdensome to them. "*But Jonah had gone down into the lower room of the ship, and had there fallen fast asleep;*" not, however, just at the time of the greatest danger, but before the wind had risen into a dangerous storm. The sentence is to be rendered as a circumstantial one in the pluperfect. *Yark*e*thē hass*e*phīnāh* (analogous to *yark*e*thē habbayith* in Amos vi. 10) is the innermost part of the vessel, *i.e.* the lower room of the ship. *S*e*phīnāh*, which only occurs here, and is used in the place of אֳנִיָּה, is the usual word for a ship in Arabic and Aramæan. *Nirdam:* used for deep sleep, as in Judg. iv. 21. This act of Jonah's is regarded by most commentators as a sign of an evil conscience. Marck supposes that he had lain down to sleep, hoping the better to escape either the dangers of sea and air, or the hand of God; others, that he had thrown himself down in despair, and being utterly exhausted and giving himself up for lost, had fallen asleep; or as Theodoret expresses it, being troubled with the gnawings of conscience and overpowered with mourning, he had sought comfort in sleep and fallen into a deep sleep. Jerome, on the other hand, expresses the idea that the words indicate "security of mind" on the part of the prophet: "he is not disturbed by the storm and the surrounding dangers, but has the same composed mind in the calm, or with shipwreck at hand;" and whilst the rest are calling upon their gods, and casting their things overboard, "he is so calm, and feels so safe with his tranquil mind, that he goes down to the interior of the ship and enjoys a most placid sleep." The truth probably lies between these two views. It was not an evil conscience, or despair occasioned by the threatening danger, which induced him to lie down to sleep; nor was it his fearless composure in the midst of the dangers of the storm, but the careless self-security with which he had embarked on the ship to flee from God, without considering that the hand of God could reach him even on the sea, and punish him for his disobedi-

ence. This security is apparent in his subsequent conduct.—
Ver. 6. When the danger was at its height, the *upper-steersman,*
or ship's captain (*rabh hachōbhēl,* the chief of the ship's governors; *chōbhēl* with the article is a collective noun, and a *denom.*
from *chebhel,* a ship's cable, hence the one who manages, steers,
or guides the ship), wakes him with the words, "*How canst
thou sleep soundly? Arise, and call upon thy God; perhaps God*
(*hā' ĕlōhīm* with the article, ' the true God') *will think of us,
that we may not perish.*" The meaning of יִתְעַשֵּׁת is disputed.
As עָשֵׁת is used in Jer. v. 28 in the sense of shining (viz. of
fat), Calvin and others (last of all, Hitzig) have maintained
that the *hithpael* has the meaning, shown himself shining, *i.e.*
bright (propitious); whilst others, including Jerome, prefer
the meaning *think again,* which is apparently better supported
than the former, not only by the Chaldee, but also by the
nouns עֶשְׁתּוּת (Job xii. 5) and עֶשְׁתֹּן (Ps. cxlvi. 4). God's thinking of a person involves the idea of active assistance. For the
thought itself, compare Ps. xl. 18. The fact that Jonah obeyed
this awakening call is passed over as self-evident; and in ver. 7
the narrative proceeds to relate, that as the storm had not
abated in the meantime, the sailors, firmly believing that some
one in the ship had committed a crime which had excited the
anger of God that was manifesting itself in the storm, had
recourse to the lot to find out the culprit. בַּאֲשֶׁר לְמִי = בְּשֶׁלְּמִי
(ver. 8), as שֶׁ is the vulgar, and in conversation the usual contraction for אֲשֶׁר : "*on account of whom*" (בַּאֲשֶׁר, in this that
= because, or followed by לְ, on account of). הָרָעָה, the misfortune (as in Amos iii. 6),—namely, the storm which is
threatening destruction. The lot fell upon Jonah. "The
fugitive is taken by lot, not from any virtue in lots themselves,
least of all the lots of heathen, but by the will of Him who
governs uncertain lots" (Jerome).

When Jonah had been singled out by the lot as the culprit,
the sailors called upon him to confess his guilt, asking him
at the same time about his country, his occupation, and his
parentage. The repetition of the question, on whose account
this calamity had befallen them, which is omitted in the LXX.
(Vatic.), the *Soncin.* prophets, and Cod. 195 of Kennicott, is
found in the margin in Cod. 384, and is regarded by Grimm
and Hitzig as a marginal gloss that has crept into the text.

It is not superfluous, however; still less does it occasion any confusion; on the contrary, it is quite in order. The sailors wanted thereby to induce Jonah to confess with his own mouth that he was guilty, now that the lot had fallen upon him, and to disclose his crime (Ros. and others). As an indirect appeal to confess his crime, it prepares the way for the further inquiries as to his occupation, etc. They inquired about his occupation, because it might be a disreputable one, and one which excited the wrath of the gods; also about his parentage, and especially about the land and people from which he sprang, that they might be able to pronounce a safe sentence upon his crime.— Ver. 9. Jonah begins by answering the last question, saying that he was "*a Hebrew*,"—the name by which the Israelites designated themselves in contradistinction to other nations, and by which other nations designated them (see at Gen. xiv. 13, and my *Lehrbuch der Einleitung*, § 9, Anm. 2),—and that he worshipped "*the God of heaven, who created the sea and the dry*" (*i.e.* the land).   יָרֵא has been rendered correctly by the LXX. σέβομαι, *colo, revereor;* and does not mean, "I am afraid of Jehovah, against whom I have sinned" (Abarbanel). By the statement, "I fear," etc., he had no intention of describing himself as a righteous or innocent man (Hitzig), but simply meant to indicate his relation to God,—namely, that he adored the living God who created the whole earth and, as Creator, governed the world. For he admits directly after, that he has sinned against this God, by telling them, as we may see from ver. 10, of his flight from Jehovah. He had not told them this as soon as he embarked in the ship, as Hitzig supposes, but does so now for the first time when they ask about his people, his country, etc., as we may see most unmistakeably from ver. 10*b*. In ver. 9 Jonah's statement is not given completely; but the principal fact, viz. that he was a Hebrew and worshipped Jehovah, is followed immediately by the account of the impression which this acknowledgment made upon the heathen sailors; and the confession of his sin is mentioned afterwards as a supplement, to assign the reason for the great fear which came upon the sailors in consequence. מַה־זֹּאת עָשִׂיתָ, *What hast thou done!* is not a question as to the nature of his sin, but an exclamation of horror at his flight from Jehovah, the God of heaven and earth, as the following explanatory

clauses כִּי יָדְעוּ וגו' clearly show. The great fear which came
upon the heathen seamen at this confession of Jonah may be
fully explained from the dangerous situation in which they
found themselves, since the storm preached the omnipotence of
God more powerfully than words could possibly do.

Vers. 11–16. Fearing as they did in the storm the wrath
of God on account of Jonah's sin, they now asked what they
should do, that the storm might abate, "*for the sea continued
to rage.*" שָׁתַק, to set itself, to come to a state of repose ; or
with מֵעַל, to desist from a person. הוֹלֵךְ, as in Gen. viii. 5, etc.,
expressive of the continuance of an action. With their fear of
the Almighty God, whom Jonah worshipped, they did not dare
to inflict a punishment upon the prophet, simply according to
their own judgment. As a worshipper of Jehovah, he should
pronounce his own sentence, or let it be pronounced by his
God. Jonah replies in ver. 12, " *Cast me into the sea ; for I
know that for my sake this great storm is* (come) *upon you.*"
As Jerome says, " He does not refuse, or prevaricate, or deny ;
but, having made confession concerning his flight, he willingly
endures the punishment, desiring to perish, and not let others
perish on his account." Jonah confesses that he has deserved
to die for his rebellion against God, and that the wrath of God
which has manifested itself in the storm can only be appeased
by his death. He pronounces this sentence, not by virtue of
any prophetic inspiration, but as a believing Israelite who is
well acquainted with the severity of the justice of the holy
God, both from the law and from the history of his nation.—
Ver. 13. But the men (the seamen) do not venture to carry
out this sentence at once. They try once more to reach the
land and escape from the storm, which is threatening them
with destruction, without so serious a sacrifice. יַחְתְּרוּ, lit. they
broke through, *sc.* through the waves, to bring (the ship) back
to the land, *i.e.* they tried to reach the land by rowing and
steering. *Châthar* does not mean to row, still less to twist or
turn round (Hitzig), but to break through ; here to break
through the waves, to try to overcome them, to which the παρε-
βιάζοντο of the LXX. points. As they could not accomplish
this, however, because the sea continued to rage against them
(סֹעֵר עֲלֵיהֶם, was raging against them), they prayed thus to
Jehovah : " *We beseech Thee, let us not* (אָנָּא = אַל־נָא) *perish*

for the sake of the soul of this man (בְּנֶפֶשׁ, lit. for the soul, as in 2 Sam. xiv. 7 after Deut. xix. 21), *and lay not upon us innocent blood*,"—that is to say, not "do not let us destroy an innocent man in the person of this man" (Hitzig), but, according to Deut. xxi. 8, "do not impute his death to us, if we cast him into the sea, as bloodguiltiness deserving death;" *"for Thou, O Jehovah, hast done as it pleased Thee,"*—namely, inasmuch as, by sending the storm and determining the lot, Thou hast so ordained that we must cast him into the sea as guilty, in order to expiate Thy wrath. They offer this prayer, not because they have no true conception of the guilt of Jonah, who is not a murderer or blasphemer, inasmuch as according to their notions, he is not a sinner deserving death (Hitzig), but because they regard Jonah as a prophet or servant of the Almighty God, upon whom, from fear of his God, they do not venture to lay their hand. "We see, therefore, that although they had never enjoyed the teaching of the law, they had been so taught by nature, that they knew very well that the blood of man was dear to God, and precious in His sight" (Calvin). —Vers. 15, 16. After they had prayed thus, they cast Jonah into the sea, and "*the sea stood still* (ceased) *from its raging*." The sudden cessation of the storm showed that the bad weather had come entirely on Jonah's account, and that the sailors had not shed innocent blood by casting him into the sea. In this sudden change in the weather, the arm of the holy God was so suddenly manifested, that the sailors "*feared Jehovah with great fear, and offered sacrifice to Jehovah*"—not after they landed, but immediately, on board the ship—"*and vowed vows,*" *i.e.* vowed that they would offer Him still further sacrifices on their safe arrival at their destination.

JONAH'S DELIVERANCE.—Chap. i. 17–ii. 10 (Heb. Chap. ii.).

When Jonah had been cast into the sea by the appointment of God, he was swallowed up by a great fish (ch. i. 17), in whose belly he spent three days and nights, and offered an earnest prayer to God (ch. ii. 1–9); whereupon, by command of Jehovah, the fish vomited him out upon the land (ver. 10).

Ch. i. 17 (Heb. ii. 1). "*And Jehovah appointed a great fish to swallow up Jonah.*" מִנָּה does not mean to create, but to determine, to appoint. The thought is this: Jehovah ordained that a great fish should swallow him. The great fish (LXX. κῆτος, cf. Matt. xii. 40), which is not more precisely defined, was not a whale, because this is extremely rare in the Mediterranean, and has too small a throat to swallow a man, but a large shark or sea-dog, *canis carcharias*, or *squalus carcharias L.*, which is very common in the Mediterranean, and has so large a throat, that it can swallow a living man whole.[1] The miracle consisted therefore, not so much in the fact that Jonah was swallowed alive, as in the fact that he was kept alive for three days in the shark's belly, and then vomited unhurt upon the land. The three days and three nights are not to be regarded as fully three times twenty hours, but are to be interpreted according to Hebrew usage, as signifying that Jonah was vomited up again on the third day after he had been swallowed (compare Esth. iv. 16 with v. 1 and Tob. iii. 12, 13, according to the Lutheran text).

Ch. ii. 1-9. "*Jonah prayed to Jehovah his God out of the fish's belly.*" The prayer which follows (vers. 2–9) is not a

---

[1] The *squalus carcharias L.*, the true shark, *Requin*, or rather *Requiem*, reaches, according to Cuvier, the length of 25 feet, and according to Oken the length of four fathoms, and has about 400 lance-shaped teeth in its jaw, arranged in six rows, which the animal can either elevate or depress, as they are simply fixed in cells in the skin. It is common in the Mediterranean, where it generally remains in deep water, and is very voracious, swallowing everything that comes in its way—plaice, seals, and tunny-fish, with which it sometimes gets into the fishermen's net on the coast of Sardinia, and is caught. As many as a dozen undigested tunny-fish have been found in a shark weighing three or four hundredweight; in one a whole horse was found, and its weight was estimated at fifteen hundredweight. Rondelet (Oken, p. 58) says that he saw one on the western coast of France, through whose throat a fat man could very easily have passed. Oken also mentions a fact, which is more elaborately described in Müller's *Vollständiges Natur-system des Ritters Carl v. Linné* (Th. iii. p. 268), namely, that in the year 1758 a sailor fell overboard from a frigate, in very stormy weather, into the Mediterranean Sea, and was immediately taken into the jaws of a sea-dog (*carcharias*), and disappeared. The captain, however, ordered a gun, which was standing on the deck, to be discharged at the shark, and the cannon-ball struck it, so that it vomited up again the sailor that it had swallowed, who was then taken up alive, and very little hurt, into the boat that had been lowered for his rescue.

petition for deliverance, but thanksgiving and praise for deliverance already received. It by no means follows from this, however, that Jonah did not utter this prayer till after he had been vomited upon the land, and that ver. 10 ought to be inserted before ver. 2; but, as the earlier commentators have shown, the fact is rather this, that when Jonah had been swallowed by the fish, and found that he was preserved alive in the fish's belly, he regarded this as a pledge of his deliverance, for which he praised the Lord. Luther also observes, that "he did not actually utter these very words with his mouth, and arrange them in this orderly manner, in the belly of the fish; but that he here shows what the state of his mind was, and what thoughts he had when he was engaged in this conflict with death." The expression "his God" (אֱלֹהָיו) must not be overlooked. He prayed not only to Jehovah, as the heathen sailors also did (ch. i. 14), but to Jehovah as his God, from whom he had tried to escape, and whom he now addresses again as his God when in peril of death. "He shows his *faith* by adoring Him as *his* God" (Burk). The prayer consists for the most part of reminiscences of passages in the Psalms, which were so exactly suited to Jonah's circumstances, that he could not have expressed his thoughts and feelings any better in words of his own. It is by no means so "atomically compounded from passages in the Psalms" that there is any ground for pronouncing it "a later production which has been attributed to Jonah," as Knobel and De Wette do; but it is the simple and natural utterance of a man versed in the Holy Scripture and living in the word of God, and is in perfect accordance with the prophet's circumstances and the state of his mind. Commencing with the confession, that the Lord has heard his crying to Him in distress (ver. 2), Jonah depicts in two strophes (vers. 3 and 4, 5–7) the distress into which he had been brought, and the deliverance out of that destruction which appeared inevitable, and closes in vers. 8, 9 with a vow of thanksgiving for the deliverance which he had received.

Ver. 2. *I cried to Jehovah out of my distress, and He heard me;*
    Out of the womb of hell I cried: Thou heardest my
    voice!

The first clause recals to mind Ps. xviii. 7 and cxx. 1; but it also shows itself to be an original reproduction of the expression מְצֻלָה לִּי, which expresses the prophet's situation in a more pointed manner than בַּצַּר־לִי in Ps. xviii. and בְּצָרָתָה לִּי in Ps. cxx. The distress is still more minutely defined in the second hemistich by the expression מִבֶּטֶן שְׁאוֹל, "out of the womb of the nether world." As a throat or swallow is ascribed to $sh^e\bar{o}l$ in Isa. v. 14, so here it is spoken of as having a בטן, or belly. This is not to be taken as referring to the belly of the shark, as Jerome supposes. The expression is a poetical figure used to denote the danger of death, from which there is apparently no escape; like the encompassing with snares of death in Ps. xviii. 5, and the bringing up of the soul out of sheol in Ps. xxx. 3. In the last clause the words pass over very appropriately into an address to Jehovah, which is brought out into still greater prominence by the omission of the copula *Vav.*

> Ver. 3. *Thou castedst me into the deep, into the heart of*
>   *the seas,*
>   *And the stream surrounded me;*
>   *All Thy billows and Thy waves went over me.*
>   4. *Then I said, I am thrust away from Thine eyes,*
>   *Yet I will look again to Thy holy temple.*

The more minute description of the peril of death is attached by *Vav consec.*, to express not sequence in time, but sequence of thought. *Jehovah* cast him into the depth of the sea, because the seamen were merely the executors of the punishment inflicted upon him by Jehovah. *M^{e}tsûlâh*, the deep, is defined by "the heart of the seas" as the deepest abyss of the ocean. The plural *yammîm* (seas) is used here with distinct significance, instead of the singular, "into the heart of the *sea*" (*yâm*) in Ex. xv. 8, to express the idea of the boundless ocean (see Dietrich, *Abhandlung zur hebr. Grammatik*, pp. 16, 17). The next clauses are circumstantial clauses, and mean, so that the current of the sea surrounded me, and all the billows and waves of the sea, which Jehovah had raised into a storm, went over me. *Nâhâr*, a *river* or *stream*, is the streaming or current of the sea, as in Ps. xxiv. 2. The words of the second hemistich are a reminiscence of Ps. xlii. 8. What the Korahite singer of that psalm had experienced spiritually, viz. that one wave of trouble after another swept over him, that had the prophet literally experienced. Jonah " does not say, The waves and the billows of the sea went over me; but *Thy* waves and *Thy* billows, because he felt in his conscience that the sea with its waves and billows was the servant of God and of His wrath, to punish sin" (Luther).   Ver. 4 contains the apodosis to ver. 3*a*: " When Thou castedst me into the deep, then I said (*sc.* in my heart, *i.e.* then I thought) that I was banished from the sphere of Thine eyes, *i.e.* of Thy protection and care." These words are formed from a reminiscence of Ps. xxxi. 23, נִגְרַשְׁתִּי being substituted for the נִגְרַזְתִּי of the psalm. The second hemistich is attached adversatively.   אַךְ, which there is no necessity to alter into אַךְ = אֵיךְ, as Hitzig supposes, introduces the antithesis in an energetic manner, like אָכֵן elsewhere, in the sense of nevertheless, as in Isa. xiv. 15, Ps. xlix. 16, Job xiii. 15 (cf. Ewald, § 354, *a*).   The thought that it is all over with him is met by the confidence of faith that he will still look to the holy temple of the Lord, that is to say, will once more approach the presence of the Lord, to worship before Him in His temple,—an assurance which recals Ps. v. 8.

The thought that by the grace of the Lord he has been once more miraculously delivered out of the gates of death, and brought to the light of the world, is carried out still further in the following strophe, in entirely new turns of thought.

Ver. 5. *Waters surrounded me even to the soul: the flood encompassed me,*
    Sea-grass was wound round my head.
    6. *I went down to the foundations of the mountains;*
    The earth, its bolts were behind me for ever:
    Then raisedst Thou my life out of the pit, O Jehovah my God.
    7. *When my soul fainted within me, I thought of Jehovah;*
    And my prayer came to Thee into Thy holy temple.

This strophe opens, like the last, with a description of the peril of death, to set forth still more perfectly the thought of miraculous deliverance which filled the prophet's mind. The first clause of the fifth verse recals to mind Ps. xviii. 5 and lxix. 2 ; the words " the waters pressed (בָּאוּ) even to the soul" (Ps. lxix. 2) being simply strengthened by אֲפָפוּנִי after Ps. xviii. 5.

The waters of the sea girt him round about, reaching even to the soul, so that it appeared to be all over with his life. *T^ehōm*, the unfathomable flood of the ocean, surrounded him. *Sūph*, sedge, *i.e.* sea-grass, which grows at the bottom of the sea, was bound about his head; so that he had sunk to the very bottom. This thought is expressed still more distinctly in ver. 6a. קִצְבֵי הָרִים, "the ends of the mountains" (from *qâtsabh*, to cut off, that which is cut off, then the place where anything is cut off), are their foundations and roots, which lie in the depths of the earth, reaching even to the foundation of the sea (cf. Ps. xviii. 16). When he sank into the deep, the earth shut its bolts behind him (הָאָרֶץ is placed at the head absolutely). The figure of bolts of the earth that were shut behind Jonah, which we only meet with here (בְּעַד from the phrase סָגַר הַדֶּלֶת בְּעַד, to shut the door behind a person: Gen. vii. 16; 2 Kings iv. 4, 5, 33; Isa. xxvi. 20), has an analogy in the idea which occurs in Job xxxviii. 10, of bolts and doors of the ocean. The bolts of the sea are the walls of the sea-basin, which set bounds to the sea, that it cannot pass over. Consequently the bolts of the earth can only be such barriers as restrain the land from spreading over the sea. These barriers are the weight and force of the waves, which prevent the land from encroaching on the sea. This weight of the waves, or of the great masses of water, which pressed upon Jonah when he had sunk to the bottom of the sea, shut or bolted against him the way back to the earth (the land), just as the bolts that are drawn before the door of a house fasten up the entrance into it; so that the reference is neither to "the rocks jutting out above the water, which prevented any one from ascending from the sea to the land," nor " *densissima terræ compages, qua abyssus tecta Jonam in hac constitutum occludebat*" (Marck). Out of this grave the Lord " brought up his life." *Shachath* is rendered φθορά, *corruptio*, by the early translators (LXX., Chald., Syr., Vulg.) ; and this rendering, which many of the more modern translators entirely reject, is unquestionably the correct one in Job xvii. 14, where the meaning "pit" is quite unsuitable. But it is by no means warranted in the present instance. The similarity of thought to Ps. xxx. 4 points rather to the meaning pit = cavern or grave, as in Ps. xxx. 10, where *shachath* is used interchangeably with בּוֹר and שְׁאוֹל in ver. 4 as being perfectly synonymous. Ver. 7a is formed after Ps. cxlii. 4 or cxliii. 4, except that נַפְשִׁי is used instead of רוּחִי, because Jonah is not speaking of the covering of the spirit with faintness, but of the plunging of the life into night and the darkness of death by drowning in the water. הִתְעַטֵּף, lit. to veil or cover one's self, hence to sink into night and faintness, to pine away. עָלָי, upon or in me, inasmuch as the *I*, as a person, embraces the soul or life (cf. Ps. xlii. 5). When his soul was about to sink into the night of death, he thought of Jehovah in prayer, and his prayer reached to God in His holy temple, where Jehovah is enthroned as God and King of His people (Ps. xviii. 7, lxxxviii. 3).

But when prayer reaches to God, then He helps and also saves. This awakens confidence in the Lord, and impels to praise and thanksgiving. These thoughts form the last strophe, with which the Psalm of thanksgiving is appropriately closed.

Ver. 8. *They who hold to false vanities*
Forsake their own mercy.
9. *But I will sacrifice to Thee with the call of thanksgiving.*
I will pay what I have vowed.
Salvation is with Jehovah.

In order to express the thought emphatically, that salvation and deliverance are only to be hoped for from Jehovah the living God, Jonah points to the idolaters, who forfeit their mercy. מְשַׁמְּרִים הַבְלֵי־שָׁוְא is a reminiscence of Ps. xxxi. 7. הַבְלֵי־שָׁוְא, worthless vanities, are all things which man makes into idols or objects of trust. הֲבָלִים are, according to Deut. xxxii. 21, false gods or idols. *Shâmar*, to keep, or, when applied to false gods, to keep to them or reverence them; in Hos. iv. 10 it is also applied to Jehovah. חַסְדָּם signifies neither *pietatem suam* nor *gratiam a Deo ipsis exhibitam*, nor " all the grace and love which they might receive" (Hitzig) ; but refers to God Himself, as He whose government is pure grace (*vid.* Gen. xxiv. 27), and might become the grace even of the idolatrous. Jonah, on the contrary, like all the righteous, would sacrifice to the Lord *b⁽e⁾qōl tōdâh*, " with the voice, or cry, of thanksgiving," *i.e.* would offer his sacrifices with a prayer of sincere thanksgiving (cf. Ps. xlii. 5), and pay the vow which he had made in his distress (cf. Ps. l. 14, 23). These utterances are founded upon the hope that his deliverance will be effected (Hitzig) ; and this hope is based upon the fact that "salvation is Jehovah's," *i.e.* is in His power, so that He only can grant salvation.

Ver. 10. *" Then Jehovah spake to the fish, and it vomited Jonah upon the dry land."* The nature of God's speaking, or commanding, may be inferred from the words וַיֹּאמֶר וגו׳. Cyril explains the thought correctly thus : " The whale is again impelled by a certain divine and secret power of God, being moved to that which seems good to Him." The land upon which Jonah was vomited was, of course, the coast of Palestine, probably the country near Joppa. According to ver. 1, this took place on the third day after he had been swallowed by the fish. On the prophetico-typical character of the miracle, see the remarks at p. 385 sqq.

JONAH'S PREACHING IN NINEVEH.—Chap. III.

After Jonah had been punished for his disobedience, and miraculously delivered from death by the mercy of God, he obeyed the renewed command of Jehovah, and preached to the city of Nineveh that it would be destroyed within forty days on account of its sins (vers. 1-4). But the Ninevites believed in God, and repented in sackcloth and ashes, to avert the threatened destruction (vers. 5-9); and the Lord spared the city (ver. 10).

Vers. 1-4. The word of the Lord came to Jonah the second time, to go to Nineveh and proclaim to that city what Jehovah would say to him. קְרִיאָה : that which is called out, the proclamation, τὸ κήρυγμα (LXX.). Jonah now obeyed the word of Jehovah. But Nineveh was *a great city to God* (*lē'lōhīm*), *i.e.* it was regarded by God as a great city. This remark points to the motive for sparing it (cf. ch. iv. 11), in case its inhabitants hearkened to the word of God. Its greatness amounted to "a three days' walk." This is usually supposed to refer to the circumference of the city, by which the size of a city is generally determined. But the statement in ver. 4, that " Jonah began to enter into the city the walk of a day," *i.e.* a day's journey, is apparently at variance with this. Hence Hitzig has come to the conclusion that the diameter or length of the city is intended, and that, as the walk of a day in ver. 4 evidently points to the walk of three days in ver. 3, the latter must also be understood as referring to the length of Nineveh. But according to Diod. ii. 3 the length of the city was 150 stadia, and Herodotus (v. 53) gives just this number of stadia as a day's journey. Hence Jonah would not have commenced his preaching till he had reached the opposite end of the city. This line of argument, the intention of which is to prove the absurdity of the narrative, is based upon the perfectly arbitrary assumption that Jonah went through the entire length of the city in a straight line, which is neither probable in itself, nor implied in בּוֹא בָעִיר. This simply means to enter, or go into the city, and says nothing about the direction of the course he took within the city. But in a city, the diameter of which was 150 stadia, and the circumference 480 stadia, one might easily walk for a whole day without reaching the other end, by winding about from one street into another. And Jonah would have to do this to find a suitable place for his preaching, since we are not warranted in assuming that it lay exactly in the geographical centre, or at the end of the street which led from the gate into the city. But if Jonah wandered about in different directions, as Theodoret says, "not going straight through the city, but strolling through market-places, streets, etc.," the distance of a day's journey over which he travelled must not be understood as relating to the diameter or length of the city; so that the objection to the general opinion, that the three days' journey given as the size of the city refers to the circumference, entirely falls to the ground. Moreover, Hitzig has quite overlooked the word וַיָּחֶל in his argument. The text does not affirm that Jonah went a day's journey into the city, but that he "began to go into the city a day's journey, and cried out." These words do not affirm that he did not begin to preach till after he had gone a whole day's journey, but simply that he had commenced his day's journey in the city when he found a suitable place and a fitting opportunity for his proclamation. They leave the distance that he had really gone, when he began his preaching, quite indefinite; and by no means necessitate the assumption that he only began to preach in the evening, after his day's journey was ended. All that they distinctly affirm is, that he did not preach directly he

entered the city, but only after he had commenced a day's
journey, that is to say, had gone some distance into the city.
And this is in perfect harmony with all that we know about
the size of Nineveh at that time. The circumference of the
great city Nineveh, or the length of the boundaries of the city
of Nineveh in the broadest sense, was, as Niebuhr says (p. 277),
"nearly ninety English miles, not reckoning the smaller wind-
ings of the boundary; and this would be just three days'
travelling for a good walker on a long journey." "Jonah,"
he continues, "begins to go a day's journey into the city, then
preaches, and the preaching reaches the ears of the king (cf.
ver. 6). He therefore came very near to the citadel as he went
along on his first day's journey. At that time the citadel was
probably in Nimrud (*Calah*). Jonah, who would hardly have
travelled through the desert, went by what is now the ordinary
caravan road past Amida, and therefore entered the city at
Nineveh. And it was on the road from Nineveh to Calah, not
far off the city, possibly in the city itself, that he preached.
Now the distance between Calah and Nineveh (not reckoning
either city), measured in a straight line upon the map, is $18\frac{1}{2}$
English miles." If, then, we add to this, (1) that the road
from Nineveh to Calah or Nimrud hardly ran in a perfectly
straight line, and therefore would be really longer than the
exact distance between the two parts of the city according to
the map, and (2) that Jonah had first of all to go through
Nineveh, and possibly into Calah, he may very well have
walked twenty English miles, or a short day's journey, before
he preached. The main point of his preaching is all that is
given, viz. the threat that Nineveh should be destroyed, which
was the point of chief importance, so far as the object of the
book was concerned, and which Jonah of course explained by
denouncing the sins and vices of the city. The threat ran
thus : " Yet forty days, and Nineveh will be destroyed." נֶהְפָּךְ,
lit. overturned, *i.e.* destroyed from the very foundations, is the
word applied to the destruction of Sodom and Gomorrah. The
respite granted is fixed at forty days, according to the number
which, even as early as the flood, was taken as the measure for
determining the delaying of visitations of God.[1]

[1] The LXX., however, has τρεῖς ἡμέρας, probably from a peculiar and
arbitrary combination, and not merely from an early error of the pen. The

Vers. 5-9. The Ninevites believed in God, since they hearkened to the preaching of the prophet sent to them by God, and humbled themselves before God with repentance. They proclaimed a fast, and put on sackcloth (penitential garments: see at Joel i. 13, 14; 1 Kings xxi. 27, etc.), "*from their great one even to their small one,*" *i.e.* both old and young, all without exception. Even the king, when the matter (*haddâbhâr*) came to his knowledge, *i.e.* when he was informed of Jonah's coming, and of his threatening prediction, descended from his throne, laid aside his royal robe ('*addereth*, see at Josh. vii. 21), wrapt himself in a sackcloth, and sat down in ashes, as a sign of the deepest mourning (compare Job ii. 8), and by a royal edict appointed a general fast for man and beast. וַיַּזְעֵק, he caused to be proclaimed. וַיֹּאמֶר, *and said,* viz. through his heralds. מִטַּעַם הַמ', *ex decreto,* by command of the king and his great men, *i.e.* his ministers (טַעַם = טְעֵם, Dan. iii. 10, 29, a technical term for the edicts of the Assyrian and Babylonian kings). "Man and beast (viz. oxen and sheep) are to taste nothing; they are not to pasture (the cattle are not to be driven to the pasture), and are to drink no water." אַל, for which we should expect לֹא, may be explained from the fact that the command is communicated directly. Moreover, man and beast are to be covered with mourning clothes, and cry to God *bᵉchozqâh, i.e.* strongly, mightily, and to turn every one from his evil ways: so "*will God perhaps* (מִי יוֹדֵעַ) *turn and repent* (*yâshûbh vᵉnicham,* as in Joel ii. 14), *and desist from the fierceness of His anger* (cf. Ex. xxxii. 12), *that we perish not.*" This verse (ver. 9) also belongs to the king's edict. The powerful impression made upon the Ninevites by Jonah's preaching, so that the whole city repented in sackcloth and ashes, is quite intelligible, if we simply bear in mind the great susceptibility of Oriental races to emotion, the awe of one Supreme Being which is peculiar to all the heathen religions of Asia, and the great esteem in which soothsaying and oracles were held in Assyria from the very earliest times (*vid.* Cicero, *de divinat.* i. 1); and if we also take into calculation the circumstance that the appearance of a foreigner, who, without any conceivable personal interest, and with the most fearless

other Greek translators (Aquil., Symm., and Theodot.) had, according to Theodoret, the number *forty;* and so also had the Syriac.

boldness, disclosed to the great royal city its godless ways, and
announced its destruction within a very short period with the
confidence so characteristic of the God-sent prophets, could not
fail to make a powerful impression upon the minds of the
people, which would be all the stronger if the report of the
miraculous working of the prophets of Israel had penetrated
to Nineveh. There is just as little to surprise us in the circumstance that the signs of mourning among the Ninevites
resemble in most respects the forms of penitential mourning
current among the Israelites, since these outward signs of
mourning are for the most part the common human expressions
of deep sorrow of heart, and are found in the same or similar
forms among all the nations of antiquity (see the numerous
proofs of this which are collected in Winer's *Real-wörterbuch*,
art. *Trauer ;* and in Herzog's *Cyclopædia*).   Ezekiel (xxvi. 16)
depicts the mourning of the Tyrian princes over the ruin of
their capital in just the same manner in which that of the king
of Nineveh is described here in ver. 6, except that, instead of
sackcloth, he mentions trembling as that with which they wrap
themselves round.   The garment of haircloth (*saq*) worn as
mourning costume reaches as far back as the patriarchal age
(cf. Gen. xxxvii. 34 ; Job xvi. 15).   Even the one feature which
is peculiar to the mourning of Nineveh—namely, that the
cattle also have to take part in the mourning—is attested by
Herodotus (ix. 24) as an Asiatic custom.[1]   This custom originated in the idea that there is a biotic *rapport* between man
and the larger domestic animals, such as oxen, sheep, and
goats, which are his living property.   It is only to these
animals that there is any reference here, and not to " horses,
asses, and camels, which were decorated at other times with

---

[1] Herodotus relates that the Persians, when mourning for their general,
Masistios, who had fallen in the battle at Platea, shaved off the hair from
their horses, and adds, " Thus did the barbarians, *in their way*, mourn for
the deceased Masistios."   Plutarch relates the same thing (Aristid. 14 fin.
Compare Brissonius, *de regno Pers. princip.* ii. p. 206 ; and Periz. *ad
Æliani Var. hist.* vii. 8).   The objection made to this by Hitzig—namely,
that the mourning of the cattle in our book is not analogous to the case
recorded by Herodotus, because the former was an expression of repentance—has no force whatever, for the simple reason that in all nations the
outward signs of penitential mourning are the same as those of mourning
for the dead.

costly coverings," as Marck, Rosenmüller, and others erroneously
assume. Moreover, this was not done "with the intention of
impelling the men to shed hotter tears through the lowing and
groaning of the cattle" (Theodoret); or "to set before them
as in a mirror, through the sufferings of the innocent brutes,
their own great guilt" (Chald.); but it was a manifestation of
the thought, that just as the animals which live with man are
drawn into fellowship with his sin, so their sufferings might
also help to appease the wrath of God. And although this
thought might not be free from superstition, there lay at the
foundation of it this deep truth, that the irrational creature is
made subject to vanity on account of man's sin, and sighs
along with man for liberation from the bondage of corruption
(Rom. viii. 19 sqq.). We cannot therefore take the words
"cry mightily unto God" as referring only to the men, as
many commentators have done, in opposition to the context;
but must regard "man and beast" as the subject of this clause
also, since the thought that even the beasts cry to or call upon
God in distress has its scriptural warrant in Joel i. 20.

Ver. 10. But however deep the penitential mourning of
Nineveh might be, and however sincere the repentance of the
people, when they acted according to the king's command;
the repentance was not a lasting one, or permanent in its
effects. Nor did it evince a thorough conversion to God, but
was merely a powerful incitement to conversion, a waking up
out of the careless security of their life of sin, an endeavour to
forsake their evil ways which did not last very long. The statement in ver. 10, that "God saw their doing, that they turned
from their evil ways; and He repented of the evil that He had
said that He would do to them, and did it not" (cf. Ex. xxxii. 14),
can be reconciled with this without difficulty. The repentance
of the Ninevites, even if it did not last, showed, at any rate, a
susceptibility on the part of the heathen for the word of God,
and their willingness to turn and forsake their evil and ungodly
ways; so that God, according to His compassion, could extend
His grace to them in consequence. God always acts in this
way. He not only forgives the converted man, who lays aside
his sin, and walks in newness of life; but He has mercy also
upon the penitent who confesses and mourns over his sin, and
is willing to amend. The Lord also directed Jonah to preach

repentance to Nineveh; not that this capital of the heathen
world might be converted at once to faith in the living God,
and its inhabitants be received into the covenant of grace which
He had made with Israel, but simply to give His people Israel
a practical proof that He was the God of the heathen also, and
could prepare for Himself even among them a people of His
possession.   Moreover, the readiness, with which the Ninevites hearkened to the word of God that was proclaimed to
them and repented, showed that with all the depth to which
they were sunken in idolatry and vice they were at that time
not yet ripe for the judgment of extermination.   The punishment was therefore deferred by the long-suffering of God, until
this great heathen city, in its further development into a God-
opposing imperial power, seeking to subjugate all nations, and
make itself the mistress of the earth, had filled up the measure
of its sins, and had become ripe for that destruction which
the prophet Nahum predicted, and the Median king Cyaxares
inflicted upon it in alliance with Nabopolassar of Babylonia.

JONAH'S DISCONTENT AND CORRECTION.—CHAP. IV.

Vers. 1–5. Jonah, provoked at the sparing of Nineveh,
prayed in his displeasure to Jehovah to take his soul from him,
as his proclamation had not been fulfilled (vers. 1–3). וַיֵּרַע אֶל י',
it was evil for Jonah, i.e. it vexed, irritated him, not merely it
displeased him, for which יֵרַע בְּעֵינָיו is generally used. The construction with אֶל resembles that with לְ in Neh. ii. 10, xiii. 8.
רָעָה גְדוֹלָה, "a great evil," serves simply to strengthen the idea
of יֵרַע. The great vexation grew even to anger (יִחַר לוֹ; cf. Gen.
xxx. 2, etc.).   The fact that the predicted destruction of Nineveh had not taken place excited his discontent and wrath.   And
he tried to quarrel with God, by praying to Jehovah.[1]   "*Alas*
(אָנָּא as in ch. i. 14), *Jehovah, was not this my word* (*i.e.* did I

---

[1] Calvin observes upon this : " He prayed in a tumult, as if reproving
God. We must necessarily recognise a certain amount of piety in this
prayer of Jonah, and at the same time many faults. There was so far
piety in it, that he directed his complaints to God. For hypocrites, even
when they address God, are nevertheless hostile to Him. But Jonah,

not say so to myself) *when I was still in my land* (in Palestine)?" What his word or his thought then was, he does not say; but it is evident from what follows: viz. that Jehovah would not destroy Nineveh, if its inhabitants repented. '*Al-kēn*, therefore, *sc.* because this was my saying. קִדַּמְתִּי, προέφθασα, *I prevented to flee to Tarshish, i.e.* I endeavoured, by a flight to Tarshish, to prevent, *sc.* what has now taken place, namely, that Thou dost not fulfil Thy word concerning Nineveh, *because I know that Thou art a God gracious and merciful*, etc. (compare Ex. xxxiv. 6 and xxxii. 14, as in Joel ii. 13). The prayer which follows, "*Take my life from me*," calls to mind the similar prayer of Elijah in 1 Kings xix. 4; but the motive assigned is a different one. Whilst Elijah adds, "for I am not better than my fathers," Jonah adds, "*for death is better to me than life*." This difference must be distinctly noticed, as it brings out the difference in the state of mind of the two prophets. In the inward conflict that had come upon Elijah he wished for death, because he did not see the expected result of his zeal for the Lord of Sabaoth; in other words, it was from spiritual despair, caused by the apparent failure of his labours. Jonah, on the other hand, did not wish to live any longer, because God had not carried out His threat against Nineveh. His weariness of life arose, not like Elijah's from stormy zeal for the honour of God and His kingdom, but from vexation at the non-fulfilment of his prophecy. This vexation was not occasioned, however, by offended dignity, or by anxiety or fear lest men should regard him as a liar or babbler (ψευδο-επής τε καὶ βωμολόχος, Cyr. Al.; ψεύστης, Theodoret; *vanus et mendax*, Calvin and others); nor was he angry, as Calvin supposes, because he associated his office with the honour of God, and was unwilling that the name of God should be exposed to the scoffing of the heathen, *quasi de nihilo terreret*, or "because he saw that it would furnish material for impious blasphemies if God changed His purpose, or if He did not abide by His word;" but, as Luther observes (in his remarks on Jonah's flight), "he was hostile to the city of Nineveh, and

when he complains, although he does not keep within proper bounds, but is carried away by a blind and vicious impulse, is nevertheless prepared to submit himself to God, as we shall presently see. This is the reason why he is said to have prayed."

still held a Jewish and carnal view of God" (for the further development of this view, see the remarks above, at p. 392). That this was really Jonah's view, is proved by Luther from the fact that God reproves his displeasure and anger in these words, " Should I not spare Nineveh?" etc. (ver. 11). " He hereby implies that Jonah was displeased at the fact that God had spared the city, and was angry because He had not destroyed it as he had preached, and would gladly have seen." Offended vanity or unintelligent zeal for the honour of God would have been reproved by God in different terms from those in which Jonah was actually reproved, according to the next verse (ver. 4), where Jehovah asks the prophet, " *Is thine anger justly kindled?*" הֵיטֵב is adverbial, as in Deut. ix. 21, xiii. 15, etc., *bene, probe, recte,* δικαίως (Symm.).

Then Jonah went out of Nineveh, sat down on the east of the city, where Nineveh was bounded by the mountains, from which he could overlook the city, made himself a hut there, and sat under it in the shade, till he saw what would become of the city, *i.e.* what fate would befal it (ver. 5). This verse is regarded by many commentators as a supplementary remark, וַיֵּצֵא, with the verbs which follow, being rendered in the pluperfect : "Jonah had gone out of the city," etc. We grant that this is grammatically admissible, but it cannot be shown to be necessary, and is indeed highly improbable. If, for instance, Jonah went out of Nineveh before the expiration of the forty days, to wait for the fulfilment of his prophecy, in a hut to the east of the city, he could not have been angry at its non-fulfilment before the time arrived, nor could God have reproved him for his anger before that time. The divine correction of the dissatisfied prophet, which is related in vers. 6–11, cannot have taken place till the forty days had expired. But this correction is so closely connected with Jonah's departure from the city and settlement to the east of it, to wait for the final decision as to its fate (ver. 5), that we cannot possibly separate it, so as to take the verbs in ver. 5 as pluperfects, or those in vers. 6–11 as historical imperfects. There is no valid ground for so forced an assumption as this. As the expression וַיֵּרַע אֶל יוֹנָה in ch. iv. 1, which is appended to וְלֹא עָשָׂה in ch. iii. 10, shows that Jonah did not become irritated and angry till after God had failed to carry out His threat concerning Nineveh, and that it was then that he poured out his discontent in a reproachful prayer to God (ver. 2), there is nothing whatever to force us to the assumption that Jonah had left Nineveh before the fortieth day.[1] Jonah had no reason to be afraid of perishing with the city. If he had faith, which we cannot deny, he could rely upon it that God would not order him, His own servant, to perish with the ungodly, but when the proper time arrived, would direct him to leave the city. But when forty days elapsed, and nothing occurred to indicate the immediate or speedy fall of the city, and he was reproved by God for his anger on that account in these words, " Art thou rightly or justly angry?" the answer from God determined him to leave the city and wait outside, in front of it, to see what fate would befal it. For since this answer still left it open, as a possible thing, that the judgment might burst upon the city, Jonah interpreted it in harmony with his own inclination, as signifying that the judgment was only postponed, not removed, and therefore resolved to wait in a hut outside the city, and watch for the issue of the whole affair.[2] But his hope was disappointed, and his remaining there became, quite contrary to his intention, an occasion for completing his correction.

Vers. 6–11. Jehovah-God appointed a *Qiqayon*, which grew up over Jonah, to give him shade over his head, " *to deliver him from his evil.*" The *Qiqayon*, which Luther renders gourd (*Kürbiss*) after the LXX., but describes in his commentary on the book of Jonah as the *vitis alba*, is, according to Jerome, the shrub called *Elkeroa* in Syriac, a very common shrub in Pales-

---

[1] There is no hold in the narrative for Marck's conjecture, that God had already communicated to him His resolution not to destroy Nineveh, because of the repentance of the people, and that this was the reason for his anger.

[2] Theod. Mops. correctly observes, that " when he reflected upon the greatness of the threat, he imagined that something might possibly occur after all." And Calvin better still, that " although forty days had passed, Jonah stood as if fastened to the spot, because he could not yet believe that what he had proclaimed according to the command of God would fail to be effected. . . . This was the cause, therefore, of his still remaining, viz. because he thought, that although the punishment from God had been suspended, yet his preaching had surely not been in vain, but the destruction of the city would take place. This was the reason for his waiting on after the time fixed, as though the result were still doubtful."

tine, which grows in sandy places, having broad leaves that throw a pleasant shadow, and which shoots up to a considerable height in a very few days.[1]   The *Elkeroa*, however, which Niebuhr also saw at Basra (*Beschreib. v. Arab.* p. 148) and describes in a similar manner, is the *ricinus* or *palma Christi*, the miraculous tree ; and, according to Kimchi and the Talmudists, it was the *Kik* or *Kiki* of the Egyptians, from which an oil was obtained according to Herodotus (ii. 94) and Pliny (*Hist. n.* xv. 7), as was the case according to Niebuhr with the *Elkeroa*.   Its rapid growth is also mentioned by Pliny, who calls it *ricinus* (see *Ges. thes.* p. 1214).   God caused this shrub to grow up with miraculous rapidity, to such a height that it cast a shade upon Jonah's head, to procure him deliverance (לְהַצִּיל לוֹ) " from his evil," *i.e.* not from the burning heat of the sun (*ab æstu solis*), from which he suffered in the hut which he had run up so hastily with twigs, but from his displeasure or vexation, the evil from which he suffered according to ver. 3 (Rosenmüller, Hitzig).   The variation in the names of the Deity in vers. 6–9 is worthy of notice.   The creation of the miraculous tree to give shade to Jonah is ascribed to *Jehovah-Elohim* in ver. 6.   This composite name, which occurs very rarely except in Gen. ii. and iii. (see comm. on Gen. ii. 4), is chosen here to help the transition from *Jehovah* in ver. 4 to *Elohim* in vers. 7, 8. *Jehovah*, who replies to the prophet concerning his discontented complaint (ver. 4) as *Elohim*, *i.e.* as the divine creative power, causes the miraculous tree to spring up, to heal Jonah of his chagrin.   And to the same end *hâ-Elohim*, *i.e.* the personal God, prepares the worm which punctures the miraculous tree and causes it to wither away (ver. 7); and this is also helped by the east wind appointed by *Elohim*, *i.e.* the Deity ruling over nature (ver. 8), to bring about the correction of the prophet, who was murmuring against God.   Hence the different names of God are employed with thoughtful deliberation.   Jonah rejoiced exceedingly at the miraculous growth of the shrub which pro-

---

[1] Jerome describes it thus : " A kind of bush or shrub, having broad leaves like vine leaves, casting a very dense shadow, and sustaining itself by its trunk, which grows very abundantly in Palestine, and chiefly in sandy places. If placed in sowing land, being quickly nourished, it grows up into a tree, and in a very few days what you saw as nothing but a herb you now look upon as a small tree."

vided shade for him, because he probably saw therein a sign of
the goodness of God and of the divine approval of his intention
to wait for the destruction of Nineveh. But this joy was not
to last long.—Ver. 8. On the rising of the dawn of the very
next day, God appointed a worm, which punctured the miraculous tree so that it withered away; and when the sun arose
He also appointed a sultry east wind, and the sun smote upon
Jonah's head, so that he fainted away. *Chărīshīth*, from *chârash*,
to be silent or quiet, is to be taken when used of the wind in
the sense of sultry, as in the Chaldee (LXX. συγκαίων). The
meaning *ventus, qualis flat tempore arandi*, derived from *chârish*,
the ploughing (Abulw.), or autumnal east wind (Hitzig), is far
less suitable. When Jonah fainted away in consequence of the
sun-stroke (for *hith'allēph*, see at Amos viii. 13), he wished himself dead, since death was better for him than life (see ver. 3).
יִשְׁאַל אֶת־נַפְשׁוֹ לָמוּת, as in 1 Kings xix. 4, " he wished that his
soul might die," a kind of accusative with the infinitive (cf.
Ewald, § 336, *b*). But God answered, as in ver. 4, by asking
whether he was justly angry. Instead of Jehovah (ver. 4) we
have *Elohim* mentioned here, and *Jehovah* is not introduced as
speaking till ver. 9. We have here an intimation, that just as
Jonah's wish to die was simply an expression of the feelings of
his mind, so the admonitory word of God was simply a divine
voice within him setting itself against his murmuring. It was
not till he had persisted in his ill-will, even after this divine
admonition within, that Jehovah pointed out to him how wrong
his murmuring was. Jehovah's speaking in ver. 9 is a manifestation of the divine will by supernatural inspiration. Jehovah
directs Jonah's attention to the contradiction into which he has
fallen, by feeling compassion for the withering of the miraculous tree, and at the same time murmuring because God has had
compassion upon Nineveh with its many thousands of living
beings, and has spared the city for the sake of these souls, many
of whom have no idea whatever of right or wrong. *Chastâ*:
" *Thou hast pitied the Qiqayon, at which thou hast not laboured,
and which thou hast not caused to grow; for* (אֲשֶׁר = בֶּן שֶׁבִּן) *son
of a night*"—*i.e.* in a night, or over night—"*has it grown, and
over night perished, and I should not pity Nineveh?*" וַאֲנִי is
a question; but this is only indicated by the tone. If Jonah
feels pity for the withering of a small shrub, which he neither

planted nor tended, nor caused to grow, shall God not have
pity with much greater right upon the creatures whom He has
created and has hitherto sustained, and spare the great city
Nineveh, in which more than 120,000 are living, who cannot
distinguish their right hand from the left, and also much cattle?
Not to be able to distinguish between the right hand and the
left is a sign of mental infancy. This is not to be restricted,
however, to the very earliest years, say the first three, but must
be extended to the age of seven years, in which children first
learn to distinguish with certainty between right and left, since,
according to M. v. Niebuhr (p. 278), "the end of the seventh
year is a very common division of age (it is met with, for
example, even among the Persians), and we may regard it as
certain that it would be adopted by the Hebrews, on account of
the importance they attached to the number seven." A hundred and twenty thousand children under seven years of age
would give a population of six hundred thousand, since, according to Niebuhr, the number of children of the age mentioned
is one-fifth of the whole population, and there is no ground for
assuming that the proportion in the East would be essentially
different. This population is quite in accordance with the size
of the city.[1] Children who cannot distinguish between right
and left, cannot distinguish good from evil, and are not yet
accountable. The allusion to the multitude of unaccountable
children contains a fresh reason for sparing the city: God

---

[1] "Nineveh, in the broader sense," says M. v. Niebuhr, " covers an area of
about 400 English square miles. Hence there were about 40,000 persons
to the square mile. Jones (in a paper on Nineveh) estimates the population of the chief city, according to the area, at 174,000 souls. So that we may
reckon the population of the four larger walled cities at 350,000. There
remain, therefore, for the smaller places and the level ground, 300,000 men
on about sixteen square miles; that is to say, nearly 20,000 men upon the
square mile." He then shows, from the agricultural conditions in the district of Elberfeld and the province of Naples, how thoroughly this population suits such a district. In the district of Elberfeld there are, in round
numbers, 22,000 persons to the square mile, or, apart from the two large
towns, 10,000. And if we take into account the difference in fertility, this
is about the same density of population as that of Nineveh. The province
of Naples bears a very great resemblance to Nineveh, not only in the kind
of cultivation, but also in the fertility of the soil. And there, in round
numbers, 46,000 are found to the square mile, or, exclusive of the capital,
22,000 souls.

would have been obliged to destroy so many thousand innocent ones along with the guilty. Besides this, there was "much cattle" in the city. "Oxen were certainly superior to shrubs. If Jonah was right in grieving over one withered shrub, it would surely be a harder and more cruel thing for so many innocent animals to perish" (Calvin). "What could Jonah say to this? He was obliged to keep silence, defeated, as it were, by his own sentence" (Luther). The history, therefore, breaks off with these words of God, to which Jonah could make no reply, because the object of the book was now attained,—namely, to give the Israelites an insight into the true nature of the compassion of the Lord, which embraces all nations with equal love. Let us, however, give heed to the sign of the prophet Jonah, and hold fast to the confession of Him who could say of Himself, "Behold, a greater than Jonah is here!"

MICAH

INTRODUCTION.

1.   PERSON OF THE PROPHET. — *Micah*, מִיכָה, an abbreviated form of מִיכָיָה (Micaiah), as he is called in Jer. xxvi. 18, which is also a contraction of מִיכָיְהוּ, " who is as Jehovah ? "—*i.e.* one dedicated to Jehovah the incomparable God (Greek, Μιχαίας; Vulg. *Michæas* or *Micha*, Neh. xi. 17)—is called *hammorashtī*, the Morashtite, *i.e.* sprung from Moresheth-Gath in the plain of Judah (see at ch. i. 14), to distinguish him from the elder prophet Micah the son of Imlah (1 Kings xxii. 8 sqq.), as well as from other persons of the same name, of whom ten are met with in the Old Testament, apart from Maacah the wife of Rehoboam, a grand-daughter of Absalom (1 Kings xv. 2, 10, 13; 2 Chron. xi. 20 sqq.), who is also called מִיכָיְהוּ in 2 Chron. xiii. 2 (see Caspari on Micha, p. 3 sqq.). Our Micah was therefore a Judæan, and prophesied, according to the heading to his book, in the reigns of Jotham, Ahaz, and Hezekiah, kings of Judah ; so that he was contemporaneous with Isaiah. He prophesied " concerning Samaria and Jerusalem," the capitals of the two kingdoms, that is to say, concerning all Israel, the fate of which was determined by the circumstances and fates of the two capitals. The correctness of this statement, and at the same time the genuineness of the heading, are confirmed by the contents of the book. Micah not only predicts, in ch. i. 6, 7, the destruction of Samaria, which took place in the sixth year of Hezekiah ; but he also mentions Asshur, the great enemy of Israel at that time, as the representative of the power of the world in its hostility to the kingdom of God (ch. v. 4) ; and he agrees so thoroughly with Isaiah in his description of the prevailing moral corruption, as well as in his Messianic

prophecies, that we are warranted in inferring the contemporaneous labours of the two prophets (compare Mic. ii. 11 with
Isa. xxviii. 7 ; Mic. iii. 5–7 with Isa. xxix. 9–12 ; Mic. iii. 12
with Isa. xxxii. 13, 14 ; and Mic. iv. 1–5 with Isa. ii. 2–5 ;
Mic. v. 2–4 with Isa. vii. 14 and ix. 5). To this we may add
the account in Jer. xxvi. 18, 19, that certain men of the elders
of Judah, when seeking to vindicate Jeremiah, who was condemned to death on account of his prophecies concerning the
destruction of Jerusalem, quoted word for word Mic. iii. 12,
to show that in the days of Hezekiah Micah had predicted the
destruction of Jerusalem, without having been put to death by
king Hezekiah and all Judah. It is true that Hitzig, Ewald,
and others, have founded an argument upon this against the
correctness of the heading to our book, according to which
Micah prophesied not only under Hezekiah, but also under
Jotham and Ahaz, interpreting it as meaning that the elders
of Judah knew from good historical tradition the time when
the particular words in Mic. iii.–v. had first been uttered.
But they are wrong in this. For even if Micah had uttered
this prophecy for the first time in the reign of Hezekiah, it
would by no means follow that he had not also prophesied
before that, namely, in the reign of Hezekiah. The relation
in which Mic. iv. 1–5 stands to Isa. ii. 2–5 is sufficient of itself
to point to the times of Jotham (see at ch. iv. 1). Again,
Mic. vi. 16 does not suit the times of Hezekiah, but only those
of Ahaz, who walked to such an extent in the ways of the kings
of Israel (2 Kings xvi. 3 ; 2 Chron. xxviii. 2), that Judah could
be charged with holding by the statutes of Omri and all the
deeds of the house of Ahab. Moreover, the assumption that
the elders of Judah in the time of Jehoiakim knew from good
traditional authority the precise time in which Micah uttered
that threat, is quite an unfounded one. They simply knew
that Micah's prophetic writings sprang from the time of
Hezekiah ; and of the kings under whom Micah prophesied
according to the statement of the writings themselves (ch. i. 1),
they mention only Hezekiah, because he was the only one who
" constituted a spiritual authority " (Hengstenberg). But the
fact that Micah's prophecies were committed to writing in the
time of Hezekiah by no means precludes the supposition that
either the prophecies themselves, or certain portions of them,

were uttered orally to the people before that time. Hitzig's attempt to prove that all the three addresses in our book were composed in the time of Hezekiah, is founded upon a false historical interpretation, and upon unscriptural ideas of the nature of prophecy.

We know nothing more about the circumstances of Micah's life, than what may be gathered from his writings. According to these, he no doubt prophesied in Jerusalem, the capital of his native land. This is evident from the fact that he chiefly condemns the moral corruption of the great and mighty men of the kingdom, and makes Zion and Jerusalem for the most part the centre of his prophecies. There is not sufficient ground for Ewald's assertion, that there are many signs which indicate an inhabitant of the plain. The introduction of the names of particular places in Judah in ch. i. 10–15 furnishes no proof of any "peculiar interest in the Jewish country, more especially the Jewish lowland, as being his home." Only a portion of the places mentioned in this passage were situated in the lowland. Moreover, Isaiah also enumerates a whole list of places in Judah (Isa. x. 28–32), and is minutely acquainted with the circumstances of Zebulun and Naphtali, and the neighbourhood of the Sea of Galilee (ch. viii. 23), although he was settled in Jerusalem, and had probably been born there. Still more precarious is the inference that has been drawn from Micah's somewhat rough and rugged style. For all that can be adduced in support of this is confined to the rapid and abrupt transitions from threatening to promise, in which he resembles Hosea (vid. ch. ii. 1–11, 12, 13, iii. 9–12, iv. 1 sqq.), and generally from one subject to another (e.g. ch. vii. 1–7, vii. 11–13), but more especially from one person to another, or from one number and gender to another (ch. i. 10, vi. 16, vii. 15–19). This may be all explained from the vivacity of his own individuality, and the excited state of his mind; and simply indicates the boldness of his words, but not any want of culture in his style. His words are never deficient in clearness or evenness; whilst in abundance of figures, similes (ch. i. 8, 16, ii. 12, 13, iv. 9, etc.), and rhetorical tropes, as well as in speciality, paronomasia, in play upon words (ch. i. 10–15), and dialogue (ch. ii. 7–11, vi. 1–8, vii. 7–20), his style resembles that of his highly cultivated contemporary Isaiah. The traditional accounts respecting his descent from the tribe of Ephraim, his death, and his grave, contained in Ps. Dorotheus and Ps. Epiphanius (collected in Carpzovii, *Introd.* iii. pp. 373–4), have partly originated in the confounding of our Micah with the elder Micah the son of Imlah, who lived in the reign of Ahab, and are partly inferences from the heading to our book.

2. THE BOOK OF MICAH.—The contents of the book consist of three prophetic addresses, which are clearly distinguished from one another in form by similarity of introduction (all three commencing with שִׁמְעוּ, ch. i. 2, iii. 1, vi. 1), and substantially by their contents, which pass through the various stages of reproof, threat, and promise, and are thereby rounded off ; so that all attempts at any other division, such as that of Ewald to connect ch. iii. with the first address, or to arrange the book in two parts (ch. i.–v. and vi. vii.), are obviously arbitrary. Ch. iii. can only be connected with ch. i. and ii. so as to form one address, on the groundless assumption that ch. ii. 12, 13 are a later gloss that has crept into the text; and though the וְאֹמַר before שִׁמְעוּ־נָא in ch. iii. 1 does indeed connect the second address more closely with the first than with the third, it by no means warrants our dividing the whole book into two parts. In the three addresses, ch. i. ii., iii.–v., and vi. vii., we have not " three prophecies of Micah, delivered to the people at three different times," as Hitzig and Maurer still suppose, but merely a condensation rhetorically arranged of the essential contents of his verbal utterances, as committed to writing by Micah himself at the end of his prophetic course in the time of Hezekiah. For these addresses are proved to be merely portions or sections of a single whole, by the absence of all reference to the concrete circumstances of any particular portion of time, and still more by their organic combination, as seen in the clearly marked and carefully planned progressive movement apparent in their contents. In the *first* address, after a general announcement of judgment on account of the sins of Israel (ch. i. 2–5), Micah predicts the destruction of Samaria (vers. 6, 7), and the devastation of Judah with the deportation of its inhabitants (vers. 8–16), and justifies this threat by an earnest and brief reproof of the existing acts of injustice and violence on the part of the great men (ch. ii. 1–5), and a sharp correc-

tion of their abettors the false prophets (vers. 6–11) ; after which this address closes with a brief promise of the eventual restoration of the remnant of Israel to favour (vers. 12, 13). The *second* address spreads itself out still more elaborately in the first half (ch. iii.) over the sins and crimes of the heads of the nation, viz. the princes, the false prophets, the unjust judges and bad priests ; and because of these sins threatens the destruction and utter devastation of Zion, and the temple hill. As an antithesis to this threat, the second half (ch. iv. and v.) contains a promise, commencing with the opening of a prospect of the glorification of Zion and Israel at the end of the days (ch. iv. 1–7), advancing to an assurance of the restoration of the former dominion of the daughter of Zion, after the people have first been carried away to Babel, and rescued again out of the hand of their enemies, and of her triumph in the last conflict with the nations of the world (vers. 8–14), and culminating in the announcement of the birth of the great Ruler in Israel, who will arise out of Bethlehem, and feed His people in the majesty of Jehovah (ch. v. 1–5), and not only protect the rescued remnant of Jacob against the attacks of the imperial kingdom, but exalt it into a beneficent, and at the same time fearful, power to the heathen nations (vers. 6–8), and establish a kingdom of blessed peace (vers. 9–14). The *third* address sets forth the way to salvation in the dramatic dress of a law-suit between Jehovah and His people, by exhibiting the divine benefits for which Israel had repaid its God with ingratitude, and by a repeated allusion to the prevailing sins and unrighteousness which God must punish (ch. vi.), and also by showing how the consciousness of misery will lead to the penitential confession of guilt and to conversion, and by encouraging to believing trust in the compassion or fidelity of the Lord, who will once more have compassion upon His people, rebuild Zion, and humble the foe, and by renewing the miracles of the olden time fill all nations with fear of His omnipotence (ch. vii. 1–17); after which the prophet closes his book with praise for the sin-forgiving grace of the Lord (vers. 18–20).

From this general survey of the contents of the three addresses, their internal connection may be at once perceived. In the first the threatening of judgment predominates; in the second the announcement of the Messianic salvation; in the third there follows the *parænesis* or admonition to repentance and humiliation under the chastising hand of the Lord, in order to participate in the promised salvation. As this admonition rests upon the threat of judgment and promise of salvation in the two previous addresses, so does the allusion to the judgment contained in the words, "Then will they cry to Jehovah, and He will not answer them" (ch. iii. 4), presuppose the announcement in ch. i. of the judgment about to burst upon the land, without which it would be perfectly unintelligible. Consequently there can be no doubt whatever that Micah has simply concentrated the quintessence of his oral discourses into the addresses contained in his book. This quintessence, moreover, shows clearly enough that our prophet was not at all behind his contemporary Isaiah, either in the clearness and distinctness of his Messianic announcements, or in the power and energy with which he combated the sins and vices of the nation. There is simply this essential difference, so far as the latter point is concerned, that he merely combats the religious and moral corruptness of the rulers of the nation, and does not touch upon their conduct on its political side. (For the exegetical literature, see my *Lehrbuch der Einleitung*, p. 296.)

EXPOSITION.

I. ISRAEL'S BANISHMENT INTO EXILE, AND RESTORATION.—
CHAP. I. AND II.

The prophet's first address is throughout of a threatening and punitive character; it is not till quite the close, that the sun of divine grace breaks brightly shining through the thunder clouds of judgment. The announcement of the judgment upon Samaria as well as upon the kingdom of Judah and Jerusalem forms the first part (ch. i. 2–16); the reproof of the sins, especially of the unrighteousness of the great and mighty of the nation, the second part (ch. ii. 1–11); and a brief but very comprehensive announcement of the salvation that will dawn upon the remnant of all Israel after the judgment, the conclusion of the address (ch. ii. 12, 13).

THE JUDGMENT UPON SAMARIA AND JUDAH.—CHAP. I.

Micah, commencing with the appeal to all nations to observe the coming of the Lord for judgment upon the earth (vers. 2–4), announces to the people of Israel, on account of its sins and its apostasy from the Lord, the destruction of Samaria (vers. 5–7) and the spreading of the judgment over Judah; and shows how, passing from place to place, and proceeding to Jerusalem, and even farther, it will throw the kingdom into deep lamentation on account of the carrying away of its inhabitants.

Vers. 1–7. The heading in ver. 1 has been explained in the introduction. Vers. 2–4 form the introduction to the prophet's address. Ver. 2. "*Hear, all ye nations: observe, O earth, and that which fills it: and let the Lord Jehovah be a witness against you, the Lord out of His holy palace. Ver. 3. For, behold, Jehovah cometh forth from His place, and cometh down, and marcheth over the high places of the earth. Ver. 4. And the mountains will melt under Him, and the valleys split, like wax before the fire, like water poured out upon a slope.*" The introductory words, "Hear, ye nations all," are taken by Micah from his earlier namesake the son of Imlah (1 Kings xxii. 28). As the latter, in his attack upon the false prophets, called all nations as witnesses to confirm the truth of his prophecy, so does Micah the Morashtite commence his prophetic testimony with the same appeal, so as to announce his labours at the very outset as a continuation of the activity of his predecessor who had been so zealous for the Lord. As the son of Imlah had to contend against the false prophets as seducers of the nation, so has also the Morashtite (compare ch. ii. 6, 11, iii. 5, 11); and as the former had to announce to both kingdoms the judgment that would come upon them on account of their sins, so has also the latter; and he does it by frequently referring to the prophecy of the elder Micah, not only by designating the false prophets as those who walk after the *rūăch* and lie, *sheqer* (ch. ii. 11), which recals to mind the *rūăch sheqer* of the prophets of Ahab (1 Kings xxii. 22, 23), but also in his use of the figures of the horn of iron in ch. iv. 13, 14 (compare the horns of iron of the false prophet Zedekiah in 1 Kings xxii. 11), and of the smiting upon the cheek in ch. iv. 14 (compare 1 Kings xxii. 14). '*Ammīm kullām* does not mean all the

tribes of Israel; still less does it mean warlike nations. ʽ*Ammīm*
never has the second meaning, and the first it has only in the
primitive language of the Pentateuch.   But here both these
meanings are precluded by the parallel אֶרֶץ וּמְלֹאָהּ; for this
expression invariably signifies the whole earth, with that which
fills it, except in such a case as Jer. viii. 16, where *'erets* is
restricted to the land of Israel by the preceding *hâʼârets*, or
Ezek. xii. 19, where it is so restricted by the suffix *'artsâh*.
The appeal to the earth and its fulness is similar to the appeals
to the heaven and the earth in Isa. i. 2 and Deut. xxxii. 1.
All nations, yea the whole earth, and all creatures upon it, are
to hear, because the judgment which the prophet has to announce to Israel affects the whole earth (vers. 3, 4), the judgment upon Israel being connected with the judgment upon all
nations, or forming a portion of that judgment.   In the second
clause of the verse, "the Lord Jehovah be witness against
you," it is doubtful who is addressed in the expression " against
you."   The words cannot well be addressed to all nations and
to the earth, because the Lord only rises up as a witness against
the man who has despised His word and transgressed His
commandments.   For being a witness is not equivalent to
witnessing or giving testimony by words,—say, for example, by
the admonitory and corrective address of the prophet which
follows, as C. B. Michaelis supposes,—but refers to the practical
testimony given by the Lord in the judgment (vers. 3 sqq.), as
in Mal. iii. 5 and Jer. xlii. 5.   Now, although the Lord is described as the Judge of the world in vers. 3 and 4, yet, according
to vers. 5 sqq., He only comes to execute judgment upon Israel.
Consequently we must refer the words " to you" to Israel, or
rather to the capitals Samaria and Jerusalem mentioned in ver. 1,
just as in Nahum i. 8 the suffix simply refers to the Nineveh
mentioned in the heading, to which there has been no further
allusion in vers. 2–7.   This view is also favoured by the fact
that Micah summons all nations to hear his word, in the same
sense as his earlier namesake in 1 Kings xxii. 28.   What the
prophet announces in word, the Lord will confirm by deed,—
namely, by executing the predicted judgment,—and indeed
"the Lord out of His holy temple," *i.e.* the heaven where He
is enthroned (Ps. xi. 4); for (ver. 3) the Lord will rise up
from thence, and striding over the high places of the earth, *i.e.*

as unbounded Ruler of the world (cf. Amos iv. 13 and Deut. xxxii. 13), will come down in fire, so that the mountains melt before Him, that is to say, as Judge of the world. The description of this theophany is founded upon the idea of a terrible storm and earthquake, as in Ps. xviii. 8 sqq. The mountains melt (Judg. v. 4 and Ps. lxviii. 9) with the streams of water, which discharge themselves from heaven (Judg. v. 4), and the valleys split with the deep channels cut out by the torrents of water. The similes, "like wax," etc. (as in Ps. lxviii. 3), and "like water," etc., are intended to express the complete dissolution of mountains and valleys. The actual facts answering to this description are the destructive influences exerted upon nature by great national judgments.

This judicial interposition on the part of God is occasioned by the sin of Israel. Ver. 5. *"For the apostasy of Jacob* (is) *all this, and for the sins of the house of Israel. Who is Jacob's apostasy? is it not Samaria? And who Judah's high places? is it not Jerusalem?* Ver. 6. *Therefore I make Samaria into a stone-heap of the field, into plantations of vines; and I pour her stones into the valley, and I will lay bare her foundations.* Ver. 7. *And all her stone images will be beaten to pieces, and all her lovers' gifts be burned with fire, and all her idols will I make into a waste: for she has gathered them of prostitute's hire, and to prostitute's hire shall they return."* "All this" refers to the coming of Jehovah to judgment announced in vers. 3, 4. This takes place on account of the apostasy and the sins of Israel. בְּ (for) used to denote reward or wages, as in 2 Sam. iii. 27 compared with ver. 30. Jacob and Israel in ver. 5a are synonymous, signifying the whole of the covenant nation, as we may see from the fact that in ver. 5b Jacob and not Israel is the epithet applied to the ten tribes in distinction from Judah. מִי, who?—referring to the author. The apostasy of Israel originates with Samaria; the worship on the high places with Jerusalem. The capitals of the two kingdoms are the authors of the apostasy, as the centres and sources of the corruption which has spread from them over the kingdoms. The allusion to the *bâmōth* of the illegal worship of the high places, which even the most godly kings were unable to abolish (see at 1 Kings xv. 14), shows, moreover, that פֶּשַׁע denotes that religious apostasy from Jehovah which was formally sanctioned in the

kingdom of the ten tribes by the introduction of the calf-worship. But because this apostasy commenced in the kingdom
of the ten tribes, the pnnishment would fall upon this kingdom
first, and Samaria would be utterly destroyed. Stone-heaps of
the field and vineyard plantations harmonize badly, in Hitzig's
view : he therefore proposes to alter the text. But there is no
necessity for this. The point of comparison is simply that
Samaria will be so destroyed, that not a single trace of a city
will be left, and the site thereof will become like a ploughed
field or plain. הַשָּׂדֶה is added to עִי, a heap of ruins or stones,
to strengthen it. Samaria shall become like a heap, not of
ruins or building stones, but of stones collected from the field.
לְמַטָּעֵי כֶרֶם, i.e. into arable land upon which you can plant vineyards. The figure answers to the situation of Samaria upon
a hill in a very fruitful region, which was well adapted for
planting vineyards (see at Amos iii. 9). The situation of the
city helps to explain the casting of its stones into the valley.
Laying bare the foundations denotes destruction to the very
foundation (cf. Ps. cxxxvii. 7). On the destruction of the city
all its idols will be annihilated. *P*ᵉ*sīlīm*, idols, as in Isa. x. 10 ;
not wooden idols, however, to which the expression *yukkattū*,
smitten to pieces, would not apply, but stone idols, from *pâsal*
(Ex. xxxiv. 1). By the lovers' gifts ('*ethnân*, see at Hos. ix. 1)
we are to understand, not "the riches of the city or their possessions, inasmuch as the idolaters regarded their wealth and
prosperity as a reward from their gods, according to Hos. ii.
7, 14" (Rashi, Hitzig, and others), but the temple gifts, "gifts
suspended in the temples and sacred places in honour of the
gods" (Rosenmüller), by which the temple worship with its
apparatus were maintained; so that by '*ethnân* we may understand the entire apparatus of religious worship. For the parallelism of the clauses requires that the word should be restricted
to this. עֲצַבִּים are also idolatrous images. "To make them
into a waste," i.e. not only to divest them of their ornament,
but so utterly to destroy them that the place where they
once stood becomes waste. The next clause, containing the
reason, must not be restricted to the '*ătsabbīm*, as Hitzig
supposes, but refers to the two clauses of the first hemistich,
so that *p*ᵉ*sīlīm* and '*ătsabbīm* are to be supplied as objects to
qibbâtsâh (she gathered), and to be regarded as the subject to

yâshûbhû (shall return).   Samaria gathered together the entire
apparatus of her idolatrous worship from prostitute's gifts (the
wages of prostitution), namely, through gifts presented by
the idolaters.   The acquisition of all this is described as the
gain of prostitute's wages, according to the scriptural view that
idolatry was spiritual whoredom.   There is no ground for
thinking of literal wages of prostitution, or money which
flowed into the temples from the voluptuous worship of Aphro-
dite, because Micah had in his mind not literal (heathenish)
idolatry, but simply the transformation of the Jehovah-worship
into idolatry by the worship of Jehovah under the symbols of
the golden calves.   These things return back to the wages of
prostitution, *i.e.* they become this once more (cf. Gen. iii. 19)
by being carried away by the enemies, who conquer the city and
destroy it, and being applied to their idolatrous worship.   On
the capture of cities, the idols and temple treasures were carried
away (cf. Isa. xlvi. 1, 2 ; Dan. i. 3).

Vers. 8–16. The judgment will not stop at Samaria, however, but spread over Judah.   The prophet depicts this by
saying that he will go about mourning as a prisoner, to set
forth the misery that will come upon Judah (vers. 8, 9) ; and
then, to confirm this, he announces to a series of cities the fate
awaiting them, or rather awaiting the kingdom, by a continued
play upon words founded upon their names (vers. 10–15) ; and
finally he summons Zion to deep mourning (ver. 16).   Ver. 8.
" *Therefore will I lament and howl, I will go spoiled and naked :
I will keep lamentation like the jackals, and mourning like the
ostriches.   Ver. 9. For her stripes are malignant ; for it comes
to Judah, reaches to the gate of my people, to Jerusalem.*" עַל־זאת
points back to what precedes, and is then explained in ver. 9.
The prophet will lament over the destruction of Samaria,
because the judgment which has befallen this city will come
upon Judah also.   Micah does not speak in his own name here
as a patriot (Hitzig), but in the name of his nation, with which
he identifies himself as being a member thereof.   This is indisputably evident from the expression אֵילְכָה שִׁילָל וְעָרוֹם, which
describes the costume of a prisoner, not that of a mourner.
The form אילכה with ' appears to have been simply suggested
by אֵילִילָה. שִׁילָל is formed like הֵידָד in Isa. xvi. 9, 10, and other
similar words (see Olshausen, *Gramm.* p. 342).   The Masoretes

have substituted שֹׁלָל, after Job xii. 17, but without the slightest
reason. It does not mean "barefooted," ἀνυπόδετος (LXX.),
for which there was already יָחֵף in the language (2 Sam. xv.
30; Isa. xx. 2, 3; Jer. ii. 25), but plundered, spoiled. עָרוֹם,
naked, *i.e.* without upper garment (see my comm. on 1 Sam.
xix. 24), not merely *vestitu solido et decente privatus.* Mourners
do indeed go barefooted (*yâchēph,* see 2 Sam. xv. 30), and in
deep mourning in a hairy garment (*saq,* 2 Sam. iii. 31; Gen.
xxxvii. 34, etc.), but not plundered and naked. The assertion,
however, that a man was called '*ârōm* when he had put on a
mourning garment (*saq,* sackcloth) in the place of his upper
garment, derives no support from Isa. xx. 2, but rather a refutation. For there the prophet does not go about '*ârōm v⁼yâchēph,*
i.e. in the dress of a prisoner, to symbolize the captivity of
Egypt, till after he has loosened the hairy garment (*saq*) from
his loins, *i.e.* taken it off. And here also the plundering of the
prophet and his walking naked are to be understood in the
same way. Micah's intention is not only to exhibit publicly his
mourning for the approaching calamity of Judah, but also to
set forth in a symbolical form the fate that awaits the Judæans.
And he can only do this by including himself in the nation,
and exhibiting the fate of the nation in his own person. Wailing like jackals and ostriches is a loud, strong, mournful cry,
those animals being distinguished by a mournful wail; see the
comm. on Job xxx. 29, which passage may possibly have floated
before the prophet's mind. Thus shall Judah wail, because the
stroke which falls upon Samaria is malignant, *i.e.* incurable (the
suffix attached to מַכּוֹתֶיהָ refers to *Shōm⁼rōn,* Samaria, in vers.
6 and 7. For the singular of the predicate before a subject
in the plural, see Ewald, § 295, *a,* and 317, *a*). It reaches to
Judah, yea, to Jerusalem. Jerusalem, as the capital, is called
the "gate of my people," because in it *par excellence* the people
went out and in. That עַד is not exclusive here, but inclusive,
embracing the *terminus ad quem,* is evident from the parallel
"even to Judah;" for if it only reached to the border of Judah,
it would not have been able to come to Jerusalem; and still
more clearly so from the description in vers. 10 sqq. The fact
that Jerusalem is not mentioned till after Judah is to be interpreted rhetorically, and not geographically. Even the capital,
where the temple of Jehovah stood, would not be spared.

The penetration of the judgment into Judah is now clearly depicted by an individualizing enumeration of a number of cities which will be smitten by it. Ver. 10. " *Go not to Gath to declare it; weeping, weep not. At Beth-Leafra (dust-home) I have strewed dust upon myself.* Ver. 11. *Pass thou away, O inhabitress of Shafir (beautiful city), stripped in shame. The inhabitress of Zaanan (departure) has not departed; the lamentation of Beth-Haëzel (near-house) takes from you the standing near it.* Ver. 12. *For the inhabitress of Maroth (bitterness) writhes for good; for evil has come down from Jehovah to the gate of Jerusalem.*" The description commences with words borrowed from David's elegy on the death of Saul and Jonathan (2 Sam. i. 20), "Publish it not in Gath," in which there is a play upon the words in *b°gath* and *taggīdū.* The Philistines are not to hear of the distress of Judah, lest they should rejoice over it. There is also a play upon words in בָּכוֹ אַל־תִּבְכּוּ. The sentence belongs to what precedes, and supplies the fuller definition, that they are not to proclaim the calamity in Gath with weeping, *i.e.* not to weep over it there.[1] After this reminiscence of the mourning of David for Saul, which expresses the greatness of the grief, and is all the more significant, because in the approaching catastrophe Judah is also to lose its king (cf. iv. 9), so that David is to experience the fate of Saul

---

[1] On the ground of the Septuagint rendering, καὶ οἱ Ἐνακεὶμ μὴ ἀνοικοδομεῖτε, most of the modern expositors follow Reland (*Palæst. ill.* p. 534 sqq.) in the opinion that בְּכוֹ is the name of a city, a contraction of בְּעַכּוֹ, " and weep not *at Acco.*" There is no force in the objection brought against this by Caspari (*Mich.* p. 110), namely, that in that case the inhabitants of both kingdoms must have stood out before the prophet's mind in hemistich *a*, which, though not rendered actually impossible by ver. 9*a*, and the expression עַל־זֹאת in ver. 8, is hardly reconcilable with the fact that from ver. 11 onwards Judah only stands out before his mind, and that in vers. 8–10 the distress of his people, in the stricter sense (*i.e.* of Judah), is obviously the pre-eminent object of his mourning. For Acco would not be taken into consideration as a city of the kingdom of Israel, but as a city inhabited by heathen, since, according to Judg. i. 31, the Canaanites were not driven out of Acco, and it cannot be shown from any passage of the Old Testament that this city ever came into the actual possession of the Israelites. It is evidently a more important objection to the supposed contraction, that not a single analogous case can be pointed out. The forms נִשְׁקָה for נִשְׁקְעָה (Amos viii. 8) and בָּלָה for בָּעֲלָה (Josh. xix. 3 and xv. 29) are of a different kind; and the blending of the prepo-

(Hengstenberg), Micah mentions places in which Judah will mourn, or, at any rate, experience something very painful. From ver. 10*b* to ver. 15 he mentions ten places, whose names, with a very slight alteration, were adapted for *jeux de mots*, with which to depict what would happen to them or take place within them. The number ten (the stamp of completeness, pointing to the fact that the judgment would be a complete one, spreading over the whole kingdom) is divided into twice five by the statement, which is repeated in ver. 12, that the calamity would come to the gate of Jerusalem; five places being mentioned before Jerusalem (vers. 10–12), and five after (vers. 13–15). This division makes Hengstenberg's conjecture a very natural one, viz. that the five places mentioned before Jerusalem are to be sought for to the north of Jerusalem, and the others to the south or south-west, and that in this way Micah indicates that the judgment will proceed from the north to the south. On the other hand, Caspari's opinion, that the prophet simply enumerates certain places in the neighbourhood of More-sheth, his own home, rests upon no firm foundation. בֵּית לְעַפְרָה is probably the *Ophra* of Benjamin (עָפְרָה, Josh. xviii. 23), which was situated, according to Eusebius, not far from Bethel (see comm. on Josh. *l.c.*). It is pointed with *pathach* here for the sake of the paronomasia with עָפָר. The *chethib* הִתְפַּלָּשְׁתִּי is the correct reading, the *keri* הִתְפַּלָּשִׁי being merely an emen-

sition בְּ with the noun עָבוֹ, by dropping the עָ, so as to form one word, is altogether unparalleled. The Septuagint translation furnishes no sufficient authority for such an assumption. All that we can infer from the fact that Eusebius has adopted the reading 'Ενακείμ in his *Onom.* (ed. Lars. p. 188), observing at the same time that this name occurs in Micah, whilst Aq. and Symm. have ἐν κλαυθμῷ (*in fletu*) instead, is that these Greek fathers regarded the Ενακείμ of the LXX. as the name of a place; but this does not in the smallest degree prove the correctness of the LXX. rendering. Nor does the position of בְּכוֹ before אַל furnish any tenable ground for maintaining that this word cannot be the inf. abs. of בְּכָה, but must con-tain the name of a place. The assertion of Hitzig, that "if the word were regarded as an inf. abs., neither the inf. itself nor אַל for לֹא would be admissible in a negative sentence (Jer. xxii. 10)," has no grammatical foundation. It is by no means a necessary consequence, that because אַל cannot be connected with the inf. abs. (Ewald, § 350, *a*), therefore the inf. abs. could not be written before a finite verb with אַל for the sake of emphasis.

dation springing out of a misunderstanding of the true meaning. הִתְפַּלֵּשׁ does not mean to revolve, but to bestrew one's self. Bestrewing with dust or ashes was a sign of deep mourning (Jer. vi. 26; 2 Sam. xiii. 19). The prophet speaks in the name of the people of what the people will do. The inhabitants of Shafir are to go stripped into captivity. עֲבָר, to pass by, here in the sense of moving forwards. The plural לָכֶם is to be accounted for from the fact that *yōshebheth* is the population. *Shâphīr*, *i.e.* beautiful city, is not the same as the *Shâmīr* in Josh. xv. 48, for this was situated in the south-west of the mountains of Judah; nor the same as the *Shâmīr* in the mountains of Ephraim (Judg. x. 1), which did not belong to the kingdom of Judah; but is a place to the north of Jerusalem, of which nothing further is known. The statement in the *Onomast. s.v.* Σαφείρ—ἐν γῇ ὀρεινῇ between Eleutheropolis and Askalon—is probably intended to apply to the *Shâmīr* of Joshua; but this is evidently erroneous, as the country between Eleutheropolis and Askalon did not belong to the mountains of Judah, but to the Shephelah. עֶרְיָה־בֹשֶׁת, a combination like עֶנְוָה־צֶדֶק in Ps. xlv. 5, equivalent to stripping which is shame, shame-nakedness = ignominious stripping. עֶרְיָה is an accusative defining the manner in which they would go out. The next two clauses are difficult to explain. צַאֲנָן, a play upon words with יָצְאָה, is traceable to this verb, so far as its meaning is concerned. The primary meaning of the name is uncertain; the more modern commentators combine it with צֹאן, in the sense of rich in flocks. The situation of *Zaanan* is quite unknown. The supposed identity with *Zenân* (see at Josh. xv. 37) must be given up, as *Zenân* was in the plain, and *Zaanan* was most probably to the north of Jerusalem. The meaning of the clause can hardly be any other than this, that the population of Zaanan had not gone out of their city to this war from fear of the enemy, but, on the contrary, had fallen back behind their walls (Ros., Casp., Hitzig). בֵּית הָאֵצֶל is most likely the same as אָצֵל in Zech. xiv. 5, a place in the neighbourhood of Jerusalem, to the east of the Mount of Olives, as *Beth* is frequently omitted in the names of places (see Ges. *Thes.* p. 193). *Etsel* signifies side, and as an adverb or preposition, "by the side of." This meaning comes into consideration here. The thought of the words *mispad bēth*, etc., might be:

" The lamentation of *Beth-Haezel* will take away its standing
(the standing by the side of it, *'etslō*) from you (Judæans), *i.e.*
will not allow you to tarry there as fugitives (cf. Jer. xlviii. 45).
The distress into which the enemy staying there has plunged
Beth-Haezel, will make it impossible for you to stop there"
(Hitzig, Caspari). But the next clause, which is connected by
כִּי, does not suit this explanation (ver. 12*b*). The only way in
which this clause can be made to follow suitably as an explanation is by taking the words thus : " The lamentation of Beth-
Haezel will take its standing (the stopping of the calamity or
judgment) from you, *i.e.* the calamity will not stop at Beth-
Haezel (at the near house), *i.e.* stop near it, as we should expect
from its name ; for (ver. 12) Maroth, which stands further off,
will feel pain," etc. With this view, which Caspari also suggests,
Hengstenberg (on Zech. xiv. 5) agrees in the main, except that
he refers the suffix in עֶמְדָתוֹ to מִסְפֵּד, and renders the words thus :
" The lamentation of Beth-Haezel will take its stopping away
from you, *i.e.* will not allow you the stopping of the lamentation." Grammatically considered, this connection is the more
natural one; but there is this objection, that it cannot be shown
that עָמַד is used in the sense of the stopping or ceasing of a
lamentation, whereas the supposition that the suffix refers to
the calamity simply by *constructio ad sensum* has all the less
difficulty, inasmuch as the calamity has already been hinted at
in the verb נָגַע in ver. 9, and in ver. 10*a* also it forms the object
to be supplied in thought. *Maroth* (lit. something bitter, bitter-
nesses) is quite unknown ; it is simply evident, from the explanatory clause כִּי יָרַד וגו׳, that it was situated in the immediate
neighbourhood of Jerusalem. The inhabitants of Maroth
writhe (*châlâh*, from *chûl*, to writhe with pain, like a woman
in child-birth), because they are also smitten with the calamity,
when it comes down to the gate of Jerusalem. לְטוֹב, " on
account of the good," which they have lost, or are about to
lose.

And the judgment will not even stop at Jerusalem, but
will spread still further over the land. This spreading is depicted in vers. 13–15 in the same manner as before. Ver. 13.
" *Harness the horse to the chariot, O inhabitress of Lachish !* It
*was the beginning of sin to the daughter Zion, that the iniquities
of Israel were found in her.* Ver. 14. *Therefore wilt thou give*

*dismissal-presents to Moresheth-Gath (i.e. the betrothed of Gath);
the houses of Achzib (lying fountain) become a lying brook for
Israel's kings.* Ver. 15. *I will still bring thee the heir, O inhabitress of Mareshah (hereditary city); the nobility of Israel
will come to Adullam.* Ver. 16. *Make thyself bald, and shave
thyself upon the sons of thy delights: spread out thy baldness
like the eagle; for they have wandered away from thee."* The
inhabitants of Lachish, a fortified city in the Shephelah, to the
west of Eleutheropolis, preserved in the ruins of *Um Lakis*
(see at Josh. x. 3), are to harness the horses to the chariot
(*rekhesh*, a runner; see at 1 Kings v. 8: the word is used as
ringing with *lâkhîsh*), namely, to flee as rapidly as possible before
the advancing foe. רְתם, ἀπ. λεγ. "to bind . . . the horse to the
chariot," answering to the Latin *currum jungere equis.* Upon
this city will the judgment fall with especial severity, because
it has grievously sinned. It was the beginning of sin to the
daughter of Zion, *i.e.* to the population of Jerusalem; it was
the first to grant admission to the iniquities of Israel, *i.e.* to the
idolatry of the image-worship of the ten tribes (for פִּשְׁעֵי יִשְׂרָאֵל,
see ver. 5 and Amos iii. 14), which penetrated even to the
capital. Nothing more is known of this, as the historical books
contain no account of it. For this reason, namely, because the
sin of Israel found admission into Jerusalem, she (the daughter
Zion) will be obliged to renounce Moresheth-Gath. This is
the thought of ver. 14*a*, the drapery of which rests upon the
resemblance in sound between *Moresheth* and *mᵉʾorâsâh*, the
betrothed (Deut. xxii. 23). *Shillûchîm*, dismissal, denotes anything belonging to a man, which he dismisses or gives up for a
time, or for ever. It is applied in Ex. xviii. 2 to the sending
away of wife and children to the father-in-law for a time; and
in 1 Kings ix. 16 to a dowry, or the present which a father
gives to his daughter when she is married and leaves his house.
The meaning "divorce," *i.e. sēpher kᵉrîthuth* (Deut. xxiv. 1, 3),
has been arbitrarily forced upon the word. The meaning is
not to be determined from *shilleăch* in Jer. iii. 8, as Hitzig
supposes, but from 1 Kings ix. 16, where the same expression
occurs, except that it is construed with ל, which makes no material difference. For נָתַן עַל signifies to give to a person, either
to lay upon him or to hand to him; ל נָתַן, to give to him. The
object given by Zion to Moresheth as a parting present is not

mentioned, but it is really the city itself; for the meaning is
simply this: Zion will be obliged to relinquish all further claim
to Moresheth, to give it up to the enemy. *Mōresheth* is not an
appellative, as the old translators suppose, but the proper name
of Micah's home; and Gath is a more precise definition of its
situation—" by Gath," viz. the well-known Philistian capital,
analogous to Bethlehem-Judah in Judg. xvii. 7–9, xix. 1, or
Abel-Maim (Abel by the water) in 2 Chron. xvi. 4. According
to Jerome (comm. in Mich. *Prol.*), *Morasthi, qui usque hodie
juxta Eleutheropolin, urbem Palæstinæ, haud grandis est viculus*
(cf. Robinson, *Pal.* ii. p. 423). The context does not admit
of our taking the word in an appellative sense, " possession of
Gath," since the prophet does not mean to say that Judah will
have to give up to the enemy a place belonging to Gath, but
rather that it will have to give up the cities of its own possession. For, as Maurer correctly observes, " when the enemy
is at the gate, men think of defending the kingdom, not of
enlarging it." But if the addition of the term *Gath* is not
merely intended to define the situation of Moresheth with
greater minuteness, or to distinguish it from other places of the
same name, and if the play upon words in *Moresheth* was intended to point to a closer relation to Gath, the thought expressed could only be, that the place situated in the neighbourhood of Gath had frequently been taken by the Philistines, or
claimed as their property, and not that they were in actual
possession of Gath at this time. The play upon words in the
second clause of the verse also points to the loss of places in
Judæa: "the houses of *Achzib* will become *Achzab* to the
kings of Israel." אַכְזָב, a lie, for נַחַל אַכְזָב, is a stream which
dries up in the hot season, and deceives the expectation of the
traveller that he shall find water (Jer. xv. 18; cf. Job vi. 15
sqq.). *Achzib*, a city in the plain of Judah, whose name has
been preserved in the ruins of *Kussabeh*, to the south-west of
Beit-Jibrin (see at Josh. xv. 44). The houses of Achzib are
mentioned, because they are, properly speaking, to be compared to the contents of the river's bed, whereas the ground on
which they stood, with the wall that surrounded them, answered
to the river's bed itself (Hitzig), so that the words do not denote
the loss or destruction of the houses so much as the loss of
the city itself. The " kings of Israel" are not the kings of

Samaria and Judah, for Achzib belonged to the kingdom of Judah alone, but the kings of Judah who followed one another (cf. Jer. xix. 13); so that the plural is to be understood as relating to the monarchy of Israel (Judah). *Mareshah* will also pass into other hands. This is affirmed in the words, " I will bring the heir to thee again" (אָבִי for אָבִיא, as in 1 Kings xxi. 29). The first heir of Mareshah was the Israelites, who received the city, which had been previously occupied by the Canaanites, for their possession on the conquest of the land. The second heir will be the enemy, into whose possession the land is now to pass. *Mareshah*, also in the lowland of Judah, has been preserved, so far as the name is concerned, in the ruins of *Marash* (see at Josh. xv. 44, and Tobler, *Dritte Wanderung*, pp. 129, 142-3). To the north of this was *Adullam* (see at Josh. xii. 15), which has not yet been discovered, but which Tobler (p. 151) erroneously seeks for in *Bét Dûla*. Micah mentions it simply on account of the cave there (1 Sam. xxii. 1), as a place of refuge, to which the great and glorious of Israel would flee (" the glory of Israel," as in Isa. v. 13). The description is rounded off in ver. 16, by returning to the thought that Zion would mourn deeply over the carrying away of the people, with which it had first set out in ver. 8. In קָרְחִי וָגֹזִּי Zion is addressed as the mother of the people. קָרַח, to shave smooth, and גָּזַז, to cut off the hair, are synonyms, which are here combined to strengthen the meaning. The children of thy delights, in whom thou hast thy pleasure, are the members of the nation. Shaving the head bald, or shaving a bald place, was a sign of mourning, which had been handed down as a traditional custom in Israel, in spite of the prohibition in Deut. xiv. 1 (see at Lev. xix. 28). The bald place is to be made to spread out like that of a *nesher*, *i.e.* not the true eagle, but the vulture, which was also commonly classed in the eagle family,—either the bearded vulture, *vultur barbatus* (see Oedmann, *Verm. Samml.* i. p. 54 sqq.), or more probably the carrion vulture, *vultur percnopterus L.*, common in Egypt, and also in Palestine, which has the front part of the head completely bald, and only a few hairs at the back of the head, so that a bald place may very well be attributed to it (see Hasselquist, *Reise*, p. 286 sqq.). The words cannot possibly be understood as referring to the yearly moulting of the eagle itself.

If we inquire still further as to the fulfilment of the prophecy concerning Judah (vers. 8–16), it cannot be referred, or speaking more correctly, it must not be restricted, to the Assyrian invasion, as Theod., Cyril, Marck, and others suppose. For the carrying away of Judah, which is hinted at in ver. 11, and clearly expressed in ver. 16, was not effected by the Assyrians, but by the Chaldeans; and that Micah himself did not expect this judgment from the Assyrians, but from Babel, is perfectly obvious from ch. iv. 10, where he mentions Babel as the place to which Judah was to be carried into exile. At the same time, we must not exclude the Assyrian oppression altogether; for Sennacherib had not only already conquered the greater part of Judah, and penetrated to the very gates of Jerusalem (2 Kings xviii. 13, 14, xix.; Isa. xxxvi.-xxxviii.), but would have destroyed the kingdom of Judah, as his predecessor Shalmaneser had destroyed the kingdom of Israel, if the Lord had not heard the prayer of His servant Hezekiah, and miraculously destroyed Sennacherib's army before the walls of Jerusalem. Micah prophesies throughout this chapter, not of certain distinct judgments, but of judgment in general, without any special allusions to the way in which it would be realized; so that the proclamation embraces all the judgments that have fallen upon Judah from the Assyrian invasion down to the Roman catastrophe.

GUILT AND PUNISHMENT OF ISRAEL. ITS FUTURE RESTORATION.—CHAP. II.

After having prophesied generally in ch. i. of the judgment that would fall upon both kingdoms on account of their apostasy from the living God, Micah proceeds in ch. ii. to condemn, as the principal sins, the injustice and oppressions on the part of the great (vers. 1, 2), for which the nation was to be driven away from its inheritance (vers. 3–5). He then vindicates this threat, as opposed to the prophecies of the false prophets, who confirmed the nation in its ungodliness by the lies that they told (vers. 6–11); and then closes with the brief but definite promise, that the Lord would one day gather together the remnant of His people, and would multiply it greatly, and make it His kingdom (vers. 12, 13). As this promise applies to all Israel of the twelve tribes, the reproof and threat of punishment are also addressed to the house of Jacob as such (ver. 7), and apply to both kingdoms. There are no valid grounds for restricting them to Judah, even though Micah may have had the citizens of that kingdom more particularly in his mind.

Vers. 1–5. The violent acts of the great men would be punished by God with the withdrawal of the inheritance of His people, or the loss of Canaan. Ver. 1. " *Woe to those who devise mischief, and prepare evil upon their beds! In the light of the morning they carry it out, for their hand is their god.* Ver. 2. *They covet fields and plunder them, and houses and take them; and oppress the man and his house, the man and his inheritance.*" The woe applies to the great and mighty of the nation, who by acts of injustice deprive the common people of the inheritance conferred upon them by the Lord (cf. Isa. v. 8). The prophet describes them as those who devise plans by night upon their beds for robbing the poor, and carry them out as soon as the day dawns. חָשַׁב אָוֶן denotes the sketching out of plans (see Ps. xxxvi. 5); and פָּעַל רָע, to work evil, the preparation of the ways and means for carrying out their wicked plans. פָּעַל, the preparation, is distinguished from עָשָׂה, the execution, as in Isa. xli. 4, for which יָצַר and עָשָׂה are also used (*e.g.* Isa. xliii. 7). "Upon their beds," *i.e.* by night, the time of quiet reflection (Ps. iv. 5; cf. Job iv. 13). "By the light of the morning," *i.e.* at daybreak, without delay. כִּי יֶשׁ וגו', lit. "for their hand is for a god," *i.e.* their power passes as a god to them; they know of no higher power than their own arm; whatever they wish it is in their power to do (cf. Gen. xxxi. 29; Prov. iii. 27; Hab. i. 11; Job xii. 6). Ewald and Rückert weaken the thought by adopting the rendering, "because it stands free in their hand;" and Hitzig's rendering, "if it stands in their hand," is decidedly false. *Kî* cannot be a conditional particle here, because the thought would thereby be weakened in a manner quite irreconcilable with the context. In ver. 2 the evil which they plan by night, and carry out by day, is still more precisely defined. By force and injustice they seize upon the property (fields, houses) of the poor, the possessions which the Lord has given to His people for their inheritance. *Chámad* points to the command against coveting (Ex. xx. 14 (17); cf. Deut. v. 18). The second half of the verse (ver. 2) contains a conclusion drawn from the first: "and so they practise violence upon the man and his property." *Bêth* answers to *bottîm*, and *nachălâh* to the *Sâdôth*, as their hereditary portion in the land—the portion of land which each family received when Canaan was divided.

Ver. 3. "*Therefore thus saith Jehovah, Behold, I devise evil concerning this family, from which ye shall not withdraw your necks, and not walk loftily, for it is an evil time.* Ver. 4. *In that day will men raise against you a proverb, and lament a lamentation. It has come to pass, they say; we are waste, laid waste; the inheritance of my people he exchanges: how does he withdraw it from me! To the rebellious one he divides our field.*" The punishment introduced with *lâkhēn* (therefore) will correspond to the sin. Because they reflect upon evil, to deprive their fellow-men of their possessions, Jehovah will bring evil upon this generation, lay a heavy yoke upon their neck, out of which they will not be able to draw their necks, and under which they will not be able to walk loftily, or with extended neck. הַמִּשְׁפָּחָה הַזֹּאת is not this godless family, but the whole of the existing nation, whose corrupt members are to be exterminated by the judgment (see Isa. xxix. 20 sqq.). The yoke which the Lord will bring upon them is subjugation to the hostile conqueror of the land and the oppression of exile (see Jer. xxvii. 12). *Hâlakh rōmâh*, to walk on high, *i.e.* with the head lifted up, which is a sign of pride and haughtiness. *Rōmâh* is different from קוֹמְמִיּוּת, an upright attitude, in Lev. xxvi. 13. כִּי עֵת רָעָה, as in Amos v. 13, but in a different sense, is not used of moral depravity, but of the distress which will come upon Israel through the laying on of the yoke. Then will the opponents raise derisive songs concerning Israel, and Israel itself will bewail its misery. The verbs *yissâ'*, *nâhâh*, and *'âmar* are used impersonally. *Mâshâl* is not synonymous with *nᵉhî*, a mournful song (Ros.), but signifies a figurative saying, a proverb-song, as in Isa. xiv. 4, Hab. ii. 6. The subject to יִשָּׂא is the opponents of Israel, hence עֲלֵיכֶם; on the other hand, the subject to *nâhâh* and *'âmar* is the Israelites themselves, as נְשַׁדֻּנוּ teaches. נִהְיָה is not a feminine formation from נְהִי, a mournful song, *lamentum lamenti*, *i.e.* a mournfully mournful song, as Rosenmüller, Umbreit, and the earlier commentators suppose; but the *niphal* of הָיָה (cf. Dan. viii. 27): *actum est!* it is all

over !—an exclamation of despair (Le de Dieu, Ewald, etc.) ;
and it is written after *'âmar*, because נִהְיָה as an exclamation
is equivalent in meaning to an object. The omission of the
copula *Vav* precludes our taking *'âmar* in connection with what
follows (Maurer). The following clauses are a still further
explanation of נִהְיָה : we are quite laid waste. The form נְשַׁדֻּנוּ
for נָשַׁדּוֹנוּ is probably chosen simply to imitate the tone of
lamentation better (Hitzig). The inheritance of my people, *i.e.*
the land of Canaan, He (Jehovah) changes, *i.e.* causes it to pass
over to another possessor, namely, to the heathen. The words
receive their explanation from the clauses which follow : How
does He cause (*sc.* the inheritance) to depart from me ! Not
how does He cause me to depart. לְשׁוֹבֵב is not an infinitive,
ad reddendum, or *restituendum,* which is altogether unsuitable,
but *nomen verbale,* the fallen or rebellious one, like שׁוֹבֵבָה in
Jer. xxxi. 22, xlix. 4. This is the term applied by mourning
Israel to the heathenish foe, to whom Jehovah apportions the
fields of His people. The withdrawal of the land is the just
punishment for the way in which the wicked great men have
robbed the people of their inheritance

Ver. 5. " *Therefore wilt thou have none to cast a measure for
the lot in the congregation of Jehovah.*" With *lâkhēn* (therefore) the threat, commenced with *lâkhēn* in ver. 3, is resumed
and applied to individual sinners. The whole nation is not
addressed in לְךָ, still less the prophet, as Hitzig supposes, but
every individual among the tyrannical great men (vers. 1, 2).
The singular is used instead of the plural, to make the address
more impressive, that no one may imagine that he is excepted
from the threatened judgment. For a similar transition from
the plural to the singular, see ch. iii. 10. The expression, to
cast the measure *b^egōrâl, i.e.* in the nature of a lot (equivalent
to for a lot, or as a lot), may be explained on the ground that
the land was divided to the Israelites by lot, and then the portion that fell to each tribe was divided among the different
families by measure. The words are not to be taken, however,
as referring purely to the future, as Caspari supposes, *i.e.* to
the time when the promised land would be divided afresh
among the people on their return. For even if the prophet
does proclaim in vers. 12, 13 the reassembling of Israel and
its restoration to its hereditary land, this thought cannot be

arbitrarily taken for granted here. We therefore regard the
words as containing a general threat, that the ungodly will
henceforth receive no further part in the inheritance of the
Lord, but that they are to be separated from the congregation
of Jehovah.

Vers. 6–11. As such a prophecy as this met with violent
contradiction, not only from the corrupt great men, but also
from the false prophets who flattered the people, Micah indicates it by showing that the people are abusing the long-suffering and mercy of the Lord; and that, by robbing the peaceable
poor, the widows, and the orphans, they are bringing about the
punishment of banishment out of the land. Ver. 6. "*Drip
not (prophesy not), they drip: if they drip not this, the shame
will not depart.* Ver. 7. *Thou, called house of Jacob, is the
patience of Jehovah short, then? or is this His doing? Are not
my words good to him that walketh uprightly?*" הִטִּיף, to drip,
to cause words to flow, used of prophesying, as in Amos vii. 16.
The speakers in ver. 6a are not the Jews generally, or the rich
oppressors who have just been punished and threatened. The
word *yattīphū* does not agree with this, since it does not mean
to chatter, but to prophesy, as ver. 11 and also the primary
passage Deut. xxxii. 2 show. But Micah could not call the
rich men's speaking prophesying. It is rather false prophets
who are speaking,—namely, those who in the word '*al-tattīphū*
(prophesy not) would prohibit the true prophets from predicting the judgments of the Lord. The second hemistich is
rendered by most of the modern commentators, "they are not
to chatter (preach) of such things; the reproaches cease not,"
or "there is no end to reproaching" (Ewald, Hitzig, Maurer,
and Caspari). But this is open to the following objections:
(1) That הִטִּיף לְ in ver. 11 means to prophesy to a person (not
concerning or of anything); (2) that *sūg* or *nâsag* means to
depart, not to cease; (3) that even the thought, "the reproaches do not cease," is apparently unsuitable, since Micah
could not well call a prohibition against prophesying an inces-
sant reproach; and to this we may add, (4) the grammatical
harshness of taking לֹא יַטִּפוּ as an imperative, and the following
לֹא יִסַּג as an indicative (a simple declaration). Still less can
the rendering, "they (the true prophets) will not chatter about
this, yet the reproach will not depart" (Ros., Rückert), be

vindicated, as such an antithesis as this would necessarily be indicated by a particle. The only course that remains, therefore, is that adopted by C. B. Michaelis and Hengstenberg, viz. to take the words as conditional: if they (the true prophets) do not prophesy to these (the unrighteous rich in vers. 1, 2: Hengstenberg), or on account of these things (Michaelis), the shame will not depart, *i.e.* shameful destruction will burst incessantly upon them. On the absence of the conditional אִם, see Ewald, p. 357, *b*. Such addresses as these do not please the corrupt great men; but they imagine that such threats are irreconcilable with the goodness of Jehovah. This is the connection of ver. 7, in which the prophet meets the reproach cast upon his threatening words with the remark, that God is not wrathful, and has no love for punishing, but that He is stirred up to wrath by the sins of the nation, and obliged to punish. הֶאָמוּר is not an exclamation, " O, what is said ! = O for such talk as this !" (Ewald, Umbreit, Caspari); for it cannot be shown that the participle is ever used in this way, and it cannot be supported from הָפְכְּכֶם in Isa. xxix. 16, especially as here a second vocative would follow. Nor is it a question: "*Num dicendum? Dare one say this?*" (Hitzig.) For although הֲ might be an interrogative particle (cf. Ezek. xxviii. 9), the passive participle cannot express the idea of daring, in support of which Hitzig is quite wrong in appealing to Lev. xi. 47 and Ps. xxii. 32. הֶאָמוּר is no doubt a vocative, but it is to be taken in connection with *bēth-Yaʿaqōb* : thou who art called house of Jacob. There is very little force in the objection, that this would have required הֶאָמוּר לְךָ ב' יׁ', since אָמַר, when used in the sense of being called or being named, is always construed with לְ of the person bearing the name. The *part. paül* of *'âmar* only occurs here; and although the *niphal*, when used in this sense, is generally construed with לְ, the same rule may apply to אָמַר as to קָרָא in the sense of naming,—namely, that in the passive construction the לְ may either be inserted or omitted (cf. Isa. lvi. 7, liv. 5; Deut. iii. 13), and הֶאָמוּר may just as well be used in the sense of *dicta* (*domus*) as הַנִּקְרָאִים in Isa. xlviii. 1 in the sense of *vocati* = *qui appellantur*. The whole nation is addressed, although the address points especially to the unrighteous great men. Is Jehovah indeed wrathful? *i.e.* has He not patience, does He not exercise long-suffering? *Qātsar rûăch* must not be explained according to Ex. vi. 9, but according to Prov. xiv. 29. Or are these (*'ēlleh*, the punishments threatened) His deeds? *i.e.* is He accustomed, or does He only like to punish? The answer to these questions, or speaking more correctly, their refutation, follows in the next question, which is introduced with the assuring הֲלוֹא, and in which Jehovah speaks: My words deal kindly with him that walks uprightly. The Lord not only makes promises to the upright, but He also grants His blessing. The words of the Lord contain their fulfilment within themselves. In הַיָּשָׁר הוֹלֵךְ, it is for the sake of emphasis that *yâshâr* stands first, and the article properly belongs to *hōlēkh;* but it is placed before *yâshâr* to bind together the two words into one idea. The reason why the Lord threatens by His prophets is therefore to be found in the unrighteousness of the people.

Ver. 8. "*But yesterday my people rises up as an enemy: off from the garment ye draw the cloak from those who pass by carelessly, averted from war. Ver. 9. The women of my people ye drive away out of the house of their delights; from their children ye take my ornament for ever.*" *'Ethmūl*, yesterday, lately, not = long ago, but, as *y^eqōmēm* shows, denoting an action that is repeated, equivalent to "again, recently." קוֹמֵם is not used here in a causative sense, "to set up," but as an intensified *kal*, to take a standing = to stand up or rise up. The causative view, They set up my people as an enemy (Ewald), yields no fitting sense; and if the meaning were, "My people causes me to rise up as its enemy" (Caspari), the suffixes could not be omitted. If this were the thought, it would be expressed as clearly as in Isa. lxiii. 10. There is no valid ground for altering the text, as Hitzig proposes. It is not stated against whom the people rise up as an enemy, but according to the context it can only be against Jehovah. This is done by robbing the peaceable travellers, as well as the widows and orphans, whereby they act with hostility towards Jehovah and excite His wrath (Ex. xxii. 21 sqq.; Deut. xxvii. 19). מִמּוּל שַׂלְמָה, from before, *i.e.* right away from, the garment. *Salmâh* is the upper garment; אַדֶּרֶת = אֶדֶר the broad dress-cloak. They take this away from those who pass carelessly by. שׁוּבֵי is an intransitive participle: averted from the war, averse to conflict, *i.e.* peaceably disposed (see Ps. cxx. 7). We have not only to think of open highway robbery, but also of their taking away the cloak in the public street from their own poor debtors, when they are walking peaceably along, suspecting nothing, for the purpose of repaying themselves. The "wives of my people" are *widows*, whom they deprive of house and home, and indeed widows of the people of Jehovah, in whose person Jehovah is injured. These children are fatherless orphans (עֹלָלֶיהָ with a singular suffix: the children of the widow). *Hădârî*, my ornament, *i.e.* the ornament which I have given them. The reference, as מֵעַל shows, is to the garment or upper coat. The expression "for ever" may be explained from the evident allusion to the Mosaic law in Ex. xxii. 25, according to which the coat taken from the poor as a pledge was to be returned before sunset, whereas ungodly creditors retained it for ever.

Such conduct as this must be followed by banishment from the land. Ver. 10. "*Rise up, and go ; for this is not the place of rest : because of the defilement which brings destruction, and mighty destruction. Ver. 11. If there were a man, walking after wind, who would lie deceit, 'I will prophesy to thee of wine and strong drink,' he would be a prophet of this people.*" The prophet having overthrown in vers. 7–9 the objection to his threatening prophecies, by pointing to the sins of the people, now repeats the announcement of punishment, and that in the form of a summons to go out of the land into captivity, because the land cannot bear the defilement consequent upon such abominations. The passage is based upon the idea contained in Lev. xviii. 25, 28, that the land is defiled by the sins of its inhabitants, and will vomit them out because of this defilement, in connection with such passages as Deut. xii. 9, 10, where coming to Canaan is described as coming to rest. זֹאת (this) refers to the land. This (the land in which ye dwell) is not the place of rest (*hammᵉnŭchâh*, as in Zech. ix. 1 and Ps. cxxxii. 14). If "*this*" were to be taken as referring to their sinful conduct, in the sense of "this does not bring or cause rest," it would be difficult to connect it with what follows, viz. "because of the defilement ;" whereas no difficulty arises if we take "this" as referring to the land, which the expression "rise up and go" naturally suggests. טָמְאָה = טֻמְאָה, defilement ; תְּחַבֵּל is to be taken in a relative sense, "which brings

destruction," and is strengthened by וְחֶבֶל, with an explanatory
וֹ: and indeed terrible destruction. חֶבֶל, *perditio ;* and נִמְרָץ as
in 1 Kings ii. 8. The destruction consists in the fact that the
land vomits out its inhabitants (Lev. xviii. 25). Such prophecies
are very unwelcome to the corrupt great men, because they do
not want to hear the truth, but simply what flatters their wicked
heart. They would like to have only prophets who prophesy
lies to them. הֹלֵךְ רוּחַ, walking after the wind; the construction is the same as הֹלֵךְ צְדָקוֹת in Isa. xxxiii. 15, and *rŭăch* is a
figure signifying what is vain or worthless, as in Isa. xxvi. 18,
xli. 29, etc. The words אַטִּיף לְךָ וגו' are the words of a false
prophet: I prophesy to thee with regard to wine. The meaning is not "that there will be an abundant supply of wine," or
"that the wine will turn out well" (Rosenmüller and others);
but wine and strong drink (for *shēkhâr,* see Delitzsch on Isa.
v. 11) are figures used to denote earthly blessings and sensual
enjoyments, and the words refer to such promises as Lev. xxvi.
4, 5, 10, Deut. xxviii. 4, 11, Joel ii. 24, iv. 18 sqq., which
false prophets held out to the people without any regard to
their attitude towards God. "This people," because the great
men represent the nation. With this explanation pointing
back to ver. 6, the threatening is brought to a close.

In vers. 12, 13 there follows, altogether without introduction, the promise of the future reassembling of the people from
their dispersion. Ver. 12. "*I will assemble, assemble thee all
together, O Jacob; gather together, gather together the remnant of
Israel; I will bring him together like the sheep of Bozrah, like a
flock in the midst of their pasture: they will be noisy with men.*
Ver. 13. *The breaker through comes up before them; they break
through, and pass along through the gate, and go out by it; and
their King goes before them, and Jehovah at their head.*" Micah
is indeed not a prophet, prophesying lies of wine and strong
drink; nevertheless he also has salvation to proclaim, only not
for the morally corrupt people of his own time. They will be
banished out of the land; but the captivity and dispersion are
not at an end. For the remnant of Israel, for the nation when
sifted and refined by the judgments, the time will come when
the Lord will assemble them again, miraculously multiply them,
and redeem them as their King, and lead them home. The
sudden and abrupt transition from threatening to promise, just

as in Hos. ii. 2, vi. 1, xi. 9, has given rise to this mistaken
supposition, that vers. 12, 13 contain a prophecy uttered by
the lying prophets mentioned in ver. 10 (Abenezra, Mich.,
Ewald, etc.). But this supposition founders not only on
the שְׁאֵרִית יִשְׂרָאֵל, inasmuch as the gathering together of the
remnant of Israel presupposes the carrying away into exile,
but also on the entire contents of these verses. Micah could
not possibly introduce a false prophet as speaking in the name
of Jehovah, and saying, "I will gather;" such a man would
at the most have said, "Jehovah will gather." Nor could he
have put a true prophecy like that contained in vers. 12, 13
into the mouth of such a man. For this reason, not only
Hengstenberg, Caspari, and Umbreit, but even Maurer and
Hitzig, have rejected this assumption; and the latter observes,
among other things, quite correctly, that "the idea expressed
here is one common to the true prophets (see Hos. ii. 2), which
Micah himself also utters in ch. iv. 6." The emphasis lies upon
the assembling, and hence אָסֹף אֶאֱסֹף and קַבֵּץ אֲקַבֵּץ are strengthened by
infinitive absolutes. But the assembling together presupposes
a dispersion among the heathen, such as Micah has threatened
in ch. i. 11, 16, ii. 4. And the Lord will gather together all
Jacob, not merely a portion, and yet only the remnant of Israel.
This involves the thought, that the whole nation of the twelve
tribes, or of the two kingdoms, will be reduced to a remnant
by the judgment. *Jacob* and *Israel* are identical epithets
applied to the whole nation, as in ch. i. 5, and the two clauses
of the verse are synonymous, so that יַעֲקֹב כֻּלָּךְ coincides in
actual fact with שְׁאֵרִית יִשְׂרָאֵל. The further description rests
upon the fact of the leading of Israel out of Egypt, which is
to be renewed in all that is essential at a future time. The
following clauses also predict the miraculous multiplication of
the remnant of Israel (see Hos. ii. 1, 2 ; Jer. xxxi. 10), as experienced by the people in the olden time under the oppression
of Egypt (Ex. i. 12). The comparison to the flock of Bozrah
presupposes that Bozrah's wealth in flocks was well known.
Now, as the wealth of the Moabites in flocks of sheep is very
evident from 2 Kings iii. 4, many have understood by בָּצְרָה not
the Edomitish Bozrah, but the Moabitish Bostra (*e.g.* Hengstenberg). Others, again, take *botsráh* as an appellative noun
in the sense of hurdle or fold (see Hitzig, Caspari, and Dietrich

in Ges. *Lex.* after the Chaldee). But there is not sufficient ground for either. The Bostra situated in the Hauran does not occur at all in the Old Testament, not even in Jer. xlviii. 24, and the appellative meaning of the word is simply postulated for this particular passage. That the Edomites were also rich in flocks of sheep is evident from Isa. xxxiv. 6, where the massacre which Jehovah will inflict upon Edom and Bozrah is described as a sacrificial slaughtering of lambs, he-goats, rams, and oxen; a description which presupposes the wealth of Bozrah in natural flocks. The comparison which follows, "like a flock in the midst of its pasture," belongs to the last verse, and refers to the multiplication, and to the noise made by a densely packed and numerous flock. The same tumult will be made by the assembled Israelites on account of the multitude of the men. For the article in הַדְּבְרוֹ, which is already determined by the suffix, see at Josh. vii. 21. In ver. 13 the redemption of Israel out of exile is depicted under the figure of liberation from captivity. Was Egypt a slave-house (ch. vi. 4; cf. Ex. xx. 2); so is exile a prison with walls and gates, which must be broken through. הַפֹּרֵץ, the breaker through, who goes before them, is not Jehovah, but, as the counterpart of Moses the leader of Israel out of Egypt, the captain appointed by God for His people, answering to the head which they are said to choose for themselves in Hos. ii. 2, a second Moses, viz. Zerubbabel, and in the highest sense Christ, who opens the prison-doors, and redeems the captives of Zion (*vid.* Isa. xlii. 7). Led by him, they break through the walls, and march through the gate, and go out through it out of the prison. "The three verbs, they break through, they march through, they go out, describe in a pictorial manner progress which cannot be stopped by any human power" (Hengstenberg). Their King Jehovah goes before them at their head (the last two clauses of the verse are synonymous). Just as Jehovah went before Israel as the angel of the Lord in the pillar of cloud and fire at the exodus from Egypt (Ex. xiii. 21), so at the future redemption of the people of God will Jehovah go before them as King, and lead the procession (see Isa. lii. 12).

The fulfilment of this prophecy commenced with the gathering together of Israel to its God and King by the preaching of the gospel, and will be completed at some future time when the Lord shall redeem Israel, which is now pining in dispersion, out of the fetters of its unbelief and life of sin. We must not exclude all allusion to the deliverance of the Jewish nation out of the earthly Babylon by Cyrus; at the same time, it is only in its typical significance that this comes into consideration at all,—namely, as a preliminary stage and pledge of the redemption to be effected by Christ out of the spiritual Babylon of this world.

II. ZION'S DEEPEST DEGRADATION AND HIGHEST EXALTATION.—Chap. iii.-v.

The prophet's second address is of a predominantly Messianic character. The announcement of the utter desolation of Zion on account of the corruption of both the civil rulers and the spiritual leaders of the nation, with which this address opens in ch. iii., serves to a certain extent simply as a foil for the prophecy which follows in ch. iv. and v. of the salvation with which the remnant of Israel, that has been rescued throughout the judgment, will be blessed in the future. This salvation is depicted first of all in all its fulness (ch. iv. 1–7); then in its gradual development, in the re-erection of the former dominion of the daughter of Zion, by her redemption out of Babylon, and her victory over the powers of the world (ch. iv. 8–14); and lastly, in its realization by the Ruler proceeding out of Bethlehem, and by the power and blessing of His rule (ch. v.).

SINS OF THE LEADERS OF THE NATION, AND DESTRUCTION OF JERUSALEM.—CHAP. III.

The threatening of punishment contained in this chapter is specially directed against the heads and leaders of Israel, and proclaims, in three strophes of four verses each, (a) to the princes, who turn right into wrong and flay the people (vers. 1–4), and (b) to the false prophets, who lead the people astray, and confirm them in their sin by lying prophecies of peace (vers. 5–8), retribution for their wicked conduct; and (c) to all three classes of the divinely-appointed chiefs of the nation —the princes, the priests, and the prophets—the destruction of Jerusalem, and the turning of Zion and the temple mountain into a ploughed field and wooded heights on account of their degeneracy (vers. 9–12).

Vers. 1–4. First strophe.—Ver. 1. *" And I said, Hear ye, O heads of Jacob, and princes of the house of Israel: Is it not for you to know the right? Ver. 2. Ye who hate good, and love evil; who draw off their skin from them, and their flesh from their bones. Ver. 3. And who have eaten the flesh of my people, and stripped off their skin from them; and broken their bones, and cut them in pieces, as if in the pot, and like flesh in the midst of the caldron. Ver. 4. Then will they cry to Jehovah, and He will not hearken; and let Him hide His face from them at the same time, as they have made their actions evil."* By the expression " And I said" (*vâ'ōmar*), the following address is indicated as a continuation of the preceding one. The reproofs of this chapter are also a still further expansion of the woe pronounced in ch. ii. 1, 2 upon the godless chiefs of the nation. The heads of Jacob are addressed, that is to say, the princes of the tribes and families of Israel, and the *qᵉtsīnīm*, lit. deciders

(answering to the Arabic قاضى, a judge) of the house of Israel, *i.e.* the heads of families and households, upon whom the administration of justice devolved (cf. Isa. i. 10, xxii. 3). הֲלוֹא לָכֶם, is it not your duty and your office to know justice? *Da'ath* is practical knowledge, which manifests itself in practice; *mishpât*, the public administration of justice. Instead of this, they do the opposite. The description of this conduct is appended by participles, in the form of apposition to the heads and princes addressed in ver. 1. Hating good and loving evil refer to the disposition, and indicate the radical corruption of these men. רָעָה, generally misfortune, here evil; hence the Masoretes have altered it into רָע; but the very fact that it deviates from the ordinary rule shows that it is the original word. Instead of administering justice to the people, they take off their skin, and tear the flesh from the bones. The suffixes attached to עֹרָם and שְׁאֵרָם point back to בֵּית־יִשְׂרָאֵל in ver. 1. The words answer to the German expression, " to pull the skin over the ears." In

ver. 3 the expression is still stronger; but the address is continued in the form of a simple description, and instead of the
participles, אֲשֶׁר is used with the finite verb. They not only
flay the people, *i.e.* rob them of all their means of subsistence,
but even devour them—treat them like cattle, which men first
of all flay, then break their bones, cut the flesh into pieces, and
boil it in the pot. In this figure, which is carried out into the
most minute details, we must not give any special meaning to
the particular features, such as that "the skin, and boiling
portions, which are cut up and put into the pot, are figures
signifying the pledged clothing and coveted fields (ii. 2, 8)."
The prophet paints in very glaring colours, to make an impression upon the ungodly. Therefore, in the time of judgment,
God will not hear their crying to Him for help, but will hide
His face from them, *i.e.* withdraw His mercy from them. אָז
and בָּעֵת הַהִיא point back to the evil time announced in ch. ii. 3.
For ver. 4*a*, compare Prov. i. 28. *V*ᵉ*yastēr* in ver. 4*b* is an
optative. The prophet continues the announcement of the
punishment in the form of a desire. כַּאֲשֶׁר, as = according to
the way in which, as in 1 Sam. xxviii. 18, Num. xxvii. 14, etc.,
i.e. answering to their evil doings.

Vers. 5-8. In the second strophe, Micah turns from the
godless princes and judges to the prophets who lead the people
astray, with whom he contrasts the true prophets and their
ways. Ver. 5. "*Thus saith Jehovah concerning the prophets
who lead my people astray, who bite with their teeth, and preach
peace; and whoever should put nothing into their mouths, against
him they sanctify war. Ver. 6. Therefore night to you because
of the visions, and darkness to you because of the soothsaying!
and the sun will set over the prophets, and the day blacken itself
over them. Ver. 7. And the seers will be ashamed, and the
soothsayers blush, and all cover their beard, because (there is)
no answer of God. Ver. 8. But I, I am filled with power,
with the Spirit of Jehovah, and with judgment and strength, to
show to Jacob his transgression, and to Israel his sin.*" As the
first strophe attaches itself to ch. ii. 1, 2, so does the second to
ch. ii. 6 and 11, carrying out still further what is there affirmed
concerning the false prophets. Micah describes them as people
who predict peace and prosperity for a morsel of bread, and
thereby lead the people astray, setting before them prosperity

and salvation, instead of preaching repentance to them, by charging them with their sins. Thus they became accomplices of the wicked rulers, with whom they are therefore classed in ver. 11, together with the wicked priests. הַמַּתְעִים, *leading astray* (cf. Isa. iii. 12, ix. 15) my people, namely, by failing to charge them with their sins, and preach repentance, as the true prophets do, and predicting prosperity for bread and payment. The words, " who bite with their teeth," are to be connected closely with the next clause, " and they preach peace," in the sense of " who preach peace if they can bite with their teeth," *i.e.* if they receive something to bite (or eat). This explanation, which has already been expressed by the Chaldee, is necessarily required by the antithesis, " but whoever puts nothing into their mouth," *i.e.* gives them nothing to eat, notwithstanding the fact that in other passages *nâshakh* only signifies to bite, in the sense of to wound, and is the word generally applied to the bite of a snake (Amos v. 19 ; Gen. xlix. 17 ; Num. xxi. 6, 8). If, however, we understand the biting with the teeth as a figurative representation of the words of the prophets who always preach prosperity, and of the injury they do to the real welfare of the people (Ros., Casp., and others), the obvious antithesis of the two double clauses of ver. 5*b* is totally destroyed. The harsh expression, to " bite with the teeth," in the sense of " to eat," is perfectly in harmony with the harsh words of vers. 2 and 3. *Qiddēsh milchâmâh*, to sanctify war, *i.e.* to preach a holy war (cf. Joel iv. 9), or, in reality, to proclaim the vengeance of God. For this shall night and darkness burst upon them. Night and darkness denote primarily the calamity which would come upon the false prophets (*unto you*) in connection with the judgment (ch. ii. 4). The sun which sets to them is the sun of salvation or prosperity (Amos viii. 9 ; Jer. xv. 9) ; and the day which becomes black over them is the day of judgment, which is darkness, and not light (Amos v. 18). This calamity is heightened by the fact that they will then stand ashamed, because their own former prophecies are thereby proved to be lies, and fresh, true prophecies fail them, because God gives no answer. " Convicted by the result, they are thus utterly put to shame, because God does not help them out of their trouble by any word of revelation " (Hitzig). *Bōsh*, to be ashamed, when connected with *châphēr* (cf. Jer. xv. 9; Ps. xxxv. 26 sqq., etc.), signifies to become pale with shame; *châphēr*, to blush, with *min causœ*, to denote the thing of which a man is ashamed. *Qōsͤmīm* (diviners) alternates with *chōzīm* (seers), because these false prophets had no visions of God, but only divinations out of their own hearts. '*Atâh sâphâm:* to cover the beard, *i.e.* to cover the face up to the nose, is a sign of mourning (Lev. xiii. 45), here of trouble and shame (cf. Ezek. xxiv. 17), and is really equivalent to covering the head (Jer. xiv. 4; Esth. vi. 12). *Ma'ănēh*, the construct state of the substantive, but in the sense of the participle; some codd. have indeed מַעֲנֶה. In ver. 8 Micah contrasts himself and his own doings with these false prophets, as being filled with power by the Spirit of Jehovah (*i.e.* through His assistance) and with judgment. *Mishpât*, governed by מָלֵא, is the divine justice which the prophet has to proclaim, and *gͤbhūrâh* strength, manliness, to hold up before the people their sins and the justice of God. In this divine strength he can and must declare their unrighteousness to all ranks of the people, and predict the punishment of God (vers. 9–12).

Vers. 9–12. Third strophe.—Ver. 9. "*Hear this, I pray, O ye heads of the house of Jacob, and princes of the house of Israel, who abhor right, and bend all that is straight. Ver. 10. Building Zion with blood, and Jerusalem with wickedness. Ver. 11. Their heads, they judge for reward; and their priests, they teach for hire; and their prophets, they divine for money, and lean upon Jehovah, saying, Is not Jehovah among us? evil will not come upon us.*" With the words "Hear this, I pray," the address returns to its starting-point in ver. 1, but only to announce to the leaders of the people the threat of punishment for which the way has been prepared by vers. 2–7. To this end their God-forgetting conduct is briefly summed up once more in vers. 10, 11. The summons to hear is really attached to the end of ver. 8. They are to hear the sin of Jacob (vers. 9–11); but they are also to hear the punishment for their sin, to which the word "this" points. The civil rulers only are addressed in ver. 9,—namely, those who were charged with the administration of justice and of the affairs of the state, but who did the very opposite, who abhorred justice, and made the straight crooked, because they passed sentence for bribes (ver. 11).

They thereby build Zion with blood, etc., *i.e.* obtain the means of erecting splendid buildings by cruel extortions, and partly also by actual judicial murders, as Ahab (1 Kings xxi. compared with Mic. vi. 16), and after him Jehoiakim, had done (Jer. xxii. 13-17). The Chaldeans built with blood in a different sense (Hab. ii. 12). The participle *bōneh* (building) is also in apposition to *rā'shē bēth* (heads of the house, etc.), and the singular without the article is to be taken collectively. They do not, however, truly build the city by this, they simply labour for its destruction (ver. 12). But before saying this, Micah once more sums up briefly all the sins of the leading ranks. The teaching of the priests for reward refers to the fact that they had to give instruction as to the ritual requirements of the law, and were to do this gratuitously (cf. Lev. x. 11 ; Deut. xvii. 11, xxxiii. 10), and that in disputed cases the judges were to pronounce sentence accordingly. At the same time, these men (not the prophets merely, but also the priests and the heads of the nation as the administrators of justice) placed their reliance upon Jehovah, upon the assurance that He was in the midst of them enthroned in His temple at Jerusalem, and that He would protect the city and its inhabitants from misfortune, without ever reflecting that Jehovah as the Holy One demands sanctification of life, and exterminates the sinners out of His people.

Ver. 12. "*Therefore will Zion for your sake be ploughed as a field, and Jerusalem become stone heaps, and the mountain of the house become forest heights.*" *Lākhēn* (therefore) applies primarily to ver. 11, directing the threat of punishment by בִּגְלַלְכֶם to all the sinners mentioned there ; but it also points back to vers. 9, 10, expressing what is there indicated by "this." *Zion* is not "the site on which the city stood," or *Jerusalem,* "the mass of houses in the city," as Maurer and Caspari suppose ; but Zion is that portion of the city which contained the royal palace, and Jerusalem the rest of the city (cf. ch. iv. 8). The mountain of the house, *i.e.* the temple hill, is also specially mentioned, for the purpose of destroying all false trust in the temple (cf. Jer. vii. 4). The predicates are divided rhetorically, and the thought is this : the royal palace, the city, and the temple shall be so utterly destroyed, that of all the houses and palaces only heaps of rubbish will remain, and the ground upon which the city stood will be partly used as a ploughed field, and partly overgrown with bushes (cf. Isa. xxxii. 13, 14). On *sâdeh* as an accusative of effect (as a field = becoming a field), see Ewald, § 281, *e;* and for the plural form ‏עִיִּין‎, see Ewald, § 177, *a.* *Habbayith* (the house) is probably chosen intentionally instead of *bêth Yᵉhôvâh* (the house of Jehovah), because the temple ceased to be the dwelling-place of Jehovah as soon as it was destroyed. Hence in Ezekiel (x. 18 sqq., xi. 22 sqq.) the Schechinah departs before the Babylonians destroy it. With regard to the fulfilment of this threat, see the points discussed at ch. iv. 10.

GLORIFICATION OF THE HOUSE OF THE LORD, AND RESTORATION OF THE DOMINION OF ZION.—CHAP. IV.

Zion will eventually be exalted from the deepest degradation to the highest glory. This fundamental thought of the announcement of salvation contained in ch. iv. and v. is carried out thus far in ch. iv. : the first section (vers. 1–7) depicts the glorification of the temple mountain by the streaming of the heathen nations to it to hear the law of the Lord, and the blessing which Israel and the nations will derive therefrom ; and the second section (vers. 8–14) describes the restoration of the dominion of Zion from its fallen condition through the redemption of the nation out of Babel, and its victorious conflict with the nations of the world.

Vers. 1–5. The promise of salvation opens, in closest connection with the destruction of Jerusalem and of the temple, with a picture of the glory awaiting in the remotest future the temple mountain, which has now become a wild forest-height. Ver. 1. "*And it comes to pass at the end of the days, that the mountain of Jehovah's house will be established on the head of the mountains, and it will be exalted above the hills, and nations stream to it. Ver. 2. And many nations go, and say, Up, let us go up to the mountain of Jehovah, and to the house of the God of Jacob, that He may teach us of His ways, and we may walk in His paths : for from Zion will law go forth, and the word of Jehovah from Jerusalem. Ver. 3. And He will judge between many nations, and pronounce sentence on strong nations afar off ; and they forge their swords into coulters, and their spears into*

*pruning-hooks : nation will not lift up sword against nation, nor
will they learn war any more.* Ver. 4. *And they will sit, every
one under his vine, and under his fig-tree, and no one will make
them afraid : for the mouth of Jehovah of hosts hath spoken it.*"[1]
By the phrase " at the end of the days," which always denotes
the Messianic era when used by the prophets (see at Hos. iii. 5),
the predicted exaltation of the temple mountain is assigned to
the period of the completion of the kingdom of God. The
mountain of the house of Jehovah is the temple mountain,
strictly speaking, Moriah, as the distinction made between the
mountain of the house and Zion in ch. iii. 12 clearly shows ;
but as a subordinate peak of Zion, it is embraced along with
Zion in what follows (compare ver. 2 with ver. 7) as the seat
of Jehovah's rule, from which the law proceeds. נָכוֹן does not
mean placed or set up, but established, founded. By connecting
the participle with יִהְיֶה, the founding is designated as a permanent one. בְּרֹאשׁ הֶהָרִים, upon (not at) the top of the mountains,
as in Judg. ix. 7, 1 Sam. xxvi. 13, Ps. lxxii. 16 ; whereas such
passages as ch. ii. 13, Amos vi. 7, and 1 Kings xxi. 9 are of a
different character, and have no bearing upon the point. The
temple mountain, or Zion, will be so exalted above all the
mountains and hills, that it will appear to be founded upon
the top of the mountains. This exaltation is of course not
a physical one, as Hofmann, Drechsler, and several of the
Rabbins suppose, but a spiritual (ethical) elevation above all
the mountains. This is obvious from ver. 2, according to
which Zion will tower above all the mountains, because the
law of the Lord issues from it. The assumption of a physical
elevation cannot be established from Ezek. xl. 2 and Rev. xxi.
10, for in the visions described in both these passages the
earthly elevation is a symbol of a spiritual one. " Through a
new revelation of the Lord, which is made upon it, and which
leaves the older revelations far behind, whether made upon
Sinai or upon itself, Zion becomes the greatest and loftiest

---

[1] This promise is placed by Isaiah (ch. ii. 2–4) at the head of his
prophecy of Zion's way through judgment from the false glory to the true.
The originality of the passage in Micah is open to no question. Delitzsch
acknowledges this, and has given the principal arguments in its favour in
the *Commentary on Isaiah.* For still more elaborate proofs, see Caspari's
Micha, pp. 444–5.

mountain in the world" (Caspari), and the mountain seen from afar, to which "nations" stream, and not merely the one nation of Israel. עַמִּים is more precisely defined in ver. 2 as גּוֹיִם רַבִּים. The attractive power which this mountain exerts upon the nations, so that they call upon one another to go up to it (ver. 2), does not reside in its height, which towers above that of all other mountains, but in the fact that the house of the God of Jacob stands upon it, *i.e.* that Jehovah is enthroned there, and teaches how to walk in His ways. הוֹרָה מִן, to teach out of the ways, so that the ways of God form the material from which they derive continual instruction. The desire for salvation, therefore, is the motive which prompts them to this pilgrimage; for they desire instruction in the ways of the Lord, that they may walk in them. The ways of Jehovah are the ways which God takes in His dealing with men, and by which men are led by Him; in reality, therefore, the ordinances of salvation which He has revealed in His word, the knowledge and observance of which secure life and blessedness. The words "for the law goes forth from Zion," etc., are words spoken not by the nations, but by the prophet, and assign the reason why the heathen go with such zeal to the mountain of Jehovah. The accent is laid upon מִצִּיּוֹן (from Zion), which stands at the head, and מִירוּשָׁלַם (from Jerusalem), which is parallel to it. Thence does *tōrâh,* *i.e.* instruction in the ways of God, proceed,—in other words, the law as the rule of a godly life,—and *d^ebhar Y^ehōvâh* (the word of Jehovah), or the word of revelation as the source of salvation. It is evident from this that the mountain of the house of God is not thought of here as the place of worship, but as the scene of divine revelation, the centre of the kingdom of God. Zion is the source of the law and word of the Lord, from which the nations draw instruction how to walk in the ways of God, to make it their own, take it to their homes, and walk according to it. The fruit of this adoption of the word of the Lord will be, that they will no longer fight out their disputes with weapons of war, but let Jehovah judge and settle them, and thus acknowledge Him as their King and Judge. שָׁפַט signifies to act as judge ; הוֹכִיחַ (lit. to set right), to settle and put a stop to a dispute. "Many nations," in contrast with the one nation, which formerly was alone in acknowledging Jehovah as its King and Judge. This is strengthened still further by the parallel

" strong, mighty nations afar off." In consequence of this they
will turn their weapons into instruments of peaceful agriculture,
and wage no more war; in fact, they will learn war no more, no
longer exercise themselves in the use of arms. For the words
וְכִתְּתוּ וגו׳ compare Joel iv. 10, where the summons to the nations
to a decisive conflict with the kingdom of God is described as
turning the instruments of agriculture into weapons of war.
With the cessation of war, universal peace will ensue, and
Israel will have no further enemies to fear, so that every one
will have undisturbed enjoyment of the blessings of peace, of
which Israel had had a foretaste during the peaceful reign of
Solomon. The words " sit under his vine" are taken from
1 Kings v. 5 (cf. Zech. iii. 10), and אֵין מַחֲרִיד from the promise
in Lev. xxvi. 6. All this, however incredible it might appear,
not only for the Israel of that time, but even now under the
Christian dispensation, will assuredly take place, for the mouth
of Jehovah the true God has spoken it.

It will not be through any general humanitarian ideas and
efforts, however, that the human race will reach this goal, but
solely through the omnipotence and faithfulness of the Lord.
The reason assigned for the promise points to this. Ver. 5. " For
all nations walk every man in the name of his God, but we walk
in the name of Jehovah our God for ever and ever." This verse
does not contain an exhortation, or a resolution to walk in the
name of God, which involves an exhortation, in the sense of
" if all nations walk, etc., then we will," etc.; for an admonition or a resolution neither suits the connection, in the midst of
simple promises, nor the words themselves, since we should at
any rate expect נֵלְכָה instead of נֵלֵךְ. The sameness in the form
of the verbs יֵלְכוּ and נֵלֵךְ requires that they should be understood in the same way. Walking in the name of God does
not mean regulating the conduct according to the name of a
God, i.e. according to the nature which expresses itself in the
name, or worshipping him in a manner corresponding to his
nature (Caspari), but walking in the strength of God, in which
the nature of this God is displayed. This is the meaning of
the phrase in 1 Sam. xvii. 45 and Zech. x. 12, where " I
strengthen them in Jehovah" forms the basis of " and in His
name will they walk" (compare Prov. xviii. 10, " The name of
the Lord is a strong tower"). But the gods of all the nations,

i.e. of all the heathen, are worthless beings, without life, without strength. Jehovah, on the contrary, is the only true God, the almighty Creator and Governor of the world. And the heathen, with their worthless gods, can do nothing to Him and the nation which walks in His name, His strength. If, therefore, Israel rejoices for ever and ever in the strength of its God, the heathen nations cannot disturb the peace which He will create for Israel and all who accept His word. In this way is the promise in vers. 3 and 4 explained in ver. 5. But this explanation assumes that, even at the time when many nations stream to the mountain of the Lord, there will still be nations that do not seek Jehovah and His word,—a thought which is still further expanded in ch. v. 4 sqq., and involves this consolation, that such opponents of the people of God as shall be still in existence will not be able to interfere with the salvation which has been prepared for it by its God.

Vers. 6, 7. From this salvation even the Israel that may be in misery or scattered abroad will not be excluded. Ver. 6. "*In that day, is the saying of Jehovah, will I assemble that which limps, and gather together that which has been thrust out, and which I have afflicted. Ver. 7. And I will make that which limps into a remnant, and that which is far removed into a strong nation; and Jehovah will rule over them from henceforth, even for ever.*" "In that day" points back to the end of the days in ver. 1. At the time when many nations shall go on pilgrimage to the highly exalted mountain of the Lord, and therefore Zion-Jerusalem will not only be restored, but greatly glorified, the Lord will assemble that which limps and is scattered abroad. The feminines הַצֹּלֵעָה and הַנִּדָּחָה are neuters, and to be understood collectively. Limping denotes the miserable condition into which the dispersed have been brought (cf. Ps. xxxv. 15, xxxviii. 18). And this misery is inflicted by God. The limping and dispersed are those whom Jehovah has afflicted, whom He has punished for their sins. The gathering together of the nation has already been promised in ch. ii. 12; but there the assembling of all Israel was foretold, whereas here it is merely the assembling of the miserable, and of those who are scattered far and wide. There is no discrepancy in these two promises. The difference may easily be explained from the different tendencies of the two addresses. "All Jacob" referred to the two

separate kingdoms into which the nation was divided in the
time of the prophet, viz. Israel and Judah, and it was distinctly
mentioned there, because the banishment of both had been foretold. This antithesis falls into the background here; and, on
the other hand, prominence is given, in connection with what
precedes, to the idea of happiness in the enjoyment of the
blessings of the holy land. The gathering together involves
reinstatement in the possession and enjoyment of these blessings. Hence only the miserable and dispersed are mentioned,
to express the thought that no one is to be excluded from the
salvation which the Lord will bestow upon His people in the
future, though now he may be pining in the misery of the
exile inflicted upon them. But just as the whole of the nation
of Israel to be gathered together, according to ch. ii. 12, consists
of the remnant of the nation only, so does the gathering together
referred to here point only to the restoration of the remnant,
which is to become a strong nation, over which Jehovah reigns
as King in Zion. מָלַךְ is emphatic, expressing the setting up of
the perfected monarchy, as it has never yet existed, either in the
present or the past.[1] This dominion will never be interrupted
again, as it formerly was, by the banishment of the nation into
exile on account of its sins, but will endure מֵעַתָּה (henceforth),
i.e. from the future, which is regarded as present, even for
ever.

So far as the realization of this exceedingly glorious promise
is concerned, the expression standing at the head, *b°achărîth
hayyâmîm* (at the end of the days), already points to the Messianic times; and the substance of the promise itself points to
the times of the completion of the Messianic kingdom, *i.e.* to
the establishment of the kingdom of glory (Matt. xix. 28).
The temple mountain is a type of the kingdom of God in its
New Testament form, which is described by all the prophets

---

[1] " Micah does not mention the descendants of David here, but Jehovah
Himself, not to exclude the kingdom of David, but to show that God will
prove that He was the author of that kingdom, and that all the power is
His. For although God governed the ancient people by the hand of David,
and by the hand of Josiah and Hezekiah, yet there was as it were a cloud
interposed, so that God then reigned obscurely. The prophet therefore
indicates a certain difference here between that shadowy kingdom and the
new kingdom which God will openly manifest at the advent of the Messiah."
—CALVIN.

after the forms of the Old Testament kingdom of God. Accordingly, the going of the nations to the mountain of the house of Jehovah is, as a matter of fact, the entrance of the heathen who have been brought to the faith into the kingdom of Christ. This commenced with the spread of the gospel among the Gentiles, and has been continued through all the ages of the Christian church. But however many nations have hitherto entered into the Christian church, the time has not yet come for them to be so entirely pervaded with the spirit of Christ, as to allow their disputes to be settled by the Lord as their King, or to renounce war, and live in everlasting peace. Even for Israel the time has not yet come for the limping and exiled to be gathered together and made into a strong nation, however many individual Jews have already found salvation and peace within the bosom of the Christian church. The cessation of war and establishment of eternal peace can only take place after the destruction of all the ungodly powers on earth, at the return of Christ to judgment and for the perfecting of His kingdom. But even then, when, according to Rom. xi. 25 sqq., the *pleroma* of the Gentiles shall have entered into the kingdom of God, and Israel as a nation ($\pi \hat{a} \varsigma$ 'Ισραήλ = יַעֲקֹב כֻּלּוֹ in ch. ii. 12) shall have turned to its Redeemer, and shall be assembled or saved, no physical elevation of the mountain of Zion will ensue, nor any restoration of the temple in Jerusalem, or return of the dispersed of Israel to Palestine. The kingdom of glory will be set up on the new earth, in the Jerusalem which was shown to the holy seer on Patmos in the Spirit, on a great and lofty mountain (Rev. xxi. 10). In this holy city of God there will be no temple, " for the Lord, the Almighty God, and the Lamb, are the temple thereof" (Rev. xxi. 22). The word of the Lord to the Samaritan woman concerning the time when men would neither worship God on this mountain, nor yet in Jerusalem, but worship Him in spirit and in truth (John iv. 21, 23), applies not only to the kingdom of God in its temporal development into the Christian church, but also to the time of the completion of the kingdom of God in glory.

Vers. 8–10. The prophecy turns from the highest glorification of Zion to the throne of Zion, which had been founded by David, and swept away with the destruction of Jerusalem (ch. iii. 12), and predicts its restoration in the future. Consequently the reign of Jehovah upon Mount Zion, promised in ver. 7, is still further defined as effected through the medium of the Davidico-Messianic dominion. Ver. 8. "*And thou flock-tower, hill of the daughter Zion, to thee will the former dominion reach and come, the reign over the daughter Jerusalem.*" This announcement is attached primarily to vers. 6 and 7. As the remnant of Israel gathered together out of the dispersion will become a strong nation, so shall the reign of the daughter Zion be also restored. The address to the flock-tower, the hill of the daughter Zion, shows that these two notions express the same thing, looked at from two sides, or with two different bearings, so that the flock-tower is more precisely defined as the " hill of the daughter Zion." Now, as the daughter Zion is the city of Zion personified as a virgin, the hill of the daughter Zion might be understood as denoting the hill upon which the city stood, *i.e.* Mount Zion. But this is precluded by Isa. xxxii. 14, where hill and watch-tower (*'ōphel vâbhachan*) are mentioned in parallelism with the palace (*'armōn*), as places or buildings which are to serve as dens for ever. From this it is obvious that *'ōphel* was a place either at the side or at the top of Zion. If we compare with this 2 Chron. xxvii. 3 and xxxiii. 14, according to which Jotham built much against the wall of the Ophel (*hâ'ōphel*), and Manasseh encircled the Ophel with a wall, and made it very high, Ophel must have been a hill, possibly a bastion, on the south-eastern border of Zion, the fortification of which was of great importance as a defence to the city of Zion against hostile attacks.[1] Consequently *migdal-*

---

[1] The opinion that Ophel is the whole of the southern steep rocky promontory of Moriah, from the southern end of the temple ground to its extreme point (Robinson, Schultz, Williams), viz. the *Ophla* or *Ophlas* of Josephus, as Arnold (Herzog's *Cycl.*) and Winer (*Bibl. R.W.*) suppose, would be in perfect harmony with this. At the same time, all that can be inferred with any certainty from the passages from Josephus which are cited in support of it (viz. *Wars of the Jews*, v. 6, 1; cf. vi. 6, 3 and v. 4, 2) is, that the place called *Ophla* was in the neighbourhood of the valley of Kidron and of the temple mountain. The question then arises, whether the *Ophla* of Josephus is identical with the Ophel of the Old Testament, since Josephus does not mention the Ophel in his list of the hills of Jerusalem, but simply mentions *Ophla* as a special locality (see Reland, *Pal.* p. 855). And lastly, the situation of the *Ophel*, upon which the Nethinim dwelt (Neh. iii. 26), is still a matter of dispute, Bertheau supposing it to be the habitable space to the east of the eastern side of the temple area.

'*ēder* cannot be the flock-tower in the neighbourhood of Bethlehem, which is mentioned in Gen. xxxv. 21, but can only be a (or rather the) tower of the Davidic palace, or royal castle upon Zion, namely the town mentioned in Neh. iii. 25, which stood out against the upper king's house, by the court of the prison (cf. ver. 26). For the prison, which also belonged to the king's house, according to Jer. xxxii. 2, formed a portion of the royal castle, according to the custom of the East. And that it had a lofty tower, is evident from Song of Sol. iv. 4: "Thy neck is like David's tower, built for an armoury: a thousand shields hang thereon, all heroes' weapons;" according to which the tower of the royal castle was ornamented with the weapons or shields of David's heroes (1 Chron. xii. 1). And the tower of the king's castle was so far specially adapted to represent the sovereignty of David, "that by its exaltation above Zion and Jerusalem, by the fact that it ruled the whole city, it symbolized the Davidic family, and its rule over the city and all Israel" (Caspari). This tower, which is most likely the one called *bachan* (the watch-tower) in Isaiah (*l.c.*), is called by Micah the flock-tower, probably as a play upon the flock-tower by which the patriarch Jacob once pitched his tent, because David, the ancestor of the divinely-chosen royal house, had been called from being the shepherd of a flock to be the shepherd of the nation of Israel, the flock of Jehovah (Jer. xiii. 17; cf. 2 Sam. vii. 8; Ps. lxxviii. 70). This epithet was a very natural one for the prophet to employ, as he not only describes the Messiah as a shepherd in ch. v. 3, but also represents Israel as the sheep of Jehovah's inheritance in ch. vii. 14, and the flock-tower is the place where the shepherd takes up his position to see whether any danger threatens his flock (cf. 2 Chron. xxvi. 10, xxvii. 4). עָרֶיךָ תֵּאתֶה, "unto thee shall it come."[1] עָרֶיךָ affirms more than אֵלֶיךָ, to thee: expressing the conquest of every obstacle that blocks up the way to the goal. תֵּאתֶה is separated from what follows, and exhibited as independent not only by the *athnach*, but also by the change of tense occurring in בָּאָה: "to thee will it come," *sc.* what the prophet has in his mind and mentions in the next clause, but brings into special promi-

---

[1] Luther's rendering, "thy golden rose will come," arose from his confounding עָרֶיךָ (from עַד, unto) with עֶדְיֵךְ, thine ornament.

nence in וּבָאָה. הַם' הָרִאשֹׁנָה, the former (first) reign, is the splendid rule of David and Solomon. This predicate presupposes that the sovereignty has departed from Zion, *i.e.* has been withdrawn from the Davidic family, and points back to the destruction of Jerusalem predicted in ch. iii. 12. This sovereignty is still more precisely defined as kingship over the daughter of Jerusalem (לְ before בַּת is a periphrasis of the *gen. obj.*). Jerusalem, the capital of the kingdom, represents as the object sovereignty over the whole kingdom. This is to be restored to the hill of Zion, *i.e.*, to the royal castle upon the top of it.

But before this takes place, the daughter Zion will lose her king, and wander into captivity to Babylon; but there she will be redeemed by the Lord out of the power of her enemies. Ver. 9. " *Now why dost thou cry a cry? Is there no king in thee, or is thy counsellor perished, that pangs have seized thee like the woman in labour?* Ver. 10. *Writhe and break forth, O daughter Zion, like a woman in labour! For how wilt thou go out of the city and dwell in the field, and come to Babel? there wilt thou be rescued; there will Jehovah redeem thee out of the hand of thine enemies.*" From this glorious future the prophet now turns his eye to the immediate future, to proclaim to the people what will precede this glorification, viz. first of all, the loss of the royal government, and the deportation of the people to Babylon. If Micah, after announcing the devastation of Zion in ch. iii. 12, has offered to the faithful a firm ground of hope in the approaching calamities, by pointing to the highest glory as awaiting it in the future, he now guards against the abuse which might be made of this view by the careless body of the people, who might either fancy that the threat of punishment was not meant so seriously after all, or that the time of adversity would very speedily give place to a much more glorious state of prosperity, by depicting the grievous times that are still before them. Beholding in spirit the approaching time of distress as already present, he hears a loud cry, like that of a woman in labour, and inquires the cause of' this lamentation, and whether it refers to the loss of her king. The words are addressed to the daughter Zion, and the meaning of the rhetorical question is simply this: Zion will lose her king, and be thrown into the deepest mourning in consequence. The loss of the king was a much more painful thing for Israel than for any other nation, because such glorious promises were attached to the throne, the king being the visible representative of the grace of God, and his removal a sign of the wrath of God and of the abolition of all the blessings of salvation which were promised to the nation in his person. Compare Lam. iv. 20, where Israel calls the king its vital breath (Hengstenberg). יוֹעֵץ (counsellor) is also the king; and this epithet simply gives prominence to that which the Davidic king had been to Zion (cf. Isa. ix. 5, where the Messiah is designated as "Counsellor" *par excellence*). But Zion must experience this pain: writhe and break forth. *Gōchī* is strengthened by *chūlī*, and is used intransitively, to break forth, describing the pain connected with the birth as being as it were a bursting of the whole nature (cf. Jer. iv. 31). It is not used transitively in the sense of "drive forth," as Hitzig and others suppose; for the determination that Jerusalem would submit, and the people be carried away, could not properly be represented as a birth or as a reorganization of things. With the words כִּי עַתָּה וגו׳ the prophet leaves the figure, and predicts in literal terms the catastrophe awaiting the nation. עַתָּה (now), repeated from ver. 9, is the ideal present, which the prophet sees in spirit, but which is in reality the near or more remote future. קִרְיָה, without an article, is a kind of proper name, like *urbs* for Rome (Caspari). In order to set forth the certainty of the threatened judgment, and at the same time the greatness of the calamity in the most impressive manner, Micah fills up the details of the drama: viz. *going out of the city, dwelling in the field*, without shelter, delivered up to all the chances of weather, and *coming to Babel*, carried thither without delay. Going out of the city presupposes the conquest of the city by the enemy; since going out to surrender themselves to the enemy (2 Kings xxiv. 12; 1 Sam. xi. 3) does not fit in with the prophetic description, which is not a historical description in detail. Nevertheless Israel shall not perish. There (*shâm, i.e.* even in Babel) will the Lord its God deliver it out of the hand of its foes.

The prediction that the daughter Zion, *i.e.* the nation of Israel which was governed from Zion, and had its centre in Zion —the covenant nation which, since the destruction of the kingdom of the ten tribes, existed in Judah only—should be carried

away to Babylon, and that at a time when Assyria was in the
field as the chief enemy of Israel and the representative of the
imperial power, goes so far beyond the bounds of the political
horizon of Micah's time, that it cannot be accounted for from
any natural presentiment.   It is true that it has an analogon
in Isa. xxxix. 6, 7, where Isaiah predicts to king Hezekiah in
the most literal terms the carrying away of all his treasures,
and of his sons (descendants), to Babylon.   At the same time,
this analogy is not sufficient to explain the prediction before
us ; for Isaiah's prophecy was uttered during the period immediately following the destruction of the Assyrian forces in front
of Jerusalem and the arrival of Babylonian ambassadors in
Jerusalem, and had a point of connection in these events,
which indicated the destruction of the Assyrian empire and
the rise of Babylon in its stead, at all events in the germ ;
whereas no such connecting link exists in the case of Micah's
prophecy, which was unquestionably uttered before these events.
It has therefore been thought, that in ch. iii. 12 Micah predicts
the destruction of Jerusalem, and here in ver. 10 the carrying
away of Judah to *Babylon* by the *Assyrians ;* and this opinion,
that Micah expected the judgment upon Jerusalem and Judah
to be executed by the Assyrians, and not by the Babylonians,
has been supported partly by such passages as ch. v. 4, 5, and
Jer. xxvi. 18, 19, and partly by the circumstance that Micah
threatens his own corrupt contemporaries with the judgment
which he predicts on account of their sins ; whereas in his time
the Assyrians were the only possible executors of a judgment
upon Israel who were then standing on the stage of history
(Caspari).   But these arguments are not decisive.   All that
can be inferred from ch. v. 4, 5, where Asshur is mentioned as
the representative of all the enemies of Israel, and of the power
of the world in its hostility to the people of God in the Messianic times, is that at the time of Micah the imperial power in
its hostility to the kingdom of God was represented by Assyria;
but it by no means follows that Assyria would always remain
the imperial power, so that it could only be from her that Micah
could expect the destruction of Jerusalem, and the carrying
away of Judah to Babylon.   Again, Jer. xxvi. 18, 19—where the
chief men of Judah, in order to defend the prophet Jeremiah,
quote Micah's prophecy, with the remark that king Hezekiah did

not put him to death in consequence, but feared the Lord and besought His face, so that the Lord repented of the evil which He had spoken concerning Jerusalem—simply proves that these chief men referred Micah's words to the Assyrians, and attributed the non-fulfilment of the threatened judgment by the Assyrians to Hezekiah's penitence and prayer, and that this was favoured by the circumstance that the Lord answered the prayer of the king, by assuring him that the Assyrian army should be destroyed (Isa. xxxvii. 21 sqq.). But whether the opinion of these chief men as to the meaning and fulfilment of Micah's prophecy (ch. iii. 12) was the correct one or not, cannot be decided from the passage quoted. Its correctness is apparently favoured, indeed, by the circumstance that Micah threatened the people of his own time with the judgment (*for your sakes* shall Zion be ploughed into a field, etc.). Now, if he had been speaking of a judgment upon Judah through the medium of the Babylonians, " he would (so Caspari thinks) not only have threatened his contemporaries with a judgment which could not fall upon them, since it was not possible till after their time, inasmuch as the Assyrians were on the stage in his day ; but he would also have been most incomprehensibly silent as to the approaching Assyrian judgment, of which Isaiah spoke again and again." This argument falls to the ground with the untenable assumptions upon which it is founded. Micah neither mentions the Assyrians nor the Babylonians as executing the judgment, nor does he say a word concerning the time when the predicted devastation or destruction of Jerusalem will occur. In the expression בִּגְלַלְכֶם, for your sakes (ch. iii. 12), it is by no means affirmed that it will take place in his time through the medium of the Assyrians. The persons addressed are the scandalous leaders of the house of Israel, *i.e.* of the covenant nation, and primarily those living in his own time, though by no means those only, but all who share their character and ungodliness, so that the words apply to succeeding generations quite as much as to his contemporaries. The only thing that would warrant our restricting the prophecy to Micah's own times, would be a precise definition by Micah himself of the period when Jerusalem would be destroyed, or his expressly distinguishing his own contemporaries from their sons and descendants. But as he has done neither the one nor the other, it cannot be said that, inasmuch as the destruction of Jerusalem and the carrying away of the people was not effected by the Assyrians, but by the Babylonians (Chaldæans), he would have been altogether silent as to the approaching Assyrian judgment, and only threatened them with the Chaldæan catastrophe, which did not take place till a long time afterwards. His words refer to all the judgments, which took place from his own time onwards till the utter destruction of Jerusalem and the carrying away of the people to Babylon by Nebuchadnezzar. The onesided reference of the prophecy to the Assyrians is simply based upon an incorrect idea of the nature of prophecy, and its relation to the fulfilment, and involves the prophet Micah in an irreconcilable discrepancy between himself and his contemporary the prophet Isaiah, who does indeed predict the severe oppression of Judah by the Assyrians, but at the same time foretels the failure of the plans of these foes to the people of Jehovah, and the total destruction of their army.

This contradiction, with the consequence to which it would inevitably lead,—namely, that if one of the prophets predicted the destruction of Jerusalem by the Assyrians, whereas the other prophesied that it would not be destroyed by them, the two contemporary prophets would necessarily lead the people astray, and render both the truth of their contradictory utterances and their own divine mission doubtful,—cannot be removed by the assumption that Isaiah uttered the prophecies in ch. xxviii.–xxxii. at a somewhat later period, after Micah had published his book, and the terribly severe words of Micah in ch. iii. 12 had produced repentance. For Isaiah had predicted that the Assyrian would not conquer Jerusalem, but that his army would be destroyed under its walls, not only in ch. xxviii.–xxxii., at the time when the Assyrians are approaching with threatening aspect under Shalmaneser or Sennacherib, but much earlier than that,—namely, in the time of Ahaz, in ch. x. 5–xii. 6. Moreover, in Isa. xxviii.–xxxii. there is not a single trace that Micah's terrible threatening had produced such repentance, that the Lord was able to withdraw His threat in consequence, and predict through Isaiah the rescue of Jerusalem from the Assyrian. On the contrary, Isaiah scourges the evil judges and false prophets quite as severely in ch. xxviii. 7 sqq. and xxix. 9–12 as Micah does in ch. iii. 1–3 and

5-8. And lastly, although the distinction between conditional prophecies and those uttered unconditionally is, generally speaking, correct enough, and is placed beyond all doubt by Jer. xviii. 7–10 ; there is nothing in the addresses and threatenings of the two prophets to indicate that Micah uttered his threats conditionally, *i.e.* in case there should be no repentance, whereas Isaiah uttered his unconditionally. Moreover, such an explanation is proved to be untenable by the fact, that in Micah the threat of the destruction of Jerusalem and of the desolation of the temple mountain (ch. iii. 12) stands in the closest connection with the promise, that at the end of the days the mountain of God's house will be exalted above all mountains, and Jehovah reign on Zion as king for ever (ch. iv. 1–3 and 7). If this threat were only conditional, the promise would also have only a conditional validity; and the final glorification of the kingdom of God would be dependent upon the penitence of the great mass of the people of Israel,—a view which is diametrically opposed to the real nature of the prophecies of both, yea, of all the prophets. The only difference between Isaiah and Micah in this respect consists in the fact that Isaiah, in his elaborate addresses, brings out more distinctly the attitude of the imperial power of Assyria towards the kingdom of God in Israel, and predicts not only that Israel will be hard pressed by the Assyrians, but also that the latter will not overcome the people of God, but will be wrecked upon the foundation-stone laid by Jehovah in Zion; whereas Micah simply threatens the sinners with judgment, and after the judgment predicts the glorification of Zion in grand general terms, without entering more minutely into the attitude of the Assyrians towards Israel. In the main, however, Micah goes hand in hand with his contemporary Isaiah. In Isa. xxxii. 14, Isaiah also foretels the devastation, or rather the destruction, of Jerusalem, notwithstanding the fact that he has more than once announced the deliverance of the city of God from Asshur, and that without getting into contradiction with himself. For this double announcement may be very simply explained from the fact that the judgments which Israel had yet to endure, and the period of glory to follow, lay, like a long, deep diorama, before the prophet's mental eye; and that in his threatenings he plunged sometimes more, sometimes less, deeply into those judgments which lay in perspective before him (see Delitzsch on *Isaiah*, ii. p. 55). The same thing applies to Micah, who goes to a great depth both in his threats and promises, not only predicting the judgment in all its extremity,—namely, the utter destruction of Jerusalem, and the carrying away of the people to Babel,—but also the salvation in its ultimate perfection, viz. the glorification of Zion. We must therefore not restrict his threats in ch. iii. 12 and iv. 10 even to the Chaldæan catastrophe, nor the promise of Israel's deliverance in Babel out of the hands of its foes to the liberation of the Jews from Babylon, which was effected by Cyrus, and their return to Palestine under Zerubbabel and Ezra; but must also extend the threat of punishment to the destruction of Jerusalem by the Romans and the attendant dispersion of the Jews over all the world, and the redemption out of Babel promised in ch. iv. 10 to that deliverance of Israel which, in the main, is in the future still. These two judgments and these two deliverances are comprehended in an undivided unity in the words of the prophet, Babel being regarded not only in its historical character, but also in its typical significance, as the beginning and the hearth of the kingdom of the world. Babel has this double significance in the Scriptures from the very commencement. Even the building of the city with a tower intended to reach to heaven was a work of human pride, and an ungodly display of power (Gen. xi. 4 sqq.); and after its erection Babel was made by Nimrod the beginning of the empire of the world (Gen. x. 10). It was from these two facts that Babel became the type of the imperial power, and not because the division of the human race into nations with different languages, and their dispersion over the whole earth, had their origin there (see A. Ch. Lämmert, *Babel, das Thier und der falsche Prophet*. Goth. 1862, p. 36 sqq.); and it is in this typical significance of Babel that we have to seek not only for the reason for the divine purpose to banish the people of God to Babel, when they were given up to the power of the kingdom of the world, but also for a point of connection for the prophetic announcement when this purpose had been communicated to the prophet's mind. Micah accordingly predicts the carrying away of the daughter Zion to Babel, and her deliverance there out of the power of her enemies, not because Babel

along with Nineveh was the metropolis of the world-empire
of his time, or a chief city of that empire, but because Babel,
from its very origin, was a type and symbol of the imperial
power. That the words of Micah, in their deepest sense, should
be so interpreted, is not only warranted, but necessitated, by the
announcement which follows in vers. 11–13 of the victorious
conflict of Zion with many nations, which points far beyond the
conflicts of the Jews in the times succeeding the captivity.

Vers. 11–13. The daughter Zion, when rescued from Babel,
overcomes all hostile powers in the strength of her God. Ver.
11. "*And now many nations have assembled together against thee,
who say, Let her be profaned, and let our eyes look upon Zion.*
Ver. 12. *But they know not the thoughts of Jehovah, and understand not His counsel; for He has gathered them together like
sheaves for the threshing-floor.* Ver. 13. *Rise up and thresh, O
daughter Zion: for I make thy horn iron, and I make thy hoofs
brass; and thou wilt crush many nations: and I ban their gain
to Jehovah, and their substance to the Lord of the whole earth.*"
With וְעַתָּה, corresponding to עַתָּה in ver. 9, there commences
a new scene, which opens to the prophet's mental eye. Many
nations have assembled together against the daughter Zion
(עָלַיִךְ pointing back to בַּת צִיּוֹן in ver. 10), with the intention of
profaning her, and feasting their eyes upon the profaned one.
It is the holiness of Zion, therefore, which drives the nations to
attack her. תֶּחֱנָף, let her be or become profaned: not by the
sins or bloodguiltiness of her inhabitants (Jer. iii. 2; Isa. xxiv.
5), for this is not appropriate in the mouths of heathen; but
through devastation or destruction let her holiness be taken
from her. They want to show that there is nothing in her
holiness, and to feast their eyes upon the city thus profaned.
חָזָה with בְּ, to look upon a thing with interest, here with malicious pleasure. On the singular *tachaz*, followed by the subject
in the plural, see Ewald § 317, *a*. To this design on the part
of the heathen, the prophet (ver. 12) opposes the counsel of the
Lord. Whilst the heathen assemble together against Zion,
with the intention of profaning her by devastation, the Lord
has resolved to destroy them in front of Zion. The destruction which they would prepare for Zion will fall upon themselves, for the Lord gathers them together like sheaves upon
the threshing-floor, to thresh, *i.e.* destroy, them. כִּי does not

mean "that," but "for." The sentence explains the assertion
that they do not understand the counsel of the Lord. כֶּעָמִיר,
with the generic article, equivalent to "like sheaves." This
judgment Zion is to execute upon the heathen. The figurative
expression, "Rise up, and thresh," etc., rests upon the oriental
custom of threshing out corn with oxen, *i.e.* of having it trodden
out with their hoofs (see Paulsen, *Ackerbau der Morgenländer*,
§ 41). In this, of course, only the strength of the hoofs was
considered. But as the horn of the ox is a figure frequently
used for destructive power (see Deut. xxxiii. 17, 1 Kings xxii.
11, Amos vi. 13, etc.), the prophet combines this figure, to
strengthen the idea of crushing power, and express the thought
that the Lord will equip Zion perfectly with the strength requisite to destroy the nations. וְהַחֲרַמְתִּי is the first person, and
must not be altered into or regarded as the second, as it has
been in the LXX. and Syriac, and by Jerome. The prophet
does not speak in the name of the theocratic nation, as Jerome
supposes, but continues to represent Jehovah as speaking, as in
אָשִׂים, with which, however, instead of לִי, the noun לַיהוָה is used,
to give greater clearness to the thought that it is Jehovah, the
God and Lord of the whole earth, who will destroy the nations
that have rebelled against Him and His kingdom, wresting
their possessions from them, and taking them back to Himself.
For everything laid under the ban belonged to the Lord, as
being most holy (Lev. xxvii. 28). חַיִל, property, wealth, the
sum and substance of the possessions. Israel is not to enrich
itself by plundering the defeated foe, but Jehovah will sanctify
the possessions of the heathen to Himself, to whom they belong
as Lord of the whole earth, by laying them under the ban: that
is to say, He will apply them to the glorification of His kingdom.

There has been a diversity of opinion as to the historical
allusion, or the fulfilment of these verses. So much, however,
is obvious at the very outset, namely, that they cannot be made
to refer to the same event as ver. 9, that is to say, to the siege
of Jerusalem by the Assyrians, without bringing the prophet
into the most striking contradiction to himself. For, since ver.
10 predicts not a partial deportation, but the complete carrying
away of Israel to Babel, and ver. 13 the perfect deliverance of
Jerusalem, the people wandering out of Jerusalem into captivity (ver. 10) cannot possibly be the enemies who lead it away,

beating it utterly before Jerusalem, and banning their possessions to the Lord. There is more to favour the allusion to the
victorious conflicts of the Maccabees with the Syrians, for which
Theodoret, Calvin, Hengstenberg, and others decide, since these
conflicts occurred in the period intervening between the return
of the Jews from the Babylonian captivity (ver. 10) and the
coming of the Messiah (ch. v. 1). But even this allusion corresponds far too little to the words of the promise for us to be
able to regard it as correct. Although, for example, the war of
the Maccabees was a religious war in the strict sense of the
word, since the Syrians, and with them the small neighbouring nations of the Jews, set themselves to attack Judah as
the nation of God, and to exterminate Judaism, the *gōyīm
rabbīm*, who have assembled against Zion, and whom the Lord
gathers together thither (vers. 11, 12), point to a much greater
event than the attacks made by the Syrians and the surrounding tribes upon Jerusalem in the time of the Maccabees.
Gōyīm rabbīm (many nations) points back to *gōyīm rabbīm* and
'ammīm rabbīm in vers. 2 and 3, so that, both here and there,
all the nations of the world that are hostile to God are included.
Again, the defeat which they suffer before Jerusalem is much
greater than the victory which the Maccabees achieved over
their enemies. On the other hand, the circumstance that the
Babylonian captivity is predicted in ver. 10, and the birth of
the Messiah in ch. v. 1, 2, and that the victorious conflicts of
the Maccabees with the Syrians and the heathen neighbours of
the Jews lie in the interim between these events, furnishes no
sufficient proof that these conflicts must be referred to in vers.
11–13, simply because the assumption that, in vers. 9–14, the
attacks of the Chaldæans, the Græco-Syrians, and the Romans
upon Zion are foretold in the order in which they followed one
another in history, has no firm basis in the threefold recurrence
of *'attâh* (now) in vers. 9, 11, and 14. As an event is introduced with *'attâh* in ver. 9, which does not follow the one predicted in ver. 8 in chronological sequence, but, on the contrary,
the prophet comes back in *vᵉ'attâh* from the more remote to the
more immediate future, it cannot be inferred from the *'attâh* in
ver. 14 that the oppression mentioned there must follow the
victory over many nations predicted in vers. 11–13 in chronological order, or that the siege and capture of Jerusalem by the

Romans are referred to in ver. 14. Moreover, the proclamation in ver. 10 already goes beyond the Chaldæan catastrophe,
and the liberation of the Jews from the Chaldæan exile, so that
if the $v^{e'}att\hat{a}h$ in ver. 12 announces a conflict with Zion which
will follow the events predicted in vers. 9 and 10, we must not
restrict the conflict to the wars of the Maccabees. We must
therefore understand these verses as referring to the events
already predicted by Joel (ch. iii.), and afterwards by Ezekiel
(xxxviii. 39) and Zechariah (xii.), and in Rev. xx. 8 sqq. : *i.e.*
to the last great attack which the nations of the world will make
upon the church of the Lord, that has been redeemed from
Babel and sanctified, with the design of exterminating the holy
city of God from the face of the earth, and to which the attacks
of the Syrians, and the rest of the nations surrounding Judah,
upon the covenant nation in the times of the Maccabees, furnished but a feeble prelude. This view is favoured by the
unmistakeable similarity between our verses and both Joel and
Ezekiel. The נֶאֶסְפוּ עָלַיִךְ גּוֹיִם רַבִּים in ver. 11, compared with
קִבְּצָם in ver. 12, points clearly back to וְקִבַּצְתִּי אֶת־כָּל־הַגּוֹיִם in Joel
iii. 2, compared with וְנִקְבְּצוּ in ver. 11 ; and the figure in ver.
12, of the gathering together of the nations like sheaves for
the threshing-floor, to the similar figures of the ripening of the
harvest and the treading of the full wine-press in Joel iii. 13.
And the use of *gōyīm rabbīm* in Micah is no reason for supposing that it differs in meaning from the *kol-haggōyīm* of Joel,
since Micah uses *gōyīm rabbīm* in vers. 2 and 3 for the totality
of the nations of the world. Ezekiel, also, simply speaks of
gōyīm rabbīm as assembling together with Gog to attack the
mountains of Israel (ch. xxxviii. 6, 9, 15) ; and in his case also,
this attack of the nations upon Jerusalem is appended to the
redemption of Israel effected at Babel. Again, the issue of this
attack is the same in Micah as in Joel, Ezekiel, and Zechariah,
—namely, the complete overthrow of the hostile nations by the
people of Israel, who fight in the strength of the Lord, by which
Jehovah manifests Himself to all nations as Lord of the whole
earth, and proves Himself to be the Holy One (compare ver. 13
with Joel iii. 12, 13, and Ezek. xxxviii. 16, xxxix. 3 sqq.).
Lastly, a decisive proof of the correctness of this allusion is to
be found in the circumstance, that the attack of the nations is
directed against Zion, which has now become holy, that it pro-

ceeds from hatred and enmity to His holiness, and has for its
object the desecration of the city of God. This feature is by
no means applicable to Jerusalem and Judah in the time of the
Maccabees, but can only apply to the time when Israel, redeemed from Babel, forms a holy church of God, *i.e.* to the last
period of the development of the kingdom of God, which began
with Christ, but has not yet reached its fullest manifestation.
"From the fact, however, that Zion, when sanctified, is to be
delivered out of much greater danger than that from which it
will not be delivered in the immediate future, and also that the
refined and sanctified Zion will conquer and destroy an incomparably greater hostile force than that to which it will now soon
succumb, it follows, in the clearest and most conclusive way,
that in the nearest future it must be given up to the power of
the world, because it is now unholy" (Caspari). This thought
prepares the way for the transition to ch. v. 1, where the
prophecy returns to the oppression foretold in vers. 9 and 10.

Ch. v. 1 (Heb. Bib. iv. 14). "*Now wilt thou gather in
troops, thou daughter of troops ; they lay siege against us ; with
the staff they smite the judge of Israel upon the cheek.*" With
'*attâh* (now) the prophet's address turns once more to the object
introduced with '*attâh* in ch. iv. 9. For we may see clearly
enough from the omission of the cop. *Vav,* which could not be
left out if it were intended to link on ch. v. 1 to ch. iv. 11–13,
that this '*attâh* points back to iv. 9, and is not attached to the
ve'attâh in iv. 11, for the purpose of introducing a fresh
occurrence to follow the event mentioned in iv. 11–13. "The
prophecy in ch. iv. 11–13 explains the ground of that in vers.
9, 10, and the one in ch. v. 1 sounds like a conclusion drawn
from this explanation. The explanation in vers. 11–13 is
enclosed on both sides by that which it explains. By returning in ch. v. 1 to the thoughts expressed in ch. iv. 9, the
prophet rounds off the strophe in iv. 9–v. 1 " (Caspari). The
words are addressed to the daughter Zion, who alone is
addressed with every '*attâh*, and generally throughout the
entire section. *Bath-ge'dûd,* daughter of the troop, might mean:
thou nation accustomed or trained to form troops, thou warlike
Zion. But this does not apply to what follows, in which a
siege alone is mentioned. This turn is given to the expression,
rather "for the purpose of suggesting the thought of a crowd

of people pressing anxiously together, as distinguished from *gᵉdūd*, an invading troop." The verb *hithgōdēd* does not mean here to scratch one's self or make incisions (Deut. xiv. 1, etc.), but, as in Jer. v. 7, to press or crowd together; and the thought is this: Now crowd together with fear in a troop, for he (*sc.* the enemy) sets, or prepares, a siege against us. In עָלֵינוּ the prophet includes himself in the nation as being a member of it. He finds himself in spirit along with the people in besieged Zion. The siege leads to conquest; for it is only in conse-quence of this that the judge of Israel can be smitten with the rod upon the cheek, *i.e.* be shamefully ill treated (compare 1 Kings xxii. 24; Ps. iii. 8; Job xvi. 10). The judge of Israel, whether the king or the Israelitish judges comprehended in one, cannot be thought of as outside the city at the time when the city is besieged. Of all the different effects of the siege of the city the prophet singles out only this one, viz. the ill-treatment of the judge, because "nothing shows more clearly how much misery and shame Israel will have to endure for its present sins" (Caspari). " The judge of Israel" is the person holding the highest office in Israel. This might be the king, as in Amos ii. 3 (cf. 1 Sam. viii. 5, 6, 20), since the Israelitish king was the supreme judge in Israel, or the true possessor of the judicial authority and dignity. But the expression is hardly to be restricted to the king, still less is it meant in distinction from the king, as pointing back to the time when Israel had no king, and was only governed by judges; but the judge stands for the king here, on the one hand with reference to the threat in ch. iii. 1, 9, 11, where the heads and princes of Israel are described as unjust and ungodly judges, and on the other hand as an antithesis to *mōshēl* in ver. 2. As the Messiah is not called king there, but *mōshēl*, ruler, as the possessor of supreme authority; so here the possessor of judicial authority is called *shōphēt*, to indicate the reproach which would fall upon the king and the leaders of the nation on account of their unrighteousness. The threat in this verse does not refer, however, to the Roman invasion. Such an idea can only be connected with the assumption already refuted, that ch. iv. 11–13 point to the times of the Maccabees, and no valid argument can be adduced to support it. In the verse before us the prophet reverts to the oppression predicted in ch. iv. 9 and 10, so that the remarks already made in iv. 10 apply to the fulfilment of what is predicted here. The principal fulfilment occurred in the Chaldæan period; but the fulfilment was repeated in every succeeding siege of Jerusalem until the destruction of the city by the Romans. For, according to ver. 3, Israel will be given up to the power of the empire of the world until the coming of the Messiah; that is to say, not merely till His birth or public appearance, but till the nation shall accept the Messiah, who has appeared as its own Redeemer.

BIRTH OF THE RULER IN ISRAEL, AND HIS PEACEFUL RULE. —CHAP. V. 2–15 (HEB. BIB. 1–14).

At the time of Zion's deepest degradation the ruler in Israel will arise out of Bethlehem, who will not only secure for His people deliverance from their foes, but raise them into a beneficent and yet dreaded power to all nations, founding a kingdom of peace, and glorifying Israel into a holy nation.

Vers. 2–4. The previous announcement of the glory to which Zion is eventually to attain, is now completed by the announcement of the birth of the great Ruler, who through His government will lead Israel to this, the goal of its divine calling. Ver. 2. " *And thou, Bethlehem Ephratah, too small to be among the thousands of Judah, out of thee will He come forth to me who will be Ruler over Israel; and His goings forth are from the olden time, from the days of eternity.*" The וְאַתָּה, with which this new section of the proclamation of salvation opens, corresponds to the וְאַתָּה in ch. iv. 8. Its former government is to return to Zion (ch. iv. 8), and out of little Bethlehem is the possessor of this government to proceed, viz. the Ruler of Israel, who has sprung from eternity. This thought is so attached to ver. 1, that the divine exaltation of the future Ruler of Israel is contrasted with the deepest degradation of the judge. The names *Bethlehem Ephratah* ('*Ephrâth* and '*Ephrâthâh, i.e.* the fertile ones, or the fruit-fields, being the earlier name; by the side of which *Bêth-lechem,* bread-house, had arisen even in the patriarchal times: see Gen. xxxv. 19, xlviii. 7; Ruth iv. 11) are connected together to give greater solemnity to the address, and not to distinguish the Judæan Bethlehem from the one in Zebulun (Josh. xix. 15), since the

following words, " among the thousands of Judah," provide
sufficiently for this.   In the little town the inhabitants are
addressed ; and this explains the masculines אַתָּה, צָעִיר, and מִמְּךְ,
as the prophet had them in his mind when describing the smallness of the little town, which is called κώμη in John vii. 42.
צָעִיר לִהְיוֹת, literally " small with regard to the being among the
'ălâphīm of Judah," *i.e.* too small to have a place among them.
Instead of the more exact מֵהְיוֹת, לִהְיוֹת is probably chosen,
simply because of the following לִהְיוֹת.¹ 'Alâphīm, thousands—an
epithet used as early as Num. i. 16, x. 4, to denote the families,
mishpâchōth, *i.e.* larger sections into which the twelve tribes
of Israel were divided (see the comm. on Num. i. 16 and Ex.
xviii. 25)—does not stand for *sârē 'ălâphīm*, the princes of the
families ; since the thought is simply this, that Bethlehem is too
small for its population to form an independent '*eleph*. We must
not infer from this, however, that it had not a thousand inhabitants, as Caspari does ; since the families were called '*ălâphīm*,
not because the number of *individuals* in them numbered a
thousand, but because the number of their families or heads
of families was generally somewhere about a thousand (see my
biblische Archäologie, § 140).   Notwithstanding this smallness,
the Ruler over Israel is to come forth out of Bethlehem. יֵצֵא מִן
does not denote descent here, as in Gen. xvii. 6 for example, so
that Bethlehem would be regarded as the father of the Messiah,
as Hofmann supposes, but is to be explained in accordance with
Jer. xxx. 21, "A Ruler will go forth out of the midst of it" (cf.
Zech. x. 4) ; and the thought is simply this, " Out of the population of the little Bethlehem there will proceed and arise."
לִי (to me) refers to Jehovah, in whose name the prophet speaks,
and expresses the thought that this coming forth is subservient
to the plan of the Lord, or connected with the promotion of
His kingdom, just as in the words of God to Samuel in 1 Sam.

The omission of the article before צָעִיר, and the use of לִהְיוֹת instead of
מֵהְיוֹת, do not warrant the alteration in the text which Hitzig proposes,
viz. to strike out לִהְיוֹת as erroneous, and to separate the ה from אפרתה
and connect it with צָעִיר = אֶפְרָת הַצָּעִיר ; for the assertion that צָעִיר, if used
in apposition, must have the article, is just as unfounded as the still further
remark, that " to say that Bethlehem was too small to be among the '*ălâphīm* of Judah is incorrect and at variance with 1 Sam. xx. 6, 29," since
these passages by no means prove that Bethlehem formed an '*eleph* by itself.

xvi. 1, "I have provided me a King among his sons," to which Micah most probably alluded for the purpose of showing the typical relation of David to the Messiah. לִהְיוֹת מֹשֵׁל is really the subject to יֵצֵא, the infinitive לִהְיוֹת being used as a relative clause, like לִכְסוֹת in Hos. ii. 11, in the sense of "who is destined to be ruler." But instead of simply saying יֵצֵא מֹשֵׁל יִשְׂרָאֵל, Micah gives the sentence the turn he does, for the purpose of bringing sharply out the contrast between the natural smallness of Bethlehem and the exalted dignity to which it would rise, through the fact that the Messiah would issue from it. בְּיִשְׂרָאֵל, not in, but over Israel, according to the general meaning of מָשַׁל בּ. The article is omitted before *môshêl*, because the only thing of primary importance was to give prominence to the idea of ruling; and the more precise definition follows immediately afterwards in וּמוֹצָאֹתָיו וגו׳. The meaning of this clause of the verse depends upon our obtaining a correct view not only of מוֹצָאוֹת, but also of the references to time which follow. מוֹצָאָה, the fem. of מוֹצָא, may denote the place, the time, the mode, or the act of going out. The last meaning, which Hengstenberg disputes, is placed beyond all doubt by Hos. vi. 3, 1 Kings x. 28, Ezek. xii. 4, and 2 Sam. iii. 25. The first of these senses, in which מוֹצָא occurs most frequently, and in which even the form מוֹצָאוֹת is used in the *keri* in 2 Kings x. 27, which is the only other passage in which this form occurs, does not suit the predicate מִימֵי עוֹלָם here, since the *days* of eternity cannot be called *places* of departure; nor is it required by the correlate מִפְּךָ, *i.e.* out of Bethlehem, because the idea which predominates in Bethlehem is that of the population, and not that of the town or locality; and in general, the antithesis between hemistich *a* and *b* does not lie in the idea of place, but in the insignificance of Bethlehem as a place of exit for Him whose beginnings are in the days of eternity. We take מוֹצָאוֹת in the sense of goings forth, exits, as the meaning "times of going forth" cannot be supported by a single passage. Both קֶדֶם and יְמֵי עוֹלָם are used to denote hoary antiquity; for example in ch. vii. 14 and 20, where it is used of the patriarchal age. Even the two together are so used in Isa. li. 9, where they are combined for the sake of emphasis. But both words are also used in Prov. viii. 22 and 23 to denote the eternity preceding the creation of the world, because man, who lives in

time, and is bound to time in his mode of thought, can only
picture eternity to himself as time without end. Which of
these two senses is the one predominating here, depends upon
the precise meaning to be given to the whole verse.

It is now generally admitted that the Ruler proceeding from
Bethlehem is the Messiah, since the idea that the words refer
to Zerubbabel, which was cherished by certain Jews, according
to the assertion of Chrysostom, Theodoret, and others, is too
arbitrary to have met with any acceptance. Coming forth out
of Bethlehem involves the idea of descent. Consequently we
must not restrict מוֹצָאֹתָיו (His goings forth) to the appearance
of the predicted future Ruler in the olden time, or to the revelations of the Messiah as the Angel of Jehovah even in the
patriarchal age, but must so interpret it that it at least affirms
His origin as well. Now the origin of the Angel of the Lord,
who is equal to God, was not in the olden time in which He
first of all appeared to the patriarchs, but before the creation
of the world—in eternity. Consequently we must not restrict
מִקֶּדֶם מִימֵי עוֹלָם (from of old, from the days of eternity) to the
olden time, or exclude the idea of eternity in the stricter sense.
Nevertheless Micah does not announce here the eternal proceeding of the Son from the Father, or of the Logos from God,
the *generatio filii æterna*, as the earlier orthodox commentators
supposed. This is precluded by the plural מוֹצָאֹתָיו, which cannot be taken either as the *plur. majestatis*, or as denoting the
abstract, or as an indefinite expression, but points to a repeated
going out, and forces us to the assumption that the words
affirm both the origin of the Messiah before all worlds and His
appearances in the olden time, and do not merely express the
thought, that "from an inconceivably remote and lengthened
period the Ruler has gone forth, and has been engaged in coming, who will eventually issue from Bethlehem" (Hofmann,
Schriftbeweis, ii. 1, p. 9).[1] The announcement of the origin of

---

[1] We must reject in the most unqualified manner the attempts that
have been made by the Rabbins in a polemical interest, and by rationalistic commentators from a dread of miracles, to deprive the words of their
deeper meaning, so as to avoid admitting that we have any supernatural
prediction here, whether by paraphrasing "His goings forth" into "the
going forth of His name" (we have this even in the Chaldee), or the eternal
origin into an eternal predestination (Calv.), or by understanding the going
forth out of Bethlehem as referring to His springing out of the family of

this Ruler as being before all worlds unquestionably presupposes His divine nature; but this thought was not strange to the prophetic mind in Micah's time, but is expressed without ambiguity by Isaiah, when he gives the Messiah the name of "the Mighty God" (Isa. ix. 5; see Delitzsch's comm. *in loc.*). We must not seek, however, in this affirmation of the divine nature of the Messiah for the full knowledge of the Deity, as first revealed in the New Testament by the fact of the incarnation of God in Christ, and developed, for example, in the prologue to the Gospel of John. Nor can we refer the "goings forth" to the eternal proceeding of the Logos from God, as showing the inward relation of the Trinity within itself, because this word corresponds to the יָצָא of the first hemistich. As this expresses primarily and directly nothing more than His issuing from Bethlehem, and leaves His descent indefinite, מוֹצָאֹתָיו can only affirm the going forth from God at the creation of the world, and in the revelations of the olden and primeval times.

The future Ruler of Israel, whose goings forth reach back into eternity, is to spring from the insignificant Bethlehem, like His ancestor, king David. The descent of David from Bethlehem forms the substratum not only for the prophetic announcement of the fact that the Messiah would come forth out of this small town, but also for the divine appointment that Christ was born in Bethlehem, the city of David. He was thereby to be made known to the people from His very birth as the great promised descendant of David, who would take possession of the throne of His father David for ever. As the coming forth from Bethlehem implies birth in Bethlehem, so do we see from Matt. ii. 5, 6, and John vii. 42, that the old Jewish synagogue unanimously regarded this passage as containing a prophecy of the birth of the Messiah in Bethlehem.

David, which belonged to Bethlehem (Kimchi, Abarb., and all the later Rabbins and more modern Rationalists). According to this view, the olden time and the days of eternity would stand for the primeval family; and even if such a *quid pro quo* were generally admissible, the words would contain a very unmeaning thought, since David's family was not older than any of the other families of Israel and Judah, whose origin also dated as far back as the patriarchal times, since the whole nation was descended from the twelve sons of Jacob, and through them from Abraham. (See the more elaborate refutation of these views in Hengstenberg's *Christology*, i. p. 486 sqq. translation, and Caspari's *Micha*, p. 216 sqq.)

The correctness of this view is also confirmed by the account in Matt. ii. 1–11; for Matthew simply relates the arrival of the Magi from the East to worship the new-born King in accordance with the whole arrangement of his Gospel, because he saw in this event a fulfilment of Old Testament prophecies.[1]

Ver. 3. "*Therefore will He give them up until the time when a travailing woman hath brought forth, and the remnant of His brethren will return, together with the sons of Israel.* Ver. 4. *And He will stand and feed in the strength of Jehovah, in the majesty of the name of Jehovah His God, and they will dwell, for now will He be great to the ends of the earth.*" "Therefore" (*lâkhēn*) : *i.e.* "because the great divine Ruler of Israel, from whom alone its redemption can proceed, will spring from the little Bethlehem, and therefore from the degraded family of

---

[1] In the quotation of this verse in Matt. ii. 6, the substance is given freely from memory : Καὶ σὺ Βεθλεέμ, γῆ Ἰούδα, οὐδαμῶς ἐλαχίστη εἶ ἐν τοῖς ἡγεμόσιν Ἰούδα· ἐκ σοῦ γὰρ ἐξελεύσεται ἡγούμενος, ὅστις ποιμανεῖ τὸν λαόν μου, τὸν Ἰσραήλ. The deviations from the original text may be accounted for from the endeavour to give the sense clearly, and bring out into more distinct prominence the allusion in the words to David. The γῆ Ἰούδα, in the place of the *Ephrata* of the original, has sprung from 1 Sam. xvii. 12, where Bethlehem is distinguished from the town of the same name in Zebulun in the account of the anointing of David as king, as it frequently is in the Old Testament, by the addition of the word *Judah;* and γῆ Ἰούδα, "land of Judah," is attached loosely in apposition to the name Bethlehem, in the place of the more precise definition, "in the land of Judah." The alteration of the expression, "too small to be among the thousands of Judah," into οὐδαμῶς ἐλαχίστη, κ.τ.λ., does not constitute a discrepancy, but simply alters the thought with an allusion to the glorification which Bethlehem would receive through the fact of the Messiah's springing from it. "Micah, looking at its outward condition, calls it little; but Matthew, looking at the nativity of Christ, by which this town had been most wondrously honoured and rendered illustrious, calls it very little indeed" (C. B. Mich.). The interpretation of בְּאַלְפֵי (among the thousands) by ἐν τοῖς ἡγεμόσιν (among the princes) was very naturally suggested by the personification of Bethlehem, and still more by the thought of the ἡγούμενος about to follow ; and it does not alter the idea, since the families ('ălâphīm) had their heads, who represented and led them. The last clause, ὅστις ποιμανεῖ, κ.τ.λ., is simply a paraphrase of בְּיִשְׂרָאֵל, probably taken from ver. 3, and resting upon 2 Sam. v. 2, and pointing to the typical relation existing between the David born in Bethlehem and the second David, viz. the Messiah. The second hemistich of the verse is omitted, because it appeared superfluous so far as the immediate object of the quotation was concerned.

David" (Caspari). This is the correct explanation; for the reason why Israel is to be given up to the power of the nations of the world, and not to be rescued earlier, does not lie in the appearance of the Messiah as such, but in His springing from little Bethlehem. The birth of the Messiah in Bethlehem, and not in Jerusalem the city of David, presupposes that the family of David, out of which it is to spring, will have lost the throne, and have fallen into poverty. This could only arise from the giving up of Israel into the power of its enemies. Micah had already stated clearly enough in what precedes, that this fate would fall upon the nation and the royal house of David, on account of its apostasy from the Lord; so that he could overlook this here, and give prominence to the other side alone, namely to the fact that, according to the counsel of God, the future Deliverer and Ruler of Israel would also resemble His royal ancestor David in the fact that He was not to spring from Zion the royal city built on high, but from the insignificant country town of Bethlehem, and that for this very reason Israel was to remain so long under the power of the nations of the world. The suffix attached to יִתְּנֵם points to יִשְׂרָאֵל in ver. 1; and נָתַן is applied, as in 1 Kings xiv. 16, to the surrender of Israel into the power of its enemies as a punishment for its sins. This surrender is not the last of many oppressions, which are to take place in the period before the birth of the Messiah (the Roman oppression), but a calamity lasting from the present time, or the coming of the judgment threatened in ch. iii., until the time of the Messiah's coming; and יִתְּנֵם points back not merely to ver. 1, but also to ch. iv. 9, 10. The travailing woman (yōlēdâh) is not the community of Israel (Theodoret, Calvin, Vitringa, and others), but the mother of the Messiah (Cyril, and most of the Christian expositors, including even Ewald and Hitzig). The supposition that the congregation is personified here, is precluded not only by the fact that in the very same sentence the *sons of Israel* are spoken of in the plural, but still more by the circumstance that in that case the bringing forth would be only a figurative representation of the joy following the pain, in which the obvious allusion in the words to the Messiah, which is required by the context, and especially by the suffix to אֶחָיו, which refers to the Messiah, and presupposes that His birth is referred to in יוֹלֵדָה יָלָדָה, would

entirely fall away. But Micah had all the more ground for
speaking of this, inasmuch as Isaiah had already predicted the
birth of the Messiah (Isa. vii. 14). יֹלֵדָה has no article, and
the travailing woman is thereby left indefinite, because the
thought, "till He is born," or "till a mother shall bring Him
forth," upon which alone the whole turns, did not require any
more precise definition.

In the second clause of the verse there commences the description of the blessing, which the birth of the Messiah will
bring to Israel. The first blessing will be the return of those
that remain of Israel to the Lord their God. אֶחָיו, the brethren
of the Ruler born at Bethlehem, are the Judæans as the members of the Messiah's own tribe; just as, in 2 Sam. xix. 13,
David calls the Judæans his brethren, his flesh and bone, in
contrast with the rest of the Israelites. יֶתֶר אֶחָיו, the remnant
of his brethren, are those who are rescued from the judgment
that has fallen upon Judah; *yether*, as in Zeph. ii. 9 and Zech.
xiv. 2, denoting the remnant, in distinction from those who
have perished (= שְׁאֵרִית, ch. ii. 12, iv. 7, etc.). יְשׁוּבוּן, to return,
not from exile to Canaan, but to Jehovah, *i.e.* to be converted.
עַל־בְּנֵי יִשׂ׳, not "to the sons of Israel;" for although שׁוּב, construed with עַל, is met with in the sense of outward return (*e.g.*
Prov. xxvi. 11) as well as in that of spiritual return to the Lord
(2 Chron. xxx. 9), the former explanation would not give any
suitable meaning here, not only because "the sons of Israel,"
as distinguished from the brethren of the Messiah, could not
possibly denote the true members of the nation of God, but also
because the thought that the Judæans are to return, or be converted, to the Israelites of the ten tribes, is altogether unheard
of, and quite at variance with the idea which runs through all
the prophetic Scriptures of the Old Testament,—namely, that
after the division of the kingdom, Judah formed the kernel of
the covenant nation, with which the rebellious Israelites were
to be united once more. עַל signifies here together with, at the
same time as (Hofmann, Caspari), as in Jer. iii. 18 with the
verb יֵלְכוּ, and in Ex. xxxv. 22 with בּוֹא; and "the sons of
Israel" are the Israelites of the ten tribes, and, in this connection, those that are left of the ten tribes. There is no ground
for the objection offered by Hengstenberg to this explanation,
namely, that "it is absurd that the ten tribes should appear to

be the principal persons redeemed;" for this is not implied in the words. The meaning "together with," for עַל, is not derived from the primary meaning, thereupon, in addition to, *insuper*, as Ewald supposes (§ 217, *i*), nor from the idea of accompanying, as Ges. and Dietrich maintain. The persons introduced with עַל are never the principal objects, as the two passages quoted sufficiently prove. The women in Ex. xxxv. 22 (עַל הַנָּשִׁים) are not the principal persons, taking precedence of the men ; nor is the house of Israel placed above the house of Judah in Jer. iii. 18. The use of עַל in the sense of together with has been developed rather from the idea of protecting, shielding, as in Gen. xxxii. 12, slaying the mothers upon, *i.e.* together with, the children, the mothers being thought of as screening the children, as Hos. x. 14 and other passages clearly show. Consequently the person screening the other is the principal person, and not the one covered or screened. And so here, the brethren of the Messiah, like the sons of Judah in Jer. iii. 18, which passage is generally so like the one before us that it might be regarded as an exposition of it, are those who first receive the blessing coming from the Messiah ; and the sons of Israel are associated with them as those to whom this blessing only comes in fellowship with them. In ver. 3 there follows what the Messiah will do for Israel when it has returned to God. He will feed it (עָמַד simply belongs to the pictorial description, as in Isa. lxi. 5) in the strength of Jehovah. The feeding, as a frequent figure for governing, reminds of David, whom the Lord had called from the flock to be the shepherd of His people (2 Sam. v. 2). This is done in the strength of Jehovah, with which He is invested, to defend His flock against wolves and robbers (see John x. 11, 12).[1] This strength is not merely the divine authority with which earthly rulers are usually endowed (1 Sam. ii. 10), but גָּאוֹן, *i.e.* the exaltation or majesty of the name of Jehovah, the majesty in which Jehovah

---

[1] The word " feed" expresses what Christ is towards His people, the flock committed to His care. He does not rule over the church like a formidable tyrant, who oppresses his people by fear; but He is a shepherd, and leads His sheep with all the gentleness to be desired. And inasmuch as we are surrounded on all sides by enemies, the prophet adds, " He will feed in the strength," etc. ; *i.e.*, as much power as there is in God, so much protection will there be in Christ, whenever it shall be necessary to defend the church, and guard it against its foes (Calvin).

manifests His deity on earth. The Messiah is *El gibbŏr* (the Mighty God, Isa. ix. 5), and equipped with the spirit of might (*rŭăch g͏ᵉbhŭrăh*, Isa. xi. 2). "Of His God;" for Jehovah is the God of this Shepherd or Ruler, *i.e.* He manifests Himself as God to Him more than to any other; so that the majesty of Jehovah is revealed in what He does. In consequence of this feeding, they (the sons of Israel) sit (*yâshâbhŭ*), without being disturbed (cf. ch. iv. 4; Lev. xxvi. 5, 6; 2 Sam. vii. 10), *i.e.* will live in perfect undisturbed peace under His pastoral care. For He (the Messiah) will now (עַתָּה, now, referring to the time when He feeds Israel, in contrast with the former oppression) be great (*auctoritate et potentia valebit* : Maurer) to the ends of the earth, *i.e.* His authority will extend over the whole earth. Compare the expression in Luke i. 32, οὗτος ἔσται μέγας, which has sprung from the passage before us, and the parallel in Mal. i. 14.

Vers. 5 and 6. Under His rule Israel will attain to perfect peace. Ver. 5. "*And He will be peace. When Asshur shall come into our land, and when he shall tread in our palaces, we set up against him seven shepherds and eight princes of men.* Ver. 6. *And they feed the land of Asshur with the sword, and the land of Nimrod in his gates; and He rescues from Asshur when he comes into our land and enters into our border.*" זֶה (this man), viz. He who feeds His people in the majesty of God, will be peace, *i.e.* not merely *pacis auctor*, but He who carries peace within Himself, and gives it to His people. Compare Eph. ii. 14, "He is our peace," which points back to this passage. In this relation the Messiah is called the Prince of peace in Isa. ix. 5, as securing peace for Israel in a higher and more perfect sense than Solomon. But in what manner? This is explained more fully in what follows : viz. (1) by defending Israel against the attacks of the imperial power (vers. 5*b*, 6); (2) by exalting it into a power able to overcome the nations (vers. 7–9); and (3) by exterminating all the materials of war, and everything of an idolatrous nature, and so preventing the possibility of war (vers. 10–15). Asshur is a type of the nations of the world by which the people of the Lord are attacked, because in the time of the prophet this power was the imperial power by which Israel was endangered. Against this enemy Israel will set up seven, yea eight princes, who, under the chief command of the Messiah, *i.e.* as His subordinates, will drive it back, and press victoriously into its land. (On the combination of the numbers seven and eight, see the discussions at Amos i. 3.) Seven is mentioned as the number of the works proceeding from God, so that seven shepherds, *i.e.* princes, would be quite sufficient; and this number is surpassed by the eight, to express the thought that there might be even more than were required. נְסִיכֵי אָדָם, not anointed of men, but installed and invested, from *nâsakh*, to pour out, to form, to appoint; hence Josh. xiii. 21, vassals, here the under-shepherds appointed by the Messiah as the upper-shepherd. The meaning " anointed," which is derived from *sûkh*, neither suits Josh. xiii. 21 nor Prov. viii. 23 (see Delitzsch on Ps. ii. 6). On the figurative expression " feed with the sword," for rule, see Ps. ii. 9 and Rev. ii. 27 ; רְעוּ from רָעָה, not from רָעַע. The land of Asshur is called the land of Nimrod, after the founder of the first empire (Gen. x. 9 sqq.), to indicate the character of the imperial power with its hostility to the kingdom of God. בִּפְתָחֶיהָ, in his gates, *i.e.* cities and fortresses; gates for cities, as in Isa. iii. 26, xiii. 2, etc.: not at his gates = on his borders, where the Assyrians stream together for defence (Hitzig, Caspari, etc.). The borders of a land are never called gates; nor could a land be devastated or governed from the border, to say nothing of the fact that בפתחיה corresponds to "in thy palaces" in ver. 4, and leads to the thought that Asshur is to be fully repaid for what it has done to the kingdom of God. The thought is rounded off with וְהִצִּיל מֵאַשּׁוּר וגו', and so He saves from Asshur, etc., not merely by the fact that Asshur is driven back to his own border, and watched there, but by the fact that he is fed in his own territory with the sword. This victorious conflict with the imperial power must not be restricted to the spiritual victory of the kingdom of God over the kingdoms of the world, as Hengstenberg supposes, appealing to vers. 10 sqq., according to which the Lord will make His people outwardly defenceless before it becomes fully victorious in Christ (Hengstenberg). For the extermination of the instruments of war announced in ver. 10 refers not to the period of the exaltation of the people of God into the world-conquering power, but to the time of consummation, when the hostile powers shall be overcome. Before the people of God reach this goal, they have not only to carry on spiritual conflicts, but to fight for existence and recognition even with the force of arms. The prediction of this conflict and victory is not at variance with the announcement in ch. iv. 2, 3, that in the Messianic times all nations will go on pilgrimage to Zion, and seek for adoption into the kingdom of God. Both of these will proceed side by side. Many nations, *i.e.* great crowds out of all nations, will seek the Lord and His gospel, and enter into His kingdom ; but a great multitude out of all nations will also persist in their enmity to the Lord and His kingdom and people, and summon all their power to attack and crush it. The more the gospel spreads among the nations, the more will the enmity of unbelief and ungodliness grow, and a conflict be kindled, which will increase till the Lord shall come to the last judgment, and scatter all His foes.

Vers. 7–9. But the Messiah will prove Himself to be peace to His people, not only by the fact that He protects and saves it from the attacks of the imperial power represented by Asshur, but also by the fact that He endows His rescuing people with the power to overcome their enemies, both spiritually and bodily also. Ver. 7. "*And the remnant of Jacob will be in the midst of many nations like dew from Jehovah, like drops of rain upon grass, which tarrieth not for man, nor waiteth for children of men. Ver. 8. And the remnant of Jacob will be among the nations, in the midst of many nations, like the lion among the beasts of the forest, like the young lion among the flocks of sheep ; which, when it goes through, treads down, and tears in pieces, without deliverer. Ver. 9. High be thy hand above thine oppressors, and may all thine enemies be rooted out.*" Two things are predicted here. In the first place (ver. 7), Israel will come upon many nations, like a refreshing dew from Jehovah, which falls plentifully in drops upon the grass, and will produce and promote new and vigorous life among them. Dew is here, as indeed everywhere else, a figurative expression for refreshing, stimulating, enlivening (cf. Ps. cx. 3, cxxxiii. 3, and lxxii. 6 ; Hos. xiv. 6 ; Deut. xxxiii. 2). The spiritual dew, which Jacob will bring to the nations, comes from Jehovah, and falls in rich abundance without the co-operation of men. Without the spiritual dew from above, the nations are grass (cf. Isa. xl. 6–8). אֲשֶׁר before לֹא יְקַוֶּה does not refer to עֵשֶׂב, but to the principal idea of the preceding clause, viz. to טַל, to

which the explanatory וּרְבִיבִים וגו׳ is subordinate. As the falling of the dew in rain-drops upon the grass does not depend
upon the waiting of men, but proceeds from Jehovah; so will
the spiritual blessing, which will flow over from Israel upon the
nations, not depend upon the waiting of the nations, but will
flow to them against and beyond their expectation. This does
not deny the fact that the heathen wait for the salvation of
Jehovah, but simply expresses the thought that the blessings
will not be measured by their expectation. Secondly (vers. 8, 9),
the rescued Israel will prove itself a terrible power among the
nations, and one to which they will be obliged to succumb.
No proof is needed that vers. 8, 9 do not state in what way
Israel will refresh the heathen, as Hitzig supposes. The refreshing dew and the rending lion cannot possibly be synonymous figures. The similarity of the introduction to vers. 7 and
8 points of itself to something new. To the nations Christ is
set for the rising and falling of many (compare Luke ii. 34,
Rom. ix. 33, with Isa. viii. 14 and xxviii. 16). The people of
God shows itself like a lion, trampling and rending the sheep
among the nations of the world which oppose its beneficent
work. And over these may it triumph. This wish (*târôm* is
optative) closes the promise of the attitude which Israel will
assume among the nations of the world. For *târôm yâd* (high
be the hand), compare Isa. xxvi. 11. High is the hand which
accomplishes mighty deeds, which smites and destroys the foe.

Vers. 10-15. But if Israel conquer the nations in such a
way as this, then will Jehovah fulfil the peace of His people
by the destruction of all the instruments of war, and the extermination of everything of an idolatrous nature, as well as by
the judgment of wrath upon all resisting nations. Ver. 10.
"*And it comes to pass in that day, is the saying of Jehovah,
that I will destroy thy horses out of the midst of thee, and
annihilate thy chariots. Ver. 11. And I shall destroy the
cities of thy land, and throw down all thy fortresses. Ver. 12.
And I shall destroy the witchcrafts out of thy hand; and cloud-
interpreters shall not be left to thee. Ver. 13. And I shall
destroy thy graven images and thy statutes out of the midst of
thee; and thou wilt no more worship the work of thy hands.
Ver. 14. And I shall root out thine idol-groves out of the midst
of thee, and destroy thy cities. Ver. 15. And I shall execute*

vengeance in wrath and fury upon the nations which have not heard." These verses do not explain ver. 8*b*, or state how the extermination of the enemy is to take place, or how Israel is made into a lion destroying the nations that are hostile to it, namely, by the fact that the Lord eradicates from its heart all confidence in horses, chariots, and fortifications, in witchcraft and idolatry (Caspari). This assumption is at variance with the words themselves, and with the strophic arrangement of the chapter. There is nothing about trust in horses, etc., but simply about the extermination of the horses, and everything else in which the idolatrous nation had sought its strength. Moreover, the expression וְהָיָה בַיּוֹם הַהוּא, when compared with וְהָיָה in vers. 4 and 6, shows at once that these verses are intended to depict the last and greatest effect produced by the coming of the Prince of peace in Israel, and overthrows Hengstenberg's assumption, that the prophet here foretels the destructive work of the Lord in Israel, which will precede the destruction of the enemy predicted in ver. 10. In that case בַּיּוֹם הַהוּא would mean "before that day," a meaning which it can never have. The prophet passes rather from the attitude of Israel among the nations, to the description of the internal perfection of the kingdom of God, which does indeed stand in a reciprocal relation to the former and proceed simultaneously with it, but which will not be completed till after the victorious suppression of the foe. Only when the people of God shall have gained the supremacy over all their enemies, will the time have arrived for all the instruments of war to be destroyed. When the world shall be overcome, then will all war cease. The ancient Israel did indeed put its trust in war-horses, and war-chariots, and fortifications (cf. Isa. ii. 7); but the Messianic Israel, or the true people of the Lord, will only put its trust in such things so far as it is not yet pervaded by the power of the peace brought by the Messiah. And the more it appropriates the spiritual power of the Prince of peace, the more will the trust in horses and chariots disappear; so that they will be destroyed, because all war comes to an end (compare Isa. ix. 4–6). And the extermination of everything of an idolatrous nature will go hand in hand with this. Two kinds are mentioned in vers. 12 and 13, viz. witchcraft and the worship of idols of their own making. As objects of witchcraft there are mentioned *kʰshâphīm*, lit. witchcrafts of differents kinds, but the expression מִיָדְךָ limits them to such as are performed with the hand, and *mᵉʿōnᵉnīm* (= ʿōnᵉnīm in Isa. ii. 6), lit. cloud-interpreters, or cloud, *i.e.* storm makers, from ʿânan, a kind of witchcraft which cannot be more precisely defined (see Delitzsch on *Isaiah, l.c.*). Of the objects of the idolatrous worship there are mentioned (after Lev. xxvi. 1) *pᵉsīlīm*, idols made of wood or metal; and מַצֵּבוֹת, stone-images, or stones dedicated to idols (see at 1 Kings xiv. 23). For ver. 12*b*, compare Isa. ii. 8.—Ver. 14 sums up the objects enumerated in vers. 10–13, which are to be exterminated, for the purpose of rounding off the description; the only objects of idolatrous worship mentioned being the 'ashērim, and the only materials of war, the cities as means of defence. אֲשֵׁירִים, written with *scriptio plena*, as in Deut. vii. 5 and 2 Kings xvii. 16, lit. stems of trees or posts standing upright or set up as idols, which were dedicated to the Canaanitish goddess of nature (see at Ex. xxxiv. 13). עָרִים, cities with walls, gates, and bolts. These two rather subordinate objects are mentioned *instar omnium*, to express the entire abolition of war and idolatry. We must not infer from this, however, that the nation of God will still have images made by human hands and worship them, during the stage of its development described in vers. 10–14; but must distinguish between the thought and its formal dress. The gross heathen idolatry, to which Israel was addicted under the Old Testament, is a figure denoting that more refined idolatry which will exist even in the church of Christ so long as sin and unbelief endure. The extermination of every kind of heathen idolatry is simply the Old Testament expression for the purification of the church of the Lord from everything of an idolatrous and ungodly nature. To this there is appended in ver. 15 a promise that the Lord will take vengeance, and wrath, and fury upon the nations which have not heard or have not observed the words and acts of the Lord, *i.e.* have not yielded themselves up to conversion. In other words, He will exterminate every ungodly power by a fierce judgment, so that nothing will ever be able to disturb the peace of His people and kingdom again.

III. THE WAY TO SALVATION.—Chap. vi. and vii.

Micah having declared to the people of Israel not only the judgment that will burst upon Zion on account of its sins, but also the salvation awaiting in the future the remnant saved and purified through the judgment, now proceeds, in the third and last address, to point out the way to salvation, by showing that they bring punishment upon themselves by their ingratitude and resistance to the commandments of God, and that it is only through sincere repentance that they can participate in the promised covenant mercies.

EXHORTATION TO REPENTANCE, AND DIVINE THREATENING.
—CHAP. VI.

In the form of a judicial contest between the Lord and His people, the prophet holds up before the Israelites their ingratitude for the great blessings which they have received from God (vers. 1–5), and teaches them that the Lord does not require outward sacrifices to appease His wrath, but righteousness, love, and humble walk with God (vers. 6–8), and that He must inflict severe punishment, because the people practise violence, lying, and deceit instead (vers. 9–14).

Vers. 1 and 2. Introduction.—Announcement of the lawsuit which the Lord will have with His people.—Ver. 1. *" Hear ye, then, what Jehovah saith ; Rise up, contend with the mountains, and let the hills hear thy voice ! Ver. 2. Hear ye, O mountains, Jehovah's contest ; and ye immutable ones, ye foundations of the earth ! For Jehovah has a contest with His people ; and with Israel will He contend."* In ver. 1 the nation of Israel is addressed in its several members. They are to hear what the Lord says to the prophet,—namely, the summons addressed to the mountains and hills to hear Jehovah's contest with His people. The words " strive with the mountains " cannot be understood here as signifying that the mountains are the objects of the accusation, notwithstanding the fact that רִיב אֶת־פּ׳ signifies to strive or quarrel with a person (Judg. viii. 1 ; Isa. l. 8 ; Jer. ii. 9) ; for, according to ver. 2, they are to hear the contest of Jehovah with Israel, and therefore are to be merely witnesses on the occasion. Consequently אֵת can only express the idea of fellowship here, and רִיב אֵת must be distinguished from רִיב עִם in ver. 2 and Hos. iv. 1, etc. The mountains and hills are to hearken to the contest (as in Deut. xxxii. 1 and Isa. i. 2), as witnesses, " who have seen what the Lord has done for Israel throughout the course of ages, and how Israel has rewarded Him for it all" (Caspari), to bear witness on behalf of the Lord, and against Israel. Accordingly the mountains are called הָאֵתָנִים, the constantly enduring, immutable ones, which have been spectators from time immemorial, and מוֹסְדֵי אָרֶץ, foundations of the earth, as being subject to no change on account of their strength and firmness. In this respect they are often called " the everlasting mountains" (e.g. Gen. xlix. 26; Deut. xxxiii. 15; Ps. xc. 2; Hab. iii. 6). Israel is called 'ammī (Jehovah's people) with intentional emphasis, not only to indicate the right of Jehovah to contend with it, but to sharpen its own conscience, by pointing to its calling. Hithvakkach, like hivvâkhach in the niphal in Isa. i. 18.

Vers. 3-5 open the suit. Ver. 3. " My people ! what have I done unto thee, and with what have I wearied thee ? Answer me. Ver. 4. Yea, I have brought thee up out of the land of Egypt, redeemed thee out of the slave-house, and sent before thee Moses, Aaron, and Miriam. Ver. 5. My people ! remember now what Balak the king of Moab consulted, and what Balaam the son of Beor answered him from Shittim to Gilgal ; that thou mayest discern the righteous acts of Jehovah." The Lord opens the contest with the question, what He has done to the nation, that it has become tired of Him. The question is founded upon the fact that Israel has fallen away from its God, or broken the covenant. This is not distinctly stated, indeed ; but it is clearly implied in the expression מֶה הֶלְאֵתִיךְ, What have I done, that thou hast become weary of me ? לָאָה, in the hiphil, to make a person weary, more particularly to weary the patience of a person, either by demands of too great severity (Isa. xliii. 23), or by failing to perform one's promises (Jer. ii. 31). עֲנֵה בִּי, answer against me, i.e. accuse me. God has done His people no harm, but has only conferred benefits upon them. Of these He mentions in ver. 4 the bringing up out of Egypt and the guidance through the Arabian desert, as being the greatest manifestations of divine grace, to which Israel owes its exalta-

tion into a free and independent nation (cf. Amos ii. 10 and
Jer. ii. 6). The *kî* (for) may be explained from the unex-
pressed answer to the questions in ver. 3 : " Nothing that could
cause dissatisfaction with me ;" *for* I have done nothing but
confer benefits upon thee. To set forth the leading up out of
Egypt as such a benefit, it is described as redemption out of
the house of bondage, after Ex. xx. 2. Moreover, the Lord had
given His people prophets, men entrusted with His counsels
and enlightened by His Spirit, as leaders into the promised
land : viz. Moses, with whom He talked mouth to mouth, as a
friend to his friend (Num. xii. 8) ; and Aaron, who was not
only able as high priest to ascertain the counsel and will of
the Lord for the sake of the congregation, by means of the
" light and right," but who also, along with Moses, represented
the nation before God (Num. xii. 6, xiv. 5, 26, xvi. 20, xx. 7
sqq., and 29). Miriam, the sister of the two, is also mentioned
along with them, inasmuch as she too was a prophetess (Ex.
xv. 20). In ver. 5 God also reminds them of the other great
display of grace, viz. the frustration of the plan formed by the
Moabitish king Balak to destroy Israel by means of the curses
of Balaam (Num. xxii.–xxiv.). יָעַץ refers to the plan which
Balak concocted with the elders of Midian (Num. xxii. 3 sqq.) ;
and עָנָה, Balaam's answering, to the sayings which this sooth-
sayer was compelled by divine constraint to utter against his
will, whereby, as Moses says in Deut. xxiii. 5, 6, the Lord
turned the intended curse into a blessing. The words " from
Shittim (Israel's last place of encampment beyond Jordan, in
the steppes of Moab ; see at Num. xxii. 1 and xxv. 1) to Gilgal"
(the first place of encampment in the land of Canaan ; see at
Josh. iv. 19, 20, and v. 9) do not depend upon זְכָר־נָא, adding
a new feature to what has been mentioned already, in the sense
of " think of all that took place from Shittim to Gilgal," in
which case זְכָר־נָא would have to be repeated in thought ; but
they are really attached to the clause וּמֶה עָנָה וגו׳, and indicate
the result, or the confirmation of Balaam's answer. The period
of Israel's journeying from Shittim to Gilgal embraces not only
Balak's advice and Balaam's answer, by which the plan invented for the destruction of Israel was frustrated, but also
the defeat of the Midianites, who attempted to destroy Israel
by seducing it to idolatry, the miraculous crossing of the

Jordan, the entrance into the promised land, and the circumcision at Gilgal, by which the generation that had grown up in the desert was received into the covenant with Jehovah, and the whole nation reinstated in its normal relation to its God. Through these acts the Lord had actually put to shame the counsel of Balak, and confirmed the fact that Balaam's answer was inspired by God.[1] By these divine acts Israel was to discern the *tsidqōth Y°hōvâh*; *i.e.* not the mercies of Jehovah, for *ts°dâqâh* does not mean mercy, but "the righteous acts of Jehovah," as in Judg. v. 11 and 1 Sam. xii. 7. This term is applied to those miraculous displays of divine omnipotence in and upon Israel, for the fulfilment of His counsel of salvation, which, as being emanations of the divine covenant faithfulness, attested the righteousness of Jehovah.

Vers. 6–8. Israel cannot deny these gracious acts of its God. The remembrance of them calls to mind the base ingratitude with which it has repaid its God by rebelling against Him; so that it inquires, in vers. 6, 7, with what it can appease the Lord, *i.e.* appease His wrath. Ver. 6. "*Wherewith shall I come to meet Jehovah, bow myself before the God of the high place? Shall I come to meet Him with burnt-offerings, with yearling calves?* Ver. 7. *Will Jehovah take pleasure in thousands of rams, in ten thousands of rivers of oil? Shall I give up my first-born for my transgression, the fruit of my body for the sin of my soul?*" As Micah has spoken in vers. 3–5 in the name of Jehovah, he now proceeds, in vers. 6, 7, to let the congregation speak; not, however, by turning directly to God, since it recognises itself as guilty before Him, but by asking the prophet, as the interpreter of the divine will, what it is to do to repair the bond of fellowship which has been rent in pieces by its guilt. קָדֵם does not here mean to anticipate, or come before, but to come to meet, as in Deut. xxiii. 5. Coming to meet, however, can only signify humble prostration (*kâphaph*) before the divine majesty. The God of the high place is the God dwelling in the high place (Isa. xxxiii. 5, lvii. 15), or enthroned in heaven (Ps. cxv. 3). It is only with sacrifices, the means

---

[1] With this view, which has already been suggested by Hengstenberg, the objections offered by Ewald, Hitzig, and others, to the genuineness of the words "from Shittim to Gilgal," the worthlessness of which has been demonstrated by Caspari, fall to the ground.

appointed by God Himself for the maintenance of fellowship with Him, that any man can come to meet Him These the people offer to bring ; and, indeed, burnt-offerings. There is no reference here to sin-offerings, through which disturbed or interrupted fellowship could be restored, by means of the expiation of their sins ; because the people had as yet no true knowledge of sin, but were still living under the delusion that they were standing firmly in the covenant with the Lord, which they themselves had practically dissolved. As burnt-offerings, they would bring calves and rams, not because they formed the only material, but because they were the material most usually employed ; and, indeed, calves of a year old, because they were regarded as the best, not because no others were allowed to be offered, as Hitzig erroneously maintains ; for, according to the law, calves and lambs could be offered in sacrifice even when they were eight days old (Lev. xxii. 27 ; Ex. xxii. 29). In the case of the calves the value is heightened by the quality, in that of the rams by the quantity : thousands of rams ; and also myriads of rivers of oil (for this expression, compare Job xx. 17). Oil not only formed part of the daily *minchah*, but of the *minchah* generally, which could not be omitted from any burnt-offering (compare Num. xv. 1–16 with ch. xxviii. and xxix.), so that it was offered in very large quantities. Nevertheless, in the consciousness that these sacrifices might not be sufficient, the people would offer the dearest thing of all, viz. the first-born son, as an expiation for their sin. This offer is founded, no doubt, upon the true idea that sacrifice shadows forth the self-surrender of man to God, and that an animal is not a sufficient substitute for a man ; but this true idea was not realized by literal (bodily) human sacrifices : on the contrary, it was turned into an ungodly abomination, because the surrender which God desires is that of the spirit, not of the flesh. Israel could and should have learned this, not only from the sacrifice of Isaac required by God (Gen. xxii.), but also from the law concerning the consecration or sanctification of the first-born (Ex. xiii. 12, 13). Hence this offer of the nation shows that it has no true knowledge of the will of its God, that it is still entangled in the heathen delusion, that the wrath of God can be expiated by human sacrifices (cf. 2 Kings iii. 27, xvi. 3).

 The prophet therefore proceeds in ver. 8 to overthrow these

outward means of reconciliation with God, and reminds the people of the moral demands of the law. Ver. 8. " *They have told thee, O man, what is good, and what Jehovah requires of thee, simply to do right, and love good, and walk humbly with thy God.*" הִגִּיד, impersonal, " one has told," or they have told thee, namely Moses in the law. The opinion that Jehovah should be supplied as the subject is a very improbable one, for the simple reason that Jehovah is expressly mentioned in the second dependent clause. The use of כִּי אִם, *nisi*, as in the similar connection of thought in Deut. x. 12, may be accounted for from the retrospective allusion to the gifts mentioned by the people : not outward sacrifices of any kind, *but only* the fulfilment of the three following duties : namely, above all things, doing righteousness and exercising love. These two embrace all the commandments of the second table, of whose fulfilment Israel thought so little, that it was addicted to the very opposite, —namely, injustice, oppression, and want of affection (*vid.* ch. ii. 1, 2, 8, iii. 2, 3, 9 sqq., vi. 10 sqq.). There is also a third : humble walk with God, *i.e.* in fellowship with God, as Israel, being a holy priestly nation, ought to walk. Without these moral virtues, sacrificial worship was a spiritless *opus operatum*, in which God had no pleasure (see at 1 Sam. xv. 22 and Hos. vi. 6).

Vers. 9–16. But because Israel is altogether wanting in these virtues, the Lord must threaten and punish. Ver. 9. " *The voice of Jehovah, to the city it cries, and wisdom has thy name in its eye; hear ye the rod, and who appoints it!*" With these words Micah introduces the threatening and reproachful words of the Lord. קוֹל יְהוָה is not to be taken by itself, as an exclamation, " Hark! voice of the Lord!" as in Isa. xiii. 4, xl. 6, etc. (Umbreit), but must be connected with what follows, in accordance with the accents. Whilst the prophet tells the people in ver. 8 what Jehovah requires, he introduces the following threat with " voice of Jehovah," etc., to give the greater emphasis to the reproof, by intimating that it is not his own voice, but Jehovah's, which is speaking now. "To the city," *i.e.* to the chief city of the kingdom, viz. Jerusalem. The sentence which follows, and which has been explained in very different ways, has the same object. תּוּשִׁיָּה, a word borrowed from the Chokmah-literature (Proverbs and Job), both here and Isa. xxviii. 29, formed from יֵשׁ or the

root שֵׁי (וְשָׁה), in the sense of *subsistentia, substantia,* then mostly
vera et realis sapientia (see Delitzsch on Job xxvi. 3). יִרְאֶה שְׁמֶךָ
is taken by many as a relative clause, "Blessed is he who sees
Thy name," *i.e.* gives heed to Thy revelation, Thy government
of the universe; but if this were the sense, the relative could not
have been omitted, or the infinitive רְאֹת must have been used.
תּוּשִׁיָּה is rather to be taken as the object, and שְׁמֶךָ as the subject:
Thy name sees wisdom, *i.e.* has the true wisdom of life in sight
(רָאָה as in Gen. xx. 10 and Ps. lxvi. 18). There is no necessity
for the conjecture יִרְאֶה for יִרְאָה (Ewald and Hitzig); and notwithstanding the fact that יְרָא is adopted in all the ancient
versions, it is unsuitable, since the thought "wisdom is to fear
Thy name" would be a very strange one in this connection,
unless we could paraphrase the *name* into "word of the person
speaking." For other explanations, see Caspari. Hear ye, *i.e.*
observe, the rod, viz. the judgment threatened by the Lord, and
appointed for His rebellious nation. The reference is to the
imperial power of Assyria, which Isaiah also describes in Isa.
x. 5, 24, as the *matteh* and *shēbhet* by which Israel is smitten.
The suffix to יְעָדָהּ refers to שֵׁבֶט, which is construed here as a
feminine; יָעַד denotes the appointment of an instrument of
punishment, as in Jer. xlvii. 7.

The threatening words commence in ver. 10; vers. 10–12
containing a condemnation of the prevailing sins. Ver. 10.
"*Are there yet in the house of the unjust treasures of injustice, and the ephah of consumption, the cursed one?* Ver. 11.
*Can I be clean with the scale of injustice, and with a purse with
stones of deceit?* Ver. 12. *That their rich men are full of
wickedness, and their inhabitants speak deceit, and their tongue is
falseness in their mouth.*" The reproof is dressed up in the form
of a question. In the question in ver. 10 the emphasis is laid
upon the עוֹד, which stands for that very reason before the
interrogative particle, as in Gen. xix. 12, the only other place
in which this occurs. אִשׁ, a softened form for יֵשׁ, as in 2 Sam.
xiv. 19. Treasures of wickedness are treasures acquired through
wickedness or acts of injustice. The meaning of the question
is not, Are the unjust treasures not yet removed out of the
house, not yet distributed again? but, as vers. 10*b* and 11
require, Does the wicked man still bring such treasures into
the house? does he still heap up such treasures in his house?

The question is affirmative, and the form of a question is chosen
to sharpen the conscience, as the unjust men to whom it is
addressed cannot deny it. אֵיפַת רָזוֹן, ephah of consumption or
hungriness, analogous to the German expression "a hungry
purse," is too small an ephah (cf. Deut. xxv. 14; Amos viii. 5);
the opposite of א' שְׁלֵמָה (Deut. xxv. 15) or א' צֶדֶק (Lev. xix.
36), which the law prescribed. Hence Micah calls it זְעוּמָה =
זְעוּם יְהֹוָה in Prov. xxii. 14, that which is smitten by the wrath
of God (equivalent to cursed; cf. Num. xxiii. 7, Prov. xxiv. 24).
Whoever has not a full ephah is, according to Deut. xxv. 16,
an abomination to the Lord. If these questions show the
people that they do not answer to the demands made by the
Lord in ver. 8, the questions in ver. 11 also teach that, with
this state of things, they cannot hold themselves guiltless. The
speaker inquires, from the standpoint of his own moral consciousness, whether he can be pure, i.e. guiltless, if he uses
deceitful scales and weights,—a question to which every one
must answer No. It is difficult, however, to decide who the
questioner is. As ver. 9 announces words of God, and in
ver. 10 God is speaking, and also in vers. 12, 13, it appears
as though Jehovah must be the questioner here. But אֶזְכֶּה
does not tally with this. Jerome therefore adopts the rendering numquid justificabo stateram impiam; but זָכָה in the kal has
only the meaning to be pure, and even in the piel it is not used
in the sense of niqqâh, to acquit. This latter fact is sufficient
to overthrow the proposal to alter the reading into piel. Moreover, "the context requires the thought that the rich men
fancy they can be pure with deceitful weights, and a refutation
of this delusive idea" (Caspari). Consequently the prophet
only can raise this question, namely as the representative of
the moral consciousness; and we must interpret this transition,
which is so sudden and abrupt to our ears, by supplying the
thought, "Let every one ask himself," Can I, etc. Instead of רֶשַׁע
we have the more definite mirmâh in the parallel clause. Scales
and a bag with stones belong together; 'ăbhânîm are the stone
weights (cf. Lev. xix. 36; Deut. xxv. 13) which were carried
in a bag (Prov. xvi. 11). In ver. 12 the condemnation of injustice is widened still further. Whereas in the first clause
the rich men of the capital (the suffix pointing back to עִיר in
ver. 9), who are also to be thought of in ver. 10, are expressly

mentioned, in the second clause the inhabitants generally are referred to. And whilst the rich are not only charged with injustice or fraud in trade, but with *châmâs*, violence of every kind, the inhabitants are charged with lying and deceit of the tongue. *L^eshōnâm* (their tongue) is not placed at the head absolutely, in the sense of "As for their tongue, deceit is," etc. Such an emphasis as this is precluded by the fact that the preceding clause, " speaking lies," involves the use of the tongue. *L^eshōnâm* is the simple subject : Their tongue is deceit or falsehood in their mouth; *i.e.* their tongue is so full of deceit, that it is, so to speak, resolved into it. Both clauses express the thought, that " the inhabitants of Jerusalem are a population of liars and cheats" (Hitzig). The connection in which the verse stands, or the true explanation of אֲשֶׁר, has been a matter of dispute. We must reject both the combination of vers. 12 and 13 (" Because their rich men, etc., therefore I also," etc.), and also the assumption that ver. 12 contains the answer to the question in ver. 10, and that אֲשֶׁר precedes the direct question (Hitzig) : the former, because ver. 12 obviously forms the conclusion to the reproof, and must be separated from what precedes it ; the latter, because the question in ver. 11 stands between vers. 10 and 12, which is closely connected with ver. 10, and ver. 12 also contains no answer to ver. 10, so far as the thought is concerned, even if the latter actually required an answer. We must rather take אֲשֶׁר as a relative, as Caspari does, and understand the verse as an exclamation, which the Lord utters in anger over the city : " She, whose rich men are full," etc. " Angry persons generally prefer to speak *of* those who have excited their wrath, instead of addressing their words *to* them."

The threat of punishment follows in vers. 13–16. Ver. 13. " *So also now do I smite thee incurably, laying waste because of thy sins.* Ver. 14. *Thou wilt eat, and not be satisfied; and thine emptiness remains in thee; and thou wilt remove, and not save; and what thou savest I will give to the sword.* Ver. 15. *Thou wilt sow, and not reap; thou wilt tread olives, and not anoint thyself with oil; new wine, and not drink wine.*" With וְנַם־אֲנִי the threatened punishment is represented as the consequence of, or retribution for, the sins of the people. הֶחֱלֵיתִי הכ' : literally, I have made the smiting thee sick, *i.e.* smitten thee with incurable sickness (for הֶחְלָה, see at Nah. iii. 19 and Jer. xxx. 12; and for the fact itself, Isa. i. 5, 6). The perfect expresses the certainty of the future. The suffix refers to the people, not of the capital only, but, as we may see from ver. 16, of the whole of the kingdom of Judah. *Hashmēm* (an uncontracted form; see Ges. § 67, Anm. 10), *devastando*, is attached to the preceding verb in an adverbial sense, as a practical exemplification, like the שֶׁבַע in Lev. xxvi. 18, 24, 28, which Micah had in his eye at the time. For the individualizing of the punishment, which follows, rests upon Lev. xxvi. 25, 26, and Deut. xxviii. 39, 40. The land is threatened with devastation by the foe, from which the people flee into fortresses, the besieging of which occasions starvation. For the fulfilment of this, see Jer. lii. 6 (cf. 2 Kings vi. 25). יֶשַׁח, ἀπ. λεγ., hollowness, or emptiness of stomach. וְתַסֵּג, thou mayest remove, *i.e.* carry off thy goods and family, yet wilt thou not save; but even if thou shouldst save anything, it will fall into the hands of the enemy, and be destroyed by his sword (*vid.* Jer. l. 37). The enemy will also partly consume and partly destroy the corn and field-fruit, as well as the stores of oil and wine (*vid.* Amos v. 11). וְלֹא תָסוּךְ שֶׁמֶן is taken verbatim from Deut. xxviii. 40.

This trouble the people bring upon themselves by their ungodly conduct. With this thought the divine threatening is rounded off and closed. Ver. 16. "*And they observe the statutes of Omri, and all the doings of the house of Ahab, and so ye walk in their counsels; that I may make thee a horror, and her inhabitants a hissing, and the reproach of my people shall ye bear.*" The verse is attached loosely to what precedes by Vav. The first half corresponds to vers. 10–12, the second to vers. 13–15, and each has three clauses. הִשְׁתַּמֵּר, as an intensive form of the *piel*, is the strongest expression for שָׁמַר, and is not to be taken as a passive, as Ewald and others suppose, but in a reflective sense: "It (or one) carefully observes for itself the statutes of Omri instead of the statutes of the Lord" (Lev. xx. 23; Jer. x. 3). All that is related of Omri, is that he was worse than all his predecessors (1 Kings xvi. 25). His statutes are the Baal-worship which his son and successor Ahab raised into the ruling national religion (1 Kings xvi. 31, 32), and the introduction of which is attributed to Omri as the founder of the dynasty. In the same sense is Athaliah, who was a daughter of Jezebel, called a daughter of Omri in 2 Chron. xxii. 2. All the doing of the house of Ahab: *i.e.* not only its Baal-worship, but also its persecution of the Lord's prophets (1 Kings xviii. 4, xxii. 27), and the rest of its sins, *e.g.* the robbery and murder committed upon Naboth (1 Kings xxi.). With וַתֵּלְכוּ the description passes over into a direct address; not into the preterite, however, for the imperfect with *Vav rel.* does not express here what has been the custom in both the past and present, but is simply the logical deduction from what precedes, "that which continually occurs." The suffix attached to בְּמֹעֲצוֹתָם refers to Ahab and Omri. By לְמַעַן the punishment is represented as intentionally brought about by the sinners themselves, to give prominence to the daring with which men lived on in godlessness and unrighteousness. In אֹתְךָ the whole nation is addressed: in the second clause, the inhabitants of the capital as the principal sinners; and in the third, the nation again in its individual members. שַׁמָּה does not mean devastation here; but in parallelism with שְׁרֵקָה, horror, or the object of horror, as in Deut. xxviii. 37, Jer. xxv. 9, li. 37, and 2 Chron. xxix. 8. *Cherpath 'ammi:* the shame which the nation of God, as such, have to bear from the heathen, when they are given up into their power (see Ezek. xxxvi. 20). This shame will have to be borne by the several citizens, the present supporters of the idea of the nation of God.

THE CHURCH'S PENITENTIAL PRAYER, AND THE DIVINE PROMISE.—CHAP. VII.

The prophet responds to the threatening of the Lord (ch. vi. 9–16) in the name of the believing church with a penitential prayer, in which it sorrowfully confesses the universality of the deep moral corruption, and painfully bemoans the necessity for the visitation of God (vers. 1–6); after which it rises, through belief in the fidelity of God, to the confidential hope that the Lord will cause the light of His grace to rise again upon the church, which is bearing the merited punishment, and will not let its enemies triumph over it, but will procure it justice, and deeply humble the foe (vers. 7–13); and to this it appends a prayer for the renewal of the former manifestations of grace (ver. 14). The Lord answers this prayer with the promise that He will renew for His people the wonders of the olden time (vers. 15–17); whereupon the prophet closes by praising the mercy and grace of the Lord (vers. 18–20).

Vers. 1-6. That the prophet is speaking in vers. 1 sqq. not in his own name, but in the name of the church, which confesses and bemoans its rebellion against the Lord, is indisputably evident from vers. 7 sqq., where, as all the expositors admit, the church speaks of itself in the first person, and that not "the existing corrupt Israelitish church," as Caspari supposes, but the penitential, believing church of the future, which discerns in the judgment the chastising hand of its God, and expresses the hope that the Lord will conduct its conflict with its foe, etc. The contents of vers. 1-6, also, do not point to the prophet in distinction from the congregation, but may be understood throughout as the confession of sin on the part of the latter. Ver. 1. " *Woe to me! for I have become like a gathering of fruit, like a gleaning of the vintage : Not a grape to eat! an early fig, which my soul desired.*" אַלְלַי, which only occurs again in Job x. 15, differs from הוֹי, and is " *vox dolentis, gementis, et ululantis magis quam minantis*" (Marck); and כִּי is not " that," but " for," giving the reason for אַלְלַי. The meaning of הָיִיתִי כְאָסֹף is not, " it has happened to me as it generally happens to those who still seek for early figs at the fruit gathering, or for bunches of grapes at the gleaning of the vintage" (Caspari and others); for כְּאָסְפֵּי קַיִץ does not mean as *at* the fruit-gathering, but *like* the fruit-gathering. The nation or the church resembles the fruit-gathering and gleaning of the vineyard, namely, in this fact, that the fruit-gathering yields no more early figs, and the gleaning of the vintage yields no more grapes to eat; that is to say, its condition resembles that of an orchard in the time of the fruit-gathering, when you may find fruit enough indeed, but not a single early fig, since the early figs ripen as early as June, whereas the fruit-gathering does not take place till August (see at Isa. xxviii. 4). The second simile is a still simpler one, and is very easily explained. אָסְפֵּי is not a participle, but a noun— אֹסֶף the gathering (Isa. xxxii. 10); and the plural is probably used simply because of עֹלֵלֹת, the gleaning, and not with any allusion to the fact that the gleaning lasts several days, as Hitzig supposes, but because what is stated applies to all gatherings of

fruit.   קַיִן, fruit ; see at Amos viii. 1.   אֹוְתָהּ is to be taken in
a relative sense, and the force of אֵין still extends to בִּכּוּרָה (compare Gen. xxx. 33).   The figure is explained in vers. 2 sqq.

Ver. 2. " *The godly man has disappeared from the earth, and
there is no more a righteous man among men.   All lie in wait for
blood, they hunt every man his brother with the net.   Ver. 3.
Their hands are after evil, to make it good.   The prince asks, and
the judge is for reward ; and the great man, he speaks the evil of
his soul : and they twist it together.*"   The grape and the early
fig signify the good and the righteous man.   חָסִיד is not the
God-fearing man, but, according to the context, the man who
cherishes love and fidelity.   אָבַד, not "to have perished," but to
be lost, to have disappeared.   מִן הָאָרֶץ, not "out of the land,"
but, as the parallel בָּאָדָם shows, from the earth, out of the world.
For the fact itself, compare Ps. xii. 2 and Isa. lvii. 1.   They all
lie in wait for blood, *i.e.* not that they all go about committing
murder, but simply that they set their minds upon quarrels,
cheating, and treachery, that they may rob their neighbour of
his means of existence, so that he must perish (cf. ch. iii. 2, 3,
ii. 1, 2) ; at the same time, even murderous thoughts are not
excluded.   The same thing is implied in the hunting with the
net.   אָח, the brother, is the fellow-countryman (for this figure,
compare Ps. x. 9, xxxv. 7, 8, etc.).   In ver. 3 the words from
עַל הָרַע to לְהֵיטִיב are not to be joined to what follows so as to
form one sentence.   Such a combination is not only opposed to
the accents, but is at variance with the structure of the whole
verse, which consists of several short clauses, and it does not
even yield a natural thought ; consequently Ewald proposes to
alter the text (שֹׁואֵל).   הָרַע is hardly the *inf. hiph.* "to do evil,"
but most likely a noun with the article, "the evil ;" and the
thought is therefore either "both hands are (*sc.* busy) with evil,"
or " both hands are stretched out to evil," to make it good, *i.e.*
to carry out the evil well (הֵיטִיב as in Jer. ii. 33), or to give
evil such a form that it shall appear to be good, or right.   This
thought is then made special : the prince, the judge, and the
great man, *i.e.* the rich man and mighty man (Lev. xix. 15;
1 Sam. xxv. 2), weave a thing to make evil good.   עָבַת, to weave,
to twist together, after עֲבֹות, twist or string.   The subject to
וַיְעַבְּתֻהָ is to be found in the three classes already named, and
not merely in the judge and the great man.   There is just as

little reason for this limitation as for the assumption that the great man and the prince are one person. The way in which the three twist the thing or the evil plan together is indicated in the statements of the three previous clauses. The prince asks, *sc.* for the condemnation of a righteous or innocent man; and the judge grants this for recompense against compensation; and the rich man co-operates by speaking *havvath naphshō. Havvâh* in most passages is universally allowed to signify hurt, mischief, destruction; and the only question is, whether this meaning is to be traced to הוה = אוה, to breathe (Hupfeld on Ps. v. 10), or to הוה, to occur, an occurrence, then specially an evil occurrence (Hengstenberg, *Diss. on the Pentateuch*, vol. i. p. 252). Only in Prov. x. 3 and the passage before us is *havvâh* said to signify desire in a bad sense, or evil lust. But, as Caspari has shown, the meaning is neither necessary nor established in either of these two passages. In Prov. x. 3 the meaning *ærumna activa aliisque inferenda* is quite sufficient; and C. B. Michaelis has adopted it for the present passage: "The great man speaks the mischief of his soul," *i.e.* the injury or destruction of another, for which he cherishes a desire. *Nephesh*, the soul as the seat of desire. הוא is not introduced to strengthen the suffix attached to נַפְשׁוֹ, "of his, yea of his soul" (Ewald, Hitzig, Umbreit); for not only are the accents against this, but also the thought, which requires no such strengthening. It is an emphatic repetition of the subject *haggâdōl.* The great man weaves evil with the king and judge, by desiring it, and expressing the desire in the most open manner, and thereby giving to the thing an appearance of right.

And even the best men form no exception to the rule. Ver. 4. "*Their best man is like a briar; the upright man more than a hedge: the day of thy spies, thy visitation cometh, then will their confusion follow. Ver. 5. Trust not in the neighbour, rely not upon the intimate one; keep the doors of thy mouth before her that is thy bosom friend. Ver. 6. For the son despiseth the father, the daughter rises up against her mother, the daughter-in-law against her mother-in-law; a man's enemies are the people of his own house.*" טוֹבָם, the good man among them, *i.e.* the best man, resembles the thorn-bush, which only pricks, hurts, and injures. In יָשָׁר the force of the suffix still continues: the most righteous man among them; and מִן before מִמְּסוּכָה is used in a comparative sense: " is more, *i.e.* worse, than a thorn-hedge." The corruption of the nation has reached such a terrible height, that the judgment must burst in upon them. This thought comes before the prophet's mind, so that he interrupts the description of the corrupt condition of things by pointing to the day of judgment. The " day of thy watchmen," *i.e.* of thy prophets (Jer. vi. 17; Ezek. iii. 17, xxxiii. 7), is explained in the apposition *pᵉqŭddâthᵉkhâ* (thy visitation). The perfect בָּאָה is prophetic of the future, which is as certain as if it were already there. עַתָּה, now, *i.e.* when this day has come (really therefore = " then "), will their confusion be, *i.e.* then will the wildest confusion come upon them, as the evil, which now envelopes itself in the appearance of good, will then burst forth without shame and without restraint, and everything will be turned upside down. In the same sense as this Isaiah also calls the day of divine judgment a day of confusion (Isa. xxii. 5). In the allusion to the day of judgment the speaker addresses the people, whereas in the description of the corruption he speaks of them. This distinction thus made between the person speaking and the people is not at variance with the assumption that the prophet speaks in the name of the congregation, any more than the words " *thy* watchmen, *thy* visitation," furnish an objection to the assumption that the prophet was one of the watchmen himself. This distinction simply proves that the penitential community is not identical with the mass of the people, but to be distinguished from them. In ver. 5 the description of the moral corruption is continued, and that in the form of a warning not to trust one another any more, neither the companion (רֵעַ) with whom one has intercourse in life, nor the confidential friend ('*allūph*), nor the most intimate friend of all, viz. the wife lying on the husband's bosom. Even before her the husband was to beware of letting the secrets of his heart cross his lips, because she would betray them. The reason for this is assigned in ver. 6, in the fact that even the holiest relations of the moral order of the world, the deepest ties of blood-relationship, are trodden under foot, and all the bonds of reverence, love, and chastity are loosened. The son treats his father as a fool (*nibbēl*, as in Deut. xxxii. 15). " The men of his house " (the subject of the last clause) are servants dwelling in the house, not relations (cf. Gen. xvii. 23, 27, xxxix. 14; 2 Sam. xii. 17, 18). This verse is applied by Christ to the period of the κρίσις which will attend His coming, in His instruction to the apostles in Matt. x. 35, 36 (cf. Luke xii. 53). It follows from this, that we have not to regard vers. 5 and 6 as a simple continuation of the description in vers. 2–4*a*, but that these verses contain the explanation of עַתָּה תִהְיֶה מְבוּכָתָם, in this sense, that at the outbreak of the judgment and of the visitation the faithlessness will reach the height of treachery to the nearest friends, yea, even of the dissolution of every family tie (cf. Matt. xxiv. 10, 12).

Vers. 7–13. " This confession of sin is followed by a confession of faith on the part of the humiliated people of God" (Schlier.). Ver. 7. "*But I, for Jehovah will I look out; I will wait for the God of my salvation; my God will hear me.* Ver. 8. *Rejoice not over me, O mine enemy! for am I fallen, I rise again; for do I sit in darkness, Jehovah is light to me.*" By וַאֲנִי what follows is attached adversatively to the preceding words. Even though all love and faithfulness should have vanished from among men, and the day of visitation should have come, the church of the faithful would not be driven from her confidence in the Lord, but would look to Him and His help, and console itself with the assurance that its God would hear it, *i.e.* rescue it from destruction. As the looking out (*tsâphâh*) for the Lord, whether He would not come, *i.e.* interpose to judge and aid, involves in itself a prayer for help, though it is not exhausted by it, but also embraces patient waiting, or the manifestation of faith in the life; so the hearing of God is a practical hearing, in other words, a coming to help and to save. The God of my salvation, *i.e.* from whom all my salvation comes (cf. Ps. xxvii. 9; Isa. xvii. 10). Her enemy, *i.e.* the heathen power of the world, represented in Micah's time by Asshur, and personified in thought as daughter Asshur, is not to rejoice over Zion. כִּי, for, not " if:" the verb *náphaltî* is rather to be taken conditionally, " for have I fallen;" *náphal* being used, as in Amos v. 2, to denote the destruction of the power and of the kingdom. The church is here supposed to be praying out of the midst of the period when the judgment has fallen upon it for its sins, and the power of the world is triumphing over it. The prophet could let her speak thus, because he had already predicted the destruction of the kingdom and the carrying away of the people into exile as a judgment that was inevitable (ch. iii. 12, vi. 16). Sitting in darkness, *i.e.* being in distress and poverty (cf. Isa. ix 1, xlii. 7; Ps. cvii. 10). In this darkness the Lord is light to the faithful, *i.e.* He is their salvation, as He who does indeed chasten His own people, but who even in wrath does not violate His grace, or break the promises which He has given to His people.

Ver. 9. " *The wrath of Jehovah shall I bear, for I have sinned against Him, till He shall fight my fight, and secure my right. He will bring me forth to the light; I shall behold His righteousness.* Ver. 10. *And may my enemy see it, and shame cover her, who hath said to me, Where is Jehovah thy God? Mine eyes will see it; now will she be for a treading down, like mire of the streets.*" Confidence in the help of the Lord flows from the consciousness, that the wretchedness and sufferings are a merited punishment for the sins. This consciousness and feeling generate patience and hope: patience to bear the wrath of God manifesting itself in the sufferings; hope that the sufferings, as inflicted by the righteous God, will cease as soon as the divine justice has been satisfied. *Za'aph: lit.* the foaming up of wrath (Isa. xxx. 30); hence strong wrath. This the church will bear, till the Lord conducts its conflict and secures its rights. רִיבִי is the judicial conflict between Israel and the heathen power of the world. Although, for example, God had given up His nation to the power of its enemies, the nations of the world, on account of its sins, so that they accomplished the will of God, by destroying the kingdoms of Israel and Judah, and carrying away the people into exile; yet they grew proud of their own might in so doing, and did not recognise themselves as instruments of punishment in the hand of the Lord, but attributed their victories to the power of their own arm, and even aimed at the destruction of Israel, with scornful defiance of the living God (cf. Isa. x. 5–15; Hab. i. 11). Thus they violated the rights of Israel, so that the Lord was obliged to conduct the contest of His people with the heathen, and secure the rights of Israel by the overthrow of the heathen power of the world. For רִיב רִיבִי, see Ps. xliii. 1; for עָשָׂה מִשְׁפָּט, Ps. ix. 4, 5; and for the fact itself, Isa. xlix. 25, li. 22. *Mishpât* is Israel's right, in opposition to the powers of the world, who would destroy it. The following word יוֹצִיאֵנִי is not governed by עַד אֲשֶׁר, as the absence of the copula *Vav* shows. With these words the hope takes the form of the certain assurance that the Lord will remove the distress, and let Israel see His righteousness. *Ts^edâqâh* is the righteousness of God revealing itself in the forgiveness and restoration of Israel to favour; like *ts^edâqōth* in ch. vi. 5 : in actual fact, the salvation of Israel about to be secured, regarded as an emanation of the righteousness of the covenant God ; hence parallel to אוֹר. רָאָה with בְּ, to look at, so that one penetrates, as it were, into an object, seeing with feasting of the eyes (so also in ver. 10). This exaltation of Israel to new salvation it is hoped that the enemy will see (וְתֵרֶא, opt.), and be covered with shame ; for the power of the world is overthrown, in order that Israel may be redeemed out of its power. This desire is a just one, because the enemy has despised the Lord God. For the expression, "Where is Jehovah thy God?" compare Joel ii. 17. And Israel will see its fulfilment (תִּרְאֶינָּה with *Nun* doubled after a sharpened *é*; see Ewald, § 198, *a*). *'Attâh,* now (seeing the future in spirit, as having already come), the enemy will be trodden down like mire of the streets (for this figure, see Isa. x. 6).

The confident expectation rises in vers. 11 sqq. into an assurance of the promise ; the words of the prophet in the name of the church rising into an address to Zion, to confirm its hope by the promise of the restoration of Zion, and the entrance of crowds of people into the city of God. Ver. 11. " *A day to build thy walls (cometh)* ; *in that day will the ordinance be far away.* Ver. 12. *In that day will they come to thee from Asshur and the cities of Egypt, and from Egypt to the river, and (to) sea from sea, and (from) mountain to mountain.* Ver. 13. *And the earth will become a desert because of its inhabitants, for the fruit of their doings.*" Ver. 11 consists of two clauses ; for we may easily supply to *yōm* " is " or " will be " = come. The daughter Zion is addressed (cf. ch. iv. 8) not as a church, but as a city, as the centre and representative of the kingdom of God. As such, she is compared to a vineyard, as in Isa. v. 1–7, xxvii. 2–4, Ps. lxxx. 9, 10. The word *gâdēr*, which is generally used for the hedge or wall around a vineyard, points to this (see Isa. v. 5 ; Num. xxii. 24 ; Eccles.

x. 8). יוֹם הַהוּא is an adverbial accusative; in that day will חק
be far away. The meaning of this word is very difficult to
find, and can hardly be settled with any certainty. The explanation of *chŏq*, as signifying the law imposed upon Israel by
the heathen oppressors (Chald., Hengstenberg, etc.), cannot
be sustained, as this meaning cannot be established from Ps.
civ. 20, and is not suggested by the context. So, again, the
explanation, " On that day will the goal set (for Israel), or
the boundary fixed (for it), be a far distant one (*i.e.* then will
the boundaries of the land of Israel lie in the far distance, or
be advanced to the remotest distance:" Hitzig, Caspari, and
others), introduces a meaning into the words which they do not
possess. Even if *chŏq* does denote a fixed point or a limit of
either space or time, it never signifies the boundary of a nation;
and *râchaq*, to be far off, is not equivalent to being advanced
to a great distance. *Chŏq* is apparently used here for the
ordinance or limit which God has appointed to separate Israel
from the nations; not a land-boundary, but the law of Israel's
separation from the nations. This law will be far away, *i.e.*
will be removed or set aside (*yirchaq* is only chosen for the sake
of the assonance with *chŏq*), inasmuch as numerous crowds, as
is added in ver. 12 by way of explanation, will then stream to
Zion, or come to the people of God, out of all lands (cf. ch. iv.
1, 2). For this is what ver. 12 refers to, and not the return
to Zion of the Israelites who have been scattered in the heathen
lands. יָבוֹא (impersonal), one comes, they come: not "return,"
יָשׁוּב, which must have been the expression used if the return
of the Israelites out of their captivity had been meant. The
heathen who cherish a desire for the God of Zion and His law
(ch. iv. 2) will come to Israel; not to Israel as still living in
their midst (Caspari), but to the Israel that has already returned, and whose walls have been rebuilt (ver. 11). The
building of the walls of Zion involves the gathering together
of the dispersed nation, or rather presupposes it. Heathen
will come " from Asshur and the cities of Egypt," *i.e.* from the
two mightiest empires in the time of the prophet. *Mâtsŏr*, the
poetical name of Egypt, as in Isa. xix. 6, xxxvii. 25; and " cities
of Egypt," because that land or kingdom was especially rich in
cities. The further definitions individualize the idea of the
totality of the lands and provinces, the correlative members

being transposed and incomplete in the last two sentences, so that the preposition עַד must be supplied to יָם, and the preposition מִן to הָהָר. From Egypt to the river (Euphrates) includes the lands lying between these two terminal points; and in the expressions, " sea from sea, and mountain to mountain," seas and mountains are mentioned in the most general manner, as the boundaries of lands and nations; so that we have not to think of any particular seas and mountains, say the Western (or Mediterranean) Sea, and the Eastern (the Dead or the Galilean) Sea, as being the western and eastern boundaries of Palestine, and of Lebanon and Sinai as the northern and southern boundaries, but must adhere firmly to the general character of the expression: " from one sea and one mountain to another sea and mountain," *i.e.* from every land situated between seas and mountains, that is to say, from all the lands and provinces of the earth. The coming out of all lands is not to be understood as denoting simply passing visits to Canaan or Zion, but as coming to connect themselves with the people of God, to be received into fellowship with them. There is a parallel to this promise in the promise contained in Isa. xix. 18–25, that in the Messianic times Egypt and Asshur will turn to Jehovah. This takes place because the earth will become a desert, on account of the evil deeds of its inhabitants. Whilst Zion is rebuilt, and the people of God are multiplied, by the addition of the godly Gentiles out of all the countries of the earth, the judgment falls upon the sinful world. This statement of ver. 13 is simply attached to what precedes it by וְהָיְתָה, in order to complete the promise of the restoration of Zion, by adding the fate which will befal the earth (*i.e.* the earth outside Canaan); but it actually contains the motive for the coming of the crowds to Zion. הָאָרֶץ cannot be the land of Israel (Canaan) here, in support of which appeal has been made to Lev. xxvi. 33 and Isa. i. 7; for the context neither leads to any such limitation as that הָאָרֶץ could be taken in the sense of אַרְצְכֶם (in Leviticus and Isaiah), nor allows of our thinking of the devastation of Canaan. When the day shall have come for the building of the walls of Zion, the land of Israel will not become a desert then; but, on the contrary, the devastation will cease. If the devastation of Canaan were intended here, we should have either to take והיתה as a pluperfect, in violation of the rules

of the language, or arbitrarily to interpolate " previously,"
as Hitzig proposes.   עַל יֹשְׁבֶיהָ is defined more precisely by
מִפְּרִי מַעַלְלֵיהֶם   The doings are of course evil ones, and the
deeds themselves are the fruit (cf. Isa. iii. 10).

Vers. 14–17. The promise of salvation impels the congregation to pray that it may be granted (ver. 14) ; whereupon
the Lord assures it that His covenant mercies shall be renewed,
and promises the thorough humiliation of the hostile nations of
the world (vers. 15–17).   Ver. 14. " *Feed thy people with thy
staff, the sheep of thine inheritance, dwelling apart, in the wood,
in the midst of Carmel : let them feed in Bashan and Gilead, as
in the days of the olden time.*"   The question in dispute among
commentators, whether this prayer is addressed to the Lord by
the prophet on behalf of the nation, or whether the prophet is
still speaking in the name of the believing church, is decided
in favour of the latter by the answer addressed to the church
in ver. 15.   The Lord is addressed as the shepherd of Israel,
the title by which Jacob addressed Him in Gen. xlix. 24 (cf.
Ps. lxxx. 2, xxiii. 1 sqq.).   The prayer is related to the promise in ch. v. 3 sqq., viz. that the ruler coming forth out of
Bethlehem will feed in the strength of Jehovah, and involves
the prayer for the sending of this ruler.   " With this staff,"
i.e. the shepherd's staff (cf. Lev. xxvii. 32 ; Ps. xxiii. 4), is
added pictorially ; and as a support to the prayer, it designates
the people as the sheep of Jehovah's inheritance.   צֹאן נַחֲלָה,
instead of עַם נַחֲלָה, which occurs more frequently, is occasioned by the figure of the shepherd.   As the sheep need
the protection of the shepherd, lest they should perish, so
Israel needs the guidance of its God, that it may not be
destroyed by its foes.   The following apposition שֹׁכְנִי לְבָדָד
determines the manner of the feeding more precisely ; so
that we may resolve it into the clause, " so that thy people
may dwell apart."   The words contain an allusion to Num.
xxiii. 9, where Balaam describes Israel as a people separated
from the rest of the nations ; and to Deut. xxxiii. 28, where
Moses congratulates it, because it dwells in safety and alone
(*bâdâd*, separate), under the protection of its God, in a land
full of corn, new wine, etc.   The church asks for the fulfilment of this blessing from Jehovah its shepherd, that it may
dwell separate from the nations of the world, so that they may

not be able to do it any harm; and that "in the wood in the midst of Carmel," that promontory abounding in wood and pasture land (*lœtis pascuis abundat:* Jerome on Amos i. 2). The wood is thought of here as shutting off the flock from the world without, withdrawing it from its sight, and affording it security; and the fact that dangerous wild beasts have their home in the forest (Jer. v. 6; Ps. lxxx. 14) is overlooked here, because Israel is protected from them by its own shepherd. יִרְעוּ, which follows, is not future, but optative, corresponding to the imperative רְעֵה. Gilead and Bashan are also named as portions of the land that were rich in pasture (cf. Num. xxxii. 1 sqq.), namely, of the land to the east of the Jordan, Carmel belonging to the western portion of Canaan. These three portions individualize the whole of the territory which Israel received for its inheritance, and not merely the territory of the kingdom of the ten tribes. The simple reason why no districts in the kingdom of Judah are mentioned, is that Judah possessed no woody districts abounding in grass and pasture resembling those named. Moreover, the prayer refers to the whole of Israel, or rather to the remnant of the whole nation that has been rescued from the judgment, and which will form an undivided flock under the Messiah (cf. ch. v. 2; Isa. xi. 13; Ezek. xxxvii. 15 sqq.). יְמֵי עוֹלָם, "the days of old," are the times of Moses and Joshua, when the Lord brought Israel with His mighty arm into the possession of the promised land.

The Lord answers this prayer, by promising, according to His abundant goodness, more than the church has asked. Ver. 15. "*As in the days of thy going out of the land of Egypt will I cause it to see wonders.* Ver. 16. *Nations will see it, and be ashamed of all their strength: they will lay the hand upon the mouth, their ears will become deaf.* Ver. 17. *They will lick dust like the snake, like the reptiles of the earth they come trembling out of their castles: they will go trembling to Jehovah our God, and before thee will they fear.*" The wonders (*niphlá'ōth;* cf. Ex. iii. 20, xv. 11; Ps. lxxviii. 11) with which the Lord formerly smote Egypt, to redeem His people out of the bondage of that kingdom of the world, will the Lord renew for His people. In צֵאתְךָ the nation is addressed, whilst the suffix of the third pers. attached to אַרְאֶנּוּ points back to עַמְּךָ in ver. 14. The miraculous deeds will make such an impression, that the heathen

nations who see them will stand ashamed, dumb and deaf with
alarm and horror. Ashamed of all their strength, *i.e.* because
all their strength becomes impotence before the mighty acts of
the Almighty God. Laying the hand upon the mouth is a
gesture expressive of reverential silence from astonishment and
admiration (cf. Judg. xviii. 19; Job xxi. 5, etc.). Their ears
shall become deaf " from the thunder of His mighty acts, Job
xxvi. 14, the *qōl hâmōn* of Isa. xxxiii. 8 " (Hitzig). With this
description of the impression made by the wonderful works of
God, the words of God pass imperceptibly into words of the
prophet, who carries out the divine answer still further in an
explanatory form, as we may see from ver. 17*b*. The heathen
will submit themselves to Jehovah in the humblest fear. This
is stated in ver. 17. Licking the dust like the serpent contains
an allusion to Gen. iii. 14 (cf. Ps. lxxii. 9 and Isa. xlix. 23).
זֹחֲלֵי אֶרֶץ, earth-creepers, *i.e.* snakes, recals the זֹחֲלֵי עָפָר of Deut.
xxxii. 24. Like snakes, when they are driven out of their
hiding-place, or when charmers make them come out of their
holes, so will the nations come trembling out of their castles
(*misgᵉrōth* as in Ps. xviii. 46), and tremble to Jehovah, *i.e.* flee
to Him with trembling, as alone able to grant help (see Hos.
iii. 5), and fear before thee. With מִמְּךָ the prayer passes into
an address to Jehovah, to attach to this the praise of God with
which he closes his book.

Ver. 18. " *Who is a God like Thee? removing guilt and passing over iniquity to the remnant of His inheritance. He retaineth
not His anger for ever, for He delighteth in mercy.* Ver. 19. *He
will have compassion upon us again, tread down our transgressions; and Thou wilt cast all their sins into the depths of the sea.*
Ver. 20. *Mayest Thou show truth to Jacob, mercy to Abraham,
which Thou hast sworn to our fathers from the days of old.*"
מִי אֵל כָּמוֹךָ looks back to Ex. xv. 11; but whether Micah also
plays upon his own name is doubtful. Like the first redemption of Isràel out of Egypt, the second or still more glorious
redemption of the people of God furnishes an occasion for
praising the incomparable nature of the Lord. But whereas
in the former Jehovah merely revealed Himself in His incomparable exaltation above all gods, in the restoration of the
nation which had been cast out among the heathen because of
its sins, and its exaltation among the nations, He now reveals

His incomparable nature in grace and compassion. The words
נֹשֵׂא עָוֹן וגו׳ are formed after Ex. xxxiv. 6, 7, where the Lord,
after the falling away of Israel from Him by the worship of the
golden calf, reveals Himself to Moses as a gracious and merciful
God, who forgives guilt and sin. But this grace and compassion are only fully revealed in the restoration and blessing
of the remnant of His nation by Jesus Christ. (For ver. 18*b*,
see Ps. ciii. 9.) As One who delighteth in mercy, He will have
compassion upon Israel again (*yâshûbh* used adverbially, as in
Hos. xiv. 8, etc.), will tread down its sins, *i.e.* conquer their
power and tyranny by His compassion, and cast them into the
depths of the sea, as He once conquered the tyrant Pharaoh
and drowned him in the depths of the sea (Ex. xv. 5, 10).
This believing assurance then closes with the prayer (*tittēn* is
optative) that the Lord will give His rescued nation truth and
mercy ('*ĕmeth* and *chesed*, after Ezek. xxxiv. 6), *i.e.* give them
to enjoy, or bestow upon them, what He had sworn to the
patriarchs (Gen. xxii. 16). Abraham and Jacob are mentioned
instead of their family (cf. Isa. xli. 8).

With this lofty praise of the Lord, Micah closes not only the
last words, but his whole book. The New Testament parallel,
as Hengstenberg has correctly observed, is Rom. xi. 33–36;
and the μυστήριον made known by the apostle in Rom. xi.
25 sqq. gives us a view of the object and end of the ways of
the Lord with His people.

END OF VOL. I.

BIBLICAL COMMENTARY

ON

THE OLD TESTAMENT

BY

C. F. KEIL, D.D., AND F. DELITZSCH, D.D.,

PROFESSORS OF THEOLOGY.

THE TWELVE MINOR PROPHETS.

By CARL FRIEDRICH KEIL, D.D.

Translated from the German
BY
THE REV. JAMES MARTIN, B.A.,

CONTENTS

NAHUM.

HABAKKUK.

ZEPHANIAH.

HAGGAI.

ZECHARIAH.

NAHUM

INTRODUCTION.

1. **P**ERSON OF THE PROPHET.—All that we know of *Nahum* (*Nachūm, i.e.* consolation or comforter, *consolator,* Gr. Ναούμ) is, that he sprang from the place called *Elkosh;* since the epithet *hâ'elqōshī,* in the heading to his book, is not a patronymic, but the place of his birth. *Elkosh* is not to be sought for in Assyria, however, viz. in the Christian village of *Alkush,* which is situated on the eastern side of the Tigris, to the north-west of Khorsabad, two days' journey from Mosul, where the tomb of the prophet Nahum is shown in the form of a simple plaster box of modern style, and which is held in great reverence, as a holy place, by the Christians and Mohammedans of that neighbour-hood (see Layard, *Nineveh and its Remains,* i. 233), as Michaelis, Eichhorn, Ewald, and others suppose. For this village, with its pretended tomb of the prophet, has not the smallest trace of antiquity about it, and is mentioned for the first time by a monk of the sixteenth century, in a letter to *Assemani* (*Biblioth. or.* i. 525, iii. 1, p. 352). Now, as a tomb of the prophet Jonah is also shown in the neighbourhood of Nineveh, the assumption is a very natural one, that the name *Elkush* did not come from the village into the book, but passed from the book to the village (Hitzig). The statement of Jerome is older, and much more credible,—namely, that " Elkosh was situated in Galilee, since there is to the present day a village in Galilee called Helcesæi (others Helcesei, Elcesi), a very small one indeed, and containing in its ruins hardly any traces of ancient buildings, but one which is well known to the Jews, and was also pointed out to me by my guide,"—inasmuch as he does not simply base his statement upon the word of his guide, but describes the place as well known to the Jews. This Jewish tradition of the

birth of Nahum in the Galilæan *Elkosh*, or Ἐλκεσέ, is also
supported by Cyril of Alex., Ps. Epiphanius, and Ps. Dorotheus, although the more precise accounts of the situation of
the place are confused and erroneous in the two last named.
We have indeed no further evidence that Nahum sprang out
of Galilee. The name of the Elkesaites furnishes just as
little proof of the existence of a place called Elkosh, as the
name Capernaum, *i.e.* village of Nahum, of the fact that our
prophet lived there. Whether the sect of the Elkesaites really
derived their name from a founder named Elxai or Elkesai, is
just as questionable as the connection between this Elxai and
the place called Elkosh ; and the conjecture that Capernaum
received its name from our prophet is altogether visionary.
But Jerome's statement is quite sufficient, since it is confirmed
by the contents of Nahum's prophecy. Ewald indeed imagines
that he can see very clearly, from the general colouring of the
little book, that Nahum did not live in Palestine, but in Assyria,
and must have seen with his own eyes the danger which threatened Nineveh, from an invasion by powerful foes, as being one
of the descendants of the Israelites who had formerly been
transported to Assyria. " It moves," he says, " for example,
round about Nineveh only, and that with a fulness such as we
do not find in any other prophecy relating to a foreign nation ;
and it is quite in a casual manner that it glances at Judah in
ch. i. 13–ii. 3. There is not a single trace of its having been
written by Nahum in Judah ; on the contrary, it follows most
decidedly, from the form given to the words in ch. ii. 1 (ch. i.
15), as compared with Isa. lii. 7, that he was prophesying at a
great distance from Jerusalem and Judah." But why should
not an earlier prophet, who lived in the kingdom of Israel or
that of Judah, have been able to utter a special prophecy concerning Nineveh, in consequence of a special commission from
God ? Moreover, it is not merely in a casual manner that
Nahum glances at Judah ; on the contrary, his whole prophecy
is meant for Judah ; and his glance at Judah, notwithstanding
its brevity, assumes, as Umbreit has correctly observed, a very
important and central position. And the assertion, that there
is not a single trace in the whole prophecy of Nahum's having
been in Judah, has been contested with good reason by Maurer,
Hitzig, and others, who appeal to ch. i. 4 and i. 13–ii. 3, where

such traces are to be found. On the other hand, if the book had been written by a prophet living in exile, there would surely be some allusions to the situation and circumstances of the exiles; whereas we look in vain for any such allusions in Nahum. Again, the acquaintance with Assyrian affairs, to which Ewald still further appeals, is no greater than that which might have been possessed by any prophet, or even by any inhabitant of Judah in the time of Hezekiah, after the repeated invasions of Israel and Judah by the Assyrians. " The liveliness of the description runs through the whole book. Chap. i. 2–14 is not less lively than ch. ii.; and yet no one would infer from the former that Nahum must have seen with his own eyes all that he sets before our eyes in so magnificent a picture in ch. i. 2 sqq." (Nägelsbach; Herzog's *Cycl.*) It is no more a fact that " ch. ii. 6 contains such special acquaintance with the locality of Nineveh, as could only be derived from actual inspection," than that " ch. ii. 7 contains the name of the Assyrian queen (Huzzab)." Moreover, of the words that are peculiar to our prophet, *taphsar* (ch. iii. 17) is the only one that is even probably Assyrian; and this is a military term, which the Judæans in Palestine may have heard from Assyrians living there. The rest of the supposed Aramæisms, such as the suffixes in גִּבּוֹרֵיהוּ (ch. ii. 4) and מַלְאָכֵכֶה (ch. ii. 14), and the words נָהַג, to sigh = הָנֵה (ch. ii. 8), דָּהַר (ch. iii. 2), and פְּלָדוֹת (ch. ii. 4), may be accounted for from the Galilæan origin of the prophet. Consequently there is no tenable ground whatever for the assumption that Nahum lived in exile, and uttered his prophecy in the neighbourhood of Nineveh. There is much greater reason for inferring, from the many points of coincidence between Nahum and Isaiah (see pp. 6, 7), that he was born in Galilee during the Assyrian invasions, and that he emigrated to Judæa, where he lived and prophesied. Nothing whatever is known of the circumstances of his life. The notices in Ps. Epiphan. concerning his miracles and his death (see O. Strauss, *Nahumi de Nino vaticin. expl.* p. xii. sq.) can lay no claim to truth. Even the period of his life is so much a matter of dispute, that some suppose him to have prophesied under Jehu and Jehoahaz, whilst others believe that he did not prophesy till the time of Zedekiah; at the same time it is possible to decide this with tolerable certainty from the contents of the book.

2. THE BOOK OF NAHUM contains one extended prophecy concerning Nineveh, in which the ruin of that city and of the Assyrian world-power is predicted in three strophes, answering to the division into chapters; viz. in ch. i. the divine purpose to inflict judgment upon this oppressor of Israel; in ch. ii. the joyful news of the conquest, plundering, and destruction of Nineveh; and in ch. iii. its guilt and its inevitable ruin. These are all depicted with pictorial liveliness and perspicuity. Now, although this prophecy neither closes with a Messianic prospect, nor enters more minutely into the circumstances of the Israelitish kingdom of God in general, it is rounded off within itself, and stands in such close relation to Judah, that it may be called a prophecy of consolation for that kingdom. The fall of the mighty capital of the Assyrian empire, that representative of the godless and God-opposing power of the world, which sought to destroy the Israelitish kingdom of God, was not only closely connected with the continuance and development of the kingdom of God in Judah, but the connection is very obvious in Nahum's prophecy. Even in the introduction (ch. i. 2 sqq.) the destruction of Nineveh is announced as a judgment, which Jehovah, the zealous God and avenger of evil, executes, and in which He proves Himself a refuge to those who trust in Him (ch. i. 7). But "those who trust in Him" are not godly Gentiles here; they are rather the citizens of His kingdom, viz. the Judæans, upon whom Asshur had laid the yoke of bondage, which Jehovah would break (ch. i. 13), so that Judah could keep feasts and pay its vows to Him (ch. i. 15). On the destruction of Nineveh the Lord returns to the eminence of Israel, which the Assyrians have overthrown (ch. ii. 2). Consequently Nineveh is to fall, and an end is to be put to the rule and tyranny of Asshur, that the glory of Israel may be restored.

The unity and integrity of the prophecy are not open to any well-founded objection. It is true that Eichhorn, Ewald, and De Wette, have questioned the genuineness of the first part of the heading (the *Massâ'* of Nineveh), but without sufficient reason, as even Hitzig observes. For there is nothing that can possibly astonish us in the fact that the object of the prophecy is mentioned first, and then the author. Moreover, the words משׂא נינוה cannot possibly have been added at a later period, because the whole of the first half of the prophecy would be unintelligible without them; since Nineveh is not mentioned by name till ch. ii. 8, and yet the suffix attached to מְקוֹמָהּ in ch. i. 8 refers to Nineveh, and requires the introduction of the name of that city in the heading. There is just as little force in the arguments with which Hitzig seeks to prove that the allusion to the conquest of No-Amon in ch. iii. 8–10 is a later addition. For the assertion that, if an Assyrian army had penetrated to Upper Egypt and taken that city, Nahum, when addressing Nineveh, could not have related to the Assyrians what had emanated from themselves, without at least intimating this, would obviously be well founded only on the supposition that the words " Art thou better than No-Amon," etc., could be taken quite prosaically as news told to the city of Nineveh, and loses all its force, when we see that this address is simply a practical turn, with which Nahum describes the fate of No-Amon not to the Ninevites, but to the Judæans, as a practical proof that even the mightiest and most strongly fortified city could be conquered and fall, when God had decreed its ruin. From the lively description of this occurrence, we may also explain the change from the third person to the second in ch. iii. 9b, at which Hitzig still takes offence. His other arguments are so subjective and unimportant, that they require no special refutation.

With regard to the date of the composition of our prophecy, it is evident from the contents that it was not written before, but after, the defeat of Sennacherib in front of Jerusalem in the reign of Hezekiah, since that event is not only clearly assumed, but no doubt furnished the occasion for the prophecy. Asshur had overrun Judah (ch. i. 15), and had severely afflicted it (ch. i. 9, 12), yea plundered and almost destroyed it (ch. ii. 2). Now, even if neither the words in ch. i. 11, " There is one come out of thee, who imagined evil against Jehovah," etc., nor those of ch. i. 12b, according to the correct interpretation, contain any special allusion to Sennacherib and his defeat, and if it is still less likely that ch. i. 14 contains an allusion to his death or murder (Isa. xxxvii. 38), yet the affliction (tsârâh) which Assyria had brought upon Judah (ch. i. 9), and the invasion of Judah mentioned in ch. i. 15 and ii. 2, can only refer to Sennacherib's expedition, since he was the only one of all the kings of Assyria who so severely oppressed Judah as to bring it to the very verge of ruin. Moreover, ch. ii. 13, " The voice of thy messengers shall no more be heard," is peculiarly applicable to the messengers whom Sennacherib sent to Hezekiah, according to Isa. xxxvi. 13 sqq. and xxxvii. 9 sqq., to compel the surrender of Jerusalem and get Judah completely into his power. But if this is established, it cannot have been a long time after the defeat of Sennacherib before Jerusalem, when Nahum prophesied ; not only because that event was thoroughly adapted to furnish the occasion for such a prophecy as the one contained in our prophet's book, and because it was an omen of the future and final judgment upon Asshur, but still more, because the allusions to the affliction brought upon Judah by Sennacherib are of such a kind that it must have still continued in the most vivid recollection of the prophet and the men of his time. We cannot do anything else, therefore, than subscribe to the view expressed by Vitringa, viz. that " the date of Nahum must be fixed a very short time after Isaiah and Micah, and therefore in the reign of Hezekiah, not only after the carrying away of the ten tribes, but also after the overthrow of Sennacherib (ch. i. 11, 13), from which the argument of the prophecy is taken, and the occasion for preaching the complete destruction of Nineveh and the kingdom of Assyria" (*Typ. doctr. prophet.* p. 37). The date of the composition of our book cannot be more exactly determined. The assumption that it was composed before the murder of Sennacherib, in the temple of his god Nisroch (Isa. xxxvii. 38 ; 2 Kings xix. 37), has no support in ch. i. 14. And it is equally impossible to infer from ch. i. 13 and i. 15 that our prophecy was uttered in the reign of Manasseh, and occasioned by the carrying away of the king to Babylon (2 Chron. xxxiii. 11).

The relation which exists between this prophecy and those of Isaiah is in the most perfect harmony with the composition of the former in the second half of the reign of Hezekiah. The resemblances which we find between Nahum iii. 5 and Isa. xlvii. 2, 3, ch. iii. 7, 10 and Isa. li. 19, 20, ch. i. 15 and Isa. lii. 1 and 7, are of such a nature that Isaiah could just as well have alluded to Nahum as Nahum to Isaiah. If Nahum composed his prophecy not long after the overthrow of Senna-

cherib, we must assume that the former was the case. The
fact that in Nahum i. 8, 13 and iii. 10 there are resemblances
to Isa. x. 23, 27 and xiii. 16, where our prophet is evidently
the borrower, furnishes no decisive proof to the contrary. For
the relation in which prophets who lived and laboured at the
same time stood to one another was one of mutual giving and
receiving; so that it cannot be immediately inferred from the
fact that our prophet made use of a prophecy of his predecessor
for his own purposes, that he must have been dependent upon
him in all his kindred utterances. When, on the other hand,
Ewald and Hitzig remove our prophecy to a much later period,
and place it in the time of the later Median wars with Assyria,
either the time of Phraortes (Herod. i. 102), or that of
Cyaxares and his first siege of Nineveh (Herod. i. 103), they
found this opinion upon the unscriptural assumption that it was
nothing more than a production of human sagacity and political conjecture, which could only have been uttered " when a
threatening expedition against Nineveh was already in full
operation" (Ewald), and when the danger which threatened
Nineveh was before his eyes,—a view which has its roots in
the denial of the supernatural character of the prophecy, and
is altogether destitute of any solid foundation.

   The style of our prophet is not inferior to the classical
style of Isaiah and Micah, either in power and originality of
thought, or in clearness and purity of form; so that, as. R.
Lowth (*De sacr. poësi Hebr.* § 281) has aptly observed, *ex
omnibus minoribus prophetis nemo videtur æquare sublimitatem,
ardorem et audaces spiritus Nahumi;* whereas Ewald, according
to his preconceived opinion as to the prophet's age, " no longer
finds in this prophet, who already formed one of the later
prophets, so much inward strength, or purity and fulness of
thought." For the exegetical writings on the book of Nahum,
see my *Lehrbuch der Einleitung,* § 299, 300.

EXPOSITION.

THE JUDGMENT UPON NINEVEH DECREED BY GOD.—Chap. i.

Jehovah, the jealous God and avenger of evil, before whose manifestation of wrath the globe trembles (vers. 2–6), will prove Himself a strong tower to His own people by destroying Nineveh (vers. 7–11), since He has determined to break the yoke which Asshur has laid upon Judah, and to destroy this enemy of His people (vers. 12–14).

Ver. 1. The heading runs thus: "*Burden concerning Nineveh; book of the prophecy of Nahum of Elkosh.*" The first sentence gives the substance and object, the second the form and author, of the proclamation which follows. מַשָּׂא signifies a burden, from נָשָׂא, to lift up, to carry, to heave. This meaning has very properly been retained by Jonathan, Aquila, Jerome, Luther, and others, in the headings to the prophetic oracle. Jerome observes on Hab. i. 1: "Massa never occurs in the title, except when it is evidently grave and full of weight and labour." On the other hand, the LXX. have generally rendered it λῆμμα in the headings to the oracles, or even ὅρασις, ὅραμα, ῥῆμα (Isa. xiii. sqq., xxx. 6); and most of the modern commentators since Cocceius and Vitringa, following this example, have attributed to the word the meaning of "utterance," and derived it from נָשָׂא, *effari.* But נשא has no more this meaning than נָשָׂא קוֹל can mean to utter the voice, either in Ex. xx. 7 and xxiii. 1, to which Hupfeld appeals in support of it, or in 2 Kings ix. 25, to which others appeal. The same may be said of מַשָּׂא, which never means *effatum,* utterance, and is never placed before simple announcements of salvation, but only before oracles of a threatening nature. Zech. ix. 1 and xii. 1 form no exception to this rule. Delitzsch (on Isa. xiii. 1) observes, with regard to the latter passage, that the promise has at least a dark foil, and in ch. ix. 1 sqq. the heathen nations of the Persian and Macedonian world-monarchy are threatened with a divine judgment which will break in pieces their imperial glory, and through which they are to be brought to conversion to Jehovah; "and it is just in this that the burden consists, which the word of God lays upon these nations, that they may be brought to conversion through such a judgment from God" (Kliefoth). Even in Prov. xxx. 1 and xxxi. 1 *Massâ'* does not mean utterance. The words of Agur in Prov. xxx. 1 are a heavy burden, which is rolled upon the natural and conceited reason; they are punitive in their character, reproving human forwardness in the strongest terms; and in ch. xxxi. 1 *Massâ'* is the discourse with which king Lemuel reproved his mother. For the thorough vindication of this meaning of *Massâ'*, by an exposition of all the passages which have been adduced in support of the rendering "utterance," see Hengstenberg, *Christology*, on Zech. ix. 1, and O. Strauss on this passage. For *Nineveh*, see the comm. on Jonah i. 2. The burden, *i.e.* the threatening words, concerning Nineveh are defined in the second clause as *sēpher châzōn*, book of the seeing (or of the seen) of Nahum, *i.e.* of that which Nahum saw in spirit and prophesied concerning Nineveh. The unusual combination of *sēpher* with *châzōn*, which only occurs here, is probably intended to show that Nahum simply committed his prophecy concerning Nineveh to writing, and did not first of all announce it orally before the people. On *hâ'elqōshī* (the Elkoshite), see the Introduction.

Vers. 2–6. The description of the divine justice, and its judicial manifestation on the earth, with which Nahum introduces his prophecy concerning Nineveh, has this double object : first of all, to indicate the connection between the destruction of the capital of the Assyrian empire, which is about to be predicted, and the divine purpose of salvation ; and secondly, to cut off at the very outset all doubt as to the realization of this judgment. Ver. 2. "*A God jealous and taking vengeance is Jehovah; an avenger is Jehovah, and Lord of wrathful fury ; an avenger is Jehovah to His adversaries, and He is One keeping wrath to His enemies. Ver. 3. Jehovah is long-suffering and of great strength, and He does not acquit of guilt. Jehovah, His way is in the storm and in the tempest, and clouds are the dust of His feet.*" The prophecy commences with the words with which God expresses the energetic character of His holiness in the decalogue (Ex. xx. 5, cf. xxxiv. 14 ; Deut. iv. 24, v. 9 ; and Josh. xxiv. 19), where we find the form קַנּוֹא for קַנָּא. Jehovah is a jealous God, who turns the burning zeal of His wrath against them that hate Him (Deut. vi. 15). His side of the energy of the divine zeal predominates here, as the following predicate,

the three-times repeated נֹקֵם, clearly shows. The strengthening
of the idea of *nōqēm* involved in the repetition of it three times
(cf. Jer. vii. 4, xxii. 29), is increased still further by the
apposition *ba'al chēmáh*, possessor of the wrathful heat, equivalent to the wrathful God (cf. Prov. xxix. 22, xxii. 24). The
vengeance applies to His adversaries, towards whom He bears
ill-will. *Nátar*, when predicated of God, as in Lev. xix. 18
and Ps. ciii. 9, signifies to keep or bear wrath. God does not
indeed punish immediately; He is long-suffering (אֶרֶךְ אַפַּיִם,
Ex. xxxiv. 6, Num. xiv. 18, etc.). His long-suffering is not
weak indulgence, however, but an emanation from His love and
mercy; for He is *gᵉdōl-kōắch*, great in strength (Num. xiv. 17),
and does not leave unpunished (נַקֵּה וגו' after Ex. xxxiv. 7 and
Num. xiv. 18; see at Ex. xx. 7). His great might to punish
sinners, He has preserved from of old; His way is in the storm
and tempest. With these words Nahum passes over to a description of the manifestations of divine wrath upon sinners in
great national judgments which shake the world (שְׂעָרָה as in
Job ix. 17 = סְעָרָה, which is connected with סוּפָה in Isa. xxix.
6 and Ps. lxxxiii. 16). These and similar descriptions are
founded upon the revelations of God, when bringing Israel out
of Egypt, and at the conclusion of the covenant at Sinai, when
the Lord came down upon the mountain in clouds, fire, and
vapour of smoke (Ex. xix. 16–18). Clouds are the dust of His
feet. The Lord comes down from heaven in the clouds. As
man goes upon the dust, so Jehovah goes upon the clouds.

Ver. 4. "*He threateneth the sea, and drieth it up, and maketh
all the rivers dry up. Bashan and Carmel fade, and the blossom
of Lebanon fadeth.* Ver. 5. *Mountains shake before Him, and
the hills melt away; the earth heaveth before Him, and the globe,
and all the inhabitants thereon.* Ver. 6. *Before His fury who
may stand? and who rise up at the burning of His wrath? His
burning heat poureth itself out like fire, and the rocks are rent in
pieces by Him.*" In the rebuking of the sea there is an allusion
to the drying up of the Red Sea for the Israelites to pass through
(cf. Ps. cvi. 9); but it is generalized here, and extended to
every sea and river, which the Almighty can smite in His
wrath, and cause to dry up. וַיַּבִּשֵׁהוּ for וַיְיַבְּשֵׁהוּ, the vowelless י of
the third pers. being fused into one with the first radical sound,
as in וַיְדוּ in Lam. iii. 53 (cf. Ges. § 69, Anm. 6, and Ewald

§ 232–3). Bashan, Carmel, and Lebanon are mentioned as very fruitful districts, abounding in a vigorous growth of vegetation and large forests, the productions of which God could suddenly cause to fade and wither in His wrath. Yea more : the mountains tremble and the hills melt away (compare the similar description in Mic. i. 4, and the explanation given there). The earth lifts itself, *i.e.* starts up from its place (cf. Isa. xiii. 13), with everything that dwells upon the surface of the globe. תִּשָּׂא from נָשָׂא, used intransitively, " to rise," as in Ps. lxxxix. 10 and Hos. xiii. 1 ; not *conclamat s. tollit vocem* (J. H. Michaelis, Burk, Strauss). תֵּבֵל, *lit.* the fertile globe, always signifies the whole of the habitable earth, ἡ οἰκουμένη ; and יֹשְׁבֵי בָהּ, not merely the men (Ewald), but all living creatures:(cf. Joel i. 18, 20). No one can stand before such divine wrath, which pours out like consuming fire (Deut. iv. 24), and rends rocks in pieces (1 Kings xix. 11 ; Jer. xxiii. 29 ; cf. Jer. x. 10 ; Mal. iii. 2).

Vers. 7–11. But the wrath of God does not fall upon those who trust in the Lord ; it only falls upon His enemies. With this turn Nahum prepares the way in vers. 7 sqq. for proclaiming the judgment of wrath upon Nineveh. Ver. 7. "*Good is Jehovah, a refuge in the day of trouble ; and He knoweth those who trust in Him.* Ver. 8. *And with an overwhelming flood will He make an end of her place, and pursue His enemies into darkness.*" Even in the manifestation of His wrath God proves His goodness ; for the judgment, by exterminating the wicked, brings deliverance to the righteous who trust in the Lord, out of the affliction prepared for them by the wickedness of the world. The predicate טוֹב is more precisely defined by the apposition לְמָעוֹז וגו׳, for a refuge = a refuge in time of trouble. The goodness of the Lord is seen in the fact that He is a refuge in distress. The last clause says to whom : viz. to those who trust in Him. They are known by Him. " To know is just the same as not to neglect ; or, expressed in a positive form, the care or providence of God in the preservation of the faithful" (Calvin). For the fact, compare Ps. xxxiv. 9, xlvi. 2, Jer. xvi. 19. And because the Lord is a refuge to His people, He will put an end to the oppressor of His people, viz. Nineveh, the capital of the Assyrian empire, and that with an overwhelming flood. *Sheteph,* overwhelming, is a figure denoting the judgment sweeping over a land or kingdom, through the invasion of hostile armies (cf. Isa. viii. 7; Dan. xi. 26, 40). עָבַר, overflowed by a river (cf. Isa. viii. 8; Hab. iii. 10; Dan. xi. 40). עָשָׂה כָלָה, to put an end to anything, as in Isa. x. 23. מְקוֹמָהּ is the accusative of the object: make her place a vanishing one. כָּלָה, the fem. of כָּלֶה, an adjective in a neuter sense, that which is vanishing away. The suffix in מְקוֹמָהּ refers to *Nineveh* in the heading (ver. 1): either Nineveh, personified as a queen (ch. ii. 7, iii. 4), is distinguished from her seat (Hitzig); or what is much more simple, the city itself is meant, and "her place" is to be understood in this sense, that with the destruction of the city even the place where it stood would cease to be the site of a city, with which Marck aptly compares the phrase, "its place knoweth man no more" (Job vii. 10, viii. 18, xx. 9). אֹיְבָיו are the inhabitants of Nineveh, or the Assyrians generally, as the enemies of Israel. יְרַדֶּף־חֹשֶׁךְ, not darkness will pursue its enemies; for this view is irreconcilable with the *makkeph*: but to pursue with darkness, *chōshekh* being an accusative either of place or of more precise definition, used in an instrumental sense. The former is the simpler view, and answers better to the parallelism of the clauses. As the city is to vanish and leave no trace behind, so shall its inhabitants perish in darkness.

The reason for all this is assigned in vers. 9 sqq. Ver. 9. "*What think ye of Jehovah? He makes an end; the affliction will not arise twice.* Ver. 10. *For though they be twisted together like thorns, and as if intoxicated with their wine, they shall be devoured like dry stubble.* Ver. 11. *From thee has one come out, who meditated evil against Jehovah, who advised worthlessness.*" The question in ver. 9*a* is not addressed to the enemy, viz. the Assyrians, as very many commentators suppose: "What do ye meditate against Jehovah?" For although *châshabh 'el* is used in Hos. vii. 15 for a hostile device with regard to Jehovah, the supposition that *'el* is used here for *'al*, according to a later usage of the language, is precluded by the fact that חָשַׁב עַל is actually used in this sense in ver. 11. Moreover, the last clause does not suit this view of the question. The words, "the affliction will not stand up, or not rise up a second time," cannot refer to the Assyrians, or mean that the infliction of a second judgment upon Nineveh will be unnecessary, because the city will utterly fall to the ground in the first judgment, and completely vanish from the earth (Hitzig). For צָרָה points back to בְּיוֹם צָרָה, and therefore must be the calamity which has fallen upon Judah, or upon those who trust in the Lord, on the part of Nineveh or Asshur (Marck, Maurer, and Strauss). This is confirmed by ver. 11 and ch. i. 15, where this thought is definitely expressed. Consequently the question, "What think ye with regard to Jehovah?" can only be addressed to the Judæans, and must mean, "Do ye think that Jehovah cannot or will not fulfil His threat upon Nineveh?" (Cyr., Marck, Strauss.) The prophet addresses these words to the anxious minds, which were afraid of fresh invasions on the part of the Assyrians. To strengthen their confidence, he answers the question proposed, by repeating the thought expressed in ver. 8. He (Jehovah) is making an end, *sc.* of the enemy of His people; and he gives a further reason for this in ver. 10. The participial clauses עַד סִירִים to סְבוּאִים are to be taken conditionally: are (or were) they even twisted like thorns. עַד סִירִים, to thorns = as thorns (עַד is given correctly by J. H. Michaelis: *eo usque ut spinas perplexitate æquent;* compare Ewald, § 219). The comparison of the enemy to thorns expresses "*firmatum callidumque nocendi studium*" (Marck), and has been well explained by Ewald thus: "crisp, crafty, and cunning; so that one would rather not go near them, or have anything to do with them" (cf. 2 Sam. xxiii. 6 and Mic. vii. 4). כְּסָבְאָם סְבוּאִים, not "wetted like their wet" (Hitzig), nor "as it were drowned in wine, so that fire can do no more harm to them than to anything else that is wet" (Ewald); for סָבָא neither means to wet nor to drown, but to drink, to carouse; and סָבוּא means drunken, intoxicated. סֹבֶא is strong unmixed wine (see Delitzsch on Isa. i. 22). "Their wine" is the wine which they are accustomed to drink. The simile expresses the audacity and hardiness with which the Assyrians regarded themselves as invincible, and applies very well to the gluttony and revelry which prevailed at the Assyrian court; even if the account given by Diod. Sic. (ii. 26), that when Sardanapalus had three times defeated the enemy besieging Nineveh, in his great confidence in his own good fortune, he ordered a drinking carousal, in the midst of which the enemy, who had been made acquainted with the fact, made a fresh attack, and conquered Nineveh, rests upon a legendary dressing up of the facts. אֻכְּלוּ, devoured by fire, is a figure signifying utter destruction ; and the perfect is prophetic, denoting what will certainly take place. Like dry stubble : cf. Isa. v. 24, xlvii. 14, and Joel ii. 5. מָלֵא is not to be taken, as Ewald supposes (§ 279, a), as strengthening יָבֵשׁ, "fully dry," but is to be connected with the verb adverbially, and is simply placed at the end of the sentence for the sake of emphasis (Ges., Maurer, and Strauss). This will be the end of the Assyrians, because he who meditates evil against Jehovah has come forth out of Nineveh. In מִמֵּךְ Nineveh is addressed, the representative of the imperial power of Assyria, which set itself to destroy the Israelitish kingdom of God. It might indeed be objected to this explanation of the verse, that the words in vers. 12b and 13 are addressed to Zion or Judah, whereas Nineveh or Asshur is spoken of both in what precedes (vers. 8 and 10) and in what follows (ver. 12a) in the third person. On this ground Hoelem. and Strauss refer מִמֵּךְ also to Judah, and adopt this explanation : " from thee (Judah) will the enemy who has hitherto oppressed thee have gone away" (taking יָצָא as fut. exact., and מִן יָצָא as in Isa. xlix. 17). But this view does not suit the context. After the utter destruction of the enemy has been predicted in ver. 10, we do not expect to find the statement that it will have gone away from Judah, especially as there is nothing said in what precedes about any invasion of Judah. The meditation of evil against Jehovah refers to the design of the Assyrian conquerors to destroy the kingdom of God in Israel, as the Assyrian himself declares in the blasphemous words which Isaiah puts into the mouth of Rabshakeh (Isa. xxxvi. 14-20), to show the wicked pride of the enemy. This address merely expresses the feeling cherished at all times by the power of the world towards the kingdom of God. It is in the plans devised for carrying this feeling into action that the יֹעֵץ בְּלִיַּעַל, the advising of worthlessness, consists. This is the only meaning that בְּלִיַּעַל has, not that of destruction.

Vers. 12-14. The power of Nineveh will be destroyed, to break the yoke laid upon Judah. Ver. 12. " *Thus saith Jehovah, Though they be unconsumed, and therefore numerous, yet are they thus mowed down, and have passed away. I have bowed thee down, I will bow thee down no more.* Ver. 13. *And now shall I break his yoke from off thee, and break thy fetters in pieces.* Ver. 14. *And Jehovah hath given commandment concerning thee, no more of thy name will be sown : from the house of thy God I cut off graven image and molten work: I prepare thy grave; for thou art found light."* To confirm the threat expressed in vers. 8—11, Nahum explains the divine purpose more fully. Jehovah hath spoken : the completeness and strength of her army will be of no help to Nineveh. It is mowed down, because Judah is to be delivered from its oppressor. The words שְׁלֵמִים to וְעָבָר refer to the enemy, the warlike hosts of Nineveh, which are to be destroyed notwithstanding their great and full number. *Shâlēm, integer,* with strength undiminished, both outwardly and inwardly, *i.e.* both numerous and strong. וְכֵן רַבִּים, and so, *i.e.* of such a nature, just because they are of full number, or numerous. וְכֵן נָגוֹזּוּ, and so, *i.e.* although of such a nature, they will nevertheless be mowed down. גּוֹז, taken from the mowing of the meadows, is a figure denoting complete destruction. וְעָבָר is not impersonal, *actum est, sc. de iis,* but signifies it is away, or has vanished. The singular is used with special emphasis, the numerous army being all embraced in the unity of one man : "he paints the whole people as vanishing away, just as if one little man were carried off" (Strauss). With וְעִנִּתִךְ the address turns to Judah. The words are not applicable to the Assyrians, to whom Abarbanel, Grotius, Ewald, and Hitzig refer this clause; for Asshur is not only bowed down or chastened, but utterly destroyed. עִנִּתִךְ refers to the oppression which Judah had suffered from the Assyrians in the time of Ahaz and Hezekiah. This shall not be repeated, as has already been promised in ver. 9b. For now will the Lord break the yoke which this enemy has laid upon Judah. וְעַתָּה, but now, is attached adversatively to עִנִּתִךְ. The suffix to מֹטֵהוּ refers to the enemy, which has its seat in Nineveh. For the figure of the yoke, cf. Lev. xxvi. 13, Jer. xxvii. 2, xxviii. 10, Ezek. xxxiv. 27, etc.; and for the fact itself, Isa. x. 27. The words do not refer to the people of the ten tribes, who were pining like slaves in exile (Hitzig); for Nahum makes no allusion to them at all, but to Judah (cf. ch. i. 15), upon whom the Assyrians had laid the yoke of tribute from the time of Ahaz. This was first of all shaken off in the reign of Hezekiah, through the overthrow of Sennacherib; but it was not yet completely broken, so long as there was a possibility that Assyria might rise again with new power, as in fact it did in the reign of Manasseh, when Assyrian generals invaded Judah and carried off this king to Babylon (2 Chron. xxxiii. 11). It was only broken when the Assyrian power was overthrown through the conquest and destruction of Nineveh. This view, which is required by the futures *'eshbōr* and *'ănattēq*, is confirmed by ver. 14, for there the utter extermination of Assyria is clearly expressed. *V^etsivvâh* is not a perfect with *Vav rel.;* but the *Vav* is a simple copula: "*and* (= for) Jehovah has commanded." The perfect refers to the divine purpose, which has already been formed, even though its execution is still in the future. This purpose runs thus: "Of thy seed shall no more be sown, *i.e.* thou wilt have no more descendants" ("the people and name are to become extinct," Strauss; cf. Isa. xiv. 20). It is not the king of Assyria who is here addressed, but the Assyrian power personified as a single man, as we may see from what follows, according to which the idols are to be rooted out along with the seed from the house of God, *i.e.* out of the idol temples (cf. Isa. xxxvii. 38, xliv. 13). *Pesel* and *massēkhâh* are combined, as in Deut. xxvii. 15, to denote every kind of idolatrous image. For the idolatry of Assyria, see Layard's *Nineveh and its Remains,* ii. p. 439 sqq. אָשִׂים קִבְרֶךָ cannot mean, "I make the temple of thy god into a grave," although this meaning has already been expressed in the Chaldee and Syriac; and the Masoretic accentuation, which connects the words with what precedes, is also founded upon this view. If an object had to be supplied to אָשִׂים from the context, it must be *pesel ūmassēkhâh;* but there would be no sense in "I make thine idol into a grave." There is no other course left, therefore, than to take קִבְרֶךָ as the nearest and only object to אָשִׂים, "I lay, *i.e.* prepare thy grave," כִּי קַלּוֹתָ, because, when weighed according to thy moral worth (Job xxxi. 6), thou hast been found light (cf. Dan. v. 27). Hence the widespread opinion, that the murder of Sennacherib (Isa. xxxvii. 38; 2 Kings xix. 37) is predicted here, must be rejected as erroneous and irreconcilable with the words, and not even so far correct as that Nahum makes any allusion to that event. He simply announces the utter destruction of the Assyrian power, together with its idolatry, upon which that power rested.

Jehovah has prepared a grave for the people and their idols, because they have been found light when weighed in the balances of righteousness.

CONQUEST, PLUNDERING, AND DESTRUCTION OF NINEVEH.—
CHAP I. 15–II. 13 (HEB. BIB. CHAP. II.).

Jehovah sends a powerful and splendid army against Nineveh, to avenge the disgrace brought upon Judah and restore its glory (i. 15–ii. 4). The city is conquered; its inhabitants flee or wander into captivity; the treasures are plundered (vers. 5–10); and the powerful city perishes with all its glory, and leaves not a trace behind (vers. 11–13).

Ch. i. 15–ii. 4. Judah hears the glad tidings, that its oppressor is utterly destroyed. A warlike army marches against Nineveh, which that city cannot resist, because the Lord will put an end to the oppression of His people. Ch. i. 15. " *Behold, upon the mountains the feet of the messengers of joy, proclaiming salvation! Keep thy feasts, O Judah; pay thy vows: for the worthless one will no more go through thee; he is utterly cut off.*" The destruction of the Assyrian, announced in ch. i. 14, is so certain, that Nahum commences the description of its realization with an appeal to Judah, to keep joyful feasts, as the miscreant is utterly cut off. The form in which he utters this appeal is to point to messengers upon the mountains, who are bringing the tidings of peace to the kingdom of Judah. The first clause is applied in Isa. lii. 7 to the description of the Messianic salvation. The messengers of joy appear upon the mountains, because their voice can be heard far and wide from thence. The mountains are those of the kingdom of Judah, and the allusion to the feet of the messengers paints as it were for the eye the manner in which they hasten on the mountains with the joyful news. מְבַשֵּׂר is collective, every one who brings the glad tidings. *Shâlōm*, peace and salvation: here both in one. The summons, to keep feasts, etc., proceeds from the prophet himself, and is, as Ursinus says, " *partim gratulatoria, partim exhortatoria.*" The former, because the feasts could not be properly kept during the oppression by the enemy, or at any rate could not be visited by those who lived at a distance from the temple; the latter, because the *chaggīm*, *i.e.* the great yearly feasts, were feasts of thanksgiving for the blessings of salvation, which Israel owed to the Lord, so that the summons to celebrate these feasts involved the admonition to thank the Lord for His mercy in destroying the hostile power of the world. This is expressed still more clearly in the summons to pay their vows. בְּלִיַּעַל, abstract for concrete = אִישׁ בְּלִ', as in 2 Sam. xxiii. 6 and Job xxxiv. 18. נִכְרָת is not a participle, but a perfect in pause.

With ch. ii. 1 the prophecy turns to Nineveh. Ver. 1. "*A dasher in pieces comes against thee. Keep thy fortress! Look out upon the way, fortify the loins, exert thy strength greatly!* Ver. 2. *For Jehovah returneth to the eminence of Jacob as to the eminence of Israel; for plunderers have plundered them, and their vines have they thrown to the ground.*" עַל־פָּנַיִךְ cannot be addressed to Judah, as in i. 15 (Chald., Rashi, etc.). It cannot indeed be objected that in ch. i. 15 the destruction of Asshur has already been announced, since the prophet might nevertheless have returned to the time when Asshur had made war upon Judah, in order to depict its ruin with greater precision. But such an assumption does not agree with the second clause of the verse as compared with ver. 2, and still less with the description of the approaching enemy which follows in ver. 3, since this is unquestionably, according to ver. 5, the power advancing against Nineveh, and destroying that city. We must therefore assume that we have here a sudden change in the person addressed, as in ch. i. 11 and 12, 13 and 14. The enemy is called מֵפִיץ, " a dasher in pieces;" not a war-hammer (cf. Prov. xxv. 18), because עָלָה, the standing expression for the advance of a hostile army, does not agree with this. עַל־פָּנַיִךְ, against thy face, *i.e.* pitching his tent opposite to the city (there is no good reason for altering the suffix into פָּנֶיךָ, as Ewald and Hitzig propose). Against this enemy Nineveh is to bring all possible power of resistance. This is not irony, but simply a poetical turn given to the thought, that Nineveh will not be able to repulse this enemy any more. The *inf. abs. nâtsōr* stands emphatically for the imperative, as is frequently the case, and is continued in the imperative. *Meªtsûrâh* is the enclosure of a city, hence the wall or fortification. צַפֵּה־דֶרֶךְ, looking watchfully upon the way by which the enemy comes, to repulse it or prevent it from entering the city. חַזֵּק מ', make the loins strong, *i.e.* equip thyself with strength, the loins being the seat of strength. The last clause expresses the same thought, and is merely added to strengthen the meaning. The explanatory *kī* in ver. 2 (3) does not follow upon ver. 1*b* in the sense of "summon up all thy strength, *for* it is God in whose strength the enemy fights" (Strauss), but to ver. 1*a* or ch. i. 15*b*. The train of thought is the following: Asshur will be utterly destroyed by the enemy advancing against Nineveh, for Jehovah will re-establish the glory of Israel, which Asshur has destroyed. שָׁב (perf. proph.) has not the force of the *hiphil, reducere, restituere,* either here or in Ps. lxxxv. 5 and Isa. lii. 8, and other passages, where the modern lexicons give it, but means to turn round, or return to a person, and is construed with the accusative, as in Num. x. 36, Ex. iv. 20, and Gen. l. 14, although in actual fact the return of Jehovah to the eminence of Jacob involves its restoration. גְּאוֹן יַעֲקֹב, that of which Jacob is proud, *i.e.* the eminence and greatness or glory accruing to Israel by virtue of its election to be the nation of God, which the enemy into whose power it had been given up on account of its rebellion against God had taken away (see at Amos vi. 8). *Jacob* does not stand for Judah, nor *Israel* for the ten tribes, for Nahum never refers to the ten tribes in distinction from Judah; and Ob. 18, where Jacob is distinguished from the house of Joseph, is of a totally different character. Both names stand here for the whole of Israel (of the twelve tribes), and, as Cyril has shown, the distinction is this: Jacob is the natural name which the people inherited from their forefather, and Israel the spiritual name which they had received from God. Strauss gives the meaning correctly thus: Jehovah will so return to the eminence of His people, who are named after Jacob, that this eminence shall become the eminence of Israel, *i.e.* of the people of God; in other words, He will exalt the nation once more to the lofty eminence of its divine calling (כְּ used in the same manner as in 1 Sam. xxv. 36). This will He do, because plunderers have plundered (*bâqaq, evacuare*) them (the Israelites), and destroyed their vines, cast them to the ground; that He may avenge the reproach cast upon His people. The plunderers are the heathen nations, especially the Assyrians. The vines are the Israelites; Israel as a people or kingdom is the vineyard (Isa. v. 1; Jer. xii. 10; Ps. lxxx. 9 sqq.); the vines are the families, and the branches (*z͞emōrīm* from *z͞emōrāh*) the members.

After assigning this reason for the divine purpose concerning Asshur, the prophet proceeds in vers. 3 sqq. to depict the army advancing towards Nineveh, viz. in ver. 3 its appearance, and in ver. 4 the manner in which it sets itself in motion for battle. Ver. 3. " *The shield of His heroes is made red, the valiant men are clothed in crimson : in the fire of the steel-bosses are the chariots, on the day of His equipment ; and the cypresses are swung about.* Ver. 4. *The chariots rave in the streets, they run over one another on the roads; their appearance is like the torches, they run about like lightning.*" The suffix attached to *gibbōrēhū* (His heroes) might be taken as referring to *mēphīts* in ver. 1 (2); but it is more natural to refer it to Jehovah in ver. 2 (3), as having summoned the army against Nineveh (cf. Isa. xiii. 3). The shields are reddened, *i.e.* not radiant (Ewald), but coloured with red, and that not with the blood of enemies who have been slain (Aberbanel and Grotius), but either with red colour with which they are painted, or what is still more probable, with the copper with which they are overlaid: see Josephus, *Ant.* xiii. 12, 5 (Hitzig). אַנְשֵׁי־חַיִל are not fighting men generally, *i.e.* soldiers, but brave men, heroes (cf. Judg. iii. 29, 1 Sam. xxxi. 12, 2 Sam. xi. 16, equivalent to *b͞enē chayil* in 1 Sam. xviii. 17, etc.). מְתֻלָּעִים, ἀπ. λεγ., a denom. of תּוֹלָע, *coccus:* clothed in coccus or crimson. The fighting dress of the nations of antiquity was frequently blood-red (see Æliani, *Var. hist.* vi. 6).[1] The ἀπ. λεγ. *p͞elādōth* is certainly not used for *lappīdīm,* torches ; but in both Arabic and Syriac *paldāh* signifies steel (see Ges. *Lex.*). But *p͞elādōth* are not scythes, which would suggest the idea of scythe-chariots (Michaelis, Ewald, and others) ; for scythe-chariots were first introduced by Cyrus, and were unknown before his time to the Medes, the Syrians, the Arabians, and also to the ancient Egyptians (see at Josh. xvii. 16). *P͞elādōth* probably denotes the steel covering of the chariots, as the Assyrian war-chariots were

---

[1] Valerius observes on this : " They used Poenic tunics in battle, to disguise and hide the blood of their wounds, not lest the sight of it should fill them with alarm, but lest it should inspire the enemy with confidence."

adorned according to the monuments with ornaments of metal.[1]
The army of the enemy presents the appearance described
בְּיוֹם הֲכִינוֹ, in the day of his equipment. הֵכִין, to prepare, used
of the equipping of an army for an attack or for battle, as
in Jer. xlvi. 14, Ezek. vii. 14, xxxviii. 7. The suffix refers
to Jehovah, like that in גִּבּוֹרֵיהוּ ; compare Isa. xiii. 4, where
Jehovah raises an army for war with Babylon. *Habbᵉrōshīm*,
the cypresses, are no doubt lances or javelins made of cypress-
wood (Grotius and others), not *magnates* (Chald., Kimchi, and
others), or *viri hastati*. הָרְעָלוּ, to be swung, or brandished, in
the hands of the warriors equipped for battle. The army
advances to the assault (ver. 4), and presses into the suburbs.
The chariots rave (go mad) in the streets. הִתְהוֹלֵל, to behave
one's self foolishly, to rave, used here as in Jer. xlvi. 9 for mad
driving, or driving with insane rapidity (see 2 Kings ix. 20).
יִשְׁתַּקְשְׁקוּן, *lithpalel* of שָׁקַק, to run (Joel ii. 9) ; in the intensive
form, to run over one another, *i.e.* to run in such a way that
they appear as though they would run over one another. חוּצוֹת
and רְחֹבוֹת are roads and open spaces, not outside the city, but
inside (cf. Amos v. 16 ; Ps. cxliv. 13, 14 ; Prov. i. 20), and,
indeed, as we may see from what follows, in the suburbs surrounding the inner city or citadel. Their appearance (viz.
that of the chariots as they drive raving about) is like torches.
The feminine suffix to מַרְאֵיהֶן can only refer to הָרֶכֶב, notwithstanding the fact that elsewhere רֶכֶב is always construed as a
masculine, and that it is so here in the first clauses. For the
suffix cannot refer to רְחֹבוֹת (Hoelem. and Strauss), because
הָרֶכֶב is the subject in the following clause as well as in the
two previous ones. The best way probably is to take it as a
neuter, so that it might refer not to the chariots only, but to
everything in and upon the chariots. The appearance of the

[1] "The chariots of the Assyrians," says Strauss, " as we see them on
the monuments, glare with shining things, made either of iron or steel,
battle-axes, bows, arrows, and shields, and all kinds of weapons ; the horses
are also ornamented with crowns and red fringes, and even the poles of the
carriages are made resplendent with shining suns and moons : add to these
the soldiers in armour riding in the chariots ; and it could not but be the
case, that when illumined by the rays of the sun above them, they would
have all the appearance of flames as they flew hither and thither with
great celerity." Compare also the description of the Assyrian war-
chariots given by Layard in his *Nineveh and its Remains*, vol. ii. p. 348.

chariots, as they drove about with the speed of lightning,
richly ornamented with bright metal (see on ver. 3), and
occupied by warriors in splendid clothes and dazzling armour,
might very well be compared to torches and flashing lightning.
רוֹצֵץ, *pilel* of רוּץ (not *poel* of רָצַץ, Judg. x. 8), *cursitare*, used of
their driving with lightning-speed.

Vers. 5–10. The Assyrian tries to repel this attack, but
all in vain. Ver. 5. " *He remembers his glorious ones: they
stumble in their paths; they hasten to the wall of it, and the
tortoise is set up.* Ver. 6. *The gates are opened in the rivers,
and the palace is dissolved.* Ver. 7. *It is determined: she is
laid bare, carried off, and her maids groan like the cry of doves,
smiting on their breasts.*" On the approach of the war-chariots
of the enemy to the attack, the Assyrian remembers his generals
and warriors, who may possibly be able to defend the city and
drive back the foe. That the subject changes with *yizkōr*, is
evident from the change in the number, *i.e.* from the singular
as compared with the plurals in vers. 3 and 4, and is placed
beyond the reach of doubt by the contents of vers. 5 sqq., which
show that the reference is to the attempt to defend the city.
The subject to *yizkōr* is the Assyrian (בְּלִיַּעַל, ver. 1), or the king
of Asshur (ch. iii. 18). He remembers his glorious ones, *i.e.*
remembers that he has '*addīrīm, i.e.* not merely generals (μεγισ-
τᾶνες, LXX.), but good soldiers, including the generals (as in
ch. iii. 18, Judg. v. 13, Neh. iii. 5). He sends for them, but
they stumble in their paths. From terror at the violent assault
of the foe, their knees lose their tension (the plural *hălīkhōth* is
not to be corrected into the singular according to the *keri*, as
the word always occurs in the plural). They hasten to the wall
of it (Nineveh); there is הַסֹּכֵךְ set up: *i.e.* literally the covering
one, not the defender, *præsidium militare* (Hitzig), but the
tortoise, *testudo*.[1] The prophet's description passes rapidly from

---

[1] Not, however, the tortoise formed by the shields of the soldiers, held
close together above their heads (Liv. xxxiv. 9), since these are never
found upon the Assyrian monuments (*vid.* Layard), but a kind of battering-ram, of which there are several different kinds, either a moveable
tower, with a battering-ram, consisting of a light framework, covered with
basket-work, or else a framework without any tower, either with an ornamented covering, or simply covered with skins, and moving upon four or
six wheels. See the description, with illustrations, in Layard's *Nineveh*, ii.
pp. 366–370, and Strauss's commentary on this passage.

the assault upon the city wall to the capture of the city itself (ver. 6). The opened or opening gates of the rivers are neither those approaches to the city which were situated on the bank of the Tigris, and were opened by the overflowing of the river, in support of which appeal has been made to the statement of Diodor. Sic. ii. 27, that the city wall was destroyed for the space of twenty stadia by the overflowing of the Tigris; for " gates of the rivers" cannot possibly stand for gates opened by rivers. Still less can it be those roads of the city which led to the gates, and which were flooded with people instead of water (Hitzig), or with enemies, who were pressing from the gates into the city like overflowing rivers (Ros.); nor even gates through which rivers flow, *i.e.* sluices, namely those of the concentric canals issuing from the Tigris, with which the palace could be laid under water (Vatabl., Burck, Hitzig, ed. 1); but as Luther renders it, " gates on the waters," *i.e.* situated on the rivers, or gates in the city wall, which were protected by the rivers; " gates most strongly fortified, both by nature and art" (Tuch, *de Nino urbe*, p. 67, Strauss, and others), for *n°hârōth* must be understood as signifying the Tigris and its tributaries and canals. At any rate, there were such gates in Nineveh, since the city, which stood at the junction of the Khosr with the Tigris, in the slope of the (by no means steep) rocky bank, was to some extent so built in the alluvium, that the natural course of the Khosr had to be dammed off from the plain chosen for the city by three stone dams, remnants of which are still to be seen; and a canal was cut above this point, which conducted the water to the plain of the city, where it was turned both right and left into the city moats, but had a waste channel through the city. To the south, however, another small collection of waters helped to fill the trenches. " The wall on the side towards the river consisted of a slightly curved line, which connected together the mouths of the trenches, but on the land side it was built at a short distance from the trenches. The wall on the river side now borders upon meadows, which are only flooded at high water; but the soil has probably been greatly elevated, and at the time when the city was built this was certainly river" (see M. v. Niebuhr, *Geschichte Assurs u. Babels*, p. 280; and the outlines of the plan of the ground on which Nineveh stood, p. 284). The words of the prophet are not to be understood as referring to any particular gate, say the western, either alone, or *par excellence*, as Tuch supposes, but apply quite generally to the gates of the city, since the rivers are only mentioned for the purpose of indicating the strength of the gates. As Luther has correctly explained it, " the gates of the rivers, however firm in other respects, and with no easy access, will now be easily occupied, yea, have been already opened." The palace melts away, not, however, from the floods of water which flow through the open gates. This literal rendering of the words is irreconcilable with the situation of the palaces in Nineveh, since they were built in the form of terraces upon the tops of hills, either natural or artificial, and could not be flooded with water. The words are figurative. *Mûg*, to melt, dissolve, *i.e.* to vanish through anxiety and alarm ; and הֵיכָל, the palace, for the inhabitants of the palace. " When the gates, protected by the rivers, are broken open by the enemy, the palace, *i.e.* the reigning Nineveh, vanishes in terror" (Hitzig). For her sway has now come to an end. הֻצַּב : the *hophal* of נָצַב, in the *hiphil*, to establish, to determine (Deut. xxxii. 8 ; Ps. lxxiv. 17 ; and Chald. Dan. ii. 45, vi. 13) ; hence it is established, *i.e.* is determined, *sc.* by God : she will be made bare ; *i.e.* Nineveh, the queen, or mistress of the nations, will be covered with shame. גֻּלְּתָה is not to be taken as interchangeable with the *hophal* הָגְלָה, to be carried away, but means to be uncovered, after the *piel* to uncover, *sc.* the shame or nakedness (ch. iii. 5 ; cf. Isa. xlvii. 2, 3 ; Hos. ii. 12). הֹעֲלָה, for הֶעֱלָה (see Ges. § 63, Anm. 4), to be driven away, or led away, like the *niph.* in Jer. xxxvii. 11, 2 Sam. ii. 27.[1] The laying bare and carrying away denote the complete destruction of Nineveh. אַמְהֹתֶיהָ, *ancillæ ejus*, *i.e. Nini.* The " maids" of the city of Nineveh personified as a queen are not the states

---

[1] Of the different explanations that have been given of this hemistich, the supposition, which dates back as far as the Chaldee, that *huzzab* signifies the queen, or is the name of the queen (Ewald and Rückert), is destitute of any tenable foundation, and is no better than Hitzig's fancy, that we should read וְהַצָּב, " and the lizard is discovered, fetched up," and that this " reptile" is Nineveh. The objection offered to our explanation, viz. that it would only be admissible if it were immediately followed by the *decretum divinum* in its full extent, and not merely by one portion of it, rests upon a misinterpretation of the following words, which do not contain merely a portion of the purpose of God.

subject to her rule (Theodor., Cyr., Jerome, and others),—for throughout this chapter Nineveh is spoken of simply as the capital of the Assyrian empire,—but the inhabitants of Nineveh, who are represented as maids, mourning over the fate of their mistress. *Nâhag,* to pant, to sigh, for which *hâgâh* is used in other passages where the cooing of doves is referred to (cf. Isa. xxxviii. 14, lix. 11). כְּקוֹל יוֹנִים instead of כַּיּוֹנִים, probably to express the loudness of the moaning. *Tôphēph,* to smite, used for the smiting of the timbrels in Ps. lxviii. 26; here, to smite upon the breast. Compare *pectus pugnis cædere,* or *palmis infestis tundere* (*e.g.* Juv. xiii. 167; Virg. *Æn.* i. 481, and other passages), as an expression of violent agony in deep mourning (cf. Luke xviii. 13, xxiii. 27). לבבהן for לְבָבְהֶן is the plural, although this is generally written לְבּוֹת; and as the י is frequently omitted as a sign of the plural (cf. Ewald, § 258, *a*), there is no good ground for reading לְבָבְהֶן, as Hitzig proposes.

Vers. 8–10. At the conquest of Nineveh the numerous inhabitants flee, and the rich city is plundered. Ver. 8. *"And Nineveh like a water-pond all her days. And they flee! Stand ye, O stand! and no one turns round. Ver. 9. Take silver as booty, take ye gold! And no end to the furnishing with immense quantity of all kinds of ornamental vessels. Ver. 10. Emptying and devastation! and the heart has melted, and trembling of the knees, and labour pain in all loins, and the countenance of every one withdraws its ruddiness."* Nineveh is compared to a pool, not merely with reference to the multitude of men who had gathered together there, but, as water is everywhere an element of life, also with reference to the wealth and prosperity which accrued to this imperial city out of the streaming together of so many men and so many different peoples. Compare Jer. li. 13, where Babel is addressed as "Thou that dwellest on many waters, art rich in many treasures." מִימֵי הִיא, since the days that she exists. הִיא = אֲשֶׁר הִיא, the relation being indicated by the construct state; מִן הוּא in Isa. xviii. 2 is different. *But they flee.* The subject to נָסִים is not the waters, although *nûs* is applied to water in Ps. civ. 7, but, as what follows shows, the masses of men who are represented as water. These flee away without being stopped by the cry "Stand ye" (*i.e.* remain), or even paying any attention to it. *Hiphnâh,* lit. "to turn the back" ('*ōreph,* Jer. xlviii. 39), to flee, but when applied to a person already fleeing, to turn round (cf. Jer. xlvi. 5). In ver. 9 the conquerors are summoned to plunder, not by their generals, but by God, who speaks through the prophet. The fact is hereby indicated, " that this does not happen by chance, but because God determines to avenge the injuries inflicted upon His people" (Calvin). With וְאֵין קֵצֶה the prophecy passes into a simple description. There is no end *latt*ᵉ*khūnâh*, to the furnishing with treasures. *T*ᵉ*khūnâh*, from *kūn*, not from *tâkhan*, lit. the setting up, the erection of a building (Ezek. xliii. 11); here the furnishing of Nineveh as the dwelling-place of the rulers of the world, whilst in Job xxiii. 3 it is applied to the place where the throne of God has been established. In כָּבֹד the ל might be thought of as still continuing in force (Ewald, Hitzig), but it answers better to the liveliness of the description to take כָּבֹד as beginning a fresh sentence. כָּבֹד written defectively, as in Gen. xxxi. 1 : glory, equivalent to the great amount of the wealth, as in Genesis (*l.c.*). *K*ᵉ*lê chemdâh*, gold and silver vessels and jewels, as in Hos. xiii. 15. That there were immense treasures of the precious metals and of costly vessels treasured up in Nineveh, may be inferred with certainty from the accounts of ancient writers, which border on the fabulous.[1] Of all these treasures nothing was left but desolate emptiness. This is expressed by the combination of three synonymous words. *Būqâh* and *m*ᵉ*bhūqâh* are substantive formations from *būq* = *bâqaq*, to empty out, and are combined to strengthen the idea, like similar combinations in Zeph. i. 15, Ezek. xxxiii. 29, and Isa. xxix. 2 sqq. *M*ᵉ*bhullâqâh* is a synonymous noun formed from the participle *pual*, and signifying devastation (cf. Isa. xxiv. 1, where even *bâlaq* is combined with *bâqaq*). In ver. 11*b* the horror of the vanquished at the

---

[1] For proofs, see Layard's *Nineveh*, ii. 415 sqq., and Movers, *Phönizier* (iii. 1, pp. 40, 41). After quoting the statements of Ctesias, the latter observes that "these numbers are indeed fabulous; but they have their historical side, inasmuch as in the time of Ctesias the riches of Nineveh were estimated at an infinitely greater amount than the enormous treasures accumulated in the treasuries of the Persian empire. That the latter is quite in accordance with truth, may be inferred from the fact that the conquerors of Nineveh, the Medes and Chaldæans, of whose immense booty, in the shape of gold, silver, and other treasures, even the prophet Nahum speaks, furnished Ecbatana and Babylon with gold and silver from the booty of Nineveh to an extent unparalleled in all history."

total devastation of Nineveh is described, also in short substantive clauses : " melted heart" (*nâmēs* is a participle), *i.e.* perfect despondency (see Isa. xiii. 7 ; Josh. vii. 5) ; trembling of the knees, so that from terror men can hardly keep upon their feet (*pīq* for *pūq*; it only occurs here). *Chalchâlâh* formed by reduplication from *chīl:* spasmodic pains in all loins, like the labour pains of women in childbirth (cf. Isa. xxi. 3). Lastly, the faces of all turning pale (see at Joel ii. 6).

Vers. 11–13. Thus will the mighty city be destroyed, with its men of war and booty. Ver. 11. " *Where is the dwelling of the lions and the feeding-place of the young lions, where the lion walked, the lioness, the lion's whelp, and no one frightened?* Ver. 12. *The lion robbing for the need of his young ones, and strangling for his lionesses, and he filled his dens with prey, and his dwelling-places with spoil.* Ver. 13. *Behold, I come to thee, is the saying of Jehovah of hosts, and I cause her chariots to burn in smoke, and thy young lions the sword devours; and I cut off thy prey from the earth, and the voice of thy messengers shall be heard no more.*" The prophet, beholding the destruction in spirit as having already taken place, looks round for the site on which the mighty city once stood, and sees it no more. This is the meaning of the question in ver. 11. He describes it as the dwelling-place of lions. The point of comparison is the predatory lust of its rulers and their warriors, who crushed the nations like lions, plundering their treasures, and bringing them together in Nineveh. To fill up the picture, the epithets applied to the lions are grouped together according to the difference of sex and age. אַרְיֵה is the full-grown male lion ; לָבִיא, the lioness ; כְּפִיר, the young lion, though old enough to go in search of prey ; גּוּר אַרְיֵה, *catulus leonis*, the lion's whelp, which cannot yet seek prey for itself. וּמִרְעֶה הוּא, lit. " and a feeding-place is it," *sc.* the dwelling-place (הוּא pointing back to מָעוֹן) in this sense: " Where is the dwelling-place which was also a feeding-place for the young lions?" By the apposition the thought is expressed, that the city of lions was not only a resting-place, but also afforded a comfortable living. אֲשֶׁר is to be taken in connection with the following שָׁם: in the very place where; and *hâlakh* signifies simply to walk, to walk about, not " to take exercise," in which case the *kal* would stand for *piel*. The more precise definition follows in וְאֵין מַחֲרִיד, without any one

terrifying, hence in perfect rest and security, and undisturbed
might (cf. Mic. iv. 4; Lev. xxvi. 6; Deut. xxviii. 26, etc.).
Under the same figure ver. 12 describes the tyranny and predatory lust of the Assyrians in their wars. This description is
subordinate in sense to the leading thought, or to the question
contained in the previous verse. Where is the city now, into
which the Assyrians swept together the booty of the peoples
and kingdoms which they had destroyed? In form, however,
the verse is attached poetically in loose apposition to ver. 12b.
The lion, as king of the beasts, is a very fitting emblem of the
kings or rulers of Assyria. The lionesses and young lions are
the citizens of Nineveh and of the province of Assyria, the
tribe-land of the imperial monarchy of Assyria, and not the
queens and princes, as the Chaldee explains it. *Gōrōth* with
the *o*-inflection for *gŭrōth*, as in Jer. li. 38. *Chŏrīm*, holes for
hiding-places, or caves, not only applies to the robbers, in which
character the Assyrians are exhibited through the figure of the
lion (Hitzig), but also to the lions, which carry their prey into
caves (cf. Bochart, *Hieroz*. i. 737). This destruction of Nineveh
will assuredly take place; for Jehovah the Almighty God has
proclaimed it, and He will fulfil His word. The word of God
in ver. 14 stamps the foregoing threat with the seal of confirmation. הִנְנִי אֵלַיִךְ, behold I (will) to thee (Nineveh). We have
not to supply אָבוֹא here, but simply the *verb. copul.*, which is
always omitted in such sentences. The relation of the subject
to the object is expressed by אֶל (cf. ch. iii. 5; Jer. li. 25).
הִבְעַרְתִּי בֶעָשָׁן, I burn into smoke, *i.e.* so that it vanishes into
smoke (cf. Ps. xxxvii. 20). רִכְבָּהּ, her war-chariots, stands
synecdochically for the whole of the apparatus of war (Calvin).
The suffix in the third person must not be altered; it may easily
be explained from the poetical variation of prophetic announcement and direct address. The young lions are the warriors;
the echo of the figure in the previous verse still lingers in this
figure, as well as in טַרְפֵּךְ. The last clause expresses the complete destruction of the imperial might of Assyria. The messengers of Nineveh are partly heralds, as the carriers of the
king's commands; partly halberdiers, or delegates who fulfilled
the ruler's commands (cf. 1 Kings xix. 2; 2 Kings xix. 23).
The suffix in מַלְאָכֵכֵה is in a lengthened form, on account of the
tone at the end of the section, analogous to אֹתָכָה in Ex. xxix.

35, and is not to be regarded as an Aramæism or a dialectical variation (Ewald, § 258, a). The *tsere* of the last syllable is occasioned by the previous *tsere*. Jerome has summed up the meaning very well as follows : " Thou wilt never lay countries waste any more, nor exact tribute, nor will thy messengers be heard throughout thy provinces." (On the last clause, see Ezek. xix. 9.)

NINEVEH'S SINS AND INEVITABLE DESTRUCTION.—Chap. iii.

The announcement of the destruction awaiting Nineveh is confirmed by the proof, that this imperial city has brought this fate upon itself by its sins and crimes (vers. 1–7), and will no more be able to avert it than the Egyptian No-Amon was (vers. 8–13), but that, in spite of all its resources, it will be brought to a terrible end (vers. 14–19).

Vers. 1–7. The city of blood will have the shame, which it has inflicted upon the nations, repaid to it by a terrible massacre. The prophet announces this with the woe which opens the last section of this threatening prophecy. Ver. 1. *" Woe to the city of blood! She all full of deceit and murder; the prey departs not."* '*Ir dâmîm*, city of drops of blood, *i.e.* of blood shed, or of murders. This predicate is explained in the following clauses : she all full of lying and murder. *Cachash* and *pereq* are asyndeton, and accusatives dependent upon מְלֵאָה. *Cachash*, lying and deceit : this is correctly explained by Abarbanel and Strauss as referring to the fact that " she deceived the nations with vain promises of help and protection." *Pereq*, tearing in pieces for murder,—a figure taken from the lion, which tears its prey in pieces (Ps. vii. 3). לֹא יָמִישׁ, the prey does not depart, never fails. *Mûsh :* in the *hiphil* here, used intransitively, " to depart," as in Ex. xiii. 22, Ps. lv. 12, and not in a transitive sense, " to cause to depart," to let go ; for if '*ir* (the city) were the subject, we should have *tâmîsh*.

This threat is explained in vers. 2 sqq., by a description of the manner in which a hostile army enters Nineveh and fills the city with corpses. Ver. 2. *" The cracking of whips, and noise of the rattling of wheels, and the horse in galloping, and chariots flying high.* Ver. 3. *Riders dashing along, and flame of the sword, and flashing of the lance, and multitude of slain men and mass of dead men, and no end of corpses; they stumble over their corpses.* Ver. 4. *For the multitude of the whoredoms of the harlot, the graceful one, the mistress of witchcrafts, who sells nations with her whoredoms, and families with her witchcrafts."* Nahum sees in spirit the hostile army bursting upon Nineveh. He hears the noise, *i.e.* the cracking of the whips of the charioteers, and the rattling (*raʿash*) of the chariot-wheels, sees horses and chariots driving along (*dâhar*, to hunt, cf. Judg. v. 22; *riqqēd*, to jump, applied to the springing up of the chariots as they drive quickly along over a rugged road), dashing riders (*maʿăleh*, lit. to cause to ascend, *sc.* the horse, *i.e.* to make it prance, by driving the spur into its side to accelerate its speed), flaming swords, and flashing lances. As these words are well adapted to depict the attack, so are those which follow to describe the consequence or effect of the attack. Slain men, fallen men in abundance, and so many corpses, that one cannot help stumbling or falling over them. כֹּבֶד, the heavy multitude. The *chethib* יכשלו is to be read יִכָּשְׁלוּ (*niphal*), in the sense of stumbling, as in ch. ii. 6. The *keri* וְכָשְׁלוּ is unsuitable, as the sentence does not express any progress, but simply exhibits the infinite number of the corpses (Hitzig). גְוִיָּתָם, their (the slain men's) corpses. This happens to the city of sins because of the multitude of its whoredoms. Nineveh is called *Zōnâh,* and its conduct *zᵉnûnîm,* not because it had fallen away from the living God and pursued idolatry, for there is nothing about idolatry either here or in what follows; nor because of its commercial intercourse, in which case the commerce of Nineveh would appear here under the perfectly new figure of love-making with other nations (Ewald), for commercial intercourse as such is not love-making; but the love-making, with its parallel " witchcrafts " (*kᵉshâphîm*), denotes " the treacherous friendship and crafty politics with which the coquette in her search for conquests ensnared the smaller states" (Hitzig, after Abarbanel, Calvin, J. H. Michaelis, and others). This policy is called whoring or love-making, " inasmuch as it was that selfishness which wraps itself up in the dress of love, and under the appearance of love seeks simply the gratification of its own lust" (Hengstenberg on the Rev.). The *zōnâh* is described still more minutely as טוֹבַת חֵן, beautiful with grace. This refers to the splendour and brilliancy of Nineveh, by which this city dazzled and ensnared the nations, like a graceful coquette. *Ba'ălath k͏eshâphĭm*, devoted to witchcrafts, mistress of them. *K͏eshâphĭm* (witchcrafts) connected with *z͏enūnĭm*, as in 2 Kings ix. 22, are "the secret wiles, which, like magical arts, do not come to the light in themselves, but only in their effects" (Hitzig). מָכַר, to sell nations, *i.e.* to rob them of liberty and bring them into slavery, to make them tributary, as in Deut. xxxii. 30, Judg. ii. 14, iii. 8, etc. (not = כמר from כבר, to entangle: Hitzig). בִּזְנוּנֶיהָ, with (not for) their whoredoms. *Mishpâchōth*, families, synonymous with עַמִּים, are smaller peoples or tribes (cf. Jer. xxv. 9; Ezek. xx. 32).

The Lord will plunge Nineveh into shameful misery in consequence. Ver. 5. "*Behold, I come to thee, is the saying of Jehovah of hosts; and uncover thy skirts over thy face, and let nations see thy nakedness, and kingdoms thy shame. Ver. 6. And cast horrible things upon thee, and shame thee, and make thee a gazing-stock. Ver. 7. And it comes to pass, every one who sees thee will flee before thee, and say, Is Nineveh laid waste? Who will bewail her? whence do I seek comforters for thee?*" Ver. 5a as in ch. ii. 13a. The punishment of Nineveh will correspond to her conduct. Her coquetry shall be repaid to her by the uncovering of her nakedness before the nations (cf. Jer. xiii. 26; Isa. xlvii. 3; Hos. ii. 5). *Gillâh*, to uncover. *Shūlĭm*, *fimbriæ*, the skirts, borders, or lower end of the long sweeping dress (cf. Ex. xxviii. 33, 34; Isa. vi. 1). עַל פָּנַיִךְ, over thy countenance, so that the train when lifted up is drawn over the face. מַעַר, a contraction of מַעֲרֶה, from עָרָה, signifies in 1 Kings vii. 36 an empty space, here nakedness or shame equivalent to עֶרְוָה. This thought is carried out still further in literal terms in vers. 6, 7. *Shiqqutsĭm*, objects of abhorrence, is used most frequently of idols; but here it is used in a more general sense for unclean or repulsive things, dirt and filth. Throwing dirt upon any one is a figurative expression for the most ignominious treatment or greatest contempt. *Nibbēl*, to treat contemptuously, not with words, as in Mic. vii. 6, but with deeds, equivalent to insult or abuse (cf. Jer. xiv. 21). To make it כְּרֹאִי, the object of sight, *i.e.* to give up to open shame, παραδειγματίζειν (Matt. i. 19). רֹאִי, a pausal form of

רְאִי, the seeing, here the spectacle, like θέατρον in 1 Cor. iv. 9. This is evident from ver. 7, where רֹאַיִךְ contains a play upon רֹאִי. Every one who looks at her will flee from her as an object of disgust. שָׁדְּדָה, a rare form of the *pual* for שֻׁדְּדָה (for the fact, compare Jer. xlviii. 20). The last two clauses express the thought that no one will take pity upon the devastated city, because its fate is so well deserved; compare Isa. li. 19, where the same words are used of Jerusalem. Nineveh will not be able to protect herself from destruction even by her great power. The prophet wrests this vain hope away from her by pointing in vers. 8 sqq. to the fall of the mighty Thebes in Egypt.

Vers. 8–10. Nineveh will share the fate of No-Amon.— Ver. 8. "*Art thou better than No-Amon, that sat by rivers, waters round about her, whose bulwark was the sea, her wall of sea?* Ver. 9. *Ethiopians and Egyptians were (her) strong men, there is no end; Phut and Libyans were for thy help.* Ver. 10. *She also has gone to transportation, into captivity; her children were also dashed in pieces at the corners of all roads; upon her nobles they cast the lot, and all her great men were bound in chains.*" הֲתֵיטְבִי for הֲתִיטְבִי, for the sake of euphony, the imperfect *kal* of יָטַב, to be good, used to denote prosperity in Gen. xii. 13 and xl. 14, is applied here to the prosperous condition of the city, which was rendered strong both by its situation and its resources. נֹא אָמוֹן, *i.e.* probably "dwelling (נֹא contracted from נוֹא, cf. נְאוֹת) of Amon," the sacred name of the celebrated city of *Thebes* in Upper Egypt, called in Egyptian *P-amen*, *i.e.* house of the god *Amun*, who had a celebrated temple there (Herod. i. 182, ii. 42; see Brugsch, *Geogr. Inschr.* i. p. 177). The Greeks called it Διὸς πόλις, generally with the predicate ἡ μεγάλη (Diod. Sic. i. 45), or from the profane name of the city, which was *Apet* according to Brugsch (possibly a throne, seat, or bank), and with the feminine article prefixed, *Tapet*, or *Tape*, or *Tepe*, Θήβη, generally used in the plural Θῆβαι. This strong royal city, which was described even by Homer (*Il.* ix. 383) as ἑκατόμπυλος, and in which the Pharaohs of the 18th to the 20th dynasties, from Amosis to the last Rameses, resided, and created those works of architecture which were admired by Greeks and Romans, and the remains of which still fill the visitor with astonishment, was situated on both banks of the river Nile, which was 1500 feet in breadth at that point, and was built upon a broad plain formed by the falling back of the Libyan and Arabian mountain wall, over which there are now scattered nine larger or smaller fellah-villages, including upon the eastern bank Karnak and Luxor, and upon the western Gurnah and Medinet Abu, with their plantations of date-palms, sugar-canes, corn, etc. הַיֹּשְׁבָה בַּיְאֹרִים, who sits there, *i.e.* dwells quietly and securely, on the streams of the Nile. The plural יְאֹרִים refers to the Nile with its canals, which surrounded the city, as we may see from what follows: "water round about her." אֲשֶׁר־חֵיל, not which is a fortress of the sea (Hitzig), but whose bulwark is sea. חֵיל (for חֵילָה) does not mean the fortified place (Hitzig), but the fortification, bulwark, applied primarily to the moats of a fortification, with the wall belonging to it; then, in the broader sense, the defence of a city in distinction from the actual wall (cf. Isa. xxvi. 1; Lam. ii. 8). מַיִם, consisting of sea is its wall, *i.e.* its wall is formed of sea. Great rivers are frequently called *yâm*, sea, in rhetorical and poetical diction: for example, the Euphrates in Isa. xxvii. 1, Jer. li. 36; and the Nile in Isa. xviii. 2, xix. 5, Job xli. 23. The Nile is still called by the Beduins *bahr*, *i.e.* sea, and when it overflows it really resembles a sea. To the natural strength of Thebes there was also added the strength of the warlike nations at her command. *Cush*, *i.e.* Ethiopians in the stricter sense, and *Mitsraim*, Egyptians, the two tribes descended from Ham, according to Gen. x. 6, who formed the Egyptian kingdom before the fall of Thebes, and under the 25th (Ethiopian) dynasty. עָצְמָה, as in Isa. xl. 29, xlvii. 9, for עֹצֶם, strength; it is written without any suffix, which may easily be supplied from the context. The corresponding words to עָצְמָה in the parallel clause are וְאֵין קֵצֶה (with *Vav cop.*): Egyptians, as for them there is no number; equivalent to an innumerable multitude. To these there were to be added the auxiliary tribes: *Put*, *i.e.* the Libyans in the broader sense, who had spread themselves out over the northern part of Africa as far as Mauritania (see at Gen. x. 6); and *Lubim* = *L'hâbhîm*, the Libyans in the narrower sense, probably the *Libyægyptii* of the ancients (see at Gen. x. 13). In בְּעֶזְרָתֵךְ (cf. Ps. xxxv. 2) Nahum addresses No-Amon itself, to give greater life to the description. Notwithstanding all this might,

No-Amon had to wander into captivity. *Laggōlâh* and *bas-shebhī* are not tautological. *Laggōlâh,* for emigration, is strengthened by *basshebhī* into captivity. The perfect הָלְכָה is obviously not to be taken prophetically. The very antithesis of גַּם־הִיא הָלְכָה and גַּם־אַתְּ תִּשְׁכְּרִי (ver. 11) shows of itself that הָלְכָה refers to the past, as תִּשְׁכְּרִי does to the future; yea, the facts themselves require that Nahum should be understood as point-ing to the fate which the powerful city of Thebes had already experienced. For it must be an event that has already occurred, and not something still in the future, which he holds up before Nineveh as a mirror of the fate that is awaiting it. The clauses which follow depict the cruelties that were gene-rally associated with the taking of an enemy's cities. For עֹלְלֶיהָ וגו', see Hos. xiv. 1, Isa. xiii. 16, and 2 Kings viii. 12; and for יַדּוּ גוֹרָל, Joel iv. 3 and Ob. 11. *Nikhbaddīm, nobiles;* cf. Isa. xxiii. 8, 9. *Gᵉdōlīm, magnates;* cf. Jonah iii. 7. It must be borne in mind, however, that the words only refer to cruelties connected with the conquest and carrying away of the inhabitants, and not to the destruction of No-Amon.

We have no express historical account of this occurrence; but there is hardly any doubt that, after the conquest of Ashdod, *Sargon* the king of Assyria organized an expedition against Egypt and Ethiopia, conquered No-Amon, the resi-dence of the Pharaohs at that time, and, as Isaiah prophesied (Isa. xx. 3, 4), carried the prisoners of Egypt and Ethiopia into exile. According to the Assyrian researches and their most recent results (*vid.* Spiegel's *Nineveh and Assyria* in Herzog's *Cyclopædia*), the king Sargon mentioned in Isa. xx. 1 is not the same person as Shalmaneser, as I assumed in my commentary on 2 Kings xvii. 3, but his successor, and the predecessor of Sennacherib, who ascended the throne during the siege of Samaria, and conquered that city in the first year of his reign, leading 27,280 persons into captivity, and appoint-ing a vicegerent over the country of the ten tribes. In Assyrian *Sargon* is called *Sar Kin, i.e.* essentially a king. He was the builder of the palace at Khorsabad, which is so rich in monu-ments; and, according to the inscriptions, he carried on wars in Susiana, Babylon, the borders of Egypt, Melitene, Southern Armenia, Kurdistan, and Media; and in all his expeditions he resorted to the removal of the people in great numbers, as one means of securing the lasting subjugation of the lands (see Spiegel, *l.c.* p. 224). In the great inscription in the palace-halls of Khorsabad, Sargon boasts immediately after the conquest of Samaria of a victorious conflict with Pharaoh Sebech at Raphia, in consequence of which the latter became tributary, and also of the dethroning of the rebellious king of Ashdod; and still further, that after another king of Ashdod, who had been chosen by the people, had fled to Egypt, he besieged Ashdod with all his army, and took it. Then follows a difficult and mutilated passage, in which Rawlinson (*Five Great Monarchies*, ii. 416) and Oppert (*Les Sargonides*, pp. 22, 26, 27) find an account of the complete subjugation of Sebech (see Delitzsch on Isaiah, vol. i. p. 374). There is apparently a confirmation of this in the monuments recording the deeds of Esarhaddon's successor, whose name is read *Assur-bani-pal*, according to which that king carried on tedious wars in Egypt against Tirhaka, who had conquered Memphis, Thebes, and sundry other Egyptian cities during the illness of Esarhaddon, and according to his own account, succeeded at length in completely overcoming him, and returned home with rich booty, having first of all taken hostages for future good behaviour (see Spiegel, p. 225). If these inscriptions have been read correctly, it follows from them that from the reign of Sargon the Assyrians made attempts to subjugate Egypt, and were partially successful, though they could not maintain their conquests. The struggle between Assyria and Egypt for supremacy in Hither Asia may also be inferred from the brief notices in the Old Testament (2 Kings xvii. 4) concerning the help which the Israelitish king Hosea expected from So the king of Egypt, and also concerning the advance of Tirhaka against Sennacherib.[1]

Vers. 11–13. The same, or rather a worse fate than No-

---

[1] From the modern researches concerning ancient Egypt, not the smallest light can be obtained as to any of these things. "The Egyptologists (as J. Bumüller observes, p. 245) have hitherto failed to fill up the gaps in the history of Egypt, and have been still less successful in restoring the chronology; for hitherto we have not met with a single well-established date, which we have obtained from a monumental inscription; nor have the monuments enabled us to assign to a single Pharaoh, from the 1st to the 21st, his proper place in the years or centuries of the historical chronology."

Amon suffered, is now awaiting Nineveh. Ver. 11. *"Thou also wilt be drunken, shalt be hidden; thou also wilt seek for a refuge from the enemy. Ver. 12. All thy citadels are fig-trees with early figs; if they are shaken, they fall into the mouth of the eater. Ver. 13. Behold thy people, women in the midst of thee; the gates of thy land are thrown quite open to thine enemies; fire consumes thy bolts."* גַּם־אַתְּ corresponds to גַּם־הִיא in ver. 10 : as she, so also thou. "The fate of No-Amon is a prophecy of thine own " (Hitzig). תִּשְׁכְּרִי, thou wilt be drunken, viz. from the goblet of divine wrath, as at Ob. 16. תְּהִי נַעֲלָמָה might mean, "thou wilt be hiding thyself;" but although this might suit what follows, it does not agree with תִּשְׁכְּרִי, since an intoxicated person is not in the habit of hiding himself. Moreover, נֶעְלָם always means "hidden," *occultus;* so that Calvin's interpretation is the correct one : "Thou wilt vanish away as if thou hadst never been ; the Hebrews frequently using the expression being hidden for being reduced to nothing." This is favoured by a comparison both with ch. i. 8 and ii. 12, and also with the parallel passage in Ob. 16, "They will drink, and be as if they had not been." This is carried out still further in what follows : "Thou wilt seek refuge from the enemy," *i.e.* in this connection, seek it in vain, or without finding it ; not, "Thou wilt surely demand salvation from the enemy by surrender" (Strauss), for מֵאוֹיֵב does not belong to תְּבַקְשִׁי, but to מָעוֹז (cf. Isa. xxv. 4). All the fortifications of Nineveh are like fig-trees with early figs (עִם in the sense of subordination, as in Song of Sol. iv. 13), which fall into the mouth of the eater when the trees are shaken. The *tertium compar.* is the facility with which the castles will be taken and destroyed by the enemy assaulting them (cf. Isa. xxviii. 4). We must not extend the comparison so far, however, as to take the figs as representing cowardly warriors, as Hitzig does. Even in ver. 13a, where the people are compared to women, the point of comparison is not the cowardliness of the warriors, but the weakness and inability to offer any successful resistance into which the nation of the Assyrians, which was at other times so warlike, would be reduced through the force of the divine judgment inflicted upon Nineveh (compare Isa. xix. 16 ; Jer. l. 37, li. 30). לְאֹיְבַיִךְ belongs to what follows, and is placed first, and pointed with *zakeph-katon* for the sake of emphasis. The gates of the land

are the approaches to it, the passes leading into it, which were
no doubt provided with castles. Tuch (p. 35) refers to the
mountains on the north, which Pliny calls impassable. The
bolts of these gates are the castles, through which the approaches
were closed. Jeremiah transfers to Babel what is here said of
Nineveh (see Jer. li. 30).

Vers. 14–19. In conclusion, the prophet takes away from the
city so heavily laden with guilt the last prop to its hope,—namely,
reliance upon its fortifications, and the numerical strength of
its population.—Ver. 14. *" Draw thyself water for the siege !
Make thy castles strong ! tread in the mire, and stamp in the
clay ! prepare the brick-kiln !* Ver. 15. *There will the fire devour thee, the sword destroy thee, devour thee like the lickers. Be
in great multitude like the lickers, be in great multitude like the
locusts ?* Ver. 16. *Thou hast made thy merchants more than the
stars of heaven ; the licker enters to plunder, and flies away.*
Ver. 17. *Thy levied ones are like the locusts, and thy men like an
army of grasshoppers which encamp in the hedges in the day of
frost ; if the sun rises, they are off, and men know not their
place : where are they ?"* Water of the siege is the drinking
water necessary for a long-continued siege. Nineveh is to
provide itself with this, because the siege will last a long while.
It is also to improve the fortifications (*chizzēq* as in 2 Kings
xii. 8, 13). This is then depicted still more fully. *Tīt* and
chōmer are used synonymously here, as in Isa. xli. 25. *Tīt*,
lit. dirt, slime, then clay and potter's clay (Isa. *l.c.*). *Chōmer*,
clay or mortar (Gen. xi. 3), also dirt of the streets (Isa. x. 6,
compared with Mic. vii. 10). הֶחֱזִיק, to make firm, or strong,
applied to the restoration of buildings in Neh. v. 16 and Ezek.
xxvii. 9, 27 ; here to restore, or to put in order, the brick-kiln
(*malbēn*, a denom. from *lᵉbhēnâh*, a brick), for the purpose of
burning bricks. The Assyrians built with bricks sometimes
burnt, sometimes unburnt, and merely dried in the sun. Both
kinds are met with on the Assyrian monuments (see Layard,
vol. ii. p. 36 sqq.). This appeal, however, is simply a rhetorical turn for the thought that a severe and tedious siege is
awaiting Nineveh. This siege will end in the destruction of
the great and populous city. שָׁם, there, *sc.* in these fortifications
of thine, will fire consume thee ; fire will destroy the city with
its buildings, and the sword destroy the inhabitants. The

destruction of Nineveh by fire is related by ancient writers
(Herod. i. 106, 185; Diod. Sic. ii. 25–28; Athen. xii. p. 529),
and also confirmed by the ruins (cf. Str. *ad h. l.*). It devours
thee like the locust. The subject is not fire *or* sword, either
one or the other, but rather both embraced in one. יֶלֶק, like
the *licker; yeleq*, a poetical epithet applied to the locust (see at
Joel i. 4), is the nominative, not the accusative, as Calvin,
Grotius, Ewald, and Hitzig suppose. For the locusts are not
devoured by the fire or the sword, but it is they who devour
the vegetables and green of the fields, so that they are everywhere used as a symbol of devastation and destruction. It is
true that in the following sentences the locusts are used figuratively for the Assyrians, or the inhabitants of Nineveh; but it
is also by no means a rare thing for prophets to give a new
turn and application to a figure or simile. The thought is this:
fire and sword will devour Nineveh and its inhabitants like the
all-consuming locusts, even though the city itself, with its mass
of houses and people, should resemble an enormous swarm of
locusts. הִתְכַּבֵּד may be either an inf. abs. used instead of the
imperative, or the imperative itself. The latter seems the more
simple; and the use of the masculine may be explained on the
assumption that the prophet had the people floating before his
mind, whereas in הִתְכַּבְּדִי he was thinking of the city. *Hith-
kabbēd*, to show itself heavy by virtue of the large multitude;
similar to כָּבֵד in ch. ii. 10 (cf. כָּבֵד in Gen. xiii. 2, Ex. viii. 20,
etc.). The comparison to a swarm of locusts is carried still
further in vers. 16 and 17, and that so that ver. 16 explains
the תֹּאכְלֵךְ כַּיֶּלֶק in ver. 15. Nineveh has multiplied its traders
or merchants, even more than the stars of heaven, *i.e.* to an
innumerable multitude. The *yeleq, i.e.* the army of the enemy,
bursts in and plunders. That Nineveh was a very rich commercial city may be inferred from its position,—namely, just
at the point where, according to oriental notions, the east and
west meet together, and where the Tigris becomes navigable, so
that it was very easy to sail from thence into the Persian Gulf;
just as afterwards Mosul, which was situated opposite, became
great and powerful through its widely-extended trade (see
Tuch, *l.c.* p. 31 sqq., and Strauss, *in loc.*).[1] The meaning of

[1] " The point," says O. Strauss (*Nineveh and the Word of God*, Berl
1855, p. 19), " at which Nineveh was situated was certainly the culmi-

this verse has been differently interpreted, according to the explanation given to the verb *pâshat*. Many, following the ὥρμησε and *expansus est* of the LXX. and Jerome, give it the meaning, to spread out the wing; whilst Credner (on *Joel*, p. 295), Maurer, Ewald, and Hitzig take it in the sense of undressing one's self, and understand it as relating to the shedding of the horny wing-sheaths of the young locusts. But neither the one nor the other of these explanations can be grammatically sustained. *Pâshat* never means anything else than to plunder, or to invade with plundering; not even in such passages as Hos. vii. 1, 1 Chron. xiv. 9 and 13, which Gesenius and Dietrich quote in support of the meaning, to spread; and the meaning forced upon it by Credner, of the shedding of the wing-sheaths by locusts, is perfectly visionary, and has merely been invented by him for the purpose of establishing his false interpretation of the different names given to the locusts in Joel i. 4. In the passage before us we cannot understand by the *yeleq*, which " plunders and flies away" (*pâshat vayyâʿōph*), the innumerable multitude of the merchants of Nineveh, because they were not able to fly away in crowds out of the besieged city. Moreover, the flying away of the merchants would be quite contrary to the meaning of the whole description, which does not promise deliverance from danger by flight, but threatens destruction. The *yeleq* is rather the innumerable army of the enemy, which plunders everything, and hurries away with its booty. In ver. 17 the last two clauses of ver. 15 are explained, and the warriors of Nineveh compared to an army of locusts. There is some difficulty caused by the two words מִנְּזָרַיִךְ and טַפְסְרַיִךְ, the first of which only occurs here, and the second only once more, viz. in Jer. li. 27, where we meet with it in the singular. That they both denote warlike companies appears to be tolerably certain; but the real meaning cannot be exactly determined. מִנְּזָרִים with *dagesh dir.*, as for example in מִקְדָּשׁ in Ex. xv. 17, is probably derived from *nâzar*, to separate, and not directly from *nezer*, a diadem, or *nâzīr*, the crowned person, from which the lexicons, following

nating point of the three quarters of the globe—Europe, Asia, and Africa; and from the very earliest times it was just at the crossing of the Tigris by Nineveh that the great military and commercial roads met, which led into the heart of all the leading known lands."

Kimchi's example, have derived the meaning princes, or persons ornamented with crowns; whereas the true meaning is those levied, selected (for war), analogous to *bâchūr*, the picked or selected one, applied to the soldiery. The meaning princes or captains is at variance with the comparison to *'arbeh*, the multitude of locusts, since the number of the commanders in an army, or of the war-staff, is always a comparatively small one. And the same objection may be offered to the rendering warchiefs or captains, which has been given to *taphsar*, and which derives only an extremely weak support from the Neo-Persian

تَاوُسِ, although the word might be applied to a commander-inchief in Jer. li. 27, and does signify an angel in the TargumJonathan on Deut. xxviii. 12. The different derivations are all untenable (see Ges. *Thes.* p. 554); and the attempt of Böttcher (*N. Krit. Æhrenl.* ii. pp. 209–10) to trace it to the Aramæan verb טפס, *obedivit*, with the inflection רְ— for הָ—, in the sense of *clientes*, vassals, is precluded by the fact that *ar* does not occur as a syllable of inflection. The word is probably Assyrian, and a technical term for soldiers of a special kind, though hitherto it has not been explained. גּוֹב גּוֹבַי, locusts upon locusts, *i.e.* an innumerable swarm of locusts. On גּוֹבַי, see at Amos vii. 1; and on the repetition of the same word to express the idea of the superlative, see the comm. on 2 Kings xix. 23 (and Ges. § 108, 4). *Yōm qârâh*, day (or time) of cold, is either the night, which is generally very cold in the East, or the winter-time. To the latter explanation it may be objected, that locusts do not take refuge in walls or hedges during the winter; whilst the expression *yōm*, day, for night, may be pleaded against the former. We must therefore take the word as relating to certain cold days, on which the sky is covered with clouds, so that the sun cannot break through, and *zârach* as denoting not the rising of the sun, but its shining or breaking through. The wings of locusts become stiffened in the cold; but as soon as the warm rays of the sun break through the clouds, they recover their animation and fly away. *Nōdad* (*poal*), has flown away, viz. the Assyrian army, which is compared to a swarm of locusts, so that its place is known no more (cf. Ps. ciii. 16), *i.e.* has perished without leaving a trace behind. אַיָּם contracted from אַיֵּה הֵם. These words depict in the most striking manner the complete annihilation of the army on which Nineveh relied.

Such an end will come to the Assyrian kingdom on the overthrow of Nineveh. Ver. 18. *" Thy shepherds have fallen asleep, king Asshur: thy glorious ones are lying there: thy people have scattered themselves upon the mountains, and no one gathers them. Ver. 19. No alleviation to thy fracture, thy stroke is grievous: all who hear tidings of thee clap the hand over thee: for over whom hath not thy wickedness passed continually?"* The king of Asshur addressed in ver. 18 is not the last historical king of that kingdom, but a rhetorical personification of the holder of the imperial power of Assyria. His shepherds and glorious ones (*'addīrīm*, as in ch. ii. 6) are the princes and great men, upon whom the government and defence of the kingdom devolved, the royal counsellors, deputies, and generals. *Nâmū*, from *nūm*, to slumber, to sleep, is not a figurative expression for carelessness and inactivity here; for the thought that the people would be scattered, and the kingdom perish, through the carelessness of the rulers (Hitzig), neither suits the context, where the destruction of the army and the laying of the capital in ashes are predicted, nor the object of the whole prophecy, which does not threaten the fall of the kingdom through the carelessness of its rulers, but the destruction of the kingdom by a hostile army. *Nūm* denotes here, as in Ps. lxxvi. 6, the sleep of death (cf. Ps. xiii. 4; Jer. li. 39, 57: Theodoret, Hesselb., Str., and others). *Shâkhan*, a synonym of *shâkhabh*, to have lain down, to lie quietly (Judg. v. 17), used here of the rest of death. As the shepherds have fallen asleep, the flock (*i.e.* the Assyrian people) is scattered upon the mountains and perishes, because no one gathers it together. Being scattered upon the mountains, is easily explained from the figure of the flock (cf. Num. xxvii. 17; 1 Kings xxii. 17; Zech. xiii. 7), and implies destruction. The mountains are mentioned with evident reference to the fact that Nineveh is shut in towards the north by impassable mountains. *Kēhâh*, a noun formed from the adjective, the extinction of the wound (cf. Lev. xiii. 6), *i.e.* the softening or anointing of it. *Shebher*, the fracture of a limb, is frequently applied to the collapse or destruction of a state or kingdom (*e.g.* Ps. lx. 4; Lam. ii. 11). נַחְלָה מַכָּתֶךְ, *i.e.* dangerously bad, incurable is the stroke which has fallen upon thee (cf. Jer. x. 19, xiv. 17, xxx. 12). Over thy destruction will all rejoice who hear thereof. שִׁמְעֵךְ, the tidings of thee, *i.e.* of that which has befallen thee. Clapping the hands is a gesture expressive of joy (cf. Ps. xlvii. 2 ; Isa. lv. 12). *All :* because they all had to suffer from the malice of Asshur. רָעָה, malice, is the tyranny and cruelty which Assyria displayed towards the subjugated lands and nations.

Thus was Nineveh to perish. If we inquire now how the prophecy was fulfilled, the view already expressed by Josephus (*Ant.* x. 2), that the fall of the Assyrian empire commenced with the overthrow of Sennacherib in Judah, is not confirmed by the results of the more recent examinations of the Assyrian monuments. For according to the inscriptions, so far as they have been correctly deciphered, Sennacherib carried out several more campaigns in Susiana and Babylonia after that disaster, whilst ancient writers also speak of an expedition of his to Cilicia. His successor, Esarhaddon, also carried on wars against the cities of Phœnicia, against Armenia and Cilicia, attacked the Edomites, and transported some of them to Assyria, and is said to have brought a small and otherwise unknown people, the *Bikni,* into subjection ; whilst we also know from the Old Testament (2 Chron. xxxiii. 11) that his generals led king Manasseh in chains to Babylon. Like many of his predecessors, he built himself a palace at Kalah or Nimrud ; but before the internal decorations were completely finished, it was destroyed by so fierce a fire, that the few monuments preserved have suffered very considerably. His successor is the last king of whom we have any inscriptions, with his name still legible upon them (viz. *Assur-bani-pal*). He carried on wars not only in Susiana, but also in Egypt, viz. against Tirhaka, who had conquered Memphis, Thebes, and other Egyptian cities, during the illness of Esarhaddon ; also on the coast of Syria, and in Cilicia and Arabia; and completed different buildings which bear his name, including a palace in Kouyunjik, in which a room has been found with a library in it, consisting of clay tablets. Assur-bani-pal had a son, whose name was written *Asur-emid-ilin,* and who is regarded as the *Sarakos* of the ancients, under whom the Assyrian empire perished, with the conquest and destruction of Nineveh (see Spiegel in Herzog's *Cycl.*). But if, according to these testimonies, the might of the

Assyrian empire was not so weakened by Sennacherib's overthrow in Judah, that any hope could be drawn from that,
according to human conjecture, of the speedy destruction of
that empire; the prophecy of Nahum concerning Nineveh,
which was uttered in consequence of that catastrophe, cannot
be taken as the production of any human combination : still
less can it be taken, as Ewald supposes, as referring to " the
first important siege of Nineveh, under the Median king
Phraortes (Herod. i. 102)." For Herodotus says nothing about
any siege of Nineveh, but simply speaks of a war between
Phraortes and the Assyrians, in which the former lost his life.
Nineveh was not really besieged till the time of Cyaxares
(Uwakhshatra), who carried on the war with an increased
army, to avenge the death of his father, and forced his way to
Nineveh, to destroy that city, but was compelled, by the invasion of his own land by the Scythians, to relinquish the siege,
and hasten to meet that foe (Her. i. 103). On the extension of
his sway, the same Cyaxares commenced a war with the Lydian
king Alyattes, which was carried on for five years with alter-
nating success and failure on both sides, and was terminated
in the sixth year by the fact, that when the two armies were
standing opposite to one another, drawn up in battle array, the
day suddenly darkened into night, which alarmed the armies,
and rendered the kings disposed for peace. This was brought
about by the mediation of the Cilician viceroy Syennesis and
the Babylonian viceroy Labynetus, and sealed by the establishment of a marriage relationship between the royal families of
Lydia and Media (Her. i. 74). And if this Labynetus was the
same person as the Babylonian king *Nabopolassar,* which there
is no reason to doubt, it was not till after the conclusion of this
peace that Cyaxares formed an alliance with Nabopolassar to
make war upon Nineveh; and this alliance was strengthened
by his giving his daughter Amuhea in marriage to Nabopolassar's son Nebuchadnezzar (Nabukudrossor). The combined
forces of these two kings now advanced to the attack upon
Nineveh, and conquered it, after a siege of three years, the
Assyrian king *Saracus* burning himself in his palace as the
besiegers were entering the city. This is the historical kernel
of the capture and destruction of Nineveh, which may be taken
as undoubted fact from the accounts of Herodotus (i. 106) and

Diod. Sic. (ii. 24–28), as compared with the extract from Abydenus in Euseb. *Chron. Armen.* i. p. 54; whereas it is impossible to separate the historical portions from the legendary and in part mythical decorations contained in the elaborate account givon by Diodorus (*vid.* M. v. Niebuhr, *Geschichte Assurs*, p. 200 sqq.; Duncker, *Geschichte des Alterthums.* i. p. 793 sqq.; and Bumüller, *Gesch. d. Alterth.* i. p. 316 sqq.).

The year of the conquest and destruction of Nineveh has been greatly disputed, and cannot be exactly determined. As it is certain that Nabopolassar took part in the war against Nineveh, and this is indirectly intimated even by Herodotus, who attributes the conquest of it to Cyaxares and the Medes (*vid.* i. 106), Nineveh must have fallen between the years 625 and 606 B.C. For according to the canon of Ptolemy, Nabopolassar was king of Babylon from 625 to 606; and this date is astronomically established by an eclipse of the moon, which took place in the fifth year of his reign, and which actually occurred in the year 621 B.C. (*vid.* Niebuhr, p. 47). Attempts have been made to determine the year of the taking of Nineveh, partly with reference to the termination of the Lydio-Median war, and partly from the account given by Herodotus of the twenty-eight years' duration of the Scythian rule in Asia. Starting from the fact, that the eclipse of the sun, which put an end to the war between Cyaxares and Alyattes, took place, according to the calculation of Altmann, on the 30th September B.C. 610 (see Ideler, *Handbuch der Chronologie,* i. p. 209 sqq.), M. v. Niebuhr (pp. 197–8) has assumed that, at the same time as the mediation of peace between the Lydians and Medes, an alliance was formed between Cyaxares and Nabopolassar for the destruction of Nineveh; and as this treaty could not possibly be kept secret, the war against Assyria was commenced at once, according to agreement, with their united forces. But as it was impossible to carry out extensive operations in winter, the siege of Nineveh may not have commenced till the spring of 609; and as it lasted three years according to Ctesias, the capture may not have been effected before the spring of 606 B.C. It is true that this combination is apparently confirmed by the fact, that during that time the Egyptian king Necho forced his way into Palestine and Syria, and after subduing all Syria, advanced to the Euphrates; since this advance of the Egyptian is most easily explained on the supposition that Nabopolassar was so occupied with the war against Nineveh, that he could not offer any resistance to the enterprise of Necho. And the statement in 2 Kings xxiii. 29, that Necho had come up to fight against the king of Asshur on the Euphrates, appears to favour the conclusion, that at that time (*i.e.* in the year of Josiah's death, 610 B.C.) the Assyrian empire was not yet destroyed. Nevertheless there are serious objections to this combination. In the first place, there is the double difficulty, that Cyaxares would hardly have been in condition to undertake the war against Nineveh in alliance with Nabopolassar, directly after the conclusion of peace with Alyattes, especially after he had carried on a war for five years, without being able to defeat his enemy ; and secondly, that even Nabopolassar, after a fierce three years' conflict with Nineveh, the conquest of which was only effected in consequence of the wall of the city having been thrown down for the length of twenty stadia, would hardly possess the power to take the field at once against Pharaoh Necho, who had advanced as far as the Euphrates, and not only defeat him at Carchemish, but pursue him to the frontier of Egypt, and wrest from him all the conquests that he had effected, as would necessarily be the case, since the battle at Carchemish was fought in the year 606 ; and the pursuit of the defeated foe by Nebuchadnezzar, to whom his father had transferred the command of the army because of his own age and infirmity, even to the very border of Egypt, is so distinctly attested by the biblical accounts (2 Kings xxiv. 1 and 7 ; Jer. xlvi. 2), and by the testimony of Berosus in Josephus (*Ant.* x. 11, 1, and *c. Ap.* i. 19), that these occurrences are placed beyond the reach of doubt (see comm. on 2 Kings xxiv. 1). These difficulties would not indeed be sufficient in themselves to overthrow the combination mentioned, provided that the year 610 could be fixed upon with certainty as the time when the Lydio-Median war was brought to a close. But that is not the case ; and this circumstance is decisive. The eclipse of the sun, which alarmed Cyaxares and Alyattes, and made them disposed for peace, must have been total, or nearly total, in Central Asia and Cappadocia, to produce the effect described. But it has been proved by exact astronomical calculations, that on the 30th September 610 B.C., the shadow of the moon did not fall upon those portions of Asia Minor, whereas it did so on the 18th May 622, after eight o'clock in the morning, and on the 28th May 585 (*vid.* Bumüll. p. 315, and M. v. Niebuhr, pp. 48, 49). Of these two dates the latter cannot come into consideration at all, because Cyaxares only reigned till the year 594 ; and therefore, provided that peace had not been concluded with Alyattes before 595, he would not have been able to carry on the war with Nineveh and conquer that city. On the other hand, there is no valid objection that can be offered to our transferring the conclusion of peace with the Lydian king to the year 622 B.C. Since, for example, Cyaxares became king as early as the year 634, he might commence the war with the Lydians as early as the year 627 or 628 ; and inasmuch as Nabopolassar was king of Babylon from 625 to 605, he might very well help to bring about the peace between Cyaxares and Alyattes in the year 622. In this way we obtain the whole space between 622 and 605 B.C. for the war with Nineveh ; so that the city may have been taken and destroyed as early as the years 615–610.

Even the twenty-eight years' duration of the Scythian supremacy in Asia, which is recorded by Herodotus (i. 104, 106, cf. iv. 1), cannot be adduced as a well-founded objection. For if the Scythians invaded Media in the year 633, so as to compel Cyaxares to relinquish the siege of Nineveh, and if their rule in Upper Asia lasted for twenty-eight years, the expedition against Nineveh, which led to the fall of that city, cannot have taken place after the expulsion of the Scythians in the year 605, because the Assyrian empire had passed into the hands of the Chaldæans before that time, and Nebuchadnezzar had already defeated Necho on the Euphrates, and was standing at the frontier of Egypt, when he received the intelligence of his father's death, which led him to return with all speed to Babylon. There is no other alternative left, therefore, than either to assume, as M. v. Niebuhr does (pp. 119, 120), that the war of Cyaxares with the Lydians, and also the last war against Nineveh, and probably also the capture of Nineveh, and the greatest portion of the Median conquests between Ararat and Halys, fell within the period of the Scythian sway, so that Cyaxares extended his power as a vassal of the Scythian Great Khan as soon as he had recovered from the first blow received from these wild hordes, inasmuch as that sovereign allowed his dependent to do just as he liked, provided that he paid the tribute, and did not disturb the hordes in their pasture grounds; or else to suppose that Cyaxares drove out the Scythian hordes from Media at a much earlier period, and liberated his own country from their sway; in which case the twenty-eight years of Herodotus would not indicate the period of their sway over Media and Upper Asia, but simply the length of time that they remained in Hither Asia generally, or the period that intervened between their first invasion and the complete disappearance of their hordes. If Cyaxares had driven the Scythians out of his own land at a much earlier period, he might extend his dominion even while they still kept their position in Hither Asia, and might commence the war with the Lydians as early as the year 628 or 627, especially as his wrath is said to have been kindled because Alyattes refused to deliver up to him a Scythian horde, which had first of all submitted to Cyaxares, and then fled into Lydia to Alyattes (Herod. i. 73). Now, whichever of these two combinations be the correct one, they both show that the period of the war commenced by Cyaxares against Nineveh, in alliance with Nabopolassar, cannot be determined by the statement made by Herodotus with regard to the twenty-eight years of the Scythian rule in Asia; and this Scythian rule, generally, does not compel us to place the taking and destruction of Nineveh, and the dissolution of the Assyrian empire, as late as the year 605 B.C., or even later.

At this conquest Nineveh was so utterly destroyed, that, as Strabo (xvi. 1, § 3) attests, the city entirely disappeared immediately after the dissolution of the Assyrian kingdom (ἡ μὲν οὖν Νῖνος πόλις ἠφανίσθη παραχρῆμα μετὰ τὴν τῶν Σύρων κατάλυσιν). When Xenophon entered the plain of Nineveh, in the year 401, on the retreat of the ten thousand Greeks, he found the ruins of two large cities, which he calls Larissa and Mespila, and by the side of the first a stone pyramid of 200 feet in height and 100 feet in breadth, upon which many of the inhabitants of the nearest villages had taken refuge, and heard from the inhabitants that it was only by a miracle that it had been possible for the Persians to conquer those cities with their strong walls (Xenoph. *Anab.* iii. 4, 7 sqq.). These ruined cities had been portions of the ancient Nineveh : Larissa was *Calah ;* and Mespila, *Kouyunjik.* Thus Xenophon passed by the walls of Nineveh without even learning its name. Four hundred years after (according to Tacitus, *Annal.* xii. 13), a small fortress stood on this very spot, to guard the crossing of the Tigris; and the same fortress is mentioned by *Abul-Pharaj* in the thirteenth century (*Hist. Dynast.* pp. 266, 289, 353). Opposite to this, on the western side of the Tigris, Mosul had risen into one of the first cities of Asia, and the ruins of Nineveh served as quarries for the building of the new city, so that nothing remained but heaps of rubbish, which even Niebuhr took to be natural heights in the year 1766, when he was told, as he stood by the Tigris bridge, that he was in the neighbourhood of ancient Nineveh. So completely had this mighty city vanished from the face of the earth ; until, in the most recent times, viz. from 1842 onwards, Botta the French consul, and the two Englishmen Layard and Rawlinson, instituted excavations in the heaps, and brought to light numerous remains of the palaces and state-buildings of the Assyrian rulers of the world. Compare the general survey of these researches, and their results, in Herm. J. C. Weissenborn's *Ninive u. sein Gebiet.*, Erfurt 1851, and 56, 4.

But if Nahum's prophecy was thus fulfilled in the destruction of Nineveh, even to the disappearance of every trace of its existence, we must not restrict it to this one historical event, but must bear in mind that, as the prophet simply saw in Nineveh the representative for the time of the power of the world in its hostility to God, so the destruction predicted to Nineveh applied to all the kingdoms of the world which have risen up against God since the destruction of Asshur, and which will still continue to do so to the end of the world.

HABAKKUK

INTRODUCTION.

1. PERSON OF THE PROPHET.—Nothing certain is known as to the circumstances of Habakkuk's life. The name חֲבַקּוּק, formed from חָבַק, to fold the hands, *piel* to embrace, by a repetition of the last radical with the vowel *u*, like נַעֲצוּץ from נָעַץ, שְׁעַרוּרָה from שָׁעַר, etc., and a reduplication of the penultimate (cf. Ewald, § 157, *a*), signifies embracing; and as the name of a person, either one who embraces, or one who is embraced. Luther took the name in the first sense. " Habakkuk," he says, " signifies an embracer, or one who embraces another, or takes him to his arms," and interpreted it thus in a clever although not perfectly appropriate manner : " He embraces his people, and takes them to his arms, *i.e.* he comforts them and holds (lifts) them up, as one embraces a weeping child or person, to quiet it with the assurance that if God will it shall be better soon." The LXX. wrote the name Ἀμβακούμ, taking the word as pronounced חַבָּקוּק, and compensating for the doubling of the ב by the liquid μ, and changing the closing ק into μ. Jerome in his translation writes the name *Habacuc*. In the headings to his book (ch. i. 1 and iii. 1) Habakkuk is simply described by the epithet הַנָּבִיא, as a man who held the office of a prophet. From the conclusion to the psalm in ch. iii., " To the leader in the accompaniment to my playing upon stringed instruments" (ver. 19), we learn that he was officially qualified to take part in the liturgical singing of the temple, and therefore belonged to one of the Levitical families, who were charged with the maintenance of the temple music, and, like the prophets Jeremiah and Ezekiel, who sprang from priestly households, belonged to the tribe of Levi. This is supported by the superscription of the apocryphon of Bel and the dragon at

Babel, ἐκ προφητείας Ἀμβακοὺμ υἱοῦ Ἰησοῦ ἐκ τῆς φυλῆς Λευΐ, which has been preserved in the Cod. Chisian. of the LXX. from Origen's tetrapla, and has passed into the Syrio-hexaplar. version; even if this statement should not be founded upon tradition, but simply inferred from the subscription to ch. iii. 19. For even in that case it would prove that בִּנְגִינוֹתָי was understood in ancient times as signifying that the prophet took part in the liturgical singing of the temple.[1] On the other hand, the rest of the legends relating to our prophet are quite worthless: viz. the circumstantial account in the apocryphal book of Bel and the Dragon of the miraculous way in which Habakkuk was transported to Daniel, who had been cast into the lions' den, which is also found in a MS. of the Midrash Bereshit rabba; and also the statements contained in the writings of Ps. Doroth. and Ps. Epiph. de vitis prophet., that Habakkuk sprang from the tribe of Simeon; that he was born at Βηθ-ζοχήρ (Sozomenus, Χαφὰρ Ζαχαρία, the talmudic כְּפַר דְּכְרִין), a hamlet to the north of Lydda, near to Maresha on the mountains; that when Nebuchadnezzar came to Jerusalem, he fled to Ostrakine (on the promontory now called Ras Straki, situated in the neighbourhood of Arabia Petræa); and that he died on his native soil two years after the return of the people from Babylon, and was buried at the spot between Keila and Gabatha, where his grave was still shown in the time of Eusebius and Jerome (cf. Onomast. ed. Lars. et Parthey, pp. 128-9).

[1] There is not much probability in this conjecture, however, since the LXX. have not understood the subscription in this sense, but have rendered it incorrectly τοῦ νικῆσαι ἐν τῇ ᾠδῇ αὐτοῦ, which has led the fathers to take the words as belonging to the psalm itself, and to understand it as relating to the songs of praise which the church would raise to God for the deliverance which it had received. Theod. Mops. explains it in this way: "He sets us higher than all the rest, so that nothing else becomes us than to continue in the songs and hymns which are due to God, because, against all human hope, He has given us the victory over our enemies." Cyril of Alex. and Theodoret give similar explanations. Even Jerome, in his rendering "et super excelsa mea deducet me victori in psalmis canentem," connects the words with the preceding sentence, and interprets them as referring to the songs of praise which "every righteous man who is worthy of the election of God" will raise at the end of the world to the great conqueror "Jesus, who was the first to conquer in the fight." With such an explanation of the words as these, it was impossible to see any intimation of the Levitical descent of the prophet in the expression בִּנְגִינוֹתָי.

For further particulars as to the apocryphal legends, see Delitzsch, *De Habacuci proph. vita atque ætate commentat.*, ed. ii., Lps. 1842.

These legends do not even help us to fix the date of Habakkuk's life. All that can be gathered with any certainty from his own writings is that he prophesied before the arrival of the Chaldæans in Palestine, *i.e.* before the victory gained by Nebuchadnezzar over Pharaoh Necho at Carchemish in the fourth year of Jehoiakim (Jer. xlvi. 2), since he announces the bringing up of this people to execute judgment upon Judah as something still in the future (ch. i. 5 sqq.). Opinions are divided as to the precise date at which he lived. Leaving out of sight the opinions of those who deny the supernatural character of prophecy, and therefore maintain that the prophet did not prophesy till the Chaldæans were coming against Jerusalem after the defeat of Necho, or had already arrived there, the only question that can arise is, whether Habakkuk lived and laboured in the reign of Josiah or in the closing years of Manasseh. Many have found a decisive proof that he lived in the reign of Josiah in ch. i. 5, viz. in the fact that the prophet there foretels the Chaldæan judgment as a work which God will perform during the lifetime of the persons to whom his words are addressed ("in your days"); and they have inferred from this that we must not at any rate go beyond Josiah's reign, because the prophet is not speaking to the children, but to the adults, *i.e.* to those who have reached the age of manhood. But the measure of time by which to interpret בִּימֵיכֶם cannot be obtained either from Joel i. 2, where the days of the persons addressed are distinguished from the days of the fathers and grandchildren, or from Jer. xvi. 9 and Ezek. xii. 25; but this expression is quite a relative one, especially in prophetic addresses, and may embrace either a few years only, or a complete lifetime, and even more. Now, as there were only thirty-eight years between the death of Manasseh and the first invasion of the Chaldæans, the Chaldæan judgment might very well be announced during the last years of that king to the then existing generation as one that would happen in their days. We are precluded from placing the announcement in the time immediately preceding the appearance of the Chaldæans in Hither Asia, say in the first years of Jehoiakim or the closing

years of Josiah's reign, by the fact that Habakkuk represents
this work of God as an incredible one : " Ye would not believe
it, if it were told you" (ch. i. 5). Moreover, it is expressly related in 2 Kings xxi. 10–16 and 2 Chron. xxxiii. 10, that in the
time of Manasseh Jehovah caused His prophets to announce the
coming of such a calamity, "that both ears of all who heard it
would tingle"—namely, the destruction of Jerusalem and rejection of Judah. In all probability, one of these prophets was
Habakkuk, who was the first of all the prophets known to us
to announce this horrible judgment. Zephaniah and Jeremiah
both appeared with the announcement of the same judgment
in the reign of Josiah, and both took notice of Habakkuk in
their threatenings. Thus Zephaniah quite as certainly borrowed the words הַס מִפְּנֵי אֲדֹנָי יְהוָֹה in ch. i. 7 from Hab. ii. 20,
as Zechariah did the words הַס כָּל־בָּשָׂר מִפְּנֵי יְהוָֹה in ch. ii. 17;
and Jeremiah formed the expressions קַלּוּ מִנְּשָׁרִים סוּסָיו in ch.
iv. 13 and וְאֵב עֲרָבוֹת in ch. v. 6 on the basis of קַלּוּ מִנְּמֵרִים סוּסָיו
וְחַדּוּ מִזְּאֵבֵי עֶרֶב in Hab. i. 8, not to mention other passages of
Jeremiah that have the ring of our prophet, which Delitzsch
has collected in his *Der Proph. Hab. ausgelegt* (p. xii.). This
decidedly upsets the theory that Habakkuk did not begin to
prophesy till the reign of Jehoiakim; although, as such resemblances and allusions do not preclude the contemporaneous
ministry of the prophets, there still remains the possibility that
Habakkuk may not have prophesied till the time of Josiah, and
indeed not before the twelfth year of Josiah's reign, when he
commenced the extermination of idolatry and the restoration of
the worship of Jehovah, since Habakkuk's prayer, which was
intended according to the subscription for use in the temple,
presupposes the restoration of the Jehovah-worship with the
liturgical service of song. But the possibility is not yet raised
into a certainty by these circumstances. Manasseh also caused
the idols to be cleared away from the temple after his return
from imprisonment in Babylon, and not only restored the altar
of Jehovah, and ordered praise-offerings and thank-offerings
to be presented upon it, but commanded the people to serve
Jehovah the God of Israel (2 Chron. xxxiii. 15, 16). Consequently Habakkuk might have composed his psalm at that time
for use in the temple service. And this conjecture as to its age
acquires extreme probability when we look carefully at the

contents and form of the prophecy. Apart from the rather more distinct and special description of the wild, warlike, and predatory nature of the Chaldæans, the contents retain throughout an ideal character, without any allusion to particular historical relations, such as we find for example in great abundance in Jeremiah, who prophesied in the thirteenth year of Josiah, and which are not altogether wanting in Zephaniah, notwithstanding the comprehensive character of his prophecy. If we look at the form, Habakkuk's prophecy still bears completely the antique stamp of the earlier prophetic literature. "His language," to use the words of Delitzsch, "is classical throughout, full of rare and select words and turns, which are to some extent exclusively his own, whilst his view and mode of presentation bear the seal of independent force and finished beauty. Notwithstanding the violent rush and lofty soaring of the thoughts, his prophecy forms a finely organized and artistically rounded whole. Like Isaiah, he is, comparatively speaking, much more independent of his predecessors, both in contents and form, than any other of the prophets. Everything reflects the time when prophecy was in its greatest glory, when the place of the sacred lyrics, in which the religious life of the church had hitherto expressed itself, was occupied, through a still mightier interposition on the part of God, by prophetic poetry with its trumpet voice, to reawaken in the church, now spiritually dead, the consciousness of God which had so utterly disappeared." On the other hand, the turning-point came as early as Zechariah, and from that time forwards the poetic swing of the prophetic addresses declines and gradually disappears, the dependence upon the earlier predecessors becomes more predominant; and even with such thoroughly original natures as Ezekiel and Zechariah, their style of composition cannot rise very far above simple prose.

2. THE BOOK OF HABAKKUK contains neither a collection of oracles, nor the condensation into one discourse of the essential contents of several prophetic addresses, but one single prophecy arranged in two parts. In the *first* part (ch. i. and ii.), under the form of a conversation between God and the prophet, we have first of all an announcement of the judgment which God is about to bring upon the degenerate covenant

nation through the medium of the Chaldæans; and *secondly*, an
announcement of the overthrow of the Chaldæan, who has lifted
himself up even to the deification of his own power. To this
there is appended in ch. iii., as a second part, the prophet's
prayer for the fulfilment of the judgment; and an exalted
lyric psalm, in which Habakkuk depicts the coming of the
Lord in the terrible glory of the Almighty, at whose wrath the
universe is terrified, to destroy the wicked and save His people
and His anointed, and gives utterance to the feelings which
the judgment of God will awaken in the hearts of the righteous.
The whole of the prophecy has an ideal and universal stamp.
Not even Judah and Jerusalem are mentioned, and the Chaldæans who are mentioned by name are simply introduced as the
existing possessors of the imperial power of the world, which
was bent upon the destruction of the kingdom of God, or as
the sinners who swallow up the righteous man. The announcement of judgment is simply a detailed expansion of the thought
that the unjust man and the sinner perish, whilst the just will
live through his faith (ch. ii. 4). This prophecy hastens on
towards its fulfilment, and even though it should tarry, will
assuredly take place at the appointed time (ch. ii. 2, 3).
Through the judgment upon the godless ones in Judah and
upon the Chaldæans, the righteousness of the holy God will be
manifested, and the earth will be filled with the knowledge of
the glory of the Lord (ch. ii. 14). Although the fact that the
Chaldæans are mentioned by name leaves no doubt whatever
that the judgment will burst upon Judah through this wild
conquering people, the prophecy rises immediately from this
particular judgment to a view of the universal judgment upon
all nations, yea, upon the whole of the ungodly world, to proclaim their destruction and the dawning of salvation for the
people of the Lord and the Lord's anointed; so that the trembling at the terrors of judgment is resolved at the close into
joy and exultation in the God of salvation. There can be no
doubt as to the unity of the book; and the attempt to interpret
the threat of judgment in ch. ii. by applying it to particular
historical persons and facts, has utterly failed.

For the exegetical works on Habakkuk, see my *Einleitung
in das alte Testament*, § 302–3.

EXPOSITION.

THE JUDGMENT UPON THE WICKED.—CHAP. I. AND II.

CHASTISEMENT OF JUDAH THROUGH THE CHALDÆANS.— CHAP. I.

The lamentation of the prophet over the dominion of wickedness and violence (vers. 2–4) is answered thus by the Lord : He will raise up the Chaldæans, who are to execute the judgment, as a terrible, world-conquering people, but who will offend by making their might into their god (vers. 5–11) ; whereupon the prophet, trusting in the Lord, who has proved Himself to His people from time immemorial to be a holy and righteous God, expresses the hope that this chastisement will not lead to death, and addresses the question to God, whether with His holiness He can look calmly upon the wickedness of this people, in gathering men into their net like fishes, and continuing in the most unsparing manner to slay the nations (vers. 12–17).

Ver. 1 contains the heading not only to ch. i. and ii., but to the whole book, of which ch. iii. forms an integral part. On the special heading in ch. iii. 1, see the comm. on that verse. The prophet calls his writing a *massá'*, or burden (see at Nahum i. 1), because it announces heavy judgments upon the covenant nation and the imperial power.

Vers. 2–4. The prophet's lamentation. Ver. 2. *" How long, Jehovah, have I cried, and Thou hearest not ? I cry to Thee, Violence ; and Thou helpest not !* Ver. 3. *Why dost Thou let me see mischief, and Thou lookest upon distress ? devastation and violence are before me : there arises strife, and contention lifts itself up.* Ver. 4. *Therefore the law is benumbed, and justice comes not forth for ever : for sinners encircle the righteous man ; therefore justice goes forth perverted."* This complaint, which involves a petition for help, is not merely an expression of the prophet's personal desire for the removal of the prevailing unrighteousness ; but the prophet laments, in the name of the righteous, *i.e.* the believers in the nation, who had to suffer

under the oppression of the wicked; not, however, as Rosenmüller and Ewald, with many of the Rabbins, suppose, over
the acts of wickedness and violence which the Chaldæans performed in the land, but over the wicked conduct of the ungodly
of his own nation.   For it is obvious that these verses refer
to the moral depravity of Judah, from the fact that God
announces His purpose to raise up the Chaldæans to punish it
(vers. 5 sqq.).   It is true that, in vers. 9 and 13, wickedness
and violence are attributed to the Chaldæans also; but all that
can be inferred from this is, that " in the punishment of the
Jewish people a divine *talio* prevails, which will eventually fall
upon the Chaldæans also" (Delitzsch).   The calling for help
(שִׁוֵּעַ) is described, in the second clause, as crying over wickedness.   חָמָס is an accusative, denoting what he cries, as in Job
xix. 7 and Jer. xx. 8, viz. the evil that is done.   Not hearing is
equivalent to not helping.   The question עַד־אָנָה indicates that
the wicked conduct has continued a long time, without God
having put a stop to it.   This appears irreconcilable with the
holiness of God.   Hence the question in ver. 3: Wherefore dost
Thou cause me to see mischief, and lookest upon it Thyself?
which points to Num. xxiii. 21, viz. to the words of Balaam,
" God hath not beheld iniquity (*'áven*) in Jacob, neither hath
He seen perverseness (*'ámál*) in Israel."   This word of God, in
which Balaam expresses the holiness of Israel, which remains
true to the idea of its divine election, is put before the Lord in
the form of a question, not only to give prominence to the
falling away of the people from their divine calling, and their
degeneracy into the very opposite of what they ought to be,
but chiefly to point to the contradiction involved in the fact, that
God the Holy One does now behold the evil in Israel and leave
it unpunished.   God not only lets the prophet see iniquity, but
even looks at Himself.   This is at variance with His holiness.
אָוֶן, nothingness, then worthlessness, wickedness (cf. Isa. i. 13).
עָמָל, labour, then distress which a man experiences or causes to
others (cf. Isa. x. 1).   הִבִּיט, to see, not to cause to see.   Ewald
has revoked the opinion, that we have here a fresh *hiphil*,
derived from a *hiphil*.   With וּגו' שֹׁד the address is continued in
the form of a simple picture.   *Shōd v*ᵉ*châmâs* are often connected (*e.g.* Amos iii. 10; Jer. vi. 7, xx. 8; Ezek. xlv. 9).
Shōd is violent treatment causing desolation.   *Châmâs* is mali-

cious conduct intended to injure another. וַיְהִי, it comes to
pass, there arises strife (rîbh) in consequence of the violent
and wicked conduct. יִשָּׂא, to rise up, as in Hos. xiii. 1, Ps.
lxxxix. 10. The consequences of this are relaxation of the
law, etc. עַל־כֵּן, therefore, because God does not interpose to
stop the wicked conduct. פּוּג, to relax, to stiffen, i.e. to lose
one's vital strength, or energy. Tôrâh is " the revealed law in
all its substance, which was meant to be the soul, the heart of
political, religious, and domestic life" (Delitzsch). Right does
not come forth, i.e. does not manifest itself, lânetsach, lit. for
a permanence, i.e. for ever, as in many other passages, e.g. Ps.
xiii. 2, Isa. xiii. 20. לָנֶצַח belongs to לֹא, not for ever, i.e. never
more. Mishpât is not merely a righteous verdict, however ; in
which case the meaning would be : There is no more any righteous verdict given, but a righteous state of things, objective
right in the civil and political life. For godless men (רָשָׁע,
without an article, is used with indefinite generality or in a collective sense) encircle the righteous man, so that the righteous
cannot cause right to prevail. Therefore right comes forth
perverted. The second clause, commencing with עַל־כֵּן, completes the first, adding a positive assertion to the negative.
The right, which does still come to the light, is מְעֻקָּל, twisted,
perverted, the opposite of right. To this complaint Jehovah
answers in vers. 5–11 that He will do a marvellous work,
inflict a judgment corresponding in magnitude to the prevailing
injustice.

Ver. 5. " *Look ye among the nations, and see, and be amazed,
amazed! for I work a work in your days : ye would not believe
it if it were told you.*" The appeal to see and be amazed is
addressed to the prophet and the people of Judah together. It
is very evident from ver. 6 that Jehovah Himself is speaking
here, and points by anticipation to the terrible nature of the
approaching work of His punitive righteousness, although פֹּעֵל
is written indefinitely, without any pronoun attached. Moreover, as Delitzsch and Hitzig observe, the meaning of the
appeal is not, " Look round among the nations, whether any
such judgment has ever occurred ;" but, " Look about among
the nations, for it is thence that the terrible storm will burst
that is about to come upon you" (cf. Jer. xxv. 32, xiii. 20).
The first and ordinary view, in support of which Lam. i. 12,

Jer. ii. 10 and xviii. 13, are generally adduced, is precluded
by the fact, (1) that it is not stated for what they are to look
round, namely, whether anything of the kind has occurred
here or there (Jer. ii. 10); (2) that the unparalleled occurrence has not been mentioned at all yet; and (3) that what
they are to be astonished or terrified at is not their failure
to discover an analogy, but the approaching judgment itself.
The combination of the *kal*, *tâmâh*, with the *hiphil* of the same
verb serves to strengthen it, so as to express the highest degree
of amazement (cf. Zeph. ii. 1, Ps. cxviii. 11, and Ewald, § 313, *c*).
כִּי, *for*, introduces the reason not only for the amazement, but
also for the summons to look round. The two clauses of the
second hemistich correspond to the two clauses of the first half
of the verse. They are to look round, because Jehovah is
about to perform a work; they are to be amazed, or terrified,
because this work is an amazing or a terrible one. The participle פֹּעֵל denotes that which is immediately at hand, and is
used absolutely, without a pronoun. According to ver. 6, אֲנִי
is the pronoun we have to supply. For it is not practicable
to supply הוּא, or to take the participle in the sense of the third
person, since God, when speaking to the people, cannot speak
of Himself in the third person, and even in that case יְהֹוָה could
not be omitted. Hitzig's idea is still more untenable, namely,
that *põʻal* is the subject, and that *põʻ ēl* is used in an intransitive
sense: the work produces its effect. We must assume, as
Delitzsch does, that there is a proleptical ellipsis, *i.e.* one in
which the word immediately following is omitted (as in Isa.
xlviii. 11, Zech. ix. 17). The admissibility of this assumption
is justified by the fact that there are other cases in which the
participle is used and the pronoun omitted; and that not merely
the pronoun of the third person (*e.g.* Isa. ii. 11, Jer. xxxviii.
23), but that of the second person also (1 Sam. ii. 24, vi. 3,
and Ps. vii. 10). On the expression בִּימֵיכֶם (in your days), see
the Introduction, p. 51. לֹא תַאֲמִינוּ, ye would not believe it if it
were told you, namely, as having occurred in another place or
at another time, if ye did not see it yourselves (Delitzsch and
Hitzig). Compare Acts xiii. 41, where the Apostle Paul
threatens the despisers of the gospel with judgment in the
words of our verse.

Vers. 6–11. Announcement of this work.—Ver. 6. "*For,*

behold, I cause the Chaldæans to rise up, the fierce and vehement nation, which marches along the breadths of the earth, to take possession of dwelling-places that are not its own. Ver. 7. *It is alarming and fearful: its right and its eminence go forth from it.* Ver. 8. *And its horses are swifter than leopards, and more sudden than evening wolves: and its horsemen spring along; and its horsemen, they come from afar; they fly hither, hastening like an eagle to devour.* Ver. 9. *It comes all at once for wickedness; the endeavour of their faces is directed forwards, and it gathers prisoners together like sand.* Ver. 10. *And it, kings it scoffs at, and princes are laughter to it; it laughs at every stronghold, and heaps up sand, and takes it.* Ver. 11. *Then it passes along, a wind, and comes hither and offends: this its strength is its god."* הִנְנִי מֵקִים, *ecce suscitaturus sum.* הִנֵּה before the participle always refers to the future. הֵקִים, to cause to stand up or appear, does not apply to the elevation of the Chaldæans into a nation or a conquering people,—for the picture which follows and is defined by the article הַגּוֹי וגו׳ presupposes that it already exists as a conquering people,—but to its being raised up against Judah, so that it is equivalent to מֵקִים עֲלֵיכֶם in Amos vi. 14 (cf. Mic. v. 4, 2 Sam. xii. 11, etc.). *Hakkasdīm,* the Chaldæans, sprang, according to Gen. xxii. 22, from *Kesed* the son of Nahor, the brother of Abraham; so that they were a Semitic race. They dwelt from time immemorial in Babylonia or Mesopotamia, and are called a primeval people, *gōi mĕ'ōlâm,* in Jer. v. 15. Abram migrated to Canaan from *Ur* of the Chaldees, from the other side of the river (Euphrates: Gen. xi. 28, 31, compared with Josh. xxiv. 2); and the *Kasdīm* in Isaiah, Jeremiah, and Ezekiel are inhabitants of Babel or Babylonia (Isa. xliii. 14, xlvii. 1, xlviii. 14, 20; Jer. xxi. 9, xxxii. 4, 24, etc.; Ezek. xxiii. 23). Babylonia is called *'erets Kasdīm* (Jer. xxiv. 5, xxv. 12; Ezek. xii. 13), or simply *Kasdīm* (Jer. l. 10, li. 24, 35; Ezek. xvi. 29, xxiii. 16). The modern hypothesis, that the Chaldæans were first of all transplanted by the Assyrians from the northern border mountains of Armenia, Media, and Assyria to Babylonia, and that having settled there, they afterwards grew into a cultivated people, and as a conquering nation exerted great influence in the history of the world, simply rests upon a most precarious interpretation of an obscure passage in Isaiah (Isa. xxiii. 18), and

has no higher value than the opinion of the latest Assyri-
ologists that the Chaldæans are a people of Tatar origin,
who mingled with the Shemites of the countries bordering
upon the Euphrates and Tigris (see Delitzsch on Isa. xxiii. 13).
Habakkuk describes this people as *mar*, bitter, or rough,
and, when used to denote a disposition, fierce (*mar nephesh*,
Judg. xviii. 25, 2 Sam. xvii. 8); and *nimhâr*, heedless or rash
(Isa. xxxii. 4), here violent, and as moving along the breadths
of the earth (ἐπὶ τὰ πλάτη τῆς γῆς, LXX.: cf. Rev. xx. 9),
i.e. marching through the whole extent of the earth (Isa. viii. 8) :
terram quam late patet (Ros.).   לְ is not used here to denote the
direction or the goal, but the space, as in Gen. xiii. 17 (Hitzig,
Delitzsch).   To take possession of dwelling-places that are not
his own (אֲשֶׁר לֹא־לוֹ = לֹא־לוֹ), *i.e.* to take possession of foreign
lands that do not belong to him.   In ver. 7 the fierce disposition of this people is still further depicted, and in ver. 8 the
violence with which it advances.   אָיֹם, *formidabilis*, exciting
terror ; נוֹרָא, *metuendus*, creating alarm.   מִמֶּנּוּ וּגו', from it, not
from God (cf. Ps. xvii. 2), does its right proceed, *i.e.* it determines right, and the rule of its conduct, according to its own
standard ; and שְׂאֵתוֹ, its eminence (Gen. xlix. 3 ; Hos. xiii. 1),
" its δόξα (1 Cor. xi. 7) above all other nations" (Hitzig),
making itself lord through the might of its arms.   Its horses
are lighter, *i.e.* swifter of foot, than panthers, which spring with
the greatest rapidity upon their prey (for proofs of the swiftness
of the panther, see Bochart, *Hieroz.* ii. p. 104, ed. Ros.), and
חַדּוּ, *lit.* sharper, *i.e.* shooting sharply upon it.   As *qâlal* represents swiftness as a light rapid movement, which hardly
touches the ground, so *châdad*, ὀξὺν εἶναι, describes it as a hasty
precipitate dash upon a certain object (Delitzsch).   The first
clause of this verse has been repeated by Jeremiah (iv. 13),
with the alteration of one letter (viz. מִנְּשָׁרִים for מִנְּמֵרִים).
Wolves of the evening (cf. Zeph. iii. 3) are wolves which go
out in the evening in search of prey, after having fasted
through the day, not " wolves of Arabia (עֶרֶב = עֲרָב, LXX.) or
of the desert" (עֲרָבָה, Kimchi).   *Pâshû* from *push*, after the

Arabic فاش, *med. Ye,* to strut proudly ; when used of a horse

and its rider, to spring along, to gallop ; or of a calf, to hop or
jump (Jer. l. 11 ; Mal. iii. 20).   The connection between this

and *pūsh* (Nah. iii. 18), *niphal* to disperse or scatter one's self, is questionable. Delitzsch (on Job xxxv. 15) derives *pūsh* in this verse and the passage cited from فاس, *med. Vav*, in the sense of swimming upon the top, and apparently traces *pūsh* in Nah. iii., as well as *pash* in Job xxxv. 15, to فش (when used of water: to overflow its dam); whilst Freytag (in the *Lexicon*) gives, as the meaning of فش II., *dissolvit, dissipavit. Pârâshīm* are horsemen, not riding-horses. The repetition of פָּרָשָׁיו does not warrant our erasing the words וּפָשׁוּ פָּרָשָׁיו as a gloss, as Hitzig proposes. It can be explained very simply from the fact, that in the second hemistich Habakkuk passes from the general description of the Chaldæans to a picture of their invasion of Judah. מֵרָחוֹק, from afar, *i.e.* from Babylonia (cf. Isa. xxxix. 3). Their coming from afar, and the comparison of the rushing along of the Chaldæan horsemen to the flight of an eagle, points to the threat in Deut. xxviii. 49, " Jehovah shall bring against thee a nation from far, from the end of the earth, as swift as the eagle flieth," which is now about to be fulfilled. Jeremiah frequently uses the same comparison when speaking of the Chaldæans, viz. in Jer. iv. 13, xlviii. 40, xlix. 22, and Lam. iv. 19 (cf. 2 Sam. i. 23). The ἅπ. λεγ. מְגַמָּה may mean a horde or crowd, after the Hebrew גֻּם, and the Arabic جَمَّة, or snorting, endeavouring, striving, after جَم, and جَام, *appetivit*, in which case גמם would be connected with גמא, to swallow. But the first meaning does not suit פְּנֵיהֶם קָדִימָה, whereas the second does. קָדִימָה, not eastwards, but according to the primary meaning of קֶדֶם, to the front, forwards. Ewald renders it incorrectly: " the striving of their face is to storm, *i.e.* to mischief;" for *qâdīm*, the east wind, when used in the sense of storm, is a figurative expression for that which is vain and worthless (Hos. xii. 2 ; cf. Job xv. 2), but not for mischief. For וַיֶּאֱסֹף, compare Gen. xli. 49 and Zech. ix. 3 ; and for כַּחוֹל, like sand of the sea, Hos. ii. 1. In ver. 10 וְהוּא and הוּא are introduced, that the words בַּמְּלָכִים and לְכָל־מִבְצָר, upon which the emphasis lies, may be placed first. It, the Chaldæan nation,

scoffs at kings and princes, and every stronghold, *i.e.* it ridi-
cules all the resistance that kings and princes offer to its
advance, by putting forth their strength, as a perfectly fruitless
attempt. *Mischâq*, the object of laughter. The words, it
heaps up dust and takes it (the fortress), express the facility
with which every fortress is conquered by it. To heap up dust:
denoting the casting up an embankment for attack (2 Sam. xx.
15, etc.). The feminine suffix attached to יִלְכְּדָה refers *ad
sensum* to the idea of a city (עִיר), implied in מִבְצָר, the latter
being equivalent to עִיר מִבְצָר in 1 Sam. vi. 18, 2 Kings iii. 19,
etc. Thus will the Chaldæan continue incessantly to overthrow
kings and conquer kingdoms with tempestuous rapidity, till he
offends, by deifying his own power. With this gentle hint
at the termination of his tyranny, the announcement of the
judgment closes in ver. 11. אָז, *there*, *i.e.* in this appearance
of his, as depicted in vers. 6–10: not " then," in which case
ver. 11 would affirm to what further enterprises the Chaldæans
would proceed after their rapidly and easily effected conquests.
The perfects חָלַף and וַיַּעֲבֹר are used prophetically, representing
the future as occurring already. חָלַף and עָבַר are used synonymously: to pass along and go further, used of the wind or
tempest, as in Isa. xxi. 1; here, as in Isa. viii. 8, of the hostile
army overflowing the land; with this difference, however, that
in Isaiah it is thought of as a stream of water, whereas here it
is thought of as a tempest sweeping over the land. The subject
to *châlaph* is not *rūăch*, but the Chaldæan (הוּא, ver. 10); and
rūăch is used appositionally, to denote the manner in which it
passes along, viz. " like a tempestuous wind" (*rūăch* as in Job
xxx. 15, Isa. vii. 2). וְאָשֵׁם is not a participle, but a perfect
with *Vav rel.*, expressing the consequence, "and so he offends."
In what way is stated in the last clause, in which זוּ does not
answer to the relative אֲשֶׁר, in the sense of " he whose power,"
but is placed demonstratively before the noun כֹּחוֹ, like זֶה in
Ex. xxxii. 1, Josh. ix. 12, 13, and Isa. xxiii. 13 (cf. Ewald,
§ 293, *b*), pointing back to the strength of the Chaldæan,
which has been previously depicted in its intensive and extensive greatness (Delitzsch). This its power is god to it, *i.e.* it
makes it into its god (for the thought, compare Job xii. 6, and
the words of the Assyrian in Isa. x. 13). The ordinary explanation of the first hemistich is, on the other hand, untenable

(then its courage becomes young again, or grows), since רוּחַ
cannot stand for רוּחוֹ, and עָבַר without an object given in the
context cannot mean to overstep, *i.e.* to go beyond the proper
measure.

Ver. 12. On this threatening announcement of the judgment by God, the prophet turns to the Lord in the name of
believing Israel, and expresses the confident hope that He as
the Holy One will not suffer His people to perish. Ver. 12.
"*Art Thou not from olden time, O Jehovah, my God, my Holy
One? We shall not die. Jehovah, for judgment hast Thou
appointed it; and, O Rock, founded it for chastisement.*" However terrible and prostrating the divine threatening may sound,
the prophet draws consolation and hope from the holiness of
the faithful covenant God, that Israel will not perish, but that
the judgment will be only a severe chastisement.[1] The supplicatory question with which he soars to this hope of faith is
closely connected with the divine and threatening prophecy in
ver. 11. The Chaldæan's god is his own strength; but Israel's
God is Jehovah, the Holy One. On the interrogative form of
the words (" art Thou not?"), which requires an affirmative
reply, Luther has aptly observed that "he speaks to God inter-
rogatively, asking whether He will do this and only punish; not
that he has any doubt on the subject, but that he shows how
faith is sustained in the midst of conflicts,—namely, that it
appears as weak as if it did not believe, and would sink at once,
and fall into despair on account of the great calamity which
crushes it. For although faith stands firm, yet it cracks, and
speaks in a very different tone when in the midst of the conflict from what it does when the victory is gained." But as
the question is sure to receive an affirmative reply, the prophet
draws this inference from it: "we shall not die," we Thy
people shall not perish. This hope rests upon two foundations:
viz. (1) from time immemorial Jehovah is Israel's God; and

[1] "Therefore," says Calvin, "whoever desires to fight bravely with
the ungodly, let him first settle the matter with God Himself, and, as it
were, confirm and ratify that treaty which God has set before us, namely,
that we are His people, and He will be a God to us in return. And because God makes a covenant with us in this manner, it is necessary that
our faith should be well established, that we may go forth to the conflict
with all the ungodly."

(2) He is the Holy One of Israel, who cannot leave wickedness unpunished either in Israel or in the foe. This leads to
the further conclusion, that Jehovah has simply appointed the
Chaldæan nation to execute the judgment, to chastise Israel,
and not to destroy His people. The three predicates applied
to God have equal weight in the question. The God to
whom the prophet prays is *Jehovah*, the absolutely constant
One, who is always the same in word and work (see at Gen.
ii. 4) ; He is also *Elohai, my, i.e.* Israel's, God, who from time
immemorial has proved to the people whom He had chosen as
His possession that He is their God ; and קְדֹשִׁי, the Holy One
of Israel, the absolutely Pure One, who cannot look upon evil,
and therefore cannot endure that the wicked should devour the
righteous (ver. 13). לֹא נָמוּת is not a supplicatory wish : Let us
not die therefore ; but a confident assertion : " We shall not
die."[1] In the second half of the verse, *Yᵉhōvâh* and *tsūr*
(rock) are vocatives. *Tsūr*, as an epithet applied to God, is
taken from Deut. xxxii. 4, 15, 18, and 37, where God is first
called the Rock of Israel, as the unchangeable refuge of His
people's trust. *Lammishpât, i.e.* to accomplish the judgment :
comp. Isa. x. 5, 6, where Asshur is called the rod of Jehovah's
wrath. In the parallel clause we have לְהוֹכִיחַ instead : " to
chastise," namely Israel, not the Chaldæans, as Ewald supposes.

The believing confidence expressed in this verse does not
appear to be borne out by what is actually done by God. The
prophet proceeds to lay this enigma before God in vers. 13–17,

---

[1] According to the Masora, לֹא נָמוּת stands as תִּקּוּן סוֹפְרִים, *i.e. correctio
scribarum* for לֹא תָמוּת, thou wilt not die. These *tikkune sophrim*, however,
of which the Masora reckons eighteen, are not alterations of original readings proposed by the *sophrim*, but simply traditional definitions of what the
sacred writers originally intended to write, though they afterwards avoided
it or gave a different turn. Thus the prophet intended to write here :
" Thou (God) wilt not die ; " but in the consciousness that this was at
variance with the divine decorum, he gave it this turn, " We shall not
die." But this rabbinical conjecture rests upon the erroneous assumption
that מִקֶּדֶם is a predicate, and the thought of the question is this : " Thou
art from of old, Thou Jehovah my God, my Holy One," according to which
לֹא תָמוּת would be an exegesis of מִקֶּדֶם, which is evidently false. For
further remarks on the *tikkune sophrim*, see Delitzsch's *Commentary on Hab.
l.c.*, and the Appendix, p. 206 sqq.

and to pray for his people to be spared during the period of the Chaldæan affliction. Ver. 13. " *Art Thou too pure of eye to behold evil, and canst Thou not look upon distress? Wherefore lookest Thou upon the treacherous? and art silent when the wicked devours one more righteous than he?* Ver. 14. *And Thou hast made men like fishes of the sea, like reptiles that have no ruler.* Ver. 15. *All of them hath he lifted up with the hook; he draws them into his net, and gathers them in his fishing net; he rejoices thereat, and is glad.* Ver. 16. *Therefore he sacrifices to his net, and burns incense to his landing net; for through them is his portion rich, and his food fat.* Ver. 17. *Shall he therefore empty his net, and always strangle nations without sparing?*" In ver. 13, טְהוֹר עֵינַיִם, with the two clauses dependent upon it, stands as a vocative, and טָהוֹר followed by מִן as a comparative: purer of eyes than to be able to see. This epithet is applied to God as the pure One, whose eyes cannot bear what is morally unclean, *i.e.* cannot look upon evil. The purity of God is not measured here by His seeing evil, but is described as exalted above it, and not coming at all into comparison with it. On the relation in which these words stand to Num. xxiii. 21, see the remarks on ver. 3. In the second clause the infinitive construction passes over into the finite verb, as is frequently the case; so that אֲשֶׁר must be supplied in thought: who canst not look upon, *i.e.* canst not tolerate, the distress which the wicked man prepares for others. Wherefore then lookest Thou upon treacherous ones, namely, the Chaldæans? They are called בּוֹגְדִים, from their faithlessly deceptive and unscrupulously rapacious conduct, as in Isa. xxi. 2, xxiv. 16. That the seeing is a quiet observance, without interposing to punish, is evident from the parallel תַּחֲרִישׁ: Thou art silent at the swallowing of the צַדִּיק מִמֶּנּוּ. The more righteous than he (the ungodly one) is not the nation of Israel as such, which, if not perfectly righteous, was relatively more righteous than the Chaldæans. This rabbinical view is proved to be erroneous, by the fact that in vers. 2 and 3 the prophet describes the moral depravity of Israel in the same words as those which he here applies to the conduct of the Chaldæans. The persons intended are rather the godly portion of Israel, who have to share in the expiation of the sins of the ungodly, and suffer when they are punished (Delitzsch). This fact, that the righteous is swallowed

along with the unrighteous, appears irreconcilable with the
holiness of God, and suggests the inquiry, how God can possibly let this be done. This strange fact is depicted still further
in vers. 14–16 in figures taken from the life of a fisherman.
The men are like fishes, whom the Chaldæan collects together
in his net, and then pays divine honour to his net, by which he
has been so enriched. וַתַּעֲשֶׂה is not dependent upon לָמָּה, but
continues the address in a simple picture, in which the imperfect
with *Vav convers.* represents the act as the natural consequence
of the silence of God: "and so Thou makest the men like fishes,"
etc. The point of comparison lies in the relative clause לֹא־מֹשֵׁל בּוֹ,
"which has no ruler," which is indeed formally attached to
כְּרֶמֶשׂ alone, but in actual fact belongs to דְּגֵי הַיָּם also. "No
ruler," to take the defenceless under his protection, and shelter
and defend them against enemies. Then will Judah be taken
prisoner and swallowed up by the Chaldæans. God has given
it helplessly up to the power of its foes, and has obviously
ceased to be its king. Compare the similar lamentation in
Isa. lxiii. 19: "are even like those over whom Thou hast never
ruled." רֶמֶשׂ, the creeping thing, the smaller animals which
exist in great multitudes, and move with great swiftness, refers
here to the smaller water animals, to which the word *remes* is
also applied in Ps. civ. 25, and the verb *râmas* in Gen. i. 21
and Lev. xi. 46. כֻּלֹּה, pointing back to the collective *'âdâm*, is
the object, and is written first for the sake of emphasis. The
form הֶעֱלָה, instead of הֵעֲלָה, is analogous to the *hophal* הָעֳלָה in
Nahum ii. 8 and Judg. vi. 28, and also to הֶעֱבַרְתָּ in Josh. vii. 7:
to take up out of the water (see Ges. § 63, Anm. 4). יְגֹרֵהוּ
from גָּרַר, to pull, to draw together. *Chakkâh* is the hook,
cherem the net generally, *mikhmereth* the large fishing-net
(σαγήνη), the lower part of which, when sunk, touches the
bottom, whilst the upper part floats on the top of the water.
These figures are not to be interpreted with such speciality as
that the net and fishing net answer to the sword and bow; but
the hook, the net, and the fishing net, as the things used for
catching fish, refer to all the means which the Chaldæans
employ in order to subdue and destroy the nations. Luther
interprets it correctly. "These hooks, nets, and fishing nets,"
he says, "are nothing more than his great and powerful armies,
by which he gained dominion over all lands and people, and

brought home to Babylon the goods, jewels, silver, and gold, interest and rent of all the world." He rejoices over the success of his enterprises, over this capture of men, and sacrifices and burns incense to his net, *i.e.* he attributes to the means which he has employed the honour due to God. There is no allusion in these words to the custom of the Scythians and Sauromatians, who are said by Herodotus (iv. 59, 60) to have offered sacrifices every year to a sabre, which was set up as a symbol of Mars. What the Chaldæan made into his god, is expressed in ver. 11, namely, his own power. " He who boasts of a thing, and is glad and joyous on account of it, but does not thank the true God, makes himself into an idol, gives himself the glory, and does not rejoice in God, but in his own strength and work" (Luther). The Chaldæan sacrifices to his net, for thereby (בְּחֶרְמָה, by net and yarn) his portion (*chelqō*) is fat, *i.e.* the portion of this booty which falls to him, and fat is his food (בְּרִאָה is a neuter substantive). The meaning is, that he thereby attains to wealth and prosperity. In ver. 17 there is appended to this the question embracing the thought: Shall he therefore, because he rejoices over his rich booty, or offers sacrifice to his net, empty his net, *sc.* to throw it in afresh, and proceed continually to destroy nations in so unsparing a manner? In the last clause the figure passes over into a literal address. The place of the imperfect is now taken by a periphrastic construction with the infinitive: Shall he constantly be about to slay? On this construction, see Ges. § 132, 3, Anm. 1, and Ewald, § 237, *c.* לֹא יַחְמוֹל is a subordinate clause appended in an adverbial sense : unsparingly, without sparing.

DESTRUCTION OF THE UNGODLY WORLD-POWER.—CHAP. II.

After receiving an answer to this supplicatory cry, the prophet receives a command from God : to write the oracle in plain characters, because it is indeed certain, but will not be immediately fulfilled (vers. 1–3). Then follows the word of God, that the just will live through his faith, but he that is proud and not upright will not continue (vers. 4, 5); accompanied by a fivefold woe upon the Chaldæan, who gathers all nations to himself with insatiable greediness (vers. 6–20).

Vers. 1–3 form the introduction to the word of God, which

the prophet receives in reply to his cry of lamentation addressed
to the Lord in ch. i. 12–17. Ver. 1. "*I will stand upon my watch-
tower, and station myself upon the fortress, and will watch to see
what He will say in me, and what I answer to my complaint.*
Ver. 2. *Then Jehovah answered me, and said, Write the vision, and
make it plain upon the tables, that he may run who reads it.* Ver. 3.
*For the vision is yet for the appointed end, and strives after the end,
and does not lie: if it tarry, wait for it; for it will come, it does
not fail.*" Ver. 1 contains the prophet's conversation with himself.
After he has poured out his trouble at the judgment announced,
in a lamentation to the Lord (ch. i. 12–17), he encourages
himself—after a pause, which we have to imagine after ch.
i. 17—to wait for the answer from God. He resolves to place
himself upon his observatory, and look out for the revelation
which the Lord will give to his questions. *Mishmereth,* a place
of waiting or observing; *mâtsōr,* a fortress, *i.e.* a watch-tower
or spying-tower. Standing upon the watch, and stationing
himself upon the fortification, are not to be understood as
something external, as Hitzig supposes, implying that the
prophet went up to a steep and lofty place, or to an actual
tower, that he might be far away from the noise and bustle of
men, and there turn his eyes towards heaven, and direct his
collected mind towards God, to look out for a revelation. For
nothing is known of any such custom as this, since the cases
mentioned in Ex. xxxiii. 21 and 1 Kings xix. 11, as extraordinary preparations for God to reveal Himself, are of a totally
different kind from this; and the fact that Balaam the sooth-
sayer went up to the top of a bare height, to look out for a
revelation from God (Num. xxiii. 3), furnishes no proof that
the true prophets of Jehovah did the same, but is rather a
heathenish feature, which shows that it was because Balaam
did not rejoice in the possession of a firm prophetic word, that
he looked out for revelations from God in significant phenomena
of nature (see at Num. xxiii. 3, 4). The words of our verse
are to be taken figuratively, or internally, like the appointment
of the watchman in Isa. xxi. 6. The figure is taken from the
custom of ascending high places for the purpose of looking into
the distance (2 Kings ix. 17; 2 Sam. xviii. 24), and simply
expresses the spiritual preparation of the prophet's soul for
hearing the word of God within, *i.e.* the collecting of his mind

by quietly entering into himself, and meditating upon the
word and testimonies of God. Cyril and Calvin bring out the
first idea. Thus the latter observes, that "the watch-tower is
the recesses of the mind, where we withdraw ourselves from the
world;" and then adds by way of explanation, "The prophet,
under the name of the watch-tower, implies that he extricates
himself as it were from the thoughts of the flesh, because there
would be no end or measure, if he wished to judge according to his own perception;" whilst others find in it nothing
more than firm continuance in reliance upon the word of
God.[1] *Tsippâh*, to spy or watch, to wait for the answer from
God. "This *watching* was lively and assiduous diligence on
the part of the prophet, in carefully observing everything that
took place *in the spirit of his mind,* and presented itself either
to be seen or heard" (Burk). יְדַבֶּר־בִּי, to speak in me, not
merely to or with me; since the speaking of God to the
prophets was an internal speaking, and not one that was perceptible from without. What I shall answer to my complaint
('*al tŏkhachtî*), namely, first of all to myself and then to the
rest. *Tŏkhachath,* lit. correction, contradiction. Habakkuk
refers to the complaint which he raised against God in ch.
i. 13–17, namely, that He let the wicked go on unpunished.
He will wait for an answer from God to this complaint, to
quiet his own heart, which is dissatisfied with the divine administration. Thus he draws a sharp distinction between his own
speaking and the speaking of the Spirit of God within him.
Jehovah gives the answer in what follows, first of all (vers. 2, 3)
commanding him to write the vision (*châzôn,* the revelation
from God to be received by inward intuition) upon tables, so
clearly, that men may be able to read it in running, *i.e.* quite
easily. בָּאֵר as in Deut. xxvii. 8; see at Deut. i. 5. The article
attached to הַלֻּחוֹת does not point to the tables set up in the
market-places for public notices to be written upon (Ewald),

---

[1] Theodoret very appropriately compares the words of Asaph in Ps.
lxxiii. 16 sqq., "When I thought to know this, it was too painful for me,
until I entered into the sanctuaries of God, and gave heed to their end;"
and observes, "And there, says the prophet, will I remain as appointed,
and not leave my post, but, standing upon such a rock as that upon which
God placed great Moses, watch with a prophet's eyes for the solution of
the things that I seek."

but simply means, make it clear on the tables on which thou shalt write it, referring to the noun implied in כְּתֹב (write), though not expressed (Delitzsch). קוֹרֵא בוֹ may be explained from קָרָא בְסֵפֶר in Jer. xxxvi. 13. The question is a disputed one, whether this command is to be understood literally or merely figuratively, " simply denoting the great importance of the prophecy, and the consequent necessity for it to be made accessible to the whole nation" (Hengstenberg, *Dissertation,* vol. i. p. 460). The passages quoted in support of the literal view, *i.e.* of the actual writing of the prophecy which follows upon tables, viz. Isa. viii. 1, xxx. 8, and Jer. xxx. 2, are not decisive. In Jer. xxx. 2 the prophet is commanded to write all the words of the Lord in a book (*sēpher*) ; and so again in Isa. xxx. 8, if כָּתְבָה עַל־לוּחַ is synonymous with עַל־סֵפֶר חֻקָּה. But in Isa. viii. 1 there are only two significant words, which the prophet is to write upon a large table after having taken witnesses. It does not follow from either of these passages, that *luchōth,* tables, say wooden tables, had been already bound together into books among the Hebrews, so that we could be warranted in identifying the writing plainly upon tables with writing in a book. We therefore prefer the figurative view, just as in the case of the command issued to Daniel, to shut up his prophecy and seal it (Dan. xii. 4), inasmuch as the literal interpretation of the command, especially of the last words, would require that the table should be set up or hung out in some public place, and this cannot for a moment be thought of. The words simply express the thought, that the prophecy is to be laid to heart by all the people on account of its great importance, and that not merely in the present, but in the future also. This no doubt involved the obligation on the part of the prophet to take care, by committing it to writing, that it did not fall into oblivion. The reason for the writing is given in ver. 3. The prophecy is לַמּוֹעֵד, for the appointed time ; *i.e.* it relates to the period fixed by God for its realization, which was then still (עוֹד) far off. לְ denotes direction towards a certain point either of place or time. The vision had a direction towards a point, which, when looked at from the present, was still in the future. This goal was the end (הַקֵּץ) towards which it hastened, *i.e.* the " last time" (מוֹעֵד קֵץ, Dan. viii. 19 ; and עֵת קֵץ, Dan. viii. 17, xi. 35), the Messianic times, in which the

judgment would fall upon the power of the world. יָפֵחַ לַקֵּץ, it
pants for the end, *inhiat fini*, *i.e.* it strives to reach the end, to
which it refers. " True prophecy is inspired, as it were, by an
impulse to fulfil itself " (Hitzig). יָפֵחַ is not an adjective, as in
Ps. xxvii. 12, but the third pers. imperf. *hiphil* of *pûŭch*; and
the contracted form (יָפֵחַ for יָפִיחַ), without a voluntative meaning, is the same as we frequently meet with in the loftier style
of composition. וְלֹא יְכַזֵּב, " and does not deceive," *i.e.* will
assuredly take place. If it (the vision) tarry, *i.e.* be not fulfilled immediately, wait for it, for it will surely take place (the
inf. abs. בּוֹא to add force, and בֹּא applying to the fulfilment of
the prophecy, as in 1 Sam. ix. 6 and Jer. xxviii. 9), will not
fail; אָחַר, to remain behind, not to arrive (Judg. v. 28 ; 2 Sam.
xx. 5).[1]

Vers. 4, 5. With these verses the prophecy itself commences; namely, with a statement of the fundamental thought,
that the presumptuous and proud will not continue, but the
just alone will live. Ver. 4. " *Behold, puffed up, his soul is not
straight within him: but the just, through his faith will he live.*
Ver. 5. *And moreover, the wine is treacherous: a boasting man,
he continues not; he who has opened his soul as wide as hell, and
is like death, and is not satisfied, and gathered all nations to himself, and collected all peoples to himself.*" These verses, although
they contain the fundamental thought, or so to speak the heading of the following announcement of the judgment upon the
Chaldæans, are nevertheless not to be regarded as the sum and
substance of what the prophet was to write upon the tables.
For they do indeed give one characteristic of two classes of
men, with a brief intimation of the fate of both, but they contain no formally rounded thought, which could constitute the
motto of the whole; on the contrary, the description of the

---

[1] The LXX. have rendered כִּי בֹא יָבֹא, ὅτι ἐρχόμενος ἥξει, which the
author of the Epistle to the Hebrews (Heb. x. 37) has still further defined
by adding the article, and, connecting it with μικρὸν ὅσον ὅσον of Isa.
xxvi. 20 (LXX.), has taken it as Messianic, and applied to the speedy
coming of the Messiah to judgment ; not, however, according to the exact
meaning of the words, but according to the fundamental idea of the prophetic announcement. For the vision, the certain fulfilment of which is
proclaimed by Habakkuk, predicts the judgment upon the power of the
world, which the Messiah will bring to completion.

insatiable greediness of the Chaldæan is attached in ver. 5*b* to
the picture of the haughty sinner, that the two cannot be separated.   This picture is given in a subjective clause, which is
only completed by the filling up in vers. 6 sqq.   The sentence
pronounced upon the Chaldæan in vers. 4, 5, simply forms the
preparatory introduction to the real answer to the prophet's
leading question.   The subject is not mentioned in ver. 4*a*, but
may be inferred from the prophet's question in ch. i. 12–17.
The Chaldæan is meant.   His soul is puffed up.   עֻפְּלָה, perf.
pual of עָפַל, of which the *hiphil* only occurs in Num. xiv. 44,
and that as synonymous with הֵזִיד in Deut. i. 43.   From this,
as well as from the noun עֹפֶל, a hill or swelling, we get the
meaning, to be swollen up, puffed up, proud ; and in the *hiphil*,
to act haughtily or presumptuously.   The thought is explained
and strengthened by לֹא יָשְׁרָה, " his soul is not straight."   יָשַׁר, to
be straight, without turning and trickery, *i.e.* to be upright.
בּוֹ does not belong to נַפְשׁוֹ (his soul in him, equivalent to his inmost soul), but to the verbs of the sentence.   The early translators and commentators have taken this hemistich differently.
They divide it into protasis and apodosis, and take עֻפְּלָה either
as the predicate or as the subject.   Luther also takes it in the
latter sense : " He who is stiff-necked will have no rest in his
soul."   Burk renders it still more faithfully : *ecce quæ effert se,
non recta est anima ejus in eo.*   In either case we must supply
נֶפֶשׁ אֲשֶׁר after עֻפְּלָה.   But such an ellipsis as this, in which not
only the relative word, but also the noun supporting the relative clause, would be omitted, is unparalleled and inadmissible,
if only because of the tautology which would arise from supplying *nephesh*.   This also applies to the hypothetical view of
הִנֵּה עֻפְּלָה, upon which the Septuagint rendering, ἐὰν ὑποστεί-
ληται, οὐκ εὐδοκεῖ ἡ ψυχή μου ἐν αὐτῷ, is founded.   Even
with this view *nephesh* could not be omitted as the subject of
the protasis, and בּוֹ would have no noun to which to refer.
This rendering is altogether nothing more than a conjecture,
עפל being confounded with עלף, and נפשׁו altered into נפשׁי.   Nor
is it proved to be correct, by the fact that the author of the
Epistle to the Hebrews (Heb. x. 38) makes use of the words of
our verse, according to this rendering, to support his admonitions to stedfastness.   For he does not introduce the verse as
a quotation to prove his words, but simply clothes his own

thoughts in these words of the Bible which floated before his mind, and in so doing transposes the two hemistichs, and thereby gives the words a meaning quite in accordance with the Scriptures, which can hardly be obtained from the Alexandrian version, since we have there to take the subject to ὑπο-στείληται from the preceding ἐρχόμενος, which gives no sense, whereas by transposing the clauses a very suitable subject can be supplied from ὁ δίκαιος.

The following clause, וְצַדִּיק וגו׳, is attached adversatively, and in form is subordinate to the sentence in the first hemistich in this sense, "whilst, on the contrary, the righteous lives through his faith," notwithstanding the fact that it contains a very important thought, which intimates indirectly that pride and want of uprightness will bring destruction upon the Chaldæan. בֶּאֱמוּנָתוֹ belongs to יִחְיֶה, not to צַדִּיק. The *tiphchah* under the word does not show that it belongs to *tsaddīq*, but simply that it has the leading tone of the sentence, because it is placed with emphasis before the verb (Delitzsch). אֱמוּנָה does not denote "an honourable character, or fidelity to conviction" (Hitzig), but (from *'âman*, to be firm, to last) firmness (Ex. xvii. 12); then, as an attribute of God, trustworthiness, unchangeable fidelity in the fulfilment of His promises (Deut. xxxii. 4; Ps. xxxiii. 4, lxxxix. 34); and, as a personal attribute of man, fidelity in word and deed (Jer. vii. 28, ix. 2; Ps. xxxvii. 3); and, in his relation to God, firm attachment to God, an undisturbed confidence in the divine promises of grace, *firma fiducia* and *fides*, so that in *'ĕmūnâh* the primary meanings of *ne'ĕmân* and *he'ĕmīn* are combined. This is also apparent from the fact that Abraham is called *ne'ĕmân* in Neh. ix. 8, with reference to the fact that it is affirmed of him in Gen. xv. 6 that הֶאֱמִן בַּיהוָה, "he trusted, or believed, the Lord;" and still more indisputably from the passage before us, since it is impossible to mistake the reference in צַדִּיק בֶּאֱמוּנָתוֹ יִחְיֶה to Gen. xv. 6, "he believed (*he'ĕmīn*) in Jehovah, and He reckoned it to him *lits*e*dâqâh*." It is also indisputably evident from the context that our passage treats of the relation between man and God, since the words themselves speak of a waiting (*chikkâh*) for the fulfilment of a promising oracle, which is to be preceded by a period of severe suffering. "What is more natural than that life or deliverance from destruction should be promised to that faith which adheres

faithfully to God, holds fast by the word of promise, and con-
fidently waits for its fulfilment in the midst of tribulation ?   It
is not the sincerity, trustworthiness, or integrity of the righteous man, regarded as being virtues in themselves, which are
in danger of being shaken and giving way in such times of
tribulation, but, as we may see in the case of the prophet himself, his *faith*.   To this, therefore, there is appended the great
promise expressed in the one word יִחְיֶה" (Delitzsch).   And in
addition to this, *'ĕmūnáh* is opposed to the pride of the Chaldæan, to his exaltation of himself above God; and for that very
reason it cannot denote integrity in itself, but simply some
quality which has for its leading feature humble submission to
God, that is to say, faith, or firm reliance upon God.   The
Jewish expositors, therefore, have unanimously retained this
meaning here, and the LXX. have rendered the word quite
correctly πίστις, although by changing the suffix, and giving
ἐκ πίστεώς μου instead of αὐτοῦ (or more properly ἑαυτοῦ:
Aquila and the other Greek versions), they have missed, or
rather perverted, the sense.   The deep meaning of these words
has been first fully brought out by the Apostle Paul (Rom. i. 17;
Gal. iii. 11: see also Heb. x. 38), who omits the erroneous μου
of the LXX., and makes the declaration ὁ δίκαιος ἐκ πίστεως
ζήσεται the basis of the New Testament doctrine of justification by faith.—Ver. 5 is closely connected with ver. 4a, not
only developing still further the thought which is there expressed, but applying it to the Chaldæan.   אַף כִּי does not mean
" really if" (Hitzig and others), even in Job ix. 14, xxxv. 14,
Ezek. xv. 5, or 1 Sam. xxi. 6 (see Delitzsch on Job xxxv. 14),
but always means " still further," or "yea also, that;" and
different applications are given to it, so that, when used as an
emphatic assurance, it signifies " to say nothing of the fact
that," or when it gives emphasis to the thing itself, " all the
more because," and in negative sentences " how much less"
(*e.g.* 1 Kings viii. 27).   In the present instance it adds a new
and important feature to what is stated in ver. 4a, " And add
to this that wine is treacherous;" *i.e.* to those who are addicted
to it, it does not bring strength and life, but leads to the way to
ruin (for the thought itself, see Prov. xxiii. 31, 32).   The application to the Chaldæan is evident from the context.   The fact
that the Babylonians were very much addicted to wine is at-

tested by ancient writers. Curtius, for example (v. 1), says, "*Babylonii maxime in vinum et quæ ebrietatem sequuntur effusi sunt;*" and it is well known from Dan. v. that Babylon was conquered while Belshazzar and the great men of his kingdom were feasting at a riotous banquet. The following words גֶּבֶר יָהִיר are not the object to בּוֹגֵד, but form a fresh sentence, parallel to the preceding one: a boasting man, he continueth not. וְלֹא introduces the apodosis to גבר יהיר, which is written absolutely. יָהִיר only occurs again in Prov. xxi. 24, and is used there as a parallel to זֵד: ἀλαζών (LXX.), swaggering, boasting. The allusion to the Chaldæan is evident from the relative clause which follows, and which Delitzsch very properly calls an individualizing exegesis to גבר יהיר. But looking to what follows, this sentence forms a protasis to ver. 6, being written first in an absolute form, "He, the widely opened one, etc., upon him will all take up," etc. *Hirchîbh naphshō*, to widen his soul, *i.e.* his desire, parallel to *pá'ar peh*, to open the mouth (Isa. v. 14), is a figure used to denote insatiable desire. כִּשְׁאוֹל, like Hades, which swallows up every living thing (see Prov. xxvii. 20, xxx. 15, 16). The comparison to death has the same meaning. וְלֹא יִשְׂבָּע does not refer to מָוֶת, but to the Chaldæan, who grasps to himself in an insatiable manner, as in ch. i. 6, 7, and 15–17. The *imperff. consecc.* express the continued gathering up of the nations, which springs out of his insatiable desire.

In vers. 6–20 the destruction of the Chaldæan, which has been already intimated in vers. 4, 5, is announced in the form of a song composed of threatening sentences, which utters woes in five strophes consisting of three verses each: (1) upon the rapacity and plundering of the Chaldæan (vers. 6–8); (2) upon his attempt to establish his dynasty firmly by means of force and cunning (vers. 9–11); (3) upon his wicked ways of building (vers. 12–14); (4) upon his base treatment of the subjugated nations (vers. 15–17); and (5) upon his idolatry (vers. 18–20). These five strophes are connected together, so as to form two larger divisions, by a *refrain* which closes the first and fourth, as well as by the promise explanatory of the threat in which the third and fifth strophes terminate; of which two divisions the first threatens the judgment of retribution upon the insatiableness of the Chaldæan in three woes (ver. 5*b*), and the second in two woes the judgment of retribution upon his

pride. Throughout the whole of the threatening prophecy the
Chaldæan nation is embraced, as in vers. 4, 5, in the ideal
person of its ruler.[1]

Vers. 6–8. Introduction of the ode and first strophe.—Ver.
6. *" Will not all these lift up a proverb upon him, and a song, a
riddle upon him? And men will say, Woe to him who increases
what is not his own! For how long? and who loadeth himself
with the burden of pledges.* Ver. 7. *Will not thy biters rise up
suddenly, and thy destroyers wake up, and thou wilt become booty
to them?* Ver. 8. *For thou hast plundered many nations, all the
rest of the nations will plunder thee, for the blood of men and
wickedness on the earth, the city, and all its inhabitants."* הֲלוֹא
is here, as everywhere else, equivalent to a confident assertion.

[1] The unity of the threatening prophecy, which is brought out in the
clearest manner in this formal arrangement, has been torn in pieces in the
most violent manner by Hitzig, through his assumption that the oracle of
God includes no more than vers. 4–8, and that a second part is appended
to it in vers. 9–20, in which the prophet expresses his own thoughts and
feelings, first of all concerning king Jehoiakim (vers. 9–14), and then concerning the Egyptians (vers. 15–20). This hypothesis, of which Maurer
observes quite correctly, *Qua nulla unquam excogitata est infelicior*, rests
upon nothing more than the dogmatic assumption, that there is no such
thing as prophecy effected by supernatural causality, and therefore Habakkuk cannot have spoken of Nebuchadnezzar's buildings before they were
finished, or at any rate in progress. The two strophes in vers. 9–14 contain nothing whatever that would not apply most perfectly to the Chaldæan,
or that is not covered by what precedes and follows (compare ver. 9*a* with
6*b* and 8*a*, and ver. 10 with 5*b* and 8*a*). " The strophe in vers. 9–11 contains the same fundamental thought as that expressed by Isaiah in Isa.
xiv. 12–14 respecting the Chaldæan, viz. the description of his pride, which
manifests itself in ambitious edifices founded upon the ruins of the prosperity of strangers" (Delitzsch). The resemblance between the contents
of this strophe and the woe pronounced upon Jehoiakim by Jeremiah in
Jer. xxii. 13–17 may be very simply explained from the fact that Jehoiakim, like the Chaldæan, was a tyrant who occupied himself with the
erection of large state buildings and fortifications, whereas the extermination of many nations does not apply in any respect to Jehoiakim. Lastly,
there is no plausible ground whatever for referring the last two strophes
(vers. 15–20) to the Egyptian, for the assertion that Habakkuk could not
pass over the Egyptian in silence, unless he meant to confine himself to the
Chaldæan, is a pure *petitio principii*; and to any unprejudiced mind the
allusion to the Chaldæan in this verse is placed beyond all possible doubt
by Isa. xiv. 8, where the devastation of Lebanon is also attributed to him,
just as it is in ver. 17 of our prophecy.

"*All these :*" this evidently points back to "all nations" and "all people." Nevertheless the nations as such, or *in pleno*, are not meant, but simply the believers among them, who expect Jehovah to inflict judgment upon the Chaldæans, and look forward to that judgment for the revelation of the glory of God. For the ode is prophetical in its nature, and is applicable to all times and all nations. *Mâshâl* is a sententious poem, as in Mic. ii. 4 and Isa. xiv. 4, not a derisive song, for this subordinate meaning could only be derived from the context, as in Isa. xiv. 4 for example; and there is nothing to suggest it here. So, again, *m^elitsâh* neither signifies a satirical song, nor an obscure enigmatical discourse, but, as Delitzsch has shown, from the first of the two primary meanings combined in the verb לִיץ, *lucere* and *lascivire*, a brilliant oration, *oratio splendida*, from which מֵלִיץ is used to denote an interpreter, so called, not from the obscurity of the speaking, but from his making the speech clear or intelligible. חִידוֹת לוֹ is in apposition to מְלִיצָה and מָשָׁל, adding the more precise definition, that the sayings contain enigmas relating to him (the Chaldæan). The enigmatical feature comes out more especially in the double meaning of עַבְטִיט in ver. 6*b*, נֹשְׁכֶיךָ in ver. 7*a*, and קִיקָלוֹן in ver. 16*b*. וְיֹאמַר serves, like לֵאמֹר elsewhere, as a direct introduction to the speech. The first woe applies to the insatiable rapacity of the Chaldæan. הַמַּרְבֶּה לֹּא־לוֹ, who increases what does not belong to him, *i.e.* who seizes upon a large amount of the possessions of others. עַד־מָתַי, for how long, *sc.* will he be able to do this with impunity; not "how long has he already done this" (Hitzig), for the words do not express exultation at the termination of the oppression, but are a sigh appended to the woe, over the apparently interminable plunderings on the part of the Chaldæan. וּמַכְבִּיד is also dependent upon *hôi*, since the defined participle which stands at the head of the cry of woe is generally followed by participles undefined, as though the former regulated the whole (cf. Isa. v. 20 and x. 1). At the same time, it might be taken as a simple declaration in itself, though still standing under the influence of the *hôi;* in which case הוּא would have to be supplied in thought, like וְחֹטֵא in ver. 10. And even in this instance the sentence is not subordinate to the preceding one, as Luther follows Rashi in assuming ("and still only heaps much slime upon

himself"); but is co-ordinate, as the parallelism of the clauses
and the meaning of עַבְטִיט require. The ἀπ. λεγ. עַבְטִיט is
probably chosen on account of the resemblance in sound to
מַכְבִּיד, whilst it also covers an enigma or *double entendre*. Being
formed from עָבַט (to give a pledge) by the repetition of the
last radical, עַבְטִיט signifies the mass of pledges (*pignorum cap-
torum copia:* Ges., Maurer, Delitzsch), not the load of guilt,
either in a literal or a tropico-moral sense. The quantity of
foreign property which the Chaldæan has accumulated is represented as a heavy mass of pledges, which he has taken from
the nations like an unmerciful usurer (Deut. xxiv. 10), to point
to the fact that he will be compelled to disgorge them in due
time. הִכְבִּיד, to make heavy, *i.e.* to lay a heavy load upon a
person. The word עַבְטִיט, however, might form two words so
far as the sound is concerned : עָב טִיט, cloud (*i.e.* mass) of dirt,
which will cause his ruin as soon as it is discharged. This is
the sense in which the Syriac has taken the word ; and Jerome
does the same, observing, *considera quam eleganter multiplicatas
divitias densum appellaverit lutum,* no doubt according to a
Jewish tradition, since Kimchi, Rashi, and Ab. Ezra take the
word as a composite one, and merely differ as to the explanation of עָב. Grammatically considered, this explanation is indeed untenable, since the Hebrew language has formed no
appellative *nomina composita;* but the word is nevertheless
enigmatical, because, when heard from the lips, it might be
taken as two words, and understood in the sense indicated. In
ver. 7 the threatening *hōi* is still further developed. Will not
thy biters arise ? נֹשְׁכִים אֹתָךְ = נֹשְׁכֶיךָ, those who bite thee. In
the description here given of the enemy as savage vipers (cf.
Jer. viii. 17) there is also an enigmatical *double entendre,* which
Delitzsch has admirably interpreted thus : "הַמַּרְבֶּה," he says,
" pointed to תַּרְבִּית (interest). The latter, favoured by the idea
of the Chaldæan as an unmerciful usurer, which is concentrated in עַבְטִיט, points to נֶשֶׁךְ, which is frequently connected
with תַּרְבִּית, and signifies usurious interest ; and this again
to the striking epithet נֹשְׁכִים, which is applied to those who
have to inflict the divine retribution upon the Chaldæan. The
prophet selected this to suggest the thought that there would
come upon the Chaldæan those who would demand back with
interest (*neshek*) the capital of which he had unrighteously

taken possession, just as he had unmercifully taken the goods of the nations from them by usury and pawn." יָקֵצוּ, from יָקַץ; they will awake, viz. מְזַעְזְעֶיךָ, those who shake or rouse thee up. זוע, *pilel* of זוע, σείω, is used in Arabic of the wind (to shake the tree); hence, as in this case, it was employed to denote shaking up or scaring away from a possession, as is often done, for example, by a creditor (Hitzig, Delitzsch). מְשִׁסּוֹת is an intensive plural.

So far as this threat applies to the Chaldæans, it was executed by the Medes and Persians, who destroyed the Chaldæan empire. But the threat has a much more extensive application. This is evident, apart from other proofs, from ver. 8 itself, according to which the whole of the remnant of the nations is to inflict the retribution. *Gōyīm rabbīm,* "many nations:" this is not to be taken as an antithesis to *kol-haggōyīm* (all nations) in ver. 5*b*, since "all nations" are simply many nations, as *kol* is not to be taken in its absolute sense, but simply in a relative sense, as denoting all the nations that lie within the prophet's horizon, as having entered the arena of history. Through יְשָׁלּוּךָ, which is placed at the head of the concluding clause without a copula, the antithesis to שַׁלּוֹתָ is sharply brought out, and the idea of the righteous retaliation distinctly expressed. כָּל־יֶתֶר עַמִּים, the whole remnant of the nations, is not all the rest, with the exception of the one Chaldæan, for *yether* always denotes the remnant which is left after the deduction of a portion; nor does it mean all the rest of the nations, who are spared and not subjugated, in distinction from the plundered and subjugated nations, as Hitzig with many others imagine, and in proof of which he adduces the fact that the overthrow of the Chaldæans was effected by nations that had not been subdued. But, as Delitzsch has correctly observed, this view makes the prophet contradict not only himself, but the whole of the prophetic view of the world-wide dominion of Nebuchadnezzar. According to ver. 5*b*, the Chaldæan has grasped to himself the dominion over all nations, and consequently there cannot be any nations left that he has not plundered. Moreover, the Chaldæan, or Nebuchadnezzar as the head of the Chaldæan kingdom, appears in prophecy (Jer xxvii. 7, 8), as he does in history (Dan. ii. 38, iii. 31, v. 19) throughout, as the ruler of the world in the highest sense, who has subjugated all nations and kingdoms round about, and compelled them to serve him. These nations include the Medes and Elamites (= Persians), to whom the future conquest of Babylon is attributed in Isa. xiii. 17, xxi. 2, Jer. li. 11, 28. They are both mentioned in Jer. xxv. 25 among the nations, to whom the prophet is to reach the cup of wrath from the hand of Jehovah; and the kingdom of Elam especially is threatened in Jer. xlix. 34 sqq. with the destruction of its power, and dispersion to all four winds. In these two prophecies, indeed, Nebuchadnezzar is not expressly mentioned by name as the executor of the judgment of wrath; but in Jer. xxv. this may plainly be inferred from the context, partly from the fact that, according to ver. 9, Judah with its inhabitants, and all nations round about, are to be given into the hand of Nebuchadnezzar, and partly from the fact that in the list of the nations enumerated in vers. 18–26a the king of Sesach (*i.e.* Babel) is mentioned as he who is to drink the cup "after them" (ver. 26b). The expression '*achărēhem* (after them) shows very clearly that the judgment upon the nations previously mentioned, and therefore also upon the kings of Elam and Media, is to occur while the Chaldæan rule continues, *i.e.* is to be executed by the Chaldæans. This may, in fact, be inferred, so far as the prophecy respecting Elam in Jer. xlix. 34 sqq. is concerned, from the circumstance that Jeremiah's prophecies with regard to foreign nations in Jer. xlvi.–li. are merely expansions of the summary announcement in ch. xxv. 19–26, and is also confirmed by Ezek. xxxii. 24, inasmuch as Elam is mentioned there immediately after Asshur in the list of kings and nations that have sunk to the lower regions before Egypt. And if even this prophecy has a much wider meaning, like that concerning Elam in Jer. xlix. 34, and the elegy over Egypt, which Ezekiel strikes up, is expanded into a threatening prophecy concerning the heathen generally (see Kliefoth, *Ezech.* p. 303), this further reference presupposes the historical fulfilment which the threatening words of prophecy have received through the judgment inflicted by the Chaldæans upon all the nations mentioned, and has in this its real foundation and soil.

History also harmonizes with this prophetic announcement. The arguments adduced by Hävernick (*Daniel*, p. 547 sqq.)

to prove that Nebuchadnezzar did not extend his conquests to Elam, and neither subdued this province nor Media, are not conclusive. The fact that after the fall of Nineveh the conquerors, Nabopolassar of Babylonia, and Cyaxares the king of Media, divided the fallen Assyrian kingdom between them, the former receiving the western provinces, and the latter the eastern, does not preclude the possibility of Nebuchadnezzar, the founder of the Chaldæan empire, having made war upon the Median kingdom, and brought it into subjection. There is no historical testimony, however, to the further assertion, that Nebuchadnezzar was only concerned to extend his kingdom towards the west, that his conquests were all of them in the lands situated there, and gave him so much to do that he could not possibly think of extending his eastern frontier. It is true that the opposite of this cannot be inferred from Strabo, xvi. 1, 18 ;[1] but it may be inferred, as M. v. Niebuhr (*Gesch. Assurs*, pp. 211–12) has said, from the fact that according to Jer. xxvii. and xxviii., at the beginning of Zedekiah's reign, and therefore not very long after Nebuchadnezzar had conquered Jerusalem in the time of Jehoiachin, and restored order in southern Syria in the most energetic manner, the kings of Edom, Moab, Ammon, Tyre, and Zidon, entered into negotiations with Zedekiah for a joint expedition against Nebuchadnezzar. M. v. Niebuhr infers from this that troublous times set in at that period for Nebuchadnezzar, and that this sudden change in the situation of affairs was connected with the death of Cyaxares, and leads to the conjecture that Nebuchadnezzar, who had sworn fealty to Cyaxares, refused at his death to do homage to his successor ; for fidelity to a father-in-law, with whose help the kingdom was founded, would assume a very different character if it was renewed to his successor. Babel was too powerful to accept any such enfeoffment as this. And even if Nebuchadnezzar was not a vassal, there could not be a more suitable opportunity for war with Media than that afforded

---

[1] This passage is quoted by Hitzig (*Ezech.* p. 251) as a proof that Elam made war upon the Babylonians, and, indeed, judging from Jer. xlix. 34, an unsuccessful war. But Strabo speaks of a war between the Elymæans (Elamites) and the Babylonians and Susians, which M. v. Niebuhr (p. 210) very properly assigns to the period of the alliance between Media (as possessor of Susa) and Babylon.

by a change of government, since kingdoms in the East are so easily shaken by the death of a great prince. And there certainly was no lack of inducement to enter upon a war with Media. Elam, for example, from its very situation, and on account of the restlessness of its inhabitants, must have been a constant apple of discord. This combination acquires extreme probability, partly from the fact that Jeremiah's prophecy concerning Elam, in which that nation is threatened with the destruction of its power and dispersion to all four winds, was first uttered at the commencement of Zedekiah's reign (Jer. xlix. 34), whereas the rest of his prophecies against foreign nations date from an earlier period, and that against Babel is the only one which falls later, namely, in the fourth year of Zedekiah (Jer. li. 59), which appears to point to the fact that at the commencement of Zedekiah's reign things were brewing in Elam which might lead to his ruin. And it is favoured in part by the account in the book of Judith of a war between Nabuchodonosor (Nebuchadnezzar) and Media, which terminated victoriously according to the *Rec. vulg.* in the twelfth year of his reign, since this account is hardly altogether a fictitious one. These prophetic and historical testimonies may be regarded as quite sufficient, considering the universally scanty accounts of the Chaldæan monarchy given by the Greeks and Romans, to warrant us in assuming without hesitation, as M. v. Niebuhr has done, that between the ninth and twentieth years of Nebuchadnezzar's reign—namely, at the commencement of Zedekiah's reign—the former had to make war not only with Elam, but with Media also, and that it is to this eastern war that we should have to attribute the commotion in Syria.

From all this we may see that there is no necessity to explain "all the remnant of the nations" as relating to the remainder of the nations that had not been subjugated, but that we may understand it as signifying the remnant of the nations plundered and subjugated by the Chaldæans (as is done by the LXX., Theodoret, Delitzsch, and others), which is the only explanation in harmony with the usage of the language. For in Josh. xxiii. 12 *yether haggōyim* denotes the Canaanitish nations left after the war of extermination; and in Zech. xiv. 2 *yether hâ'âm* signifies the remnant of the nation left after the previous conquest of the city, and the carrying

away of half its inhabitants. In Zeph. ii. 9 *yether gōi* is synonymous with שְׁאֵרִית עַמִּי, and our יֶתֶר עַמִּים is equivalent to שְׁאֵרִית
הַגּוֹיִם in Ezek. xxxvi. 3, 4. מִדְּמֵי אָדָם: on account of the human
blood unjustly shed, and on account of the wickedness on the
earth (*chămas* with the gen. obj. as in Joel iv. 19 and Ob. 10).
'*Erets* without an article is not the holy land, but the earth
generally; and so the city (*qiryâh*, which is still dependent
upon *chămas*) is not Jerusalem, nor any one particular city,
but, with indefinite generality, " cities." The two clauses are
parallel, cities and their inhabitants corresponding to men and
the earth. The Chaldæan is depicted as one who gathers men
and nations in his net (ch. i. 14–17). And so in Jer. l. 23 he
is called a hammer of the whole earth, in li. 7 a cup of reeling,
and in li. 25 the destroyer of the whole earth.

Vers. 9–11. The second woe is pronounced upon the wickedness of the Chaldæan, in establishing for himself a permanent
settlement through godless gain. Ver. 9. " *Woe to him who
getteth a godless gain for his house, to set his nest on high, to save
himself from the hand of calamity.* Ver. 10. *Thou hast consulted shame to thy house, destruction of many nations, and in-
volvest thy soul in guilt.* Ver. 11. *For the stone out of the wall
will cry, and the spar out of the wood will answer it.*" To the
Chaldæan's thirst for robbery and plunder there is attached
quite simply the base avarice through which he seeks to procure strength and durability for his house. בֹּצֵעַ בֶּצַע, to get
gain, has in itself the subordinate idea of unrighteous gain
or sinful covetousness, since בָּצַע denotes cutting or breaking
something off from another's property, though here it is still
further strengthened by the predicate רַע, evil (gain). בֵּיתוֹ
(his house) is not the palace, but the royal house of the Chaldæan, his dynasty, as ver. 10 clearly shows, where בַּיִת evidently
denotes the king's family, including the king himself. How
far he makes בֶּצַע for his family, is more precisely defined by
קִנּוֹ לָשׂוּם וְגוּ'. קִנּוֹ, his (the Chaldæan's) nest, is neither his capital
nor his palace or royal castle; but the setting up of his nest
on high is a figure denoting the founding of his government,
and securing it against attacks. As the eagle builds its nest
on high, to protect it from harm (cf. Job xxxix. 27), so does
the Chaldæan seek to elevate and strengthen his rule by robbery and plunder, that it may never be wrested from his family

again. We might here think of the buildings erected by Nebuchadnezzar for the fortification of Babylon, and also of the
building of the royal palace (see Berosus in *Jos. c. Ap.* i. 19).
We must not limit the figurative expression to this, however,
but must rather refer it to all that the Chaldæan did to establish his rule. This is called the setting on high of his nest, to
characterize it as an emanation from his pride, and the lofty
thoughts of his heart. For the figure of the nest, see Num.
xxiv. 21, Ob. 4, Jer. xlix. 16. His intention in doing this is
to save himself from the hand of adversity. רָע is not masculine, the evil man ; but neuter, adversity, or " the hostile fate,
which, so far as its ultimate cause is God (Isa. xlv. 7), is inevitable and irreversible" (Delitzsch). In ver. 10 the result
of his heaping up of evil gain is announced : he has consulted
shame to his house. יָעַץ, to form a resolution. His determination to establish his house, and make it firm and lofty by
evil gain, will bring shame to his house, and instead of honour
and lasting glory, only shame and ruin. קְצוֹת, which has been
variously rendered, cannot be the plural of the noun קָצֶה, " the
ends of many nations," since it is impossible to attach any
intelligent meaning to this. It is rather the infinitive of the
verb קָצָה, the occurrence of which Hitzig can only dispute by
an arbitrary alteration of the text in four different passages,
and is equivalent to קָצַץ, to cut off, hew off, which occurs in
the *piel* in 2 Kings x. 32 and Prov. xxvi. 6, but in the *kal* only
here. The infinitive construct does not stand for the inf. abs.,
or for לִקְצוֹת, *exscindendo*, but is used substantively, and is
governed by יָעַצְתָּ, which still retains its force from the previous
clause. Thou hast consulted (resolved upon) the cutting off,
or destruction, of many nations. וְחוֹטֵא, and sinnest against
thy soul thereby, *i.e.* bringest retribution upon thyself, throwest
away thine own life. On the use of the participle in the sense
of the second person without אַתָּה, see at ch. i. 5. חָטָא, with
the accusative of the person, as in Prov. xx. 2 and viii. 36,
instead of חָטָא בְנַפְשׁוֹ. The participle is used, because the reference is to a present, which will only be completed in the
future (Hitzig and Delitzsch). The reason for this verdict,
and also for the *hôi* which stands at the head of this strophe,
follows in ver. 11. The stone out of the wall and the spar
out of the woodwork will cry, *sc.* because of the wickedness

which thou hast practised in connection with thy buildings
(ch. i. 2), or for vengeance (Gen. iv. 10), because they have
been stolen, or obtained from stolen property. The apparently
proverbial expression of the crying of stones is applied in a
different way in Luke xix. 40. קִיר does not mean the wall of
a room here, but, as distinguished from עֵץ, the outside wall,
and עֵץ, the woodwork or beams of the buildings. The ἀπ.
λεγ. כָּפִיס, lit. that which binds, from כפס in the Syriac and
Targum, to bind, is, according to Jerome, "the beam which is
placed in the middle of any building to hold the walls together,
and is generally called ἱμάντωσις by the Greeks." The explanation given by Suidas is, δέσις ξύλων ἐμβαλλομένων ἐν τοῖς
οἰκοδομήσασι, hence rafters or beams. יַעֲנֶנָּה, will answer, sc.
the stone, i.e. join in its crying (cf. Isa. xxxiv. 14).

Vers. 12–14. The third woe refers to the building of cities
with the blood and property of strangers. Ver. 12. " *Woe to
him who buildeth cities with blood, and foundeth castles with
injustice.* Ver. 13. *Is it not, behold, from Jehovah of hosts
that the peoples weary themselves for fire, and nations exhaust
themselves for vanity?* Ver. 14. *For the earth will be filled with
knowledge of the glory of Jehovah, as the waters cover the sea.*"
The earnest endeavour of the Chaldæan to found his dynasty
in permanency through evil gain, manifested itself also in the
building of cities with the blood and sweat of the subjugated
nations. עִיר and קִרְיָה are synonymous, and are used in the
singular with indefinite generality, like קִרְיָה in ver. 8. The
preposition בְּ, attached to דָּמִים and עַוְלָה, denotes the means
employed to attain the end, as in Mic. iii. 10 and Jer. xxii. 13.
This was murder, bloodshed, transportation, and tyranny of
every kind. *Kōnēn* is not a participle with the *Mem* dropped,
but a perfect; the address, which was opened with a participle,
being continued in the finite tense (cf. Ewald, § 350, a). With
ver. 13 the address takes a different turn from that which it
has in the preceding woes. Whereas there the woe is always
more fully expanded in the central verse by an exposition of
the wrong, we have here a statement that it is of Jehovah, i.e.
is ordered or inflicted by Him, that the nations weary themselves for the fire. The וּ before יִיגְעוּ introduces the declaration of what it is that comes from Jehovah. הֲלוֹא הִנֵּה (is it
not? behold!) are connected together, as in 2 Chron. xxv. 26,

to point to what follows as something great that was floating
before the mind of the prophet. בְּדֵי אֵשׁ, literally, for the need
of the fire (compare Nah. ii. 13 and Isa. xl. 16). They labour
for the fire, *i.e.* that the fire may devour the cities that have
been built with severe exertion, which exhausts the strength of
the nations. So far they weary themselves for vanity, since
the buildings are one day to fall into ruins, or be destroyed.
Jeremiah (li. 58) has very suitably applied these words to
the destruction of Babylon. This wearying of themselves for
vanity is determined by Jehovah, for (ver. 14) the earth shall
be filled with the knowledge of the glory of Jehovah. That
this may be the case, the kingdom of the world, which is hostile
to the Lord and His glory, must be destroyed. This promise
therefore involves a threat directed against the Chaldæan. His
usurped glory shall be destroyed, that the glory of Jehovah of
Sabaoth, *i.e.* of the God of the universe, may fill the whole
earth. The thought in ver. 14 is formed after Isa. xi. 9, with
trifling alterations, partly substantial, partly only formal. The
choice of the *niphal* תִּמָּלֵא instead of the מָלְאָה of Isaiah refers
to the actual fact, and is induced in both passages by the different turn given to the thought. In Isaiah, for example, this
thought closes the description of the glory and blessedness of
the Messianic kingdom in its perfected state. The earth is
then full of the knowledge of the Lord, and the peace throughout all nature which has already been promised is one fruit of
that knowledge. In Habakkuk, on the other hand, this knowledge is only secured through the overthrow of the kingdom
of the world, and consequently only thereby will the earth be
filled with it, and that not with the knowledge of Jehovah (as
in Isaiah), but with the knowledge of His glory (כְּבוֹד יְיָ), which
is manifested in the judgment and overthrow of all ungodly
powers (Isa. ii. 12–21, vi. 3, compared with the primary passage, Num. xiv. 21). כְּבוֹד יְיָ is "the δόξα of Jehovah, which
includes His right of majesty over the whole earth" (Delitzsch).
יְכַסּוּ עַל־יָם is altered in form, but not in sense, from the לַיָּם מְכַסִּים
of Isaiah; and יְכַסּוּ is to be taken relatively, since כְּ is only
used as a preposition before a noun or participle, and not like
a conjunction before a whole sentence (comp. Ewald, § 360, *a*,
with § 337, *c*). לְדַעַת is an infinitive, not a noun, with the preposition לְ; for יִמָּלֵא, מָלֵא, is construed with the *accus. rei*, lit. the

earth will be filled with the acknowledging. The water of the sea is a figure denoting overflowing abundance.

Vers. 15–17. The fourth woe is an exclamation uttered concerning the cruelty of the Chaldæan in the treatment of the conquered nations. Ver. 15. "*Woe to him that giveth his neighbour to drink, mixing thy burning wrath, and also making drunk, to look at their nakedness.* Ver. 16. *Thou hast satisfied thyself with shame instead of with honour; then drink thou also, and show the foreskin. The cup of Jehovah's right hand will turn to thee, and the vomiting of shame upon thy glory.* Ver. 17. *For the wickedness at Lebanon will cover thee, and the dispersion of the animals which frightened them; for the blood of the men and the wickedness on the earth, upon the city and all its inhabitants.*" The description in vers. 15 and 16 is figurative, and the figure is taken from ordinary life, where one man gives another drink, so as to intoxicate him, for the purpose of indulging his own wantonness at his expense, or taking delight in his shame. This helps to explain the מַשְׁקֵה רֵעֵהוּ, who gives his neighbour to drink. The singular is used with indefinite generality, or in a collective, or speaking more correctly, a distributive sense. The next two circumstantial clauses are subordinate to הוֹי מַשְׁקֵה, defining more closely the mode of the drinking. סָפַּח does not mean to pour in, after the Arabic سفح; for this, which is another form for سفك, answers to the Hebrew שָׁפַךְ, to pour out (compare שָׁפַךְ חֲמָתוֹ, to pour out, or empty out His wrath: Ps. lxxix. 6; Jer. x. 25), but has merely the meaning to add or associate, with the sole exception of Job xiv. 19, where it is apparently used to answer to the Arabic سفح; consequently here, where drink is spoken of, it means to mix wrath with the wine poured out. Through the suffix חֲמָתְךָ the woe is addressed directly to the Chaldæan himself,—a change from the third person to the second, which would be opposed to the genius of our language. The thought is sharpened by וְאַף שַׁכֵּר, " and also (in addition) making drunk " (*shakkēr*, inf. abs.). To look upon their nakednesses: the plural מְעוֹרֵיהֶם is used because רֵעֵהוּ has a collective meaning. The prostrate condition of the drunken man is a figurative representation of the overthrow of a conquered nation (Nah. iii. 11), and the uncovering of the shame a figure denoting the

ignominy that has fallen upon it (Nah. iii. 5 ; Isa. xlvii. 3).
This allegory, in which the conquest and subjugation of the
nations are represented as making them drink of the cup of
wrath, does not refer to the open violence with which the
Chaldæan enslaves the nations, but points to the artifices with
which he overpowers them, " the cunning with which he en-
tices them into his alliance, to put them to shame" (Delitzsch).
But he has thereby simply prepared shame for himself, which
will fall back upon him (ver. 16). The perfect שָׂבַעְתָּ does
not apply prophetically to the certain future ; but, as in the
earlier strophes (vers. 8 and 10) which are formed in a similar
manner, to what the Chaldæan has done, to bring upon himself
the punishment mentioned in what follows. The shame with
which he has satisfied himself is the shamefulness of his conduct ; and שָׂבַע, to satisfy himself, is equivalent to revelling in
shame. מִכָּבוֹד, far away from honour, *i.e.* and not in honour.
מִן is the negative, as in Ps. lii. 5, in the sense of וְלֹא, with which
it alternates in Hos. vi. 6. For this he is now also to drink
the cup of wrath, so as to fall down intoxicated, and show himself as having a foreskin, *i.e.* as uncircumcised (הֵעָרֵל from
עָרְלָה). This goblet Jehovah will hand to him. *Tissōbh*, he will
turn, עַל (upon thee, or to thee). This is said, because the cup
which the Chaldæan had reached to other nations was also
handed over to him by Jehovah. The nations have hitherto
been obliged to drink it out of the hand of the Chaldæan.
Now it is his turn, and he must drink it out of the hand of
Jehovah (see Jer. xxv. 26). וְקִיקָלוֹן, and shameful vomiting,
(*sc.* יִהְיֶה) will be over thine honour, *i.e.* will cover over thine
honour or glory, *i.e.* will destroy thee. The ἅπ. λεγ. קִיקָלוֹן is
formed from the *pilpal* קִלְקֵל from קָלַל, and softened down from
קְלַקְלוֹן, and signifies extreme or the greatest contempt. This
form of the word, however, is chosen for the sake of the play
upon קִיא קָלוֹן, vomiting of shame, *vomitus ignominiæ* (Vulg. ;
cf. קִיא צֹאָה in Isa. xxviii. 8), and in order that, when the word
was heard, it should call up the subordinate meaning, which
suggests itself the more naturally, because excessive drinking is
followed by vomiting (cf. Jer. xxv. 26, 27). This threat is
explained in ver. 17, in the statement that the wickedness
practised by the Chaldæan on Lebanon and its beasts will cover
or fall back upon itself. Lebanon with its beasts is taken by

most commentators allegorically, as a figurative representation
of the holy land and its inhabitants.   But although it may
be pleaded, in support of this view, that Lebanon, and indeed
the summit of its cedar forest, is used in Jer. xxii. 6 as a symbol
of the royal family of Judæa, and in Jer. xxii. 23 as a figure
denoting Jerusalem, and that in Isa. xxxvii. 24, and probably
also in Zech. xi. 1, the mountains of Lebanon, as the northern
frontier of the Israelitish land, are mentioned synecdochically
for the land itself, and the hewing of its cedars and cypresses
may be a figurative representation of the devastation of the
land and its inhabitants ; these passages do not, for all that,
furnish any conclusive evidence of the correctness of this view,
inasmuch as in Isa. x. 33, 34, Lebanon with its forest is also a
figure employed to denote the grand Assyrian army and its
leaders, and in Isa. lx. 13 is a symbol of the great men of the
earth generally ; whilst in the verse before us, the allusion to
the Israelitish land and nation is neither indicated, nor even
favoured, by the context of the words.   Apart, for example,
from the fact that such a thought as this, " the wickedness
committed upon the holy land will cover thee, because of the
wickedness committed upon the earth," not only appears lame,
but would be very difficult to sustain on biblical grounds, inasmuch as the wickedness committed upon the earth and its
inhabitants would be declared to be a greater crime than that
committed upon the land and people of the Lord ; this view
does not answer to the train of thought in the whole of the
ode, since the previous strophes do not contain any special
allusion to the devastation of the holy land, or the subjugation and ill-treatment of the holy people, but simply to the
plundering of many nations, and the gain forced out of their
sweat and blood, as being the great crime of the Chaldæan (cf.
vers. 8, 10, 13), for which he would be visited with retribution
and destruction.   Consequently we must take the words literally,
as referring to the wickedness practised by the Chaldæan upon
nature and the animal world, as the glorious creation of God,
represented by the cedars and cypresses of Lebanon, and the
animals living in the forests upon those mountains.   Not satis
fied with robbing men and nations, and with oppressing and
ill-treating them, the Chaldæan committed wickedness upon the
cedars and cypresses also, and the wild animals of Lebanon,

cutting down the wood either for military purposes or for state
buildings, so that the wild animals were unsparingly exterminated. There is a parallel to this in Isa. xiv. 8, where the
cypresses and cedars of Lebanon rejoice at the fall of the
Chaldæan, because they will be no more hewn down. *Shōd
bᵉhēmōth*, devastation upon (among) the animals (with the *gen.
obj.*, as in Isa. xxii. 4 and Ps. xii. 6). יְחִיתַן is a relative clause,
and the subject, *shōd*, the devastation which terrified the
animals. The form יְחִיתַן for יְחִתֵּן, from יֵחַת, *hiphil* of חָתַת, is
anomalous, the syllable with *dagesh* being resolved into an
extended one, like הֵתִימְךָ for הֵתִמְּךָ in Isa. xxxiii. 1; and the
tsere of the final syllable is exchanged for *pathach* because of
the pause, as, for example, in הִתְעַלָּם in Ps. lv. 2 (see Olshausen,
Gramm. p. 576). There is no necessity to alter it into יְחִתֶּךָ
(Ewald and Olshausen after the LXX., Syr., and Vulg.), and
it only weakens the idea of the *talio*. The second hemistich is
repeated as a refrain from ver. 8*b*.

Vers. 18–20. Fifth and last strophe.—Ver. 18. " *What
profiteth the graven image, that the maker thereof hath carved it;
the molten image and the teacher of lies, that the maker of his
image trusteth in him to make dumb idols?* Ver. 19. *Woe to him
that saith to the wood, Wake up; Awake, to the hard stone.
Should it teach? Behold, it is encased in gold and silver, and
there is nothing of breath in its inside.* Ver. 20. *But Jehovah is
in His holy temple: let all the world be silent before Him.*"
This concluding strophe does not commence, like the preceding
ones, with *hōi*, but with the thought which prepares the way
for the *woe*, and is attached to what goes before to strengthen
the threat, all hope of help being cut off from the Chaldæan.
Like all the rest of the heathen, the Chaldæan also trusted in the
power of his gods. This confidence the prophet overthrows in
ver. 18 : " What use is it?" equivalent to " The idol is of no
use" (cf. Jer. ii. 11; Isa. xliv. 9, 10). The force of this question
still continues in *massēkhâh* : " Of what use is the molten
image?" *Pesel* is an image carved out of wood or stone; *massēkhâh* an image cast in metal. הוֹעִיל is the perfect, expressing
a truth founded upon experience, as a fact : What profit has it
ever brought? *Mōreh sheqer* (the teacher of lies) is not the
priest or prophet of the idols, after the analogy of Mic. iii. 11
and Isa. ix. 14; for that would not suit the following explana

tory clause, in which עָלָיו (in him) points back to *mōreh sheqer* :
" that the maker of idols trusteth in him (the teacher of lies)."
Consequently the *mōreh sheqer* must be the idol itself; and it is
so designated in contrast with the true God, the teacher in the
highest sense (cf. Job xxxvi. 22). The idol is a teacher of
lying, inasmuch as it sustains the delusion, partly by itself and
partly through its priests, that it is God, and can do what men
expect from God; whereas it is nothing more than a dumb
nonentity ('*elîl 'illēm* : compare εἴδωλα ἄφωνα, 1 Cor. xii. 2).
Therefore woe be to him who expects help from such lifeless
wood or image of stone. עֵץ is the block of wood shaped into
an idol. *Hâqîtsâh*, awake ! *sc.* to my help, as men pray to the
living God (Ps. xxxv. 23, xliv. 24, lix. 6 ; Isa. li. 9). הוּא יוֹרֶה
is a question of astonishment at such a delusion. This is required by the following sentence : it is even encased in gold.
Tâphas : generally to grasp ; here to set in gold, to encase in
gold plate (*zâhâbh* is an accusative). כָּל אֵין: there is not at all.
רוּחַ, breath, the spirit of life (cf. Jer. x. 14). Vers. 18 and 19
contain a concise summary of the reproaches heaped upon
idolatry in Isa. xliv. 9-20 ; but they are formed quite inde-
pendently, without any evident allusions to that passage. In
ver. 20 the contrast is drawn between the dumb lifeless idols
and the living God, who is enthroned in His holy temple, *i.e.*
not the earthly temple at Jerusalem, but the heavenly temple,
or the temple as the throne of the divine glory (Isa. lxvi. 1),
as in Mic. i. 2, whence God will appear to judge the world, and
to manifest His holiness upon the earth, by the destruction of
the earthly powers that rise up against Him. This thought is
implied in the words, " He is in His holy temple," inasmuch as
the holy temple is the palace in which He is enthroned as Lord
and Ruler of the whole world, and from which He observes the
conduct of men (Ps. xi. 4). Therefore the whole earth, *i.e.* all
the population of the earth, is to be still before Him, *i.e.* to
submit silently to Him, and wait for His judgment. Compare
Zeph. i. 7 and Zech. ii. 17, where the same command is borrowed
from this passage, and referred to the expectation of judgment.
הַס is hardly an *imper. apoc.* of הָסָה, but an interjection, from
which the verb *hâsâh* is formed. But if the whole earth must
keep silence when He appears as Judge, it is all over with the
Chaldæan also, with all his glory and might.

PRAYER FOR COMPASSION IN THE MIDST OF THE JUDGMENT.—Chap. iii.

In this chapter, which is called a prayer in the heading, the prophet expresses the feelings which the divine revelation of judgment described in ch. i. and ii. had excited in his mind, and ought to excite in the congregation of believers, so that this supplicatory psalm may be called an echo of the two answers which the prophet had received from the Lord to his complaints in ch. i. 2–4 and 12–17 (*vid.* ch. i. 5–11 and ii. 2–20). Deeply agitated as he was by the revelation he had received concerning the terrible judgment, which the Lord would execute first of all upon Judah, through the wild and cruel Chaldæan nation, and then upon the Chaldæan himself, because he deified his own power, the prophet prays to the Lord that He will carry out this work of His " within years," and in the revelation of His wrath still show mercy (ver. 2). He then proceeds in vers. 3–15 to depict in a majestic theophany the coming of the Lord to judge the world, and bring salvation to His people and His anointed ; and secondly, in vers. 16–19, to describe the fruit of faith which this divine manifestation produces, namely, first of all fear and trembling at the day of tribulation (vers. 16, 17), and afterwards joy and rejoicing in the God of salvation (vers. 18 and 19). Consequently we may regard ver. 2 as the theme of the psalm, which is distributed thus between the two parts. In the first part (vers. 3–15) we have the prayer for the accomplishment of the work (ver. 2a) announced by God in ch. i. 5, expressed in the form of a prophetico-lyric description of the coming of the Lord to judgment; and in the second part (vers. 16–19), the prayer in wrath to remember mercy (ver. 2b), expanded still more fully in the form of a description of the feelings and state of mind excited by that prayer in the hearts of the believing church.

The song has a special heading, after the fashion of the psalms, in which the contents, the author, and the poetical character of the ode are indicated. The contents are called *t^ephillâh*, a prayer, like Ps. xvii., lxxxvi., xc., cii., and cxlii., not merely with reference to the fact that it commences with a prayer

to God, but because that prayer announces the contents of the
ode after the manner of a theme, and the whole of the ode is
simply the lyrical unfolding of that prayer. In order, however,
to point at the same time to the prophetic character of the
prayer, that it may not be regarded as a lyrical effusion of the
subjective emotions, wishes, and hopes of a member of the
congregation, but may be recognised as a production of the
prophets, enlightened by the Spirit of Jehovah, the name of
the author is given with the predicate "the prophet;" and to
this there is added עַל שִׁגְיֹנוֹת, to indicate the poetico-subjective
character, through which it is distinguished from prophecy in
the narrower sense. The expression "upon Shigionoth" cannot
refer to the contents or the object of the ode; for although
shiggâyōn, according to its etymon *shâgâh* = *shâgag*, to trans-
gress by mistake, to sin, might have the meaning transgression
in a moral sense, and consequently might be referred to the
sins of transgressors, either of the Judæans or the Chaldæans,
such an assumption is opposed both to the use of *shiggâyōn* in
the heading to Ps. vii., and also to the analogy between *'al
shigyōnōth*, and such headings to the psalms as *'al haggittīth,
'al neginōth*, and other words introduced with *'al*. Whilst
shiggâyōn in Ps. vii. 1 indicates the style of poetry in which
the psalm is composed, all the notices in the headings to the
psalms that are introduced with *'al* refer either to the melody
or style in which the psalms are to be sung, or to the musical
accompaniment with which they are to be introduced into the
worship of God. This musico-liturgical signification is to be
retained here also, since it is evident from the subscription
in ver. 19, and the repetition of *Selah* three times (vers. 3,
9, 13), that our hymn was to be used with musical accompaniment. Now, as *shâgâh*, to err, then to reel to and fro, is
applied to the giddiness both of intoxication and of love (Isa.
xxviii. 7; Prov. xx. 1, v. 20), *shiggâyōn* signifies reeling, and
in the terminology of poetry a reeling song, *i.e.* a song delivered in the greatest excitement, or with a rapid change
of emotion, *dithyrambus* (see Clauss on Ps. vii. 1; Ewald,
Delitzsch, and others); hence עַל שִׁגְיֹנוֹת, after dithyrambs, or
"after the manner of a stormy, martial, and triumphal ode"
(Schmieder).

Ver. 2. "*Jehovah, I have heard Thy tidings, am alarmed.*

Jehovah, Thy work, in the midst of the years call it to life, in the midst of the years make it known; in wrath remember mercy." שְׁמַע is the tidings (ἀκοή) of God; what the prophet has heard of God, *i.e.* the tidings of the judgment which God is about to inflict upon Judah through the Chaldæans, and after that upon the Chaldæans themselves. The prophet is alarmed at this. The word יָרֵאתִי (I am alarmed) does not compel us to take what is heard as referring merely to the judgment to be inflicted upon Judah by the Chaldæans. Even in the over-throw of the mighty Chaldæan, or of the empire of the world, the omnipotence of Jehovah is displayed in so terrible a manner, that this judgment not only inspires with joy at the destruction of the foe, but fills with alarm at the omnipotence of the Judge of the world. The prayer which follows, " Call Thy work to life," also refers to this twofold judgment which God revealed to the prophet in ch. i. and ii. פָּעָלְךָ, placed absolutely at the head for the sake of emphasis, points back to the work (*po'al*) which God was about to do (ch. i. 5); but this work of God is not limited to the raising up of the Chaldæan nation, but includes the judgment which will fall upon the Chaldæan after he has offended (ch. i. 11). This assumption is not at variance even with חַיֵּיהוּ. For the opinion that חִיָּה never means to call a non-existent thing to life, but always signifies either to give life to an inorganic object (Job xxxiii. 4), or to keep a living thing alive, or (and this most frequently) to restore a dead thing to life, and that here the word must be taken in the sense of restoring to life, because in the description which follows Habakkuk looks back to Ps. lxxvii. and the *po'al* depicted there, viz. the deliverance out of Egyptian bondage, is not correct. חִיָּה does not merely mean to restore to life and keep alive, but also to give life and call to life. In Job xxxiii. 4, where תְּחַיֵּנִי is parallel to עֲשָׂתְנִי, the reference is not to the impartation of life to an inorganic object, but to the giving of life in the sense of creating; and so also in Gen. vii. 3 and xix. 32, חִיָּה זֶרַע means to call seed to life, or raise it up, *i.e.* to call a non-existent thing to life. Moreover, the resemblances in the theophany depicted in what follows to Ps. lxxvii. do not require the assumption that Habakkuk is praying for the renewal of the former acts of God for the redemption of His people, but may be fully explained on the ground that the saving acts of God on behalf of His people are essentially the same in all ages, and that the prophets generally were accustomed to describe the divine revelations of the future under the form of imagery drawn from the acts of God in the past. There is special emphasis in the use of בְּקֶרֶב שָׁנִים twice, and the fact that in both instances it stands at the head. It has been interpreted in very different ways; but there is an evident allusion to the divine answer in ch. ii. 3, that the oracle is for an appointed time, etc. "In the midst of the years," or within years, cannot of course mean by itself "within a certain number, or a small number, of years," or "within a brief space of time" (Ges., Ros., and Maurer); nevertheless this explanation is founded upon a correct idea of the meaning. When the prophet directs his eye to the still remote object of the oracle (ch. ii.), the fulfilment of which was to be delayed, but yet assuredly to come at last (ch. ii. 3), the interval between the present time and the *mō'ēd* appointed by God (ch. ii. 3) appears to him as a long series of years, at the end only of which the judgment is to come upon the oppressors of His people, namely the Chaldæans. He therefore prays that the Lord will not delay too long the work which He designs to do, or cause it to come to life only at the end of the appointed interval, but will bring it to life within years, *i.e.* within the years, which would pass by if the fulfilment were delayed, before that *mō'ēd* arrived. Grammatically considered, *qerebh shânîm* cannot be the centre of the years of the world, the boundary-line between the Old and New Testament æons, as Bengel supposes, who takes it at the same time, according to this explanation, as the starting-point for a chronological calculation of the whole course of the world. Moreover, it may also be justly argued, in opposition to this view and application of the words, that it cannot be presupposed that the prophets had so clear a consciousness as this, embracing all history by its calculus; and still less can we expect to find in a lyrical ode, which is the outpouring of the heart of the congregation, a revelation of what God Himself had not revealed to him according to ch. ii. 3. Nevertheless the view which lies at the foundation of this application of our passage, viz. that the work of God, for the manifestation of which the prophet is praying, falls in the centre of the years of the world, has this deep truth, that it exhibits the overthrow not only of the im-

perial power of Chaldæa, but that of the world-power generally,
and the deliverance of the nation from its power, and forms
the turning-point, with which the old æon closes and the new
epoch of the world commences, with the completion of which
the whole of the earthly development of the universe will reach
its close. The repetition of בְּקֶרֶב שָׁנִים is expressive of the earnest
longing with which the congregation of the Lord looks for the
tribulation to end. The object to תּוֹדִיעַ, which is to be taken
in an optative sense, answering to the imperative in the parallel
clause, may easily be supplied from the previous clause. To
the prayer for the shortening of the period of suffering there
is appended, without the copula *Vav*, the further prayer, in
wrath to remember mercy. The wrath (*rōgez*, like *râgaz* in
Isa. xxviii. 21 and Prov. xxix. 9) in which God is to remember
mercy, namely for His people Israel, can only be wrath over
Israel, not merely the wrath manifested in the chastisement of
Judah through the Chaldæans, but also the wrath displayed in
the overthrow of the Chaldæans. In the former case God
would show mercy by softening the cruelty of the Chaldæans;
in the latter, by accelerating their overthrow, and putting a
speedy end to their tyranny. This prayer is followed in vers.
3–15 by a description of the work of God which is to be called
to life, in which the prophet expresses confidence that his
petition will be granted.

Vers. 3–15. *Coming of the Lord to judge the nations and
to redeem His people.* The description of this theophany rests
throughout upon earlier lyrical descriptions of the revelations
of God in the earlier times of Israel. Even the introduction
(ver. 3) has its roots in the song of Moses in Deut. xxxiii. 2 ;
and in the further course of the ode we meet with various
echoes of different psalms (compare ver. 6 with Ps. xviii. 8 ;
ver. 8 with Ps. xviii. 10 ; ver. 19 with Ps. xviii. 33, 34 ; also
ver. 5 with Ps. lxviii. 25 ; ver. 8 with Ps. lxviii. 5, 34). The
points of contact in vers. 10–15 with Ps. lxxvii. 17–21, are still
more marked, and are of such a kind that Habakkuk evidently
had the psalm in his mind, and not the writer of the psalm the
hymn of the prophet, and that the prophet has reproduced in
an original manner such features of the psalm as were adapted
to his purpose. This is not only generally favoured by the
fact that Habakkuk's prayer is composed throughout after the

poetry of the Psalms, but still more decidedly by the circumstance that Habakkuk depicts a coming redemption under figures borrowed from that of the past, to which the singer of this psalm looks back from his own mournful times, comforting himself with the picture of the miraculous deliverance of his people out of Egypt (see Hengstenberg and Delitzsch on Ps. lxxvii.). For it is very evident that Habakkuk does not describe the mighty acts of the Lord in the olden time, in order to assign a motive for his prayer for the deliverance of Israel out of the affliction of exile which awaits it in the future, as many of the earlier commentators supposed, but that he is predicting a future appearance of the Lord to judge the nations, from the simple fact that he places the future יָבוֹא (ver. 3) at the head of the whole description, so as to determine all that follows; whilst it is placed beyond the reach of doubt by the impossibility of interpreting the theophany historically, *i.e.* as relating to an earlier manifestation of God.

Ver. 3. "*Eloah comes from Teman, and the Holy One from the mountains of Paran. Selah. His splendour covers the sky, and the earth is full of His glory. Ver. 4. And brightness appears like sunlight, rays are at His hand, and there His power is concealed. Ver. 5. Before Him goes the plague, and pestilence follows His feet.*" As the Lord God once came down to His people at Sinai, when they had been redeemed out of Egypt, to establish the covenant of His grace with them, and make them into a kingdom of God, so will He appear in the time to come in the terrible glory of His omnipotence, to liberate them from the bondage of the power of the world, and dash to pieces the wicked who seek to destroy the poor. The introduction to this description is closely connected with Deut. xxxiii. 2. As Moses depicts the appearance of the Lord at Sinai as a light shining from Seir and Paran, so does Habakkuk also make the Holy One appear thence in His glory; but apart from other differences, he changes the preterite בָּא (Jehovah came from Sinai) into the future יָבוֹא, He will come, or comes, to indicate at the very outset that he is about to describe not a past, but a future revelation of the glory of the Lord. This he sees in the form of a theophany, which is fulfilled before his mental eye; hence יָבוֹא does not describe what is future, as being absolutely so, but is something progressively unfolding itself from the

present onwards, which we should express by the present tense.
The coming one is called *Eloah* (not *Jehovah*, as in Deut.
xxxiii. 2, and the imitation in Judg. v. 4), a form of the name
Elohim which only occurs in poetry in the earlier Hebrew
writings, which we find for the first time in Deut. xxxii. 15,
where it is used of God as the Creator of Israel, and which is
also used here to designate God as the Lord and Governor of
the whole world.   *Eloah,* however, comes as the Holy One
(*qâdōsh*), who cannot tolerate sin (ch. i. 13), and who will
judge the world and destroy the sinners (vers. 12–14).   As
Eloah and *Qâdōsh* are names of one God; so "from Teman" and
"from the mountain of Paran" are expressions denoting, not
two starting-points, but simply two localities of one single starting-point for His appearance, like Seir and the mountains of
Paran in Deut. xxxiii. 2.   Instead of *Seir*, the poetical name
of the mountainous country of the Edomites, *Teman,* the
southern district of the Edomitish land, is used *per synecdochen*
for Idumæa generally, as in Ob. 9 and Amos i. 12 (see vol.
i. p. 248).   The mountains of *Paran* are not the Et-Tih mountains, which bounded the desert of Paran towards the south,
but the high mountain-land which formed the eastern half of
that desert, and the northern portion of which is now called,
after its present inhabitants, the mountains of the *Azazimeh*
(see comm. on Num. x. 12).   The two localities lie opposite to
one another, and are only separated by the Arabah (or deep
valley of the Ghor).   We are not to understand the naming
of these two, however, as suggesting the idea that God was
coming from the Arabah, but, according to the original passage in Deut. xxxiii. 2, as indicating that the splendour of the
divine appearance spread over Teman and the mountains of
Paran, so that the rays were reflected from the two mountainous
regions.   The word *Selâh* does not form part of the subject-
matter of the text, but shows that the music strikes in here
when the song is used in the temple, taking up the lofty
thought that God is *coming,* and carrying it out in a manner
befitting the majestic appearance, in the prospect of the speedy
help of the Lord.   The word probably signified *elevatio*, from
sâlâh = sâlal, and was intended to indicate the strengthening
of the musical accompaniment, by the introduction, as is supposed, of a blast from the trumpets blown by the priests,

corresponding therefore to the musical *forte*. (For further remarks, see Hävernick's *Introduction to the Old Testament*, iii. p. 120 sqq., and Delitzsch on Ps. iix.) In ver. 3*b* the glory of the coming of God is depicted with reference to its extent, and in ver. 4 with reference to its intensive power. The whole creation is covered with its splendour. Heaven and earth reflect the glory of the coming one. הוֹדוֹ, His splendour or majesty, spreads over the whole heaven, and His glory over the earth. *T°hillâh* does not mean the praise of the earth, *i.e.* of its inhabitants, here (Chald., Ab. Ezr., Ros., and others); for there is no allusion to the manner in which the coming of God is received, and according to ver. 6 it fills the earth with trembling; but it denotes the object of the praise or fame, the glory, ἡ δόξα, like *hâdâr* in Job xl. 10, or *kâbhôd* in Isa. vi. 3, xlii. 8, and Num. xiv. 21. Grammatically considered, תְּהִלָּתוֹ is the accusative governed by מָלְאָה, and הָאָרֶץ is the subject.—Ver. 4. A splendour shines or arises like the light. תִּהְיֶה does not point back to תְּהִלָּתוֹ, "splendour like the sun will His glory be" (Hitzig); but it is the predicate to *nōgah* in the sense of to become, or to arise. הָאוֹר is the light of the sun. Like this light, or like the rising sun, when the Lord comes, there arises (spreads) a brilliant light, from which the rays emanate on its two sides. קַרְנַיִם, according to קֶרֶן in Ex. xxxiv. 29, 30, is to be taken in the sense of rays; and this meaning has developed itself from a comparison of the first rays of the rising sun, which shoot out above the horizon, to the horns or antlers of the gazelle, which is met with in the Arabian poets. מִיָּדוֹ, from His hand, *i.e.* since the hand is by the side, "at His side" (after the analogy of מִימִינוֹ and מִשְּׂמֹאלוֹ), and indeed "His hand" in a general sense, as signifying the hand generally, and not one single hand, equivalent therefore to "on both sides" (Delitzsch). As the disc of the sun is surrounded by a splendid radiance, so the coming of God is enclosed by rays on both sides. לוֹ refers to God. "Such a radiant splendour (קַרְנַיִם) surrounding God is presupposed when it is affirmed of Moses, that on coming from the presence of Jehovah his face was radiant, or emitted rays" (קָרַן, Ex. xxxiv. 29, 30). This interpretation of the words is established beyond all doubt, not only by the מִימִינוֹ of the original passage in Deut. xxxiii. 2, but also by the expressions which follow in ver. 5, viz. לְפָנָיו (before him) and לְרַגְלָיו (behind him); and consequently the interpretation "rays (emanating) from His hand are to Him," with the idea that we are to think of flashes of lightning darting out of God's hand (Schnur., Ros., Hitzig, Maurer, etc.), is proved to be untenable. According to Hebrew notions, flashes of lightning do not proceed from the hand of God (in Ps. xviii. 9, which has been appealed to in support of this explanation, we have מִמֶּנּוּ); and קַרְנַיִם does not occur either in Arabic or the later Hebrew in the sense of flashes of lightning, but only in the sense of the sun's rays. וְשָׁם חֶבְיוֹן עֻזֹּה, and there—namely, in the sun-like splendour, with the rays emanating from it—is the hiding of His omnipotence, *i.e.* the place where His omnipotence hides itself; in actual fact, the splendour forms the covering of the Almighty God at His coming, the manifestation of the essentially invisible God. The cloudy darkness is generally represented as the covering of the glory of God (Ex. xx. 21; 1 Kings viii. 12), not merely when His coming is depicted under the earthly substratum of a storm (Ps. xviii. 12, 13), but also when God was manifested in the pillar of cloud and fire (Ex. xiii. 21) on the journey of the Israelites through the desert, where it was only by night that the cloud had the appearance of fire (Num. ix. 15, 16). Here, on the contrary, the idea of the splendour of the rising sun predominates, according to which light is the garment in which God clothes Himself (Ps. civ. 2, cf. 1 Tim. vi. 16), answering to His coming as the Holy One (ver. 3). For the sun-light, in its self-illumining splendour, is the most suitable earthly element to serve as a symbol of the spotless purity of the Holy One, in whom there is no variation of light and darkness (Jas. i. 17; see at Ex. xix. 6). The alteration of וְשָׂם into וְשָׁם (he provides or contrives the concealment of His power), which Hitzig proposes after the LXX. (Aq., Symm., and Syr.), must be rejected, inasmuch as in that case the object, which he makes into the covering (cf. Ps. xviii. 12), could not be omitted; and this thought is by no means suitable here, and has merely been brought into the text on the assumption that God appears in a storm. As the Holy One, God comes to judgment upon the unholy world (ver. 5). Before Him goes *debher*, plague, and after His feet, *i.e.* behind Him, *resheph*, lit. burning heat, or a

blaze (Song of Sol. viii. 6), here the burning heat of the pestilence, fever-heat, as in Deut. xxxii. 24. Plague and pestilence,
as proceeding from God, are personified and represented as
satellites ; the former going before Him, as it were, as a shield-
bearer (1 Sam. xvii. 7), or courier (2 Sam. xv. 1) ; the latter
coming after Him as a servant (1 Sam. xxv. 42). This verse
prepares the way for the description, which commences with
ver. 6, of the impression produced by the coming of God upon
the world and its inhabitants.

Ver. 6. *" He stands, and sets the earth reeling : He looks,
and makes nations tremble ; primeval mountains burst in pieces,
the early hills sink down : His are ways of the olden time.*
Ver. 7. *I saw the tents of Cushan under affliction : the cur-
tains of the land of Midian tremble."* God coming from
afar has now drawn near and taken His stand, to smite the
nations as a warlike hero (cf. vers. 8, 9, and 11, 12). This is
affirmed in עָמַד, He has stationed Himself, not " He steps forth
or appears." This standing of Jehovah throws the earth and
the nations into trembling. יְמֹדֶד cannot mean to measure
here, for there is no thought of any measuring of the earth,
and it cannot be shown that *mâdad* is used in the sense of
measuring with the eye (Ros. and Hitzig). Moreover, the
choice of the *poel*, instead of the *piel*, would still remain unexplained, and the parallelism of the clauses would be dis-
regarded. We must therefore follow the Chaldee, Ges., Delitzsch, and others, who take מֹדֵד as the *poel* of מוּט = מוּד, to
set in a reeling motion. It is only with this interpretation
that the two parallel clauses correspond, in which יַתֵּר, the
hiphil of נָתַר, to cause to shake or tremble, answers to יְמֹדֵד.
This explanation is also required by what follows. For just
as ver. 7 unquestionably gives a further expansion of יַתֵּר גּוֹיִם,
so does עוֹלָם . . . יִתְפֹּצְצוּ contain the explanation of יְמֹדֵד אֶרֶץ.
The everlasting hills crumble (יִתְפֹּצְצוּ from פּוּץ), *i.e.* burst and
resolve themselves into dust, and the hills sink down, pass
away, and vanish (compare the similar description in Nahum
i. 5 and Mic. i. 4). הַרְרֵי־עַד (= הַרְרֵי קֶדֶם, Deut. xxxiii. 15)
in parallelism with גִּבְעוֹת עוֹלָם are the primeval mountains, as
being the oldest and firmest constituents of the globe, which
have existed from the beginning (מִנִּי עַד, Job xx. 4), and were
formed at the creation of the earth (Ps. xc. 2 ; Job xv. 7 ;

Prov. viii. 25). לוֹ עוֹלָם הֲלִיכוֹת is not to be taken relatively, and connected with what precedes, "which are the old paths," according to which the hills of God are called everlasting ways (Hitzig) ; because this does not yield a sense in harmony with the context. It is a substantive clause, and to be taken by itself : everlasting courses or goings are to Him, *i.e.* He now goes along, as He went along in the olden time. הֲלִיכָה, the going, advancing, or ways of God, analogous to the עוֹלָם דֶּרֶךְ, the course of the primitive world (Job xxii. 15). The prophet had Ps. lxviii. 25 floating before his mind, in which *hălīkhōth 'ĕlōhīm* denote the goings of God with His people, or the ways which God had taken from time immemorial in His guidance of them. As He once came down upon Sinai in the cloudy darkness, the thunder, lightning, and fire, to raise Israel up to be His covenant nation, so that the mountains shook (cf. Judg. v. 5) ; so do the mountains and hills tremble and melt away at His coming now. And as He once went before His people, and the tidings of His wondrous acts at the Red Sea threw the neighbouring nations into fear and despair (Ex. xv. 14–16) ; so now, when the course of God moves from Teman to the Red Sea, the nations on both sides of it are filled with terror. Of these, two are individualized in ver. 7, viz. Cushan and Midian. By *Cushan* we are not to understand the Mesopotamian king named Cushan Rishathaim, who subjugated Israel for eight years after the death of Joshua (Judg. iii. 8 sqq.) ; for this neither agrees with אָהֳלֵי, nor with the introduction of Midian in the parallel clause. The word is a lengthened form for *Cush*, and the name of the African Ethiopians. The *Midianites* are mentioned along with them, as being inhabitants of the Arabian coast of the Red Sea, which was opposite to them (see at Ex. ii. 15). כ' אָהֳלֵי, the tents with their inhabitants, the latter being principally intended. The same remark applies to יְרִיעוֹת, lit. the tent-curtains of the land of Midian, *i.e.* of the tents pitched in the land of Midian.

To the impression produced upon the nations by the coming of the Lord to judge the world, there is now appended in vers. 8 sqq. a description of the execution of the judgment. Ver. 8. " *Was it against rivers, O Jehovah, against the rivers that Thy wrath was kindled? that Thou ridest hither upon Thy horses, Thy chariots of salvation.* Ver. 9. *Thy bow lays itself bare; rods are sworn by word. Selah. Thou splittest the earth into rivers.*" The ode, taking a new turn, now passes from the description of the coming of God, to an address to God Himself. To the mental eye of the prophet, God presents Himself as Judge of the world, in the threatening attitude of a warlike hero equipped for conflict, so that he asks Him what is the object of His wrath. The question is merely a poetical turn given to a lively composition, which expects no answer, and is simply introduced to set forth the greatness of the wrath of God, so that in substance it is an affirmation. The wrath of God is kindled over the rivers, His fury over the sea. The first clause of the question is imperfect; Jehovah is not the subject, but a vocative, or an appeal, since *chârâh*, when predicated of God, is construed with בְּ. The subject follows in the double clause, into which the question divides itself, in אַפֶּךָ and עֶבְרָתֶךָ. Here the indefinite בְּנְהָרִים is defined by בַּנְּהָרִים. *Hann^e hârīm, the* rivers, are not any particular rivers, such as the arms of the Nile in Lower Egypt, or the rivers of Ethiopia, the Nile and Astaboras, the *nahărē Khūsh* (Isa. xviii. 1; Zeph. iii. 10: see Delitzsch), but the rivers of the earth generally; and "the sea" (*hayyâm*) is not the Red Sea, but the world-sea, as in Nahum i. 4 (cf. Ps. lxxxix. 10, Job xxxviii. 8). It is true that this description rests upon the two facts of the miraculous dividing of the Red Sea and of the Jordan (Ex. xv. 18; Ps. cxiv. 3, 5); but it rises far above these to a description of God as the Judge of the world, who can smite in His wrath not only the sea of the world, but all the rivers of the earth. עֶבְרָה is stronger than אַף, the wrath which passes over, or breaks through every barrier. *Kī, quod,* explaining and assigning the reason for the previous question. The riding upon horses is not actual riding, but driving in chariots with horses harnessed to them, as the explanatory words "thy chariots" (מַרְכְּבֹתֶיךָ) clearly shows, and as *rákhabh* (to ride) always signifies when predicated of God (cf. Deut. xxxiii. 26, Ps. lxviii. 34, civ. 3). *Y^e shū'âh* is governed by *mark^e bhōthekhâ*, with the freedom of construction allowed in poetry, as in 2 Sam. xxii. 33, Ps. lxxi. 7, whereas in prose the noun is generally repeated in the construct state (*vid.* Gen. xxxvii. 23, and Ewald, § 291, *b*). *Y^e shū'âh* signifies salvation, even in this case, and not victory,—a meaning which it never has, and which

is all the more inapplicable here, because *yᵉshûʿâh* is interpreted in ver. 13 by לְיֵשַׁע. By describing the chariots of God
as chariots of salvation, the prophet points at the outset to the
fact, that the riding of God has for its object the salvation or
deliverance of His people.—Ver. 9. God has already made
bare the bow, to shoot His arrows at the foe. תֵּעוֹר, third pers.
imperf. *niph.* of עוּר, equivalent to עָרַר (Isa. xxxii. 11), and the
more usual עָרָה, to be naked. To strengthen the thought, the
noun עֶרְיָה is written before the verb instead of the inf. abs.
(cf. Mic. i. 11). The bow is made bare, not by the shooting
of the arrows, but by its covering (γωρυτός, *corytus*) being
removed, in order to use it as a weapon. The reference is to
the bow used in war, which God carries as a warrior; so that
we are not to think of the rainbow, even if the chariots might
be understood as signifying the clouds, as in Isa. xix. 1 and
Ps. civ. 3, since the rainbow is a sign of peace and of the
covenant, whereas God is represented as attacking His enemies.
The next clause, שְׁבֻעוֹת מַטּוֹת אֹמֶר, is very obscure, and has not
yet been satisfactorily explained. Of the two meanings which
may be given to *mattôth*, viz. branches, rods, or staffs, and
tribes of the people of Israel, the latter can hardly be thought
of here, since *mattôth* would certainly have been defined by
either a suffix or some determining clause, if the tribes of
Israel were intended. On the other hand, the meaning staffs
or sticks is very naturally suggested both by the context—viz.
the allusion to the war-bow—and also by ver. 14, where *mattīm*
unquestionably signifies staves or lances. At the same time,
the meaning spears or darts cannot be deduced from either
ver. 14 or 2 Sam. xviii. 14. In both passages the meaning
staves, used as lances or weapons, is quite sufficient. *Matteh*, a
stick or staff with which blows were struck, might stand, as an
instrument of chastisement, for the punishment or chastisement
itself (cf. Isa. ix. 3, x. 5), and in Mic. vi. 9 it denotes the rod.
שְׁבֻעוֹת may be either the plural construct of שָׁבֻעַ, the seventh,
the heptad, or the plural of שְׁבוּעָה, an oath, or the passive participle of שָׁבַע, to be sworn, like שְׁבֻעֵי שְׁבֻעוֹת in Ezek. xxi. 28.
There is no material difference in the meaning obtained from
the last two; and the view we take of the word אֹמֶר must
decide between them and the first explanation. This word,
which is peculiar to poetry, denotes a discourse or a word, and

in Job xxii. 28 the affair, or the occasion, like דָּבָר. Here, at
any rate, it signifies the address or word of God, as in Ps.
lxviii. 12, lxxvii. 9, and is either a genitive dependent upon
mattōth or an adverbial accusative. The Masoretic pointing,
according to which *mattōth* is separated from '*ōmer* by *tiphchah*,
and the latter joined to *selâh* by *munach*, is connected with the
evidently false rabbinical rendering of *selah* as eternity (*in
sempiternum*), and being decidedly erroneous, cannot be taken
into consideration at all. But the interpretation of שְׁבֻעוֹת as
the seventh, does not suit either of these two possible views of
'*ōmer*. We therefore prefer the second meaning, chastising
rods or chastisements. אֹמֶר, however, cannot be a genitive
dependent upon *mattōth;* since chastisements of speech would
hardly stand for chastisements which God had spoken, but,
according to the analogy of שֵׁבֶט פִּיו in Isa. xi. 4, would point to
chastisements consisting in words, and this does not agree with
the present train of thought. '*Omer* is rather an adverbial
accusative, and belongs to שְׁבֻעוֹת, indicating the instrument or
media employed in the swearing : sworn with the word or
through the word, like חַרְבְּךָ in Ps. xvii. 13 (for the use of
the accusative to describe the substance or the instrumental
medium of an action, see Ewald, § 282, *c*). Hence שְׁבֻעוֹת cannot
be a noun, but must be a passive participle,. sworn. The expression, " chastising rods (chastisements) are sworn through
the word," points to the solemn oath with which God promised
in Deut. xxxii. 40–42 to take vengeance upon His enemies,
and avenge the blood of His servants : " For I lift up my hand
to heaven, and say, As I live for ever, when I have sharpened
my glittering sword, and my hand grasps for judgment, I will
render vengeance to mine adversaries, and repay them that
hate me. I will make mine arrows drunk with blood, and my
sword will eat flesh ; from the blood of the slain and the captives, from the hairy head of the enemy." That Habakkuk
had in his mind this promise of the vengeance of God upon His
enemies, which is strengthened by a solemn oath, is unmistakeably evident, if we compare בְּרַק חֲנִיתֶךָ in ver. 11 with בְּרַק חַרְבִּי
in Deut. xxxii. 41, and observe the allusion in רֹאשׁ מִבֵּית רָשָׁע
and רֹאשׁ פַּרְעוֹת in vers. 13 and 14 to רֹאשׁ פַּרְעוֹת אוֹיֵב in Deut.
xxxii. 42. From this promise the words of the prophet, which
are so enigmatical in themselves, obtain the requisite light to

render them intelligible. Gesenius (*Thes.* p. 877) has explained the prophet's words in a similar manner, *jurejurando firmatæ sunt castigationes promissæ* (the threatened rods, *i.e.* chastisements, are sworn), even without noticing the allusion to Deut. xxxii. 40 sqq. upon which these words are founded. Delitzsch was the first to call attention to the allusion to Deut. xxxii. 40 sqq.; but in his explanation, " the darts are sworn through his word of power (*jurejurando adstricta sunt tela verbo tuo*)," the swearing is taken in a sense which is foreign to Deuteronomy, and therefore conceals the connection with the original passage. Of the other explanations not one can be vindicated. The rabbinical view which we find in the Vulgate, *juramenta tribubus quæ locutus es*, is overthrown by the fact that שְׁבֻעוֹת without a preposition cannot mean *per*, or *ob*, or *juxta juramenta*, as we should have to render it, and as Luther actually has rendered it in his version ("as Thou hadst sworn to the tribes"). Ewald's rendering, " sevenfold darts of the word," is precluded by the combination of ideas, "darts of the word," which is quite foreign to the context. According to our explanation, the passage does indeed form simply a parenthesis in the description of the judicial interposition of God, but it contains a very fitting thought, through which the description gains in emphasis. In the last clause of the verse the description is continued in the manner already begun, and the effect indicated, which is produced upon the world of nature by the judicial interposition of God : " Thou splittest the earth into rivers." בָּקַע is construed with a double accusative, as in Zech. xiv. 4. This may be understood either as signifying that the earth trembles at the wrath of the Judge, and rents arise in consequence, through which rivers of water burst forth from the deep, or so that at the quaking of the earth the sea pours its waves over the land and splits it into rivers. The following verses point to an earthquake through which the form of the earth's surface is changed.

Ver. 10. " *The mountains see Thee, they writhe : a shower of waters passes along : the abyss lifts up its voice, it lifts up its hands on high.* Ver. 11. *Sun, moon, enter into their habitation at the light of Thine arrows which shoot by, at the shining of the lightning of Thy spear.*" The effect of the coming of God upon the mountains was already referred to in ver. 6. There they crumbled into ruins, here they writhe with terror. This difference is to be explained from the fact that there (ver. 6) the general effect of the omnipotence of God upon nature was intended, whereas here (vers. 10, 11) the special effect is described, which is produced upon nature by the judgment about to be executed by God upon the nations. The perfects in the description represent this effect as following immediately upon the coming of God. But in the first clause of ver. 10 the perfect רָאוּךָ is followed by the imperfect יָחִילוּ, because the writhing is a lasting condition. The force of the description is heightened by the omission of the copula before the clauses and the particular objects. The two verbs of the first clause stand in the relation of cause and effect to one another: when the mountains have seen Thee, they writhe with terror. The further description is not founded upon the idea of a terrible storm; for there is no reference to thunder, nor even to lightnings, but only to the arrows (ver. 11), which may be explained from the idea of God, as a warlike hero, making bare His bow. The colours and different features of the description are borrowed from the judgment of the flood. Ver. 10 (a and b) points to this divine judgment of the olden time, both the coming of the showers of water (geshem as in Gen. vii. 12 and viii. 2, and strengthened by mayim, analogous to hammabbūl hâyâh mayim in Gen. vii. 6; 'âbhar as in Nah. iii. 19, Ps. xlviii. 5), and also the nâthan tᵉhōm qōlō, the raging outburst of the abyss. Tᵉhōm is the mass of water in the abyss, not merely that of the ocean, but that of the subterranean waters also (Gen. xlix. 25; Deut. xxxiii. 13), the "great deep" (tᵉhōm rabbâh), whose fountains were broken up at the flood (Gen. vii. 11); and not the ocean of heaven, as Hitzig erroneously infers from Gen. vii. 11, viii. 2, and Prov. viii. 27. To this mass of water, which is called tᵉhōm from its roaring depth, the prophet attributes a voice, which it utters, to express the loud, mighty roaring of the waters as they rush forth from the bursting earth. As at the time of the flood, which was a type of the last judgment (Isa. xxiv. 18), the windows of heaven and the fountains of the deep were opened, so that the upper and lower waters, which are divided by the firmament, rushed together again, and the earth returned, as it were, to its condition before the second day of creation; so

here also the rivers of earth and rain-showers of heaven come
together, so that the abyss roars up with a loud noise (Delitzsch).
This roaring outburst of the mass of waters from the heart of
the earth is then represented as a lifting up of the hands to
heaven, with reference to the fact that the waves are thrown
up. *Rōm = rūm* (Prov. xxv. 3, xxi. 4) is an accusative of
direction, like *mârōm* in 2 Kings xix. 22. יָדֵיהוּ, for יָדָיו, a
full-sounding and more extended form, possibly to express by
the rhythm the greatness of the prodigy, how *magna vi brachii
tollunt* (Delitzsch). The lifting up of the hands is not a gesture denoting either an oath or rebellion ; but it is an involuntary utterance of terror, of restlessness, of anguish, as it were,
with a prayer for help (Delitzsch).—Ver. 11. The chaotic
condition into which the earth has been brought is heightened
by the darkness in which the heaven clothes itself. Sun and
moon, which give light to day and night, have put themselves,
or entered, into their habitation. זְבֻל with ה local, a dwelling-
place, is, according to oriental view, the place from which the
stars come out when they rise, and to which they return when
they set. Nevertheless it is not actual setting that is spoken
of here, but simply their obscuration, which is not the effect of
heavy clouds that pour out their water in showers of rain, but
is caused by the shining of the arrows of God (לְ in לְאוֹר and
לְנֹגַהּ denoting the outward cause or occasion). It is not, however, that they " turn pale in consequence of the surpassing
brilliancy of the lightnings" (Ewald), but that they " withdraw
altogether, from the fear and horror which pervade all nature,
and which are expressed in the mountains by trembling, in the
waters by roaring, and in the sun and moon by obscuration "
(Delitzsch). The idea that this verse refers to the standing
still of the sun and moon at the believing word of Joshua (Josh.
x. 12 sqq.), in which nearly all the earlier commentators agreed,
is quite untenable, inasmuch as עָמַד זְבֻלָה cannot mean to stand
still in the sky. The arrows and spear (*chănīth*) of God are
not lightnings, as in Ps. lxxvii. 18, 19, xviii. 15, etc., because
this theophany is not founded upon the idea of a storm, but
the darts with which God as a warrior smites down His foes,
as the instruments and effects of the wrath of God. A brilliant splendour is attributed to them, because they emanate
from Him whose coming, like the sunlight, pours out its rays

on both sides (ver. 4). בְּרַק חֲנִית has the same meaning here
as in Nah. iii. 3 : the flashing, because naked and sharpened,
spear. And just as we cannot understand the "bright sword"
of Nah. iii. 3 as signifying flashes of lightning, so here we cannot take the arrows as lightnings. יְהַלֵּכוּ is to be taken relatively,
"which pass along, or shoot by."

In ver. 12 there follows a description of the judgment upon
the nations for the rescue of the people of God. Ver. 12. "*In
fury Thou walkest through the earth, in wrath Thou stampest
down nations.* Ver. 13. *Thou goest out to the rescue of Thy
people, to the rescue of Thine anointed one; Thou dashest in
pieces the head from the house of the wicked one, laying bare the
foundation even to the neck. Selah.* Ver. 14. *Thou piercest
with his spears the head of his hordes, which storm hither to
beat me to powder, whose rejoicing is, as it were, to swallow the
poor in secret.* Ver. 15. *Thou treadest upon the sea : Thy horses,
upon the heap of great waters.*" The Lord, at whose coming in
the terrible glory of the majesty of the Judge of the world all
nature trembles and appears to fall into its primary chaotic
state, marches over the earth, and stamps or tramples down the
nations with His feet (compare the kindred figure of the treader
of the winepress in Isa. lxiii. 1-6). Not all nations, however,
but only those that are hostile to Him ; for He has come forth
to save His people and His anointed one. The perfects in
vers. 13-15 are prophetic, describing the future in spirit as
having already occurred. יָצָא, referring to the going out of
God to fight for His people, as in Judg. v. 4, 2 Sam. v. 24,
Isa. xlii. 13, etc. יֵשַׁע, rescue, salvation, is construed the second
time with an accusative like an inf. constr. (see Ewald, § 239, *a*).
The anointed of God is not the chosen, consecrated nation
(Schnur., Ros., Hitzig, Ewald, etc.) ; for the nation of Israel
is never called the anointed one (*hammâshĭăch*) by virtue of
its calling to be "a kingdom of priests" (*mamlekheth kohănīm*,
Ex. xix. 6), neither in Ps. xxviii. 8 nor in Ps. lxxxiv. 10,
lxxxix. 39. Even in Ps. cv. 15 it is not the Israelites who are
called by God "my anointed" (*meshĭchai*), but the patriarchs,
as princes consecrated by God (Gen. xxiii. 6). And so here
also מְשִׁיחֶךָ is the divinely-anointed king of Israel ; not, however, this or that historical king—say Josiah, Jehoiakim, or
even Jehoiachin—but the Davidic king absolutely, including

the Messiah, in whom the sovereignty of David is raised to an
eternal duration, "just as by the Chaldæan king here and in
ch. ii. we must understand the Chaldæan kings generally"
(Delitzsch), since the prophecy spreads from the judgment
upon the Chaldæans to the universal judgment upon the
nations, and the Chaldæan is merely introduced as the possessor
of the imperial power. The Messiah as the Son of David is
distinguished from Jehovah, and as such is the object of divine
help, just as in Zech. ix. 9, where He is called נוֹשָׁע in this
respect, and in the royal Messianic psalms. This help God
bestows upon His people and His anointed, by dashing in
pieces the head from the house of the wicked one. The *râshâ'*
(wicked one) is the Chaldæan, not the nation, however, which
is spoken of for the first time in ver. 14, but the Chaldæan
king, as chief of the imperial power which is hostile to the
kingdom of God. But, as the following clause clearly shows,
the house is the house in the literal sense, so that the "head,"
as part of the house, is the gable. A distinction is drawn
between this and *y^esôd*, the foundation, and צַוָּאר, the neck, *i.e.*
the central part looking from the gable downwards. The
destruction takes place both from above and below at once, so
that the gable and the foundation are dashed in pieces with one
blow, and that even to the neck, *i.e.* up to the point at which
the roof or gable rests upon the walls. עַד, inclusive, embracing
the part mentioned as the boundary; not exclusive, so as to leave
the walls still rising up as ruins. The description is allegorical,
the house representing the Chaldæan dynasty, the royal family
including the king, but not "including the exalted Chaldæan
kingdom in all its prosperity" (Hitzig). עָרוֹת, a rare form of
the inf. abs., like שָׁתוֹת in Isa. xxii. 13 (cf. Ewald, § 240, *b*),
from עָרָה, to make bare, to destroy from the very foundation,
the infinitive in the sense of the gerund describing the mode
of the action. The warlike nation meets with the same fate
as the royal house (ver. 14). The meaning of the first clause
of the verse depends upon the explanation to be given to the
word *p^erâzâv.* There is no foundation for the meaning leaders
or judges, which has been claimed for the word *p^erâzîm* ever
since the time of Schrœder and Schnur. In Hebrew usage
p^erâzî signifies the inhabitant of the plain (Deut. iii. 5; 1 Sam.
vi. 18), and *p^erâzôth* the plains, the open flat land, as distin-

guished from walled cities (Ezek. xxxviii. 11). *P'rázōn* has the
same meaning in Judg. v. 7 and 11. Consequently Delitzsch
derives *p'rázáv* from a segholate noun *perez* or *pĕrez*, in the
sense of the population settled upon the open country, the
villagers and peasantry, whence the more general signification
of a crowd or multitude of people, and here, since the context
points to warriors, the meaning hordes, or hostile companies,
which agrees with the Targum, Rashi, and Kimchi, who explain the word as signifying warriors or warlike troops. רֹאשׁ,
the head of his hordes, cannot be the leader, partly because
of what follows, "who come storming on," which presupposes
that not the leader only, but the hordes or warriors, will be
destroyed, and partly also because of the preceding verse, in
which the destruction of the king is pronounced, and also
because the distinction between the king and the leader of the
army is at variance with the complex character of the prophetic description. We must take רֹאשׁ in the literal sense, but
collectively, "heads." The prophet was led to the unusual figure
of the piercing of the head by the reminiscence of the piercing of
Sisera's head by Jael (Judg. v. 26). The suffixes in בְּמַטָּיו and
פְּרָזוֹ refer back to רָשָׁע. מַטָּיו, sticks, for lances or spears, after
2 Sam. xviii. 14. The meaning of the words is this: with the
spear of the king God pierces the heads of his warlike troops;
and the thought expressed is, that the hostile troops will slay
one another in consequence of the confusion, as was the case
in the wars described in 1 Sam. xiv. 20 and 2 Chron. xx.
23, 24, and as, according to prophecy, the last hostile power
of the world is to meet with its ruin when it shall attack the
kingdom of God (Ezek. xxxviii. 21; Zech. xiv. 13). יִסְעֲרוּ לַהֲפ׳
is to be taken relatively: "which storm hither (*sá'ar*, approach
with the swiftness and violence of a storm) to destroy me."
The prophet includes himself along with the nation, and uses
hēphīts with reference to the figure of the dispersion or powder-
ing of the chaff by a stormy wind (Isa. xli. 16; Jer. xiii. 24,
xviii. 17). עֲלִיצֻתָם forms a substantive clause by itself: "their
rejoicing is," for they who rejoice, as if to swallow, *i.e.* whose
rejoicing is directed to this, to swallow the poor in secret. The
enemies are compared to highway murderers, who lurk in dark
corners for the defenceless traveller, and look forward with rejoicing for the moment when they may be able to murder him.

עָנִי forms the antithesis to רָשָׁע. Inasmuch as "the wicked"
denotes the Chaldæan; "the poor" is the nation of Israel, *i.e.*
the congregation of the righteous, who are really the people of
God. To devour the poor, *i.e.* to take violent possession of
his life and all that he has (cf. Prov. xxx. 14, and for the fact
itself, Ps. x. 8–10), is, when applied to a nation, to destroy it
(*vid.* Deut. vii. 16 and Jer. x. 25).

In order that these enemies may be utterly destroyed, God
passes through the sea. This thought in ver. 15 connects the
conclusion of the description of the judicial coming of God
with what precedes. The drapery of the thought rests upon
the fact of the destruction of Pharaoh and his horsemen in the
Red Sea (Ex. xiv.). The sea, the heap of many waters, is not
a figurative expression for the army of the enemy, but is to
be taken literally. This is required by דָּרַכְתָּ בַיָּם, since דָּרַךְ
with בְּ, to tread upon a place, or enter into it (cf. Mic. v. 4,
Isa. lix. 8, Deut. xi. 24, 25), does not suit the figurative interpretation; and it is required still more by the parallel passages,
viz. Ps. lxxvii. 20 (בַּיָּם דַּרְכֶּךָ), which floated before the prophet's
mind, and Zech. x. 11. Just as God went through the Red
Sea in the olden time to lead Israel through, and to destroy the
Egyptian army, so will He in the future go through the sea
and do the same, when He goes forth to rescue His people out
of the power of the Chaldæan. The prophet does not express
the latter indeed, but it is implied in what he says. סוּסֶיךָ is
an accusative, not *instrumenti*, however, but of more precise
definition: thou, namely, according to thy horses; for " with
thy horses," as in Ps. lxxxiii. 19, xliv. 3 (אַתָּה יָדְךָ); cf. Ewald,
§ 281, *c*, and 293, *c*. The horses are to be taken, as in ver. 8,
as harnessed to the chariots; and they are mentioned here with
reference to the horses and chariots of Pharaoh, which were
destroyed by Jehovah in the sea. *Chōmer*, in the sense of
heap, as in Ex. viii. 10, is not an accusative, but is still dependent upon the בְּ of the parallel clause. The expression
" heap of many waters" serves simply to fill up the picture, as
in Ps. lxxvii. 20.

Vers. 16–19 form the second part of the psalm, in which
the prophet describes the feelings that are produced within
himself by the coming of the Lord to judge the nations, and
to rescue His own people; viz. first of all, fear and trembling

at the tribulation (vers. 16, 17); then exulting joy, in his confident trust in the God of salvation (vers. 18, 19). Ver. 16. *" I heard it, then my belly trembled, at the sound my lips yelled; rottenness forces itself into my bones, and I tremble under myself, that I am to wait quietly for the day of tribulation, when he that attacketh it approacheth the nation.* Ver. 17. *For the fig-tree will not blossom, and there is no yield on the vines; the produce of the olive-tree disappoints, and the corn-fields bear no food; the flock is away from the fold, and no ox in the stalls."* שָׁמַעְתִּי is not connected with the theophany depicted in vers. 3–15, since this was not an audible phenomenon, but was an object of inward vision, " a spectacle which presented itself to the eye." " I heard" corresponds to " I have heard" in ver. 2, and, like the latter, refers to the report heard from God of the approaching judgment. This address goes back to its starting-point, to explain the impression which it made upon the prophet, and to develop still how he " was afraid." The alarm pervades his whole body, belly, and bones, *i.e.* the softer and firmer component parts of the body; lips and feet, *i.e.* the upper and lower organs of the body. The lips cried *l^eqōl*, at the voice, the sound of God, which the prophet heard. *Ts̆âlal* is used elsewhere only of the ringing of the ears (1 Sam. iii. 11; 2 Kings xxi. 12; Jer. xix. 3); but here it is applied to the chattering sound produced by the lips, when they smite one another before crying out, not to the chattering of the teeth. Into the bones there penetrates *râqâbh*, rottenness, inward consumption of the bones, as an effect of alarm or pain, which paralyzes all the powers, and takes away all firmness from the body (cf. Prov. xii. 4, xiv. 30). *Tachtai*, under me, *i.e.* in my lower members, knees, feet: not as in Ex. xvi. 29, 2 Sam. ii. 23, on the spot where I stand (cf. Ewald, § 217, *k*). אֲשֶׁר אָנוּחַ might mean, " I who was to rest;" but it is more appropriate to take *'ăsher* as a relative conjunction, " that I," since the clause explains the great fear that had fallen upon him. אֲשֶׁר is used in a similar way, viz. as a conjunction with the verb in the first person, in Ezek. xxix. 29. *Nŭăch*, to rest, not to rest in the grave (Luther and others), nor to bear quietly or endure (Ges., Maurer), but to wait quietly or silently. For it could hardly occasion such consuming pain to a God-fearing man as that which the prophet experienced, to bear misfortune quietly, when it has already come, and cannot be averted ; but it might be to wait quietly and silently, in constant anticipation. *Tsârâh,* the trouble which the Chaldæans bring upon Judah. לַעֲלוֹת is not subordinate to לְיוֹם צָרָה, but co-ordinate with it, and is still dependent upon אָנוּחַ ; and יְגוּדֶנּוּ, as a relative clause (who oppresses it), is the subject to לַעֲלוֹת : " that I am to wait quietly for him that attacketh to approach my nation." For if לַעֲלוֹת were dependent upon לְיוֹם, it would be necessary to supply יוֹם as the subject : " when it (the day) comes." But this is precluded by the fact that עָלָה is not used for the approach or breaking of day. לְעַם, to the people, *dativ. incomm.*, is practically equivalent to עַל עָם, against the people. עָם, used absolutely, as in Isa. xxvi. 11, xlii. 6, is the nation of Israel. *Gūd,* as in Gen. xlix. 19, 20, *i.e. gâdad,* to press upon a person, to attack him, or crowd together against him (cf. Ps. xciv. 21). In ver. 17 the trouble of this day is described ; and the sensation of pain, in the anticipation of the period of calamity, is thereby still further accounted for. The plantations and fields yield no produce. Folds and stalls are empty in consequence of the devastation of the land by the hostile troops and their depredations : " a prophetic picture of the devastation of the holy land by the Chaldæan war" (Delitzsch). Fig-tree and vine are mentioned as the noblest fruit-trees of the land, as is frequently the case (see Joel i. 7 ; Hos. ii. 14 ; Mic. iv. 4). To this there is added the olive-tree, as in Mic. vi. 15, Deut. vi. 11, viii. 8, etc. *Ma'asēh zayith* is not the shoot, but the produce or fruit of the olive-tree, after the phrase עָשָׂה פְרִי, to bear fruit. *Kichēsh,* to disappoint, namely the expectation of produce, as in Hos. ix. 2. *Shᵉdēmōth,* which only occurs in the plural, corn-fields, is construed here as in Isa. xvi. 8, with the verb in the singular, because, so far as the sense was concerned, it had become almost equivalent to *sâdeh,* the field (see Ewald, § 318, *a*). *Gâzar,* to cut off, used here in a neuter sense : to be cut off or absent. מִכְלָה, contracted from מִכְלָאָה : fold, pen, an enclosed place for sheep. *Repheth, ἁπ. λεγ.*, the rack, then the stable or stall.

Although trembling on account of the approaching trouble, the prophet will nevertheless exult in the prospect of the salvation that he foresees. Ver. 18. "*But I, in Jehovah will I rejoice, will shout in the God of my salvation.* Ver. 19. *Jehovah the*

Lord is my strength, and makes my feet like the hinds, and causes me to walk along upon my high places." The turning-point is introduced with וַאֲנִי, as is frequently the case in the Psalms. For this exaltation out of the sufferings of this life to believing joy in God, compare Ps. v. 8, xiii. 6, xxxi. 15, etc. עָלַז, a softened form of עָלַץ, to rejoice in God (cf. Ps. v. 12), *i.e.* so that God is the inexhaustible source and infinite sphere of the joy, because He is the God of salvation, and rises up to judgment upon the nations, to procure the salvation of His people (ver. 13). *Elōhē yish'ī* (the God of my salvation), as in Ps. xviii. 47, xxv. 5 (see at Mic. vii. 7). The thoughts of the 19th verse are also formed from reminiscences of Ps. xviii.: the first clause, " the Lord is my strength," from ver. 33. " God, who girdeth me with strength," *i.e.* the Lord gives me strength to overcome all tribulation (cf. Ps. xxvii. 1 and 2 Cor. xii. 9). The next two clauses are from Ps. xviii. 34, " He maketh my feet like hinds'," according to the contracted simile common in Hebrew for "hinds' feet;" and the reference is to the swiftness of foot, which was one of the qualifications of a thorough man of war (2 Sam. i. 23 ; 1 Chron. xii. 8), so as to enable him to make a sudden attack upon the enemy, and pursue him vigorously. Here it is a figurative expression for the fresh and joyous strength acquired in God, which Isaiah calls rising up with eagles' wings (Isa. xl. 29–31). Causing to walk upon the high places of the land, was originally a figure denoting the victorious possession and government of a land. It is so in Deut. xxxii. 13 and xxxiii. 29, from which David has taken the figure in Ps. xviii., though he has altered the high places of the earth into " my high places" (*bâmōthai*). They were the high places upon which the Lord had placed him, by giving him the victory over his enemies. And Habakkuk uses the figurative expression in the same sense, with the simple change of יַעֲמִידֵנִי into יַדְרִכֵנִי after Deut. xxxiii. 29, to substitute for the bestowment of victory the maintenance of victory corresponding to the blessing of Moses. We have therefore to understand *bâmōthai* neither as signifying the high places of the enemy, nor the high places at home, nor high places generally. The figure must be taken as a whole ; and according to this, it simply denotes the ultimate triumph of the people of God over all oppression on the part of the power of the world, altogether apart from the local standing which the kingdom of God will have upon the earth, either by the side of or in antagonism to the kingdom of the world. The prophet prays and speaks throughout the entire ode in the name of the believing congregation. His pain is their pain; his joy their joy. Accordingly he closes his ode by appropriating to himself and all believers the promise which the Lord has given to His people and to David His anointed servant, to express the confident assurance that the God of salvation will keep it, and fulfil it in the approaching attack on the part of the power of the world upon the nation which has been refined by the judgment.

The last words, לַמְנַצֵּחַ בִּנְגִינוֹתַי, do not form part of the contents of the supplicatory ode, but are a subscription answering to the heading in ver. 1, and refer to the use of the ode in the worship of God, and simply differ from the headings לַמְנַצֵּחַ בִּנְגִינוֹת in Ps. iv., vi., liv., lv., lxvii., and lxxvi., through the use of the suffix in בִּנְגִינוֹתַי. Through the words, " *to the president* (of the temple-music, or the conductor) *in accompaniment of my stringed playing,*" the prophet appoints his psalm for use in the public worship of God accompanied by his stringed playing. Hitzig's rendering is grammatically false, " to the conductor of my pieces of music;" for בְּ cannot be used as a periphrasis for the genitive, but when connected with a musical expression, only means *with* or *in the accompaniment of* (בְּ *instrumenti* or *concomitantiæ*). Moreover, נְגִינוֹת does not mean pieces of music, but simply a song, and the playing upon stringed instruments, or the stringed instrument itself (see at Ps. iv.). The first of these renderings gives no suitable sense here, so that there only remains the second, viz. "playing upon stringed instruments." But if the prophet, by using this formula, stipulates that the ode is to be used in the temple, accompanied by stringed instruments, the expression *bingīnōthai*, with *my* stringed playing, affirms that he himself will accompany it with his own playing, from which it has been justly inferred that he was qualified, according to the arrangements of the Israelitish worship, to take part in the public performance of such pieces of music as were suited for public worship, and therefore belonged to the Levites who were entrusted with the conduct of the musical performance of the temple.

ZEPHANIAH

INTRODUCTION.

1. **P**ERSON OF THE PROPHET.—*Zephaniah's* family is traced back in the heading to his book through four members, namely, to his great-great-grandfather *Hezekiah;* from which it has been justly inferred, that inasmuch as the father only is mentioned as a general rule, Hezekiah must have been a celebrated man, and that in all probability the king of that name is intended. For the only other person of such a name mentioned in the earlier history is an Ephraimite called *Y^ehizkiyâh* in 2 Chron. xxviii. 12, and he can hardly be the person intended. The circumstance that Hezekiah is not described as the king of that name by the predicate *hammelekh* or *melekh Y^ehûdâh,* furnishes no decided argument against this assumption, but may probably be explained on the ground that the predicate "king of Judah" follows immediately afterwards in connection with Josiah's name. There is still less force in the objection, that in the genealogy of the kings only two generations occur between Hezekiah and Josiah, inasmuch as Manasseh reigned for fifty-five years, that is to say, for nearly two generations. The name Zephaniah (*Ts^ephanyâh*), *i.e.* he whom Jehovah hides or shelters, not "*speculator et arcanorum Dei cognitor*," as Jerome explains it according to an erroneous derivation from *tsâphâh* instead of *tsâphan,* occurs again as the name of a priest (Jer. xxi. 1, xxix. 25, etc.), as well as of other persons (cf. Zech. vi. 10, 14, 1 Chron. vi. 21). The LXX. write it Σοφονίας, *Sophonias,* according to their usual custom of expressing צ by σ, and the Sheva by a short vowel which is regulated by the full vowel that follows; they have also changed the *a* into *o,* as in the case of Γοδολίου for *G^edalyâh* in ch. i. 1. Nothing further is known concerning the prophet's life. The state-

ment in Ps. Doroth. and Ps. Epiph., that he sprang "from the
tribe of Simeon, from the mountain of Sarabathá" (al. Baratha
or Sabartharam), is quite worthless. The date at which he
lived is determined by the statement in the heading to his
book, to the effect that he prophesied under king Josiah the
son of Amos, who reigned from 641 to 610 B.C. This agrees
both with the place assigned to his book in the series of the
minor prophets, namely, between Habakkuk and Haggai, and
also by the contents of his prophecies. According to ch. ii.
13 sqq., where he predicts the destruction of the kingdom of
Asshur and the city of Nineveh, the Assyrian empire was still
in existence in his time, and Nineveh was not yet conquered,
which took place, according to our discussions on Nahum
(p. 44 sqq.), at the earliest, in the closing years of Josiah's reign,
and possibly not till after his death. Moreover, his description
of the moral depravity which prevailed in Jerusalem coincided
in many respects with that of Jeremiah, whose labours as a
prophet commenced in the thirteenth year of Josiah. Along
with the worship of Jehovah (ch. i. 5; cf. Jer. vi. 20), he speaks
of idolatry (ch. i. 4, 5; cf. Jer. vii. 17, 18), of false swearing
by Jehovah, and swearing by the idols (ch. i. 5b; Jer. v. 2,
vii. 9, and v. 7, xii. 16), of the wicked treatment of the *thorâh*
(ch. iii. 4; Jer. viii. 8, 9), of the fruitlessness of all the admonitions that have hitherto been addressed to Judah (ch. iii. 2;
Jer. ii. 30, vii. 28), and of the deep moral corruption that has
pervaded all ranks—the royal family, the princes, the prophets,
and the priests (ch. i. 4, 8, 9, iii. 3, 4; cf. Jer. ii. 8, 26). He
describes the nation as a shameless one (ch. ii. 1, iii. 5; cf.
Jer. iii. 3, vi. 15, viii. 12), and Jerusalem as a rebellious city
(מוֹרָאָה, ch. iii. 1; cf. Jer. iv. 17, v. 23), as stained with blood
and the abominations of idolatry (ch. iii. 1; cf. Jer. ii. 22, 23,
34), and as oppressive towards widows and orphans, and with
its houses full of unrighteous possessions (ch. iii. 1 and i. 9;
cf. Jer. v. 27, 28, vi. 6).

The only point open to dispute is whether Zephaniah's
prophecy belonged to the first or the second half of the thirty-
first year of Josiah's reign. Whilst Ewald supposes that
Zephaniah wrote at a time when "not even any preparation
had yet been made in Jerusalem for that important and thorough
reformation of religion which king Josiah attempted with such

energetic decision and such good results in the second half of his reign" (2 Kings xxii. xxiii.), most of the other commentators infer from ch. i. 4, where the extermination of the remnant of Baal is predicted, and with greater propriety, that Josiah's reformation of religion had already commenced, and that the outward predominance of idolatry was already broken down when Zephaniah uttered his prophecies. For the prophet could not well speak of a remnant of Baal before the abolition of the idolatry introduced into the kingdom by Manasseh and Amon had really commenced. But Ewald and Hävernick reply to this, that the prophet announces that even the remnant and the name of idolatry are to disappear, so that nothing at all will remain, and that this presupposes that in the time of the prophet not only the remnant of the worship of Baal was in existence, but the Baal-worship itself. But however correct the former remark may be, there is no ground for the conclusion drawn from it. The destruction of Baal, even to the very remnant and name, does not warrant the assumption that the worship of Baal still existed in undiminished power and extent at the time when the threat was uttered, but could be fully explained if there were only remnants of it left to which the expression "remnant of Baal" primarily refers. If nothing had been hitherto done for the abolition of idolatry, Zephaniah would certainly have spoken differently and more strongly than he does in ch. i. 4, 5, concerning the abomination of it. If, for example, according to ch. i. 5, sacrifices were still offered upon the roofs to the army of heaven, the existence of the Jehovah-worship is also presupposed in the reproof in ch. iii. iv., "the priests pollute the sanctuary;" and in the words "them that swear by Jehovah, and swear by their king" (ch. i. 5), Jehovah-worship and idolatry are mentioned as existing side by side. We cannot therefore regard the opinion, that "throughout the whole of the prophecy there is no trace of any allusion to Josiah's reformation," as a well-founded one. According to the more precise account given in the Chronicles, Josiah commenced the reformation of worship in the twelfth year of his reign (2 Chron. xxxiv. 3–7), and in the eighteenth year he had the temple repaired. It was then that the book of the law was discovered, the reading of which affected the king so much, that he not only appointed a solemn passover, but after the feast was over had all the remaining traces of idolatry in Jerusalem and Judah completely obliterated (2 Kings xxiii. 24). Now, as Zephaniah's prophecy presupposes the maintenance of the temple-worship, it can only have been uttered after the purification of the temple from the abominations of idolatry that were practised in its courts, and in all probability was not uttered till after the completion of the repairs of the temple, and the celebration of the solemn passover in the eighteenth year of Josiah's reign. The time cannot be determined more exactly. The threat in ch. i. 8, that the judgment shall fall upon the princes, and even upon the king's sons, does not warrant us in concluding that the sons of Josiah had reached a sufficient age to have occasioned the announcement of punishment, by sinful acts for which they themselves were accountable, which would not apply to the twelfth year of the king's reign, when Jehoiakim was six years old, Jehoahaz four years, and when Zedekiah was not yet born, but only to the eighteenth year, when Jehoiakim had reached his twelfth year and Jehoahaz his tenth. For "the king's sons" are not necessarily the sons of the reigning sovereign only, but may also include the sons of the deceased kings, Manasseh and Amon; and this general threat of judgment announced against all ranks may be understood without hesitation as relating to all princes or persons of royal blood. The character of the prophecy as a whole also furnishes no decisive points bearing upon the question, whether it was uttered or composed before or after the eighteenth year of Josiah's reign. For the tendency to promote the work of religious reformation which had already commenced, by means of strong prophetic encouragements, in order that it might lead to a division, and therefore to decision for the Lord (ch. ii. 1–3), which Hävernick and several other commentators claim for our prophecy, can no more be proved to exist in the writing before us, than the conjecture expressed by Delitzsch in Herzog's *Cyclopædia*, that the prophet did not come forward with his threat till the efforts of the pious king to exterminate utterly the worship of Baal had reached their highest point, without securing their end; inasmuch as it is in accordance with the position of things and the character of prophecy, that when human efforts have done their utmost without securing the desired result, Jehovah interposes and threatens what still remains of Baal with His outstretched arm of punishment. For however correct the remark (of Delitzsch) may be, that in the form in which the prophecy lies before us it contains no trace of any intention to promote the work taken in hand by the king, and that the state of the nation as reflected therein is not a progressive one in process of reformation, but appears rather to be a finished one and ripe for judgment; the latter only applies to the mass of the nation, who were incorrigible, and therefore ripe for judgment, and does not preclude the existence of a better kernel, to which the prophet could still preach repentance, and cry, " Seek ye the Lord, seek humility; perhaps ye may be hidden in the day of Jehovah" (ch. ii. 3). But the nation was in this state not only after the eighteenth year of Josiah's reign, but also before it; and the efforts of the pious king to exterminate idolatry, and to raise and revive the worship of Jehovah, could effect no further alteration in this, than that individuals out of the corrupt mass were converted, and were saved from destruction. The measure of the sin, which was inevitably followed by the destruction of the kingdom of Judah, had been already filled by Manasseh, and Josiah's reformation could only effect a postponement, and not avert the threatened judgment (compare 2 Kings xxi. 10-16 with xxiii. 26, 27).

2. THE BOOK OF ZEPHANIAH does not contain two or three prophetic addresses, but the quintessence of the oral proclamations of the prophet condensed into one lengthened prophecy, commencing with the threat of judgment (ch. i.), proceeding to an exhortation to repentance (ch. ii.–iii. 8), and concluding with a promise of the salvation which would flourish for the remnant of Israel after the termination of the judgment (ch. iii. 9-20). This is arranged in three sections. The first section consists of the first chapter; the second reaches from ch. ii. 1 to ch. iii. 8; and the third comprises ch. iii. 9–20. This division is indicated by both the contents and the form of the announcement: by the contents, since the first two parts threaten the judgment and assign the reason, whilst the third follows with the promise; by the form, inasmuch as the thought in ch. i. 18, " All the earth shall be devoured by the fire of His jealousy," is repeated as a *refrain* in ch. iii. 8, and the *hōi* in

ch. ii. 5 answers to the *hōi* in ch. iii. 1, the former announcing the judgment upon the nations, the latter the judgment upon Jerusalem, which assigns the motive for the summons to repentance in ch. ii. 1–4. Zephaniah proclaims the judgment upon the whole earth, upon all the heathen nations, and upon Judah and Jerusalem, in the following order: In the first part of his prophecy he threatens the near approach of the judgment upon the whole earth (ch. i. 2–7) and upon Judah (ch. i. 8–13), and depicts its terrible character (ch. i. 14–18); and in the second part (ch. ii.–iii. 8) he exhorts the people to repent, and the righteous to persevere (ch. ii. 1–3), and assigns a reason for this exhortation, by announcing that the Lord will judge the heathen nations both near at hand and far off for the reproach which they have cast upon His people, and by destroying their power lead them to reverence His name (ch. ii. 4–15), and will also bring His righteousness to light in Jerusalem and Judah by the destruction of the ungodly (ch. iii. 1–8). Then (the announcement of salvation commences thus in ch. iii. 9, 10) will the nations serve Jehovah with one accord, and lead His scattered people to Him. The remnant of Israel will be made into a humble nation of God by the destruction of the wicked one out of the midst of it; and being sheltered by its God, it will rejoice in undisturbed happiness, and be exalted to "a name and praise" among all the nations of the earth (ch. iii. 11–20).

Zephaniah's prophecy has a more general character, embracing both judgment and salvation in their totality, so as to form one complete picture. It not only commences with the announcement of a universal judgment upon the whole world, out of which the judgment rises that will fall upon Judah on account of its sins, and upon the world of nations on account of its hostility to the people of Jehovah; but it treats throughout of the great and terrible day of Jehovah, on which the fire of the wrath of God consumes the whole earth (ch. i. 14–18, ii. 2, iii. 8). But the judgment, as a revelation of the wrath of God on account of the general corruption of the world, does not form the centre of gravity or the sole object of the whole of the predictions of our prophet. The end and goal at which they aim are rather the establishment of divine righteousness in the earth, and the judgment is simply the means and the way by which this the aim of all the development of the world's history is to be realized. This comes clearly out in the second and third sections. Jehovah will manifest Himself terribly to the nations, to destroy all the gods of the earth, that all the islands of the nations may worship Him (ch. ii. 11). By pouring out His wrath upon nations and kingdoms, He will turn to the peoples a pure lip, so that they will call upon His name and serve Him with one shoulder (iii. 8, 9). The idolaters, the wicked, and the despisers of God will be destroyed out of Judah and Jerusalem, that the righteousness of Jehovah may come to the day (iii. 1–7). The humble, who do God's righteousness, are to seek Jehovah, to strive after righteousness and humility, and to wait for the Lord, for the day when He will arise, to procure for Himself worshippers of His name among the nations through the medium of the judgment, and to gather together His dispersed people, and make the remnant of Israel into a sanctified and blessed people of God (iii. 11–20).

It is in this comprehensive character of his prophecy that we find the reason why Zephaniah neither names, nor minutely describes, the executors of the judgment upon Judah, and even in the description of the judgment to be inflicted upon the heathen nations (ch. ii. 4–15) simply individualizes the idea of "*all* the nations of the earth," by naming the nearer and more remote nations to the west and east, the south and north of Judah. He does not predict either this or that particular judgment, but extends and completes in comprehensive generality the judgment, by which God maintains His kingdom on the earth. This peculiarity in Zephaniah's prophecy has been correctly pointed out by Bucer (in his commentary, 1528), when he says of the book before us: " If any one wishes all the secret oracles of the prophets to be given in a brief compendium, let him read through this brief Zephaniah." There are many respects in which Zephaniah links his prophecy to those of the earlier prophets, both in subject-matter and expression ; not, however, by resuming those prophecies of theirs which had not been fulfilled, or were not exhausted, during the period of the Assyrian judgment upon the nations, and announcing a fresh and more perfect fulfilment of them by the Chaldæans, but by reproducing in a compendious form the fundamental thoughts

of judgment and salvation which are common to all the prophets, that his contemporaries may lay them to heart; in
doing which he frequently appropriates striking words and
pregnant expressions taken from his predecessors, and applies
them to his own purpose. Thus, for example, the expression
in ch. i. 7 is compiled from earlier prophetic words : " Be silent
before the Lord Jehovah (from Hab. ii. 20), for the day of
Jehovah is at hand (Joel i. 15 and others); for Jehovah has
prepared a sacrificial slaughter (Isa. xxxiv. 6), has consecrated
His invited ones (Isa. xiii. 3)." (For further remarks on this
point, see my *Lehrbuch der Einleitung*, p. 307.) In this respect Zephaniah opens the series of the less original prophets
of the Chaldæan age of judgment, who rest more upon the
earlier types; whilst in more material respects his predecessor
Habakkuk acted as pioneer to the prophets of this period.

Ewald's view bears evidence of a strong misapprehension
of the nature of prophecy generally, and of the special peculiarities of the prophecy before us. " The book of Zephaniah,"
he says, " must have originated in a great commotion among the
nations, which threw all the kingdoms round about Judah far
and wide into a state of alarm, and also threatened to be very
dangerous to Jerusalem,"—namely, on account of the invasion
of Upper and Hither Asia by the Scythians, which is mentioned
by Herodotus in i. 15, 103-6, iv. 10 sqq. For there is not a
trace discoverable in the whole book of any great commotion
among the nations. The few allusions to the fact that a
hostile army will execute the judgment upon Jerusalem and
Judah (in ch. i. 12, 13, 16, and iii. 15) do not presuppose anything of the kind; and in the threatening of the judgment
upon Philistia, Moab and Ammon, Cush, and Asshur with
Nineveh, Jehovah only is named as executing it (ch. ii. 4-15).
Moreover, neither Herodotus nor the historical books of the
Old Testament mention any conquest of Jerusalem by the
Scythians; whilst, even according to the account given by
Herodotus, the Scythian hordes neither destroyed Nineveh nor
made war upon the Cushites (Æthiopians), as would be predicted by Zephaniah (ii. 12-15), if he had the Scythians in
his eye; and lastly, Jeremiah, upon whose prophecies Ewald,
Hitzig, and Bertheau have principally based their Scythian
hypothesis, knows nothing of the Scythians, but simply expects

and announces that the judgment upon Judah and Jerusalem will come from the Chaldæans. Zephaniah found the historical occasion for his prophecy in the moral depravity of Judah and Jerusalem, in the depth to which his people had fallen in idolatry, and in their obstinate resistance to all the efforts made by the prophets and the pious king Josiah to stem the corruption, and thus avert from Judah the judgment threatened even by Moses and the earlier prophets, of the dispersion of the whole nation among the heathen. On the ground of the condition of his people, and the prophetic testimonies of his predecessors, Zephaniah, under the impulse of the Spirit of God, predicted the near approach of the great and terrible day of Jehovah, which came upon Judah and the heathen nations far and wide through the instrumentality of the Chaldæans. For Nebuchadnezzar laid the foundation of the empire which devastated Judah, destroyed Jerusalem with its temple, and led the degenerate covenant nation into exile. This empire was perpetuated in the empires of the Persians, the Macedonians, and the Romans, which arose after it and took its place, and in whose power Judah continued, even after the return of one portion of the exiles to the land of their fathers, and after the restoration of the temple and the city of Jerusalem during the Persian rule; so that the city of God was trodden down by the heathen even to the time of the destruction of Jerusalem by the Romans, whereby the desolation of the holy land, which continues to the present day, was produced, and the dispersion of the Jews to all quarters of the globe accomplished, and both land and people were laid under the ban, from which Israel can only be liberated by its conversion to Jesus Christ, the Saviour of all nations, and from which it will assuredly be redeemed by virtue of the promise of the faithful covenant God. For the exegetical literature, see my *Lehrbuch der Einleitung*, pp. 305-6.

EXPOSITION.

THE JUDGMENT UPON ALL THE WORLD, AND UPON JUDAH IN PARTICULAR.—Chap. i.

The judgment will come upon all the world (vers. 2, 3), and will destroy all the idolaters and despisers of God in Judah and Jerusalem (vers. 4–7), and fall heavily upon sinners of every rank (vers. 8–13). The terrible day of the Lord will burst irresistibly upon all the inhabitants of the earth (vers. 14–18).

Ver. 1 contains the heading, which has been explained in the introduction. Vers. 2 and 3 form the preface.—Ver. 2. "*I will sweep, sweep away everything from the face of the earth, is the saying of Jehovah.* Ver. 3. *I will sweep away man and cattle, sweep away the fowls of heaven, and the fishes of the sea, and the offences with the sinners, and I cut off men from the face of the earth, is the saying of Jehovah.*" The announcement of the judgment upon the whole earth not only serves to sharpen the following threat of judgment upon Judah and Jerusalem in this sense, "Because Jehovah judges the whole world, He will punish the apostasy of Judah all the more;" but the judgment upon the whole world forms an integral part of his prophecy, which treats more fully of the execution of the judgment in and upon Judah, simply because Judah forms the kingdom of God, which is to be purified from its dross by judgment, and led on towards the end of its divine calling. As Zephaniah here opens the judgment awaiting Judah with an announcement of a judgment upon the whole world, so does he assign the reason for his exhortation to repentance in ch. ii., by showing that all nations will succumb to the judgment; and then announces in ch. iii. 9 sqq., as the fruit of the judgment, the conversion of the nations to Jehovah, and the glorification of the kingdom of God. The way to salvation leads through judgment, not only for the world with its enmity against God, but for the degenerate theocracy also. It is only through judgment that the sinful world can be renewed and glorified. The verb אָסֵף, the *hiphil* of *sûph*, is strengthened by the inf. abs. אָסֹף, which is formed from the verb אָסַף, a verb of kindred meaning. *Sūph* and *'âsaph* signify to take away, to sweep away, *hiph.* to put an end, to destroy. *Kōl*, everything, is specified in ver. 3 : men and cattle, the birds of heaven, and the fishes of the sea ; the verb *'âsēph* being repeated before the two principal members. This specification stands in unmistakeable relation to the threatening of God : to destroy all creatures for the wickedness of men, from man to cattle, and to creeping things, and even to the fowls of the heaven (Gen. vi. 7). By playing upon this threat, Zephaniah intimates that the approaching judgment will be as general over the earth, and as terrible, as the judgment of the flood. Through this judgment God will remove or destroy the offences (stumbling-blocks) together with the sinners. אֵת before הָרְשָׁעִים cannot be the sign of the accusative, but can only be a preposition, with, together with, since the objects to אָסֵף are all introduced without the sign of the accusative ; and, moreover, if אֶת־הֽרֹשׁ׳ were intended for an accusative, the copula *Vâv* would not be omitted. *Hammakhshēlôth* does not mean houses about to fall (Hitzig), which neither suits the context nor can be grammatically sustained, since even in Isa. iii. 6 *hammakhshēlâh* is not the fallen house, but the state brought to ruin by the sin of the people ; and *makhshēlâh* is that against which or through which a person meets with a fall. *Makhshēlōth* are all the objects of coarser and more refined idolatry, not merely the idolatrous images, but all the works of wickedness, like τὰ σκάνδαλα in Matt. xiii. 41. The judgment, however, applies chiefly to men, *i.e.* to sinners, and hence in the last clause the destruction of men from off the earth is especially mentioned. The irrational creation is only subject to φθορά, on account of and through the sin of men (Rom. viii. 20 sqq.).

Vers. 4–7. The judgment coming upon the whole earth with all its inhabitants will fall especially upon Judah and Jerusalem. Ver. 4. "*And I stretch my hand over Judah, and over all the inhabitants of Jerusalem, and cut off from this place the remnant of Baal, the name of the consecrated servants, together with the priests.* Ver. 5. *And those who worship the army of heaven upon the roofs, and the worshippers who swear to Jehovah, and who swear by their king.* Ver. 6. *And those who draw back from Jehovah, and who did not seek Jehovah, and did not inquire*

for Him." God stretches out His hand (יָד) or His arm (זְרוֹעַ)
to smite the ungodly with judgments (compare ch. vi. 6, Deut.
iv. 34, v. 15, with Isa. v. 25, ix. 11, 16, 20, x. 4, xiv. 26 sqq.).
Through the judgment upon Judah and Jerusalem He will cut
off שְׁאָר הַבַּעַל, the remnant of Baal, *i.e.* all that remains of Baal
and of idolatry; for Baal or the Baal-worship stands *per synecdochen* for idolatry of every kind (see at Hos. ii. 10). The
emphasis lies upon "the remnant," all that still exists of the
Baal-worship or idolatry, even to the very last remnant; so that
the emphasis presupposes that the extermination has already
begun, that the worship of Baal no longer exists in undiminished force and extent. It must not be limited, however,
to the complete abolition of the outward or grosser idolatry,
but includes the utter extermination of the grosser as well as
the more refined Baal-worship. That the words should be so
understood is required by the parallel clause : the name of the
consecrated servants together with the priests. *K^emârîm* are
not prophets of Baal, but, as in 2 Kings xxiii. 5 and Hos. x. 5,
the priests appointed by the kings of Judah for the worship of
the high places and the idolatrous worship of Jehovah (for the
etymology of the word, see at 2 Kings xxiii. 5). The *kōhănîm*,
as distinguished from these, are idolatrous priests in the stricter
sense of the word (*i.e.* those who conducted the literal idolatry).
The names of both the idolatrous priests of Jehovah and the
literal priests of the idols are to be cut off, so that not only
the persons referred to will disappear, but even their names
will be heard no more. Along with the idols and their priests,
the worshippers of idols are also to be destroyed. Just as in
ver. 4 two classes of priests are distinguished, so in ver. 5 are
two classes of worshippers, viz. (1) the star-worshippers, and
(2) those who tried to combine the worship of Jehovah and
the worship of idols; and to these a third class is added in
ver. 6. The worship of the stars was partly Baal-worship, the
sun, moon, and stars being worshipped as the bearers of the
powers of nature worshipped in Baal and Asherah (see at
2 Kings xxiii. 5); and partly Sabæism or pure star-worship, the
stars being worshipped as the originators of all growth and
decay in nature, and the leaders and regulators of all sublunary
things (see at 2 Kings xxi. 3). The worship took place upon
the roofs, *i.e.* on altars erected upon the flat roofs of the houses,

chiefly by the burning of incense (Jer. xix. 13), but also by the offering of sacrifices (2 Kings xxiii. 12 ; see the comm. *in loc.*). "They offered the sacrifices upon the roofs, that they might be the better able to see the stars in the heavens" (Theodoret). Along with the star-worshippers as the representatives of literal idolatry, Zephaniah mentions as a second class the worshippers who swear partly to Jehovah, and partly by their king, *i.e.* who go limping on two sides (1 Kings xviii. 21), or try to combine the worship of Jehovah with that of Baal. *Malkâm*, their king, is Baal, who is distinctly called king in the inscriptions (see Movers, *Phönizier*, i. pp. 171–2), and not the "earthly king of the nation," as Hitzig has erroneously interpreted the Masoretic text, in consequence of which he proposes to read *milkōm*, *i.e.* Moloch. נִשְׁבַּע with לְ signifies to take an oath to Jehovah, *i.e.* to bind one's self on oath to His service; whereas נִשְׁבַּע with בְּ (to swear by a person) means to call upon Him as God when taking an oath. The difference between the two expressions answers exactly to the religious attitude of the men in question, who pretended to be worshippers of Jehovah, and yet with every asseveration took the name of Baal into their mouth. In ver. 6 we have not two further classes mentioned, viz. "the vicious and the irreligious," as Hitzig supposes; but the persons here described form only one single class. Retiring behind Jehovah, drawing back from Him, turning the back upon God, is just the same as not seeking Jehovah, or not inquiring after Him. The persons referred to are the religiously indifferent, those who do not trouble themselves about God, the despisers of God.

This judgment will speedily come. Ver. 7. "*Be silent before the Lord Jehovah! For the day of Jehovah is near, for Jehovah has prepared a slaying of sacrifice, He has consecrated His called.*" The command, "Be silent before the Lord," which is formed after Hab. ii. 20, and with which the prophet summons to humble, silent submission to the judgment of God, serves to confirm the divine threat in vers. 2–6. The reason for the commanding Hush! (keep silence) is given in the statement that the day of Jehovah is close at hand (compare Joel i. 15), and that God has already appointed the executors of the judgment. The last two clauses of the verse are formed from reminiscences taken from Isaiah. The description of the judg-

ment as *zebhach*, a sacrifice, is taken from Isa. xxxiv. 6 (cf.
Jer. xlvi. 10 and Ezek. xxxix. 17). The sacrifice which God
has prepared is the Jewish nation; those who are invited to
this sacrificial meal ("called," 1 Sam. ix. 13) are not beasts
and birds of prey, as in Ezek. xxxix. 17, but the nations which
He has consecrated to war that they may consume Jacob (Jer.
x. 25). The extraordinary use of the verb *hiqdīsh* (consecrated)
in this connection may be explained from Isa. xiii. 3, where the
nations appointed to make war against Babel are called *mᵉqud-
dâshīm*, the sanctified of Jehovah (cf. Jer. xxii. 7).

Vers. 8–13. The judgment will fall with equal severity upon
the idolatrous and sinners of every rank (vers. 8–11), and no one
in Jerusalem will be able to save himself from it (vers. 12, 13).
In three double verses Zephaniah brings out three classes of
men who differ in their civil position, and also in their attitude
towards God, as those who will be smitten by the judgment:
viz. (1) the princes, *i.e.* the royal family and superior servants
of the king, who imitate the customs of foreigners, and oppress
the people (vers. 8, 9); (2) the merchants, who have grown
rich through trade and usury (vers. 10, 11); (3) the irreligious
debauchees (vers. 12, 13). The first of these he threatens
with visitation. Ver. 8. "*And it will come to pass in the day
of Jehovah's sacrifice, that I visit the princes and the king's sons,
and all who clothe themselves in foreign dress. Ver. 9. And I
visit every one who leaps over the threshold on that day, those
who fill the Lord's house with violence and deceit.*" The enumeration of those who are exposed to the judgment commences
with the *princes, i.e.* the heads of the tribes and families, who
naturally filled the higher offices of state; and the *king's sons*,
not only the sons of Josiah, who were still very young (see
the Introduction, p. 120), but also the sons of the deceased
kings, the royal princes generally. The king himself is not
named, because Josiah walked in the ways of the Lord, and
on account of his piety and fear of God was not to live to see
the outburst of the judgment (2 Kings xxii. 19, 20; 2 Chron.
xxxiv. 27, 28). The princes and king's sons are threatened
with punishment, not on account of the high position which
they occupied in the state, but on account of the ungodly disposition which they manifested. For since the clauses which
follow not only mention different classes of men, but also point

out the sins of the different classes, we must also expect this
in the case of the princes and the king's sons, and consequently
must refer the dressing in foreign clothes, which is condemned
in the second half of the verse, to the princes and king's sons
also, and understand the word "all" as relating to those who
imitated their manners without being actually princes or king's
sons. *Malbūsh nokhrī* (foreign dress) does not refer to the
clothes worn by the idolaters in their idolatrous worship (Chald.,
Rashi, Jer.), nor to the dress prohibited in the law, viz. "women
dressing in men's clothes, or men dressing in women's clothes"
(Deut. xxii. 5, 11), as Grotius maintains, nor to clothes stolen
from the poor, or taken from them as pledges; but, as *nokhrī*
signifies a foreigner, to foreign dress. Drusius has already
pointed this out, and explains the passage as follows: "I think
that the reference is to all those who betrayed the levity of
their minds by wearing foreign dress. For I have no doubt
that in that age some copied the Egyptians in their style of
dress, and others the Babylonians, according as they favoured
the one nation or the other. The prophet therefore says, that
even those who adopted foreign habits, and conformed themselves to the customs of the victorious nation, would not be
exempt." The last allusion is certainly untenable, and it
would be more correct to say with Strauss: "The prophets did
not care for externals of this kind, but it was evident to them
that 'as the dress, so the heart;' that is to say, the clothes were
witnesses in their esteem of the foreign inclinations of the
heart." In ver. 9a many commentators find a condemnation
of an idolatrous use of foreign customs; regarding the leaping
over the threshold as an imitation of the priests of Dagon,
who adopted the custom, according to 1 Sam. v. 5, of leaping
over the threshold when they entered the temple of that idol.
But an imitation of that custom could only take place in temples
of Dagon, and it appears perfectly inconceivable that it should
have been transferred to the threshold of the king's palace,
unless the king was regarded as an incarnation of Dagon,—a
thought which could never enter the minds of Israelitish idolaters, since even the Philistian kings did not hold themselves to be
incarnations of their idols. If we turn to the second hemistich,
the thing condemned is the filling of their masters' houses with
violence; and this certainly does not stand in any conceivable

relation to that custom of the priests of Dagon; and yet the
words " who fill," etc., are proved to be explanatory of the first
half of the verse, by the fact that the second clause is appended
without the copula *Vav*, and without the repetition of the preposition עַל. Now, if a fresh sin were referred to here, the
copula *Vav*, at all events, could not have been omitted. We
must therefore understand by the leaping over the threshold a
violent and sudden rushing into houses to steal the property of
strangers (Calvin, Ros., Ewald, Strauss, and others), so that
the allusion is to " dishonourable servants of the king, who
thought that they could best serve their master by extorting
treasures from their dependants by violence and fraud" (Ewald).
אֲדֹנֵיהֶם, of their lord, *i.e.* of the king, not " of their lords:" the
plural is in the *pluralis majestatis*, as in 1 Sam. xxvi. 16, 2 Sam.
ii. 5, etc.

Even the usurers will not escape the judgment. Ver. 10.
" *And it will come to pass in that day, is the saying of Jehovah,
voice of the cry from the fish-gate, and howling from the lower
city, and great destruction from the hills.* Ver. 11. *Howl,
inhabitants of the mortar, for all the people of Canaan are destroyed ; cut off are all that are laden with silver.*" In order to
express the thought that the judgment will not spare any one
class of the population, Zephaniah depicts the lamentation
which will arise from all parts of the city. קוֹל צְעָקָה, voice of
the cry, *i.e.* a loud cry of anguish will arise or resound. The
fish-gate (according to Neh. iii. 3, xii. 39; cf. 2 Chron. xxxiii. 14)
was in the eastern portion of the wall which bounded the lower
city on the north side (for further details on this point, see at
Neh. iii. 3). הַמִּשְׁנֶה (= הָעִיר מִשְׁנֶה, Neh. xi. 9), the second part
or district of the city, is the lower city upon the hill Acra (see
at 2 Kings xxii. 14). *Shebher, fragor,* does not mean a cry of
murder, but the breaking to pieces of what now exists, not
merely the crashing fall of the buildings, like *za'ăqath shebher*
in Isa. xv. 5, the cry uttered at the threatening danger of utter
destruction. In order to heighten the terrors of the judgment,
there is added to the crying and howling of the men the tumult
caused by the conquest of the city. "From the hills," *i.e.*
" not from Zion and Moriah," but from the hills surrounding
the lower city, viz. Bezetha, Gareb (Jer. xxxi. 39), and others.
For Zion, the citadel of Jerusalem, is evidently thought of as

the place where the howling of the men and the noise of the
devastation, caused by the enemy pressing in from the north
and north-west, are heard. *Hammakhtēsh*, the mortar (Prov.
xxvii. 22), which is the name given in Judg. xv. 19 to a hollow
place in a rock, is used here to denote a locality in Jerusalem,
most probably the depression which ran down between Acra
on the west and Bezetha and Moriah on the east, as far as the
fountain of Siloah, and is called by Josephus " the cheese-
maker's valley," and by the present inhabitants *el-Wâd, i.e.* the
valley, and also the mill-valley. The name " mortar " was probably coined by Zephaniah, to point to the fate of the merchants
and men of money who lived there. They who dwell there
shall howl, because " all the people of Canaan " are destroyed.
These are not Canaanitish or Phœnician merchants, but Judæan
merchants, who resembled the Canaanites or Phœnicians in
their general business (see at Hos. xii. 8), and had grown rich
through trade and usury. *Netīl keseph*, laden with silver.

The debauchees and rioters generally will also not remain
free from punishment. Ver. 12. " *And at that time it will come
to pass, that I will search Jerusalem with candles, and visit the
men who lie upon their lees, who say in their heart, Jehovah does
no good, and no evil.* Ver. 13. *Their goods will become plunder,
and their houses desolation : they will build houses, and not dwell
(therein), and plant vineyards, and not drink their wine.*" God
will search Jerusalem with candles, to bring out the irreligious debauchees out of their hiding-places in their houses,
and punish them. The visitation is effected by the enemies
who conquer Jerusalem. Jerome observes on this passage :
"Nothing will be allowed to escape unpunished. If we read the
history of *Josephus*, we shall find it written there, that princes
and priests, and mighty men, were dragged even out of the
sewers, and caves, and pits, and tombs, in which they had hidden
themselves from fear of death." Now, although what is stated
here refers to the conquest of Jerusalem by Titus, there can
be no doubt that similar things occurred at the Chaldæan conquest. The expression to search with candles (cf. Luke xv. 8)
is a figure denoting the most minute search of the dwellings
and hiding-places of the despisers of God. These are described
as men who sit drawn together upon their lees (קָפָא, lit. to draw
one's self together, to coagulate). The figure is borrowed from

old wine, which has been left upon its lees and not drawn off, and which, when poured into other vessels, retains its flavour, and does not alter its odour (Jer. xlviii. 11), and denotes perseverance or confirmation in moral and religious indifference, "both external quiet, and carelessness, idleness, and spiritual insensibility in the enjoyment not only of the power and possessions bestowed upon them, but also of the pleasures of sin and the worst kinds of lust" (Marck). Good wine, when it remains for a long time upon its lees, becomes stronger; but bad wine becomes harsher and thicker. *Sh^emârîm*, lees, do not denote "sins in which the ungodly are almost stupefied" (Jerome), or "splendour which so deprives a man of his senses that there is nothing left either pure or sincere" (Calvin), but "the impurity of sins, which were associated in the case of these men with external good" (Marck). In the carnal repose of their earthly prosperity, they said in their heart, *i.e.* they thought within themselves, there is no God who rules and judges the world; everything takes place by chance, or according to dead natural laws. They did not deny the existence of God, but in their character and conduct they denied the working of the living God in the world, placing Jehovah on the level of the dead idols, who did neither good nor harm (Isa. xli. 23; Jer. x. 5), whereby they really denied the being of God.[1] To these God will show Himself as the ruler and judge of the world, by giving up their goods (*chēlâm, opes eorum*) to plunder, so that they will experience the truth of the punishments denounced in His word against the despisers of His name (compare Lev. xxvi. 32, 33, Deut. xxviii. 30, 39, and the similar threats in Amos v. 11, Mic. vi. 15).

Vers. 14–18. This judgment will not be delayed. To terrify the self-secure sinners out of their careless rest, Zephaniah now carries out still further the thought only hinted at in ver. 7 of the near approach and terrible character of the

---

[1] "For neither the majesty of God, nor His government or glory, consists in any imaginary splendour, but in those attributes which so meet together in Him that they cannot be severed from His essence. It is the property of God to govern the world, to take care of the human race, to distinguish between good and evil, to relieve the wretched, to punish all crimes, to restrain unjust violence. And if any one would deprive God of these, he would leave nothing but an idol."—CALVIN.

judgment. Ver. 14. "*The great day of Jehovah is near, near and hasting greatly. Hark! the day of Jehovah, bitterly crieth the hero there.* Ver. 15. *A day of fury is this day, a day of anguish and pressure, a day of devastation and desert, a day of darkness and gloom, a day of cloud and cloudy night.* Ver. 16. *A day of the trumpet and battering, over the fortified cities and high battlements.*" The day of Jehovah is called "the great day" with reference to its effects, as in Joel ii. 11. The emphasis lies primarily, however, upon the *qârōbh* (is near), which is therefore repeated and strengthened by מַהֵר מְאֹד. מַהֵר is not a *piel* participle with the *Mem* dropped, but an adjective form, which has sprung out of the adverbial use of the inf. abs. (cf. Ewald, § 240, *e*). In the second hemistich the terrible character of this day is described. קוֹל before *yōm Yᵉhōvâh* (the day of Jehovah), at the head of an interjectional clause, has almost grown into an interjection (see at Isa. xiii. 4). The hero cries bitterly, because he cannot save himself, and must succumb to the power of the foe. *Shâm, adv. loci*, has not a temporal signification even here, but may be explained from the fact that in connection with the day the prophet is thinking of the field of battle, on which the hero perishes while fighting. In order to depict more fully the terrible character of this day, Zephaniah crowds together in vers. 15 and 16 all the words supplied by the language to describe the terrors of the judgment. He first of all designates it as *yōm ʿebhrâh*, the day of the overflowing wrath of God (cf. ver. 18); then, according to the effect which the pouring out of the wrath of God produces upon men, as a day of distress and pressure (cf. Job xv. 24), of devastation (שֹׁאָה and מְשׁוֹאָה combined, as in Job xxxviii. 27, xxx. 3), and of the darkest cloudy night, after Joel ii. 2; and lastly, in ver. 16, indicating still more closely the nature of the judgment, as a day of the trumpet and the trumpet-blast, *i.e.* on which the clangour of the war-trumpets will be heard over all the fortifications and castles, and the enemy will attack, take, and destroy the fortified places amidst the blast of trumpets (cf. Amos ii. 2). *Pinnōth* are the corners and battlements of the walls of the fortifications (2 Chron. xxvi. 15).

In the midst of this tribulation the sinners will perish without counsel or help. Ver. 17. "*And I make it strait for men, and they will walk like blind men, because they have sinned against*

Jehovah ; and their blood will be poured out like dust, and their flesh like dung. Ver. 18. *Even their silver, even their gold, w'll not be able to save them on the day of Jehovah's fury, and in the fire of His wrath will the whole earth be devoured ; for He will make an end, yea a sudden one, to all the inhabitants of the earth."* וַהֲצֵרֹתִי reminds of the threat of Moses in Deut. xxviii. 52, to which Zephaniah alluded in ver. 16. And in הָלְכוּ כַעִוְרִים the allusion to Deut. xxviii. 29 is also unmistakeable. To walk like the blind, *i.e.* to seek a way out of the trouble without finding one. This distress God sends, because they have sinned against Him, by falling away from Him through idolatry and the transgression of His commandments, as already shown in vers. 4–12. But the punishment will be terrible. Their blood will be poured out like dust. The point of comparison is not the quantity, as in Gen. xiii. 16 and others, but the worthlessness of dust, as in 2 Kings xiii. 7 and Isa. xlix. 23. The blood is thought as little of as the dust which is trodden under foot. *L'chūm,* which occurs again in Job xx. 23, means flesh (as in the Arabic), not food. The verb *shâphakh,* to pour out, is also to be taken *per zeugma* in connection with this clause, though without there being any necessity to associate it with 2 Sam. xx. 10, and regard *l'chūm* as referring to the bowels. For the fact itself, compare 1 Kings xiv. 10 and Jer. ix. 21. In order to cut off all hope of deliverance from the rich and distinguished sinners, the prophet adds in ver. 18 : Even with silver and gold will they not be able to save their lives. The enemy will give no heed to this (cf. Isa. xiii. 17 ; Jer. iv. 30 ; Ezek. vii. 19) in the day that the Lord will pour out His fury upon the ungodly, to destroy the whole earth with the fire of His wrathful jealousy (cf. Deut. iv. 24). By *kol-hâ'ârets* we might understand the whole of the land of Judah, if we looked at what immediately precedes it. But if we bear in mind that the threat commenced with judgment upon the whole earth (vers. 2, 3), and that it here returns to its starting-point, to round off the picture, there can be no doubt that the whole earth is intended. The reason assigned for this threat in ver. 18*b* is formed after Isa. x. 23 ; but the expression is strengthened by the use of אַךְ־נִבְהָלָה instead of וְנֶחֱרָצָה, the word found in Isaiah. *Kâlâh :* the finishing stroke, as in Isa. *l.c.* (see at Nah. i. 8). אַךְ, only, equivalent to " not otherwise than," *i.e.* assuredly. נְבְהֲלָה is used as a substantive, and is synonymous with *behâlâh,* sudden destruction, in Isa. lxv. 23. The construction with *'êth accus.* as in Nah. i. 8.

EXHORTATION TO REPENTANCE IN VIEW OF THE JUDGMENT.
⸺Chap. ii. 1–iii. 8.

Zephaniah, having in the previous chapter predicted the judgment upon the whole world, and Judah especially, as being close at hand, now summons his people to repent, and more especially exhorts the righteous to seek the Lord and strive after righteousness and humility, that they may be hidden in the day of the Lord (vers. 1–3). The reason which he gives for this admonition to repentance is twofold : viz. (1) that the Philistines, Moabites, and Ammonites will be cut off, and Israel will take possession of their inheritances (vers. 4–10), that all the gods of the earth will be overthrown, and all the islands brought to worship the Lord, since He will smite the Cushites, and destroy proud Asshur and Nineveh (vers. 11–15) ; and (2) that even blood-stained Jerusalem, with its corrupt princes, judges, and prophets, will endure severe punishment. Accordingly, the call to repentance is not simply strengthened by the renewed threat of judgment upon the heathen and the ungodly in Judah, but is rather accounted for by the introduction of the thought, that by means of the judgment the heathen nations are to be brought to acknowledge the name of the Lord, and the rescued remnant of Israel to be prepared for the reception of the promised salvation.

Vers. 1–3. Call to conversion.—Ver. 1. " *Gather yourselves together, and gather together, O nation that dost not grow pale.* Ver. 2. *Before the decree bring forth (the day passes away like chaff), before the burning wrath of Jehovah come upon you, before the day of Jehovah's wrath come upon you.* Ver. 3. *Seek Jehovah, all ye humble of the land, who have wrought His right ; seek righteousness, seek humility, perhaps ye will be hidden in the day of Jehovah's wrath.*" The summons in ver. 1 is addressed to the whole of Judah or Israel. The verb *qôshêsh,* possibly a *denom.* from *qash,* signifies to gather stubble (Ex. v. 7, 12), then generally to gather together or collect, *e.g.* branches of wood (Num. xv. 32, 33 ; 1 Kings xvii. 10) ; in the *hithpoel*, to gather one's self together, applied to that spiritual gathering which leads to self-examination, and is the first condition of conversion. The attempts of Ewald and Hitzig to prove, by means of doubtful etymological combinations from the Arabic, that the word possesses the meanings, to grow pale, or to purify one's self, cannot be sustained. The *kal* is combined with the *hiphil* for the purpose of strengthening it, as in Hab. i. 5 and Isa. xxix. 9. *Nikhsâph* is the perf. *niphal* in pause, and not a participle, partly because of the לא which stands before it (see however Ewald, § 286, *g*), and partly on account of the omission of the article ; and *nikhsâph* is to be taken as a relative, " *which* does not turn pale." *Kâsaph* has the meaning " to long," both in the *niphal* (*vid.* Gen. xxxi. 30, Ps. lxxxiv. 3) and *kal* (cf. Ps. xvii. 12, Job xiv. 15). This meaning is retained by many here. Thus Jerome renders it, " *gens non amabilis, i.e. non desiderata a Deo ;*" but this is decidedly unsuitable. Others render it " not possessing strong desire," and appeal to the paraphrase of the Chaldee, " a people not wishing to be converted to the law." This is apparently the view upon which the Alex. version rests : ἔθνος ἀπαίδευτον. But although *nikhsâph* is used to denote the longing of the soul for fellowship with God in Ps. lxxxiv. 3, this idea is not to be found in the word itself, but simply in the object connected with it. We therefore prefer to follow Grotius, Gesenius, Ewald, and others, and take the word in its primary sense of turning pale at anything, becoming white with shame (cf. Isa. xxix. 22), which is favoured by ch. iii. 15. The reason for the appeal is given in ver. 2, viz. the near approach of the judgment. The resolution brings forth, when that which is resolved upon is realized (for *yâlad* in this figurative sense, see Prov. xxvii. 1). The figure is explained in the second hemistich. The next clause וגו׳ כְּמֹץ does not depend upon בְּטֶרֶם, for in that case the verb would stand at the head with *Vav* cop., but it is a parenthesis inserted to strengthen the admonition : the day comes like chaff, *i.e.* approaches with the greatest rapidity, like chaff driven by the wind: not " the time passes by like chaff " (Hitzig) ; for it cannot be shown that *yōm* was ever used for time in this sense. *Yōm* is the day of judgment mentioned in ch. i. 7, 14, 15; and עָבַר here is not to pass by, but to approach, to come near, as in Nah. iii. 19. For the figure of the chaff, see Isa. xxix. 5. In the second hemistich בְּטֶרֶם is strengthened by לֹא; and חֲרוֹן אַף, the burning of wrath in the last clause, is explained by יוֹם אַף יְיָ, the day of the revelation of the wrath of God.—Ver. 3. But because the judgment will so speedily burst upon them, all the pious especially—'anvē hā'ârets, the quiet in the land, οἱ πραεῖς (Amos ii. 7; Isa. xi. 4; Ps. xxxvii. 11)—are to seek the Lord. The humble ('ănâvîm) are described as those who do Jehovah's right, i.e. who seek diligently to fulfil what Jehovah has prescribed in the law as right. Accordingly, seeking Jehovah is explained as seeking righteousness and humility. The thought is this: they are to strive still more zealously after Jehovah's right, viz. righteousness and humility (cf. Deut. xvi. 20; Isa. li. 1, 7); then will they probably be hidden in the day of wrath, i.e. be pardoned and saved (cf. Amos v. 15). This admonition is now still further enforced from ver. 4 onwards by the announcement of the coming of judgment upon all the heathen, that the kingdom of God may attain completion.

Vers. 4–7. Destruction of the Philistines.—Ver. 4. "For Gaza will be forgotten, and Ashkelon become a desert; Ashdod, they drive it out in broad day, and Ekron will be ploughed out. Ver. 5. Woe upon the inhabitants of the tract by the sea, the nation of the Cretans! The word of Jehovah upon you, O Canaan, land of the Philistines! I destroy thee, so that not an inhabitant remains. Ver. 6. And the tract by the sea becomes pastures for shepherds' caves, and for folds of sheep. Ver. 7. And a tract will be for the remnant of the house of Judah; upon them will they feed: in the houses of Ashkelon they encamp in the evening; for Jehovah their God will visit them, and turn their captivity." The fourth verse, which is closely connected by kī (for) with the exhortation to repentance, serves as an introduction to the threat of judgment commencing with hŏi in ver. 5. As the mentioning of the names of the four Philistian capitals (see at Josh. xiii. 3) is simply an individualizing periphrasis for the Philistian territory and people, so the land and people of Philistia are mentioned primarily for the purpose of individualizing, as being the representatives of the heathen world by which Judah was surrounded; and it is not till afterwards, in the further development of the threat, that the enumeration of certain near and remote heathen nations is appended, to express more clearly the idea of the heathen world as a whole. Of the names of the Philistian cities Zephaniah makes use of two, *'Azzâh* and *'Eqrōn*, as a play upon words, to express by means of paronomasia the fate awaiting them. *'Azzâh*, Gaza, will be *'ăzŭbhâh*, forsaken, desolate. *'Eqrōn*, Ekron, will be *tēʿâqēr*, rooted up, torn out of its soil, destroyed. To the other two he announces their fate in literal terms, the *shᵉmâmâh* threatened against Ashkelon corresponding to the *'ăzŭbhâh*, and the *gârēsh* predicated of Ashdod preparing the way for Ekron's *tēʿâqēr*. בַּצָּהֳרַיִם, at noon, *i.e.* in broad day, might signify, when used as an antithesis to night, " with open violence" (Jerome, Kimchi); but inasmuch as the expulsion of inhabitants is not effected by thieves in the night, the time of noon is more probably to be understood, as v. Cölln and Rosenmüller suppose, as denoting the time of day at which men generally rest in hot countries (2 Sam. iv. 5), in the sense of unexpected, unsuspected expulsion ; and this is favoured by Jer. xv. 8, where the devastation at noon is described as a sudden invasion. The omission of Gath may be explained in the same manner as in Amos i. 6-8, from the fact that the parallelism of the clauses only allowed the names of four cities to be given ; and this number was amply sufficient to individualize the whole, just as Zephaniah, when enumerating the heathen nations, restricts the number to four, according to the four quarters of the globe : viz. the Philistines in the west (vers. 5-7) ; the Moabites and Ammonites comprised in one in the east (vers. 8-10) ; the Cushites in the south (vers. 11, 12); and Asshur, with Nineveh, in the north (north-east), (vers. 13-15). The woe with which the threat is commenced in ver. 5 applies to the whole land and people of the Philistines. *Chebhel*, the measure, then the tract of land measured out or apportioned (see at Deut. iii. 4, xxxii. 9, etc.). The tract of the sea is the tract of land by the Mediterranean Sea which was occupied by the Philistines (*chebhel hayyâm* = *'erets Pᵉlishtīm*). Zephaniah calls the inhabitants *gōi Kᵉrēthīm*, nation of the Cretans, from the name of one branch of the Philistian people which was settled in the southwest of Philistia, for the purpose of representing them as a people devoted to *kârath*, or extermination. The origin of this

name, which is selected both here and in Ezek. xxv. 16 with a
play upon the appellative signification, is involved in obscurity;
for, as we have already observed at 1 Sam. xxx. 14, there is no
valid authority for the derivation which is now current, viz.
from the island of *Crete* (see Stark, *Gaza*, pp. 66 and 99 sqq.).
דְּבַר יי׳ עֲלֵיכֶם forms an independent sentence : The word of the
Lord cometh over you.　The nature of that word is described
in the next sentence : I will destroy thee.　The name *Kenaʿan*
is used in the more limited sense of Philistia, and is chosen to
indicate that Philistia is to share the lot of Canaan, and lose its
inhabitants by extermination.—Ver. 6.　The tract of land thus
depopulated is to be turned into "pastures (*nevōth*, the construct
state plural of *nâveh*) of the excavation of shepherds," *i.e.* where
shepherds will make excavations or dig themselves huts under
the ground as a protection from the sun.　This is the simplest explanation of the variously interpreted *kerōth* (as an inf.
of *kârâh*, to dig), and can be grammatically sustained.　The
digging of the shepherds stands for the excavations which they
make.　Bochart (*Hieroz.* i. p. 519, ed. Ros.) has already given
this explanation : " *Caulæ s. caulis repletus erit effossionis pas-
torum, i.e. caulæ a pastoribus effossæ in cryptis subterraneis ad
vitandum solis æstum.*"　On the other hand, the derivation
from the noun *kērâh*, in the sense of cistern, cannot be sustained ; and there is no proof of it in the fact that *kârâh* is
applied to the digging of wells.　Still less is it possible to
maintain the derivation from יכר (Arab. كَرِ), by which Ewald
would support the meaning nests for *kērōth*, *i.e.* " the small
houses or carts of the shepherds."　And Hitzig's alteration of
the text into כָּרִים = כְּרֹת, pastures, so as to obtain the tautology
" meadows of the pastures," is perfectly unwarranted.　The
word *chebhel* is construed in ver. 6 as a feminine *ad sensum*,
with a retrospective allusion to *'erets Pelishtīm* ; whereas in ver.
7 it is construed, as it is everywhere else, as a masculine.　Moreover, the noun *chebhel*, which occurs in this verse without the
article, is not the subject ; for, if it were, it would at least have
had the article.　It is rather a predicate, and the subject must
be supplied from ver. 6 : " The Philistian tract of land by the
sea will become a tract of land or possession for the remnant of
the house of Judah, the portion of the people of God rescued

from the judgment. Upon them, viz. these pastures, will they
feed." The plural עֲלֵיהֶם does not stand for the neuter, but is
occasioned by a retrospective glance at נְוֹת רֹעִים. The subject
is, those that are left of the house of Judah. They will there
feed their flocks, and lie down in the huts of Ashkelon. For
the prophet adds by way of explanation, Jehovah their God
will visit them. *Pâqad*, to visit in a good sense, *i.e.* to take them
under His care, as is almost always the meaning when it is construed with an accusative of the person. It is only in Ps. lix. 6
that it is used with an *acc. pers.* instead of with עַל, in the sense
of to chastise or punish. שׁוּב שְׁבוּת as in Hos. vi. 11 and Amos
ix. 14. The *keri* שְׁבִית has arisen from a misinterpretation. On
the fulfilment, see what follows.

Vers. 8–10. The judgment upon Moab and Ammon.—Ver.
8. " *I have heard the abuse of Moab, and the revilings of the sons
of Ammon, who have abused my nation, and boasted against its
boundary.* Ver. 9. *Therefore, as I live, is the saying of Jehovah
of hosts, the God of Israel : Yea, Moab shall become like Sodom,
and the sons of Ammon like Gomorrha, an inheritance of nettles
and salt-pits, and desert for ever. The remnant of my nation will
plunder them, the residue of my nation will inherit them.* Ver. 10.
*Such to them for their pride, that they have despised and boasted
against the nation of Jehovah of hosts.*" The threat now turns
from the Philistines in the west to the two tribes to the east,
viz. the Moabites and Ammonites, who were descended from
Lot, and therefore blood-relations, and who manifested hostility
to Israel on every possible occasion. Even in the time of Moses,
the Moabitish king Balak sought to destroy Israel by means of
Balaam's curses (Num. xxii.), for which the Moabites were
threatened with extermination (Num. xxiv. 17). In the time
of the judges they both attempted to oppress Israel (Judg. iii.
12 sqq. and x. 7 sqq. ; cf. 1 Sam. xi. 1–5 and 2 Sam. x.–xii.), for
which they were severely punished by Saul and David (1 Sam.
xiv. 47, and 2 Sam. viii. 2, xii. 30, 31). The reproach of
Moab and the revilings of the Ammonites, which Jehovah had
heard, cannot be taken, as Jerome, Rashi, and others suppose,
as referring to the hostilities of those tribes towards the Judæans
during the Chaldæan catastrophe ; nor restricted, as v. Cölln
imagines, to the reproaches heaped upon the ten tribes when
they were carried away by the Assyrians, since nothing is known

of any such reproaches. The charge refers to the hostile attitude assumed by both tribes at all times towards the nation of
God, which they manifested both in word and deed, as often as
the latter was brought into trouble and distress. Compare Jer.
xlviii. 26, 27 ; and for *giddēph*, to revile or blaspheme by actions,
Num. xv. 30, Ezek. xx. 27 ; also for the fact itself, the remarks
on Amos i. 13–ii. 3. יַנְדִּילוּ עַל גב׳, they did great things against
their (the Israelites') border (the suffix in *gᵉbhūlām, their* border,
refers to *'ammī*, my people). This great doing consisted in
their proudly violating the boundary of Israel, and endeavouring to seize upon Israelitish territory (cf. Amos i. 13). Pride
and haughtiness, or high-minded self-exaltation above Israel as
the nation of God, is charged against the Moabites and Ammonites by Isaiah and Jeremiah also, as a leading feature in their
character (cf. Isa. xvi. 6, xxv. 11 ; Jer. xlviii. 29, 30). Moab
and Ammon are to be utterly exterminated in consequence. The
threat of punishment is announced in ver. 8 as irrevocable by
a solemn oath. It shall happen to them as to Sodom and
Gomorrha. This simile was rendered a very natural one by the
situation of the two lands in the neighbourhood of the Dead
Sea. It affirms the utter destruction of the two tribes, as the
appositional description shows. Their land is to become the
possession of nettles, *i.e.* a place where nettles grow. *Mimshâq*,
ἀπ. λεγ., from the root *mâshaq*, which was not used, but from
which *mesheq* in Gen. xv. 2 is derived. *Chârūl:* the stinging
nettle (see at Job xxx. 7), which only flourishes in waste places.
Mikhrēh melach : a place of salt-pits, like the southern coast of
the Dead Sea, which abounds in rock-salt, and to which there
is an allusion in the threat of Moses in Deut. xxix. 22. " A
desert for ever :" the emphasis lies upon *'ad 'ōlâm* (for ever)
here. The people, however, *i.e.* the Moabites and Ammonites
themselves, will be taken by the people of Jehovah, and be
made their possession. The suffixes attached to יְבֻזּוּם and יִנְחָלוּם
can only refer to the people of Moab and Ammon, because a
land turned into an eternal desert and salt-steppe would not be
adapted for a *nachălâh* (possession) for the people of God. The
meaning is not, they will be their heirs through the medium of
plunder, but they will make them into their own property, or
slaves (cf. Isa. xiv. 2, lxi. 5). גּוֹי is גּוֹיִ with the suffix of the first
person, only one of the two being written. In ver. 10 the

threat concludes with a repetition of the statement of the guilt which is followed by such a judgment.

The fulfilment or realization of the threat pronounced upon Philistia, Moab, and Ammon, we have not to look for in the particular historical occurrences through which these tribes were conquered and subjugated by the Chaldæans, and to some extent by the Jews after the captivity, until they eventually vanished from the stage of history, and their lands became desolate, as they still are. These events can only come into consideration as preliminary stages of the fulfilment, which Zephaniah completely passes by, since he only views the judgment in its ultimate fulfilment. We are precluded, moreover, from taking the words as relating to that event by the circumstance, that neither Philistia on the one hand, nor Moabites and Ammonites on the other, were ever taken permanent possession of by the Jews; and still less were they ever taken by Judah, as the nation of God, for His own property. Judah is not to enter into such possession as this till the Lord turns the captivity of Judah (ver. 7); that is to say, not immediately after the return from the Babylonish captivity, but when the dispersion of Israel among the Gentiles, which lasts till this day, shall come to an end, and Israel, through its conversion to Christ, be reinstated in the privileges of the people of God. It follows from this, that the fulfilment is still in the future, and that it will be accomplished not literally, but spiritually, in the utter destruction of the nations referred to as heathen nations, and opponents of the kingdom of God, and in the incorporation of those who are converted to the living God at the time of the judgment, into the citizenship of the spiritual Israel. Until the eventual restoration of Israel, Philistia will remain an uninhabited shepherds' pasture, and the land of the Moabites and Ammonites the possession of nettles, a place of salt-pits and a desert; just as the land of Israel will for the very same time be trodden down by the Gentiles. The curse resting upon these lands will not be entirely removed till the completion of the kingdom of God on earth. This view is proved to be correct by the contents of ver. 11, with which the prophet passes to the announcement of the judgment upon the nations of the south and north.

Ver. 11. " *Fearful is Jehovah over them, for He destroyeth*

*all the gods of the earth; that all the islands of the nations, every
one from its place, may worship Him."* Whilst עֲלֵיהֶם refers to
what precedes, the next clause in the reason assigned points to
the announcement of judgment upon the remaining nations of
the earth in vers. 12 sqq.; so that ver. 11 cannot be taken
either as the conclusion of the previous threat, or as the commencement of the following one, but leads from the one to the
other. Jehovah is terrible when He reveals Himself in the
majesty of Judge of the world. The suffix appended to עֲלֵיהֶם
does not refer to עַם יְהֹוָה, but to the לָהֶם in ver. 10, answering
to the Moabites and Ammonites. Jehovah proves Himself
terrible to these, because He has resolved to destroy all the gods
of the earth. *Râzâh*, to make lean; hence to cause to vanish,
to destroy. He causes the gods to vanish, by destroying the
nations and kingdoms who relied upon these gods. He thereby
reveals the nothingness of the gods, and brings the nations to
acknowledge His sole deity (Mic. v. 12). The fall of the false
gods impels to the worship of the one true God. וְיִשְׁתַּחֲווּ לוֹ is
the consequence, the fruit, and the effect of Jehovah's proving
Himself terrible to the nations and their gods. אִיֵּי הַגּוֹיִם, islands
of the Gentiles, is an epithet taken from the islands and coast-
lands of Europe, to denote the whole of the heathen world (see
at Isa. xli. 1). The distributive אִישׁ מִמְּקוֹמוֹ refers to *haggōyīm*
as the principal idea, though not in the sense of "every nation,"
but in that of every individual belonging to the nations. *Mim-
m^eqōmō*, coming from his place: the meaning is not that the
nations will worship Jehovah at their own place, in their own
lands, in contradistinction to Mic. iv. 1, Zech. xiv. 16, and
other passages, where the nations go on pilgrimage to Mount
Zion (Hitzig); but their going to Jerusalem is implied in the
min (from), though it is not brought prominently out, as being
unessential to the thought. With regard to the fulfilment,
Bucer has correctly observed, that " the worship of Jehovah
on the part of the heathen is not secured without sanguinary
wars, that the type may not be taken for the fact itself, and the
shadow for the body. . . . But the true completion of the whole
in the kingdom of Christ takes place here in spirit and in faith,
whilst in the future age it will be consummated in all its reality
and in full fruition." Theodoret, on the other hand, is too
one-sided in his view, and thinks only of the conversion of

the heathen through the preaching of the gospel. " This prophecy," he says, " has received its true fulfilment through the
holy apostles, and the saints who have followed them ; . . . and
this takes place, not by the law, but by the teaching of the
gospel."

Vers. 12–15. After this statement of the aim of the judgments of God, Zephaniah mentions two other powerful heathen
nations as examples, to prove that the whole of the heathen
world will succumb to the judgment. Ver. 12. " *Ye Cushites
also, slain of my sword are they. Ver. 13. And let him stretch
out his hand toward the south, and destroy Asshur ; and make
Nineveh a barren waste, a dry place, like the desert. Ver. 14.
And herds lie down in the midst of it, all kinds of beasts in
crowds: pelicans also and hedgehogs will lodge on their knobs;
the voice of the singer in the window ; heaps upon the threshold :
for their cedar-work hath He made bare. Ver. 15. This the city,
the exulting one, the safely dwelling one, which said in her heart,
I, and no more : how has she become a desolation, a lair of
beasts! Every one that passeth by it will hiss, swing his hand."*
As a representative of the heathen dwelling in the south,
Zephaniah does not mention Edom, which bordered upon
Judah, or the neighbouring land of Egypt, but the remote
Ethiopia, the furthest kingdom or people in the south that was
known to the Hebrews. The Ethiopians will be slain of the
sword of Jehovah. הֵמָּה does not take the place of the copula
between the subject and predicate, any more than הוּא in Isa.
xxxvii. 16 and Ezra v. 11 (to which Hitzig appeals in support
of this usage : see Delitzsch, on the other hand, in his *Comm.
on Isaiah, l.c.*), but is a predicate. The prophecy passes suddenly from the form of address (in the second person) adopted
in the opening clause, to a statement concerning the Cushites
(in the third person). For similar instances of sudden transition, see ch. iii. 18, Zech. iii. 8, Ezek. xxviii. 22.[1] חַלְלֵי חַרְבִּי is
a reminiscence from Isa. lxvi. 16 : slain by Jehovah with the
sword. Zephaniah says nothing further concerning this distant
nation, which had not come into any hostile collision with Judah
in his day; and only mentions it to exemplify the thought that

[1] Calvin correctly says : " The prophet commences by driving them, in
the second person, to the tribunal of God, and then adds in the third person, ' They will be,' etc."

all the heathen will come under the judgment. The fulfilment commenced with the judgment upon Egypt through the Chaldæans, as is evident from Ezek. xxx. 4, 9, as compared with Josephus, *Ant.* x. 11, and continues till the conversion of that people to the Lord, the commencement of which is recorded in Acts viii. 27–38. The prophet dwells longer upon the heathen power of the north, the Assyrian kingdom with its capital Nineveh, because Assyria was then the imperial power, which was seeking to destroy the kingdom of God in Judah. This explains the fact that the prophet expresses the announcement of the destruction of this power in the form of a wish, as the use of the contracted forms *yēt* and *yāsēm* clearly shows. For it is evident that Ewald is wrong in supposing that וְיֵט stands for וַיֵּט, or should be so pointed, inasmuch as the historical tense, "there He stretched out His hand," would be perfectly out of place. נָטָה יָד (to stretch out a hand), as in ch. i. 4. '*Al tsâphōn*, over (or against) the north. The reference is to Assyria with the capital Nineveh. It is true that this kingdom was not to the north, but to the north-east, of Judah; but inasmuch as the Assyrian armies invaded Palestine from the north, it is regarded by the prophets as situated in the north. On Nineveh itself, see at Jonah i. 2 (vol. i. p. 390); and on the destruction of this city and the fall of the Assyrian empire, at Nah. iii. 19 (p. 42). *Lishmâmâh* is strengthened by the apposition *tsiyyâh kammidbâr*. Nineveh is not only to become a steppe, in which herds feed (Isa. xxvii. 10), but a dry, desolate waste, where only desert animals will make their home. *Tsiyyâh*, the dry, arid land—the barren, sandy desert (cf. Isa. xxxv. 1). בְּתוֹכָהּ, in the midst of the city which has become a desert, there lie flocks, not of sheep and goats (צֹאן, ver. 6; cf. Isa. xiii. 20), but כָּל־חַיְתוֹ־גוֹי, literally of all the animals of the (or a) nation. The meaning can only be, "all kinds of animals in crowds or in a mass." גּוֹי is used here for the mass of animals, just as it is in Joel i. 6 for the multitude of locusts, and as עַם is in Prov. xxx. 35, 36 for the ant-people; and the genitive is to be taken as in apposition. Every other explanation is exposed to much greater objections and difficulties. For the form חַיְתוֹ, see at Gen. i. 24. Pelicans and hedgehogs will make their homes in the remains of the ruined buildings (see at Isa. xxxiv. 11, on

which passage Zephaniah rests his description). בְּכַפְתֹּרֶיהָ, upon
the knobs of the pillars left standing when the palaces were
destroyed (*kaphtōr ;* see at Amos ix. 1). The reference to the
pelican, a marsh bird, is not opposed to the *tsiyyâh* of ver. 13,
since Nineveh stood by the side of streams, the waters of which
formed marshes after the destruction of the city. קוֹל יְשׁוֹרֵר
cannot be rendered " a voice sings," for *shōrēr*, to sing, is not
used for tuning or resounding; but *y⁵shōrēr* is to be taken relatively, and as subordinate to קוֹל, the voice of him that sings
will be heard in the window. Jerome gives it correctly: *vox
canentis in fenestra.* There is no necessity to think of the cry
of the owl or hawk in particular, but simply of birds generally,
which make their singing heard in the windows of the ruins.
The sketching of the picture of the destruction passes from the
general appearance of the city to the separate ruins, coming
down from the lofty knobs of the pillars to the windows, and
from these to the thresholds of the ruins of the houses. Upon
the thresholds there is *chōrebh*, devastation (= rubbish), and no
longer a living being. This is perfectly appropriate, so that
there is no necessity to give the word an arbitrary interpretation, or to alter the text, so as to get the meaning a raven or a
crow. The description closes with the explanatory sentence :
" for He has laid bare the cedar-work," *i.e.* has so destroyed
the palaces and state buildings, that the costly panelling of the
walls is exposed. *'Arzâh* is a collective, from *'erez*, the cedar-
work, and there is no ground for any such alteration of the text
as Ewald and Hitzig suggest, in order to obtain the trivial
meaning " hews or hacks in pieces," or the cold expression,
" He destroys, lays bare." In ver. 15 the picture is rounded
off. " This is the city," *i.e.* this is what happens to the exulting
city. עַלִּיזָה, exulting, applied to the joyful tumult caused by
the men—a favourite word with Isaiah (cf. Isa. xxii. 2, xxiii. 7,
xxiv. 8, xxxii. 13). The following predicates from הַיּוֹשֶׁבֶת to עוֹד
are borrowed from the description of Babel in Isa. xlvii. 8, and
express the security and self-deification of the mighty imperial
city. The *Yod* in *'aphsī* is not paragogical, but a pronoun in
the first person ; at the same time, *'ephes* is not a preposition,
" beside me," since in that case the negation " not one" could
not be omitted, but " the non-existence," so that אֵינִי=אַפְסִי, I am
absolutely no further (see at Isa. xlvii. 8). But how has this

self-deifying pride been put to shame! אֵיךְ, an expression of
amazement at the tragical turn in her fate. The city filled
with the joyful exulting of human beings has become the lair
of wild beasts, and every one that passes by expresses his malicious delight in its ruin. *Shâraq*, to hiss, a common manifestation of scorn (cf. Mic. vi. 16; Jer. xix. 8). הֵנִיעַ יָד, to swing
the hand, embodying the thought, " Away with her, she has
richly deserved her fate."

Ch. iii. 1–8. To give still greater emphasis to his exhortation to repentance, the prophet turns to Jerusalem again, that
he may once more hold up before the hardened sinners the
abominations of this city, in which Jehovah daily proclaims
His right, and shows the necessity for the judgment, as the
only way that is left by which to secure salvation for Israel
and for the whole world. Ver. 1. " *Woe to the refractory and
polluted one, the oppressive city !* Ver. 2. *She has not hearkened
to the voice; not accepted discipline; not trusted in Jehovah; not
drawn near to her God.* Ver. 3. *Her princes are roaring lions in
the midst of her; her judges evening wolves, who spare not for the
morning.* Ver. 4. *Her prophets boasters, men of treacheries :
her priests desecrate that which is holy, do violence to the law.*"
The woe applies to the city of Jerusalem. That this is intended in ver. 1 is indisputably evident from the explanation
which follows in vers. 2–4 of the predicates applied to the
city addressed in ver. 1. By the position of the indeterminate
predicates מוֹרְאָה and נִגְאָלָה before the subject to which the *hôi*
refers, the threat acquires greater emphasis. מוֹרְאָה is not
formed from the *hophal* of רָאָה (ἐπιφανής, LXX., Cyr., Cocc.),
but is the participle *kal* of מָרָא = מָרָה or מָרַר, to straighten one's
self, and hold one's self against a person, hence to be rebellious
(see Delitzsch on *Job*, vol. ii. p. 2, note). נִגְאָלָה, stained with
sins and abominations (cf. Isa. lix. 3). *Yōnâh* does not mean
columba, but oppressive (as in Jer. xlvi. 16, l. 16, and xxv. 38),
as a participle of *yânâh* to oppress (cf. Jer. xxii. 3). These
predicates are explained and vindicated in vers. 2–4, viz. first
of all מוֹרְאָה in ver. 2. She gives no heed to the voice, *sc.* of
God in the law and in the words of the prophets (compare
Jer. vii. 28, where קוֹל יְהוָֹה occurs in the repetition of the first
hemistich). The same thing is affirmed in the second clause,
" she accepts no chastisement." These two clauses describe the

attitude assumed towards the legal contents of the word of God,
the next two the attitude assumed towards its evangelical contents, *i.e.* the divine promises. Jerusalem has no faith in these,
and does not allow them to draw her to her God. The whole
city is the same, *i.e.* the whole of the population of the city.
Her civil and spiritual rulers are no better. Their conduct
shows that the city is oppressive and polluted (vers. 3 and 4).
Compare with this the description of the leaders in Mic. iii.
The princes are lions, which rush with roaring upon the poor
and lowly, to tear them in pieces and destroy them (Prov.
xxviii. 15; Ezek. xix. 2; Nah. ii. 12). The judges resemble
evening wolves (see at Hab. i. 8), as insatiable as wolves, which
leave not a single bone till the following morning, of the prey
they have caught in the evening. The verb *gâram* is a denom.
from *gerem*, to gnaw a bone, *piel* to crush them (Num. xxiv. 8);
to gnaw a bone for the morning, is the same as to leave it to
be gnawed in the morning. *Gâram* has not in itself the meaning to reserve or lay up (Ges. *Lex.*). The prophets, *i.e.* those
who carry on their prophesying without a call from God (see
Mic. ii. 11, iii. 5, 11), are *pōchăzīm*, vainglorious, boasting,
from *pâchaz*, to boil up or boil over, and when applied to
speaking, to overflow with frivolous words. Men of treacheries,
bōgᵉdōth, a subst. verb, from *bâgad*, the classical word for faithless adultery or apostasy from God. The prophets proved
themselves to be so by speaking the thoughts of their own
hearts to the people as revelations from God, and thereby
strengthening it in its apostasy from the Lord. The priests
profane that which is holy (*qōdesh*, every holy thing or act),
and do violence to the law, namely, by treating what is holy
as profane, and perverting the precepts of the law concerning
holy and unholy (cf. Ezek. xxii. 26).

Jerusalem sins in this manner, without observing that
Jehovah is constantly making known to it His own righteousness. Ver. 5. "*Jehovah is just in the midst of her; does no
wrong: morning by morning He sets His justice in the light, not
failing; but the unjust knoweth no shame. Ver. 6. I have cut
off nations: their battlements are laid waste; I have devastated
their streets, so that no one else passeth over: their cities are laid
waste, that there is no man there, not an inhabitant more.*" Ver. 5
is attached adversatively to what precedes without a particle, in

this sense : And yet Jehovah is just *b^eqirbâh*, *i.e.* in the midst of the city filled with sinners. The words recal to mind the description of the divine administration in Deut. xxxii. 4, where Jehovah is described as אֵין עָוֶל and יָשָׁר. It follows from this that *tsaddîq* is not to be referred to the fact that God does not leave the sins of the nation unpunished (Ros.), but to the fact that He commits no wrong : so that לֹא יַעֲשֶׂה עַוְלָה is only a negative paraphrase of *tsaddîq*. His justice, *i.e.* the righteous-ness of His conduct, He puts in the light every morning (*babbōqer babbōqer*, used distributively, as in Ex. xvi. 21, Lev. vi. 5, etc.), not by rewarding virtue and punishing wickedness (Hitzig, Strauss, after the Chaldee, Jerome, Theodoret, and Cyril), according to which *mishpât* would signify judgment ; but by causing His law and justice to be proclaimed to the nation daily " by prophets, whose labour He employs to teach the nation His laws, and who exert themselves diligently by exhorting and admonishing every day, to call it to bring forth better fruit, but all in vain (Ros., Ewald, etc.; cf. Hos. vi. 5). It is at variance with the context to take these words as refer-ring to the judgments of God. These are first spoken of in ver. 6, and the correspondence between these two verses and vers. 7 and 8 shows that we must not mix up together ver. 5*b* and ver. 6, or interpret ver. 5*b* from ver. 6. Just as the judgment is threatened there (ver. 8) because the people have accepted no correction, and have not allowed themselves to be moved to the fear of Jehovah, so also in vers. 5 and 6 the prophet demonstrates the righteousness of God from His double administration : viz. first, from the fact that He causes His justice to be proclaimed to the people, that they may accept correction ; and secondly, by pointing to the judgments upon the nations. לֹא נֶעְדָּר paraphrases the idea of "infallibly;" the literal meaning is, that there is no morning in which the justice is wanting. Hitzig, Strauss, and others have rendered it quite unsuitably, " God does not suffer Himself to be want-ing," *i.e.* does not remain absent. But the perverse one, viz. the nation sunk in unrighteousness, knows no disgrace, to make it ashamed of its misdeeds. In ver. 6 Jehovah is introduced as speaking, to set before the nations in the most impressive manner the judgments in which He has manifested His righteousness. The two hemistichs are formed uniformly, each consisting of two clauses, in which the direct address alternates with an indefinite, passive construction: I have cut off nations, their battlements have been laid waste, etc. *Gōyīm* are neither those nations who are threatened with ruin in ch. ii. 4–15, nor the Canaanites, who have been exterminated by Israel, but nations generally, which have succumbed to the judgments of God, without any more precise definition. *Pinnōth*, the battlements of the fortress-walls and towers (i. 16), stand *per synecdochen* for castles or fortifications. *Chūtsōth* are not streets of the city, but roads, and stand synecdochically for the flat country. This is required by the correspondence of the clauses. For just as the cities answer to the castles, so do *chūtsōth* to the nations. *Nitsdū*, from *tsâdâh*, not in the sense of waylaying (Ex. xxi. 13; 1 Sam. xxiv. 12), but in accordance with Aramæan usage, to lay waste, answering to *nâshammū*, for which Jeremiah uses *nittᵉtsū* in ch. iv. 26.

In vers. 7 and 8 the prophet sums up all that he has said in vers. 1–6, to close his admonition to repentance with the announcement of judgment. Ver. 7. "*I said, Only do thou fear me, do thou accept correction, so will their dwelling not be cut off, according to all that I have appointed concerning them: but they most zealously destroyed all their doings. Ver. 8. Therefore wait for me, is the saying of Jehovah, for the day when I rise up to the prey; for it is my right to gather nations together, to bring kingdoms in crowds, to heap upon them my fury, all the burning of my wrath: for in the fire of my zeal will the whole earth be devoured.*" God has not allowed instruction and warning to be wanting, to avert the judgment of destruction from Judah; but the people have been getting worse and worse, so that now He is obliged to make His justice acknowledged on earth by means of judgments. אָמַרְתִּי, not I thought, but I said. This refers to the strenuous exertions of God to bring His justice to the light day by day (ver. 5), and to admonitions of the prophets in order to bring the people to repentance. תִּירְאִי and תִּקְחִי are cohortatives, chosen instead of imperatives, to set forth the demand of God by clothing it in the form of entreating admonition as an emanation of His love. *Lâqach mūsâr* as in ver. 2. The words are addressed to the inhabitants of Jerusalem personified as the daughter of Zion (ver. 11); and מְעוֹנָהּ, her dwelling, is the city of Jerusalem, not the temple, which is called the dwelling-place of Jehovah indeed, but never the dwelling-place of the nation, or of the inhabitants of Jerusalem. The clause which follows, and which has been very differently interpreted, כֹּל אֲשֶׁר פָּקַדְתִּי עָלֶיהָ, can hardly be taken in any other way than that in which Ewald has taken it, viz. by rendering *kōl* as the accusative of manner : according to all that I have appointed, or as I have appointed everything concerning them. For it is evidently impracticable to connect it with what precedes as *asyndeton*, because the idea of יָבוֹא cannot be taken *per zeugma* from יִכָּרֵת, and we should necessarily have to supply that idea. For *hikkârēth* does not in any way fit in with אֲשֶׁר פָּקַדְתִּי, whether we take פָּקַד עַל in the sense of charge, command, appoint (after Job xxxiv. 13, xxxvi. 23), or in that of correct, punish. For the thought that God will cut off all that He has appointed concerning Jerusalem, would be just as untenable as the thought that He will exterminate the sins that have been punished in Jerusalem. But instead of repenting, the people have only shown themselves still more zealous in evil deeds. *Hishkīm*, to rise early, then in connection with another verb, adverbially : early and zealously. *Hishchīth*, to act corruptly ; and with *'ălîlōth*, to complete corrupt and evil deeds (cf. Ps. xiv. 1). Jehovah must therefore interpose with punishment.— Ver. 8. With the summons *chakkū lī*, wait for me, the prophecy returns to its starting-point in vers. 2 and 3, to bring it to a close. The persons addressed are *kol 'anvē hâ'ârets*, whom the prophet has summoned in the introduction to his exhortation to repentance (ch. ii. 3), to seek the Lord and His righteousness. The Lord calls upon them, to wait for Him. For the nation as such, or those who act corruptly, cannot be addressed, since in that case we should necessarily have to take *chakkū lī* as ironical (Hitzig, Maurer) ; and this would be at variance with the usage of the language, inasmuch as *chikkâh lay'hōvâh* is only used for waiting in a believing attitude for the Lord and His help (Ps. xxxiii. 20 ; Isa. viii. 17, xxx. 18, lxiv. 3). The *lī* is still more precisely defined by לְיוֹם וגו׳, for the day of my rising up for prey. לְעַד does not mean εἰς μαρτύριον = לְעֵד (LXX., Syr.), or for a witness (Hitzig), which does not even yield a suitable thought apart from the alteration in the pointing, unless we " combine with the witness the accuser and judge" (Hitzig), or, to speak more correctly, make the witness into a judge; nor does לְעַד stand for לְעַד, *in perpetuum*, as Jerome has interpreted it after Jewish commentators, who referred the words to the coming of the Messiah, "who as they hope will come, and, as they say, will devour the earth with the fire of His zeal when the nations are gathered together, and the fury of the Lord is poured out upon them." For "the rising up of Jehovah for ever" cannot possibly denote the coming of the Messiah, or be understood as referring to the resurrection of Christ, as Cocceius supposes, even if the judgment upon the nations is to be inflicted through the Messiah. לְעַד means "for prey," that is to say, it is a concise expression for taking prey, though not in the sense suggested by Calvin : "Just as lions seize, tear in pieces, and devour ; so will I do with you, because hitherto I have spared you with too much humanity and paternal care." This neither suits the expression *chakkū lī*, according to the only meaning of *chikkâh* that is grammatically established, nor the verses which follow (vers. 9, 10), according to which the judgment to be inflicted upon the nations by the Lord is not an exterminating but a refining judgment, through which He will turn to the nations pure lips, to call upon His name. The prey for which Jehovah will rise up, can only consist, therefore, in the fact, that through the judgment He obtains from among the nations those who will confess His name, so that the souls from among the nations which desire salvation fall to Him as prey (compare Isa. liii. 12 with lii. 15 and xlix. 7). It is true that, in order to gain this victory, it is necessary to exterminate by means of the judgment the obstinate and hardened sinners. "For my justice (right) is to gather this." *Mishpât* does not mean *judicium*, judgment, here ; still less does it signify *decretum*, a meaning which it never has ; but justice or right, as in ver. 5. My justice, *i.e.* the justice which I shall bring to the light, consists in the fact that I pour my fury upon all nations, to exterminate the wicked by judgments, and to convert the penitent to myself, and prepare for myself worshippers out of all nations. לְשָׁפֵּךְ is governed by לֶאֱסֹף וגו'. God will gather together the nations, to sift and convert them by severe judgments. To give the reason for the terrible character and universality of the judgment, the thought is repeated from ch. i. 18 that "all the earth shall be devoured

in the fire of His zeal." In what follows, the aim and fruit of
the judgment are given; and this forms an introduction to the
announcement of salvation.

PROMISE OF THE CONVERSION OF THE NATIONS AND
GLORIFICATION OF ISRAEL.—Chap. iii. 9-20.

The confessors of His name, whom the Lord will procure
for Himself among the nations through the medium of the
judgment, will offer to Him His dispersed nation as a sacrifice
(vers. 9, 10). And the rescued remnant of Israel, in their
humility, will trust in the Lord, and under the pastoral fidelity
of their God have no more foe to fear, but rejoicing in the
blessed fellowship of the Lord, be highly favoured and glorified (vers. 11-20).

Ver. 9. *"For then will I turn to the nations a pure lip, that
they may all call upon the name of Jehovah, to serve Him with
one shoulder.* Ver. 10. *From beyond the rivers of Cush will
they bring my worshippers, the daughter of my dispersed ones, as
a meat-offering to me."* By the explanatory *kî* the promise is
connected with the threat of judgment. The train of thought
is this: the believers are to wait for the judgment, for it will
bring them redemption. The first clause in ver. 9 is explained
in different ways. Many commentators understand by *sâphâh
bheṛûrâh* the lip of God, which He will turn to the nations
through His holy servants. According to this view, Luther
has adopted the rendering: "Then will I cause the nations to
be preached to otherwise, with friendly lips, that they may all
call upon the name of the Lord." But this view, which has
been defended by Cocceius, Mark, and Hofmann (*Schriftbeweis*, ii. 2, pp. 573-4), would only be admissible if *bârûr*
signified clear, evident,—a meaning which Hofmann assumes
as the ground of his explanation: "A clear, easily intelligible,
unmistakeable language does God turn to the nations, to call
them all in the name of Jehovah, that they may serve Him as
one man." But, apart from the inadmissible rendering of
קְרֹא בְשֵׁם יי, this explanation is proved to be erroneous by the
fact that *bârûr* does not mean clear, intelligible; that even in

Job xxxiii. 3 it has not this meaning; but that it simply means pure, purified, sinless; and that *sâphâh bh°rûrâh*, the opposite of טְמֵא שְׂפָתַיִם in Isa. vi. 5, cannot be used at all of the lip or language of God, but simply of the lip of a man who is defiled by sin. Consequently הָפַךְ אֶל must be explained according to 1 Sam. x. 9, since the circumstance that we have הָפַךְ לְ in this passage does not make any material difference in the meaning. The construction in both passages is a pregnant one. God turns to the nations a pure lip, by purifying their sinful lips, *i.e.* He converts them, that they may be able to call upon Him with pure lips. Lip does not stand for language, but is mentioned as the organ of speech, by which a man expresses the thoughts of his heart, so that purity of the lips involves or presupposes the purification of the heart. The lips are defiled by the names of the idols whom they have invoked (cf. Hos. ii. 19, Ps. xvi. 4). The fruit of the purification is this, that henceforth they call upon the name of Jehovah, and serve Him. קָרָא בְשֵׁם יי, when used of men, always signifies to call solemnly or heartily upon the name of Jehovah. To serve *sh°khem 'echâd*, with one shoulder, is to serve together or with unanimity. The metaphor is taken from bearers who carry a burden with even shoulders; cf. Jer. xxxii. 39. As an example of the way in which they will serve the Lord, it is stated in ver. 10 that they will offer the widely scattered members of the Israelitish church as a sacrifice to the Lord. Compare Isa. lxvi. 20, where this thought is applied to the heathen of all quarters of the globe; whereas Zephaniah, while fixing his eye upon that passage, has given it more briefly, and taken the expression "from beyond the rivers of Cush" from Isa. xviii. 1, for the purpose of naming the remotest heathen nations *instar omnium*. The rivers of Cush are the Nile and the Astaboras, with their different tributaries. עֲתָרַי בַּת פּוּצַי is the accusative of the nearest object, and מִנְחָתִי that of the more remote. *'Athâr* does not mean fragrance (Ges., Ewald, Maurer), but worshipper, from *'âthar*, to pray, to entreat. The worshippers are more precisely defined by *bath pûtsai*, the daughter of my dispersed ones (*pûts*, part. pass.), *i.e.* the crowd or congregation consisting of the dispersed of the Lord, the members of the Israelitish congregation of God scattered about in all the world. They are presented to the Lord by the converted Gentiles as *minchâh,* a meat-offering, *i.e.* according to Isa. lxvi. 20, just as the children of Israel offered a meat-offering. In the symbolism of religious worship, the presentation of the meat-offering shadowed forth diligence in good works as the fruit of justification. The meaning is therefore the following: The most remote of the heathen nations will prove that they are worshippers of Jehovah, by bringing to Him the scattered members of His nation, or by converting them to the living God. We have here in Old Testament form the thought expressed by the Apostle Paul in Rom. xi., namely, that the Gentiles have been made partakers of salvation, that they may incite to emulation the Israelites who have fallen away from the call of divine grace. The words of the prophet treat of the blessing which will accrue, from the entrance of the Gentiles into the kingdom of God, to the Israelites who have been rejected on account of their guilt, and refer not only to the missionary work of Christians among the Jews in the stricter sense of the term, but to everything that is done, both directly and indirectly, through the rise and spread of Christianity among the nations, for the conversion of the Jews to the Saviour whom they once despised. Their complete fulfilment, however, will only take place after the *pleroma* of the Gentiles has come in, when the πώρωσις, which in part has happened to Israel, shall be removed, and " all Israel" shall be saved (Rom. xi. 25, 26). On the other hand, Mark, Hitzig, and others, have taken ʽăthârai bath pūtsai as the subject, and understand it as referring to the heathen who have escaped the judgment by flying in all directions to their own homes, for example even to Cush, and who having become converted, offer to the Lord the gift that is His due. But, apart from the parallel passage in Isa. lxvi. 20, which alone is quite decisive, this view is proved to be untenable by *bath pūtsai,* daughter of *my* dispersed ones. The thought that Jehovah disperses the heathen, either at the judgment or through the judgment, is foreign to the whole of the Old Testament, as Hitzig himself appears to have felt, when he changed *pūts,* to disperse, into its very opposite—namely, to come home. The thought, on the other hand, that God will disperse His people Israel among all nations on account of their sins, and will hereafter gather them together again, is a truth expressed even in the song of Moses, and one which recurs in all the prophets, so that every hearer or reader of our prophet must think at once of the Israel scattered abroad in connection with the expression " my (*i.e.* Jehovah's) dispersed ones." The objection, that Judah is first spoken of in ver. 11 (Hitzig), is thereby deprived of all its significance, even if this really were the case. But the objection is also incorrect, since the Judæans have been already addressed in ver. 8 in the expression חַכּוּ לִי.

Ver. 11. "*In that day wilt thou not be ashamed of all thy doings, wherewith thou hast transgressed against me; for then will I remove from the midst of thee those that rejoice in thy pride, and thou wilt no more pride thyself upon my holy mountain.* Ver. 12. *And I leave in the midst of thee a people bowed down and poor, and they trust in the name of Jehovah.* Ver. 13. *The remnant of Israel will not do wrong, and not speak lies, and there will not be found in their mouth a tongue of deceit; for they will feed and rest, and no one will terrify them.*" The congregation, being restored to favour, will be cleansed and sanctified by the Lord from every sinful thing. The words of ver. 11 are addressed to the Israel gathered together from the dispersion, as the daughter of Zion (cf. ver. 14). "In that day" refers to the time of judgment mentioned before, viz. to the day when Jehovah rises up for prey (ver. 8). לֹא תֵבוֹשִׁי, thou wilt not need to be ashamed of all thine iniquities; because, as the explanatory clauses which follow clearly show, they occur no more. This is the meaning of the words, and not, as Ewald imagines, that Jerusalem will no more be bowed down by the recollection of them. The perfect אֲשֶׁר פָּשַׁעַתְּ does indeed point to the sins of former times; not to the recollection of them, however, but to the commission of them. For the proud and sinners will then be exterminated from the congregation. עַלִּיזֵי גַּאֲוָה is taken from Isa. xiii. 3, where it denotes the heroes called by Jehovah, who exult with pride caused by the intoxication of victory; whereas here the reference is to the haughty judges, priests, and prophets (vers. 3 and 4), who exult in their sinful ways. גַּבְהָה a feminine form of the infinitive, like *moshcháh* in Ex. xxix. 29, etc. (cf. Ges. § 45, 1, *b*, and Ewald, § 236, *a*). גָּבַה, to be haughty, as in Isa. iii. 16. The prophet mentions pride as the root of all sins. The holy mountain is not Canaan as a mountainous country, but the temple mountain, as in the parallel passage, Isa. xi. 9. The people left by the Lord, *i.e.* spared in the judgment, and gathered together again out of the dispersion, will be ʿânī and *dal.* The two words are often connected together as synonyms, *e.g.* Isa. xxvi. 6 and Job xxxiv. 28. עָנִי is not to be confounded with עָנָו, gentle or meek, but signifies bowed down, oppressed with the feeling of impotence for what is good, and the knowledge that deliverance is due to the compassionate grace of God alone; it is therefore the opposite of proud, which trusts in its own strength, and boasts of its own virtue. The leading characteristic of those who are bowed down will be trust in the Lord, the spiritual stamp of genuine piety. This remnant of Israel, the ἐκλογή of the people of God, will neither commit injustice, nor practise wickedness and deceit with word and tongue, will therefore be a holy nation, answering to its divine calling (Ex. xix. 6), just as God does no wrong (ver. 5), and the servant of Jehovah has no deceit in his mouth (Isa. liii. 9). What is stated here can, of course, not refer to those who were brought back from Babylon, as Calvin supposes, taking the words comparatively, because there were many hypocrites among the exiles, and adding, "because the Lord will thus wipe away all stains from His people, that the holiness may then appear all the purer." The prophetic announcement refers to the time of perfection, which commenced with the coming of Christ, and will be completely realized at His return to judgment. Strauss very appropriately compares the words of John, "Whatsoever is born of God doth not commit sin" (1 John iii. 9). Zephaniah explains what he says, by adding the assurance of the blessing which is promised in the law as the reward of faithful walk in the commandments of the Lord. This reason rests upon the assumption that they only rejoice in the promised blessing who walk in the commandments of God. In this respect the enjoyment of the blessing yields a practical proof that wrong and wickedness occur no more. The words יִרְעוּ וְרָבְצוּ may be explained from the comparison of the remnant of Israel to a flock both in Mic. vii. 14 and Luke xii. 32 ("little flock;" for the fact itself, compare Mic. iv. 4). This blessing is still further developed in what follows, first of all by a reference to the removal of the judgments of God (vers. 14–17), and secondly by the promise of God that

all the obstacles which prevent the enjoyment of the blessing
are to be cleared away (vers. 18–20).

Ver. 14. "*Exult, O daughter Zion; shout, O Israel! rejoice
and exult with all the heart, O daughter Jerusalem.* Ver. 15.
*Jehovah has removed thy judgments, cleared away thine enemy;
the King of Israel, Jehovah, is in the midst of thee: thou
wilt see evil no more.* Ver. 16. *In that day will men say to
Jerusalem, Fear not, O Zion; let not thy hands drop.* Ver. 17.
*Jehovah thy God is in the midst of thee, a hero who helps: He
rejoices over thee in delight, He is silent in His love, exults over
thee with rejoicing.*" The daughter Zion, *i.e.* the reassembled
remnant of Israel, is to exult and shout at the fulness of the
salvation prepared for it. The fulness is indicated in the
heaping up of words for exulting and rejoicing. The greater
the exultation, the greater must the object be over which men
exult. הָרִיעוּ, to break out into a cry of joy, is a plural, because
the Israel addressed is a plurality. The re-establishment of the
covenant of grace assigns the reason for the exultation. God
has removed the judgments, and cleared away the enemies,
who served as the executors of His judgments. *Pinnâh, piel,*
to put in order (*sc.* a house), by clearing away what is lying
about in disorder (Gen. xxiv. 31; Lev. xiv. 36), hence to
sweep away or remove. '*Oyēbh:* with indefinite generality,
every enemy. Now is Jehovah once more in the midst of the
daughter Zion as King of Israel, whereas, so long as Israel
was given up to the power of the enemy, He had ceased to be
its King. *Yᵉhōváh* is in apposition to *melekh Yisrá'ēl*, which
is placed first for the sake of emphasis, and not a predicate.
The predicate is merely בְּקִרְבֵּךְ (in the midst of thee). The
accent lies upon the fact that Jehovah is in the midst of His
congregation as King of Israel (cf. ver. 17). Because this is
the case, she will no more see, *i.e.* experience, evil (רָאָה as in
Jer. v. 12, Isa. xliv. 16, etc.), and need not therefore any
longer fear and despair. This is stated in ver. 16: They will
say to Jerusalem, Fear not. She will have so little fear, that
men will be able to call her the fearless one. צִיּוֹן is a vocative
of address. It is simpler to assume this than to supply לְ from
the previous clause. The falling of the hands is a sign of
despair through alarm and anxiety (cf. Isa. xiii. 7). This
thought is still further explained in ver. 17. Jehovah, the

God of Zion, is within her, and is a hero who helps or saves ;
He has inward joy in His rescued and blessed people (cf. Isa.
lxii. 5, lxv. 19). יַחֲרִישׁ בְּאַהֲבָתוֹ appears unsuitable, since we
cannot think of it as indicating silence as to sins that may
occur (cf. Ps. l. 21, Isa. xxii. 14), inasmuch as, according to
ver. 13, the remnant of Israel commits no sin. Ewald and
Hitzig would therefore read *yachădish;* and Ewald renders it
" he will grow young again," which Hitzig rejects as at variance with the language, because we should then have יִתְחַדֵּשׁ.
He therefore takes *yachădish* as synonymous with יַעֲשֶׂה חֲדָשׁוֹת,
he will do a new thing (Isa. xliii. 19). But this rendering
cannot be justified by the usage of the language, and does not
even yield a thought in harmony with the context. Silence in
His love is an expression used to denote love deeply felt, which
is absorbed in its object with thoughtfulness and admiration,[1]
and forms the correlate to rejoicing with exultation, *i.e.* to the
loud demonstration of one's love. The two clauses contain
simply a description, drawn from man's mode of showing love,
and transferred to God, to set forth the great satisfaction
which the Lord has in His redeemed people, and are merely a
poetical filling up of the expression, " He will rejoice over thee
with joy." This joy of His love will the Lord extend to all
who are troubled and pine in misery.

Ver. 18. " *I gather together those that mourn for the festive
meeting; they are of thee; reproach presses upon them.* Ver. 19.
*Behold, at that time I will treat with all thine oppressors, and will
save the limping, and gather together that which is dispersed, and
make them a praise and a name in every land of their shame.*
Ver. 20. *At that time will I bring you and gather you in time;
for I will make you a name and a praise among all the nations
of the earth, when I turn your captivity before your eyes, saith
Jehovah.*" The salvation held up in prospect before the remnant of Israel, which has been refined by the judgments and
delivered, was at a very remote distance in Zephaniah's time.

---

[1] " He assumes the person of a mortal man, because, unless He stam-
mers in this manner, He cannot sufficiently show how much He loves us.
Thy God will therefore be quiet in His love, i.e. this will be the greatest
delight of thy God, this His chief pleasure, when He shall cherish thee.
As a man caresses his dearest wife, so will God then quietly repose in thy
love."—CALVIN.

The first thing that awaited the nation was the judgment, through which it was to be dispersed among the heathen, according to the testimony of Moses and all the prophets, and to be refined in the furnace of affliction. The ten tribes were already carried away into exile, and Judah was to share the same fate immediately afterwards. In order, therefore, to offer to the pious a firm consolation of hope in the period of suffering that awaited them, and one on which their faith could rest in the midst of tribulation, Zephaniah mentions in conclusion the gathering together of all who pine in misery at a distance from Zion, and who are scattered far and wide, to assure even these of their future participation in the promised salvation. Every clause of ver. 18 is difficult. נוּגֵי is a *niphal* participle of יָגָה, with ו instead of י, as in Lam. i. 4, in the sense of to mourn, or be troubled. *Mōʿēd*, the time of the feast, when all Israel gathered together to rejoice before Jehovah, as in Hos. xii. 10, except that the word is not to be restricted to the feast of tabernacles, but may be understood as relating to all the feasts to which pilgrimages were made. The preposition *min* is taken by many in the sense of far from; in support of which Hitzig appeals to Lam. i. 4. But that passage is rather opposed to the application of the meaning referred to, inasmuch as we have מִבְּלִי there, in which *min* denotes the cause. And this causal signification is to be retained here also, if only because of the close connection between נוּגֵי and מִמּוֹעֵד, according to which the dependent word can only denote the object or occasion of the *nōgāh*. Those who are troubled for the festal meeting are they who mourn because they cannot participate in the joy of assembling before the face of the Lord, namely, on account of their banishment into foreign lands. *Mimmēkh hāyū*, from thee were they, *i.e.* they have been thine (*min* expressing descent or origin, as in Isa. lviii. 12, Ezra ii. 59, Ps. lxviii. 27; and the whole clause containing the reason for their meeting). The explanation given by Anton and Strauss is unsuitable and forced: " They will be away from thee, namely, separated from thee as mourners." In the last clause it is a matter of dispute to what the suffix in עָלֶיהָ refers. The explanation of Strauss, that it refers to Zion, is precluded by the fact that Zion is itself addressed, both in what precedes and what follows, and the thought does not require so rapid a change of persons. It is more natural to refer it to נוּגֵי, in which case the singular suffix is used collectively as a neuter, like the feminines הַצֹּלֵעָה and הַנִּדָּחָה; and the meaning takes this form : a burden upon them, viz. those who mourned for the feasts, was the reproach, *sc.* of slavery among the heathen (compare ver. 19, at the close). Consequently the clause assigns a still further reason for the promise, that they are to be gathered together. In ver. 19, עָשָׂה with אֵת signifies neither to handle in an evil sense, nor *comprimere, conculcare,* but to treat or negotiate with a person, as in Ezek. xxiii. 25 and xvii. 17, where אוֹת, according to a later usage of the language, is a preposition, and not a sign of the accusative. The more precise definition of the procedure, or of the kind of negotiation, is evident from the context. The reference is to a punitive procedure, or treating in wrath. מְעַנַּיִךְ as in Ps. lx. 14, the heathen nations who had subjugated Israel. What follows is taken almost *verbatim* from Mic. iv. 6; and the last clause points back to Deut. xxvi. 19, to tell the people that the Lord will assuredly realize the glorification promised to the people of His possession, and make Israel an object of praise to the whole earth. בְּכָל־הָאָרֶץ בָּשְׁתָּם, in all lands, where they have suffered shame. *Boshtâm* is epexegetical of *hâ'ârets,* which governs it; this explains the use of the article with the *nomen regens* (cf. Ewald, § 290, *d*). In order to paint the glory of the future salvation in still more vivid colours before the eyes of the people, the Lord ends by repeating this promise once more, with a slight change in the words. At that time will I lead you. The indefinite אָבִיא might be expounded from the context, by supplying the place to which God will lead them, after such passages as Isa. xiv. 2, xliii. 5. But it is more natural to think of the phrase, to lead out and in, according to Num. xxvii. 17, and to take אָבִיא as an abbreviation of הוֹצִיא וְהֵבִיא, picturing the pastoral fidelity with which the Lord will guide the redeemed. The following words קַבְּצִי אֶתְכֶם point to this : compare Isa. xl. 11, where the gathering of the lambs is added to the feeding of the flock, to give prominence to the faithful care of the shepherds for the weak and helpless. קַבְּצִי is the infinitive : my gathering you, *sc.* will take place. The choice of this form is to be traced, as Hitzig supposes, to the endeavour to secure uniformity in the clauses. A fresh reason is then assigned for

the promise, by a further allusion to the glorification appointed
for the people of God above all the nations of the earth,
coupled with the statement that this will take place at the
turning of their captivity, *i.e.* when God shall abolish the
misery of His people, and turn it into salvation (" turn the
captivity," as in ch. ii. 7), and that " before your eyes ;" *i.e.*,
not that " ye yourselves shall see the salvation, and not merely
your children, when they have closed your eyes" (Hitzig)—for
such an antithesis would be foreign to the context—but as
equivalent to " quite obviously, so that the turn in events stands
out before the eye," analogous to " ye will see eye to eye"
(Isa. lii. 8 ; cf. Luke ii. 30). This will assuredly take place,
for Jehovah has spoken it.

On the fulfilment of this promise, Theodoret observes that
" these things were bestowed upon those who came from Babylon, and have been offered to all men since then." This no
doubt indicates certain points of the fulfilment, but the principal fulfilment is generalized too much. For although the
promise retains its perfect validity in the case of the Christian
church, which is gathered out of both Jews and Gentiles, and will
receive its final accomplishment in the completion of the kingdom of heaven founded by Christ on the earth, the allusion to
the Gentile Christians falls quite into the background in the
picture of salvation in vers. 11–20, and the prophet's eye is
simply directed towards Israel, and the salvation reserved for
the rescued ἐκλογὴ τοῦ Ἰσραήλ. But inasmuch as Zephaniah
not only announces the judgment upon the whole earth, but
also predicts the conversion of the heathen nations to Jehovah
the living God (ch. iii. 9, 10), we must not restrict the description of salvation in ch. iii. 11–20 to the people of Israel who
were lineally descended from Abraham, and to the remnant of
them ; but must also regard the Gentiles converted to the
living God through Christ as included among them, and must
consequently say that the salvation which the Lord will procure
through the judgment for the daughter Zion or the remnant of
Israel, commenced with the founding of the Christian church
by the apostles for Judah and the whole world, and has been
gradually unfolded more and more through the spread of the
name of the Lord and His worship among all nations, and will
be eventually and fully realized at the second coming of Christ

to the last judgment, and to perfect His kingdom in the establishment of the New Jerusalem (Rev. xxi. and xxii.). It is true that both the judgment and the salvation of the remnant of Israel seeking Jehovah and His righteousness commenced even before Christ, with the giving up of Judah, together with all the tribes and kingdoms falling within the horizon of Old Testament prophecy, into the hand of Nebuchadnezzar and the imperial rulers who followed him ; but so far as the question of the fulfilment of our prophecy is concerned, these events come into consideration merely as preliminary stages of and preparations for the times of decision, which commenced with Christ not only for the Jews, but for all nations.

HAGGAI

INTRODUCTION.

1. PERSON OF THE PROPHET.—We have no further information concerning *Haggai* (*Chaygai, i.e.* the festal one, formed from *châg*, with the adjective termination *ai*: cf. Ewald, § 164, *c*, and 273, *e*; LXX. 'Aγγαῖος, Vulg. *Aggæus*) than that obtained from the headings to his prophetic addresses (ch. i. 1, ii. 1, 10, 20), and confirmed by Ezra v. 1,—namely, that he commenced his prophesying in the second year of Darius Hystaspes, and by means of his prophecies caused the work of building the temple, which had been suspended in consequence of the machinations of the *Cuthæans* (Samaritans), to be resumed, and in common with the prophet Zechariah, who commenced his labours two months later, ensured the continuance of that work. The extra-biblical accounts of the circumstances of his life have no evidence at all to support them. This is the case, for example, with the statement of Ps. Dorotheus and Ps. Epiphanius, that Haggai came from Babylon to Jerusalem when quite a young man, and that he survived the rebuilding of the temple, and was buried in honour near the burial-place of the priests, to say nothing of the strange opinion which was tolerably general in the times of Jerome and Cyril of Alexandria, and which arose from a misinterpretation of the word מַלְאַךְ in ch. i. 13, viz. that Haggai was an angel who appeared in human shape. And Ewald's conjecture, that Haggai had seen the temple of Solomon, cannot be inferred from ch. ii. 3. In that case he would have been about eighty years old when he commenced his labours as a prophet.

2. THE BOOK OF HAGGAI contains four words of God uttered by the prophet in the second year of the reign of Darius

Hystaspes, which had for their object the furtherance of the
building of the temple, and in all probability simply reproduce
the leading thought of His oral addresses. In the first prophecy, delivered on the new moon's day of the sixth month of
the year named (ch. i.), he condemns the indifference of the
people concerning the building of the temple, and represents
the failure of the crops and the curse under which the people
were suffering as a divine punishment for the neglect of that
work. In consequence of this admonition the building was
resumed. The three following prophecies in ch. ii. encourage
the people to continue the work they have begun. The
second, which was delivered only twenty-four days after the
first (ch. ii. 1-9), consoles those who are desponding on account
of the poverty of the new building, by promising that the Lord
will keep the covenant promise made to His people when they
came out of Egypt, and by shaking the whole world and all
the heathen, will give the new temple even greater glory than
that of Solomon had. The last two words of God were delivered to the people on the twenty-fourth day of the ninth month
of the same year. They predict in the first place the cessation
of the previous curse, and the return of the blessings of nature
promised to the church which had remained faithful to the
covenant (vers. 10-19); and in the second place, the preservation of the throne of Israel, represented in the person and
attitude of Zerubbabel, among the tempests which will burst
upon the kingdoms of this world, and destroy their might and
durability (vers. 20-23).

In order to understand clearly the meaning of these prophecies and promises in relation to the development of the Old
Testament kingdom of God, we must look at the historical circumstances under which Haggai was called by God to labour
as a prophet. Haggai was the first prophet who rose up after
the exile in the midst of the congregation of Judah that had
returned from Babylon, to proclaim to it the will and saving
purposes of its God. Between him and Zephaniah there lay
the seventy years' exile, and the labours of the great prophets
Jeremiah, Ezekiel, and Daniel. What all the earlier prophets
had foretold, and Jeremiah especially, in a comprehensive and
most impressive manner—namely, that the Lord would thrust
out Judah also among the heathen, on account of its obstinate

idolatry and resistance to the commandments of God, and would cause it to be enslaved by them—had been fulfilled. As the ten tribes had been carried away by the Assyrians long before, so had the inhabitants of Judah and Jerusalem been also carried into exile by the Chaldæans through Nebuchadnezzar. The Lord had now banished all His people from before His face, and sent them away among the heathen, but He had not cast them off entirely and for ever. He had indeed suspended His covenant with Israel, but He had not entirely abolished it. Even to the people pining in exile He had not only renewed the ancient promises through the prophet Ezekiel, after the dissolution of the kingdom of Judah and the destruction of Jerusalem and the temple, viz. that He would restore the nation to favour again, when it should come to the knowledge of its grievous sins, and turn to Him with penitence, and that He would redeem it from exile, lead it back to its own land, and exalt it to great glory; but He had also caused the might and duration of the kingdoms of the world to be proclaimed through Daniel, and their eventual overthrow through the kingdom of God from heaven. The seventy years, during which the land of Judah was to lie waste and the nation to serve Babel (Jer. xxv. 11), had now passed away. The Babylonian empire had fallen, and Koresh (Cyrus), the founder of the Persian empire, had given the Jews permission to return to their own land in the first year of his sole dominion, and had commanded that the temple of Jehovah in Jerusalem should be rebuilt. In consequence of this, a considerable number of the captives of Judah and Benjamin, viz. 42,360 freemen, with 7337 men-servants and maid-servants, led by Zerubbabel prince of Judah, a descendant of David, who was appointed governor in Judah, and by the high priest Joshua,. had returned to their homes (Ezra i. and ii.). Having arrived there, they had restored Jehovah's altar of burnt-offering in the seventh month of the year, and re-established the sacrificial worship prescribed in the law. They had also so far made preparations for the rebuilding of the temple, that even in the second month of the second year after their return they were able solemnly to lay the foundation for the new temple (Ezra iii.).

They had hardly commenced building, however, when the

Samaritans came with a request that they might take part in the building of the temple, because they also sought the God of the Jews. Now, when the chiefs of Judah refused to grant them this request, as being a mixed people, composed of the heathen colonists who had been transplanted into the kingdom of the ten tribes and a few Israelites who were left behind in the land, whilst their worship of God was greatly distorted by heathenism (see at 2 Kings xvii. 24–41), they endeavoured to disturb the work already begun, and to prevent its continuation and completion. They made the hands of the people of Judah idle, as we read in Ezra iv. 4, 5, frightening them while building, and hiring counsellors against them to frustrate their design, the whole of the still remaining time of Cyrus, and even till the reign of king Darius of Persia, so that the work at the house of God at Jerusalem ceased and was suspended till the second year of the reign of this king (Ezra iv. 24). But even if these machinations of the adversaries of Judah furnished the outward occasion for the interruption and suspension of the work they had begun, we must not seek for the sole and sufficient reason for the breaking off of the work in these alone. Nothing is recorded of any revocation of the edict issued by Cyrus during his reign; and even if the letter to Artachsata given in Ezra iv. 7 sqq. referred, as is generally assumed, to the building of the temple, and the reply of this king, which prohibited the continuation of the building, was issued by *Pseudo-Smerdis*, this only took place under the second successor of Cyrus, twelve years after the laying of the foundation-stone of the temple. What the enemies of Judah had previously undertaken and accomplished consisted simply in the fact that they made the hands of the Jewish people idle, frightening them while building, and frustrating their enterprise by hiring counsellors.[1] The latter they would hardly have succeeded in, if the Jews themselves had taken real

---

[1] So much is evident from the account in the book of Ezra, concerning the machinations of the Samaritans to frustrate the building. The more precise determination of what they did—namely, whether they obtained a command from the king to suspend the building—depends upon the explanation given to the section in Ezra (iv. 6–23), into which we need not enter more minutely till we come to our exposition of the book itself, inasmuch as it is not important to decide this question in order to understand our prophet.

pleasure in the continuation of the work, and had had firm confidence in the assistance of God. These were wanting. Even at the ceremony of laying the foundation-stone, many of the old priests, Levites and heads of tribes, who had seen the first temple, spoiled the people's pleasure by loud weeping. This weeping can hardly be explained merely from the recollection of the trials and sufferings of the last fifty years, which came involuntarily into their mind at that moment of solemn rejoicing, but was no doubt occasioned chiefly by the sight of the miserable circumstances under which the congregation took this work in hand, and in which they could not help saying to themselves, that the execution of the work would not correspond to the hopes which might have been cherished from the restoration of the house of God. But such thoughts as these would of necessity greatly detract from their pleasure in building, and as soon as outward difficulties were also placed in their way, would supply food to the doubt whether the time for carrying on this work had really come. Thus the zeal for building the house of God so cooled down, that they gave it up altogether, and simply began to provide for their own necessities, and to establish themselves comfortably in the land of their fathers, so far as the circumstances permitted (Hag. i. 4). This becomes perfectly intelligible, if we add that, judging from the natural character of sinful men, there were no doubt a considerable number of men among those who had returned, who had been actuated to return less by living faith in the Lord and His word, than by earthly hopes of prosperity and comfort in the land of their fathers. As soon as they found themselves disappointed in their expectations, they became idle and indifferent with regard to the house of the Lord. And the addresses of our prophet show clearly enough, that one principal reason for the suspension of the work is to be sought for in the lukewarmness and indifference of the people.

The contents and object of these addresses, viz. the circumstance that they are chiefly occupied with the command to build the temple, and attach great promises to the performance of this work, can only be explained in part, however, from the fact that the fidelity of the nation towards its God showed itself in zeal for the house of God. The deeper and truer explanation is to be found in the significance which the temple possessed in relation to the kingdom of God in its Old Testament form. The covenant of grace, made by the God of heaven and earth with the nation of Israel which He had chosen for His own peculiar possession, required, as a visible pledge of the real fellowship into which Jehovah had entered with Israel, a place where this fellowship could be sustained. For this reason, directly after the conclusion of the covenant at Sinai, God commanded the tabernacle to be erected, for a sanctuary in which, as covenant God, He would dwell among His people in a visible symbol; and, as the sign of the fulfilment of this divine promise, at the dedication of the tabernacle, and also of the temple of Solomon which took its place, the glory of Jehovah in the form of a cloud filled the sanctuary that had been built for His name. Hence the continuance of the ancient covenant, or of the kingdom of God in Israel, was bound up with the temple. When this was destroyed the covenant was broken, and the continuance of the kingdom of God suspended. If, therefore, the covenant which had been dissolved during the exile was to be renewed, if the kingdom of God was to be re-established in its Old Testament form, the rebuilding of the temple was the first and most important prerequisite for this; and the people were bound to pursue the work of building it with all possible zeal, that they might thereby practically attest their desire and readiness to resume the covenant fellowship which had been interrupted for a time. After the people had thus fulfilled the duty that devolved upon them, they might expect from the faithfulness of the Lord, their covenant God, that He would also restore the former gracious connection in all its completeness, and fulfil all His covenant promises. It is in this that the significance of *Haggai's* prophecies consists, so far as they have regard to the furthering of the work of building the temple. And this object was attained. The building of the temple was resumed in consequence of his admonition, and at the end of four years and a half—namely, in the sixth year of the reign of Darius— the work was finished (Ezra vi. 14, 15). But at its dedication the new temple was not filled with the cloud of the glory of Jehovah; yea, the most essential feature in the covenant made at Sinai was wanting, viz. the ark with the testimony, *i.e.* the tables of the law, which no man could restore, inasmuch as the ten words of the covenant had been written upon the tables by God Himself. The old covenant was not to be restored in its Sinaitic form ; but according to the promise made through Jeremiah (xxxi. 31 sqq.), the Lord would make a new covenant with the house of Israel and Judah ; He would put His law into their heart, and write it in their minds. The people, however, were not sufficiently prepared for this. Therefore those who had returned from Babylon were still to continue under the rule of the heathen powers of the world, until the time had arrived for the conclusion of the new covenant, when the Lord would come to His temple, and the angel of the covenant would fill it with the glory of the heathen. Thus the period of Zerubbabel's temple was a time of waiting for Judah, and a period of preparation for the coming of the promised Saviour. To give the people a pledge during that period of the certainty of the fulfilment of the covenant grace of God, was the object of Haggai's two promises of salvation.

So far as the form is concerned, the prophecies of Haggai have not the poetical swing of the earlier prophetical diction. They are written in the simplest rhetorical style, and never rise very far above the level of good prose, although vivacity is given to the delivery by the frequent use of interrogatives (cf. ch. i. 4, 9, ii. 3, 12, 13, 19), and it by no means infrequently opens into full oratorical rhythm (cf. ch. i. 6, 9–11, ii. 6–8, 22). One characteristic of Haggai's mode of description is the peculiar habit to which Nægelsbach has called attention—namely, of uttering the main thought with concise and nervous brevity, after a long and verbose introduction (cf. ch. i. 2b, i. 12b, ii. 5b, ii. 19b) ; so that it might be said that he is accustomed "to conceal a small and most intensive kernel under a broad and thick shell." His language is tolerably free from Chaldæisms.

For the exegetical literature, see my *Lehrbuch der Einleitung*, p. 308 ; to which add Aug. Koehler's *die Weissagungen Haggai's erklärt*, Erlangen 1860.

EXPOSITION.

ADMONITION TO BUILD THE TEMPLE, AND ITS RESULT.—
Chap. i.

Haggai, having reproved the people for their indifference with regard to the rebuilding of the temple, and pointed to the failure of their crops for want of rain as a divine chastisement consequent upon it, admonishes Zerubbabel the governor, Joshua the high priest, and the people generally, to resume the building of the temple (vers. 2–11), and then describes the way in which his appeal was responded to (vers. 12–15).

In ver. 1 this address is introduced by a statement of the time at which it had been delivered, and the persons to whom it was addressed. The word of Jehovah was uttered through the prophet in the second year of king Darius, on the first day of the sixth month. דָּרְיָוֶשׁ answers to the name *Dâryavush* or *Dârayavush* of the arrow-headed inscriptions; it is derived from the Zendic *dar*, Sanskrit *dhri*, contracted into *dhar*, and is correctly explained by Herodotus (vi. 98) as signifying ἑρξείης = *coërcitor*. It is written in Greek Δαρεῖος (*Darius*). The king referred to is the king of Persia (Ezra iv. 5, 24), the first of that name, *i.e. Darius Hystaspes*, who reigned from 521 to 486 B.C. That this is the king meant, and not *Darius Nothus*, is evident from the fact that Zerubbabel the Jewish prince, and Joshua the high priest, who had led back the exiles from Babylon to Judæa in the reign of Cyrus, in the year 536 (Ezra i. 8, ii. 2), might very well be still at the head of the returned people in the second year of the reign of Darius Hystaspes, *i.e.* in the year 520, but could not have been still living in the reign of Darius Nothus, who did not ascend the throne till 113 years after the close of the captivity. Moreover, in ch. ii. 3, Haggai presupposes that many of his contemporaries had seen the temple of Solomon. Now, as that temple had been destroyed in the year 588 or 587, there might very well be old men still living under Darius Hystaspes, in the year 520, who had seen that temple in their early days; but that could not be the case under Darius Nothus, who

ascended the Persian throne in the year 423. The prophet
addresses his word to the temporal and spiritual heads of the
nation, to the governor *Zerubbabel* and the high priest *Joshua.*
זְרֻבָּבֶל is written in many codd. זְרוּבָבֶל, and is either formed
from זְרוּי בָּבֶל, *in Babyloniam dispersus,* or as the child, if born
before the dispersion in Babylonia, would not have received
this name proleptically, probably more correctly from זְרוּעַ בָּבֶל,
in Babylonia satus s. genitus, in which case the ע was assimi-
lated to the ב when the two words were joined into one, and
ב received a *dagesh.* Zerubbabel (LXX. Ζοροβάβελ) was
the son of *Shealtiël.* שְׁאַלְתִּיאֵל is written in the same way in
ch. ii. 23, 1 Chron. iii. 17, Ezra iii. 2, and Neh. xii. 1 ; whereas
in vers. 12 and 14, and ch. ii. 2, it is contracted into שַׁלְתִּיאֵל.
She'altī'ēl, i.e. the prayer of God, or one asked of God in
prayer, was, according to 1 Chron. iii. 17, if we take *'assir* as
an appellative, a son of *Jeconiah* (Jehoiachin), or, if we take
'assir as a proper name, a son of Assir the son of Jeconiah,
and therefore a grandson of Jehoiachin. But, according to
1 Chron. iii. 19, Zerubbabel was a son of *Pedaiah,* a brother
of Shealtiel. And lastly, according to the genealogy in Luke
iii. 27, Shealtiel was not a son of either Assir or Jeconiah, but
of *Neri,* a descendant of David through his son Nathan. These
three divergent accounts, according to which Zerubbabel was
(1) a son of Shealtiël, (2) a son of Pedaiah, the brother of
Shealtiël, and a grandson of Assir or Jeconiah, (3) a son of
Shealtiël and grandson of Neri, may be brought into harmony
by means of the following combinations, if we bear in mind
the prophecy of Jeremiah (Jer. xxii. 30), that Jeconiah would
be childless, and not be blessed with having one of his seed
sitting upon the throne of David and ruling over Judah.
Since this prophecy of Jeremiah was fulfilled, according to
the genealogical table given by Luke, inasmuch as Shealtiël's
father there is not Assir or Jeconiah, a descendant of David
in the line of Solomon, but Neri, a descendant of David's son
Nathan, it follows that neither of the sons of Jeconiah mentioned in 1 Chron. iii. 17, 18 (Zedekiah and Assir) had a son,
but that the latter had only a daughter, who married a man
of the family of her father's tribe, according to the law of
the heiresses, Num. xxvii. 8, xxxvi. 8, 9—namely Neri, who
belonged to the tribe of Judah and family of David. From

this marriage sprang Shealtiël, Malkiram, Pedaiah, and others. The eldest of these took possession of the property of his maternal grandfather, and was regarded in law as his (legitimate) son. Hence he is described in 1 Chron. iii. 17 as the son of Assir the son of Jeconiah, whereas in Luke he is described, according to his lineal descent, as the son of Neri. But Shealtiël also appears to have died without posterity, and simply to have left a widow, which necessitated a Levirate marriage on the part of one of the brothers (Deut. xxv. 5–10; Matt. xxii. 24–28). Shealtiël's second brother Pedaiah appears to have performed his duty, and to have begotten Zerubbabel and Shimei by this sister-in-law (1 Chron. iii. 19), the former of whom, Zerubbabel, was entered in the family register of the deceased uncle Shealtiël, passing as his (lawful) son and heir, and continuing his family. Koehler holds essentially the same views (see his comm. on ch. ii. 23). Zerubbabel was *pechâh*, a Persian governor. The real meaning of this foreign word is still a disputed point.[1] In addition to his Hebrew name, Zerubbabel also bore the Chaldæan name *Sheshbazzar*, as an officer of the Persian king, as we may see by comparing Ezra i. 8, 11, v. 14, 16, with Ezra ii. 2, iii. 2, 8, and v. 2. For the prince of Judah, Sheshbazzar, to whom Koresh directed the temple vessels brought from Jerusalem by Nebuchadnezzar to be delivered, and who brought them back from Babylon to Jerusalem (Ezra i. 8, 11, v. 14), and who laid the foundation for the house of God, according to ch. v. 16, is

---

[1] Prof. Spiegel (in Koehler on Mal. i. 8) objects to the combination attempted by Benfey, and transferred to the more modern lexicons, viz. with the Sanscrit *paksha*, a companion or friend (see at 1 Kings x. 15), on the ground that this word (1) signifies *wing* in the Vedas, and only received the meaning *side*, *party*, *appendix*, at a later period, and (2) does not occur in the Eranian languages, from which it must necessarily have been derived. Hence Spiegel proposes to connect it with *pâvan* (from the root *pâ*, to defend or preserve : compare F. Justi, *Hdb. der Zendsprache*, p. 187), which occurs in Sanscrit and Old Persian (cf. *Khsatrapâvan* = Satrap) at the end of composite words, and in the Avesta as an independent word, in the contracted form *pavan*. " It is quite possible that the dialectic form *pagvan* (cf. the plural *pachăvōth* in Neh. ii. 7, 9) may have developed itself from this, like *dregvat* from *drevat*, and *hvôgva* from *hvôva*." Hence *pechâh* would signify a keeper of the government, or of the kingdom (*Khsatra*).

called Zerubbabel in Ezra ii. 2, as the leader of the procession, who not only laid the foundation for the temple, along with Joshua the high priest, according to Ezra iii. 2, 8, but also resumed the building of the temple, which had been suspended, in connection with the same Joshua during the reign of Darius. The high priest *Joshua* (*Y^ehōshuá*, in Ezra iii. 2, 8, iv. 3, contracted into *Yeshuá*) was a son of Jozadak, who had been carried away by the Chaldæans to Babylon (1 Chron. v. 41), and a grandson of the high priest Seraiah, whom Nebuchadnezzar had caused to be executed at Riblah in the year 588, after the conquest of Jerusalem (2 Kings xxv. 18-21 ; Jer. lii. 24-27). The time given, " in the sixth month," refers to the ordinary reckoning of the Jewish year (compare Zech. i. 7 and vii. 1, and Neh. i. 1 with Neh. ii. 1, where the name of the month is given as well as the number). The first day, therefore, was the new moon's day, which was kept as a feast-day not only by a special festal sacrifice (Num. xxviii. 11 sqq.), but also by the holding of a religious meeting at the sanctuary (compare Isa. i. 13 and the remarks on 2 Kings iv. 23). On this day Haggai might expect some susceptibility on the part of the people for his admonition, inasmuch as on such a day they must have been painfully and doubly conscious that the temple of Jehovah was still lying in ruins (Hengstenberg, Koehler).

Vers. 2-6. The prophet begins by charging the people with their unconcern about building the house of God. Ver. 2. "*Thus saith Jehovah of hosts : This people saith, It is not time to come, the time for the house of Jehovah to be built.*" הָעָם הַזֶּה, *iste populus,* not my people, or Jehovah's people, but *hazzeh* (this) in a contemptuous sense. Of the two clauses, (*a*) " It is not time to come," and (*b*) " The time of the house of Jehovah," the latter gives the more precise definition of the former, the בּא (to come) being explained as meaning the time to build the house of Jehovah. The meaning is simply this : the time has not yet arrived to come and build the house of Jehovah; for לֹא in this connection signifies " not yet," as in Gen. ii. 5, Job xxii. 16. A distinction is drawn between coming to the house of Jehovah and building the house, as in ver. 14. There is no ground, therefore, for altering the text, as Hitzig proposes, inasmuch as the defective mode of writing the infinitive בּא is by no means rare (compare, for example, Ex. ii. 18, Lev. xiv. 48, Num. xxxii. 9, 1 Kings xiv. 28, Isa. xx. 1); and there is no foundation whatever for the absurd rendering of the words of the text, " It is not the time of the having arrived of the time of the house," etc. (Hitzig).

The word of Jehovah is opposed in ver. 4 to this speech of the people ; and in order to give greater prominence to the antithesis, the introductory formula, " *The word of Jehovah came by Haggai the prophet thus*," is repeated in ver. 3. In order to appeal to the conscience of the people, God meets them with the question in ver. 4 : " *Is it time for you yourselves to live in your houses wainscoted, whilst this house lies waste ?*" The הַ before עֵת is not the article, but ה interr. אַתֶּם is added to strengthen the pronoun (cf. Ges. § 121, 3). *S*ᵉ*phūnīm* without the article is connected with the noun, in the form of an apposition : in your houses, they being wainscoted, *i.e.* with the inside walls covered or inlaid with costly wood-work. Such were the houses of the rich and of the more distinguished men (cf. Jer. xxii. 14; 1 Kings vii. 7). Living in such houses was therefore a sign of luxury and comfort. וְהַבַּיִת וגו' is a circumstantial clause, which we should express by " *whilst* this house," etc. With this question the prophet cuts off all excuse, on the ground that the circumstances of the times, and the oppression under which they suffered, did not permit of the rebuilding of the temple. If they themselves lived comfortably in wainscoted houses, their civil and political condition could not be so oppressive, that they could find in that a sufficient excuse for neglecting to build the temple. Even if the building of the temple had been prohibited by an edict of *Pseudo-Smerdes*, as many commentators infer from Ezra iv. 8-24, the reign of this usurper only lasted a few months; and with his overthrow, and the ascent of the throne by Darius Hystaspes, a change had taken place in the principles of government, which might have induced the heads of Judah, if the building of the house of God had rested upon their hearts as it did upon the heart of king David (2 Sam. vii. 2 ; Ps. cxxxii. 2-5), to take steps under the new king to secure the revocation of this edict, and the renewal of the command issued by Cyrus.

After rebutting the untenable grounds of excuse, Haggai calls attention in vers. 5, 6 to the curse with which God has

punished, and is still punishing, the neglect of His house.
Ver. 5. "*And now, thus saith Jehovah of hosts, Set your heart
upon your ways.* Ver. 6. *Ye have sowed much, and brought
in little: ye eat, and not for satisfaction; drink, and not to be
filled with drink: ye clothe yourselves, and it does not serve for
warming; and the labourer for wages works for wages into a
purse pierced with holes.*" שִׂימוּ לְבַבְכֶם, a favourite formula with
Haggai (cf. ver. 7 and ch. ii. 15, 18). To set the heart upon
one's ways, *i.e.* to consider one's conduct, and lay it to heart.
The ways are the conduct, with its results. J. H. Michaelis
has given it correctly, "To your designs and actions, and their
consequences." In their ways, hitherto, they have reaped no
blessing: they have sowed much, but brought only a little into
their barns. הָבֵא, inf. abs., to bring in what has been reaped,
or bring it home. What is here stated must not be restricted
to the last two harvests which they had had under the reign of
Darius, as Koehler supposes, but applies, according to ch. ii.
15–17, to the harvests of many years, which had turned out
very badly. The inf. abs., which is used in the place of the
finite verb and determined by it, is continued in the clauses
which follow, אָכוֹל, etc. The meaning of these clauses is, not that
the small harvest was not sufficient to feed and clothe the people
thoroughly, so that they had to "cut their coat according to
their cloth," as Maurer and Hitzig suppose, but that even in
their use of the little that had been reaped, the blessing of God
was wanting, as is not only evident from the words themselves,
but placed beyond the possibility of doubt by ver. 9.[1] What
they ate and drank did not suffice to satisfy them; the clothes
which they procured yielded no warmth; and the wages which
the day-labourer earned vanished just as rapidly as if it had
been placed in a bag full of holes (cf. Lev. xxvi. 26; Hos. iv.
10; Mic. vi. 14). לוֹ after לָהֶם refers to the individual who

---

[1] Calvin and Osiander see a double curse in ver. 6. The former says,
"We know that God punishes men in both ways, both by withdrawing
His blessing, so that the earth is parched, and the heaven gives no rain,
and also, even when there is a good supply of the fruits of the earth, by
preventing their satisfying, so that there is no real enjoyment of them.
It often happens that men collect what would be quite a sufficient quantity for food, but for all that, are still always hungry. This kind of curse
is seen the more plainly when God deprives the bread and wine of their
true virtue, so that eating and drinking fail to support the strength."

clothes himself, and is to be explained from the phrase לִי חַם,
" I am warm" (1 Kings i. 1, 2, etc.).

Vers. 7–11. After this allusion to the visitation of God, the
prophet repeats the summons in vers. 7, 8, to lay to heart their
previous conduct, and choose the way that is well-pleasing to
God. Ver. 7. *" Thus saith Jehovah of hosts, Direct your heart
upon your ways.* Ver. 8. *Go up to the mountains and fetch wood
and build the house, and I will take pleasure therein and glorify
myself, saith Jehovah."* Hâhâr (the mountain) is not any particular mountain, say the temple mountain (Grotius, Maurer,
Ros.), or Lebanon (Cocceius, Ewald, etc.); but the article is
used generically, and hâhâr is simply the mountain regarded as
the locality in which wood chiefly grows (cf. Neh. viii. 15).
Fetching wood for building is an individualizing expression for
providing building materials; so that there is no ground for the
inference drawn by Hitzig and many of the Rabbins, that
the walls of the temple had been left standing when it was
destroyed, so that all that had to be done was to renew the
wood-work,—an inference at variance not only with the reference made to the laying of the foundation of the temple in
ch. ii. 18 and Ezra iii. 10, but also to the express statement in
the account sent by the provincial governor to king Darius in
Ezra v. 8, viz. that the house of the great God was built with
square stones, and that timber was laid in the walls. וְאֶרְצֶה־בּוֹ,
so will I take pleasure in it (the house); whereas so long as it lay
in ruins, God was displeased with it. וְאֶכָּבֵד, and I will glorify
myself, *sc.* upon the people, by causing my blessing to flow to
it again. The *keri* וְאֶכָּבְדָה is an unnecessary emendation, inasmuch as, although the voluntative might be used (cf. Ewald,
§ 350, *a*), it is not required, and has not been employed, both
because it is wanting in אֶרְצֶה, for the simple reason that the
verbs ל"ה do not easily admit of this form (Ewald, § 228, *a*),
and also because it is not used in other instances, where the
same circumstances do not prevail (*e.g.* Zech. i. 3).[1] Ewald

[1] The later Talmudists, indeed, have taken the omission of the ה, which
stands for 5 when used as a numeral, as an indication that there were five
things wanting in the second temple: (1) the ark of the covenant, with
the atoning lid and the cherubim; (2) the sacred fire; (3) the shechinah;
(4) the Holy Spirit; (5) the Urim and Thummim (compare the Babylonian
tract *Joma* 21*b*, and *Sal. ben Melech, Miclal Jophi* on Hag. i. 8).

and Hitzig adopt this rendering, " that I may feel myself honoured," whilst Maurer and Rückert translate it as a passive, " that I may be honoured." But both of these views are much less in harmony with the context, since what is there spoken of is the fact that God will then turn His good pleasure to the people once more, and along with that His blessing. How thoroughly this thought predominates, is evident from the more elaborate description, which follows in vers. 9–11, of the visitation from God, viz. the failure of crops and drought.

Ver. 9. " *Ye looked out for much, and behold (it came) to little ; and ye brought it home, and I blew into it.   Why ? is the saying of Jehovah of hosts.   Because of my house, that it lies waste, whereas ye run every man for his house.* Ver. 10. *Therefore the heaven has withheld its dew on your account, that no dew fell, and the earth has withheld her produce.* Ver. 11. *And I called drought upon the earth, and upon the mountains, and upon the corn, and upon the new wine, and upon the oil, and upon everything that the ground produces, and upon men, and upon cattle, and upon all the labour of the hands.*" The meaning of ver. 9a is evident from the context.   The inf. abs. *pânōh* stands in an address full of emotion in the place of the perfect, and, as the following clause shows, for the second person plural. Ye have turned yourselves, fixed your eye upon much, *i.e.* upon a rich harvest, וְהִנֵּה־לִמְעָט, and behold the desired much turned to little.   Ye brought into the house, ye fetched home what was reaped, and I blew into it, *i.e.* I caused it to fly away, like chaff before the wind, so that there was soon none of it left. Here is a double curse, therefore, as in ver. 6 : instead of much, but little was reaped, and the little that was brought home melted away without doing any good.   To this exposition of the curse the prophet appends the question יַעַן מֶה, why, *sc.* has this taken place ? that he may impress the cause with the greater emphasis upon their hardened minds.   For the same reason he inserts once more, between the question and the answer, the words " is the saying of Jehovah of hosts," that the answer may not be mistaken for a subjective view, but laid to heart as a declaration of the God who rules the world. The choice of the form מֶה for מָה was probably occasioned by the guttural ע in the יַעַן, which is closely connected with it, just as the analogous use of עַל־מֶה instead of עַל־מָה in Isa. i. 5,

Ps. x. 13, and Jer. xvi. 10, where it is not followed by a word commencing with ע as in Deut. xxix. 23, 1 Kings ix. 8, Jer. xxii. 8. The former have not been taken into account at all by Ewald in his elaborate *Lehrbuch* (cf. § 182, *b*). In the answer given by God, "because of my house" (*ya'an bêthî*) is placed first for the sake of emphasis, and the more precise explanation follows. אֲשֶׁר הוּא, "because it," not "that which." וְאַתֶּם וגו׳ is a circumstantial clause. רָצִים . . . לְבֵיתוֹ, not "every one runs to his house," but "runs for his house," לְ denoting the object of the running, as in Isa. lix. 7 and Prov. i. 16. "When the house of Jehovah was in question, they did not move from the spot; but if it concerned their own house, they ran" (Koehler). In vers. 10 and 11, the curse with which God punished the neglect of His house is still further depicted, with an evident play upon the punishment with which transgressors are threatened in the law (Lev. xxvi. 19, 20; Deut. xi. 17 and xxviii. 23, 24). עֲלֵיכֶם is not a *dat. incomm.* (Hitzig), which is never expressed by עַל; but עַל is used either in a causal sense, "on your account" (Chald.), or in a local sense, "over you," after the analogy of Deut. xxviii. 23, שָׁמֶיךָ אֲשֶׁר עַל רֹאשְׁךָ, in the sense of "the heaven over you will withhold" (Ros., Koehl.). It is impossible to decide with certainty between these two. The objection to the first, that "on your account" would be superfluous after עַל־כֵּן, has no more force than that raised by Hitzig against the second, viz. that *super* would be מֵעַל. There is no tautology in the first explanation, but the עֲלֵיכֶם, written emphatically at the commencement, gives greater intensity to the threat : "on account of you," you who only care for your own houses, the heaven withholds the dew. And with the other explanation, מֵעַל would only be required in case עֲלֵיכֶם were regarded as the object, upon which the dew ought to fall down from above. כָּלָא, not "to shut itself up," but in a transitive sense, with the derivative meaning to withhold or keep back; and *mittâl*, not partitively "of the dew," equivalent to "a portion of it," but *min* in a privative sense, "away from," *i.e.* so that no dew falls ; for it is inadmissible to take *mittâl* as the object, "to hold back along with the dew," after the analogy of Num. xxiv. 11 (Hitzig), inasmuch as the accusative of the person is wanting, and in the parallel clause כָּלָא is construed with the *accus. rei.* וָאֶקְרָא in ver. 11 is still dependent upon עַל־כֵּן. The word *chōrebh*, in the sense of drought, applies strictly speaking only to the land and the fruits of the ground, but it is also transferred to men and beasts, inasmuch as drought, when it comes upon all vegetation, affects men and beasts as well; and in this clause it may be taken in the general sense of devastation. The word is carefully chosen, to express the idea of the *lex talionis.* Because the Jews left the house of God *chârēbh,* they were punished with *chōrebh.* The last words are comprehensive: "all the labour of the hands" had reference to the cultivation of the soil and the preparation of the necessities of life.

Vers. 12–15. The result of this reproof.—Ver. 12. "*Zerubbabel, and Joshua, and the whole of the remnant of the people, hearkened to the voice of Jehovah their God, and according to the words of Haggai the prophet, as Jehovah their God had sent him; and the people feared before Jehovah.*" "All the remnant of the people" does not mean the rest of the nation besides Zerubbabel and Joshua, in support of which Koehler refers to Jer. xxxix. 3 and 1 Chron. xii. 38, either here or in ver. 14 and ch. ii. 2, inasmuch as Zerubbabel as the governor and prince of Judah, and Joshua as the high priest, are not embraced under the idea of the "people" (*'âm*), as is the case in the passages quoted, where those who are described as the *sh⁰'ērīth,* or remnant, are members or portions of the whole in question. The "remnant of the people," as in Zech. viii. 6, is that portion of the nation which had returned from exile as a small gleaning of the nation, which had once been much larger. שָׁמַע בְּקוֹל, to hearken to the voice, *i.e.* to lay to heart, so as to obey what was heard. בְּקוֹל יי is still more minutely defined by וְעַל־דִּבְרֵי וגו': "and (indeed) according to the words of Haggai, in accordance with the fact that Jehovah had sent him." This last clause refers to דִּבְרֵי, which he had to speak according to the command of God (Hitzig); cf. Mic. iii. 4. The first fruit of the hearing was, that the people feared before Jehovah; the second is mentioned in ver. 14, namely, that they resumed the neglected building of the temple. Their fearing before Jehovah presupposes that they saw their sin against God, and discerned in the drought a judgment from God.

This penitential state of mind on the part of the people and their rulers was met by the Lord with the promise of His assistance, in order to elevate this disposition into determination and deed. Ver. 13. " *Then spake Haggai, the messenger of Jehovah, in the message of Jehovah to the people, thus: I am with you, is the saying of Jehovah.* Ver. 14. *And Jehovah stirred up the spirit of Zerubbabel, and the spirit of Joshua, and the spirit of all the remnant of the nation ; and they came and did work at the house of Jehovah of hosts, their God.*" The prophet is called מַלְאָךְ in ver. 13, *i.e.* messenger (not "angel," as many in the time of the fathers misunderstood the word as meaning), as being sent by Jehovah to the people, to make known to them His will (compare Mal. ii. 7, where the same epithet is applied to the priest). As the messenger of Jehovah, he speaks by command of Jehovah, and not in his own name or by his own impulse. אֲנִי אִתְּכֶם, I am with you, will help you, and will remove all the obstacles that stand in the way of your building (cf. ch. ii. 4). This promise Jehovah fulfilled, first of all by giving to Zerubbabel, Joshua, and the people, a willingness to carry out the work. הֵעִיר רוּחַ, to awaken the spirit of any man, *i.e.* to make him willing and glad to carry out His resolutions (compare 1 Chron. v. 26 ; 2 Chron. xxi. 16; Ezra i. 1, 5). Thus filled with joyfulness, courage, and strength, they began the work on the twenty-fourth day of the sixth month, in the second year of king Darius (ver. 15), that is to say, twenty-three days after Haggai had first addressed his challenge to them. The interval had been spent in deliberation and counsel, and in preparations for carrying out the work. In several editions and some few MSS. in Kennicott, in Tischendorf's edition of the LXX., in the Itala and in the Vulgate, ver. 15 is joined to the next chapter. But this is proved to be incorrect by the fact that the chronological statements in ver. 15 and ch. ii. 1 are irreconcilable with one another. Ver. 15 is really so closely connected with ver. 14, that it is rather to be regarded as the last clause of that verse.

THE GLORY OF THE NEW TEMPLE, AND THE BLESSINGS OF THE NEW ERA.—CHAP. II.

This chapter contains three words of God, which Haggai published to the people in the seventh and ninth months of the second year of Darius, to strengthen them in their zeal for the building of the temple, and to preserve them from discouragement. The first of these words (vers. 1–9) refers to the relation in which the new temple would stand to the former one, and was uttered not quite four weeks after the building of the temple had been resumed.

Vers. 1–9. GLORY OF THE NEW TEMPLE.—Vers. 1 and 2. *" In the seventh month, on the twenty-first day of the month, the word of the Lord came through Haggai,"* viz. to Zerubbabel, Joshua, and the remnant of the nation, that is to say, to the whole of the congregation that had returned from exile; whereas the first appeal was only addressed to Zerubbabel and Joshua (see the introduction to ch. i. 1), although it also applied to the whole nation. Just as in the second year of the return from Babylon, when the foundation for the temple, which was about to be rebuilt, was laid in the reign of Cyrus, many old men, who had seen the temple of Solomon, burst out into loud weeping when they saw the new foundation (Ezra iii. 10 sqq.); a similar feeling of mourning and despair appears to have taken possession of the people and their rulers immediately after the work had been resumed under Darius, and doubts arose whether the new building was really well-pleasing to the Lord, and ought to be carried on. The occasion for this despondency is not to be sought, as Hitzig supposes, in the fact that objections were made to the continuance of the building (Ezra v. 3), and that the opinion prevailed in consequence that the works ought to be stopped till the arrival of the king's authority. For this view not only has no support whatever in our prophecy, but is also at variance with the account in the book of Ezra, according to which the governor and his companions, who had made inquiries concerning the command to build, did not stop the building while they sent word of the affair to the king (Ezra v. 5). Moreover, the conjecture that the people had been seized with a feeling of sadness, when the work had so far advanced that they were able to institute a comparison between the new temple and the earlier one (Hengstenberg), does not suffice to explain the rapid alteration which took place in the feelings of the people. The building could not have been so far advanced in three weeks and a half as that the contrast between the new temple and the former one could be clearly seen, if it had not been noticed from the very first; a fact, however, to which Ezra iii. 12 distinctly refers. But although it had been seen from the very beginning that the new building would not come up to the glory of the former temple, the people could not from the very outset give up the hope of erecting a building which, if not quite equal to the former one in glory, would at all events come somewhat near to it. Under these circumstances, their confidence in the work might begin to vanish as soon as the first enthusiasm flagged, and a time arrived which was more favourable for the quiet contemplation of the general condition of affairs. This explanation is suggested by the time at which the second word of God was delivered to the congregation through the prophet. The twenty-first day of the seventh month was the seventh day of the feast of tabernacles (cf. Lev. xxiii. 34 sqq.), the great festival of rejoicing, on which Israel was to give practical expression to its gratitude for the gracious guidance which it had received through the wilderness, as well as for the blessing of the ingathering of all the fruits of the ground, which ended with the gathering of the orchard-fruits and with the vintage, by the presentation of numerous burnt-offerings and other sacrifices (see my *biblische Archäologie*, i. p. 415 sqq.). The return of this festal celebration, especially after a harvest which had turned out very miserably, and showed no signs of the blessing of God, could not fail to call up vividly before the mind the difference between the former times, when Israel was able to assemble in the courts of the Lord's house, and so to rejoice in the blessings of His grace in the midst of abundant sacrificial meals, and the present time, when the altar of burnt-sacrifice might indeed be restored again, and the building of the temple be resumed, but in which there was no prospect of erecting a building that would in any degree answer to the glory of the former temple; and when the prophecies of an Isaiah or an Ezekiel were remembered,

according to which the new temple was to surpass the former
one in glory, it would be almost sure to produce gloomy thoughts,
and supply food for doubt whether the time had really come
for rebuilding the temple, when after all it would be only a
miserable hut. In this gloomy state of mind consolation was
very necessary, if the hardly awakened zeal for the building
of the house of God was not to cool down and vanish entirely
away. To bring this consolation to those who were in despair
was the object of the second word of God, which Haggai was
to publish to the congregation. It runs as follows:

Ver. 3. " *Who is left among you. that saw this house in its
former glory? and how do ye see it now? Is it not as nothing
in your eyes?* Ver. 4. *And now be comforted, Zerubbabel, is
the saying of Jehovah; and be comforted, Joshua son of Jozadak,
thou high priest; and be comforted all the people of the land, is
the saying of Jehovah, and work: for I am with you, is the
saying of Jehovah of hosts.* Ver. 5. *The word that I concluded
with you at your coming out of Egypt, and my Spirit, stand in
the midst of you; fear ye not.*" The prophet, admitting the
poverty of the new building in comparison with the former one,
exhorts them to continue the work in comfort, and promises
them that the Lord will be with them, and fulfil His covenant
promises. The question in ver. 3 is addressed to the old men,
who had seen Solomon's temple in all its glory. There might
be many such men still living, as it was only sixty-seven or sixty-
eight years since the destruction of the first temple. הַנִּשְׁאָר is
the predicate to the subject מִי, and has the article because it is
defined by the reflex action of the relative clause which follows
(compare Ewald, § 277, *a*). The second question, וּמָה אַתֶּם וגו',
et qualem videtis, In what condition do ye see it now? is appended to the last clause of the first question: the house which
ye saw in its former glory. There then follows with הֲלוֹא, in
the form of a lively assurance, the statement of the difference
between the two buildings. כָּמֹהוּ כְּאַיִן, which has been interpreted in very different ways, may be explained from the
double use of the כ in comparisons, which is common in
Hebrew, and which answers to our *as—so:* here, however, it is
used in the same way as in Gen. xviii. 25 and xliv. 18; that is
to say, the object to be compared is mentioned first, and the
object with which the comparison is instituted is mentioned

afterwards, in this sense, " so is it, as having no existence," in
which case we should either leave out the first particle of comparison, or if it were expressed, should have to reverse the order
of the words: " as not existing (nothing), so is it in your eyes."
Koehler gives this correct explanation ; whereas if כָּמֹהוּ be explained according to Joel ii. 2, its equal, or such an one, we
get the unsuitable thought, that it is not the temple itself, but
something like the temple, that is compared to nothing. Even in
Gen. xliv. 18, to which Ewald very properly refers as containing a perfectly equivalent phrase, it is not a man equal to Joseph,
but Joseph himself, who is compared to Pharaoh, and described
as being equal to him. Nevertheless they are not to let their
courage fail, but to be comforted and to work. *Cházaq*, to be
inwardly strong, *i.e.* to be comforted. *Asâh*, to work or procure, as in Ruth ii. 19 and Prov. xxxi. 13, in actual fact, to
continue the work of building bravely, without there being any
necessity to supply מְלָאכָה from ch. i. 14. For Jehovah will be
with them (cf. ch. i. 13). In confirmation of this promise the
Lord adds, that the word which He concluded with them on
their coming out of Egypt, and His Spirit, will continue among
them. " The word" (*'eth-haddâbhâr*) cannot be either the
accusative of the object to the preceding verb *'âsû* (ver. 4), or
to any verb we may choose to supply, or the preposition *'ēth*,
with, or the accusative of norm or measure (Luther, Calvin,
and others). To connect it with *'âsû* yields no suitable meaning. It is not the word, which they vowed to the Lord, at the
conclusion of the covenant, that they are to do now, but the
work which they had begun, viz. the building of the temple,
they are now to continue. It is perfectly arbitrary to supply
the verb *zikhrū*, remember (Ewald and Hengstenberg), and to
understand the prophet as reminding them of the word " fear
not" (Ex. xx. 17 (20)). That word, " fear not," with which
Moses, not God, infused courage into the people, who were
alarmed at the terrible phenomenon with which Jehovah came
down upon Sinai, has no such central significance as that
Haggai could point to it without further introduction, and say
that Jehovah had concluded it with them on their coming out
of Egypt. The word which the Lord concluded with Israel
when He led it out of Egypt, can only be the promise which
established the covenant, to the fulfilment of which God bound

Himself in relation to the people, when He led them out of Egypt, namely, the word that He would make Israel into His own property out of all nations (Ex. xix. 5, 6 ; Deut. vii. 6 ; cf. Jer. vii. 22, 23, and xi. 4). It would quite agree with this to take *'ēth* as the accusative of the norm, and also to connect it as a preposition, if this could only be shown to be in accordance with the rules of the language. But although the accusative in Hebrew is often used, in the relation of free subordination, " to express more precisely the relation of measure and size, space and time, mode and kind" (cf. Ewald, § 204–206), it is impossible to find any example of such an accusative of norm as is here assumed, especially with *'ēth* preceding it. But if *'ēth* were a preposition instead of אִתְּכֶם, we should have עִמָּכֶם, inasmuch as the use of אֶת־הַדָּבָר, as a parallel to אִתְּכֶם, makes the words clumsy and awkward. The thought which Haggai evidently wishes to express requires that *haddâbhâr* should stand upon the same line with *rūchī*, so that *'eth-haddâbhâr* is actually the subject to *'ōmedeth*, and *'ēth* is simply used to connect the new declaration with the preceding one, and to place it in subjection to the one which follows, in the sense of " as regards," *quoad* (Ewald, § 277, *d*, pp. 683–4), in which case the choice of the accusative in the present instance may either be explained from a kind of attraction (as in the Latin, *urbem quam statuo vestra est*), as Hitzig supposes, or from the blending together of two constructions, as Koehler maintains ; that is to say, Haggai intended to write אֶת־הַדָּבָר וְרוּחִי הֶעֱמַדְתִּי, but was induced to alter the proposed construction by the relative clause אֲשֶׁר כָּרַתִּי וגו' attaching itself to הַדָּבָר. Consequently *'ōmedeth*, as predicate, not only belongs to *rūchī*, but also to *haddâbhâr*, in the sense of to have continuance and validity ; and according to a later usage of the language, עָמַד is used for קוּם, to stand fast (compare Isa. xl. 8 with Dan. xi. 14). The word, that Israel is the property of Jehovah, and Jehovah the God of Israel, still stands in undiminished force ; and not only so, but His Spirit also still works in the midst of Israel. *Rūăch*, in parallelism with the word containing the foundation of the covenant, is neither the spirit of prophecy (Chald., J. D. Mich.), nor the spirit which once filled Bezaleel and his companions (Ex. xxxi. 1 sqq., xxxvi. 1 sqq.), enabling them to erect the tabernacle in a proper manner, and one well-pleasing to God

(Luc., Osiander, and Koehler). Both views are too narrow; *rūăch* is the divine power which accompanies the word of promise and realizes it in a creative manner, *i.e.* not merely " the virtue with which God will establish their souls, that they may not be overcome by temptations" (Calvin), but also the power of the Spirit working in the world, which is able to remove all the external obstacles that present themselves to the realization of the divine plan of salvation. This Spirit is still working in Israel (" in the midst of you") ; therefore they are not to fear, even if the existing state of things does not correspond to human expectations. The omnipotence of God can and will carry out His word, and glorify His temple. This leads to the further promise in vers. 6-9, which gives the reason for the exhortation, " Fear ye not."

Ver. 6. " *For thus saith Jehovah of hosts, Once more, in a short time it comes to pass, I shake heaven and earth, and the sea, and the dry.* Ver. 7. *And I shake all nations, and the costly of all nations will come, and I shall fill this house with glory, saith Jehovah of hosts.* Ver. 8. *Mine is the silver, and mine the gold, is the saying of Jehovah of hosts.* Ver. 9. *The last glory of this house will be greater than the first, saith Jehovah of hosts; and in this place shall I give peace, is the saying of Jehovah of hosts.*" Different explanations have been given of the definition of the time עוֹד אַחַת מְעַט הִיא. Luther, Calvin, and others, down to Ewald and Hengstenberg, follow the Chaldee and Vulgate, and either take *achath* in the sense of the indefinite article or as a numeral, " *adhuc unum modicum est,*" or "it is yet a little thither." But if *achath* belonged to מְעַט as a numeral adjective, either in the one sense or the other, according to the arrangement adopted without exception in Hebrew (for *'echâd* is not an adjective in Dan. viii. 13), it could not stand before מְעַט, but must be placed after it. The difference of gender also precludes this combination, inasmuch as מְעַט is not construed as a feminine in a single passage. We must therefore take מְעַט הִיא as forming an independent clause of itself, *i.e.* as a more precise definition of עוֹד אַחַת. But *'achath* does not mean one = one time, or a short space of time (Burk, Hitzig, Hofmann) ; nor does it acquire this meaning from the clause מְעַט הִיא ; nor can it be sustained by arbitrarily supplying עֵת. *'Achath* is used as a neuter in the sense of " once," as in Ex. xxx. 10, 2 Kings

vi. 10, Job xl. 5 (cf. Ewald, § 269, *b*). מְעַט הִיא, a little, *i.e.* a short time is it, equivalent to "soon," in a short time will it occur (cf. Hos. viii. 10; Ps. xxxvii. 10). The LXX. have rendered it correctly ἔτι ἅπαξ, only they have left out מְעַט הִיא. The words, "once more and indeed in a short time I shake," etc., have not the meaning which Koehl. attaches to the correct rendering, viz. "Once, and only once, will Jehovah henceforth shake heaven and earth," in which the עוֹד standing at the head is both moved from its place, and taken, not in the sense of repetition or of continuance from the present to the future, but simply in the sense of an allusion to the future; in other words, it is completely deprived of its true meaning. For עוֹד never loses its primary sense of repetition or return any more than the German *noch* (still or yet), so as to denote an occurrence in the future without any allusion whatever to an event that has already happened or is in existence still, not even in 2 Sam. xix. 36 and 2 Chron. xvii. 6, with which Koehler endeavours to support his views, without observing that in these passages עוֹד is used in a very different sense, signifying in 2 Sam. *prœterea*, and in 2 Chron. "moreover." In the verse before us it is used with reference to the previous shaking of the world at the descent of Jehovah upon Sinai to establish the covenant with Israel, to which the author of the Epistle to the Hebrews has quite correctly taken it as referring (Heb. xii. 26). On the other hand, the objection offered by Koehler, that that shaking did not extend beyond Sinai and the Sinaitic region, either according to the historical account in Ex. xix. 16–18, or the poetical descriptions in Judg. v. 4, 5, and Ps. lxviii. 8, 9, is incorrect. For not only in the two poetical descriptions referred to, but also in Hab. iii. 6, the manifestation of God upon Sinai is represented as a trembling or shaking of the earth, whereby the powers of the heaven were set in motion, and the heavens dropped down water. The approaching shaking of the world will be much more violent; it will affect the heaven and the earth in all their parts, the sea and the solid ground, and also the nations. Then will the condition of the whole of the visible creation and of the whole of the world of nations be altered. The shaking of the heaven and the earth, *i.e.* of the universe, is closely connected with the shaking of all nations. It is not merely a figurative representation or symbol, however, of great political agitations, but is quite as real as the shaking of the nations, and not merely follows this and is caused by it, but also precedes it and goes side by side with it, and only in its completion does it form the conclusion to the whole of the shaking of the world. For earthquakes and movements of the powers of heaven are heralds and attendants of the coming of the Lord to judgment upon the whole earth, through which not only the outward form of the existing world is altered, but the present world itself will finally be reduced to ruins (Isa. xxiv. 18–20), and out of the world thus perishing there are to be created a new heaven and a new earth (Isa. lxv. 17, lxvi. 22 ; 2 Pet. iii. 10–13). But if the shaking of heaven and earth effects a violent breaking up of the existing condition of the universe, the shaking of all nations can only be one by which an end is put to the existing condition of the world of nations, by means of great political convulsions, and indeed, according to the explanation given in ver. 22, by the Lord's overthrowing the throne of the kingdoms, annihilating their power, and destroying their materials of war, so that one falls by the sword of the other, that is to say, by wars and revolutions, by which the might of the heathen world is broken and annihilated. It follows from this, that the shaking of the heathen is not to be interpreted spiritually, either as denoting " the marvellous, supernatural, and violent impulse by which God impels His elect to betake themselves to the fold of Christ" (Calvin), or " the movement to be produced among the nations through the preaching of the gospel, with the co-operation of the Holy Spirit." The impulse given by the preaching of the gospel and the operation of the Holy Spirit to such souls among the nations as desire salvation, to seek salvation from the living God, is only the fruit of the shaking of the heathen world, and is not to be identified with it ; for the coming of the *chemdath kol-haggōyīm* is defined by וּבָאוּ with the *Vav consec.* as a consequence of the shaking of the nations.

By *chemdath kol-haggōyīm* most of the earlier orthodox commentators understood the Messiah, after the example of the Vulgate, *et veniet desideratus gentibus*, and Luther's " consolation of the Gentiles." But the plural בָּאוּ is hardly reconcilable with this. If, for example, *chemdath* were the subject of the clause, as most of the commentators assume, we should have

the singular נבא. For the rule, that in the case of two nouns
connected together in the construct state, the verb may take
the number of the governed noun, applies only to cases in
which the governed noun contains the principal idea, so that
there is a *constructio ad sensum ;* whereas in the case before us
the leading idea would be formed, not by *kol-haggōyĭm,* but by
chemdath, desideratus, or consolation, as a designation of the
Messiah. Hence Cocc., Mark, and others, have taken *chemdath*
as the accusative of direction : " that they (*sc.* the nations)
may come to the desire of all nations—namely, to Christ." It
cannot be objected to this, as Koehler supposes, that to designate
Christ as the desire of all nations would be either erroneous,
inasmuch as in the time of Haggai only a very few heathen
knew anything about Israel's hope of a Messiah, or perfectly
unintelligible to his contemporaries, especially if the meaning
of the epithet were that the heathen would love Him at some
future time. For the latter remark is at once proved to be
untenable by the prophecy of Isaiah and Micah, to the effect
that all nations will flow to the mountain of God's house.
After such prophecies, the thought that the heathen would one
day love the Messiah could not be unintelligible to the contemporaries of our prophet; and there is not the smallest proof
of the first assertion. In the year 520 B.C., when the ten tribes
had already been scattered among the heathen for 200 years,
and the Judæans for more than seventy years, the Messianic
hope of Israel could not be any longer altogether unknown to
the nations. It may with much better reason be objected to the
former view, that if *chemdâh* were the accusative of direction,
we should expect the preposition *'el* in order to avoid ambiguity
But what is decisive against it is the fact, that the coming of the
nations to the Messiah would be a thought completely foreign
to the context, since the Messiah cannot without further explanation be identified with the temple. *Chemdâh* signifies desire
(2 Chron. xxi. 20), then the object of desire, that in which a
man finds pleasure and joy, valuables. *Chemdath haggōyĭm* is
therefore the valuable possessions of the heathen, or according
to ver. 8 their gold and silver, or their treasures and riches;
not the best among the heathen (Theod. Mops., Capp., Hitzig).
Hence *chemdath* cannot be the accusative of direction, since
the thought that the heathen come to the treasures of all the

heathen furnishes no suitable meaning; but it is the nominative or subject, and is construed as a collective word with the verb in the plural. The thought is the following : That shaking will be followed by this result, or produce this effect, that all the valuable possessions of the heathen will come to fill the temple with glory. Compare Isa. lx. 5, where the words, " the possessions (riches) of the heathen (*chēl gōyĭm*) will come to thee," *i.e.* be brought to Jerusalem, express the same thought; also Isa. lx. 11. With the valuable possessions of the heathen the Lord will glorify His temple, or fill it with *kâbhōd*. *Kâbhōd* without the article denotes the glory which the temple will receive through the possessions of the heathen presented there. The majority of the commentators have referred these words to the glorification of the temple through the appearance of Jesus in it, and appeal to Ex. xl. 34, 35, 1 Kings viii. 10, 11, 2 Chron. v. 13, 14, according to which passages the glory of Jehovah filled the tabernacle and Solomon's temple at their dedication, so that they identify *kâbhōd* (glory) with *kᵉbhōd Yᵉhōvâh* (glory of Jehovah) without reserve. But this is impracticable, although the expression *kâbhōd* is chosen by the prophet with a reference to those events, and the fulfilment of our prophecy did commence with the fact that Jehovah came to His temple in the person of Jesus Christ (Mal. iii. 1).— Ver. 8. Jehovah can fill this house with glory, because the silver and gold which the heathen nations possess belong to Him. By shaking all kingdoms He can induce the nations to present their treasures to Him as gifts for the glorification of His house. Thus (the promise closes with this in ver. 9), the later glory of this house will be greater than the former was. *Hâachărōn* might be regarded as belonging to *habbayith hazzeh*, in the sense of " the glory of this latter house ;" and the majority of the commentators have taken it so, after the Itala, Vulgate, and Peschito. But it is quite as admissible to connect it with *kâbhōd*, in the sense of " the later glory of this house," inasmuch as when one substantive is determined by another which is connected with it in the construct state, the adjective belonging to the *nomen regens* follows with the article (cf. 2 Sam. xxiii. 1; 1 Chron. xxiii. 27 ; and Ewald, § 289, *a*). This is the rendering adopted by Michaelis, Maurer, Hitzig, and others, after the LXX. According to the first construction, the distinction would be drawn between a former and a later house ; according to the second, simply between the earlier and later glory of the same house ; and the passage would be based upon the idea, that through all ages there was only one house of Jehovah in Jerusalem existing under different forms. Ver. 3 is decisive in favour of the second view, for there an earlier glory is attributed to this house, and contrasted with its present miserable condition. The first or former glory is that of Solomon's temple, the later or last that of Zerubbabel's. The difference of opinion as to the true rendering of the words has no material influence upon the matter itself ; except that, if the latter view be adopted, the question so often discussed by earlier writers—namely, whether by the second temple we are to understand the temple of Zerubbabel or the temple as altered by Herod, which many have erroneously taken to be the third— falls to the ground as perfectly unmeaning. The final glory of the temple will also be a lasting one. This is implied in the closing words of the promise : " And in this place will I give peace." "This place" is not the temple, but Jerusalem, as the place where the temple is built; and the "peace" is not spiritual peace, but external peace, which does indeed in its perfect form include spiritual peace as well. This is perfectly evident from the parallel passages, Mic. v. 4, Joel iv. 17, and Isa. lx. 18.

If we also take up the question as to the fulfilment of this prophecy, we must keep the two features quite distinct—(a) the shaking of heaven and earth and all nations; (b) the consequence of this shaking, the coming of the heathen with their possessions to the glorification of the temple—although they both stand in close connection. The earlier commentators were no doubt generally right, when they sought for the fulfilment in the establishment of the new covenant through Christ ; they simply erred in referring the predicted shaking of the nations and the promised glorification of the temple in too one-sided and exclusive a manner to the coming of Christ in the flesh, to His teaching in the temple, and to the establishment of the kingdom of heaven through the preaching of the gospel. They were thereby compelled, on the one hand, to force upon the prophecy a meaning irreconcilable with the words themselves, and, on the other hand, to seek for its fulfilment in historical particulars to some extent of very subordinate importance.

Even the predicted nearness of the time ("it is a little while")
does not suit the exclusive reference to the establishment of
the new covenant, or the founding of the Christian church.
The period of 520 years, which elapsed before the birth of
Christ, cannot be called a little or short time, as Calovius
supposes, "in comparison with the time that had passed since
either the promulgation of the law or the promulgation of the
protevangelium," inasmuch as five hundred are not מְעַט in
relation to fifteen hundred, and the proposal to go back to the
protevangelium is evidently merely a loophole of perplexity.
Nor can מְעַט הִיא be explained on the hypothesis that the
measure of time here is not a human one, but the divine
measure, according to which a thousand years are equal to
one day. "For whoever speaks to men, must speak of things
according to a human method of thinking; or if he do not, he
must make it clear that this is the case. The prophet lays
stress upon the brevity of the time, for the purpose of comforting. And only what is short in the eyes of men is fitted
for this" (Hengstenberg). The shaking of the heathen world
did not first begin with the birth of Christ, but commenced
shortly after the time of Haggai. It is true that under Darius
Hystaspes the Persian empire was still standing at the summit
of its power; but its shaking began under his successor
Xerxes, and came very plainly to light in his war against
Greece. "Even then there were forebodings that the time of
this empire would soon be accomplished, and the rapid conquests of Alexander gave fulfilment to this foreboding. And
even his power, which seemed destined to last for ever, very
speedily succumbed to the lot of all temporal things. *Inde*
(says Livy) *morte Alexandri distractum in multa regna, dum
ad se quisque opes rapiunt lacerantes viribus, a summo culmine
fortunæ ad ultimum finem centum quinquaginta annos stetit.*
The two most powerful kingdoms that grew out of the monarchy of Alexander, viz. the Syrian and Egyptian, destroyed
one another. The Romans now attained to the government
of the world; but at the very time when they appeared to be
at the summit of their greatness, their shaking had very considerably advanced" (Hengstenberg). The circumstance that
the prophet mentions the shaking of heaven and earth before
the shaking of all the heathen, cannot furnish any valid ground

for objecting to these allusions; nor can it force us to the conclusion that the words are only to be understood as denoting
"great political shakings, whereby the power of the heathen
would be broken, their pride humbled, and so the susceptibility
for salvation be evoked among them." For even if such events
do shake the world, and are poetically represented as earthquakes, even if they were regarded by the nations as heralds
of the approaching destruction of the world, because the impression they produced upon the mind was as if heaven and
earth were falling to pieces; all this does not satisfy the words,
which do not express the subjective emotion, but announce
real facts. The shaking of heaven and earth, of the sea and
of the dry land, is indeed partially effected by violent earthquakes and wonderful signs in the sky, and was typified by
such judgments as the flood; but it is only fully accomplished
at the breaking up of the present condition of the world in
the destruction of this heaven and this earth. The prophet
mentions at the very outset the utmost and the last that God
will do, to clear away all existing hindrances to the completion
of His kingdom in glory, and then passes on to the shakings
of the world of nations which prepare the way for and lead
on to this result, just as Micah in ch. iv. comes back from the
most remote future to the less remote, and then to the immediate future. For the shakings of the heathen, by which their
power will be broken and the dissolution of heathenism and
of the ungodly power of the world will be effected, do not
reach their end with the coming of Christ and the establishment of the Christian church: but just as the kingdom of the
world maintains its standing by the side of the kingdom of
heaven established by Christ upon the earth, until the return
of our Lord to judgment; so does the shaking of the heathen
and of the kingdoms of the nations continue till every power
which rises against the Almighty God and His Christ is
broken, and the world which has been thrown into confusion
by the sin of men, and is made subject to corruptibility on
their account, shall perish, and the new heaven and new earth
wherein dwelleth righteousness, for which we are looking, shall
be established (2 Pet. iii. 12, 13).[1]

[1] Aug. Koehler also assumes that the ultimate fulfilment of our prophecy will not take place till the second coming of Christ, although he is

But if the shaking of the heathen commenced before the coming of Christ in the flesh, and will continue till His second coming in glory, we must not restrict the fulfilment of the predicted moral consequences of this shaking—namely, that the heathen come and consecrate their possessions to the Lord for the glorification of His house, to the conversion of the heathen to Christ, and their entrance into the Christian church —but must also regard the desire for the living God, awakened by the decay of heathendom and its religions, which was manifested in the adoption of Judaism by the more pious heathen, as a prelude to the fulfilment which commenced with the spread of the gospel among the Gentiles, and must include not only the presentation of dedicatory offerings τῶν ἀλλυφύλων and of gifts τῶν ἔξωθεν ἐθνῶν, with which the temple was adorned according to Josephus, *de Bell. Jud.* ii. 17, 3, but also the presents of king Artaxerxes and his counsellors, which Ezra received on his return to Jerusalem to carry with him for the

of opinion that, generally speaking, it has not been fulfilled in the manner originally intended. Starting, for example, with the fact that the fulfilment of the events predicted by Haggai and the coming of the day of Jehovah are one and the same, and that according to Mal. iii. 1, 23 the day of Jehovah was to be preceded by the coming of a messenger, to prepare the way for Jehovah to come to His temple, Koehler assumes that the fulfilment of these events ought to have taken place with the coming of Jesus of Nazareth, to establish the new covenant as the Messiah. But, inasmuch as Israel was still without such moral preparation as would allow of the coming of Jehovah being a blessing to it, and rejected its Messiah, there occurred an event in connection with this rejection of Jesus on the part of Israel, which not only put a stop to the fulfilment of the prophecies, the realization of which had commenced with the coming of Jesus, but introduced a partial modification. "The new covenant," he says, "which was established by the Lord in His incarnation, was not at first a blessing to Israel, but to the heathen world. Instead of setting up His kingdom over the earth, with Zion as the centre, the Lord returned to heaven, and there took possession of the throne above all thrones. But Israel was smitten with the ban, and scattered among the heathen nations. The sacred places which were to be glorified by the valuables of all the heathen, had become unclean through Israel's sin, and were given up to destruction in consequence." In his opinion there is a coming of Jehovah still in the future. Jesus will return from heaven again, but not till Israel shall have been converted to the Messiah it rejected. Then will the prophecies of Haggai that remained unfulfilled at the first coming of Jesus be accomplished, but in the only way that is still possible, since the former holy

temple (Ezra vii. 15 sqq.).[1] Yea, even the command of king
Darius Hystaspes to his vicegerent, which no doubt reached
Jerusalem after our prophecy had been uttered, not only to
allow the work at this house of God to continue, but also to
deliver to the elders of Judah what was required for the building as well as for the requirements of the daily sacrificial worship out of the moneys raised by taxation on this side the river
(Ezra vi. 6–10), may at any rate be regarded as a pledge of
the certain fulfilment of the divine promise uttered by Haggai.
But whilst the honour paid to the temple of Zerubbabel on the
part of the heathen and heathen princes by the presentation of
sacrifices and dedicatory offerings must not be overlooked, as
preludes to the promised filling of this house with the riches of
the Gentiles, we must not look to this outward glorification of
the temple at Jerusalem for the true fulfilment of our prophecy, even if it had exceeded Solomon's temple in glory.
This first took place with the coming of Christ, and that not

places of Israel have been destroyed, and the heathen world has already
participated in the new covenant, and has at any rate in part already
become the people of God. Consequently the events predicted by Haggai
(ii. 6–9) have not been fulfilled; for the valuable possessions of all the
heathen have not been applied to the glorification of the sanctuary of
Jehovah built by Zerubbabel, and there has not been a place of peace
created there in the midst of the judgments that were to fall upon the
heathen world. But the fault of this rests purely upon Israel. And so
also it is in the impenitence of Israel that we have to look for the reason
why the shaking of the heaven and the earth, and all the heathen, which
Haggai announced as מְעַט הִיא, has been postponed for more than 500
years. This is Koehler's view. But if there had really been any foundation in the Scriptures for this view, and the predictions of our prophet had
not been fulfilled in the manner intended, the fault would not rest entirely
in the impenitence of Israel, but would fall in part upon God Himself, for
having sent His Son, not at the proper time, or when the time was accomplished, but too early, namely, before Israel was in that moral condition
which would allow of the coming of the Messiah to become a blessing to it,
whether God was mistaken as to the proper time for sending His Son, or
in His judgment as to the moral condition of Israel. If Koehler had put
this clearly to his own mind, he would certainly have hesitated before he
built up a view on the basis of an erroneous idea of the day of the Lord
which necessarily leads to the denial not only of the divine prescience or
the πρόγνωσις τοῦ Θεοῦ, but also of the supernatural character of the Old
Testament prophecy.

[1] We must not, however, include the additions to Zerubbabel's temple

in the fact that Jesus visited the temple and taught in it, and
as the incarnate *Logos*, in whom the "glory of Jehovah"
that filled the temple of Solomon dwelt in its truest essence
as δόξα ὡς μονογενοῦς παρὰ πατρός, glorified the temple of
stone with His presence, but by the fact that Christ raised up
the true temple of God not built with human hand (John
ii. 19), *i.e.* that He exalted the kingdom of God shadowed
forth in the temple at Jerusalem to its true essence. We
must draw a distinction between the substance and form,
the kernel and the shell, of the prophecy. The temple, as
the place where the Lord dwelt in the midst of Israel in a
visible symbol of His gracious presence, was the seat and
concentration of the kingdom of God, which had its visible
embodiment in the temple so long as the old covenant lasted.
In this respect the rebuilding of the temple that had been
destroyed was a sign and pledge of the restoration of the
kingdom of God, which had been broken up through the

undertaken by Herod the Great for the sake of beautifying it, because,
although Herod was a Gentile by descent, the work was not undertaken
from any love to the Lord, but (as Calvin; and Hengstenberg, *Christol.* iii.
pp. 289–90, have already observed) with the intention of securing the fulfilment of Haggai's prophecy, in order to prevent the coming of the kingdom
of God, his fear of which was that it would put an end to his earthly
sway. His intention is obvious enough from the address communicated by
Josephus (*Ant.* xv. 11, 1), through which Herod endeavoured to win over
the people to his plan. After telling them that the temple built after the
return of the fathers from exile was still sixty cubits lower than that of
Solomon, which he proposed to add, he proceeded thus: "But since I am
now by God's will your governor, and I have had peace a long time, and
have gained great riches and large revenues, and, what is the principal
thing of all, I am at amity with and well regarded by the Romans, who, if
I may so say, are the rulers of the whole world," etc. The allusion to
our prophecy, as Hengstenberg says, is unmistakeable here. He tries to
prove that all the conditions which it lays down for the glorifying of the
temple have now been realized. "All nations," by whom the building of
the temple is to be promoted, are equivalent in his esteem to "the Romans,
who are the rulers of the whole world." He whom God has called to the
government has gold and silver enough. And the words "in this place
will I give peace" are now fulfilled. The manner in which he strained
every nerve to fulfil the words "the glory will be greater," is evident from
§ 3, where it is stated that "he laid out larger sums of money upon them
than had been done before him, till it seemed that no one else had so
greatly adorned the temple as he had done."

banishment of Israel among the heathen, and the attitude of those who returned from exile towards the building of the temple was a sign of their internal attitude towards the Lord and His kingdom. If, then, the old men who had seen the temple in its former glory wept aloud at the laying of the foundation of the new building, because in comparison with the former it was as nothing in their eyes, this mourning was occasioned not so much by the fact that the new temple would not be so beautiful and majestic a building as that of Solomon had been, as by the fact that the poverty of the new building set before their eyes the wretched condition of the kingdom of God. This true or deeper ground for their mourning, which might very well give rise to the question whether the Lord would restore His former gracious relation to Israel, or at any rate would restore it now, is met by the divine promise published by Haggai to the people, which attaches itself in form to the existing circumstances, and accordingly promises for the future a glorification of the temple which will outshine the glory of the former one. If we look at the thought itself which is expressed in this form, it is the following : The Lord will one day exalt His kingdom, which is so deeply degraded and despised, to a glory which will far surpass the glory of the kingdom of God at the time of Solomon, and that by the fact that all the heathen nations will dedicate their possessions to it. This glorification of the house of God commenced with the introduction of the kingdom of heaven, which Jesus Christ preached, and of which He laid the foundation in His church. And whilst the stone-temple at Jerusalem built by Zerubbabel and splendidly finished by Herod fell into ruins, because the Jews had rejected their Saviour, and crucified Him, this has been carried on through the spread of the kingdom of God among the nations of the earth, and will be completed at the end of the course of this world; not, however, by the erection of a new and much more glorious temple in Jerusalem, but in the founding of the new Jerusalem coming down out of heaven from God upon the new earth, after the overthrow of all the powers of the world that are hostile to God. This holy city will have the glory of God ($\dot{\eta}$ $\delta\acute{o}\xi\alpha$ $\tau o\hat{v}$ $\Theta\epsilon o\hat{v}$ = כְּבוֹד יְהוָה), but no temple; because the Lord God Almighty and the Lamb are the temple of it. Into this holy city of God will the kings of the earth bring their glory and honour, and the heathen who are saved will walk therein (Rev. xxi. 10, 11, 22–24). Thus the promise covers the entire development of the kingdom of God to the end of days.

This was the sense in which the author of the Epistle to the Hebrews (Heb. xii. 26, 27) understood our prophecy. In order, namely, to give emphasis to his admonition, not to expose themselves to still severer punishment than fell upon those who hardened themselves under the Old Testament against the incomplete revelation of God, by rejecting the far more perfect revelation of God in Christ, he quotes our prophecy, and shows from it (ver. 26), that at the founding of the old covenant only a comparatively small shaking of the earth took place; whereas for the times of the new covenant there had been predicted a shaking not only of the earth, but also of the heaven, which indicated that what was moveable was to be altered, as made for that purpose, that the immoveable might remain. The author of this epistle consequently brings out the fundamental thought of our prophecy, in which its fulfilment culminates, viz. that everything earthly must be shaken and altered, that the immoveable, *i.e.* the βασιλεία ἀσάλευτος, may remain, or in other words, that the whole of the earthly creation must perish, in order that the kingdom of God may be shown to be immoveably permanent. He does not, however, thereby represent the predicted shaking of heaven and earth " as still in the future," as Koehler supposes; but, as his words in ver. 28 (cf. ver. 22), "Wherefore we, receiving a kingdom which cannot be moved, let us have grace," clearly show, he takes it as having already commenced, and looks upon the whole period, from the coming of Christ in the flesh till His coming again in glory, as one *continuum.*

Vers. 10–19. RETURN OF THE BLESSINGS OF NATURE.— Ver. 10. On the 24th day of the ninth month of the same year, that is to say, exactly three months after the congregation had resumed the building of the temple (cf. ch. i. 15), and about two months after the second prophecy (ch. ii. 1), a new word of the Lord was uttered through Haggai to the people. It was now time, since the despondency which had laid hold of the people a few weeks after the recommencement of the building had been dispelled by the consolatory promises in vers. 6–9, and the work was vigorously pursued, to confirm the people in the fidelity which they had manifested, by bestowing upon them the blessing which had been withdrawn. To this end Haggai received the commission to make it perfectly clear to the people, that the curse which had rested upon them since the building of the temple had been neglected, had been nothing but a punishment for their indolence in not pushing forward the work of the Lord, and that from that time forth the Lord would bestow His blessing upon them again. The ninth month (*Khislēv*) corresponds very nearly to the period between the middle of November and the middle of December, when the sowing of the winter crops, that commenced after the feast of tabernacles, was finished, and the autumnal rain (early rain) had set in, so that in the abundant fall of this rain they might discern a trace of the divine blessing. The word of God was as follows: Ver. 11. "*Thus saith Jehovah of hosts, Ask now the priests for instruction, saying,* Ver. 12. *Behold, one carries holy flesh in the lappet of his garment, and touches with his lappet the bread, and that which is boiled, the wine, and the oil, and any kind of food: does it then become holy? And the priests answered and said, No.* Ver. 13. *And Haggai said, If one who is unclean on account of a corpse touches all this, does it become unclean? And the priests answered and said, It does become unclean.* Ver. 14. *Then Haggai answered and said, So is this people, and so this nation before my face, is the saying of Jehovah; and so is all the work of their hands, and what they offer to me there: it is unclean.*" In order to impress most earnestly upon the hearts of the people the fact that it was through their sin that they brought upon themselves the failure of crops that had hitherto prevailed, viz. as a punishment from God, the prophet proposes two questions concerning holy and clean for the priests to answer, in order that he may make an application of the answer they give to the moral condition of the nation. *Tōrâh* in ver. 11, without the article, is used in its primary signification of instruction, and is governed by אֵת, *accus. rei:* to ask a person anything, for to ask or solicit anything from him. The first question has reference to the communication of the holiness of holy objects to other objects brought into contact with them: whether, if a person carried holy flesh in

the lappet of his garment,[1] and touched any food with the
lappet, it would become holy in consequence. *Hēn*, behold,
pointing to an action as possible, has almost the force of a conditional particle, " if," as in Isa. liv. 15, Jer. iii. 1 (cf. Ewald,
§ 103, *g*). " Holy flesh" is flesh of animals slain as sacrifices,
as in Jer. xi. 15. *Nâzīd*, that which is boiled, boiled food
(Gen. xxv. 29 ; 2 Kings iv. 38 sqq.). The priests answer the
question laid before them quite correctly with " No ;" for,
according to Lev. vi. 20, the lappet of the dress itself was made
holy by the holy flesh, but it could not communicate this holiness any further. The second question (ver. 13) has reference
to the spread of legal defilement. טְמֵא נֶפֶשׁ is not one who is
unclean in his soul ; but, as Lev. xxii. 4 shows, it is synonymous with טְמֵא לָנֶפֶשׁ in Num. v. 2, ix. 10, " defiled on a soul ;"
and this is a contraction of טְמֵא לְנֶפֶשׁ אָדָם, or טְמֵא לְנֶפֶשׁ מֵת,
in Num. ix. 6, 7, " defiled on (through) the soul of a dead
man" (Num. vi. 6 ; Lev. xxi. 11 : see at Lev. xix. 28), hence
one who has been defiled through touching a dead body. This
uncleanness was one of the strongest kinds ; it lasted seven
days, and could only be removed by his being twice purified
with sprinkling water, prepared from the ashes of the red cow
(see at Num. xix.). This question the priests also answered
correctly. According to Num. xix. 22, he who was defiled by
touching a dead body made everything unclean that he touched.
The prophet now applies these provisions of the law to the
ethical relation in which the people stood to Jehovah. " So is
this people before me, saith Jehovah." הַגּוֹי is quite synonymous
with הָעָם, as in Zeph. ii. 9, without any subordinate meaning of
a contemptuous kind, which could at the most be contained in
hazzeh (this), but in that case would apply to *hâ'âm* just as
well. *Kēn, ita*, refers to the substance of the two legal questions
in vers. 12 and 13. The nation, in its attitude towards the
Lord, resembles, on the one hand, a man who carries holy flesh
in the lappet of his garment, and on the other hand, a man

---

[1] Luther : " in the *geren* of his dress." The *gehren*, or *gehre*, middle
high German *gêre*, old high German *kêro* (English *goar*), is a triangular
piece, forming the gusset of a dress or shirt, then that portion of the dress
in which it is inserted, viz. below the waist, probably derived from the
Gothic *gáis*, and the conjectural root *geisan* = to thrust or strike (Weigand,
Germ. Dict.).

who has become unclean through touching a corpse. "Israel also possesses a sanctuary in the midst of its land,—namely, the place which Jehovah has chosen for His own abode, and favoured with many glorious promises. But just as no kind of food, neither bread nor vegetables, neither wine nor oil, is sanctified by the fact that a man touches it with his sanctified garment, so will all this not be rendered holy by the fact that it is planted in the soil of the land which surrounds and encloses the sanctuary of Jehovah. For though the land itself becomes a holy land in consequence, it cannot spread this holiness any further, nor communicate it to what grows upon it. All that Israel raises on its holy land, whether corn, wine, or oil, remains unholy or common. No special blessing rests upon the fruits of this land, on account of the holiness of the land itself, so as of necessity to produce fruitfulness as its result; nor, on the other hand, does it in itself communicate any curse. But if, as experience shows, a curse is resting notwithstanding upon the productions of this land, it arises from the fact that they are unclean because Israel has planted them. For Israel is utterly unclean on account of its neglect of the house of Jehovah, like a man who has become unclean through touching a corpse. Everything that Israel takes hold of, or upon which it lays its hand, everything that it plants and cultivates, is from the very first affected with the curse of uncleanness; and consequently even the sacrifices which it offers there upon the altar of Jehovah are unclean" (Koehler). *Shâm*, there, *i.e.* upon the altar built immediately after the return from Babylon (Ezra iii. 3).

The prophet explains these words in vers. 15–19 by representing the failure of the crops, and the curse that has hitherto prevailed, as a punishment from God for having been wanting in faithfulness to the Lord (vers. 15–17), and promises that from that time forward the blessing of God shall rest upon them again (vers. 18, 19). Ver. 15. "*And now, direct your heart from this day and onward, before stone was laid to stone at the temple of Jehovah.* Ver. 16. *Before this was, did one come to the heap of sheaves of twenty (in measure), there were ten: did he come to the vat to draw fifty buckets, there were twenty.* Ver. 17. *I have smitten you with blasting, and with mildew, and with hail, all the work of your hands; and not one of you (turned) to me, is the saying of Jehovah.*" The object to which they are

to direct their heart, *i.e.* to give heed, is not to be supplied
from ch. i. 5, 7, "to your ways" (Ros. and others), but is
contained substantially in vers. 16 and 17, and is first of all
indicated in the words "from this day," etc. They are to
notice what has taken place from this day onwards. וָמַ֫עְלָה,
lit. upwards, then further on. Here it is used not in the sense
of forwards into the future, but, as the explanatory clause
which follows (from before, etc.) clearly shows, in that of backwards into the past. *Mitterem*, literally "from the not yet of
the laying . . . onwards," *i.e.* onwards from the time when stone
was laid upon stone at the temple; in other words, when the
building of the temple was resumed, backwards into the past;
in reality, therefore, the time before the resuming of the building of the temple : for *min* in *mitterem* cannot be taken in any
other sense than in the parallel מִיּוֹם which precedes it, and
מִהְיוֹתָם which follows in ver. 16. The objection which Koehler
raises to this cannot be sustained. מִהְיוֹתָם, from their existence
(backwards). Most of the modern commentators take the suffix
as referring to a noun, *yâmîm* (days), to be supplied from
ver. 15; but it appears much simpler to take it as a neuter,
as Mark and others do, in the sense of "before these things
were or were done, viz. this day, and this work of laying stone
upon stone," etc. The meaning is not doubtful, viz. looking
backwards from the time when the building of the temple
was resumed, in other words, before the point of time. בָּא
commences a new sentence, in which facts that they had experienced are cited, the verb בָּא being used conditionally, and
forming the protasis, the apodosis to which is given in וְהָיְתָה.
If one came to a heap of sheaves of twenty measures (*sᵉʾâh* is
probably to be supplied : LXX. σάτα), they became ten. A
heap of sheaves (*ʾărēmâh* as in Ruth iii. 7), from which they
promised themselves twenty measures, yielded, when threshed,
no more than ten, *i.e.* only the half of what they expected.
They experienced just the same at the pressing of the grapes.
Instead of fifty buckets, which they expected, they obtained
only twenty. *Yeqebh* was the vat into which the juice flowed
when pressed out of the grapes. *Châsaph*, lit. to lay bare, here
to draw out, as in Isa. xxx. 14; and *pûrâh*, in Isa. lxiii. 3,
the pressing-trough, here a measure, probably the measure
which was generally obtained from one filling of the wine-

press with grapes (LXX. μετρητής). Ver. 17 gives the reason why so small a result was yielded by the threshing-floor and wine-press. Jehovah smote you with blasting and mildew. These words are a reminiscence of Amos iv. 9, to which passage the last words of the verse also refer. To the disease of the corn there is also added the hail which smote the vines, as in Ps. lxxviii. 47. *'Eth kol-ma'ăsēh*, all the labour of the hands, *i.e.* all that they had cultivated with great toil, is a second accusative, "which mentions the portion smitten" (Hitzig). The perfectly unusual construction אֵין־אֶתְכֶם אֵלַי does not stand for 'אֵין בָּכֶם א, *non fuit in vobis qui* (Vulg.), nor is אֶתְכֶם used for אִתְּכֶם, "with you;" but אֵין־אֶתְכֶם either stands for אֵינְכֶם, the suffix which was taken as a verbal suffix used as an accusative being resolved into the accusative (cf. Ewald, § 262, *d*); or it is the accusative used in the place of the subject, that is to say, אֵת is to be taken in the sense of "as regards," *quoad* (Ewald, § 277, p. 683): "as far as you are concerned, there was not (one) turning himself to me." אֵלַי, to me, *sc.* turning himself or being converted; though there is no necessity to supply שָׁבִים, as the idea is implied in the word אֶל, as in Hos. iii. 3 and 2 Kings vi. 11.

After this appeal to lay to heart the past time during which the blessing had been withheld, Haggai called upon the people in vers. 18 and 19 to fix their eyes upon the time which was commencing with that very day. Ver. 18. "*Direct your heart, then, from this day and onward, from the four and twentieth day of the ninth (month); namely, from the day when the foundation of the temple of Jehovah was laid, direct your heart.* Ver. 19. *Is the seed still in the granary? and even to the vine, and pomegranate, and olive-tree, it has not borne: from this day forward will I bless.*" The twenty-fourth day of the ninth month was the day on which Haggai uttered this word of God (ver. 10). Hence וָמָעְלָה in ver. 18 is to be understood as denoting the direction towards the future (Itala, Vulg., and many comm.). This is evident partly from the fact, that only in that case can the repetition of שִׂימוּ לְבַבְכֶם in ver. 18 (end), and the careful announcement of the point of time (from the twenty-fourth day, etc.), be simply and naturally explained, and partly from the fact that *min hayyōm hazzeh* (from this day) is not explained here, as in ver. 15, by a clause pointing back to the past (like *mitterem sūm* in ver. 15), but simply by a precise notice of the day referred to, and that in the last clause of ver. 19 this day is clearly described as the commencement of a new era. For there can be no doubt whatever that in *min hayyōm hazzeh* in ver. 19 the *terminus a quo* mentioned in ver. 18*a* is resumed. But the time mentioned in ver. 18, "from the day that the foundation of the temple was laid," etc., and also the contents of the first two clauses of ver. 19, to the effect that there was no more seed in the granary, and that the vine, etc., had not borne, do not appear to harmonize with this. To remove the first of these difficulties, Ros., Maurer, Ewald, and others have taken לְמִן־הַיּוֹם אֲשֶׁר־יֻסַּד as the *terminus ad quem*, and connected it with the foregoing *terminus a quo*: "observe the time," which reaches back from the present day, the twenty-fourth of the ninth month, to the day when the foundation of the temple was laid in the reign of Cyrus (Ezra iii. 10). They have thus taken לְמִן in the sense of וְעַד. But it is now generally admitted that this is at variance with the usage of the language; even Ewald and Gesenius acknowledge this (see Ew., *Lehrbuch*, § 218, *b*, and Ges. *Thes.* p. 807). לְמִן is never equivalent to עַד or וְעַד, but invariably forms the antithesis to it (compare, for example, Judg. xix. 30, 2 Sam. vii. 6, and Mic. vii. 12). Now, since *l'min hayyōm* cannot mean "to the time commencing with the laying of the foundation of the temple," but must mean "from the day when the foundation of the temple was laid," Hitzig and Koehler have taken לְמִן הַיּוֹם וגו' as an explanatory apposition to מִיּוֹם עֶשְׂרִים וגו', and assume that through this apposition the twenty-fourth day of the ninth month, in the second year of Darius, is expressly designated as the day on which the foundation was laid for the temple of Jehovah. But this assumption is not only in direct contradiction to Ezra iii. 10, where it is stated that the foundation of the temple was laid in the reign of Cyrus, in the second year after the return from Babylon, but also makes the prophet Haggai contradict himself in a manner which can only be poorly concealed by any *quid pro quo* at variance with the language, viz. (*a*) by identifying the words of ver. 15, "when stone was laid to stone at the temple of Jehovah," which, according to their simple meaning, express the carrying on or continuance of the building, with the laying of the foundation-

stone; secondly (*b*), by understanding the statement, "they
did work at the house of Jehovah on the twenty-fourth day
of the sixth month" (ch. i. 14, 15), not according to its natural
meaning as relating to their building upon the foundation
already laid, but as signifying the removal of the rubbish and
the procuring of wood and stone, that is to say, as referring
to the preparations for building; and lastly (*c*), by explaining
אֲשֶׁר יֻסַּד וגו' in ver. 19 as signifying the laying of a fresh
or second foundation. These assumptions are so forced, that
if there were not a simpler and easier way of removing the
difficulty raised, we would rather assume that there had been
a corruption of the text. But the thing is not so desperate
as this. In the first place, we must pronounce the opinion
that לְמִן הַיּוֹם וגו' is an explanatory apposition to מִיּוֹם עֶשְׂרִים וגו'
an unfounded one. The position of the *athnach* in וָמַעְלָה furnishes no tenable proof of this. Nor can the assumption
that *l^emin* is synonymous with *min* be sustained. In support
of the statement, "that *l^emin* only differs from *min* in the
greater emphasis with which it is spoken," Ewald (§ 218, *b*)
has merely adduced this passage, Hag. ii. 18, which is supposed to exhibit this with especial clearness, but in which,
as we have just shown, such an assumption yields no appropriate meaning. לְמִן followed by עַד or וְעַד does indeed occur
in several instances in such a connection, that it appears to be
used instead of the simple *min*. But if we look more closely
at the passages (*e.g.* Ex. xi. 7 ; Judg. xix. 30 ; 2 Sam. vii. 6),
the לְ is never superfluous; and *l^emin* is simply used in cases
where the definition so introduced is not closely connected with
what goes before, but is meant to be brought out as an independent assertion or additional definition, so that in all such
cases the לְ "has the peculiar force of a brief allusion to something not to be overlooked, a retrospective glance at the separate parts, or a rapid summary of the whole, like our 'with
regard to,' 'as regards' (Lat. *quoad*);" and it only fails to
correspond entirely to this, "from the fact that לְ is only ex-
pressible in the softest manner, and indeed in our language
can hardly be expressed in words at all, though it quite per-
ceptibly yields this sense" (Ewald, § 310). לְמִקְצָת is also used
in this sense in Dan. i. 18 instead of מִקְצָת (ver. 15), whilst
in other cases (*e.g.* in לְמֵרָחוֹק in 2 Sam. vii. 19) it indicates the

direction to a place or towards an object (Ewald, § 218, b).[1] In the verse before us, the לְ before מִן corresponds exactly to the German *anlangend, betreffend,* concerning, as to, *sc.* the time, from the day when the foundation of the temple was laid, and is used to give prominence to this assertion, and by the prominence given to it to preclude any close connection between the defini- tion of the time so introduced and what goes before, and to point to the fact that the following definition contains a fresh subject of discourse. The expression שִׂימוּ לְבַבְכֶם, which closes the sentence commencing with לְמִן הַיּוֹם, and which would be somewhat tautological and superfluous, if the day of the laying of the foundation of the temple coincided with the twenty- fourth day of the ninth month, also points to this. What space of time it is to which Haggai gives prominence in these words, as one which they are to lay to heart, is shown in ver. 19, "Is the seed still in the granary?" etc. That this question is not to be taken in the sense of a summons to proceed now with good heart to sow the summer crops, which were not sown till January, and therefore were still in the granary, as Hitzig sup- poses, has been pointed out by Koehler, who also correctly observes that the prophet first of all reminds his hearers of the mournful state of things in the past (not "in the present," as he says), that they may thoroughly appreciate the promise for the future. For even if the question to be answered with "no," viz. whether the corn is still in the granary, were to be referred to the present, what follows, viz. that the fruit-trees have not borne, would not suit this, since not having borne is a past thing, even if it merely related to the last year, although there is no ground for any such limitation of the words. And if in ver. 19 the prophet directs the attention of his hearers to the past, we must also understand the chronological datum immediately preceding as relating to the past as well, and must assume that the words

---

[1] Koehler's objection to this explanation of *l'mērâchōq,* viz. that with the verb *dibber,* the object concerning which a person is spoken to, is never introduced with the preposition לְ, is groundless. "With verbs of speaking לְ yields the same double meaning as אֶל, according to the con- text," *i.e.* it can denote the person spoken to, and the person or thing to which the speaking refers, or about which a person is speaking (cf. Gen. xxi. 7 ; Num. xxiii. 23 ; Isa. v. 1 ; Mic. ii. 6 ; Jer. xxiii. 9 ; Ps. iii. 3, xi. 1, xxvii. 8 ; and Ewald, § 217, c).

from לְמִן הַיּוֹם in ver. 18 to לֹא נָשָׂא in ver. 19 contain a parenthetical thought; that is to say, we must assume that the prophet, in order to set clearly before their minds the difference
between the past when the building of the temple was suspended, and the future commencing with that very day, before
promising the blessing of God to be enjoyed in the future,
directs another look at the past, and that from the time of the
laying of the foundation of the temple in the reign of Cyrus
to his own time, and reminds them once more of the want of
blessing which they had experienced from that time forth even
to the present time. Koehler's objection to this view cannot
be sustained. He says, " The Jews are to observe the time from
that day forward, namely, from the twenty-fourth day of the
ninth month (backwards); the time from the laying of the
foundation of the temple in the reign of Cyrus (forwards). . . .
Such a mode of expression seems utterly out of place." But
this only affects the erroneous assumption, that the definition
"from the day of the laying of the foundation of the temple"
is merely a more precise explanation of the previous definition,
from the twenty-fourth day of the ninth month, and falls to
the ground of itself as soon as these two definitions are separated, as the expression and the matter in hand require. The
second objection—namely, that the day of the laying of the
foundation of the temple in the reign of Cyrus does not suit
as a *terminus a quo* for the commencement of the withdrawal
of the divine favour, or for the infliction of a curse upon the
people, inasmuch as the Jews were not punished because they
laid the foundation for the house of Jehovah, but simply because they neglected the house of God, that is to say, because
they desisted from the building they had already begun—is
one that would have some force if an interval of at least one or
more years had elapsed between the laying of the foundation
of the temple and the suspension of the building. But if the
work of building was interrupted immediately after the foundation had been laid, as is evident from Ezra iii. 10, as compared with ch. iv., Haggai might with perfect propriety describe
the whole time from the laying of the foundation of the temple
in the reign of Cyrus to the twenty-fourth day of the ninth
month of the second year of Darius as a time without blessing,
without there being any necessity for him expressly to deduct

the few weeks which elapsed between the laying of the foundation-stone and the suspension of the work of building, any more than the last three months, in which the work had been resumed again. The last three months could hardly be taken into account, because they fell for the most part in the period after the last harvest; so that if this had proved to be a bad one, the cause would be still in force. The prophet could therefore very properly inquire whether the seed was still in the granary, to which they would be obliged to answer No, because the miserable produce of the harvest was already either consumed for the supply of their daily wants, or used up for the sowing which was just ended. זֶרַע, seed, is not what is sown, but what the sowing yields, the corn, as in Lev. xxvii. 30, Isa. xxiii. 3, Job xxxix. 12. *Mᵉgūráh* = *mammᵉgūráh* in Joel i. 17, a barn or granary, from *gūr*, ἀγείρεσθαι, *congregari*. The following words, 'וְעַד־הַגֶּפֶן וגו, are really appended to the thought contained *implicite* in the first clause : the corn has not borne, and even to the vine, etc., it has borne nothing. נָשָׂא is indefinite : it has not borne = has borne nothing. It shall be different in future. From this day, *i.e.* from the twenty-fourth day of the ninth month, Jehovah will bless again, *i.e.* grant a blessing, namely, so that fruitful seasons will come again, and fields and fruit-trees bear once more. There is no necessity to supply a definite object to אֲבָרֵךְ.

Vers. 20–23. Renewal of the Promise of Salvation. —Ver. 20. On the same day on which the Lord promised to the people the return of the blessings of nature, Haggai received a second revelation, which promised to the community the pre- servation and care of the Davidic monarchy, represented for the time by Zerubbabel, in the midst of the storms that were about to burst upon the power of the world. Ver. 21. "*Speak to Zerubbabel the governor of Judah thus: I shake the heaven and the earth.* Ver. 22. *And I will overthrow the throne of the king- doms; and destroy the might of the kingdoms of the nations; and will overthrow the war-chariots, and those who ride in them : and horses and their riders shall fall, one by the sword of the other.* Ver. 23. *On that day, is the saying of Jehovah of hosts, will I take thee, Zerubbabel son of Shealtiel, my servant, is the saying of Jehovah, and make thee as a signet-ring : for I have chosen thee, is the saying of Jehovah of hosts.*" אֲנִי מַרְעִישׁ does not stand for הִנְנִי מַרְעִישׁ, but the participial clause is to be taken as a circumstantial clause : If I shake heaven and earth, I overthrow (cf. Ewald, § 341, c and d). The words point back to the shaking of the world predicted in vers. 6, 7. When this shaking takes place, then shall the throne of the kingdoms be thrown down, and their might be destroyed. The singular כִּסֵּא is used collectively, or rather distributively : "every throne of the kingdoms." The throne is the symbol of the monarchy, or of the government (cf. Dan. vii. 27) ; not in this sense, however, that "the prophet regarded all the kingdoms of the earth as one combined power in contradistinction to the people of God, or as a single power, as the power of the world, which was sitting as mistress at the time upon the throne of the earth" (Koehler). The plural *mamlâkhôth* does not agree with this, since every kingdom had both a king and a throne. The continuance of this throne rests upon the strength (*chōzeq*) of the heathen kingdoms, and this again upon their military power, their war-chariots, horses, and riders. These are to be overthrown and fall to the ground, and indeed by one another's swords. One hostile kingdom will destroy another, and in the last conflict the heathen hosts will annihilate one another (compare Ezek. xxxviii. 21 ; Zech. xiv. 13). At that time, when the dominion of the heathen had thus collapsed, Jehovah would take Zerubbabel and set or make him as a signet-ring. The verb *'eqqach* (will I take) simply serves to introduce the following act as one of importance, as for example in Deut. iv. 20 and 2 Kings xiv. 21. The meaning of the figurative expression, to make Zerubbabel as a signet-ring, is evident from the importance of the signet-ring in the eyes of an oriental, who is accustomed to carry his signet-ring constantly about with him, and to take care of it as a very valuable possession. It is introduced with the same idea in the Song of Sol. viii. 6, "Lay me as a signet-ring upon thy breast, as a signet-ring in thine arms ;" and it is in the same sense that Jehovah says of Jehoiachin in Jer. xxii. 24, " Though Coniah the son of Jehoiakim were even a signet-ring upon my right hand, *i.e.* a possession from which it would be thought impossible that I should separate myself, yet would I tear thee away from thence." Hence we obtain this thought for our present passage, namely, that on the

day on which Jehovah would overthrow the kingdoms of the
nations, He would make Zerubbabel like a signet-ring, which
is inseparable from its possessor; that is to say, He would
give him a position in which he would be and remain inseparably connected with Him (Jehovah), would therefore not
cast him off, but take care of him as His valuable possession.   This is the explanation given by Koehler (after Calvin,
Osiander, and others); and he has also refuted the various
explanations that differ from it.   But in order clearly to understand the meaning of this promise, we must look at the position
which Zerubbabel occupied in the community of Israel on its
return from exile.   For we may at the outset assume that the
promise did not apply to his own particular person, but rather
to the official post he held, from the fact that what is here
predicted was not to take place till after the overthrow of the
throne and might of all the kingdoms of the heathen, and
therefore could not take place in Zerubbabel's lifetime, inasmuch as, although the fall of this or the other kingdom might
be looked for in the course of one generation, the overthrow
of all kingdoms and the coming of all the heathen to fill the
temple of the Lord with their possessions (ver. 7) certainly could
not.   Zerubbabel was (Persian) governor in Judah, and had no
doubt been selected for this office because he was prince of
Judah (Ezra i. 8), and as son of Shealtiel was a descendant of
the family of David (see at ch. i. 1).   Consequently the sovereignty of David in its existing condition of humiliation, under
the sovereignty of the imperial power, was represented and
preserved in his appointment as prince and governor of Judah,
so that the fulfilment of the divine promise of the eternal perpetuation of the seed of David and his kingdom was then
associated with Zerubbabel, and rested upon the preservation
of his family.   Hence the promise points to the fact, that at the
time when Jehovah would overthrow the heathen kingdoms,
He would maintain and take good care of the sovereignty of
David in the person of Zerubbabel.   For Jehovah had chosen
Zerubbabel as His servant.   With these words the Messianic
promise made to David was transferred to Zerubbabel and his
family among David's descendants, and would be fulfilled in
his person in just the same way as the promise given to David,
that God would make him the highest among the kings of the

earth (Ps. lxxxix. 27). The fulfilment culminates in Jesus Christ, the son of David and descendant of Zerubbabel (Matt. i. 12 ; Luke iii. 27), in whom Zerubbabel was made the signet-ring of Jehovah. Jesus Christ has raised up the kingdom of His father David again, and of His kingdom there will be no end (Luke i. 32, 33). Even though it may appear oppressed and deeply humiliated for the time by the power of the kingdoms of the heathen, it will never be crushed and destroyed, but will break in pieces all these kingdoms, and destroy them, and will itself endure for ever (Dan. ii. 44 ; Heb. xii. 28 ; 1 Cor. xv. 24).

ZECHARIAH

INTRODUCTION.

1. THE Prophet.—*Zechariah,* זְכַרְיָה—*i.e.* not μνήμη Κυρίου, *memoria Domini,* remembrance of God (Jerome and others), nor God's renown (Fürst), but he whom God remembers (LXX. Ζαχαρίας, Vulg. Zacharias)—is a name of frequent occurrence in the Old Testament. Our prophet, like Jeremiah and Ezekiel, was of priestly descent,—a son of *Berechiah,* and grandson of Iddo (ch. i. 1, 7), the chief of one of the priestly families, that returned from exile along with Zerubbabel and Joshua (Neh. xii. 4). He followed his grandfather in that office under the high priest Jehoiakim (Neh. xii. 16), from which it has been justly concluded that he returned from Babylon while still a youth, and that his father died young. This also probably serves to explain the fact that Zechariah is called *bar 'Iddo',* the son (grandson) of Iddo, in Ezra v. 1 and vi. 14, and that his father is passed over. He commenced his prophetic labours in the second year of Darius Hystaspes, only two months later than his contemporary Haggai, in common with whom he sought to stimulate the building of the temple (Ezra v. 1, vi. 14), and that while he was still of youthful age, as we may infer partly from the facts quoted above, and partly from the epithet הַנַּעַר הַלָּז (the young man) in ch. ii. 8 (4), which refers to him. On the other hand, the legends handed down by the fathers, which are at variance with the biblical accounts, to the effect that Zechariah returned from Chaldæa at an advanced age, that he had previously predicted to Jozadak the birth of his son Joshua, and to Shealtiel the birth of Zerubbabel, and had shown to Cyrus his victory over Crœsus and Astyages by means of a miracle (Ps. Dor., Ps. Epiph., Hesych., and others), are not worth noticing. It is impossible to determine how long

his prophetic labours lasted. We simply know from ch. vii. 1, that in the fourth year of Darius he announced a further revelation from God to the people, and that his last two oracles (ch. ix.–xiv.) fall within a still later period. All that the fathers are able to state with regard to the closing portion of his life is, that he died at an advanced age, and was buried near to Haggai; whilst the contradictory statement, in a Cod. of Epiph., to the effect that he was slain under Joash king of Judah, between the temple and the altar, has simply arisen from our prophet being confounded with the Zechariah mentioned in 2 Chron. xxiv. 20–23.

2. THE BOOK OF ZECHARIAH contains, besides the brief word of God, which introduces his prophetic labours (ch. i. 1-6), four longer prophetic announcements: viz. (1) a series of seven visions, which Zechariah saw during the night, on the twenty-fourth day of the eleventh month, in the second year of Darius (ch. i. 7–vi. 8), together with a symbolical transaction, which brought the visions to a close (vi. 9–15); (2) the communication to the people of the answer of the Lord to a question addressed to the priests and prophets by certain Judæans as to their continuing any longer to keep the day appointed for commemorating the burning of the temple and Jerusalem by the Chaldæans as a fast-day, which took place in the fourth year of Darius (ch. vii. and viii.); (3) a burden, i.e. a prophecy of threatening import, concerning the land of Hadrach, the seat of the ungodly world-power (ch. ix.–xi.); and (4) a burden concerning Israel (ch. xii.–xiv.). The last two oracles, which are connected together by the common epithet massâ', are distinguished from the first two announcements not only by the fact that the headings contain neither notices as to the time, nor the prophet's name, but also by the absence of express allusions to the circumstances of Zechariah's own times, however unmistakeably the circumstances of the covenant nation after the captivity form the historical background of these prophecies also; whilst there is in general such a connection between their contents and the prophetic character of the night-visions, that ch. ix.–xiv. might be called a prophetic description of the future of the kingdom of God, in its conflict with the kingdoms of the world, as seen in the night-visions. For example, in the night-visions, as a sequel

to Haggai, who had predicted two months before the overthrow of the might of all the kingdoms of the world and the preservation of Zerubbabel in the midst of that catastrophe (Hag. ii. 20–23), the future development of the kingdom of God is unfolded to the prophet in its principal features till its final completion in glory. The *first* vision shows that the shaking of the kingdoms of the world predicted by Haggai will soon occur, notwithstanding the fact that the whole earth is for the time still quiet and at rest, and that Zion will be redeemed from its oppression, and richly blessed (ch. i. 7–17). The realization of this promise is explained in the following visions: in the *second* (ii. 1–4), the breaking in pieces of the kingdoms of the world, by the four smiths who threw down the horns of the nations; in the *third* (ch. ii. 5–17), the spread of the kingdom of God over the whole earth, through the coming of the Lord to His people; in the *fourth* (ch. iii.), the restoration of the church to favour, through the wiping away of its sins; in the *fifth* (ch. iv.), the glorifying of the church through the communication of the gifts of the Spirit; in the *sixth* (ch. v.), the sifting out of sinners from the kingdom of God; in the *seventh* (ch. vi. 1–8), the judgment, through which God refines and renews the sinful world; and *lastly*, in the symbolical transaction which closes the visions (ch. vi. 9–15), the completion of the kingdom of God by the Sprout of the Lord, who combines in His own person the dignity of both priest and king. If we compare with these the last two oracles, in ch. ix.-xi. we have first of all a picture of the judgment upon the kingdoms of the world, and of the establishment of the Messianic kingdom, through the gathering together of the scattered members of the covenant nation, and their exaltation to victory over the heathen (ch. ix. x.), and secondly, a more minute description of the attitude of the Lord towards the covenant nation and the heathen world (ch. xi.); and in ch. xii.-xiv. we have an announcement of the conflict of the nations of the world with Jerusalem, of the conversion of Israel to the Messiah, whom it once rejected and put to death (ch. xii. xiii.); and lastly, of the final attack of the heathen world upon the city of God, with its consequences,—namely, the purification and transfiguration of Jerusalem into a holy dwelling-place of the Lord, as King over the whole earth (ch. xiv.); so that in both oracles the development of the Old Testament kingdom of God is predicted until its completion in the kingdom of God, which embraces the whole earth. The revelation from God, which stands between these two principal parts, concerning the continuance of the fast-days (ch. vii. viii.), does indeed divide the two from one another, both chronologically and externally; but substantially it forms the connecting link between the two, inasmuch as this word of God impresses upon the people the condition upon which the attainment of the glorious future set before them in the night-visions depends, and thereby prepares them for the conflicts which Israel will have to sustain according to the announcement in ch. ix.–xiv., until the completion of the kingdom of God in glory.

Thus all the parts of the book hang closely together; and the objection which modern critics have offered to the unity of the book has arisen, not from the nature of the last two longer oracles (ch. ix.–xiv.), but partly from the dogmatic assumption of the rationalistic and naturalistic critics, that the biblical prophecies are nothing more than the productions of natural divination, and partly from the inability of critics, in consequence of this assumption, to penetrate into the depths of the divine revelation, and to grasp either the substance or form of their historical development, so as to appreciate it fully.[1] The current opinion of these critics, that the chapters in question date from the time before the captivity—viz. ch. ix.–xi. from a contemporary of Isaiah, and ch. xii.–xiv. from the last period before the destruction of the kingdom of Judah —is completely overthrown by the circumstance, that even in these oracles the condition of the covenant nation after the captivity forms the historical ground and starting-point for the proclamation and picture of the future development of the kingdom of God. The covenant nation in its two parts, into which it had been divided since the severance of the kingdom at the death of Solomon, had been dispersed among the heathen like a flock without a shepherd (ch. x. 2). It is true that Judah had already partially returned to Jerusalem and the cities of Judah; but the daughter Zion had still " prisoners of

---

[1] For the history of these attacks upon the genuineness of the last part of Zechariah, and of the vindication of its genuineness, with the arguments *pro* and *con*, see my *Lehrbuch der Einleitung*, § 103, and Koehler's *Zechariah*, ii. p. 297 sqq.

hope" waiting for release (ch. ix. 11, 12, compared with ch. ii. 10, 11), and the house of Joseph or Ephraim was still to be gathered and saved (ch. x. 6–10). Moreover, the severance of Judah and Ephraim, which lasted till the destruction of both kingdoms, had ceased. The eye of Jehovah is now fixed upon *all* the tribes of Israel (ch. ix. 1); Judah and Ephraim are strengthened by God for a common victorious conflict with the sons of Javan (ix. 13); the Lord their God grants salvation to His people as a flock (ix. 16 compared with viii. 13); the shepherd of the Lord feeds them both as a single flock, and only abolishes the brotherhood between Judah and Israel by the breaking of his second staff (ch. xi. 14). Hence the jealousy between Judah and Ephraim, the cessation of which was expected in the future by the prophets before the captivity (cf. Isa. xi. 13; Hos. ii. 2; Ezek. xxxvii. 15 sqq.), is extinct; and all that remains of the severance into two kingdoms is the epithet house of Judah or house of Israel, which Zechariah uses not only in ch. ix.–xi., but also in the appeal in ch. viii. 13, which no critic has called in question. All the tribes form one nation, which dwells in the presence of the prophet in Jerusalem and Judah. Just as in the first part of our book Israel consists of Judah and Jerusalem (i. 19, cf. ii. 12), so in the second part the burden pronounced upon Israel (xii. 1) falls upon Jerusalem and Judah (xii. 2, 5 sqq., xiv. 2, 14); and just as, according to the night-visions, the imperial power has its seat in the land of the north and of the south (ch. vi. 6), so in the last oracles Asshur (the north land) and Egypt (the south land) are types of the heathen world (ch. x. 10). And when at length the empire of the world which is hostile to God is more precisely defined, it is called Javan,—an epithet taken from Dan. viii. 21, which points as clearly as possible to the times after the captivity, inasmuch as the sons of Javan never appear as enemies of the covenant nation before the captivity, even when the Tyrians and Philistines are threatened with divine retribution for having sold to the Javanites the prisoners of Judah and Jerusalem (Joel iii. 6).

On the other hand, the differences which prevail between the first two prophecies of Zechariah and the last two are not of such a character as to point to two or three different prophets. It is true that in ch. ix.–xiv. there occur no visions, no

angels taking an active part, no Satan, no seven eyes of God;
but Amos also, for example, has only visions in the second
part, and none in the first; whilst the first part of Zechariah
contains not only visions, but also, in ch. i. 1-6, ch. vii. and
viii., simple prophetic addresses, and symbolical actions not
only in ch. vi. 9-15, but also in ch. xi. 4-17. The angels and
Satan, which appear in the visions, are also absent from ch.
vii. and viii.; whereas the angel of Jehovah is mentioned in
the last part in ch. xii. 8, and the saints in ch. xiv. 5 are angels.
The seven eyes of God are only mentioned in two visions (ch.
iii. 9 and iv. 10); and the providence of God is referred to in
ch. ix. 1, 8, under the epithet of the eye of Jehovah. This
also applies to the form of description and the language employed in the two parts. The visionary sights are described in
simple prose, as the style most appropriate for such descriptions.
The prophecies in word are oratorical, and to some extent are
rich in bold figures and similes. This diversity in the prophetic modes of presentation was occasioned by the occurrence
of peculiar facts and ideas, with the corresponding expressions
and words; but it cannot be proved that there is any constant
diversity in the way in which the same thing or the same idea
is described in the two parts, whereas there are certain unusual
expressions, such as מֵעֹבֵר וּמִשָּׁב (in ch. vii. 14 and ix. 8) and
הֶעֱבִיר in the sense of *removere* (in ch. iii. 4 and xiii. 2), which
are common to both parts. Again, the absence of any notice
as to the time in the headings in ch. ix. 1 and xii. 1 may be
explained very simply from the fact, that these prophecies of
the future of the kingdom are not so directly associated with
the prophet's own time as the visions are, the first of which
describes the condition of the world in the second year of
Darius. The omission of the name of the author from the
headings no more disproves the authorship of the Zechariah
who lived after the captivity, than the omission of the name
from Isa. xv. 1, xvii. 1, xix. 1, disproves Isaiah's authorship in
the case of the chapters named. All the other arguments that
have been brought against the integrity or unity of authorship
of the entire book, are founded upon false interpretations and
misunderstandings; whereas, on the other hand, the integrity of
the whole is placed beyond the reach of doubt by the testimony
of tradition, which is to be regarded as of all the greater value

in the case of Zechariah, inasmuch as the collection of the
prophetic writings, if not of the whole of the Old Testament
canon, was completed within even less than a generation after
the prophet's death.

Zechariah's mode of prophesying presents, therefore, according to the cursory survey just given, a very great variety.
Nevertheless, the crowding together of visions is not to be
placed to the account of the times after the captivity; nor can
any foreign, particularly Babylonian, colouring be detected in
the visions or in the prophetic descriptions. The habit of
leaning upon the prophecies of predecessors is not greater in
his case than in that of many of the prophets before the
captivity. The prophetic addresses are to some extent rich in
repetitions, especially in ch. vii. and viii., and tolerably uniform; but in the last two oracles they rise into very bold and
most original views and figures, which are evidently the production of a lively and youthful imagination. This abundance
of very unusual figures, connected with much harshness of
expression and transitions without intermediate links, makes
the work of exposition a very difficult one; so that Jerome and
the rabbins raise very general, but still greatly exaggerated,
lamentations over the obscurity of this prophet. The diction
is, on the whole, free from Chaldaisms, and formed upon the
model of good earlier writers. For the proofs of this, as well
as for the exegetical literature, see my *Lehrbuch der Einleitung*,
p. 310 sqq.

EXPOSITION.

INTRODUCTORY ADMONITION.—CHAP. I. 1–6.

The first word of the Lord was addressed to the prophet
Zechariah in the eighth month of the second year of the reign
of Darius, and therefore about two months after Haggai's first
prophecy and the commencement of the rebuilding of the
temple, which that prophecy was intended to promote (compare
ver. 1 with Hag. i. 1 and 15), and a few weeks after Haggai's
prophecy of the great glory which the new temple would

receive (Hag. ii. 1–9). Just as Haggai encouraged the chiefs and the people of Judah to continue vigorously the building that had been commenced by this announcement of salvation, so Zechariah opens his prophetic labours with the admonition to turn with sincerity to the Lord, and with the warning not to bring the same punishment upon themselves by falling back into the sins of the fathers. This exhortation to repentance, although it was communicated to the prophet in the form of a special revelation from God, is actually only the introduction to the prophecies which follow, requiring thorough repentance as the condition of obtaining the desired salvation, and at the same time setting before the impenitent and ungodly still further heavy judgments.[1] Ver. 1. *Bachōdesh hassh{e}mīnī* does not mean "on the eighth new moon" (Kimchi, Chr. B. Mich., Koehl.); for *chōdesh* is never used in chronological notices for the new moon, or the first new moon's day (see at Ex. xix. 1). The day of the eighth month is left indefinite, because this was of no importance whatever to the contents of this particular address. The word of the Lord was as follows : Ver. 2. " *Jehovah was angry with wrath concerning your fathers.* Ver. 3. *And thou shalt say to them, Thus saith Jehovah of hosts, Return ye to me, is the saying of Jehovah of hosts, so will I return to you, saith Jehovah of hosts.* Ver. 4. *Be not like your fathers, to whom the former prophets cried, Thus saith Jehovah of hosts, Turn now from your evil ways, and from your evil actions ! But they hearkened not, and paid no attention to me, is the saying of Jehovah.*" The statement in ver. 2 contains the ground for the summons to turn, which the prophet is to address to the people, and is therefore placed before וְאָמַרְתָּ in ver. 3, by which this summons is introduced. Because the Lord was very angry concerning the fathers, those who are living now are to repent with sincerity of heart. The noun *qetseph* is added as the object to the verb, to give it greater force. The nation had experienced the severe anger of God at the destruction of the kingdom of Judah, and of Jerusalem

---

[1] "The prophet is thus instructed by God, that, before exhibiting to the nation the rich blessings of God for them to look at under the form of symbolical images, he is to declare the duty of His people, or the condition upon which it will be becoming in God to grant them an abundant supply of these good things."—VITRINGA, *Comm. in Sach.* p. 76.

and the temple, and also in exile. The statement in ver. 15, that Jehovah was angry מְעָט, is not at variance with this; for מְעָט does not refer to the strength of the anger, but to its duration. וְאָמַרְתָּ is the *perf.* with *Vav consec.*, and is used for the imperative, because the summons to repentance follows as a necessary consequence from the fact stated in ver. 2 (cf. Ewald, § 342, *b* and *c*). אֲלֵהֶם does not refer to the fathers, which might appear to be grammatically the simplest interpretation, but to the contemporaries of the prophet, addressed in the pronoun *your* fathers, the existing generation of Judah. שׁוּבוּ אֵלַי does not presuppose that the people had just fallen away from the Lord again, or had lost all their pleasure in the continuance of the work of building the temple, but simply that the return to the Lord was not a perfect one, not a thorough conversion of heart. So had Jehovah also turned to the people again, and had not only put an end to the sufferings of exile, but had also promised His aid to those who had returned (compare אֲנִי אִתְּכֶם in Hag. i. 13); but the more earnestly and the more thoroughly the people turned to Him, the more faithfully and the more gloriously would He bestow upon them His grace and the promised salvation. This admonition is shown to be extremely important by the threefold " saith the Lord of Zebaoth," and strengthened still further in ver. 4 by the negative turn not to do like the fathers, who cast the admonitions of the prophets to the winds. The " earlier prophets" are those before the captivity (cf. ch. vii. 7, 12). The predicate רִאשֹׁנִים points to the fact that there was a gap between Zechariah and his predecessors, namely the period of the exile, so that Daniel and Ezekiel, who lived in exile, are overlooked; the former because his prophecies are not admonitions addressed to the people, the latter because the greater part of his ministry fell in the very commencement of the exile. Moreover, when alluding to the admonitions of the earlier prophets, Zechariah has not only such utterances in his mind as those in which the prophets summoned the people to repentance with the words שׁוּבוּ ונו' (*e.g.* Joel ii. 13; Hos. xiv. 2, 3; Isa. xxxi. 6; Jer. iii. 12 sqq., vii. 13, etc.), but the admonitions, threatenings, and reproofs of the earlier prophets generally (compare 2 Kings xvii. 13 sqq.). The *chethib* מעליליכם is to be read מֵעֲלִילֵיכֶם, a plural form עֲלִילִים from עֲלִילָה, and is to be retained, since the

preposition *min* is wanting in the *keri;* and this reading has
probably only arisen from the offence taken at the use of the
plural form *ʿălīlīm,* which does not occur elsewhere, in the place
of *ʿălīlōth,* although there are many analogies to such a formation, and feminine forms frequently have plurals in ‏ים-‏, either
instead of those in ‏ות‏ or in addition to them.

A reason for the warning not to resist the words of the
Lord, like the fathers, is given in vers. 5, 6, by an allusion to
the fate which they brought upon themselves through their
disobedience. Ver. 5. " *Your fathers, where are they? And
the prophets, can they live for ever?* Ver. 6. *Nevertheless my
words and my statutes, which I commanded my servants the
prophets, did they not overtake your fathers, so that they turned
and said, As Jehovah purposed to do to us according to our
ways and our actions, so has He done to us?*" The two questions in ver. 5 are meant as denials, and are intended to
anticipate the objection which the people might have raised
to the admonitions in ver. 4, to the effect that not only the
fathers, but also the earlier prophets, had died long ago; and
therefore an allusion to things that had long since passed by
could have no force at all for the present generation. Zechariah neutralizes this objection by saying: Your fathers have
indeed been long dead, and even the prophets do not, or cannot,
live for ever; but notwithstanding this, the words of the earlier
prophets were fulfilled in the case of the fathers. The words
and decrees of God uttered by the prophets did reach the
fathers, so that they were obliged to confess that God had
really done to them what He threatened, *i.e.* had carried out
the threatened punishment. ‏אַךְ‏, only, in the sense of a limitation of the thing stated: yet, nevertheless (cf. Ewald, § 105, *d*).
‏דְּבָרַי‏ and ‏חֻקַּי‏ are not the words of ver. 4, which call to repentance, but the threats and judicial decrees which the earlier
prophets announced in case of impenitence.   ‏דְּבָרַי‏ as in Ezek.
xii. 28, Jer. xxxix. 16.   ‏חֻקַּי‏, the judicial decrees of God, like
chōq in Zeph. ii. 2.   *Hissīg,* to reach, applied to the threatened
punishments which pursue the sinner, like messengers sent
after him, and overtake him (cf. Deut. xxviii. 15, 45). Biblical
proofs that even the fathers themselves did acknowledge that
the Lord had fulfilled His threatenings in their experience,
are to be found in the mournful psalms written in captivity

(though not exactly in Ps. cxxvi. and cxxxvii., as Koehler supposes), in Lam. ii. 17 (זמם אשר יהוה עשׂה, upon which Zechariah
seems to play), and in the penitential prayers of Daniel
(ix. 4 sqq.) and of Ezra (ix. 6 sqq.), so far as they express the
feeling which prevailed in the congregation.

I. THE NIGHT-VISIONS.—CHAP. I. 7–VI. 15.

Three months after his call to be a prophet through the
first word of God that was addressed to him, Zechariah received
a comprehensive revelation concerning the future fate of the
people and kingdom of God, in a series of visions, which were
given him to behold in a single night, and were interpreted by
an angel. This took place, according to ver. 7, " *on the twenty-
fourth day of the eleventh month, i.e. the month Shebat, in the
second year of Darius,*" that is to say, exactly five months
after the building of the temple had been resumed (Hag. i. 15),
with which fact the choice of the day for the divine revelation
was evidently connected, and two months after the last promise
issued through Haggai to the people, that the Lord would from
henceforth bless His nation, and would glorify it in the future
(Hag. ii. 10–23). To set forth in imagery this blessing and
glorification, and to exhibit the leading features of the future
conformation of the kingdom of God, was the object of these
visions, which are designated in the introduction as " word of
Jehovah," because the pictures seen in the spirit, together with
their interpretation, had the significance of verbal revelations,
and are to some extent still further explained by the addition of
words of God (cf. i. 14 sqq., ii. 10–17). As they were shown
to the prophet one after another in a single night, so that
in all probability only short pauses intervened between the
different views ; so did they present a substantially connected
picture of the future of Israel, which was linked on to the
then existing time, and closed with the prospect of the ultimate
completion of the kingdom of God.

FIRST VISION: THE RIDER AMONG THE MYRTLES.
—CHAP. I. 8–17.

Ver. 8. "*I saw by night, and behold a man riding upon a red horse, and he stood among the myrtles which were in the hollow; and behind him red, speckled, and white horses.* Ver. 9. *And I said, What are these, my lord? Then the angel that talked with me said to me, I will show thee what these are.* Ver. 10. *And the man who stood among the myrtles answered and said, These are they whom Jehovah hath sent to go through the earth.* Ver. 11. *And they answered the angel of Jehovah who stood among the myrtles, and said, We have gone through the earth, and, behold, the whole earth sits still, and at rest.* Ver. 12. *Then the angel of Jehovah answered and said, Jehovah of hosts, how long wilt Thou not have compassion upon Jerusalem and the cities of Judah, with whom Thou hast been angry these seventy years?* Ver. 13. *And Jehovah answered the angel that talked with me good words, comforting words.* Ver. 14. *And the angel that talked with me said to me, Preach, and say, Thus saith Jehovah of hosts, I have been jealous for Jerusalem and Zion with great jealousy,* (Ver. 15) *and with great wrath I am angry against the nations at rest: for I had been angry for a little, but they helped for harm.* Ver. 16. *Therefore thus saith Jehovah, I turn again to Jerusalem with compassion: my house shall be built in it, is the saying of Jehovah of hosts, and the measuring line shall be drawn over Jerusalem.* Ver. 17. *Preach as yet, and say, Thus saith Jehovah of hosts, My cities shall yet swell over with good, and Jehovah will yet comfort Zion, and will yet choose Jerusalem.*" The prophet sees, during the night of the day described in ver. 7 (הַלַּיְלָה is the accusative of duration), in an ecstatic vision, not in a dream but in a waking condition, a rider upon a red horse in a myrtle-bush, stopping in a deep hollow, and behind him a number of riders upon red, speckled, and white horses (*sūsīm* are horses with riders, and the reason why the latter are not specially mentioned is that they do not appear during the course of the vision as taking any active part, whilst the colour of their horses is the only significant feature). At the same time he also sees, in direct proximity to himself, an angel who interprets the vision, and farther off (ver. 11) the angel of Jehovah also standing or stopping among the myrtle-bushes,

and therefore in front of the man upon a red horse, to whom
the riders bring a report, that they have gone through the
earth by Jehovah's command and have found the whole earth
quiet and at rest; whereupon the angel of Jehovah addresses
a prayer to Jehovah for pity upon Jerusalem and the cities of
Judah, and receives a good consolatory answer, which the interpreting angel conveys to the prophet, and the latter publicly
proclaims in vers. 14–17. The rider upon the red horse is not
to be identified with the angel of Jehovah, nor the latter with
the *angelus interpres*. It is true that the identity of the rider
and the angel of Jehovah, which many commentators assume,
is apparently favoured by the circumstance that they are both
standing among the myrtles (*'ōmēd*, stood; see vers. 8, 10, and
11); but all that follows from this is that the rider stopped at
the place where the angel of Jehovah was standing, *i.e.* in front
of him, to present a report to him of the state of the earth,
which he had gone through with his retinue. This very circumstance rather favours the diversity of the two, inasmuch
as it is evident from this that the rider upon the red horse was
simply the front one, or leader of the whole company, who is
brought prominently forward as the spokesman and reporter.
If the man upon the red horse had been the angel of Jehovah
Himself, and the troop of horsemen had merely come to bring
information to the man upon the red horse, the troop of horsemen could not have stood behind him, but would have stood
either opposite to him or in front of him. And the different
epithets applied to the two furnish a decisive proof that the
angel of the Lord and "the angel that talked with me" are
not one and the same. The angel, who gives or conveys to the
prophet the interpretation of the vision, is constantly called
"the angel that talked with me," not only in ver. 9, where it is
preceded by an address on the part of the prophet to this same
angel, but also in vers. 13 and 14, and in the visions which
follow (ch. ii. 2, 7, iv. 1, 4, v. 5, 10, vi. 4), from which it is
perfectly obvious that הַדֹּבֵר בִּי denotes the function which this
angel performs in these visions (*dibber b^e*, signifying the speaking of God or of an angel within a man, as in Hos. i. 2, Hab.
ii. 1, Num. xii. 6, 8). His occupation, therefore, was to interpret the visions to the prophet, and convey the divine revelations, so that he was only an *angelus interpres* or *collocutor*.

This angel appears in the other visions in company with other angels, and receives instructions from them (ch. ii. 5–8); and his whole activity is restricted to the duty of conveying higher instructions to the prophet, and giving him an insight into the meaning of the visions, whereas the angel of Jehovah stands on an equality with God, being sometimes identified with Jehovah, and at other times distinguished from Him. (Compare the remarks upon this subject in the comm. on Genesis, *Pent.* i. p. 185 sqq.) In the face of these facts, it is impossible to establish the identity of the two by the arguments that have been adduced in support of it. It by no means follows from ver. 9, where the prophet addresses the mediator as " my lord," that the words are addressed to the angel of the Lord ; for neither he nor the *angelus interpres* has been mentioned before ; and in the visions persons are frequently introduced as speaking, according to their dramatic character, without having been mentioned before, so that it is only from what they say or do that it is possible to discover who they are. Again, the circumstance that in ver. 12 the angel of the Lord presents a petition to the Supreme God on behalf of the covenant nation, and that according to ver. 13 Jehovah answers the *angelus interpres* in good, comforting words, does not prove that he who receives the answer must be the same person as the intercessor : for it might be stated in reply to this, as it has been by Vitringa, that Zechariah has simply omitted to mention that the answer was first of all addressed to the angel of the Lord, and that it was through him that it reached the mediating angel ; or we might assume, as Hengstenberg has done, that " Jehovah addressed the answer directly to the mediating angel, because the angel of the Lord had asked the question, not for his own sake, but simply for the purpose of conveying consolation and hope through the mediator to the prophet, and through him to the nation generally."

There is no doubt that, in this vision, both the locality in which the rider upon the red horse, with his troop, and the angel of the Lord had taken up their position, and also the colour of the horses, are significant. But they are neither of them easy to interpret. Even the meaning of *mᵉtsullâh* is questionable. Some explain it as signifying a " shady place," from צל, a shadow ; but in that case we should expect the form *m^etsillâh*. There is more authority for the assumption that *m^etsullâh* is only another form for *m^etsūlâh*, which is the reading in many codd., and which ordinarily stands for the depth of the sea, just as in Ex. xv. 10 *tsâlal* signifies to sink into the deep. The Vulgate adopts this rendering : *in profundo.* Here it signifies, in all probability, a deep hollow, possibly with water in it, as myrtles flourish particularly well in damp soils and by the side of rivers (see Virgil, *Georg.* ii. 112, iv. 124). The article in *bamm^etsullâh* defines the hollow as the one which the prophet saw in the vision, not the ravine of the fountain of Siloah, as Hofmann supposes (*Weissagung u. Erfüllung*, i. p. 333). The hollow here is not a symbol of the power of the world, or the abyss-like power of the kingdoms of the world (Hengstenberg and M. Baumgarten), as the author of the Chaldee paraphrase *in Babele* evidently thought ; for this cannot be proved from such passages as ch. x. 16, Isa. xliv. 27, and Ps. cvii. 24. In the myrtle-bushes, or myrtle grove, we have no doubt a symbol of the theocracy, or of the land of Judah as a land that was dear and lovely in the estimation of the Lord (cf. Dan. viii. 9, xi. 16), for the myrtle is a lovely ornamental plant. Hence the hollow in which the myrtle grove was situated, can only be a figurative representation of the deep degradation into which the land and people of God had fallen at that time. There is a great diversity of opinion as to the significance of the colour of the horses, although all the commentators agree that the colour is significant, as in ch. vi. 2 sqq. and Rev. vi. 2 sqq., and that this is the only reason why the horses are described according to their colours, and the riders are not mentioned at all. About two of the colours there is no dispute. אָדֹם, red, the colour of the blood ; and לָבָן, white, brilliant white, the reflection of heavenly and divine glory (Matt. xvii. 2, xxviii. 3 ; Acts i. 10), hence the symbol of a glorious victory (Rev. vi. 2). The meaning of *s^eruqqīm* is a disputed one. The LXX. have rendered it ψαροὶ καὶ ποικίλοι, like בְּרֻדִּים אֲמֻצִּים in ch. vi. 3 ; the Itala and Vulgate, *varii;* the Peshito, *versicolores.* Hence *sūsīm s^eruqqīm* would correspond to the ἵππος χλωρός of Rev. vi. 8. The word *s^eruqqīm* only occurs again in the Old Testament in Isa. xvi. 8, where it is applied to the tendrils or branches of the vine, for which *sōrēq* (Isa. v. 2 ; Jer. ii. 21) or *s^erēqâh* (Gen. xlix. 11) is used elsewhere.　On the other hand, Gesenius (*Thes. s.v.*) and others defend the meaning red, after the Arabic اِشْقَر, the red horse, the fox, from شَقَ, to be bright red; and Koehler understands by *sūsīm s*'*ruqqīm*, bright red, fire-coloured, or bay horses.　But this meaning cannot be shown to be in accordance with Hebrew usage: for it is a groundless conjecture that the vine branch is called *sōrēq* from the dark-red grapes (Hitzig on Isa. v. 2); and the incorrectness of it is evident from the fact, that even the Arabic شَقَ does not denote dark-red, but bright, fiery red.　The Arabic translator has therefore rendered the Greek πυῤῥός by اِشْقَ in Cant. v. 9; but πυῤῥός answers to the Hebrew אָדֹם, and the LXX. have expressed *sūsīm 'ădummīm* by ἵπποι πυῤῥοί both here and in ch. vi. 2. If we compare this with ch. vi. 2, where the chariots are drawn by red ('*ădummīm*, πυῤῥοί), black (*sh*'*chōrīm*, μέλανες), white (*l*'*bhānīm*, λευκοί), and speckled (*b*'*ruddīm*, ψαροί) horses, and with Rev. vi., where the first rider has a white horse (λευκός), the second a red one (πυῤῥός), the third a black one (μέλας), the fourth a pale horse (χλωρός), there can be no further doubt that three of the colours of the horses mentioned here occur again in the two passages quoted, and that the black horse is simply added as a fourth; so that the *s*'*ruqqīm* correspond to the *b*'*ruddīm* of ch. vi. 3, and the ἵππος χλωρός of Rev. vi. 8, and consequently *sārōq* denotes that starling kind of grey in which the black ground is mixed with white, so that it is not essentially different from *bārōd*, speckled, or black covered with white spots (Gen. xxxi. 10, 12).

By comparing these passages with one another, we obtain so much as certain with regard to the meaning of the different colours,—namely, that the colours neither denote the lands and nations to which the riders had been sent, as Hävernick, Maurer, Hitzig, Ewald, and others suppose; nor the three imperial kingdoms, as Jerome, Cyril, and others have attempted to prove.　For, apart from the fact that there is no foundation whatever for the combination proposed, of the red colour with the south as the place of light, or of the white with the west, the fourth quarter of the heavens would be altogether wanting. Moreover, the riders mentioned here have unquestionably gone through the earth in company, according to vers. 8 and 11, or at any rate there is no intimation whatever of their having gone through the different countries separately, according to the colour of their respective horses; and, according to ch. vi. 6, not only the chariot with the black horses, but that with the white horses also, goes into the land of the south. Consequently the colour of the horses can only be connected with the mission which the riders had to perform. This is confirmed by Rev. vi., inasmuch as a great sword is there given to the rider upon the red horse, to take away peace from the earth, that they may kill one another, and a crown to the rider upon the white horse, who goes forth conquering and to conquer (ver. 2), whilst the one upon the pale horse receives the name of Death, and has power given to him to slay the fourth part of the earth with sword, famine, and pestilence (ver. 8). It is true that no such effects as these are attributed to the riders in the vision before us, but this constitutes no essential difference. To the prophet's question, *mâh-'ēlleh*, what are these? *i.e.* what do they mean? the *angelus interpres*, whom he addresses as " my lord" (*'ădōnī*), answers, " I will show thee what these be ;" whereupon the man upon the red horse, as the leader of the company, gives this reply : " These are they whom Jehovah hath sent to go through the earth ;" and then proceeds to give the angel of the Lord the report of their mission, viz. " We have been through the earth, and behold all the earth sitteth still and at rest." The man's answer (*vayya'an,* ver. 10) is not addressed to the prophet or to the *angelus interpres,* but to the angel of the Lord mentioned in ver. 11, to whom the former, with his horsemen (hence the plural, " they answered," in ver. 11), had given a report of the result of their mission. The verb *'ânâh,* to answer, refers not to any definite question, but to the request for an explanation contained in the conversation between the prophet and the interpreting angel. הָאָרֶץ, in vers. 10 and 11, is not the land of Judah, or any other land, but the earth. The answer, that the whole earth sits still and at rest (יֹשֶׁבֶת וְשֹׁקָטֶת denotes the peaceful and secure condition of a land and its inhabitants, undisturbed by any foe ; cf. ch. vii. 7, 1 Chron. iv. 40, and Judg. xviii. 27), points back to Hag. ii. 7, 8, 22, 23. God had there announced that for a little He would shake heaven and earth, the whole world and all nations, that the nations would come and fill His temple with glory. The riders sent out by God now return and report that the earth is by no means shaken and in motion, but the whole world sits quiet and at rest. We must not, indeed, infer from this account that the riders were all sent for the simple and exclusive purpose of obtaining information concerning the state of the earth, and communicating it to the Lord. For it would have been quite superfluous and unmeaning to send out an entire troop, on horses of different colours, for this purpose alone. Their mission was rather to take an active part in the agitation of the nations, if any such existed, and guide it to the divinely appointed end, and that in the manner indicated by the colour of their horses; viz. according to Rev. vi., those upon the red horses by war and bloodshed; those upon the starling-grey, or speckled horses, by famine, pestilence, and other plagues; and lastly, those upon the white horses, by victory and the conquest of the world.

In the second year of Darius there prevailed universal peace; all the nations of the earlier Chaldæan empire were at rest, and lived in undisturbed prosperity. Only Judæa, the home of the nation of God, was still for the most part lying waste, and Jerusalem was still without walls, and exposed in the most defenceless manner to all the insults of the opponents of the Jews. Such a state of things as this necessarily tended to produce great conflicts in the minds of the more godly men, and to confirm the frivolous in their indifference towards the Lord. As long as the nations of the world enjoyed undisturbed peace, Judah could not expect any essential improvement in its condition. Even though Darius had granted permission for the building of the temple to be continued, the people were still under the bondage of the power of the world, without any prospect of the realization of the glory predicted by the earlier prophets (Jer. xxxi. seq.; Isa. xl. sqq.), which was to dawn upon the nation of God when redeemed from Babylon. Hence the angel of the Lord addresses the intercessory prayer to Jehovah in ver. 12: How long wilt Thou not have compassion upon Jerusalem, etc.? For the very fact that the angel of the Lord, through whom Jehovah had formerly led His people and

brought them into the promised land and smitten all the enemies before Israel, now appears again, contains in itself one
source of consolation. His coming was a sign that Jehovah
had not forsaken His people, and His intercession could not
fail to remove every doubt as to the fulfilment of the divine
promises. The circumstance that the angel of Jehovah addresses an intercessory prayer to Jehovah on behalf of Judah,
is no more a disproof of his essential unity with Jehovah, than
the intercessory prayer of Christ in John xvii. is a disproof of
His divinity. The words, "over which Thou hast now been
angry for seventy years," do not imply that the seventy years
of the Babylonian captivity predicted by Jeremiah (Jer. xxv.
11 and xxix. 10) were only just drawing to a close. They had
already expired in the first year of the reign of Cyrus (2 Chron.
xxxvi. 22 ; Ezra i. 1). At the same time, the remark made by
Vitringa, Hengstenberg, and others, must not be overlooked,—
namely, that these seventy years were completed twice, inasmuch as there were also (not perhaps quite, but nearly) seventy
years between the destruction of Jerusalem and of the temple,
and the second year of Darius. Now, since the temple was
still lying in ruins in the second year of Darius, notwithstanding the command to rebuild it that had been issued by Cyrus
(Hag. i. 4), it might very well appear as though the troubles
of the captivity would never come to an end. Under such
circumstances, the longing for an end to be put to the mournful condition of Judah could not fail to become greater and
greater; and the prayer, " Put an end, O Lord, put an end to
all our distress," more importunate than ever. Jehovah replied
to the intercession of the angel of the Lord with good and
comforting words. *D^ebhârîm tôbhîm* are words which promise
good, *i.e.* salvation (cf. Josh. xxiii. 14 ; Jer. xxix. 10). So far
as they set before the people the prospect of the mitigation of
their distress, they are *nichummîm*, consolations. The word
nichummîm is a substantive, and in apposition to *d^ebhârîm*.
Instead of the form *nichummîm*, the *keri* has the form *nichumîm*,
which is grammatically the more correct of the two, and which
is written still more accurately *nichûmîm* in some of the codd.
in Kennicott. The contents of these words, which are addressed
to the interpreting angel either directly or through the medium
of the angel of Jehovah, follow in the announcement which

the latter orders the prophet to make in vers. 14–17. קְרָא (ver.
14) as in Isa. xl. 6. The word of the Lord contains two things:
(1) the assurance of energetic love on the part of God towards
Jerusalem (vers. 14, 15); and (2) the promise that this love
will show itself in the restoration and prosperity of Jerusalem
(vers. 16, 17). קִנֵּא, to be jealous, applied to the jealousy of
love as in Joel ii. 18, Num. xxv. 11, 13, etc., is strengthened
by קִנְאָה גְדוֹלָה. Observe, too, the use of the perfect קִנֵּאתִי, as
distinguished from the participle קֹצֵף. The perfect is not
merely used in the sense of "I have become jealous," expressing the fact that Jehovah was inspired with burning jealousy,
to take Jerusalem to Himself (Koehler), but includes the
thought that God has already manifested this zeal, or begun
to put it in action, namely by liberating His people from exile.
Zion, namely the mountain of Zion, is mentioned along with
Jerusalem as being the site on which the temple stood, so that
Jerusalem only comes into consideration as the capital of the
kingdom. Jehovah is also angry with the self-secure and
peaceful nations. The participle qôtsēph designates the wrath
as lasting. Sha'ănân, quiet and careless in their confidence in
their own power and prosperity, which they regard as secured
for ever. The following word, אֲשֶׁר, quod, introduces the reason
why God is angry, viz. because, whereas He was only a little
angry with Israel, they assisted for evil. מְעַט refers to the duration, not to the greatness of the anger (cf. Isa. liv. 8). עָזְרוּ לְרָעָה,
they helped, so that evil was the result (לְרָעָה as in Jer. xliv.
11), i.e. they assisted not only as the instruments of God for
the chastisement of Judah, but so that harm arose from it, inasmuch as they endeavoured to destroy Israel altogether (cf. Isa.
xlvii. 6). It is no ground of objection to this definition of the
meaning of the words, that לְרָעָה in that case does not form an
appropriate antithesis to מְעַט, which relates to time (Koehler);
for the fact that the anger only lasted a short time, was in
itself a proof that God did not intend to destroy His people.
To understand עָזְרוּ לְרָעָה as only referring to the prolonged oppression and captivity, does not sufficiently answer to the words.
Therefore (lâkhēn, ver. 16), because Jehovah is jealous with
love for His people, and very angry with the heathen, He has
now turned with compassion towards Jerusalem. The perfect
שַׁבְתִּי is not purely prophetic, but describes the event as having

already commenced, and as still continuing. This compassion
will show itself in the fact that the house of God is to be built
in Jerusalem, and the city itself restored, and all the obstacles
to this are to be cleared out of the way. The measuring line
is drawn over a city, to mark off the space it is to occupy, and
the plan upon which it is to be arranged. The *chethib* קוה,
probably to be read קָוֶה, is the obsolete form, which occurs
again in 1 Kings vii. 23 and Jer. xxxi. 39, and was displaced
by the contracted form קָו (*keri*). But the compassion of God
will not be restricted to this. The prophet is to proclaim still
more ("cry yet," ver. 17, referring to the "cry" in ver. 14).
The cities of Jehovah, *i.e.* of the land of the Lord, are still to
overflow with good, or with prosperity. *Pūts*, to overflow, as
in Prov. v. 16; and תְּפוּצֶנָה for תְּפוּצֶינָה (*vid.* Ewald, § 196, *c*).
The last two clauses round off the promise. When the Lord
shall restore the temple and city, then will Zion and Jerusalem
learn that He is comforting her, and has chosen her still. The
last thought is repeated in ch. ii. 16 and iii. 2.

In this vision it is shown to the prophet, and through him
to the people, that although the immediate condition of things
presents no prospect of the fulfilment of the promised restoration and glorification of Israel, the Lord has nevertheless already
appointed the instruments of His judgment, and sent them out
to overthrow the nations of the world, that are still living at
rest and in security, and to perfect His Zion. The fulfilment
of this consolatory promise is neither to be transferred to the
end of the present course of this world, as is supposed by Hofmann (*Weiss. u. Erfüll.* i. 335), who refers to ch. xiv. 18, 19
in support of this, nor to be restricted to what was done in the
immediate future for the rebuilding of the temple and of the city
of Jerusalem. The promise embraces the whole of the future
of the kingdom of God; so that whilst the commencement
of the fulfilment is to be seen in the fact that the building
of the temple was finished in the sixth year of Darius, and
Jerusalem itself was also restored by Nehemiah in the reign
of Artaxerxes, these commencements of the fulfilment simply
furnished a pledge that the glorification of the nation and
kingdom of God predicted by the earlier prophets would quite
as assuredly follow.

SECOND VISION : THE FOUR HORNS AND THE FOUR SMITHS.—
CHAP. I. 18–21 (HEB. BIB. CHAP. II. 1–4).

The second vision is closely connected with the first, and
shows how God will discharge the fierceness of His wrath upon
the heathen nations in their self-security (ch. i. 15). Ver. 18.
*"And I lifted up mine eyes, and saw, and behold four horns. Ver.
19. And I said to the angel that talked with me, What are these?
And he said to me, These are the horns which have scattered
Judah, Israel, and Jerusalem. Ver. 20. And Jehovah show'ed
me four smiths. Ver. 21. And I said, What come these to do?
And He spake to me thus : These are the horns which have scattered Judah, so that no one lifted up his head; these are now come
to terrify them, to cast down the horns of the nations which have
lifted up the horn against the land of Judah to scatter it."* The
mediating angel interprets the four horns to the prophet first
of all as the horns which have scattered Judah ; then literally,
as the nations which have lifted up the horn against the land
of Judah to scatter it. The horn is a symbol of power (cf.
Amos vi. 13). The horns therefore symbolize the powers of
the world, which rise up in hostility against Judah and hurt it.
The number four does not point to the four quarters of the
heaven, denoting the heathen foes of Israel in all the countries
of the world (Hitzig, Maurer, Koehler, and others). This view
cannot be established from ver. 10, for there is no reference to
any dispersion of Israel to the four winds there. Nor does it
follow from the perfect זֵרוּ that only such nations are to be
thought of, as had already risen up in hostility to Israel and
Judah in the time of Zechariah ; for it cannot be shown that
there were four such nations. At that time all the nations
round about Judah were subject to the Persian empire, as they
had been in Nebuchadnezzar's time to the Babylonian. Both
the number four and the perfect *zērū* belong to the sphere of
inward intuition, in which the objects are combined together
so as to form one complete picture, without any regard to the
time of their appearing in historical reality. Just as the prophet in ch. vi. sees the four chariots all together, although they
follow one another in action, so may the four horns which are
seen simultaneously represent nations which succeeded one

another. This is shown still more clearly by the visions in
Dan. ii. and vii., in which not only the colossal image seen in
a dream by Nebuchadnezzar (ch. ii.), but also the four beasts
which are seen by Daniel to ascend simultaneously from the
sea, symbolize the four empires, which rose up in succession
one after the other. It is to these four empires that the four
horns of our vision refer, as Jerome, Abarb., Hengstenberg, and
others have correctly pointed out, since even the picturing of
nations or empires as horns points back to Dan. vii. 7, 8, and
viii. 3–9. Zechariah sees these in all the full development of their
power, in which they have oppressed and crushed the people
of God (hence the perfect *zērū*), and for which they are to be
destroyed themselves. *Zârâh*, to scatter, denotes the dissolution of the united condition and independence of the nation of
God. In this sense all four empires destroyed Judah, although
the Persian and Grecian empires did not carry Judah out of
their own land. The striking combination, "Judah, Israel,
and Jerusalem," in which not only the introduction of the
name of Israel between Judah and Jerusalem is to be noticed,
but also the fact that the *nota acc.* אֵת is only placed before
Yᵉhūdâh and *Yisrâ'ēl*, and not before *Yᵉrūshâlaim* also, is not
explained on the ground that Israel denotes the kingdom of the
ten tribes, Judah the southern kingdom, and Jerusalem the
capital of the kingdom (Maurer, Umbreit, and others), for in
that case *Israel* would necessarily have been repeated before
Judah, and *'ēth* before *Yᵉrūshâlaim*. Still less can the name
Israel denote the rural population of Judah (Hitzig), or the
name *Judah* the princely house (Neumann). By the fact that
'ēth is omitted before *Yᵉrūshâlaim*, and only *Vav* stands before
it, Jerusalem is connected with Israel and separated from
Judah; and by the repetition of *'ēth* before *Yisrâ'ēl*, as well
as before *Yᵉhūdâh*, Israel with Jerusalem is co-ordinated with
Judah. Kliefoth infers from this that "the heathen had dispersed on the one hand Judah, and on the other hand Israel
together with Jerusalem," and understands this as signifying
that in the nation of God itself a separation is presupposed,
like the previous separation into Judah and the kingdom of the
ten tribes. "When the Messiah comes," he says, "a small portion of the Israel according to the flesh will receive Him, and
so constitute the genuine people of God and the true Israel, *the*

Judah; whereas the greater part of the Israel according to the
flesh will reject the Messiah at first, and harden itself in unbelief, until at the end of time it will also be converted, and
join the true Judah of Christendom." But this explanation,
according to which *Judah* would denote the believing portion
of the nation of twelve tribes, and *Israel* and *Jerusalem* the
unbelieving, is wrecked on the grammatical difficulty that the
cop. ו is wanting before אֶת־יִשְׂרָאֵל. If the names *Judah* and
Israel were intended to be co-ordinated with one another as
two different portions of the covenant nation as a whole, the
two parts would necessarily have been connected together by
the cop. *Vav.* Moreover, in the two co-ordinated names *Judah*
and *Israel,* the one could not possibly stand in the spiritual sense,
and the other in the carnal. The co-ordination of *'eth-Yᵉhūdáh*
with *'eth-Yisrâ'ēl* without the cop. *Vav* shows that Israel is really
equivalent to the *Jerusalem* which is subordinated to it, and does
not contain a second member (or part), which is added to it,—
in other words, that Israel with Jerusalem is merely an interpretation or more precise definition of *Yᵉhūdáh;* and Hengstenberg has hit upon the correct idea, when he takes Israel as the
honourable name of Judah, or, more correctly, as an honourable name for the covenant nation as then existing in Judah.
This explanation is not rendered questionable by the objection
offered by Koehler: viz. that after the separation of the two
kingdoms, the expression Israel always denotes either the kingdom of the ten tribes, or the posterity of Jacob without regard
to their being broken up, because this is not the fact. The
use of the name Israel for Judah after the separation of the
kingdoms is established beyond all question by 2 Chron. xii. 1,
xv. 17, xix. 8, xxi. 2, 4, xxiii. 2, xxiv. 5, etc.[1]

Jehovah then showed the prophet four *chârâshīm,* or work-
men, *i.e.* smiths; and on his putting the question, "What have

[1] Gesenius has correctly observed in his *Thesaurus,* p. 1339, that
"from this time (*i.e.* from the severance of the kingdom) the name of
Israel began to be usurped by the whole nation that was then in existence,
and was used chiefly by the prophets Jeremiah, Ezekiel, and Deutero(?)-
Isaiah, and after the captivity by Ezra and Nehemiah; from which it came
to pass, that in the *Paralipomena,* even when allusion is made to an earlier
period, *Israel* stands for Judah," although the proofs adduced in support
of this from the passages quoted from the prophets need considerable
sifting.

these come to do?" gave him this reply : "To terrify those," etc. For the order of the words מָה אֵלֶּה בָאִים לַעֲשׂוֹת, instead of מָה לַעֲשׂוֹת אֵלֶּה בָּאִים, see Gen. xlii. 12, Neh. ii. 12, Judg. ix. 48. אֵלֶּה הַקְּרָנוֹת is not a nominative written absolutely at the head of the sentence in the sense of "these horns," for that would require הַקְּרָנוֹת הָאֵלֶּה; but the whole sentence is repeated from ver. 2, and to that the statement of the purpose for which the smiths have come is attached in the form of an apodosis: "these are the horns, etc., and they (the smiths) have come." At the same time, the earlier statement as to the horns is defined more minutely by the additional clause כְּפִי אִישׁ וגו׳, according to the measure, *i.e.* in such a manner that no man lifted up his head any more, or so that Judah was utterly prostrate. *Hachărid*, to throw into a state of alarm, as in 2 Sam. xvii. 2. *Them* (*ŏthâm*): this refers *ad sensum* to the nations symbolized by the horns. *Yaddŏth*, inf. *piel* of *yâdâh*, to cast down, may be explained as referring to the power of the nations symbolized by the horns. *'Erets Yᵉhūdâh* (the land of Judah) stands for the inhabitants of the land. The four smiths, therefore, symbolize the instruments "of the divine omnipotence by which the imperial power in its several historical forms is overthrown" (Kliefoth), or, as Theod. Mops. expresses it, "the powers that serve God and inflict vengeance upon them from many directions." The vision does not show what powers God will use for this purpose. It is simply designed to show to the people of God, that every hostile power of the world which has risen up against it, or shall rise up, is to be judged and destroyed by the Lord.

THIRD VISION: THE MAN WITH THE MEASURING LINE.— CHAP. II. (HEB. CHAP. II. 5–17.)

Whilst the second vision sets forth the destruction of the powers that were hostile to Israel, the third (ch. ii. 1–5) with the prophetic explanation (vers. 6–13) shows the development of the people and kingdom of God till the time of its final glory. The vision itself appears very simple, only a few of the principal features being indicated; but in this very brevity it presents many difficulties so far as the exposition is concerned. It is as follows: Ver. 1. "*And I lifted up my eyes, and saw, and behold a man, and in his hand a measuring line.* Ver. 2. *Then*

I said, Whither goest thou? And he said to me, To measure Jerusalem, to see how great its breadth, and how great its length. Ver. 3. *And, behold, the angel that talked with me went out, and another angel went out to meet him.* Ver. 4. *And he said to him, Run, speak to this young man thus: Jerusalem shall lie as an open land for the multitude of men and cattle in the midst of it.* Ver. 5. *And I shall be to it, is the saying of Jehovah, a fiery wall round about; and I shall be for glory in the midst of it.*" The man with the measuring line in his hand is not the interpreting angel (C. B. Mich., Ros., Maurer, etc.); for it was not his duty to place the events upon the stage, but simply to explain to the prophet the things which he saw. Moreover, this angel is clearly distinguished from the man, inasmuch as he does not go out (ver. 3) till after the latter has gone to measure Jerusalem (ver. 2). At the same time, we cannot regard the measuring man as merely " a figure in the vision," since all the persons occurring in these visions are significant; but we agree with those who conjecture that he is the angel of Jehovah, although this conjecture cannot be distinctly proved. The task which he is preparing to perform —namely, to measure Jerusalem—leads unquestionably to the conclusion that he is something more than a figure. The measuring of the breadth and length of Jerusalem presupposes that the city is already in existence; and this expression must not be identified with the phrase, to draw the measure over Jerusalem, in ch. i. 16. Drawing the measure over a place is done for the purpose of sketching a plan for its general arrangement, or the rebuilding of it. But the length and breadth of a city can only be measured when it is already in existence; and the object of the measuring is not to see how long and how broad it is to be, but what the length and breadth actually are. It is true that it by no means follows from this that the city to be measured was the Jerusalem of that time; on the contrary, the vision shows the future Jerusalem, but it exhibits it as a city in actual existence, and visible to the spiritual eye. While the man goes away to measure the city, the interpreting angel goes out: not out of the myrtle thicket, for this only occurs in the first vision; but he goes away from the presence of the prophet, where we have to think of him as his interpreter, in the direction of the man with the measuring line, to find out what he is going to do, and bring back word to the prophet. At the very same time another angel comes out to meet *him,* viz. the *angelus interpres,* not the man with the measuring line. For one person can only come to meet another when the latter is going in the direction from which the former comes. Having come to meet him, he (the second angel) says to him (the *angelus interpres*), "Run, say to this young man," etc. The subject to וַיֹּאמֶר can only be the second angel; for if, on grammatical grounds, the *angelus interpres* might be regarded as speaking to the young man, such an assumption is proved to be untenable, by the fact that it was no part of the office of the *angelus interpres* to give orders or commissions to another angel. On the other hand, there is nothing at all to preclude another angel from revealing a decree of God to the *angelus interpres* for him to communicate to the prophet; inasmuch as this does not bring the *angelus interpres* into action any further than his function requires, so that there is no ground for the objection that this is at variance with his standing elsewhere (Kliefoth). But the other angel could not give the instructions mentioned in ver. 4 to the *angelus interpres,* unless he were either himself a superior angel, viz. the angel of Jehovah, or had been directed to do so by the man with the measuring line, in which case this "man" would be the angel of Jehovah. Of these two possibilities we prefer the latter on two grounds: (1) because it is impossible to think of any reason why the "other angel" should not be simply called מַלְאַךְ יְהוָֹה, if he really were the angel of the Lord; and (2) because, according to the analogy of Ezek. xl. 3, the man with the measuring line most probably was the angel of Jehovah, with whose dignity it would be quite in keeping that he should explain his purpose to the *angelus interpres* through the medium of another (inferior) angel. And if this be established, so far as the brevity of the account will allow, we cannot understand by the "young man" the man with the measuring line, as Hitzig, Maurer, and Kliefoth do. The only way in which such an assumption as this could be rendered tenable or in harmony with the rest, would be by supposing that the design of the message was to tell the man with the measuring line that "he might desist from his useless enterprise" (Hitzig), as Jerusalem could not be measured at all, on account of the

number of its inhabitants and its vast size (Theod. Mops.,
Theodoret, Ewald, Umbreit, etc.); but Kliefoth has very
justly replied to this, that "if a city be ever so great, inasmuch as it is a city, it can always be measured, and also
have walls." If, then, the symbolical act of measuring, as
Kliefoth also admits, expresses the question how large and
how broad Jerusalem will eventually be, and if the words of
vers. 4, 5 contain the answer to this question, viz. Jerusalem
will in the first place (ver. 4) contain such a multitude of men
and cattle that it will dwell like *p⁶rázōth;* this answer, which
gives the meaning of the measuring, must be addressed not to
the measuring man, but simply to the prophet, that he may
announce to the people the future magnitude and glory of the
city. The measuring man was able to satisfy himself of this
by the measuring itself. We must therefore follow the majority
of both the earlier and later expositors, and take the "young
man" as being the prophet himself, who is so designated on
account of his youthful age, and without any allusion whatever to "human inexperience and dim short-sightedness"
(Hengstenberg), since such an allusion would be very remote
from the context, and even old men of experience could not
possibly know anything concerning the future glory of Jerusalem without a revelation from above. *Hallâz,* as in Judg. vi.
20 and 2 Kings iv. 25, is a contraction of *hallâzeh,* and formed
from *lâzeh,* there, thither, and the article *hal,* in the sense
of the (young man) there, or that young man (cf. Ewald, §
103, *a,* and 183, *b*; Ges. § 34, Anm. 1). He is to make haste
and bring this message, because it is good news, the realization
of which will soon commence. The message contains a double
and most joyful promise. (1) Jerusalem will in future dwell,
i.e. be built, as *p⁶rázōth.* This word means neither "without
walls," nor *loca aperta,* but strictly speaking the *plains,* and is
only used in the plural to denote the open, level ground, as
contrasted with the fortified cities surrounded by walls: thus
ʿ*árē p⁶rázōth,* cities of the plain, in Esth. ix. 19, as distinguished
from the capital Susa; and *'erets p⁶rázōth* in Ezek. xxxviii. 11,
the land where men dwell "without walls, bolts, and gates;"
hence *p⁶rázī,* inhabitant of the plain, in contrast with the
inhabitants of fortified cities with high walls (Deut. iii. 5;
1 Sam. vi. 18). The thought is therefore the following:

Jerusalem is in future to resemble an open country covered with unwalled cities and villages; it will no longer be a city closely encircled with walls; hence it will be extraordinarily enlarged, on account of the multitude of men and cattle with which it will be blessed (cf. Isa. xlix. 19, 20; Ezek. xxxviii. 11) Moreover, (2) Jerusalem will then have no protecting wall surrounding it, because it will enjoy a superior protection. Jehovah will be to it a wall of fire round about, that is to say, a defence of fire which will consume every one who ventures to attack it (cf. Isa. iv. 5; Deut. iv. 24). Jehovah will also be the glory in the midst of Jerusalem, that is to say, will fill the city with His glory (cf. Isa. lx. 19). This promise is explained in the following prophetic words which are uttered by the angel of Jehovah, as vers. 8, 9, and 11 clearly show. According to these verses, for example, the speaker is sent by Jehovah, and according to ver. 8 to the nations which have plundered Israel, "after glory," *i.e.* to smite these nations and make them servants to the Israelites. From this shall Israel learn that Jehovah has sent him. The fact that, according to vers. 3, 4, another angel speaks to the prophet, may be easily reconciled with this. For since this angel, as we have seen above, was sent by the angel of Jehovah, he speaks according to his instructions, and that in such a manner that his words pass imperceptibly into the words of the sender, just as we very frequently find the words of a prophet passing suddenly into the words of God, and carried on as such. For the purpose of escaping from this simple conclusion, Koehler has forcibly broken up this continuous address, and has separated the words of vers. 8, 9, and 11, in which the angel says that Jehovah has sent him, from the words of Jehovah proclaimed by the angel, as being interpolations, but without succeeding in explaining them either simply or naturally.

The prophecy commences thus in vers. 6–9 : Ver. 6. " *Ho, ho, flee out of the land of the north, is the saying of Jehovah ; for I spread you out as the four winds of heaven, is the saying of Jehovah.* Ver. 7. *Ho, Zion, save thyself, thou that dwellest with the daughter Babel.* Ver. 8. *For thus saith Jehovah of hosts, After glory hath he sent me to the nations that have plundered you ; for whoever toucheth you, toucheth the apple of His eye.* Ver. 9. *For, behold, I swing my hand over them, and they*

*become a spoil to those who served them; and ye will see that
Jehovah of hosts hath sent me.*" The summons to flee out of
Babylon, in vers. 6 and 7, is addressed to the Israelites, who
are all included in the one name Zion in ver. 7; and shows
that the address which follows is not a simple continuation of
the promise in vers. 4 and 5, but is intended both to explain it,
and to assign the reason for it. The summons contains so far
a reason for it, that the Israelites are directed to flee out of
Babylon, because the judgment is about to burst upon this
oppressor of the people of God. The words *nūsū*, flee, and
himmâlᵉtī, save thyself or escape, both point to the judgment,
and in ver. 9 the judgment itself is clearly spoken of. The
land of the north is Babylon (cf. Jer. i. 14, vi. 22, x. 22; and
for the fact itself, Isa. xlviii. 20). The reason for the exclamation " Flee" is first of all given in the clause, " for like the
four winds have I spread you out," not " dispersed you" (Vulg.,
C. B. Mich., Koehler). For apart from the fact that *pērēs*
almost always means to spread out, and has the meaning to
disperse at the most in Ps. lxviii. 15 and Ezek. xvii. 21, this
meaning is altogether unsuitable here. For if Israel had been
scattered like the four winds, it would of necessity have been
summoned to return, not only from the north, but from all
quarters of the globe (Hitzig, Kliefoth). Moreover, we should
then have לְאַרְבַּע, *into* the four winds; and the method suggested
by Koehler for reconciling כְּאַרְבַּע with his view, viz. by assuming that " like the four winds" is equivalent to " as chaff is
pounded and driven away from its place by the four winds,"
according to which the winds would be mentioned in the place
of the chaff, will hardly meet with approval. The explanation
is rather that the perfect *pērastī* is used prophetically to denote
the purpose of God, which had already been formed, even if
its realization was still in the future. To spread out like the
four winds is the same as to spread out just as the four winds
spread out to all quarters of· the globe. Because God has resolved upon spreading out His people in this manner, they are
to flee out of Babel, that they may not suffer the fate of Babel.
That this thought lies at the foundation of the motive assigned,
is evident from the further reasons assigned for the summons
in vers. 8 and 9. *Zion* stands for the inhabitants of Zion,
namely the people of God, who are for the time being still

yōshebheth bath Bâbel, dwelling with the daughter Babel. As *Zion* does not mean the city or fortress of Jerusalem, but the inhabitants, so the "daughter Babel" is not the city of Babylon or country of Babylonia personified, but the inhabitants of Babel; and יָשַׁב is construed with the *accusative* of the person, as in Ps. xxii. 4 and 2 Sam. vi. 2. What Jehovah states in explanation of the twofold call to flee out of Babel, does not commence with ver. 9 (Ewald), or with כִּי הַנֹּגֵעַ in ver. 8*b* (Koehler), but with אַחַר כָּבוֹד וגו׳. The incorrectness of the two former explanations is seen first of all in the fact that כִּי only introduces a speech in the same manner as ὅτι, when it follows directly upon the introductory formula; but not, as is here assumed, when a long parenthesis is inserted between, without the introduction being resumed by לֵאמֹר. And secondly, neither of these explanations furnishes a suitable meaning. If the words of God only followed in ver. 9, עֲלֵיהֶם in the first clause would be left without any noun to which to refer; and if they commenced with כִּי הַנֹּגֵעַ (for he that toucheth), the thought "he that toucheth you," etc., would assign no reason for the call to flee and save themselves. For if Israel is defended or valued by God as a pupil of the eye, there can be no necessity for it to flee. And lastly, it is impossible to see what can be the meaning or object of the parenthesis, "After glory hath He sent me," etc. If it treated "of the execution of the threat of punishment upon the heathen" (Koehler), it would be inserted in an unsuitable place, since the threat of punishment would not follow till afterwards. All these difficulties vanish if Jehovah's words commence with *'achar kâbhōd* (after glory), in which case *shᵉlâchanī* (He hath sent me) may be very simply explained from the fact that the address is introduced, not in a direct form, but indirectly: Jehovah says, He has sent me after glory. The sender is Jehovah, and the person sent is not the prophet, but the angel of the Lord. *Achar kâbhōd:* behind glory, after glory; not however "after the glory of success" (Hitzig, Ewald, etc.), still less "with a glorious commission," but to get glory upon the heathen, *i.e.* to display the glory of God upon the heathen through the judgment by which their power is broken, and the heathen world is made to serve the people of God. The manner in which the next two clauses, commencing with *kī* (for), are attached, is the following: The

first assigns the subjective motive; that is to say, states the
reason why God has sent him to the heathen, namely, because
they have plundered His people, and have thereby touched the
apple of His eye. בָּבַת עַיִן, the apple of the eye (*lit.* the gate,
the opening in which the eye is placed, or more probably the
pupil of the eye, *pupilla*, as being the object most carefully
preserved), is a figure used to denote the dearest possession or
good, and in this sense is applied to the nation of Israel as early
as Deut. xxxii. 10. The second explanatory clause in ver. 9
adds the practical ground for this sending after glory. The
speaker is still the angel of the Lord; and his acting is identical with the acting of God. Like Jehovah, he swings his
hand over the heathen nations which plundered Israel (cf. Isa.
xi. 15, xix. 16), and they become (וְהָיוּ expressing the consequence), *i.e.* so that they become, booty to the Israelites, who
had previously been obliged to serve them (cf. Isa. xiv. 2). In
what way the heathen would serve Israel is stated in ver. 11.
By the execution of this judgment Israel would learn that
Jehovah had sent His angel, namely to execute upon the
heathen His saving purposes for Israel. This is the meaning
of these words, not only here and in ver. 11, but also in ch.
iv. 9 and vi. 15, where this formula is repeated, not however
in the sense imagined by Koehler, namely that he had spoken
these words in consequence of a command from Jehovah, and
not of his own accord, by which the " sending" is changed into
" speaking."

Vers. 10–13. The daughter Zion is to rejoice at this sending
of the angel of the Lord. Ver. 10. " *Exult and rejoice, O
daughter Zion: for, behold, I come, and dwell in the midst of thee,
is the saying of Jehovah. Ver. 11. And many nations will attach
themselves to Jehovah in that day, and become a people to me: and
I dwell in the midst of thee; and thou wilt know that Jehovah of
hosts hath sent me to thee.*" The daughter Zion, or the church
of the Lord, delivered out of Babel, is to rejoice with joy,
because her glorification is commencing now. The Lord comes
to her in His angel, in whom are His name (Ex. xxiii. 21) and
His face (Ex. xxxiii. 14), *i.e.* the angel of His face (Isa. lxiii. 9),
who reveals His nature, to dwell in the midst of her. This
dwelling of Jehovah, or of His angel, in the midst of Zion, is
essentially different from the dwelling of Jehovah in the Most

Holy Place of His temple. It commences with the coming of the Son of God in the flesh, and is completed by His return in glory (John i. 14 and Rev. xxi. 3). Then will many, or powerful, nations, attach themselves to Jehovah, and become His people (cf. ch. viii. 20, 21; Isa. xiv. 1). This kingdom of God, which has hitherto been restricted to Israel, will be spread out and glorified by the reception of the heathen nations which are seeking God (Mic. iv. 2). The repetition of the expression, "I dwell in the midst of thee," merely serves as a stronger asseveration of this brilliant promise; and the same remark applies to the repetition of וְיָדַעַתְּ וגו׳ (and thou shalt know): see at ver. 13. Jerusalem will thereby receive the expansion shown to the prophet in ver. 4; and through the dwelling of God in the midst of her, the promise in ver. 5 will also be fulfilled. The next verse refers to this.

Ver. 12. "*And Jehovah will take possession of Judah as His portion in the holy land, and will yet choose Jerusalem. Ver. 13. Be still, all flesh, before Jehovah; for He has risen up out of His holy habitation.*" The first hemistich of ver. 12 rests upon Deut. xxxii. 9, where Israel, as the chosen nation, is called the *chēleq* and *nachălăh* of Jehovah. This appointment of Israel to be the possession of Jehovah will become perfect truth and reality in the future, through the coming of the Lord. *Y*ᵉ*hūdăh* is Judah as delivered, *i.e.* the remnant of the whole of the covenant nation. This remnant, after being gathered out of Babel, will dwell upon holy ground, or in a holy land, as the possession of the Lord. The holy land is the land of Jehovah (Hos. ix. 3); but this is not to be set down without reserve as identical with Palestine. On the contrary, every place where Jehovah may be is holy ground (cf. Ex. iii. 5); so that even Palestine is only holy when the Lord dwells there. And we must not limit the idea of the holy land in this passage to Palestine, because the idea of the people of God will be so expanded by the addition of many nations, that it will not have room enough within the limits of Palestine; and according to ver. 4, even Jerusalem will no longer be a city with limited boundaries. The holy land reaches just as far as the nations, which have become the people of Jehovah by attaching themselves to Judah, spread themselves out over the surface of the earth. The words "choose Jerusalem again" round off the promise, just as in ch. i. 17;

but in ver. 13 the admonition is added, to wait in reverential
silence for the coming of the Lord to judgment, after Hab. ii.
20; and the reason assigned is, that the judgment will soon
begin. נֵעוֹר, *niphal* of עוּר (compare Ewald, § 140, *a;* Ges. § 72,
Anm. 9), to wake up, or rise up from His rest (cf. Ps. xliv. 24).
מְעוֹן קָדְשׁוֹ, the holy habitation of God, is heaven, as in Deut.
xxvi. 15, Jer. xxv. 30. The judgment upon the heathen world-
power began to burst in a very short time. When Babylon
revolted against the king of Persia, under the reign of Darius,
a great massacre took place within the city after its re-capture,
and its walls were destroyed, so that the city could not rise
again to its ancient grandeur and importance. Compare with
this the remark made in the comm. on Haggai (p. 196), concerning the overthrow of the Persian empire and those which
followed it. We have already shown, at p. 107, note, what
a groundless hypothesis the opinion is, that the fulfilment was
interrupted in consequence of Israel's guilt; and that as the
result of this, the completion of it has been deferred for centuries, or even thousands of years.

THE FOURTH VISION: THE HIGH PRIEST JOSHUA IN THE PRESENCE OF THE ANGEL OF THE LORD.—CHAP. III.

In this and the following visions the prophet is shown the
future glorification of the church of the Lord. Ver. 1. "*And
he showed me Joshua the high priest standing before the angel
of Jehovah, and Satan stood at his right hand to oppose him.
Ver. 2. And Jehovah said to Satan, Jehovah rebuke thee, O
Satan; and Jehovah who chooseth Jerusalem rebuke thee. Is not
this a brand saved out of the fire? Ver. 3. And Joshua was
clothed with filthy garments, and stood before the angel. Ver. 4.
And he answered and spake to those who stood before him thus:
Take away the filthy garments from him. And he said to him,
Behold, I have taken away thy guilt from thee, and clothe thee in
festal raiment. Ver. 5. And I said, Let them put a clean mitre
upon his head. Then they put the clean mitre upon his head, and
clothed him with garments. And the angel of Jehovah stood by.*"
The subject to וַיַּרְאֵנִי is Jehovah, and not the mediating angel,
for his work was to explain the visions to the prophet, and
not to introduce them; nor the angel of Jehovah, because he

appears in the course of the vision, although in these visions he is sometimes identified with Jehovah, and sometimes distinguished from Him. The scene is the following: Joshua stands as high priest before the angel of the Lord, and Satan stands at his (Joshua's) right hand as accuser. Satan (*hassâtân*) is the evil spirit so well known from the book of Job, and the constant accuser of men before God (Rev. xii. 10), and not Sanballat and his comrades (Kimchi, Drus., Ewald). He comes forward here as the enemy and accuser of Joshua, to accuse him in his capacity of high priest. The scene is therefore a judicial one, and the high priest is not in the sanctuary, the building of which had commenced, or engaged in supplicating the mercy of the angel of the Lord for himself and the people, as Theodoret and Hengstenberg suppose. The expression עֹמֵד לִפְנֵי furnishes no tenable proof of this, since it cannot be shown that this expression would be an inappropriate one to denote the standing of an accused person before the judge, or that the Hebrew language had any other expression for this. Satan stands on the right side of Joshua, because the accuser was accustomed to stand at the right hand of the accused (cf. Ps. cix. 6). Joshua is opposed by Satan, however, not on account of any personal offences either in his private or his domestic life, but in his official capacity as high priest, and for sins which were connected with his office, or for offences which would involve the nation (Lev. iv. 3); though not as the bearer of the sins of the people before the Lord, but as laden with his own and his people's sins. The dirty clothes, which he had on, point to this (ver. 3). But Jehovah, *i.e.* the angel of Jehovah, repels the accuser with the words, "Jehovah rebuke thee; ... Jehovah who chooseth Jerusalem."[1] The words are repeated for the sake of emphasis, and with the repetition the motive which led Jehovah to reject the accuser

---

[1] The application made in the Epistle of Jude (ver. 9) of the formula "Jehovah rebuke thee," namely, that Michael the archangel did not venture to execute upon Satan the κρίσις βλασφημίας, does not warrant the conclusion that the angel of the Lord places himself below Jehovah by these words. The words "Jehovah rebuke thee" are a standing formula for the utterance of the threat of a divine judgment, from which no conclusion can be drawn as to the relation in which the person using it stood to God. Moreover, Jude had not our vision in his mind, but another event, which has not been preserved in the canonical Scriptures.

is added. Because Jehovah has chosen Jerusalem, and maintains His choice in its integrity (this is implied in the participle
bōchĕr). He must rebuke Satan, who hopes that his accusation will have the effect of repealing the choice of Jerusalem,
by deposing the high priest. For if any sin of the high priest,
which inculpated the nation, had been sufficient to secure his removal or deposition, the office of high priest would have ceased
altogether, because no man is without sin. גְּעַר, to rebuke, does
not mean merely to nonsuit, but to reprove for a thing; and
when used of God, to reprove by action, signifying to sweep
both him and his accusation entirely away. The motive for
the repulse of the accuser is strengthened by the clause which
follows: Is he (Joshua) not a brand plucked out of the fire?
i.e. one who has narrowly escaped the threatening destruction
(for the figure, see Amos iv. 11). These words, again, we
must not take as referring to the high priest as an individual;
nor must we restrict their meaning to the fact that Joshua
had been brought back from captivity, and reinstated in the
office of high priest. Just as the accusation does not apply
to the individual, but to the office which Joshua filled, so do
these words also apply to the supporter of the official dignity.
The fire, out of which Joshua had been rescued as a brand,
was neither the evil which had come upon Joshua through
neglecting the building of the temple (Koehler), nor the guilt
of allowing his sons to marry foreign wives (Targ., Jerome,
Rashi, Kimchi): for in the former case the accusation would
have come too late, since the building of the temple had been
resumed five months before (Hag. i. 15, compared with Zech.
i. 7); and in the latter it would have been much too early,
since these misalliances did not take place till fifty years afterwards. And, in general, guilt which might possibly lead to
ruin could not be called a fire; still less could the cessation
or removal of this sin be called deliverance out of the fire.
Fire is a figurative expression for punishment, not for sin.
The fire out of which Joshua had been saved like a brand was
the captivity, in which both Joshua and the nation had been
brought to the verge of destruction. Out of this fire Joshua
the high priest had been rescued. But, as Kliefoth has aptly
observed, "the priesthood of Israel was concentrated in the
high priest, just as the character of Israel as the holy nation

was concentrated in the priesthood. The high priest represented the holiness and priestliness of Israel, and that not merely in certain official acts and functions, but so that as a particular Levite and Aaronite, and as the head for the time being of the house of Aaron, he represented in his own person that character of holiness and priestliness which had been graciously bestowed by God upon the nation of Israel." This serves to explain how the hope that God must rebuke the accuser could be made to rest upon the election of Jerusalem, *i.e.* upon the love of the Lord to the whole of His nation. The pardon and the promise do not apply to Joshua personally any more than the accusation; but they refer to him in his official position, and to the whole nation, and that with regard to the special attributes set forth in the high priesthood— namely, its priestliness and holiness. We cannot, therefore, find any better words with which to explain the meaning of this vision than those of Kliefoth. "The character of Israel," he says, "as the holy and priestly nation of God, was violated —violated by the general sin and guilt of the nation, which God had been obliged to punish with exile. This guilt of the nation, which neutralized the priestliness and holiness of Israel, is pleaded by Satan in the accusation which he brings before the *Maleach* of Jehovah against the high priest, who was its representative. A nation so guilty and so punished could no longer be the holy and priestly nation: its priests could no longer be priests; nor could its high priests be high priests any more. But the *Maleach* of Jehovah sweeps away the accusation with the assurance that Jehovah, from His grace, and for the sake of its election, will still give validity to Israel's priesthood, and has already practically manifested this purpose of His by bringing it out of its penal condition of exile."

After the repulse of the accuser, Joshua is cleansed from the guilt attaching to him. When he stood before the angel of the Lord he had dirty clothes on. The dirty clothes are not the costume of an accused person (Drus., Ewald); for this Roman custom (Lev. ii. 54, vi. 20) was unknown to the Hebrews. Dirt is a figurative representation of sin; so that dirty clothes represent defilement with sin and guilt (cf. Isa. lxiv. 5, iv. 4; Prov. xxx. 12; Rev. iii. 4, vii. 14). The Lord had indeed refined His nation in its exile, and in His grace had

preserved it from destruction ; but its sin was not thereby
wiped away. The place of grosser idolatry had been taken by
the more refined idolatry of self-righteousness, selfishness, and
conformity to the world. And the representative of the nation
before the Lord was affected with the dirt of these sins, which
gave Satan a handle for his accusation. But the Lord would
cleanse His chosen people from this, and make it a holy and
glorious nation. This is symbolized by what takes place in
vers. 4 and 5. The angel of the Lord commands those who
stand before Him, *i.e.* the angels who serve Him, to take off
the dirty clothes from the high priest, and put on festal clothing ; and then adds, by way of explanation to Joshua, Behold,
I have caused thy guilt to pass away from thee, that is to say,
I have forgiven thy sin, and justified thee (cf. 2 Sam. xii. 13,
xxiv. 10), and clothe thee with festal raiment. The inf. abs.
halbēsh stands, as it frequently does, for the finite verb, and
has its norm in הֶעֱבַרְתִּי (see at Hag. i. 6). The last words are
either spoken to the attendant angels as well, or else, what is
more likely, they are simply passed over in the command given
to them, and mentioned for the first time here. *Machălâtsōth,*
costly clothes, which were only worn on festal occasions (see at
Isa. iii. 22). They are not symbols of innocence and righteousness (Chald.), which are symbolized by clean or white raiment
(Rev. iii. 4, vii. 9); nor are they figurative representations of joy
(Koehler), but are rather symbolical of glory. The high priest,
and the nation in him, are not only to be cleansed from sin,
and justified, but to be sanctified and glorified as well.—Ver. 5.
At this moment the prophet feels compelled to utter the prayer
that they may also put a clean mitre upon Joshua's head, which
prayer is immediately granted. The prayer appears at first to
be superfluous, inasmuch as the mitre would certainly not be
forgotten when the dirty clothes were taken away and the festal
dress was put on. Nevertheless, the fact that it is granted
shows that it was not superfluous. The meaning of the prayer
was hardly that the high priest might be newly attired from
head to foot, as Hengstenberg supposes, but is rather connected
with the significance of the mitre. *Tsânîph* is not a turban,
such as might be worn by anybody (Koehler), but the head-
dress of princely persons and kings (Job xxix. 14 ; Isa. lxii. 3),
and is synonymous with *mitsnepheth,* the technical word for the

tiara prescribed for the high priest in the law (Ex. and Lev.), as we may see from Ezek. xxi. 31, where the regal diadem, which is called *tsânîph* in Isa. lxii. 3, is spoken of under the name of *mitsnepheth*. The turban of the high priest was that portion of his dress in which he carried his office, so to speak, upon his forehead ; and the clean turban was the substratum for the golden plate that was fastened upon it, and by which he was described as holy to the Lord, and called to bear the guilt of the children of Israel (Ex. xxviii. 38). The prayer for a clean mitre to be put upon his head, may therefore be accounted for from the wish that Joshua should not only be splendidly decorated, but should be shown to be holy, and qualified to accomplish the expiation of the people. Purity, as the earthly type of holiness, forms the foundation for glory. In the actual performance of the matter, therefore, the putting on of the clean mitre is mentioned first, and then the clothing with festal robes. This took place in the presence of the angel of the Lord. That is the meaning of the circumstantial clause, " and the angel of the Lord stood" (*ritum tanquam herus imperans, probans et præsentia sua ornans*, C. B. Mich.), and not merely that the angel of the Lord, who had hitherto been sitting in the judge's seat, rose up from his seat for the purpose of speaking while the robing was going on (Hofmann, Koehler). עָמַד does not mean to stand up, but simply to remain standing.

Vers. 6–10. In these verses there follows a prophetic address, in which the angel of the Lord describes the symbolical action of the re-clothing of the high priest, according to its typical significance in relation to the continuance and the future of the kingdom of God. Ver. 6. " *And the angel of the Lord testified to Joshua, and said,* Ver. 7. *Thus saith Jehovah of hosts, If thou shalt walk in my ways, and keep my charge, thou shalt both judge my house and keep my courts, and I will give thee ways among these standing here.* Ver. 8. *Hear then, thou high priest Joshua, thou, and thy comrades who sit before thee : yea, men of wonder are they : for, behold, I bring my servant Zemach (Sprout).* Ver. 9. *For behold the stone which I have laid before Joshua ; upon one stone are seven eyes : behold I engrave its carving, is the saying of Jehovah of hosts, and I clear away the iniquity of this land in one day.* Ver. 10. *In that day, is the saying of Jehovah of hosts, ye will invite one another under the vine and under the fig-tree."* In ver. 7 not only is the high priest confirmed in his office, but the perpetuation and glorification of his official labours are promised. As Joshua appears in this vision as the supporter of the office, this promise does not apply to Joshua himself so much as to the office, the continuance of which is indeed bound up with the fidelity of those who sustain it. The promise in ver. 7 therefore begins by giving prominence to this condition: If thou wilt walk in my ways, etc. Walking in the ways of the Lord refers to the personal attitude of the priests towards the Lord, or to fidelity in their personal relation to God; and keeping the charge of Jehovah, to the faithful performance of their official duties (*shâmar mishmartî,* noticing what has to be observed in relation to Jehovah; see at Lev. viii. 35). The apodosis begins with וְגַם אַתָּה, and not with וְנָתַתִּי. This is required not only by the emphatic *'attâh,* but also by the clauses commencing with *vᵉgam;* whereas the circumstance, that the tense only changes with *vᵉnáthattî,* and that *tâdîn* and *tishmōr* are still imperfects, has its simple explanation in the fact, that on account of the *gam,* the verbs could not be linked together with *Vav,* and placed at the head of the clauses. Taken by themselves, the clauses *vᵉgam tâdîn* and *vᵉgam tishmōr* might express a duty of the high priest quite as well as a privilege. If they were taken as apodoses, they would express an obligation; but in that case they would appear somewhat superfluous, because the obligations of the high priest are fully explained in the two previous clauses. If, on the other hand, the apodosis commences with them, they contain, in the form of a promise, a privilege which is set before the high priest as awaiting him in the future—namely, the privilege of still further attending to the service of the house of God, which had been called in question by Satan's accusation. דִּין אֶת־בֵּיתִי, to judge the house of God, *i.e.* to administer right in relation to the house of God, namely, in relation to the duties devolving upon the high priest in the sanctuary as such; hence the right administration of the service in the holy place and the holy of holies. This limitation is obvious from the parallel clause, to keep the courts, in which the care of the ordinary performance of worship in the courts, and the keeping of everything of an idolatrous nature from the house of God, are transferred to him. And to this a new and important promise is added in the last clause (וְנָתַתִּי וגו'). The meaning of this depends upon the explanation given to the word מַהְלְכִים. Many commentators regard this as a Chaldaic form of the *hiphil* participle (after Dan. iii. 25, iv. 34), and take it either in the intransitive sense of "those walking" (LXX., Pesh., Vulg., Luth., Hofm., etc.), or in the transitive sense of those conducting the leaders (Ges., Hengst., etc.). But apart from the fact that the *hiphil* of הָלַךְ in Hebrew is always written either הוֹלִיךְ or הֵילִיךְ, and has never anything but a transitive meaning, this view is precluded by the בְּ, for which we should expect מִבֵּין or מִן, since the meaning could only be, "I give thee walkers or leaders between those standing here," *i.e.* such as walk to and fro between those standing here (Hofmann), or, "I will give thee leaders among (from) these angels who are standing here" (Hengstenberg). In the former case, the high priest would receive a promise that he should always have angels to go to and fro between himself and Jehovah, to carry up his prayers, and bring down revelations from God, and supplies of help (John i. 52 ; Hofmann). This thought would be quite a suitable one ; but it is not contained in the words, "since the angels, even if they walk between the standing angels and in the midst of them, do not go to and fro between Jehovah and Joshua" (Kliefoth). In the latter case the high priest would merely receive a general assurance of the assistance of superior angels ; and for such a thought as this the expression would be an extremely marvellous one, and the בְּ would be used incorrectly. We must therefore follow Calvin and others, who take מַהְלְכִים as a substantive, from a singular מַהֲלָךְ, formed after מַחֲלָב, מִסְמָר, מַזְלֵג, or else as a plural of מַהֲלָךְ, to be pointed מַהְלָכִים (Ros., Hitzig, Kliefoth). The words then add to the promise, which ensured to the people the continuance of the priesthood and of the blessings which it conveyed, this new feature, that the high priest would also receive a free access to God, which had not yet been conferred upon him by his office. This points to a time when the restrictions of the Old Testament will be swept away. The further address, in vers. 8 and 9, announces how God will bring about this new time or future. To show the importance of what follows, Joshua is called upon to "hear." It is doubtful where what

he is to hear commences; for the idea, that after the summons
to attend, the successive, chain-like explanation of the reason
for this summons passes imperceptibly into that to which he is
to give heed, is hardly admissible, and has only been adopted
because it was found difficult to discover the true commencement of the address. The earlier theologians (Chald., Jerome,
Theod. Mops., Theodoret, and Calvin), and even Hitzig and
Ewald, take כִּי הִנְנִי מֵבִיא (for behold I will bring forth). But
these words are evidently explanatory of אַנְשֵׁי מוֹפֵת הֵמָּה (men
of wonder, etc.). Nor can it commence with *ūmashtī* (and I
remove), as Hofmann supposes (*Weiss. u. Erfüll.* i. 339), or
with ver. 9, " for behold the stone," as he also maintains in his
Schriftbeweis (ii. 1, pp. 292–3, 508–9). The first of these is
precluded not only by the fact that the address would be cut
far too short, but also by the cop. *Vav* before *mashtī;* and the
second by the fact that the words, " for behold the stone," etc.,
in ver. 9, are unmistakeably a continuation and further explanation of the words, " for behold I will bring forth my servant
Zemach," in ver. 8. The address begins with " thou and thy
fellows," since the priests could not be called upon to hear,
inasmuch as they were not present. Joshua's comrades who sit
before him are the priests who sat in the priestly meetings in
front of the high priest, the president of the assembly, so that
yōshēbh liphnē corresponds to our " assessors." The following
kī introduces the substance of the address; and when the
subject is placed at the head absolutely, it is used in the sense
of an asseveration, " yea, truly" (cf. Gen. xviii. 20; Ps. cxviii.
10–12, cxxviii. 2; and Ewald, § 330, *b*). *'Anshē mōphēth*, men
of miracle, or of a miraculous sign, as *mōphēth*, τὸ τέρας, *por-
tentum, miraculum*, embraces the idea of אוֹת, σημεῖον (cf. Isa.
viii. 18), are men who attract attention to themselves by something striking, and are types of what is to come, so that *mōphēth*
really corresponds to τύπος τῶν μελλόντων (see at Ex. iv. 21,
Isa. viii. 18). הֵמָּה stands for אַתֶּם, the words passing over from
the second person to the third on the resuming of the subject,
which is placed at the head absolutely, just as in Zeph. ii. 12, and
refers not only to רֵעֶיךָ, but to Joshua and his comrades. They
are men of typical sign, but not simply on account of the office
which they hold, viz. because their mediatorial priesthood points
to the mediatorial office and atoning work of the Messiah, as most

of the commentators assume. For " this applies, in the first place, not only to Joshua and his priests, but to the Old Testament priesthood generally; and secondly, there was nothing miraculous in this mediatorial work of the priesthood, which must have been the case if they were to be *mōphēth*. The miracle, which is to be seen in Joshua and his priests, consists rather in the fact that the priesthood of Israel is laden with guilt, but by the grace of God it has been absolved, and accepted by God again, as the deliverance from exile shows," and Joshua and his priests are therefore brands plucked by the omnipotence of grace from the fire of merited judgment (Kliefoth). This miracle of grace which has been wrought for them, points beyond itself to an incomparably greater and better act of the sin-absolving grace of God, which is still in the future. This is the way in which the next clause, " for I bring my servant Zemach," which is explanatory of *'anshē mōphēth* (men of miracle), attaches itself. The word *Tsemach* is used by Zechariah simply as a proper name of the Messiah; and the combination ʿabhdī *Tsemach* (my servant Tsemach) is precisely the same as ʿabhdī *Dâvid* (my servant David) in Ezek. xxxiv. 23, 24, xxxvii. 24, or " my servant Job" in Job i. 8, ii. 3, etc. The objection raised by Koehler—namely, that if *tsemach*, as a more precise definition of ʿabhdī (my servant), or as an announcement what servant of Jehovah is intended, were used as a proper name, it would either be construed with the article (הַצֶּמַח), or else we should have עַבְדִּי צֶמַח שְׁמוֹ as in ch. vi. 12—is quite groundless. For " if poets or prophets form new proper names at pleasure, such names, even when deprived of the article, easily assume the distinguishing sign of most proper names, like *bâgōdâh* and *mᵉshûbhâh* in Jer. iii." (Ewald, § 277, c.) It is different with שְׁמוֹ in ch. vi. 12 ; there *shᵉmō* is needed for the sake of the sense, as in 1 Sam. i. 1 and Job i. 1, and does not serve to designate the preceding word as a proper name, but simply to define the person spoken of more precisely by mentioning his name. Zechariah has formed the name *Tsemach*, Sprout, or Shoot, primarily from Jer. xxiii. 5 and xxxiii. 15, where the promise is given that a righteous Sprout (*tsemach tsaddīq*), or a Sprout of righteousness, shall be raised up to Jacob. And Jeremiah took the figurative description of the great descendant of David, who will create righteousness upon the earth, as

a *tsemach* which Jehovah will raise up, or cause to shoot up
to David, from Isa. xi. 1, 2, liii. 2, according to which the
Messiah is to spring up as a rod out of the stem of Jesse that
has been hewn down, or as a root-shoot out of dry ground.
Tsemach, therefore, denotes the Messiah in His origin from
the family of David that has fallen into humiliation, as a
sprout which will grow up from its original state of humiliation to exaltation and glory, and answers therefore to the train
of thought in this passage, in which the deeply humiliated
priesthood is exalted by the grace of the Lord into a type of
the Messiah. Whether the designation of the *sprout* as "my
servant" is taken from Isa. lii. 13 and liii. 11 (cf. xlii. 1, xlix. 3),
or formed after "my servant David" in Ezek. xxxiv. 24, xxxvii.
24, is a point which cannot be decided, and is of no importance
to the matter in hand. The circumstance that the removal of
iniquity, which is the peculiar work of the Messiah, is mentioned in ver. 9*b*, furnishes no satisfactory reason for deducing
'*abhdī tsemach* pre-eminently from Isa. liii. For in ver. 9 the
removal of iniquity is only mentioned in the second rank, in the
explanation of Jehovah's purpose to bring His servant *Tsemach*.
The first rank is assigned to the stone, which Jehovah has laid
before Joshua, etc. The answer to the question, what this
stone signifies, or who is to be understood by it, depends upon
the view we take of the words עֵינָיִם . . . עַל אֶבֶן. Most of the
commentators admit that these words do not form a parenthesis
(Hitzig, Ewald), but introduce a statement concerning הִנֵּה הָאֶבֶן.
Accordingly, הִנֵּה הָאֶבֶן וגו' is placed at the head absolutely, and
resumed in עַל אֶבֶן אַחַת. This statement may mean, either upon
one stone are seven eyes (visible or to be found), or seven eyes
are directed upon one stone. For although, in the latter case,
we should expect אֶל instead of עַל (according to Ps. xxxiii. 18,
xxxiv. 16), שִׂים עַיִן עַל does occur in the sense of the exercise of
loving care (Gen. xliv. 21; Jer. xxxix. 12, xl. 4). But if the
seven eyes were to be seen upon the stone, they could only be
engraved or drawn upon it. And what follows, הִנְנִי מְפַתֵּחַ וגו',
does not agree with this, inasmuch as, according to this, the
engraving upon the stone had now first to take place instead
of having been done already, since *hinnēh* followed by a participle never expresses what has already occurred, but always
what is to take place in the future. For this reason we must

decide that the seven eyes are directed towards the stone, or watch over it with protecting care. But this overthrows the view held by the expositors of the early church, and defended by Kliefoth, namely, that the stone signifies the Messiah, after Isa. xxviii. 16 and Ps. cxviii. 22,—a view with which the expression *nâthattî*, "given, laid before Joshua," can hardly be reconciled, even if this meant that Joshua was to see with his own eyes, as something actually present, that God was laying the foundation-stone. Still less can we think of the foundation-stone of the temple (Ros., Hitz.), since this had been laid long ago, and we cannot see for what purpose it was to be engraved; or of the stone which, according to the Rabbins, occupied the empty place of the ark of the covenant in the most holy place of the second temple (Hofmann); or of a precious stone in the breastplate of the high priest. The stone is the symbol of the kingdom of God, and is laid by Jehovah before Joshua, by God's transferring to him the regulation of His house and the keeping of His courts (before, *liphnē*, in a spiritual sense, as in 1 Kings ix. 6, for example). The seven eyes, which watch with protecting care over this stone, are not a figurative representation of the all-embracing providence of God; but, in harmony with the seven eyes of the Lamb, which are the seven Spirits of God (Rev. v. 6), and with the seven eyes of Jehovah (Zech. iv. 10), they are the sevenfold radiations of the Spirit of Jehovah (after Isa. xi. 2), which show themselves in vigorous action upon this stone, to prepare it for its destination. This preparation is called *pittēăch pittuchâh* in harmony with the figure of the stone (cf. Ezek. xxviii. 9, 11). "I will engrave the engraving thereof," *i.e.* engrave it so as to prepare it for a beautiful and costly stone. The preparation of this stone, *i.e.* the preparation of the kingdom of God established in Israel, by the powers of the Spirit of the Lord, is one feature in which the bringing of the *tsemach* will show itself. The other consists in the wiping away of the iniquity of this land. *Mūsh* is used here in a transitive sense, to cause to depart, to wipe away. הָאָרֶץ הַהִיא (that land) is the land of Canaan or Judah, which will extend in the Messianic times over the whole earth. The definition of the time, *b'yōm 'echâd*, cannot of course mean "on one and the same day," so as to affirm that the communication of the true nature to Israel, namely, of one well pleasing to God, and

the removal of guilt from the land, would take place simultaneously (Hofmann, Koehler) ; but the expression " in one day "
is substantially the same as ἐφάπαξ in Heb. vii. 27, ix. 12, x. 10,
and affirms that the wiping away of sin to be effected by the
Messiah (*tsemach*) will not resemble that effected by the typical
priesthood, which had to be continually repeated, but will be
all finished at once. This one day is the day of Golgotha.
Accordingly, the thought of this verse is the following :
Jehovah will cause His servant *Tsemach* to come, because He
will prepare His kingdom gloriously, and exterminate all the
sins of His people and land at once. By the wiping away of
all guilt and iniquity, not only of that which rests upon the
land (Koehler), but also of that of the inhabitants of the land,
i.e. of the whole nation, all the discontent and all the misery
which flow from sin will be swept away, and a state of blessed
peace will ensue for the purified church of God. This is the
thought of the tenth verse, which is formed after Mic. iv. 4
and 1 Kings v. 5, and with which the vision closes. The next
vision shows the glory of the purified church.

THE FIFTH VISION : THE CANDLESTICK WITH THE TWO OLIVE TREES.—CHAP. IV.

Ver. 1. "*And the angel that talked with me returned and
waked me, like a man who is waked out of his sleep.*" After the
prophet has seen four visions one after another, probably with
very short intervals, and has heard the marvellous interpretation of them, he is so overpowered by the impression produced
by what he has seen and heard, that he falls into a state of
spiritual exhaustion resembling sleep, just as Peter and his
companions were unable to keep awake at the transfiguration
of Christ (Luke ix. 32). He has not only fallen back into
the state of ordinary human consciousness, but his ordinary
spiritual consciousness was so depressed that he resembled a
man asleep, and had to be waked out of this sleep-like state
by the mediating angel, in order to be qualified for further
seeing. It is evident from the expression וַיָּשָׁב (and he returned)
that the *angelus interpres* had left the prophet after the termination of the previous visions, and now came back to him
again. The fresh vision which presents itself to his spiritual

intuition, is described according to its principal features in vers. 2 and 3. Ver. 2. "*And he said to me, What seest thou? And I said, I see, and behold a candlestick all of gold, and its oil-vessel up above it, and its seven lamps upon it, seven pipes each for the lamps upon the top of it.* Ver. 3. *And two olive trees* (oil trees) *by it, one to the right of the oil-vessel, and one to the left of it.*" The second ויאמר (*chethib*) in ver. 2 might, if necessary, be explained in the way proposed by L. de Dieu, Gusset., and Hofmann, viz. by supposing that the mediating angel had no sooner asked the prophet what he saw, than he proceeded, without waiting for his answer, to give a description himself of what was seen. But this is at variance with the analogy of all the rest of the visions, where the visions seen by the prophet are always introduced with רָאִיתִי or וָאֶרְאֶה followed by וְהִנֵּה (cf. ch. i. 8, ii. 1, 5, v. 1, vi. 1), and it remains quite inflexible; so that we must accept the *keri* וָאֹמַר, which is adopted by the early translators, and found in many codd., as being the true reading, and pronounce ויאמר a copyist's error. On the combination מְנוֹרַת זָהָב כֻּלָּהּ, in which the last two words are construed as a relative clause in subordination to *m⁰nōrath*, see Ewald, § 332, c. The visionary candlestick, all of gold, with its seven lamps, is unquestionably a figurative representation of the seven-branched golden candlestick in the tabernacle, and differs from this only in the three following additions which are peculiar to itself : (1) That it has its *gullâh* (גֻּלָּהּ for גֻּלָּתָהּ, with the feminine termination resolved; cf. Hos. xiii. 2, and Ewald, § 257, *d*), *i.e.* a can or round vessel for the oil, which was omitted altogether from the candlestick of the holy place, when the lamps were filled with oil by the priests, "at the top of it" (עַל־רֹאשָׁהּ); (2) That it had seven *mūtsâqōth* (pipes) each for the lamps, that is to say, tubes through which the oil poured from the *gullâh* into the lamps, or was conducted to them, whereas the candlestick of the tabernacle had no pipes, but only seven arms (*qânīm*), for the purpose of holding the lamps, which of course could not be wanting in the case of the visionary candlestick, and are merely omitted from the description as being self-evident. The number of the pipes is also a disputed point, viz. whether שִׁבְעָה וְשִׁבְעָה means seven and seven, *i.e.* fourteen, or whether it is to be taken distributively, seven each for the lamps, *i.e.* seven for each lamp, and therefore forty-nine for the seven. The distributive view is disputed by Hitzig and Koehler as at variance with the usage of the language : the former proposing to alter the text, so as to obtain seven pipes, *i.e.* one for each lamp ; and the latter, on the other hand, assuming that there were fourteen pipes, and inferring from the statement " seven and seven," instead of fourteen, that the second seven are to be sought in a different place from the first, that is to say, that the first seven led from the oil-vessel to the seven different lamps, whilst the second seven connected the seven lamps with one another, which would have been a very strange and perfectly useless provision. But there is no foundation whatever for the assertion that it is at variance with the usage of the language. For although a distributive relation is certainly expressed as a rule by the simple repetition of the number without any connecting *Vav*, such passages as 2 Sam. xxi. 20 and 1 Chron. xx. 6 show quite indisputably that the repetition of the same number with the *Vav cop.* between is also to be taken distributively. When, for example, it is stated in 2 Sam. xxi. 20, with regard to the hero of Gath, that the fingers of his hands and the fingers (toes) of his feet were " *shēsh vâshēsh*, four-and-twenty in number," it is evident that *shēsh vâshēsh* cannot mean " six and six," because six and six do not make twenty-four ; and a division of the *shēsh* between the hands and feet is also untenable, because his two hands had not six fingers on them, but twelve, and so his two feet had not six toes on them, but twelve. Consequently *shēsh vâshēsh* must be taken distributively : the fingers of his (two) hands and the toes of his (two) feet were six each ; for it is only $2+2 \ (=4) \times 6$ that can give 24. This is shown still more clearly in 1 Chron. xx. 6 : " and his fingers were *shēsh vâshēsh*, four-and-twenty." It is in this distributive sense, which is thus thoroughly established, so far as the usage of the language is concerned, that שִׁבְעָה וְשִׁבְעָה מוּצָ֯' is to be taken : seven pipes each for the lamps, *i.e.* forty-nine for the seven lamps ; inasmuch as if fourteen pipes were meant, it would be impossible to imagine any reason why " seven and seven " should be written instead of fourteen. And we cannot be shaken in this conviction, either by the objection " that if there was any proportion between the pipes and the size of the oil-vessel, such a number of pipes could not possibly (?) spring from one oil-can "

(Koehler), or by the statement that "forty-nine would be quite as much at variance with the *original* as fourteen, since that had only one pipe for every lamp" (Hitzig). For the supposed original for the pipes had no existence, inasmuch as the Mosaic candlestick had no pipes at all; and we can form no opinion as to the possibility of forty-nine pipes issuing from one oil-vessel, because we have no information as to the size either of the oil-vessel or of the pipes. (3) The third peculiarity in the visionary candlestick consists in the olive trees on the right and left of the oil-vessel, which supplied it with oil, and whose connection with the candlestick is first described in ver. 12. These three additions which were made to the golden candlestick seen by Zechariah, as contrasted with the golden candlestick of the tabernacle, formed the apparatus through which it was supplied with the oil required to light it continually without the intervention of man.

The interpretation of this vision must therefore be founded upon the meaning of the golden candlestick in the symbolism of the tabernacle, and be in harmony with it. The prophet receives, first of all, the following explanation, in reply to his question on this point: Ver. 4. *"And I answered and spake to the angel that talked with me, What are these, my lord?* Ver. 5. *And the angel that talked with me answered and said to me, Knowest thou not what these are? And I said, No, my lord.* Ver. 6. *Then he answered and spake to me thus: This is the word of Jehovah to Zerubbabel, saying, Not by might, and not by power, but by my Spirit, saith Jehovah of hosts.* Ver. 7. *Who art thou, O great mountain before Zerubbabel? Into a plain! And He will bring out the top-stone amidst shoutings, Grace, grace unto it!"* The question addressed by the prophet to the mediating angel, "What are these?" (*mâh 'ēlleh,* as in ch. ii. 2) does not refer to the two olive trees only (Umbreit, Kliefoth), but to everything described in vers. 2 and 3. We are not warranted in assuming that the prophet, like every other Israelite, knew what the candlestick with its seven lamps signified; and even if Zechariah had been perfectly acquainted with the meaning of the golden candlestick in the holy place, the candlestick seen by him had other things beside the two olive trees which were not to be found in the candlestick of the temple, viz. the *gullâh* and the pipes for the lamps, which might easily make the meaning of the visionary candlestick a doubtful thing. And the counter-question of the angel, in which astonishment is expressed, is not at variance with this. For that simply presupposes that the object of these additions is so clear, that their meaning might be discovered from the meaning of the candlestick itself. The angel then gives him the answer in ver. 6: "This (the vision as a symbolical prophecy) is the word of the Lord to Zerubbabel: Not by might," etc. That is to say, through this vision Zerubbabel is informed that it—namely, the work which Zerubbabel has taken in hand or has to carry out—will not be effected by human strength, but by the Spirit of God. The work itself is not mentioned by the angel, but is referred to for the first time in ver. 7 in the words, "He will bring out the top-stone," and then still more clearly described in the word of Jehovah in ver. 9: "The hands of Zerubbabel have laid the foundation of this house (the temple), and his hands will finish it." It by no means follows from this that the candlestick, with its seven lamps, represented Zerubbabel's temple (Grotius, Hofmann); for whilst it is impossible that the candlestick, as one article of furniture in the temple, should be a figurative representation of the whole temple, what could the two olive trees, which supplied the candlestick with oil, signify with such an interpretation? Still less can the seven lamps represent the seven eyes of God (ver. 10), according to which the candlestick would be a symbol of God or of the Spirit (Hitzig, Maurer, Schegg). The significance of the candlestick in the holy place centred, as I have shown in my *biblische Archäologie* (i. p. 107), in its seven lamps, which were lighted every evening, and burned through the night. The burning lamps were a symbol of the church or of the nation of God, which causes the light of its spirit, or of its knowledge of God, to shine before the Lord, and lets it stream out into the night of a world estranged from God. As the disciples of Christ were called, as lights of the world (Matt. v. 14), to let their lamps burn and shine, or, as candlesticks in the world (Luke xii. 35; Phil. ii. 15), to shine with their light before men (Matt. v. 16), so was the church of the Old Testament also. The correctness of this explanation of the meaning of the candlestick is placed beyond all doubt by Rev. i. 20, where the seven λυχνίαι, which

John saw before the throne of God, are explained as being the seven ἐκκλησίαι, which represent the new people of God, viz. the Christian church. The candlestick itself merely comes into consideration here as the stand which carried the lamps, in order that they might shine, and as such was the divinely appointed form for the realization of the purpose of the shining lamps. In this respect it might be taken as a symbol of the kingdom of God on its formal side, *i.e.* of the divinely appointed organism for the perpetuation and life of the church. But the lamps received their power to burn from the oil, with which they had to be filled before they could possibly burn. Oil, regarded according to its capacity to invigorate the body and increase the energy of the vital spirits, is used in the Scriptures as a symbol of the Spirit of God, not in its transcendent essence, but so far as it works in the world, and is indwelling in the church; and not merely the anointing oil, as Kliefoth supposes, but also the lamp oil, since the Israelites had no other oil than olive oil even for burning, and this was used for anointing also.[1] And in the case of the candlestick, the oil comes into consideration as a symbol of the Spirit of God. There is no force in Kliefoth's objection—namely, that inasmuch as the oil of the candlestick was to be presented by the people, it could not represent the Holy Spirit with its power and grace, as coming from God to man, but must rather

[1] The distinction between lamp oil and anointing oil, upon which Kliefoth founds his interpretation of the visionary candlestick, and which he tries to uphold from the language itself, by the assertion that the anointing oil is always called *shemen*, whereas the lamp oil is called *yitshâr*, is shown to be untenable by the simple fact that, in the minute description of the preparation of the lamp oil for the sacred candlestick, and the repeated allusion to this oil in the Pentateuch, the term *yitshâr* is never used, but always *shemen*, although the word *yitshâr* is by no means foreign to the Pentateuch, but occurs in Num. xviii. 12, Deut. vii. 13, xi. 14, xii. 17, and other passages. According to Ex. xxvii. 20, the lamp oil for the candlestick was to be prepared from *shemen zayith zâkh kâthîth*, pure, beaten olive oil (so also according to Lev. xxiv. 2); and according to Ex. xxx. 24, *shemen zayith*, olive oil, was to be used for anointing oil. Accordingly the lamp oil for the candlestick is called *shemen lammâ'ōr* in Ex. xxv. 6, xxxv. 8, 28, and *shemen hammâ'ōr* in Ex. xxxv. 14, xxxix. 37, and Num. iv. 16; and the anointing oil is called *shemen hammishchâh* in Ex. xxix. 7, xxxi. 11, xxxv. 15, xxxix. 38, xl. 9, Lev. viii. 2, 10, and other passages; and *shemen mishchath-qōdesh* in Ex. xxx. 25. Apart from

represent something human, which being given up to God, is
cleansed by God through the fire of His word and Spirit ; and
being quickened thereby, is made into a shining light. For,
apart from the fact that the assumption upon which this argument is founded—namely, that in the oil of the candlestick the
Spirit of God was symbolized by the altar fire with which it
was lighted—is destitute of all scriptural support, since it is
not mentioned anywhere that the lamps of the candlestick were
lighted with fire taken from the altar of burnt-offering, but
it is left quite indefinite where the light or fire for kindling
the lamps was to be taken from; apart, I say, from this, such
an argument proves too much (*nimium, ergo nihil*), because
the anointing oil did not come directly from God, but was
also presented by the people. Supposing, therefore, that this
circumstance was opposed to the symbolical meaning of the
lamp oil, it would also be impossible that the anointing oil
should be a symbol of the Holy Ghost, since not only the oil,
but the spices also, which were used in preparing the anointing
oil, were given by the people (Ex. xxv. 6). We might indeed
say, with Kliefoth, that " the oil, as the fatness of the fruit of
the olive tree, is the last pure result of the whole of the vital
process of the olive tree, and therefore the quintessence of its
nature ; and that man also grows, and flourishes, and bears
fruit like an olive tree; and therefore the fruit of his life's fruit,

---

ver. 14 of the chapter before us, *yitshâr* is never used for the lamp oil as
such, but simply in the enumeration of the productions of the land, or of
the tithes and first-fruits, when it occurs in connection with *tīrōsh*, must or
new wine (Num. xviii. 12 ; Deut. vii. 13, xi. 14, xiv. 23, xviii. 4, xxviii. 51 ;
2 Chron. xxxi. 5, xxxii. 28 ; Neh. v. 11, x. 40, xiii. 12 ; Hos. ii. 10, 24;
Joel i. 10, ii. 19, 24 ; Jer. xxxi. 12 ; Hag. i. 11), but never in connection
with *yayin* (wine), with which *shemen* is connected (1 Chron. xix. 40 ;
2 Chron. ii. 14, xi. 11 ; Prov. xxi. 17; Jer. xl. 10).   It is evident from
this that *yitshâr*, the shining, bears the same relation to *shemen*, fatness, as
tīrōsh, must, to *yayin*, wine,—namely, that *yitshâr* is applied to oil as the
juice of the olive, *i.e.* as the produce of the land, from its shining colour,
whilst *shemen* is the name given to it when its strength and use are considered. Hengstenberg's opinion, that *yitshâr* is the rhetorical or poetical
name for oil, has no real foundation in the circumstance that *yitshâr* only
occurs once in the first four books of the Pentateuch (Num. xviii. 12)
and *shemen* occurs very frequently ; whereas in Deuteronomy *yitshâr* is
used more frequently than *shemen*, viz. the former six times, and the latter
four.

the produce of his personality and of the unfolding of his life, may be compared to oil." But it must also be added (and this Kliefoth has overlooked), that the olive tree could not grow, flourish, and bear fruit, unless God first of all implanted or communicated the power to grow and bear fruit, and then gave it rain and sunshine and the suitable soil for a prosperous growth. And so man also requires, for the production of the spiritual fruits of life, not only the kindling of this fruit by the fire of the word and Spirit of God, but also the continued nourishment and invigoration of this fruit through God's word and Spirit, just as the lighting and burning of the lamps are not effected simply by the kindling of the flame, but it is also requisite that the oil should possess the power to burn and shine. In this double respect the candlestick, with its burning and shining lamps, was a symbol of the church of God, which lets the fruit of its life, which is not only kindled but also nourished by the Holy Spirit, shine before God. And the additions made to the visionary candlestick indicate generally, that the church of the Lord will be supplied with the conditions and requirements necessary to enable it to burn and shine perpetually, *i.e.* that the daughter of Zion will never fail to have the Spirit of God, to make its candlestick bright. (See at ver. 14.)

There is no difficulty whatever in reconciling the answer of the angel in ver. 6 with the meaning of the candlestick, as thus unfolded according to its leading features, without having to resort to what looks like a subterfuge, viz. the idea that ver. 6 does not contain an exposition, but passes on to something new, or without there being any necessity to account, as Koehler does, for the introduction of the candlestick, which he has quite correctly explained (though he weakens the explanation by saying that it applies primarily to Zerubbabel), namely, by assuming that " it was intended, on the one hand, to remind him what the calling of Israel was; and, on the other hand, to admonish him that Israel could never reach this calling by the increase of its might and the exaltation of its strength, but solely by suffering itself to be filled with the Spirit of Jehovah." For the candlestick does not set forth the object after which Israel is to strive, but symbolizes the church of God, as it will shine in the splendour of the light received through the Spirit

of God. It therefore symbolizes the future glory of the people
of God. Israel will not acquire this through human power
and might, but through the Spirit of the Lord, in whose power
Zerubbabel will accomplish the work he has begun. Ver. ,
does not contain a new promise for Zerubbabel, that if he lays
to heart the calling of Israel, and acts accordingly, *i.e.* if he re-
sists the temptation to bring Israel into a free and independent
position by strengthening its external power, the difficulties
which have lain in the way of the completion of the building
of the temple will clear away of themselves by the command
of Jehovah (Koehler). For there is not the slightest intimation
of any such temptation as that supposed to have presented
itself to Zerubbabel, either in the vision itself or in the historical and prophetical writings of that time. Moreover, ver. 7
has not at all the form of a promise, founded upon the laying
to heart of what has been previously mentioned. The contents of the verse are not set forth as anything new either by
נְאֻם יְהֹוָה (saith Jehovah), or by any other introductory formula.
It can only be a further explanation of the word of Jehovah,
which is still covered by the words "saith Jehovah of hosts"
at the close of ver. 6. The contents of the verse, when properly understood, clearly lead to this. The great mountain
before Zerubbabel is to become a plain, not by human power,
but by the Spirit of Jehovah. The meaning is given in the
second hemistich: He (Zerubbabel) will bring out the top-
stone. וְהוֹצִיא is not a simple preterite, "he has brought out
the foundation-stone" (viz. at the laying of the foundation of
the temple), as Hengstenberg supposes; but a future, "he
will bring out," as is evident from the *Vav consec.*, through
which הוֹצִיא is attached to the preceding command as a consequence to which it leads. Moreover, אֶבֶן הָרֹאשָׁה does not mean
the foundation-stone, which is called אֶבֶן פִּנָּה, *lit.* corner-stone
(Job xxxviii. 6; Isa. xxviii. 16; Jer. li. 26), or רֹאשׁ פִּנָּה, the
head-stone of the corner (Ps. cxviii. 22), but the stone of the
top, *i.e.* the finishing or gable stone (הָרֹאשָׁה with *raphe* as a
feminine form of רֹאשׁ, and in apposition to הָאֶבֶן). הוֹצִיא, to
bring out, namely out of the workshop in which it had been
cut, to set it in its proper place in the wall. That these words
refer to the finishing of the building of the temple which
Zerubbabel had begun, is placed beyond all doubt by ver. 9.

The great mountain, therefore, is apparently "a figure denoting the colossal difficulties, which rose up mountain high at the
continuation and completion of the building of the temple."
Koehler adopts this explanation in common with "the majority
of commentators." But, notwithstanding this appearance, we
must adhere to the view adopted by the Chald., Jerome, Theod.
Mops., Theodoret, Kimchi, Luther, and others, that the great
mountain is a symbol of the power of the world, or the imperial power, and see no difficulty in the "unwarrantable consequence" spoken of by Koehler, viz. that in that case the
plain must be a symbol of the kingdom of God (see, on the
contrary, Isa. xl. 4). For it is evident from what follows, that
the passage refers to something greater than this, namely to
the finishing of the building of the temple that has already
begun, or to express it briefly and clearly, that the building of
the temple of stone and wood is simply regarded as a type of
the building of the kingdom of God, as ver. 9 clearly shows.
There was a great mountain standing in the way of this building of Zerubbabel's—namely the power of the world, or the
imperial power—and this God would level to a plain. Just as,
in the previous vision, Joshua is introduced as the representative of the high-priesthood, so here Zerubbabel, the prince of
Judah, springing from the family of David, comes into consideration not as an individual, but according to his official rank
as the representative of the government of Israel, which is now
so deeply humbled by the imperial power. But the government
of Israel has no reality or existence, except in the government
of Jehovah. The family of David will rise up into a new royal
power and glory in the *Tsemach*, whom Jehovah will bring
forth as His servant (ch. iii. 8). This servant of Jehovah will
fill the house of God, which Zerubbabel has built, with glory.
In order that this may be done, Zerubbabel must build the
temple, because the temple is the house in which Jehovah
dwells in the midst of His people. On account of this importance of the temple in relation to Israel, the opponents of
Judah sought to throw obstacles in the way of its being built;
and these obstacles were a sign and prelude of the opposition
which the imperial power of the world, standing before Zerubbabel as a great mountain, will offer to the kingdom of God.
This mountain is to become a plain. What Zerubbabel the

governor of Judah has begun, he will bring to completion;
and as he will finish the building of the earthly temple, so will
the true Zerubbabel, the Messiah, *Tsemach*, the servant of
Jehovah, build the spiritual temple, and make Israel into a
candlestick, which is supplied with oil by two olive trees, so
that its lamps may shine brightly in the world. In this sense
the angel's reply gives an explanation of the meaning of the
visionary candlestick. Just as, according to the economy of
the Old Testament, the golden candlestick stood in the holy
place of the temple before the face of Jehovah, and could only
shine there, so does the congregation, which is symbolized by
the candlestick, need a house of God, that it may be able to
cause its light to shine. This house is the kingdom of God
symbolized by the temple, which was to be built by Zerubbabel,
not by human might and power, but by the Spirit of the Lord.
In this building the words " He will bring forth the top-stone"
find their complete and final fulfilment. The finishing of this
building will take place תְּשֻׁאוֹת חֵן חֵן לָהּ, *i.e.* amidst loud cries of
the people, " Grace, grace unto it." תְּשֻׁאוֹת is an accusative of
more precise definition, or of the attendant circumstances (cf.
Ewald, § 204, *a*), and signifies noise, tumult, from שָׁאָה = שׁוֹא,
a loud cry (Job xxxix. 7 ; Isa. xxii. 2). The suffix לָהּ refers,
so far as the form is concerned, to הָאֶבֶן הָרֹאשָׁה, but actually to
habbayith, the temple which is finished with the gable-stone.
To this stone (so the words mean) may God direct His favour
or grace, that the temple may stand for ever, and never be
destroyed again.

A further and still clearer explanation of the angel's answer
(vers. 6 and 7) is given in the words of Jehovah which follow
in vers. 8–10. Ver. 8. " *And the word of Jehovah came to me
thus :* Ver. 9. *The hands of Zerubbabel have laid the foundation of this house, and his hands will finish it ; and thou wilt
know that Jehovah of hosts hath sent me to you.* Ver. 10. *For
who despiseth the day of small things ? and they joyfully behold
the plummet in the hand of Zerubbabel, those seven : the eyes of
Jehovah, they sweep through the whole earth.*" This word of
God is not addressed to the prophet through the *angelus interpres*, but comes direct from Jehovah, though, as ver. 9*b* clearly
shows when compared with ch. ii. 9*b* and 11*b*, through the
Maleach Jehovah. Although the words " the hands of Zerub-

babel have laid the foundation of this house" unquestionably refer primarily to the building of the earthly temple, and announce the finishing of that building by Zerubbabel, yet the apodosis commencing with "and thou shalt know" shows that the sense is not thereby exhausted, but rather that the building is simply mentioned here as a type of the spiritual temple (as in ch. vi. 12, 13), and that the completion of the typical temple simply furnishes a pledge of the completion of the true temple. For it was not by the finishing of the earthly building, but solely by the carrying out of the kingdom of God which this shadowed forth, that Judah could discern that the angel of Jehovah had been sent to it. This is also apparent from the reason assigned for this promise in ver. 10, the meaning of which has been explained in very different ways. Many take וְשָׂמְחוּ וגו׳ as an apodosis, and connect it with כִּי מִי בַז as the protasis : "for whoever despises the day of small things, they shall see with joy," etc. (LXX., Chald., Pesh., Vulg., Luth., Calv., and others) ; but מִי can hardly be taken as an indefinite pronoun, inasmuch as the introduction of the apodosis by *Vav* would be unsuitable, and it has hitherto been impossible to find a single well-established example of the indefinite מִי followed by a perfect with *Vav consec.* And the idea that *v*ᵉ*sâm*ᵉ*chū* is a circumstantial clause, in the sense of "whereas they see with joy" (Hitzig, Koehler), is equally untenable, for in a circumstantial clause the verb never stands at the head, but always the subject ; and this is so essential, that if the subject of the minor (or circumstantial) clause is a noun which has already been mentioned in the major clause, either the noun itself, or at any rate its pronoun, must be repeated (Ewald, § 341, *a*), because this is the only thing by which the clause can be recognised as a circumstantial clause. We must therefore take מִי as an interrogative pronoun : Who has ever despised the day of the small things? and understand the question in the sense of a negation, "No one has ever despised," etc. The perfect *baz* with the syllable sharpened, for *bâz*, from *būz* (like *tach* for *tâch* in Isa. xliv. 18 ; cf. Ges. § 72, Anm. 8), expresses a truth of experience resting upon facts. The words contain a perfect truth, if we only take them in the sense in which they were actually intended,—namely, that no one who hopes to accomplish, or does accomplish, anything great, despises the day of the small things. *Yōm q'tannōth*, a day on which only small things occur (cf. Num. xxii. 18). This does not merely mean the day on which the foundation-stone of the temple was first laid, and the building itself was still in the stage of its small beginnings, according to which the time when the temple was built up again in full splendour would be the day of great things (Koehler and others). For the time when Zerubbabel's temple was finished—namely, the sixth year of Darius—was just as miserable as that in which the foundation was laid, and the building that had been suspended was resumed once more. The whole period from Darius to the coming of the Messiah, who will be the first to accomplish great things, is a day of small things, as being a period in which everything that was done for the building of the kingdom of God seemed but small, and in comparison with the work of the Messiah really was small, although it contained within itself the germs of the greatest things. The following perfects, וְשָׂמְחוּ וְרָאוּ, have *Vav consec.*, and express the consequence, though not " the necessary consequence, of their having despised the day of small beginnings," as Koehler imagines, who for that reason properly rejects this view, but the consequence which will ensue if the day of small things is not despised. The fact that the clause beginning with *v'sâm'chū* is attached to the first clause of the verse in the form of a consequence, may be very simply explained on the ground that the question " who hath despised," with its negative answer, contains an admonition to the people and their rulers not to despise the small beginnings. If they lay this admonition to heart, the seven eyes of God will see with delight the plumb-lead in the hand of Zerubbabel. In the combination וְשָׂמְחוּ וְרָאוּ the verb *sâm'chū* takes the place of an adverb (Ges. § 142, 3, *a*). אֶבֶן הַבְּדִיל is not a stone filled up with lead, but an *'ebhen* which is lead, *i.e.* the plumb-lead or plummet. A plummet in the hand is a sign of being engaged in the work of building, or of superintending the erection of a building. The meaning of the clause is therefore, " Then will the seven eyes of Jehovah look with joy, or with satisfaction, upon the execution," not, however, in the sense of " They will find their pleasure in this restored temple, and look upon it with protecting care" (Kliefoth); for if this were the meaning, the introduction of the plummet in the hand of Zerubbabel would be a very superfluous addition. Zerubbabel is still simply the type of the future Zerubbabel—namely, the Messiah—who will build the true temple of God; and the meaning is the following: Then will the seven eyes of God help to carry out this building. שִׁבְעָה אֵלֶּה cannot be grammatically joined to עֵינֵי יְהֹוָה in the sense of "these seven eyes," as the position of 'ēlleh (these) between the numeral and the noun precludes this; but עֵינֵי יְהֹוָה is an explanatory apposition to שִׁבְעָה אֵלֶּה: "those (well-known) seven, (viz.) the eyes of Jehovah." The reference is to the seven eyes mentioned in the previous vision, which are directed upon a stone. These, according to ch. iii. 9, are the sevenfold radiations or operations of the Spirit of the Lord. Of these the angel of the Lord says still further here: They sweep through the whole earth, i.e. their influence stretches over all the earth. These words also receive their full significance only on the supposition that the angel of Jehovah is speaking of the Messianic building of the house or kingdom of God. For the eyes of Jehovah would not need to sweep through the whole earth, in order to see whatever could stand in the way and hinder the erection of Zerubbabel's temple, but simply to watch over the opponents of Judah in the immediate neighbourhood and the rule of Darius.

This gave to the prophet a general explanation of the meaning of the vision; for the angel had told him that the house (or kingdom) of God would be built and finished by the Spirit of Jehovah, and the church of the Lord would accomplish its mission, to shine brightly as a candlestick. But there is one point in the vision that is not yet quite clear to him, and he therefore asks for an explanation in vers. 11–14. Ver. 11. "And I answered and said to him, What are these two olive-trees on the right of the candlestick, and on the left? Ver. 12. And I answered the second time, and said to him, What are the two branches (ears) of the olive-trees which are at the hand of the two golden spouts, which pour the gold out of themselves? Ver. 13. And he spake to me thus: Knowest thou not what these are? and I said, No, my lord. Ver. 14. Then said he, These are the two oil-children, which stand by the Lord of the whole earth." The meaning of the olive-trees on the right and left sides of the candlestick ('al, over, because the olive-trees rose above the

candlestick on the two sides) is not quite obvious to the prophet.
He asks about this in ver. 11; at the same time, recognising
the fact that their meaning is bound up with the two *shibbălē
hazzēthīm*, he does not wait for an answer, but gives greater
precision to his question, by asking the meaning of these two
branches of the olive-trees. On שְׁתֵּי the Masora observes, that
the *dagesh forte conjunct.*, which is generally found after the
interrogative pronoun *mâh*, is wanting in the שׁ, and was probably omitted, simply because the שׁ has not a full vowel, but a
sheva, whilst the ת which follows has also a *dagesh*. These
branches of the olive-trees were *b*ʿ*yad*, " at the hand of" (*i.e.*
close by, as in Job xv. 23) the two golden *tsant*ʿ*rōth*, which
poured the gold from above into the *gullâh* of the candlestick.
*Tsant*ʿ*rōth* (ἁπ. λεγ.) is supposed by Aben Ezra and others to
stand for oil-presses; but there is no further ground for this
than the conjecture that the olive-trees could only supply the
candlestick with oil when the olives were pressed. The older
translators render the word by spouts or " channels" (LXX.
μυξωτῆρες, Vulg. *rostra*, Pesh. *noses*). It is probably related
in meaning to *tsinnōr*, channel or waterfall, and to be derived
from *tsânar*, to rush : hence spouts into which the branches of
the olive-trees emptied the oil of the olives, so that it poured
with a rush out of them into the oil vessel. The latter is
obviously implied in the words *hamm*ʿ*rīqīm*, etc., which empty
out the gold from above themselves, *i.e.* the gold which comes
to them from above. *Hazzâhâbh*, the gold which the *tsant*ʿ*rōth*
empty out, is supposed by most commentators to signify the
golden-coloured oil. Hofmann (*Weiss. u. Erf.* i. 344–5) and
Kliefoth, on the contrary, understand by it real gold, which
flowed out of the spouts into the candlestick, so that the latter
was thereby perpetually renewed. But as the candlestick is
not now for the first time in process of formation, but is represented in the vision as perfectly finished, and as the gold comes
from the branches of the olive-trees, it is impossible to think of
anything else than the oil which shines like gold. Accordingly
the oil (*yitshâr*, lit. shining) is called *zâhâbh*, as being, as it
were, liquid gold. Hence arises the play upon words : the
spouts are of gold, and they pour gold from above themselves
into the candlestick (Hitzig and Koehler). The angel having
expressed his astonishment at the prophet's ignorance, as he

does in ver. 5, gives this answer : These (the two bushes of the olive-tree, for which the olive-trees stood there) are the two *b⁽e⁾nē yitshâr*, sons of oil, *i.e.* endowed or supplied with oil (cf. Isa. v. 1), which stand by the Lord of the whole earth, namely as His servants (on *'âmad 'al*, denoting the standing posture of a servant, who rises above his master when seated, see 1 Kings xxii. 19, also Isa. vi. 2). The two children of oil cannot be the Jews and Gentiles (Cyril), or Israel and the Gentile world in their fruitful branches, *i.e.* their believing members (Kliefoth), because the candlestick is the symbol of the church of the Lord, consisting of the believers in Israel and also in the Gentile world. This is just as clear as the distinction between the olive-trees and the candlestick, to which they conduct the oil. Others think of the prophets Haggai and Zechariah (J. D. Mich., Hofm., Baumg., etc.) ; but although there is no force in Koehler's objection, that in that case there would be a double order of prophets in Israel, since two prophets, both influenced by the Spirit of God, would not imply a double order of prophets, this explanation is decidedly precluded by the fact that two mortal men could not convey to the church for all ages the oil of the Spirit of God. The two sons of oil can only be the two media, anointed with oil, through whom the spiritual and gracious gifts of God were conveyed to the church of the Lord, namely, the existing representatives of the priesthood and the regal government, who were at that time Joshua the high priest and the prince Zerubbabel. These stand by the Lord of the whole earth, as the divinely appointed instruments through whom the Lord causes His Spirit to flow into His congregation. Israel had indeed possessed both these instruments from the time of its first adoption as the people of Jehovah, and both were consecrated to their office by anointing. So far the fact that the olive-trees stand by the side of the candlestick does not appear to indicate anything that the prophet could not have interpreted for himself ; and hence the astonishment expressed in the question of the angel in ver. 13. Moreover, the vision was not intended to represent an entirely new order of things, but simply to show the completion of that which was already contained and typified in the old covenant. The seven-armed candlestick was nothing new in itself. All that was new in the candlestick seen by Zechariah was the apparatus through

which it was supplied with oil that it might give light, namely,
the connection between the candlestick and the two olive-trees,
whose branches bore olives like bunches of ears, to supply it
abundantly with oil, which was conveyed to each of its seven
lamps through seven pipes.   The candlestick of the tabernacle
had to be supplied every day with the necessary oil by the hands
of the priests.   This oil the congregation had to present ; and
to this end the Lord had to bestow His blessing, that the fruits
of the land might be made to prosper, so that the olive-tree
should bear its olives, and yield a supply of oil.   But this
blessing was withdrawn from the nation when it fell away from
its God (cf. Joel i. 10).   If, then, the candlestick had two olive-
trees by its side, yielding oil in such copious abundance, that
every one of the seven lamps received its supply through seven
pipes, it could never fail to have sufficient oil for a full and
brilliant light.   This was what was new in the visionary candlestick ; and the meaning was this, that the Lord would in future
bestow upon His congregation the organs of His Spirit, and
maintain them in such direct connection with it, that it would
be able to let its light shine with sevenfold brilliancy.

SIXTH VISION : THE FLYING ROLL, AND THE WOMAN IN THE EPHAH.—CHAP. V.

These two figures are so closely connected, that they are
to be taken as *one* vision.   The circumstance, that a pause is
introduced between the first and second view, in which both
the ecstatic elevation and the interpreting angel leave the
prophet, so that it is stated in ver. 5 that " the angel came
forth," furnishes no sufficient reason for the assumption that
there were two different visions.   For the figure of the ephah
with the woman sitting in it is also divided into two views,
since the prophet first of all sees the woman and receives the
explanation (vers. 5–8), and the further development of the
vision is then introduced in ver. 9 with a fresh introductory
formula, " And I lifted up my eyes, and saw."   And just as
this introductory formula, through which new and different
visions are introduced in ch. ii. 1 and 5, by no means warrants
us in dividing what is seen here into two different visions ; so
there is nothing in the introduction in ver. 5 to compel us to

separate the vision of the flying roll (vers. 1–4) from the following vision of the ephah, since there is no such difference in the actual contents of the two as to warrant such a separation. They neither stand in such a relation to one another, as that the first sets forth the extermination of sinners out of the holy land, and the second the extermination of sin itself, as Maurer supposes; nor does the one treat of the fate of the sinners and the other of the full measure of the sin; but the vision of the flying roll prepares the way for, and introduces, what is carried out in the vision of the ephah (vers. 5–11), and the connection between the two is indicated formally by the fact that the suffix in עֵינָם in ver. 6 refers back to vers. 3 and 4.

Ver. 1. "*And I lifted up my eyes again, and saw, and behold a flying roll. Ver. 2. And he said to me, What seest thou? And I said, I see a flying roll; its length twenty cubits, and its breadth ten cubits. Ver. 3. And he said to me, This is the curse that goeth forth over the whole land: for every one that stealeth will be cleansed away from this side, according to it; and every one that sweareth will be cleansed away from that side, according to it. Ver. 4. I have caused it to go forth, is the saying of Jehovah of hosts, and it will come into the house of the thief, and into the house of him that sweareth by my name for deceit: and it will pass the night in the midst of his house, and consume both its beams and its stones.*" The person calling the prophet's attention to the vision, and interpreting it, is the *angelus interpres.* This is not specially mentioned here, as being obvious from what goes before. The roll (book-scroll, *megillâh* = *megillath sēpher,* Ezek. ii. 9) is seen flying over the earth unrolled, so that its length and breadth can be seen. The statement as to its size is not to be regarded as "an approximative estimate," so that the roll would be simply described as of considerable size (Koehler), but is unquestionably significant. It corresponds both to the size of the porch of Solomon's temple (1 Kings vi. 3), and also to the dimensions of the holy place in the tabernacle, which was twenty cubits long and ten cubits broad. Hengstenberg, Hofmann, and Umbreit, following the example of Kimchi, assume that the reference is to the porch of the temple, and suppose that the roll has the same dimensions as this porch, to indicate that the judgment is "a consequence of the theocracy," or was to issue from the sanctuary of Israel, where the people assembled before the Lord. But the porch of the temple was neither a symbol of the theocracy, nor the place where the people assembled before the Lord, but a mere architectural ornament, which had no significance whatever in relation to the worship. The people assembled before the Lord in the court, to have reconciliation made for them with God by sacrifice; or they entered the holy place in the person of their sanctified mediators, the priests, as cleansed from sin, there to appear before God and engage in His spotless worship. The dimensions of the roll are taken from the holy place of the tabernacle, just as in the previous vision the candlestick was the Mosaic candlestick of the tabernacle. Through the similarity of the dimensions of the roll to tnose of the holy place in the tabernacle, there is no intention to indicate that the curse proceeds from the holy place of the tabernacle or of the temple; for the roll would have issued from the sanctuary, if it had been intended to indicate this. Moreover, the curse or judgment does indeed begin at the house of God, but it does not issue or come from the house of God. Kliefoth has pointed to the true meaning in the following explanation which he gives: "The fact that the writing, which brings the curse upon all the sinners of the earth, has the same dimensions as the tabernacle, signifies that the measure will be meted out according to the measure of the holy place;" and again, "the measure by which this curse upon sinners will be meted out, will be the measure of the holy place." With this measure would all sinners be measured, that they might be cut off from the congregation of the Lord, which appeared before God in the holy place. The flight of the roll symbolized the going forth of the curse over the whole land. כָּל־הָאָרֶץ is rendered by Hofmann, Neumann, and Kliefoth "the whole earth," because "it evidently signifies the whole earth in ch. iv. 10, 14, and vi. 5" (Kliefoth). But these passages, in which the Lord of the whole earth is spoken of, do not prove anything in relation to our vision, in which כָּל־הָאָרֶץ is unmistakeably limited to the land of Canaan (Judah) by the antithesis in ver. 11, "the land of Shinar." If the sinners who are smitten by the curse proceeding over כָּל־הָאָרֶץ are to be carried into the land of *Shinar*, the former must be a definite land, and not the earth as the sum of all lands. It

cannot be argued in opposition to this, that the sin of the land
in which the true house of God and the true priesthood were,
was wiped away by expiation, whereas the sin of the whole
world would be brought into the land of judgment, when its
measure was concluded by God; for this antithesis is foreign
not only to this vision, but to the Scriptures universally. The
Scriptures know nothing of any distribution or punishment of
sins according to different lands, but simply according to the
character of the sinners, viz. whether they are penitent or
hardened. At the same time, the fact that כָּל־הָאָרֶץ denotes
the whole of the land of Israel, by no means proves that our
vision either treats of the " carrying away of Israel into exile,"
which had already occurred (Ros.), or " sets before them a
fresh carrying away into exile, and one still in the future "
(Hengstenberg), or that on the coming of the millennial kingdom the sin and the sinners will be exterminated from the
whole of the holy land, and the sin thrown back upon the rest
of the earth, which is still under the power of the world (Hofmann). The vision certainly refers to the remote future of
the kingdom of God; and therefore "the whole land" cannot
be restricted to the extent and boundaries of Judæa or Palestine, but reaches as far as the spiritual Israel or church of
Christ is spread over the earth; but there is no allusion in our
vision to the millennial kingdom, and its establishment within
the limits of the earthly Canaan. The curse falls upon all
thieves and false swearers. הַנִּשְׁבָּע in ver. 3 is defined more
precisely in ver. 4, as swearing in the name of Jehovah for
deceit, and therefore refers to perjury in the broadest sense of
the word, or to all abuse of the name of God for false, deceitful swearing. Thieves are mentioned for the sake of individualizing, as sinners against the second table of the decalogue;
false swearers, as sinners against the first table. The repetition of מִזֶּה כָּמוֹהָ points to this; for mizzeh, repeated in correlative clauses, signifies hinc et illinc, hence and thence, i.e. on
one side and the other (Ex. xvii. 12; Num. xxii. 24; Ezek.
xlvii. 7), and can only refer here to the fact that the roll was
written upon on both sides, so that it is to be taken in close connection with כָּמוֹהָ: " on this side . . . and on that, according to
it " (the roll), i.e. according to the curse written upon this side
and that side of the roll. We have therefore to picture the

roll to ourselves as having the curse against the thieves written upon the one side, and that against the perjurers upon the other. The supposition that *mizzeh* refers to כָּל־הָאָרֶץ is precluded most decidedly, by the fact that *mizzeh* does not mean "thence," *i.e.* from the whole land, but when used adverbially of any place, invariably signifies "hence," and refers to the place where the speaker himself is standing. Moreover, the double use of *mizzeh* is at variance with any allusion to *hâ'ârets*, as well as the fact that if it belonged to the verb, it would stand after כָּמֹהָ, whether before or after the verb. *Niqqâh*, the *niphal*, signifies here to be cleaned out, like καθαρίζεσθαι in Mark vii. 19 (cf. 1 Kings xiv. 10; Deut. xvii. 12). This is explained in ver. 4 thus: Jehovah causes the curse to go forth and enter into the house of the thief and perjurer, so that it will pass the night there, *i.e.* stay there (*lâneh* third pers. perf. of *lūn*, from *lânâh*, to be blunted, like *zûreh* in Isa. lix. 5, and other verbal formations); it will not remain idle, however, but work therein, destroying both the house and sinners therein, so that beams and stones will be consumed (cf. 1 Kings xviii. 38). The suffix in כִּלַּתּוּ (for כִּלַּתְהוּ, cf. Ges. § 75, Anm. 19) refers to the house, of course including the inhabitants. The following nouns introduced with וְאֶת are in explanatory apposition: both its beams and its stones. The roll therefore symbolizes the curse which will fall upon sinners throughout the whole land, consuming them with their houses, and thus sweeping them out of the nation of God.

To this there is appended in vers. 5–11 a new view, which exhibits the further fate of the sinners who have been separated from the congregation of the saints. Ver. 5. *"And the angel that talked with me went forth, and said to me, Lift up now thine eyes, and see, what is this that goeth out there? Ver. 6. And I said, What is it? And he said, This is the ephah going out. And he said, This is their aspect in all the land. Ver. 7. And behold a disk of lead was lifted up, and there was a woman sitting in the midst of the ephah. Ver. 8. And he said, This is wickedness; and he cast it into the midst of the ephah, and cast the leaden weight upon its mouth."* With the disappearing of the previous vision, the *angelus interpres* had also vanished from the eyes of the prophet. After a short pause he comes out again, calls the prophet's attention to a new figure which emerges out of the cloud, and so comes within the range of vision (הַיּוֹצֵאת הַזֹּאת), and informs him with regard to it: "This is the ephah which goeth out." יָצָא, to go out, in other words, to come to view. The *ephah* was the greatest measure of capacity which really existed among the Hebrews for dry goods, and was about the size of a cubic foot; for the *chōmer*, which contained ten ephahs, appears to have had only an ideal existence, viz. for the purpose of calculation. The meaning of this figure is indicated generally in the words זֹאת עֵינָם בכ', the meaning of which depends upon the interpretation to be given to עֵינָם. The suffix of this word can only refer to the sinners mentioned before, viz. the thieves and perjurers; for it is contrary to the Hebrew usage to suppose that the words refer to the expression appended, בְּכָל־הָאָרֶץ, in the sense of "all those who are in the whole land" (Koehler). Consequently עַיִן does not mean the eye, but *adspectus*, appearance, or shape, as in Lev. xiii. 55, Ezek. i. 4 sqq; and the words have this meaning: The ephah (bushel) is the shape, *i.e.* represents the figure displayed by the sinners in all the land, after the roll of the curse has gone forth over the land, *i.e.* it shows into what condition they have come through that anathema (Kliefoth). The point of comparison between the ephah and the state into which sinners have come in consequence of the curse, does not consist in the fact that the ephah is carried away, and the sinners likewise (Maurer), nor in the fact that the sin now reaches its full measure (Hofm., Hengstenberg); for "the carrying away of the sinners does not come into consideration yet, and there is nothing at all here about the sin becoming full." It is true that, according to what follows, sin sits in the ephah as a woman, but there is nothing to indicate that the ephah is completely filled by it, so that there is no further room in it; and this thought would be generally out of keeping here. The point of comparison is rather to be found in the explanation given by Kliefoth: "Just as in a bushel the separate grains are all collected together, so will the individual sinners over the whole earth be brought into a heap, when the curse of the end goes forth over the whole earth." We have no hesitation in appropriating this explanation, although we have not rendered הָאָרֶץ "the earth," inasmuch as at the final fulfilment of the vision the holy land will extend over all the earth. Immediately

afterwards the prophet is shown still more clearly what is in
the ephah. A covering of lead (*kikkâr*, a circle, a rounding
or a circular plate) rises up, or is lifted up, and then he sees
a woman sitting in the ephah (*'achath* does not stand for the
indefinite article, but is a numeral, the sinners brought into a
heap appearing as a unity, *i.e.* as *one* living personality, instead
of forming an atomistic heap of individuals). This woman,
who had not come into the ephah now for the first time, but
was already sitting there, and was only seen now that the lid
was raised, is described by the angel as *mirsha'ath*, ungodliness,
as being wickedness embodied, just as in 2 Chron. xxiv. 7 this
name is given to godless Jezebel. Thereupon he throws her
into the ephah, out of which she had risen up, and shuts it with
the leaden lid, to carry her away, as the following vision shows,
out of the holy land.

Ver. 9. "*And I lifted up my eyes, and saw, and behold
there came forth two women, and wind in their wings, and they
had wings like a stork's wings; and they carried the ephah between
earth and heaven.* Ver. 10. *And I said to the angel that talked
with me, Whither are these taking the ephah?* Ver. 11. *And he
said to me, To build it a dwelling in the land of Shinar: and it
will be placed and set up there upon its stand.*" The meaning
of this new scene may easily be discovered. The ephah with
the woman in it is carried away between earth and heaven, *i.e.*
through the air. Women carry it because there is a woman
inside; and two women, because two persons are required to
carry so large and heavy a measure, that they may lay hold of it
on both sides (תִּשֶּׂנָה with the א dropped; cf. Ges. § 74, Anm. 4).
These women have wings, because it passes through the air;
and a stork's wings, because these birds have broad pinions,
and not because the stork is a bird of passage or an unclean
bird. The wings are filled with wind, that they may be able to
carry their burden with greater velocity through the air. The
women denote the instruments or powers employed by God to
carry away the sinners out of His congregation, without any
special allusion to this or the other historical nation. This is
all that we have to seek for in these features, which only serve
to give distinctness to the picture. But the statement in ver.
11 is significant: "to build it a house in the land of Shinar."
The pronoun לָהּ with the suffix softened instead of לָהּ, as in Ex.

ix. 18, Lev. xiii. 4 (cf. Ewald, § 247, *d*), refers grammatically to הָאֵיפָה; but so far as .the sense is concerned, it refers to the woman sitting in the ephah, since a house is not built for a measure, but only for men to dwell in. This also applies to the feminine form הִנִּיחָה, and to the suffix in מְכֻנָתָהּ. The building of a house indicates that the woman is to dwell there permanently, as is still more clearly expressed in the second hemistich. הוּכַן refers to בַּיִת, and is not to be taken hypothetically, in the sense of " as soon as the house shall be restored," but is a perfect with *Vav consec.*; and *hûkhan*, the *hophal* of *kûn*, is not to be taken in the sense of restoring, but, in correspondence with *m^ekhunâh*, in the sense of establishing or building on firm foundations. *M^ekhunâh:* the firmly established house. In this the woman of sin is brought to rest. The land in which the woman of sin carried away out of the holy land is permanently to dwell, is the land of *Shinar*. This name is not to be identified with *Babel*, so as to support the conclusion that it refers to a fresh removal of the people of Israel into exile; but according to Gen. x. 10 and xi. 2, *Shinar* is the land in which Nimrod founded the first empire, and where the human race built the tower of Babel which was to reach to the sky. The name is not to be taken geographically here as an epithet applied to Mesopotamia, but is a notional or real definition, which affirms that the ungodliness carried away out of the sphere of the people of God will have its permanent settlement in the sphere of the imperial power that is hostile to God. The double vision of this chapter, therefore, shows the separation of the wicked from the congregation of the Lord, and their banishment into and concentration within the ungodly kingdom of the world. This distinction and separation commenced with the coming of the Messiah, and runs through all the ages of the spread and development of the Christian church, until at the time of the end they will come more and more into outward manifestation; and the evil, having been sifted out by the judicial power of God and His Spirit, will form itself into a Babel of the last days, as Ezek. xxxviii. and xxxix. clearly show, and attempt a last struggle with the kingdom of God, in which it will be overcome and destroyed by the last judgment.

SEVENTH VISION : THE FOUR CHARIOTS.—CHAP. VI. 1–8.

Ver. 1. *" And again I lifted up my eyes, and saw, and behold four chariots coming forth between the two mountains, and the mountains were mountains of brass.* Ver. 2. *In the first chariot were red horses, and in the second chariot black horses.* Ver. 3. *And in the third chariot white horses, and in the fourth chariot speckled powerful horses.* Ver. 4. *And I answered and said to the angel that talked with me, What are these, my lord?* Ver. 5. *And the angel answered and said to me, These are the four winds of heaven going out, after having stationed themselves by the Lord of the whole earth.* Ver. 6. *Those in which the black horses are, go out into the land of the north, and the white have gone out behind them, and the speckled have gone out into the land of the south.* Ver. 7. *And the powerful ones have gone out, and sought to go, to pass through the earth ; and he said, Go ye, and pass through the earth ; and they passed through the earth.* Ver. 8. *And he called to me, and spake to me thus : Behold, those which go out into the land of the north let down my spirit in the land of the north."* The four chariots are explained in ver. 5 by the interpreting angel to be the four winds of heaven, which go forth after they have taken their stand by the Lord of the whole earth, *i.e.* have appeared before Him in the attitude of servants, to lay their account before Him, and to receive commands from Him (הִתְיַצֵּב עַל, as in Job i. 6, ii. 1). This addition shows that the explanation is not a real interpretation ; that is to say, the meaning is not that the chariots represent the four winds ; but the less obvious figure of the chariots is explained through the more obvious figure of the winds, which answers better to the reality. Since, for example, according to ver. 8, the chariots are designed to carry the Spirit (*rŭăch*) of God, there was nothing with which they could be more suitably compared than the winds (*rŭăch*) of heaven, for these are the most appropriate earthly substratum to symbolize the working of the Divine Spirit (cf. Jer. xlix. 36 ; Dan. vii. 2). This Spirit, in its judicial operations, is to be borne by the chariots to the places more immediately designated in the vision. As they go out, after having appeared before God, the two mountains, between which they go out or come forth, can only be sought in the place where God's dwelling is. But the mountains are of brass, and therefore are not earthly mountains; but they are not therefore mere symbols of the might of God with which His church is defended (Hengst., Neumann), or allusions to the fact that the dwelling-place of God is immoveable and unapproachable (Koehler), or symbols of the imperial power of the world and the kingdom of God (Kliefoth), according to which the power of the world would be just as immoveable as the kingdom of God. The symbol has rather a definite geographical view as its basis. As the lands to which the chariots go are described geographically as the lands of the north and south, the starting-point of the chariots must also be thought of geographically, and must therefore be a place or country lying between the northern and southern lands: this is the land of Israel, or more especially Jerusalem, the centre of the Old Testament kingdom of God, where the Lord had His dwelling-place. It is therefore the view of Jerusalem and its situation that lies at the foundation of the vision; only we must not think of the mountains Zion and Moriah (as Osiander, Maurer, Hofmann, and Umbreit do), for these are never distinguished from one another in the Old Testament as forming two separate mountains; but we have rather to think of Zion and the Mount of Olives, which stood opposite to it towards the east. Both are named as places where or from which the Lord judges the world, viz. the Mount of Olives in ch. xiv. 4, and Zion very frequently, *e.g.* in Joel iii. 16. The place between the two mountains is, then, the valley of Jehoshaphat, in which, according to Joel iii. 2 sqq., the Lord judges the nations. In the vision before us this valley simply forms the starting-point for the chariots, which carry the judgment from the dwelling-place of God into the lands of the north and south, which are mentioned as the seat of the imperial power; and the mountains are of brass, to denote the immoveable firmness of the place where the Lord dwells, and where He has founded His kingdom.

The colour of the horses, by which the four chariots are distinguished, is just as significant here as in ch. i. 8; and indeed, so far as the colour is the same, the meaning is also the same here as there. Three colours are alike, since *b'ruddîm*, speckled, is not essentially different from *s'ruqqîm*, star-

ling-grey, viz. black and white mixed together (see at ch. i. 8).
The black horses are added here. Black is the colour of grief
(cf. "black as sackcloth of hair," Rev. vi. 12). The rider
upon the black horse in Rev. vi. 5, 6, holds in his hand the
emblem of dearness, the milder form of famine. Consequently
the colours of the horses indicate the destination of the chariots,
to execute judgment upon the enemies of the kingdom of God.
Red, as the colour of blood, points to war and bloodshed; the
speckled colour to pestilence and other fatal plagues; and the
black colour to dearness and famine: so that these three chariots symbolize the three great judgments, war, pestilence, and
hunger (2 Sam. xxiv. 11 sqq.), along with which "the noisome
beast" is also mentioned in Ezek. xiv. 21 as a fourth judgment.
In the vision before us the fourth chariot is drawn by white
horses, to point to the glorious victories of the ministers of the
divine judgment. The explanation of the chariots in this
vision is rendered more difficult by the fact, that on the one
hand the horses of the fourth chariot are not only called
bᵉruddīm, but אֲמֻצִּים also; and on the other hand, that in the
account of the starting of the chariots the red horses are
omitted, and the speckled are distinguished from the אֲמֻצִּים
instead, inasmuch as it is affirmed of the former that they
went forth into the south country, and of the latter, that "they
sought to go that they might pass through the whole earth,"
and they passed through with the consent of God. The commentators have therefore attempted in different ways to identify
הָאֲמֻצִּים in ver. 7 with אֲדֻמִּים. Hitzig and Maurer assume that
אמצים is omitted from ver. 6 by mistake, and that אמצים in
ver. 7 is a copyist's error for אדמים, although there is not a
single critical authority that can be adduced in support of this.
Hengstenberg and Umbreit suppose that the predicate אֲמֻצִּים,
strong, in ver. 3 refers to all the horses in the four chariots,
and that by the "strong" horses of ver. 7 we are to understand the "red" horses of the first chariot. But if the horses
of all the chariots were strong, the red alone cannot be so
called, since the article not only stands before אֲמֻצִּים in ver. 7,
but also before the three other colours, and indicates nothing
more than that the colours have been mentioned before. Moreover, it is grammatically impossible that אֲמֻצִּים in ver. 3 should
refer to all the four teams; as "we must in that case have had

אֲמֻצִּים כֻּלָּם" (Koehler). Others (*e.g.* Abulw., Kimchi, Calvin, and Koehler) have attempted to prove that אֲמֻצִּים may have the sense of אֲדֻמִּים; regarding אָמֹץ as a softened form of חָמֹץ, and explaining the latter, after Isa. lxiii. 1, as signifying bright red. But apart from the fact that it is impossible to see why so unusual a word should have been chosen in the place of the intelligible word *'ǎdummīm* in the account of the destination of the red team in ver. 7, unless אֲמֻצִּים were merely a copyist's error for *'ǎdummīm,* there are no satisfactory grounds for identifying אָמֹץ with חָמֹץ, since it is impossible to adduce any well-established examples of the change of ח into א in Hebrew. The assertion of Koehler, that the Chaldee verb אֲלַם, *robustus fuit,* is חָלַם in Hebrew in Job xxxix. 4, is incorrect; for we find חָלַם in the sense of to be healthy and strong in the Syriac and Talmudic as well, and the Chaldaic אֲלַם is a softened form of עָלַם, and not of חָלַם. The fact that in 1 Chron. viii. 35 we have the name תַּאְרֵעַ in the place of תַּחְרֵעַ in 1 Chron. ix. 41, being the only instance of the interchange of א and ח in Hebrew, is not sufficient of itself to sustain the alteration, amidst the great mass of various readings in the genealogies of the Chronicles. Moreover, *châmūts,* from *châmēts,* to be sharp, does not mean red (= *'ǎdōm*), but a glaring colour, like the Greek ὀξύς; and even in Isa. lxiii. 1 it has simply this meaning, *i.e.* merely "denotes the unusual redness of the dress, which does not look like the purple of a king's talar, or the scarlet of a chlamys" (Delitzsch); or, speaking more correctly, it merely denotes the glaring colour which the dress has acquired through being sprinkled over with red spots, arising either from the dark juice of the grape or from blood. All that remains therefore is to acknowledge, in accordance with the words of the text, that in the interpretation of the vision the departure of the team with the red horses is omitted, and the team with speckled powerful horses divided into two teams —one with speckled horses, and the other with black. We cannot find any support in this for the interpretation of the four chariots as denoting the four imperial monarchies of Daniel, since neither the fact that there are four chariots nor the colour of the teams furnishes any tenable ground for this. And it is precluded by the angel's comparison of the four chariots to the four winds, which point to four quarters of the

globe, as in Jer. xlix. 36 and Dan. vii. 2, but not to four
empires rising one after another, one of which always took
the place of the other, so that they embraced the same lands,
and were merely distinguished from one another by the fact
that each in succession spread over a wider surface than its
predecessor. The colour of the horses also does not favour,
but rather opposes, any reference to the four great empires.
Leaving out of sight the arguments already adduced at ch.
i. 8 against this interpretation, Kliefoth himself admits that,
so far as the horses and their colour are concerned, there is a
thorough contrast between this vision and the first one (ch.
i. 7–17),—namely, that in the first vision the colour assigned
to the horses corresponds to the kingdoms of the world to
which they are sent, whereas in the vision before us they have
the colour of the kingdoms from which they set out to convey
the judgment to the others ; and he endeavours to explain this
distinction, by saying that in the first vision the riders procure
information from the different kingdoms of the world as to
their actual condition, whereas in the vision before us the
chariots have to convey the judgment to the kingdoms of the
world. But this distinction furnishes no tenable ground for
interpreting the colour of the horses in the one case in accordance with the object of their mission, and in the other case in
accordance with their origin or starting-point. If the intention
was to set forth the stamp of the kingdoms in the colours, they
would correspond in both visions to the kingdoms upon or in
which the riders and the chariots had to perform their mission.
If, on the other hand, the colour is regulated by the nature
and object of the vision, so that these are indicated by it, it
cannot exhibit the character of the great empires.

If we look still further at the statement of the angel as to
the destination of the chariots, the two attempts made by Hofmann and Kliefoth to combine the colours of the horses with
the empires, show most distinctly the untenable character of
this view. According to both these expositors, the angel says
nothing about the chariot with the red horses, because the
Babylonian empire had accomplished its mission to destroy the
Assyrian empire. But the Perso-Median empire had also
accomplished its mission to destroy the Babylonian, and therefore the team with the black horses should also have been left

unnoticed in the explanation. On the other hand, Kliefoth asserts, and appeals to the participle יֹצְאִים in ver. 6 in support of his assertion, that the chariot with the horses of the imperial monarchy of Medo-Persia goes to the north country, viz. Mesopotamia, the seat of Babel, to convey the judgment of God thither ; that the judgment was at that very time in process of execution, and the chariot was going in the prophet's own day. But although the revolt of Babylon in the time of Darius, and its result, furnish an apparent proof that the power of the Babylonian empire was not yet completely destroyed in Zechariah's time, this intimation cannot lie in the participle as expressing what is actually in process, for the simple reason that in that case the perfects יָצְאוּ which follow would necessarily affirm what had already taken place; and consequently not only would the white horses, which went out behind the black, *i.e.* the horses of the imperial monarchy of Macedonia, have executed the judgment upon the Persian empire, but the speckled horses would have accomplished their mission also, since the same יָצְאוּ is affirmed of both. The interchange of the participle with the perfect does not point to any difference in the time at which the events occur, but simply expresses a distinction in the idea. In the clause with יֹצְאִים the mission of the chariot is expressed through the medium of the participle, according to its idea. The expression " the black horses are going out" is equivalent to, " they are appointed to go out;" whereas in the following clauses with יָצְאוּ the going out is expressed in the form of a fact, for which we should use the present.

A still greater difficulty lies in the way of the interpretation of the colours of the horses as denoting the great empires, from the statement concerning the places to which the teams go forth. Kliefoth finds the reason why not only the black horses (of the Medo-Persian monarchy), but also the white horses (of the Græco-Macedonian), go forth to the north country (Mesopotamia), but the latter after the former, in the fact that not only the Babylonian empire had its seat there, but the Medo-Persian empire also. But how does the going forth of the speckled horses into the south country (Egypt) agree with this ? If the fourth chariot answered to the fourth empire in Daniel, *i.e.* to the Roman empire, since this empire executed the judgment upon the Græco-Macedonian monarchy, this

chariot must of necessity have gone forth to the seat of that
monarchy. But that was not Egypt, the south country, but
Central Asia or Babylon, where Alexander died in the midst
of his endeavours to give a firm foundation to his monarchy.
In order to explain the going out of the (fourth) chariot with
the speckled horses into the south country, Hofmann inserts
between the Græco-Macedonian monarchy and the Roman the
empire of Antiochus Epiphanes as a small intermediate empire,
which is indicated by the speckled horses, and thereby brings
Zechariah into contradiction not only with Daniel's description
of the empires, but also with the historical circumstances, according to which, as Kliefoth has already observed, "Antiochus
Epiphanes and his power had not the importance of an imperial
monarchy, but were merely an offshoot of another imperial
monarchy, namely the Græco-Macedonian."[1] Kliefoth's attempt
to remove this difficulty is also a failure. Understanding by
the spotted strong horses the Roman empire, he explains the
separation of the spotted from the powerful horses in the
angel's interpretation from the peculiar character of the imperial monarchy of Rome,—namely, that it will first of all appear
as an actual and united empire, but will then break up into ten
kingdoms, i.e. into a plurality of kingdoms embracing the whole

---

[1] Kliefoth (Sach. p. 90) adds, by way of still further argument in
support of the above: "The way in which Antiochus Epiphanes is introduced in Dan. viii. is in perfect accordance with these historical circumstances. The third monarchy, the Græco-Macedonian, represented as a
he-goat, destroys the Medo-Persian empire; but its first great horn, Alexander, breaks off in the midst of its victorious career: four horns or
kingdoms grow out of the Græco-Macedonian, and one of these offshoots
of the Macedonian empire is Antiochus Epiphanes, the 'little horn,' the
bold and artful king." But Zechariah would no more agree with this
description in Daniel than with the historical fulfilment, if he had intended
the speckled horses to represent Antiochus Epiphanes. For whereas, like
Daniel, he enumerates four imperial monarchies, he makes the spotted
horses appear not with the third chariot, but with the fourth, and expressly
combines the spotted horses with the powerful ones, which, even according
to Hofmann, were intended to indicate the Romans, and therefore unquestionably connects the spotted horses with the Roman empire. If, then, he
wished the spotted horses to be understood as referring to Antiochus
Epiphanes, he would represent Antiochus Epiphanes not as an offshoot of
the third or Græco-Macedonian monarchy, but as the first member of the
fourth or Roman, in direct contradiction to the book of Daniel and to the
historical order of events.

earth, and finally pass over into the kingdom of Antichrist. Accordingly, the spotted horses go out first of all, and carry the spirit of wrath to the south country, Egypt, which comes into consideration as the kingdom of the Ptolemies, and as that most vigorous offshoot of the Græco-Macedonian monarchy, which survived Antiochus Epiphanes himself. The powerful horses harnessed to the same chariot as the Roman horses go out after this, and wander over the whole earth. They are the divided kingdoms of Daniel springing out of the Roman empire, which are called the powerful ones, not only because they go over the whole earth, but also because Antichrist with his kingdom springs out of them, to convey the judgments of God over the whole earth. But however skilful this interpretation is, it founders on the fact, that it fails to explain the going forth of the speckled horses into the land of the south in a manner corresponding to the object of the vision and the historical circumstances. If the vision represented the judgment, which falls upon the empires in such a manner that the one kingdom destroys or breaks up the other, the speckled horses, which are intended to represent the actual and united Roman empire, would of necessity have gone out not merely into the south country, but into the north country also, because the Roman empire conquered and destroyed not only the one offshoot of the Græco-Macedonian empire, but all the kingdoms that sprang out of that empire. Kliefoth has given no reason for the exclusive reference to the southern branch of this imperial monarchy, nor can any reason be found. The kingdom of the Ptolemies neither broke up the other kingdoms that sprang out of the monarchy of Alexander, nor received them into itself, so that it could be mentioned as *pars pro toto*, and it had no such importance in relation to the holy land and nation as that it could be referred to on that account. If the angel had simply wished to mention a vigorous offshoot of the Græco-Macedonian empire instead of mentioning the whole, he would certainly have fixed his eye upon the kingdom of the Seleucidæ, which developed itself in Antiochus Epiphanes into a type of Antichrist, and have let the speckled horses also go to the north, *i.e.* to Syria. This could have been explained by referring to Daniel; but not their going forth to the south country from the fact that the south country is mentioned in Dan. xi. 5, as Kliefoth supposes, inasmuch as in this prophecy of Daniel not only the king of the south, but the king of the north is also mentioned, and that long-continued conflict between the two described, which inflicted such grievous injury upon the holy land.

To obtain a simple explanation of the vision, we must consider, above all things, that in all these visions the interpretations of the angel do not furnish a complete explanation of all the separate details of the vision, but simply hints and expositions of certain leading features, from which the meaning of the whole may be gathered. This is the case here. All the commentators have noticed the fact, that the statement in ver. 8 concerning the horses going forth into the north country, viz. that they carry the Spirit of Jehovah thither, also applies to the rest of the teams—namely, that they also carry the Spirit of Jehovah to the place to which they go forth. It is also admitted that the angel confines himself to interpreting single features by individualizing. This is the case here with regard to the two lands to which the chariots go forth. The land of the north, *i.e.* the territory covered by the lands of the Euphrates and Tigris, and the land of the south, *i.e.* Egypt, are mentioned as the two principal seats of the power of the world in its hostility to Israel: Egypt on the one hand, and Asshur-Babel on the other, which were the principal foes of the people of God, not only before the captivity, but also afterwards, in the conflicts between Syria and Egypt for the possession of Palestine (Dan. xi.). If we observe this combination, the hypothesis that our vision depicts the fate of the four imperial monarchies, is deprived of all support. Two chariots go into the north country, which is one representative of the heathen world-power: viz. first of all the black horses, to carry famine thither, as one of the great plagues of God with which the ungodly are punished: a plague which is felt all the more painfully, in proportion to the luxury and excess in which men have previously lived. Then follow the white horses, indicating that the judgment will lead to complete victory over the power of the world. Into the south country, *i.e.* to Egypt, the other representative of the heathen world-power, goes the chariot with the speckled horses, to carry the manifold judgment of death by sword, famine, and pestilence, which is indicated by this colour. After what has been said concerning

the team that went forth into the north country, it follows as
a matter of course that this judgment will also execute the
will of the Lord, so that it is quite sufficient for a chariot to
be mentioned. On the other hand, it was evidently important
to guard against the opinion that the judgment would only
affect the two countries or kingdoms that are specially mentioned, and to give distinct prominence to the fact that they
are only representatives of the heathen world, and that what
is here announced applies to the whole world that is at enmity
against God. This is done through the explanation in ver. 7
concerning the going out of a fourth team, to pass through
the whole earth. This mission is not received by the red
horses, but by the powerful ones, as the speckled horses are
also called in the vision, to indicate that the manifold judgments indicated by the speckled horses will pass over the earth
in all their force. The going forth of the red horses is not
mentioned, simply because, according to the analogy of what
has been said concerning the other teams, there could be no
doubt about it, as the blood-red colour pointed clearly enough
to the shedding of blood. The object of the going forth of
the chariots is to let down the Spirit of Jehovah upon the
land in question. הֵנִיחַ רוּחַ יי׳, to cause the Spirit of Jehovah
to rest, *i.e.* to let it down, is not identical with הֵנִיחַ חֵמָתוֹ, to let
out His wrath, in Ezek. v. 13, xvi. 42 ; for *rūăch* is not equivalent to *chēmâh*, wrath or fury ; but the Spirit of Jehovah is
rūăch mishpât (Isa. iv. 4), a spirit of judgment, which not only
destroys what is ungodly, but also quickens and invigorates
what is related to God. The vision does not set forth the
destruction of the world-power, which is at enmity against God,
but simply the judgment by which God purifies the sinful
world, exterminates all that is ungodly, and renews it by His
Spirit. It is also to be observed, that vers. 6 and 7 are a continuation of the address of the angel, and not an explanation
given by the prophet of what has been said by the angel in
ver. 5. The construction in ver. 6a is anakolouthic, the horses
being made the subject in יֹצְאִים, instead of the chariot with
black horses, because the significance of the chariots lay in
the horses. The object to וַיֹּאמֶר in ver. 7b is "the Lord of the
whole earth" in ver. 5, who causes the chariots to go forth ;
whereas in וַיַּזְעֵק אֹתִי in ver. 8 it is the interpreting angel again.

By יָּיָעַק, lit. he cried to him, *i.e.* called out to him with a loud voice, the contents of the exclamation are held up as important to the interpretation of the whole.

THE CROWN UPON JOSHUA'S HEAD.—CHAP. VI. 9–15.

The series of visions closes with a symbolical transaction, which is closely connected with the substance of the night-visions, and sets before the eye the figure of the mediator of salvation, who, as crowned high priest, or as priestly king, is to build the kingdom of God, and raise it into a victorious power over all the kingdoms of this world, for the purpose of comforting and strengthening the congregation. The transaction is the following: Ver. 9. *"And the word of Jehovah came to me thus:* Ver. 10. *Take of the people of the captivity, of Cheldai, of Tobijah, and of Jedahyah, and go thou the same day, go into the house of Josiah the son of Zephaniah, whither they have come from Babel;* Ver. 11. *And take silver and gold, and make crowns, and set them upon the head of Joshua the son of Jozadak the high priest."* By the introduction, "The word of the Lord came to me," the following transaction is introduced as a procedure of symbolical importance. It is evident from vers. 10 and 11 that messengers had come to Jerusalem from the Israelites who had been left behind in Babel, to offer presents of silver and gold, probably for supporting the erection of the temple, and had gone to the house of Josiah the son of Zephaniah. The prophet is to go to them, and to take silver and gold from them, to have a crown made for Joshua the high priest. The construction in vers. 10 and 11 is somewhat broad and dragging. The object is wanting to the inf. absol. לָקוֹחַ, which is used instead of the imperative; and the sentence which has been begun is interrupted by וּבָאתָ וגו׳, so that the verb which stands at the head is resumed in the וְלָקַחְתָּ of ver. 11, and the sentence finished by the introduction of the object. This view is the simplest one. For it is still more impracticable to take לָקוֹחַ in an absolute sense, and either supply the object from the context, or force it out by alterations of the text (Hitzig). If, for example, we were to supply as the object, "that which they are bringing," this meaning would result: "accept what they are bringing, do not refuse it," without there being any ground for the assumption that there had been any unwillingness to accept the presents.   The alteration of מֶחֶלְדָּי into מַחֲמַדִּי, "my jewels," is destitute of any critical support, and מֶחֶלְדָּי is defended against critical caprice by the לְחֵלֶם in ver. 14.   Nor can מֵאֵת הַגּוֹלָה be taken as the object to לָקוֹחַ, "take (some) from the emigration," because this thought requires מִן, and is irreconcilable with מֵאֵת, "from with."   *Haggōlâh*, lit. the wandering into exile, then those who belong to the wandering, or to the exiled, not merely those who are still in exile, but very frequently also those who have returned from exile.   This is the meaning here, as in Ezra iv. 1, vi. 19, etc.   *Mēcheldai* is an abbreviation for מֵאֵת חֶלְדָּי. *Cheldai*, *Tobiyah*, and *Yedahyah*, were the persons who had come from Babylon to bring the present.   This is implied in the words אֲשֶׁר בָּאוּ מב׳, whither they have come from Babel. אֲשֶׁר is an *accus. loci*, pointing back to בֵּית.   We are not warranted in interpreting the names of these men symbolically or typically, either by the circumstance that the names have an appellative meaning, like all proper names in Hebrew, or by the fact that *Cheldai* is written *Chēlem* in ver. 14, and that instead of *Josiah* we have there apparently *chēn*.   For *chēn* is not a proper name (see at ver. 14), and *chēlem, i.e.* strength, is not materially different from *Cheldai, i.e.* the enduring one ; so that it is only a variation of the name, such as we often meet with.   The definition " on that day" can only point back to the day mentioned in ch. i. 7, on which Zechariah saw the night-visions, so that it defines the chronological connection between this symbolical transaction and those night-visions. For, with the explanation given by C. B. Michaelis, " *die isto quo scil. facere debes quæ nunc mando,*" the definition of the time is unmeaning.   If God had defined the day more precisely to the prophet in the vision, the prophet would have recorded it.   Zechariah is to have given to him as much of the silver and gold which they have brought with them as is required to make ʿătârōth.   The plural ʿătârōth does indeed apparently point to at least two crowns, say a silver and a golden one, as C. B. Michaelis and Hitzig suppose.   But what follows cannot be made to harmonize with this.   The prophet is to put the ʿătârōth upon Joshua's head.   But you do not put two or more crowns upon the head of one man ; and the indifference

with which Ewald, Hitzig, and Bunsen interpolate the words
וּבְרֹאשׁ זְרֻבָּבֶל after בְּרֹאשׁ, without the smallest critical authority,
is condemned by the fact that in what follows only *one* wearer
of a crown is spoken of, and in ver. 13, according to the correct
interpretation, there is no " sharp distinction made between the
priest and the Messiah." The plural *ʿătârōth* denotes here one
single splendid crown, consisting of several gold and silver
twists wound together, or rising one above another, as in Job
xxxi. 36, and just as in Rev. xix. 12 (ἐπὶ τὴν κεφαλὴν αὐτοῦ
διαδήματα πολλά) Christ is said to wear, not many separate
diadems, but a crown consisting of several diadems twisted
together, as the insignia of His regal dignity.

The meaning of this is explained in vers. 12-15. Ver. 12.
" *And speak to him, saying, Thus speaketh Jehovah of hosts,
saying, Behold a man, His name is Tsemach (Sprout), and from
His place will He sprout up, and build the temple of Jehovah.
Ver. 13. And He will build the temple of Jehovah, and He will
carry loftiness, and will sit and rule upon His throne, and will
be a priest upon His throne, and the counsel of peace will be
between them both. Ver. 14. And the crown will be to Chelem,
and to Tobijah, and to Jedahjah, and the favour of the son of
Zephaniah, for a memorial in the temple of Jehovah. Ver. 15.
And they that are far off will come and build at the temple of
Jehovah; then will ye know that Jehovah of hosts hath sent me
to you; and it will come to pass, if ye hearken to the voice of
Jehovah your God.*' Two things are stated in these verses
concerning the crown : (1) In vers. 12 and 13 the meaning is
explained of the setting of the crown upon the head of Joshua
the high priest; and (2) in vers. 14, 15, an explanation is
given of the circumstance, that the crown had been made of
silver and gold presented by men of the captivity. The
crowning of Joshua the high priest with a royal crown, which
did not properly belong to the high priest as such, as his head-
dress is neither called a crown (*ʿătârâh*) nor formed part of
the insignia of royal dignity and glory, had a typical significance. It pointed to a man who would sit upon his throne as
both ruler and priest, that is to say, would combine both royalty
and priesthood in his own person and rank. The expression
" Speak thou to him" shows that the words of Jehovah are
addressed to Joshua, and to him alone (אֵלָיו is singular), and

therefore that Zerubbabel must not be interpolated into ver. 11 along with Joshua. The man whom Joshua is to represent or typify, by having a crown placed upon his head, is designated as the Messiah, by the name *Tsemach* (see at ch. iii. 8) ; and this name is explained by the expression מִתַּחְתָּיו יִצְמָח. These words must not be taken impersonally, in the sense of " under him will it sprout" (LXX., Luth., Calov., Hitzig, Maurer, and others) ; for this thought cannot be justified from the usage of the language, to say nothing of its being quite remote from the context, since we have מִתַּחְתָּיו, and not תַּחְתָּיו (under him) ; and moreover, the change of subject in יִצְמָח and וּבָנָה would be intolerably harsh. In addition to this, according to Jer. xxxiii. 15, the Messiah is called *Tsemach*, because Jehovah causes a righteous growth to spring up to David, so that *Tsemach* is the sprouting one, and not he who makes others or something else to sprout. מִתַּחְתָּיו, " from under himself," is equivalent to " from his place" (Ex. x. 23), *i.e.* from his soil ; and is correctly explained by Alting in Hengstenberg thus : " both as to his nation and as to his country, of the house of David, Judah, and Abraham, to whom the promises were made." It also contains an allusion to the fact that He will grow from below upwards, from lowliness to eminence. This Sprout will build the temple of the Lord. That these words do not refer to the building of the earthly temple of stone and wood, as Ros. and Hitzig with the Rabbins suppose, is so obvious, that even Koehler has given up this view here, and understands the words, as Hengstenberg, Tholuck, and others do, as relating to the spiritual temple, of which the tabernacle and the temples of both Solomon and Zerubbabel were only symbols, the temple which is the church of God itself (Hos. viii. 1 ; 1 Pet. ii. 5 ; Heb. iii. 6 ; and Eph. ii. 21, 22). Zechariah not only speaks of this temple here, but also in ch. iv. 9, as Haggai had done before him, in Hag. ii. 6–9, which puts the correctness of our explanation of these passages beyond the reach of doubt. The repetition of this statement in ver. 13*a* is not useless, but serves, as the emphatic וְהוּא before this and the following sentence shows, to bring the work of the *Tsemach* into connection with the place He will occupy, in other words, to show the glory of the temple to be built. The two clauses are to be linked together thus : " He who will build the temple, the same will carry eminence." There is no " antithesis to the building of the temple by Joshua and Zerubbabel" (Koehler) in וְהוּא; but this is quite as foreign to the context as another view of the same commentator, viz. that ver. 13 interrupts the explanation of what the shoot is to be. הוֹד, eminence, is the true word for regal majesty (cf. Jer. xxii. 18 ; 1 Chron. xxix. 25 ; Dan. xi. 21). In this majesty He will sit upon His throne and rule, also using His regal dignity and power for the good of His people, and will be a Priest upon His throne, *i.e.* will be at once both Priest and King upon the throne which He assumes. The rendering, " And there will be a priest upon His throne" (Ewald and Hitzig), is precluded by the simple structure of the sentences, and still more by the strangeness of the thought which it expresses ; for the calling of a priest in relation to God and the people is not to sit upon a throne, but to stand before Jehovah (cf. Judg. xx. 28 ; Deut. xvii. 12). Even the closing words of this verse, " And a counsel of peace will be between them both," do not compel us to introduce a priest sitting upon the throne into the text by the side of the *Tsemach* ruling upon His throne. שְׁנֵיהֶם cannot be taken as a neuter in the sense of " between the regal dignity of the Messiah and His priesthood" (Capp., Ros.), and does not even refer to the *Tsemach* and *Jehovah,* but to the *Mōshēl* and *Kōhēn,* who sit upon the throne, united in one person, in the *Tsemach.* Between these two there will be *'ătsath shâlōm.* This does not merely mean, " the most perfect harmony will exist" (Hofmann, Umbreit), for that is a matter of course, and does not exhaust the meaning of the words. *'Atsath shâlōm,* counsel of peace, is not merely peaceful, harmonious consultation, but consultation which has peace for its object ; and the thought is the following : The Messiah, who unites in Himself royalty and priesthood, will counsel and promote the peace of His people.

This is the typical meaning of the crowning of the high priest Joshua. But another feature is added to this. The crown, which has been placed upon the head of Joshua, to designate him as the type of the Messiah, is to be kept in the temple of the Lord after the performance of this act, as a memorial for those who bring the silver and gold from the exiles in Babel, and לְחֵן בֶּן־צ׳, *i.e.* for the favour or grace of the son of Zephaniah. *Chēn* is not a proper name, or another name for Josiah, but an appellative in the sense of favour, or a favourable disposition, and refers to the favour which the son of Zephaniah has shown to the emigrants who have come from Babylon, by receiving them hospitably into his house. For a memorial of these men, the crown is to be kept in the temple of Jehovah. The object of this is not merely " to guard it against profanation, and perpetuate the remembrance of the givers" (Kliefoth) ; but this action has also a symbolical and prophetic meaning, which is given in ver. 15 in the words, " Strangers will come and build at the temple of the Lord." Those who have come from the far distant Babylon are types of the distant nations who will help to build the temple of the Lord with their possessions and treasures. This symbolical proceeding therefore furnishes a confirmation of the promise in Hag. ii. 7, that the Lord will fill His temple with the treasures of all nations. By the realization of what is indicated in this symbolical proceeding, Israel will perceive that the speaker has been sent to them by the Lord of hosts ; that is to say, not that Zechariah has spoken by the command of God, but that the Lord has sent the angel of Jehovah. For although in what precedes, only the prophet, and not the angel of Jehovah, has appeared as acting and speaking, we must not change the " sending" into " speaking" here, or take the formula וִידַעְתֶּם כִּי וגו' in any other sense here than in ch. ii. 13, 15, and iv. 9. We must therefore assume, that just as the words of the prophet pass imperceptibly into words of Jehovah, so here they pass into the words of the angel of Jehovah, who says concerning himself that Jehovah has sent him. The words conclude with the earnest admonition to the hearers, that they are only to become partakers of the predicted good when they hearken to the voice of their God. The sentence commencing with וְהָיָה does not contain any *aposiopesis ;* there is no valid ground for such an assumption as this in the simple announcement, which shows no trace of excitement ; but *v^ehâyâh* may be connected with the preceding thought, " ye will know," etc., and affirms that they will only discern that the angel of Jehovah has been sent to them when they pay attention to the voice of their God. Now, although the recognition of the sending of the angel of the Lord involves participation in the Messianic salvation, the fact that this recognition is made to

depend upon their giving heed to the word of God, by no means
implies that the coming of the Messiah, or the participation of
the Gentiles in His kingdom, will be bound up with the fidelity
of the covenant nation, as Hengstenberg supposes; but the
words simply declare that Israel will not come to the knowledge
of the Messiah or to His salvation, unless it hearkens to the
voice of the Lord.   Whoever intentionally closes his eyes, will
be unable to see the salvation of God.

The question whether the prophet really carried out the
symbolical action enjoined upon him in vers. 10 sqq., externally or not, can neither be answered in the affirmative nor
with a decided negative.   The statement in ver. 11, that the
prophet, who was hardly a goldsmith, was to make the crown,
is no more a proof that it was not actually done, than the
talmudic notice in *Middoth* iii., concerning the place where
the crown was hung up in the temple, is a proof that it
was.   For עָשִׂיתָ in ver. 11 may also express causing to be
made; and the talmudic notice referred to does not affirm
that this crown was kept in the temple, but simply states that
in the porch of the temple there were beams stretching from
one wall to the other, and that golden chains were fastened to
them, upon which the priestly candidates climbed up and saw
crowns; and the verse before us is then quoted, with the
formula שׁנאמר as a confirmation of this.

II. THE ANSWER TO THE QUESTION CONCERNING THE
FASTING.—CHAP. VII. AND VIII.

In reply to a question addressed to the priests and prophets
in Jerusalem by the messengers of Bethel, whether the day on
which Jerusalem and the temple were reduced to ashes by the
Chaldæans is still to be kept as a day of mourning and fasting
(ch. vii. 1–3), the Lord declares to the people through Zechariah,
that He does not look upon fasting as a service well-pleasing
to Him, but that He desires obedience to His word (vers. 4–7),
and that He has only been obliged to scatter Israel among the
nations on account of its obstinate resistance to the commandments of righteousness, love, and truth made known to them

through the prophets (vers. 8–14), but that now He will turn again to Zion and Jerusalem with great warmth of love, and will bless His people with abundant blessings if they will only perform truth, just judgment, faithfulness, and love one towards another (ch. viii. 1–17). Then will He make the previous fast-days into days of joy and delight to them, and so glorify Himself upon Jerusalem, that many and powerful nations will come to seek and worship the Lord of hosts there (ch. viii. 18–23).

THE FAST-DAYS OF ISRAEL, AND OBEDIENCE TO THE WORD OF GOD.—CHAP. VII.

Vers. 1–3 describe the occasion for this instructive and consolatory " word of God," which was addressed to Zechariah in the fourth year of Darius, *i.e.* two years after the building of the temple was resumed, and two years before its completion, and therefore at a time when the building must have been far advanced, and the temple itself was possibly already finished in the rough. Ver. 1. "*It came to pass in the fourth year of king Darius, that the word of Jehovah came to Zechariah, on the fourth (day) of the ninth month, in Kislev.*" In this definition of the time we are surprised first of all at the circumstance, that, according to the Masoretic accentuation, and the division of the verses, the statement of the time is torn into two halves, and the notice of the year is placed after וַיְהִי, whilst that of the month does not follow till after הָיָה דְבַר יי; and secondly, at the fact that the introduction of the occurrence which led to this word of God is appended with the imperfect *c. Vav rel.* (*vayyishlach*), which would then stand in the sense of the pluperfect in opposition to the rule. On these grounds we must give up the Masoretic division of the verses, and connect the notice of the month and day in ver. 1*b* with ver. 2, so that ver. 1 contains merely the general statement that in the fourth year of king Darius the word of the Lord came to Zechariah. What follows will then be appended thus : On the fourth day of the ninth month, in Kislev, Bethel sent, etc. Thus the more precise definition of the time is only given in connection with the following occurrence, because it was self-evident that the word of God which was addressed to the prophet in consequence of that event, could not have been addressed to him before it occurred. The rendering of the words in ver. 2a is also a disputed point. We adopt the following : Ver. 2. *" Then Bethel sent Sharezer and Regem-melech, and his people, to entreat the face of Jehovah,* (ver. 3) *to speak to the priests who were at the house of Jehovah of hosts, and to the prophets, thus : Shall I weep, abstaining in the fifth month as I have now done so many years?"* As *Bēth-ēl* may either signify the house of God, or be the name of the town of Bethel, it may be taken either as *accus. loci,* or as the subject of the sentence. Against the first explanation, which is very widely spread, viz. "it sent to the house of God, or to Bethel, Sharezer," etc., or "they sent to the house of God Sharezer," etc., it may be argued not only that the prophet, in order to make himself intelligible, ought either to have written *'el Bēth-'ēl,* or to have placed *Bēth-'ēl* after the object, but also that *bēth-'ēl* cannot be shown to have been ever applied to the temple of Jehovah, and that it would have been altogether out of place to speak of sending to Bethel, because Jehovah could not be prayed to in Bethel after the captivity. We must therefore take *bēth-'ēl* as the subject, and understand it as denoting the population of Bethel, and not as a name given to the church of the Lord, since there are no conclusive passages to support any such use, as *bēth Yᵉhōvâh* only is used for the church of God (see at Hos. viii. 1), and here there could be no inducement to employ so unusual an epithet to denote the nation. A considerable number of the earlier inhabitants of Bethel had already returned with Zerubbabel, according to Ezra ii. 28 and Neh. vii. 32 ; and, according to Neh. xi. 31, the little town appears to have been soon rebuilt. The inhabitants of this city sent an embassy to Jerusalem, namely Sharezer and Rechem-Melech, and his men. The omission of the *nota accus.* אֵת has indeed been adduced as an objection to this interpretation of the names as the object, and the names have been therefore taken as the subject, and regarded as in apposition to *Bēth-ēl :* "Bethel, namely Sharezer and Rechem, etc., sent ;" that is to say, two men are mentioned in connection with Bethel, who are supposed to have acted as leaders of the embassy. But there is something so harsh and inflexible in the assumption of such an apposition as this, that in spite of the omission of the אֵת we prefer to regard the names as accusatives. The name *Sharezer* is evidently Assyrian (cf. Isa. xxxvii

38; Jer. xxxix. 3, 13), so that the man was probably born in Babylonia. The object of sending these men is given first of all in general terms : viz. 'י אֶת־פְּנֵי לְחַלּוֹת, *lit.* to stroke the face of Jehovah,—an anthropomorphic expression for affectionate entreaty (see at Ps. cxix. 58), and then defined more precisely in ver. 3, where it is stated that they were to inquire of the priests and prophets, *i.e.* through their mediation, to entreat an answer from the Lord, whether the mourning and fasting were to be still kept up in the fifth month. Through the clause אֲשֶׁר לְבֵית יי the priests are described as belonging to the house of Jehovah, though not in the sense supposed by Kliefoth, namely, "because they were appointed to serve in His house along with the Levites, in the place of the first-born, who were the possession of Jehovah" (Num. iii. 41; Deut. x. 8, 9). There is no such allusion here ; but the meaning is simply, "as the persons in the temple, who by virtue of their mediatorial service were able to obtain an answer from Jehovah to a question addressed to Him in prayer." The connection with the prophets points to this. The question הַאֶבְכֶּה is defined by the inf. absol. הִנָּזֵר, as consisting in weeping or lamentation connected with abstinence from food and drink, *i.e.* with fasting. On this use of the *inf. abs.*, see Ewald, § 280, *a;* הִנָּזֵר, to abstain (in this connection from meat and drink), is synonymous with צוּם in ver. 5. זֶה כַּמֶּה שָׁנִים : "these how many years," for which we should say, "so many years." *Kammeh* suggests the idea of an incalculably long duration. זֶה, in this and other similar combinations with numerical *data*, has acquired the force of an adverb : now, already (cf. ch. i. 12, and Ewald, § 302, *b*). The subject to אֶבְכֶּה is the population of Bethel, by which the men had been delegated. The question, however, had reference to a subject in which the whole community was interested, and hence the answer from God is addressed to all the people (ver. 5). So far as the circumstances themselves are concerned, we can see from ver. 5 and ch. viii. 19, that during the captivity the Israelites had adopted the custom of commemorating the leading incidents in the Chaldæan catastrophe by keeping fast-days in the fifth, seventh, fourth, and tenth months. In the fifth month (*Ab*), on the tenth day, because, according to Jer. lii. 12, 13, that was the day on which the temple and the city of Jerusalem were destroyed by fire in the nineteenth year of Nebuchadnezzar, though the seventh day of that month is the date given in 2 Kings xxv. 8, 9 (see the comm. *in loc.*). In the seventh month, according to Jewish tradition, they fasted on the third day, on account of the murder of the governor Gedaliah, and the Judæans who had been left in the land (2 Kings xxv. 25, 26; Jer. xli. 1 sqq.). In the fourth month (*Tammuz*) they fasted on the ninth day, on account of the conquest of Jerusalem by Nebuchadnezzar in the eleventh year of Zedekiah (Jer. xxxix. 2, lii. 6, 7). And lastly, in the tenth month, a fast was kept on the tenth day on account of the commencement of the siege of Jerusalem by Nebuchadnezzar on that day, in the ninth year of Zedekiah (2 Kings xxv. 1 and Jer. xxxix. 1).[1] The question put by the delegates referred simply to the fasting in the fifth month, in commemoration of the destruction of the temple. And now that the rebuilding of the temple was rapidly approaching completion, it appeared no longer in character to continue to keep this day, especially as the prophets had proclaimed on the part of God, that the restoration of the temple would be a sign that Jehovah had once more restored His favour to the remnant of His people. If this fast-day were given up, the others would probably be also relinquished. The question actually involved the prayer that the Lord would continue permanently to bestow upon His

---

[1] The later Jews kept the 9th Ab as the day when both the first and second temples were destroyed by fire; and in *Mishna Taanit* iv. 6, five disasters are enumerated, which had fallen upon Israel on that day : viz. (1) the determination of God not to suffer the fathers to enter the promised land ; (2 and 3) the destruction of the first and second temples ; (4) the conquest of the city of Bether in the time of *Bar-Cochba* ; (5) the destruction of the holy city, which Rashi explains from Mic. iii. 12 and Jer. xxvi. 18, but which others refer to the fact that *Turnus Rufus* (either *Turannius Rufus* or *T. Annius Rufus*: cf. Schöttgen, *Horæ hebr. et talm.* ii. 953 sqq., and Jost, *Gesch. des Judenthums*, ii. 77) ploughed over the foundation of the temple. Also, on the seventeenth of the fourth month (*Tammuz*), according to *Mishna Taan.* iv. 6, five disasters are said to have befallen Israel : (1) the breaking of the tables of the law (Ex. xxxii.) ; (2) the cessation of the daily sacrifice in the first temple from the want of sacrificial lambs (cf. Jer. lii. 6) ; (3) the breach made in the city walls ; (4) the burning of the law by *Apostemus;* and (5) the setting up of the abomination, *i.e.* of an idol, in the temple (Dan. xi. 31, xii. 13). *Vid.* Lundius, *Codex talm. de jejunio,* Traj. ad Rhen. 1694, p. 55 sqq. ; also in abstract in *Mishna ed. Surenhus.* ii. pp. 382–3

people the favour which He had restored to them, and not only bring to completion the restoration of the holy place, which was already begun, but accomplish generally the glorification of Israel predicted by the earlier prophets. The answer given by the Lord through Zechariah to the people refers to this, since the priests and prophets could give no information in the matter of their own accord.

The answer from the Lord divides itself into two parts, ch. vii. 4–14 and ch. viii. In the first part He explains what it is that He requires of the people, and why He has been obliged to punish them with exile : in the second He promises them the restoration of His favour and the promised salvation. Each of these parts is divisible again into two sections, ch. vii. 4–7 and ch. vii. 8–14, ch. viii. 1–17 and ch. viii. 18–23 ; and each of these sections opens with the formula, " The word of Jehovah (of hosts) came to me (Zechariah), saying."

Vers. 4–7. The first of these four words of God contains an exposure of what might be unwarrantable in the question and its motives, and open to disapproval. Ver. 4. " *And the word of Jehovah of hosts came to me thus,* Ver. 5. *Speak to all the people of the land, and to the priests, saying, When ye fasted and mourned in the fifth and in the seventh (month), and that for seventy years, did ye, when fasting, fast to me ?* Ver. 6. *And when ye eat, and when ye drink, is it not ye who eat, and ye who drink ?* Ver. 7. *Does it not concern the words, which Jehovah has preached through the former prophets, when Jerusalem was inhabited and satisfied, and her towns round about her, and the south country and the low land were inhabited ?* " The thought of vers. 6 and 7 is the following : It is a matter of indifference to God whether the people fast or not. The true fasting, which is well pleasing to God, consists not in a pharisaical abstinence from eating and drinking, but in the fact that men observe the word of God and live thereby, as the prophets before the captivity had already preached to the people. This overthrew the notion that men could acquire the favour of God by fasting, and left it to the people to decide whether they would any longer observe the previous fast-days ; it also showed what God would require of them if they wished to obtain the promised blessings. For the inf. absol. see at Hag. i. 6. The fasting in the seventh month was not the fast on the day of atonement which was prescribed in the law (Lev. xxiii.), but, as has been already observed, the fast in commemoration of the murder of Gedaliah. In the form צַמְתֻּנִי the suffix is not a substitute for the dative (Ges. § 121, 4), but is to be taken as an accusative, expressive of the fact that the fasting related to God (Ewald, § 315, *b*). The suffix is strengthened by אָנִי for the sake of emphasis (Ges. § 121, 3). In ver. 7 the form of the sentence is elliptical. The verb is omitted in the clause הֲלוֹא אֶת־הַדְּבָרִים, but not the subject, say זֶה, which many commentators supply, after the LXX., the Peshito, and the Vulgate ("Are these not the words which Jehovah announced?"), in which case אֶת would have to be taken as *nota nominativi*. The sentence contains an *aposiopesis*, and is to be completed by supplying a verb, either "should ye not do or give heed to the words which," etc.? or "do ye not know the words?" יֹשֶׁבֶת, as in ch. i. 11, in the sense of sitting or dwelling; not in a passive sense, "to be inhabited," although it might be so expressed. שְׁלֵוָה is synonymous with שֹׁקֶטֶת in ch. i. 11. יֹשֵׁב, in the sense indicated at the close of the verse, is construed in the singular masculine, although it refers to a plurality of previous nouns (cf. Ges. § 148, 2). In addition to Jerusalem, the following are mentioned as a periphrasis for the land of Judah: (1) her towns round about; these are the towns belonging to Jerusalem as the capital, towns of the mountains of Judah which were more or less dependent upon her: (2) the two rural districts, which also belonged to the kingdom of Judah, viz. the *negeb*, the south country (which Koehler erroneously identifies with the mountains of Judah; compare Josh. xv. 21 with xv. 48), and the *shᵉphēlâh*, or lowland along the coast of the Mediterranean (see at Josh. xv. 33).

Vers. 8–14. The second word of the Lord recals to the recollection of the people the disobedience of the fathers, and its consequences, viz. the judgment of exile, as a warning example. The introduction of the prophet's name in the heading in ver. 8 does not warrant the strange opinion held by Schmieder and Schlier—namely, that our prophet is here reproducing the words of an earlier Zechariah who lived before the captivity—but is merely to be attributed to a variation in the form of expression. This divine word was as follows:

Ver. 9. "*Thus hath Jehovah of hosts spoken, saying, Execute judgment of truth, and show love and compassion one to another.* Ver. 10. *And widows and orphans, strangers and destitute ones, oppress not; and meditate not in your heart the injury of every brother.* Ver. 11. *But they refused to attend, and offered a rebellious shoulder, and hardened their ears that they might not hear.* Ver. 12. *And they made their heart diamond, that they might not hear the law and the words which Jehovah of hosts sent through His Spirit by means of the former prophet, so that great wrath came from Jehovah of hosts.*" כֹּה אָמַר is to be taken as a preterite here, referring to what Jehovah had caused to be proclaimed to the people before the captivity. The kernel of this announcement consisted in the appeal to the people, to keep the moral precepts of the law, to practise the true love of the neighbour in public life and private intercourse. *Mishpat 'ĕmeth,* judgment of truth (cf. Ezek. xviii. 8), is such an administration of justice as simply fixes the eye upon the real circumstances of any dispute, without any personal considerations whatever, and decides them in accordance with truth. For the fact itself, compare Ex. xxii. 20, 21, xxiii. 6–9 ; Lev. xix. 15–18 ; Deut. x. 18, 19, xxiv. 14 ; Isa. i. 17 ; Jer. vii. 5, 6, xxii. 3 ; Ezek. xviii. 8 ; Hos. xii. 7, etc. רָעַת אִישׁ אָחִיו, the injury of a man who is his brother (as in Gen. ix. 5) ; not "injury one towards another," which would suppose a transposition of the אִישׁ = אִישׁ רָעַת אָחִיו. In vers. 11 and 12 the attitude of the people towards these admonitions of God is described. *Nâthan kâthēph sōrereth:* to give or offer a rebellious shoulder, as in Neh. ix. 29. The figure is borrowed from an ox, which will not allow a yoke to be placed upon its neck (cf. Hos. iv. 16). To make the ears heavy (*hikhbīd*), away from hearing, *i.e.* so that they do not hear (cf. Isa. vi. 10). To make the heart diamond (*shâmīr*), *i.e.* as hard as diamond. A stony heart is a heart not susceptible to impressions (cf. Ezek. xi. 19). The relative אֲשֶׁר before *shâlach* refers to the two nouns named before, viz. *tōrâh* and *dĕbhârīm,* though we need not on that account take *tōrâh* in the general sense of instruction. God also sent the law to the people through the prophets, *i.e.* caused them to preach it and impress it upon their hearts. The consequence of this obduracy of the people was, that "there arose great wrath from Jehovah" (cf. ch. i. 2 ; 2 Kings iii. 27).

This wrath is described in vers 13, 14. Ver. 13. "*It came to pass : as he cried and they did not hear, so will they cry and I shall not hear, said Jehovah of hosts.* Ver. 14. *And I will scatter them with a whirlwind over all nations, who did not know them, and the land is laid waste behind them, so that no one passes to and fro. And thus they made the choice land a desert.*" The form of the address changes in ver. 13. Whereas in the protasis the prophet is still speaking of Jehovah in the third person, in the apodosis he introduces Jehovah as speaking (so will they cry, and I, etc.) and announcing the punishment, which He will inflict upon the rebellious and has already inflicted in their captivity. This address of God is continued in ver. 14 as far as וּמִשָּׁב. The opinion, that the address terminates with לֹא יְדָעוּם, and that וְהָאָרֶץ commences the account of the accomplishment of the purpose to punish, is not so much at variance with the circumstance, that in that case the last two clauses of ver. 14 would say essentially the same thing, as with the fact that וְהָאָרֶץ וגו' cannot, from its very form, be taken as an account of the accomplishment of the divine purpose. The perfect *nâshammâh* in this clause does not preclude our connecting it with the preceding one, but is used to set forth the devastation as a completed fact : the land will be (not become) waste. The infliction of the punishment is expressed in ver. 13 in the form of a divine *talio*. As they have not hearkened to the word of God, so will God, when they call upon Him, namely in distress (cf. Hos. v. 15), also not hear (cf. Jer. xi. 11), but whirl them like a tempest over the nations. The form אֲסָעֲרֵם is the first pers. imperf. *piel* for אֲסָעֲרֵם or אֲסָעֲרֵם, and Aramaic (cf. Ges. § 52, 2, Anm. 2). On the nations whom they do not know, and who will therefore have no pity and compassion upon them, compare Jer. xxii. 28, xvi. 13. מֵעֹבֵר וּמִשָּׁב (cf. ix. 8), that not one goes to and fro in the desolate land; lit. goes away from a place and returns again (cf. Ex. xxxii. 27). In the clause וַיָּשִׂימוּ וגו' the result of the stiff-necked obstinacy of the fathers is briefly stated : They have made the choice land a desert ('*erets chemdâh*, as in Jer. iii. 19 and Ps. cvi. 24), so that they have brought upon the land all the calamity which is now bewailed upon the fast-days.

RENEWAL AND COMPLETION OF THE COVENANT OF GRACE.—
CHAP. VIII.

In this chapter we have the second half of the Lord's
answer to the question concerning the fast-days, which promises
to the people the restitution of the former relation of grace, and
the future glorification of Israel, on the simple condition of their
observing the moral precepts of the law. This double promise
is contained in two words of God, each of which is divided
into a number of separate sayings, containing the separate
details of the salvation bestowed by the formula 'צ יְיָ אָמַר כֹּה
(thus saith Jehovah of hosts): the first into seven (vers. 2, 3,
4–5, 6, 7, and ch. viii. 9–13, 14–17), the second into three
(vers. 19, 20–22, and 23). Jerome observes, with reference
to this : " By the separate words and sentences, in which Israel
is promised not only prosperity, but things almost incredible in
their magnitude, the prophet declares, 'Thus saith the Almighty
God ;' saying, in other words, Do not imagine that the things
which I promise are my own, and so disbelieve me as only a
man ; they are the promises of God which I unfold."

Vers. 1–17. Restoration and completion of the covenant
relation.—Ver. 1. "*And the word of Jehovah of hosts came,
saying,* Ver. 2. *Thus saith Jehovah of hosts, I am jealous for
Zion with great jealousy, and with great fury I am jealous for
her.*" The promise commences with the declaration of the
Lord, that He has resolved to give active expression once more
to the warmth of His love to Zion. The perfects are used
prophetically of that which God had resolved to do, and was
now about to accomplish. For the fact itself, compare ch. i.
14, 15. This warmth of the love of God towards Zion, and
of His wrath towards the nations that were hostile to Zion,
will manifest itself in the facts described in ver. 3 : " *Thus
saith Jehovah, I return to Zion, and shall dwell in the midst of
Jerusalem; and Jerusalem will be called city of truth, and the
mountain of Jehovah of hosts the holy mountain.*" When Jerusalem was given up into the power of its foes, the Lord had
forsaken His dwelling-place in the temple. Ezekiel saw the
glory of the Lord depart from the temple (ch. ix. 3, x. 4, 18,
xi. 22, 23). Now He is about to resume His abode in Jeru-

salem once more. The difference between this promise and
the similar promise in ch. ii. 14–17, is not that in the latter
passage Jehovah's dwelling in the midst of His people is to
be understood in an ideal and absolute sense, whereas here
it simply denotes such a dwelling as had taken place before, as
Koehler supposes. This is not implied in שָׁבְתִּי, nor is it in
harmony with the statement that Jerusalem is to be called a
city of truth, and the temple hill the holy mountain. 'Ir 'ĕmeth
does not mean " city of security," but city of truth or fidelity,
i.e. in which truth and fidelity towards the Lord have their
home. The temple mountain will be called the holy mountain, i.e. will be so, and will be recognised and known as being
so, from the fact that Jehovah, the Holy One of Israel, will
sanctify it by His dwelling there. Jerusalem did not acquire
this character in the period after the captivity, in which, though
not defiled by gross idolatry, as in the times before the captivity,
it was polluted by other moral abominations no less than it
had been before. Jerusalem becomes a faithful city for the
first time through the Messiah, and it is through Him that the
temple mountain first really becomes the holy mountain. The
opinion, that there is nothing in the promises in vers. 3–13
that did not really happen to Israel in the period from Zerubbabel to Christ (Kliefoth, Koehler, etc.), is proved to be incorrect by the very words, both of this verse and also of vers. 6,
7, 8, which follow. How could the simple restoration of the
previous covenant relation be described in ver. 6 as something
that appeared miraculous and incredible to the nation ? There
is only so much correctness in the view in question, that the
promise does not refer exclusively to the Messianic times, but
that feeble commencements of its fulfilment accompanied the
completion of the work of building the temple, and the restoration of Jerusalem by Nehemiah. But the saying which
follows proves that these commencements do not exhaust the
meaning of the words.

Ver. 4. " *Thus saith Jehovah of hosts, Yet will there sit old
men and women in the streets of Jerusalem, every one with his
staff in his hand, for the multitude of the days of his life.* Ver. 5.
*And the streets of the city will be full of boys and girls playing
in their streets.*" Long life, to an extreme old age, and a plentiful number of blooming children, were theocratic blessings,

which the Lord had already promised in the law to His people, so far as they were faithful to the covenant. Consequently there does not appear to be any Messianic element in this promise. But if we compare this fourth verse with Isa. lxv. 20, we shall see that extreme old age also belonged to the blessings of the Messianic times. And as Israel had almost always to suffer most grievously from wars and other calamities, which swept off the people at an untimely age, during the time which extended from Zerubbabel to Christ; it must be admitted, notwithstanding the description of the prosperous times which Israel enjoyed under the government of Simon (1 Macc. xiv. 4–15), that this promise also was only fulfilled in a very meagre measure, so far as Jerusalem was concerned, before the coming of Christ.

Ver. 6. "*Thus saith Jehovah of hosts, If it be marvellous in the eyes of the remnant of this nation in those days, will it also be marvellous in my eyes? is the saying of Jehovah of hosts.*" The second clause of this verse is to be taken as a question with a negative answer, גַּם for הֲגַם, as in 1 Sam. xxii. 7, and the meaning is the following: If this (what is promised in vers. 3–5) should appear marvellous, *i.e.* incredible, to the people in those days when it shall arrive, it will not on that account appear marvellous to Jehovah Himself, *i.e.* Jehovah will for all that cause what has been promised actually to occur. This contains an assurance not only of the greatness of the salvation set before them, but also of the certainty of its realization. "The remnant of the nation," as in Hag. i. 12–14.

Ver. 7. "*Thus saith Jehovah of hosts, Behold, I save my people out of the land of the rising and out of the land of the setting of the sun.* Ver. 8. *And I bring them hither, and they will dwell in the midst of Jerusalem, and will be my people, and I shall be their God, in truth and righteousness.*" The deliverance of the people of God out of the heathen lands did indeed commence with the return of a body of exiles from Babylon under the guidance of Zerubbabel, but their deliverance out of all the countries of the earth is still in the future. Instead of all countries, the land of the rising (the east) and the land of the setting (the west) are individualized (cf. Ps. l. 1, cxiii. 3; Isa. lix. 19; Mal. i. 11). This deliverance is first effected through the Messiah. This is indisputably evident from the words, "I bring them to Jerusalem," by which of course we cannot understand the earthly Jerusalem, since that would not furnish space enough for the Jews scattered throughout all the world, but the open and enlarged Jerusalem mentioned in ch. ii. 8, *i.e.* the Messianic kingdom of God. Then will those who have been gathered together out of all the countries of the earth become in truth God's nation. Israel was the nation of Jehovah, and Jehovah was also Israel's God from the time of the establishment of the old covenant at Sinai (Ex. xxiv.). This relation is to be restored in the future, "in truth and righteousness." This is the new feature by which the future is to be distinguished from the present and the past. The words "in truth and righteousness" belong to the two clauses, "they shall be" and "I will be." For the fact itself, compare Hos. ii. 21, 22; and for the expression, Isa. xlviii. 1 and 1 Kings iii. 6.

After these promises the prophet admonishes the people to be of good courage, because the Lord will from henceforth bestow His blessing upon them Ver. 9. " *Thus saith Jehovah of hosts, Let your hands be strong, ye that hear in these days these words from the mouth of the prophets, on the day that the foundation of the house of Jehovah of hosts was laid, the temple, that it may be built.* Ver. 10. *For before those days there were no wages for the men, and no wages of cattle; and whoever went out and in had no peace because of the oppressor: and I drove all men, one against the other.* Ver. 11. *But now I am not as in the former days to the remnant of this people, is the saying of Jehovah of hosts.* Ver. 12. *But the seed of peace, the vine, shall yield its fruit, and the land shall yield its produce, and the heaven give its dew; and to the remnant of this people will I give all this for an inheritance.*" Having the hands strong, is the same as taking good courage for any enterprise (thus in Judg. vii. 11, 2 Sam. ii. 7, and Ezek. xxii. 14). This phrase does not refer specially to their courageous continuation of the building of the temple, but has the more general meaning of taking courage to accomplish what the calling of each required, as vers. 10–13 show. The persons addressed are those who hear the words of the prophets in these days. This suggests a motive for taking courage. Because they hear these words, they are to look forward with comfort to the future, and do what their calling

requires. The words of the prophets are the promises which
Zechariah announced in vers. 2–8, and his contemporary
Haggai in ch. ii. It will not do to take the plural נְבִיאִים in a
general sense, as referring to Zechariah alone. For if there
had been no prophet at that time beside Zechariah, he could
not have spoken in general terms of prophets. By the defining phrase, who are or who rose up at the time when the
foundation of the temple was laid, these prophets are distinguished from the earlier ones before the captivity (ch. vii. 7, 12,
i. 4), and their words are thereby limited to what Haggai and
Zechariah prophesied from that time downwards. בַּיּוֹם does
not stand for מִיּוֹם (Hitzig), but *yōm* is used in the general
sense of the time at which anything does occur or has occurred.
As a more precise definition of יוֹם יֻסַּד the word לְהִבָּנוֹת is
added, to show that the time referred to is that in which the
laying of the foundation of the temple in the time of Cyrus
became an eventful fact through the continuation of the
building. In vers. 10 sqq. a reason is assigned for the admonition to work with good courage, by an exhibition of the
contrast between the present and the former times. Before
those days, *sc.* when the building of the temple was resumed
and continued, a man received no wages for his work, and
even the cattle received none, namely, because the labour of
man and beast, *i.e.* agricultural pursuits, yielded no result, or
at any rate a most meagre result, by no means corresponding
to the labour (cf. Hag. i. 6, 9–11, ii. 16, 19). The feminine
suffix attached to אֵינֶנָּה refers with inexactness to the nearest
word הַבְּהֵמָה, instead of the more remote שָׂכָר (cf. Ewald,
§ 317, *c*). In addition to this, on going out and coming in,
i.e. when pursuing their ordinary avocations, men came everywhere upon enemies or adversaries, and therefore there was an
entire absence of civil peace. הַצָּר is not an abstract noun, " oppression" (LXX., Chald., Vulg.), but a concrete, " adversary,"
oppressor, though not the heathen foe merely, but, as the last
clause of ver. 10 shows, the adversaries in their own nation
also. In וַאֲשַׁלַּח the ו is not a simple copula, but the ו *consec.*
with the compensation wanting, like וָאֶגְרֹשׁ in Judg. vi. 9 (cf.
Ewald, § 232, *h*) ; and שִׁלַּח, to send, used of a hostile nation, is
here transferred to personal attacks on the part of individuals.
—Vers. 11 sqq. But now the Lord will act differently to His

remaining people, and bless it again with a fruitful harvest of
the fruits of the field and soil. כִּי in ver. 12, "for," after a
negative clause, "but." זֶרַע הַשָּׁלוֹם, not the seed will be secure
(Chald., Pesh.), but the seed of peace, viz. the vine. This is
so designated, not because there is a *berâkhâh* in the grape
(Isa. lxv. 8); but because the vine can only flourish in peaceful times, and not when the land is laid waste by enemies
(Koehler). On the words which follow, compare Lev. xxvi. 4
sqq., Ps. lxvii. 7, Hag. i. 10, ii. 19. "Future abundance will
compensate for the drought and scarcity of the past" (Jerome).

The whole blessing is finally summed up in one expression
in ver. 13: "*And it will come to pass, as ye were a curse among
the nations, O house of Judah and house of Israel, so will I
endow you with salvation, that ye may be a blessing. Fear not, let
your hands be strong.*" The formula, to be a curse among the
nations, is to be interpreted according to Jer. xxiv. 9, xxv. 9,
xlii. 18, 2 Kings xxii. 19, as equivalent to being the object of a
curse, *i.e.* so smitten by God as to serve as the object of curses.
In harmony with this, the phrase to "become a blessing" is
equivalent to being so blessed as to be used as a benedictory
formula (cf. Gen. xlviii. 22; Jer. xxix. 22). This promise is
made to the remnant of Judah and Israel, and therefore of all
the twelve tribes, who are to become partakers of the future
salvation in undivided unity (cf. ch. ix. 10, 13, x. 6, xi. 14).
Israel is therefore to look forward to the future without alarm.

The ground upon which this promise rests is given in vers.
14 and 15, and it is closed in vers. 16 and 17 by the addition
of the condition upon which it is to be fulfilled.   Ver. 14.
"*For thus saith Jehovah of hosts: As I thought to do evil to you,
when your fathers were angry with me, saith Jehovah of hosts, and
repented not;* Ver. 15. *So have I purposed again in these days to
do good to Jerusalem and to the house of Judah. Fear ye not.*
Ver. 16. *These are the words that ye are to do: speak truth every
one to his neighbour; truth and judgment of peace judge ye in
your gates.* Ver. 17. *And let not one devise the evil of his neighbour, and love not the oath of deceit: for all this, I hate it, is
the saying of Jehovah.*"   As the time of punishment by exile
came upon Israel through the decree of God, so is it now a
decree of the Lord to show good to Judah.   In שַׁבְתִּי זָמַמְתִּי
the שַׁבְתִּי takes the place of the adverbial idea "again."   The

people have therefore no need to fear, if they are only diligent in practising truth, righteousness, and love to their neighbour. God required the same of the fathers (ch. vii. 9, 10). *Mishpat shâlôm* is such an administration of justice as tends to promote peace and establish concord between those who are at strife. "In your gates," where courts of justice were held (cf. Deut. xxi. 19, xxii. 15, etc.). The אֵת before כָּל־אֵלֶּה in ver. 17 may be accounted for from a kind of attraction, inasmuch as by the insertion of אֲשֶׁר the object "all this" is separated from the verb, to bring it out with emphasis: "As for all this, it is what I hate." Compare the similar use of *'êth* in Hag. ii. 5, and Ewald, § 277, *d*.

Vers. 18–23. The last word of God gives, in connection with what precedes, the direct answer to the inquiry concerning the fast-days, and consists of three sayings, vers. 19, 20, and 23, of which the second and third explain the contents of the first more clearly. Ver. 18 is the same as vers. 1 and 7 and ch. iv. 8. Ver. 19. "*Thus saith Jehovah of hosts : The fasting of the fourth, and the fasting of the fifth, and the fasting of the seventh, and the fasting of the tenth (months), will become pleasure and joy to the house of Judah, and good feasts. But truth and peace ye should love.*" On the fast-days mentioned, compare the exposition of ch. vii. 3. These fast-days the Lord will turn into days of joy and cheerful feast-days—namely, by bestowing upon them such a fulness of salvation, that Judah will forget to commemorate the former mournful events, and will only have occasion to rejoice in the blessings of grace bestowed upon it by God; though only when the condition mentioned in vers. 16 and 17 has been fulfilled.[1]

Ver. 20. "*Thus saith Jehovah of hosts : Yet will nations come, and inhabitants of many cities.* Ver. 21. *And the inhabitants of one (city) will go to another, and say, 'We will go, go away, to supplicate the face of Jehovah, and to seek Jehovah*

---

[1] Luther aptly observes : " Keep only what I command, and let fasting alone. Yea, if ye keep my commandments, not only shall such fasts be over and come to an end ; but because I will do so much good to Jerusalem, all the affliction, for which ye have chosen and kept such fasting, shall be so forgotten, that ye will be transported with joy when ye think of your fasting, and of the heart's grief on account of which ye fasted for the time," etc.

of hosts.' 'I will also go.' Ver. 22. *And many peoples and
strong nations will come, to seek Jehovah of hosts in Jerusalem,
and to supplicate the face of Jehovah.*" These verses do not
announce a further or second glorification, which God has
designed for His people, but simply indicate the nature and
magnitude of the salvation appointed for Israel, through which
its fast-days will be turned into days of joy. Hitherto Israel
had kept days of mourning and fasting on account of the
destruction of Jerusalem and the temple; but in the future
the Lord will so glorify His city and His house, that not only
will Israel keep joyful feasts there, but many and strong
heathen nations will go to the house of God, to seek and
worship the God of hosts. עֹד is used with emphasis, so that
it resembles a sentence : "It will still come to pass, that," etc.
This is how אֲשֶׁר in vers. 21 and 23 is to be taken, and not
as the introduction to the saying preceded energetically by עֹד,
for which Hitzig is wrong in referring to Mic. vi. 10.   For
the fact itself, compare Mic. iv. 1 sqq., Isa. ii. 2 sqq., Jer.
xvi. 19. In ver. 21 the thought is individualized. The inhabitants of one city call upon those of another. נֵלְכָה הָלוֹךְ "we
will *go* to supplicate," etc.; and the population of the other
city responds to the summons by saying, "I also will go."
חַלּוֹת אֶת־פְּנֵי, as in ch. vii. 2.

Ver. 23. "*Thus saith Jehovah of hosts : In those days ten
men out of all languages of the nations take hold ; they will take
hold of the skirt of a Jewish man, saying, We will go with you;
for we have heard God is with you.*" Not only will the heathen
then flow to Jerusalem to seek the God of Israel, but they will
crowd together to Israel and Judah to be received into fellowship with them as a nation. Ten men from the heathen nations
to one Jewish man : so great will be the pressure of the heathen.
Ten is used as an indefinite number, denoting a great and complete multitude, as in Gen. xxxi. 7, Lev. xxvi. 26, Num. xiv. 22,
and 1 Sam. i. 8. For the figure, compare Isa. iv. 1. וְהֶחֱזִיקוּ is
a resumption of יַחֲזִיקוּ in the form of an apodosis. The unusual
combination כֹּל לְשֹׁנוֹת הַגּוֹיִם, "all the tongues of the nations,"
is formed after Isa. lxvi. 18 (הַגּוֹיִם וְהַלְּשֹׁנוֹת, "all nations and
tongues," *i.e.* nations of all languages), and on the basis of
Gen. x. 20 and 31. For נֵלְכָה עִמָּכֶם, compare Ruth i. 16; and
for אֱלֹהִים עִמָּכֶם, 2 Chron. xv. 9.

The promise, that the Lord would change the fast-days in the future into days of rejoicing and cheerful feasts, if Israel only loved truth and peace (ver. 20), when taken in connection with what is said in ch. vii. 5, 6 concerning fasting, left the decision of the question, whether the fast-days were to be given up or to be still observed, in the hands of the people. We have no historical information as to the course adopted by the inhabitants of Judah in consequence of the divine answer. All that we know is, that even to the present day the Jews observe the four disastrous days as days of national mourning. The talmudic tradition in *Rosh-hashana* (f. 18, *a*, *b*), that the four fast-days were abolished in consequence of the answer of Jehovah, and were not restored again till after the destruction of the second temple, is not only very improbable, but is no doubt erroneous, inasmuch as, although the restoration of the days for commemorating the destruction of Jerusalem and the burning of the temple could easily be explained, on the supposition that the second destruction occurred at the same time as the first, it is not so easy to explain the restoration of the fast-days in commemoration of events for which there was no link of connection whatever in the destruction of Jerusalem by the Romans. In all probability, the matter stands rather thus: that after the receipt of this verbal answer, the people did not venture formally to abolish the fast-days before the appearance of the promised salvation, but let them remain, even if they were not always strictly observed; and that at a later period the Jews, who rejected the Messiah, began again to observe them with greater stringency after the second destruction of Jerusalem, and continue to do so to the present time, not because "the prophecy of the glory intended for Israel (vers. 18–23) is still unfulfilled" (Koehler), but because "blindness in part is happened to Israel," so that it has not discerned the fulfilment, which commenced with the appearance of Christ upon earth.

III. FUTURE OF THE WORLD-POWERS, AND OF THE KINGDOM OF GOD.—Chaps. ix.-xiv.

The two longer prophecies, which fill up the last part of our book (ch. ix.-xi. and xii.-xiv.), show by their headings, as well as by their contents, and even by their formal arrangement, that they are two corresponding portions of a greater whole. In the headings, the fact that they have both the common character of a threatening prophecy or proclamation of judgment, is indicated by the application of the same epithet, *Massâ' d^ebhar Y^ehōvâh* (burden of the word of Jehovah), whilst the objects, "land of Hadrach" (ch. ix. 1) and "Israel" (ch. xii. 1), point to a contrast, or rather to a conflict between the lands of Hadrach and Israel. This contrast or conflict extends through the contents of both. All the six chapters treat of the war between the heathen world and Israel, though in different ways. In the first oracle (ch. ix.-xi.), the judgment, through which the power of the heathen world over Israel is destroyed and Israel is endowed with strength to overcome all its enemies, forms the fundamental thought and centre of gravity of the prophetic description. In the second (ch. xii.-xiv.), the judgment through which Israel, or Jerusalem and Judah, is sifted in the war with the heathen nations, and translated into the holy nation of the Lord by the extermination of its spurious members, is the leading topic. And lastly, in a formal respect the two oracles resemble one another, in the fact that in the centre of each the announcement suddenly takes a different tone, without any external preparation (ch. xi. 1 and xiii. 7), so that it is apparently the commencement of a new prophecy; and it is only by a deeper research into the actual fact, that the connection between the two is brought out, and the relation between the two clearly seen,—namely, that the second section contains a more minute description of the manner in which the events announced in the first section are to be realized. In the threatening word concerning the land of Hadrach, ch. ix. and x. form the first section, ch. xi. the second; in that concerning Israel, the first section extends from ch. xii. 1 to xiii. 6, and the second from ch. xiii. 7 to the end of the book.

FALL OF THE HEATHEN WORLD, AND DELIVERANCE AND
GLORIFICATION OF ZION.—CHAP. IX. AND X.

Whilst the judgment falls upon the land of Hadrach, upon
Damascus and Hamath, and upon Phœnicia and Philistia, so
that these kingdoms are overthrown and the cities laid waste
and the remnant of their inhabitants incorporated into the
nation of God (ch. ix. 1–7), Jehovah will protect His people,
and cause His King to enter Zion, who will establish a kingdom of peace over the whole earth (vers. 8–10). Those
members of the covenant nation who are still in captivity are
redeemed, and endowed with victory over the sons of Javan
(vers. 11–17), and richly blessed by the Lord their God to
overcome all enemies in His strength (ch. x.). The unity of
the two chapters, which form the first half of this oracle, is
evident from the close substantial connection between the
separate sections. The transitions from one complex of thought
to the other are so vanishing, that it is a matter of dispute, in
the case of ch. x. 1 and 2, for example, whether these verses
should be connected with ch. ix., or retained in connection with
ch. x. 4 sqq.

Ch. ix. 1–10. JUDGMENT UPON THE LAND OF HADRACH;
AND ZION'S KING OF PEACE.—Ver. 1. The true interpretation
of this section, and, in fact, of the whole prophecy, depends
upon the explanation to be given to the heading contained
in this verse. The whole verse reads thus: " *Burden of the
word of Jehovah over the land of Hadrach, and Damascus is its
resting-place; for Jehovah has an eye upon the men, and upon
all the tribes of Israel.*" There is a wide divergence of opinion
concerning the land of חַדְרָךְ. We need not stop to give any
elaborate refutation to the opinion that *Hadrach* is the name
of the Messiah (as some Rabbins suppose), or that it is the
name of an unknown Syrian king (Ges., Bleek), or of an
Assyrian fire-god, *Adar* or *Asar* (Movers), or of a deity of
Eastern Aramæa (Babylonia), as Hitzig maintained, since there
is no trace whatever of the existence of such a king or deity;
and even Hitzig himself has relinquished his own conjecture.
And the view defended by J. D. Mich. and Rosenmüller, that

Hadrach is the name of an ancient city, situated not far from
Damascus, is destitute of any tenable basis, since Hengstenberg (*Christol.* iii. p. 372, transl.) has proved that the historical
testimonies adduced in support of this rest upon some confusion
with the ancient Arabian city of *Drâa, Adrâa,* the biblical
Edrei (Deut. i. 4). As the name *Hadrach* or *Chadrach* never
occurs again, and yet a city which gives its name to a land,
and occurs in connection with Damascus, Hamath, Tyre, and
Sidon, could not possibly have vanished so completely, that even
the earlier Jewish and Christian commentators heard nothing
of it, *Chadrach* can only be a symbolical name formed by the
prophet himself (as Jerome maintained, according to a Jewish
tradition), from *chad, acris,* sharp, brave, ready for war (in

Arabic, ‎حَدَّ‎, *vehemens fuit, durus in ira, pugna*), and *râkh,* soft,

tender, in the sense of sharp-soft, or strong-tender, after the
analogy of the symbolical names, *Dumah* for Edom, in Isa. xxi.
11; *Sheshach* for Babylon, in Jer. xxv. 26, li. 41; *Ariel* for
Jerusalem, in Isa. xxix. 1, 2, 7. This view can no more be
upset by the objection of Koehler, that the interpretation of the
name is a disputed point among the commentators, and that it
is doubtful why the prophet should have chosen such a symbolical epithet, than by the circumstance that the rabbinical
interpretation of the word as a name for the Messiah is evidently false, and has long ago been given up by the Christian
commentators. That *Hadrach* denotes a land or kingdom, is
raised above all reach of doubt by the fact that '*erets* (the
land) is placed before it. But what land? The statement
in the following sentence by no means compels us to think of
a province of Syria, as Hitzig, Koehler, and others suppose.
As the cities and lands which follow are quoted under their
ordinary names, it is impossible to imagine any reason for
the choice of a symbolical name for another district of Syria
bordering upon Damascus and Hamath. The symbolical
name rather points to the fact that the land of *Hadrach*
denotes a territory, of which Damascus, Hamath, Tyre, Sidon,
and Philistia formed the several parts. And this is favoured
by the circumstance that the words, " Burden of the word of
Jehovah upon the land of *Hadrach*," form the heading to
the oracle, in which the preposition ‎ב‎ is used as in the ex-

pression מַשָּׂא בַּעְרָב in Isa. xxi. 13, and is to be explained from
the phrase נָפַל דָּבָר בְּ in Isa. ix. 7 : The burdensome word falls,
descends upon the land of Hadrach. The remark of Koehler
in opposition to this, to the effect that these words are not a
heading, but form the commencement of the exposition of the
word of Jehovah through the prophet, inasmuch as the following clause is appended with ו, is quite groundless. The clause
in Isa. xiv. 28, "In the year that king Ahaz died was this
burden," is also a heading; and the assertion that the ו before
דַּמֶּשֶׂק is not a ו explic., but an actual ו conjunct., rests upon
the assumption that the cities and lands mentioned in the
course of this prophecy have not already been all embraced by
the expression אֶרֶץ חַדְרָךְ,—an assumption which has not been
sustained by any proofs. On the contrary, the fact that not
only is Damascus mentioned as the resting-place of the word
of Jehovah, but Hamath and also the capitals of Phœnicia
and Philistia are appended, proves the very opposite. This
evidently implies that the burden resting upon the land of
Hadrach will affect all these cities and lands. The exposition
of the burden announced upon the land of *Hadrach* commences
with וְדַמֶּשֶׂק. This is attached to the heading with *Vav*, because,
so far as the sense is concerned, *massâ'* is equivalent to " it
presses as a burden." The exposition, however, is restricted,
so far as Damascus and Hamath are concerned, to the simple
remark that the burdensome word upon Hadrach will rest upon
it, *i.e.* will settle permanently upon it. (The suffix in מְנֻחָתוֹ
refers to מַשָּׂא דְבַר יי.) It is only with the lands which stood in
a closer relation to Judah, viz. Tyre, Sidon, and the provinces
of Philistia, that it assumes the form of a specially prophetic
description. The contents of the heading are sustained by the
thought in the second hemistich : "Jehovah has an eye upon
men, and upon all the tribes of Israel." עֵין אָדָם with the *genit.*
obj. signifies an eye *upon* man, analogous to אֲסִירֵי הַתִּקְוָה in
ver. 12. אָדָם, as distinguished from "all the tribes of Israel,"
signifies the rest of mankind, *i.e.* the heathen world, as in Jer.
xxxii. 20, where "Israel" and "men" are opposed to one
another. The explanatory clause, according to which the
burden of Jehovah falls upon the land of Hadrach, and rests
upon Damascus, because the eye of Jehovah looks upon mankind and all the tribes of Israel, *i.e.* His providence stretches

over the heathen world as well as over Israel, is quite sufficient in itself to overthrow the assumption of Hofmann and Koehler, that by the land of Hadrach we are to understand the land of Israel. For if the explanatory clause were understood as signifying that the burden, *i.e.* the judgment, would not only fall upon Hamath as the representative of the human race outside the limits of Israel, but also upon the land of Hadrach as the land of all the tribes of Israel, this view would be precluded not only by the circumstance that in what follows heathen nations alone are mentioned as the objects of the judgment, whereas salvation and peace are proclaimed to Israel, but also by the fact that no ground whatever can be discovered for the application of so mysterious an epithet to the land of Israel. According to Hofmann (*Schriftb.* ii. 2, p. 604), אֶרֶץ חַדְרָךְ signifies the whole of the territory of the kingdom of David, which is so called as "the land of Israel, which, though weak in itself, was, through the strength of God, as sharp as a warrior's sword." But if a judgment of destruction, which Hofmann finds in our prophecy, were announced "to all the nations dwelling within the bounds of what was once the Davidic kingdom," the judgment would fall upon Israel in the same way as upon the heathen nations that are named, since the tribes of Israel formed the kernel of the nations who dwelt in what was once the Davidic kingdom, and Israel would therefore show itself as a sharp-soft people. Hence Koehler has modified this view, and supposes that only the heathen dwelling within the limits of the nation of the twelve tribes are threatened with Jehovah's judgment,—namely, all the heathen within the land which Jehovah promised to His people on their taking possession of Canaan (Num. xxxiv. 1-12). But apart from the unfounded assumption that *Hadrach* is the name of a district of Syria on the border of Damascus and Hamath, this loophole is closed by the fact that, according to Num. xxxiv. 1 sqq., Hamath and Damascus are not included in the possession promised to Israel. According to Num. xxxiv. 8, the northern boundary of the land of Israel was to extend to Hamath, *i.e.* to the territory of the kingdom of Hamath, and Damascus is very far beyond the eastern boundary of the territory assigned to the Israelites (see the exposition of Num. xxxiv. 1-12). Now, if the land of Hadrach, Damascus, and

Hamath were not within the ideal boundaries of Israel, and if Hamath and Hadrach did not belong to the Israelitish kingdom in the time of David, the other lands or cities mentioned in our oracle cannot be threatened with the judgment on account of their lying within the Mosaic boundaries of the land of Israel, or being subject to the Israelites for a time, but can only come into consideration as enemies of Israel whose might was to be threatened and destroyed by the judgment. Consequently the land of *Hadrach* must denote a land hostile to the covenant nation or the kingdom of God, and can only be a symbolical epithet descriptive of the Medo-Persian empire, which is called sharp-soft or strong-weak on account of its inwardly divided character, as Hengstenberg and Kliefoth assume. Now, however difficult it may be satisfactorily to explain the reason why Zechariah chose this symbolical name for the Medo-Persian monarchy, so much is certain, that the choice of a figurative name was much more suitable in the case of the dominant empire of that time, than in that of any small country on the border of Damascus or Hamath. All the cities and lands enumerated after " the land of Hadrach," as losing their glory at the same time, belonged to the Medo-Persian monarchy. Of these the prophet simply refers to Damascus and Hamath in general terms; and it is only in the case of the Phœnician and Philistian cities that he proceeds to a special description of their fall from their lofty eminence, because they stood nearest to the kingdom of Israel, and represented the might of the kingdom of the world, and its hostility to the kingdom of God, partly in the worldly development of their own might, and partly in their hostility to the covenant nation. The description is an individualizing one throughout, exemplifying general facts by particular cities. This is also evident from the announcement of salvation for Zion in vers. 8–10, from which we may see that the overthrow of the nations hostile to Israel stands in intimate connection with the establishment of the Messianic kingdom; and it is also confirmed by the second half of our chapter, where the conquest of the imperial power by the people of God is set forth in the victories of Judah and Ephraim over the sons of Javan. That the several peoples and cities mentioned by name are simply introduced as representatives of the imperial power, is evident from the distinction made in this verse between (the rest of) mankind and all the tribes of Israel.

Ver. 2. "*And Hamath also, which borders thereon; Tyre and Sidon, because it is very wise.* Ver. 3. *And Tyre built herself a stronghold, and heaped up silver like dust, and gold like dirt of the streets.* Ver. 4. *Behold, the Lord will cause it to be taken, and smite its might in the sea, and she will be consumed by fire.*" *Chămáth* is appended to Damascus by *v°gam* (and also). *Tigbol-báh* is to be taken as a relative clause; and *báh* refers to *chămáth*, and not to *'erets chadrákh* (the land of Hadrach). "*Hamath also,*" *i.e.* 'Επιφάνεια on the Orontes, the present *Hamah* (see at Gen. x. 18), which borders on Damascus, *i.e.* which has its territory touching the territory of Damascus, *sc.* will be a resting-place of the burden of Jehovah. The relative clause connects *Hamath* with *Damascus*, and separates it from the names which follow. Damascus and Hamath represent Syria. Tyre and Sidon, the two capitals of Phœnicia, are connected again into a pair by the explanatory clause כִּי חָכְמָה מְאֹד. For although חָכְמָה is in the singular, it cannot be taken as referring to *Sidon* only, because Tyre is mentioned again in the very next verse as the subject, and the practical display of its wisdom is described. The singular חָכְמָה cannot be taken distributively in this sense, that being wise applies in just the same manner to both the cities (Koehler); for the cases quoted by Gesenius (§ 146, 4) are of a totally different kind, since there the subject is in the plural, and is construed with a singular verb; but צִידוֹן is subordinate to צֹר, "Tyre with Sidon," Sidon being regarded as an annex of Tyre, answering to the historical relation in which the two cities stood to one another, —namely, that Tyre was indeed originally a colony of Sidon, but that it very soon overshadowed the mother city, and rose to be the capital of all Phœnicia (see the comm. on Isa. xxiii.), so that even in Isaiah and Ezekiel the prophecies concerning Sidon are attached to those concerning Tyre, and its fate appears interwoven with that of Tyre (cf. Isa. xxiii. 4, 12; Ezek. xxviii. 21 sqq.). Hence we find Tyre only spoken of here in vers. 3 and 4. This city showed its wisdom in the fact that it built itself a fortress, and heaped up silver and gold like dust and dirt of the streets. Zechariah has here in his mind the insular Tyre, which was built about three or four stadia from the mainland, and thirty stadia to the north of *Palœ-tyrus*, and which is called מָעוֹז הַיָּם in Isa. xxiii. 4, because, although very small in extent, it was surrounded by a wall a hundred and fifty feet high, and was so strong a fortification, that Shalmaneser besieged it for five years without success, and Nebuchadnezzar for thirteen years, and apparently was unable to conquer it (see Delitzsch on *Isaiah*, vol. i. p. 416). This fortification is called *mâtsōr*. Here Tyre had heaped up immense treasures. *Chârūts* is shining gold (Ps. lxviii. 14, etc.). But the wisdom through which Tyre had acquired such might and such riches (cf. Ezek. xxviii. 4, 5) would be of no help to it. For it was the wisdom of this world (1 Cor. i. 20), which ascribes to itself the glory due to God, and only nourishes the pride out of which it sprang. The Lord will take the city. *Hōrīsh* does not mean to drive from its possession—namely, the population (Hitzig) —for the next two clauses show that it is not the population of Tyre, but the city itself, which is thought of as the object; ncr does it mean to " give as a possession"—namely, their treasures (Calv., Hengst., etc.)—but simply to take possession, to take, to conquer, as in Josh. viii. 7, xvii. 12, Num. xiv. 24 (Maurer, Koehler). And will smite in the sea חֵילָה, not " her bulwarks:" for חֵיל, when used of fortifications, neither denotes the city wall nor earthworks, but the moat, including the small outer wall (2 Sam. xx. 15) as distinguished from the true city wall (*chōmâh*, Isa. xxvi. 1, Lam. ii. 8), and this does not apply to the insular Tyre; moreover, חֵיל cannot be taken here in any other sense than in Ezek. xxviii. 4, 5, which Zechariah follows. There it denotes the might which Tyre had acquired through its wisdom, not merely warlike or military power (Koehler), but might consisting in its strong situation and artificial fortification, as well as in the wealth of its resources for defence. This will be smitten in the sea, because Tyre itself stood in the sea. And finally, the city will be destroyed by fire.

Ver. 5. "*Ashkelon shall see it, and fear; Gaza, and tremble greatly; and Ekron, for her hope has been put to shame; and the king will perish out of Gaza, and Ashkelon will not dwell.* Ver. 6. *The bastard will dwell in Ashdod; and I shall destroy the pride of the Philistines.* Ver. 7. *And I shall take away his blood out of his mouth, and his abominations from between his teeth; and he will also remain to our God, and will be as a*

tribe-prince in Judah, and Ekron like the Jebusite." From the
Phœnicians the threat turns against the Philistines. The fall
of the mighty Tyre shall fill the Philistian cities with fear and
trembling, because all hope of deliverance from the threatening
destruction is thereby taken away (cf. Isa. xxiii. 5). תֵּרֶא is
jussive. The effect, which the fall of Tyre will produce upon
the Philistian cities, is thus set forth as intended by God. The
description is an individualizing one in this instance also. The
several features in this effect are so distributed among the different cities, that what is said of each applies to all. They will
not only tremble with fear, but will also lose their kingship, and be
laid waste. Only four of the Philistian capitals are mentioned,
Gath being passed over, as in Amos i. 6, 8, Zeph. ii. 4, and
Jer. xxv. 20; and they occur in the same order as in Jeremiah,
whose prophecy Zechariah had before his mind. To וְעֵזָה we
must supply תֵּרֶא from the parallel clause; and to עֶקְרוֹן not only
תֵּרֶא, but also וְתִירָא. The reason for the fear is first mentioned
in connection with *Ekron*,—namely, the fact that the hope is
put to shame. הוֹבִישׁ is the *hiphil* of בּוֹשׁ (Ewald, § 122, *e*), in
the ordinary sense of this *hiphil*, to be put to shame. מִבָּט
with *seghol* stands for מַבָּט (Ewald, § 88, *d*, and 160, *d*), the
object of hope or confidence. Gaza loses its king. *Melekh*
without the article is the king as such, not the particular king
reigning at the time of the judgment; and the meaning is,
" Gaza will henceforth have no king," *i.e.* will utterly perish,
answering to the assertion concerning Ashkelon : לֹא תֵשֵׁב, she
will not dwell, *i.e.* will not come to dwell, a poetical expression
for be inhabited (see at Joel iii. 20). The reference to a king
of Gaza does not point to times before the captivity. The
Babylonian and Persian emperors were accustomed to leave to
the subjugated nations their princes or kings, if they would
only submit as vassals to their superior control. They therefore bore the title of "kings of kings" (Ezek. xxvi. 7; cf.
Herod. iii. 15; Stark, *Gaza*, pp. 229, 230; and Koehler, *ad
h. l.*). In Ashdod will *mamzēr* dwell. This word, the etymology of which is obscure (see at Deut. xxiii. 3, the only other
passage in which it occurs), denotes in any case one whose
birth has some blemish connected with it; so that he is not an
equal by birth with the citizens of a city or the inhabitants of
a land. Hengstenberg therefore renders it freely, though not

inappropriately, by *Gesindel* (rabble). The dwelling of the
bastard in Ashdod is not at variance with the fact that Ashkelon " does not dwell," notwithstanding the individualizing
character of the description, according to which what is affirmed
of one city also applies to the other. For the latter simply
states that the city will lose its native citizens, and thus forfeit
the character of a city. The dwelling of bastards or rabble in
Ashdod expresses the deep degradation of Philistia, which is
announced in literal terms in the second hemistich. The pride
of the Philistines shall be rooted out, *i.e.* everything shall be
taken from them on which as Philistines they based their pride,
viz. their power, their fortified cities, and their nationality.
" These words embrace the entire contents of the prophecy
against the Philistines, affirming of the whole people what had
previously been affirmed of the several cities" (Hengstenberg).
A new and important feature is added to this in ver. 7. Their
religious peculiarity—namely, their idolatry—shall also be
taken from them, and their incorporation into the nation of
God brought about through this judgment. The description in
ver. 7 is founded upon a personification of the Philistian nation.
The suffixes of the third pers. sing. and the pronoun הוּא in ver.
7*a* do not refer to the *mamzēr* (Hitzig), but to *pᵉlishtīm* (the
Philistines), the nation being comprehended in the unity of a
single person. This person appears as an idolater, who, when
keeping a sacrificial feast, has the blood and flesh of the sacrificial animals in his mouth and between his teeth. *Dâmīm* is
not human blood, but the blood of sacrifices; and *shiqqutsīm*,
abominations, are not the idols, but the idolatrous sacrifices,
and indeed their flesh. Taking away the food of the idolatrous
sacrifices out of their mouth denotes not merely the interruption
of the idolatrous sacrificial meals, but the abolition of idolatry
generally. He also (the nation of the Philistines regarded as
a person) will be left to our God. The *gam* refers not to the
Phœnicians and Syrians mentioned before, of whose being left
nothing was said in vers. 1–4, but to the idea of " Israel" implied
in לֵאלֹהֵינוּ, *our* God. Just as in the case of Israel a " remnant "
of true confessors of Jehovah is left when the judgment falls
upon it, so also will a remnant of the Philistines be left for
the God of Israel. The attitude of this remnant towards the
people of God is shown in the clauses which follow. He will

be like an *'alluph* in Judah. This word, which is applied in the earlier books only to the tribe-princes of the Edomites and Horites (Gen. xxxvi. 15, 16; Ex. xv. 15; 1 Chron. i. 51 sqq.), is transferred by Zechariah to the tribe-princes of Judah. It signifies literally not a phylarch, the head of an entire tribe (*matteh*, φυλή), but a chiliarch, the head of an *'eleph*, one of the families into which the tribes were divided. The meaning "friend," which Kliefoth prefers (cf. Mic. vii. 5), is unsuitable here; and the objection, that "all the individuals embraced in the collective והוא cannot receive the position of tribe-princes in Judah" (Kliefoth), does not apply, because והוא is not an ordinary collective, but the remnant of the Philistines personified as a man. Such a remnant might very well assume the position of a chiliarch of Judah. This statement is completed by the addition "and Ekron," *i.e.* the Ekronite "will be like the Jebusite." The Ekronite is mentioned for the purpose of individualizing in the place of all the Philistines. "Jebusite" is not an epithet applied to the inhabitants of Jerusalem, but stands for the former inhabitants of the citadel of Zion, who adopted the religion of Israel after the conquest of this citadel by David, and were incorporated into the nation of the Lord. This is evident from the example of the Jebusite Araunah, who lived in the midst of the covenant nation, according to 2 Sam. xxiv. 16 sqq., 1 Chron. xxi. 15 sqq., as a distinguished man of property, and not only sold his threshing-floor to king David as a site for the future temple, but also offered to present the oxen with which he had been ploughing, as well as the plough itself, for a burnt-offering. On the other hand, Koehler infers, from the conventional mode of expression employed by the subject when speaking to his king, "*thy* God," and the corresponding words of David, "*my* God" instead of our God, that Araunah stood in the attitude of a foreigner towards the God of Israel; but he is wrong in doing so. And there is quite as little ground for the further inference drawn by this scholar from the fact that the servants of Solomon and the Nethinim are reckoned together in Ezra ii. 58 and Neh. vii. 60, in connection with the statement that Solomon had levied bond-slaves for his buildings from the remnants of the Canaanitish population (1 Kings ix. 20), viz. that the Jebusites reappeared in the Nethinim of the later historical books, and that the Nethinim "given by David and the princes" were chiefly Jebusites, according to which "Ekron's being like a Jebusite is equivalent to Ekron's not only meeting with reception into the national fellowship of Israel through circumcision, but being appointed, like the Jebusites, to service in the sanctuary of Jehovah." On the contrary, the thought is simply this: The Ekronites will be melted up with the people of God, like the Jebusites with the Judæans. Kliefoth also observes quite correctly, that "there is no doubt that what is specially affirmed of the Philistians is also intended to apply to the land of Chadrach, to Damascus, etc., as indeed an absolute generalization follows expressly in ver. 10. . . . Just as in what precedes, the catastrophe intended for all these lands and nations is specially described in the case of Tyre alone; so here conversion is specially predicted of the Philistines alone."

If we inquire now into the historical allusion or fulfilment of this prophecy, it seems most natural to think of the divine judgment, which fell upon Syria, Phœnicia, and Philistia through the march of Alexander the Great from Asia Minor to Egypt. After the battle at Issus in Cilicia, Alexander sent one division of his army under Parmenio to Damascus, to conquer this capital of Cœle-Syria. On this expedition Hamath must also have been touched and taken. Alexander himself marched from Cilicia direct to Phœnicia, where Sidon and the other Phœnician cities voluntarily surrendered to him; and only Tyre offered so serious a resistance in its confidence in its own security, that it was not till after a seven months' siege and very great exertions that he succeeded in taking this fortified city by storm. On his further march the fortified city of Gaza also offered a prolonged resistance, but it too was eventually taken by storm (cf. Arrian, ii. 15 sqq.; Curtius, iv. 12, 13, and 2-4; and Stark, *Gaza*, p. 237 sqq.). On the basis of these facts, Hengstenberg observes (*Christol.* iii. p. 369), as others have done before him, that "there can be no doubt that in vers. 1-8 we have before us a description of the expedition of Alexander as clear as it was possible for one to be given, making allowance for the difference between prophecy and history." But Koehler has already replied to this, that the prophecy in ver. 7 was not fulfilled by the deeds of Alexander, since neither the remnant of the Phœnicians nor the other heathen dwelling in the midst of Israel were converted to Jehovah through the calamities connected with Alexander's expedition; and on this ground he merely regards the conquests of Alexander as the commencement of the fulfilment, which was then continued throughout the calamities caused by the wars of succession, the conflicts between the Egyptians, Syrians, and Romans, until it was completed by the fact that the heathen tribes within the boundaries of Israel gradually disappeared as separate tribes, and their remnants were received into the community of those who confessed Israel's God and His anointed. But we must go a step further, and say that the fulfilment has not yet reached its end, but is still going on, and will until the kingdom of Christ shall attain that complete victory over the heathen world which is foretold in vers. 8 sqq.

Vers. 8–10. Whilst the heathen world falls under the judgment of destruction, and the remnant of the heathen are converted to the living God, the Lord will protect His house, and cause the King to appear in Jerusalem, who will spread out His kingdom of peace over all the earth. Ver. 8. "*I pitch a tent for my house against military power, against those who go to and fro, and no oppressor will pass over them any more ; for now have I seen with my eyes. Ver. 9. Exult greatly, O daughter Zion ; shout, daughter Jerusalem : behold, thy King will come to thee : just and endowed with salvation is He ; lowly and riding upon an ass, and that upon a foal, the she-ass's son. Ver. 10. And I cut off the chariots out of Ephraim, and the horses out of Jerusalem, and the war-bow will be cut off : and peace will He speak to the nations ; and His dominion goes from sea to sea, and from the river to the ends of the earth.*" *Chânâh*, to encamp, to pitch a tent. לְבֵיתִי, *dat. commod.* " for my house," for the good of my house. The house of Jehovah is not the temple, but Israel as the kingdom of God or church of the Lord, as in Hos. viii. 1, ix. 15, Jer. xii. 7, and even Num. xii. 7, from which we may see that this meaning is not founded upon the temple, but upon the national constitution given to Israel, *i.e.* upon the idea of the house as a family. In the verse before us we cannot think of the temple, for the simple reason that the temple was not a military road for armies on the march either while it was standing, or, as Koehler supposes, when it was in ruins. מִצָּבָה stands, according to the Masora, for מִצָּבָא = מִן־צָבָא, not however in the sense of without an army, but " on account of (against) a hostile troop," protecting His house from them. But Böttcher, Koehler, and others, propose to follow the LXX. and read מַצָּבָה, military post, after 1 Sam. xiv. 12, which is the rendering given by C. B. Michaelis and Gesenius to מִצָּבָה. But this does not apply to חָנָה, for a post (מַצָּבָה, that which is set up) stands up, and does not lie down. מִצָּבָה is more precisely defined by מֵעֹבֵר וּמִשָּׁב, as going through and returning, *i.e.* as an army marching to and fro (cf. ch. vii. 14). There will come upon them no more (עֲלֵיהֶם, *ad sensum*, referring to בֵּיתִי) *nōgēs*, *lit.* a bailiff or taskmaster (Ex. iii. 7), then generally any oppressor of the nation. Such oppressors were Egypt, Asshur, Babel, and at the present time the imperial power of Persia. This promise is explained by the last clause: Now have I seen with mine eyes. The object is wanting, but it is implied in the context, viz. the oppression under which my nation sighs (cf. Ex. ii. 25, iii. 7). 'Attâh (now) refers to the ideal present of the prophecy, really to the time when God interposes with His help; and the perfect רָאִיתִי is prophetic. God grants help to His people, by causing her King to come to the daughter Zion. To show the magnitude of this salvation, the Lord calls upon the daughter Zion, *i.e.* the personified population of Jerusalem as a representative of the nation of Israel, namely the believing members of the covenant nation, to rejoice. Through מַלְכֵּךְ, *thy* King, the coming one is described as the King appointed for Zion, and promised to the covenant nation. That the Messiah is intended, whose coming is pre dicted by Isaiah (ix. 5, 6), Micah (v. 1 sqq.), and other pro phets, is admitted with very few exceptions by all the Jewish and Christian commentators.[1] לָךְ, not only to thee, but also for thy good. He is *tsaddîq*, righteous, *i.e.* not one who has right, or the good cause (Hitzig), nor merely one righteous in character, answering in all respects to the will of Jehovah (Koehler), but animated with righteousness, and maintaining in His government this first virtue of a ruler (cf. Isa. xi. 1–4 ; Jer. xxiii. 5, 6, xxxiii. 15, 16, etc.). For He is also נוֹשָׁע, *i.e.* not σώζων, *salvator*, helper (LXX., Vulg., Luth.), since the *niphal* has not the active or transitive sense of the *hiphil* (מוֹשִׁיעַ),

---

[1] See the history of the exposition in Hengstenberg's *Christology.*

nor merely the passive σωζόμενος, salvatus, delivered from suffering; but the word is used in a more general sense, endowed
with יֵשַׁע, salvation, help from God, as in Deut. xxxiii. 29, Ps.
xxxiii. 16, or furnished with the assistance of God requisite for
carrying on His government. The next two predicates describe
the character of His rule. עָנִי does not mean gentle, πραΰς
(LXX. and others) = עָנָו, but lowly, miserable, bowed down,
full of suffering. The word denotes "the whole of the lowly,
miserable, suffering condition, as it is elaborately depicted in
Isa. liii." (Hengstenberg.) The next clause answers to this,
"riding upon an ass, and indeed upon the foal of an ass."
The ו before עַל עַיִר is epexegetical (1 Sam. xvii. 40), describing
the ass as a young animal, not yet ridden, but still running behind the she-asses. The youthfulness of the animal is brought
out still more strongly by the expression added to עַיִר, viz.
בֶּן־אֲתֹנוֹת, i.e. a foal, such as asses are accustomed to bear (אֲתֹנוֹת
is the plural of the species, as in כְּפִיר אֲרָיוֹת, Judg. xiv. 5;
שְׂעִיר הָעִזִּים, Gen. xxxvii. 31, Lev. iv. 23). "Riding upon an
ass" is supposed by most of the more modern commentators to
be a figurative emblem of the peacefulness of the king, that
He will establish a government of peace, the ass being regarded
as an animal of peace in contrast with the horse, because on
account of its smaller strength, agility, and speed, it is less
adapted for riding in the midst of fighting and slaughter than
a horse. But, in the first place, this leaves the heightening of
the idea of the ass by the expression "the young ass's foal"
quite unexplained. Is the unridden ass's foal an emblem of
peace in a higher degree than the full-grown ass, that has
already been ridden?[1] And secondly, it is indeed correct that
the ass was only used in war as the exception, not the rule, and
when there were no horses to be had (cf. Bochart, *Hieroz.* i.
p. 158, ed. Ros.); and also correct that in the East it is of a
nobler breed, and not so despised as it is with us; but it is also a

---

[1] We may see how difficult it is to reconcile the emphasis laid upon the
ass's foal with this explanation of the significance of the ass, from the
attempts made by the supporters of it to bring them into harmony. The
assertion made by Ebrard, that עַיִר denotes an ass of noble breed, and
בֶּן־אֲתֹנוֹת signifies that it is one of the noblest breed, has been already
proved by Koehler to be a fancy without foundation ; but his own attempt
to deduce the following meaning of this riding upon a young ass from the

fact that in the East, and more especially among the Israelites, it was only in the earlier times, when they possessed no horses as yet, that distinguished persons rode upon asses (Judg. v. 10, x. 4, xii. 14; 2 Sam. xvii. 23, xix. 27), whereas in the time of David the royal princes and kings kept mules for riding instead of asses (2 Sam. xiii. 29, xviii. 9; 1 Kings i. 33, xxxviii. 44); and from the time of Solomon downwards, when the breeding of horses was introduced, not another instance occurs of a royal person riding upon an ass, although asses and mules are still constantly used in the East for riding and as beasts of burden; and lastly, that in both the ancient and modern East the ass stands much lower than the horse, whilst in Egypt and other places (Damascus for example), Christians and Jews were, and to some extent still are, only allowed to ride upon asses, and not upon horses, for the purpose of putting them below the Mohammedans (for the proofs, see Hengstenberg's *Christology*, iii. pp. 404–5). Consequently we must rest satisfied with this explanation, that in accordance with the predicate עָנִי the riding of the King of Zion upon the foal of an ass is an emblem, not of peace, but of lowliness, as the Talmudists themselves interpreted it. "For the ass is not a more peaceful animal than the horse, but a more vicious one" (Kliefoth).—Ver. 10. Just as the coming of the King does not contain within itself a sign of earthly power and exaltation, so will His kingdom not be established by worldly power. The war-chariots and horses, in which the kingdoms of the world seek their strength, will be exterminated by Jehovah out of Ephraim and Jerusalem (cf. Mic. v. 9). And so also will the war-chariots, for which "the battle-bow" stands synecdochically. Ephraim denotes the former kingdom of the ten tribes, and Jerusalem is mentioned as the capital in the place of the kingdom of Judah. Under the Messiah will the two kingdoms that were formerly divided be united once more, and through the destruction of their

precepts concerning the sacrifices, viz. that the future king is riding in the service of Israel, and therefore comes in consequence of a mission from Jehovah, can be proved to fail, from the fact that he is obliged to collect together the most heterogeneous precepts, of which those in Num. xix. 2, Deut. xxi. 3, and 1 Sam. vi. 7, that for certain expiatory purposes animals were to be selected that had never borne a yoke, have a much more specific meaning than that of simple use in the service of Jehovah.

military power will their nature be also changed, the covenant
nation be divested of its political and worldly character, and
made into a spiritual nation or kingdom. The rule of this King
will also extend far beyond the limits of the earthly Canaan.
He will speak peace to the nations, *i.e.* will not command peace
through His authoritative word (Hitzig, Koehler, etc.), but
bring the contests among the nations to an end (Mic. iv. 3) ;
for *dibbēr shâlōm* does not mean to command peace, but it
either simply denotes such a speaking as has peace for its subject, giving an assurance of peace and friendship, *i.e.* uttering
words of peace (a meaning which is inapplicable here), or
signifies to speak peace for the purpose of bringing disputes to
an end (Esth. x. 3).   But this is done not by authoritative
commands, but by His gaining the nations over through the
spiritual power of His word, or establishing His spiritual kingdom in the midst of them.   It is only as thus interpreted, that
the statement concerning the extension of His kingdom harmonizes with the rest.   This statement rests upon Ps. lxxii. 8,
"from sea to sea," as in Amos viii. 12 and Mic. vii. 12, viz.
from the sea to the other end of the world where sea begins
again.   "From the river :" *i.e.* from the Euphrates, which is
intended here by *nâhâr* without the article, as in Mic. vii. 12
and Isa. vii. 20, and is mentioned as the remotest eastern
boundary of the land of Israel, according to Gen. xv. 18, Ex.
xxiii. 31, as being the *terminus a quo*, to which the ends of the
earth are opposed as the *terminus ad quem*.

The leading thought in the promise (vers. 8–10) is therefore the following : When the catastrophe shall burst upon the
Persian empire, Israel will enjoy the marvellous protection of
its God, and the promised King will come for Zion, endowed
with righteousness and salvation, but in outward humiliation ;
and through the extermination of the materials of war out of
Israel, as well as by the peaceful settlement of the contests of
the nations, He will establish a kingdom of peace, which will
extend over all the earth.   On the fulfilment of this prophecy,
we learn from the gospel history, that when Jesus took His
last journey to Jerusalem, He so arranged His entrance into
this city, that our prophecy (ver. 9), "Say ye to the daughter
Zion, Behold, thy King cometh," etc., was fulfilled (cf. Matt.
xxi. 2 sqq., Mark xi. 2 sqq., Luke xix. 30 sqq., and John xii.

14 sqq.). The exact agreement between the arrangement made by Jesus on this occasion and our prophecy is especially evident from the account given by Matthew, according to which Jesus ordered not only the ass's foal (πῶλον, ὀνάριον), upon which He rode into Jerusalem, to be brought, as Mark, Luke, and John relate, but a she-ass and a foal with her (Matt. xxi. 2 and 7), "that it might be fulfilled which was spoken by the prophet" (ver. 4), although He could really only ride upon one animal. The she-ass was to follow, to set forth Zechariah's figurative description with greater completeness. For we see, from the corresponding accounts of the other three evangelists, that Jesus only mounted the ass's foal. John, even when quoting our prophecy, only mentions the "sitting on an ass's colt" (ver. 15), and then adds in ver. 16, that the allusion in this act of Jesus to the Old Testament prophecy was only understood by the disciples after Jesus was glorified. By this mode of entering Jerusalem before His death, Jesus intended to exhibit Himself to the people as the King foretold by the prophets, who, coming in lowliness, would establish His kingdom through suffering and dying, so as to neutralize the carnal expectations of the people as to the worldly character of the Messianic kingdom. The fulfilment, however, which Jesus thereby gave to our prophecy is not to be sought for in this external agreement between His act and the words of the prophet. The act of Jesus was in itself simply an embodiment of the thought lying at the basis of the prophecy,—namely, that the kingdom of the Messiah would unfold itself, through lowliness and suffering, to might and glory; that Jesus, as the promised Messiah, would not conquer the world by the force of arms, and so raise His people to political supremacy, but that He would found His kingdom by suffering and dying,—a kingdom which, though not of this world, would nevertheless overcome the world. The figurative character of the prophetic picture, according to which "riding upon an ass" merely serves to individualize עָנִי, and set forth the lowliness of the true King of Zion under appropriate imagery, has been already pointed out by Calvin[1] and Vitringa; and the latter has also

---

[1] Calvin says: "I have no doubt that the prophet added this clause (viz. 'riding upon an ass,' etc.) as an appendix to the word עָנִי, as much as to say: The King of whom I speak will not be illustrious for His magni-

correctly observed, that the prophecy would have been fulfilled in Christ, even if He had not made His entry into Jerusalem in this manner.[1] Hengstenberg and Koehler adopt the same view. Nevertheless, this entry of Christ into Jerusalem forms the commencement of the fulfilment of our prophecy, and that not merely inasmuch as Jesus thereby declared Himself to be the promised Messiah and King of Zion, and set forth in a living symbol the true nature of His person and of His kingdom in contrast with the false notions of His friends and foes, but still more in this respect, that the entry into Jerusalem formed the commencement of the establishment of His kingdom, since it brought to maturity the resolution on the part of the Jewish rulers to put Him to death; and His death was necessary to reconcile the sinful world to God, and restore the foundation of peace upon which His kingdom was to be built. With the spread of His kingdom over the earth, treated of in ver. 10, the fulfilment continues till the annihilation of all the ungodly powers, after which all war will cease. But this end can only be reached through severe conflicts and victory. This is the subject of the following section.

Vers. 11–17.—ISRAEL'S REDEMPTION FROM CAPTIVITY, AND VICTORY OVER THE HEATHEN.—Ver. 11. "*Thou also, for the sake of thy covenant blood, I release thy captives out of the pit wherein there is no water.* Ver. 12. *Return to the fortress, ye prisoners of hope. Even to-day I proclaim: Double will I repay to thee.*" This is addressed to the daughter Zion, *i.e.* to all Israel, consisting of Ephraim and Judah. We not only learn this from the context, since both of them are spoken

ficent and splendid state, as earthly princes generally are." He then gives this explanation of the riding upon the ass: "He will not prevail by His great exaltation; nor will He be conspicuous for arms, riches, splendour, the number of his soldiers, or even the royal insignia, which attract the eyes of the people."

[1] Vitringa says, on Isa. liii. 4: "In that passage of Zechariah, indeed, according to its spiritual and mystical sense, his meaning would have been evident without this accident of the entry of Christ into Jerusalem; but when God would put all the emphasis of which the words are capable upon the predictions uttered by the prophets, His own providence took care that this accident should also occur, so that no part of the machinery might be wanting here."

of before (ver. 10) and afterwards (ver. 13); but it is also
obvious from the expression *b⁰dam b⁰rīthēkh*, since the covenant
blood belonged to all Israel of the twelve tribes (Ex. xxiv. 8).
נַּם־אַתְּ stands at the head absolutely, on account of the emphasis
lying upon the אַתְּ.   But as the following clause, instead of
being directly attached to אַתְּ, is so constructed that the pronoun אַתְּ is continued with suffixes, the question arises, to
what the נַּם is to be taken as referring, or which is the antithesis indicated by נַּם.   The answer may easily be obtained if
we only make it clear to ourselves which of the two words,
with the second pers. suffix, forms the object of the assertion
made in the entire clause.   This is not בְּדַם־בְּרִיתֵךְ, but אֲסִירַיִךְ:
thou also (=thee)—namely, thy prisoners—I release.   But the
emphasis intended by the position in which נַּם־אַתְּ is placed
does not rest upon the prisoners of Israel in contrast with
any other prisoners, but in contrast with the Israel in Jerusalem, the daughter Zion, to which the King is coming.   Now,
although נַּם actually belongs to אֲסִירַיִךְ, it refers primarily to
the אַתְּ to which it is attached, and this only receives its more
precise definition afterwards in אֲסִירַיִךְ.   And the allusion intended by נַּם is simply somewhat obscured by the fact, that
before the statement to which it gives emphasis בְּדַם־בְּרִיתֵךְ is
inserted, in order from the very first to give a firm pledge
of the promise to the people, by declaring the motive which
induced God to make this fresh manifestation of grace to
Israel.   This motive also acted as a further reason for placing the pronoun אַתְּ at the head absolutely, and shows that
אַתְּ is to be taken as an address, as for example in Gen.
xlix. 8.   בְּדַם־בְּרִיתֵךְ: literally, being in thy covenant blood,
because sprinkled therewith, the process by which Israel was
expiated and received into covenant with God (Ex. xxiv. 8).
"The covenant blood, which still separates the church and the
world from one another, was therefore a certain pledge to the
covenant nation of deliverance out of all trouble, so long, that
is to say, as it did not render the promise nugatory by wickedly
violating the conditions imposed by God" (Hengstenberg).
The new matter introduced by נַּם־אַתְּ in ver. 11 is therefore
the following: The pardon of Israel will not merely consist
in the fact that Jehovah will send the promised King to the
daughter Zion; but He will also redeem such members of His

nation as shall be still in captivity out of their affliction. The perfect *shillachtī* is prophetic. Delivering them out of a pit without water is a figure denoting their liberation out of the bondage of exile. This is represented with an evident allusion to the history of Joseph in Gen. xxxvii. 22, as lying in a pit wherein there is no water, such as were used as prisons (cf. Jer. xxxviii. 6). Out of such a pit the captive could not escape, and would inevitably perish if he were not drawn out. The opposite of the pit is בִּצָּרוֹן, a place cut off, *i.e.* fortified, not the steep height, although fortified towns were generally built upon heights. The prisoners are to return where they will be secured against their enemies ; compare Ps. xl. 3, where the rock is opposed to the miry pit, as being a place upon which it is possible to stand firmly. "Prisoners of hope" is an epithet applied to the Israelites, because they possess in their covenant blood a hope of redemption. גַּם־הַיּוֹם, also to-day, *i.e.* even to-day or still to-day, "notwithstanding all threatening circumstances" (Ewald, Hengstenberg). I repay thee double, *i.e.*, according to Isa. lxi. 7, a double measure of glory in the place of the sufferings.

This thought is supported in vers. 13 sqq. by a picture of the glory intended for Israel. Ver. 13. "*For I stretch Judah as my bow, fill it with Ephraim, and stir up thy sons, O Zion, against thy sons, O Javan, and make thee like the sword of a hero.* Ver. 14. *And Jehovah will appear above them, and like the lightning will His arrow go forth; and the Lord Jehovah will blow the trumpets, and will pass along in storms of the south.* Ver. 15. *Jehovah of hosts will shelter above them, and they will eat and tread down sling-stones, and will drink, make a noise, as if with wine, and become full, like the sacrificial bowls, like the corners of the altar.*" The double recompense which the Lord will make to His people, will consist in the fact that He not only liberates them out of captivity and bondage, and makes them into an independent nation, but that He helps them to victory over the power of the world, so that they will tread it down, *i.e.* completely subdue it. The first thought is not explained more fully, because it is contained *implicite* in the promise of return to a strong place ; the " double" only is more distinctly defined, namely, the victory over Javan. The expression, " I stretch," etc., implies that the Lord will subdue the enemies by Judah and Ephraim, and therefore Israel will carry on this conflict in the power of its God. The figurative description is a bold one. Judah is the extended bow; Ephraim the arrow which God shoots at the foe. קֶשֶׁת is indeed separated from יְהוּדָה by the accents; but the LXX., Targ., Vulg., and others, have taken it more correctly, as in apposition to יְהוּדָה; because with the many meanings that דֶּרֶךְ possesses, the expression דֶּרֶךְ יְהוּדָה needs a more precise definition; whereas there is no difficulty in supplying in thought the noun *qesheth*, which has been mentioned only just before, to the verb מִלֵּאתִי (I fill). מִלֵּאתִי is to be understood as signifying the laying of the arrow upon the bow, and not to be explained from 2 Kings ix. 24, " to fill the hand with the bow." A bow is filled when it is supplied with the arrow for shooting. We must bear in mind that the matter is divided rhetorically between the parallel members; and the thought is this: Judah and Ephraim are bow and arrow in the hand of Jehovah. עוֹרַרְתִּי, I stir up, not I swing thy children as a lance (Hitzig and Koehler); for if עוֹרֵר had this meaning, חֲנִית could not be omitted. The sons of Zion are Judah and Ephraim, the undivided Israel, not the Zionites living as slaves in Javan (Hitzig). The sons of Javan are the Greeks, as the world-power, the Græco-Macedonian monarchy (cf. Dan. viii. 21), against which the Lord will make His people into a hero's sword. This took place in weak beginnings, even in the wars between the Maccabees and the Seleucidæ, to which, according to Jerome, the Jews understood our prophecy to refer; but it must not be restricted to this, as the further description in vers. 14, 15 points to the complete subjugation of the imperial power. Jehovah appears above them, *i.e.* coming from heaven as a defence, to fight for them (the sons of Zion), as a mighty man of war (Ps. xxiv. 8). His arrow goes out like the lightning (כְ the so-called כ *veritatis*; for the fact described, compare Hab. iii. 11). Marching at the head of His people, He gives the signal of battle with a trumpet-blast, and attacks the enemy with terribly devastating violence. The description rests upon the poetical descriptions of the coming of the Lord to judgment, the colours of which are borrowed from the phenomena of a storm (cf. Ps. xviii. and Hab. iii. 8 sqq.). Storms of the south are the most violent storms, as they come from the Arabian desert, which bounds Canaan on the

south (Isa. xxi. 1; cf. Hos. xiii. 15). But Jehovah not only
fights for His people; He is also a shield to them in battle,
covering them against the weapons of the foe. This is affirmed
in עֲלֵיהֶם יָגֵן in ver. 15. Hence they are able to destroy their
enemies, and, like devouring lions, to eat their flesh and drink
their blood. That this figure lies at the foundation cf the horrible picture of וְאָכְלוּ, is evident from Num. xxiii. 24, which was
the passage that Zechariah had in his mind: "Behold a people
like the lioness; it rises up, and like the lion does it lift itself
up: it lies not down till it devour the prey, and drink the blood
of the slain." Hence the object to אָכְלוּ is not the possessions
of the heathen, but their flesh. אַבְנֵי קֶלַע כָּבְשׁוּ does not mean,
they tread down (subdue) the enemy with sling-stones (LXX.,
Vulg., Grot.); for אַבְנֵי ק׳ cannot, when considered grammatically, be taken in an instrumental sense, and is rather an *accus.
obj.*; but they tread down sling-stones. The sling-stones might
be used *per synecdochen* to signify darts, which the enemy hurls
at them, and which they tread down as perfectly harmless
(Kliefoth). But the comparison of the Israelites to the stones
of a crown, in ver. 16, leads rather to the conclusion that the
sling-stones are to be taken as a figure denoting the enemy, who
are trampled under the feet like stones (Hitzig, Hengstenberg).
Only we cannot speak of eating sling-stones, as Koehler would
interpret the words, overlooking כָּבְשׁוּ, and appealing to the
parallel member: they will drink, reel as if from wine, which
shows, in his opinion, that it is the sling-stones that are to be
eaten. But this shows, on the contrary, that just as there no
mention is made of what is to be drunk, so here what is to be
eaten is not stated. It is true that wine and sacrificial blood
point to the blood of the enemy; but wine and blood are
drinkable, whereas sling-stones are not edible. The description
of the enemy as sling-stones is to be explained from the figure
in 1 Sam. xxv. 29, to hurl away the soul of the enemy. They
drunk (*sc.* the blood of the enemy) even to intoxication, making
a noise, as if intoxicated with wine (כְּמוֹ יָיִן, an abbreviated
comparison; cf. Ewald, § 221, *a*, and 282, *e*), and even to
overflowing, so that they become full, like the sacrificial bowls
in which the blood of the sacrificial animals was caught, and
like the corners of the altar, which were sprinkled with the
sacrificial blood. זָוִית are corners, not the horns of the altar.

The sacrificial blood was not sprinkled upon these ; they were
simply smeared with a little blood applied with the finger, in
the case of the expiatory sacrifices. According to the law
(Lev. i. 5, 11, iii. 2, etc.), the blood was to be swung against
the altar. This was done, according to rabbinical tradition
(*Mishn. Seb.* v. 4 sqq., and Rashi on Lev. i. 5), in such a manner, that with two sprinklings all the four sides of the altar
were wetted,—a result which could only be ensured by swinging
the bowls filled with blood, so as to strike the corners of the
altar.

Through this victory over the world-power Israel will attain
to glory. Ver. 16. "*And Jehovah their God will endow them
with salvation in that day, like a flock His people; for stones of a
crown are they, sparkling in His land.* Ver. 17. *For how great
is its goodness, aud how great its beauty! Corn will make youths
to sprout, and new wine maidens.*" הוֹשִׁיעַ does not mean to help
or deliver here ; for this would affirm much too little, after what
has gone before. When Israel has trodden down its foes, it no
longer needs deliverance. It denotes the granting of positive
salvation, which the explanatory clause that follows also requires.
The motive for this is indicated in the clause, " like a flock His
people." Because Israel is His (Jehovah's) people, the Lord
will tend it as a shepherd tends his flock. The blessings which
Jehovah bestows upon His people are described by David in
Ps. xxiii. The Lord will do this also, because they (the Israelites) are crown-stones, namely as the chosen people, which
Jehovah will make a praise and glory for all nations (Zeph. iii.
19, 20). To the predicate אַבְנֵי נֵזֶר the subject הֵמָּה may easily
be supplied from the context, as for example in מַגִּיד in ver. 12.
To this subject מִתְנוֹסְסוֹת וגו' attaches itself. This verb is connected with *nēs*, a banner, in Ps. lx. 6, the only other passage
in which it occurs ; but here it is used in the sense of *nâtsats*,
to glitter or sparkle. The meaning, to lift up, which is given
by the lexicons, has no foundation, and is quite unsuitable
here. For crown-stones do not lift themselves up, but sparkle ;
and the figure of precious stones, which sparkle upon the land,
denotes the highest possible glory to which Israel can attain.
The suffix attached to אַדְמָתוֹ refers to *Jehovah*, only we must
not identify the land of Jehovah with Palestine. The application of this honourable epithet to Israel is justified in ver. 17,

by an allusion to the excellence and beauty to which it will
attain. The suffixes in טוּבוֹ and יָפְיוֹ cannot refer to *Jehovah*,
as Ewald and Hengstenberg suppose, but refer to עַמּוֹ, the
people of Jehovah. יָפְי is quite irreconcilable with an allusion
to Jehovah, since this word only occurs in connection with men
and the Messianic King (Ps. xlv. 3; Isa. xxxiii. 17); and even
if it were used of Jehovah, it would still be unsuitable here.
For though the vigorous prosperity of the nation is indeed a
proof of the goodness of God, it is not a proof of the beauty of
God. *Mâh* is an exclamation of amazement: " how great!"
(Ewald, § 330, *a*). טוּב, when affirmed of the nation, is not
moral goodness, but a good appearance, and is synonymous with
יָפְי, beauty, as in Hos. x. 11. This prosperity proceeds from
the blessings of grace, which the Lord causes to flow down
to His people. Corn and new wine are mentioned as such
blessings, for the purpose of individualizing, as indeed they
frequently are (*e.g.* Deut. xxxiii. 28; Ps. lxxii. 16), and are
distributed rhetorically between the youths and the maidens.

Chap. x. COMPLETE REDEMPTION OF THE PEOPLE OF
GOD.—This chapter contains no new promise, but simply a
further expansion of the previous section, the condition on
which salvation is to be obtained being mentioned in the introduction (vers. 1 and 2); whilst subsequently, more especially
from ver. 6 onwards, the participation of Ephraim in the salvation in prospect is more elaborately treated of. The question
in dispute among the commentators, viz. whether vers. 1 and 2
are to be connected with the previous chapter, so as to form the
conclusion, or whether they form the commencement of a new
address, or new turn in the address, is to be answered thus: The
prayer for rain (ver. 1) is indeed occasioned by the concluding
thought in ch. ix. 17, but it is not to be connected with the
preceding chapter as though it were an integral part of it, inasmuch as the second hemistich of ver. 2 can only be separated
with violence from ver. 3. The close connection between ver.
2*b* and ver. 3 shows that ver. 1 commences a new train of
thought, for which preparation is made, however, by ch. ix. 17.
    Ver. 1. " *Ask ye of Jehovah rain in the time of the latter
rain; Jehovah createth lightnings, and showers of rain will He
give them, to every one vegetation in the field.* Ver. 2. *For the*

*teraphim have spoken vanity, and the soothsayers have seen a lie,
and speak dreams of deceit; they comfort in vain: for this they
have wandered like a flock, they are oppressed because there is no
shepherd.*" The summons to prayer is not a mere turn of the
address expressing the readiness of God to give (Hengstenberg),
but is seriously meant, as the reason assigned in ver. 2 clearly
shows. The church of the Lord is to ask of God the blessings
which it needs for its prosperity, and not to put its trust in
idols, as rebellious Israel has done (Hos. ii. 7). The prayer for
rain, on which the successful cultivation of the fruits of the
ground depends, simply serves to individualize the prayer for
the bestowal of the blessings of God, in order to sustain both
temporal and spiritual life; just as in ch. ix. 17 the fruitfulness of the land and the flourishing of the nation are simply
a concrete expression, for the whole complex of the salvation
which the Lord will grant to His people (Kliefoth). This
view, which answers to the rhetorical character of the exhortation, is very different from allegory. The time of the latter
rain is mentioned, because this was indispensable to the ripening
of the corn, whereas elsewhere the early and latter rain are
connected together (*e.g.* Joel ii. 23; Deut. xi. 13–15). The
lightnings are introduced as the harbingers of rain (cf. Jer.
x. 13; Ps. cxxxv. 7). *M*ᵉ*tar geshem*, rain of the rain-pouring,
i.e. copious rain (compare Job xxxvii. 6, where the words are
transposed). With *láhem* (to them) the address passes into the
third person: to them, *i.e.* to every one who asks. עֵשֶׂב is not
to be restricted to grass or herb as the food of cattle, as in
Deut. xi. 15, where it is mentioned in connection with the corn
and the fruits of the field; but it includes these, as in Gen.
i. 29 and Ps. civ. 14, where it is distinguished from *châtsîr*.
The exhortation to pray to Jehovah for the blessing needed to
ensure prosperity, is supported in ver. 2 by an allusion to the
worthlessness of the trust in idols, and to the misery which
idolatry with its consequences, viz. soothsaying and false
prophecy, have brought upon the nation. The *tᵉráphîm* were
house-deities and oracular deities, which were worshipped as the
givers and protectors of the blessings of earthly prosperity (see
at Gen. xxxi. 19). Along with these קוֹסְמִים are mentioned, *i.e.*
the soothsayers, who plunged the nation into misery through
their vain and deceitful prophesyings. חֲלֹמוֹת is not the subject

of the sentence, for in that case it would have the article like הַקּוֹסְמִים; but it is the object, and הַקּוֹסְמִים is also the subject to יְדַבֵּרוּ and יְנַחֵמוּ. "Therefore," *i.e.* because Israel had trusted in teraphim and soothsayers, it would have to wander into exile. נָסַע, to break up, applied to the pulling up of the pegs, to take down the tent, involves the idea of wandering, and in this connection, of wandering into exile. Hence the perfect נָסְעוּ, to which the imperfect יַעֲנוּ is suitably appended, because their being oppressed, *i.e.* the oppression which Israel suffered from the heathen, still continued. The words apply of course to all Israel (Ephraim and Judah); compare ch. ix. 13 with ch. x. 4, 6. Israel is bowed down because it has no shepherd, *i.e.* no king, who guards and provides for his people (cf. Num. xxvii. 17; Jer. xxiii. 4), having lost the Davidic monarchy when the kingdom was overthrown.

To this there is appended in vers. 3 sqq. the promise that Jehovah will take possession of His flock, and redeem it out of the oppression of the evil shepherds. Ver. 3. " *My wrath is kindled upon the shepherds, and the goats shall I punish; for Jehovah of hosts visits His flock, the house of Judah, and makes it like His state-horse in the war.* Ver. 4. *From Him will be corner-stone, from Him the nail, from Him the war-bow; from Him will every ruler go forth at once.*" When Israel lost its own shepherds, it came under the tyranny of bad shepherds. These were the heathen governors and tyrants. Against these the wrath of Jehovah is kindled, and He will punish them. There is no material difference between רֹעִים, shepherds, and עַתּוּדִים, leading goats. '*Attūdīm* also signifies rulers, as in Isa. xiv. 9. The reason assigned why the evil shepherds are to be punished, is that Jehovah visits His flock. The perfect *pâqad* is used prophetically of what God has resolved to do, and will actually carry out; and *pâqad c. acc. pers.* means to visit, *i.e.* to assume the care of, as distinguished from *pâqad* with '*al pers.*, to visit in the sense of to punish (see at Zeph. ii. 7). The house of Judah only is mentioned in ver. 3, not in distinction from Ephraim, however (cf. ver. 6), but as the stem and kernel of the covenant nation, with which Ephraim is to be united once more. The care of God for Judah will not be limited to its liberation from the oppression of the bad shepherds; but Jehovah will also make Judah into a victorious people. This is the meaning of

the figure "like a state-horse," *i.e.* a splendid and richly ornamented war-horse, such as a king is accustomed to ride. This
figure is not more striking than the description of Judah and
Ephraim as a bow and arrow (ch. ix. 13). This equipment of
Judah as a warlike power overcoming its foes is described in
ver. 4, namely in 4*a*, in figures taken from the firmness and
furnishing of a house with everything requisite, and in 4*b*,
etc., in literal words. The verb יֵצֵא of the fourth clause cannot
be taken as the verb belonging to the מִמֶּנּוּ in the first three
clauses, because יֵצֵא is neither applicable to *pinnâh* nor to
yâthēd. We have therefore to supply יִהְיֶה. From (out of)
Him will be *pinnâh*, corner, here corner-stone, as in Isa. xxviii.
16, upon which the whole building stands firmly, and will be
built securely,—a suitable figure for the firm, stately foundation which Judah is to receive. To this is added *yâthēd*, the
plug. This figure is to be explained from the arrangement
of eastern houses, in which the inner walls are provided with
a row of large nails or plugs for hanging the house utensils
upon. The plug, therefore, is a suitable figure for the supports
or upholders of the whole political constitution, and even in
Isa. xxii. 23 was transferred to persons. The war-bow stands
synecdochically for weapons of war and the military power.
It is a disputed point, however, whether the suffix in *mimmennū*
(out of him) refers to *Judah* or *Jehovah*. But the opinion of
Hitzig and others, that it refers to Jehovah, is overthrown by
the expression יֵצֵא מִמֶּנּוּ in the last clause. For even if we
could say, Judah will receive its firm foundation, its internal
fortification, and its military strength from *Jehovah*, the expression, "Every military commander will go out or come forth out
of Jehovah," is unheard-of and unscriptural. It is not affirmed
in the Old Testament even of the Messiah that He goes forth
out of God, although His "goings forth" are from eternity
(Mic. v. 1), and He Himself is called *El gibbōr* (Isa. ix. 5).
Still less can this be affirmed of *every* ruler (*kol-nōgēs*) of
Judah. In this clause, therefore, *mimmennū* must refer to
Judah, and consequently it must be taken in the same way
in the first three clauses. On יָצָא מִן, see Mic. v. 1. *Nōgēs*,
an oppressor or taskmaster, is not applied to a leader or ruler
in a good sense even here, any more than in Isa. iii. 12
and lx. 17 (see the comm. on these passages). The fact that

negus in Ethiopic is the name given to the king (Koehler),
proves nothing in relation to Hebrew usage. The word has
the subordinate idea of oppressor, or despotic ruler, in this
instance also; but the idea of harshness refers not to the
covenant nation, but to its enemies (Hengstenberg), and the
words are used in antithesis to ch. ix. 8. Whereas there the
promise is given to the nation of Israel that it will not fall
under the power of the *nōgēs* any more, it is here assured that
it is to attain to the position of a *nōgēs* in relation to its foes
(Kliefoth). כָּל־נוֹגֵשׂ is strengthened by יַחְדָּו: every oppressor
together, which Judah will require in opposition to its foes.

Thus equipped for battle, Judah will annihilate its foes.
Ver. 5. "*And they will be like heroes, treading street-mire in the
battle: and will fight, for Jehovah is with them, and the riders
upon horses are put to shame.* Ver. 6. *And I shall strengthen
the house of Judah, and grant salvation to the house of Joseph,
and shall make them dwell; for I have had compassion upon
them: and they will be as if I had not rejected them: for I am
Jehovah their God, and will hear them.* Ver. 7. *And Ephraim
will be like a hero, and their heart will rejoice as if with wine:
and their children will see it, and rejoice; their heart shall rejoice
in Jehovah.*" In ver. 5, *bōsīm* is a more precise definition of
kegibbōrīm, and the house of Judah (ver. 3) is the subject of
the sentence. They will be like heroes, namely, treading upon
mire. *Bōsīm* is the *kal* participle used in an intransitive sense,
since the form with *o* only occurs in verbs with an intransitive
meaning, like *bōsh*, *lōt*, *qōm*; and *būs* in *kal* is construed in
every other case with the accusative of the object: treading
upon mire = treading or treading down mire. Consequently
the object which they tread down or trample in pieces is expressed by בְּטִיט חוּצוֹת; and thus the arbitrary completion of
the sentence by "everything that opposes them" (C. B. Mich.
and Koehler) is set aside as untenable. Now, as "treading
upon mire" cannot possibly express merely the firm tread of a
courageous man (Hitzig), we must take the dirt of the streets
as a figurative expression for the enemy, and the phrase
"treading upon street-mire" as a bold figure denoting the
trampling down of the enemy in the mire of the streets (Mic.
vii. 10; 2 Sam. xxii. 43), analogous to their "treading down
sling-stones," ch. ix. 15. For such heroic conflict will they be

fitted by the help of Jehovah, that the enemy will be put to shame before them. The riders of the horses are mentioned for the purpose of individualizing the enemy, because the principal strength of the Asiatic rulers consisted in cavalry (see Dan. xi. 40). הוֹבִישׁ intransitive, as in ch. ix. 5. This strength for a victorious conflict will not be confined to Judah, but Ephraim will also share it. The words, " and the house of Ephraim will I endow with salvation," have been taken by Koehler as signifying " that Jehovah will deliver the house of Ephraim by granting the victory to the house of Judah in conflict with its own foes and those of Ephraim also;" but there is no ground for this. We may see from ver. 7, according to which Ephraim will also fight as a hero, as Judah will according to ver. 5, that הוֹשִׁיעַ does not mean merely to help or deliver, but to grant salvation, as in ch. ix. 16. The circumstance, however, " that in the course of the chapter, at any rate from ver. 7 onwards, it is only Ephraim whose deliverance and restoration are spoken of," proves nothing more than that Ephraim will receive the same salvation as Judah, but not that it will be delivered by the house of Judah. The abnormal form הוֹשֵׁבוֹתִים is regarded by many, who follow Kimchi and Aben Ezra, as a *forma composita* from הוֹשַׁבְתִּים and הֲשִׁיבוֹתִי : " I make them dwell, and bring them back." But this is precluded by the fact that the bringing back would necessarily precede the making to dwell, to say nothing of the circumstance that there is no analogy whatever for such a composition (cf. Jer. xxxii. 37). The form is rather to be explained from a confusion of the verbs ע״וּ and פ״וּ, and is the *hiphil* of יָשַׁב for הוֹשַׁבְתִּים (LXX., Maurer, Hengstenberg ; comp. Olshausen, *Grammat.* p. 559), and not a *hiphil* of שׁוּב, in which a transition has taken place into the *hiphil* form of the verbs פ״וּ (Ewald, § 196, *b*, Not. 1 ; Targ., Vulg., Hitzig, and Koehler). For " bringing back " affirms too little here. הוֹשַׁבְתִּים, " I make them dwell," corresponds rather to " they shall be as if they had not been cast off," without needing any further definition, since not only do we meet with יָשַׁב without anything else, in the sense of peaceful, happy dwelling (*e.g.* Mic. v. 3), but here also the manner of dwelling is indicated in the appended clause כַּאֲשֶׁר לֹא־זְנַחְתִּים, " as before they were cast off" (cf. Ezek. xxxvi. 11). אֶעֱנֵם is also not to be taken as referring to the answering of the prayers, which Ephraim addressed to Jehovah out of its distress, out of its imprisonment (Koehler), but is to be taken in a much more general sense, as in ch. xiii. 9, Isa. lviii. 9, and Hos. ii. 23. Ephraim, like Judah, will also become a hero, and rejoice as if with wine, *i.e.* fight joyfully like a hero strengthened with wine (cf. Ps. lxxviii. 65, 66). This rejoicing in conflict the sons will see, and exult in consequence; so that it will be a lasting joy.

In order to remove all doubt as to the realization of this promise, the deliverance of Ephraim is described still more minutely in vers. 8–12. Ver. 8. "*I will hiss to them, and gather them; for I have redeemed them: and they will multiply as they have multiplied.* Ver. 9. *And I will sow them among the nations: and in the far-off lands will they remember me; and will live with their sons, and return.* Ver. 10. *And I will bring them back out of the land of Egypt, and gather them out of Asshur, and bring them into the land of Gilead and of Lebanon; and room will not be found for them.*" That these verses do not treat of a fresh (second) dispersion of Ephraim, or represent the carrying away as still in the future (Hitzig), is evident from the words themselves, when correctly interpreted. Not only are the enticing and gathering together (ver. 8) mentioned before the sowing or dispersing (ver. 9), but they are both expressed by similar verbal forms (אֶשְׁרְקָה and אֶזְרָעֵם); and the misinterpretation is thereby precluded, that events occurring at different times are referred to. We must also observe the voluntative form אֶשְׁרְקָה, "I will (not I shall) hiss to them, *i.e.* entice them" (*sháraq* being used for alluring, as in Isa. v. 26 and vii. 18), as well as the absence of a copula. They both show that the intention here is simply to explain with greater clearness what is announced in vers. 6, 7. The perfect פְּדִיתִים is prophetic, like רִחַמְתִּים in ver. 6. The further promise, "they will multiply," etc., cannot be taken as referring either merely to the multiplication of Israel in exile (Hengst., Koehler, etc.), or merely to the future multiplication after the gathering together. According to the position in which the words stand between אֲקַבְּצֵם and אֶזְרָעֵם, they must embrace both the multiplication during the dispersion, and the multiplication after the gathering together. The perfect כְּמוֹ רָבוּ points to the increase which Israel experienced in the olden time under the oppression of Egypt (Ex. i. 7, 12). This increase, which is also promised in Ezek. xxxvi. 10, 11, is effected by God's sowing them broadcast among the nations. זָרַע does not mean to scatter, but to sow, to sow broadcast (see at Hos. ii. 25). Consequently the reference cannot be to a dispersion of Israel inflicted as a punishment. The sowing denotes the multiplication (cf. Jer. xxxi. 27), and is not to be interpreted, as Neumann and Kliefoth suppose, as signifying that the Ephraimites are to be scattered as seed-corn among the heathen, to spread the knowledge of Jehovah among the nations. This thought is quite foreign to the context; and even in the words, "in far-off lands will they remember me," it is neither expressed nor implied. These words are to be connected with what follows: Because they remember the Lord in far-off lands, they will live, and return with their children. In ver. 10a the gathering together and leading back of Israel are more minutely described, and indeed as taking place out of the land of Asshur and out of Egypt. The fact that these two lands are mentioned, upon which modern critics have principally founded their arguments in favour of the origin of this prophecy before the captivity, cannot be explained " from the circumstance that in the time of Tiglath-pileser and Shalmaneser many Ephraimites had fled to Egypt" (Koehler and others); for history knows nothing of this, and the supposition is merely a loophole for escaping from a difficulty. Such passages as Hos. viii. 13, ix. 3, 6, xi. 11, Mic. vii. 12, Isa. xi. 11, xxvii. 13, furnish no historical evidence of such thing. Even if certain Ephraimites had fled to Egypt, these could not be explained as relating to a return or gathering together of the Ephraimites or Israelites out of Egypt and Assyria, because the announcement presupposes that the Ephraimites had been transported to Egypt in quite as large numbers as to Assyria,—a fact which cannot be established either in relation to the times before or to those after the captivity. Egypt, as we have already shown at Hos. ix. 3 (cf. viii. 13), is rather introduced in all the passages mentioned simply as a type of the land of bondage, on account of its having been the land in which Israel lived in the olden time, under the oppression of the heathen world. And Asshur is introduced in the same way, as the land into which the ten tribes had been afterwards exiled. This typical significance is placed beyond all doubt by ver. 11, since the redemption of Israel out of the countries named is there exhibited under the type of the liberation of Israel out of the bondage of Egypt under the guidance of Moses. (Compare also Delitzsch on Isa. xi. 11.) The Ephraimites are to return into the land of Gilead and Lebanon; the former representing the territory of the ten tribes in the olden time to the east of the Jordan, the latter that to the west (cf. Mic. vii. 14). לֹא יִמָּצֵא, there is not found for them, *sc.* the necessary room : equivalent to, it will not be sufficient for them (as in Josh. xvii. 16).

Ver. 11. "*And he goes through the sea of affliction, and smites the waves in the sea, and all the depths of the river dry up; and the pride of Asshur will be cast down, and the staff of Egypt will depart.* Ver. 12. *And I make them strong in Jehovah; and they will walk in His name, is the saying of Jehovah.*" The subject in ver. 11 is Jehovah. He goes, as once He went in the pillar of cloud as the angel of the Lord in the time of Moses, through the sea of affliction. צָרָה, which has been interpreted in very different ways, we take as in apposition to יָם, though not as a permutative, "through the sea, viz. the affliction" (C. B. Mich., Hengst.) ; but in this sense, "the sea, which caused distress or confinement," so that the simple reason why צָרָה is not connected with יָם in the construct state, but placed in apposition, is that the sea might not be described as a straitened sea, or sea of anxiety. This apposition points to the fact which floated before the prophet's mind, namely, that the Israelites under Moses were so confined by the Red Sea that they thought they were lost (Ex. xiv. 10 sqq.). The objection urged by Koehler against this view—namely, that צָרָה as a noun is not used in the sense of local strait or confinement—is proved to be unfounded by Jonah ii. 3 and Zeph. i. 15. All the other explanations of *tsârâh* are much more unnatural, being either unsuitable, like the suggestion of Koehler to take it as an exclamation, "O distress!" or grammatically untenable, like the rendering adopted by Maurer and Kliefoth, after the Chaldæan usage, "he splits." The smiting of the waves in the sea does indeed play upon the division of the waves of the sea when the Israelites passed through the Red Sea (Ex. xiv. 16, 21 ; cf. Josh. iii. 13, Ps. lxxvii. 17, cxiv. 5);

but it affirms still more, as the following clause shows, namely, a binding or constraining of the waves, by which they are annihilated, or a drying up of the floods, like הֶחֱרִים in Isa. xi. 15. Only the floods of the Nile (יְאֹר) are mentioned, because the allusion to the slavery of Israel in Egypt predominates, and the redemption of the Israelites out of all the lands of the nations is represented as bringing out of the slave-house of Egypt. The drying up of the flood-depths of the Nile is therefore a figure denoting the casting down of the imperial power in all its historical forms; Asshur and Egypt being mentioned by name in the last clause answering to the declaration in ver. 10, and the tyranny of Asshur being characterized by גָּאוֹן, pride, haughtiness (cf. Isa. x. 7 sqq.), and that of Egypt by the rod of its taskmasters. In ver. 12 the promise for Ephraim is brought to a close with the general thought that they will obtain strength in the Lord, and walk in the power of His name. With וְגִבַּרְתִּים the address reverts to its starting-point in ver. 6. בַּיהוָה stands for בִּי, to point emphatically to the Lord, in whom Israel as the people of God had its strength. Walking in the name of Jehovah is to be taken as in Mic. iv. 5, and to be understood not as relating to the attitude of Israel towards God, or to the "self-attestation of Israel" (Koehler), but to the result, viz. walking in the strength of the Lord.

If, in conclusion, we survey the whole promise from ch. ix. 11 onwards, there are two leading thoughts developed in it: (a) That those members of the covenant nation who were still scattered among the heathen should be redeemed out of their misery, and gathered together in the kingdom of the King who was coming for Zion, i.e. of the Messiah; (b) That the Lord would endow all His people with power for the conquest of the heathen. They were both fulfilled, in weak commencements only, in the times immediately following and down to the coming of Christ, by the return of many Jews out of captivity and into the land of the fathers, particularly when Galilee was strongly peopled by Israelites; and also by the protection and care which God bestowed upon the people in the contests between the powers of the world for supremacy in Palestine. The principal fulfilment is of a spiritual kind, and was effected through the gathering of the Jews into the kingdom of Christ, which commenced in the times of the apostles, and will continue till the remnant of Israel is converted to Christ its Saviour.

ISRAEL UNDER THE GOOD SHEPHERD AND THE FOOLISH ONE.—CHAP. XI.

In the second half of the " burden " upon the world-power, which is contained in this chapter, the thought indicated in ch. x. 3—namely, that the wrath of Jehovah is kindled over the shepherds when He visits His flock, the house of Judah— is more elaborately developed, and an announcement is made of the manner in which the Lord visits His people, and rescues it out of the hands of the world-powers who are seeking to destroy it, and then, because it repays His pastoral fidelity with ingratitude, gives it up into the hands of the foolish shepherd, who will destroy it, but who will also fall under judgment himself in consequence. The picture sketched in ch. ix. 8-10, 12, of the future of Israel is thus completed, and enlarged by the description of the judgment accompanying the salvation ; and through this addition an abuse of the proclamation of salvation is prevented. But in order to bring out into greater prominence the obverse side of the salvation, there is appended to the announcement of salvation in ch. x. the threat of judgment in vers. 1–3, without anything to explain the transition ; and only after that is the attitude of the Lord towards His people and the heathen world, out of which the necessity for the judgment sprang, more fully described. Hence this chapter divides itself into three sections : viz. the threat of judgment (vers. 1–3) ; the description of the good shepherd (vers. 4–14) ; and the sketch of the foolish shepherd (vers. 15–17).

Vers. 1–3. THE DEVASTATION OF THE HOLY LAND.— Ver. 1. *" Open thy gates, O Lebanon, and let fire devour thy cedars ! Ver. 2. Howl, cypress ; for the cedar is fallen, for the glory is laid waste ! Howl, ye oaks of Bashan ; for the inaccessible forest is laid low ! Ver. 3. A loud howling of the shepherds ; for their glory is laid waste ! A loud roaring of the young lions ; for the splendour of Jordan is laid waste !"* That these verses do not form the commencement of a new prophecy, having no connection with the previous one, but that they are simply a new turn given to that prophecy, is evident not only from the omission of any heading or of any indication whatever which could point to the commencement of a fresh word of God, but still more so from the fact that the allusion to Lebanon and Bashan and the thickets of Judah points back unmistakeably to the land of Gilead and of Lebanon (ch. x. 10), and shows a connection between ch. xi. and x., although this retrospect is not decided enough to lay a foundation for the view that vers. 1–3 form a conclusion to the prophecy in ch. x., to which their contents by no means apply. For let us interpret the figurative description in these verses in what manner we will, so much at any rate is clear, that they are of a threatening character, and as a threat not only form an antithesis to the announcement of salvation in ch. x., but are substantially connected with the destruction which will overtake the "flock of the slaughter," and therefore serve as a prelude, as it were, to the judgment announced in vers. 4–7. The undeniable relation in which Lebanon, Bashan, and the Jordan stand to the districts of Gilead and Lebanon, also gives us a clue to the explanation; since it shows that Lebanon, the northern frontier of the holy land, and Bashan, the northern part of the territory of the Israelites to the east of the Jordan, are synecdochical terms, denoting the holy land itself regarded in its two halves, and therefore that the cedars, cypresses, and oaks in these portions of the land cannot be figurative representations of heathen rulers (Targ., Eph. Syr., Kimchi, etc.); but if powerful men and tyrants are to be understood at all by these terms, the allusion can only be to the rulers and great men of the nation of Israel (Hitzig, Maurer, Hengst., Ewald, etc.). But this allegorical interpretation of the cedars, cypresses, and oaks, however old and widely spread it may be, is not so indisputable as that we could say with Kliefoth: "The words themselves do not allow of our finding an announcement of the devastation of the holy land therein." For even if the words themselves affirm nothing more than "that the very existence of the cedars, oaks, shepherds, lions, is in danger; and that if these should fall, Lebanon will give way to the fire, the forest of Bashan will fall, the thicket of Jordan be laid waste;" yet through the destruction of the cedars, oaks, etc., the soil on which these trees grow is also devastated and laid waste. The picture is a dramatic one. Instead of the devastation of Lebanon being announced, it is summoned to open its gates, that the fire may be able to enter in and devour its cedars. The cypresses, which hold the second place among the celebrated woods of Lebanon, are then called upon to howl over the fall of the cedars, not so much from sympathy as because the same fate is awaiting them. The words אֲשֶׁר אַדִּירִם שֻׁדָּדוּ contain a second explanatory clause. אֲשֶׁר is a conjunction (for, because), as in Gen. xxx. 18, xxxi. 49. *'Addīrīm* are not the glorious or lofty ones among the people (Hengst., Kliefoth), but the glorious ones among the things spoken of in the context,—namely, the noble trees, the cedars and cypresses. The oaks of Bashan are also called upon to howl, because they too will fall like "the inaccessible forest," *i.e.* the cedar forest of Lebanon. The *keri habbâtsīr* is a needless correction, because the article does not compel us to take the word as a substantive. If the adjective is really a participle, the article is generally attached to it alone, and omitted from the noun (cf. Ges. § 111, 2, *a*). קוֹל יְלָלַת, voice of howling, equivalent to a loud howling. The shepherds howl, because *'addartâm*, their glory, is laid waste. We are not to understand by this their flock, but their pasture, as the parallel member גְּאוֹן הַיַּרְדֵּן and the parallel passage Jer. xxv. 36 show, where the shepherds howl, because their pasture is destroyed. What the pasture, *i.e.* the good pasture ground of the land of Bashan, is to the shepherds, that is the pride of Jordan to the young lions,—namely, the thicket and reeds which grew so luxuriantly on the banks of the Jordan, and afforded so safe and convenient a lair for lions (cf. Jer. xii. 5, xlix. 19, l. 44). Ver. 3 announces in distinct terms a devastation of the soil or land. It follows from this that the cedars, cypresses, and oaks are not figures representing earthly rulers. No conclusive arguments can be adduced in support of such an allegory. It is true that in Isa. x. 34 the powerful army of Assyria is compared to Lebanon; and in Jer. xxii. 6 the head of the cedar forest is a symbol of the royal house of Judah; and that in Jer. xxii. 23 it is used as a figurative term for Jerusalem (see at Hab. ii. 17); but neither men generally, nor individual earthly rulers in particular, are represented as cedars or oaks. The cedars and cypresses of

Lebanon and the oaks of Bashan are simply figures denoting what is lofty, glorious, and powerful in the world of nature and humanity, and are only to be referred to persons so far as their lofty position in the state is concerned. Consequently we get the following as the thought of these verses : The land of Israel, with all its powerful and glorious creatures, is to become desolate. Now, inasmuch as the desolation of a land also involves the desolation of the people living in the land, and of its institutions, the destruction of the cedars, cypresses, etc., does include the destruction of everything lofty and exalted in the nation and kingdom ; so that in this sense the devastation of Lebanon is a figurative representation of the destruction of the Israelitish kingdom, or of the dissolution of the political existence of the ancient covenant nation. This judgment was executed upon the land and people of Israel by the imperial power of Rome. This historical reference is evident from the description which follows of the facts by which this catastrophe is brought to pass.

Vers. 4–14. This section contains a symbolical act. By the command of Jehovah the prophet assumes the office of a shepherd over the flock, and feeds it, until he is compelled by its ingratitude to break his shepherd's staff, and give up the flock to destruction. This symbolical act is not a poetical fiction, but is to be regarded in strict accordance with the words, as an internal occurrence of a visionary character and of prophetical importance, through which the faithful care of the Lord for His people is symbolized and exhibited. Ver. 4. " *Thus said Jehovah my God: Feed the slaughtering-flock ;* Ver. 5. *whose purchasers slay them, and bear no blame, and their sellers say, Blessed be Jehovah ! I am getting rich, and their shepherds spare them not.* Ver. 6. *For I shall no more spare the inhabitants of the earth, is the saying of Jehovah ; and behold I cause the men to fall into one another's hands, and into the king's hand ; and they will smite the land, and I shall not deliver out of their hand.*" The person who receives the commission to feed the flock is the prophet. This is apparent, both from the expression " my God" (ver. 5, comp. with vers. 7 sqq.), and also from ver. 15, according to which he is to take the instruments of a foolish shepherd. This latter verse also shows clearly enough, that the prophet does not come forward here as performing these acts in his own person, but that he represents another, who does things in vers. 8, 12, and 13, which in truth neither Zechariah nor any other prophet ever did, but only God through His Son, and that in ver. 10 He is identified with God, inasmuch as here the person who breaks the staff is the prophet, and the person who has made the covenant with the nations is God. These statements are irreconcilable, both with Hofmann's assumption, that in this symbolical transaction Zechariah represents the prophetic office, and with that of Koehler, that he represents the mediatorial office. For apart from the fact that such abstract notions are foreign to the prophet's announcement, these assumptions are overthrown by the fact that neither the prophetic office nor the mediatorial office can be identified with God, and also that the work which the prophet carries out in what follows was not accomplished through the prophetic office. " The destruction of the three shepherds, or world-powers (ver. 8), is not effected through the prophetic word or office ; and the fourth shepherd (ver. 15) is not instituted through the prophetic office and word" (Kliefoth). The shepherd depicted by the prophet can only be Jehovah Himself, or the angel of Jehovah, who is equal in nature to Himself, *i.e.* the Messiah. But since the angel of Jehovah, who appears in the visions, is not mentioned in our oracle, and as the coming of the Messiah is also announced elsewhere as the coming of Jehovah to His people, we shall have in this instance also to understand Jehovah Himself by the shepherd represented in the prophet. He visits His flock, as it is stated in ch. x. 3 and Ezek. xxxiv. 11, 12, and assumes the care of them. The distinction between the prophet and Jehovah cannot be adduced as an argument against this; for it really belongs to the symbolical representation of the matter, according to which God commissions the prophet to do what He Himself intends to do, and will surely accomplish. The more precise definition of what is here done depends upon the answer to be given to the question, Who are the slaughtering flock, which the prophet undertakes to feed? Does it denote the whole of the human race, as Hofmann supposes ; or the nation of Israel, as is assumed by the majority of commentators ? צֹאן הַהֲרֵגָה, flock of slaughtering, is an expression that may be applied either to a flock that is being slaughtered, or to one that is destined to be slaughtered in the future. In

support of the latter sense, Kliefoth argues that so long as the
sheep are being fed, they cannot have been already slaughtered,
or be even in process of slaughtering, and that ver. 6 expressly
states, that the men who are intended by the flock of slaughtering will be slaughtered in future when the time of sparing is
over, or be treated in the manner described in ver. 5. But the
first of these arguments proves nothing at all, inasmuch as,
although feeding is of course not equivalent to slaughtering,
a flock that is being slaughtered by its owners might be transferred to another shepherd to be fed, so as to rescue it from the
caprice of its masters. The second argument rests upon the
erroneous assumption that יֹשְׁבֵי הָאָרֶץ in ver. 6 is identical with
the slaughtering flock. The epithet צֹאן הַהֲרֵנָה, i.e. lit. flock of
strangling—as hârag does not mean to slay, but to strangle—is
explained in ver. 5. The flock is so called, because its present
masters are strangling it, without bearing guilt, to sell it for the
purpose of enriching themselves, and its shepherds treat it in an
unsparing manner; and ver. 6 does not give the reason why
the flock is called the flock of strangling or of slaughtering
(as Kliefoth supposes), but the reason why it is given up by
Jehovah to the prophet to feed. לֹא יֶאְשָׁמוּ does not affirm that
those who are strangling it do not think themselves to blame—
this is expressed in a different manner (cf. Jer. l. 7): nor that
they do not actually incur guilt in consequence, or do not repent
of it; for Jehovah transfers the flock to the prophet to feed,
because He does not wish its possessors to go on strangling
it, and אָשֵׁם never has the meaning, to repent. לֹא יֶאְשָׁמוּ refers
rather to the fact that these men have hitherto gone unpunished, that they still continue to prosper. So that 'âshêm
means to bear or expiate the guilt, as in Hos. v. 15, xiv. 1 (Ges.,
Hitzig, Ewald, etc.). What follows also agrees with this,—
namely, that the sellers have only their own advantage in view,
and thank God that they have thereby become rich. The
singular יֹאמַר is used distributively: every one of them says
so. וַאַעְשִׁר, a syncopated form for וְאַעְשִׁר (Ewald, § 73, b), and
ו expressing the consequence, that I enrich myself (cf. Ewald,
§ 235, b). רֹעֵיהֶם are the former shepherds. The imperfects
are not futures, but express the manner in which the flock was
accustomed to be treated at the time when the prophet undertook to feed it. Jehovah will put an end to this capricious

treatment of the flock, by commanding the prophet to feed it. The reason for this He assigns in ver. 6 : For I shall not spare the inhabitants of the earth any longer. יֹשְׁבֵי הָאָרֶץ cannot be the inhabitants of the land, *i.e.* those who are described as the " flock of slaughtering" in ver. 4 ; for in that case " feeding" would be equivalent to slaughtering, or making ready for slaughtering. But although a flock is eventually destined for slaughtering, it is not fed for this purpose only, but generally to yield profit to its owner. Moreover, the figure of feeding is never used in the Scriptures in the sense of making ready for destruction, but always denotes fostering and affectionate care for the preservation of anything; and in the case before us, the shepherd feeds the flock entrusted to him, by slaying the three bad shepherds ; and it is not till the flock has become weary of his tending that he breaks the shepherd's staves, and lays down his pastoral office, to give them up to destruction. Consequently the יֹשְׁבֵי הָאָרֶץ are different from the צֹאן הַהֲרֵגָה, and are those in the midst of whom the flock is living, or in whose possession and power it is. They cannot be the inhabitants of a land, however, but since they have kings (in the plural), as the expression " every one into the hand of his king" clearly shows, the inhabitants of the earth, or the world-powers ; from which it also follows that the " flock of slaughtering" is not the human race, but the people of Israel, as we may clearly see from what follows, especially from vers. 11–14. Israel was given up by Jehovah into the hands of the nations of the world, or the imperial powers, to punish it for its sin. But as these nations abused the power entrusted to them, and sought utterly to destroy the nation of God, which they ought only to have chastised, the Lord takes charge of His people as their shepherd, because He will no longer spare the nations of the world, *i.e.* will not any longer let them deal with His people at pleasure, without being punished. The termination of the sparing will show itself in the fact that God causes the nations to destroy themselves by civil wars, and to be smitten by tyrannical kings. הִמְצִיא בְּיַד ר', to cause to fall into the hand of another, *i.e.* to deliver up to his power (cf. 2 Sam. iii. 8). הָאָדָם is the human race ; and מַלְכּוֹ, the king of each, is the king to whom each is subject. The subject of כִּתְּתוּ is רֵעֵהוּ and מַלְכּוֹ, the men and the kings who tyrannize over the others. These smite them in pieces, *i.e.* devastate the earth by civil war and tyranny, without any interposition on the part of God to rescue the inhabitants of the earth, or nations beyond the limits of Israel, out of their hand, or to put any restraint upon tyranny and self-destruction.

From ver. 7 onwards the feeding of the flock is described. Ver. 7. *" And I fed the slaughtering flock, therewith the wretched ones of the sheep, and took to myself two staves: the one I called Favour, the other I called Bands; and so I fed the flock.* Ver. 8a. *And I destroyed three of the shepherds in one month."* The difficult expression לָכֵן, of which very different renderings have been given (lit. with the so-being), is evidently used here in the same sense as in Isa. xxvi. 14, lxi. 7, Jer. ii. 33, etc., so as to introduce what occurred *eo ipso* along with the other event which took place. When the shepherd fed the slaughtering flock, he thereby, or at the same time, fed the wretched ones of the sheep. עֲנִיֵּי הַצֹּאן, not the most wretched of the sheep, but the wretched ones among the sheep, like צְעִירֵי הַצֹּאן in Jer. xlix. 20, l. 45, the small, weak sheep. עֲנִיֵּי הַצֹּאן therefore form one portion of the צֹאן הַהֲרֵגָה, as Hofmann and Kliefoth have correctly explained; whereas, if they were identical, the whole of the appended clause would be very tautological, since the thought that the flock was in a miserable state was already expressed clearly enough in the predicate הֲרֵגָה, and the explanation of it in ver. 5. This view is confirmed by ver. 11, where עֲנִיֵּי הַצֹּאן is generally admitted to be simply one portion of the flock. To feed the flock, the prophet takes two shepherds' staves, to which he gives names, intended to point to the blessings which the flock receives through his pastoral activity. The fact that he takes two staves does not arise from the circumstance that the flock consists of two portions, and cannot be understood as signifying that he feeds one portion of the flock with the one staff, and the other portion with the other. According to ver. 7, he feeds the whole flock with the first staff; and the destruction to which, according to ver. 9, it is to be given up when he relinquishes his office, is only made fully apparent when the two staves are broken. The prophet takes two staves for the simple purpose of setting forth the double kind of salvation which is bestowed upon the nation through the care of the good shepherd. The first staff he calls נֹעַם, *i.e.*

loveliness, and also favour (cf. Ps. xc. 17, נֹעַם יְהֹוָה). It is in the latter sense that the word is used here ; for the shepherd's staff shows what Jehovah will thereby bestow upon His people. The second staff he calls חֹבְלִים, which is in any case a *kal* participle of חָבַל. Of the two certain meanings which this verb has in the *kal*, viz. to bind (hence *chebhel*, a cord or rope) and to ill-treat (cf. Job xxxiv. 31), the second, upon which the rendering staff-woe is founded, does not suit the explanation which is given in ver. 14 of the breaking of this staff. The first is the only suitable one, viz. the binding ones, equivalent to the bandage or connection. Through the staff *nōʻam* (Favour), the favour of God, which protects it from being injured by the heathen nations, is granted to the flock (ver. 10) ; and through the staff *chōbhᵉlīm* the wretched sheep receive the blessing of fraternal unity or binding (ver. 14). The repetition of the words וָאֶרְעֶה אֶת־הַצֹּאן (end of ver. 7) expresses the idea that the feeding is effected with both staves. The first thing which the shepherd appointed by God does for the flock is, according to ver. 8, to destroy three shepherds. הִכְחִיד, the *hiphil* of כָּחַד, signifies ἀφανίζειν, to annihilate, to destroy (as in Ex. xxiii. 23). אֶת־שְׁלֹשֶׁת הָרֹעִים may be rendered, the three shepherds (τοὺς τρεῖς ποιμένας, LXX.), or three of the shepherds, so that the article only refers to the genitive, as in Ex. xxvi. 3, 9, Josh. xvii. 11, 1 Sam. xx. 20, Isa. xxx. 26, and as is also frequently the case when two nouns are connected together in the construct state (see Ges. § 111, Anm.). We agree with Koehler in regarding the latter as the only admissible rendering here, because in what precedes shepherds only have been spoken of, and not any definite number of them. The shepherds, of whom three are destroyed, are those who strangled the flock according to ver. 5, and who are therefore destroyed in order to liberate the flock from their tyranny. But who are these three shepherds ? It was a very widespread and ancient opinion, and one which we meet with in Theodoret, Cyril, and Jerome, that the three classes of Jewish rulers are intended,— namely, princes (or kings), priests, and prophets. But apart from the fact that in the times after the captivity, to which our prophecy refers, prophesying and the prophetic office were extinct, and that in the vision in ch. iv. 14 Zechariah only mentions two classes in the covenant nation who were represented by the prince Zerubbabel and the high priest Joshua; apart, I say, from this, such a view is irreconcilable with the words themselves, inasmuch as it requires us to dilute the destruction into a deposition from office, or, strictly speaking, into a counteraction of their influence upon the people; and this is quite sufficient to overthrow it. What Hengstenberg says in vindication of it—namely, that "an actual extermination cannot be intended, because the shepherds appear immediately afterwards as still in existence"—is founded upon a false interpretation of the second half of the verse. So much is unquestionably correct, that we have not to think of the extermination or slaying of three particular individuals,[1] and that not so much because it cannot be shown that three rulers or heads of the nation were ever destroyed in the space of a month, either in the times before the captivity or in those which followed, as because the persons occurring in this vision are not individuals, but classes of men. As the רעים mentioned in ver. 5 as not sparing the flock are to be understood as signifying heathen rulers, so here the three shepherds are heathen liege-lords of the covenant nation. Moreover, as it is unanimously acknowledged by modern commentators that the definite number does not stand for an indefinite plurality, it is natural to think of the three imperial rulers into whose power Israel fell, that is to say, not of three rulers of one empire, but of the rulers of the three empires. The statement as to time, "in one month," which does not affirm that the three were shepherds within one month, as Hitzig supposes, but that the three shepherds were destroyed in one month, may easily be reconciled with this, if we only observe that, in a symbolical transaction, even the distinctions of time are intended to be interpreted symbolically. There can be no doubt whatever

---

[1] The attempts of rationalistic commentators to prove that the three shepherds are three kings of the kingdom of the ten tribes, have completely broken down, inasmuch as of the kings Zechariah, Shallum, and Menahem (2 Kings xv. 8–14), Shallum alone reigned an entire month, so that not even the ungrammatical explanation of Hitzig, to the effect that בְּיֶרַח אֶחָד refers to the reign of these kings, and not to their destruction, furnishes a sufficient loophole; whilst Maurer, Bleek, Ewald, and Bunsen felt driven to invent a third king or usurper, in order to carry out their view.

that "a month" signifies a comparatively brief space of time. At the same time, it is equally impossible to deny that the assumption that "in a month" is but another way of saying in a very short time, is not satisfactory, inasmuch as it would have been better to say "in a week," if this had been the meaning; and, on the other hand, a year would not have been a long time for the extermination of three shepherds. Nor can Hofmann's view be sustained,—namely, that the one month (= 30 days) is to be interpreted on the basis of Dan. ix. 24, as a prophetical period of $30 \times 7 = 210$ years, and that this definition of the time refers to the fact that the Babylonian, Medo-Persian, and Macedonian empires were destroyed within a period of 210 years. For there is no tenable ground for calculating the days of a month according to sabbatical periods, since there is no connection between the *yerach* of this verse and the שָׁבֻעִים of Daniel, to say nothing of the fact that the time which intervened between the conquest of Babylon and the death of Alexander the Great was not 210 years, but 215. The only way in which the expression "in one month" can be interpreted symbolically is that proposed by Kliefoth and Koehler,—namely, by dividing the month as a period of thirty days into three times ten days according to the number of the shepherds, and taking each ten days as the time employed in the destruction of a shepherd. Ten is the number of the completion or the perfection of any earthly act or occurrence. If, therefore, each shepherd was destroyed in ten days, and the destruction of the three was executed in a month, *i.e.* within a space of three times ten days following one another, the fact is indicated, on the one hand, that the destruction of each of these shepherds followed directly upon that of the other; and, on the other hand, that this took place after the full time allotted for his rule had passed away. The reason why the prophet does not say three times ten days, nor even thirty days, but connects the thirty days together into a month, is that he wishes not only to indicate that the time allotted for the duration of the three imperial monarchies is a brief one, but also to exhibit the unwearied activity of the shepherd, which is done more clearly by the expression "one month" than by "thirty days."

The description of the shepherd's activity is followed, from ver. 8*b* onwards, by a description of the attitude which the flock assumed in relation to the service performed on its behalf. Ver. 8*b*. "*And my soul became impatient over them, and their soul also became weary of me.* Ver. 9. *Then I said, I will not feed you any more ; what dieth may die, and what perisheth may perish ; and those which remain may devour one another's flesh.* Ver. 10. *And I took my staff Favour, and broke it in pieces, to destroy my covenant which I had made with all nations.* Ver. 11. *And it was destroyed in that day ; and so the wretched of the sheep, which gave heed to me, perceived that it was the word of Jehovah.*" The way in which ver. 8*a* and ver. 8*b* are connected in the Masoretic text, has led the earlier commentators, and even Hengstenberg, Ebrard, and Kliefoth, to take the statement in ver. 8*b* as also referring to the shepherds. But this is grammatically impossible, because the imperfect *c. Vav consec.* וַתִּקְצַר in this connection, in which the same verbal forms both before and after express the sequence both of time and thought, cannot be used in the sense of the pluperfect. And this is the sense in which it must be taken, if the words referred to the shepherds, because the prophet's becoming impatient with the shepherds, and the shepherds' dislike to the prophet, must of necessity have preceded the destruction of the shepherds. Again, it is evident from ver. 9, as even Hitzig admits, that the prophet " did not become disgusted with the three shepherds, but with his flock, which he resolved in his displeasure to leave to its fate." As the suffix אֶתְכֶם in ver. 9 is taken by all the commentators (except Kliefoth) as referring to the flock, the suffixes בָּהֶם and נַפְשָׁם in ver. 8 must also point back to the flock (הַצֹּאן, ver. 7). קָצְרָה נֶפֶשׁ, to become impatient, as in Num. xxi. 4. בָּחֲל, which only occurs again in Prov. xx. 21 in the sense of the Arabic بَخِلَ, to be covetous, is used here in the sense of the Syriac, to experience vexation or disgust. In consequence of the experience which the shepherd of the Lord had had, according to ver. 8*b*, he resolves to give up the feeding of the flock, and relinquish it to its fate, which is described in ver. 9*b* as that of perishing and destroying one another. The participles מֵתָה, נִכְחֶדֶת, and נִשְׁאָרוֹת are present participles, that which dies is destroyed (perishes) and remains ; and the imperfects תָּמוּת, תִּכָּחֵד, and תֹּאכַלְנָה are not jussive, as the form

תְּמוּתָה clearly proves, but are expressive of that which can be or may happen (Ewald, § 136, *d*, *b*). As a sign of this, the shepherd breaks one staff in pieces, viz. the *nōʻam*, to intimate that the good which the flock has hitherto received through this staff will be henceforth withdrawn from it; that is to say, that the covenant which God has made with all nations is to be repealed or destroyed. This covenant is not the covenant made with Noah as the progenitor of all men after the flood (Kliefoth), nor a relation entered into by Jehovah with all the nationalities under which each nationality prospered, inasmuch as the shepherd continued again and again to remove its flock-destroying shepherds out of the way (Hofmann, *Schriftbeweis*, ii. 2, p. 607). For in the covenant with Noah, although the continuance of this earth was promised, and the assurance given that there should be no repetition of a flood to destroy all living things, there was no guarantee of protection from death or destruction, or from civil wars; and history has no record of any covenant made by Jehovah with the nationalities, which secured to the nations prosperity on the one hand, or deliverance from oppressors on the other. The covenant made by God with all nations refers, according to the context of this passage, to a treaty made with them by God in favour of His flock the nation of Israel, and is analogous to the treaty made by God with the beasts, according to Hos. ii. 20, that they should not injure His people, and the treaty made with the stones and the beasts of the field (Job v. 23, cf. Ezek. xxxiv. 25) This covenant consisted in the fact that God imposed upon the nations of the earth the obligation not to hurt Israel or destroy it, and was one consequence of the favour of Jehovah towards His people. Through the abrogation of this covenant Israel is delivered up to the nations, that they may be able to deal with Israel again in the manner depicted in ver. 5. It is true that Israel is not thereby delivered up at once or immediately to that self-immolation which is threatened in ver. 9, nor is this threat carried into effect through the breaking in pieces of one staff, but is only to be fully realized when the second staff is broken, whereby the shepherd entirely relinquishes the feeding of the flock. So long as the shepherd continues to feed the flock with the other staff, so long will utter destruction be averted from it, although by the breaking of the staff Favour,

protection against the nations of the world is withdrawn
from it. Ver. 11. From the abrogation of this covenant the
wretched among the sheep perceived that this was Jehovah's
word. בֵּן, so, i.e. in consequence of this. The wretched sheep
are characterized as הַשֹּׁמְרִים אֹתִי, "those which give heed to me."
אֹתִי refers to the prophet, who acts in the name of God, and
therefore really to the act of God Himself. What is affirmed
does not apply to one portion, but to all, עֲנִיֵּי הַצֹּאן, and proves
that we are to understand by these the members of the covenant nation who give heed to the word of God. What these
godly men recognised as the word of Jehovah, is evident from
the context, viz. not merely the threat expressed in ver. 9, and
embodied in the breaking of the staff Favour, but generally
speaking the whole of the prophet's symbolical actions, including both the feeding of the flock with the staves, and the
breaking of the one staff. The two together were an embodied
word of Jehovah; and the fact that it was so was discerned,
i.e. discovered by the righteous, from the effect produced upon
Israel by the breaking of the staff Favour, i.e. from the consequences of the removal of the obligation imposed upon the
heathen nations to do no hurt to Israel.

With the breaking of the staff Favour, the shepherd of the
Lord has indeed withdrawn one side of his pastoral care from
the flock that he had to feed, but his connection with it is not
yet entirely dissolved. This takes place first of all in vers.
12–14, when the flock rewards him for his service with base
ingratitude. Ver. 12. "*And I said to them, If it seem good to
you, give me my wages; but if not, let it alone : and they weighed
me as wages thirty silverlings.* Ver. 13. *Then Jehovah said to
me, Throw it to the potter, the splendid price at which I am
valued by them; and so I took the thirty silverlings, and threw it
into the house of Jehovah to the potter.* Ver. 14. *And I broke
my second staff Bands, to destroy the brotherhood between Judah
and Israel.*" אֲלֵיהֶם (to them), so far as the grammatical construction is concerned, might be addressed to the wretched
among the sheep, inasmuch as they were mentioned last. But
when we bear in mind that the shepherd began to feed not
only the wretched of the sheep, but the whole flock, and that
he did not give up any one portion of the flock by breaking
the staff Favour, we are forced to the conclusion that the words

are addressed to the whole flock, and that the demand for
wages is only intended to give the flock an opportunity for
explaining whether it is willing to acknowledge his feeding,
and appreciate it rightly. The fact that the prophet asks for
wages from the sheep may be explained very simply from the
fact that the sheep represent men. The demand for wages is
not to be understood as implying that the shepherd intended
to lay down his office as soon as he had been paid for his
service ; for in that case he would have asked for the wages
before breaking the first staff. But as he does not ask for it
till afterwards, and leaves it to the sheep to say whether they
are willing to give it or not ("if it seem good to you"), this
demand cannot have any other object than to call upon the
sheep to declare whether they acknowledge his service, and
desire it to be continued. By the wages the commentators
have very properly understood repentance and faith, or piety
of heart, humble obedience, and heartfelt, grateful love. These
are the only wages with which man can discharge his debt to
God. They weighed him now as wages thirty shekels of silver
(on the omission of *sheqel* or *keseph*, see Ges. § 120, 4, Anm. 2).
"Thirty,"—not to reward him for the one month, or for thirty
days—that is to say, to give him a shekel a day for his service
(Hofm., Klief.) : for, in the first place, it is not stated in ver. 8
that he did not feed them longer than a month ; and secondly,
a shekel was not such very small wages for a day's work, as
the wages actually paid are represented as being in ver. 13.
They rather pay him thirty shekels, with an allusion to the
fact that this sum was the compensation for a slave that had
been killed (Ex. xxi. 32), so that it was the price at which a
bond-slave could be purchased (see at Hos. iii. 2). By paying
thirty shekels, they therefore gave him to understand that
they did not estimate his service higher than the labour of a
purchased slave. To offer such wages was in fact "more
offensive than a direct refusal" (Hengstenberg). Jehovah
therefore describes the wages ironically as "a splendid value
that has been set upon me." As the prophet fed the flock
in the name of Jehovah, Jehovah regards the wages paid to
His shepherd as paid to Himself, as the value set upon His
personal work on behalf of the nation, and commands the
prophet to throw this miserable sum to the potter. Both the

verb *hishlīkh* (throw) and the contemptuous expression used in relation to the sum paid down, prove unmistakeably that the words "throw to the potter" denote the actual casting away of the money. And this alone is sufficient to show that the view founded upon the last clause of the verse, "I threw it into the house of Jehovah to the potter," viz. that *hayyōtsēr* signifies the temple treasury, and that *yōtsēr* is a secondary form or a copyist's error for אוֹצָר, is simply a mistaken attempt to solve the real difficulty. God could not possibly say to the prophet, The wages paid for my service are indeed a miserable amount, yet put it in the temple treasury, for it is at any rate better than nothing. The phrase "throw to the potter" (for the use of *hishlīkh* with 'el pers. compare 1 Kings xix. 19) is apparently a proverbial expression for contemptuous treatment (= to the knacker), although we have no means of tracing the origin of the phrase satisfactorily. Hengstenberg's assumption, that "to the potter" is the same as to an unclean place, is founded upon the assumption that the potter who worked for the temple had his workshop in the valley of Ben-Hinnom, which, having been formerly the scene of the abominable worship of Moloch, was regarded with abhorrence as an unclean place after its defilement by Josiah (2 Kings xxiii. 10), and served as the slaughter-house for the city. But it by no means follows from Jer. xviii. 2 and xix. 2, that this potter dwelt in the valley of Ben-Hinnom; whereas Jer. xix. 1 and 2 lead rather to the opposite conclusion. If, for example, God there says to Jeremiah, "Go and buy a pitcher of the potter (ver. 1), and go out into the valley of Ben-Hinnom, which lies in front of the potter's gate" (ver. 2), it follows pretty clearly from these words that the pottery itself stood within the city gate. But even if the potter had had his workshop in the valley of Ben-Hinnom, which was regarded as unclean, he would not have become unclean himself in consequence, so that men could say "to the potter," just as we should say "*zum Schinder*" (to the knacker); and if he had been looked upon as unclean in this way, he could not possibly have worked for the temple, or supplied the cooking utensils for use in the service of God— namely, for boiling the holy sacrificial flesh. The attempts at an explanation made by Grotius and Hofmann are equally unsatisfactory. The former supposes that throwing anything before the potter was equivalent to throwing it upon the heap of potsherds; the latter, that it was equivalent to throwing it into the dirt. But the potter had not to do with potsherds only, and potter's clay is not street mire. The explanation given by Koehler is more satisfactory; namely, that the meaning is, "The amount is just large enough to pay a potter for the pitchers and pots that have been received from him, and which are thought of so little value, that men easily comfort themselves when one or the other is broken." But this does not do justice to *hishlīkh*, since men do not *throw* to a potter the money for his wares, but put it into his hand. The word *hishlīkh* involves the idea of contempt, and earthen pots were things of insignificant worth. The execution of the command, "I threw it (*ōthō*, the wages paid me) into the house of Jehovah to the potter," cannot be understood as signifying "into the house of Jehovah, that it might be taken thence to the potter" (Hengstenberg). If this were the meaning, it should have been expressed more clearly. As the words read, they can only be understood as signifying that the potter was in the house of Jehovah when the money was thrown to him; that he had either some work to do there, or that he had come there to bring some earthenware for the temple kitchens (cf. xiv. 20). This circumstance is no doubt a significant one; but the meaning is not merely to show that it was as the servant of the Lord, or in the name and by the command of Jehovah, that the prophet did this, instead of keeping the money (Koehler); for Zechariah could have expressed this in two or three words in a much simpler and clearer manner. The house of Jehovah came into consideration here rather as the place where the people appeared in the presence of their God, either to receive or to solicit the blessings of the covenant from Him. What took place in the temple, was done before the face of God, that God might call His people to account for it. Ver. 14. In consequence of this shameful payment for his service, the shepherd of the Lord breaks his second staff, as a sign that he will no longer feed the ungrateful nation, but leave it to its fate. The breaking of this staff is interpreted, in accordance with its name, as breaking or destroying the brotherhood between Judah and Israel. With these words, which are chosen with reference to the former division of the nation into two hostile kingdoms, the dissolution of the fraternal unity of the nation is depicted, and the breaking up of the nation into parties opposing and destroying one another is represented as the result of a divine decree. Hofmann, Ebrard (*Offenbarung Johannis*), and Kliefoth have erroneously supposed that this relates to the division of the covenant nation into two parties, one of which, answering to the earlier Judah, would receive Christ, and remain the people of God; whilst the other, answering to the Ephraim or Israel of the times after Solomon, would reject Christ, and therefore be exposed to hardening and judgment. According to the evident meaning of the symbolical representation, the whole flock paid the good shepherd wages, which were tantamount to a rejection of his pastoral care, and was therefore given up by him; so that by falling into parties it destroyed itself, and, as the shepherd tells it in ver. 9, one devoured the flesh of the other. This is not at variance with the fact that by this self-destroying process they did not all perish, but that the miserable ones among the sheep who gave heed to the Lord, *i.e.* discerned their Saviour in the shepherd, and accepted Jesus Christ as the Messiah, were saved. This is simply passed over in our description, which treats of the fate of the whole nation as such, as for example in Rom. ix. 31, xi. 11–15, because the number of these believers formed a vanishing minority in comparison with the whole nation. The breaking up of the nation into parties manifested itself, however, in a terrible manner soon after the rejection of Christ, and accelerated its ruin in the Roman war.

There is this difference, however, in the interpretation which has been given to this symbolical prophecy, so far as the historical allusion or fulfilment is concerned, by expositors who believe in revelation, and very properly understand it as referring to the times of the second temple: namely, that some regard it as setting forth the whole of the conduct of God towards the covenant nation under the second temple; whilst others take it to be merely a symbol of one single attempt to save the nation when on the verge of ruin, namely, that of the pastoral office of Christ. Hengstenberg, with many of the older commentators, has decided in favour of the latter view. But all that he adduces in proof of the exclusive correctness of this explanation does not touch the fact itself, but simply answers weak arguments by which the first view has been defended by its earlier supporters; whilst the main argument which he draws from ver. 8, to prove that the symbolical action of the prophet sets forth one single act of pastoral fidelity on the part of the Lord, to be accomplished in a comparatively brief space of time, rests upon a false interpretation of the verse in question. By the three shepherds, which the shepherd of Jehovah destroyed in a month, we are to understand, as we have shown at ver. 8, not the three classes of Jewish rulers, but the three imperial rulers, in whose power Israel continued from the times of the captivity to the time of Christ. But the supposition that this section refers exclusively to the work of Christ for the salvation of Israel during His life upon earth, is quite irreconcilable with this. We cannot therefore come to any other conclusion than that the first view, which has been defended by Calvin and others, and in the most recent times by Hofmann, Kliefoth, and Koehler, is the correct one, though we need not therefore assume with Calvin that the prophet "represents in his own person all the shepherds, by whose hand God ruled the people;" or discern, as Hofmann does, in the shepherd of the Lord merely a personification of the prophetic order; or, according to the form in which Koehler expresses the same view, a representation of the mediatorial work in the plan of salvation, of which Daniel was the first representative, and which was afterwards exhibited on the one hand by Haggai and Zechariah, and on the other hand by Zerubbabel and his successors, as the civil rulers of Israel, and by Joshua and those priests who resumed the duties of their office along with him. For the extermination or overthrow of the three imperial rulers or imperial powers was no more effected or carried out by the prophets named, than by the civil rulers and priesthood of Israel. The destruction was effected by Jehovah without the intervention of either the prophets, the priests, or the civil authorities of the Jews; and what Jehovah accomplished in this respect as· the Shepherd of His people, was wrought by Him in that form of revelation by which He prepared the way for His coming to His people in the incarnation of Jesus Christ, namely as the Angel of Jehovah, although this form is not more precisely indicated in the symbolical action described in the chapter before us. In that action the shepherd, to whom thirty silverlings are weighed out as his wages, is so far from being regarded as distinct from Jehovah, that Jehovah Himself speaks of these wages as the price at which He was valued by the people; and it is only from the gospel history that we learn that it was not Jehovah the super-terrestrial God, but the Son of God, who became incarnate in Christ, *i.e.* the Messiah, who was betrayed and sold for such a price as this.

What the Evangelist Matthew observes in relation to the fulfilment of vers. 12 and 13, presents various difficulties. After describing in ch. xxvi. the betrayal of Jesus by Judas, the taking of Jesus, and His condemnation to death by the Roman governor Pontius Pilate at the instigation of the high priests and elders of the Jews; and having still further related that Judas, feeling remorse at the condemnation of Jesus, brought back to the high priests and elders the thirty silver-lings paid to him for the betrayal, with the confession that he had betrayed innocent blood, and that having thrown down the money in the temple, he went and hanged himself, whereupon the high priests resolved to apply the money to the purchase of a potter's field as a burial-ground for pilgrims; he adds in ch. xxvii. 9, 10: "Then was fulfilled that which was spoken by Jeremiah the prophet, saying, And they took the thirty pieces of silver, the price of him that was valued, whom they of the children of Israel did value, and gave them for the potter's field, as the Lord appointed me." The smallest difficulty of all is occasioned by the fact that the thirty silverlings were weighed, according to the prophecy, as wages for the shepherd; whereas, according to the fulfilment, they were paid to Judas for the betrayal of Jesus. For, as soon as we trace back the form of the prophecy to its idea, the difference is resolved into harmony. The payment of the wages to the shepherd in the prophetical announcement is simply the symbolical form in which the nation manifests its ingratitude for the love and fidelity shown towards it by the shepherd, and the sign that it will no longer have him as its shepherd, and therefore a sign of the blackest ingratitude, and of hard-heartedness in return for the love dis-played by the shepherd. The same ingratitude and the same hardness of heart are manifested in the resolution of the representatives of the Jewish nation, the high priests and elders, to put Jesus their Saviour to death, and to take Him prisoner by bribing the betrayer. The payment of thirty silverlings to the betrayer was in fact the wages with which the Jewish nation repaid Jesus for what He had done for the salvation of Israel; and the contemptible sum which they paid to the betrayer was an expression of the deep contempt which they felt for Jesus. There is also no great importance in this difference, that here the prophet throws the money into the house of Jehovah to the potter; whereas, according to Matthew's account, Judas threw the silverlings into the temple, and the high priests would not put the money into the divine treasury, because it was blood-money, but applied it to the purchase of a potter's field, which received the name of a field of blood. For by this very fact not only was the prophecy almost literally fulfilled; but, so far as the sense is concerned, it was so exactly fulfilled, that every one could see that the same God who had spoken through the prophet, had by the secret operation of His omnipotent power, which extends even to the ungodly, so arranged the matter that Judas threw the money into the temple, to bring it before the face of God as blood-money, and to call down the vengeance of God upon the nation, and that the high priest, by purchasing the potter's field for this money, which received the name of "field of blood" in consequence "unto this day" (Matt. xxvii. 8), perpetuated the memorial of the sin committed against their Messiah. Matthew indicates this in the words "as the Lord commanded me," which correspond to וַיֹּאמֶר יְהוָה אֵלַי in ver. 13 of our prophecy; on which H. Aug. W. Meyer has correctly observed, "that the words 'as the Lord commanded me' express the fact, that the application of the wages of treachery to the purchase of the potter's field took place '*in accordance with the purpose of God*,' whose command the prophet had received. As God had directed the prophet (μοι) how to proceed with the thirty silverlings, so was it with the antitypical fulfilment of the prophecy by the high priests, and thus was the purpose of the divine will accomplished." The other points in which the quotation in Matthew differs from the original text (for the LXX. have adopted a totally different rendering) may be explained from the fact that the passage is quoted *memoriter*, and that the allusion to the mode of fulfilment has exerted some influence upon the choice of words. This involuntary allusion shows itself in the reproduction of וָאֶקְחָה וגו׳, "*I* took the thirty silverlings, and threw them to the potter," by "*they* took the thirty pieces of silver, . . . and gave them for the potter's field;" whilst "the price of him that was valued" is only a free rendering of אֶדֶר הַיְקָר, and "of the children of Israel" an explanation of מֵעֲלֵיהֶם.

The only real and important difficulty in the quotation is to be found in the fact that Matthew quotes the words of *Zechariah* as "that which was spoken by *Jeremy* the prophet," whereas all that he quotes is taken simply and solely from the prophet Zechariah. The reading Ἱερεμίου in Matthew is critically unassailable; and the assumption that Matthew refers to some lost scripture, or to a saying of Jeremiah handed down by oral tradition, and others of a similar kind, are simply arbitrary loopholes, which cannot come into any further consideration at all. On the other hand, the attempts made to explain the introduction of Jeremiah's name in the place of that of Zechariah, on the ground that, so far as the principal features are concerned, our prophecy is simply a resumption of the prophecy in Jer. xix., and that Zechariah announces a second fulfilment of this prophecy (Hengstenberg), or that it rests upon the prophecy of Jer. xviii., in which the potter is also introduced, and that its fulfilment goes beyond Zechariah's prophecy in those features which deviate from the words of Zechariah, so that Jer. xviii. xix. was fulfilled at the same time (Kliefoth), are deserving of serious consideration. Matthew, it is supposed, intended to point to this relation by mentioning Jeremiah instead of Zechariah. We would support this view without reserve, if the connection assumed to exist between our prophecy and the prophecies of Jer. xviii. and xix. could only be shown to be a probable one. But the proof adduced by Hengstenberg that our prophecy rests upon Jer. xviii. reduces itself to these two remarks: (1) That the potter, of whom Jeremiah purchased a pot (ch. xix.) to break it in the valley of Ben-Hinnom, had his workshop in this valley, which was regarded with abhorrence, as being unclean; and (2) that Zechariah was to throw the bad wages into the valley of Ben-Hinnom precisely at the spot where this potter's workshop was.

This he supposes to have taken place with a distinct allusion to the prophecy in Jer. xix., and with the assumption that the readers would have this prophecy before their minds. But in our exposition of ver. 13 we have already shown that Jeremiah did not purchase his pot in the valley of Ben-Hinnom, but of the potter who dwelt within the city gate; and also that the words of Zechariah, "I threw it into the house of Jehovah to the potter," do not affirm that the prophet threw the wages paid him into the valley of Ben-Hinnom. But with these false assumptions, the view founded upon them—namely, that our prophecy is a resumption of that of Jeremiah—necessarily falls to the ground. The symbolical action enjoined upon Jeremiah, and carried out by him, viz. the breaking to pieces in the valley of Ben-Hinnom of the pot purchased of the potter in the city, does not stand in any perceptible relation to the word of the Lord to Zechariah, to throw the wages paid to him into the house of Jehovah to the potter, so as to lead us to take this word as a resumption of that prophecy of Jeremiah. Kliefoth appears to have seen this also, inasmuch as he gives up the idea of finding the proof that our prophecy rests upon that of Jeremiah in the prophecy itself. He therefore bases this view upon the simple fact that Matthew (xxvii. 9) does not quote our passage as a word of Zechariah, but as a word of Jeremiah, and therefore at any rate regarded it as such; and that our passage has nothing independent in its contents, but is rather to be completed or explained from Jeremiah, though not from Jer. xix., but from Jer. xviii., where the potter who makes a pot, and breaks it in pieces because it is marred, repre-sents God, who is doing just the same with Israel as the potter with the pot that is marred. Consequently even in Zechariah we are to understand by the potter, to whom the prophet throws the wages in the temple, Jehovah Himself, who dwells in the temple. But apart from the impossibility of understanding the words of God in ver. 13, "Throw the splendid price at which I have been valued by them to the potter," as meaning "Throw this splendid price *to me*," this view founders on the simple fact that it necessitates the giving up of the agreement between the prophecy and its historical fulfilment, inasmuch as in the fulfilment the price of the betrayal of Jesus is paid, not to the potter, Jehovah, but to a common potter for his field in the valley of Ben-Hinnom. If, therefore, it is impossible to show any connection between our prophecy and the prophecies of Jeremiah, there is no other course left than to follow the example of Luther,—namely, either to attribute the introduction of Jeremiah's name in Matt. xxvii. 9 in the place of that of Zechariah to a failure of memory, or to regard it as a very old copyist's error, of a more ancient date than any of the critical helps that have come down to us.[1]

Vers. 15–17.—THE FOOLISH SHEPHERD.—Ver. 15. "*And Jehovah said to me, Take to thee yet the implement of a foolish shepherd.* Ver. 16. *For, behold, I raise up to myself a shepherd in the land: that which is perishing will he not observe, that which is scattered will he not seek, and that which is broken will he not heal; that which is standing will he not care for; and the flesh of the fat one will he eat, and tear their claws in pieces.* Ver. 17. *Woe to the worthless shepherd, who forsakes the flock! sword over his arm, and over his right eye: his arm shall wither, and his right eye be extinguished.*" After Israel has compelled the good shepherd to lay down his shepherd's office, in consequence of its own sin, it is not to be left to itself, but to be given into the hand of a foolish shepherd, who will destroy it. This is the thought in the fresh symbolical action. By עוֹד, "yet (again) take the instruments," etc., this action is connected with the previous one (vers. 4 sqq.); for עוֹד implies that the prophet had already taken a shepherd's instruments once before in his hand. The shepherd's instruments are the shepherd's staff, and taking it in his hand is a figurative representation of the feeding of a flock. This time he is to take the im-

---

[1] Luther says, in his *Commentary on Zechariah*, of the year 1528: "This chapter gives rise to the question, Why did Matthew attribute the text concerning the thirty pieces of silver to the prophet Jeremiah, whereas it stands here in Zechariah? This and other similar questions do not indeed trouble me very much, because they have but little bearing upon the matter; and Matthew does quite enough by quoting a certain scripture, although he is not quite correct about the name, inasmuch as he quotes prophetic sayings in other places, and yet does not even give the words as they stand in the Scripture. The same thing may occur now; and if it does not affect the sense that the words are not quoted exactly, what is to hinder his not having given the name quite correctly, since the words are of more importance than the name?"

plement of a foolish shepherd, *i.e.* to set forth the action of a foolish shepherd. Whether the pastoral staff of the foolish shepherd was of a different kind from that of the good shepherd, is a matter of indifference, so far as the meaning of the symbol is concerned. Folly, according to the Old Testament view, is synonymous with ungodliness and sin (cf. Ps. xiv. 1 sqq.). The reason for the divine command is given in ver. 16 by a statement of the meaning of the new symbolical action. God will raise up a shepherd over the land, who will not tend, protect, and care for the flock, but will destroy it. That we are not to understand by this foolish shepherd all the evil native rulers of the Jewish people collectively, as Hengstenberg supposes, is as evident from the context as it possibly can be. If the good shepherd represented by the prophet in vers. 4–14 is no other than Jehovah in His rule over Israel, the foolish shepherd who is raised up over the land in the place of the good shepherd, who had been despised and rejected, can only be the possessor of the imperial power, into whose power the nation is given up after the rejection of the good shepherd sent to it in Christ, *i.e.* the Roman empire, which destroyed the Jewish state. The rule of the foolish shepherd is depicted not only as an utter neglect, but as a consuming of the flock, as in Ezek. xxxiv. 3, 4, Jer. xxiii. 1, 2. The perishing sheep he will not seek, *i.e.* will not take charge of them (cf. ver. 9). הַנַּעַר cannot be the young or tender one; for not only is *na'ar*, the boy, not used of animals, but even when used of men it has not the meaning tender or weak. The word is a substantive formation from *nâ'ar*, to shake, *piel* to disperse, used in the sense of *dispulsio*, and the abstract being used for the concrete, the dispersed, the scattered, as the early translators rendered it. *Hannishbereth*, that which is broken, *i.e.* injured through the fracture of a limb. The opposite of *nishbereth* is הַנִּצָּבָה, that which stands upon its feet, and therefore is still strong. But not only will he neglect the flock: he will also seize upon it, and utterly consume it, not only devouring the flesh of the fat one, but even tearing in pieces the claws of the sheep. Not indeed by driving them along bad and stony roads (Tarn., Ewald, Hitzig), for this does no great harm to sheep, but so that when he consumes the sheep, he even splits or tears in pieces the claws, to seize upon and swallow the last morsel of flesh or fat. But this tyrant will also receive his punishment for doing so. The judgment which is to fall upon him is set forth in accordance with the figure of the shepherd, as punishment through the loss of the arm and of the right eye. These two members are mentioned, because with the arm he ought to have protected and provided for the flock, and with the eye to have watched over them. The *Yod* in רֹעִי and עֹזְבִי is not the suffix of the first person, but the so-called *Yod compaginis* with the construct state (see at Hos. x. 11). הָאֱלִיל is a substantive, as in Job xiii. 4; it does not mean worthlessness, however, but nothingness. A worthless shepherd is one who is the opposite of what the shepherd should be, and will be: one who does not feed the flock, but leaves it to perish (עֹזְבִי הַצֹּאן). The words from *cherebh* to *yeminō* are a sentence in the form of a proclamation. The sword is called to come upon the arm and the right eye of the worthless shepherd, *i.e.* to hew off his arm, to smite his right eye. The further threat that the arm is to wither, the eye to become extinct, does not appear to harmonize with this. But the sword is simply mentioned as the instrument of punishment, and the connecting together of different kinds of punishment simply serves to exhibit the greatness and terrible nature of the punishment. With this threat, the threatening word concerning the imperial power of the world (ch. ix.–xi.) is very appropriately brought to a close, inasmuch as the prophecy thereby returns to its starting-point.

ISRAEL'S CONFLICT AND VICTORY, CONVERSION AND SANCTIFICATION.—CHAP. XII. 1–XIII. 6.

This section forms the first half of the second prophecy of Zechariah concerning the future of Israel and of the nations of the world, viz. the prophecy contained in ch. xii.–xiv., which, as a side-piece to ch. ix.–xi., treats of the judgment by which Israel, the nation of God, will be refined, sifted, and led on to perfection through conflict with the nations of the world. This first section announces how the conflict against Jerusalem and Judah will issue in destruction to the nations of the world (ch. xii. 1–4). Jehovah will endow the princes of Judah and inhabitants of Jerusalem with marvellous strength to overcome all

their foes (vers. 5–9), and will pour out His Spirit of grace
upon them, so that they will bitterly repent the death of the
Messiah (vers. 10–14), and purify themselves from all ungodliness (ch. xiii. 1–6).

Ver. 1. *"Burden of the word of Jehovah over Israel. Saying
of Jehovah, who stretches out the heaven, and lays the foundation
of the earth, and forms the spirit of man within him."* This
heading, which belongs to the whole prophecy in ch. xii.–xiv.,
corresponds in form and contents to that in ch. ix. 1. The
burden of Jehovah over Israel stands by the side of the burden
of Jehovah over the land of Hadrach, the seat of the heathen
power of the world (ch. ix. 1). And as the reason assigned
for the latter was that the eye of Jehovah looks at mankind
and all the tribes of Israel, so the former is explained here by
an allusion to the creative omnipotence of Jehovah. Only
there is nothing in our heading to answer to the words "and
Damascus is his rest," which are added to the explanation of
the symbolical name Hadrach in ch. ix. 1, because Israel, as
the name of the covenant nation, needed no explanation. The
other formal differences are very inconsiderable. עַל answers
substantially to the בְּ (in בְּאֶרֶץ, ch. ix. 1), and signifies, notwithstanding the fact that *massa'* announces a threatening word,
not "against," but "over," as we may see by comparing it with
מַשָּׂא אֶל יִשְׂ' in Mal. i. 1. The reason for the *massa'* announced
is given here in the form of an apposition, נְאֻם יְהוָֹה standing
first like a heading, as in Ps. cx. 1, 2 Sam. xxiii. 1, Num. xxiv.
3, 15. The predicates of God are formed after Isa. xlii. 5 (see
also Amos iv. 13), and describe God as the creator of the universe, and the former of the spirits of all men, to remove all
doubt as to the realization of the wonderful things predicted
in what follows. יֹצֵר רוּחַ וגו', the forming of the spirit within
man, does not refer to the creation of the spirits or souls
of men once for all, but denotes the continuous creative
formation and guidance of the human spirit by the Spirit
of God. Consequently we cannot restrict the stretching out
of the heaven and the laying of the foundation of the earth
to the creation of the universe as an act accomplished once
for all at the beginning of all things (Gen. ii. 1), but must
take these words also as referring to the upholding of the
world as a work of the continuously creative providence of

God. According to the biblical view (cf. Ps. civ. 2–4), "God stretches out the heavens every day afresh, and every day He lays the foundation of the earth, which, if His power did not uphold it, would move from its orbit, and fall into ruin" (Hengst.).

Ver. 2. "*Behold, I make Jerusalem a reeling-basin for all the nations round about, and upon Judah also will it be at the siege against Jerusalem.* Ver. 3. *And it will come to pass on that day, I will make Jerusalem a burden-stone to all nations: all who lift it up will tear rents for themselves; and all the nations of the earth will gather together against it.* Ver. 4. *In that day, is the saying of Jehovah, will I smite every horse with shyness, and its rider with madness, and over the house of Judah will I open my eyes, and every horse of the nations will I smite with blindness.*" These verses allude to an attack on the part of the nations upon Jerusalem and Judah, which will result in injury and destruction to those who attack it. The Lord will make Jerusalem a reeling-basin to all nations round about. *Saph* does not mean threshold here, but basin, or a large bowl, as in Ex. xii. 22. רַעַל is equivalent to תַּרְעֵלָה in Isa. li. 17 and Ps. lx. 5, viz. reeling. Instead of the goblet, the prophet speaks of a basin, because many persons can put their mouths to this at the same time, and drink out of it (Schmieder). The "cup of reeling," *i.e.* a goblet filled with intoxicating drink, is a figure very frequently employed to denote the divine judgment, which intoxicates the nations, so that they are unable to stand any longer, and therefore fall to the ground and perish (see at Isa. li. 17).—Ver. 2*b* has been explained in very different ways. It is an old and widespread view, that the words "also upon Judah will it be," etc., express the participation of Judah in the siege of Jerusalem. The Chaldee and Jerome both adopt this explanation, that in the siege of Jerusalem Judah will be constrained by the nations to besiege the capital of its own land. The grammatical reason assigned for this view is, that we must either take הָיָה with עַל in the sense of obligation (it will also be the duty of Judah: Mich., Ros., Ewald), or supply סַף־רַעַל as the subject to יִהְיֶה: the reeling-basin will also come upon Judah. But there is great harshness in both explanations. With the former, לְהִלָּחֵם, or some other infinitive, would hardly have been omitted; and with the latter, the preposition

לְ would stand before יְהוּדָה, instead of עַל. Moreover, in what
follows there is no indication whatever of Judah's having made
common cause with the enemy against Jerusalem; on the
contrary, Judah and Jerusalem stand together in opposition
to the nations, and the princes of Judah have strength in the
inhabitants of Jerusalem (ver. 5), and destroy the enemy to
save Jerusalem (ver. 6). Moreover, it is only by a false interpretation that any one can find a conflict between Judah
and Jerusalem indicated in ch. xiv. 14. And throughout it
is incorrect to designate the attitude of Judah towards Jerusalem in these verses as "opposition,"—a notion upon which
Ebrard (*Offenb. Joh.*) and Kliefoth have founded the marvellous view, that by Jerusalem with its inhabitants and the
house of David we are to understand the unbelieving portion
of Israel; and by Judah with its princes, Christendom, or the
true people of God, formed of believing Israelites, and increased
by believing Gentiles. Judah is not opposed to Jerusalem,
but simply distinguished from it, just as the Jewish kingdom
or people is frequently designated by the prophets as Jerusalem
and Judah. The גַם, which does not separate, but adds, is of
itself inapplicable to the idea of opposition. Consequently we
should expect the words וְגַם עַל יה׳ to express the thought, that
Judah will be visited with the same fate as Jerusalem, as
Luther, Calvin, and many others follow the Peshito in supposing that they do. הָיָה עַל has then the meaning to happen,
to come over a person; and the only question is, What are we
to supply in thought as the subject? The best course is probably to take it from the previous clause, "that which passes
over Jerusalem;" for the proposal of Koehler to supply *mâtsōr*
as the subject is precluded by the circumstance that *mâtsōr*, a
siege, can only affect a city or fortress (cf. Deut. xx. 20), and
not a land. The thought is strengthened in ver. 3. Jerusalem
is to become a burden-stone for all nations, which inflicts con-
tusions and wounds upon those who try to lift it up or carry
it away ("experiencing no hurt itself, it causes great damage
to them:" Marck). The figure is founded upon the idea of
the labour connected with building, and not upon the custom,
which Jerome speaks of as a very common one in his time
among the youth of Palestine, of testing and exercising their
strength by lifting heavy stones. There is a gradation in the

thought, both in the figure of the burdensome stone, which wounds whoever tries to lift it, whilst intoxicating wine only makes one powerless and incapable of any undertaking, and also in the description given of the object, viz. in ver. 2 all nations round about Jerusalem, and in ver. 3 all peoples and all nations of the earth. It is only in the last clause of ver. 3 that the oppression of Jerusalem indicated in the two figures is more minutely described, and in ver. 4 that its overthrow by the help of God is depicted. The Lord will throw the mind and spirit of the military force of the enemy into such confusion, that instead of injuring Jerusalem and Judah, it will rush forward to its own destruction. Horses and riders individualize the warlike forces of the enemy. The rider, smitten with madness, turns his sword against his own comrades in battle (cf. ch. xiv. 3, Judg. vii. 22, 1 Sam. xiv. 20). On the other hand, Jehovah will open His eyes upon Judah for its protection (1 Kings viii. 29; Neh. i. 6; Ps. xxxii. 8). This promise is strengthened by the repetition of the punishment to be inflicted upon the enemy. Not only with alarm, but with blindness, will the Lord smite their horses. We have an example of this in 2 Kings vi. 18, where the Lord smote the enemy with blindness in answer to Elisha's prayer, *i.e.* with mental blindness, so that, instead of seizing the prophet, they fell into the hands of Israel. The three plagues, *timmâhōn*, *shiggāʿōn*, and *ʿivvârōn*, are those with which rebellious Israelites are threatened in Deut. xxviii. 28. The "house of Judah" is the covenant nation, the population of Judah including the inhabitants of Jerusalem, as we may see from what follows.

Ver. 5. "*And the princes of Judah will say in their hearts, The inhabitants of Jerusalem are strength to me, in Jehovah of hosts their God.* Ver. 6. *On that day will I make the princes of Judah as a basin of fire under logs of wood, and like a torch of fire under sheaves; and they will devour all nations round about, on the right and on the left; and Jerusalem will dwell still further in its place, at Jerusalem.* Ver. 7. *And Jehovah will save the tents of Judah first, that the splendour of the house of David and the splendour of the inhabitants of Jerusalem may not lift itself up over Judah.*" The princes of Judah are mentioned as the leaders of the people in war. What they say is the conviction of the whole nation ('*allûph*, as in ch. ix. 7).

אָמְצָה (in this form ἁπ. λεγ.) is a substantive = אֹמֶץ, strength
(Job xvii. 9). The singular *lī* (to *me*) expresses the fact that
every individual says or thinks this, as with the expression
"should *I* weep" in ch. vii. 3. The princes of Judah recognise in the inhabitants of Jerusalem their strength or might,
not in this sense, that Judah, being crowded together before
Jerusalem, expects help against the foe from the strength of
the city and the assistance of its inhabitants, as Hofmann and
Koehler maintain, for "their whole account of the inhabitants
of the land being shut up in the city (or crowded together
before the walls of Jerusalem, and covered by them) is a pure
invention" (Koehler), and has no foundation in the text; but
in this sense, that the inhabitants of Jerusalem are strong
through Jehovah their God, *i.e.* through the fact that Jehovah
has chosen Jerusalem, and by virtue of this election will save
the city of His sanctuary (compare x. 12 with iii. 2, i. 17,
ii. 16). Because the princes of Judah put their trust in the
divine election of Jerusalem, the Lord makes them into a
basin of fire under logs of wood, and a burning torch under
sheaves, so that they destroy all nations round about like flames
of fire, and Jerusalem therefore remains unconquered and
undestroyed in its place at Jerusalem. In this last sentence
Jerusalem is first of all the population personified as a woman,
and in the second instance the city as such. From the fact
that Jerusalem is still preserved, in consequence of the destruction of the enemy proceeding from the princes of Judah, it is
very evident that the princes of Judah are the representatives
of the whole nation, and that the whole of the covenant nation
(Judah with Jerusalem) is included in the house of Judah in
ver. 4. And ver. 7 may easily be reconciled with this. The
statement that the Lord will "save the tents of Judah first,
that the splendour of the house of David may not lift itself up
above Judah," contains the simple thought that the salvation
will take place in such a manner that no part of the nation
will have any occason to lift itself up above another, and that
because the salvation is effected not by human power, but by
the omnipotence of God alone. "The tents of Judah, *i.e.*
its huts, form an antithesis to the splendid buildings of the
capital, and probably (?) also point to the defenceless condition
of Judah, through which it was absolutely cast upon the help

of God" [1] (Hengstenberg). תִּפְאֶרֶת, the splendour or glory, not the boasting. The house of David is the royal line, which was continued in Zerubbabel and his family, and culminated in Christ. Its splendour consists in the glorification promised in ch. iv. 6–10 and 14, and Hag. ii. 23; and the splendour of the inhabitants of Jerusalem is the promises which this city received through its election to be the city of God, in which Jehovah would be enthroned in His sanctuary, and also through the future glorification predicted for it in consequence (ch. i. 16, 17, ii. 8, 14, sqq.). The antithesis between Jerusalem and the house of David on the one hand, and the tents of Judah on the other, does not serve to express the thought that "the strong ones will be saved by the weak, in order that the true equilibrium may arise between the two" (Hengst.), for Judah cannot represent the weak ones if its princes consume the enemy like flames of fire; but the thought is simply this: At the deliverance from the attack of the foe, Jerusalem will have no pre-eminence over Judah; but the promises which Jerusalem and the house of David have received will benefit Judah, i.e. the whole of the covenant nation, in like manner. This thought is expressed in the following way: The defenceless land will be delivered sooner than the well-defended capital, that the latter may not lift itself up above the former, but that both may humbly acknowledge "that the victory in both cases is the Lord's" (Jerome); for, according to ver. 8, Jerusalem will enjoy in the fullest measure the salvation of God.

Ver. 8. "*On that day Jehovah will shelter the inhabitants of Jerusalem; and he that stumbleth among them will be as David on that day; and the house of David as God, as the angel of Jehovah before them. Ver. 9. And it will come to pass on that day, I will seek to destroy all the nations that come against Jerusalem.*" In the conflict with the heathen nations, the Lord will endow the inhabitants of Jerusalem with marvellous strength with which to overcome all their foes. The population of Jerusalem is divided into two classes, the weak and the strong. The weak are designated as *hannikhshâl*, the stumbling one, who cannot stand firmly upon his feet (1 Sam.

---

[1] Calvin observes: "In my opinion, the prophet applies the term 'tents' to huts which cannot protect their guests or inhabitants. We have thus a tacit contrast between huts and fortified cities."

ii. 4). These are to become like David, the bravest hero of
Israel (cf. 1 Sam. xvii. 34 sqq., 2 Sam. xvii. 8). The strong
ones, designated as the house, *i.e.* the household or family of
David, are to be like *Elohim*, *i.e.* not angels, but God, the
Deity, *i.e.* a superhuman being (cf. Ps. viii. 6), yea, like the
angel of Jehovah, who goes before Israel (לִפְנֵיהֶם), or the
revealer of the invisible God, who is essentially the equal of
Jehovah (see at ch. i. 8). The point of comparison lies in
the power and strength, not in moral resemblance to God, as
Kliefoth supposes, who takes *Elohim* as equivalent to *Jehovah*,
and identifies it with the angel of Jehovah, as some of the
earlier commentators have done, and places the graduation of
Elohim into the angel of Jehovah in the appearance of God in
human form, in which case, however, לִפְנֵיהֶם has no meaning.
This shows rather that the "angel of Jehovah" is simply
referred to here in connection with his appearance in the
history of Israel, when he went at the head of Israel and
smote the Egyptians and all the enemies of Israel (Ex. xxiii.
20 sqq.; Josh. v. 13 sqq.). This is evident from the antithesis
in ver. 9. Whilst Jehovah endows the inhabitants of Jerusalem with supernatural strength, He will seek to destroy all
the nations which attack Jerusalem. *Biqqēsh*, followed by
an infinitive with *Lamed*, to strive after anything, as in ch.
vi. 7. בּוֹא עַל applied to the advance of the enemy against a
city (= עָלָה עַל, Isa. vii. 1).

Vers. 10–14. But the Lord will do still more than this for
His people. He will renew it by pouring out His spirit of
grace upon it, so that it will come to the knowledge of the
guilt it has incurred by the rejection of the Saviour, and will
bitterly repent of its sin. Ver. 10. "*And I will pour out upon
the house of David, and upon the inhabitants of Jerusalem, the
spirit of grace and of supplication; and they will look upon me,
whom they have pierced, and will mourn over him like the
mourning over an only one, and will grieve bitterly over him, as
one grieves bitterly over the first-born.*" This new promise is
simply attached to the previous verse by ו *consec.* (וְשָׁפַכְתִּי).
Through this mode of attachment such connections as that
suggested by Kliefoth, "But such glory can only be enjoyed
by rebellious Israel when it is converted, and acknowledges
and bewails Him whom it has rejected," are precluded, as at

variance with the text. There is not a word in the text about conversion as the condition on which the glory set before them in vers. 3–9 was to be obtained; on the contrary, conversion is represented as one fruit of the outpouring of the spirit of prayer upon the nation; and this outpouring of the Spirit is introduced by וְשָׁפַכְתִּי, which corresponds to אֲבַקֵּשׁ in ver. 9, as a new feature in the salvation, to be added to the promise of the destruction of the nations which fight against Jerusalem. The fact that only the inhabitants of Jerusalem are named, and not those of Judah also, is explained correctly by the commentators from the custom of regarding the capital as the representative of the whole nation. And it follows *eo ipso* from this, that in ver. 8 also the expression "inhabitants of Jerusalem" is simply an individualizing epithet for the whole of the covenant nation. But just as in ver. 8 the house of David is mentioned emphatically along with these as the princely family and representative of the ruling class, so is it also in ver. 10, for the purpose of expressing the thought that the same salvation is to be enjoyed by the whole nation, in all its ranks, from the first to the last. The outpouring of the Spirit points back to Joel iii. 1 sqq., except that there the Spirit of Jehovah generally is spoken of, whereas here it is simply the spirit of grace and of supplication. *Chēn* does not mean "prayer," nor emotion, or goodness, or love (Hitzig, Ewald), but simply grace or favour; and here, as in ch. iv. 7, the grace of God; not indeed in its objectivity, but as a principle at work in the human mind. The spirit of grace is the spirit which produces in the mind of man the experience of the grace of God. But this experience begets in the soul of sinful man the knowledge of sin and guilt, and prayer for the forgiveness of sin, *i.e.* supplication; and this awakens sorrow and repentance. הִבִּיטוּ אֵלַי, they look upon me. *Hibbīt*, used of bodily sight as well as spiritual (cf. Num. xxi. 9). The suffix in אֵלַי (to *me*) refers to the speaker. This is *Jehovah*, according to ver. 1, the creator of the heaven and the earth. אֵת־אֲשֶׁר דָּקָרוּ, not "Him whom they pierced," but simply "whom they pierced." אֵת, that is to say, is not governed by *hibbītū* as a second object, but simply refers to אֵלַי, to me, "whom they pierced." אֵת־אֲשֶׁר is chosen here, as in Jer. xxxviii. 9, in the place of the simple אֲשֶׁר, to mark אֲשֶׁר more clearly as an accu-

sative, since the simple אֲשֶׁר might also be rendered " who
pierced (me) :" cf. Ges. § 123, 2, Not. 1.   *Dâqar* does not
mean to ridicule, or scoff at, but only to pierce, thrust through,
and to slay by any kind of death whatever (cf. Lam. iv. 9).
And the context shows that here it signifies to put to death.
With reference to the explanation proposed by Calvin, " whom
they have harassed with insults," Hitzig has very properly
observed : " If it were nothing more than this, wherefore such
lamentation over him, which, according to the use of סָפַד,
with עַל governing the person, and from the similes employed,
is to be regarded as a lamentation for the dead ?"   It is true
that we have not to think of a slaying of Jehovah, the creator
of the heaven and the earth, but simply of the slaying of
the *Maleach* Jehovah, who, being of the same essence with
Jehovah, became man in the person of Jesus Christ.   As
Zechariah repeatedly represents the coming of the Messiah as
a coming of Jehovah in His *Maleach* to His people, he could,
according to this view, also describe the slaying of the *Maleach*
as the slaying of Jehovah.   And Israel having come to the
knowledge of its sin, will bitterly bewail this deed.   עָלָיו does
not mean thereat, *i.e.* at the crime, but is used personally, over
him whom they have pierced.   Thus the transition from the
first person (אֵלַי) to the third (עָלָיו) points to the fact that the
person slain, although essentially one with Jehovah, is personally distinct from the Supreme God.   The lamentation for the
only son (*yâchîd :* cf. Amos viii. 10) and for the first-born is
the deepest and bitterest death-wail.   The *inf. abs. hâmēr*,
which is used in the place of the finite verb, signifies making
bitter, to which *mispēd* is to be supplied from the previous
sentence (cf. מִסְפַּד הַמְּרוּרִים, Jer. vi. 26).

The historical fulfilment of this prophecy commenced with
the crucifixion of the Son of God, who had come in the flesh.
The words הִבִּיטוּ אֵלַי אֵת־אֲשֶׁר דָּקָרוּ are quoted in the Gospel of
John (xix. 37), according to the Greek rendering ὄψονται εἰς
ὃν ἐξεκέντησαν, which probably emanated not from the LXX.,
but from Aquila, or Theodotion, or Symmachus, as having
been fulfilled in Christ, by the fact that a soldier pierced His
side with a lance as He was hanging upon the cross (*vid.* John
xix. 34).   If we compare this quotation with the fact mentioned in ver. 36, that they did not break any of His bones,

there can be no doubt that John quotes this passage with distinct allusion to this special circumstance; only we must not infer from this, that the evangelist regarded the meaning of the prophecy as exhausted by this allusion. The piercing with the spear is simply looked upon by him as the climax of all the mortal sufferings of Christ; and even with Zechariah the piercing is simply an individualizing expression for putting to death, the instrument used and the kind of death being of very subordinate importance. This is evident from a comparison of our verse with ch. xiii. 7, where the sword is mentioned as the instrument employed, whereas *dâqar* points rather to a spear. What we have observed at p. 337 respecting the fulfilment of ch. ix. 9 by the entry of Christ into Jerusalem, also applies to this special fulfilment, viz. that the so to speak literal fulfilment in the outward circumstances only served to make the internal concatenation of the prophecy with its historical realization so clear, that even unbelievers could not successfully deny it. Luke (xxiii. 48) indicates the commencement of the fulfilment of the looking at the slain one by these words: " And all the people that came together to that sight, beholding the things which were done, smote their breasts." (For the smiting of the breasts, comp. Isa. xxxii. 12, סֹפְדִים עַל שָׁדַיִם.) " The crowds, who had just before been crying out, Crucify him, here smite upon their breasts, being overpowered with the proofs of the superhuman exaltation of Jesus, and lament over the crucified one, and over their own guilt" (Hengst.). The true and full commencement of the fulfilment, however, shows itself in the success which attended the preaching of Peter on the first day of Pentecost,—namely, in the fact that three thousand were pricked in their heart with penitential sorrow on account of the crucifixion of their Saviour, and were baptized in the name of Jesus Christ for the forgiveness of sins (Acts ii. 37–41), and in the further results which followed the preaching of the apostles for the conversion of Israel (Acts iii.–v.). The fulfilment has continued with less striking results through the whole period of the Christian church, in conversions from among the Jews; and it will not terminate till the remnant of Israel shall turn as a people to Jesus the Messiah, whom its fathers crucified. On the other hand, those who continue obstinately in unbelief will see Him at last when He returns in the clouds of heaven, and shriek with despair (Rev. i. 7 ; Matt. xxiv. 30).

In vers. 11–14 the magnitude and universality of the mourning are still further depicted. Ver. 11. "*In that day the mourning in Jerusalem will be great, like the mourning of Hadad-rimmon in the valley of Megiddo.* Ver. 12. *And the land will mourn, every family apart ; the family of the house of David apart, and their wives apart ; the family of the house of Nathan apart, and their wives apart.* Ver. 13. *The family of the house of Levi apart, and their wives apart ; the family of the Shimeite apart, and their wives apart.* Ver. 14. *All the rest of the families, every family apart, and their wives apart.*" In ver. 11, the depth and bitterness of the pain on account of the slain Messiah are depicted by comparing it to the mourning of Hadad-rimmon. Jerome says with regard to this : " Adad-remmon is a city near Jerusalem, which was formerly called by this name, but is now called Maximianopolis, in the field of Mageddon, where the good king Josiah was wounded by Pharaoh Necho." This statement of Jerome is confirmed by the fact that the ancient Canaanitish or Hebrew name of the city has been preserved in *Rümuni*, a small village three-quarters of an hour to the south of Lejun (*Legio = Megiddo :* see at Josh. xii. 21 ; and V. de Velde, *Reise*, i. p. 267). The mourning of Hadad-rimmon is therefore the mourning for the calamity which befel Israel at Hadad-rimmon in the death of the good king Josiah, who was mortally wounded in the valley Megiddo, according to 2 Chron. xxxv. 22 sqq., so that he very soon gave up the ghost. The death of this most pious of all the kings of Judah was bewailed by the people, especially the righteous members of the nation, so bitterly, that not only did the prophet Jeremiah compose an elegy on his death, but other singers, both male and female, bewailed him in dirges, which were placed in a collection of elegiac songs, and preserved in Israel till long after the captivity (2 Chron. xxxv. 25). Zechariah compares the lamentation for the putting of the Messiah to death to this great national mourning. All the other explanations that have been given of these words are so arbitrary, as hardly to be worthy of notice. This applies, for example, to the idea mentioned by the Chald., that the reference is to the death of the wicked Ahab, and also to Hitzig's hypothesis, that *Hadad-rimmon* was one name of the god *Adonis*. For, apart from the fact that it is only from this passage that Movers has inferred that there ever was an idol of that name, a prophet of Jehovah could not possibly have compared the great lamentation of the Israelites over the death of the Messiah to the lamentation over the death of Ahab the ungodly king of Israel, or to the mourning for a Syrian idol. But the mourning will not be confined to Jerusalem; the land (*há'árets*), *i.e.* the whole nation, will also mourn. This universality of the lamentation is individualized in vers. 12–14, and so depicted as to show that all the families and households of the nation mourn, and not the men only, but also the women. To this end the prophet mentions four distinct leading and secondary families, and then adds in conclusion, "all the rest of the families, with their wives." Of the several families named, two can be determined with certainty,— namely, the family of the house of David, *i.e.* the posterity of king David, and the family of the house of Levi, *i.e.* the posterity of the patriarch Levi. But about the other two families there is a difference of opinion. The rabbinical writers suppose that *Nathan* is the well known prophet of that name, and the family of *Shimei* the tribe of Simeon, which is said, according to the rabbinical fiction, to have furnished teachers to the nation.[1] But the latter opinion is overthrown, apart from any other reason, by the fact that the patronymic of *Simeon* is not written שִׁמְעִי, but שִׁמְעֹנִי, in Josh. xxi. 4, 1 Chron. xxvii. 16. Still less can the Benjamite Shimei, who cursed David (2 Sam. xvi. 5 sqq.), be intended. מִשְׁפַּחַת הַשִּׁמְעִי is the name given in Num. iii. 21 to the family of the son of Gershon and the grandson of Levi (Num. iii. 17 sqq.). This is the family intended here, and in harmony with this *Nathan* is not the prophet of that name, but the son of David, from whom Zerubbabel was descended (Luke iii. 27, 31). Luther adopted this explanation: "Four families," he says, "are enumerated, two from the royal line, under the names of David and Nathan,

---

[1] Jerome gives the Jewish view thus: "In David the regal tribe is included, *i.e.* Judah. In Nathan the prophetic order is described. Levi refers to the priests, from whom the priesthood sprang. In Simeon the teachers are included, as the companies of masters sprang from that tribe. He says nothing about the other tribes, as they had no special privilege or dignity."

and two from the priestly line, as Levi and Shimei; after which he embraces all together." Of two tribes he mentions one leading family and one subordinate branch, to show that not only are all the families of Israel in general seized with the same grief, but all the separate branches of those families. Thus the word *mishpâchâh* is used here, as in many other cases, in the wider and more restricted meaning of the leading and the subordinate families.

Chap. xiii. 1–6. The penitential supplication of Israel will lead to a thorough renewal of the nation, since the Lord will open to the penitent the fountain of His grace for the cleansing away of sin and the sanctifying of life. Ver. 1. *" In that day will a fountain be opened to the house of David, and to the inhabitants of Jerusalem, for sin and uncleanness."* As the Lord Himself pours out the spirit of supplication upon Israel, so does He also provide the means of purification from sin. A fountain is opened, when its stream of water bursts forth from the bosom of the earth (see Isa. xli. 18, xxxv. 6). The water, which flows from the fountain opened by the Lord, is a water of sprinkling, with which sin and uncleanness are removed. The figure is taken partly from the water used for the purification of the Levites at their consecration, which is called מֵי חַטָּאת, sin-water, or water of absolution, in Num. viii. 7, and partly from the sprinkling-water prepared from the sacrificial ashes of the red heifer for purification from the defilement of death, which is called מֵי נִדָּה, water of uncleanness, *i.e.* water which removed uncleanness, in Num. xix. 9. Just as bodily uncleanness is a figure used to denote spiritual uncleanness, the defilement of sin (cf. Ps. li. 9), so is earthly sprinkling-water a symbol of the spiritual water by which sin is removed. By this water we have to understand not only grace in general, but the spiritual sprinkling-water, which is prepared through the sacrificial death of Christ, through the blood that He shed for sin, and which is sprinkled upon us for the cleansing away of sin in the gracious water of baptism. The blood of Jesus Christ cleanseth us from all sin (1 John i. 7; compare v. 6).

The house of David and the inhabitants of Jerusalem represent the whole nation here, as in ch. xii. 10. This cleansing will be followed by a new life in fellowship with God, since the Lord will remove everything that could hinder sanctification. This renewal of life and sanctification is described in vers. 2-7. Ver. 2. "*And it will come to pass in that day, is the saying of Jehovah of hosts, I will cut off the names of the idols out of the land, they shall be remembered no more; and the prophets also and the spirit of uncleanness will I remove out of the land.* Ver. 3. *And it will come to pass, if a man prophesies any more, his father and his mother, they that begat him, will say to him, Thou must not live, for thou hast spoken deceit in the name of Jehovah: and his father and his mother, they that begat him, will pierce him through because of his prophesying.* Ver. 4. *And it will come to pass on that day, the prophets will be ashamed every one of his vision, at his prophesying, and will no more put on a hairy mantle to lie.* Ver. 5. *And he will say, I am no prophet, I am a man who cultivates the land; for a man bought me from my youth.* Ver. 6. *And if they shall say to him, What scars are these between thy hands? he will say, These were inflicted upon me in the house of my loves.*" The new life in righteousness and holiness before God is depicted in an individualizing form as the extermination of idols and false prophets out of the holy land, because idolatry and false prophecy were the two principal forms in which ungodliness manifested itself in Israel. The allusion to idols and false prophets by no means points to the times before the captivity; for even if gross idolatry, and therefore false prophecy, did not spread any more among the Jews after the captivity, such passages as Neh. vi. 10, where lying prophets rise up, and even priests contract marriages with Canaanitish and other heathen wives, from whom children sprang who could not even speak the Jewish language (Ezra ix. 2 sqq.; Neh. xiii. 23), show very clearly that the danger of falling back into gross idolatry was not a very remote one. Moreover, the more refined idolatry of pharisaic self-righteousness and work-holiness took the place of the grosser idolatry, and the prophets generally depict the future under the forms of the past. The cutting off of the names of the idols denotes utter destruction (cf. Hos. ii. 19). The prophets are false prophets, who either uttered the thoughts of their hearts as divine inspiration, or stood under the demoniacal influence of the spirit of darkness. This is evident from the fact that they are associated not only with idols, but with the "spirit of uncleanness." For this, the opposite of

the spirit of grace (ch. xii. 10), is the evil spirit which culminates in Satan, and works in the false prophets as a lying spirit
(1 Kings xxii. 21–23; Rev. xvi. 13, 14). The complete extermination of this unclean spirit is depicted thus in vers. 3–6,
that not only will Israel no longer tolerate any prophet in the
midst of it (ver. 3), but even the prophets themselves will be
ashamed of their calling (vers. 4–6). The first case is to
be explained from the law in Deut. xiii. 6–11 and xviii. 20,
according to which a prophet who leads astray to idolatry, and
one who prophesies in his own name or in the name of false
gods, are to be put to death. This commandment will be
carried out by the parents upon any one who shall prophesy
in the future. They will pronounce him worthy of death as
speaking lies, and inflict the punishment of death upon him
(dâqar, used for putting to death, as in ch. xii. 10). This
case, that a man is regarded as a false prophet and punished
in consequence, simply because he prophesies, rests upon the
assumption that at that time there will be no more prophets,
and that God will not raise them up or send them any more.
This assumption agrees both with the promise, that when
God concludes a new covenant with His people and forgives
their sins, no one will teach another any more to know the
Lord, but all, both great and small, will know Him, and all
will be taught of God (Jer. xxxi. 33, 34; Isa. liv. 13); and
also with the teaching of the Scriptures, that the Old Testament prophecy reached to John the Baptist, and attained its
completion and its end in Christ (Matt. xi. 13; Luke xvi. 16,
cf. Matt. v. 17). At that time will those who have had to
do with false prophecy no longer pretend to be prophets, or
assume the appearance of prophets, or put on the hairy garment of the ancient prophets, of Elias for example, but rather
give themselves out as farm-servants, and declare that the marks
of wounds inflicted upon themselves when prophesying in the
worship of heathen gods are the scars of wounds which they
have received (vers. 4–6). בּוֹשׁ מִן, to be ashamed on account of
(cf. Isa. i. 29), not to desist with shame. The form הִנָּבְאֹתוֹ in
ver. 4 instead of הִנָּבֵא (ver. 3) may be explained from the fact
that the verbs ל״א and ל״ה frequently borrow forms from one
another (Ges. § 75, Anm. 20–22). On אַדֶּרֶת שֵׂעָר, see at 2 Kings
i. 8. לְמַעַן כַּחֵשׁ, to lie, i.e. to give themselves the appearance of

prophets, and thereby to deceive the people. The subject to וְאָמַר
in ver. 5 is אִישׁ from ver. 4; and the explanation given by the
man is not to be taken as an answer to a question asked by
another concerning his circumstances, for it has not been preceded by any question, but as a confession made by his own spontaneous impulse, in which he would repudiate his former calling.
The verb הִקְנָה is not a *denom.* of מִקְנֶה, *servum facere, servo uti*
(Maurer, Koehler, and others), for *miqneh* does not mean slave,
but that which has been acquired, or an acquisition. It is a
simple *hiphil* of *qânâh* in the sense of acquiring, or acquiring
by purchase, not of selling. That the statement is an untruth-
ful assertion is evident from ver. 6, the two clauses of which
are to be taken as speech and reply, or question and answer.
Some one asks the prophet, who has given himself out as a
farm-servant, where the stripes (*makkōth*, strokes, marks of
strokes) between his hands have come from, and he replies that
he received them in the house of his lovers. אֲשֶׁר הֻכֵּיתִי, ἅς (*sc.*
πληγὰς) ἐπλήγην: cf. Ges. § 143, 1. The questioner regards
the stripes or wounds as marks of wounds inflicted upon himself, which the person addressed had made when prophesying,
as is related of the prophets of Baal in 1 Kings xviii. 28 (see
the comm.). The expression "between the hands" can hardly
be understood in any other way than as relating to the palms
of the hands and their continuation up the arms, since, according to the testimony of ancient writers (Movers, *Phöniz.* i. p.
682), in the self-mutilations connected with the Phrygian,
Syrian, and Cappadocian forms of worship, the arms were
mostly cut with swords or knives. The meaning of the answer
given by the person addressed depends upon the view we take
of the word מְאַהֲבִים. As this word is generally applied to paramours, Hengstenberg retains this meaning here, and gives the
following explanation of the passage: namely, that the person
addressed confesses that he has received the wounds in the
temples of the idols, which he had followed with adulterous
love, so that he admits his former folly with the deepest shame.
But the context appears rather to indicate that this answer is
also nothing more than an evasion, and that he simply pretends
that the marks were scars left by the chastisements which he
received when a boy in the house of either loving parents or
some other loving relations.

JUDGMENT OF REFINEMENT FOR ISRAEL, AND GLORIOUS END
OF JERUSALEM.—CHAP. XIII. 7–XIV. 21.

The prophecy takes a new turn at ver. 7, and announces
the judgment, through which Israel will be refined from the
dross still adhering to it, and transformed into the truly holy
people of the Lord by the extermination of its spurious and
corrupt members. This second half of the prophecy is really
an expansion of the first (xii. 1–xiii. 6). Whereas the first
announces how the Lord will protect Israel and Jerusalem
against the pressure of the powers of the world, how He will
smite the enemy, and not only endow His people with miraculous power which ensures their victory, but also by pouring
out His Spirit of grace, lead it to a knowledge of the guilt it
has contracted by putting the Messiah to death, and to repentance and renovation of life; the second half depicts the judgment which will fall upon Jerusalem, to sever the ungodly
from the righteous, to exterminate the former out of the land
of the Lord, to purify and preserve the latter, and by completing this separation, to perfect His kingdom in glory. This
second half is divisible again into two parts, the former of
which (ch. xiii. 7–9) gives a summary of the contents, whilst
the latter (ch. xiv.) expands it into fuller detail.

Ver. 7. "*Arise, O sword, over my shepherd, and over the man
who is my neighbour, is the saying of Jehovah of hosts: smite
the shepherd, that the sheep may be scattered; and I will bring
back my hand over the little ones.* Ver. 8. *And it will come to
pass in all the land, is the saying of Jehovah; two parts therein
shall be cut off, shall die, and the third remains therein.* Ver. 9.
*And the third will I bring into the fire, and melt them as silver
is melted, and will refine them as gold is refined: it will call upon
my name, and I will answer it; I say, It is my people; and it
will say, Jehovah my God.*" The summons addressed to the
sword, to awake and smite, is a poetical turn to express the
thought that the smiting takes place with or according to the
will of God. For a similar personification of the sword, see
Jer. xlvii. 6. רֹעִי is the shepherd of Jehovah, since the summons comes from Jehovah. In what sense the person to be
smitten is called the shepherd of Jehovah, we may see from
the clause עַל־גֶּבֶר עֲמִיתִי. The word עָמִית, which only occurs in

the Pentateuch and in Zechariah, who has taken it thence, is only used as a synonym of אָח (cf. Lev. xxv. 15) in the concrete sense of the nearest one. And this is the meaning which it has in the passage before us, where the construct state expresses the relation of apposition, as for example in אִישׁ חֲסִידֶךָ (Deut. xxxiii. 8; cf. Ewald, § 287, e), the man who is my nearest one. The shepherd of Jehovah, whom Jehovah describes as a man who is His next one (neighbour), cannot of course be a bad shepherd, who is displeasing to Jehovah, and destroys the flock, or the foolish shepherd mentioned in ch. xi. 15-17, as Grotius, Umbr., Ebrard, Ewald, Hitzig, and others suppose; for the expression " man who is my nearest one" implies much more than unity or community of vocation, or that he had to feed the flock like Jehovah. No owner of a flock or lord of a flock would call a hired or purchased shepherd his 'âmīth. And so God would not apply this epithet to any godly or ungodly man whom He might have appointed shepherd over a nation. The idea of nearest one (or fellow) involves not only similarity in vocation, but community of physical or spiritual descent, according to which he whom God calls His neighbour cannot be a mere man, but can only be one who participates in the divine nature, or is essentially divine. The shepherd of Jehovah, whom the sword is to smite, is therefore no other than the Messiah, who is also identified with Jehovah in ch. xii. 10; or the good shepherd, who says of Himself, " I and my Father are one" (John x. 30). The masculine form הַךְ in the summons addressed to the sword, although חֶרֶב itself is feminine, may be accounted for from the personification of the sword; compare Gen. iv. 7, where sin (חַטָּאת, fem.) is personified as a wild beast, and construed as a masculine. The sword is merely introduced as a weapon used for killing, without there being any intention of defining the mode of death more precisely. The smiting of the shepherd is also mentioned here simply for the purpose of depicting the consequences that would follow with regard to the flock. The thought is therefore merely this: Jehovah will scatter Israel or His nation by smiting the shepherd; that is to say, He will give it up to the misery and destruction to which a flock without a shepherd is exposed. We cannot infer from this that the shepherd himself is to blame; nor does the circumstance that the smiting of the shepherd is represented as the execution of a divine command, necessarily imply that the death of the shepherd proceeds directly from God. According to the biblical view, God also works, and does that which is done by man in accordance with His counsel, and will, and even that which is effected through the sin of men. Thus in Isa. liii. 10 the mortal sufferings of the Messiah are described as inflicted upon Him by God, although He had given up His soul to death to bear the sin of the people. In the prophecy before us, the slaying of the shepherd is only referred to so far as it brings a grievous calamity upon Israel ; and the fact is passed over, that Israel has brought this calamity upon itself by its ingratitude towards the shepherd (cf. ch. xi. 8, 12). The flock, which will be dispersed in consequence of the slaying of the shepherd, is the covenant nation, *i.e.* neither the human race nor the Christian church as such, but the flock which the shepherd in ch. xi. 4 sqq. had to feed. At the same time, Jehovah will not entirely withdraw His hand from the scattered flock, but " bring it back over the small ones." The phrase הֵשִׁיב יָד עַל, to bring back the hand over a person (see at 2 Sam. viii. 3), *i.e.* make him the object of his active care once more, is used to express the employment of the hand upon a person either for judgment or salvation. It occurs in the latter sense in Isa. i. 25 in relation .to the grace which the Lord will manifest towards Jerusalem, by purifying it from its dross ; and it is used here in the same sense, as vers. 8, 9 clearly show, according to which the dispersion to be inflicted upon Israel will only be the cause of ruin to the greater portion of the nation, whereas it will bring salvation to the remnant. Vers. 8*b* and 9 add the real explanation of the bringing back of the hand over the small ones. צֹעֲרִים (lit. a participle of צָעַר, which only occurs here) is synonymous with צָעִיר or צָעוּר (Jer. xiv. 3, xlviii. 4, *chethib*), the small ones in a figurative sense, the miserable ones, those who are called עֲנִיֵּי הַצֹּאן in ch. xi. 7. It naturally follows from this, that the צֹעֲרִים are not identical with the whole flock, but simply form a small portion of it, viz. " the poor and righteous in the nation, who suffer injustice" (Hitzig). " The assertion that the flock is to be scattered, but that God will bring back His hand to the small ones, evidently implies that the small ones are included as one portion of the entire flock, for which God will prepare a different fate from that of the larger whole which is about to be dispersed" (Kliefoth).

On the fulfilment of this verse, we read in Matt. xxvi. 31, 32, and Mark xiv. 27, that the bringing back of the hand of the Lord over the small ones was realized first of all in the case of the apostles. After the institution of the Lord's Supper, Christ told His disciples that that same night they would all be offended because of Him; for it was written, " I will smite the shepherd, and the sheep of the flock shall be scattered abroad. But after I am risen again, I will go before you into Galilee." The quotation is made freely from the original text, the address to the sword being resolved into its actual meaning, " I will smite." The offending of the disciples took place when Jesus was taken prisoner, and they all fled. This flight was a prelude to the dispersion of the flock at the death of the shepherd. But the Lord soon brought back His hand over the disciples. The promise, " But after my resurrection I will go before you into Galilee," is a practical exposition of the bringing back of the hand over the small ones, which shows that the expression is to be understood here in a good sense, and that it began to be fulfilled in the gathering together of the disciples by the risen Saviour. This special fulfilment did not indeed exhaust the meaning of the verses before us; but they had a much more general fulfilment in the whole of the nation of Israel, to which we shall afterwards return. This more general sense of the words is placed beyond the reach of doubt by vers. 8 and 9; for ver. 8 depicts the misery which the dispersion of the flock brings upon Israel, and ver. 9 shows how the bringing back of the hand upon the small ones will be realized in the remnant of the nation. The dispersion of the flock will deliver two-thirds of the nation in the whole land to death, so that only one-third will remain alive. כָּל־הָאָרֶץ is not the whole earth, but the whole of the holy land, as in ch. xiv. 9, 10; and הָאָרֶץ, in ch. xii. 12, the land in which the flock, fed by the shepherds of the Lord, i.e. the nation of Israel, dwells. פִּי־שְׁנַיִם is taken from Deut. xxi. 17, as in 2 Kings ii. 9; it is used there for the double portion inherited by the first-born. That it is used here to signify two-thirds, is evident from the remaining הַשְּׁלִישִׁית. " The whole of the Jewish nation," says Hengstenberg, " is introduced here, as an inheritance left by the shep-

berd who has been put to death, which inheritance is divided
into three parts, death claiming the privileges of the first-born,
and so receiving *two* portions, and life one,—a division similar
to that which David made in the case of the Moabites (2 Sam.
viii. 2)." יִגְוָעוּ is added to יִכָּרְתוּ, to define יִכָּרֵת more precisely, as
signifying not merely a cutting off from the land by transportation (cf. ch. xiv. 2), but a cutting off from life (Koehler). גָוַע,
exspirare, is applied both to natural and violent death (for the
latter meaning, compare Gen. vii. 21, Josh. xxii. 20). The
remaining third is also to be refined through severe afflictions,
to purify it from everything of a sinful nature, and make it
into a truly holy nation of God. For the figure of melting and
refining, compare Isa. i. 25, xlviii. 10, Jer. ix. 6, Mal. iii. 3,
Ps. lxvi. 10. For the expression in ver. 9*b*, compare Isa. lxv.
24; and for the thought of the whole verse, ch. viii. 8, Hos.
ii. 25, Jer. xxiv. 7, xxx. 22. The cutting off of the two-
thirds of Israel commenced in the Jewish war under Vespasian
and Titus, and in the war for the suppression of the rebellion
led by the pseudo-Messiah *Bar Cochba*. It is not to be restricted to these events, however, but was continued in the
persecutions of the Jews with fire and sword in the following
centuries. The refinement of the remaining third cannot be
taken as referring to the sufferings of the Jewish nation during
the whole period of its present dispersion, as C. B. Michaelis
supposes, nor generally to the tribulations which are necessary
in order to enter into the kingdom of God, to the seven conflicts which the true Israel existing in the Christian church
has to sustain, first with the two-thirds, and then and more
especially with the heathen (ch. xii. 1–9, 14). For whilst
Hengstenberg very properly objects to the view of Michaelis,
on the ground that in that case the unbelieving portion of
Judaism would be regarded as the legitimate and sole continuation of Israel; it may also be argued, in opposition to the
exclusive reference in the third to the Christian church, that it
is irreconcilable with the perpetuation of the Jews, and the
unanimous entrance of all Israel into the kingdom of Christ, as
taught by the Apostle Paul. Both views contain elements of
truth, which must be combined, as we shall presently show.

Chap. xiv. All nations will be gathered together by the Lord
against Jerusalem, and will take the city and plunder it, and

lead away the half of its inhabitants into captivity (vers. 1, 2).
The Lord will then take charge of His people; He will appear
upon the Mount of Olives, and by splitting this mountain,
prepare a safe way for the rescue of those that remain, and
come with all His saints (vers. 3–5) to complete His kingdom.
From Jerusalem a stream of salvation and blessing will pour
over the whole land (vers. 6–11); the enemies who have come
against Jerusalem will be miraculously smitten, and destroy
one another (vers. 12–15). The remnant of the nations, however, will turn to the Lord, and come yearly to Jerusalem, to
keep the feast of Tabernacles (vers. 16–19); and Jerusalem
will become thoroughly holy (vers. 20, 21). From this brief
description of the contents, it is perfectly obvious that our
chapter contains simply a further expansion of the summary
announcement of the judgment upon Israel, and its refinement
(xiii. 7–9). Vers. 1, 2 show how the flock is dispersed, and for
the most part perishes; vers. 2*b*–5, how the Lord brings back
His hand over the small ones; vers. 6–21, how the rescued
remnant of the nation is endowed with salvation, and the kingdom of God completed by the reception of the believers out of
the heathen nations. There is no essential difference in the
fact that the nation of Israel is the object of the prophecy in
ch. xiii. 7–9, and Jerusalem in ch. xiv. Jerusalem, as the
capital of the kingdom, is the seat of Israel, the nation of
God; what happens to it, happens to the people and kingdom
of God.

Vers. 1–5. The judgment and the deliverance.—Ver. 1.
" *Behold, a day cometh for Jehovah, and thy spoil is divided in the
midst of thee. Ver. 2. And I will gather all nations against
Jerusalem to war; and the city will be taken, and the houses
plundered, and the women ravished, and half the city will go out
into captivity; but the remnant of the nation will not be cut off
out of the city.*" A day comes to the Lord, not inasmuch as He
brings it to pass, but rather because the day belongs to Him,
since He will manifest His glory upon it (cf. Isa. ii. 12). This
day will at first bring calamity or destruction upon Israel; but
this calamity will furnish occasion to the Lord to display His
divine might and glory, by destroying the enemies of Israel
and saving His people. In the second hemistich of ver. 1,
Jerusalem is addressed. "Thy spoil" is the booty taken by the

enemy in Jerusalem. The prophet commences directly with
the main fact, in a most vivid description, and only gives the
explanation afterwards in ver. 2. The *Vav consec.* attached to
וְאָסַפְתִּי is also a *Vav explicativum.* The Lord gathers all nations
together to war against Jerusalem, and gives up the city into
their power, that they may conquer it, and let loose all their
barbarity upon it, plundering the houses and ravishing the
women (cf. Isa. xiii. 16, where the same thing is affirmed of
Babylon). Just as in the Chaldæan conquest the people had
been obliged to wander into captivity, so will it be now, though
not all the people, but only the half of the city. The remaining portion will not be cut off out of the city, *i.e.* be transported
thence, as was the case at that time, when even the remnant
of the nation was carried into exile (2 Kings xxv. 22). It is
obvious at once from this, that the words do not refer to the
destruction of Jerusalem by the Romans, as Theodoret, Jerome,
and others have supposed.

This time the Lord will come to the help of His people.
Ver. 3. "*And Jehovah will go forth and fight against those
nations, as in His day of battle, on the day of slaughter. Ver. 4.
And His feet will stand in that day upon the Mount of Olives,
which lies to the east before Jerusalem; and the Mount of Olives
will split in the centre from east to west into a very great valley,
and half of the mountain will remove to the north, and its (other)
half to the south. Ver. 5. And ye will flee into the valley of my
mountains, and the valley of the mountains will reach to Azel,
and ye will flee as ye fled before the earthquake in the days of
Uzziah king of Judah. And Jehovah my God will come, all the
saints with Thee.*" Against those nations which have conquered
Jerusalem the Lord will fight כַּיּוֹם וגו׳, as the day, *i.e.* as on
the day, of His fighting, to which there is added, for the
purpose of strengthening the expression, "on the day of the
slaughter." The meaning is not "according to the day when
He fought in the day of the war," as Jerome and many others
suppose, who refer the words to the conflict between Jehovah
and the Egyptians at the Red Sea (Ex. xiv. 14); for there
is nothing to support this special allusion. According to the
historical accounts in the Old Testament, Jehovah went out
more than once to fight for His people (cf. Josh. x. 14, 42,
xxiii. 3; Judg. iv. 15; 1 Sam. vii. 10; 2 Chron. xx. 15).

The simile is therefore to be taken in a more general sense, as signifying " as He is accustomed to fight in the day of battle and slaughter," and to be understood as referring to all the wars of the Lord on behalf of His people. In vers. 4 and 5 we have first of all a description of what the Lord will do to save the remnant of His people. He appears upon the Mount of Olives, and as His feet touch the mountain it splits in half, so that a large valley is formed. The splitting of the mountain is the effect of the earthquake under the footsteps of Jehovah, before whom the earth trembles when He touches it (cf. Ex. xix. 18; Judg. v. 5; Ps. lxviii. 8; Nah. i. 5, etc.). The more precise definition of the situation of the Mount of Olives, viz. " before Jerusalem eastwards," is not introduced with a geographical purpose—namely, to distinguish it from other mountains upon which olive trees grow—but is connected with the means employed by the Lord for the salvation of His people, for whom He opens a way of escape by splitting the mountain in two. The mountain is split מֵחֶצְיוֹ מִזְרָחָה וָיָמָּה, from the half (*i.e.* the midst) of it to the east and to the west, *i.e.* so that a chasm ensues, which runs from the centre of the mountain both eastwards and westwards; so that the mountain is split latitudinally, one half (as is added to make it still more clear) removing to the south, the other to the north, and a great valley opening between them. Into this valley the half of the nation that is still in Jerusalem will flee. גֵּיא הָרַי is the accusative of direction (Luther and others render it incorrectly, " before the valley of my mountains"). This valley is not the valley of the *Tyropœon*, or the valley between Moriah and Zion (Jerome, Drus., Hofm.), but the valley which has been formed by the splitting of the Mount of Olives; and Jehovah calls the two mountains which have been formed through His power out of the Mount of Olives *hârai*, " my mountains." Nor is it connected with the valley of Jehoshaphat; for the opinion that the newly-formed valley is merely an extension of the valley of Jehoshaphat has no foundation in the text, and is not in harmony with the direction taken by the new valley—namely, from east to west. The explanatory clause which follows, " for the (newly-formed) valley of the mountains will reach אֶל אָצַל," shows that the flight of the people into the valley is not to be understood as signifying that the valley will merely

furnish the fugitives with a level road for escape, but that they
will find a secure place of shelter in the valley. *'El 'Atsal* has
been taken by different commentators, after Symm. and Jerome,
in an appellative sense, " to very near," which Koehler interprets as signifying that the valley will reach to the place where
the fugitives are. This would be to Jerusalem, for that was
where the fugitives were then. But if Zechariah had meant
to say this, he could not have spoken more obscurely. *'Atsal,*
the form in pause for *'âtsēl,* as we may see by comparing
1 Chron. viii. 38 and ix. 44 with 1 Chron. viii. 39 and ix. 43
(cf. Olsh. *Gramm.* § 91, *d*), is only met with elsewhere in the
form אֵצֶל, not merely as a preposition, but also in the name
בֵּית־הָאֵצֶל, and is here a proper name, as most of the ancient
translators perceived,—namely, a contracted form of בֵּית־הָאֵצֶל,
since בֵּית is frequently omitted from names of places constructed
with it (see Ges. *Thes.* p. 193). This place is to be sought for,
according to Mic. i. 11, in the neighbourhood of Jerusalem,
and according to the passage before us to the east of the
Mount of Olives, as Cyril states, though from mere hearsay,
κώμη δὲ αὕτη πρὸς ἐσχατιαῖς, ὡς λόγος, τοῦ ὄρους κειμένη.
The fact that Jerome does not mention the place is no proof
that it did not exist. A small place not far from Jerusalem,
on the other side of the Mount of Olives, might have vanished
from the earth long before this father lived. The comparison
of the flight to the flight from the earthquake in the time of
king Uzziah, to which reference is made in Amos i. 1, is intended to express not merely the swiftness and universality of
the flight, but also the cause of the flight,—namely, that they do
not merely fly from the enemy, but also for fear of the earthquake which will attend the coming of the Lord. In the last
clause of ver. 5 the object of the coming of the Lord is indicated. He has not only gone forth to fight against the enemy
in Jerusalem, and deliver His people; but He comes with His
holy angels, to perfect His kingdom by means of the judgment,
and to glorify Jerusalem. This coming is not materially different from His going out to war (ver. 3); it is not another
or a second coming, but simply a visible manifestation. For
this coming believers wait, because it brings them redemption
(Luke xxi. 28). This joyful waiting is expressed in the address " my God " The holy ones are the angels (cf. Deut.

xxxiii. 2, 3 ; Dan. vii. 9, 10 ; Matt. xxv. 31), not believers, or
believers as well as the angels. In what follows, Zechariah
depicts first of all the completion secured by the coming of the
Lord (vers. 6–11), and then the judgment upon the enemy
(vers. 12–15), with its fruits and consequences (vers. 16–21).

Vers. 6–11. Complete salvation.—Ver. 6. *" And it will
come to pass on that day, there will not be light, the glorious ones
will melt away.* Ver. 7. *And it will be an only day, which will
be known to Jehovah, not day nor night : and it will come to pass,
at evening time it will be light."* The coming of the Lord will
produce a change on the earth. The light of the earth will
disappear. The way in which לֹא יִהְיֶה אוֹר is to be understood
is indicated more precisely by יְקָרוֹת יִקְפָּאוּן. These words have
been interpreted, however, from time immemorial in very different ways. The difference of gender in the combination of
the feminine יְקָרוֹת with the masculine verb יִקְפָּאוּן, and the
rarity with which the two words are met with, have both contributed to produce the *keri* וְקִפָּאוֹן יְקָרוֹת, in which יְקָרוֹת has
either been taken as a substantive formation from קָרַר, or the
reading וְקָרוֹת with *Vav cop.* has been adopted in the sense of
cold, and קִפָּאוֹן (contraction, rigidity) taken to signify ice. The
whole clause has then been either regarded as an antithesis to
the preceding one, " It will not be light, but (*sc.* there will be)
cold and ice" (thus Targ., Pesh., Symm., Itala, Luther, and
many others) ; or taken in this sense, " There will not be light,
and cold, and ice, *i.e.* no alternation of light, cold, and ice will
occur" (Ewald, Umbr., Bunsen). But there is intolerable harshness in both these views : in the first, on account of the insertion of יִהְיֶה without a negation for the purpose of obtaining an
antithesis ; in the second, because the combination of light,
cold, and ice is illogical and unparalleled in the Scriptures,
and cannot be justified even by an appeal to Gen. viii. 22,
since light is no more equivalent to day and night than cold
and ice are to frost and heat, or summer and winter. We
must therefore follow Hengstenberg, Hofmann, Koehler, and
Kliefoth, who prefer the *chethib* יקפאון, and read it יִקְפָּאוּן, the
imperf. *kal* of קָפָא. קָפָא signifies to congeal, or curdle, and
is applied in Ex. xv. 8 to the heaping up of the waters as
it were in solid masses. יְקָרוֹת, the costly or splendid things
are the stars, according to Job xxxi. 26, where the moon is

spoken of as יְקַר הוֹלֵךְ, walking in splendour. The words therefore describe the passing away or vanishing of the brightness
of the shining stars, answering to the prophetic announcement,
that on the day of judgment, sun, moon, and stars will lose
their brightness or be turned into darkness (Joel iv. 15 ; Isa.
xiii. 10 ; Ezek. xxxii. 7, 8 ; Matt. xxiv. 29 ; Rev. vi. 12).   In
ver. 7 this day is still more clearly described : first, as solitary
in its kind; and secondly, as a marvellous day, on which the
light dawns at evening time.   The four clauses of this verse
contain only two thoughts ; each so expressed in two clauses
that the second explains the first. יוֹם אֶחָד, *unus dies*, is not equivalent to *tempus non longum* (Cocceius, Hengst.), nor to "only
one day, not two or more" (Koehler), but solitary in its kind,
unparalleled by any other, because no second of the kind ever
occurs (for the use of *'echâd* in this sense, compare ver. 9, Ezek.
vii. 5, Song of Sol. vi. 9).   It is necessary to take the words
in this manner on account of the following clause, "it will be
known to the Lord;" *i.e.* not "it will be singled out by Jehovah
in the series of days as the appropriate one" (Hitzig and
Koehler), nor "it stands under the supervision and guidance
of the Lord, so that it does not come unexpectedly, or interfere with His plans" (Hengstenberg), for neither of these is
expressed in נוֹדָע; but simply, it is known to the Lord according to its true nature, and therefore is distinguished above
all other days.   The following definition, "not day and not
night," does not mean that "it will form a turbid mixture of
day and night, in which there will prevail a mongrel condition
of mysterious, horrifying twilight and gloom" (Koehler) ; but
it will resemble neither day nor night, because the lights of
heaven, which regulate day and night, lose their brightness,
and at evening time there comes not darkness, but light.   The
order of nature is reversed : the day resembles the night, and
the evening brings light.   At the time when, according to the
natural course of events, the dark night should set in, a bright
light will dawn.   The words do not actually affirm that the
alternation of day and night will cease (Jerome, Neumann,
Kliefoth) ; but this may be inferred from a comparison of
Rev. xxi. 23 and 25.

Ver. 8. "*And it will come to pass in that day, that living
waters will go out from Jerusalem ; by half into the eastern sea,*

and by half into the western sea: in summer and in winter will it be. Ver. 9. *And Jehovah will be King over all the land; in that day will Jehovah be one, and His name one.* Ver. 10. *The whole land will turn as the plain from Geba to Rimmon, south of Jerusalem; and this will be high, and dwell in its place, from the gate of Benjamin to the place of the first gate, to the corner gate, and from the tower of Chananeel to the king's wine-presses.* Ver. 11. *And men will dwell therein, and there will be no more curse (ban); and Jerusalem will dwell securely.*" The living water which issues from Jerusalem, and pours over the land on both sides, flowing both into the eastern or Dead Sea, and into the hinder (*i.e.* western) or Mediterranean Sea (see at Joel ii. 20), is, according to Joel iii. 18 and Ezek. xlvii. 1–12, a figurative representation of the salvation and blessing which will flow out of Jerusalem, the centre of the kingdom of God, over the holy land, and produce vigorous life on every hand. According to Joel and Ezekiel, the water issues from the temple (see at Joel iii. 18). Zechariah adds, that this will take place in summer and winter, *i.e.* will proceed without interruption throughout the whole year, whereas natural streams dry up in summer time in Palestine. To this blessing there is added the higher spiritual blessing, that Jehovah will be King over all the land, and His name alone will be mentioned and revered. כָּל־הָאָרֶץ does not mean the whole earth, but, as in vers. 8 and 10, the whole of the land of Canaan or of Israel, which is bounded by the Dead Sea and the Mediterranean. It by no means follows from this, however, that Zechariah is simply speaking of a glorification of Palestine. For Canaan, or the land of Israel, is a type of the kingdom of God in the full extent which it will have on the earth in the last days depicted here. Jehovah's kingship does not refer to the kingdom of nature, but to the kingdom of grace,—namely, to the perfect realization of the sovereignty of God, for which the old covenant prepared the way; whereas the old Israel continually rebelled against Jehovah's being King, both by its sin and its idolatry. This rebellion, *i.e.* the apostasy of the nation from its God, is to cease, and the Lord alone will be King and God of the redeemed nation, and be acknowledged by it; His name alone will be mentioned, and not the names of idols as well. The earthly soil of the kingdom of God will then experience a change. The whole land will be levelled into a plain, and Jerusalem will be elevated in consequence; and Jerusalem, when thus exalted, will be restored in its fullest extent. יִסֹּב (imperf. *kal*, not *niphal*; see Ges. § 67, 5), to change like the plain, *i.e.* to change so as to become like the plain. הָעֲרָבָה is not a plain generally, in which case the article would be used generically, but *the* plain, so called κατ᾽ ἐξοχήν, the plain of the Jordan, or the Ghor (see at Deut. i. 1). The definition "from Geba to Rimmon" does not belong to כָּעֲרָבָה (Umbreit, Neum., Klief.), but to כָּל־הָאָרֶץ; for there was no plain between Geba and Rimmon, but only an elevated, hilly country. *Geba* is the present *Jeba*, about three hours to the north of Jerusalem (see at Josh. xviii. 24), and was the northern frontier city of the kingdom of Judah (2 Kings xxiii. 8). *Rimmon*, which is distinguished by the clause "to the south of Jerusalem" from the Rimmon in Galilee, the present *Rummaneh* to the north of Nazareth (see at Josh. xix. 13), and from the rock of Rimmon, the present village of *Rummon*, about fifteen Roman miles to the north of Jerusalem (see Judg. xx. 45), is the *Rimmon* situated on the border of Edom, which was given up by the tribe of Judah to the Simeonites (Josh. xv. 32, xix. 7), probably on the site of the present ruins of *Um er Rummanim*, four hours to the north of Beersheba (see at Josh. xv. 32). To וְרָאֲמָה וגו׳ we must supply as the subject *Jerusalem*, which has been mentioned just before. ראמה is probably only an outwardly expanded form of רָמָה from רוּם, like קָאם in Hos. x. 14. The whole land will be lowered, that Jerusalem alone may be high. This is, of course, not to be understood as signifying a physical elevation caused by the depression of the rest of the land; but the description is a figurative one, like the exaltation of the temple mountain above all the mountains in Mic. iv. 1. Jerusalem, as the residence of the God-King, is the centre of the kingdom of God; and in the future this is to tower high above all the earth. The figurative description is attached to the natural situation of Jerusalem, which stood upon a broad mountain ridge, and was surrounded by mountains, which were loftier than the city (see Robinson, *Palestine*). The exaltation is a figurative representation of the spiritual elevation and glory which it is to receive. Moreover, Jerusalem is to dwell on its ancient site (יֵשַׁב תַּחְתֶּיהָ, as in ch. xii. 6). The meaning of this is not that the exaltation above the surrounding land will be the only alteration that will take place in its situation (Koehler); but, as a comparison with Jer. xxxi. 38 clearly shows, that the city will be restored or rebuilt in its former extent, and therefore is to be completely recovered from the ruin brought upon it by conquest and plunder (ver. 1). The boundaries of the city that are mentioned here cannot be determined with perfect certainty. The first definitions relate to the extent of the city from east to west. The starting-point (for the use of לְמִן, see Hag. ii. 18) is Benjamin's gate, in the north wall, through which the road to Benjamin and thence to Ephraim ran, so that it was no doubt the same as Ephraim's gate mentioned in 2 Kings xiv. 13 and Neh. viii. 16. The *terminus ad quem*, on the other hand, is doubtful, viz. "to the place of the first gate, to the corner gate." According to the grammatical construction, עַד־שַׁעַר הַפִּנִּים is apparently in apposition to עַד־מְקוֹם שַׁעַר הר', or a more precise description of the position of the first gate; and Hitzig and Kliefoth have taken the words in this sense. Only we cannot see any reason why the statement "to the place of the first gate" should be introduced at all, if the other statement "to the corner gate" describes the very same terminal point, and that in a clearer manner. We must therefore assume, as the majority of commentators have done, that the two definitions refer to two different terminal points; in other words, that they define the extent both eastwards and westwards from the Benjamin's gate, which stood near the centre of the north wall. The corner gate (*sha'ar happinnīm* is no doubt the same as *sha'ar happinnâh* in 2 Kings xiv. 13 and Jer. xxxi. 38) was at the western corner of the north wall. "The first gate" is supposed to be identical with שַׁעַר הַיְשָׁנָה, the gate of the old (city), in Neh. iii. 6 and xii. 39, and its place at the north-eastern corner of the city. The definitions which follow give the extent of the city from north to south. We must supply מִן before מִגְדַּל The tower of *Hananeel* (Jer. xxxi. 38; Neh. iii. 1, xii. 39) stood at the north-east corner of the city (see at Neh. iii. 1). The king's wine-presses were unquestionably in the king's gardens at the south side of the city (Neh. iii. 15). In the city so glorified the inhabitants dwell (יָשְׁבוּ) in contrast to going

out as captives or as fugitives, vers. 2 and 5), and that as a
holy nation, for there will be no more any ban in the city.
The ban presupposes sin, and is followed by extermination as a
judgment (cf. Josh. vi. 18). The city and its inhabitants will
therefore be no more exposed to destruction, but will dwell
safely, and have no more hostile attacks to fear (cf. Isa. lxv.
18 sqq. and Rev. xxii. 3).

Vers. 12–15. Punishment of the hostile nations.—Ver. 12.
" *And this will be the stroke wherewith Jehovah will smite all the
nations which have made war upon Jerusalem : its flesh will rot
while it stands upon its feet, and its eyes will rot in their sockets,
and its tongue will rot in their mouth.* Ver. 13. *And it will come
to pass in that day, the confusion from Jehovah will be great among
them, and they will lay hold of one another's hand, and his hand
will rise up against the hand of his neighbour.* Ver. 14. *And
Judah will also fight at Jerusalem, and the riches of all nations
will be gathered together round about, gold and silver and clothes
in great abundance.* Ver. 15. *And so will be the stroke of the
horse, of the mule, of the camel, and of the ass, and of all the
cattle, that shall be in the same tents, like this stroke.*" To the
description of the salvation there is appended here as the obverse
side the execution of the punishment upon the foe, which was
only indicated in ver. 3. The nations which made war against
Jerusalem shall be destroyed partly by the rotting away of
their bodies even while they are alive (ver. 12), partly by
mutual destruction (ver. 13), and partly by Judah's fighting
against them (ver. 14). To express the idea of their utter
destruction, all the different kinds of plagues and strokes by
which nations can be destroyed are grouped together. In the
first rank we have two extraordinary strokes inflicted upon them
by God. *Maggēphâh* always denotes a plague or punishment
sent by God (Ex. ix. 14 ; Num. xiv. 37 ; 1 Sam. vi. 4). הָמֵק,
the inf. abs. *hiphil* in the place of the finite verb: "He (Jehovah)
makes its flesh rot while it stands upon its feet," *i.e.* He causes
putrefaction to take place even while the body is alive. The
singular suffixes are to be taken distributively : the flesh of
every nation or every foe. To strengthen the threat there is
added the rotting of the eyes which spied out the nakednesses
of the city of God, and of the tongue which blasphemed God
and His people (cf. Isa. xxxvii. 6). The other kind of destruc-

tion is effected by a panic terror, through which the foes are thrown into confusion, so that they turn their weapons against one another and destroy one another,—an occurrence of which several examples are furnished by the Israelitish history (com- pare Judg. vii. 22, 1 Sam. xiv. 20, and especially that in 2 Chron. xx. 23, in the reign of Jehoshaphat, to which the description given by our prophet refers). The grasp of the other's hand is a hostile one in this case, the object being to seize him, and, having lifted his hand, to strike him dead. Ver. 14a is translated by Luther and many others, after the Targum and Vulgate, "Judah will fight *against* Jerusalem," on the ground that נִלְחַם בְּ generally signifies "to fight against a person." But this by no means suits the context here, since those who fight against Jerusalem are "all the heathen" (ver. 2), and nothing is said about any opposition between Jerusalem and Judah. בְּ is used here in a local sense, as in Ex. xvii. 8, with נִלְחַם, and the thought is this: Not only will Jehovah smite the enemies miraculously with plagues and confusion, but Judah will also take part in the conflict against them, and fight against them in Jerusalem, which they have taken. *Judah* denotes the whole of the covenant nation, and not merely the inhabitants of the country in distinction from the inhabitants of the capital. Thus will Judah seize as booty the costly possessions of the heathen, and thereby visit the heathen with ample retribution for the plundering of Jerusalem (ver. 2). And the destruction of the enemy will be so complete, that even their beasts of burden, and those used in warfare, and all their cattle, will be destroyed by the same plague as the men ; just as in the case of the ban, not only the men, but also their cattle, were put to death (cf. Josh. vii. 24). Moreover, there is hardly any need for the express remark, that this description is only a rhetorically individualizing amplification of the thought that the enemies of the kingdom of God are to be utterly destroyed, —namely, those who do not give up their hostility and turn unto God. For the verses which follow show very clearly that it is only to these that the threat of punishment refers.

Vers. 16–19. Conversion of the heathen.—Ver. 16. "*And it will come to pass, that every remnant of all the nations which came against Jerusalem will go up year by year to worship the King Jehovah of hosts, and to keep the feast of tabernacles.* Ver.

17. *And it will come to pass, that whoever of the families of the earth does not go up to Jerusalem to worship the King Jehovah of hosts, upon them there will be no rain.* Ver. 18. *And if the family of Egypt go not up, and come not, then also not upon them; there will be (upon them) the plague with which Jehovah will plague all nations which do not go up to keep the feast of tabernacles.* Ver. 19. *This will be the sin of Egypt, and the sin of all the nations, which do not go up to keep the feast of tabernacles.*" The heathen will not be all destroyed by the judgment; but a portion of them will be converted. This portion is called " the whole remnant of those who marched against Jerusalem" (עַל בּוֹא as in ch. xii. 9). It will turn to the worship of the Lord. The construction in ver. 16 is anacolouthic: כָּל־הַנּוֹתָר, with its further definition, is placed at the head absolutely, whilst the predicate is attached in the form of an apodosis with וְעָלוּ. The entrance of the heathen into the kingdom of God is depicted under the figure of the festal journeys to the sanctuary of Jehovah, which had to be repeated year by year. Of the feasts which they will keep there every year (on מִדֵּי, see Delitzsch on Isa. lxvi. 23), the feast of tabernacles is mentioned, not because it occurred in the autumn, and the autumn was the best time for travelling (Theod. Mops., Theodoret, Grot., Ros.), or because it was the greatest feast of rejoicing kept by the Jews, or for any other outward reason, but simply on account of its internal significance, which we must not seek for, however, as Koehler does, in its agrarian importance as a feast of thanksgiving for the termination of the harvest, and of the gathering in of the fruit; but rather in its historical allusion as a feast of thanksgiving for the gracious protection of Israel in its wanderings through the desert, and its introduction into the promised land with its abundance of glorious blessings, whereby it foreshadowed the blessedness to be enjoyed in the kingdom of God (see my *bibl. Archäologie,* i. p. 414 sqq.). This feast will be kept by the heathen who have come to believe in the living God, to thank the Lord for His grace, that He has brought them out of the wanderings of this life into the blessedness of His kingdom of peace. With this view of the significance of the feast of tabernacles, it is also possible to harmonize the punishment threatened in ver. 17 for neglecting to keep this feast,—namely, that the rain will not be (come)

upon the families of the nations which absent themselves from this feast. For rain is an individualizing expression denoting the blessing of God generally, and is mentioned here with reference to the fact, that without rain the fruits of the land, on the enjoyment of which our happiness depends, will not flourish. The meaning of the threat is, therefore, that those families which do not come to worship the Lord, will be punished by Him with the withdrawal of the blessings of His grace. The Egyptians are mentioned again, by way of example, as those upon whom the punishment will fall. So far as the construction of this verse is concerned, וְלֹא בָאָה is added to strengthen לֹא תַעֲלֶה, and עֲלֵיהֶם לֹא contains the apodosis to the conditional clause introduced with אִם, to which יִהְיֶה הַגֶּשֶׁם is easily supplied from ver. 17. The positive clause which follows is then appended as an asyndeton: It (the fact that the rain does not come) will be the plague, etc. The prophet mentions Egypt especially, not because of the fact in natural history, that this land owes its fertility not to the rain, but to the overflowing of the Nile, —a notion which has given rise to the most forced interpretations; but as the nation which showed the greatest hostility to Jehovah and His people in the olden time, and for the purpose of showing that this nation was also to attain to a full participation in the blessings of salvation bestowed upon Israel (cf. Isa. xix. 19 sqq.). In ver. 19 this thought is rounded off by way of conclusion. זֹאת, this, namely the fact that no rain falls, will be the sin of Egypt, etc. חַטַּאת, the sin, including its consequences, or in its effects, as in Num. xxxii. 23, etc. Moreover, we must not infer from the way in which this is carried out in vers. 17–19, that at the time of the completion of the kingdom of God there will still be heathen, who will abstain from the worship of the true God; but the thought is simply this: there will then be no more room for heathenism within the sphere of the kingdom of God. To this there is appended the thought, in vers. 20 and 21, that everything unholy will then be removed from that kingdom.

Ver. 20. " *In that day there will stand upon the bells of the horses, Holy to Jehovah; and the pots in the house of Jehovah will be like the sacrificial bowls before the altar.* Ver. 21. *And every pot in Jerusalem and Judah will be holy to Jehovah of hosts, and all who sacrifice will come and take of them, and boil*

*therein; and there will be no Canaanite any more in the house of
Jehovah of hosts in that day."* The meaning of ver. 20*a* is not
exhausted by the explanation given by Michaelis, Ewald, and
others, that even the horses will then be consecrated to the
Lord. The words קֹדֶשׁ לַיהוָֹה were engraven upon the gold plate
on the tiara of the high priest, in the characters used in engrav-
ings upon a seal (Ex. xxviii. 36). If, then, these words are
(*i.e.* are to stand) upon the bells of the horses, the meaning is,
that the bells of the horses will resemble the head-dress of the
high priest in holiness.[1] This does not merely express the fact
that the whole of the ceremonial law will be abolished, but also
that the distinction between holy and profane will cease, inasmuch as even the most outward things, and things having no
connection whatever with worship, will be as holy as those
objects formerly were, which were dedicated to the service of
Jehovah by a special consecration. In vers. 20*b* and 21*a*, the
graduated distinction between the things which were more or
less holy is brought prominently out. The pots in the sanctuary, which were used for boiling the sacrificial flesh, were
regarded as much less holy than the sacrificial bowls in which
the blood of the sacrificial animals was received, and out of
which it was sprinkled or poured upon the altar. In the future
these pots will be just as holy as the sacrificial bowls; and
indeed not merely the boiling pots in the temple, but all the
boiling pots in Jerusalem and Judah, which have hitherto been
only clean and not holy, so that men will use them at pleasure for boiling the sacrificial flesh. In this priestly-levitical
drapery the thought is expressed, that in the perfected kingdom
of God not only will everything without exception be holy, but
all will be equally holy. The distinction between holy and
profane can only cease, however, when the sin and moral defilement which first evoked this distinction, and made it necessary
that the things intended for the service of God should be set
apart, and receive a special consecration, have been entirely
removed and wiped away. To remove this distinction, to pre-

---

[1] It follows from this passage, that it was an Israelitish custom to hang
bells upon the horses and mules as ornaments, and probably also for other
purposes, as with us. This custom was a very common one in antiquity
(see the proofs which have been so diligently collected in *Dougtæi Analecta
sacr.* p. 296 sqq.).

pare the way for the cleansing away of sin, and to sanctify once more that which sin had desecrated, was the object of the sacred institutions appointed by God. To this end Israel was separated from the nations of the earth ; and in order to train it up as a holy nation, and to secure the object described, a law was given to it, in which the distinction between holy and profane ran through all the relations of life. And this goal will be eventually reached by the people of God ; and sin with all its consequences be cleansed away by the judgment. In the perfected kingdom of God there will be no more sinners, but only such as are righteous and holy. This is affirmed in the last clause : there will be no Canaanite any more in the house of Jehovah. The Canaanites are mentioned here, not as merchants, as in Zeph. i. 11, Hos. xii. 8 (as Jonathan, Aquila, and others suppose), but as a people laden with sin, and under the curse (Gen. ix. 25 ; Lev. xviii. 24 sqq. ; Deut. vii. 2, ix. 4, etc.), which has been exterminated by the judgment. In this sense, as the expression עוֹד לֹא implies, the term Canaanite is used to denote the godless members of the covenant nation, who came to the temple with sacrifices, in outward self-righteousness. As עוֹד presupposes that there were Canaanites in the temple of Jehovah in the time of the prophet, the reference cannot be to actual Canaanites, because they were prohibited by the law from entering the temple, but only to Israelites, who were Canaanites in heart. Compare Isa. i. 10, where the princes of Judah are called princes of Sodom (Ezek. xvi. 3, xliv. 9). The " house of Jehovah" is the temple, as in the preceding verse, and not the church of Jehovah, as in ch. ix. 8, although at the time of the completion of the kingdom of God the distinction between Jerusalem and the temple will have ceased, and the whole of the holy city, yea, the whole of the kingdom of God, will be transformed by the Lord into a holy of holies (see Rev. xxi. 22, 27).

Thus does our prophecy close with a prospect of the completion of the kingdom of God in glory. All believing commentators are agreed that the final fulfilment of vers. 20 and 21 lies before us in Rev. xxi. 27 and xxii. 15, and that even ch. xii. neither refers to the Chaldæan catastrophe nor to the Maccabæan wars, but to the Messianic times, however they may differ from one another in relation to the historical events which the prophecy foretels. Hofmann and Koehler, as well as Ebrard and Kliefoth, start with the assumption, that the prophecy in ch. xii.–xiv. strikes in where the preceding one in ch. ix.–xi. terminates; that is to say, that it commences with the time when Israel was given up to the power of the fourth empire, on account of its rejection of the good shepherd, who appeared in Christ. Now since Hofmann and Koehler understand by Israel only the chosen people of the old covenant, or the Jewish nation, and by Jerusalem the capital of this nation in Palestine, they find this prophecy in ch. xii., that when Jehovah shall eventually bring to pass the punishment of the bad shepherd, *i.e.* of the imperial power, with its hostility to God, it will assemble together again in its members the nations of the earth, to make war upon the material Jerusalem and Israel, which has returned again from its dispersion in all the world into the possession of the holy land (Palestine), and will besiege the holy city; but it will there be smitten by Jehovah, and lose its power over Israel. At that time will Jehovah also bring the previous hardening of Israel to an end, open its eyes to its sin against the Saviour it has put to death, and effect its conversion. But they differ in opinion as to ch. xiv. According to Koehler, this chapter refers to a future which is still in the distance—to a siege and conquest of Jerusalem which are to take place after Israel's conversion, through which the immediate personal appearance of Jehovah will be brought to pass, and all the effects by which that appearance is necessarily accompanied. According to Hofmann (*Schriftbeweis*, ii. p. 610 sqq.), ch. xiv. 1 sqq. refers to the same occurrence as ch. xii. 2 sqq., with this simple difference, that in ch. xii. the prophet states what that day, in which the whole of the world of nations attacks Jerusalem, will do with the people of God, and in ch. xiv. to what extremity it will be brought. Ebrard and Kliefoth, on the other hand, understand by *Israel*, with its capital Jerusalem, and the house of David (in ch. xii. 1–xiii. 6), rebellious Judaism after the rejection of the Messiah; and by *Judah* with its princes, Christendom. Hence the prophecy in this section announces what calamities will happen to Israel according to the flesh—that has become rebellious through rejecting the Messiah—from the first coming of Christ onwards, until its ultimate conversion after the fulness of the Gentiles has come in.[1] The section ch. xiii. 7–9 (the smiting of the shepherd) does not refer to the crucifixion of Christ, because this did not lead to the consequences indicated in ver. 8, so far as the whole earth was concerned, but to the " cutting off of the Messiah" predicted in Dan. ix. 26, the great apostasy which forms the beginning of the end, according to Luke xvii. 25, 2 Thess. ii. 3, 1 Tim. iv. 1, and 2 Tim. iii. 1, and through which Christ in His church is, according to the description in Rev. xiii. 17, so cut off from historical life, that it cannot be anything on earth. Lastly, chap. xiv. treats of the end of the world and the general judgment.

Of these two views, we cannot look upon either as well founded. For, in the first place, the assumption common to the two, and with which they set out, is erroneous and untenable, —namely, that the prophecy in ch. xii. sqq. strikes in where the previous one in ch. ix.–xi. terminated, and therefore that ch. xii.–xiv. is a direct continuation of ch. ix.–xi. This assumption is at variance not only with the relation in which the two prophecies stand to one another, as indicated by the correspondence in their headings, and as unfolded in ch. xii. 1 and 2 (p. 380 f., comp. p. 320), but also with the essence of the prophecy, inasmuch as it is not a historical prediction of the future according to its successive development, but simply a spiritual intuition effected by inspiration, in which only the leading features of the form which the kingdom of God would hereafter assume are set forth, and that in figures drawn from the circumstances of the present and the past. Again, the two views can only be carried out by forcing the text. If the prophecy in ch. xii. started with the period when Israel came into the power of the Roman empire after the rejection of the Messiah, it could not

---

[1] Kliefoth accordingly finds the siege of Jerusalem, predicted in ch. xii. 2, fulfilled in the siege of that city by Titus. The besieging nations then drank the reeling-cup ; for the subjection of Judah was the last act in the victory of the Roman empire over the Macedonian. Rome was then at the summit of its imperial greatness ; and from that time forth it became reeling and weak. This weakening was indeed prepared and effected through the Christian church ; but it was just the siege of Jerusalem which transferred the centre of the Christian church from Jerusalem to the Roman empire. The fulfilment of ch. xii. 3 is to be found in the Crusades, the Oriental question, the Haute Finance, and the Emancipation of the Jews. Jerusalem has thus become a burden-stone for all nations, etc.

leap so abruptly to the last days, as Hofmann and Koehler
assume, and commence with the description of a victorious
conflict on the part of Israel against the nations of the world
that were besieging Jerusalem, but would certainly first of
all predict, if not the destruction of the Jewish nation by the
Romans (which is merely indicated in ch. xi.), at all events
the gathering together of the Jews, who had been scattered by
the Romans over all the world, into Palestine and Jerusalem,
before an attack of the nations of the world upon Israel could
possibly be spoken of. Moreover, even the difference between
Hofmann and Koehler with regard to the relation between ch.
xii. 1–9 and ch. xiv. 1–5 shows that the transference of the
whole to the last times cannot be reconciled with the words
of these sections. The hypothesis of Koehler, that after the
gathering together of Israel out of its dispersion, the nations of
the world would make an attack upon Jerusalem in which they
would be defeated, and that this conflict would for the first
time bring Israel to the recognition of its guilt in putting
Christ to death, is at variance with the whole of the prophecy
and teaching of both the Old and New Testaments. For, according to these, Israel is not to be gathered together from its
dispersion among the nations till it shall return with penitence
to Jehovah, whom it has rejected. But Hofmann's statement
as to the relation between the two sections is so brief and obscure, that it is more like a concealment than a clearing up of
the difficulties which it contains. Lastly, when Hofmann correctly observes, that " by the *Israel* of the heading in ch. xii. 1
we can only understand the people of God, in contradistinction
to the world of nations, which is estranged from God," this cannot apply to the unbelieving Jews, who have been given into the
power of the last empire on account of their rejection of Christ,
or Israel according to the flesh, for that Israel is rejected by
God. The people of God exists, since the rejection of Christ,
only in Christendom, which has been formed out of believing
Jews and believing Gentiles, or the church of the New Testament, the stem and kernel of which were that portion of Israel
which believingly accepted the Messiah when He appeared,
and into whose bosom the believing Gentile peoples were received. Ebrard and Kliefoth are therefore perfectly right in
their rejection of the Jewish chiliasm of Hofmann and Koehler;

but when they understand by the Israel of the heading belonging to ch. xii.-xiv., which we find in ch. xii. 1-9, only the unbelieving carnal Israel, and by that in ch. xiv. the believing Israel which has been converted to Christ, and also introduce into ch. xii. 1-9 an antithesis between Israel and Judah, and then understand by Jerusalem and the house of David in ch. xii. the hardened Jews, and by Judah, Christendom; and, on the other hand, by Jerusalem and Judah in ch. xiv. the Christendom formed of believing Jews and believing Gentiles,—we have already shown at ch. xii. 10 (p. 387) that these distinctions are arbitrarily forced upon the text.

Our prophecy treats in both parts—ch. xii. 1-xiii. 6 and ch. xiii. 7-xiv. 21—of Israel, the people of God, and indeed the people of the new covenant, which has grown out of the Israel that believed in Christ, and believers of the heathen nations incorporated into it, and refers not merely to the church of the new covenant in the last times, when all the old Israel will be liberated by the grace of God from the hardening inflicted upon it, and will be received again into the kingdom of God, and form a central point thereof (Vitringa, C. B. Mich., etc.), but to the whole development of the church of Christ from its first beginning till its completion at the second coming of the Lord, as Hengstenberg has in the main discovered and observed. As the Israel of the heading (ch. xii. 1) denotes the people of God in contradistinction to the peoples of the world, the inhabitants of Jerusalem with the house of David, and Judah with its princes, as the representatives of Israel, are typical epithets applied to the representatives and members of the new covenant people, viz. the Christian church; and Jerusalem and Judah, as the inheritance of Israel, are types of the seats and territories of Christendom. The development of the new covenant nation, however, in conflict with the heathen world, and through the help of the Lord and His Spirit, until its glorious completion, is predicted in our oracle, not according to its successive historical course, but in such a manner that the first half announces how the church of the Lord victoriously defeats the attacks of the heathen world through the miraculous help of the Lord, and how in consequence of this victory it is increased by the fact that the hardened Israel comes more and more to the acknowledgment of its sin and to

belief in the Messiah, whom it has put to death, and is incorporated into the church; whilst the second half, on the other
hand, announces how, in consequence of the slaying of the
Messiah, there falls upon the covenant nation a judgment
through which two-thirds are exterminated, and the remainder
is tested and refined by the Lord, so that, although many do
indeed fall and perish in the conflicts with the nations of the
world, the remnant is preserved, and in the last conflict will be
miraculously delivered through the coming of the Lord, who
will come with His saints to complete His kingdom in glory
by the destruction of the enemies of His kingdom, and by the
transformation and renewal of the earth. As the believing
penitential look at the pierced One (xii. 10) will not take place
for the first time at the ultimate conversion of Israel at the end
of the days, but began on the day of Golgotha, and continues
through all the centuries of the Christian church, so did the
siege of Jerusalem by all nations (ch. xii. 1-9), *i.e.* the attack
of the heathen nations upon the church of God, commence even
in the days of the apostles (cf. Acts iv. 25 sqq.), and continues
through the whole history of the Christian church to the last
great conflict which will immediately precede the return of
our Lord to judgment. And again, just as the dispersion of
the flock after the slaying of the shepherd commenced at the
arrest and death of Christ, and the bringing back of the hand
of the Lord upon the small ones at the resurrection of Christ,
so have they both been repeated in every age of the Christian
church, inasmuch as with every fresh and powerful exaltation
of antichristian heathenism above the church of Christ, those
who are weak in faith flee and are scattered; but as soon as
the Lord shows Himself alive in His church again, they let
Him gather them together once more. And this will continue,
according to the word of the Lord in Matt. xxiv. 10 sqq., till
the end of the days, when Satan will go out to deceive the
nations in the four quarters of the earth, and to gather together
Gog and Magog to battle against the camp of the saints and
the holy city; whereupon the Lord from heaven will destroy
the enemy, and perfect His kingdom in the heavenly Jerusalem (Rev. xx.–xxii.).

So far as the relation between ch. xii. 2–9 and ch. xiv. 1–5
is concerned, it is evident from the text of both these passages

that they do not treat of two different attacks upon the church of God by the imperial power, occurring at different times; but that, whilst ch. xii. depicts the constantly repeated attack in the light of its successful overthrow, ch. xiv. describes the hostile attack according to its partial success and final issue in the destruction of the powers that are hostile to God. This issue takes place, no doubt, only at the end of the course of this world, with the return of Christ to the last judgment; but the fact that Jerusalem is conquered and plundered, and the half of its population led away into captivity, proves indisputably that the siege of Jerusalem predicted in ch. xiv. must not be restricted to the last attack of Antichrist upon the church of the Lord, but that all the hostile attacks of the heathen world upon the city of God are embraced in the one picture of a siege of Jerusalem. In the attack made upon Jerusalem by Gog and Magog, the city is not conquered and plundered, either according to Ezek. xxxviii. and xxxix., or according to Rev. xx. 7–9; but the enemy is destroyed by the immediate interposition of the Lord, without having got possession of the holy city. But to this ideal summary of the conflicts and victories of the nations of the world there is appended directly the picture of the final destruction of the ungodly power of the world, and the glorification of the kingdom of God; so that in ch. xiv. (from vers. 6 to 21) there is predicted in Old Testament form the completion of the kingdom of God, which the Apostle John saw and described in Rev. xx.–xxii. in New Testament mode under the figure of the heavenly Jerusalem.

MALACHI

INTRODUCTION.

1. **PERSON OF THE PROPHET.**—The circumstances of *Malachi's* life are so entirely unknown, that it is a disputed point whether מַלְאָכִי in the heading (ch. i. 1) is the name of a person, or merely an ideal name given to the prophet who foretels the sending of the messenger of Jehovah (מַלְאָכִי, ch. iii. 1), and whose real name has not been handed down. The LXX. rendered the בְּיַד מַלְאָכִי of the heading by ἐν χειρὶ ἀγγέλου αὐτοῦ, and therefore either had or conjectured as their reading מַלְאָכוֹ; and the Targumist *Jonathan,* who adds to בְּיַד מַלְאָכִי *cujus nomen appellatur* ESRA *scriba,* has also taken מלאכי in an ideal sense, and given the statement that Ezra the scribe is the prophetic author of our book, as a conjecture founded upon the spirit and contents of the prophecy. The notion that *Malachi* is only an official name is therefore met with in many of the fathers, and has been vigorously defended in the most recent times by Hengstenberg, who follows the lead of Vitringa, whilst Ewald lays it down as an established truth. But the arguments adduced in support of this, especially by Hengstenberg in his *Christology,* are not conclusive. The circumstance " that the heading does not contain any further personal description, whether the name of his father or the place of his birth," is not more striking in our book than in the writings of Obadiah and Habakkuk, which also contain only the name of the prophet in the heading, without any further personal descriptions. It is a striking fact, no doubt, that the LXX. and the Targumist have taken the name as an appellative; at the same time, it by no means follows from this " that nothing was known in tradition of any historical person of the name of Malachi," but simply that nothing certain had

been handed down concerning the circumstances of the prophet's life. The recollection, however, of the circumstances connected with the personal history of the prophet might easily have become extinct during the period of at least 150 or 200 years which intervened between the lifetime of the prophet and the Alexandrian version of the Old Testament, if his life was not distinguished by any other facts than the prophecies contained in his book. And *Jonathan* lived, at the earliest, 400 years after Malachi. That all recollection of the person of Malachi was not lost, however, is evident both from the notice in the Talmud to the effect that Malachi was one of the men of the great synagogue, as Haggai and Zechariah had been, and also from the statements made by Ps. Doroth., Epiph., and other fathers, to the effect that he was a Levite of the tribe of Zebulun, and was born in *Supha*, or Σοφά, or Σοφιρά (see the passages in Koehler, *Mal.* pp. 10, 11), although all these statements show that nothing certain was known as to the circumstances of his life. But the principal reason for taking the name not as a *nomen proprium*, but simply as a name adopted by the prophet for this particular prophecy, is to be found, according to Hengstenberg, in the character of the name itself, viz. in the fact that it is not formed from מַלְאָךְ and יָהּ = יְהוָה, and cannot be explained by *angelicus*. But neither the one nor the other can be regarded as established. The formation of proper names by adding the termination ־ִי to appellative nouns is by no means unusual, as the long list of examples of words formed in this manner, given by Olshausen (*Heb. Gramm.* § 218, *b*), clearly shows; and the remark that "this formation only serves to denote descent or occupation" (Hengstenberg) is beside the mark, since it does not apply to such names as גֵּרְמִי, זִכְרִי, and others. The interpretation of the name as a contraction of מַלְאָכִיָּה, messenger of Jehovah, is quite as possible as this derivation. We have an unquestionable example of a contraction of this kind in אֲבִי in 2 Kings xviii. 2, as compared with אֲבִיָּה in 2 Chron. xxix. 1. And just as the יָה is there omitted altogether in אֲבִי, so is the other name of God, אֵל, omitted in פַּלְטִי in 1 Sam. xxv. 44, which is written פַּלְטִיאֵל in 2 Sam. iii. 15. This omission of the name of God is by no means rare. "The Hebrews very often drop the names of God at the end of proper names" (Simonis, p. 11).

The formation of such a name as מַלְאָכִי would be perfectly analogous to these cases; and no objection whatever can be brought against such a name, since the ־ִ need not be taken as a suffix of the first person (*my* messenger is Jehovah), but is rather to be taken as *Yod compaginis*, like יְחִזְקִיָּה formed from יְחִזְקִי (for יְחַזֵּק) and יָה, "messenger of Jehovah." This name might very well have been given by parents to a son whom God had given them, or sent to them in fulfilment of their wishes. Which of these two derivations deserves the preference, cannot be determined with certainty; at the same time, there is more probability in the latter than in the former, partly because of the obvious play upon His name in the words הִנְנִי שֹׁלֵחַ מַלְאָכִי (ch. iii. 1), and partly because of the Greek form of the name Μαλαχίας in the heading of the book. Since, then, there is no valid argument that can be brought against the formation of such a name, there is all the more reason for regarding the name in the heading (ch. i. 1) as the real name of the prophet, from the fact that the ideal explanation would be without any distinct analogy. "All the prophets whose writings have come down to us in the canon, have given their own names in the headings to their books, that is to say, the names which they received at their birth; and the names of the rest of the prophets of the Old Testament are also their real names" (Caspari, *Micha*, p. 28). Even in the case of the names *Agur* (Prov. xxx. 1) and *Lemuel* (Prov. xxxi. 1), which Hengstenberg cites as analogies, it is still doubtful whether the first, Agur the son of Jakeh, is not a historical name; and even if the ideal use of the two were established beyond all doubt, no conclusion could be drawn from a collection of proverbs bearing upon a prophetic writing. A collection of proverbs is a poetical work, whose ethical or religious truth is not dependent upon the person of the poet. The prophet, on the contrary, has to guarantee the divinity of his mission and the truth of his prophecy by his own name or his own personality.

The period of Malachi is also a disputed point, although all are agreed that he lived and prophesied after the captivity. We may gather from his prophecy, not only that he commenced his prophetic labours after Haggai and Zechariah, since, according to ch. i. 6 sqq. and iii. 10, the temple had been rebuilt and the temple-worship had been restored for a considerable time, but also, as Vitringa has shown in his *Observ. ss.* ii. lib. 6, that he did not prophesy till after the first arrival of Nehemiah in Jerusalem, *i.e.* after the thirty-second year of Artaxerxes Longimanus. The chief reason for this is to be found in the agreement between Malachi and Nehemiah (ch. xiii.), in the reproof administered for the abuses current among the people, and even in the priesthood,—namely, the marriage of heathen wives (compare ch. ii. 11 sqq. with Neh. xiii. 23 sqq.), and the negligent payment of the tithes (compare ch. iii. 8–10 with Neh. xiii. 10–14). The first of these abuses—namely, that many even of the priests and Levites had taken heathen wives—found its way among the people even on Ezra's first arrival in Jerusalem; and he succeeded in abolishing it by vigorous measures, so that all Israel put away the heathen wives within three months (Ezra ix. and x.). But it is evidently impossible to refer the condemnation of the same abuse in Malachi to this particular case, because on the one hand the exhortation to be mindful of the law of Moses (ch. iii. 22), as well as the whole of the contents of our book which are founded upon the authority of the law, apply rather to the time when Ezra had already put forth his efforts to restore the authority of the law (Ezra vii. 14, 25, 26), than to the previous time; whilst, on the other hand, the offering of unsuitable animals in sacrifice (i. 7 sqq.), and unfaithfulness in the payment of the tithes and heave-offerings (iii. 8), can evidently be only explained on the supposition that Israel had to provide for the necessities of the temple and the support of the persons engaged in the worship; whereas in Ezra's time, or at any rate immediately after his arrival, as well as in the time of Darius (Ezra vi. 9, 10), the costs of worship were defrayed out of the royal revenues (Ezra vii. 15 -17, 20–24). But after the abolition of the heathen marriages by Ezra, and after his reformatory labours as a whole, such breaches of the law could not have spread once more among the people in the short interval between the time of Ezra and the first arrival of Nehemiah, even if Ezra had not continued his labours up to that time, as is evident from Neh. viii.-x. Moreover, Nehemiah would no doubt have attacked these abuses at that time, as he did at a later period, if he had detected them. Consequently the falling back into the old sin that had been abolished by Ezra cannot have taken place before the period of Nehemiah's return to the king's court, in the thirty-second year of Artaxerxes (Neh. xiii. 6). If, therefore, Malachi condemns and threatens with the punishment of God the very same abuses which Nehemiah found in Jerusalem on his second arrival there, and strove most energetically to exterminate, Malachi must have prophesied at that time; but whether immediately before Nehemiah's second arrival in Jerusalem, or during his presence there, so as to support the reformatory labours of Nehemiah by his prophetic testimony, cannot be decided with certainty. What Malachi says in ch. i. 8 concerning the attitude of the people towards the Persian governor does not necessarily presuppose a non-Israelitish vicegerent, but might also apply to Nehemiah, since the prophet's words may be understood as relating to free-will gifts or presents, whereas Nehemiah (v. 14, 15) simply says that he has not required from the people the governor's supplies, and has not burdened them with taxes. The circumstance, however, that Nehemiah finds the abuses still existing in undiminished force, renders the assumption that Malachi had already prophesied improbable, and favours rather the contemporaneous labours of the two; in which case the work of Malachi bore the same relation to that of Nehemiah as the work of Haggai and Zechariah to that of Zerubbabel and Joshua; and the reformatory labours of Nehemiah, which were chiefly of an outward character, were accompanied by the more inward labours of Malachi, as was very frequently the case in the history of Israel; for example, in the case of Isaiah and Hezekiah, or of Jeremiah and Josiah (see Hengstenberg, *Christology*, iv. p. 157).

2. THE BOOK OF MALACHI contains one single prophecy, the character of which is condemnatory throughout. Starting with the love which the Lord has shown to His people (i. 2–5), the prophet proves that not only do the priests profane the name of the Lord by an unholy performance of the service at the altar (i. 6, ii. 9), but the people also repudiate their divine calling both by heathen marriages and frivolous divorces (ii. 10–16), and by their murmuring at the delay of the judgment; whereas the Lord will soon reveal Himself as a just judge, and before His coming will send His messenger, the prophet Elijah,

to warn the ungodly and lead them to repentance, and then suddenly come to His temple as the expected angel of the covenant, to refine the sons of Levi, punish the sinners who have broken the covenant, and by exterminating the wicked, as well as by blessing the godly with salvation and righteousness, make the children of Israel the people of His possession (ii. 17–iv. 6). The contents of the book, therefore, arrange themselves in three sections: ch. i. 6–ii. 9; ii. 10–16; ii. 17–iv. 6. These three sections probably contain only the leading thoughts of the oral addresses of the prophet, which are so combined as to form one single prophetic address. Throughout the whole book we meet with the spirit which developed itself among the Jews after the captivity, and assumed the concrete forms of Phariseeism and Saduceeism. The outward or grosser kind of idolatry had been rendered thoroughly distasteful to the people by the sufferings of exile; and its place was taken by the more refined idolatry of dead-work righteousness, and trust in the outward fulfilment of the letter of the divine commands, without any deeper confession of sin, or penitential humiliation under the word and will of God. Because the fulness of salvation, which the earlier prophets had set before the people when restored to favour and redeemed from captivity, had not immediately come to pass, they began to murmur against God, to cherish doubts as to the righteousness of the divine administration, and to long for the judgment to fall upon the Gentiles, without reflecting that the judgment would begin at the house of God (Amos iii. 2; 1 Pet. iv. 17). Malachi fights against this spirit, and the influence of the time in which he lived is apparent in the manner in which he attacks it. This style is distinguished from the oratorical mode of address adopted by the earlier prophets, and not unfrequently rises into a lyrico-dramatical diction, by the predominance of the conversational form of instruction, in which the thought to be discussed is laid down in the form of a generally acknowledged truth, and developed by the alternation of address and reply. In this mode of developing the thought, we can hardly fail to perceive the influence of the scholastic discourses concerning the law which were introduced by Ezra; only we must not look upon this conversational mode of instruction as a sign of the defunct spirit of prophecy, since it corresponded exactly to the practical wants of the time, and prophecy did not die of spiritual exhaustion, but was extinguished in accordance with the will and counsel of God, as soon as its mission had been fulfilled. Malachi's language, considering the late period in which he lived and laboured, is still vigorous, pure, and beautiful. "Malachi," as Nägelsbach says in Herzog's *Cyclopædia*, "is like a late evening, which brings a long day to a close; but he is also the morning dawn, which bears a glorious day in its womb."

For the exegetical literature, see my *Lehrbuch der Einleitung*, p. 318; also Aug. Koehler's *Weissagungen Maleachi's erklärt*, Erl. 1865.

EXPOSITION.

GOD'S LOVE, AND THE CONTEMPT OF HIS NAME.—
CHAP. I. 1–II. 9.

The Lord has shown love to Israel (i. 2–5), but Israel refuses Him the gratitude which is due, since the priests despise His name by offering bad sacrifices, and thereby cherish the delusion that God cannot do without the sacrifices (vers. 6–14). The people are therefore punished with adversity, and the priesthood with desecration (ii. 1–9).

Vers. 1–5. The first verse contains the heading (see the introduction), "*The burden of the word of the Lord*," as in Zech. ix. 1 and xii. 1. On *massa'* (burden), see Nah. i. 1. The prophet commences his address in ver. 2, by showing the love for which Israel has to thank its God, in order that on the ground of this fact he may bring to the light the ingratitude of the people towards their God. Ver. 2. "*I have loved you, saith Jehovah; and ye say, Wherein hast Thou loved us? Is not Esau a brother of Jacob? is the saying of Jehovah: and I loved Jacob*, Ver. 3. *And I hated Esau, and made his mountains a waste, and his inheritance for jackals of the desert.* Ver. 4. *If Edom says, We are dashed to pieces, but will build up the ruins again, thus saith Jehovah of hosts: They will build, but I will pull down: and men will call them territory of wickedness, and the people with whom Jehovah is angry for ever.* Ver. 5. *And your eyes will see it; and ye will say, Great is Jehovah over the border of Israel."* These four verses form neither an independent address, nor merely the first member of the following address, but the introduction and foundation of the whole book. The love which God has shown to Israel ought to form the motive and model for the conduct of Israel towards its God. אָהֵב denotes love in its expression or practical manifestation. The question asked by the people, " Wherein hast Thou shown us love?" may be explained from the peculiarities of Malachi's style, and is the turn he regularly gives to his address, by way of introducing the discussion of the matter in hand, so that we are not to see in it any intention to disclose the hypocrisy of the people. The prophet proves the love of Jehovah towards Israel, from the attitude of God towards Israel and towards Edom. Jacob and Esau, the tribe-fathers of both nations, were twin brothers. It would therefore have been supposed that the posterity of both the Israelites and the Edomites would be treated alike by God. But this is not the case. Even before their birth Jacob was the chosen one; and Esau or Edom was the inferior, who was to serve his brother (Gen. xxv. 23, cf. Rom. ix. 10–13). Accordingly Jacob became the heir of the promise, and Esau lost this blessing. This attitude on the part of God towards Jacob and Esau, and towards the nations springing from them, is described by Malachi in these words: I (Jehovah) have loved Jacob, and hated Esau. The verbs אָהֵב, to love, and שָׂנֵא, to hate, must not be weakened down into loving more and loving less, to avoid the danger of falling into the doctrine of predestination. שָׂנֵא, to hate, is the opposite of love. And this meaning must be retained here; only we must bear in mind, that with God anything arbitrary is inconceivable, and that no explanation is given here of the reasons which determined the actions of God. Malachi does not expressly state in what the love of God to Jacob (*i.e.* Israel) showed itself; but this is indirectly indicated in what is stated concerning the hatred towards Edom. The complete desolation of the Edomitish territory is quoted as a proof of this hatred. Ver. 3*b* does not refer to the assignment of a barren land, as Rashi, Ewald, and Umbreit suppose, but to the devastation of the land, which was only utterly waste on the western mountains; whereas it was by no means barren on the eastern slopes and valleys (see at Gen. xxvii. 39). *Tannōth* is a feminine plural form of *tan = tannīm* (Mic. i. 8; Isa. xiii. 22, etc.), by which, according to the Syrio-Aramæan version, we are to understand the jackal. The meaning dwelling-places, which Gesenius and others have given to *tannōth*, after the LXX. and Peshito, rests upon a very uncertain derivation (see Roediger at Ges. *Thes.* p. 1511). " For jackals of the desert:" *i.e.* as a dwelling-place for these beasts of the desert (see Isa. xxxiv. 13). It is a disputed point when this devastation took place, and from what people it proceeded. Jahn, Hitzig, and Koehler are of opinion that it is only of the most recent date, because otherwise the Edomites would long ago have repaired the injury, which, according to ver. 4, does not appear to have been done. Ver. 4, however, simply implies that the Edomites would not succeed in the attempt to repair the injury. On the other hand, vers. 2 and 3 evidently contain the thought, that whereas Jacob had recovered, in consequence of the love of Jehovah, from the blow which had fallen upon it (through the Chaldæans), Esau's territory was still lying in ruins from the same blow, in consequence of Jehovah's hatred (Caspari, *Obad.* p. 143). It follows from this, that the devastation of Idumæa emanated from the Chaldæans. On the other hand, the objection that the Edomites appear to have submitted voluntarily to the Babylonians, and to have formed an alliance with them, does not say much, since neither the one nor the other can be raised even into a position of probability; but, on the contrary, we may infer with the greatest probability from Jer. xlix. 7 sqq., as compared with xxv. 9, 21, that the Edomites were also subjugated by Nebuchadnezzar. Maurer's assumption, that Idumæa was devastated by the Egyptians, Ammonites, and Moabites, against whom Nebuchadnezzar marched in the fifth year after the destruction of Jerusalem, is perfectly visionary. The threat in ver. 4, that if Edom attempts to rebuild its ruins, the Lord will again destroy that which is built, is equivalent to a declaration that Edom will never recover its former prosperity and power. This was soon fulfilled, the independence of the Edomites being destroyed, and their land made an eternal desert, especially from the times of the Maccabees onwards (see i. 377). The construction of אֱדוֹם as a feminine with תֹּאמַר may be explained

on the ground that the land is regarded as the mother of its
inhabitants, and stands synecdochically for the population.
Men will call them (לָהֶם, the Edomites) גְּבוּל רִשְׁעָה, territory, land
of wickedness,—namely, inasmuch as they will look upon the
permanent devastation, and the failure of every attempt on the
part of the nation to rise up again, as a practical proof that
the wrath of God is resting for ever upon both people and land
on account of Edom's sins.—Ver. 5. These ineffectual attempts
on the part of Edom to recover its standing again will Israel
see with its eyes, and then acknowledge that Jehovah is showing
Himself to be great above the land of Israel. מֵעַל לִגְבוּל does not
mean "beyond the border of Israel" (Drus., Hitzig, Ewald,
and others). מֵעַל לְ does not mean this, but simply over, above
(cf. Neh. iii. 28; Eccles. v. 7). יִגְדַּל is not a wish, "Let Him
be great, i.e. be praised," as in Ps. xxxv. 27, xl. 17, etc. The
expression מֵעַל לִגְבוּל יְ does not suit this rendering; for it is an
unnatural assumption to take this as an apposition to יְהוָה, in
the sense of: Jehovah, who is enthroned or rules over the border
of Israel. Jehovah is great, when He makes known His greatness to men, by His acts of power or grace.

Vers. 6–14. The condemnation of that contempt of the
Lord which the priests displayed by offering bad or blemished
animals in sacrifices, commences with the following verse. Ver.
6. "*A son honoureth the father, and a servant his master. And
if I am a father, where is my honour? and if I am a master,
where is my fear? saith Jehovah of hosts to you, ye priests who
despise my name, and yet say, Wherein have we despised Thy
name? Ver. 7. Ye who offer polluted bread upon my altar, and
yet say, Wherewith have we polluted thee? In that ye say, The
table of Jehovah, it is despised. Ver. 8. And if ye offer what is
blind for sacrifice, it is no wickedness; and if ye offer what is
lame and diseased, it is no wickedness. Offer it, now, to thy
governor: will he be gracious to thee, or accept thy person? saith
Jehovah of hosts. Ver. 9. And now, supplicate the face of God,
that He may have compassion upon us: of your hand has this
occurred: will He look upon a person on your account? saith
Jehovah of hosts.*" This reproof is simply directed against the
priests, but it applies to the whole nation; for in the times
after the captivity the priests formed the soul of the national
life. In order to make an impression with his reproof, the

prophet commences with a generally acknowledged truth, by which both priests and people could and ought to measure their attitude towards the Lord. The statement, that the son honours the father and the servant his master, is not to be taken as a moral demand. יְכַבֵּד is not jussive (Targ., Luth., etc.) ; for this would only weaken the prophet's argument. The imperfect expresses what generally occurs, individual exceptions which are sometimes met with being overlooked. Malachi does not even appeal to the law in Ex. xx. 12, which enjoins upon children reverence towards their parents, and in which reverence on the part of a servant towards his master is also implied, but simply lays it down as a truth which no one will call in question. To this he appends the further truth, which will also be admitted without contradiction, that Jehovah is the Father and Lord of Israel. Jehovah is called the Father of Israel in the song of Moses (Deut. xxxii. 6), inasmuch as He created and trained Israel to be His covenant nation ; compare Isa. lxiii. 16, where Jehovah is called the Father of Israel as being its Redeemer (also Jer. xxxi. 9 and Ps. c. 3). As Father, God is also Lord (*ădōnīm : plur. majest.*) of the nation, which He has made His possession. But if He is a Father, the honour which a son owes to his father is due to Him ; and if a Lord, the fear which a servant owes to his lord is also due to Him. The suffixes attached to כְּבוֹדִי and מוֹרָאִי are used in an objective sense, as in Gen. ix. 2, Ex. xx. 17, etc. In order now to say to the priests in the most striking manner that they do the opposite of this, the prophet calls them in his address despisers of the name of Jehovah, and fortifies this against their reply by proving that they exhibit this contempt in their performance of the altar service. With regard to the construction of the clauses in the last members of ver. 6, and also in ver. 7, the participle מַגִּישִׁים is parallel to בּוֹזֵי שְׁמִי, and the reply of the priests to the charge brought against them is attached to these two participial clauses by "and ye say ;" and the antithesis is exhibited more clearly by the choice of the finite tense, than it would have been by the continuation of the participle. Ver. 7aα is not an answer to the question of the priests, " Wherein have we despised Thy name ?" for the answer could not be given in the participle ; but though the clause commencing with *maggīshīm* does explain the previous rebuke, viz. that they

despise the name of Jehovah, and will not even admit that this
is true, it is not in the form of an answer to the reply of
the opponents, but by a simple reference to the conduct of the
priests. The answer is appended by בֶּאֱמָרְכֶם in ver. 7½ to the
reply made to this charge also; and this answer is explained in
ver. 8 by an allusion to the nature of the sacrificial animals,
without being followed by a fresh reply on the part of the
priests, because this fact cannot be denied. The contempt on
the part of the priests of the name of Jehovah, *i.e.* of the glory
in which God manifested Himself in Israel, was seen in the
fact that they offered polluted bread upon the altar of Jehovah.
Lechem, bread or food, does not refer to the shew-bread, for
that was not offered upon the altar, but is the sacrificial flesh,
which is called in Lev. xxi. 6, 8, 17, the food (*lechem*) of God
(on the application of this epithet to the sacrifices, see the
remarks in our comm. on Lev. iii. 11, 16). The prophet calls
this food מְגֹאָל, polluted, blemished, not so much with reference
to the fact, that the priests offered the sacrifices in a hypocritical
or impure state of mind (Ewald), as because, according to ver.
8, the sacrificial animals were affected with blemishes (*mūm*),
or had something corrupt (*moshchâth*) about them (Lev. xxii.
20–25). The reply, "Wherewith have we defiled *Thee*?" is
to be explained from the idea that either touching or eating
anything unclean would defile a person. In this sense they
regard the offering of defiled food to God as defiling God
Himself. The prophet answers: In that ye represent the table
of Jehovah as something contemptible. The table of Jehovah
is the altar, upon which the sacrifices (*i.e.* the food of God)
were laid. נִבְזֶה has the force of an adjective here: contemptible. They represent the altar as contemptible not so much
in words or speeches, as in their practice, viz. by offering up
bad, despicable sacrificial animals, which had blemishes, being
either blind, lame, or diseased, and which were unfit for sacrifices on account of these blemishes, according to the law in
Lev. xxii. 20 sqq. Thus they violated both reverence for the
altar and also reverence for Jehovah. The words אֵין רָע are
not to be taken as a question, but are used by the prophet in
the sense of the priests, and thus assume the form of bitter
irony. רָע, bad, evil, as a calumniation of Jehovah. In order
to disclose to them their wrong in the most striking manner,

the prophet asks them whether the governor (פֶּחָה : see at Hag i. 1) would accept such presents; and then in ver. 9 draws this conclusion, that God also would not hear the prayers of the priests for the people. He clothes this conclusion in the form of a challenge to supplicate the face of Jehovah (חַלָּה פְּנֵי : see at Zech. vii. 2), that God would have compassion upon the nation; but at the same time he intimates by the question, whether God would take any notice of this, that under the existing circumstances such intercession would be fruitless. פְּנֵי אֵל is selected in the place of פְּנֵי יְהוָֹה, to lay the greater emphasis upon the antithesis between God and man (the governor). If the governor would not accept worthless gifts graciously, how could they expect a gracious answer to their prayers from God when they offered such gifts to Him? The suffix in יְחָנֵּנוּ refers to the people, in which the prophet includes himself. The clause "from your hand has זֹאת (this : viz. the offering of such reprehensible sacrifices) proceeded" (cf. Isa. l. 11), is inserted between the summons to pray to God and the intimation of the certain failure of such intercession, to give still further prominence to the unlawfulness of such an act. The question הֲיִשָּׂא וגו' is appended to the principal clause חַלּוּ־נָא, and מִכֶּם פָּנִים does not stand for פְּנֵיכֶם : will He lift up your face, i.e. show you favour? but מִכֶּם is causal, "on your account" (Koehler) : "will He regard a person, that is to say, will He show favour to any one, on your account, viz. because ye pray to Him for compassion, when these are the actions ye perform?" The view of Jerome, Grotius, and Hitzig, that the challenge to seek the face of God is an earnest call to repentance or to penitential prayer, is at variance with the context. What follows, for example, is opposed to this, where the prophet says it would be better if the temple were closed, since God does not need sacrifices.

Ver. 10. "*O that there were one among you, who would shut the doors, that ye might not light mine altar to no purpose! I have no pleasure in you, saith Jehovah of hosts, and sacrificial offering does not please me from your hand.* Ver. 11. *For from the rising of the sun to the setting thereof my name is great among the nations, and in every place incense is burned and sacrifice offered, and indeed a pure sacrifice to my name; for my name is great among the nations, saith Jehovah of hosts.*

Ver. 12. *And ye desecrate it with your saying: the table of Jehovah, it is defiled, and its fruit—contemptible is its food.* Ver. 13. *And ye say: behold what a plague! and ye blow upon it, saith Jehovah of hosts, and ye bring hither what is robbed and the lame and the sick, and thus ye bring the sacrificial gift; shall I take pleasure in this from your hand? saith Jehovah."* The construction מִי בָכֶם וְיִסְגֹּר is to be explained in accordance with Job xix. 23: "Who is among you and he would shut," for "who is there who would shut?" and the question is to be taken as the expression of a wish, as in 2 Sam. xv. 4, Ps. iv. 7, etc.: "would that some one among you would shut!" The thought is sharpened by *gam*, which not only belongs to בָכֶם, but to the whole of the clause: "O that some one would shut," etc. The doors, the shutting of which is to be desired, are the folding doors of the inner court, in which the altar of burnt-offering stood; and the object of the wish is that the altar might no more be lighted up, not "by lights which burned by the side of the altar" (Ewald), but by the shining of the sacrificial fire which burned upon the altar. חִנָּם, in vain, *i.e.* without any object or use, for Jehovah had no pleasure in such priests or such worthless sacrifices. *Minchâh* here is not the meat-offering as distinguished from the slain-offering, but sacrifice generally, as in 1 Sam. ii. 17, Isa. i. 13, Zeph. iii. 10, etc. Such sacrifices God does not desire, for His name proves itself to be great among all the nations of the earth, so that pure sacrifices are offered to Him in every place. This is the simple connection between vers. 10 and 11, and one in perfect harmony with the words. Koehler's objection, that such a line of argument apparently presupposes that God needs sacrifices on the part of man for His own sake, and is only in a condition to despise the sacrifices of His nation when another nation offers Him better ones, has no force, because the expression "for His own sake," in the sense of "for His sustenance or to render the perpetuation of His being possible," with the conclusion drawn from it, is neither to be found in the words of the text, nor in the explanation referred to. God does indeed need no sacrifices for the maintenance of His existence, and He does not demand them for this purpose, but He demands them as signs of the dependence of men upon Him, or of the recognition on the part of men that they are indebted to God for life and every other blessing,

and owe Him honour, praise, and thanksgiving in return. In
this sense God needs sacrifices, because otherwise He would
not be God to men on earth ; and from this point of view the
argument that God did not want to receive the reprehensible
sacrifices of the Israelitish priests, because sacrifices were
offered to Him by the nations of the earth in all places, and
therefore His name was and remained great notwithstanding
the desecration of it on the part of Israel, was a very proper
one for attacking the delusion, that God needs sacrifices for
His own sustenance; a delusion which the Israelitish priests,
against whom Malachi was contending, really cherished, if not
in thesi, at all events *in praxi*, when they thought any sacrificial animal good enough for God.   Koehler's assumption, that
ver. 11 contains a subordinate parenthetical thought, and that
the reason for the assertion in ver. 10*b* is not given till vers.
12, 13, is opposed to the structure of the sentences, since it
necessitates the insertion of " although" after כִּי in ver. 11.

It is much more difficult to decide the question whether
ver. 11 treats of what was already occurring at the time of the
prophet himself, as Hitzig, Maurer, and Koehler suppose (after
the LXX, Ephr., Theod. Mops., etc.), or of that which would
take place in the future through the reception of the heathen
into the kingdom of God in the place of Israel, which would
be rejected for a time (Cyr., Theod., Jerome, Luther, Calvin,
and others, down to Hengstenberg and Schmieder).   Both of
these explanations are admissible on grammatical grounds ; for
such passages as Gen. xv. 14 and Joel iii. 4 show very clearly
that the participle is also used for the future.   If we take the
words as referring to the present, they can only mean that the
heathen, with the worship and sacrifices which they offer to the
gods, do worship, though ignorantly yet in the deepest sense,
the true and living God (Koehler).   But this thought is not
even expressed by the Apostle Paul in so definite or general a
form, either in Rom. i. 19, 20, where he teaches that the
heathen can discern the invisible being of God from His
works, or in Acts xvii. 23 sqq. in his address at Athens, where
he infers from the inscription upon an altar, " to the unknown
God," that the unknown God, whom the Athenians worshipped,
is the true God who made heaven and earth.   Still less is this
thought contained in our verse.   Malachi does not speak of an

" unknown God," whom all nations from the rising to the
setting of the sun, *i.e.* over all the earth, worshipped, but says
that Jehovah's name is great among the nations of the whole
earth.   And the name of God is only great among the Gentiles,
when Jehovah has proved Himself to them to be a great God,
so that they have discerned the greatness of the living God
from His marvellous works and thus have learned to fear Him
(cf. Zeph. ii. 11; Ps. xlvi. 9–11; Ex. xv. 11, 14–16).   This
experience of the greatness of God forms the substratum for
the offering of sacrifices in every place, since this offering is
not mentioned merely as the consequence of the fact that the
name of Jehovah is great among the nations; but in the clause
before the last, " the latter is also expressly placed towards the
former in the relation of cause to effect" (Koehler).   The
idea, therefore, that the statement, that incense is burned and
sacrifice offered to the name of Jehovah in every place, refers
to the sacrifices which the heathen offered to their gods, is
quite inadmissible.   At the time of Malachi the name of
Jehovah was not great from the rising to the setting of the
sun, nor were incense and sacrifice offered to Him in every
place, and therefore even Hitzig looks upon the expression
בְּכָל־מָקוֹם as " saying too much."   Consequently we must understand the words prophetically as relating to that spread of the
kingdom of God among all nations, with which the worship of
the true God would commence " in every place."   בְּכָל־מָקוֹם
forms an antithesis to the *one* place, in the temple at Jerusalem,
to which the worship of God was limited during the time of
the old covenant (Deut. xii. 5, 6).   מֻקְטָר is not a *partic. nomi-
nasc.*, incense, *suffimentum*, for this could not signify the burnt-
offering or slain-offering as distinguished from the meat-offering
(*minchâh*), but it is a *partic. verbale*, and denotes not the kindling of the sacrificial flesh upon the altar, but the kindling of
the incense (*suffitur*); for otherwise מֻגָּשׁ would necessarily stand
before מֻקְטָר, since the presentation preceded the burning upon
the altar.   The two participles are connected together *asyndetos*
and without any definite subject (see Ewald, § 295, *a*).   It is
true that *minchâh t^ehōrâh* does actually belong to *muggâsh* as
the subject, but it is attached by *Vav explic.* in the form of an
explanatory apposition: offering is presented to my name, and
indeed a sacrificial gift (*minchâh* covering every sacrifice, as

in ver. 10). The emphasis rests upon *tʰŏrâh*, pure, *i.e.* according to the requirements of the law, in contrast to sacrifices polluted by faulty animals, such as the priests of that day were accustomed to offer.[1] In the allusion to the worship, which would be paid by all nations to the name of the Lord, there is an intimation that the kingdom of God will be taken from the Jews who despise the Lord, and given to the heathen who seek God. This intimation forms the basis for the curse pronounced in ver. 14 upon the despisers of God, and shows "that the kingdom of God will not perish, when the Lord comes and smites the land with the curse (iv. 6), but that this apparent death is the way to true life" (Hengstenberg).

To this allusion to the attitude which the heathen will assume towards Jehovah when He reveals His name to them, the prophet appends as an antithesis in vers. 12, 13 a repetition of the reproof, that the priests of Israel desecrate the name of the Lord by that contempt of His name, which they display by offering faulty animals in sacrifice. Ver. 12 is only a repetition of the rebuke in ver. 7. חִלֵּל is really equivalent to בְּזֵה שֵׁם and גָּאַל in vers. 6 and 7, and מְגֹאָל to נִבְזֶה in ver. 7, which occurs in the last clause of ver. 12 as synonymous with it. The additional words וְנִיבוֹ וגו׳ serve to strengthen the opinion expressed by the priests concerning the table of the Lord. נִיבוֹ is placed at the head absolutely, and is substantially resumed in אָכְלוֹ. נִיב, *proventus*, produce, income; the suffix refers to *shulchan Yʰhŏvâh* (the table of the Lord). The revenue of the table of the Lord, *i.e.* of the altar, consisted of the sacrifices offered upon it, which are also called its food. The assumption is an erroneous one, that the sentence contains any such thought as

---

[1] In Mal. i. 11 the Romish Church finds a biblical foundation for its doctrine of the bloodless sacrifice of the New Testament, *i.e.* the holy sacrifice of the mass (see *Canones et decreta concil. Trident.* sess. 22), understanding by *minchâh* the meat-offering as distinguished from the bloody sacrifices. But even if there were any ground for this explanation of the word, which there is not, it would furnish no support to the sacrifice of the mass, since apart from the fact that the sacrifice of the mass has a totally different meaning from the meat-offering of the Old Testament, the literal interpretation of the word is precluded by the parallel "burning incense" or "frankincense." If burning incense was a symbol of prayer, as even Reincke admits, the "sacrificial offering" can only have denoted the spiritual surrender of a man to God (Rom. xii. 1).

the following : " The revenue drawn by the priests from the
altar, *i.e.* the sacrificial flesh which fell to their share, was contemptible;" according to which the priests would be represented
as declaring, that they themselves could not eat the flesh of the
sacrifices offered without disgust ; for they could not possibly
speak in this way, since it was they themselves who admitted
the faulty animals. If the flesh of blind, lame, or diseased
animals had been too bad for food in their estimation, they
would not have admitted such animals or offered them in
sacrifice (Koehler). Even in ver. 13 this thought is not implied. מַתְּלָאָה is a contraction of מַה־תְּלָאָה (cf. Ges. § 20, 2, *a*) :
What a weariness it is ! The object, which the priests declare
to be a burdensome and troublesome affair, can only be inferred
from the following expression, *v^ehippachtem 'ōthō*. *Hippēăch*
signifies here to blow away, like הֵפִיחַ בְּ in Ps. x. 5, which is
radically connected with it, *i.e.* to treat contemptuously. The
suffix אוֹתוֹ does not refer to אָכְלוֹ, but to שֻׁלְחַן יְיָ. The table of
Jehovah (*i.e.* the altar) they treat contemptuously. Consequently the service at the altar is a burden or a trouble to
them, whereas this service ought to be regarded as an honour
and a privilege. Jerome thinks that instead of אוֹתוֹ, we might
read אוֹתִי, which is found in a good number of codices ; and
according to the Masora, אוֹתוֹ has found its way into the text
as *Tikkun Sopherim* (compare the remarks at Hab. i. 12 on the
Tikkune Sopherim). But in this case also the reading in the
text is evidently original and correct. They manifest their
contempt of the altar by offering in sacrifice that which has
been stolen, etc. (cf. ver. 8). The first הֲבֵאתֶם is to be understood as referring to the bringing of the animals to the altar ;
the second to the offering of the animals upon the altar ; and
וַהֲבֵאתֶם אֶת־הַמִּנְחָה is to be interpreted thus : " And having brought
such worthless animals to the slaughter, ye then offer the sacrificial gift." There is indeed no express prohibition in the law
against offering *gázūl*, or that which has been stolen ; but it
was shut out from the class of admissible sacrifices by the simple
fact, that robbery was to be visited with punishment as a crime.
The reproof closes with the question, which is repeated from
ver. 8 (cf. ver. 10), whether God can accept such sacrifices
with pleasure. The prophet then utters the curse in the name
of God upon all who offer bad and unsuitable sacrifices.

Ver. 14. "*And cursed is he who deceives whilst there is in his flock a male animal, and he who vows and sacrifices to the Lord that which is corrupt; for I am a great King, saith Jehovah of hosts, and my name is feared among the nations.*" This verse is not attached adversatively to ver. 13*b*, but *Vav* is the simple copula, for the question in ver. 13*b* has a negative sense, or is to be answered by "No." To this answer there is attached the curse upon all the Israelites who offer such sacrifices to God as have not the characteristics required by the law. Two cases are mentioned. In the first place, that when according to the law a male animal ought to have been sacrificed, the person offering the sacrifice offered a female, *i.e.* one of less value, under the pretence that he did not possess or could not procure a male. The prophet calls this *nâkhal*, cheating. The second case refers to votive sacrifices; for which as *zebhach sh^elâmîm* (Lev. xxii. 21) both male and female animals could be used, though only such as were free from faults, inasmuch as animals having any *moshchâth* are declared in Lev. xxii. 25 to be not acceptable. *Moshchâth*, according to the Masoretic pointing, is the feminine of the *hophal* participle for מָשְׁחָת, like מְשָׁרֵת for מְשָׁרֶתֶת in 1 Kings i. 15 (cf. Ewald, § 188, *b*, and Olshausen, p. 393), according to which we should have to think of a female animal in bad condition. This pointing, however, is probably connected with the view still defended by Ewald, Maurer, and Hitzig, that the words וְנֹדֵר וְזֹבֵחַ are a continuation of the circumstantial clause וְיֵשׁ וגו׳, and that ver. 14 only refers to votive sacrifices: Cursed is the deceiver who has in his flock a male, but vows and sacrifices a corrupt female. This view, however, is evidently opposed to the meaning of the words. If וְנֹדֵר were a circumstantial clause, we should expect וְהוּא נֹדֵר. Moreover, since even female animals were admissible for votive sacrifices, the vowing and offering of a female animal could not be blamed in itself, and therefore what was reprehensible was not that a female animal was vowed and offered in sacrifice by any one, but that, instead of offering a faultless animal (*tâmîm*), he presented a blemished one. We must therefore follow the ancient translators and many commentators, who read *moshchâth* (*masc.*), according to which the curse is pronounced upon any one who vowed a sacrifice and afterwards redeemed his vow with a faulty and unsuitable animal.

An animal was *moshchâth*, corrupt, when it had any fault, which
rendered it unsuitable for sacrifice. The reason for the curse
is explained by reminding them of the greatness of God. Because Jehovah is a great King and His name is feared among
the nations, to offer a corrupt animal in sacrifice is an offence
against His majesty.

Chap. ii. 1–9. The rebuke administered to the priests for
their wicked doings is followed by an announcement of the
punishment which they will bring upon themselves in case they
should not observe the admonition, or render to the Lord the
reverence due to His name when discharging the duties of
their office. Ver. 1. " *And now, ye priests, this commandment
comes to you.* Ver. 2. *If ye do not hear and lay it to heart, to
give glory to my name, saith Jehovah of hosts, I send against
you the curse and curse your blessings, yea I have cursed them,
because ye will not lay it to heart.* Ver. 3. *Behold I rebuke
your arm, and scatter dung upon your face, the dung of your
feasts, and they will carry you away to it.* Ver. 4. *And ye will
perceive that I have sent this commandment to you, that it may
be my covenant with Levi, saith Jehovah of hosts.*" Ver. 1
introduces the threat; this is called *mitsvâh*, a command, not as
a commission which the prophet received, for the speaker is not
the prophet, but Jehovah Himself; nor as " instruction, admonition, or warning," for *mitsvâh* has no such meaning. *Mitsvâh*
is rather to be explained from *tsivvâh* in Nah. i. 14. The term
command is applied to that which the Lord has resolved to
bring upon a person, inasmuch as the execution or accomplishment is effected by earthly instruments by virtue of a
divine command. The reference is to the threat of punishment which follows in vers. 2 and 3, but which is only to be
carried out in case the priests do not hear and lay to heart,
namely, the warning which the Lord has addressed to them
through Malachi (i. 6–13), and sanctify His name by their
service. If they shall not do this, God will send the curse
against them, and that in two ways. In the first place He
will curse their blessings; in fact, He has already done so.
B^erâkhôth, blessings, are obviously not the revenues of the
priests, tithes, atonement-money, and portions of the sacrifices
(L. de Dieu, Ros., Hitzig), but the blessings pronounced by
the priests upon the people by virtue of their office. These

God will curse, *i.e.* He will make them ineffective, or turn them into the very opposite. וְגַם אָרוֹתִיהָ is not a simple, emphatic repetition, but אָרוֹתִי is a perfect, which affirms that the curse has already taken effect. The emphatic *v°gam*, and also, and indeed, also requires this. The suffix ָה attached to אָרוֹתִי is to be taken distributively: "each particular blessing." In the second place God will rebuke אֶת־הַזֶּרַע, *i.e.* the seed. But since the priests did not practise agriculture, it is impossible to see how rebuking the seed, *i.e.* causing a failure of the crops, could be a punishment peculiar to the priests. We must therefore follow the LXX., Aquila, Vulg., Ewald, and others, and adopt the pointing הַזְּרֹעַ, *i.e.* the arm. Rebuking the arm does not mean exactly "laming the arm," nor manifesting His displeasure in any way against the arm, which the priests raised to bless (Koehler). For it was not the arm but the hand that was raised to bless (Lev. ix. 22; Luke xxiv. 50), and rebuking signifies something more than the manifestation of displeasure. It is with the arm that a man performs his business or the duties of his calling; and rebuking the arm, therefore, signifies the neutralizing of the official duties performed at the altar and in the sanctuary. Moreover, God will also deliver them up to the most contemptuous treatment, by scattering dung in their faces, namely, the dung of their feasts. *Chaggīm*, feasts, is used metonymically for festal sacrifices, or the sacrificial animals slain at the festivals (cf. Ps. cxviii. 27) The dung of the sacrificial animals was to be carried away to an unclean place outside the camp and burned there, in the case of the sin-offerings, upon an ash-heap (Lev. iv. 12, xvi. 27; Ex. xxix. 14). Scattering dung in the face was a sign and figurative description of the most ignominious treatment. Through the expression "dung of your festal sacrifices," the festal sacrifices offered by these priests are described as being themselves dung; and the thought is this: the contempt of the Lord, which they show by offering blind or lame animals, or such as are blemished in other ways, He will repay to them by giving them up to the greatest ignomiмиny. The threat is strengthened by the clause וְנָשָׂא אֶתְכֶם אֵלָיו, which has been interpreted, however, in different ways. The Vulgate, Luther ("and shall remain sticking to you"), Calvin, and others take *peresh* as the subject to נָשָׂא: "the dung will draw the priests to itself, so that they will also become dung." But נָשָׂא has no such meaning; we must therefore leave the subject indefinite: they (*man*) will carry you away, or sweep you away to it, *i.e.* treat you as dung. When they should be treated in this ignominious manner, then would they perceive that the threatening had come from the Lord. " This commandment (*mitsvâh*) is the *mitsvâh* mentioned in ver. 1. The infinitive clause which follows announces the purpose of God, in causing this threat to come to pass. But the explanation of these words is a disputed point, since we may either take *b^erîthî* (my covenant) as the subject, or supply *hammitsvâh* (the commandment) from the previous clause. In the first case (" that my covenant may be with Levi ") the meaning could only be, that the covenant with Levi may continue. But although *hâyâh* does indeed mean to exist, it does not mean to continue, or be maintained. We must therefore take *hammitsvâh* as the subject, as Luther, Calvin, and others have done (" that it, viz. my purpose, may be my covenant with Levi "). Koehler adopts this, and has explained it correctly thus : " They will perceive that just as Jehovah has hitherto regulated His conduct towards Levi by the terms of His covenant, which was made with it at the time of its departure from Egypt, so will He henceforth let it be regulated by the terms of the decree of punishment which He has resolved upon now, so that this decree of punishment takes the place, as it were, of the earlier covenant." *Lêvî* is the tribe of Levi, which culminated in the priesthood. The attitude of God towards the priests is called a covenant, inasmuch as God placed them in a special relation to Himself by choosing them for the service of the sanctuary, which not only secured to them rights and promises, but imposed duties upon them, on the fulfilment of which the reception of the gifts of divine grace depended (*vid.* Deut. x. 8, 9, xxxiii. 8–10 ; Num. xviii. 1 sqq., xxv. 10 sqq.).

To explain and show the reason for this thought, the real nature of the covenant made with Levi is described in vers. 5–7 ; and vers. 8 and 9 then show how the priests have neutralized this covenant by forsaking the way of their fathers, so that God is obliged to act differently towards them now, and deliver them up to shame and ignominy. Ver. 5. "*My covenant was with him life and salvation, and I lent them to him for fear, and he feared me and trembled before my name.* Ver. 6. *Law of truth was in his mouth and there was no perversity on his lips, he walked with me in salvation and integrity, and brought back many from guilt.* Ver. 7. *For the priest's lips should keep knowledge, and men seek law from his mouth, because he is a messenger of Jehovah.*" In ver. 5a הַחַיִּים וְהַשָּׁלוֹם are the nominative of the predicate. "My covenant was with him life," etc., means, my covenant consisted in this, that life and salvation were guaranteed and granted to him. The elliptical mode of explaining it, viz. "my covenant was a covenant of life and salvation," gives the same sense, only there is no analogous example by which this ellipsis can be vindicated, since such passages as Num. xxv. 12, Gen. xxiv. 24, and Hos. xiv. 3, which Hitzig adduces in support of it, are either of a different character, or different in their meaning. *Shâlōm*, salvation (peace), is the sum of all the blessings requisite for wellbeing. Jehovah granted life and salvation to Levi, *i.e.* to the priesthood, for fear, viz. as the lever of the fear of God; and Levi, *i.e.* the priesthood of the olden time, responded to this divine intention. "He feared me." *Nichath* is the *niphal* not of *nâchath*, he descended, *i.e.* humbled himself (Ewald, Reincke), but of *châthath*, to terrify, to shake, which is frequently met with in connection with יָרֵא (*e.g.* Deut. xxxi. 8, Josh. i. 9, Jer. i. 17). Vers. 5 and 6 state how Levi preserved this fear both officially and in life. *Tōrath 'ĕmeth* (analogous to *mishpat 'ĕmeth* in Zech. vii. 9) is instruction in the law consisting in truth. Truth, which had its roots in the law of Jehovah, was the rule not only of his own conduct, but also and more especially of the instruction which he had to give to the people (cf. ver. 7). The opposite of *'ĕmeth* is *'avlâh*, perversity, conduct which is not regulated by the law of God, but by selfishness or sinful self-interest. Grammatically considered, the feminine *'avlâh* is not the subject to נִמְצָא, but is construed as the object : "they found not perversity" (cf. Ges. § 143, 1, *b* ; Ewald, § 295, *b*). Thus he walked in peace (salvation) and integrity before God. *B^eshâlōm* is not merely in a state of peace, or in peaceableness, nor even equivalent to בְּלֵבָב שָׁלֵם (2 Kings xx. 3), but according to ver. 5, "equipped with the salvation bestowed upon him by God." The *integritas vitæ* is affirmed in בְּמִישׁוֹר. הָלַךְ אֶת־יְיָ, to walk with Jehovah, denotes the most confidential intercourse with God, or walking as it were by the side of God (see at Gen. v. 22). Through this faithful discharge of the duties of his calling, Levi (*i.e.* the priesthood) brought many back from guilt or iniquity, that is to say, led many back from the way of sin to the right way, viz. to the fear of God (cf. Dan. xii. 3). But Levi did nothing more than what the standing and vocation of the priest required. For the lips of the priest should preserve knowledge. דַעַת is the knowledge of God and of His will as revealed in the law. These the lips of the priest should keep, to instruct the people therein; for out of the mouth of the priest men seek *tōrâh*, law, *i.e.* instruction in the will of God, because he is a messenger of Jehovah to the people. מַלְאָךְ, the standing epithet for the angels as the heavenly messengers of God, is here applied to the priests, as it is in Hag. i. 13 to the prophets. Whilst the prophets were extraordinary messengers of God, who proclaimed to the people the will and counsel of the Lord, the priests, by virtue of their office, were so to speak the standing or ordinary messengers of God. But the priests of that time had become utterly untrue to this vocation.

Ver. 8. "*But ye have departed from the way, have made many to stumble at the law, have corrupted the covenant of Levi, saith Jehovah of hosts. Ver. 9. Thus I also make you despised and base with all the people, inasmuch as ye do not keep my ways, and respect person in the law.*" הַדֶּרֶךְ is the way depicted in vers. 6 and 7, in which the priests ought to have walked. הִכְשַׁלְתֶּם בַּתּוֹרָה does not mean "ye have caused to fall by instruction" (Koehler); for, in the first place, *hattōrâh* (with the article) is not the instruction or teaching of the priests, but the law of God; and secondly, ב with כָּשַׁל denotes the object against which a man stumbles and which causes him to fall. Hitzig has given the correct explanation: ye have made the law to many a מִכְשׁוֹל, instead of the light of their way, through your example and through false teaching, as though the law allowed or commanded things which in reality are sin. In this way they have corrupted or overthrown the covenant with Levi. הַלֵּוִי, with the article, is not the patriarch Levi, but his posterity, really the priesthood, as the kernel of the Levites. Hence Jehovah also is no longer bound by the covenant, but withdraws from the priests what He granted to the Levi who was faithful to the covenant, viz. life and salvation (ver. 5), and makes them contemptible and base with all the people. This is simply a just retribution for the fact, that the priests depart from His ways and have respect to men. *Battōráh*, in the law, *i.e.* in the administration of the law, they act with partiality. For the fact itself compare Mic. iii. 11.

CONDEMNATION OF MARRIAGES WITH HEATHEN WOMEN AND OF DIVORCES.—Chap. II. 10–16.

This section does not stand in any close connection with the preceding one. It does not furnish an example of the stumbling upon the law mentioned in ver. 8; nor is the violation of the covenant of the fathers (ver. 10) or of the marriage covenant (ver. 14) appended to the neutralizing of the covenant of Levi on the part of the priests (vers. 8 and 4). For there is no indication in vers. 10–16 that the priests gave any impulse through their bad teaching to the breaches of the law which are here condemned; and the violation of the covenant of the fathers and of the marriage covenant forms no more a thought by which the whole is ruled, than the violation of the covenant with Levi in the previous section (Koehler). The prophet rather passes over with ver. 10 to a perfectly new object, namely, the condemnation of marriages with heathen women (vers. 10–12), and of the frivolous dissolution of marriages with Israelitish women, which was the natural consequence of the former (vers. 13–16). This sin the priests have only so far participated in, that they set a bad example to the people in their own unprincipled treatment of the law, which might easily lead to contempt of the divine ordinance of marriage.— Ver. 10. *" Have we not all one father? hath not one God created us? wherefore are we treacherous one towards another, to desecrate the covenant of our fathers?* Ver. 11. *Judah acts treacherously, and abomination has taken place in Israel and in Jerusalem; for Judah has desecrated the sanctuary of Jehovah, which He loves, and marries the daughter of a strange god.* Ver. 12. *Jehovah will cut off, to the man that doeth this, wakers and answerers out of the tents of Jacob, and him that offereth sacrifices to Jehovah of*

hosts." Malachi adopts the same course here as in the previous
rebuke, and commences with a general clause, from which the
wrongfulness of marriages with heathen women and of frivolous divorces necessarily followed. The *one* father, whom all
have, is neither Adam, the progenitor of all men, nor Abraham,
the father of the Israelitish nation, but Jehovah, who calls
Himself the Father of the nation in ch. i. 6. God is the
Father of Israel as its Creator; not, however, in the general
sense in which He is Creator of all men, but in the more
sacred sense, according to which He made Israel the people
of His possession. By the two clauses placed at the head,
Malachi intends not so much to lay emphasis upon the common descent of all the Israelites, by virtue of which they form
one united family in contrast with the heathen, as to say that
all the Israelites are children of God, and as such spiritual
brethren and sisters. Consequently every violation of the
fraternal relation, such as that of which the Israelite was
guilty who married a heathen woman, or put away an Israelitish wife, was also an offence against God, a desecration of
His covenant. The idea that the expression " one father"
refers to Abraham as the ancestor of the nation (Jerome,
Calvin, and others), is precluded by the fact, that not only the
Israelites, but also the Ishmaelites and Edomites were descended
from Abraham; and there is no ground whatever for thinking
of Jacob, because, although he had indeed given his name to
Israel, he is never singled out as its ancestor. *Nibhgad* is the
first pers. plur. imperf. *kal,* notwithstanding the fact that in
other cases *bâgad* has *cholem* in the imperfect; for the *niphal*
of this verb is never met with. The Israelite acted faithlessly
towards his brother, both when he contracted a marriage with
a heathen woman, and when he put away his Israelitish wife,
and thereby desecrated the covenant of the fathers, *i.e.* the
covenant which Jehovah made with the fathers, when He
chose them from among the heathen, and adopted them as
His covenant nation (Ex. xix. 5, 6, xxiv. 8). The reason for
this rebuke is given in ver. 11, in a statement of what has
taken place. In order the more emphatically to describe this
as reprehensible, *bâg^edáh* (hath dealt treacherously) is repeated
and applied to the whole nation. *Y^ehūdáh* (Judah), construed
as a feminine, is the land acting in its inhabitants. Then what

has taken place is described as תּוֹעֵבָה, abomination, like idolatry, witchcraft, and other grievous sins (cf. Deut. xiii. 15, xviii. 9 sqq.), in which the name *Israel* is intentionally chosen as the holy name of the nation, to indicate the contrast between the holy vocation of Israel and its unholy conduct. In addition to Israel as the national name (= Judah) Jerusalem is also mentioned, as is frequently the case, as the capital and centre of the nation. What has occurred is an abomination, because Judah desecrates קֹדֶשׁ יְיָ, *i.e.* neither the holiness of Jehovah as a divine attribute, nor the temple as the sanctuary, still less the holy state of marriage, which is never so designated in the Old Testament, but Israel as the nation which Jehovah loved. Israel is called *qōdesh*, a sanctuary or holy thing, as עַם קָדוֹשׁ, which Jehovah has chosen out of all nations to be His peculiar possession (Deut. vii. 6, xiv. 2 ; Jer. ii. 3 ; Ps. cxiv. 2 ; Ezra ix. 2 : see Targ., Rashi, Ab. Ezra, etc.). Through the sin which it had committed, Judah, *i.e.* the community which had returned from exile, had profaned itself as the sanctuary of God, or neutralized itself as a holy community chosen and beloved of Jehovah (Koehler). To this there is appended, though not till the last clause, the statement of the abomination : Judah, in its individual members, has married the daughter of a strange god (cf. Ezra ix. 2 sqq.; Neh. xiii. 23 sqq.). By the expression בַּת אֵל נֵכָר the person married is described as an idolatress (*bath*, daughter = dependent). This involved the desecration of the holy calling of the nation. It is true that in the law it is only marriages with Canaanites that are expressly forbidden (Ex. xxxiv. 16 ; Deut. vii. 3), but the reason assigned for this prohibition shows, that all marriages with heathen women, who did not give up their idolatry, were thereby denounced as irreconcilable with the calling of Israel (see at 1 Kings xi. 1, 2). This sin may God punish by cutting off every one who commits it. This threat of punishment (ver. 12) is indeed only expressed in the form of a wish, but the wish has been created by the impulse of the Holy Spirit. Very different and by no means satisfactory explanations have been given of the expression עֵר וְעֹנֶה, the waking one (עֵר the participle of עוּר) and the answering one, a proverbial description of the posterity of the wicked man formed by the combination of opposites (on the custom of expressing totality by opposites, see Dietrich, *Abhandlung zur hebr. Gramm.* p. 201 sqq.), in which, however, the meaning of the word עֵר still continues a matter of dispute. The rabbinical explanation, which is followed by Luther, viz. teacher and scholar, is founded upon the meaning *excitare* given to the verb עוּר, and the *excitans* is supposed to be the teacher who stimulates by questioning and admonishing. But apart from all other reasons which tell against this explanation, it does not suit the context; for there is not a single word to indicate that the prophet is speaking only of priests who have taken foreign wives; on the contrary, the prophet accuses Judah and Jerusalem, and therefore the people generally, of being guilty of this sin. Moreover, it was no punishment to an Israelite to have no rabbi or teacher of the law among his sons. The words are at any rate to be taken more generally than this. The best established meaning is *vigil et respondens*, in which עֵר is taken transitively, as in Job xli. 2 in the *chethib*, and in the Chaldee עֵר, watcher (Dan. iv. 10 (13) and 14 (17)), in the sense of *vivus quisque*. In this case the proverbial phrase would be taken from the night-watchman (J. D. Mich., Ros., Ges. *Thes.* p. 1004). It is no conclusive objection to this, that the words which follow, וּמַגִּישׁ מִנְחָה, evidently stand upon the same line as עֵר וְעֹנֶה and must form part of the same whole, and therefore that עֵר וְעֹנֶה cannot of itself embrace the whole. For this conclusion is by no means a necessary one. If the two expressions referred to portions of the same whole, they could not well be separated from one another by מֵאָהֳלֵי יַעֲקֹב. Moreover, the limitation of עֵר וְעֹנֶה to the age of childhood founders upon the artificial interpretation which it is necessary to give to the two words. According to Koehler עֵר denotes the child in the first stage of its growth, in which it only manifests its life by occasionally waking up from its ordinary state of deep, death-like slumber, and עֹנֶה the more advanced child, which is able to speak and answer questions. But who would ever think of calling a child in the first weeks of its life, when it sleeps more than it wakes, a waker? Moreover, the sleep of an infant is not a "deep, death-like slumber." The words " out of the tents of Jacob," *i.e.* the houses of Israel, belong to יַכְרֵת. The last clause adds the further announcement, that whoever commits such abominations shall have no one to offer a sacrificial gift to the Lord.

These words are not to be taken as referring to the priestly caste, as Hitzig supposes; but Jerome has given the correct meaning: "and whoever is willing to offer a gift upon the altar for men of this description." The meaning of the whole verse is the following: "May God not only cut off every descendant of such a sinner out of the houses of Israel, but any one who might offer a sacrifice for him in expiation of his sin."

Ver. 13. "*And this ye do a second time: cover the altar of Jehovah with tears, with weeping and sighs, so that He does not turn any more to the sacrifice, and accept the well-pleasing thing at your hand.* Ver. 14. *And ye say, Wherefore? Because Jehovah has been witness between thee and the wife of thy youth, towards whom thou hast acted treacherously; whereas she is nevertheless thy companion, and the wife of thy covenant.* Ver. 15. *And not one did so who had still a remnant of spirit. And what (did) the one? He sought seed of God. Therefore shall ye take heed for your spirit, and deal not faithlessly to the·wife of thy youth.* Ver. 16. *For I hate divorce, saith Jehovah, the God of Israel; and he will cover wickedness over his garment, saith Jehovah of hosts. Thus shall ye take heed to your spirit, and not deal treacherously.*" In these verses the prophet condemns a second moral transgression on the part of the people, viz. the putting away of their wives. By *shēnīth* (as a second thing, *i.e.* for the second time) this sin is placed in the same category as the sin condemned in the previous verses. Here again the moral reprehensibility of the sin is described in ver. 11, before the sin itself is named. They cover the altar of Jehovah with tears, namely, by compelling the wives who have been put away to lay their trouble before God in the sanctuary. The inf. constr. introduces the more minute definition of זֹאת; and בְּכִי וַאֲנָקָה is a supplementary apposition to דִּמְעָה, added to give greater force to the meaning. מֵאֵין עוֹד, so that there is no more a turning (of Jehovah) to the sacrifice, *i.e.* so that God does not graciously accept your sacrifice any more (cf Num. xvi. 15). The following infinitive וְלָקַחַת is also dependent upon מֵאֵין, but on account of the words which intervene it is attached with לְ. רָצוֹן, the good pleasure or satisfaction, used as *abstractum pro concreto* for the well-pleasing sacrifice. Ver. 14. This sin also the persons addressed will not recognise. They inquire the reason why God will no more graciously accept their sacrifices, whereupon the prophet discloses their sin in the plainest terms. עַל־אֲשֶׁר = עַל־כִּי, as in Deut. xxxi. 17, Judg. iii. 12, etc. The words, "because Jehovah was a witness between thee and the wife of thy youth," cannot be understood as Ges., Umbreit, and Koehler assume, in accordance with ch. iii. 5, as signifying that Jehovah had interposed between them as an avenging witness; for in that case הֵעִיד would necessarily be construed with בְּ, but they refer to the fact that the marriage took place before the face of God, or with looking up to God; and the objection that nothing is known of any religious benediction at the marriage, or any mutual vow of fidelity, is merely an *argumentum a silentio*, which proves nothing. If the marriage was a *b⁰rīth 'Elōhīm* (a covenant of God), as described in Prov. ii. 17, it was also concluded before the face of God, and God was a witness to the marriage. With the expression "wife of thy youth" the prophet appeals to the heart of the husband, pointing to the love of his youth with which the marriage had been entered into; and so also in the circumstantial clause, through which he brings to the light the faithless treatment of the wife in putting her away: "Yet she was thy companion, who shared thy joy and sorrow, and the wife of thy covenant, with whom thou didst make a covenant for life." In ver. 15*a* the prophet shows still further the reprehensible character of the divorce, by rebutting the appeal to Abraham's conduct towards Hagar as inapplicable. The true interpretation of this hemistich, which has been explained in very different, and to some extent in very marvellous ways, is obvious enough if we only bear in mind that the subordinate clause וּשְׁאָר רוּחַ לוֹ, from its very position and from the words themselves, can only contain a more precise definition of the subject of the principal clause. The affirmation "a remnant of spirit is (was) to him" does not apply to God, but only to man, as L. de Dieu has correctly observed. *Rūăch* denotes here, as in Num. xxvii. 18, Josh. v. 1, 1 Kings x. 5, not so much intelligence and consideration, as the higher power breathed into man by God, which determines that moral and religious life to which we are accustomed to give the name of virtue. By *'echâd* (one), therefore, we cannot understand God, but only a man; and לֹא אֶחָד (not any one = no one, not one man) is the subject of the sen-

tence, whilst the object to עָשָׂה must be supplied from the previous sentence : " No man, who has even a remnant of reason,
or of sense for right and wrong, has done," *sc.* what ye are
doing, namely, faithlessly put away the wife of his youth.
To this there is appended the objection : " And what did the
one do ?" which the prophet adduces as a possible exception
that may be taken to his statement, for the purpose of refuting
it.   The words וּמָה הָאֶחָד are elliptical, the verb עָשָׂה, which
may easily be supplied from the previous clause, being omitted
(cf. Eccl. ii. 12). הָאֶחָד, not *unus aliquis*, but the well-known
one, whom it was most natural to think of when the question
in hand was that of putting away a wife, viz. Abraham, who
put away Hagar, by whom he had begotten Ishmael, and who
was therefore also his wife (Gen. xxi.). The prophet therefore
replies, that Abraham sought to obtain the seed promised him
by God, *i.e.* he dismissed Hagar, because God promised to give
him the desired posterity, not in Ishmael through the maid
Hagar, but through Sarah in Isaac, so that in doing this he
was simply acting in obedience to the word of God (Gen.
xxi. 12). After meeting this possible objection, Malachi warns
his contemporaries to beware of faithlessly putting away their
wives.   The *Vav* before *nishmartem* is the *Vav rel.*, through
which the perfect acquires the force of a cohortative as a
deduction from the facts before them, as in וְעָשִׂיתָ in 1 Kings
ii. 6 (see Ewald, § 342, *c*). נִשְׁמַר בְּרוּחוֹ is synonymous with
נִשְׁמַר בְּנַפְשׁוֹ in Jer. xvii. 21, and this is equivalent to נִשְׁמַר לְנַפְשׁוֹ
in Deut. iv. 15 and Josh. xxiii. 11. The instrumental view
of בְ (" by means of the Spirit :" Koehler) is thus proved to be
inadmissible. "Take heed to your spirit," *i.e.* beware of losing
your spirit. We need not take *rŭăch* in a different sense here
from that in which it is used in the clause immediately preceding; for with the loss of the spiritual and moral *vis vitæ*,
which has been received from God, the life itself perishes.
What it is that they are to beware of is stated in the last
clause, which is attached by the simple copula (*Vav*), and in
which the address passes from the second person into the third,
to express what is affirmed as applying to every man. This
interchange of *thou* (in wife of thy youth) and *he* (in יִבְגֹּד) in
the same clause appears very strange to our mode of thought
and speech ; but it is not without analogy in Hebrew (*e.g.* in

Isa. i. 29; cf. Ewald, § 319, *a*), so that we have no right to
alter יִבְגֹּד into תִּבְגֹּד, since the ancient versions and the readings
of certain codices do not furnish sufficient critical authority for
such a change.   The subject in יִבְגֹּד is naturally thought of as
indefinite : any one, men.   This warning is accounted for in
ver. 16, first of all in the statement that God hates putting
away.   שַׁלַּח is the inf. constr. *piel* and the object to שֹׂנֵא :
"the sending away (of a wife), divorce."   שֹׂנֵא is a participle,
the pronominal subject being omitted, as in *maggîd* in Zech.
ix. 12, because it may easily be inferred from the following
words : אָמַר יי׳ (saith the Lord of hosts).   The thought is not
at variance with Deut. xxiv. 1 sqq., where the putting away of
a wife is allowed; for this was allowed because of the hardness
of their hearts, whereas God desires that a marriage should be
kept sacred (cf. Matt. xix. 3 sqq. and the comm. on Deut.
xxiv. 1-5).   A second reason for condemning the divorce is
given in the words וְכִסָּה חָמָס עַל לְ׳, which do not depend upon
כִּי שֹׂנֵא, but form a sentence co-ordinate to this.   We may either
render these words, "he (who puts away his wife) covers his
garment with sin," or "sin covers his garment."   The meaning
is the same in either case, namely, that wickedness will adhere
irremoveably to such a man.   The figurative expression may
be explained from the idea that the dress reflects the inward
part of a man, and therefore a soiled garment is a symbol of
uncleanness of heart (cf. Zech. iii. 4; Isa. lxiv. 5; Rev. iii. 4,
vii. 14).   With a repetition of the warning to beware of this
faithlessness, the subject is brought to a close.

THE DAY OF THE LORD.—Chap. ii. 17–iv. 6.

   In this section the prophet's words are directed against the
spirit of discontent and murmuring which prevailed among the
people, who lost faith in all the promises of God, because
the expected manifestation of the glory of the Lord for the
good of His people did not take place at once, and in their
despair called even the holiness and justice of God in question,
and began to deny the coming of the Lord to judge the world.
The prophet lets the feelings of the people express themselves

in ch. ii. 17, for the purpose of meeting them with an announcement of the day of the Lord and its true nature, in ch. iii. and
iv. Before His coming the Lord will send a messenger, to
prepare the way for Him. He Himself will then suddenly
come, and that to refine His people by the fire of judgment
and to exterminate the sinners (ch. iii. 1–6). The people are
retarding the revelation of the promised salvation through their
unfaithfulness to God (vers. 7–12), and preparing destruction
for themselves by their impatient murmuring; for in the day
of judgment none but the righteous find mercy : the judgment
will make manifest the distinction between the righteous and
the wicked (vers. 13–18), and bring destruction to the wicked,
and salvation to the godly (ch. iv. 1–3). The prophecy then
closes with the admonition to lay to heart the law of Moses,
and with an announcement that the Lord will send the prophet
Elijah before the day of His coming, to call the degenerate
nation to repentance, in order that when He appears the land
may not be smitten with the curse (vers. 4–6).

Ch. ii. 17. " *Ye weary Jehovah with your words, and say,
Wherewith do we weary? In that ye say, Every evil-doer is good
in the eyes of Jehovah, and He takes pleasure in them, or where
is the God of judgment?*" The persons who are introduced as
speaking here are neither the pious Israelites, who were not
only pressed down by the weight of their heavy afflictions, but
indignant at the prosperity of their godless countrymen, and
were thus impelled to give utterance to despairing complaints,
and doubts as to the justice of God (Theodoret) ; nor a middle
class between the truly pious and perfectly godless, consisting
of those who were led by a certain instinctive need to adopt
the faith inherited from the fathers, and sought to fulfil the
commandments of the moral law of God, but the foundations
of whose faith and piety were not deep enough for them
humbly to submit themselves to the marvellous ways of God,
so that whenever the dealings of God did not correspond to
their expectations, they lost their faith in Him and turned
their backs upon Him (Koehler). The whole of the contents
of this section are opposed to the first assumption. Those who
murmured against God were, according to ch. iii. 7 sqq., such
as had departed like the fathers from the law of God and
defrauded God in the tithes and heave-offerings, and with

whom those who feared God are contrasted in vers. 16 sqq. Moreover, the reproach brought against them in ch. ii. 17, "Ye weary Jehovah with your words," and in ch. iii. 13, "Your words put constraint upon me," show that they do not belong to the righteous, who, while bending under the burden of temptation, appear to have raised similar complaints; as we read for example in Ps. xxxvii., xlix., and lxxiii. The second view is precluded by the absence, not only of every trace of the nation being divided into three classes, but also of every indication that those who murmured thus had endeavoured to fulfil the commandments of the moral law of God. The answer of the Lord to this murmuring is addressed to the whole nation as one which had departed from His commandments, and defrauded God with the tithes and sacrifices (ch. iii. 7, 8). The judgment which they wanted to see would fall, according to ch. iii. 5, upon the sorcerers, adulterers, and other gross sinners; and in ch. iii. 16–18 the only persons distinguished from these are the truly righteous who remember the name of the Lord. It clearly follows from this, that the feelings expressed in ch. ii. 17 and iii. 13 were not cherished by the whole nation without exception, but only by the great mass of the people, in contrast with whom the small handful of godly men formed a vanishing minority, which is passed over in the attack made upon the spirit prevailing in the nation. This disposition vents itself in the words: Every one who does evil is good in the eyes of God, and Jehovah takes pleasure in the wicked. By עֹשֵׂה רָע the murmurers mean, not notorious sinners in their midst, but the heathen who enjoyed undisturbed prosperity. To give a reason for this fancy, they inquire, Where is the God of judgment? אֹו, "or," i.e. if this be not the case, as in Job xvi. 3, xxii. 11, why does not God punish the ungodly heathen? why does He not interpose as judge, if He has no pleasure in the wicked? Such speeches as these the prophet calls הֹוגַע, a wearying of God (cf. Isa. xliii. 23, 24).

Ch. iii. 1–6. Coming of the Lord to judgment. Ver. 1. "Behold, I send my messenger, that he may prepare the way before me; and the Lord, whom ye seek, will suddenly come to His temple, and the angel of the covenant, whom ye desire; behold he comes, saith Jehovah of hosts." To the question, Where is or remains the God of judgment? the Lord Himself replies that He will suddenly come to His temple, but that before His coming He will send a messenger to prepare the way for Him. The announcement of this messenger rests upon the prophecy in Isa. xl. 3 sqq., as the expression וּפִנָּה דֶרֶךְ, which is borrowed from that passage, clearly shows. The person whose voice Isaiah heard calling to make the way of Jehovah in the desert, that the glory of the Lord might be revealed to all flesh, is here described as מַלְאָךְ, whom Jehovah will send before Him, *i.e.* before His coming. This *mal'âkh* is not a heavenly messenger, or spiritual being (Rashi, Kimchi), nor the angel of Jehovah κατ᾽ ἐξοχήν, who is mentioned afterwards and called *mal'akh habb'rîth*, but an earthly messenger of the Lord, and indeed the same who is called the prophet Elijah in ver. 23, and therefore not " an ideal person, viz. the whole choir of divine messengers, who are to prepare the way for the coming of salvation, and open the door for the future grace" (Hengst.), but a concrete personality—a messenger who was really sent to the nation in John the Baptist immediately before the coming of the Lord. The ideal view is precluded not only by the historical fact, that not a single prophet arose in Israel during the whole period between Malachi and John, but also by the context of the passage before us, according to which the sending of the messenger was to take place immediately before the coming of the Lord to His temple. It is true that in ch. ii. 7 the priest is also called a messenger of Jehovah; but the expression הִנְנִי שֹׁלֵחַ (behold I send) prevents our understanding the term *mal'âkh* as referring to the priests, or even as including them, inasmuch as " sending" would not apply to the priests as the standing mediators between the Lord and His people. Moreover, it was because the priests did not fulfil their duty as the ordinary ambassadors of God that the Lord was about to send an extraordinary messenger. Preparing the way (פִנָּה דֶרֶךְ, an expression peculiar to Isaiah : compare Isa. xl. 3 ; also, Isa. lvii. 14 and lxii. 10), by clearing away the impediments lying in the road, denotes the removal of all that retards the coming of the Lord to His people, *i.e.* the taking away of enmity to God and of ungodliness by the preaching of repentance and the conversion of sinners. The announcement of this messenger therefore implied, that the nation in its existing moral condition was not yet prepared for the reception of the Lord, and therefore had

no ground for murmuring at the delay of the manifestation of
the divine glory, but ought rather to murmur at its own sin
and estrangement from God.   When the way shall have been
prepared, the Lord will suddenly come.   פִּתְאֹם, not *statim*,
immediately (Jerome), but unexpectedly.   "This suddenness
is repeated in all the acts and judgments of the Lord.   The
Lord of glory always comes as a thief in the night to those
who sleep in their sins" (Schmieder).   "The Lord" (*hâ'âdōn*)
is God ; this is evident both from the fact that He comes to
His temple, *i.e.* the temple of Jehovah, and also from the relative clause "whom ye seek," which points back to the question,
"Where is the God of judgment?" (ch. ii. 17.)   The Lord
comes to His temple (*hēkhâl, lit.* palace) as the God-king of
Israel, to dwell therein for ever (cf. Ezek. xliii. 7, xxxvii.
26, 27).   And He comes as the angel of the covenant, for
whom the people are longing.   The identity of the angel of
the covenant with the "Lord" (*hâ'âdōn*) is placed beyond
the reach of doubt by the parallelism of the clauses, and the
notion is thereby refuted that the "covenant angel" is identical
with the person previously mentioned as מַלְאָכִי (Hitzig, Maurer,
etc.).   This identity does not indeed exclude a distinction of
person ; but it does exclude a difference between the two, or
the opinion that the angel of the covenant is that mediator
whom Isaiah had promised (Isa. xlii. 6) as the antitype of
Moses, and the mediator of a new, perfect, and eternally-
enduring covenant relation between God and Israel (Hofmann, *Schriftbeweis*, i. p. 183).   For it was not for a second
Moses that the people were longing, or for a mediator of the
new covenant, but for the coming of God to judgment.   The
coming of the Lord to His temple is represented as a coming
of the covenant angel, with reference to the fact that Jehovah
had in the olden time revealed His glory in His *Malʾakh* in
a manner perceptible to the senses, and that in this mode of
revelation He had not only redeemed Israel out of the hand
of Egypt (Ex. iii. 6 sqq.), gone before the army of Israel (Ex.
xiv. 19), and led Israel through the desert to Canaan (Ex.
xxiii. 20 sqq., xxxiii. 14 sqq.), but had also filled the temple
with His glory.   The covenant, in relation to which the
Malʾakh, who is of one essence with Jehovah, is here called
the angel of the covenant, is not the new covenant promised

in Jer. xxxi. 31 sqq., but the covenant of Jehovah with Israel, according to which Jehovah dwells in the midst of Israel, and manifests His gracious presence by blessing the righteous and punishing the ungodly (cf. Ex. xxv. 8; Lev. xxvi. 11, 12; Deut. iv. 24; Isa. xxxiii. 14): (Koehler). The words "Behold he (the covenant angel) cometh" serve to confirm the assurance, and are still further strengthened by 'צ 'יי אָמַר (saith Jehovah of hosts). This promise was fulfilled in the coming of Christ, in whom the angel of the covenant, the Logos, became flesh, and in the sending of John the Baptist, who prepared the way for Him. (See also at ver. 24.)

With the coming of the Lord the judgment will also begin; not the judgment upon the heathen, however, for which the ungodly nation was longing, but the judgment upon the godless members of the covenant nation. Ver. 2. "*And who endures the day of His coming? and who can stand at His appearing? for He is like the smelter's fire, and like washers' lye:* Ver. 3. *And will sit smelting and purifying silver, and will purify the children of Levi, and refine like gold and silver, that they may be offering to Jehovah His sacrifice in righteousness.* Ver. 4. *And the sacrifice of Judah and Jerusalem will be pleasant, as in the days of the olden time, and as in the years of the past.*" The question "who endures the day" has a negative meaning, like מִי in Isa. liii. 1: no one endures it (for the fact itself compare Joel ii. 11). The prophet is speaking to the ungodly. The second clause is synonymous. עָמַד, to remain standing, in contrast with falling, or sinking under the burden of the judgment. The reason for this is given in the second hemistich. The Lord when He comes will be like a smelter's fire, which burns out all the corrupt ingredients that are mixed with the gold and silver (cf. Zech. xiii. 9), and like the lye or alkaline salt by which clothes are cleansed from dirt (cf. Isa. iv. 4). The double figure has but one meaning; hence only the first figure is carried out in ver. 3, a somewhat different turn being given to it, since the Lord is no longer compared to the fire, but represented as a smelter. As a smelter purifies gold and silver from the dross adhering to it, so will the Lord refine the sons of Levi, by whom the priests are principally intended. The *yâshabh* (sit) serves as a pictorial description, like *'âmad* (stand) in Mic.

v. 3. The participles *m*ᵉ*tsâreph* and *m*ᵉ*tah*ēr describe the capacity in which He sits, viz. as a smelter and purifier of silver.　זָקַק : to strain, or filter; a term transferred to metals, because in smelting the pure metal is allowed to flow off, so that the earthy ingredients are left in the crucible (Ps. xii. 7; Job xxviii. 1, etc.). The fact that the sons of Levi are named, as the object of the refining action of the Lord, is to be explained from what is mentioned in ch. i. 6 sqq. concerning their degeneracy. Since they, the supporters and promoters of the religious life of the nation, were quite corrupt, the renovation of the national life must begin with their purification. This purification, however, does not consist merely in the fact, that the individuals who are displeasing to God will be cut off from among them (Koehler), nor merely in their being cleansed from the sins and crimes adhering to them (Hitzig), but in both, so that those who are corrigible are improved, and the incorrigible cut off. This is implied in the idea of purification, and is confirmed by the result of the refining work of the Lord, as given in the last clause of the verse. They are to become to the Lord offerers of sacrifices in righteousness. *Bits*ᵉ*dâqâh* does not refer to the nature of the sacrifices, viz. righteous sacrifices, *i.e.* such as correspond to the law, but to the moral character of the offerers, viz. that they will attend to the offering of sacrifice in a proper state of heart, as in Ps. iv. 6. הָיוּ מַגִּישֵׁי is a *constructio periphr.* to denote the permanence of the action (cf. Ewald, § 168, *c*). The *tsaqeph-qaton* does not compel us to separate הָיוּ לַיהוָֹה (compare, on the contrary, Gen. i. 6*b* for example). Then, namely when the priests offer sacrifices in righteousness again, will the sacrificing of the whole nation be pleasant to the Lord, as was the case in the olden time. The days of the olden time and years of the past are the times of Moses, or the first years of the sojourn in the desert (Jer. ii. 2), possibly also the times of David and of the first years of the reign of Solomon; whereas now, *i.e.* in the time of Malachi, the sacrifices of the nation were displeasing to God, not merely on account of the sins of the people (ch. ii. 13), but chiefly on account of the badness of the sacrificing priests (i. 10, 13). Moreover, we must not infer from vers. 3 and 4, that Malachi imagined that the Old Testament worship would be continued during the Messianic times; but his words are to be explained from the custom of the prophets, of using the forms of the Old Testament worship to depict the reverence for God which would characterize the new covenant,

Ver. 5. "*And I will draw near to you to judgment, and will be a swift witness against the sorcerers, and against the adulterers, and against those who swear for deceit, and those who press down the wages of the hireling, the widow and the orphan, and bow down the foreigner, and fear not me, saith Jehovah of hosts.* Ver. 6. *For I Jehovah, I change not ; and ye sons of Israel, ye are not consumed.*" The refining which the Lord will perform at His coming will not limit itself to the priests, but become a judgment upon all sinners. This judgment is threatened against those who wanted the judgment of God to come, according to ch. ii. 17. To these the Lord will draw near to judgment, and rise up as a swift witness against all the wicked who do not fear Him. The word קָרַבְתִּי does not imply that the judgment announced will actually commence at once. The drawing near to judgment takes place in the day of His coming (ver. 2), and this is preceded by the sending of the messenger to prepare the way. The words affirm nothing as to the time of the coming, because this was not revealed to the prophet. Nor is there any intimation on this point in the word מְמַהֵר, but simply the announcement that the Lord will come with unexpected rapidity, in contrast with the murmuring of the people at the delay of judgment (ch. ii. 17). מְמַהֵר answers substantially to פִּתְאֹם in ver. 1. God comes as a practical witness against the wicked, convicting them of their guilt by punishing them. The particular sins mentioned here are such as were grievous sins in the eye of the law, and to some extent were punishable with death. On sorcerers and adulterers see Ex. xxii. 17, Lev. xx. 10, Deut. xxii. 22. That sorcery was very common among the Jews after the captivity, is evident from such passages as Acts viii. 9, xiii. 6, and from Josephus, *Ant.* xx. 6, *de bell. Jud.* ii. 12, 23 ; and the occurrence of adultery may be inferred from the condemnation of the marriages with heathen wives in ch. ii. 10-16. On false swearing compare Lev. xix. 12. The expression to press the wages of the labourer is unusual, since the only other passage in which עָשַׁק is construed with a neuter object is Mic. ii. 2, and in every other case it is applied to persons : for עָשַׁק שָׂכִיר compare Lev. xix. 13 and Deut. xxiv. 14, 15, to which the reproof refers. אַלְמָנָה וְיָתוֹם are not genitives dependent upon שָׂכָר, but further objects to עֹשְׁקֵי. For the fact itself compare Ex. xxii. 21–23, Deut. xxiv. 17, xxvii. 19. To מַטֵּי גֵר we are not to supply מִשְׁפָּט, after Deut. xxiv. 17 and xxvii. 19; but הִטָּה is used of the person as in Amos v. 12: to bow down the stranger, *i.e.* to oppress him unjustly. The words, " and fear not me," point to the source from which all these sins flowed, and refer to all the sinners mentioned before. This threat of judgment is explained in ver. 6 in the double clause : that Jehovah does not change, and the sons of Israel do not perish. Because Jehovah is unchangeable in His purposes, and Israel as the people of God is not to perish, therefore will God exterminate the wicked out of Israel by means of judgment, in order to refine it and shape it according to its true calling. The perfects are used to express established truths. The unchangeableness of God is implied in the name *Jehovah,* " who is that He is," the absolutely independent and absolutely existing One (see at Gen. ii. 4). For the fact itself compare Num. xxiii. 19, 1 Sam. xv. 29, Jas. i. 17. *Jehovah* is in apposition to *'ănĭ* (I), and not a predicate in the sense of " I am Jehovah " (Luther, Hengstenberg, etc.) ; this is evident from the parallel וְאַתֶּם בְּנֵי יַעֲקֹב (and ye, the sons of Jacob), where no one thinks of taking בני יעק (sons of Jacob) as a predicate. *Kâlâh,* to come to an end, to be destroyed, as the parallel passage, Jer. xxx. 11, which floated before the prophet's mind, clearly shows. The name " sons of Jacob " (poetical for sons of Israel) is used emphatically, denoting the true members of the people of God, who rightly bear the name of *Israel.* These do not perish, because their existence rests upon the promise of the unchangeable God (cf. Rom. xi. 28, 29).

After the Lord has announced to the murmuring people that He will suddenly draw near to judgment upon the wicked, He proceeds to explain the reason why He has hitherto withheld His blessing and His salvation. Ver. 7. " *From the days of your fathers ye have departed from mine ordinances, and have not kept them. Return to me, and I will return to you, saith Jehovah of hosts ; and ye say, Wherein shall we return?* Ver. 8. *Dare a man indeed defraud God, that ye have defrauded me? and ye say, In what have we defrauded Thee? In the tithes and the heave-offering.* Ver. 9. *Ye are cursed with the curse, and yet ye defraud me, even the whole nation.*" The reason why Israel waits in vain for the judgment and the salvation dawning with it, is not to be found in God, but in the people, in the fact, that from time immemorial they have transgressed the commandments of God (see Isa. xliii. 27; Ezek. ii. 3; Hos. x. 9). And yet they regard themselves as righteous. They reply to the call to repentance by saying, בַּמֶּה נָשׁוּב, wherein, *i.e.* in what particular, shall we turn? The prophet thereupon shows them their sin: they do what no man should presume to attempt —they try to defraud God in the tithe and heave-offering, namely, by either not paying them at all, or not paying them as they should into the house of God. קָבַע, which only occurs here and at Prov. xxii. 23, signifies to defraud, to overreach. הַמַּעֲשֵׂר והתר׳ is either an accusative of free subordination, or else we must supply the preposition בּ from the question itself. On the tithe see Lev. xxvii. 30 sqq., Num. xviii. 20 sqq., and Deut. xiv. 22 sqq. (see also my *Bibl. Ant.* i. p. 337 sqq.); and on the heave-offering (*t'rūmâh*), the portion of his income lifted off from the rest, for the purposes of divine worship, see my *Bibl. Ant.* i. p. 245. And this they do, notwithstanding the fact that God has already visited them with severe punishment, viz. with the curse of barrenness and of the failure of the harvest. We may see from vers. 10–12, that the curse with which they were smitten consisted in this. וְאֹתִי is adversative: yet ye defraud me, and indeed the whole nation, and not merely certain individuals.

Ver. 10. "*Bring ye all the tithe into the treasure-house, that there may be consumption in my house, and prove me now herewith, saith Jehovah of hosts, if I do not open you the sluices of heaven, and pour you out a blessing to superabundance. Ver. 11. And I will rebuke the devourer for you, that he may not destroy the fruit of your ground; and your vine will not miscarry in the field, saith Jehovah of hosts. Ver. 12. And all nations will call you blessed; for ye will be a land of good pleasure, saith Jehovah of hosts.*" In ver. 10a the emphasis lies upon *kol*: the *whole* of the tithe they are to bring, and not merely a portion of it, and so defraud the Lord; for the tithe was paid to Jehovah for His servants the Levites (Num. xviii. 24). It was delivered, at least after the times of the later kings, at the

sanctuary, where store-chambers were built for the purpose
(cf. 2 Chron. xxxi. 11 sqq; Neh. x. 38, 39, xii. 44, xiii. 12).
Tereph signifies here food, or consumption, as in Prov. xxxi. 15,
Ps. cxi. 5. בָּזֹאת, through this, *i.e.* through their giving to God
what they are under obligation to give Him, they are to prove
God, whether in His attitude towards them He is no longer
the holy and righteous God (ii. 17, iii. 6). Then will they also
learn, that He causes the promised blessing to flow in the
richest abundance to those who keep His commandments.
אִם לֹא is not a particle of asseveration or oath (Koehler), but
an indirect question : whether not. Opening the sluices of
heaven is a figure, denoting the most copious supply of blessing,
so that it flows down from heaven like a pouring rain (as in
2 Kings vii. 2). עַד בְּלִי דָי, till there is no more need, *i.e.* in
superabundance. This thought is individualized in ver. 11.
Everything that could injure the fruits of the land God will
take away. גָּעַר, to rebuke practically, *i.e.* to avert the intention. אֹכֵל, the devourer, is here the locust, so called from its
insatiable voracity. *Shikkēl*, to miscarry, is affirmed of the vine,
when it has set a good quantity of grapes, which perish and
drop off before they ripen. In consequence of this blessing, all
nations will call Israel blessed (ver. 12), because its land will be
an object of pleasure to every one (cf. Zech. vii. 14, viii. 13, 23).

Vers. 13–18. The impatient murmuring of the nation.—
Ver. 13. " *Your words do violence to me, saith Jehovah; and ye
say, What do we converse against Thee?* Ver. 14. *Ye say, It
is vain to serve God ; and what gain is it, that we have kept His
guard, and have gone about in deep mourning before Jehovah of
hosts?* Ver. 15. *And now we call the proud blessed : not only
have the doers of wickedness been built up, but they have also
tempted God and have been saved.*" After the Lord has disclosed to the people the cause of His withholding His blessing,
He shows them still further, that their murmuring against Him
is unjust, and that the coming day of judgment will bring to
light the distinction between the wicked and those who fear
God. חָזַק with עַל, to be strong over any one, does not mean
to be harsh or burdensome, but to do violence to a person, to
overpower him (cf. Ex. xii. 33 ; 2 Sam. xxiv. 4, etc.). The
niphal *nidbar* has a reciprocal meaning, to converse with one
another (cf. Ezek. xxxiii. 30). The conversations which they

carry on with one another take this direction, that it is useless
to serve God, because the righteous have no advantage over
sinners. For שָׁמַר מִשְׁמַרְתּוֹ see the comm. on Gen. xxvi. 5.
Hâlakh qᵉdōrannīth, to go about dirty or black, either with their
faces and clothes unwashed, or wrapped in black mourning
costume (*saq*), is a sign of mourning, here of fasting, as
mourning for sin (cf. Ps. xxxv. 13, 14, xxxviii. 7; Job xxx.
28; 1 Macc. iii. 48). מִפְּנֵי יְהֹוָה, from awe of Jehovah. The
fasting, and that in its external form, they bring into prominence as a special sign of their piety, as an act of penitence,
through which they make reparation for certain sins against
God, by which we are not to understand the fasting prescribed
for the day of atonement, but voluntary fasting, which was
regarded as a special sign of piety. What is reprehensible in
the state of mind expressing itself in these words, is not so
much the complaint that their piety brings them no gain (for
such complaints were uttered even by believing souls in their
hours of temptation; cf. Ps. lxxiii. 13), as the delusion that
their merely outward worship, which was bad enough according
to what has already been affirmed, is the genuine worship
which God must acknowledge and reward. This disposition to
attribute worth to the *opus operatum* of fasting is attacked
even by Isaiah, in Isa. lviii.; but after the captivity it continued to increase, until it reached its culminating point in
Pharisaism. How thoroughly different the persons speaking
here are from the believing souls under temptation, who also
appeal to their righteousness when calling upon God in their
trouble, is especially clear from their further words in ver. 15.
Because God does not reward their fasting with blessing and
prosperity, they begin to call the proud sinners, who have happiness and success, blessed. וְעַתָּה is the particle of inference.
The participle מְאַשְּׁרִים has the force of a *futurum instans* (cf.
Ewald, § 306, *d*), denoting what men prepare to do. *Zēdīm*,
the haughty or proud, are the heathen, as in Isa. xiii. 11, who
are called עֹשֵׂי רִשְׁעָה in the following clause. The next two
clauses are placed in a reciprocal relation to one another by
gam . . . gam (cf. Ewald, § 359). The wicked are both built
up, *i.e.* flourish (cf. Jer. xii. 16, 17; Ex. i. 21), and also, notwithstanding the fact that they have tempted God, are delivered
when they fall into misfortune. *Bâchan Elohim*, to prove or

test God, *i.e.* to call out His judgment through their wickedness.

With these foolish speeches the prophet proceeds in vers. 16
sqq. to contrast the conduct of those who fear God, pointing to
the blessing which they derive from their piety. Ver. 16.
" *Then those who feared Jehovah conversed with one another, and
Jehovah attended and heard, and a book of remembrance was
written before Him, for those who fear Jehovah and reverence
His name.* Ver. 17. *And they will be to me as a possession,
saith Jehovah of hosts, for the day that I create, and I will spare
them as a man spareth his son that serveth him.* Ver. 18. *And
ye will again perceive the difference between the righteous and
the wicked, between him that serveth God and him that serveth
Him not.*" אָז, *then*, indicates that the conversation of those
who feared God had been occasioned by the words of the
ungodly. The substance of this conversation is not described
more minutely, but may be gathered from the context, namely,
from the statement as to the attitude in which Jehovah stood
towards them. We may see from this, that they strengthened
themselves in their faith in Jehovah, as the holy God and
just Judge who would in due time repay both the wicked
and the righteous according to their deeds, and thus presented a great contrast to the great mass with their blasphemous sayings. This description of the conduct of the godly is
an indirect admonition to the people, as to what their attitude
towards God ought to be. What was done by those who feared
Jehovah ought to be taken as a model by the whole nation
which called Jehovah its God. Jehovah not only took notice
of these conversations, but had them written in a book of
remembrance, to reward them for them in due time. Writing
in a book of remembrance recals to mind the custom of the
Persians, of having the names of those who deserved well of
the king entered in a book with a notice of their merits, that
they might be rewarded for them at some future time (Esth.
vi. 1); but it rests upon the much older idea, that the names
and actions of the righteous are written in a book before God
(cf. Ps. lvi. 9, Dan. vii. 10). This book was written לְפָנָיו,
before Jehovah, *i.e.* not in His presence, but in order that it
might lie before Jehovah, and remind Him of the righteous
and their deeds. לְיִרְאֵי is a *dat. com.:* "for those who fear God,"

i.e. for their good. חָשַׁב שֵׁם, to consider or value the name of the Lord (cf. Isa. xiii. 17, xxxiii. 8). This writing was done because the Lord would make them His own on the day of His coming, and show them mercy. *Layyōm:* for the day = on the day; the *lamed* denoting the time, as in Isa. x. 3, Gen. xxi. 2, etc. The day which Jehovah makes is the day of the judgment which attends His coming. *S*e*gullâh* is the object, not to 'ōseh, as we might suppose according to the accents, but to *hâyū:* they will be my possession on the day which I create. This is evident partly from a comparison of ver. 21, where the words יוֹם אֲשֶׁר אֲנִי עֹשֶׂה recur, and partly from the original passage in Ex. xix. 5: ye will be to me *s*e*gullâh, i.e.* a valued possession (see the comm.). The righteous will then be a possession for Jehovah, because on that day the glory of the children of God will first be revealed, and the Israel of God will reach the mark of its heavenly calling (see Col. iii. 4). The Lord will spare them in the judgment as a father spares his son who serves him. The expression *to spare* may be explained from the contrast to the punishment of the ungodly. In ver. 18 the prophet bids the murmurers consider what has been said concerning the righteous, by telling them that they will then see the difference between the righteous who serve God, and the wicked who do not serve Him, that is to say, will learn that it is always profitable to serve God. שַׁבְתֶּם before רְאִיתֶם is to be taken adverbially: ye will see again. The expression "again" presupposes that the difference between those who feared God and the ungodly was to be seen before, and that the Lord had already made it manifest by former judgments. This had been the case in Egypt, where the Lord had caused such a separation to be made (Ex. xi. 7). The words do not imply that the persons addressed had previously stood in a different relation to this question from that in which they were standing then (Koehler). רָאָה בֵין does not mean to look in between (Hitzig), but בֵּין is used in the sense of a substantive, signifying that which is between the two, the difference between the two. That בֵּן was originally a noun is evident from the dual הַבֵּנַיִם in 1 Sam. xvii. 4, 23.

This admonition to the ungodly is explained in ch. iv. 1 sqq. by a picture of the separation which will be effected by the day of judgment. Ver. 1. "*For behold the day cometh*

*burning like a furnace, and all the proud and every doer of
wickedness become stubble, and the coming day will burn them,
saith Jehovah of hosts, so that it will not leave them root or
branch.* Ver. 2. *But to you who fear my name, the sun of
righteousness will rise and healing in its wings, and ye will go
out and skip like stalled calves,* Ver. 3. *And will tread down the
ungodly, for they will be ashes under the soles of your feet in the
day that I create, saith Jehovah of hosts."* The day of judgment
will be to the ungodly like a burning furnace. " A fire burns
more fiercely in a furnace than in the open air" (Hengstenberg). The ungodly will then resemble the stubble which the
fire consumes (cf. Isa. v. 24, Zeph. i. 18, Ob. 18, etc.). זֵדִים
and עֹשֵׂה רִשְׁעָה point back to ver. 15. Those who are called
blessed by the murmuring nation will be consumed by the fire,
as stubble is burned up, and indeed *all* who do wickedness, and
therefore the murmurers themselves. אֲשֶׁר before לֹא יַעֲזֹב is a
conjunction, *quod;* and the subject is not Jehovah, but the
coming day. The figure " root and branch" is borrowed from
a tree—the tree is the ungodly mass of the people (cf. Amos
ii. 9)—and denotes total destruction, so that nothing will be
left of them. To the righteous, on the other hand, the sun of
righteousness will arise. *Ts⁰dáqáh* is an epexegetical genitive
of apposition. By the sun of righteousness the fathers, from
Justin downwards, and nearly all the earlier commentators
understand *Christ,* who is supposed to be described as the rising
sun, like Jehovah in Ps. lxxxiv. 12 and Isa. lx. 19 ; and this
view is founded upon a truth, viz. that the coming of Christ
brings justice and salvation. But in the verse before us the
context does not sustain the personal view, but simply the idea
that righteousness itself is regarded as a sun. *Ts⁰dáqáh,* again,
is not justification or the forgiveness of sins, as Luther and
others suppose, for there will be no forgiving of sins on the day
of judgment, but God will then give to every man reward or
punishment according to his works. *Ts⁰dáqáh* is here, what it
frequently is in Isaiah (*e.g.* Isa. xlv. 8, xlvi. 13, li. 5, etc.),
righteousness in its consequences and effects, the sum and substance of salvation. Malachi uses *ts⁰dáqáh,* righteousness,
instead of יֶשַׁע, salvation, with an allusion to the fact, that the
ungodly complained of the absence of the judgment and righteousness of God, that is to say, the righteousness which not

only punishes the ungodly, but also rewards the good with happiness and salvation. The sun of righteousness has מַרְפֵּא, healing, in its wings. The wings of the sun are the rays by which it is surrounded, and not a figure denoting swiftness. As the rays of the sun spread light and warmth over the earth for the growth and maturity of the plants and living creatures, so will the sun of righteousness bring the healing of all hurts and wounds which the power of darkness has inflicted upon the righteous. Then will they go forth, *sc.* from the holes and caves, into which they had withdrawn during the night of suffering and where they had kept themselves concealed, and skip like stalled calves (cf. 1 Sam. xxviii. 24), which are driven from the stall to the pasture. On *pūsh*, see at Hab. i. 8. And not only will those who fear God be liberated from all oppression, but they will also acquire power over the ungodly. They will tread down the wicked, who will then have become ashes, and lie like ashes upon the ground, having been completely destroyed by the fire of the judgment (cf. Isa. xxvi. 5, 6).

Vers. 4-6.—Concluding Admonition.—Ver. 4. "*Remember ye the law of Moses, my servant, which I commanded him upon Horeb for all Israel, statutes and rights.*[1] *Ver. 5. Behold, I send you Elijah the prophet before the day of Jehovah comes, the great and terrible one. Ver. 6. And he will turn the heart of the fathers to the sons, and the heart of the sons to their fathers,*

---

[1] The LXX. have put ver. 4 at the end of the book, not to call attention to its great importance, but probably for the very same reason for which the *Masora* observes, at the close of our book, that in the תִּתְחַלֵּק, *i.e.* in the books of Isaiah, the twelve prophets, the Lamentations, and Ecclesiastes, the last verse but one of these books was to be repeated when they were read in the synagogue, namely, because the last verse had too harsh a sound. The transposition is unsuitable, inasmuch as the promise in vers. 5 and 6 does not fit on to the idea expressed in vers. 2 and 3, but only to that in ver. 4. According to the *Masora*, the ז in זִכְרוּ should be written as *litera majusc.*, although in many codd. it has the usual form; and this also is not to show the great importance of the verse, since these Masoretic indications have generally a different meaning, but in all probability it is simply to indicate that this is the only passage in the book of the twelve prophets in which the word is pronounced זִכְרוּ (cf. זְכֹר in Hos. xii. 6, xiv. 8), whereas in the other books, with the exception of Job xviii. 17, this is the only pronunciation that is met with.

that I may not come and smite the land with the curse" (*mit dem Banne*, with the ban). The admonition, " Remember ye the law of Moses," forms the conclusion not only of the last section (ch. iii. 13–iv. 3), but of the whole of the book of Malachi, and cannot be connected with ver. 3 in the sense of " Remember what Moses has written in the law concerning Christ, or concerning the judgment," as Theod. Mops. and others maintain ; nor must it be restricted to the time previous to the coming of the Messiah by the interpolation of *interim* (v. Til and Mich.). It is rather a perfectly general admonition to lay to heart and observe the law. For this is referred to here, " not according to its casual and transient form, but according to its real essence as expressing the holiness of God, just as in Matt. v. 17 " (Hengstenberg). Malachi thus closes by showing to the people what it is their duty to do, if on the day of judgment they would escape the curse with which transgressors are threatened in the law, and participate in the salvation so generally desired, and promised to those who fear God. By the expression " my servant," the law is traced back to God as its author. At the giving of the law, Moses was only the servant of Jehovah. אֲשֶׁר צִוִּיתִי אוֹתוֹ is not to be rendered " whom (אֲשֶׁר אוֹתוֹ) I charged with statutes and rights to all Israel" (Ewald, Bunsen), for we do not expect any further explanation of the relation in which Moses stood to the law, but " which I commanded him upon (to) all Israel." *Tsivváh* is construed with a double accusative, and also with עַל governing the person to whom the command refers, as in Ezra viii. 17, 2 Sam. xiv. 8, Esther iv. 5. The words *chuqqīm ūmishpâtīm* are an epexegetical definition belonging to אֲשֶׁר: " which I commanded as statutes and rights," *i.e.* consisting of these; and they recal to mind Deut. iv. 1 and viii. 14, where Moses urges upon the people the observance of the law, and also mentions *Horeb* as the place where the law was given. The whole of the admonition forms an antithesis to the rebuke in ver. 7, that from the days of their fathers they went away from the ordinances of Jehovah. These they are to be mindful to observe, that the Lord when He comes may not smite the land with the ban. In order to avert this curse from Israel, the Lord would send the prophet Elijah before His coming, for the purpose of promoting a change of heart in the nation.

The identity of the prophet Elijah with the messenger mentioned in ver. 1, whom the Lord would send before Him, is universally acknowledged. But there is a difference of opinion as to the question, who is the Elijah mentioned here? The notion was a very ancient one, and one very widely spread among the rabbins and fathers, that the prophet Elijah, who was caught up to heaven, would reappear (compare the history of the exposition of our verse in Hengstenberg's *Christology*, vol. iv. p. 217 translation). The LXX. thought of him, and rendered אֵלִיָּה הַנָּבִיא by Ἠλίαν τὸν Θεσβίτην; so also did Sirach (xlviii. 10) and the Jews in the time of Christ (John i. 21; Matt. xvii. 10); and so have Hitzig, Maurer, and Ewald in the most recent times. But this view is proved to be erroneous by such passages as Hos. iii. 5, Ezek. xxxiv. 23, xxxvii. 24, and Jer. xxx. 9, where the sending of David the king as the true shepherd of Israel is promised. Just as in these passages we cannot think of the return or resurrection of the David who had long been dead; but a king is meant who will reign over the nation of God in the mind and spirit of David; so the Elijah to be sent can only be a prophet with the spirit or power of Elijah the Tishbite. The second David was indeed to spring from the family of David, because to the seed of David there had been promised the eternal possession of the throne. The prophetic calling, on the other hand, was not hereditary in the prophet's house, but rested solely upon divine choice and endowment with the Spirit of God; and consequently by Elijah we are not to understand a lineal descendant of the Tishbite, but simply a prophet in whom the spirit and power of Elijah are revived, as Ephr. Syr., Luther, Calvin, and most of the Protestant commentators have maintained. But the reason why this prophet Elijah is named is to be sought for, not merely in the fact that Elijah was called to his work as a reformer in Israel at a period which was destitute of faith and of the true fear of Jehovah, and which immediately preceded a terrible judgment (Koehler), but also and more especially in the power and energy with which Elijah rose up to lead back the ungodly generation of his own time to the God of the fathers. The one does not exclude but rather includes the other. The greater the apostasy, the greater must be the power which is to stem it, so as to rescue those who suffer themselves to be rescued, before the judgment bursts over such as are hardened. For ver. 5*b*, compare Joel iii. 4. This Elijah, according to ver. 6, is to lead back the heart of the fathers to the sons, and the heart of the sons to their fathers. The meaning of this is not that he will settle disputes in families, or restore peace between parents and children; for the leading sin of the nation at the time of our prophet was not family quarrels, but estrangement from God. The fathers are rather the ancestors of the Israelitish nation, the patriarchs, and generally the pious forefathers, such as David and the godly men of his time. The sons or children are the degenerate descendants of Malachi's own time and the succeeding ages. "The hearts of the godly fathers and the ungodly sons are estranged from one another. The bond of union, viz. common love to God, is wanting. The fathers are ashamed of their children, the children of their fathers" (Hengstenberg). This chasm between them Elijah is to fill up. Turning the heart of the fathers to the sons does not mean merely directing the love of the fathers to the sons once more, but also restoring the heart of the fathers in the sons, or giving to the sons the fathers' disposition and affections. Then will the heart of the sons also return to their fathers, turn itself towards them, so that they will be like-minded with the pious fathers. Elijah will thereby prepare the way of the Lord to His people, that at His coming He may not smite the land with the ban. The ban involves extermination. Whoever and whatever was laid under the ban was destroyed (cf. Lev. xxvii. 28, 29; Deut. xiii. 16, 17; and my *Bibl. Archäol.* i. § 70). This threat recals to mind the fate of the Canaanites who were smitten with the ban (Deut. xx. 17, 18). If Israel resembles the Canaanites in character, it will also necessarily share the fate of that people (cf. Deut. xii. 29).

The New Testament gives us a sufficient explanation of the historical allusion or fulfilment of our prophecy. The prophet Elijah, whom the Lord would send before His own coming, was sent in the person of John the Baptist. Even before his birth he was announced to his father by the angel Gabriel as the promised Elijah, by the declaration that he would turn many of the children of Israel to the Lord their God, and go before Him in the spirit and power of Elijah to turn the hearts of the fathers to the children, and the unbelieving to the wisdom of the just (Luke i. 16, 17). This address of the angel gives at the same time an authentic explanation of vers. 5 and 6 of our prophecy : the words "and the heart of the children to their fathers" being omitted, as implied in the turning of the heart of the fathers to the sons, and the explanatory words "and the unbelieving to the wisdom of the just" being introduced in their place ; and the whole of the work of John, who was to go before the Lord in the spirit and power of Elijah, being described as "making ready a prepared people for the Lord." The appearance and ministry of John the Baptist answered to this announcement of the angel, and is so described in Matt. iii. 1-12, Mark i. 2-8, Luke iii. 2-18, that the allusion to our prophecy and the original passage (Isa. xl. 3) is obvious at once. Even by his outward appearance and his dress John announced himself as the promised prophet Elijah, who by the preaching of repentance and baptism was preparing the way for the Lord, who would come after him with the winnowing shovel to winnow His floor, and gather the wheat into His granary, but who would burn up the chaff with unquenchable fire. Christ Himself also not only assured the people (in Matt. xi. 10 sqq., Luke vii. 27 sqq.) that John was the messenger announced by Malachi and the Elijah who was to come, but also told His disciples (Matt. xvii. 11 sqq. ; Mark ix. 11 sqq.) that Elijah, who was to come first and restore all things, had already come, though the people had not acknowledged him. And even John i. 21 is not at variance with these statements. When the messengers of the Sanhedrim came to John the Baptist to ask whether he was Elias, and he answered, " I am not," he simply gave a negative reply to their question, interpreted in the sense of a personal reappearance of Elijah the Tishbite, which was the sense in which they meant it, but he also declared himself to be the promised forerunner of the Lord by applying to his own labours the prophecy contained in Isa. xl. 3.

And as the prophet Elijah predicted by Malachi appeared in John the Baptist, so did the Lord come to His temple in the appearing of Jesus Christ. The opinion, which was very widely spread among the fathers and Catholic commentators, and which has also been adopted by many of the more modern

Protestant theologians (*e.g.* Menken and H. Olshausen), viz. that our prophecy was only provisionally fulfilled in the coming of John the Baptist and the incarnation of the Son of God in Jesus Christ, and that its true fulfilment will only take place at the second coming of Christ to judge the world, in the actual appearance of the risen Elijah by which it will be preceded, is not only at variance with the statements of the Lord concerning John the Baptist, which have been already quoted, but has no tenable foundation in our prophecy itself. The prophets of the Old Testament throughout make no allusion to any second coming of the Lord to His people. The day of the Lord, which they announce as the day of judgment, commenced with the appearance on earth of Christ, the incarnate Logos; and Christ Himself declared that He had come into the world for judgment (John ix. 39, cf. iii. 19 and xii. 40), viz. for the judgment of separating the believing from the ungodly, to give eternal life to those who believe on His name, and to bring death and condemnation to unbelievers. This judgment burst upon the Jewish nation not long after the ascension of Christ. Israel rejected its Saviour, and was smitten with the ban at the destruction of Jerusalem in the Roman war; and both people and land lie under this ban to the present day. And just as the judgment commenced at that time so far as Israel was concerned, so does it also begin in relation to all peoples and kingdoms of this earth with the first preaching of Christ among them, and will continue throughout all the centuries during which the kingdom spreads upon earth, until it shall be ultimately completed in the universal judgment at the visible second coming of the Lord at the last day.

With this calling to remembrance of the law of Moses, and this prediction that the prophet Elijah will be sent before the coming of the Lord Himself, the prophecy of the Old Testament is brought to a close. After Malachi, no other prophet arose in Israel until the time was fulfilled when the Elijah predicted by him appeared in John the Baptist, and immediately afterwards the Lord came to His temple, that is to say, the incarnate Son of God to His own possession, to make all who received Him children of God, the *s*ᵉ*gullâh* of the Lord. Law and prophets bore witness of Christ, and Christ came not to destroy the law or the prophets, but to fulfil them. Upon the

Mount of Christ's Transfiguration, therefore, there appeared both Moses, the founder of the law and mediator of the old covenant, and Elijah the prophet, as the restorer of the law in Israel, to talk with Jesus of His decease which He was to accomplish in Jerusalem (Matt. xvii. 1 sqq.; Mark ix. 1 sqq.; Luke ix. 28 sqq.), for a practical testimony to the apostles and to us all, that Jesus Christ, who laid down His life for us, to bear our sin and redeem us from the curse of the law, was the beloved Son of the Father, whom we are to hear, that by believing in His name we may become children of God and heirs of everlasting life.